There are a number of reasons why I chose the beautiful painting of Mount Whitney, California by John Grossman for the end papers of this volume on the American Revolution. My first reason is that mountains are ever the symbol of government in the Bible, and this volume is about Christian civil government.

These mountains, the Sierra Nevada of California, include the highest peak in the contiguous United States, Mt. Whitney (14,495 feet, center right in the painting), but it is almost lost among the surrounding lofty peaks. To me this mountain range is representative of the Founding Father generation and the form of government which they established—Christian civil government. The many peaks representative of the leaders of that generation are all high, but one is highest. I like to equate Mt. Whitney with General George Washington.

On a somewhat negative note, I liken the distance between the desert valley and the high mountains, to the distance lying between the American Christians of 1976 and those of 1776 in comprehending Christian civil government. But I thank God we can still look up to our Founding Fathers, still read their writings, and with God's help we too can comprehend the Biblical principles of government and lift our nation to its God appointed purpose once again.

Mountains are either obstacles or opportunities. Christian civil government is either an obstacle, a "stumbling stone/block" or an opportunity to prove the power of Christ in the life of the individual.

Let us be like the early pioneers moving west to settle California. After struggling for months across the vast plains and desert, they saw these seemingly impassable mountains. But instead of being defeated by them (as the Spanish thought they would be), they used them as an opportunity to prove the power of Christ in their lives and bring California into the union—the farthest westward land for Christianity at that time. The Orient still lies west with all its challenges to Christianity. What will the American Christians of our Third Century do for America and for the world?

VERNA M. HALL

THE CHRISTIAN
HISTORY OF
THE AMERICAN
REVOLUTION

"WHERE THE SPIRIT OF THE LORD IS, THERE IS LIBERTY." II CORINTHIANS 3:17

THE CHRISTIAN HISTORY OF THE AMERICAN REVOLUTION

CONSIDER AND PONDER

A COMPILATION BY VERNA M. HALL

WITH AN INDEX OF LEADING IDEAS BY ROSALIE J. SLATER

FOUNDATION FOR AMERICAN CHRISTIAN EDUCATION

SAN FRANCISCO, CALIFORNIA

ANNO DOMINI 1976

First Edition, 1976
Second Printing, 1982
Copyright 1975 by Verna M. Hall

Published by
THE FOUNDATION FOR AMERICAN CHRISTIAN EDUCATION
Box 27035, San Francisco, California 94127

Printed by Iversen-Norman Associates
New York, New York

Designed by John Grossman
Woodacre, California

Library of Congress Catalog Card Number 75-18326
ISBN Number 0-912498-04-8

TITLE PAGE MAP:
AN ACCURATE MAP OF NORTH AMERICA (DETAIL)
EMAN BOWEN, GEOGRAPHER, AND JOHN GIBSON, ENGRAVER
PRINTED FOR ROBERT SAYER, LONDON, 1763.
FULL MAP: 40 X 45 ¾ INCHES
SCALE IN THE ORIGINAL: 1 INCH = 85.7 MILES
COURTESY OF WILLIAM L. CLEMENTS LIBRARY,
ANN ARBOR, MICHIGAN

THE HAND OF GOD IN AMERICAN HISTORY

CONSTITUTIONAL DEBATE PERIOD: 1765-1775

GENERAL GEORGE WASHINGTON IN PRAYER
AT VALLEY FORGE
BY JAMES EDWARD KELLY (AMERICAN, 1855-1933)
BRONZE BAS-RELIEF, 48 X 36 IN. 1904.
UNITED STATES SUB-TREASURY BUILDING,
NEW YORK, NEW YORK
COURTESY OF LIBRARY OF CONGRESS, WASHINGTON, D.C.

In this hour of darkness and of danger, when 'foes were strong and friends were few,' when every human prospect presented to the commander at Valley Forge was disheartening, he retires to a sequestered spot, and there laid the cause of his bleeding country AT THE THRONE OF GRACE. That country had appealed in vain to the justice of her acknowledged sovereign; HE pleads her cause before the King of kings. He had before complained to Congress that there was a deficiency in the chaplaincy of the army. But it was not the form he relied on. It was not a religous awe, as a matter of mere policy, with which he sought to imbue the minds of soldiery religiously educated. He sought to link our cause, by a sincere devotion, to the immutable throne of justice; to find wisdom to guide his own action; to place the country in the RIGHT, so that he might bring upon her prosperity, as the natural result of justice to the injured.

How full of interest is this scene! How instructive! How sublime! Let our children come up from their cradles through the remotest generations to contemplate this picture. Let parents open it to their admiring families. Let it be hung on the parlor walls, ornament the center tables, be pictured on the tapestry, be grouped with every cradle scene, recited in every nursery, that it may meet the early vision, and affect the young heart of every child who may breathe the free air of this land of freedom—'WASHINGTON IS AT PRAYER.' Well did he earn the title of 'PATRIARCH'— 'THE FATHER OF HIS COUNTRY.' As we honor him, and teach our children to give him honor, may we also love and honor, and teach our children to acknowledge the God of our fathers, who alone giveth the victory.

The Family Circle—1847

FOR ESTHER S. K. ROBERTS

AMERICAN CHRISTIAN MOTHER AND PATRIOT,

WHO EARLY SAW THE VITAL IMPORTANCE OF

AMERICAN CHRISTIAN EDUCATION

IN REBUILDING THE FOUNDATIONS OF AMERICA

THROUGH TEACHING THE RISING GENERATION

AMERICA'S CHRISTIAN HISTORY.

ACKNOWLEDGEMENTS

When one undertakes a work to call to the attention of the American Christians the vast amount of written evidence of America's Christian history, the cooperation and assistance of a number of individuals and institutions are required.

It has been my privilege and pleasure to have the assistance of dedicated Christian men and women, whose love of America is only exceeded by their love of God who gave their freedom to them. They have voluntarily given of their time, talents and funds that this volume might come forth to help those who do not yet know what God has done for us who are fortunate to live in the nation called America.

It is their prayer and mine, that this volume can be used of the Lord to awaken and stir the minds and hearts of American Christians throughout our land so they will be willing to assume their responsibility for returning America to the principles of Christian civil government. America's God-intended purpose—the propagation of the Gospel—needs the support of Christian civil government.

I want each individual listed here to know how much I value all he or she has done over the years to make this volume possible, and how their understanding patience was appreciated as the delays in publishing took place. I think we all can see now that these were divine delays, enabling this volume to appear during the Bicentennial of the American Revolution.

Mrs. Alice Bolander
Miss Kay Bullock
Mrs. Christine Detmer
Mr. and Mrs. Robert English
Mr. and Mrs. Robert Foulk
Mrs. Edwina Garfield
Miss Elizabeth Garfield
Miss Helen Louise Garfield
Mrs. Lucile Hosmer
Mr. William Hosmer
Mr. and Mrs. James Humphrey
Mrs. Lois Jenkinson
Mr. and Mrs. Curtis Kielsmeier
Mrs. Ethel Le Brun
Mrs. Gladys Marley
Mrs. Joy Nichols
Mr. and Mrs. James B. Rose
Mrs. Gladys Soule
Mrs. Marianne Stoakes
Miss Mildred Strutzel
Mrs. Mary Elaine Adams Swanson

There are two features in this volume which will bring much pleasure and satisfaction to the reader as he strives to assimilate the great amount

ACKNOWLEDGE-
MENTS

of material contained therein, namely, the thoughtfully beautiful design of the book as a whole and in its every page, and the equally thoughtful and scholarly Index of Leading Ideas.

Mr. John Grossman of Woodacre, California is the artist designer. He is now one of California's leading landscape painters, but before this was very successful in the graphic arts profession. He has served on the California Arts Commission, being chairman for two years. Mr. Grossman's charming wife, Andrea, is an artist and designer in her own right and has been willing to take the time to paste up all these pages for the photo-offset process. Both Mr. and Mrs. Grossman are rather unusual in their profession, for they understand there is a philosophy of government underlying all artistic expressions. Theirs is the American Christian philosophy of government, which shows through in their lives and in their work. I am most grateful to both of them for making this complex book readable and beautiful.

Miss Rosalie J. Slater, president of this foundation, is responsible for the Index of Leading Ideas—an unusual feature in any book, and one originated by Miss Slater especially for this volume. Through her volume *Teaching and Learning America's Christian History*, Miss Slater has produced the Scriptural alternative to progressive education, namely, the American Christian philosophy of education, known as the Principle Approach. Instead of constructing a separate book as a guide to the understanding and teaching of this volume, Miss Slater has given the reader the ways and means to grasp the richness of America's Christian history through an Index of Leading Ideas. She has also given an historical example of our Colonial education in the life of John Quincy Adams.

The quality of education in America has so deteriorated during the last one hundred years, that we now find ourselves as a people far inferior mentally and spiritually to the founding father generations. We may have more technical advantages, more material wealth, but we are not able to reason from Scripture nor to relate the "first principles" of Christianity to all areas of life, as were they. But for those American Chris-

tians who are willing to begin to rebuild the foundations of America in the sanctity of their homes, churches and Christian educational institutions by restoring this prowess to themselves and to their sphere of influence, Miss Slater's index, so thoughtfully and lovingly prepared, is handily available. It only needs to be used.

I am indeed blessed to have my professional associate willing to devote the many, many hours away from her own fields of literature and education, to produce such a unique educational tool so this volume may be of practical value to the reader.

Those readers familiar with my first volumes will recognize the work of Mrs. Mary Elaine Swanson (nee Adams) in the preparation of the short biographical sketches of the writers appearing in this volume. Once again I am the recipient of an individual's devotion to the subject of this volume—America's Christian history.

We in America are fortunate in having the written record of our beginnings in the hands of many historical societies and libraries throughout our country. The men and women staffing these institutions are most helpful to those desiring to learn of our unique history. Our founding fathers and mothers were careful to write down for posterity how they thought and acted, and these records are now being carefully preserved, although a great deal has been lost because of disinterest during a certain period of our history. I would like to pay tribute to all of these historical institutions and their staffs, by naming those with whom I have had the most occasions to require their help:

American Antiquarian Society, Worcester, Massachusetts; Boston Public Library, Boston, Massachusetts; Connecticut Historical Society, Hartford, Connecticut; Essex Institute, Salem, Massachusetts; Harvard University, Cambridge, Massachusetts; Historical Society of Pennsylvania, Philadelphia, Pennsylvania; Library Company of Philadelphia, Philadelphia, Pennsylvania; Library of Congress, Washington, D.C. Massachusetts Historical Society, Boston, Massachusetts.

VERNA M. HALL

CONTENTS

THINK ON WITH CARE

CHRISTIAN CONSTITUENTS OF THE AMERICAN REVOLUTION: LOVE OF GOD IN HOME, CHURCH, AND EDUCATION

CHRISTIAN LIBERTY "READY TO PASS TO THE AMERICAN STRAND"

God Prepares a Christian People to Establish the American Nation

Mercy Otis Warren
New England Historian Cotemporary with
the American Revolution   353

David Ramsay
Southern Historian Cotemporary with
the American Revolution   423

Arm of Flesh or Arm of the Lord

Georgia Completes the "American Chain"
Continental Fast Day, July 20, 1775   511

APPENDIX

INDEX OF LEADING IDEAS

BY ROSALIE J. SLATER

ILLUSTRATIONS

INTRODUCTION

But whoso looketh into the perfect law of liberty, and continueth therein, he being not a forgetful hearer, but a doer of the word, this man shall be blessed in his deed. (James 1:25)
So speak ye, and so do, as they that shall be judged by the law of liberty. (James 2:12)

INTERNAL CHRISTIAN LIBERTY
RELATES TO EXTERNAL
CIVIL FREEDOM

The Law of Liberty had a threefold relation to the founding of America: its colonization, the War for Independence, and the formation of the American Christian Constitution. The Law of Liberty has an equally important relation to the restoring and maintaining of our Christian civil government.

To "consider" America's Christian history, means to thoroughly "ponder" what the nation America is in the Christian era; to attentively weigh America's unique and excellent form of government; to think what an American Christian's responsibility might be to maintain the original intent of our Constitution. It is by diligently "pondering" the cause of America's history, that the American Christian begins to understand the goodness of God in bringing the nation America into being for His Gospel purpose. To "consider" America's Christian history means to behold the Hand of God in all events leading to the Declaration of Independence and the Constitutional Convention. It is more than a passing glance at our country or an occasional patriotic thought. America's Christian history should be "as a seal upon thine heart" (Song of Sol. 8:6) because it pertains to Christ—His story of civil freedom, civil government in the Christian era.

Consider the many unusual aspects in the settling of America's thirteen colonies, the enduring and winning of the seven years War for Independence, and the establishing of the first Christian Constitution the world has ever known. All these "human events" required "a peculiar people zealous of good works (Titus 2:14; I Peter 2:9).

Ponder the fact that for one hundred and fifty years, God gathered and allowed representatives from all parts of Europe and Africa to come to America until by 1775 there were almost three million people settled upon the eastern seaboard (q.v. p. 430, 437)*. Such a diversity of races, colors, and creeds had not been able to live peaceably with one another in their respective

---

* See item or article in this volume.

homelands, yet in America they were able to unite voluntarily, and, without a strong central government, defeat England, the greatest military power of the time. They were able to make the transition with surprisingly little difficulty from colonies dependent on England politically, economically, culturally, and, to a considerable degree religiously, to independent states. They were able to move in an orderly manner from a confederation to a federation—the world's first Christian republic. They established their national-federal Constitution upon the Biblical principles by which they had lived for over one hundred and fifty years, i.e. God's principle of individuality, Christian self-government, property, and voluntary union.

How did all these events happen, and why did they happen in America when they did? Was it solely man's intellectual capability which initiated and carried through these accomplishments, or was it the Providence of God working for and through His people for His purpose, and according to His time-table of events?

The Christian history of the American Revolution is not to be proved through the cotemporary Christian statements of individuals or sermons of the clergy, although there are such statements and sermons; not through public documents referring to God as the Governor of the world, although there are such documents; not even through Providential events, although there are such events. These are effects, the results of God's Law of Liberty being accepted and obeyed individually, internally.

Inasmuch as Christian liberty is individual, internal and causative, does it not follow that there should be a societal, external effect of this fact?

The phrase "America's Christian History" and the title *The Christian History of the American Revolution* is based upon the conviction that America's civil freedom, i.e. freedom for the individual, came from God through His Son, Jesus Christ, and is the result or effect of Christianity's development and westward march from Asia, through Europe and England to America.

The cause and timing of events which led to the War for American Independence, the raising up of civil and military leaders and the willingness of a diversified people to be self-governed—the cause of these aspects and many more—is attributed to the fulfillment of the promises of God to those who obey His precepts in His Word, obey His Law of Liberty in all aspects of their lives—including civil government.

THE BIBLE
AMERICA'S GOVERNMENTAL
TEXTBOOK

The Bible is the only source of man's knowledge of how to obtain and maintain Christian civil liberty, and history shows that according to the degree the Bible has been received by the individual and its contents related to all aspects of his life, has Christian civil freedom risen or declined.

To learn of salvation through Jesus Christ, and how to live the Christian life, the Bible must be opened to the individual. Therefore the *history of the Bible* in the hands of the individual is the *history of Christian civil government*. Also, because the church is the assembly or congregation of believers, whatever is reasoned from Scripture regarding church polity or government, is the precursor of civil polity or government. Thus it also can be said that the *history of church government* is the *history of Christian civil government*.

When John Wycliffe began to translate the Bible into English in 1356, he started with the Book of Revelation because he thought its contents might be of help to the people of England at that time, suffering as they were from plagues and riots. (q.v. p. 3) By 1382, he had translated the whole Bible out of Latin into English, thus becoming "the first to conceive the great idea of a translation of the whole Bible, and that for the use of the whole people."* Prior to the middle of the fourteenth century, none of the translating work with the Bible in England was "designed to make the Word of God accessible to the mass of the people, and to spread scriptural knowledge among them. The only object which was kept in view was partly to furnish aid to the clergy and to render service to the educated class." (ibid.)

But God gave Wycliffe not only the vision and ability to translate His Word into English for all the people, but He gave him the vision of the relation of the Bible to all spheres of the individual's life. As Dr. Lechler says, "Not merely in the ecclesiastical sphere and in that of religion and morals, but in the whole circle of human existence, including civil life and the State, all law, according to Wycliffe, ought to order itself

---

* *John Wycliffe*, by Professor Lechler, 1904 edition p. 230ff.

according to the law of God. Every action, every charitable deed, buying, exchange, etc., is only so far right and good as the action is in accord with the Evangelical Law; and in so far as it departs from that law, it is to the same extent wrong and invalid. Yea, he goes so far as to assert that the whole code of civil law ought to be grounded upon the Evangelical Law as a Divine Rule." (ibid.)

Consider and ponder the human events which take place when *one individual* recognizes the importance of the Bible in the hands of the individual! For down to the middle of the fourteenth century the individual was separated from the Word of God, but when Wycliffe not only saw the importance of the individual having his own Bible but began to do something about it in spite of the danger to his life, God honored him, and within forty years a translation of the whole Bible had been executed with the design of becoming available to all.

Summarily, the Bible not only had to be seen as divine, and the authority for the church, but for the individual's salvation and sufficient for every phase of his life.

Almost immediately following Wycliffe's translation of the whole Bible, God began to call forth men to develop the many scientific and economic fields which would be necessary to enable man to sail the seas, explore, and finally settle the lands across the vast Atlantic ocean. With the correlation so plain and easily documented between the Bible being made available to the individual in England, and the almost sudden development of basic inventions necessary for sailing the seas, and colonizing America, it is strange this is not better known by American Christians who have so dramatically benefitted thereby. (q.v. p. 48) God had been reserving the land we know as the original thirteen colonies to begin establishing the Christian form of civil government, until there could be a handful of "peculiar people" properly rooted and grounded in His Word.

Over a hundred years ago the importance of the Bible to mankind's progress was recognized, for we find Robert Winthrop saying in 1866, the jubilee of the American Bible Society, "Beyond all doubt, my friends, we are dealing here today with the great enginery of the world's progress, with the greatest of all instrumentalities for social advancement as well as for individual salvation." (q.v. p. 20) And during our nation's centenary celebrations we find a member of the clergy, Rev. Samuel Foljambe, reminding the lawmakers of Massachusetts of *The Hand of God in American History* when he says in the Election Sermon of that year: "Observe the hand of God in the wise and beneficent timing of events in the dawn of our history. The events of history are not accidents. There are no accidents in the lives of men or of nations. We may go back to the underlying cause of every event, and discover in each God's overruling and intervening wisdom. . . . Neither social order, moral progress, nor a Christian civilization can spring out of chance. . . . God's hand is seen in the starting, speeding, retarding, and matching such coincident and colliding influences as mark the progress and constitute the varied crises of history." (q.v. p. 46) But since 1876 we find less recognition given to the Bible as the source of America's governmental, economic, social and cultural principles. And as we reach the two hundredth anniversary of America's Declaration of Independence, we find American Christians have almost forgotten that the Bible was and is the only source of their external civil freedom. America and the world are suffering from the consequences of this ignorance.

CHRISTIANITY AND CIVIL GOVERNMENT

Christians sometimes have difficulty with the subject of America's Christian history and civil government, for it seems to them they are being asked to yoke together that which should not be yoked. They have assumed that external separation of church and state, which the United States enjoys, means the separation of Christian principles from our civil government, rather than believing as did our founding fathers, that our civil government is predicated upon, and inseparable from Christian principles. For Noah Webster writes: "the moral principles and precepts contained in the scriptures ought to form the basis of all our civil constitutions and laws. These principles and precepts have truth, immutable truth, for their foundation; and they are adapted to the wants of men in every condition of life. They are the best principles and precepts because they are exactly adapted to secure the practice of universal justice and kindness among men; and of course to prevent crimes, war, and disorders in society. No human laws dictated by different principles from those in the gospel, can ever secure these objects. All the miseries and evils which men suffer from vice, crime, ambition, injustice, oppression, slavery, and war, proceed from their despising or neglecting the precepts contained in the Bible." (q.v. 256)

Civil government is not an entity in the sense of being an individual capable of producing goods and services. Rather, *civil government is the flow of power and force in society.* The structure or form of civil government, i.e., legislative, judicial and executive, is only the means by which *power and force* operate. Of primary concern to the American Christian is the understanding of the *source and quality* of this *power and force,* and how civil government is to be used so as not to negate Biblical precepts and principles.

Government, i.e. *power and force,* has two spheres of operation—the INTERNAL and the EXTERNAL. In the former the *power and force* is called individual self-government, in the latter, civil government. Christians know that the internal sphere is causative to the external, for does not our Lord so instruct us when He says, "A good man out of the good treasure of the heart bringeth forth good things: and the evil man out of the evil treasure bringeth forth evil things" (Matt. 12:35). This statement of our Lord not only describes the term government, the flow of power or force, but tells us where the source and quality of this force or power resides—in the heart of the individual. Natural man, because of his evil nature, cannot bring forth good government, good flow of power and force. Only through Christ in the lives of citizens can this "treasure" be good, and bring forth "good things"—i.e. good government, *good flow of power* predicated upon God's Word and subject to God's Law of Liberty.

As has been stated, the heart of the individual is the source of power for good or evil in a nation's civil government. The quality of the individual's heart for good or for evil, is dependent upon whether or not he accepts the *sovereignty of God* in his life, or whether he chooses the *sovereignty of man.* The "sovereignty of the people," therefore, the source and quality of force and power, i.e. government, is only as good as their acceptance of the sovereignty of God.

Appropos of this discussion of "government" and "sovereignty" is the example of I Samuel 8:5,8, when the elders of Israel came to Samuel and for their own reasons, asked him to "Make us a king to judge us like all the nations." In spite of the warning of the Lord through Samuel, the people insisted upon having a man to rule over them, instead of God. They wanted to be like all the pagan nations even though they knew the confiscatory action the king would take in relation to their lives and their property. "And the Lord said unto Samuel, Hearken unto the voice of the people in all that they say unto thee: for they have not rejected thee, but they have rejected me, that I should not reign over them." This action on the part of Israel began the "divine right" of kings theory of government, or the supposedly "divine right" of man to rule over man. Mankind now had no other form of civil government than the sovereignty of man over man, which lasted for almost 3000 years, from 1120 B.C. until 1620 A.D.—the arrival of the Pilgrims in America. Whatever civil rights or privileges were obtained for the individual during this 3000 year period were brought about by the sovereign, be he called king, pope, or emperor, granting such privileges as part of his prerogative.

GOD REQUIRES INDIVIDUAL PREPARATION FOR CHRISTIAN CIVIL GOVERNMENT

American Christians recognize that God provided civil government in Old Testament times by speaking directly to the nation Israel through His prophets and judges, but they have not always recognized that God has also been directing the development of civil government for the civil freedom of *all* men during the Christian era, by speaking to the heart and mind of *individual Christians.* It is sometimes argued that because America was not mentioned by name in the Bible its history is not to be considered or studied in the light of the Gospel, yet America's history begins with Genesis when God placed America where He did, separated and hidden from man by wide oceans until He was ready to reveal and use it for His Gospel purpose.

One might reasonably ask, "Why did it take so long for Christianity to work a change in civil government?" for Paul tells the Corinthians, "Therefore, if any man be in Christ he is a new creature; old things are passed away; behold, all things are become new" (II Cor. 5:17). Why wasn't there an immediate change in civil government? Why did it take the "new creature" so long to effect a new form of civil government?

Part of the answer lies in the nature of Christianity and its method of working out changes in the lives of individuals and nations when properly understood and lived. As August Neander says, speaking of Christianity in the first three centuries, "That religion which aimed nowhere to produce violent and convulsive changes from without, but led to reforms by beginning in the first place within,—whose peculiar character it was to operate positively rather than negatively,—to displace and destroy no faster than it substituted something better, might, by virtue of this its law of action, suffer many of the existing customs to remain just as they were, in their old defective forms, aiming simply to infuse into them a new spirit, in trust that this would eventually throw off the unbefitting exterior, and create all things new. . . . Yet Christianity nowhere began with outward revolutions and changes, which, in all cases where they have not been prepared from within, and are not based upon conviction, fail of their salutary ends. The new creation to which Christianity gave birth, was in all respects an inward one, from which the outward effects gradually and therefore more surely and healthfully, unfolded themselves to their full extent." (q.v. p. 18)

The other part of the answer as to why it took Christianity so long to bring about a change in civil government is because the Christian's governmental textbook—the Bible, was not actually in the individual's hands until the sixteenth century, when the small Geneva Bible became available through God's providence. As the Puritans of England studied the Scriptures they gradually changed their concept of civil as well as ecclesiastical government. They began to see the error of the centuries-old beliefs about civil government, (1) sovereignty belonging to a king by a "divine right," and, (2) the laws of the land not having to be in conformity with God's Word. They were understanding the importance of each individual in God's sight and were catching a vision of what Christian civil government might be when governor and governed agreed to bow to the sovereignty of God. They were beginning to grasp the fact that all civil laws, as well as ecclesiastical laws, were to be subject to God's Law of Liberty. The vision of Wycliffe was about to come into being, now that there was no mediary between the Word of God and the individual. The individual with his Bible opened, became the root of America's Christian form of civil government—a Christian republic. The Bible was first the means of the individual's salvation, then it became the means for reforming his life, his relation not only to God, but to his neighbor. It became the basis for reforming

church government and civil government. Finally, in America, the Bible became the political textbook for establishing, maintaining and protecting Christian civil government.

THREE FORMS OF
CHURCH GOVERNMENT

In the twentieth century we forget there once were exciting debates regarding the distinctions and merits of the three forms of ecclesiastical government—congregational, presbyterian and episcopal. (q.v. 89, 106, 159) We take for granted the three forms as if they had always existed, and were but a matter of choice. On the contrary, the Puritan movement in England was not only concerned with doctrinal matter, but very much concerned with church polity and its effect in civil government. (q.v. 91, 107, 165) The development of Christian civil government in America in the colonial period and in the formation of the American Christian Constitution, is dependent upon comprehending these three forms of church government; i.e. their arrangement of authority, representation, union, flow of power, etc., for all three forms are represented in the structure of our constitution and account for its delicate balances, and need for self-governing Christians to make it operate properly.

SERMONS OF THE CLERGY—
UNITY WITH DIVERSITY

The leadership of the clergy in articulating the Biblical principles of civil government through the Election, Artillery, Fast Day and Thanksgiving sermons, which were usually printed, gave a written source for the people to study. (q.v. 183, 191, 513, 533, 536) These sermons are unique to America, and indicate one of the distinctly Christian features of our founding period. The colonial understanding of God's principle of unity with diversity preceded and made possible the civil union we know as the United States of America. Only a Christian people can give leadership to this principle. Many Christian denominations had a part and made a contribution in bringing forth American civil freedom. (q.v. p. 170) The voluntary cooperation of individuals of various denominations working out Christian civil government, is a testimony to the power of Christ in the lives of individuals, an expression of Christian "unity of the Spirit" (Eph. 4:3).

AMERICA'S MEMORIAL TO THE HAND OF GOD IN HER HISTORY

The writings contained in this volume and those to follow are to be viewed as a memorial to the Hand of God in America's history.

The quotation from Joshua 4 regarding the Children of Israel passing over Jordan, is relevant to the Pilgrims passing over the wild north Atlantic in winter. It would not, and could not have been done without God's direction and help. "And it came to pass, when all the people were clean passed over Jordan, that the Lord spake unto Joshua, saying, Take you twelve men out of the people, out of every tribe a man, And command ye them, saying, Take you hence out of the midst of Jordan, out of the place where the priests' feet stood firm, twelve stones and ye shall carry them over with you, and leave them in the lodging place, where ye shall lodge this night. Then Joshua called the twelve men, whom he had prepared of the children of Israel, out of every tribe a man: And Joshua said unto them, Pass over before the ark of the Lord your God into the midst of Jordan, and take ye up every man of you a stone upon his shoulder, according unto the number of the tribes of the children of Israel: That this may be a sign among you, that when your children ask their fathers in time to come, saying, What mean ye by these Stones? Then ye shall answer them, That the waters of Jordan were cut off before the ark of the covenant of the Lord: when it passed over Jordan, the waters of Jordan were cut off; and these stones shall be for a memorial unto the children of Israel for ever" (Joshua 4:1-7).

Matthew Henry comments on this passage, in part, "How much soever we have to do of business for ourselves, and our families, we must not neglect or omit what we have to do for the glory of God and the serving of his honour, for that is our best business. . . . God's works of wonder ought to be kept in everlasting remembrance, and means devised for the preserving of the memorial of them."

Each of our thirteen colonies has "stones" commemorative of the Hand of God in its history. These wonderful works of God are worthy of treasuring, and God requires we take pains to do so, for we must never forget it was the Lord who directed all our country's events for His glory. Man is ever prone to forget God's works, and at this Bicentennial time American Christians should remember "His works and won-ders" in their behalf (Ps. 78:11) in the establishment of America. God would have us be able to explain to the rising generation the uniqueness of America and her form of civil government, and not fail them when they ask "What mean ye by these stones?" (q.v. 255)

As each generation of Americans arose after the establishment of our Constitution, it should have been taught what the Lord had done in bringing this nation into being. But alas! we Christians failed to do so, especially after the founding fathers were gone from this scene. As a nation we became enamoured with the fruits of freedom, and like Israel of old, began to worship other gods, and forgot God's wonderful accomplishments and benevolences, "and there arose another generation after them, which knew not the Lord, nor yet the works which he had done for Israel" (Judges 2:10).

PLYMOUTH ROCK—AMERICA'S FIRST GILGAL STONE

We should solemnly remember "all the way which the Lord thy God led thee" (Deut. 8:2), and frequently call to mind the instances of God's faithfulness and tender care of our Pilgrim forefathers as they struggled to begin in 1620 what would become 150 years later, the American Christian Republic and, governmentally speaking, turn "the world upside down" (Acts 17:6). The detailed record of their Biblical reasoning and their experience has been faithfully recorded by Governor Bradford in "Of Plimoth Plantation". This first American classic, has a miraculous survival testimony itself, and the full printed text should be in each home library, so the rising generations may know there is more to the Pilgrim story than a Thanksgiving feast. December 22 is known in Plymouth, Massachusetts as Forefathers Day, being the day the Pilgrims set foot on Plymouth Rock. Hopefully the day will come when across this broad land, the clergy will remember the birth of our nation as well as they remember the birth of our Lord. (q.v. 22, 30)

THE GREAT CONSTITUTIONAL DEBATE 1765–1775

When we consider and ponder the state of the world in 1763 at the ending of the French and Indian war, we can see how unlikely it was that twenty years later the world's greatest military and naval power would be defeated by thirteen of its colonies. God would now have a new nation appear, unique in all its formative steps. God indeed rules in the affairs of men. (q.v. 263)

It is in the ten year period of 1765-1775 when the great constitutional debate took place between England and the colonies over the matter of representation and the latter's right to control their own life, liberty and property, that we see the Hand of God guiding and preparing the American people to become a separate nation, in spite of themselves, in spite of the lack of human preparedness. God works silently, both with individuals and nations, and with infinite variety in His operations. These ten years contain the fullest expression of the American Christian philosophy of government, yet these writings have not been properly used to instruct each rising generation of Americans.

HISTORIANS MERCY WARREN AND DAVID RAMSAY

Two of the foremost authors of the time are chosen to relate the details of this period, and to show the coincidence without design of their respective narrations: Mercy Warren, of the north, and David Ramsay of the south. (q.v. 357, 423) Note how they recognize the superintending providence of God, for they knew first hand how humanly impossible it was for these colonies to suddenly become a nation. As the Christian begins to study this period, he should consider how swiftly God worked in the colonies to bring internal unity of mind and heart to support and defend God's Law of Liberty. As David Ramsay describes it, ". . . the time to part being come, the Governor of the Universe, by a secret influence on their minds, disposed them to union. From whatever cause it proceeded, it is certain, that a disposition to do, to suffer, and to accommodate, spread from breast to breast, and from colony to colony, beyond the reach of human calculation. It seemed as though one mind inspired the whole". (q.v. 478)

Consider the many acts of Parliament which were enacted against the colonies with little or no reason for doing so, except the hearts of Parliament and the king were hardened against America. As a result, the colonies had no other choice than to sadly and reluctantly defend their God-given rights under God's Law of Liberty. They were willing to obey God rather than man, no matter what it cost them. David Ramsay says, "It is probable that neither party in the beginning, intended to go this far; but by the inscruta-

ble operations of Providence, each was permitted to adopt such measures as not only rent the empire, but involved them both, with their own consent, in all the calamities of a long and bloody war" (q.v. 484)

CHRISTIAN UNITY WITH DIVERSITY

Consider again the diversity of the three million people who made up the population of the thirteen colonies. Consider the diversity from any classification, i.e. political, racial, economic, cultural or religious, and there is more evidence for disunion than union. Only God could bring about Christian civil freedom, for only God knew the hearts of men and whether or not they were ready for the responsibility of self-government. Only God knew whether there were enough Christians of such faith in God, in Christ, to follow His directions as would provide the necessary leadership for those whose faith might not be as strong. As in Old Testament times, God would use whom He pleased to accomplish His purpose, so too in the establishing of Christian civil government, God used whom He pleased to accomplish His purpose, whether their qualifications were of man's liking or not. God would have us in 1976 realize that God alone brought America into being according to His ways and means, and not man's be they ever so good. As Bishop Burnet wisely wrote when noting how God had used Henry VIII for the forwarding of the Gospel, "In sum, God's ways are a great deep; who has often showed his power and wisdom in raising up unlikely and unpromising instruments to do great services in the world; not always employing the best men in them, lest good instruments should share too deep in the praises of that, which is only due to the supreme Creator and Governor of the world: and therefore he will stain the pride of all glory, that such as glory may only glory in the Lord".*

And then, ponder the Christian character of the colonists in their being able to resist the dual nature of Satan—the roaring lion of massed force, and the subtle serpent of deception. (q.v. 208/9) As individual Christians they were able to be fired upon at Lexington, April 19, 1775, thus *not* starting an aggressive war; and in the national sense the Continental Congress patiently waited over a year before reluctantly declaring independence from England.

* *The History of the Reformation of the Church of England*, by Gilbert Burnet, D.D. Vol I, p. xix, 1829.

CONTINENTAL FAST DAY—

JULY 20, 1775

When God's people turn to him in prayer for His direction in their affairs, He guides them step by step, and fights against their enemies. Perhaps the most dramatic illustration of this fact occurred on June 12, 1775. On that day two proclamations were issued, one by General Gage, Commander-in-Chief of the British forces in America, calling for martial law in the Province of Massachusetts and singling out Samuel Adams and John Hancock for capture and trial in England; the other proclamation was by the Continental Congress meeting in Philadelphia, calling for a day of fasting and prayer. This was three days before selecting the Commander-in-Chief of the Continental Army. Both Samuel Adams and John Hancock as members of this Continental Congress were calling the nation to prayer before taking the necessary steps to defend their God-given liberties. They were appealing to the Arm of the Lord for direction, rather than relying solely upon the arm of flesh. (q.v. 508, 510), When the day selected arrived, July 20, 1775, David Ramsay describes it as follows:

"Since the fast of the Ninevites, recorded in sacred writ, perhaps there has not been one, which was more generally kept, with suitable dispositions, than that of July 20th, 1775. It was no formal service. The whole body of the people felt the importance, the weight and the danger of the unequal contest, in which they were about to engage; that every thing dear to them was at stake; and that a divine blessing only could carry them through it successfully". (q.v. 506)

Is it any wonder the colonists were eventually victorious?

ELIAS BOUDINOT ON THE
AMERICAN REVOLUTION

To illustrate how the founding fathers felt about the American Revolution, excerpts are here given from an oration delivered by Dr. Elias Boudinot, President of the Continental Congress in 1783. Dr. Boudinot gave this before the New Jersey Society of the Cincinnati on July 4, 1793.

"Having devoutly paid the sacrifice of prayer to that Almighty Being, by whose favor and mercy this day is peculiarly dedicated to the commemoration of events which fill our minds with joy and gladness, it now becomes me, in obedience to the resolutions of our Society, to aim at a further improvement of this festival, by leading your reflections to the contemplation of those special privileges which attend the happy and important situation you now enjoy among the nations of the earth.

"Is there any necessity, fellow-citizens, to spend your time in attempting to convince you of the policy and propriety of setting apart this anniversary for the purpose of remembering, with gratitude, the unexampled event of our political salvation?

"The cordial testimony you have borne to this institution for seventeen years past, supersedes the necessity of an attempt of this kind; and, indeed, if this had been the first instance of our commemorating the day, the practice of all nations, and of all ages, would have given a sanction to the measure.

"The history of the world, as well sacred as profane, bears witness to the use and importance of setting apart a day as a memorial of great events, whether of a religious or political nature.

"No sooner had the great Creator of the heavens and the earth finished his almighty work, and pronounced all very good, but He set apart (not an anniversary, or one day in a year, but) one day in seven, for the commemoration of his inimitable power in producing all things out of nothing.

"The deliverance of the children of Israel from a state of bondage to an unreasonable tyrant was perpetuated by the Paschal Lamb, and enjoining it on their posterity as an annual festival for ever, with a 'remember this day, in which ye came out of Egypt, out of the house of bondage.'

"The resurrection of the Saviour of mankind is commemorated by keeping the first day of the week, not only as a certain memorial of his first coming in a state of humiliation, but the positive evidence of his future coming in glory.

"Let us then, my friends and fellow-citizens, unite all our endeavors this day to remember with reverential gratitude to our supreme Benefactor, all the wonderful things He has done for us, in our miraculous deliverance from a second Egypt—another house of bondage. 'And thou shalt show thy son on this day, saying, this day is kept as a day of joy and gladness, because of the great things the Lord hath done for us, when we were delivered from the threatening power of an invading foe. And it shall be a sign unto thee, upon thine hand, and for a memorial between thine eyes, that the law of the Lord may be in thy mouth, for with a strong hand hast thou been delivered from thine enemies. Thou shalt therefore keep this ordinance in its season, from year to year, for ever.'

"When great events are to be produced in this our world, great exertions generally become necessary; men are therefore usually raised up with talents and powers peculiarly adapted to the purposes intended by Providence, who often, by their disinterested services and extreme sufferings, become the wonder as well as the examples of their generation.

"The obligations of mankind to these worthy characters increase in proportion to the importance of the blessings purchased by their labors.

"It is not then an unreasonable expectation which, I well know, generally prevails, that this day should be usually devoted to the perpetuating and respectfully remembering the dignified characters of those great men with whom it has been our honor to claim the intimate connection of Fellow-Citizens—men who have purchased our present joyful circumstances at the invaluable price of their blood.

"But you must also acknowledge with me, that this subject has been so fully considered, and so ably handled, by those eloquent and enlightened men who have gone before me in this honorable path, that had their superior abilities fallen to my lot, I could do but little more than repeat the substance of their observations and vary their language.

"Forgive me, yet spirits of my worthy, departed fellow-citizens! Patriots of the first magnitude whose integrity no subtle arts of bribery and corruption could successfully assail; and whose fortitude and perseverance no difficulties or dangers could intimidate! whose labors and sufferings in the common cause of our country—whose exploits in the field, and wisdom in the cabinet, I have often been witness to, during a cruel and distressing war! . . .

"Were you present to direct this day's meditations, would you not point to your scarred limbs and bleeding breasts, and loudly call upon us to reward your toils and sufferings, by forcibly inculcating and improving those patriotic principles and practices which led you to those noble achievements that secured the blessings we now enjoy?

"Yes, ye martyrs to liberty! ye band of heroes! ye once worthy compatriots and fellow-citizens! we will obey your friendly suggestion, and greatly prize that freedom and independence, purchased by your united exertions, as the most invaluable gem of our earthly crown!

"The late revolution, my respected audience, in which we this day rejoice, is big with events, that are daily unfolding themselves, and pressing in thick succession to the astonishment of a wondering world!

"It has been marked with the certain characteristic of a Divine over-ruling hand, in that it was brought about and perfected against all human reasoning, and apparently against all human hope; and that in the very moment of time when all Europe seemed ready to be plunged into commotion and distress.

"Divine Providence, throughout the government of this world, appears to have impressed many great events with the undoubted evidence of his own almighty arm. He putteth down kingdoms, and He setteth up whom He pleaseth, and it has been literally verified in us, that 'no king prevaileth by the power of his own strength.'

"The first great principle established and secured by our revolution, and which since seems to be pervading all the nations of the earth; and which should be most zeaously and carefully improved and glorified by us, is the rational equality and rights of men, as men and citizens.

"I do not mean to uphold the absurd idea charged upon us, by the enemies of this valuable principle, and which contains in it inevitable destruction to every government, 'that all men are equal, as to acquired or adventitious rights.' Men must and do continually differ in their genius, knowledge, industry, integrity, and activity.

"Their natural and moral characters—their virtues and vices—their abilities, natural and acquired—together with favorable opportunities for exertion, will always make men different among themselves, and of course create a pre-eminence and superiority one over another. But the equality and rights of men here contemplated are natural, essential and unalienable; such as the security of life, liberty, and property. These should be the firm foundation of every good government, as they will apply to all nations, at all times, and may properly be called a universal law. It is apparent that every man is born with the same right to improve the talent committed to him, for the use and benefit of society, and to be respected accordingly.

"We are all the workmanship of the same Divine hand. With our Creator, abstractly considered, there are neither kings nor subjects—masters nor servants, otherwise than stewards of his appointment, to serve each other according to our different opportunities and abilities, and of course accountable for the manner in which we perform our duty—He is no respecter of persons—He beholds all with an equal eye, and although 'order is Heaven's first law,' and He has made it essential to good government and necessary for the welfare of every community, that there should be distinctions among members of the same society, yet this difference is originally designed for the service, benefit, and best good of the whole and not for their oppression or destruction.

"It is our duty then, as a people acting on principles of universal application, to convince mankind of the truth and practicability of them, by carrying them into actual exercise, for the happiness of our fellow-men, without suffering them to be perverted to oppression or licentiousness.

"The eyes of the nations of the earth are fast opening, and the inhabitants of this globe, notwithstanding it is 1700 years since the promulgation of that invaluable precept 'Thou shalt love thy neighbor as thyself,' are but just beginning to discover their brotherhood to each other, and that all men, however different with regard to nation or color, have an essential interest in each other's welfare.

"Let it then be our peculiar constant care, and vigilant attention, to inculcate this sacred principle, and to hand it down to posterity, improved by every generous and liberal practice, that while we are rejoicing in our own political and religious privileges, we may with pleasure contemplate the happy period, when all the nations of the earth shall join in the triumph of this day, and one universal anthem of praise shall arise to the Universal Creator, in return for the general joy.

"Another essential ingredient in the happiness we enjoy as a nation, and which arises from the principles of our revolution, is the right that every people have to govern themselves in such a manner as they judge best calculated for the common benefit.

"It is a principle interwoven with our Constitution, and not one of the least blessings purchased by that glorious struggle, to the commemoration of which this day is specially devoted, that every man has a natural right to be governed by laws of his own making, either in person or by his representative; and that no authority ought justly to be exercised over him that is not derived from the people, of whom he is one.

"This fellow-citizens! is a most important practicable principle, first carried into complete execution by the United States of America.

"I tremble for the event, while I glory in the subject.

"To you, ye citizens of America! do the inhabitants of the earth look with eager attention

for the success of a measure on which their happiness and prosperity so manifestly depend.

"To use the words of a famous foreigner, 'You are become the hope of human nature, and ought to become its great example. The asylum opened in your land for the oppressed of all nations must console the earth.'

"On your virtue, patriotism, integrity, and submission to the laws of your own making, and the government of your own choice, do the hopes of men rest with prayers and supplications for a happy issue.

"Be not therefore careless, indolent, or inattentive in the exercise of any right of citizenship. Let no duty, however small or seemingly of little importance, be neglected by you.

"Ever keep in mind that it is parts that form the whole, and fractions constitute the unit. Good government generally begins in the family, and if the moral character of a people once degenerate, their political character must soon follow.

"A friendly consideration of our fellow-citizens, who by our free choice become the public servants, and manage the affairs of our common country, is but a reasonable return for their diligence and care in our service.

"The most enlightened and zealous of our public servants can do little without the exertions of private citizens to perfect what they do but form, as it were, in embryo. The highest officers of our government are but the first servants of the people, and always in their power; they have therefore a just claim to a fair and candid experiment of the plans they form and the laws they enact for the public weal. Too much should not be expected from them; they are but men and of like passions and of like infirmities with ourselves; they are liable to err, though exercising the purest motives and best abilities required for the purpose.

"Times and circumstances may change, and accidents intervene to disappoint the wisest measures. Mistaken and wicked men (who cannot live but in troubled waters) are often laboring with indefatigable zeal, which sometimes proves but too successful, to sour minds and derange the best formed systems. Plausible pretensions, censorious insinuations, are always at hand to transfer the deadly poison of jealousy, by which the best citizens may for a time be deceived.

"These considerations should lead to an attentive solicitude to keep the pure, unadulterated principles of our Constitution always in view; to be religiously careful in our choice of all public officers; and as they are again in our power at very short periods, lend not too easily a patient ear to every invidious insinuation or improbable story, but prudently mark the effects of their public measures, and judge of the tree by its fruits.

"I do not wish to discourage a constant and lively attention to the conduct of our rulers. A prudent suspicion of our public measures is a great security to a republican government; but a line should be drawn between a careful and critical examination into the principles and effects of regular systems, after a fair and candid trial, and a captious, discontented, and censorious temper, which leads to find fault with every proposition in which we have not an immediate hand; and raises obstacles to rational plans of government without waiting a fair experiment. It is generally characteristic of this disposition to find fault without proposing a better plan for consideration.

"We should not forget that our country is large and our fellow-citizens of different manners, interests, and habits; that our laws, to be right, must be equal and general; of course, the differing interest must be combined, and brotherly conciliation and forbearance continually exercised, if we will judge with propriety of those measures that respect a nation at large.

"While we thus enjoy, as a community, the blessings of the social compact in its purity, and are all endeavoring to secure the valuable privileges, purchased by the blood of thousands of our brethren, who fell in the dreadful conflict, let us also be careful to encourage and promote a liberality and benevolence of mind toward those whom they have left behind, and whose unhappy fate it has been to bear a heavier proportion of the expensive purchase in the loss of husbands, parents, or children, perhaps their only support and hope in life.

"Mankind, considered as brethren, should be dear to each other; but fellow-citizens, who have together braved the common danger—who have fought side by side—who have mingled their blood together, as it were in one rich stream—who have labored and toiled with united efforts to accomplish the same glorious end, must surely be more than brethren—it is a union cemented by blood. . . .

"If we turn our attention to the strong hope of every community, the rising generation, the world has yet enjoyed nothing equal to their advantages and future prospects.

"The road to honors, riches, usefulness, and fame in this happy country is open to all. The equality of citizens in its true sense must raise the most lively hopes, prompt the noblest exer-

tions, and secure a certainty of success to all who shall excel in the service of their country, without respect of persons.

"The meanest citizen of America educates his beloved child with a well-founded hope, that if he should become equal to the task, he may rationally aspire to the command of our armies, a place in the cabinet, or even to the filling of the presidential chair: he stands on equal ground, in regard to the first honors of the state, with the richest of his fellow-citizens.

"The child of the poorest laborer, by enjoying the means of education (afforded in almost every corner of this happy land) is trained up for, and is encouraged to look forward to a share in the legislation of the Union, or of a particular State with as much confidence as the noblest subject of an established monarchy.

"This is a peculiar happiness of our highly-favored republic, among the nations of the earth, proceeding from the successful revolution in which we this day rejoice.

"Suffer me, fair daughters of New Jersey, to call on you also, in a special manner, to add your invigorating smiles to the mirth and festivity of this day. Our happiness can be but half completed if you refuse to crown the whole with your kind approbation.

"Have you not at all times, and do you not still continue to participate deeply in the multiplied blessings of our common country? Raised from the humiliating state of your sex in most other countries, you also breathe the sacred air of Freedom, and nobly unite your exertions for the general good.

"The Rights of Women are no longer strange sounds to an American ear; they are now heard as familiar terms in every part of the United States; and I devoutly hope that the day is not far distant when we shall find them dignifying, in a distinguishing code, the jurisprudence of the several States in the union.

"But in your domestic character, do you not also enjoy the most delightful contemplations, arising from the Revolution of Seventeen Hundred and Seventy-Six?

"Can you look on the children of your tenderest care, and reflect on the cheerful prospects opening upon them through life, without feeling the most lively emotions of gratitude for the inestimable privileges conferred on the citizens of America?—Are not your resolutions strengthened, and your endeavors redoubled, to furnish them with every qualification, both mental and personal, for the future service of a country thus rendered dear to you? But your share of the joy of this day does not rise from a single source. To whom are we more indebted for the origin of our present happiness than to your delicate and discerning sex.

"In vain did Columbus, our great founder and discoverer, after settling the principles of his sound philosophy, apply to the wise men of his country, in vain did he solicit, in strains of· the most suppliant humiliation, the different thrones of Europe, where kings considered themselves as God's vice gerents here below. Despised by the ignorant,—traduced by the malevolent—condemned by the great—laughed at by pretended philosophers—and trifled with by the arrogance of ministers and their hirelings; all his hopes, and those of a New World, had at last sunk in despair, and we this day might have mingled our fate with the slaves of the Old World had not the penetrating wisdom and persevering magnanimity of the fair but undaunted Isabella, the ornament of your sex and the jealousy of ours, saved this Western World from the oblivion of more than five thousand years. Did they employ the excess of useful treasures in this happy adventure? No! After the refusal of her husband—despising the appendages of brilliant royalty, when compared with the general mood of mankind, her enlarged mind, incapable of being confined, by the shackles of the age, found a resource in her costly jewels, which she freely offered as a pledge, to accomplish the glorious discovery of the Four Quarters of the Globe!

"To your sex, then, ladies, we are obliged to yield the palm. Had this great event depended altogether on our sex, it is not easy to guess what our united fate had been at this moment. Instead of our present agreeable employment, we might have been hewers of wood and drawers of water to some mighty Pharaoh, whose tender mercies would have been cruelty. Your right, then, my Fair Auditors, to a large portion of the general joy must be acknowledged to be of a superior kind.

"Do you, my worthy fellow-citizens of every description, wish for more lasting matter of pleasure and satisfaction in contemplating the great events brought to your minds this day? Extend, then, your views to a distant period of future time. Look forward a few years, and behold our extended forests (now a pathless wilderness) converted into fruitful fields and busy towns. Take into view the pleasing shores of our immense lakes, united to the Atlantic States by a thousand winding canals, and beautified with rising cities,

crowded with innumerable peaceful fleets, transporting the rich produce from one coast to another.

"Add to all this, what must most please every humane and benevolent mind, the ample provision thus made by the God of all flesh for the reception of the nations of the earth, flying from the tyranny and oppression of the despots of the Old World, and say, if the prophecies of ancient times are not hastening to a fulfillment, when this wilderness shall blossom as a rose—the heathen be given to the Great Redeemer, as his inheritance, and these uttermost parts of the earth for his possession.

"Who knows but the country for which we have fought and bled may hereafter become a theatre of greater events than yet have been known to mankind.

"May these invigorating prospects lead us to the exercise of every virtue, religious, moral, and political. May we be roused to a circumspect conduct—to an exact obedience to the laws of our own making—to the preservation of the spirit and principles of our truly invaluable constitution —to respect and attention to magistrates of our own choice; and, finally, by our example as well as precept, add to the real happiness of our fellowmen, and the particular glory of our common country.

"And may these great principles, in the end, become instrumental in bringing about that happy state of the world, when, from every human breast, joined by the grand chorus of the skies, shall arise with the profoundest reverence, that divinely celestial anthem of universal praise— 'Glory to God in the highest—Peace on earth— Good will towards men.' "

So spake one of our founding fathers in 1793.

REBUILDING THE FOUNDATIONS

As we consider and ponder the Christian qualities of character of the men and women who won for us our civil freedom, we can see how disappointed and grieved they would be if they could see how in two hundred years, American Christians have allowed the world's first Christian republic to drift into a socialist state. But infinitely more serious, is how we have grieved the Holy Spirit by our forgetfulness, our disinterestedness in the unique government He brought about in America for His glory.

As American Christians begin the third century and look at the world's attitude toward them, and the attitude of many of the people in our own nation, we are not presented with a very encouraging sight, yet when viewed against the backdrop of America's Christian history, the American Christians of 1976 are seen to have been given by God as unique a challenge and opportunity in relation to God's Law of Liberty as He gave to Mr. Boudinot and the other colonists 200 years ago. It is our turn to walk by faith and not by sight (II Cor. 5:7), faith to look back to what the Arm of the Lord hath done "in the ancient days, in the generations of Old", (Isa. 51:9) faith enough in Christ to know that even if America becomes surrounded by communist or pro-communist nations, they are not just against America, but are against America's God, who will not share His glory with another. America from the days of creation has been for God's glory and for His people, and if His people will be willing to learn what He has done for them in days past, repent and ask God's forgiveness for forgetting what He had done in bringing America into being, God will deal with their enemies within and without.

But God expects us to fight the good fight of faith for the Law of Liberty in the same degree as He expected the colonists to fight. We are as dependent upon God for the maintenance of individual liberty and freedom as for the actual gift of it in the first place. Satan has attempted to dispossess American Christians by causing them to forget their Christian history. Peter Force, the eminent historian and archivist writes: ". . . The same purity of motive, the same respect for lawful authority, the same opposition to tyranny, the same vigilance in detecting the first insidious approaches of despotism, the same stern resolution in resisting its progress, which made us a Nation, are equally essential, as the means of preserving those liberties our fathers bequeathed to us, and those institutions which they framed. (q.v. 250)

The colonists of two hundred years ago had the responsibility for establishing the model of Christian civil government as a testimony to the power of Christ in the life of the individual. We have the responsibility for rebuilding this model for the same purpose—as a testimony to the power of Christ in the life of the individual. The colonists were coming from darkness into light, governmentally speaking, for the first time in the history of mankind; we have the opportunity to come from darkness to light, governmentally speaking, as a result of a form of apostasy, backsliding and general falling away of American Christians who have turned their back upon, or

ignored, God's Hand in this nation and the relation of Christianity to civil government. It is not just this generation of American Christians who has done so, but this erosion has been going on since 1830 when American Christian parents turned the education of their children over to the state. America's Christian history cannot be taught by the state; God's providential care of America cannot be taught by the state. Seven or eight generations of American Christian parents have "forgat his works" (Ps. 106:13) in relation to America and her Christian form of civil government.

The rebuilding of America's Christian foundation and its superstructure of individual freedom, begins in the homes of American Christians, with the adults of this generation putting a stop to the ignorance of America's Christian history. The rebuilding does not begin in the legislative halls of our states or of the nation. God has provided us the Bicentennial period in which to begin, and this volume and those to follow are dedicated to those American Christian parents who will obey their God-given instructions, and take back the supervision of their children's education, which includes teaching the Hand of God in America's history. (q.v. 73, 213, 232)

The Pilgrims honored this Law of God, the parents concern for the welfare and education of their children, and God opened up America for them. The Patriots honored this same Law, as is seen in their regard for the proper and excellent education of their young, and God enabled them to form a new nation in accordance with His Law of Liberty. And even though American Christians have not been honoring this Law for a very long time, nevertheless, if we cease to grieve the Spirit of God in this manner, God will bless our efforts and restore America to her rightful course, for His own Glory.

America, through God's grace and providence has received the greatest expression of individual freedom and the resultant affluence the world has ever seen. And where God's grace is abundantly bestowed, there a greater responsibility is required. American Christians have more responsibility for preserving individual liberty, based upon God's Law of Liberty, than any other people on the face of the globe.

Because America's first Gilgal stone is Plymouth Rock, I am closing this explanation of *The Christian History of the American Revolution* by quoting from the Thanksgiving Sermon delivered December 22, 1775 at Plymouth, Massachusetts by Samuel Baldwin, pastor of the Church in Hanover.

"It remains that we should be unfeignedly thankful for every instance of past success; that we be patient under all fatigues and hardships, and that we, at the call of past providences, adequate to the redemption of our fathers, and favourable to us, persevere in the direct line of opposition to that tyranny, which is abominable in the sight of heaven, and destructive of the rights of mankind.

" 'Our fathers trusted in thee—they trusted in thee, and thou didst deliver them; they cried unto thee, and were delivered; they trusted in thee, and were not confounded' (Ps. 22:4–5).

"God has often appeared for this people in days of great darkness and distress. Such is our cause, so righteous in the sight of heaven, that it will, by no means become us to harbour one distrustful thought. How can we say, after such a series of favourable providences, in the midst of deserved affliction, that his mercies are clean gone, and that he will be favourable no more.

"For my own part, I must acknowledge, that I feel animated from this confidence, that our present noble struggle for our rights, and the unwearied exertions of the patriots, friends and benefactors of this country, will bring about a happy termination of all our troubles.

" 'In the morning sow thy seed, and in the evening withhold not thine hand: for thou knowest not whether shall prosper' (Eccl. 11:6). Let those who have begun well endure to the end, leaving our most important concerns with Him, who is the avenger of wrongs, in confidence that he will finally break and subdue the power of the oppressors of the earth, and of this Continent in particular.

"Should the deportment of this people be, according to the various providences of God, in every suitable expression of piety and patriotism, then might we all pray with the most raised expectation, that the petitions we asked of him should be granted.

"Return, oh Lord we beseech thee, and visit the vine which thine own right hand hath planted, and make it strong for thyself, and give peace in our day.

"Should this be the grant of heaven, the most pleasing and glorious prospect would open to our view.

"Then America and 'the desert shall rejoice and blossom as the rose, and the ransomed of the Lord shall return, and come to Zion with songs and everlasting joy upon their heads: they shall obtain joy and gladness, and sorrow and sighing shall flee away' (Isa. 35:10)".

Verna M. Hall

July 4, 1976
San Francisco, California

ANNO
DOMINI
I

ANNO   ANNO   ANNO   ANNO   ANNO
DOMINI DOMINI DOMINI DOMINI   DOMINI
1382   1556   1620   1776   1976

XXXVI

THINK ON WITH CARE

Know therefore this day, and consider it in thine heart,
that the Lord he is God in heaven above, and upon the earth beneath:
there is none else. (Deuteronomy 4:39)

Every way of a man is right in his own eyes:
but the Lord pondereth the hearts. (Proverbs 21:2)

Wherefore, holy brethren, partakers of the heavenly calling,
consider the Apostle and High Priest of our profession, Christ Jesus.
(Hebrews 3:1)

THE SCRIPTURE SAITH:

A New Testament Commentary for English Readers, Edited by Charles John Ellicott, D.D., Vols. I, III, London, 1884

"All scripture is given by inspiration of God, and is profitable for doctrine, for reproof, for correction, for instruction in righteousness: That the man of God may be perfect, throughly furnished unto all good works." (*II Timothy 3:16-17*)

It was significant, as an indication of what was ripening for the future, that the first book of the New Testament to be translated into English should have been the Revelation of St. John. The evils of the time were great. Men's minds were agitated by wild communistic dreams of a new social order, and by the false revelation of a so-called Everlasting Gospel, ascribed to the Abbot Joachim of Calabria (ob. A.D. 1202). It seemed to John Wycliffe, in A.D. 1356, that men would find the guidance which they needed in the Apocalypse, and with this accordingly he began. He soon formed, however, the wider plan of making the whole Bible accessible to his countrymen. . . .

What is the aim of this book? The answers given, though various, have much in common. We may take this as a key to its meaning: it proclaims Christ's coming and victory. But is it the victory of Christ over Paganism, or over degenerate forms of Christianity, or over some final and future antichristian power or person? The true answer appears to be, It is the victory of Christ over all wrong-thoughtedness, wrongheartedness, and wrong-spiritedness; the pictures given in the visions find their counterpart not in one age only, but gather their *full-filment* as the ages advance: the fall of Paganism is included in the visions, as the downfall of the world-power of Imperial Rome is included; but the picture-prophecy is not exhausted, and will not be till every form of evil of which Pagan and Imperial Rome, of which the wild beast and Babylon are types, has been overthrown.

"He comes" is the key. He comes when Paganism falls; He comes when brute world force is cast down; He comes when worldliness falls— He comes, and His coming is spreading ever over the world, shining more and more unto the perfect day. Clouds may gather, and make the epochs which are nearest the full day darker than those which preceded them, but still in every epoch leading up to the golden day; the line of conflict may advance and recede from time to time, but it is a triumphant battle-field which is pictured. It is thus the book of the advent and victory of Christ.

But is it a book affording false hopes? Is it an echo of the wish of the early Christian Church, or is it a revelation from Christ to the waiting and perhaps impatient Church? I believe it is the latter. . . . In it we are bidden to remember

3

that though the victory is sure, the victory is through suffering; we are shown scenes which betoken the prolonged sorrows of the faithful, the obstinate tenacity of evil, its subtle transformations, and the concealed powers by which it is sustained: we are thus, as it were, shown the world's drama from a heavenly view-point, not in continuous historical succession, but in its various essential features, it is in this dramatic —that it does not tell its story right on, but groups its episodes round convenient centres, bringing into special prominence successively the principles of God's world-government. It is thus an apocalypse unfolding in symbolical forms the characteristic features of the struggle between good and evil, when the power of the gospel enters the field; it is the revelation of the coming of Christ, because it shows not only that He will come, but that He does come; that He who has been revealed, is being revealed, and will yet be revealed. . . .

The book is thus a help and stay—not as yielding fruit to curiosity. It is not a manual of tiresome details: it is not meant to be a treasure-house of marvels for the prophetical archaeologist: it is a book of living principles. It exhibits the force and fortune of truth as it acts upon the great mass of human society: it shows the revolutions which are the result. It shows the decay of the outward form, the release of the true germ, which will spring up in better harvests. It shows us how the corn of wheat may fall and die, and so bring forth much fruit. It shows us how evermore, from first to last, Christ is with us—encouraging, consoling, warning, helping, and leading us onward through conflict to rest. . . .

CHRISTIAN WARFARE

"And there appeared a great wonder in heaven; a woman clothed with the sun, and the moon under her feet, and upon her head a crown of twelve stars; and she being with child cried, travailing in birth, and pained to be delivered.

"And there appeared another wonder in heaven; and behold a great red dragon, having seven heads and ten horns, and seven crowns upon his heads. And his tail drew the third part of the stars of heaven, and did cast them to the earth: and the dragon stood before the woman which was ready to be delivered, for to devour her child as soon as it was born.

And she brought forth a man child, who was to rule all nations with a rod of iron: and her child was caught up unto God, and to his throne. And the woman fled into the wilderness, where she hath a place prepared of God, that they should feed her there a thousand two hundred and threescore days.

And there was war in heaven: Michael and his angels fought against the dragon; and the dragon fought and his angels, and prevailed not; neither was their place found any more in heaven." (*Revelation xii: 1-8*)

Revelation XII deals with the spiritual conditions of the great war between evil and good; it disrobes the false appearances which deceive men; it makes manifest the thoughts of men's hearts; it shows that the great war is not merely a war between evil and good, but between an evil spirit and the Spirit of God: and that, therefore, the question is not only one between right and wrong conduct, but between true and false spiritual dispositions. Men look at the world, and they acknowledge a kind of conflict between evil and good; their sympathies are vaguely on the side of good; they admire much in Christianity; they are willing to think the martyred witnesses of the Church heroes; they think the reformers of past ages worthy of honour; they would not be averse to a Christianity without Christ or a Christianity without spirituality. They do not realise that the war which is raging round them is not a war between men morally good and men morally bad, but between spiritual powers, and that what the Gospel asks is not merely a moral life, but a life lived by faith in the Son of God, a life in which the spiritual dispositions are Godward and Christward.

The Apocalypse, in this set of visions, unveils the spiritual aspects of the conflict, that we may know that the issue is not between Christianity and un-Christianity, but between Christianity and anti-Christianity. Hitherto we have seen the more outward aspects of the great war. Now we are to see its hidden, secret, spiritual—yes supernatural aspects—that we may understand what immeasurably divergent and antagonistic principles are in conflict under various and specious aspects in the history of the world. . . . We see clearly and unmistakably the real issue which is being fought out, and we see the real spiritual work which the Church is designed to accomplish in the world. The motto of this section might well be, "He that is not with me is against me"— "He that gathereth not with me scattereth;" for only those who are truly with Christ will avoid falling under the yoke of one of the three enemies of Christ—the dragon and the two wild beasts animated and inspired by him. . . .

"Who is she that looketh forth as the morning, fair as the moon, clear as the sun, and terrible as an army with banners (or, the *heavenly host*)?" It is the picture of the bride, the Church. The beams of the divine glory clothe her; she has caught—like Moses—the radiance of her Lord, whose countenance was as the sun (Rev. 1:16); the moon is beneath her feet; she rises superior to all change, and lays all lesser lights of knowledge under tribute; she is crowned with a crown of twelve stars. . . .

All life dawns in anguish, according to the ancient fiat (Gen. 3:16); but this is not all. There is an anguish of the Church which Christ laid upon her; it is the law of her life that she must bring forth Christ to the world; it is not simply that she must encounter pain, but that she cannot work deliverance without knowing suffering. Thus the Apostles felt: the love of Christ constrained them; woe it would be to them if they did not preach the Gospel; necessity was laid upon them; they spoke of themselves as travailing in birth over their children till Christ was formed in them. This, then, is the picture, the Church fulfilling her destiny even in pain. The work was to bring forth Christ to men, and never to be satisfied till Christ was formed in them, *i.e.*, till the spirit of Christ, and the teaching of Christ, and the example of Christ were received, loved, and obeyed, and men transformed to the same image, even as by the Spirit of the Lord. But there was to be opposition; the enemy is on the watch to destroy the likeness of Christ wherever it was seen. . . .

The dragon stands for some dread and hostile power. . . . The dragon is the emblem of the evil spirit, the devil, the perpetual antagonist of good, the persecutor of the Church in all ages. . . . He is one, yet diverse; one, as an evil spirit; diverse, in the varieties of his power. The woman is but one: but her foe is multiform; she has one trust to keep, one work to do, and can but fulfil it in her Master's way: evil is bound by no law, regards no scruple, and exerts its power through any channel and by every means. . . .

The spirit of evil is represented as ever on the watch to destroy the first tokens of better things. . . .

There can be no doubt that this man child is Christ. . . . But the fact that this child is Christ must not cause us to limit the meaning of the vision to the efforts of the evil one to destroy the infant Jesus; for it is also the Christ in the Church which the wicked one hates: and wherever Christ dwells in any heart by faith, and wherever the preachers of the gospel in earnest travail for their Master, seek to lift up Christ, there will the foe be found, like the fowls of the air, ready to carry away the good seed. . . . The power of the vision reaches over a wider area, and forcibly reminds us that as there are irreconcileable principles at work in the world, so all these, when traced to their original forms, are the Spirit of Christ and the spirit of the devil. . . .

The Church may be as a weak, oppressed, and persecuted woman, but her faith rises up as a song from the lips of its members. . . .

As long as the evil one can be called the prince of this world: as long, that is, as the world refuses to recognise her true Prince, and pays homage to worldliness, and baseness, and falseness in heart, mind, or life, so long must the Church, in so far as she is faithful to Him who is true, dwell as an exile in the wilderness. . . .

The result of the war was the dragon's defeat. The whole power of the evil hosts failed them. There is an inherent weakness in evil; a spot which may be touched whereupon all its vaunted strength withers. So complete was the overthrow, that even their place knew them no more. . . .

WORSHIP OF BEAST-POWER

"And I stood upon the sand of the sea, and saw a beast rise up out of the sea, having seven heads and ten horns, and upon his horns ten crowns, and upon his heads the name of blasphemy." (Revelation 13:1)

"And I beheld another beast coming up out of the earth; and he had two horns like a lamb, and he spake as a dragon." (Revelation 13:11)

Revelation XIII describes the rise of two foes of Christ and His people. They are described as "wild beasts" in opposition to Him who is the Lamb. They are distinct from the dragon; yet they are inspired, as it were, by him. . . . They are forces and powers utilised by him in hostility to the cause of righteousness and truth. . . .

The wild beast is always the figure of the kingdoms of this world, i.e., the kingdoms which are founded on passion or selfishness. . . . The wild beast is a representative of all forms of world-power. . . .

We must notice the contrasts and resemblances between the wild beasts. They are both wild beasts; they both have horns; they both have a dragon-like inspiration; they both tyrannise over men; but, the second beast is less monstrous in appearance. He somewhat resembles a lamb; his power lies in deception as well as violence. Do not these features lead to the conclusion that the principles which the second wild beast supports are the same as those on which the former wild beast acted, but that he supports them with more subtlety, intelligence, and culture? . . . Because of this seductiveness, and of his efforts to support his mission with higher sanctions, in later chapters he is called the False Prophet. . . .

The advancing intelligence of the world, its increase in knowledge and wisdom, the wider diffusion of culture and thought, produce a change in the general fashion of life, but the spirit which animates society is unchanged. The second wild beast is that change which is a change of mode, but not of spirit—a change of manners, but not of heart; there is more refinement, more civilization, more mind, but it is still the world-power which is worshipped; it is the self-seeking adoration of pleasures, honours, occupations, influences which spring from earth and end in earth—the pursuit of powers which are worldly. . . .

All who use their knowledge, their culture, their wisdom, to teach men that there is nothing worthy of worship save what they can see, and touch, and taste, are acting the part of the second wild beast; and be they apostles of science, or apostles of culture, or apostles of logical immorality, or apostles of what is called materialism, if their teaching leads men to limit their worship to the visible and the tangible, they are making men worship the beast who is the adversary of the servants of the Lamb.

When men lose the sense of duty,—the will to ask, "Is it right?"—they become an easy prey to some specious deception. . . . Mere greatness, either of achievement or of miracle, is no guarantee of a good cause. The motto "Might is right" is the motto of worldliness: "Right is might" is the motto of faith, and those who hold it cannot worship the beast.

Whenever nations or peoples allow the secular spirit to breathe through all they do, they are not with Christ, they are against Him.

PRIMITIVE CHRISTIANS

To appreciate the providential wonder of the American Revolution, it is necessary for us to consider the life and times of the Primitive Christians, their character, wisdom and courage; for in truth the American Revolution begins with them. The standard of excellence they set was to be emulated by future generations, in greater and lesser degrees, as Christianity moved westward to fulfill God's purpose. The men and women who participated in the American Revolution approximate in many ways the character of those Primitive Christians.   Editor.

RELATION OF THE CHRISTIAN
CHURCH TO THE UNCHRISTIAN WORLD

If we contemplate the essential character of Christianity in its relation to the religious state of the world, we shall be at no loss to see what it was that tended on the one hand to further, and on the other to retard the progress of the christian faith. Our Saviour referred to the signs of the times as witnessing of him,—and, in like manner, this contemplation will disclose to us, in the movements of the intellectual world then going on, the signs which heralded the new and great epoch in the history of the world; and it will be clear to us that the same tendencies, which, singly and by themselves, presented the

stoutest opposition to Christianity, and most effectually debarred its entrance, must, when combined together, only serve to hasten its triumph. It was a fact grounded in the relation of Christianity to the point of attainment which the general life of humanity had then reached, that the obstacles opposing themselves to the power which was destined to the sovereignty of the world, were converted into means for its advancement. We must therefore contemplate both in their connection with each other.

What, in the first place, particularly served to make possible and to facilitate the introduction of such a religion everywhere, was its own peculiar character, as one raised above every kind of outward, sensible form, and hence capable of entering into all the existing forms of human society, since it was not its aim to found a kingdom of this world. How Christianity could adapt itself to all earthly relations, and, while it allowed men still to remain in them, yet by the new spirit which it gave them, the divine life which it breathed into them, how it was enabled to raise men above these relations, is distinctly set before us by a Christian living in the early part of the second century, who thus describes his contemporaries: "The Christians are not separated from other men by earthly abode, by language, or by customs. They dwell nowhere in cities by them-

General History of the Christian Religion and Church, by Dr. Augustus Neander, Vol. I, Boston, 1871

selves; they do not use a different language, or
affect a singular mode of life. They dwell in the
cities of the Greeks, and of the Barbarians, each
as his lot has been cast; and while they conform
to the usages of the country, in respect to dress,
food, and other things pertaining to the outward
life, they yet show a peculiarity of conduct wonderful and striking to all. They obey the existing
laws, and conquer the laws by their own living."

CONFLICT WITH UNGODLINESS

But this same loftier spirit, which could merge
itself in all the forms it found at hand, must yet,
while it coalesced with all the *purely human*
come into conflict with all the *ungodly* nature of
mankind, with whatever issued from it and was
connected with it. It announced itself as a power
aiming at the *renovation of the world;* and the
world sought to maintain itself in its old ungodly
character. While Christ came not to destroy but
to fulfil, so too he came not to bring peace upon
the earth, but the sword. Hence the necessary collision with prevailing modes of thinking and manners. Christianity could find entrance everywhere,
precisely because it was the religion of God's sovereignty in the heart, and excluded from itself
every political element; but to the fundamental
position of the old world, which Christianity was
to overthrow, belonged religion as an institution
of the State. The pagan religion, as such, was so
closely interwoven with the entire civil and social life, that whatever attacked the one, must
soon be brought into conflict also with the other.
This conflict might, in many cases at least, have
been avoided if the early Church, like that of
later times, had been inclined to accommodate itself to the world, more than the holiness of Christianity allowed, and to secularize itself, in order
to gain the world as a mass. But with the primitive Christians this was not the case; they were
much more inclined to a stern repulsion of everything that pertained to paganism, even of that
which had but a seeming connection with it, than
to any sort of lax accommodation; and assuredly
it was at that period far more wholesome, and
better adapted to preserve the purity of Christian
doctrine and of the Christian life, to go to an
extreme in the first of these ways than in the last.

And the religion which thus opposed itself to
these deep-rooted customs and modes of thinking,
which threatened to shake to the foundation what
had been established by ages of duration, came
from a people despised for the most part in the
cultivated world, and at first found readiest ad-

mission among the lower classes of society;—a
circumstance which sufficed of itself to make the
learned aristocracy of Rome and Greece look
down on such a religion with contempt. How
should they hope to find more in the shops of
mechanics, than in the schools of the philosophers!
Celsus, the first writer against Christianity, jeers
at the fact, that "wool-workers, cobblers, leather-
dressers, the most illiterate and vulgar of mankind, were zealous preachers of the gospel, and
addressed themselves, particularly in the outset,
to women and children." Of a faith which,
adapted to all stages of culture, presupposed a
like want in all, the men of this stamp had not
the remotest conception. Their standing objection against the Christians was, that they preached
only a blind faith; they should prove what they
advanced on philosophic grounds. And as Christianity had against it, on the one hand, the pride
of culture, and was placed in the same class with
all kinds of superstition; so, on the other, it
found in superstition itself, and in fanaticism, its
fiercest enemies. It had to contend no less with
the rudeness than with the cultivation of the
world. . . .

CONFLICT WITH SUPERSTITION

Quite at the beginning of the second century,
Celsus supposed he could account for the rapid
progress of Christianity, from the credulity of
the age; and referred to the multitude of magicians that were trying to deceive men by a pretended exhibition of supernatural powers, and
who with many found ready belief, creating a
great sensation for the moment, which however
soon subsided. . . . But the influence of such
people, of which the opponents of Christianity
themselves bear witness, presented a new obstacle
to its progress. It must force its way through the
ring of delusions, within which those people had
succeeded in charm-binding the minds of men,
before it could reach their consciences and hearts.
The examples of a Simon Magus, an Elymas,
an Alexander of Abonoteichos, show in what way
this class of people opposed the progress of the
gospel. It needed striking facts, addressed to the
outward sense, to bring men entangled in such
deceptive arts, out of their bewilderment to the
sober exercise of reason, and render them recep-
tive of higher spiritual impressions.

To this end served those supernatural effects,
which proceeded from the new creative power of
Christianity, and which were destined to accompany it, until it had entered completely into

the natural process of human development. The Apostle Paul appeals to such effects, witnessing of the power of the Divine Spirit which inspired his preaching, as well-known and undeniable facts, in epistles addressed to the churches which had beheld them; and the narratives in the Acts illustrate, with particular examples, the power of those effects, in first arresting the attention, and in dispelling those delusive influences . . . . The church teachers, until after the middle of the third century, appeal in language that shows the consciousness of truth, and often before the pagans themselves, to such extraordinary phenomena, as conducing to the spread of the faith; and however we may be disposed to distinguish the facts at bottom from the point of view in which they are contemplated by the narrator, we must still admit the facts themselves, and their effects on the minds of men. It remains, therefore, undeniable, that even subsequent to the Apostolic times, the spread of the gospel was advanced by such means. . . .

SUPERNATURAL INFLUENCES

The whole might of the ungodly, the destroying principle must be roused to action, when the healing power of the divine was to enter into humanity. The revelation of heavenly peace, bringing back all to harmony, must be preceded by the deep-felt inward disunion, which betrayed itself in such cases. There was no want, either among Pagans or Jews, of those who pretended to be able, by various methods,—perfuming with incense, embrocations, medicinal herbs, amulets, adjurations expressed in strange enigmatical formulas,—to expel those demoniacal powers. In every case, if they produced any effect, it was only to drive out one devil by means of another, and hence the true dominion of the demoniacal power must, by their means, have been much rather confirmed than weakened. The words which our Saviour himself spoke, in reference to such transactions, found here their appropriate application. *"He that is not with me, is against me."*

It so happens now that one who has vainly sought relief from such impostors, falls in with a devout Christian. The latter recognizes here the power of darkness, and thinks of looking for no other cause of the disease. But he is confident of this, that his Saviour has overcome that power, and that in whatsoever shape it may manifest itself, it must yield to him. In this confidence, he prays, and witnesses of him, who by his sufferings triumphed over the gates of Hell; and his

prayer, drawing down the powers of Heaven, works deeply upon the distracted nature of the sick man. Peace succeeds to the conflicts that had raged within; and led to the faith by this experience of a change in his own personal condition, he is now first delivered, in the full sense, from the dominion of evil,—thoroughly and permanently healed by the enlightening and sanctifying power of the truth; so that the evil spirit, returning back to the house, finds it no longer swept and garnished for his reception.

Of such effects, Justin Martyr witnesses, when, addressing himself to the pagans, he says: "That the kingdom of evil spirits has been destroyed by Jesus, you may, even at the present time, convince yourselves by what passes before your own eyes; for many of our people, of us Christians, have healed and still continue to heal, in every part of the world, and in your city (Rome), numbers possessed of evil spirits, such as could not be healed by other exorcists, simply by adjuring them in the name of Jesus Christ, who was crucified under Pontius Pilate." We learn from Iranaeus, that the cure of such disorders not unfrequently prepared the way for the conversion of men to Christianity; for he says, that often they who had been delivered from evil spirits attained to the faith, and united with the Church. The inward conflicts of a soul that could find no longer the satisfaction of its religious wants in what the old world had to offer, may have frequently been the occasion of such forms of disease; and by the Christian influence, the disorder was overcome in its cause, and not in its symptoms merely. . . . Origen recognizes in the miraculous powers still existing in his time, though already sensibly diminished, a proof of what served in the first times of the appearance of Christianity particularly to advance its progress. In his defence of Christianity against Celsus, he cites examples from his own experience, where he had been himself an eyewitness of the fact, how, by invocation of the name of God and of Jesus, in connection with the preaching of his history, many were healed of grievous diseases and states of insanity which had withstood all other means of the healing art. . . .

Such testimonies are full of instruction, since they make us acquainted with the manner in which conversions, at this period, were often brought about. We shall, indeed, have to trace these phenomena, not so much to a divine miraculous agency, operating from without, as to the power with which Christianity moved the spiritual life of the period. From the manner in which the divine principle of life in Christianity,

PRIMITIVE
CHRISTIANS

CONFLICT WITH
UNGODLINESS
AND
SUPERSTITION

—the new force that had come in among mankind,—and the principle of paganism came into collision with each other, extraordinary phenomena in the world of consciousness could not fail to result, through which the crisis in the religious life of individuals must pass, ere it arrived at its end.

Yet as each particular miracle, wrought by Christ, was but a single flash from the fullness of the Godhead dwelling in him, and was to operate simply to this end, that the immediate self-manifestation of this fullness might be brought nearer before the minds of men; so too are all succeeding miracles but single flashes, issuing forth from the immediate divine power of the gospel, and contributing to introduce the revelation of this itself into the religious consciousness. . . . It is this which the Apostle Paul places above all other kinds of evidence, above all particular miracles, and describes as the demonstration of the Spirit and of power. And as this divine power showed its efficacy on the inner life of the man, so it manifested itself, with an attractive force, in the outward appearance and actions of that life; and it was this, which, more than everything beside, wrought to the conversion of the heathen. . . .

CHRISTIAN HEROISM

The distinguished virtues of the Christians must have shone forth the more brightly, as contrasted with the prevailing vices; their severity of morals, sometimes even carried to excess, as opposed to the general depravation of the age; their hearty fraternal love, in contrast with that predominant selfishness which separated man from man, and rendered each distrustful of the other, insomuch that men could not comprehend the nature of Christian fellowship, nor sufficiently wonder at its fruits. "See,"—was the common remark,—"how they love one another." . . . Although a brotherly union of this sort excited suspicion in those who were used to watch everything with the jealous eye of police espionage, and several persecutions of the Christians were thereby occasioned; yet on all minds not narrowed by such habits or not abandoned to fanaticism, a quite different impression must have been produced, and the question could hardly fail to arise in them, "What is it, which can thus bind together the hearts of men, in other respects wholly strangers to one another?" In a time when civilization had degenerated to effeminacy, in a time of servile cowardice, the life-renovating en-

thusiasm, the heroism of faith, with which the Christians despised tortures and death, when the question was whether they would do what was contrary to conscience,—this heroism of the Christians did indeed strike many so forcibly as an appearance foreign to the age, that they were inclined to consider a character so well befitting the heroic days of antiquity, but not these more refined and gentle times, a matter of reproach.

But although the ordinary Roman statesmen, though the followers of a set worldly prudence, though the cool Stoic who required everywhere philosophic demonstration,—saw in the spirit with which the Christians, in testimony of their faith, went to death, nothing but blind enthusiasm; yet the confidence and the cheerfulness of these suffering, dying men, could not fail to make an impression on less hardened or less prejudiced minds, whereby they would be led to inquire more deeply into the cause, for which men could be thus impelled to sacrifice their all. Outward force could effect nothing against the inward power of divine truth; it could only operate to render the might of this truth more gloriously manifest. Hence Tertullian concludes his "Apology" with these words, addressed to the persecutors of the Christians: "All your refinements of cruelty can accomplish nothing; on the contrary, they serve as a lure to this sect. Our number increases, the more you destroy us. The blood of the Christians is the seed of a new harvest. Your philosophers, who exhort to the endurance of pain and death, make fewer disciples by their words, than the Christians by their deeds. That obstinacy, for which you reproach us, is a preceptor. For who that beholds it, is not impelled to inquire into the cause? And who, when he has inquired, does not embrace it; and when he has embraced it, does not himself wish to suffer for it?"

DIFFUSION OF CHRISTIANITY

Christianity appeared when the time was now fulfilled, that the glory of the "eternal city" must depart from her: for so long as that power still had dominion over the minds of men, and swallowed up all other interests, small place was left for that feeling of need which led men to Christianity. But when all was now becoming old and withered, which had hitherto been an object of enthusiastic love and had given a certain buoyancy to the soul, Christianity appeared, and called men from the sinking old world to a new creation, destined for eternity. . . . And the higher life which Christianity imparted, required no brilliant outward relations for the manifestation of its glory, like what had been wondered at as great in the old civic virtue. Into the midst of circumstances and situations the most cramping and depressing, this divine life could find its way, and cause its glory to shine forth in weak and despised vessels, and raise men above all that would bow them down to the earth, without their over-stepping the bounds of that earthly order, in which they considered themselves placed by an overruling providence. The slave, in his earthly relations, remained a slave still, and fulfilled all the duties of his place with far greater fidelity and conscientiousness than before; and yet he felt himself free within, showed an elevation of soul, an assurance, a power of faith and of resignation, which must have filled his master with amazement. Men in the lowest class of society, who had hitherto known nothing in religion but ceremonial rites and mythical stories, attained to a clear and confident religious conviction. The remarkable words, already quoted from Celsus, as well as many individual examples of these first Christian times, show us how often from women, who, as wives and mothers, let a spiritual light shine out in the midst of pagan corruption; how often from young men, boys and maidens; from slaves who put their masters to shame, Christianity was diffused through whole families. . . .

The great highways by which the knowledge of the gospel was to be diffused abroad, had already been opened by the intercourse of nations. The easy means of inter-communication within the vast Roman empire; the close relation between the Jews dispersed through all lands, and those at Jerusalem; the manner in which all parts of the Roman empire were linked in with the great capital of the world; the connection of the provinces with their metropolitan towns, and of the larger portions of the empire with the more considerable cities, were all circumstances favorable to this object. These cities, such as Alexandria, Antioch, Ephesus, Corinth, were centres of commercial, political and literary correspondence; and hence became also the principal seats, chosen for the propagation of the gospel, where the first preachers tarried longest. Commercial intercourse, which had served from the earliest times, not merely for the exchange of worldly goods, but also for transmitting the nobler treasures of the mind, could now be used as a means for diffusing the highest spiritual blessings.

As a general thing, Christianity at first made progress in the cities; for as it was needful, above all, to gain fixed seats for the propagation of the gospel, the first preachers, passing rapidly over the country, had to propose their message first in the cities, whence it might afterwards be more easily diffused through the country by native teachers. On the other hand, in the country, greater obstacles must necessarily have been encountered, owing to the entire rudeness, the blind superstition, and the heathen fanaticism of the people: oftentimes also to the want of a knowledge in the early preachers of the old provincial dialects; while in the towns, they could, for the most part, make themselves sufficiently well understood in the Greek or the Latin language. . . .

In the New Testament, we find accounts of the dissemination of Christianity in Syria, in Cilicia; probably also in the Parthian empire, at that time so widely extended; in Arabia; in Lesser Asia, and the countries adjacent; in Greece, and the bordering countries as far as Illyricum; in Italy. But we are greatly deficient in further and credible accounts, on this subject; the later traditions, growing out of the eagerness to trace each national church to an apostolic origin, deserve no examination. We confine ourselves to what can be safely credited. . . .

PERSECUTION OF THE CHRISTIAN CHURCH; ITS CAUSES

It is quite important to a just understanding of the nature of these persecutions, to be rightly informed, in the first place, of their causes. Many have been surprised, that the Romans, a people in other respects so tolerant, should exhibit so impatient and persecuting a spirit against the Christians; but whatever is said about the religious tolerance of the Romans, must be understood with considerable restriction. The ideas of man's universal rights, of universal religious freedom and liberty of conscience, were quite alien to the views of the whole ancient world. Nor could it be otherwise; since the idea of the state was the highest idea of ethics, and within that was included all actual realization of the highest good:—hence the development of all other goods pertaining to humanity was made dependent on this. Thus the *religious* element also was subordinated to the *political*. There were none but state religions and national gods. It was first and only Christianity that could overcome this principle of antiquity, release men from the bondage of the world, subvert particularism and the all-subjecting force of the political element, by its own generalizing Theism, by the awakened consciousness of the oneness of God's image in all, by the idea of the kingdom of God, as the highest good, comprehending all other goods in itself, which was substituted in place of the state as the realization of the highest good, whereby the state was necessitated to recognize a higher power over itself. Looked at from this point of view, which was the one actually taken by the ancient world, a defection from the religion of the state could not appear otherwise than as a crime against the state. . . .

The Roman civilian, Julius Paulus, cites, as one of the ruling principles of civil law in the Roman state, the following: "Whoever introduced new religions, the tendency and character of which were unknown, whereby the minds of men might be disturbed, should, if belonging to the higher rank, be banished; if to the lower, punished with death." It is easy to see, that Christianity, which produced so great, and to the Roman statesman so unaccountable an agitation in the minds of men, must fall into this class of *religiones novae*. We have the two points of view, under which Christianity came necessarily into collision with the laws of the state. *1. It induced Roman citizens to renounce the religion of the state, to the observance of which they were bound by the laws,—to refuse compliance with the "caerimonias Romanas". . . . 2. It introduced a new religion, not admitted by the laws of the state into the class of religiones licitae.* Hence the common taunt of the pagans against the Christians, according to Tertullian; non licet esse vos,—"you are not permitted by the laws"; and Celsus accuses them of secret compacts, contrary to the laws.

Without doubt, the Romans did exercise a certain religious toleration, but it was a toleration not to be separated from their polytheistic religious notions and their civil policy, and which, by its own nature, could not be applied to Christianity. They were in the habit of securing to the nations they had conquered, the free exercise of their own religions, inasmuch as they hoped by so doing to gain them over more completely to their interests, and also to make the gods of those nations their friends. The Romans, who were religiously inclined, attributed their sovereignty of the world to this policy of conciliating the gods of every nation. Even without the limits of their own country, individuals of these nations were allowed the free exercise of their opinions; and hence Rome, into which there was a constant influx of strangers from all quarters of the world, became the seat of every description of religion. . . .

CHRISTIANITY NOT A NATIONAL RELIGION

The case was altogether different with Christianity. Here was no ancient, national form of worship, as in all the other religions. Christianity appeared rather as a defection from a *religio licita,*—an insurrection against a venerable national faith. This is brought as a charge against the Christians, in the spirit of the prevailing mode of thinking, by Celsus. "The Jews," he says, "are a nation by themselves, and they observe the sacred institutions of their country,—whatever they may be,—and in so doing, act like other men. It is right for every people to reverence their ancient laws; but to desert them is a crime." Hence the very common taunt thrown out against the Christians that they were neither one thing, nor the other, neither Jews nor pagans, but *genus tertium.* A religion for mankind must have appeared,—as viewed from that position of antiquity according to which every nation, had its own particular religion,—a thing contrary to nature, threatening the dissolution of all existing order. The man that can believe it possible,—says Celsus,—for Greeks and Barbarians, in Asia, Europe and Lybia, to agree in one code of religious laws, must be quite void of understanding. But what had been held impossible, seemed more likely every day to be realized. It was now perceived, that Christianity steadily made progress among people of every rank, and threatened to overthrow the religion of the state, together with the constitution of civil society which seemed closely interwoven with the same. Nothing else remained, therefore, but to oppose the inward power, which men were unwilling to acknowledge, by outward force. As well the whole shape and form of the Christian worship, as the idea of a religion for mankind, stood in direct contradiction with the point of religious development hitherto attained. . . .

So Celsus calls it the countersign of a secret compact, of an invisible order, that the Christians alone would have no altars, images or temples. Again, the intimate brotherly union which prevailed among the Christians, the circumstance that every one among them, in every town where fellow-believers dwelt, immediately found friends, who were dearer to him than all the friends of this world—this was something that men could not comprehend. The Roman police were utterly unable to fathom the nature of the bond which so united the Christians with one another. The jealousy of despotism could everywhere easily see or fear political aims. To the Roman statesman, who had no conception of the rights of conscience, the unbending will, which could be forced by no fear and by no tortures to yield obedience to the laws of the state in reference to religion, to perform the prescribed ceremonies, appeared a blind obstinacy, *inflexibilis obstinatio,* as men called it. But such an unconquerable wilfulness must have presented itself to those rulers, who were accustomed to servile obedience, as something extremely dangerous. . . .

Whenever, on the anniversary of the emperor's accession to the throne, or at the celebration of a triumph, public festivals were appointed, in which all were expected to participate, the Christians alone kept away, to avoid that which was calculated to wound their religious or moral feelings, which was uncongenial with the temper of mind inspired by their faith. It cannot be denied that, in this case, many went to an extreme, and shrunk from joining even in such demonstrations of respect and of joy as contained in them nothing that was repugnant to Christian faith and decorum, because they were associated in their minds with the pagan religion and manners,—such, for example, as the illumination of their dwellings, and the decorating them with festoons of laurel. . . . The majority were far from approving such excess of zeal: but the mistake of *individuals* was easily laid to the charge of all. Hence the accusation, so dangerous in those times, of high treason, (*crimen majestatis,*) which was brought against the Christians. . . .

If the Christians were accused generally of morosely withdrawing themselves from the world and from the courtesies of civil and social life, this charge was grounded partly in the relation itself of Christianity to paganism, as that relation was present to each one's own consciousness; but in part also to a certain one-sided tendency, growing in the first place out of the development of the Christian life in its opposition to the pagan world. So the Christians were represented as men dead to the world, and useless for all affairs of life; dumb in public—loquacious among themselves; and it was asked, what would become of the business of life, if all were like them?

Of this kind were the causes by which the Roman state was moved to persecute the Christians; but all persecutions did not proceed from the state. *The Christians were often victims of the popular rage.* The populace saw in them the enemies of their gods; and this was the same thing as to have no religion at all. . . . There was, besides, no want of individuals who were ready to excite the popular rage against the Christians; priests, artisans and others, who, like Demetrius in the Acts, drew their gains from idolatry; magicians, who beheld their juggling tricks exposed; sanctimonious Cynics, who found their hypocrisy unmasked by the Christians. When, in the time of the emperor Marcus Aurelius, the magician whose life has been written by Lucian, Alexander of Abonoteichus, observed that his tricks had ceased to create any sensation in the cities, he exclaimed, "The Pontus is filled with atheists and Christians"; and called on the people to stone them, if they did not wish to draw down on themselves the anger of the gods. He would never exhibit his arts before the people, until he had first proclaimed, "If any Atheist, Christian or Epicurean has slipped in here as a spy, let him begone!" An appeal to popular violence seems, at this time, to have been considered the most convenient course, by the advocates of religion among the pagans. . . .

From these remarks on the causes of the persecutions, the conclusion is obvious, *that until Christianity had been received, by express laws of the State, into the class of lawful religions, (religiones licitae,) the Christians could not enjoy any general and certain tranquillity in the exercise of their religion; within the Roman empire they were constantly exposed to the rage of the populace and to the malice of individuals. . . .*

CHRISTIANS UNDER CLAUDIUS 41-54 A.D.

At first, the Christians were confounded with the Jews; consequently, the order issued under the emperor Claudius, in the year 53, for the banishment of the turbulent Jews, would involve the Christians also, if there were any at that time in Rome, and if Christianity made its first converts there among Jews, who continued to observe the Jewish customs. . . . Christianity meanwhile, had been continually making progress among the pagans in the Roman empire; and the worship of God, shaped according to the principles of the apostle Paul, rendered it no longer possible to mistake the Christians for a Jewish sect. . . . It was not the principles of the civil law of the empire,—it was this popular hate, which furnished the occasion for this first persecution of the Christians in Rome. But its immediate cause was something wholly accidental; and that precisely so reckless a monster as Nero must be the first persecutor of the Christians, was likewise owing immediately to a concurrence of accidental circumstances.

CHRISTIANS UNDER NERO 54-68 A.D.

Yet there was something intrinsically significant in the fact, that the individual by whom the renunciation of everything on the side of the divine and moral was most completely carried out, that the impersonation of creaturely will revolting against all higher order, must give the first impulse to the persecution of Christianity.

The moving cause which led Nero in the year 64, to vent his fury against the Christians, was originally nothing else than a wish to divert from himself the suspicion of being the author of the conflagration of Rome, and to fix the guilt on others; and as the Christians were already become objects of popular hatred, and the fanatic mob were prepared to believe them capable of any shameful crime that might be charged upon them, such an accusation, if brought against the Christians, would be most easily credited. He could make himself popular by the sufferings inflicted on a class of men hated by the people, and at the same time secure a new gratification for his satanic cruelty. All being seized whom the popular hate had stigmatized as Christians, and therefore profligate men, it might easily happen that some who were not really Christians would be included in the number.

Those arrested as Christians were now, by the emperor's commands, executed in the most cruel manner. Some were crucified; others sewn up in the skins of wild beasts and exposed to be torn in pieces by dogs; others, again, had their garments smeared over with some combustible material, and were then set on fire to illuminate the public gardens at night.

This persecution was not, indeed, in its immediate effects, a general one; but fell exclusively on the Christians in Rome, accused as the incendiaries of the city. Yet what had occurred in the capital, could not fail of being attended with serious consequences affecting the situation of the Christians,—whose religion, moreover, was an unlawful one, throughout all the provinces. . . .

CHRISTIANS UNDER DOMITIAN 81-96 A.D.

Since the despotic Domitian, who ascended the imperial throne in 81, was in the practice of encouraging informers, and of removing out of the way, under various pretexts, those persons who had excited his suspicions or his cupidity, the charge of embracing Christianity would, in this reign, be the most common one after that of high treason. In consequence of such accusations, many were condemned to death, or to the confiscation of their property and banishment to an island. . . .

CHRISTIANS UNDER NERVA 96-98 A.D.

The emperor Nerva, who assumed the government in the year 96, was by the natural justice and philanthropy of his character, an enemy to that whole system of information and sycophancy which had been the occasion of so much evil in the time of his predecessors. This of itself was favorable to the Christians, inasmuch as the crime of passing over to their religion had been one of the most common subjects of accusation. Nerva set at liberty those who had been condemned on charges of this nature, and recalled such as had been banished; he caused all the slaves and freedmen, who had appeared as accusers of their masters, to be executed. He forbade generally the accusations of slaves against their masters to be received. All this must have operated favorably on the Christians, as the complaints brought against them proceeded frequently from ill-disposed slaves. . . . Thus it is true, the complaints against the Christians must, during the short reign of Nerva, have been suspended; yet no lasting tranquillity was secured to them, since their religion was not recognized by any public act as a *religio licita;* and we may easily conceive, that if Christianity, during these few years, could be diffused without opposition, the fury of its enemies, which had been held in check, would break forth with fresh violence on this emperor's death.

CHRISTIANS UNDER TRAJAN 98-117 A.D.

These consequences ensued under the reign of Trajan, after the year 99; since this emperor, a statesman in the Roman sense, could not overlook the encroachments on all sides of a religious community so entirely repugnant in its character to the Roman spirit. . . . It is no matter of wonder considering the rapid and powerful spread of Christianity in this country, if the faith of many, who had come over to the religion during the peaceful times of Nerva, was of no such nature as to stand the trial of persecution. Sudden and extensive conversions of this kind are not apt to prove the most thorough. So was it in the present case; many who had embraced Christianity, or were on the point of embracing it, drew back at the threatening prospect of death, and the consequences of this change were visible in the increase of the numbers who participated in the public religious ceremonies. . . .

The change produced by the rescript of Trajan was this: Christianity, which hitherto had tacitly passed for an "unlawful religion," (*a religio illicita*) was now condemned as such by an *express law*. It was the emperor's design, that the Christians should be subjected only to legal trials; but the impulse had been now given to a movement to which no limits could be fixed. With the political opposition associated itself the religious, which exercises a vastly greater power on men's passions. The open war of paganism with the spiritual might that threatened its destruction was lighted up. The fanatical rage of the populace imagined it had found a point of union and support in the laws, and the Christians were laid bare to their assaults. These commenced in the first years of the government of Hadrian, who was elevated to the imperial throne in 117. . . .

ORIGEN'S REMARKS (244? A.D.)

The remarkable words of that great ecclesiastical teacher and writer,—Origen,—respecting the trials which the church had already encountered, and respecting her then external condition and future prospects, remarks; "As the Christians, who had been commanded not to defend themselves against their enemies by outward force, observed the mild and philanthropic injunctions; what they could not have gained, had they been ever so powerful, in case they had been permitted to wage war, *that* they *received* from the *God* who constantly *fought for them,* and who, from time to time, constrained to peace *those* who had arrayed themselves against the Christians and would have exterminated them from the earth; . . . while God has always prevented a war of extermination against the whole body of Christians, since it was his pleasure that they should remain, and that the whole earth should be filled with this saving and most holy doctrine. And yet, on the other hand, in order that the weaker brethren might breathe freely, delivered from their fear of death, God has taken care of the faithful, scattering, by his mere will, all the assaults of their enemies, so that neither emperor, nor governor, nor the populace, has been able to rage against them longer." In reference to his own times, he observes, "The number of the Christians, God has caused continually to increase, and some addition is made to it every day; he has, moreover, *given

them already the free exercise of their religion; although a thousand obstacles hindered the spread of the doctrines of Jesus in the world. But since it was God who willed that the doctrines of Jesus should become a blessing also to the heathen, the machinations of men against the Christians have all been turned to shame, and the more emperor, governor and the populace *have endeavored to destroy the Christians, the more powerful have they become.*" He says, that among the multitude who became Christians, might be found men of wealth and of high stations in the government, as also rich and noble women; that the teacher of a Christian church might now, indeed, obtain honor and respect, but that the contempt which he met with from others exceeded the respect which he enjoyed from his brethren in the faith. . . . He foresaw, that the persecutions had not yet come to an end, and the opinion that the decline of the state religion and the unceasing progress of Christianity was bringing calamity upon the Roman empire, would sooner or later, bring on another persecution of the Christians. . . .

Although Origen was too sensible and sagacious to place great confidence in the peaceful times which the Christian church then enjoyed, though he saw that new struggles must be undergone, yet he was firmly persuaded that the day was coming when Christianity, by virtue of its intrinsic, divine power, would come forth victorious out of them all, and gain the dominion over entire humanity. . . . The Apostle Paul describes Christianity as a power that should reach as well to Scythians as to Greeks, and impart the same divine life to both these national stocks, binding them together in one divine family; and Justin Martyr testifies that no barbarian or Nomadic race was to be found, in which prayers did not ascend to God in the name of the crucified. But the really new,—wherein we perceive the change which the onward progress of history, during the course of this century, had produced in the mode of thinking among Christians and in their anticipations of the future development of God's kingdom,—was, that Origen confidently avows the expectation that Christianity, *working outward from within,* would overcome and suppress every other religion, and gain the dominion of the world. Such an anticipation was foreign to the thoughts of the *older* teachers of the church. They could conceive of the Pagan state in no other relation than one of constant hostility to Christianity, and expected the triumph of the church only as the result of a supernatural interposition, at the second coming of Christ. . . .

PRIMITIVE
CHRISTIANS

CHRISTIANS
UNDER NERO,
DOMITIAN, NERVA
AND TRAJAN,
54–117 A.D.

ATTACKS ON CHRISTIANITY.
DEFENCE OF CHRISTIANITY
AGAINST THESE WRITINGS

While the ancient world, in order to maintain itself on its own religious foundation, was endeavoring to suppress Christianity by force, the culture of the age enlisted itself in the same cause and entered the contest with its writings. Intellectual weapons were combined with outward violence in attacking the new principle which had begun to reveal its power in human life. . . .

In the ferment which Christianity produced on its first appearance, many impure elements necessarily became mixed with it, which were destined to be expelled during the purifying process of its development. The crisis brought on by Christianity, which was to introduce a genuine healthfulness of the spiritual life, must needs call forth also some considerable degree of morbid action, as a necessary means of arriving at that ultimate healthy condition. Much that savored of a jealous and narrowly exclusive spirit, would naturally be engendered by that opposition to the world, in which the new faith must first display itself before it could furnish the world with the principle of its own renovation.

Now in order to judge rightly of these impure admixtures in their relation to the essence of Christianity, and to discern the higher element lying at the ground of them, it was necessary that Christianity itself should be studied and understood in its essential character. Whoever contemplated these phenomena from some outward position, and by the very peculiarity of this point of view found himself opposed to Christianity, would easily confound these accidents attending the process of its development, with the essential thing itself, and from his knowledge of the former, imagine that he comprehended the latter. This remark we shall have to apply to everything which wears the form of opposition to Christianity in these centuries.

Thus Lucian, fixing on certain accidental marks by which his attention had been caught, could place Christianity in the same class with the various appearances of fanaticism and boastful jugglery which he made the butt of his ridicule. When he heard of men who were said to possess the power of curing demoniacs, and of healing other diseases, he placed them down on the same list with the common vagabond exorcists and magicians. . . .

The stoic Arrian, who lived at a somewhat

earlier period than Lucian, judged of the Christians—as the emperor Marcus Aurelius had done before—strictly according to the relation of the stoic philosophy to Christianity. . . . It may be easily understood, respecting the relation of the *New Platonism* to the religious stage of development in the ancient world, and to Christianity, that while on one hand it might serve as a transition-point to the Christian faith, and a source from whence to borrow the scientific form to be used in the explanation and defence of Christian truth; so on the other, it would be the school from which the most numerous as well as the most formidable antagonists of the same religion would proceed. Perhaps the first man who felt sufficiently interested in the subject to attack Christianity in an express work, was from this school; viz. Celsus, who under the government of Marcus Aurelius, when it was attempted to extirpate Christianity by the sword, attacked it at the same time with the weapons of his witty and acute intellect. . . .

THE CHRISTIAN APOLOGISTS

These attacks on the Christian church were met, from the time of the Emperor Hadrian and onwards, by men who stood up for the defence of Christianity and of the Christians. . . . One class of them were expositions of Christian doctrine, designed for the use of enlightened Pagans generally; the other class had a more official character, as the authors advocated the cause of the Christians before emperors, or before the proconsuls and presidents of the provinces. As they could not obtain a personal hearing, it was necessary for them to speak through their writings. . . . We cannot wonder, however, that these apologies seldom or never produced their desired effect on the authorities of the state; for the latter would hardly give themselves the time, or find themselves in a suitable mood, to examine with calmness what these apologists had to advance. Even master-pieces of apologetic art, which these productions, written from the fullness of conviction, certainly were not, could, in this case, have effected nothing; for there was no possible way in which they could recommend Christianity so as to meet the *politico-religious* views of Roman statesmen. . . .

CHRISTIAN LIFE

Christianity, since it first entered into human nature, has operated wherever it has struck root, with the same divine power for sanctification; and this divine power cannot be weakened by the lapse of ages. In this respect, therefore, the period of the first appearance of Christianity could have no advantage over any of the following ages of the Christian church. There was but one peculiarity of this first period, viz. that the change wrought by Christianity, in the consciousness and life of those in whom it was produced, could not fail to be more strongly marked by the contrast it presented with what they had previously been, as pagans. . . . As the contrast of Christianity with paganism—which is none other than that of the old with the new man—was strongly marked in comparing different periods of the life of the same individual, so was it also, in comparing the Christian life with the pagan, as a whole; for the opposition now stood forth open and undisguised; since paganism needed not as yet to hide itself under any foreign guise. . . . The inducements to a mere outward Christianity that presented themselves in later times,—the worldly advantages connected with the profession of Christianity as the state religion; custom, which leads men without any special reasons or inward call in their own minds to abide by the religion of their fathers,—all this, in the period of which we treat—especially the early part of it—could effect nothing for the advantage of Christianity. . . .

PROMINENT VIRTUES OF THE CHRISTIANS

That which our Lord himself, in his last interview with his disciples, described as the test by which his disciples might always be distinguished,—as the mark of their fellowship with him and the Father in heaven, the mark of his glory dwelling in the midst of them,—namely that they loved one another,—precisely this constituted the prominent mark, plain and striking to the pagans themselves, of the first Christian fellowship. The names "brother" and "sister" which the Christians gave to each other, were not names without meaning. . . .

The care of providing for the support and maintenance of strangers, of the poor, the sick, the old, of widows and orphans, and of those in prison on account of their faith, devolved on the whole church. This was one of the main purposes for which the collection of voluntary contributions in the assemblies convened for public worship, was instituted; and the charity of individuals, moreover, led them to emulate each other in the same good work. In particular, it was con-

sidered as belonging to the office of the Christian matron to provide for the poor, for the brethren languishing in prison, to show hospitality to strangers. . . .

Nor did the active brotherly love of each community confine itself to what transpired in its own immediate circle, but extended itself also to the wants of the Christian communities in distant lands. On urgent occasions of this kind, the bishops made arrangements for special collections. They appointed fasts; so that what was saved, even by the poorest of the flock, from their daily food, might help to supply the common wants. . . .

That from which such works took the impress of a truly Christian character, was indeed nothing else than the temper—which here expresses itself—of Christian love simply following the impulse from within. This Christian character was no longer present in its purity, when the charitable action had reference to an outward end; when it was converted into a ground of merit before God, into a means for extinguishing sin. . . .

In times of public calamity, the contrast was strikingly displayed between the cowardly selfishness of the pagans and the self-sacrificing brotherly love of the Christians.

RELATION OF CHRISTIANITY TO GOVERNMENT

There were opposite sinful tendencies which Christianity taught men to avoid, and between which the development of the Christian life had to make good its way. In these times of despotism it was no rare thing to find, united with a servile spirit that gave to the creature the honor which is due to God alone,—with a slavish obedience that sprung only from fear, a contempt for the laws of the state where they bore hard on selfish interests and the restraint of fear was removed. But Christianity, by the *positive* spirit which went forth from it, secured men against both these errors. By it was rendered an obedience that had its root in the love of God and pointed ultimately to *him,*—therefore a free obedience, equally removed from the slavish fear of man on the one hand, and lawless self-will on the other. The same spirit of Christianity which inculcated obedience to man for the sake of God, taught also that God should be obeyed rather than man, that every consideration must be sacrificed, property and life despised, in all cases where human authority demanded an obedience contrary to the laws and ordinances of God. Here was displayed in the Christians that true spirit of freedom, against which despotic power could avail nothing. . . .

The principles by which men were bound to act in this case, could be easily laid down in theory, and easily deduced from the Holy Scriptures and from the nature of Christianity. Hence, in theory, all Christians were agreed; but there was some difficulty in applying these principles to particular cases, and in answering the question in every instance, how the line was to be drawn between what belonged to Caesar and what belonged to God,—between what might be considered, in reference to religion, matters of indifference, and what not. The pagan religion was, in truth, so closely interwoven with all the arrangements of civil and social life, that it was not always easy to separate and distinguish the barely civil or social from the religious element. . . .

Again, Christianity, from its nature, must pronounce sentence of condemnation against all ungodliness, but at the same time appropriate to itself all purely human relations and arrangements, consecrating and ennobling, instead of annihilating them. . . . Christianity having appeared as the *new leaven* in the *old* world,—and being destined to produce a *new creation* in an old one that had grown out of an entirely different principle of life, the question might the more readily occur; which of the already existing elements needed only to be transformed and ennobled, and which should be purged wholly away? . . .

That religion which aimed nowhere to produce violent and convulsive changes from without, but led to reforms by beginning in the first place within,—whose peculiar character it was to operate positively rather than negatively,—to displace and destroy no faster than it substituted something better, might, by virtue of this its law of action, suffer many of the existing customs to remain just as they were, in their old defective forms, aiming simply to infuse into them a new spirit, in trust that this would eventually throw off the unbefitting exterior, and create *all* things new. . . . Among those social relations which were alien to the nature of Christianity, and which Christianity found existing at the time of its first propagation, belonged *slavery*. . . . But Christianity brought about that change in the consciousness of humanity, from which a dissolution of this whole relation, though it could not be immediately effected, yet by virtue of the consequences resulting from that change, must eventually take place. This effect Christianity produced, first by the facts of which it was a witness; and next by the ideas which, by occasion of these facts, it set in circulation. . . .

Yet Christianity nowhere began with outward revolutions and changes, which, in all cases where they have not been prepared from within, and are not based upon conviction, fail of their salutary ends.

The new creation to which Christianity gave birth, was in all respects an inward one, from which the outward effects gradually, and therefore more surely and healthfully, unfolded themselves to their full extent. It gave servants first the true, inward freedom, without which the outward and earthly freedom is a mere show, and which, wherever it exists, can be cramped by no earthly bond, no earthly yoke.

THE BIBLE

An address delivered at the Annual Meeting of the Massachusetts Bible Society in Boston, May 28, 1849.

Undoubtedly, Sir, the first of all charities, the noblest of all philanthropies, is that which brings the Bible home to every fireside, which places its Divine truths within the range of every eye, and its blessed promises and consolations within the reach of every heart. All other charities should follow, and, indeed, they naturally do follow, in the train of this. . . .

Diffuse the knowledge of the Bible, and the hungry will be fed, and the naked clothed. Diffuse the knowledge of the Bible, and the stranger will be sheltered, the prisoner visited, and the sick ministered unto. Diffuse the knowledge of the Bible, and Temperance will rest upon a surer basis than any mere private pledge or public statute. Diffuse the knowledge of the Bible, and the peace of the world will be secured by more substantial safeguards than either the mutual fear, or the reciprocal interests, of princes or of people. Diffuse the knowledge of the Bible, and the day will be hastened, as it can be hastened in no other way, when every yoke shall be loosened, and every bond broken, and when there shall be no more leading into captivity. . . .

The world, which seems to outgrow succes-sively all other books, finds still in this an ever fresh adaptation to every change in its condition and every period in its history. Now, as a thousand years ago, it has lessons alike for individuals and for nations; for rulers and for people; for monarchies and for republics; for times of stability and for times of overthrow; for the rich and the poor; for the simplest and the wisest. . . .

OUR COUNTRY AND THE BIBLE

Mr. President, there is a striking coincidence of dates in the history of our country, and in the history of the Bible. You remember that it was about the year 1607, that King James the First, of blessed memory for this if for nothing else, gave it in charge to fifty or sixty of the most learned ministers of his realm, to prepare that version of the Holy Scriptures, which is now everywhere received and recognized among Protestant Christians as the Bible. This version was finally published in 1611, and it is from this event that the general diffusion of the Bible may fairly be said to date.

The Bible had, indeed, been more than once previously translated and previously printed. During the two preceding centuries, there had been Wickliff's version, and Tyndale's version, and Coverdale's version, and Cranmer's version,

Addresses and Speeches on Various Occasions, by Robert C. Winthrop, Vols. I, II, Boston, 1852

and the Geneva Bible, and the Douay Bible, and I know not what others; and they had all been more or less extensively circulated and read, in manuscript or in print, in churches and in families, sometimes under the sanction, and sometimes in defiance of the civil and spiritual authorities. . . .

It is, thus, only from the publication of the authorized and standard version of King James, that the general diffusion of the Holy Scriptures can be said to have commenced. It was then that the printed word of God "first began to have free course and to be glorified." And that, you remember, Mr. President, was the very date of the earliest settlement of these North American Colonies. It was just then, that the Cavaliers were found planting themselves at Jamestown in Virginia; and it was just then, that the Pilgrims, with the Bible in their hands, were seen flying over to Leyden, on their way to our own Plymouth Rock.

And now, Sir, it is not more true, in my judgment, that the first settlement of our country was precisely coincident in point of time, with the preparation and publication of this standard version of the Bible, than it is that our free institutions have owed their successful rise and progress thus far, and are destined to owe their continued security and improvement in time to come, to the influences which that preparation and publication could alone have produced.

The voice of experience and the voice of our own reason speak but one language on this point. Both unite in teaching us, that men may as well build their houses upon the sand and expect to see them stand, when the rains fall, and the winds blow, and the floods come, as to found free institutions upon any other basis than that morality and virtue, of which the Word of God is the only authoritative rule, and the only adequate sanction.

EITHER BY THE BIBLE, OR BY THE BAYONET

All societies of men must be governed in some way or other. The less they may have of stringent State Government, the more they must have of individual self-government. The less they rely on public law or physical force, the more they must rely on private moral restraint. Men, in a word, must necessarily be controlled, either by a power within them, or by a power without them; either by the word of God, or by the strong arm of man; either by the Bible, or by the bayonet. It may do for other countries and other govern-

ments to talk about the State supporting religion. Here, under our own free institutions, it is Religion which must support the State.

And never more loudly than at this moment have these institutions of ours called for such support. . . . Who does not perceive in all these circumstances that our country is threatened, more seriously than it ever has been before, with that moral deterioration, which has been the unfailing precursor of political downfall? And who is so bold a believer in any system of human checks and balances as to imagine, that dangers can be effectively counteracted or averted in any other way, than by bringing the mighty moral and religious influences of the Bible to bear in our defence.

GREAT ENGINERY OF THE WORLD'S PROGRESS

The Jubilee of the American Bible Society, New York, May 10, 1866.

Beyond all doubt, my friends, we are dealing here today with the great enginery of the world's progress, with the greatest of all instrumentalities for social advancement as well as for individual salvation. Personally or politically, whether as States and nations or as individual men and women, we can do without any thing, and without every thing, better than without the Bible. We could spare Homer from ancient literature; we could spare Shakespeare, and Milton, too, from modern literature; and there would still be something, there would still be much, left. But what an eclipse would be experienced, what an aching void would be felt, were there no Sermon on the Mount, no Gospel of St. John, no Psalms of David, no Prophecy of Isaiah, no Epistle to the Corinthians! Where would this world of ours have found itself by this time, had those Divine and matchless voices never been vouchsafed to us? Into what lower deeps, beyond the lowest depths which have ever yet been imagined, of superstition and sensuality, of vice and villany and barbarism, would it not have been plunged! How should we have realized in such a case the full import of that agony which one of the old prophets intended to portray in those memorable words:

"Behold, the days come that I will send a famine in the land, not a famine of bread, not a thirst for water, but of hearing the words of the Lord. And they shall wander from sea to sea, and from the north even to the east, they shall run to and

fro to seek the word of the Lord, and shall not find it!" (*Amos 8:11-12*) God in his mercy spare our own land from such a famine as that! Better were it for us to endure war, or pestilence, or any other variety of famine, than a famine of the Word of the Lord.

BANNER OF THE CROSS; AND FLAG OF OUR UNION

Anniversary Meeting of the American Sunday School Union in Boston, May 27, 1852.

Let the Banner of the Cross go forth side by side with the Flag of our Union wherever it is carried; let the Spirit of the Lord be invoked to accompany the Spirit of Liberty in its triumphant march; let the Bible be everywhere on the same shelf with the Constitution; let there be no region so remote, no valley so secluded, no wilderness so solitary or so desolate, that men shall be able to escape from the visible presence of Religion, as manifested in the observance of the Lord's Day, and in that most attractive and fascinating of all its forms,—the religious instruction of young children; let this be accomplished, and, depend upon it, the people of this country will have much less to fear for the stability of their institutions, and Congresses and Cabinets will have much less to do to preserve the Union. There will then, too, be no longer any doubt that we are "a power on earth;" a power for every purpose of promoting either the welfare of men, or the glory of God.

★   ★   ★   ★   ★

PRINCIPLES OF LIBERTY DRAWN FROM BIBLE

It is extremely important to our nation, in a political as well as religious view, that all possible authority and influence should be given to the scriptures; for these furnish the best principles of civil liberty, and the most effectual support of republican government. They teach the true principles of that equality of rights which belongs to every one of the human family, but only in consistency with a strict subordination to the magistrate and the law.

The scriptures were intended by God to be the *guide of human reason.* The Creator of man established the moral order of the Universe; knowing that *human reason,* left without a divine guide or rule of action, would fill the world with *disorder, crime and misery.* A great portion of mankind, ignorant of this guide or rejecting its authority, have verified the fact; and the history of three thousand years is a tissue of proof that human reason left to itself can neither preserve morals nor give duration to a free government. Human reason never has been, and unquestionably never will be, a match for ambition, selfishness, and other evil passions of man. On the other hand, opposed to the force of these passions, constitution and laws are generally found to be mere cobwebs and gossamer.

The principles of all genuine liberty, and of wise laws and administrations are to be drawn from the Bible and sustained by its authority. The man therefore who weakens or destroys the divine authority of that book may be accessory to all the public disorders which society is doomed to suffer.

In my view, there are two powers only which are sufficient to control men, and secure the rights of individuals and a peaceable administration; these are the *combined force of religion and law,* and the *force or fear of the bayonet.*

★

The Bible is the chief moral cause of all that is *good,* and the best corrector of all that is *evil,* in human society; the *best* book for regulating the temporal concerns of men, and the *only book* that can serve as an infallible guide to future felicity.

Noah Webster

Preface to The Holy Bible containing the Old and New Testaments, in the Common Version. With Amendments of the Language, by Noah Webster, LL.D. New Haven, 1833.

PILGRIM ANNIVERSARY THANKSGIVING SERMONS 1773, 1774

📖 *Anno Domini 1970 marked the three hundred and fiftieth anniversary of the landing of the Pilgrims at Plymouth Rock. This volume on* The Christian History of the American Revolution, *and those to follow, are dedicated to the Pilgrims of 1620, for they were chosen of God to begin the establishment of the first Christian Republic—America.*

I pray that Christians throughout our land will use the forthcoming decade to rededicate themselves to Christ and return America to the faith and walk of our Pilgrim Fathers, so that God's purpose for America can be fulfilled.   Editor.

DECEMBER 22ND, 1773

A Sermon Preached at Plymouth, December 22, 1773, by Charles Turner, A.M. Pastor in Duxbury

"Who hath despised the day of small things? For they shall rejoice, and shall see the plummet in the hand of Zerubbable, with those seven, they are the eyes of the Lord, which run to and fro through the whole earth." (Zech. 4:10)

That Isaiah should speak of Cyrus, as the person designed of God to restore the jewish captivity, and call him by name near two hundred years before he was born, is truly remarkable. It has been thought this extraordinary prophecy was shewn to Cyrus, by the prophet Daniel; which excited the Persian monarch to favor the resto-ration of the jewish ecclesiastical and civil state.

Zerubbable,* is supposed to have been grandson to Jeconiah King of Judah and the eldest surviving branch of the royal family of David; and for that reason appointed by the King of Persia, to be the first Governor of the returning Jews.

Many of the Jews had so little confidence as to the success of the enterprize, that they chose rather to continue still at Babylon, where they had formed connections, and some of them had acquired estates, than to engage themselves in it. And, of those who went up with the Governor to Jerusalem, some were not a little grieved and dispirited, when they saw the foundation of the temple, laid by Zerubbable, was so inferior to that of the first temple built by Solomon, which had been destroyed; nor could they flatter themselves, it would ever arise to any thing considerable. There was, moreover, this circumstance,

---

* He was called also, by the Chaldeans, Sheshbazzar, and so named, perhaps on occasion of his being promoted to be one of the King of Babylon's life-guards. It was an antient custom for Princes to give new names to those whom they saw fit to promote and distinguish; as appears by a number of instances in the old-testament; to which custom there may be an allusion in our Lord's promise to the church in Pergamos, that he would give to him that should overcome, a white stone, and in the stone a new name written.

whereby some might be disheartned, that the Jews, in their feeble state, were environed with malignant cunning enemies, who, by their wicked influence in the Persian court, for a long time obstructed the building of the house.

Zechariah (with Haggai, his contemporary, and engaged in the same laudable design) labored to animate the Jews, and encourage the progress of the work; particularly by the prophetical passage before us, the sense of which may be, that whoever had been heartless, concerning the success of their enterprize, in it's infancy, should have occasion of rejoicing, if their lives were spared, on seeing the temple rise into a noble finished structure, in spite of all opposition, under the conduct of Zerubbable, supported of God, and assisted by concurrent aids of the divine super-intending gracious universal providence.

The seven, here mentioned, are the seven eyes, before spoken of in this prophecy, to be engraved on the head-stone of the temple, as emblems of the Heavenly Angels, called the eyes of the Lord, which run to and fro through the whole earth, to signify, that he uses the instrumentality of Angels, in taking the providential oversight of the world, and that his care and government of the world, by their ministry, in concurrence with other methods, is universal.

The jewish temple and commonwealth could not rise without the blessing of providence. *Except the Lord build the house, they labor in vain that build it. This is the word of the Lord unto Zerubbable, saying, not by might, nor by power; but by my spirit* (my providence) *saith the Lord of hosts.*

The Governor of Judah, and his people, accompanied with those seven, the eyes of the Lord, i.e. aided by divine providence, might joyfully hope for prosperity; and that, by divine assistance, they should succeed, is the prophet's encouraging voice, in this passage of holy scripture. Similar, in their animating design and tendency, are the following expressions of this public spirited Man of God. *Who art thou oh great mountain? Before Zerubbable thou shalt become a plain; and he shall bring forth the head* (chief) *stone thereof with shoutings, crying,* GRACE! GRACE! *unto it,* in acknowledgment of it's denoting the Messiah, that great instance and dispenser of grace to the world,* in testimony of desire, that the divine gracious blessing might ever attend the temple service; and in demonstration of gratitude, for the favor of God, in prospering the work. *The hands of Zerubbable have laid the foundation of this house; his hands shall also finish it.*

When our fathers crossed the atlantic, to escape being subjected, either to the iron jaws of English civil and prelatical tyranny, or the insupportable difficulties of residing on the eastern continent; and settled in this place, to erect a temple of freedom and religion; it was indeed with them, in certain respects, a day of small things. In emigrating from England, maintaining themselves in Holland, and transporting themselves to these shores, their interest was diminished. Their numbers were small; their company, when they arrived, including every person pertaining to their families, scarcely exceeding one hundred people; and nearly one half of them, God saw fit to remove by death, within the space of a few months after their landing. Small were their accommodations of life, and means of subsistance; it was, at times, with great difficulty they could procure the essential necessaries of life. And small was their power, compared with that of their cruel Indian neighbors, and (I wish I could say less cruel) European persecutors.

But in other lights the day was great. Our ancestors are not to be represented as perfect; but while they were not rude in knowledge, and in doctrinals not inferior to the church of England, with regard to piety and virtue they in general deserve an excellent character. For the great and fearful name of God, and for the Lord's day, their veneration was truly great. They discovered a principle of strict justice, particularly towards the natives of the country.

Their willingness to communicate among themselves, resembled the spirit which prevailed in the primitive church, when no man said that ought that he possessed was his own; but they had all things common; a spirit which, in extraordinary situations, may be most highly virtuous. They were temperate.

They were full in the great protestant principles, concerning the right of private judgment, and making the word of God the only rule in religion. Their desire was to build not on human inventions, but on the foundation of the Apostles

---

* It has been supposed, that this head-stone with the seven eyes engraved on it, was designed to represent Jesus Christ, attended by angels, in the gracious care and government of the church and world. The thought may receive an illustration from Christ's being called, the stone which is become the head of the corner, and a chief corner stone, elect, precious, laid in Sion; as also, from the following words in Revelation, *And I beheld, and lo, in the midst of the throne and of the four beasts, and in the midst of the elders, stood a lamb as it had been slain, having seven horns and seven eyes, which are the seven spirits of God sent forth into all the earth.*

and Prophets, Jesus Christ himself being the chief corner stone. So far as they adopted the instructions and spirit of their excellent minister, Mr. Robinson, they were divested of bigotry, and friends to free inquiry. They were zealous advocates for religious liberty. If they have been thought, nevertheless, to have discovered a little too much asperity towards those who differed from them in religious sentiment, we may be disposed to make an apology for them, if not to justify them, in that regard, when we consider the exasperating things they had suffered; and how easy it was for them to judge, that severity was essential to their preservation, in their peculiar circumstances.

But if they deserve censure on this head, we shall be able to administer it with a better grace when we have so thoroughly studied and adopted the spirit of protestantism and charity, as not to attempt unscriptural impositions on our fellow christians.

Their design, in coming over to this inhospitable shore, was great and honorable; to enjoy for themselves and theirs, civil, and especially sacred freedom, to worship God, without molestation, agreeably to the dictates of their own consciences, to enlarge the Kings dominions, and to pave the way for the conversion of the heathen; They had "an inward zeal and great hope of laying some foundation, or making way for propagating the kingdom of Christ, to the remote ends of the earth; though they should be but as stepping stones to others;" And they came to remove their children, their posterity, from the snares, oppressions, and corruptions of the old world; which, however, have been permitted to follow them hither, like a flood of waters, cast forth out of the dragon's mouth.

Their ecclesiastical plan* was, in the main, ra-

---

*I have thought proper to insert it here, as I have taken it from Mr. Prince's Chronology, 91st 92d and 93d pages.

"As to ecclesiastical matters, they held the following articles to be agreeable to scripture and reason.

"1. That no particular church ought to consist of more members than can conveniently watch over one another, and usually meet and worship in one congregation.

"2. That every particular church of Christ is only to consist of such as appear to believe in, and obey him.

"3. That any competent number of such, when their consciences ablige them, have a right to embody into a church for their mutual edification.

"4. That this embodying is by some certain contract or covenant, either expressed or implied, though it ought to be by the former.

"5. That being embodied, they have a right of chusing all their officers.

"6. That the officers appointed by Christ for this embodied church, are in some respects of three sorts, in others but two, viz.

"(1.) Pastors or teaching elders, who have the power both of overseeing, teaching, administring the sacraments, and ruling too: and being chiefly to give themselves to studying, teaching and the spiritual care of the flock, are therefore to be maintained.

"(2.) Meer ruling elders, who are to help the pastors in overseeing and ruling; that their offices be not temporary, as among the Dutch and French churches, but continual; and being also qualified in some degree to teach, they are to teach only occasionally, through necessity, or in their pastor's absence or illness; but being not to give themselves to study or teaching, they have no need of maintenance.

That the elders of both sorts form the presbytery of overseers and rulers, which should be in every particular church; and are in scripture called sometimes presbyters or elders, sometimes bishops or overseers, sometimes guides, and sometimes rulers.

"(3.) Deacons, who are to take care of the poor and of the church's treasure; to distribute for the support of the pastor, the supply of the needy, the propagation of religion, and to minister at the Lord's table, &c.

"7. That these officers being chosen and ordained, have no lordly, arbitrary or imposing power; but can only rule and minister with the consent of the brethren; who ought not in contempt to be called the laity, but to be treated as men and brethren in Christ, not as slaves or minors.

"8. That no churches or church officers whatever, have any power over any other church or officers, to controul or impose upon them; but are all equal in their rights and privileges, and ought to be independant in the exercise and enjoyment of them.

"9. As to church administrations, they held, that baptism is a seal of the covenant of grace, and should be dispensed only to visible believers, with their unadult children; and this in primitive purity, as in the times of Christ, and his Apostles, without the sign of the cross, or any other invented ceremony; that the Lord's supper, should be received as it was at first even in Christ's immediate presence, in the table posture; that the elders should not be restrained from praying in public as well as private, according to the various occasions continually offering from the word or providence, and no set form should be imposed on any; that excommunication should be wholly spiritual, a meer rejecting the scandalous from the communion of the church in the holy sacraments, and those other spiritual privileges which are peculiar to the faithful; and that the church or it's officers have no authority to inflict any penalties of a temporal nature.

"10. And lastly, as for holy days, they were very strict for the observation of the Lord's day, in a pious memorial of the incarnation, birth, death, resurrection, ascension and benefits of Christ; as also solemn fastings and thanksgivings, as the state of providence requires; but all other times not prescribed in scripture they utterly relinquished; and as in general, they could not conceive any thing a part of Christ's religion which he has not required; they therefore renounced all human right of inventing, and much less of imposing it on others.

"These were the main principles of that scriptural and religious liberty, for which this people suffered in England, fled to Holland, traversed the ocean, and sought a dangerous retreat in these remote and savage desarts of North-America; that here they might fully enjoy them, and leave them to their last posterity."

tional and scriptural; it was noble, founded on the principles of the perfect law of liberty. Whether their choice of meer ruling elders, can be justified by the bible, may indeed be disputed.

Their dissapprobation of the established church, in respect to hierarchy discipline and ceremonies, we are fully persuaded was reasonable: their dissent, in respect to such things, was honorable. They have been reproached as being schismatics, with as much reason as England might be stigmatized as schismatical, for departing from the church of Rome; and no more. If the church of England was schismatical in leaving Rome, we could heartily wish they had carried their schism to a greater length. The punctilious tenacity, wherewith the church of England establishment is retained and upheld, appears the more surprizing when we reflect, that the worthy English reformers lamented that they could not carry the reformation to perfection, by reason of the peculiar difficulties of the times.

When we consider that Mr. Robinson, their minister, was a celebrated opposer of the Brownists; and "that the Brownists (at Amsterdam) would hardly hold communion with the people at Leyden," our ancestors, having been charged with Brownism appears wonderful.

They have been blamed as being independents; but we will forbear to censure them, on that score, at least till it is a little more clearly determined, that the plan of independency is disagreable to the christian institution.*

Their self-denials and deadness to the world, their magnanimity and perseverance in troubles, straits and dangers, at once command our admiration, and give us the highest pleasure. Let us reflect upon the hardships, and remarkably disheartening circumstances of their voyage, their being disappointed of their intended place of settlement, their being destitute of a public engagement for the security of that freedom which was so near their hearts, their landing at such a season as this, where the winters are more severe, than they, in their early years, had been inured to; without an house to screen them from the rigid inclemencies of the climate and season; all friendless strangers; not having, at that juncture, an European within hundreds of miles; but attended with natives, savage, and at certain times cruel as beasts of prey! Let us reflect upon their being

* The Rev. Mr. Cotton of Boston, in regard to Mr. Robinson's being called the author of independency, said, "That the new-testament was the author of it; and it was received in the times of purest, primitive antiquity, many hundreds of years before Mr. Robinson was born."   Vid. Prince's Chron. p. 90.

thrown, by their hardships, into a scene of mortal sickness; which did, at once, most sorrowfully diminish their number, and weaken them in comparison with their heathen neighbors: let us consider them moreover, as struggling through all these things, with such fortitude, such spirit and patience, that we can scarcely discern in them, so much as a symptom of discouragement, in their most perilous circumstances; and then let us be charmed with the power of christianity, and praise the gospel; let us adore the God of all grace, who was pleased to replenish them with such love to liberty, and posterity, such faith and hope, and, as the effect of these things, such astonishing firmness, in one of the grandest of causes. Mr. Robinson and Mr. Brewster spake with great sobriety, when they said of their church in Leyden, "It is not with us as with other men; whom small things can discourage, or small discontents cause to wish ourselves at home again." Had we generally inherited but a single portion of their spirits, we might not have suffered so. But it has happened to us, in some measure, as to the church in early ages; at first our graces were brightned by adversity; but when the country became more prosperous, we have grown corrupted.

The fortitude and heroism of our fore-fathers, when we consider them as surmounting the peculiar difficulties and perils of making the first settlement in New-England, appear with distinguished lustre; we do however, by no means intend by this, to derogate from the high praises which are justly due to the first planters of the Massachusetts Colony; we gladly acknowledge their accomplishments and merits, and with great respect and affection think on them, as brethren of our fathers, their companions in tribulation, and in the kingdom and patience of Jesus Christ.

In regard to wonderful appearances of providence, for the preservation and success of our ancestors, it was truly a day of great things. Contrary to their own intention, they were diverted from a place where the natives were numerous to a place where they had been a few years before greatly diminished by a wasting sickness; and though the remaining numbers of the natives in the vicinity, were sufficient to have swallowed up our infant settlement, as it were in a moment; yet possibly, that God who knows the proper means for restraining the wrath of man, by such a judgment on the savages, might abate the ferocity of such of them as survived the calamity, and render them more moderate and pacifick. Providence brought them to a place, where the woods were stored with venison, and the waters happily enlivened with fish and covered with foul, things of no trivial importance to them, in their critical circumstances. Providence brought them to a place, where the soil, very near to the shore, is good, as well as of easy culture; though the circumjacent territory is poor. Providence preserved them through a long and hazardous voyage! preserved them through the extreme perils of approaching and landing upon a coast, so dangerous at this season, that sea-men who have been the longest acquainted with it, find it sufficiently perilous to come upon it at this time of the year, notwithstanding all the hospitable arms which are open for their reception immediately in case of their arrival. Providence procured them a patent from the King, when they entertained no expectation of it. When they were ready to perish, providence ever sent them seasonable supplies. Providence was their safeguard by day and by night, and effectually prevented their being destroyed by the sword of the wilderness, to which they were exposed, in getting their bread, as well as in their sleeping hours; while it equally prevented their being ruined by insidious foes,* who crept in from Europe, among themselves. And providence has, by their means, transmitted to us this fair inheritance we now enjoy; wherein we live in ease and happiness; and though it be with pain, I must say, wherein many of us live in great degrees of God-offending excess, prophanely rioting on the dearly bought fruits of our ancestor's toils, treasures and lives; and most ungratefully requiting that benign providence, which supported them, and made them the instruments of conveying to us the blessings we thus wantonly abuse. On the whole, the spiritual grace and watchful care of Heaven, in the case of our ancestors, have gained a triumph; manifesting in how gloomy scenes people may sustain spirits, and in what extreme situations they may hope Heaven will effectually interpose for the preservation of men.

* Some of the principal of these were, Lyford a minister, and a man whose name was Oldham. Their conduct resembled that of Rehum and Shimshai, Tatnai and Shethar, Boznai and their companions the Apharsachites, in old time. They secretly wrote letters to England, to subvert the immunities of the Colony. The letters were intercepted by the vigilence of Governor Bradford. Lyford, who had before made the most pious and friendly professions, and had been received into the New-Plymouth church, made, after the discovery, as affecting an acknowledgment; and by it the church was pacified. But, in a short time, he offended again in the same way; such instances of hypocrisy the world has afforded! They were both expelled. Oldham presuming to return, was remanded off; and having passed through a guard, when each man gave him a blow, with the butt-end of his musket, he was carried down to the boat, ready to receive him.

Unless we amuse ourselves with vain ideas, concerning future excellence, the day was great, as being pregnant with empire.

In a retrospection upon the spirit wherewith God was pleased to animate our fathers; their patience in the cause of God and freedom; and the singular care he was pleased to take of them; while he intended to make them the first planters of such a country as New-England; in which we their posterity live in so much felicity; and which promises to become so glorious; every little circumstance, relating to them and their adventure, seems to contract a dignity and importance, and is dwelt upon with satisfaction; we take a pleasure in imitating, annually, the simplicity of their tables; and we glory in their very infirmities and sufferings.

Let us, in the midst of these reflections, have our hearts enlarged in thanksgiving to God, for his merciful favor to our fathers, and to us by their instrumentality. Let us piously acknowledge the hand of God, in all that has been done for them and us, and to the whole, cry, grace, grace. With what strange gloom are our hearts filled, when we make the supposition, that all our fathers had been left to perish in their attempt! Proportionable to the dreadfulness of such a supposition, let our gratitude be, to our father's God and our's. And, out of gratitude to God, let us improve the blessings of life with sobriety, and maintain our liberties with an honorable christian firmness.

May we deeply imbibe the spirit of piety, charity, and liberty, wherewith our fathers were blessed, dignified and adorned; and not, like children of wantonness, for worldly trifles relinquish those privileges, which are so sacred, and were so dearly purchased! And let us exercise such good judgment, godliness, virtue, and merited filial respect to the precious honorable memory of our fore-fathers as to abhor the most distant thought of a reversion to that politico-ecclesiastical, half reformed church, oppressive as well as unscriptural, from whose cruelty they suffered such bitter things!

It ought indeed to be noticed, to the reputation of the old Plymouth Colony, that they have not relapsed to the established church, in so great a degree, as some other parts of New-England.

Our beginnings may have been thought by some, not ill-affected towards us, to be unpromising, and in certain respects inconsiderable; while we, like the Jews on their re-settlement, have been attended with persons who have treated us and our enterprize, with envenomed contempt.

But, whosoever have despised our day of small things, if they are now alive, and are enriched with a christian spirit of benevolence, may rejoice, in seeing that we, with our associates, have indulged to us by Heaven, one of the fairest prospects that ever a community was blessed with. Saith the worthy Bishop of St. Asaph,* "Perhaps the annals of history have never afforded a more grateful spectacle to a benevolent and philosophic mind, than the growth and progress of the british Colonies in North-America."

We have a sufficient extent of territory, and variety of soils and climates. Our manufactures prosper and increase in a pleasing manner, and promise to rise to the highest perfection. Agriculture is studied. Arts and sciences in general flourish. Literature, which has been journeying westward, has made at last, a welcome visit to these shores: and perhaps having performed the tour of the globe, it may here fix a more settled residence, and arise to singular perfection. There is among us a prevalent spirit of inquiry concerning the rights of the country, and a prevalent disposition to assert them; which things afford a pleasure, proportionable to the known richness of liberty, and the known destructive nature and tendency of slavery. The rapidity of our population is surprizing. Had our New-Plymouth settlers been told, that the British North-American Colonies would contain several millions of people, before their grand-children should all of them be laid in their graves,† could they have believed the information? If it should please God to allow a population for the future, in any measure similar to what is past, some of our grand-children may live to see more people in these Colonies, than are now in Europe.

As the country has been growing more populous, godliness and friendship have decayed, and iniquities have prevailed. We trust in the God of all grace, that, on the contrary, all christian and moral accomplishments, will for the future increase with our growing numbers. We chearfully hope, that all the absurd popish doctrines and wicked devices of spiritual and civil oppression

---

* In his sermon, preached before the society for the propagation of the gospel in foreign parts. Feb. 19. 1773.

† Capt. Samuel Alden, grandson to Mr. John Alden, who was one of the signers of the covenant at Cape-Cod harbor, and was, for many years, chosen an assistant in the government of New-Plymouth, is now living in Duxbury, aged 85. His father, deacon David Alden, arrived to the age of 73. And his grandfather lived 88 years. He has a sister, now living as I suppose, in Barnstable county, whose age is equal to that of her grandfather.

will fall into utter contempt; that the spirit of liberty will be perfected; and that, as there will be constant need of such a spirit, while any sons of pride, ambition and avarice remain, so it will be perpetuated; that the country will be blessed with magistrates, who shall esteem it their greatest glory and interest to excel in piety and public virtues, and in the promotion of every thing conducive to the prosperity and happiness of society; that the clergy of the land (in the judgment of some, if one of their number may say it with decency) deserving, at present, of an excellent character, will obtain the most correct understanding of the *truth as it is in Jesus,* and arrive to all the highest ministerial accomplishments; that the plummet for adjusting the line, between the power of rulers and privileges of the people, in matters civil and ecclesiastical, will be held with a steady, wise and unerring hand; and North-America rise unto the noblest structure the sun has ever beheld; and which shall be a pattern and source of instruction and happiness to the rest of mankind. I cannot prevail with myself to censure it, as vanity and enthusiasm, to form such an alotment. There is this at least in reason to countenance it, that when God has seen fit to appear for a people, for several ages, in a remarkable manner, there is a certain degree of probability, according to the known rules of analogy, that he will continue thus remarkably to favor them. When we consider Rome, as founded by a rude uncultivated collection of people; but yet, without christian principles to form and animate the patriot, arriving to such an eminent pitch of glory among the nations, we stand amazed; and ought to consider ourselves as reproached: If God will grant that North-America, shall exceed Rome in it's highest perfection, as much as our ancestry and our advantages exceed theirs, our highest expectations will be answered; and the most sanguinary wishes of the warmest patriot will be completely gratified. Imagining such happiness to be in reserve for future generations, we may be tempted to regret that we were born so soon; but that need give us no uneasiness. Inlarged with that christian spirit, whereby the disciples of Jesus possess all things, we are transported into futurity; we live with posterity; we see all their religion, virtue, catholicism, love, peace, unity, beneficence, sobriety, learning, liberty, wealth and greatness; and enjoy all their happiness.

After all, we are not to imagine that God sets before us any prospect, which may not be blasted by our irreligion and vices; any hope, but such as may be cut off, by a neglect to pursue the proper measures for the public welfare. I rejoice in all the christian piety and holiness among us; am conscious of no malevolent inclination to exaggerate the degeneracy of the times; but confess myself unable to point out a country, founded in oeconomy industry frugality and temperance, that has arrived to such a degree of luxury, in so short a time as ours. Our singularity, in this regard, may indeed be accounted for, in a great measure, by our intaminating connections; but ought to be viewed as a most melancholy threatning circumstance. In this fluctuating earthly scene, states, when by various means they have arrived to power and wealth, are by prosperity thrown into luxury; and luxury operates slavery and political death! Such is the course of this world! No doubt, late and present dispensations of providence towards us, have been designed in part, to put us in mind of such a truth, for our warning to repent and become temperate; while they were designed also, to quicken us to a laudable inquiry, into all the proper means for establishing and perpetuating our freedom and happiness. May the divine admonition be properly regarded; and oppression, which occasioned our being planted, be made, in effect, to contribute to our safety and perfection. If no additional laws are enacted, for a check to vitious extravagancies, we hope the higher ranks of people will combine to lead in the necessary reformation. And may God pour out his spirit upon his people, and his blessing on their offspring; that the inhabitants of the land may return, to be a godly virtuous temperate community; and have the singular honor among the nations, of knowing how to abound; and the glory and happiness of pursuing that on which their deliverance depends, and in which their life consisteth. Is it impossible that there should once be a people, wise enough to withstand the temptations of affluence?

We admire at the growth of our loved country: *freedom* is a thing, which, under God, has been principally instrumental of it's arriving to be what it is; and freedom must still, in the hand of God, be one of it's main pillars; or it will fall, with as great a celerity, as ever it has risen.

In a view to the edification, and permanent liberty and happiness of our land, it must be thought of the last importance, that the *youth be educated,* as in general, in the principles of *our most holy faith;* so, particularly, in that spirit of heavenly contempt of the pleasures of sin and wages of unrighteousness, and in that spirit of freedom, which christianity naturally inspires. Liberty is the happiness, and slavery the misery,

depopulation and destruction of any land. A spirit of liberty is necessary to the preservation of the thing. And the character of the world, as to a spirit of liberty, and everything else, we cannot but perceive, is ever mainly formed by *education.**

Nor is it by any means of trivial consequence, that a laudable care be taken to prevent the establishment of an episcopal hierarchy among us. As episcopacy, in the modern sense of the word, is disagreable to the gospel; so, it is to be considered, as an engine of civil, as well as ecclesiastical slavery. NO BISHOP! NO KING! was a maxim with a British Prince, whose ideas of royal power, and what we call tyranny, appear to have been the same; and who, perhaps, had no vast regard for Bishop, church or religion, farther than he thought they might be subservient to his arbitrary views. It might not be greatly amiss if, NO BISHOP, NO TYRANT! Should be ever held a sacred maxim with this people; and a proportionable vigilence be used that episcopacy may never take place in this country.†

We please ourselves in a prospect of the future greatness and happiness of our country, and devise means for perpetuating it's liberty and felicity; but when we come to think of our present political embarrassments, together with our sinfulness, our rejoicing is damped, and our hearts are filled with concern. What further calamities may be in reserve for us, God only knows; however, if we put away our sins by repentance, in conformity to

---

* In this light it may possibly appear to gentlemen of large estates and public spirit, a disposition of the surplusage of their wealth not injudiciously made, if they should found *professorships of liberty in universities.*

† When Bishops are immediately and highly dependant on the Prince, and at the same time are Lords over the rest of the clergy, the whole power and influence of the clergy is apt to be thrown into the prerogative scale; and this, when a Prince is disposed for a stretch of power, may have a most unhappy aspect on the liberties of a land.

Moreover, to prevent the appropriation and confinement of the landed interest, and posts of honor, profit and influence, to a few particular families in the country, demands the vigilence of the patriot. If such things are not prevented, honor will be too apt to alight on those for whom it is not seemly; power will be too apt to fall into the hands of those, who want the understanding or the heart to make a good use of it; there will not be proper encouragement for the geniuses, which the God of nature scatters promiscuously among the people; hope of rising will be cut off; laudable and useful emulation will be cramped: there will not be that exertion for liberty, which may be seen, where there are great numbers of freeholders in a country, who have real estates to preserve unembarrassed: bribery in elections (if any such things as elections remain) will take place more easily and successfully, than it would if the number of freeholders was very great: there will not be such a spur to in-the disciplining intention of the rod of God; if we are believing, pious, just, holy, temperate; if we wait on God with trust and prayer, and live in his fear; if we nourish that spirit of christianity, which implies the spirit of liberty and union, and will form us to such disinterested grandeur, and persevering firmness of mind, as were possessed by our fore-fathers, we may humbly hope that God, by that gracious providence which is essential to our relief and prosperity, will appear for our deliverance out of all tribulation, so that we shall not be ruined thereby; that he will make our adversities, in effect, to serve us; and cause all things to conspire for our preservation, and becoming a great and happy people! *For the eyes of the Lord run to and fro through the whole earth, to shew himself strong in the behalf of them whose heart is perfect towards him.*

In fine, might we suppose our ancestors present, raised from the dead; and all their numerous descendants, who are now living, convened in attentive silence; it is not unnatural to think, that one of the venerable sires should, in the name of the whole, address the assembly, to the following purpose. It is, our much respected offspring, parental affection, and therefore affection which is real, that has brought us from the unseen world. We heartily congratulate you, in a reflection upon all the great things which God has done for you; and (in the sense, in which our present state of happiness will admit the exercise of sympathy) we as heartily compassionate you under your present sufferings; for the exercise of which sympathetic tenderness, we are in a better capacity,

as having learnt, by bitter experiment what oppressions mean. They are not unimportant things, wherewith we are desirous to impress your hearts. You are not insensible of the arduous difficulties we were called to encounter, the sea of troubles we waded through, as advocates for Heaven-born liberty; and that some of us lost our lives in freedom's sacred cause. It was, in a great measure, for your sakes, that we thus suffered; and, in a benevolent regard to your good, we suffered cheerfully. That the church, from whose bigotry and malevolence our sufferings chiefly proceeded, is an imperfectly reformed one, constitutionally calculated to serve the cause of spiritual and civil thraldom; and that the cause of liberty is one of the noblest that can employ human attention and care, are truths, which will endure the severest, and most impartial scrutiny of all ages. Can you reflect upon such things, and with unpained hearts relapse to the established church? Or can you sell the truth, and relinquish your birth-right liberty, for such things as captivate the children of this world? With what care, with what pains, with what self-denials and sufferings, with what tender zeal, with what alotments, did we lay up for you! We know indeed that, in such a world as this, the provision made by tender industrious frugal parents, is not seldom consumed, by the riot prodigality and dissipation of their posterity; but, considering how near you live to our time, with every other circumstance that merits attention in the case, if you are found so immersed in worldly-mindedness and sensuality, so dead to a sense of the importance of liberty, and so void of all religious and virtuous principles, as to be now ripe for squandering away the inheritance which we procured for you, we must beg leave to consider it as one of the most astonishing of all events! If it might be a means of your standing fast in the cause of liberty and dissenting religion, which is the cause of God, of truth and righteousness; if it might be instrumental of your recovery from the sinfulness into which many of you are fallen; if it might be instrumental of the universal prevalence of those real regards to Christ, on which the relief and lasting good of this our loved country, and the eternal happiness of individuals, are suspended; we say it with great sincerity, that severe as our sufferings were, we should be heartily willing to suspend our present happiness, and undergo a repetition of these sufferings, or even submit ourselves to much heavier woes. With all the respect, tenderness and fidelity of the parental breast, we say, that if an effectual, speedy check, be not given to your thriving lux-

---

dustry, as where men have a prospect of obtaining good farms, for themselves and for their children: a great part of the people will be very poor, and therefore ignorant, irreligious and vicious; they will be untaught to read, or they will have but little leisure for reading the word of God, or other useful writings; they will be callous and insensible; the friendly instructions and warnings of the patriot's pen, will not reach their understandings and hearts; they will be low lived, mean spirited and servile in their tempers, and they will be slaves.

We ask leave to subjoin, that instead of endeavoring to keep the people in ignorance, and under hard bondage, under a pretence of it's being necessary for keeping them in order, and to prevent their ruining themselves; rulers, of any kind, if they would act the truely human and christian part, should strive to enlighten them as far as possible; and, leaving them in the enjoyment of their liberty, endeavor to correct their morals, and bring them to choose that respectfulness and submission to regular government, in which their interest will forever be involved.

The care that has been taken to support more public or more private schools in New-England, is high praiseworthy, and we hope there will, in time to come, be much larger room for commendation, in this respect.

ury; but the vices, which come under that general denomination, increase among you, and in the rest of the land, in time to come, as they have done for a number of years past, you may look upon your ruin as hastening on, and not extremely distant. Your effeminacy, intemperate drinking, and other sinful extravagancies, have, in late times, occasioned a scene of venality and prostration of principle, to the no small hazard of your valuable liberties! But if you will return, penitently renouncing all your sinfulness; if you will return to hope in God through Christ, and unitedly to love and fear and serve him, with the whole heart; and to exert yourselves with honor and perseverance for the public good, he will pardon your sins, and deliver and heal your land; he will raise you to singular eminence; he will give his tutelar angels charge over you, and you will be protected free and happy, in this good land, which God, in his mercy and grace, has been pleased to make us instrumental of conveying into your possession. And, if your children forsake not the gospel; but continue in God's covenant, they will be encircled with all the blessings implied in having the divine father for their God, unto all generations. Recalling to view all the wonderful things God has done for us and you, and considering the great prospects he sets before you and yours, if you reform, and you and they follow him fully and forever, we desire you, before we part, to join with us in adopting the following sacred language: *Alleluia; salvation, and glory, and honor, and power unto the Lord our God. Alleluia: for the lord God omnipotent, reigneth. Blessing, and honor, and glory, and power be unto him that sitteth upon the throne, and unto the lamb forever and ever, Amen: blessing, and glory, and wisdom, and thanksgiving, and honor and power, and might be unto our God forever and ever, Amen.* Farewel, our dear and greatly honored progeny! Most ardently wishing, that you may enjoy the best understanding of the blessed gospel, the largest communications of spiritual grace, with the Almighty protection, and all the rich blessings of divine providence. We return, earnestly desiring that you may all follow us; in due time, to that world where the wicked cease from troubling, and the weary are at rest; where, the man who sells his conscience and his country's liberty for any worldly consideration, without repentance can never come; and where they, who have lost their lives, in a well principled assertion of the cause of freedom and of God, shall find them, in so sublime a sense, as cannot be adequately expressed by mortal language, such as we are now obliged to use.

A Sermon Preached at Plymouth

*A Sermon
Preached
at Plymouth,
December 22,
1774,* by Gad
Hitchcock, A.M.
Pastor in
Pembroke

And God saw every thing that he had made, and behold, it was very good (Genesis 1:31). Deliver me from the oppression of man: So will I keep thy precepts (Psalm 119:134th ver.).

Being assembled in the house of worship, which is erected on the ruins of paganism, and *where satan's seat once was;* to commemorate the arrival of our illustrious ancestors, under the auspices of Heaven, to this new world; and to improve an event astonishing in its rise, and progress, and in every gradation and circumstance, wearing the signatures of the divine care and providence, for the purpose of raising in our breasts sentiments of piety and gratitude towards God; the two passages of sacred writ now read, though of a dissimilar nature and aspect, may not be unsuitably chosen for the foundation of our design.

My reverend brethren, who have gone before me on this occasion, having refreshed your memory with several historic facts, relative to the removal of our fore-fathers, through great impediment, and hazard, by means of the merciless rage, and cruelty of their persecutors, from England, to Holland; their first settlement at Amsterdam; afterwards at Leyden, and their return to England, with resolutions, by the will of God, to pursue their voyage, with all convenient speed, over the Atlantic, to the uncultivated regions of America; and their landing on these distant and then savage shores, in a cold and inclement season; actuated by the same principles, that at first induced them to abandon their fair inheritance in their own country, and seek an asylum from the illiberal persecuting spirit of their fellow citizens, in the more peaceful climes of a neighbouring state.

I shall not therefore risque the censure of this

grave and intelligent audience, if I excuse myself from the repetition of such interesting particulars, and invite their attention to that part of the inspired word proposed for our present consideration; which, however, I trust, will lead us to employ our minds in sentiments not altogether foreign from the intention of this anniversary.

The first passage, in accommodation to human conception and practice, represents the supreme Being, as reviewing his works, after they were finished; and being satisfied when he saw his plan compleated; and that every thing He had made, every class and order of beings, and each individual, in regard to the diversity of their rank, power, propensity and pursuits, perfectly corresponded to the original model formed in his own mind. *God saw every thing that He had made, and behold it was very good,* framed according to his purpose, and endued with every capacity, and quality, to answer the end of it's creation.

Among the works of God, man holds a place of distinguished rank, and dignity; being made in the divine Image, and invested with dominion and superiority over the rest of the creatures. "The change of phrase, and the manner of expression used, at the formation of man, it has been observed, denotes that he is the chief, and most perfect of the works of God, in this lower world."

It is beside our design to enquire particularly, what is intended by the Image of God, in which man was at first created; about which divines have held some different opinions: But as it cannot imply less than pre-eminence of nature, and vastly superior endowments both of body and mind, as well as dominion, above any of those works which God pronounced very good; we shall dismiss the consideration of other natures, and confine our attention to his.

As God designed such a creature as man should exist at the head, and as Lord of this world; having prepared the way, and provided for his regular exercise and entertainment, by the previous formation of the earth, and the great variety of things both of the animal and vegetable kind that replenish and adorn it; his almighty fiat spake him into being.

In his exalted station, he was happy in the favour and approbation of his Creator; the superior principle of reason, and moral sense with which he was endowed, rendered him capable of discharging the duties of it; and behaving with that propriety, and dignity, as should redound to the divine glory, and his own progress, and advantage.

He had a capacity to improve in natural and moral science, and perfection; his appetites and passions were controulable by the superior principles of his nature, and his propensities carried him into acts of love, gratitude and obedience towards God. By observing the law of his nature, and those positive precepts which perfect wisdom saw fit to subjoin, he was able to make high advances in moral rectitude and happiness, and continue in the smiles and benediction of his maker.

He was a moral agent, endowed as it is commonly expressed, with freedom of will, or a self-determining power, in regard to such volitions and actions as form the moral character, and beget a likeness to the divine purity, or the contrary.

Liberty was an essential principle of his constitution, a natural quality, and a necessary spring, and incentive to all virtuous improvement.

His right to use the things provided for the supply of his necessities, or convenience, was derived from the divine grant, either explicitly made, or discovered by the light of his own understanding; subject to no restraint, but the law of his nature, which was not only consistent with, but the perfection of Liberty; obligation to obey the laws of the Creator, being only a check to licentiousness, and *abuse*.

He could not reasonably desire any change in his state, or any of his circumstances, but what his progress in holiness, and in the several pious, and social affections, would to the advantage of his felicity, necessarily produce.

Had he persevered in his natural rectitude, and attachment to God, and obedience to his laws, of which he was made capable; and posterity descended from him in his own likeness; angry contentions, oppression, and cruelty which now take place, and are the sources of so much havock and misery to the human race, would not have been known in the world.

Government of some sort, adapted to the human nature and circumstances, would indeed, probably, have been instituted among them, as from many passages of scripture we have reason to think it is among the Angels themselves; but there would have been no such laws as are made for the lawless and disobedient, for the ungodly and for sinners.

It is perhaps, necessary to the order and happiness of all created intelligences, whose understanding must be limited, to have government among them; though we need not enquire, whether in regard to created spirits, who have no bodily wants to supply, it ought to be distinct from, or more positive, than the original laws of their nature? To such beings, however, it seems necessary it should, who require bodily support and convenience, and who from their situation, and condition are capable of acquiring distinct and private property. This would have been the case with man, had he continued innocent, and become numerous, as it now is in his fallen and depraved state.

Disputes might and probably would sometimes arise, in regard to personal rights and property; not, indeed, as now from the depravity of our affections, but meerly from the imperfection of knowledge; which must be settled by some known rules, or laws established by the consent of the whole; otherwise property would in some instances, remain precarious, and undetermined.

As there would however, be no evil inclination, or design in any individual, or suspicion of it in others, to invade the property, retain the rights, or check the liberty of any; and as these disputes would take place in consequence only of those errors of the memory, misapprehension and mistake to which the human mind, from its natural imbecility, tho' innocent, must be liable; they would always be issued in the most amicable manner, and to the entire satisfaction of the parties; and every one left to the free exercise of the gifts of nature, and the unmolested enjoyment of the bounties of providence.

Making daily progress in natural and moral perfection, dignity and happiness; of which in this state of things, mankind could not fail, they would proportionably fulfil, and always be fulfilling the wise and good end of their Creation.

With great propriety, therefore, might God on the review of the make of man, finding how admirably he was qualified to answer such a purpose, and to live in perpetual freedom and happiness, be represented saying, as in our text, *Behold it is very good.*

Such was the primitive state of man—happy in the divine image and favor, and in the purity and freedom of his own faculties.

But alas! how changed! what a reverse of things did he undergo at the fall! when he violated the law of his maker, given for the tryal of his fidelity and obedience, and commenced rebel against God, what forfeiture did he make of the divine presence, and favour! what a sinful nature! What irregular propensities! What strong untoward and eccentric appetites and passions were introduced into his constitution! and how by one man's disobedience were many made sinners, and brought under the condemnation of the righteous law of God!

Mankind, however, though fallen into a disordered, and perverted state, were not suffered to perish in consequence of the one transgression; but the fore-ordained grace of God counteracted the effects of it, by bringing forward a new, and happy dispensation, founded on the obedience and righteousness of Jesus Christ.

What marvellous designs of wisdom, and love had God our heavenly Father, in view, for a lost world! and how ought our hearts to be comforted, being knit together in love, and unto all riches of the full assurance of understanding, to the acknowledgement of the mystery of God, and of the Father and of Christ!

The rational faculties of the human mind, though sadly darkened, and indisposed to moral and religious performances, were not destroyed; the passions, though depraved, were not eradicated: In every idea of the soul, but its primitive purity and rectitude, there remained the essential properties of humanity; particularly the love of Liberty; which is an original passion, not meerly innocent, but requisite both before and since the fall, to all virtuous exertions, and happy enjoyments, though now extremely liable to abuse by ourselves, and restraint from our fellowmen.

In whatever view the principle of Liberty be considered, or by whatever name distinguished, whether by natural or moral, Civil or religious Liberty; it has its rise from nature; and it appears to be the will of God that mankind should possess it, in each of these senses.

Civil liberty is indeed, immediately derived from human compact, and founded on civil government; but it more properly, though remotely, proceeds from nature, as it is the voice of reason that men, for the greater security of their persons and property, and the promotion of their happiness, should form into society, and establish government among them.

Considering men as being already so formed, I shall hereafter speak of liberty chiefly as it relates to their civil and religious affairs; though it will be difficult to discourse without sometimes blending the other senses with it; which I shall not be very careful to avoid.

The beneficial improvements both of our civil and religious rights depends on liberty.

Matters that pertain to conscience, and the worship and service of God, and the preparation of our Souls for another world, are the objects of religious liberty; and those things that relate to our present security and happiness in civil government, are the objects of civil liberty.

In this manner civil and religious liberty, are

usually distinguished; but as there is a connection between those blessings which tend to our present happiness, in civil government, and those, which are necessary to lay the foundation of that which is future and eternal, and as conscience is really concerned in both; and men can no more, without offending God, and violating the laws of society, resign, or neglect the former, than the latter; these two senses of liberty seem so far to intermix, and in a sort become one.

The human mind is so framed by its wise author, as to be greatly susceptive of disadvantageous impressions in regard to its moral state and acts of worship, from the restraints of our civil liberty, which must be allowed to be an undeniable argument that such restraints are contrary to the will of God.

Of this the royal Psalmist was deeply sensible, and it gave rise to his prayer, contained in the other passage which has been read. *Deliver me from the oppression of man, so will I keep thy precepts.*

This is an experimental declaration of one who was disposed to worship God and keep his precepts, of the extream difficulty of doing so, to any considerable advantage, while deprived of civil liberty, and oppressed, and borne down, by the superior force and cruelty of lawless persecutors.

The case of our venerable New-England forefathers, who suffered so much at home, in the reign of James the first, was in many respects similar to this, and an exemplification of the truth of it.

Things did not pass well with them, either in church or state; they were treated with rigour, and denied the liberty of the Gospel, and the enjoyment of the ordinances of God in their purity, by laws and mandates from both.

Mr. Robinson's church in particular, the seed whence this church grew, and many others have since branched, "was extremely harrassed; some cast into prison, some beset in their houses, and some forced to leave their farms, and families," as has been witnessed by one, who was no small sharer in their sufferings, both in old England, and New.

And to their pious zeal, love of liberty, and magnanimity is it chiefly owing, under the smiles and guidance of providence, that the wilds of America are now so immensely occupied by civilized and christian inhabitants.

The royal Psalmist had before prayed, in the verse preceeding our text, against all inward hindrance of duty and obedience; such as arose from evil inclination, and corrupt affections, —Order my steps in thy word, says he, and let not any iniquity have dominion over me.

But sensible of another, and common temptation to transgression, and the neglect of God, he prays against this also in the text, —*Deliver me from the oppression of man; so will I keep thy precepts.*

This he considers as a great outward impediment in the way of his duty; but at the same time he was so well perswaded of the disposition of his own heart, as to think if it was but removed, and he was delivered out of the hands of them that oppressed him, he should go on in an even chearful course of obedience to the precepts of God; though under his present circumstances, from the restraint of his liberty, it was impossible for him to do it, according to his mind and conscience.

If we take into consideration the effects produced by oppression in the human mind, —the evil consequences of it to society, and the abatements of happiness it occasions to individuals; or consult the sacred oracles, and the several dispensations of God towards mankind; we shall find that it has been his design all along, to discountenance oppression in its various forms, and encourage and promote liberty in the world.

From our natural notions of the divine character, besides what we are taught by revelation, it may be argued, that the communication of happiness, in co-incidence with his own glory, was the great end proposed by God in the creation of man.

He designed we should be happy in both worlds; and accordingly by our internal frame and furniture, and outward enjoyments, we are provided with all the materials that are necessary for this purpose; we are constituted with liberty, as well to exercise and improve our rational faculties, as to make use of the blessings and liberalities of providence.

By the principle of liberty, which is the spring and animation of our rational exertions, we maintain our supremacy among the creatures of this lower world, which otherwise would annoy us; and by it we taste the sweets of the good things of life, and improve in piety and virtue, in divine and social affections, in natural and moral science, and in all those arts and accomplishments, which perfect and adorn human nature, and make men happy.

It is, however, subject to great impediment and diminution, from various causes, but from none more, except our own lusts, than the oppressions of our fellowmen.

Though the devil is the grand tyrant of mankind, yet if we resist him, he will flee from us; but the oppression of man may be so established, and triumphant, as to admit no hope, either of overcoming it by our own strength, or escaping out of its hands.

And when this is the case, it produceth the worst effects in the human mind. It breaks its force, enervates and obscures its faculties, cramps the spirits, destroys emulation, and snaps the sinews of every exalted and virtuous design.

The tempers, and dispositions of men are strangely vitiated and changed by oppression. The brave and enterprising grow irresolute and spiritless—the social and human, turn sullen, unfeeling and vicious—the wicked pass on to higher degrees of enormity, and the righteous decay; obstructed in their course of obedience, they become heartless and unimproving.

The blessings of life—the means of natural, civil and moral improvements—the peace and tranquility of society, and the prospects of future happiness, are greatly disturbed and diminished by it. And when it is carried to its extream, and begets confirmed slavery, like soil prepared to invigorate its proper seed, it is productive of many species of vice: Falsehoods, thefts, and intemperance grow out of it; which is a demonstrative proof that the benevolent Creator never formed the human nature for oppression, or originally designed it should be subject to it.

On the contrary, it is introduced at the door of sin; and is, at once, promoted by the general depravity, and promotive of it.

Whereas liberty is innate, and original; the plant of our heavenly Father; liable indeed, like other original principles to neglect or abuse from ourselves and others; but under proper nurture and guidance, capable of accomplishing noble and beneficent purposes.

Possessed of it, men are, in a moral sense, subjects of the divine agency, capable of perswasion, of being actuated by motives, and by those influences from on high, which are adapted to their make and circumstances; and of being led to acquire, and support the character of religion and virtue.

They may be animated by it, to the noblest pursuits and highest attainments; to grow in grace, and in the knowledge of our Lord and Saviour Jesus Christ; to secure their best interest here, and to cultivate in their souls those dispositions and graces, which lay the foundation of future happiness.

But deprived of liberty, oppressed, and enslaved, men not only sink below the primitive standard of humanity; but even that which has been erected in consequence of the original transgression. They become stupid, and debased in spirit, indolent and groveling, indifferent to all valuable improvement, and hardly capable of any.

How much then does it concern mankind to preserve, and cherish the spirit of liberty! —it is their crown and diadem; and essential to human happiness.

May the body of the people in these colonies, in imitation of our renowned fore-fathers, those free born spirits, those brave christian Heroes, who in the true spirit of liberty, and for the sake of worshipping God according to conscience, forsook their native shores, and fled from the iron hand of oppression, to the remote and dark regions of America, be always ready to adopt every self-denying measure, and call forth every magnanimous exertion, that may be found necessary, to extricate themselves, from their present political evils, and continue the enjoyment of the blessing of liberty, in this new world.

And may we all have wisdom to improve it, for the advantageous purposes it is calculated to accomplish, in the diligent and faithful study of the holy Scriptures, and in cultivating the universal temper of piety and humanity; hereby enlarging the foundation, both of our present and future happiness: For so is the will of God, that with well doing ye may put to silence the ignorance of foolish men; as free, and not using your liberty for a cloke of maliciousness, but as the servants of God.

Liberty is the grand preservative of public spirit, and incentive to private virtue. How far soever the spirit of liberty has been, and still is crushed and borne down by mighty tyrants, the nimrods of the earth, it is happy for mankind that some of it yet remaineth in the world.

To this invigorating principle, are chiefly to be attributed those high advances in natural and moral philosophy, and those useful discoveries in civil and common life, which go far towards improving and embellishing human nature.

"If, says a fine writer, elegance comes short of the just standard, and is not yet arrived at its proper maturity, human life must necessarily be deprived of the enjoyment of many conveniences, of which it is capable, and the manners of mankind must incline towards fierceness and superstition. If carried no farther than the just limit, it produces a more commodious method of living, gives rise to the invention of many true refinements, heightens the splendor and magnificence of society, tends to render mankind social and humane, begets mildness and moderation in the tempers and actions of men, and helps to banish ignorance and superstition out of the world; and thus far it contributes to the perfection of human society."

Liberty is requisite to the growth of every good seed in a commonwealth.

While men are free they have suitable encouragement and spirit to improve in the arts of commerce and government, as well as those of common life—they investigate new arts, and cultivate the old—they contrive methods of just refinement —they study how errors may be rectified, and defects supplied, and how things of real use may be perfected, and rendered more excellent—they go the round of their daily occupations with alacrity, and review their enjoyments with pleasure, and thus enterprize great schemes for the good of society.

Far from confining their views to their own times, and the emoluments of the present age, or the narrow circle of a few in any, they extend them to future periods, and lay foundations of improvement and magnificence for generations yet unborn.

Animated by the spirit of liberty, men are led to attempt great things, in the day of small things; and according to their limited and very imperfect capacity and manner, to imitate the works of God himself; to whom a thousand years are as one day, "Who has an immensely large, progressive scheme, consisting of many under parts, and intermediate steps; all placed in their proper periods, and each rising upon the past, and the whole conducted in that regular gentle manner, which is best suited to the moral government of a world of intelligent free agents, and most becoming a Being of infinite wisdom, and goodness."

From such hints, which will probably be more largely considered by some successor, may be justly argued, that God made man to be free; and that in proportion as they have lost their liberty in any true sense, the benevolent purposes of the creator have some how, been impiously and injuriously counteracted in the world.

We shall come to the same conclusion if we examine the accounts of the holy scriptures: It is manifest from the dealings of God with mankind, recorded in them, that he has from the beginning, had a regard for liberty, and that tyrants, and oppressors, have been the objects of his abhorrence.

Oppression and tyranny began to work in early ages, in the person and family of Cain, and spread abroad its baneful influence, and pernicious effects among men; and when at length, by the unlawful mixtures of *Seth's* family with his elder brothers, the whole world became corrupt; and injustice, tyranny, and oppression prevailed; God manifested his displeasure against those giants in wickedness, by involving the whole human race, eight persons excepted, in one common ruin.

The miraculous deliverance of the children of *Israel* from the Egyptian Bondage, is a very signal instance of God's appearing in favour of liberty, and frowning on tyrants; and it shews how much he regards the rights of his people, and in how exemplary a manner, hard hearted tyrants, and merciless oppressors, sometimes feel his vengeance.

He had pity on his people, toiling in the service, and for the benefit of strangers, and groaning under the unreasonable weight of their burdens; and he came down and set them free.

It ought not to be forgotten, that this was done, at a time, and in a manner peculiarly calculated and intended, to be a terror and warning to the remotest nations, and all future oppressors.

In what strains of paternal tenderness, on the one hand, and indignation on the other, is the divine Being represented as speaking, on this occasion? I have surely seen the affliction of my people, which are in *Egypt,* and have heard their cry, by reason of their task-masters; for I know their sorrows, and I am come down to deliver them out of the hand of the Egyptians.

The same thing is further confirmed by the nature of the civil government of the *Jews.*

After they had been delivered out of the house of bondage, God saw fit to institute a certain form of mixed government among them, under which they were to be restored to the knowledge and practice of true religion, and the possession of their natural rights and liberties. This form was proposed to the consideration of the people, and they gave their full consent to it, and it was in all respects a free government.

The spirit of liberty breathed in every part, and was supported, defended, and promoted, by its whole constitution.

Wise laws were enacted for the preservation of Liberty, and the administration of Justice through the whole nation, and "as their lands were to descend to their posterity, and were alienable but for a limited time, a proper and natural foundation was hereby laid, for keeping up the balance of power among the several tribes, the security of the liberty of the body of the people, and the rights of each individual."

From express prohibitions of oppression, and of the sale of any Israelite for a bondman; from the release of debtors, the restoration of lands to their original owners, the general freedom of servants on sabbatical years, and times of rejoicing celebrated among the Jews, in commemoration of their deliverance out of Egypt, for all which things, particular statutes were ordained; we may see how admirably their government was calculated to keep alive a spirit of liberty, and inspire them with the love of it.

At the time of their withdraw from the government of Jehovah, when they unwisely and ungratefully desired a change in their political state, and to come under the power of earthly Kings, God did not forsake them; but on the contrary, manifested his concern for their welfare, and let them know how far, and in what respects, if they proceeded, they would be likely to be deprived of their liberties, by ordering a description of the manner of their King to be laid before them: He will take your sons and appoint them for himself; for his chariots, and to be his horsemen; and some shall run before his chariots—and he will appoint him captains over thousands, and captain over fifties, and will set them to ear his ground, and to reap his harvest, and to make his instruments of war, and instruments of his chariots; and he will take your daughters to be confectionaries, and to be cooks, and to be bakers—and he will take your fields, and your vineyards, and your olive yards, even the best of them, and give them to his servants; and he will take the tenth of your seed, and of your vineyards, and give to his officers and to his servants, and he will take your men servants, and your maid servants, and your goodliest young men, and your asses, and put them to his work, he will take the tenth of your sheep, and ye shall be his servants.

This is not a description of what their Kings would have any right or just authority to do; but of what their practice would be; if, as they requested, they had a King like the other nations; unmindful of the common good, the only end of civil authority, they would treat their subjects injuriously, and make use of them and of their wealth for their own aggrandisement and evil design, divesting them of that liberty, which they so happily enjoyed, under their former government.

The evident traces of the spirit of liberty, discoverable in the writings of the succeeding Prophets, and running through them; the frequent denunciations of the divine judgments against tyrants, and oppressors, the names and images by which they characterise them, their predictions

of their final overthrow, and of a time approaching before the end of the world, when righteousness and peace, truth and liberty, and happiness shall prevail, are other undeniable proofs of God's care to uphold the cause of liberty, and his purpose to render it finally triumphant over all the tyrants of the earth; those beasts and dragons, as the Prophets call them, that is, deceivers and destroyers of mankind.

The ancient Prophets were endowed with plentiful measures of the spirit of liberty; their breasts glowed with the sacred flame, and they had a just sense of its necessity to promote improvements both in a civil and religious view. Far from thinking it a prostitution of their sacred office, they on the contrary, considered it as part of the duty of it, to give their voice in favour of liberty, and speak as they often did, in the severest language, and warmest strains of indignant eloquence against oppressive powers and domineering tyrants.

If we will now look into the writings of the new testament, we shall find that they are friendly to the cause of liberty.

In the most perfect sense of it, intending freedom from the bondage of satan and our own lusts, it was the great object of Christ's undertaking; and agreeably He applied to himself what had been long before testified of Him, by the spirit of prophecy—the spirit of the Lord is upon me, because he hath anointed me to preach the gospel to the poor, He hath sent me to heal the broken hearted, to preach deliverance to the captives, and recovering sight to the blind, to set at liberty them that are bruised. It is said that the law of the spirit of life in Christ Jesus, maketh free from the law of sin and death; and if the Son make us free, we shall be free indeed.

'Tis allowed that when Christ was in the world working out the redemption of sinners, He did not say many things concerning civil government and political liberty: Freedom of a far more important nature employ'd his time and thoughts: and his silence in this regard, has been turned into an argument by some, that the ministers of religion depart from the duty of their office, and act out of character, when in any state of our public affairs, they make such matters subjects of their discourses from the pulpit, or even in private conversation. But besides other substantial things that might be replied, it ought to be remembered, that the Prophets before, and the Apostles after him, were not so sparing; and this I think is a solid proof, either that his silence was not intended as an example, or that some of the inspired Apostles at least misunderstood it.

There were special prudential reasons why Christ, 'till He had finished the work of his ministry, and fulfilled every thing in the scriptures concerning Him, should avoid speaking with any degree of freedom and openness of matters of government and the civil liberties of mankind. "The Jews were continually laying weight for something to accuse Him of to the Romans, tempting Him, and trying all methods to draw Him into any act, which might be construed treason, or disaffection to their government."

And considering the great wickedness of the Jews in that age, and their particular malignity against Christ, together with the usurpations and encroachments of some of the roman magistrates, had He said almost any thing of civil rights, they would have charged Him with sedition and treason. For similar reasons, He declined any direct answer, when questioned about his being the Messiah, and some other matters; and it is hoped ministers will not be blamed for treating on the messiahship of Christ, because He himself had sometimes good reasons to be cautious.

But though Christ did not think proper to decide any thing, as to civil rights in particular cases; yet from what He said, on several occasions, we may learn his sentiments on the subject of liberty, and government in general.

He not only bore testimony against spiritual tyranny, and the undue claims of power, in the Scribes and Pharisees—He not only intimated his detestation of persecution, when He advised his Apostles, to beware of men, and if they persecuted them in one city to flee to another—He not only implicitly censured the tyrannies of the Gentile world, when he said to his disciples, that the princes of the Gentiles exercise dominion over them, but it shall not be so among you: But he spake of Herod King of Galilee, with a degree of severity, when the Pharisees told him, that he would kill him. He also expressly commanded to render unto Cesar the things that are Cesar's and unto God the things that are God's; the natural sense of which precept is this, that men should give tribute and custom, respect and obedience, to those cloathed with lawful authority, as far as they are due, and necessary to answer the ends of government, but that they are to make no encroachments on the things of God, which are likewise to be given to him, things pertaining to his service, appropriated to his worship; the rights of conscience and natural rights and liberties, which are the donations of his good-

ness, and necessary to the preservation of that peace and order, and justice among men, which He hath ordained.

In this precept much is said in little, relative to civil government; such prudence is displayed, as was sufficient to avoid the snare that was laid for Him, and at the same time, the most perfect general rule is given for the guidance of magistrates and people, and rendering society happy.

Among the apostles, St. Paul in his epistle to the Romans, hath explicitly spoken of civil government, and pointed out the ends of it, duty of magistrates, and the ground of submission to their authority in the most concise and instructive manner.

His own conduct, on diverse occasions, manifested the sense he had both of civil and religious liberty; it was of a piece with his doctrine, and is the best comment upon it.

There was a remarkable display of the spirit of liberty in his behavior, when on a false accusation, and without legal process, he and Silas were, by order of the magistrates, beaten and cast into Prison, and their feet made fast in the stocks.

The magistrates, terrified by an earthquake, sent the serjeants to release them, but Paul, animated by the spirit of liberty, even in a goal, and sensible that his rights had been invaded; insisted on a practical acknowledgment of it, from the magistrates themselves—Paul said unto them, they have beaten us openly, uncondemned, being Romans, and have cast us into prison; and now do they thrust us out privily? nay verily! —but let them come themselves, and fetch us out.

The serjeants reported these words to the magistrates, and they feared when they heard they were Romans. They knew they had injured them by depriving them of liberty, who were as free as themselves, and had as good a right to the privileges and protection of the roman government; just as the Americans, by nature and character, are entitled to the same rights and liberties as Britons, or as they themselves would have enjoyed, had they been born within the realm of England.

It is, however, hard for exalted characters, who have been used to have their orders executed, to bring themselves to make concessions; but the magistrates were overawed by the earthquake, and from other considerations also, they found it necessary to come personally, and by entreaties make up the matter—they came and besought them, and brought them out.

But it may be asked; why was Paul and his companion so obstinate? why did they not come

37

out when the serjeant came with orders to let them go free? Why did they continue in confinement a moment longer than was necessary?— The keeper of the prison, it seems thought they would readily embrace the offer, and as he had now great reason to esteem them, he ran hastily with the joyful tidings, and wished them peace.

But they had good reason for their conduct; they knew the value of liberty, and its importance to mankind, and they chose rather to suffer the cruelty, and ignominy of a goal, a while longer, than not bear sufficient testimony against such magistrates as had unjustly invaded it.

Their behaviour in this affair may be considered, as having respect to themselves and others; as to themselves, they were sensible if they did not improve this opportunity, to induce the magistrates who had done the injury to make reparation; other magistrates would not be so likely to be deterred from a similar practice, nor these so effectually prevented from repeating the abuse, and perhaps carrying it to a greater extremity, when the horrors of the earthquake were gone off. —And as to other men, whose welfare they were obliged to promote, they knew if they did not bring their oppressors to acknowledge the injustice they had been guilty of, in denying them the liberties of Romans, they should set an example of ill influence to all who might afterwards be oppressed, and encourage magistrates to go any lengths in this ill treatment of subjects. But if they brought them to a practical nullifying of this instance of oppression, their example would be likely to be beneficial to mankind in future time, and induce them under similar abuses to tread in their steps, and so maintain liberty in the world.

Paul and Silas therefore, like men acquainted with their own, and the rights of society, acted this noble part, for the promotion and establishment of the cause of liberty.

No man was ever more tender of his liberties, or more desirous to continue such rich blessings in the world than the apostle Paul.

At a time when the chief captain had ordered him to be examined by scourging, and they were binding him with thongs for that purpose, with what independence of mind did he demand of the centurion, —Is it lawful for you to scourge a man that is a Roman, and uncondemned?

And when the same officers on being informed of his assuming the freedom of Rome, doubting his claim, observed that it was with a great sum he himself had obtained this freedom; how did Paul assert his own pre-eminence, —but I was

free born. And afterwards, having fallen into the hands of the high priest, who as he was pleading his cause, commanded him to be smitten on the mouth; with what a manly spirit of resentment did he reply, God shall smite thee, thou whited wall, for sittest thou to judge me after the law, and commandest me to be smitten contrary to the law?

Soon after, indeed, he recalled the reproachful language stiling the high Priest a whited wall, and said he wist not that he was the high priest, but he never retracted the sense he had of the illegal indignity that was offered him, nor his zeal against such rulers as contradicted the end of their office.

When he was brought before Felix at one time, and Festus, and King Agrippa at another, he made his defence with the same free and intrepid spirit. —He yielded no rights, he resigned no liberties into the hands of any man, however cloathed with authority, but he was always submissive to magistrates acting in their line, and ready to be governed and judged by the law.

If it should be enquired why these instances of Paul's conduct relative to civil liberty are handed down to us, since it was his chief business to instruct men in the great doctrines and duties of religion; it may be said, that among other reasons, which I need not mention, a probable one is, to let us know, the sense he had of the connection between religious and civil liberty, and that the former cannot be expected to exist, but upon the basis of the latter.

The conduct and discourses of the Apostles, whenever they had occasion to speak of civil liberty, were always friendly to its cause, and a reproof of tyranny and usurpation; —the great principle which they ever acted from themselves, and inculcated on others was, that we ought to obey God rather than man.

Although agreeable to what their Lord had said, they looked on themselves and all christians, as belonging to a society totally different from civil states, subjects of a kingdom which is not of this world; yet as the free exercise of the external offices of this peculiar kingdom, must in such a world as this, and among such inhabitants, greatly depend on the equity, impartiality and freedom of civil government, and as in this respect it was more, and in every laudable worldly respect, as much the interest of christians, as of other men, to live under such a government, they made conscience as 'tis natural to suppose they would, of speaking and acting on proper occasions, in a manner that had a tendency to recommend it to mankind. Civil liberty, which itself is an object of great moment, is sometimes spoken of by the sacred penmen, in both testaments, for its own sake; at other times on the account of its salutary influence and effects on religious liberty.

Enough has been said by the ancient Prophets, and by Christ and the Apostles, to convince us that they had a most tender regard for the natural and civil rights of mankind, and an abhorrence of all spiritual tyranny and domination.

Christ has told us that the members of his mystical body, the church, are brethren—there are to be no masters among them—no authority exercised over the faith or consciences of any—one is our master, even Christ.

The Apostle Peter, who was himself an elder, hath strictly prohibited the elders of the flock, lording it over God's heritage.

And whoever are guilty of such usurpation, though dignified among men, and distinguished by the epithets of right reverend, and even his Holiness, are liable to the reproof administred by the Prophet to the ancient shepherds of Israel; wo be to the shepherds of Israel that do feed themselves; should not the shepherds feed the flock? ye eat the fat, and ye cloath you with the wool, ye kill them that are fed; but ye feed not the flock, the diseased have ye not strengthned, neither have ye healed that which was sick, neither have ye bound up that which was broken, neither have ye bro't again that which was driven away, neither have ye sought that which was lost; but with force and with cruelty have ye ruled them.

At the time St. Paul had occasion to use friendly severity, at least with some of the Corinthians, he expressly disclaimed dominion over their faith, assigning this good reason for it, by faith ye stand.

Had we time to consider more largely the nature and genius of the religion of the Bible, its various requirements, and the principles, affections and duties it enjoins; the divine regards both to civil and religious liberty, and God's intention to promote it among men, would appear in a strong and irresistable point of light.

That temper and conduct—that love of God and man, and those divine and social virtues, every where recommended; particularly that imitation of Christ, or correspondence of heart and life to his example, which are essential parts of his religion, are admirably calculated to secure the natural and religious rights and liberties of mankind, and put an end to the miseries of op-

pression and tyranny. Christ not only set us an example of universal benevolence, but of the love of our country as consistent with it; like a true patriot he had a peculiar concern for the welfare of his own nation, and spent his life in the most beneficent actions among them, and he could not call to mind the calamities he knew they were about to suffer in consequence of their obstinacy and unbelief, but with the tenderest emotions of compassion and grief.

And so far as men partake of his spirit, and are actuated by the principles of his religion, be they magistrates or subjects, they will be led to a behaviour tending to support the general cause of liberty, and the particular freedom and prosperity of their own country.

It was, indeed, the great intention of Christ, to introduce men into a state of spiritual liberty; that being made free from sin, and become servants to God, they might have their fruit unto holiness, and the end everlasting life; but as his religion is formed to produce this effect, by reinforcing doctrines and principles, that have a tendency, to subdue those lusts and corruptions that enslave the mind, and to influence men to practise those virtues in which the freedom of the soul consists; and as the assistances and co-operations of the divine spirit are provided to break the yoke of satan and replace our souls in a state of moral strength and freedom, which is the purest and most perfect idea and condition of freedom we are capable of; so in virtue of the same influence and tendency, his religion contributes to the preservation and establishment of liberty in civil and religious societies. For, in proportion as the minds of individuals are made free from sin, and the virtues of the Gospel are practised; oppression and tyranny must cease, and liberty revive and prevail every where, both in church and state.

May therefore a deep sense of religion impress the minds, and influence the conduct of all men! and those happy times, we are taught to expect, come on! when the power of oppression shall be banished from the world; and a King shall reign and prosper, who shall execute judgment, and justice in the earth; and there shall be nothing to hurt or destroy in all God's holy mountain.

It only remains that we make a few reflections, or inferences from what has been discoursed, and conclude with them.

First, We see what reason we have to admire and adore the wisdom and goodness of God, in constituting a religion for us, which, while it provides for the moral liberty of our souls, and our everlasting happiness in another world; hath not been unmindful of the rights of conscience, and the civil liberties of society, in this.

Liberty is the spirit and genius of the sacred writings; the great thing aimed at in them, is to make men free from sin; to deliver them out of bondage to their lusts, and procure and establish the moral freedom of their minds.

But though this be their main object, yet as liberty in any important sense, civil or religious, is friendly to the cause of godliness, stands in connection with it, and has its influence into the spiritual freedom of the soul; they have taken care by enjoining self government, the generous affections and a righteous behaviour towards men, to provide for this kind of liberty in human society.

A just regard for the authority of the inspired word, will most effectually secure and promote it.

As far as the liberty of mankind has been impaired, and their rights invaded, and oppression and tyranny have prevailed in any kingdom or nation on earth; so far has there been a repugnance to, and a departure from the true spirit of the holy scriptures.

The religion of the Bible hath a regard to our benefit in both worlds, it consists of such principles, duties and virtues, as are adapted to the human nature and circumstances; it is so contrived as to deliver us from the vassalage of our lusts, and the oppression of man, by the same divine energy—it forms our tempers to the resemblance of God, and disposes us for the sublime exercises, and refined enjoyments of his heavenly Kingdom; at the same time, and by the same means, that it promotes our best interest, peace and quietness on earth—godliness hath the promise of the life that now is, and of that which is to come.

This is a consideration that demands our warmest gratitude; and while our hearts are enlarged, and our mouths filled with the praises of God for so rich and inestimable a blessing; may it be our care to devote ourselves forever to his service; and improve our religious advantages, according to their gracious design and tendency, for the promotion both of our present and future happiness.

Secondly; If religion is eminently productive of liberty, and the security of it; we are led, from the remarkable display of liberty in the great undertaking of our fore-fathers, to form a favourable judgment of their religion, and to believe it was pure and undefiled, and according to knowledge, in opposition to enthusiastic rant and fanaticism.

There have been indeed, many instances of the love of liberty among a people, whose religion has been no other than pagan; and no marvel; it is a natural passion, capable however, of being strengthened by religion; and is usually the strongest, where religion is the purest and the most divine.

Notwithstanding the names of our illustrious ancestors have been traduced, and their religion questioned, and even vilified by some, as the ravings of a disordered mind, or the effects of ignorance and superstition, an abuse which few escaped who were distinguished by the name of puritans; yet the charitable as well as probable opinion is, that they were men of real piety and godliness; and that like David of old, they desired to get out of the hands of their oppressors, that they might have more liberty to keep God's precepts, and worship and serve him according to the light of their own consciences.

I am not sensible of any bias, though I would not be too confident, from an undue veneration for antiquity, or for the superior knowledge and discernment of them whom we commonly call the Fathers; but with respect to the fathers of New England, the more I am acquainted with their history and minutely enquire into their religion and morality, and particular behaviour towards the natives of this land, the greater reason have I to be perswaded, that their religion was derived from the fountain of truth, and therefore real and substantial.

It appears to have had the marks of divinity upon it, and to have been founded on the proper basis of all religion—the love of God; and that charity to man, that bond of peace and of all virtues, made a very conspicuous part of it.

At the time of our Fathers abandoning their native country, many things were out of order in the state, and they had reason to complain of the too arbitrary and undue exercise of the powers of government. But their chief motive in it was religion; freedom of worshipping God agreeably to the rule of his word, and the dictates of their own minds.

Religion was precious in their eyes; they were willing to leave houses and lands, and many dear and valuable possessions, for the sake of enjoying it in its purity. But they were men, and like other good men they were liable to, and had their failings; its well they had no more.

When we recollect the cruel treatment they met with from their brethren at home, and their sufferings abroad; the difficulties and perils of their voyage, and the many hardships and dangers they encountered after they had arrived, in this season of the year, to these dark and unfriendly shores; their unshaken fortitude and patient suffering of affliction in the cause of religion, fill our minds with equal pleasure and astonishment.

We ought doubtless to consider it, as an argument of the love of God ruling in their hearts, and of his grace abiding with them, and supporting them with the stedfast hope of good things to come; that under such tryals, their spirits were not broken, and their tempers soured to distrust, peevishness and vice.

It may, I believe, be justly affirmed, that their devotedness to God and his cause, their regard for the holy scriptures, and love of the truth as it is in Jesus, their faithfulness to themselves and posterity, and their assiduous care and endeavours to transmit their religion uncorrupted, and their liberties unimpaired to remotest ages; are to be equalled but by few instances, and perhaps surpassed by none, since the days of inspiration.

Their history, if faithfully recorded, will shine with a peculiar lustre, in the annals of the church, down to its latest period in this militant state.

To us especially, who are entered on their labours, as our natural inheritance, and who, till of late years, have largely partaken of the happy fruits of their virtuous sufferings, and many toils, both in church and state; and believe we shall again partake of them; their names are justly venerable: But we intend no more than a decent expression of filial respect, when on this anniversary, we their children, rise up, and call them blessed.

Their example, however, as far as it was formed, by the love of religion and liberty, and the grace of God that was in them, ought to be regarded by us, and improved for the more perfect accomplishing of their great and pious designs.

In this view, we cannot but approve the late conduct of the town of Plymouth, in devoting the anniversary of our fore-fathers landing here, to a religious use, and a grateful recollection of the care of providence, in bringing about so memorable an event.

Much benefit, if I mistake not, both to ourselves, and posterity, may grow out of the design; if it be but observed with sobriety, and temperance, as a civil and religious festivity, and not suffered to degenerate into carnal mirth, and the works of darkness.

Thirdly—We learn that no man in community, of any rank or character whatever, can be uninterested in the cause of liberty; or lawfully neglect it; much less make use of his influence in opposing and bearing it down.

It is a common cause, and the right of nature. Every man that is born into the world, as Mr. Lock, that prince of philosophers hath said, "is born to it," and every member of civil and religious society has an unalienable title to, and concern in it; and is bound by the most sacred and indissoluble ties, in a just exertion of his abilities and by every adequate method, to spread the love of it among mankind, and defend it, against tyrants and oppressors.

This observation comes with too self-evident clearness, and force, to the reason of man, to admit of avowed opposition from any, but yet in the political disputes in which we are at present, unhappily involved with our fellow subjects at home, there are some in the midst of us, and hard as it may be to believe it, such as are descended from our worthy ancestors, who from a misapprehension of the nature and just extent of the ministerial office, have pretended to deny it, in regard to the clergy in particular; and have used some feeble and uncouth attempts to wrest it out of their hands. The conduct however, of the holy Prophets and Apostles, the firm and open spirit with which they delivered their sentiments, on the subject of liberty, and bare testimony against lawless oppressors, though ignorantly passed over by them, will be discerned by others, to afford example to the ordinary ministers of religion, and authorise them, in their public and private addresses to use their influence, if any they have, in supporting and cherishing the cause of liberty.

This is not barely a right that may be exercised or neglected at pleasure, but the duty of all ranks of men in society; no one is, or can be, exempted. Liberty is the cause of all, and all should be ready to spend, and be spent in its service.

Political apostates, and other paricides will not indeed admit, though they cannot deny such doctrine; it were to be wished there was no occasion to say that their unexampled behaviour, in this day of anxiety and contest, when the rights of all the colonies are the stake, is too manifestly calculated according to the weight of its influence, to cut up the liberties of America by the roots, and cool the passion, and obscure the sense of them in the breasts of their fellow countrymen. At the same time, strange to relate! They fondly assume, and by assuming prophane the respectable characters of loyalty and friends to government! Solicitous to hide from the world, and if possible from themselves, their unhallowed views of ambition and avarice, under the cover of venerable forms, as the grand apostate spirit himself is sometimes transformed into an angel of light, to accomplish the baneful designs of the kingdom of darkness. Notwithstanding, when they shall make their cordial submissions to their much injured country, and seek reconciliation with it, we may forgive, but it will be a hard thing to forget their crimes.

Fourthly, As liberty is the right of nature, confirmed to us by revelation, and essential to our happiness, we ought to be deeply humbled under the tokens of the divine resentments, in suffering so great an adversity to befal us, as that of being obliged to contend for it in opposition to measures contrived to deprive us of so rich a blessing.

When the righteous providence of God, which in the friendless and defenceless state of our pious ancestors, condescended to be their sun and shield, the vigilant and almighty guardian of their persons, families and rights, hath seen it necessary to correct the growing infidelity, immorality and prophaneness of their degenerate offspring, by permitting a thick cloud to gather over our heads, and invelope the American colonies in darkness; some humiliating reflections ought to intermix with the joy and gratitude of the day.

We justify the ways of providence in all that is come upon us—the Lord hath done right, but we have done wickedly—our sins have been the procuring moral cause of the Judgments we feel, and we ought to be humble before God, and repent and amend our ways and doings; but yet with regard to man, we are greatly injured, we have reason to complain, and may justly assert our rights, and maintain our cause against them.

A more grievous misfortune however, could not befal us than this; we deeply lament it! We deprecate a contention with the parent state! It is the burden of America, and under the weight of it we are all ready to enquire with anxious hearts, watchman, what of the night? watchman, what of the night? is there any good news from our mother country? any thing to raise the hopes of our own? can America entertain expectations from british justice or parental sympathy of a deliverance out of her distresses.

In a situation so gloomy, let us commit our cause unto him who judgest righteously, and lift up our hearts to God in the heavens, in earnest prayer and supplication—trust in him at all times, oh ye people, pour out your hearts before him. Our expectation is from God. He is our salvation and our glory, the rock of our strength, and

our refuge is in God. The great affairs of states and kingdoms, are subject to his controul and governance. He changeth times and seasons; the hearts of Kings and of all men are in his hands, and He turneth them as rivers of water are turned.

In the midst of our perplexity and fear, then let us look to God, who is high above all nations, and whose glory is above the heavens; and may we all as one man, break off our sins by repentance, and our iniquities by turning to the Lord; if we will thus penitently betake ourselves to him, though He hath smitten us, He will bind us up; his going forth is prepared as the morning, and He shall come unto us as the rain, as the latter and former rain, unto the earth.

Fifthly, Considering that the rights and liberties of the colonies are so important blessings, derived to us from the divine goodness, through the hands of our adventurous fore-fathers, it is hoped we shall not supinely suffer them to slip out of our possession, or be wanting in any instances of self-denial, and other wise and effectual means, to secure them to the present, and transmit them to future generations.

The alarm that is gone forth through the land, and the assiduous attention given to our public affairs, by all ranks, ages and sexes among us, we cannot but esteem a token for good, a symptom of vital strength, in the body politic, though some of its members are mutilated and maimed; nor can we attribute the firm union and cement of our numerous colonies, and the general agreement of their respective inhabitants in modes of opposition, to unconstitutional measures, to any principle so justly, as the efficacy of the divine influence on the minds of men.

Judging from appearances, we have reason to hope, and believe, that God himself has risen to work out our salvation.

Let us not provoke him to withdraw the influences of his providence, by our own inactivity and neglect.

God usually worketh by means and instruments, in accomplishing the great purposes of his providence among men; we have no reason from analogy, to expect a deliverance out of our political evils, by the immediate exertion of almighty power; we must work ourselves, with a due dependance on the divine energy and blessing, and then, from the justice of our cause, may we expect that God will work with us and in us, and crown our endeavours with success.

The honourable, and much esteemed American Continental Congress, whom we voluntarily constituted the guardians of our rights, have with great judgment and faithfulness, pointed us to a mode of conduct, from which, if religiously adhered to by ourselves, and followed with the divine blessing, we may entertain the strongest hopes.

It is at once calculated to procure a radical redress of American grievances, and to promote the future peace, harmony and prosperity both of Great-Britain, and the colonies. —It shews that we contend for nothing but our own, that we aim at nothing but our rights, and wish and pray for nothing more ardently in this world, then a reconciliation and lasting connection with our brethren at home: If it succeeds, we are mutually happy; if not, as the wisest schemes of men may prove abortive, thro' the corruption and wickedness of some other, it will at least manifest to the whole world, that the demands of America are just, and her disposition loyal and pacific.

And then, when the worst of events cometh, to which that respectable body have in the mean time advised us to extend our views, and be prepared for, we may with firm hope and humble reliance, implore the aids of his providence, who is the almighty avenger of wrongs, with whom is wisdom and strength, who poureth contempt upon princes, and weakneth the strength of the mighty, who leadeth councellors away spoiled, and maketh the judges fools.

To conclude, Upon a retrospective view of our fore-fathers coming over into this land, the causes moving them to it—the pious designs they had in it—the many hardships and perils attending it, and the foundation hereby laid for useful improvements in the arts of civilized life, commerce and literature; but especially in the knowledge and practice of the christian religion, where ignorance and barbarism had before prevailed for unknown ages; we ought to be very thankful to almighty God for the peculiar care and guardianship of his providence, so conspicuous in every part of this grand enterprize.

God was with them of a truth, encouraging and defending them, and carrying them through difficulties and perils in a wonderful manner, which demands our particular attention and grateful acknowledgments this day.

He had, doubtless, great and wise purposes to serve, in leading them into this barbarous and extensive wilderness, which we have reason to believe, are far from having yet been wholly accomplished.

It is remarkable, that in the many threatning dangers that beset our Fathers in early time, from the wicked machinations of open enemies, or the secret plots of treacherous and false-hearted friends, and that have since, even down to the present day, beset us, God hath always appeared on our side, and delivered us out of all our fears and distresses, and we trust he will still deliver us.

Not unto us, oh Lord, not unto us, but unto thy name be the glory.

It is not for short-sighted mortals to fathom the counsels of the most high God: His Judgments are unsearchable; and his ways past finding out.

But if it be lawful to permit our thoughts to delight us with contemplations on futurity; the American desert rejoices and blossoms as a rose, cities and empires rise, arts and sciences flourish, and the solitary places are glad. How great is the goodness of the Lord, and how great is his beauty! The time cometh, when old men and old women shall dwell in our streets, very man with his staff in his hand for very age; when corn shall make the young men cheerful, and new wine the maids, and our cities shall be full of boys and girls, playing in our streets. But above all, when the aboriginal nations shall bow the knee at the name of Jesus, and confess him to be Lord, to the glory of God the Father; and pure and undefiled religion shall prevail in the land, and there shall be one Lord, and his name one.

Amen.

A NARRATIVE OF THE PLANTING OF THE MASSACHUSETTS COLONY 1628

Joshua Scottow,
Massachusetts
Historical
Collections,
Vol. IV, Fourth
Series, 1858

It was an Ordinance of old, to Commemorate the Political Birth and Growth of a People, it may not (we hope) be unbeseeming us, to give a small account of the Genesis of this superhumane and really Divine Creation, wrought by the admirable Architect, who manifest himself most Illustriously Great in the Minimes of Created Beings.

This Colonies Foundation was not laid, by exhausting the Exchequers of Princes, Peers, or Lords of the Realm, nor by Lotteries, and such like Contrivances of Advance, as other *English* Plantations have been.

It was incomparable Minute, to what its now attain'd unto, and the rather to be observed, because of the great opposition, from those of strength it first met with, its growth must be assigned to Heavens Influence, and Blessing: It evidently proceeded from Him who rais'd up the Righteous man from the East, and called him to his Foot; the sudden mover and incliner of Hearts, both infused and guided the inclinations and motions of these worthy Patriots, with their Associates, who either attended, or followed them in great measure, parallel to that of the *Father of the Faithful,* who upon a Divine Call, left Kindred, Country and Fathers House, and went he knew not whether, to Enjoy he knew not what, both proceeding from the same Inspiration, and Instinct, drawn by the Magnetick Influence of the same Holy Spirit, and as it were by the impulse of a sacred Charm or Spell, as by its operation appeared, as if a Royal Herald, through our Nation from *Barwick* to *Cornwell* had made Proclamation, to Summon and Muster up Volunteers, to appear in *New England,* for His Sacred Majesties Service, there to attend further Orders: Such was the *Day of Christ's Power,* as an incredible number of Willing People, forthwith Listed themselves; yea many of those whose Faces were unknown to each other; the hearts of multitudes in this Design responded, as Face to Face in Water; thus the Body of this People was animated as with one soul.

That this Design was Super-humane, will be evidenced by the *Primum Mobile,* or grand Wheel thereof. Neither Spanish Gold or Silver, nor *French* or *Dutch* Trade of Peltry did Oil their Wheels; it was the Propagation of Piety and Religion to Posterity; and the secret Macedonean Call, COME OVER AND HELP US, afterward Instamp'd in the Seal of this Colony, the Setting up of Christ's Kingdom among the Heathens, in this Remote End of the Earth, was the main spring of motion, and that which gave the Name to *New-England,* and at such a time, when as Divine *Herbert* in his Temple Prophetically sang.

*Religion Stands on Tiptoe in our Land,
Ready to pass to the AMERICAN Strand.*

The agency of the great God appeared, who never lets any of his works, fall for want of materials or instruments, he raised up such as were fit to lead, and feed this People in this wilderness, such were our Famous Founders, we had our *Mose's* and *Aaron's*, our *Zorobabels,* and *Joshua's,* our *Ezrah's,* and *Nehemiahs,* so many Noble spirited persons, fitted and called of God, raised up to this great service, both to the Civil and Sacred Administration, to the Cure and Care of this flock in this wilderness.

Men of narrow spirits, of mean Capacities, and fortunes, had not been capable to officiate in so great a worke, that such, and so many Gentlemen of Ancient and Worshipful Families, of Name and Number, of Character and Quality, should Combine and Unite in so desperate and dangerous a Design, attended with such insuperable Difficulties, and Hazards, in the plucking up of their Stakes, leaving so pleasant and profitable a place as their Native Soil, parting with their Patrimonies, Inheritances, plentiful Estates, and settlement of Houses well Furnished; of Land well Stock'd, and with comfortable ways of Subsistence, which the first Planters Deserted; and not a few did leave all their worldly hopes, to come into this Desert, & unknown Land, and smoaky Cottages, to the Society of Cursed Cannibals, (as they have proved to be) and at best wild Indians; what less then a Divine Ardour could inflame a People thus circumstanced to a work so contrary to Flesh and Blood.

Infinite Wisdom and Prudence contrived and directed this Mysterious Work of Providence, Divine Courage and Resolution managed it, Superhumane Sedulity and Diligence attended it, and Angelical Swiftness and Dispatch finished it; Its Wheels stirr'd not, but according to the HOLY SPIRITS motion in them; yea there was the Involution of a Wheel within a Wheel: God's Ways were a Great Depth, and high above the Eagle or Vulturous Eye; and such its Immensity as mans Cockle-shell is infinitely unable to Emptie this Ocean.

Let us Commemorate their *Exodus* or Departure from our Nation. These Prudent Under takers sent forth their *Forlorn Hope* in two ships, Laden with Passengers, and Servants: two

years before they mov'd with their main Body, and Pattent Government, which were fully Furnished with a Pastor and Teacher, worthy *Higgison* and *Skelton,* and all Materials, for Compleating of a Church of Christ, according to Divine Institution: Who safely Arriving according to their predeterminate Design of Inlargement of Christ's Kingdom, and His Majesty of *England's* Dominion: Firstly, they set up their Standards, Dethroning Satan, they cast him out of Heaven; which beyond times memorial, he had in the Natives Consciences, and by Turf and Twig they took possession of this his large Continent, and set up the first Church in these parts, in a place they then called *Salem;* at which Convention, the Testimony which the Lord of all the Earth bore unto it, is wonderfully memorable, by a Saving Work upon a Gentleman of Quality, who afterwards was the Chieftain and Flower of *New-England's* Militia, and an Eminent Instrument both in Church and Commonwealth; he being the younger Brother of the House of an Honourable Extract, his Ambition exceeding what he could expect at home, Rambled hither: Before one Stone was laid in this Structure, or our Van-Currier's Arrival, he was no Debauchee, but of a Jocund Temper, and one of the Merry Mounts Society, who chose rather to Dance about a *May pole,* first Erected to the Honour of *Strumpet Flora,* than to hear a good Sermon; who hearing of this Meeting, though above Twenty Miles distant from it, and desirous to see the Mode and Novel of a Churches Gathering; with great studiousness, he applyed himself to be at it: where beholding their orderly procedure, and their method of standing forth, to declare the Work of God upon their Souls, being pricked at the Heart, he sprung forth among them, desirous to be one of the Society, who though otherwise well accomplished, yet divinely illiterate, was then convinc'd and judged before all; the secrets of his heart being made manifest, fell down and Worshipped God, to their astonishment, saying, *That God was in them of a Truth;* the Verity hereof, as long since it hath been affirmed by old Planters, so by his own Manuscript, found after his Death it's confirmed; he about that time Lamenting his Christless Estate, which evidenceth that it ought to be said of that Sion,

This man was Born there. . . .

THE PLANTING
OF THE
MASSACHU-
SETTS COLONY

"THIS MAN
WAS BORN THERE"

45

THE HAND OF GOD
IN AMERICAN HISTORY

*Annual Election
Sermon,
Boston, Mass.,
January 5, 1876,
by Rev.
S. W. Foljambe
of Malden*

*"The Lord our God be with us, as he was with
our fathers: let him not leave us, nor forsake us."*
(*I Kings viii. 57*)

When St. Paul stood before that famous court
of which the poets and orators of Greece tell such
proud things, he proclaimed to them the God they
knew not, filling up the inscription to the unknown God with the name of Jehovah. He tells
them more of God in a few minutes, than Plato
had done in all his life. He brings the matter
closely home to them, and makes them feel as if
in contact with God; not with an ideal merely,
but with a living, personal Being, whose providence is directed at once to the individual interests of men, and the highest interest of nations.
*"Seeing he giveth to all life, and breath, and all
things; and hath made of one blood all nations of
men for to dwell on all the face of the earth, and
hath determined the times before appointed, and
the bounds of their habitation; that they should
seek the Lord, if haply they might feel after him,
and find him"* (*Acts. 17:25-27*). Such is the
divine basis of that institution which we call the
State, and such the ultimate religious end of its
existence. . . .

The more thoroughly a nation deals with its
history, the more decidedly will it recognize and
own an overruling Providence therein, and the
more religious a nation will it become; while the
more superficially it deals with its history, seeing
only secondary causes and human agencies, the
more irreligious will it be. If the history of any
nation is the development of the latent possibilities
existing in its special nature, it is also the record
of a Divine Providence furnishing place and
scope for that development, creating its opportunities, and guiding its progress. History is not
a string of striking episodes, with no other connection but that of time. It is rather the working out of a mighty system, by means of regularly
defined principles as old as creation, and as infallible as divine wisdom. With this truth in view,
we approach our chosen theme,—THE HAND OF
GOD IN AMERICAN HISTORY.

GOD'S WISE AND BENEFICENT
TIMING OF EVENTS

Not inappropriate do we deem it, that we trace
along the line of our history how God was with
our fathers, and recall and reaffirm in this presence the truth of our increasing dependence upon
him for the continued prosperity of our country
and people.

1. Observe the hand of God in the wise and
beneficent timing of events in the dawn of our
history. The events of history are not accidents.

There are no accidents in the lives of men or of nations. We may go back to the underlying cause of every event, and discover in each God's overruling and intervening wisdom. It has been said that history is the biography of communities; in another, and profounder, sense, it is the autobiography of him *"who worketh all things after the counsel of his own will"* (*Ephesians 1:11*), and who is graciously timing all events in the interests of his Christ, and of the kingdom of God on earth. Tracing the history of men, we find the most trivial and seemingly fortuitous things issuing beyond all human expectations or intention in the sublimest events; we see men planning and working with only their own more immediate and material interests in view, and yet a power behind them is noiselessly and effectually, though possibly for generations unobserved, overruling their action to the furtherance of higher, more widely extended, and more permanent purposes.

Human freedom and human responsibility in bringing about either good or evil, are not to be pushed aside; providence is not fatalism; but, on the other hand, man's free activities do not prove the despotism of a blind chance, shifting as man's caprice may dictate. Neither social order, moral progress, nor a Christian civilization, can spring out of chance. These demand a prevision and adjustment of causes keener and mightier than man with his wisest forethought and highest intelligence can exercise. There are influences which man can wield, and should control, aright; there are others which God alone originates and shapes. There are, again, other influences which are under human management, but which become mighty for good only by their timing; and this timing is sometimes a visible, but more frequently an invisible, interposition of God's overruling care, only truly seen after many generations have passed away. God's hand is seen in the starting, speeding, retarding, and matching such coincident and colliding influences as mark the progress and constitute the varied crises of history.

DISCOVERY AND PREPARATION OF AMERICA

The discovery and preparation of this country to be the home of a great people,—the theatre of a new experiment in government, and the scene of an advancing Christian civilization,—is illustrative of this truth. Whatever may have been its prehistoric condition, for centuries it was concealed behind the mighty veil of waters from the eyes of the world. Not until the early part of the tenth century was it discovered by the Scandinavians, and only then to be hidden away again till the time should be ripe for its settlement, by a people providentially prepared for its occupancy. What a land it was, so magnificent in extent, so varied in soil and climate, so unlimited in mineral wealth and vegetable bounties; while its conformation was such as to preclude its occupants from ever being other than an united people. Harbors, and rivers, and mountain ranges link as with iron bands the far separated localities. Yet all this thorough preparation by which this continent had been builded and furnished, was not available until God's hour had come for its occupancy.

Nor was this period reached without the concurrence of great moral and social events affecting the whole progress of society. The invention of movable type at Haarlem or Mentz, half a century before the discovery of America,—and only a few years previous to that invention, the manufacture of paper from linen rags, a most indispensable help to the development of the press,—had made books available to many, where manuscripts had been available to few. A few years later still came the capture of Constantinople by the Turks, which scattered the learning of the Greeks among the nations of the West. By these conspiring influences, knowledge became distributed, and a spirit of inquiry was everywhere awakened, broader and freer than was ever known before. Then occurred the rediscovery of this continent, expanding the globe to the minds of the Old World, and stimulating a new spirit of enterprise and activity.

But neither the wonderful art of printing, nor the discovery of this transatlantic continent, had aroused with such mighty energy the mind of christendom, as did the discovery of a new world in theology by Luther, and the sudden reformation in religion which sprung up in Germany, and swiftly extended through Northern Europe. To an unreflecting mind, it would appear that the questions raised in this religious movement were purely theological, having no interest outside the Church. But this is not the case. If a man has the right to seek truth freely, he has the right to declare and communicate this truth; he has the right to associate himself with those who think as he does, and to assist them, and relieve their wants. A free Church, free education, free association, the right to speak and to write,—these are the consequences of the liberty of conscience proclaimed by the Reformers. Without knowing it, without desiring it, they brought about a revolution. The Reformation was the cause of a great forward movement in human affairs. It awakened the intellect of mankind. Science, literature, invention, social life, political reform,—all were stimulated by it. These two events, therefore, the most important in modern times, are intimately connected in their bearing on American history. God timed the physical and the spiritual discovery to each other. The new life evoked would need a new and ampler field for its unhindered development. When he had created a stalwart race, and ordained them for the settlement of this country, and for laying the foundations of a higher civilization than the world had yet seen, and when they had started on their mission of light, and freedom, and religion, then he suddenly dropped the veil from this continent, and there arose before the astonished vision of the nations the splendors of the Western World.

Take, again, the century embracing the settlement of this country, and we discover the providential timing of influences shaping our national life and character. That century was a remarkable era, a period of wondrous activity and marvellous achievement, of strenuous struggles and lofty heroisms, of transcendent genius and bold enterprise. The roots of our national existence strike down into no arid wastes of intellectual or political life. It was in a time when liberal thought was beginning to assert itself, when education was extending its influence, and when the mind, especially of Northern Europe, was full of intense stimulation. It was a period of abounding material enterprise, when inventions followed each other almost as rapidly, and with the same startling novelty, as in our own times. The telescope and the compound microscope,—the one opening up the boundlessness of God's empire, and the other revealing the delicate organism, the marvellous beauty, the infinite skill and care manifest in the minutest forms of creature life,—were the inventions of this age. Besides these, we have the mariner's compass, so improved as to become almost a new invention, the airpump, the barometer, the thermometer; while among its discoveries were those of the circulation of the blood and the nature and use of electricity. It was the era of extended research and discovery. Its navigators and explorers traversed the globe in every meridian.

It was, moreover, a period of copious learning and of distinguished genius, both in literature and art, of discursive philosophy, profound piety, and a sagacious statesmanship. Science was represented by Galileo, Tycho Brahé, and Kepler; art

by Rubens, Vandyke, and Rembrandt; literature by Tasso, Cervantes, Molière, Racine, Edmund Spenser, Ben Jonson, and Beaumont; philosophy by Francis Bacon, John Selden, Philip Sidney, and Descartes; and theology by Isaac Casaubon, the immortal Hooker, and Blaise Pascal. It was in this century that Shakespeare, the myriad-minded man, the greatest intellect who in our recorded world has left record of himself in literature, the poet of the human race, lived and wrote. It was now the strain of Milton's song was heard. Great men like these are both the ripe fruit and the creators of their times. The times could not be without them, nor are they independent of them.

They are God's gift to the world, and in their thought and work indicate the world's progress, and are its means and helpers.

It was, further, a century of startling incident and wonderful vicissitude, both in the ecclesiastical and political world. We are apt to suppose that progress and innovation are so peculiarly the features of these latter times, that it is only in them that a man of more than ordinary length of life has witnessed any remarkable change. But the period we are now considering is quite as varied in the changes presented as any other age of the world. It included the magnificent reign of Elizabeth, the great English rebellion, the ten years of the Commonwealth, and the restoration of the crown. It saw the forty years' reign of Philip II., the amazing revolt of the Netherlands, and the final establishment of a Protestant republic. It witnessed the struggles of the Huguenots in France, including the horrors of St. Bartholomew's and saw the establishment of the inquisition in Holland, persecutions by which Rome lost more than Protestants. It included in its wonderful annals the Thirty Years' War, with the sorrow and sacrifice it involved, and the remarkable energy and heroism it developed.

Such, in brief, are some of the leading features of the remarkable century out of which the earlier settlers of this continent came. These men could not fail to feel the influence of the times which, in the expressive language of the Old Testament, were going over them. While these times were partly of the earth, they were in very much of their bearing above the earth. In them God was evoking and guiding energies, awakening and developing moral forces, and working out results, which were to affect the whole race. They were the dawn of a new era, the beginning of a new life; and the men whom they produced brought with them to this new world the indomitable energy, the restless activity, the independent thought, and the power of achievement which so distinctly characterized the new era. They were plain, unassuming men, bringing with them little wealth, and unattended by the pomp of circumstance. They attracted little attention at the time. Indeed, they were guided by him, whose promise was that he would lead the blind by a way they know not (Isaiah 42:16). They saw not the vastness of the foundations they were laying. The founders of this country were truly great in their unconsciousness. But taking hold of the work immediately at hand, they proved themselves to be men knowing the times, and God was with them. Such being the providential springs of our national existence, observe—

2. The hand of God in the development of our national life. Neither nations, governments, nor yet religion itself, are sudden creations. All governments are experimental. They are growths. God simply gives us the seeds of things, and then, under the action of his truth and spirit, and the leadings of his providence, we are to see to their planting and growth. The Reformation, with the social impulse to which it had given birth, was destined to advance a second step, appearing in a purer form, but on a different soil. To escape from religious intolerance, a body of English dissenters, contemptuously called Puritans, were seen flying first to Holland, then to these American shores. Thus exiled and escaping, God watched and guided their flight. Through these men he intended to realize, in the form of permanent institutions, the ideas of religion and government which the majority of mankind but imperfectly understood, which they were poorly prepared to appreciate, and were little disposed to promote, but which, being essential to the best interests of mankind, were wrapt up in the divine purpose.

THE MEN SELECTED FOR THIS WORK

In the men selected for this work, we find, as aforetime, that *"not many wise men after the flesh, not many noble, not many mighty are called"* (*I Corinthians 1:26*). God works by the lowliest agencies, in accomplishing his purposes. The human instrumentality is graciously adapted to its service, but never permitted to hide the hand that uses it. . . . The men who came to these American shores, bringing the inspiration and impulse of the new life which had appeared in Europe, were a plain, common people. They were hardworking, Bible-reading, profoundly in earnest,

with a deep sense of God in them; but they were not so colossal, nor so perfect, as our imagination so often paints them. They needed the schooling of the times and of Providence, as we all do, that they might not drop into the old ruts, and perpetuate the evils of the old religious and political life. It is evident that a double purpose animated them. They were not unmindful, in seeking this new home, of worldly advantage. They were impelled by a spirit of material enterprise, and were far from willing to settle down to any idle, dreamy existence. At the same time, a deep religious conviction swayed their minds, and a profound religious purpose shaped their lives.

LOVE OF GOD, NOT LOVE OF MAN

It was not a love of man, but a love of God,—not a love of country, but a love of Christ, overmastering and crucifying all love of country, a personal consecration to the gospel superior to all philanthropy, to all patriotism,—that planted the germs of our national life on Plymouth Rock and Jamestown. Governed and impelled by this twofold spirit, strong in God and their own heroic patience, they commenced their battle with danger and hardship. Stepping forth upon the shore, a wild and frowning wilderness received them. Disease smote them, but they fainted not; famine overtook them, but they feasted on roots with a patient spirit. They built a house for God, then for themselves. They established education and the observance of a stern but august morality, then legislated for the smaller purposes of material interests. Thus did they lay the foundations. Soon the villages began to smile. Churches arose still farther in the depths of the wilderness. Industry multiplied her hands. Colleges were founded, and the beginning of civil order were witnessed. A decade of years passed,—Salem, Charlestown, Dorchester, Roxbury, Watertown, Cambridge, and Boston are settled,—trade is opened with the Mother Country, and the foundations of a permanent colony are laid. This colonial period was full of indomitable energy, of a busy enterprise, of advancing learning, of abounding religious and political activity. The population increased with a startling rapidity. Commerce, says Mr. Burke, extended itself "out of all proportion beyond the numbers of the people," and already the Old World began to be fed by the New; while the love of freedom deepened in the hearts of the people, and became the predominant feature distinguishing the whole body. Two things impress us, as marking the history of this period.

DEVELOPMENT OF RELIGIOUS
LIBERTY AND GROWTH OF
REPRESENTATIVE GOVERNMENT

(a.) The earnest struggles of religious freedom. It was as yet only imperfectly that some of the principles which began to be evolved in Luther's day had been wrought out. Much was gained for religious liberty when that Reformer broke with the traditional dogmatism of the Papal Church. Still more was gained when the Puritans broke with the churchly authority which they left behind them. But there was needed another break, and it was one with themselves. In the early settlement of our country, Church and State were united by law. The Church was sustained by taxation and state appropriation. In the Southern States, formal church establishments existed. In all, there existed religious tests, excluding from public office or civil franchise such as did not accept the accredited faith. While in Connecticut and Massachusetts there was no religious establishment as such,—the bare suggestion of one having drawn forth an energetic protest,—yet a forced conformity to, and support of, the congregational church system was manifestly the policy of the founders. . . . A new advance was to be made; but, like all true reform, it is to be through persecution and trial. There is to be another break from authority and religious intolerance. . . . Rhode Island, Maryland, and Pennsylvania were the first civil communities that ever incorporated religious liberty into their original constitutions, since which time the world has been led to admit the wisdom and sound policy of such a course. And as the principle has gained ascendency over the land, it has been proven that freedom of opinion is not inimical to religious growth, and that a free Church and a free State are a people's grandest opportunity for religious and political development.

(b.) A second feature of this period, is, the almost spontaneous growth of representative governments. Without any concerted action on the part of the Colonies, but, as it were, by a popular instinct, which lay at the foundation of that constitutional freedom which the fathers sought in this country, "a House of Burgesses," says Mr. Hutchinson, "broke out in Virginia, in 1620; and although there was no color for it in the charter of Massachusetts, a House of Deputies appeared suddenly in 1643." Various acts of interference were attempted to check this tendency to independent self-government, but all in vain, and only to develop that spirit of resistance which afterward broke out in the Revolution. . . . The people formed its own commonwealths,—its ultimate nation. "The people," says Mr. Bancroft, "was superior to its institutions, possessing the vital force which goes before organization, and gives to it strength and form." Under the action of this vital force the principle of self-government was nurtured, and for the space of one hundred and fifty years the work went on quietly, almost imperceptibly, until there appeared before the statesmen of the Old World a new claimant for national recognition and honors. Surely the eye that can see no indication of a Divine Providence working in such historical development, is one which, though it may discern the face of the sky, cannot discern the signs of the times (Matthew 16:3).

★　　　　★　　　　★　　　　★　　　　★

Rev. Foljambe's sermon is interrupted to insert the following excerpt from a pastor's sermon of an earlier date, also illustrating the "Hand of God in American history." *Editor*

*Thanksgiving
Sermon,
November 29,
1798,* by Rev.
Jonathan French
of Andover

FRANCE REPELLED IN 1746 THROUGH PRAYER
AND FASTING OF NEW ENGLANDERS

"Many, O Lord my God, are thy wonderful works which thou hast done, and thy thoughts which are to us-ward: They cannot be reckoned up in order unto thee: If I would declare and speak of them, they are more than can be numbered." (Psalms 40:5)

What cannot a people do when the Lord is on their side? Filled with resentment on account of the loss of Louisburgh (June 17th, 1745), France resolved to raise "a fleet and armament to recover that place, to make a conquest of Novascotia, and to lay waste the whole seacoast from Novascotia to Georgia."

Great preparations were accordingly made: "The whole fleet consisted of 14 capital ships, 20 smaller ones, together with fire ships, bombs, tenders, and transports for eight thousand troops; in the whole about seventy sail."

This great fleet, under the command of Duke d'Anville, was to have sailed the beginning of May, 1746. But the hand of that providence, which commands the winds and the seas, seemed to be visible in causing the opposing elements to retard the enterprise; for, notwithstanding they were so early ready for sea, contrary winds prevented their sailing from France, till the 22nd of June.

M. Conflans, with four ships of the line from the West Indies was to join them. This squadron arrived upon the coast sometime before the grand fleet. After a while, being severely combated by storms and fogs, and being strangers to the coast, and not finding the fleet, they grew discouraged, and returned to France.

The news of the fleet's sailing from France excited great anxiety in the minds of the people. Their fears were in some measure, however, relieved by the news of the sailing of a British fleet after them. These hopes, however, proved abortive; for Admiral Lestock put out no less than seven times from England, it is said, and was driven back by contrary winds. The French fleet having sailed, and steering too far southward fell into the hot climates in the very heat of summer. This, with the length of their passage, which was about three months, caused a mortal sickness among them, of which about thirteen hundred died at sea. The rest were much weakened and dispirited.

When the news arrived that the fleet was seen approaching the coast, the country was filled with consternation; and every face seemed to gather paleness. The streets filled with men, marching for the defence of the sea ports, and the distresses of women and children, trembling for the event, made too deep impressions upon the minds of those who remember these scenes, ever to be erased. But never did that religion, for which this country was settled, appear more important, nor prayer more prevalent, than on this occasion. A God hearing prayer, stretched forth the arm of his power, and destroyed that mighty Armament, in a manner almost as extraordinary as the drowning of Pharaoh and his host in the Red Sea.

Coming near the coast a tremendous storm threw the fleet into great distress. One vessel was cast away upon the isle of Sables, and four ships of the line, and one transport were seen in great distress, but not heard of afterwards. After the storm, they were enveloped for several days, in an uncommon fog. At length, the Admirals ship and one more, on the 12th of September got into the harbour. One got in before and three others in three days after. Finding his ships in a shattered condition, so many of his men dead, and so many sickly, the Admiral fell into discouragement and died on the sixteenth. The Vice Admiral, soon after arrived, and finding himself in such an awful condition, and struck with chagrin and disappointment, put an end to his own life with his sword. What remained of the fleet landed to recruit. But the sickness swept off one thousand, one hundred and thirty more at Chibucto (Halifax) before they left the place.

The news that Admiral Lestock with an English fleet was expected after them, hastened their determination to leave the place. They burnt one ship of the line, and several others not fit for sea; struck their tents, embarked, and on the 13th of October, put to sea with all expedition. On the 15th, they were met by another violent storm near Cape Sables, by which they were scattered and very much damaged. On the next day, the storm abating, and the weather proving more favorable, they collected their scattered fleet as well as they could, and attempted to press forward on their voyage.

On this great emergency, and day of darkness and doubtful expectation, the 16th of October was observed as a day of FASTING and PRAYER throughout the Province. And, wonderful to relate, that very night God sent upon them a more dreadful storm than either of the former, and completed their destruction. Some overset, some foundered, and a remnant only of this miserable fleet, returned to France to carry the news. Thus New England STOOD STILL, AND SAW THE SALVATION OF GOD.

★   ★   ★   ★   ★

GOD'S HAND IN REVOLUTIONARY PERIOD

(3) Passing now from the infancy of the nation to the revolutionary period of our history, when it reached its manhood, we find added illustration of God's hand in that history. The Revolution was not the result of any causes or of any spirit that had suddenly arisen. It was the necessary consequence of the previous providential training,—of the moral and political forces which had long been at work in the minds of the people . . . . It must have come sooner or later; but the attempt to deprive the Colonies of their representative system hastened the event. The passage of the Stamp Act and the Port Bill fell upon the minds of a spirited and jealous people as an act of oppression to be resisted. The presence of bodies of armed men, instead of producing the designed intimidation, only served to arouse the spirit of the people, and cement the Colonies in a common bond, for mutual support and protection. I need not stop to rehearse the story of the

Annual Election Sermon, Boston, Mass., January 5, 1876, by Rev. S. W. Foljambe of Malden

uprising and struggles of an earnest and enlightened people for independence. . . .

But, in looking over this heroic past, I see the hand of God; and this, not only in the shaping of events and directing of influences, likely to serve as motives in the minds of men, but in the unity of the people, and the unparalleled devotion of the various Colonies,—scattered as they were over a large extent of territory, and bound together, not so much by a common material interest, as by a common and all-pervading sentiment of freedom. I see that hand in the men raised up for the times. He who makes the times go over us, has always the men ready to meet them. It was so in the era of the Reformation. . . . So, for the times of Republican progress,—when a new nation is to come to its manhood, and new institutions are to be confirmed and established,—he found an Otis and a Henry, the impassioned and triumphant defenders of popular rights; a Samuel and a John Adams, the one with his profound sagacity and untiring courage, the other acute and impassioned; a Thomas Jefferson and George Mason, both sagacious and learned; a Benjamin Franklin, astute and philosophical; a Josiah Quincy, Jr., well styled "the silver-tongued orator of freedom"; a Robert Morris, who, as the skilful financier, rendered services which, though differing in form, were hardly less needful to the success of the cause than those of Washington himself, who stands peerless among the great and good of all ages. In a most emphatic sense, Washington was a man prepared by Providence for a special end. In the long and dreary war, commencing in the spring of 1775, and which was not closed for seven years, what was wanting was a permanent military chieftain, who should be possessed of the rare qualities of patience, perseverance and endurance; and all these qualities Washington had in so very high a degree, that it may be said with entire truth, that there never was his superior in such endowments. Calm, wise, incorruptible, he was preeminently the man for the times.

I see, further, the hand of God in his unmistakable help in the hour of conflict. We attained our national independence against all probabilities. Often, in the dark hours of the struggle, nothing saved the American cause from entire destruction but the divine interposition. It had its days of darkness, suffering, and reverses, when it seemed as if success were impossible. A country without resources, an army gathered on short enlistments, and without discipline, a Congress sometimes tardy in supplying the means of carrying on the war, were not the most encouraging conditions of success. It is a matter of astonishment, that the spirit of the great leader did not break down, and that the internal supports of his hope and courage did not give way. But for the firm hold he had upon first and highest principles, and the confidence that he felt in God as their defender, his spirit must have sunk within him long before the close of the war. Whether he himself recognized a Divine Providence as working in the American cause; whether he regarded his country's success as dependent upon that Providence, he would have told you, had you asked him, as he came from his knees in the forest seclusion, where he was accustomed to bow in prayer, while passing that dark winter at Valley Forge. God was as certainly in the lives of Washington, and Lafayette, and Marion, as he was in the lives of Moses, and Joshua, and Daniel; he was no more present at Megiddo and Jericho, than at White Plains and Valley Forge. The battle was the Lord's and it could not be lost.

REPUBLIC FORMED

(4) In the growth and progress of the intervening century, we discover the guiding and beneficent hand of God. The struggles of the Revolution past, the boon of independence won, a new epoch was to be entered upon, and it was one of vast moment. Failing here, all that had gone before would go for nothing. It was not enough that the country should become free from the domination of England: it was necessary that it should be erected into a nation, and that the numerous Colonies that had been converted into States should be formed into one Republic. This was a solemn hour in our history. The American cause needed men of far-sighted sagacity, of able statesmanship; it needed men of incorruptible patriotism, who would fill the offices of government, not in the interest of self, but of their country,—faithful at home, and just abroad. How adequately God furnished the men, and overruled all things in the interests of the nation, the history of the constitutional era shows. . . .

PRESENT STANDING AS A NATION

Looking, now, at our present standing as a nation, we have every reason to recognize and own the hand of God. The future chronicler of events, as he looks down on the unrolled scroll

THE HAND
OF GOD
IN AMERICAN
HISTORY

OUR SECOND
CENTURY

of time, will write down the period in which we live as part of the marvellous century in human story. The interest in history deepens as time advances, for it becomes more and more the record of intellectual and moral progress, of the advancing liberty and happiness of mankind. This is preeminently so with our history. It is the story of a wonderful growth. It is in no spirit of empty boasting or vain-glory I speak of what we are, and what we enjoy as a people; for not by the might of our power, or the wisdom of our counsel, has this nation been built, or its resources developed. Has there been wisdom in our counsels? It was by the inspiration of the Almighty. Has wealth increased? God gave us power to get wealth (*Deuteronomy 8:18*). Has freedom gained new victories? He led us in the ways of righteousness for his own name's sake. *"He hath not dealt so with any nation"* (*Psalms 147:20*).

But better than all outward and material progress have been the firm rooting and beneficent growth of our religious and political institutions . . . . We have accomplished the separation of Church and State, without any serious detriment to either; nay, with positive advantage to both. The State has not ceased to be Christian because freed from all responsibility as to religious opinions and institutions. It originated in the Christian religion, and will continue to be conserved by it. Mr. Everett declares that "all the distinctive features and superiority of our Republican institutions are derived from the teachings of Scripture." . . . I care not for any formal constitutional recognition of Christianity; indeed, the fact complained of in some quarters, that there is no such recognition in the Constitution, is, to my mind, proof of the purity of the religious spirit of its framers. The separation of State and Religion was the testimony of the fathers to the inherent power of the Christian faith, and that it had no need of any political bolstering up. But all this was far from ignoring the religious spirit in our national life; its guiding and impelling power in the lives of our people, and its formative influence in all their institutions and laws. If ever there has been a people who incorporated the Bible into themselves, and themselves into the Bible,—whose laws, customs, institutions and literature were permeated by the spirit of Christianity,—it has been our own, and this while the Constitution expressly provides that Congress shall make no law respecting an establishment of religion. . . .

Next to the growth of our religious institutions, is the development of the educational interests of our country. The founders of this government were so sagacious, as to see that the permanence of free institutions depended on the intelligence of the people; and it has been shown, by our experiment, that free institutions can give a wider education to the people, than has ever been given by an aristocracy or a monarchy. . . .

Intelligence, however, is not alone indispensable. Knowledge is power, but it may be power for evil as much as good; it has no moral quality in itself. The greatest danger of the Republic is its educated, experienced, cultivated, corrupt demagogues. Intelligence without religion is a dangerous pilot for the ship of state. Eliminate that element; take religious thought, sentiment, and aspiration from the atmosphere of our education, and men will soon become animalized, and this government sink beneath the green pool of its own corruption. It was an instinct of self-preservation that incorporated in the Bill of Rights that "religion, morality, and knowledge are necessary to good government." It is our unsectarian, popular education,—but an education as yet undivorced from the religious sentiment and spirit, —that has been the source and means of all our progress in the past, and must continue to be our defence and hope in all the future. . . .

OUR SECOND CENTURY

We enter upon our second century amid deepening responsibilities. No thoughtful man can close his eyes to the dangers which beset us, or be unmindful of the new issues constantly arising, demanding for their wise solution the most unselfish and the purest patriotism with the most enlightened Christian conscientiousness.

We need, in view of our dangers, to temper our enthusiasm with sobriety. We are menaced by a growing spirit of materialism. The eagerness of men after material prosperity tends to a practical absorption in those ends. Thus we have the greed, the excitement, the infatuation, the extravagance, and the corruption, that, to so great an extent, characterize our times. The abounding iniquity of our day is a just cause of alarm. While we ought not to forget nor undervalue much that is noble, and true, and good, in the present time, nor regard the former days as in all respects better than these, we must admit that we are living in a period of shameful prevalent corruption and crime. Each daily paper brings its fresh instalment of defalcation, fraudulent dealing, forgery, robbery, and murder. On every hand men are making void the law of God. While there is an advance of truth and religion on the one hand, there is a strengthening of the bands of wickedness, and a breaking away from the restraints of law. . . .

It is true you cannot legislate evil out of the world, but by an impartial, rigorous justice you can make it too costly for practice, and by a wise and Christian legislation you may limit its reach and remove its temptations; and for this, in its most perfect measure, and to our utmost ability, the God of righteousness holds every man responsible. But alas! not the least evil of our times is the increasing corruption in the officers of government, both national and local. . . . If today there be reason for any concern, it is not so much because of any loss of hereditary talent, or eloquence, or shrewd intelligence, but because of the decay, in too many places, of the old ancestral integrity, disinterestedness, and magnanimity. What our country needs in its leaders and legislators are the purest Christian principles, the loftiest personal character, the highest and most unselfish political aims; that they be men whom no gold can buy, no adulation of the people can mislead, and no spirit of ambition can pervert. . . .

In referring to the evils of our times, we have not spoken despondently; for there is no evil which a true Christian fidelity, and a wise and sagacious patriotism, and a pure political action, cannot lessen or remove. If, in the present season of difficulty and depression, any mind has yielded to despondency as to our future, it needs only to be remembered, as a check to this hasty despair, how much of misrule and mischief every great nation has had to survive. There never has been an auspicious day for humanity that was not one of doubt and conflict. Great evils have always confronted the world's earnest workers. Indeed, the intense light that they have flashed on them,

has tended to reveal them with greater clearness. The world does not move backward, neither is it stationary. Men may leave their work incomplete, but the work of God goes on to perfection. What trials of our faith in principles, what delays, nay, even what momentary reverses may be before us, none may foresee; but our trust is in God, whose purposes never fail. Generations may come and go, individuals may die, the great and the mighty, men wise in council and reverend in goodness, may pass away, but God's work in the regeneration of the race will go on. There will be vicissitude and change, the conflict between good and evil will deepen, the questions engrossing the thought of today will find their solution, and give place to the more absorbing questions of the future; but the country will live, its institutions perfected and perpetuated by the enlightened devotion and patriotism of the people, till our letters and our arts, our schools and our churches, our laws and our liberties, shall be carried from the arctic circle to the tropics, from the rising of the sun to the going down thereof. . . .

The interests of a citizen, as well as the sentiments of a preacher, have led me to speak of the providence of God in our history,—a history as wonderful as it is unique. With the Psalmist, we can say, "He hath not dealt so with any people." . . . Whatever is noble in the character of our people, or heroic in the annals of our history, is deeply grounded in their constant recognition of a Divine Providence in human affairs, and the immutability of moral law,—the one the object of their daily trust, the other the inspiration and rule of their daily life. . . .

"The Lord our God be with us, as he was with our fathers; let him not leave us nor forsake us." (I Kings 8:57)

Centennial Oration at Valley Forge, June 19, 1878

The Valley Forge Oration, by Henry Armitt Brown, 1878

The following oration is to serve a twofold purpose: First, show the quality and scope of oratory which still existed in our country in 1878, with the hope it will inspire young men of today to learn in comparable detail the Christian history of America and become accomplished in this art; and second, give a word-picture of the time during the war that, perhaps, most clearly shows the Christian character of the founders' generation. If the reader's soul is stirred and feeling runs deep as he realizes what this one event cost, then the true appreciation of the Revolutionary War can be gained. Editor.

One hundred years ago this country was the scene of extraordinary events and very honorable actions. . . . This anniversary, if I understand it right, has a purpose of its own. It is duty that has brought us here. The spirit appropriate to this hour is one of humility rather than of pride, of reverence rather than of exultation. We come, it is true, the representatives of forty millions of free men by ways our fathers never dreamed of, from regions of which they never heard. We come in the midst of plenty, under a sky of peace, power in our right hand and the keys of knowledge in our left. But we are here to learn rather than to teach; to worship, not to glorify. We come to contemplate the sources of our country's greatness; to commune with the honored past; to remind ourselves, and show our children that Joy can come out of Sorrow, Happiness out of Suffering, Light out of Darkness, Life out of Death. Such is the meaning of this anniversary. I cannot do it justice. . . .

Some of us bear their blood, and all alike enjoy the happiness their valor and endurance won. And if my voice be feeble, we have but to look around. The hills that saw them suffer look down on us; the ground that thrilled beneath their feet we tread today; their unmarked graves still lie in yonder field; the breastworks which they built to shelter them surround us here! Dumb witnesses of the heroic past, ye need no tongues! Face to face with you we see it all:—this soft breeze changes to an icy blast; these trees drop the glory of the summer, and the earth beneath our feet is wrapped in snow. Beside us is a village of log huts—along that ridge smoulder the fires of a camp. The sun has sunk, the stars glitter in the inky sky, the camp is hushed, the fires are out, the night is still. All are in slumber save when a lamp glimmers in a cottage window, and a passing shadow shows a tall figure pacing to and fro. The cold silence is unbroken save when on yonder rampart, crunching the crisp snow with wounded feet, a ragged sentinel keeps watch for Liberty!

55

The close of 1777 marked the gloomiest period of the Revolution. The early enthusiasm of the struggle had passed away. The doubts which the first excitements banished had returned. The novelty of war had gone, and its terrors become awfully familiar. Fire and sword had devastated some of the best parts of the country, its cities were half ruined, its fields laid waste, its resources drained, its best blood poured out in sacrifice. The struggle now had become one of endurance, and while Liberty and Independence seemed as far off as ever, men began to appreciate the tremendous cost at which they were to be purchased. The capture of Burgoyne had, after all, been only a temporary check to a powerful and still unexhausted enemy. Nor was its effect on the Americans themselves wholly beneficial. It had caused the North to relax, in a great measure, its activity and vigilance, and, combined with the immunity from invasion which the South had enjoyed, "to lull asleep two-thirds of the continent." While a few hundred ill-armed, half-clad Americans guarded the Highlands of the Hudson, a well-equipped garrison, several thousand strong, lived in luxury in the city of New York. The British fleet watched with the eyes of Argus the rebel coast. Rhode Island lay undisputed in their hands; Georgia, Virginia, and the Carolinas were open to their invasion, and as incapable of defence as Maryland had been when they landed in the Chesapeake. Drawn upon for the army, the sparse population could not half till the soil, and the savings of laborious years had all been spent. While the miserable paper currency which Congress, with a fatal folly never to be absent from the counsels of men, continued to issue and call money, obeyed natural rather than artificial laws and fell four hundred per cent., coin flowed to Philadelphia and New York, and in spite of military orders and civil edicts, the scanty produce of the country followed it. Nor could the threatened penalty of death restrain the evil. Want began to be widely felt, and the frequent proclamations of the British, accompanied with Tory intrigue and abundant gold began to have effect. To some, even of the wisest, the case was desperate. Even the elements seemed to combine against the cause. A deluge prevented a battle at the Warren Tavern; a fog robbed Washington of victory at Germantown; and at last, while the fate of America hung on the courage, the fortitude, and the patriotism of eleven thousand half-clothed, half-armed, hungry Continentals, who,

discomforted but not discouraged, beaten but not disheartened, suffering but steadfast still, lay on their firelocks on the frozen ridges of Whitemarsh, a British army, nineteen thousand five hundred strong, of veteran troops, perfectly equipped, freshly recruited from Europe, and flushed with recent victory, marched into winter quarters in the chief city of the nation.

CAPTURE OF PHILADELPHIA

Philadelphia surely had never seen such gloomy days as those which preceded the entry of the British. On the 24th of August the American army marched through the length of Front Street; on the 25th the British landed at the Head of Elk. Days of quiet anxiety ensued. On the 11th of September, as Tom Paine was writing a letter to Dr. Franklin, the sound of cannon in the southwest interrupted him. From morning until late in the afternoon people in the streets listened to the dull sound like distant thunder. About six o'clock it died away, and the straining ear could catch nothing but the soughing of the wind. With what anxiety men waited —with what suspense! The sun sank in the west, and the shadows crept over the little city. It was the universal hour for the evening meal, but who could go home to eat? Men gathered about the State House to talk, to conjecture, to consult together, and the women whispered in little groups at the doorsteps, and craned their necks out of the darkened windows to look nervously up and down the street. About eight o'clock there was a little tumult near the Coffee House. The story spread that Washington had gained a victory, and a few lads set up a cheer. But it was not traced to good authority, and disappointment followed. By nine in the evening the suspense was painful. Suddenly, far up Chestnut Street, was heard the clatter of horses' feet. Some one was galloping hard. Down Chestnut like an arrow came at full speed a single horseman. He had ridden fast, and his horse was splashed with foam. Hearts beat quickly as he dashed by; past Sixth Street, past the State House, past Fifth, and round the corner into Fourth. The crowd followed, and instantly packed around him as he drew rein at the Indian Queen. He threw a glance at the earnest faces that were turned toward his, and spoke: "A battle has been fought at the Birmingham Meeting-House, on the Brandywine; the army has been beaten; the French Marquis Lafayette shot through the leg. His Excellency has fallen back to Chester; the road below is full of stragglers." And then the crowd scattered, each one to his home, but not to sleep. A few days followed full of contradictory stories. The armies are manoeuvring on the Lancaster Road. Surely Washington will fight another battle. And then the news came and spread like lightning—Wayne has been surprised and his brigade massacred at the Paoli, and the enemy are in full march for Philadelphia; the Whigs are leaving by hundreds; the authorities are going; the Congress have gone; the British have arrived at Germantown. Who can forget the day that followed?

A sense of something dreadful about to happen hangs over the town. A third of the houses are shut and empty. Shops are unopened, and busy rumor flies about the streets. Early in the morning the sidewalks are filled with a quiet, anxious crowd. The women watch behind bowed windows with half curious, half frightened looks. The men, solemn and subdued, whisper in groups: "Will they come to-day?" "Are they here already?" "Will they treat us like a conquered people?" The morning drags along. By ten o'clock Second Street from Callowhill to Chestnut, is filled with old men and boys. There is hardly a young man to be seen. About eleven is heard the sound of approaching cavalry, and a squadron of dragoons comes galloping down the street, scattering the boys right and left. The crowd parts to let them by, and melts together again. In a few minutes far up the street there is the faint sound of martial music and something moving that glitters in the sunlight. The crowd thickens, and is full of hushed expectation. Presently one can see a red mass swaying to and fro. It becomes more and more distinct. Louder grows the music and the tramp of marching men, as waves of scarlet, tipped with steel, come moving down the street. They are now but a square off—their bayonets glancing in perfect line, and steadily advancing to the music of "God Save the King."

These are the famous grenadiers. Their pointed caps of red, fronted with silver, their white leather leggins and short scarlet coats, trimmed with blue, made a magnificent display. They are perfectly equipped and look well fed and hearty. Behind them are more cavalry. No, these must be officers. The first one is splendidly mounted and wears the uniform of a general. He is a stout man with gray hair and a pleasant countenance, in spite of the squint of an eye which disfigures it. A whisper goes through the bystanders: "It is Lord Cornwallis himself." A brilliant staff in various uniforms follows him,

and five men in civilian's dress. A glance of recognition follows these last like a wave along the street, for they are Joseph Galloway, Enoch Story, Tench Coxe, and the two Allens—father and son—Tories, who have only dared to return home behind British bayonets. Long lines of red coats follow till the Fourth, the Fortieth, and the Fifty-fifth regiments have passed by. But who are these in dark blue that come behind the grenadiers? Breeches of yellow leather, leggins of black, and tall, pointed hats of brass, complete their uniform. They wear moustaches and have a fierce foreign look, and their unfamiliar music seems to a child in that crowd to cry "Plunder! plunder! plunder!" as it times their rapid march. These are the Hessian mercenaries whom Washington surprised and thrashed so well at Christmas in '76. And now Grenadiers and Yagers, horse, foot, and artillery that rumbles along making the windows rattle, have all passed by. The Fifteenth Regiment is drawn up on High Street, near Fifth; the Forty-second Highlanders in Chestnut, below Third, and the artillery is parked in the State House yard. All the afternoon the streets are full—wagons with luggage lumbering along, officers in scarlet riding to and fro, aids and orderlies seeking quarters for their different officers. Yonder swarthy, haughty-looking man, dismounting at Norris's door, is my Lord Rawdon. Lord Cornwallis is quartered at Peter Reeve's in Second, near Spruce, and Knyphausen at Henry Lisle's, nearer to Dock Street, on the east. The younger officers are well bestowed, for Dr. Franklin's house has been taken by a certain clever Captain Andre. The time for the evening parade comes, and the well-equipped regiments are drawn up in line, while slowly to the strains of martial music the sun sinks in autumnal splendor in the west. The streets are soon in shadow, but still noisy with the trampling of soldiers and the clatter of arms. In High Street, and on the commons, fires are lit for the troops to do their cooking, and the noises of the camp mingle with the city's hum. Most of the houses are shut, but here and there one stands wide open, while brilliantly-dressed officers lounge at the windows or pass and repass in the doorway. The sound of laughter and music is heard and the brightly-lit windows of the London Coffee House and the Indian Queen tell of the parties that are celebrating there the event they think so glorious; and thus, amid sounds of revelry, the night falls on the Quaker City. In spite of Trenton and Princeton and Brandywine; in spite of the wisdom of Congress and the courage and skill of the Commander-in-chief; in spite of the bravery and fortitude of the Continental army, the forces of the king are in the Rebel capital, and the "all's well" of hostile sentinels keeping guard by her northern border passes unchallenged from the Schuylkill to the Delaware.

What matters it to Sir William Howe and his victorious army if rebels be starving and their ragged currency be almost worthless? Here is gold and plenty of good cheer. What whether they threaten to attack the British lines or disperse through the impoverished country in search of food? The ten redoubts that stretch from Fairmount to Cohoesink Creek are stout and strongly manned, the river is open, and supplies and reinforcements are on the way from England. What if the earth be wrinkled with frost? The houses of Philadelphia are snug and warm. What if the rigorous winter has begun and snow be whitening the hills? Here are mirth and music, and dancing and wine, and women and play, and the pageants of a riotous capital! And so with feasting and with revelry let the winter wear away!

THE CONTINENTAL ARMY

The wind is cold and piercing on the old Gulf Road, and the snowflakes have begun to fall. Who is this that toils up yonder hill, his footsteps stained with blood? "His bare feet peep through his worn-out shoes, his legs nearly naked from the tattered remains of an only pair of stockings, his breeches not enough to cover his nakedness, his shirt hanging in strings, his hair dishevelled, his face wan and thin, his look hungry, his whole appearance that of a man forsaken and neglected." On his shoulder he carries a rusty gun, and the hand that grasps the stock is blue with cold. His comrade is no better off, nor he who follows, for both are barefoot, and the ruts of the rough country road are deep and frozen hard. A fourth comes into view, and still another. A dozen are in sight. Twenty have reached the ridge, and there are more to come. See them as they mount the hill that slopes eastward into the Great Valley. A thousand are in sight, but they are but the vanguard of the motley company that winds down the road until it is lost in the cloud of snow-flakes that have hidden the Gulf hills. Yonder are horsemen in tattered uniforms, and behind them cannon lumbering slowly over the frozen road, half dragged, half pushed by men. They who appear to be in authority have coats of every make and color. Here

is one in a faded blue, faced with buckskin that has once been buff. There is another on a tall, gaunt horse, wrapped "in a sort of dressing-gown made of an old blanket or woollen bed cover." A few of the men wear long linen hunting shirts reaching to the knee, but of the rest no two are dressed alike—not half have shirts, a third are barefoot, many are in rags. Nor are their arms the same. Cowhorns and tin boxes they carry for want of pouches. A few have swords, fewer still bayonets. Muskets, carbines, fowling-pieces, and rifles are to be seen together side by side.

Are these soldiers that huddle together and bow their heads as they face the biting wind? Is this an army that comes straggling through the valley in the blinding snow? No martial music leads them in triumph into a captured capital. No city full of good cheer and warm and comfortable homes awaits their coming. No sound keeps time to their steps save the icy wind rattling the leafless branches and the dull tread of their weary feet on the frozen ground. In yonder forest must they find their shelter, and on the northern slope of these inhospitable hills their place of refuge. Perils shall soon assault them more threatening than any they encountered under the windows of Chew's house or by the banks of Brandywine. Trials that rarely have failed to break the fortitude of men await them here. False friends shall endeavor to undermine their virtue and secret enemies to shake their faith; the Congress whom they serve shall prove helpless to protect them, and their country herself seem unmindful of their sufferings; Cold shall share their habitations, and Hunger enter in and be their constant guest; Disease shall infest their huts by day, and Famine stand guard with them through the night; Frost shall lock their camp with icy fetters, and the snows cover it as with a garment; the storms of winter shall be pitiless—but all in vain. Danger shall not frighten nor temptation have power to seduce them. Doubt shall not shake their love of country nor suffering overcome their fortitude. The powers of evil shall not prevail against them, for they are the Continental Army, and these are the hills of Valley Forge!

VALLEY FORGE

It is not easy to-day to imagine this country as it appeared a century ago. Yonder city, which now contains one-fourth as many inhabitants as were found in those days between Maine and Georgia, was a town of but thirty thousand men, and at the same time the chief city of the continent. The richness of the soil around it had early attracted settlers, and the farmers of the Great Valley had begun to make that country the garden which it is to-day; but from the top of this hill one could still behold the wilderness under cover of which, but twenty years before, the Indian had spread havoc through the back settlements on the Lehigh and the Susquehanna. The most important place between the latter river and the site of Fort Pitt, "at the junction of the Ohio," was the frontier village of York, where Congress had taken refuge. The single road which connected Philadelphia with the Western country had been cut through the forest to Harris's Block House but forty years before. It was half a century only since its iron ore had led to the settlement of Lancaster, and little more than a quarter since a single house had marked the site of Reading. The ruins of Colonel Bull's plantation, burned by the British on their march, lay in solitude on the hills which are covered to-day with the roofs and spires of Norristown; and where yonder cloud hangs over the furnaces and foundries of Phoenixville, a man named Gordon, living in a cave, gave his name to a crossing of the river. Nor was this spot itself the same. A few small houses clustered about Potts's Forge, where the creek tumbled into the Schuylkill, and two or three near the river bank marked the beginning of a little farm. The axe had cleared much of the bottom lands and fertile fields of the Great Valley, but these hills were still wrapped in forest that covered their sides as far as the eye could reach. The roads that ascended their ridge on the south and east plunged into densest woods as they climbed the hill, and met beneath its shadow at the same spot where to-day a school-house stands in the midst of smiling fields. It is no wonder that the Baron De Kalb, as he gazed on the forest of oak and chestnut that covered the sides and summit of Mount Joy, should have described the place bitterly as "a wilderness."

But nevertheless it was well chosen. There was no town that would answer. Wilmington and Trenton would have afforded shelter, but in the one the army would have been useless, and in the other in constant danger. Reading and Lancaster were so distant that the choice of either would have left a large district open to the enemy, and both, in which were valuable stores, could be better covered by an army here. Equally distant with Philadelphia from the fords of Brandywine and the ferry into Jersey, the army could move to either point as rapidly as the Brit-

ish themselves, and while distant enough from the city to be safe from surprise or sudden attack itself, it could protect the country that lay between, and at the same time be a constant menace to the capital. Strategically, then, the General could not have chosen better. And the place was well adapted for the purpose. The Schuylkill, flowing from the Blue Hills, bent here toward the eastward. Its current was rapid, and its banks precipitous. The Valley Creek, cutting its way through a deep defile at right angles to the river, formed a natural boundary on the west. The hill called Mount Joy, at the entrance of that defile, threw out a spur which, running parallel to the river about a mile, turned at length northward and met its banks. On the one side this ridge enclosed a rolling table land; on the other it sloped sharply to the Great Valley. The engineers under Du Portail marked out a line of entrenchments four feet high, protected by a ditch six feet wide, from the entrance of the Valley Creek defile, along the crest of this ridge until it joined the bank of the Schuylkill, where a redoubt marked the eastern angle of the encampment. High on the shoulder of Mount Joy a second line girdled the mountain, and then ran northward to the river, broken only by the hollow through which the Gulf Road descended to the Forge. This hollow place was later defended by an abattis and a triangular earthwork.

A redoubt on the east side of Mount Joy commanded the Valley road, and another behind the left flank of the abattis, that which came from the river, while a star redoubt on a hill at the bank acted as a *tete-de-pont* for the bridge that was thrown across the Schuylkill. Behind the front and before the second line the troops were ordered to build huts for winter quarters. Fourteen feet by sixteen, of logs plastered with clay, these huts began to rise on every side. Placed in rows, each brigade by itself, they soon gave the camp the appearance of a little city. All day long the axe resounded among the hills, and the place was filled with the noise of hammering and the crash of falling trees. "I was there when the army first began to build huts," wrote Paine to Franklin. "They appeared to me like a family of beavers, every one busy; some carrying logs, others mud, and the rest plastering them together. The whole was raised in a few days, and it is a curious collection of buildings in the true rustic order." The weather soon became intensely cold. The Schuylkill froze over, and the roads were blocked with snow, but it was not until nearly the middle of January that the last hut was built

59

and the army settled down into winter quarters on the bare hillsides.

PROBLEMS WITH CONGRESS

The trials which have made this place so famous arose chiefly from the incapacity of Congress. It is true that the country in the neighborhood of Philadelphia was well-nigh exhausted. An active campaign over a small extent of territory had drawn heavily on the resources of this part of Pennsylvania and the adjacent Jersey. Both forces had fed upon the country, and it was not so much disaffection (of which Washington wrote) as utter exhaustion which made the farmers of the devastated region furnish so little to the army. Nor would it have been human nature in them to have preferred the badly printed, often counterfeited, depreciated promise to pay, of the Americans, for the gold which the British had to offer. In spite of the efforts of McLane's and Lee's Light Horse and the activity of Lacey, of the militia, the few supplies that were left went steadily to Philadelphia, and the patriot army remained in want. But the more distant States, north and south, could easily have fed and clothed a much more numerous army. That they did not was the fault of Congress. That body no longer contained the men who had made it famous in the years gone by. Franklin was in Paris, where John Adams was about to join him. Jay, Jefferson, Rutledge, Livingston, and Henry were employed at home. Hancock had resigned. Samuel Adams was absent in New England. Men much their inferiors had taken their places.

The period, inevitable in the history of revolutions, had arrived, when men of the second rank came to the front. With the early leaders in the struggle had disappeared the foresight, the breadth of view, the loftiness of purpose, and the self-sacrificing spirit belonging only to great minds which had marked and honored the commencement of the struggle. A smaller mind had begun to rule, a narrower view to influence, a personal feeling to animate the members. Driven from Philadelphia, they were in a measure disheartened, and their pride touched in a tender spot. Incapable of the loftier sentiments which had moved their predecessors, they could not overcome a sense of their own importance and the desire to magnify their office. Petty rivalries had sprung up among them, and sectional feeling, smothered in '74, '75, and '76, had taken breath again, and asserted itself with renewed vigor in the recent debates on the confederation. But if divided among themselves by petty jealousies, they were united in a greater jealousy of Washington and the army. They cannot be wholly blamed for this. Taught by history no less than by their own experience, of the dangers of standing armies in a free State, and wanting in modern history the single example which we have in Washington of a successful military chief retiring voluntarily into private life, they judged the leader of their forces by themselves and the ordinary rules of human nature. Their distrust was not unnatural nor wholly selfish, and must find some justification in the exceptional greatness of his character.

It was in vain that he called on them to dismiss their doubts and trust an army which had proved faithful. In vain he urged them to let their patriotism embrace, as his had learned to do, the whole country with an equal fervor. In vain he pointed out that want of organization in the army was due to want of union among them. They continued distrustful and unconvinced. In vain he asked for a single army, one and homogeneous. Congress insisted on thirteen distinct armies, each under the control of its particular State. The effect was disastrous. The personnel of the army was continually changing. Each State had its own rules, its own system of organization, its own plan of making enlistments. No two worked together—the men's terms even expiring at the most delicate and critical times. Promotion was irregular and uncertain, and the sense of duty was impaired as that of responsibility grew less. Instead of an organized army, Washington commanded a disorganized mob. The extraordinary virtues of that great man might keep the men together, but there were some things which they could not do. Without an organized quartermaster's department the men could not be clothed or fed. At first mismanaged, this department became neglected. The warnings of Washington were disregarded, his appeals in vain. The troops began to want clothing soon after Brandywine.

By November it was evident that they must keep the field without blankets, overcoats, or tents. At Whitemarsh they lay, half clad, on frozen ground. By the middle of December they were in want of the necessaries of life.

FOUR MONTHS OF SUFFERING

"We are ordered to march over the river," writes *Dr. Waldo,* of Colonel Prentice's Connecticut Regiment, at Swede's Ford, on December 12. "It snows—I'm sick—eat nothing—no whiskey—no baggage—Lord—Lord—Lord! Till sunrise crossing the river, cold and uncomfortable." "I'm sick," he goes on two days after, in his diary, discontented and out of humor. "Poor food—hard lodging—cold weather—fatigued—nasty clothes—nasty cookery—smoked out of my sense—I can't endure it. Here comes a bowl of soup, sickish enough to make a Hector ill. Away with it, boy—I'll live like the chameleon, on air." On the 19th of December they reached Valley Forge. By the 21st even such a bowl of soup had become a luxury. "A general cry," notes Waldo again, "through the camp this evening": . . . "No meat, no meat." The distant vales echoed back the melancholy sound: "No meat, no meat." It was literally true. On the next day *Washington* wrote to the President of Congress: "I do not know from what cause this alarming deficiency, or rather total failure of supplies, arises, but unless more vigorous exertions and better regulations take place in that line immediately this army must dissolve. I have done all in my power by remonstrating, by writing, by ordering the commissaries on this head, from time to time, but without any good effect, or obtaining more than a present scanty relief. Owing to this the march of the army has been delayed on more than one interesting occasion in the course of the present campaign; and had a body of the enemy crossed the Schuylkill this morning (as I had reason to expect from the intelligence I received at four o'clock last night) the divisions which I ordered to be in readiness to march and meet them could not have moved." Hardly was this written when the news did come that the enemy had come out to Darby, and the troops were ordered under arms. "Fighting," responded *General Huntington* when he got the order, "will be far preferable to starving. My brigade is out of provisions, nor can the commissary obtain any meat." "Three days successively," added *Varnum,* of Rhode Island, "we have been destitute of bread, two days we have been entirely without meat." It was impossible to stir.

And "this," wrote *Washington,* in indignation, "brought forth the only commissary in camp, and with him this melancholy and alarming truth that he had not a single hoof to slaughter, and not more than twenty-five barrels of flour." "I am now convinced beyond a doubt that unless some great and capital change suddenly takes place in that line this army must inevitably be reduced to one or other of these three things—starve, dis-

solve, or disperse, in order to obtain subsistence."

But no change was destined to take place for many suffering weeks to come. The cold grew more and more intense, and provisions scarcer every day. Soon all were alike in want. "The colonels were often reduced to two rations and sometimes even to one. The army frequently remained whole days without provisions," is the testimony of *Lafayette.* "We have lately been in an alarming state for want of provisions," says *Colonel Laurens,* on the 17th of February. "The army has been in great distress since you left," wrote *Greene* to *Knox* nine days afterwards; "the troops are getting naked. They were seven days without meat, and several days without bread. . . . We are still in danger of starving. Hundreds of horses have already starved to death." The painful testimony is full and uncontradicted. "Several brigades," wrote *Adjutant-General Scammell* to *Timothy Pickering,* early in February, "have been without their allowance of meat. This is the third day." "In yesterday's conference with the General," said the *Committee of Congress* sent to report, writing on the 12th of February, "he informed us that some brigades had been four days without meat, and that even the common soldiers had been at his quarters to make known their wants. Should the enemy attack the camp successfully, your artillery would undoubtedly fall into their hands for want of horses to remove it. But these are smaller and tolerable evils when compared with the imminent danger of your troops perishing with famine, or dispersing in search of food." "For some days past there has been little less than a famine in the camp," writes *Washington* to *Clinton;* "a part of the army has been a week without any kind of flesh, and the rest three or four days."

Famished for want of food, they were no better off for clothes. "The unfortunate soldiers were in want of everything. They had neither coats, hats, shirts, nor shoes," wrote the *Marquis de Lafayette.* "The men," said *Baron Steuben,* "were literally naked, some of them in the fullest extent of the word." " 'Tis a melancholy consideration," were the words of *Pickering,* "that hundreds of our men are unfit for duty only for want of clothes and shoes." . . .

Naked and starving in an unusually rigorous winter, they fell sick by hundreds. From want of clothes "their feet and legs froze till they became black, and it was often necessary to amputate them." Through a want of straw or materials to raise them from the wet earth, (I quote again from the Committee of Congress) "sickness and mortality have spread through their quarters to an astonishing degree. The smallpox has broken out. Notwithstanding the diligence of the physicians and surgeons, of whom we bear no complaint, the sick and dead list has increased one-third in the last week's return, which was one-third greater than the week preceding, and from the present inclement weather will probably increase in a much greater proportion." Well might *Washington* exclaim: "Our sick naked, and well naked, our unfortunate men in captivity naked. Our difficulties and distresses are certainly great, and such as wound the feelings of humanity." Nor was this all. What many had to endure beside, let Dr. Waldo tell: "When the officer has been fatiguing through wet and cold, and returns to his tent to find a letter from his wife filled with the most heart-aching complaints a woman is capable of writing, acquainting him with the incredible difficulty with which she procures a little bread for herself and children; that her money is of very little consequence to her—concluding with expressions bordering on despair of getting sufficient food to keep soul and body together through the winter, and begging him to consider that charity begins at home, and not suffer his family to perish with want in the midst of plenty—what man is there whose soul would not shrink within him? Who would not be disheartened from persevering in the best of causes —the cause of his country—when such discouragements as these lie in his way, which his country might remedy if it would?" Listen to his description of the common soldier: "See the poor soldier when in health. With what chearfullness he meets his foes, and encounters every hardship! If barefoot, he labours thro' the Mud and Cold with a Song in his mouth extolling War and Washington. If his food be bad, he eats it notwithstanding with seeming content, blesses God for a good Stomach, and Whistles it into digestion. But harkee! Patience a moment! There comes a Soldier, and crys with an air of wretchedness and dispair: 'I'm Sick; my feet lame; my legs are sore; my body cover'd with this tormenting Itch; my Cloaths are worn out; my Constitution is broken; my former Activity is exhausted by fatigue, hunger, and Cold; I fail fast; I shall soon be no more! And all the reward I shall get will be, 'Poor Will is dead!'"

AND THEY PERSEVERED—THEY KEPT FAITH

And in the midst of this they persevered! Freezing, starving, dying, rather than desert their

flag they saw their loved ones suffer, but kept the faith. And the American yeoman of the Revolution remaining faithful through that winter is as splendid an example of devotion to duty as that which the pitying ashes of Vesuvius have preserved through eighteen centuries in the figure of the Roman soldier standing at his post, unmoved amid all the horrors of Pompeii. "The Guard die, but never surrender", was the phrase invented for Cambronne. "My comrades freeze and starve, but they never forsake me," might be put into the mouth of Washington.

"Naked and starving as they are," writes one of their officers, we "cannot enough admire the incomparable patience and fidelity of the soldiery that they have not been ere this excited by their sufferings to a general mutiny and desertion." "Nothing can equal their sufferings," says the Committee, "except the patience and fortitude with which they bear them." Greene's account to Knox is touching: "Such patience and moderation as they manifested under their sufferings does the highest honor to the magnanimity of the American soldiers. The seventh day they came before their superior officers and told their sufferings as if they had been humble petitioners for special favors. They added that it would be impossible to continue in camp any longer without support." In March Thomas Wharton writes in the name of Pennsylvania: "The unparalleled patience and magnanimity with which the army under your Excellency's command have endured the hardships attending their situation, unsupplied as they have been through an uncommonly severe winter, is an honor which posterity will consider as more illustrious than could have been derived to them by a victory obtained by any sudden and vigorous exertion." "I would cherish these dear, ragged Continentals, whose patience will be the admiration of future ages, and glory in bleeding with them," cried John Laurens in the enthusiasm of youth. "The patience and endurance of both soldiers and officers was a miracle which each moment served to renew," said Lafayette in his old age. But the noblest tribute comes from the pen of him who knew them best: "Without arrogance or the smallest deviation from truth it may be said that no history now extant can furnish an instance of an army's suffering such uncommon hardships as ours has done and bearing them with the same patience and fortitude. To see men without clothes to cover their nakedness, without blankets to lie on, without shoes (for the want of which their marches might be traced by the blood from their feet), and almost as often without provisions as with them, marching through the frost and snow, and at Christmas taking up their winter quarters within a day's march of the enemy, without a house or a hut to cover them till they could be built, and submitting without a murmur, is a proof of patience and obedience which in my opinion can scarce be paralleled." Such was *Washington's* opinion of the soldiers of Valley Forge.

Americans, who have gathered on the broad bosom of these hills to-day: if heroic deeds can consecrate a spot of Earth, if the living be still sensible of the example of the dead, if Courage be yet a common virtue, and Patience in Suffering be still honorable in your sight, if Freedom be any longer precious and Faith in Humanity be not banished from among you, if Love of Country still find a refuge among the hearts of men, *"take your shoes from off your feet, for the place on which you stand is holy ground!"*

THE OFFICERS

And who are the leaders of the men whose heroism can sanctify a place like this? Descend the hill and wander through the camp. The weather is intensely cold and the smoke hangs above the huts. On the plain behind the front line a few general officers are grouped about a squad whom the new inspector, the German baron, is teaching some manoeuvre. Bodies of men here and there are dragging wagons up hill (for the horses have starved to death) or carrying fuel for fires, without which the troops would freeze. The huts are deserted save by the sick or naked, and as you pass along the street a poor fellow peeps out at the door of one and cries: "No bread, no soldier!"

These are the huts of *Huntington's* brigade of the Connecticut line, next to it those of Pennsylvanians under *Conway*. This is the Irish-Frenchman soon to disappear in a disgraceful intrigue. Here in camp there are many who whisper that he is a mere adventurer, but in Congress they still think him "a great military character." Down towards headquarters are the Southerners commanded by *Lachlin McIntosh,* in his youth "the handsomest man in Georgia." Beyond Conway, on the hill, is *Maxwell,* a gallant Irishman, commissioned by New Jersey. *Woodford* of Virginia, commands on the right of the second line, and in front of him the Virginian *Scott.* The next brigade in order are Pennsylvanians—many of them men whose homes are in this neighborhood—Chester county boys and

Quakers from the Valley turned soldiers for their country's sake. They are the children of three races—the hot Irish blood mixes with the colder Dutch in their calm English veins, and some of them—their chief, for instance—are splendid fighters. There he is at this moment riding up the hill from his quarters in the valley. A man of medium height and strong frame, he sits his horse well and with a dashing air. His nose is prominent, his eye piercing, his complexion ruddy, his whole appearance that of a man in splendid health and flowing spirits. He is just the fellow to win by his headlong valor the nickname of "The Mad." But he is more than a mere fighter. Skilful, energetic, full of resources and presence of mind, quick to comprehend and prompt to act, of sound judgment and extraordinary courage, he has in him the qualities of a great general, as he shall show many a time in his short life of one-and-fifty years. Pennsylvania, after her quiet fashion, may not make as much of his fame as it deserves, but impartial history will allow her none the less the honor of having given its most brilliant soldier to the Revolution in her *Anthony Wayne.* *Poor* of New Hampshire, is encamped next, and then *Glover,* whose regiment of Marblehead sailors and fishermen manned the boats that saved the army on the night of the retreat from Long Island. *Learned, Paterson,* and *Weedon* follow, and then at the corner of the entrenchments by the river is the Virginian brigade of *Muhlenberg.* Born at the Trappe, close by, and educated abroad, Muhlenberg was a clergyman in Virginia when the war came on, but he has doffed his parson's gown forever for the buff and blue of a brigadier. His stalwart form and swarthy face are already as familiar to the enemy as they are to his own men, for the Hessians are said to have cried, "Hier kommt Teufel Pete!" as they saw him lead a charge at Brandywine. The last brigade is stationed on the river bank, where *Varnum* and his Rhode Islanders, in sympathy with young *Laurens,* of Carolina, are busy with a scheme to raise and enlist regiments of negro troops. These are the commanders of brigades.

The major-generals: Portly *William Alexander,* of New Jersey, who claims to be the Earl of Stirling, but can fight for a republic bravely, nevertheless; swarthy *John Sullivan,* of New Hampshire, a little head-strong, but brave as a lion; *Steuben,* the Prussian martinet, who has just come to teach the army; *De Kalb*—self-sacrificing and generous De Kalb—whose honest breast shall soon bear eleven mortal wounds, received in the service of America; *Lafayette,* tall, with auburn hair, the French boy of twenty with an old man's head, just recovering from the wounds of Brandywine; and last and greatest of them all, *Nathaniel Greene,* the Quaker blacksmith from Rhode Island, in all great qualities second only to the Chief himself. Yonder is *Henry Knox* of the artillery, as brave and faithful as he is big and burly; and the Pole, *Pulaski,* a man "of hardly middle stature, of sharp countenance and lively air." Here are the Frenchmen, *Du Portail, Dubryson, Duplessis,* and *Duponceau.* Here are *Timothy Pickering* and Light Horse *Harry Lee,* destined to be famous in Senate, Cabinet and field. Here are *Henry Dearborn* and *William Hull,* whose paths in life shall one day cross again, and *John Laurens* and *Tench Tilghman,* those models of accomplished manhood, destined so soon to die!

Does that silent boy of twenty, who has just ridden by with a message from *Lord Stirling,* imagine that one day the doctrine which shall keep the American continent free from the touch of European politics shall be forever associated with the name of *James Monroe?* Does yonder tall, awkward youth in the Third Virginia, who bore a musket so gallantly at Brandywine, dream as he lies there shivering in his little hut on the slopes of Mount Joy that in the not distant future it is he that shall build up the jurisprudence of a people, and after a life of usefulness and honor bequeath to them in the fame of *John Marshall* the precious example of a great and upright Judge? Two other youths are here—both of small stature and lithe, active frame—of the same rank and almost the same age, whose ambitious eyes alike look forward already to fame and power in law and politics. But not even his own aspiring spirit can foretell the splendid rise, the dizzy elevation and the sudden fall of *Aaron Burr*—nor can the other foresee that the time will never come when his countrymen will cease to admire the genius and lament the fate of *Alexander Hamilton!*

GEORGE WASHINGTON

And what shall I say of him who bears on his heart the weight of all? Who can measure the anxieties that afflict his mind? Who weigh the burdens that he has to bear? Who but himself can ever know the responsibilities that rest upon his soul? Behold him in yonder cottage, his lamp burning steadily through half the winter night, his brain never at rest, his hand always busy, his pen ever at work; now counselling with Greene how to clothe and feed the troops, or with Steuben how to reorganize the service; now writing to Howe about exchanges, or to Livingston about the relief of prisoners, or to Clinton about supplies, or to Congress about enlistments or promotions or finances or the French Alliance; opposing foolish and rash counsels to-day, urging prompt and rigorous policies to-morrow; now calming the jealousy of Congress, now soothing the wounded pride of ill-used officers; now answering the complaints of the civil authority, and now those of the starving soldiers, whose sufferings he shares, and by his cheerful courage keeping up the hearts of both; repressing the zeal of friends to-day, and overcoming with steadfast rectitude the intrigues of enemies in Congress and in camp to-morrow; bearing criticism with patience, and calumny with fortitude, and, lest his country should suffer, answering both only with plans for her defence, of which others are to reap the glory; guarding the long coast with ceaseless vigilance, and watching with sleepless eye a chance to strike the enemy in front a blow; a soldier subordinating the military to the civil power; a dictator, as mindful of the rights of Tories as of the wrongs of Whigs; a statesman, commanding a revolutionary army; a patriot, forgetful of nothing but himself; this is he whose extraordinary virtues only have kept the army from disbanding, and saved his country's cause. Modest in the midst of Pride; Wise in the midst of Folly; Calm in the midst of Passion; Cheerful in the midst of Gloom; Steadfast among the Wavering; Hopeful among the Despondent; Bold among the Timid; Prudent among the Rash; Generous among the Selfish; True among the Faithless; Greatest among good men, and Best among the Great—such was *George Washington* at Valley Forge.

But the darkest hour of night is just before the day. In the middle of February Washington described the dreadful situation of the army and "the miserable prospects before it" as "more alarming" than can possibly be conceived, and as occasioning him more distress "than he had felt" since the commencement of the war. On the 23d of February, he whom we call Baron Steuben, rode into camp; on the 6th Franklin signed the Treaty of Alliance at Versailles.

BARON VON STEUBEN

Frederick William Augustus Baron von Steuben was a native of Magdeburg, in Prussia. Trained from early life to arms, he had been

Aide to the Great Frederick, Lieutenant-General to the Prince of Baden, Grand Marshal at the Court of one of the Hohenzollerns, and a Canon of the Church. A skilful soldier, a thorough disciplinarian, a gentleman of polished manners, a man of warm and generous heart, he had come in the prime of life and vigor to offer his services to the American people. None could have been more needed or more valuable at the time. Congress sent him to the camp, Washington quickly discerned his worth, and in a little time he was made Major-General and Inspector of the Army. In an instant there was a change in that department. A discipline unknown before took possession of the camp. Beginning with a picked company of one hundred and twenty men, the Baron drilled them carefully, himself on foot and musket in hand. These, when they became proficient, he made a model for others, and presently the whole camp had become a military school. Rising at three in the morning, he smoked a single pipe while his servant dressed his hair, drank one cup of coffee, and, with his star of knighthood gleaming on his breast, was on horseback at sunrise, and, with or without his suite, galloped to the parade. There all day he drilled the men, and at nightfall galloped back to the hut in which he made his quarters, to draw up regulations and draft instructions for the inspectors under him. And thus day after day, patient, careful, laborious, and persevering, in a few months he transformed this untrained yeomanry into a disciplined and effective army. There have been more brilliant services rendered to America than these, but few perhaps more valuable and worthier of remembrance.

Knight of the Order of Fidelity, there have been more illustrious names than thine upon our lips to-day. Like many another who labored for us, our busy age has seemed to pass thee by. But here, at least, when, after a Century, Americans gather to review their Country's history, shall they recall thy unselfish services with gratitude and thy memory with honor!

And surely at Valley Forge we must not forget what Franklin was doing for his country's cause in France. It was a happy thing for the Republican Idea that it had a distant continent for the place of its experiment. It was a fortunate thing for America that between her and her nearest European neighbor lay a thousand leagues of sea. That distance—a very different matter from what it is today—made it at the same time difficult for England to overcome us, and safe for France to lend us aid. From an early period

this alliance seemed to have been considered by the Cabinet of France. For several years secret negotiations had been going on, and in the fall of 1777 they became open and distinct, and the representatives of both nations came face to face. There was no sympathy between weak and feeble Louis and his crafty Ministers on the one side and the representatives of Democracy and Rebellion on the other; nor had France any hopes of regaining her foothold on this Continent. The desire of her rulers was simply to humiliate and injure England, and the revolution in America seemed to offer the chance. Doubtless they were influenced by the fact that the cause of America had become very popular with all classes of the French people, impressed to a remarkable degree with the character of Dr. Franklin, and stirred by the contagious and generous example of Lafayette. Nor was this popular feeling merely temporary or without foundation. Long familiar as he had been with despotism in both politics and religion, the Frenchman still retained within him a certain spirit of liberty which was stronger than he knew. His sympathies naturally went out toward a distant people engaged in a gallant struggle against his hereditary enemies, the English; but besides all that, there was in his heart something, he hardly knew what, that vibrated at the thought of a freedom for others which he had hardly dreamed of and never known. Little did he or any of his rulers foresee what that something was. . . .

Accordingly, after much doubt, delay, and intrigue, during which Franklin bore himself with rare ability and tact, Treaties of Amity, Commerce, and Alliance were prepared and signed. The Independence of America was acknowledged and made the basis of alliance, and it was mutually agreed that neither nation should lay down its arms until England had conceded it. A fleet, an army, and munitions were promised by the King, and, as a consequence, war was at once declared against Great Britain.

THE TURNING POINT

We are accustomed to regard this as the turning point in the Revolutionary struggle. And so it was. But neither the fleet of France nor her armies, gallant as they were, nor the supplies and means with which she furnished us, were as valuable to the cause of the struggling country as the moral effect, at home as well as abroad, of the Alliance. Hopes that were built upon the skill of French sailors were soon dispelled, the expectations of large contingent armies were not to be fulfilled, but the news of the French Alliance carried into every patriotic heart an assurance that never left it afterward and kept aroused a spirit that henceforward grew stronger every year. Says the historian Bancroft: "The benefit then conferred on the United States was priceless." And "so the flags of France and the United States went together into the field against Great Britain, unsupported by any other government, yet with the good wishes of all the peoples of Europe." And thus illustrious Franklin, the Philadelphia printer, earned the magnificent compliment that was paid him in the French Academy: "Eripuit fulmen coelo, sceptrumque tyrannis."

And all the while, unconscious of the event, the winter days at Valley Forge dragged by, one after another, with sleet and slush and snow, with storms of wind, and ice and beating rain. The light-horse scoured the country, the pickets watched, the sentinels paced up and down, the men drilled and practised, and starved and froze and suffered, and at last the spring-time came, and with it stirring news. Greene was appointed Quartermaster-General on the 23d of March, and under his skilful management relief and succor came. The Conciliatory Bills, offering all but independence, were received in April, and instantly rejected by Congress, under the stirring influence of a letter from Washington, declaring with earnestness that "nothing short of independence would do," and at last, on the 4th of May, at eleven o'clock at night, the news of the French treaty reached the Head-Quarters.

On the 6th, by general orders, the army, after appropriate religious services, was drawn up under arms, salutes were fired with cannon and musketry, cheers given by the soldiers for the King of France and the American States, and a banquet by the General-in-Chief to all the officers, in the open air, completed a day devoted to rejoicing. "And all the while," says the English satirist, "Howe left the famous camp of Valley Forge untouched, whilst his great, brave, and perfectly appointed army, fiddled and gambled and feasted in Philadelphia. And by Byng's countrymen triumphal arches were erected, tournaments were held in pleasant mockery of the Middle Ages, and wreaths and garlands offered by beautiful ladies to this clement chief, with fantastical mottoes and poesies announcing that his laurels should be immortal."

On the 18th of May Lafayette took post at Barren Hill, from which he escaped so brilliantly

66

two days afterwards. At last, on the 18th of June, George Roberts, of Philadelphia, came galloping up the Gulf Road covered with dust and sweat, with the news that the British had evacuated Philadelphia. Six brigades were at once in motion—the rest of the army prepared to follow with all possible despatch early on the 19th. The bridge across the Schuylkill was laden with tramping troops. Cannon rumbled rapidly down the road to the river. The scanty baggage was packed, the flag at Head-Quarters taken down, the last brigade descended the river bank, the huts were empty, the breastworks deserted, the army was off for Monmouth, and the hills of Valley Forge were left alone with their glory and their dead. The last foreign foe had left the soil of Pennsylvania forever. Yes, the last foreign foe! . . .

THEY SERVED HERE FOR POSTERITY

My countrymen: For a century the eyes of struggling nations have turned toward this spot, and lips in every language have blessed the memory of Valley Forge! The tide of battle never ebbed and flowed upon these banks. These hills never trembled beneath the tread of charging squadrons nor echoed the thunders of contending cannon. The blood that stained this ground did not rush forth in the joyous frenzy of the fight; it fell drop by drop from the heart of a suffering people. They who once encamped here in the snow fought not for conquest, not for power, not for glory, not for their country only, not for themselves alone. They served here for Posterity; they suffered here for the Human Race; they bore here the cross of all the peoples; they died here that Freedom might be the heritage of all. It was Humanity which they defended; it was Liberty herself that they had in keeping. She that was sought in the wilderness and mourned for by the waters of Babylon—that was saved at Salamis and thrown away at Chaeronea; that was fought for at Cannae and lost forever at Pharsalie and Philippi—she who confronted the Armada on the deck with Howard and rode beside Cromwell on the field of Worcester—for whom the Swiss gathered into his breast the sheaf of spears at Sempach, and the Dutchman broke the dykes of Holland and welcomed in the sea—she of whom Socrates spoke, and Plato wrote, and Brutus dreamed and Homer sung—for whom Eliot pleaded, and Sydney suffered, and Milton prayed, and Hampden fell! Driven by the persecution of centuries from the older world, she had come with Pilgrim and

Puritan, and Cavalier and Quaker, to seek a shelter in the new. Attacked once more by her old enemies, she had taken refuge here. Nor she alone. The dream of the Greek, the Hebrew's prophecy, the desire of the Roman, the Italian's prayer, the longing of the German mind, the hope of the French heart, the glory and honor of Old England herself, the yearning of all the centuries, the aspiration of every age, the promise of the Past, the fulfilment of the Future, the seed of the old time, the harvest of the new—all these were with her. And here, in the heart of America, they were safe. The last of many struggles was almost won; the best of many centuries was about to break; the time was already come when from these shores the light of a new Civilization should flash across the sea, and from this place a voice of triumph make the Old World tremble, when from her chosen refuge in the West the spirit of Liberty should go forth to meet the Rising Sun and set the people free!

Americans: A hundred years have passed away and that Civilization and that Liberty are still your heritage. But think not that such an inheritance can be kept safe without exertion. It is the burden of your Happiness, that with it Privilege and Duty go hand in hand together. You cannot shirk the Present and enjoy in the Future the blessings of the Past. Yesterday begot To-day, and To-day is the parent of To-morrow. The Old Time may be secure, but the New Time is uncertain. The dead are safe; it is the privilege of the living to be in peril. A country is benefited by great actions only so long as her children are able to repeat them. The memory of this spot shall be an everlasting honor for our fathers, but we can make it an eternal shame for ourselves if we choose to do so. The glory of Lexington and Bunker Hill and Saratoga and Valley Forge belongs not to you and me, but we can make it ours if we will. It is well for us to keep these anniversaries of great events. It is well for us to meet by thousands on these historic spots. It is well to walk by those unknown graves or follow the windings of the breastworks that encircle yonder hill. It is well for us to gather beneath yon little fort, which the storms of so many winters have tenderly spared to look down on us to-day. It is well to commemorate the past with song and eulogy and pleasant festival—but it is not enough.

If they could return, whose forms have been passing in imagination before our eyes; if in the presence of this holy hour the dead could rise and lips dumb for a century find again a tongue, might they not say to us: You do well, Countrymen, to

commemorate this time. You do well to honor those who yielded up their lives in glory here. Theirs was a perfect sacrifice, and the debt you owe them you can never pay. Your lives have fallen in a happier time. The boundaries of your Union stretch from sea to sea. You enjoy all the blessings which Providence can bestow; a peace we never knew; a wealth we never hoped for; a power of which we never dreamed. Yet think not that these things only can make a nation great. We laid the foundations of your happiness in a time of trouble, in days of sorrow and perplexity, of doubt, distress, and danger, of cold and hunger, of suffering and want. We built it up by virtue, by courage, by self-sacrifice, by unfailing patriotism, by unceasing vigilance. By those things alone did we win your liberties; by them only can you hope to keep them. Do you revere our names? Then follow our example. Are you proud of our achievements? Then try to imitate them. Do you honor our memories? Then do as we have done. You yourselves owe something to America, better than all those things which you spread before her with such lavish hand—something which she needs as much in her prosperity to-day, as ever in the sharpest crisis of her fate! For you have duties to perform as well as we. It was ours to create; it is yours to preserve. It was ours to found; it is yours to perpetuate. It was ours to organize; it is yours to purify! And what nobler spectacle can you present to mankind to-day, than that of a people honest, steadfast, and secure—mindful of the lessons of experience—true to the teachings of history—led by the loftiest examples and bound together to protect their institutions at the close of the Century, as their fathers were to win them at the beginning, by the ties of "Virtue, Honor, and Love of Country" —by that Virtue which makes perfect the happiness of a people—by that Honor which constitutes the chief greatness of a State—by that Patriotism which survives all things, braves all things, endures all things, achieves all things— and which, though it find a refuge nowhere else, should live in the heart of every true American!

We know that we are more fortunate than our fathers. We believe that our children shall be happier than we. We know that this century is more enlightened than the last. We hope that the time to come will be better and more glorious than this. We think, we believe, we hope, but we do not know. Across that threshold we may not pass; behind that veil we may not penetrate. Into that country it may not be for us to go. It may be vouchsafed to us to behold it, wonderingly, from afar, but never to enter in. It matters not. The age in which we live is but a link in the endless and eternal chain. Our lives are like the sands upon the shore; our voices like the breath of this summer breeze that stirs the leaf for a moment and is forgotten. Whence we have come and whither we shall go not one of us can tell. And the last survivor of this mighty multitude shall stay but a little while.

But in the impenetrable To Be, the endless generations are advancing to take our places as we fall. For them as for us shall the Earth roll on and the seasons come and go, the snowflakes fall, the flowers bloom, and the harvest be gathered in. For them as for us shall the Sun, like the life of man, rise out of darkness in the morning and sink into darkness in the night. For them as for us shall the years march by in the sublime procession of the ages. And here, in this place of Sacrifice, in this vale of Humiliation, in this valley of the Shadow of that Death, out of which the Life of America rose, regenerate and free, let us believe with an abiding faith, that to them Union will seem as dear and Liberty as sweet and Progress as glorious as they were to our fathers and are to you and me, and that the Institutions which have made us happy, preserved by the virtue of our children, shall bless the remotest generations of the time to come. And unto Him,

who holds in the hollow of His hand the fate of nations, and yet marks the sparrow's fall, let us lift up our hearts this day, and into His eternal care commend ourselves, our children, and our country.

★

TRAPPE, PENNSYLVANIA
MAY 7, 1778

I heard a fine example today, namely, that His Excellency General Washington rode around among his army yesterday and admonished each and every one to fear God, to put away the wickedness that has set in and become so general, and to practice the Christian virtues. From all appearances this gentleman does not belong to the so-called world of society, for he respects God's Word, believes in the atonement through Christ, and bears himself in humility and gentleness. Therefore the Lord God has also singularly, yea, marvelously, preserved him from harm in the midst of countless perils, ambuscades, fatigues, etc. and has hitherto graciously held him in his hand as a chosen vessel.

Rev. Henry Melchior Muhlenberg

The Journals of Henry Melchior Muhlenberg, Vol. III
Translated by Theodore G. Tappert and John W. Doberstein.

CHRISTIAN CONSTITUENTS OF THE AMERICAN REVOLUTION; LOVE OF GOD IN HOME, CHURCH, AND EDUCATION

Our houses being constructed of brick, stone, and wood,

though destroyed may be rebuilt;

but liberty once gone is lost forever.

Christopher Gadsden of South Carolina in Continental Congress, 1775

THE AMERICAN
CHRISTIAN HOME

I feel myself at this Moment so domestically disposed

that I could say a thousand things to you, if I had Leisure.

I could dwell on the Importance of Piety & Religion,

of Industry & Frugality, of Prudence, Economy, Regularity & even Government,

all which are essential to the Well being of a Family. But I have not Time.

I cannot however help repeating Piety, because I think it indispensable.

Religion in a Family is at once its brightest Ornament

& its best Security.

Samuel Adams to his Future Son-in-law, 1780

PATRIOTIC WOMEN
AND HOME SENTIMENT

The remarkable Christian character of the Americans preceding and during the Revolution suggests that we look for its cause, that lessons for today can be learned. We find this cause rooted in the importance given the home and the church, with education supporting both. Editor,

All Americans are accustomed to view with interest and admiration the events of the Revolution. Its scenes are vivid in their memory, and its prominent actors are regarded with the deepest veneration. But while the leading spirits are thus honored, attention should be directed to the source whence their power was derived—to the sentiment pervading the mass of the people. . . . It gave statesmen their influence, and armed heroes for victory. What could they have done but for the home-sentiment to which they appealed, and which sustained them in the hour of trial and success? . . .

The feeling which wrought thus powerfully in the community depended, in a great part, upon the women. It is always thus in times of popular excitement. Who can estimate, moreover, the controlling influence of early culture! During the years of the progress of British encroachment and colonial discontent, when the sagacious politician could discern the portentous shadow of events yet far distant, there was time for the

nurture, in the domestic sanctuary, of that love of civil liberty, which afterwards kindled into a flame, and shed light on the world. The talk of matrons, in American homes, was of the people's wrongs, and the tyranny that oppressed them, till the sons who had grown to manhood, with strengthened aspirations towards a better state of things, and views enlarged to comprehend their invaded rights, stood up prepared to defend them to the utmost. Patriotic mothers nursed the infancy of freedom. Their counsels and their prayers mingled with the deliberations that resulted in a nation's assertion of its independence. They animated the courage, and confirmed the self-devotion of those who ventured all in the common cause. They frowned upon instances of coldness or backwardness; and in the period of deepest gloom, cheered and urged onward the desponding. They willingly shared inevitable dangers and privations, relinquished without regret prospects of advantage to themselves, and parted with those they loved better than life, not knowing when they were to meet again.

It is almost impossible now to appreciate the vast influence of woman's patriotism upon the destinies of the infant republic. We have no means of showing the important part she bore in maintaining the struggle, and in laying the foundations on which so mighty and majestic a

The Women of the American Revolution, by Elizabeth F. Ellet, New York, 1849

73

structure has arisen. History can do it no justice; for history deals with the workings of the head, rather than the heart. . . . We can only dwell upon individual instances of magnanimity, fortitude, self-sacrifice, and heroism, bearing the impress of the feeling of Revolutionary days, indicative of the spirit which animated all, and to which, in its various and multiform exhibitions, we are not less indebted for national freedom, than to the swords of the patriots who poured out their blood. . . .

How the influence of women was estimated by John Adams, appears from one of his letters to his wife:

"I think I have some times observed to you in conversation, that upon examining the biography of illustrious men, you will generally find some female about them, in the relation of mother, or wife, or sister, to whose instigation a great part of their merit is to be ascribed. You will find a curious example of this in the case of Aspasia, the wife of Pericles. She was a woman of the greatest beauty, and the first genius. She taught him, it is said, his refined maxims of policy, his lofty imperial eloquence, nay, even composed the speeches on which so great a share of his reputation was founded.

"I wish some of our great men had such wives. By the account in your last letter, it seems the women in Boston begin to think themselves able to serve their country. What a pity it is that our generals in the northern districts had not Aspasias to their wives.

"I believe the two Howes have not very great women for wives. If they had, we should suffer more from their exertions than we do. This is our good fortune. A smart wife would have put Howe in possession of Philadelphia a long time ago."

The venerable Major Spalding of Georgia, writes, in reply to an application to him for information respecting the revolutionary women of his state: "I am a very old man, and have read as much as any one I know, yet I have never known, and never read of one—no, not one! —who did not owe high standing, or a great name, to his mother's blood, or his mother's training. My friend Randolph said he owed every thing to his mother. Mr. Jefferson's mother was a Randolph, and he acknowledged that he owed every thing to her rearing. General Washington, we all know, attributed every thing to his mother. Lord Bacon attributed much to his mother's training. And will any one doubt that even Alexander believed he owed more to the blood and lofty ambition of Olympia, than the wisdom or cunning of Philip?" . . .

A letter found among some papers belonging to a lady of Philadelphia, addressed to a British officer in Boston, and written before the Declaration of Independence, reads, in part:

"I will tell you what I have done. My only brother I have sent to the camp with my prayers and blessings. I hope he will not disgrace me; I am confident he will behave with honor, and emulate the great examples he has before him; and had I twenty sons and brothers they should go. I have retrenched every superfluous expense in my table and family; tea I have not drunk since last Christmas, nor bought a new cap or gown since your defeat at Lexington; and what I never did before, have learned to knit, and am now making stockings of American wool for my servants; and this way do I throw in my mite to the public good. I know this—that as free I can die but once; but as a slave I shall not be worthy of life. I have the pleasure to assure you that these are the sentiments of all my sister Americans. They have sacrificed assemblies, parties of pleasure, tea drinking and finery, to that great spirit of patriotism that actuates all degrees of people throughout this extensive continent. If these are the sentiments of females, what must glow in the breasts of our husbands, brothers, and sons! They are as with one heart determined to die or be free. It is not a quibble in politics, a science which few understand, that we are contending for; it is this plain truth, which the most ignorant peasant knows, and is clear to the weakest capacity—that no man has a right to take their money without their consent. You say you are no politician. Oh, sir, it requires no Machiavelian head to discover this tyranny and oppression. It is written with a sunbeam. Every one will see and know it, because it will make every one feel; and we shall be unworthy of the blessings of Heaven if we ever submit to it. . . . Heaven seems to smile on us; for in the memory of man, never were known such quantities of flax, and sheep without number. We are making powder fast, and do not want for ammunition."

From all portions of the country thus rose the expression of woman's ardent zeal. Under accumulated evils the manly spirit that alone could secure success, might have sunk but for the firmness and intrepidity of the weaker sex. It supplied every persuasion that could animate to perseverance, and secure fidelity. . . .

The heroism of the Revolutionary women has passed from remembrance with the generation

PATRIOTIC
WOMEN
AND HOME
SENTIMENT

MARTHA
WASHINGTON

who witnessed it; or is seen only by faint and occasional glimpses, through the gathering obscurity of tradition. . . .

To render a measure of justice—inadequate it must be—to a few of the American matrons, whose names deserve to live in remembrance—and to exhibit something of the domestic side of the Revolutionary picture—is the object of this work. As we recede from the realities of that struggle, it is regarded with increasing interest by those who enjoy its results; while the elements which were its life-giving principle, too subtle to be retained by the grave historian, are fleeting fast from apprehension. Yet without some conception of them, the Revolution cannot be appreciated. We must enter into the spirit, as well as master the letter. . . .

MARTHA WASHINGTON

None who take an interest in the history of Washington can fail to desire some knowledge of her who shared his thoughts and plans, and was associated with him in the great events of his life. Few women have been called to move, in the drama of existence, amid scenes so varied and imposing; and few have sustained their part with so much dignity and discretion. In the shades of retirement or the splendor of eminent station, she was the same unostentatious, magnanimous woman; through the gloom of adverse fortune she walked by the side of the Chief, ascending with him the difficult path Heaven had opened before him; and when standing with him on the summit, in the full light of his power and renown, the eyes of her spirit looked still upward, seeking in the smile of the Supreme a reward which earthly honors could not bestow.

Though the life of Mrs. Washington was a changeful one, and had its full measure of sorrow and joy, it affords little material for the biographer. She moved in woman's domestic sphere, to which pertain not actions that strike the public eye, but uncomplaining endurance, and continual, unnoted self-sacrifice. . . . Her education was only a domestic one, such as was given to females in those days, when there were few seminaries of instruction, and private teachers were generally employed. Her beauty and fascinating manners, with her amiable qualities of character, gained her distinction among the ladies who were accustomed to resort to Williamsburg, at that time the seat of government.

She passed the winters with her husband. . . . Her arrival at camp was an event much antici-

pated; the plain chariot, with the neat postillions in their scarlet and white liveries, was always welcomed with great joy by the army, and brought a cheering influence, which relieved the general gloom in seasons of disaster and despair. Her example was followed by the wives of other general officers.

Lady Washington, as she was always called in the army, usually remained at head-quarters till the opening of the succeeding campaign, when she returned to Mount Vernon. She was accustomed afterwards to say that it had been her fortune to hear the first cannon at the opening, and the last at the closing, of all the campaigns of the Revolutionary war. How admirably her equanimity and cheerfulness were preserved, through the sternest periods of the struggle—and how inspiring was the influence she diffused, is testified in many of the military journals. She was at Valley Forge in that dreadful winter of 1777-8; her presence and submission to privation strengthening the fortitude of those who might have complained, and giving hope and confidence to the desponding. She soothed the distresses of many sufferers, seeking out the poor and afflicted with benevolent kindness, extending relief wherever it was in her power, and with graceful deportment presiding in the Chief's humble dwelling. In a letter to Mrs. Warren she says, "The General's apartment is very small; he has had a log cabin built to dine in, which has made our quarters much more tolerable than they were at first."

Their table was but scantily furnished; but the soldiers fared still worse, sitting down at a board of rough planks, set with horn spoons and a few tumblers; the food being often salt herrings and potatoes, without other vegetables, or tea, coffee, or sugar. Their continental money was no temptation to the farmers to sell them produce. The stone jug passed round was filled with water from the nearest spring; and rare was the privilege of toddy in which to drink the health of the nation. Yet here, forgetful of herself, the patriot wife anxiously watched the aspect of affairs, and was happy when the political horizon brightened. She writes to Mrs. Warren, "It has given me unspeakable pleasure to hear that General Burgoyne and his army are in safe quarters in your State. Would bountiful Providence aim a like stroke at General Howe, the measure of my happiness would be complete." (MS letter, March 7th, 1778). . . .

The recollections of a veteran, at the age of ninety-two, bear testimony to the kindness of

Mrs. Washington towards those in the humblest sphere. One little incident occurred when she came to spend the cold season with her husband in winter-quarters. There were but two frame-houses in the settlement, and neither had a finished upper story. The General was contented with his rough dwelling, but wished to prepare for his wife a more retired and comfortable apartment. He sent for the young mechanic, and desired him and one of his fellow apprentices to fit up a room in the upper story for the accommodation of Lady Washington through the winter. She herself arrived before the work was commenced. "She came", says the narrator, "into the place—a portly-looking agreeable woman of forty-five, and said to us: "Now, young men, I care for nothing but comfort here; and should like you to fit me up a beauffet on one side of the room, and some shelves and places for hanging clothes on the other." We went to work with all our might. Every morning about eleven Mrs. Washington came up stairs with a glass of spirits for each of us; and after she and the General had dined, we were called down to eat at their table. We worked very hard, nailing smooth boards over the rough and worm-eaten planks, and stopping the crevices in the walls made by time and hard usage. Then we consulted together how we could smoothe the uneven floor, and take out, or cover over some of the huge black knots. We studied to do every thing to please so pleasant a lady, and to make some return in our humble way for the kindness of the General. On the fourth day, when Mrs. Washington came up to see how we were getting along, we had finished the work, made the shelves, put up the pegs on the wall, built the beauffet, and converted the rough garret into a comfortable apartment. As she stood looking round, I said, "Madam, we have endeavored to do the best we could; I hope we have suited you." She replied, smiling, "I am astonished! your work would do honor to an old master, and you are mere lads. I am not only satisfied, but highly gratified with what you have done for my comfort." As the old soldier repeated these words, the tears ran down his furrowed cheeks. The thrill of delight which had seventy years before penetrated his heart at the approving words of his General's lady, again animated his worn frame, sending back his thoughts to the very moment and scene. . . .

Those who read the record of her worth, dwell with interest on the loveliness of her character. To a superior mind she joined those amiable qualities and Christian virtues which best adorn the female sex, and a gentle dignity that inspired respect without creating enmity.

MARTHA WASHINGTON TO MERCY WARREN

I am still determined to be cheerful and happy in whatever situation I may be; for I have also learned from experience that the greater part of our happiness or misery depends on our dispositions and not on our circumstances. We carry the seeds of the one or the other about with us in our minds, wherever we go.—*The Pioneer Mothers of America,* Harry C. Green and Mary W. Green, 1912.

MERCY WARREN
PLYMOUTH, MASSACHUSETTS

The name of Mercy Warren belongs to American history. In the influence she exercised, she was perhaps the most remarkable woman who lived at the Revolutionary period. She was the third child of Colonel James Otis, of Barnstable, in the old colony of Plymouth; and was born there, September 25th, 1728. (This date, with that of her death, is taken from the entries in the family Bible at Plymouth.) The Otis family came to the country in 1630 or 1640, and settled first in Hingham.

The youth of Miss Otis was passed in the retirement of her home, in a routine of domestic employments, and the duties devolving upon her as the eldest daughter in a family of high respectability. Her love of reading was early manifested; and such was her economy of time, that, never neglecting her domestic cares or the duties of hospitality, she found leisure not only to improve her mind by careful study, but for various works of female ingenuity. A card-table is preserved by one of her descendants in Quincy, as a monument of her taste and industry. The design was her own, the patterns being obtained by gathering and pressing flowers from the gardens and fields. These are copied in worsted work, and form one of the most curious and beautiful specimens to be found in the country.

At that period, the opportunities for female education were extremely limited, but perhaps the more prized on that account. Miss Otis gained nothing from schools. Her only assistant, in the intellectual culture of her earlier years, was the Rev. Jonathan Russell, the minister of the parish, from whose library she was supplied with books, and by whose counsels her tastes were in a measure formed. It was from reading, in accordance with his advice, Raleigh's *History of the World,* that her attention was particularly directed to history, the branch of literature to which she afterwards devoted herself. In later years, her brother James, who was himself an excellent scholar, became her adviser and companion in literary pursuits. There existed between them a strong attachment, which nothing ever impaired. . . .

When about twenty-six, she became the wife of James Warren, then a merchant of Plymouth, Massachusetts. In him she found a partner of congenial mind. Her new avocations and cares were not allowed to impair the love of literature which had been the delight of her youth. It was while residing occasionally for a few weeks with her husband and children on a farm a few miles from the village, to which she gave the name of "Clifford," that most of her poetical productions were written. On the other hand, attached as she was to these pursuits, she never permitted them to interfere with household duties, or the attention of a devoted mother to her children. Her attainments fitted her to give them valuable instruction; and the lessons of her loving spirit of wisdom were not lost.

With this fondness for historical studies, and the companionship of such a brother and husband, it is not strange that the active and powerful intellect of Mrs. Warren should become engaged with interest in political affairs. These were now assuming an aspect that engrossed universal attention. Decision and action were called for on the part of those inclined to one or the other side. How warmly Mrs. Warren espoused the cause of her country—how deeply her feelings were enlisted—appears in her letters. . . . This rich correspondence has been preserved by her descendants. . . . It includes letters, besides those from members of her own family, from Samuel and John Adams, Jefferson, Dickinson, Gerry, Knox and others. These men asked her opinion in political matters, and acknowledged the excellence of her judgment. . . . Colonial difficulties, and the signs of the times, formed subjects of communication continually between Mrs. Warren and her female friends. . . .

"The late convulsions are only the natural struggles which ensue when the genius of *liberty* arises to assert her rights in opposition to the ghost of tyranny. I doubt not this *fell form* will ere long be driven from our land; then may the western skies behold virtue (which is generally the attendant of freedom) seated on a throne of peace, where may she ever preside over the rising

Commonwealth of America." (Letter to Mrs. E. Lothrop, 1775). . . .

The influence commanded by her talents was enhanced by her virtues, and by the deep religious feeling which governed her throughout life. . . .

LYDIA DARRAH
QUAKERESS OF PHILADELPHIA

On the second day of December, 1777, late in the afternoon, an officer in the British uniform ascended the steps of a house in Second street, Philadelphia, immediately opposite the quarters occupied by General Howe, who, at that time, had full possession of the city. The house was plain and neat in its exterior, and well known to be tenanted by William and Lydia Darrah, members of the Society of Friends. It was the place chosen by the superior officers of the army for private conferences, whenever it was necessary to hold consultations on subjects of importance; and selected, perhaps on account of the unobtrusive character of its inmates, whose religion inculcated meekness and forbearance, and forbade them to practise the arts of war.

The officer, who seemed quite familiar with the mansion, knocked at the door. It was opened; and in the neatly-furnished parlor he met the mistress, who spoke to him, calling him by name. It was the adjutant-general; and he appeared in haste to give an order. This was to desire that the back-room above stairs might be prepared for the reception that evening of himself and his friends, who were to meet there and remain late. "And be sure, Lydia," he concluded, "that your family are all in bed at an early hour. I shall expect you to attend to this request. When our guests are ready to leave the house, I will myself give you notice, that you may let us out, and extinguish the fire and candles." . . .

Having delivered this order with an emphatic manner which showed that he relied much on the prudence and discretion of the person he addressed, the adjutant-general departed. Lydia betook herself to getting all things in readiness. But the words she had heard, especially the injunction to retire early, rang in her ears; and she could not divest herself of the indefinable feeling that something of importance was in agitation. While her hands were busy in the duties that devolved upon her, her mind was no less actively at work. The evening closed in, and the officers came to the place of meeting. Lydia had ordered all her family to bed, and herself admitted the

PATRIOTIC
WOMEN
AND HOME
SENTIMENT

———

MERCY WARREN,
PLYMOUTH
LYDIA DARRAH,
PHILADELPHIA

guests, after which she retired to her own apartment, and threw herself, without undressing, upon the bed.

But sleep refused to visit her eyelids. Her vague apprehensions gradually assumed more definite shape. She became more and more uneasy, till her nervous restlessness amounted to absolute terror. Unable longer to resist the impulse—not of curiosity, but surely of a far higher feeling—she slid from the bed, and taking off her shoes, passed noiselessly from her chamber and along the entry. Approaching cautiously the apartment in which the officers were assembled, she applied her ear to the key-hole. For a few moments she could distinguish but a word or two amid the murmur of voices; yet what she did hear but stimulated her eager desire to learn the important secret of the conclave.

At length there was profound silence, and a voice was heard reading a paper aloud. It was an order for the troops to quit the city on the night of the fourth, and march out to a secret attack upon the American army, then encamped at White Marsh.

Lydia had heard enough. She retreated softly to her own room, and laid herself quietly on the bed. . . . It seemed to her that but a few moments had elapsed, when there was a knocking at her door. She knew well what the signal meant, but took no heed. It was repeated, and more loudly; still she gave no answer. Again, and yet more loudly, the knocks were repeated; and then she rose quickly, and opened the door.

It was the adjutant-general, who came to inform her they were ready to depart. Lydia let them out, fastened the house, and extinguished the lights and fire. Again she returned to her chamber, and to bed; but repose was a stranger for the rest of the night. . . . She thought of the danger that threatened the lives of thousands of her countrymen, and of the ruin that impended over the whole land. Something must be done, and that immediately, to avert this widespread destruction. Should she awaken her husband and inform him? That would be to place him in special jeopardy, by rendering him a partaker of her secret; and he might, too, be less wary and prudent than herself. No; come what might, she would encounter this risk alone. After a petition for heavenly guidance, her resolution was formed; and she waited with composure, though sleep was impossible, till the dawn of day. Then she waked her husband, and informed him flour was wanted for the use of the household, and that it was necessary she should go to Frank-

ford to procure it. This was no uncommon occurrence; and her declining the attendance of the maid-servant excited little surprise. Taking the bag with her, she walked through the snow; having stopped first at head-quarters, obtained access to General Howe, and secured his written permission to pass the British lines.

The feelings of a wife and mother—one whose religion was that of love, and whose life was but a quiet round of domestic duties—bound on an enterprise so hazardous, and uncertain whether her life might not be the forfeit, may be better imagined than described. Lydia reached Frankford, distant four or five miles, and deposited her bag at the mill. Now commenced the dangers of her undertaking; for she pressed forward with all haste towards the outposts of the American army. Her determination was to apprise General Washington of the danger.

She was met on her way by an American officer, who had been selected by General Washington to gain information respecting the movements of the enemy. . . . He immediately recognized her, and inquired whither she was going. In reply, she prayed him to alight and walk with her; which he did, ordering his men to keep in sight. To him she disclosed the secret, after having obtained from him a solemn promise not to betray her individually, since the British might take vengeance on her and her family.

The officer thanked her for her timely warning, and directed her to go to a house near at hand, where she might get something to eat. But Lydia preferred returning at once; and did so, while the officer made all haste to the commander-in-chief. Preparations were immediately made to give the enemy a fitting reception.

With a heart lightened and filled with thankfulness, the intrepid woman pursued her way homeward, carrying the bag of flour which had served as the ostensible object of her journey. None suspected the grave, demure Quakeress of having snatched from the English their anticipated victory. . . .

Time never appeared to pass so slowly as during the interval which elapsed between the marching out and the return of the British troops. . . .

A sudden and loud knocking at her door was not calculated to lessen her apprehensions. She felt that the safety of her family depended on her self-possession at this critical moment. The visitor was the adjutant-general, who summoned her to his apartment. With a pale cheek, but composed, for she placed her trust in a higher power, Lydia obeyed the summons.

PATRIOTIC
WOMEN
AND HOME
SENTIMENT

JANE THOMAS,
CHARLESTOWN

The officer's face was clouded, and his expression stern. He locked the door with an air of mystery when Lydia entered, and motioned her to a seat. After a moment of silence, he said—

"Were any of your family up, Lydia, on the night when I received company in this house?"

"No," was the unhesitating reply. "They all retired at eight o'clock."

"It is very strange". . . said the officer, and mused a few minutes. "You, I know, Lydia, were asleep; for I knocked at your door three times before you heard me—yet it is certain that we were betrayed. I am altogether at a loss to conceive who could have given the information of our intended attack to General Washington! On arriving near his encampment we found his cannon mounted, his troops under arms, and so prepared at every point to receive us, that we have been compelled to march back without injuring our enemy, like a parcel of fools."

It is not known whether the officer ever discovered to whom he was indebted for the disappointment.

But the pious quakeress blessed God for her preservation, and rejoiced that it was not necessary for her to utter an untruth in her own defence. And all who admire examples of courage and patriotism, especially those who enjoy the fruits of them, must honor the name of Lydia Darrah. . . .

JANE THOMAS
CHARLESTOWN, S. CAROLINA

The state of popular feeling after the occupation of Charlestown by the British, and during the efforts made to establish an undisputed control over the State, might be in some measure illustrated by the life of Mrs. Thomas. . . .

For many years previous to the commencement of the Revolutionary war, Mr. Thomas was a magistrate and a captain of militia. . . . Colonel Thomas led out his quota of men to repel the Indians in 1776, and shared the privations and dangers connected with the expedition under General Williamson into the heart of the Indian Territory, in the autumn of that year. . . .

It was the policy of Cornwallis, whom Sir Henry Clinton, on his departure to New York, had left in command of the royal army, to compel submission by the severest measures. The bloody slaughter under Tarleton at Waxhaw Creek, was an earnest of what those who ventured resistance might expect. This course was pursued with unscrupulous cruelty, and the unfortunate patriots were made to feel the vengeance of exasperated tyranny. He hoped thus eventually to crush and extinguish the spirit still struggling and flashing forth, like hidden fire, among the people whom the arm of power had for a season brought under subjection. But the oppressor, though he might overawe, could not subdue the spirit of a gallant and outraged people. . . .

One of the congenial co-operators in these plans of the British commander, was Colonel Ferguson. He encouraged the loyalists to take arms, and led them to desolate the homes of their neighbors. About the last of June he came into that part of the country where the family of Colonel Thomas lived, and caused great distress by the pillage and devastation of the bands of tories who hung around his camp. The whigs were robbed of their negroes, horses, cattle, clothing, bedding, and every article of property of sufficient value to take away. . . .

While her husband was a prisoner at Ninety-Six, she paid a visit to him and her two sons, who were his companions in rigorous captivity. By chance she overheard a conversation between some tory women, the purport of which deeply interested her. One said to the others: "To-morrow night the loyalists intend to surprise the rebels at Cedar Spring."

The heart of Mrs. Thomas was thrilled with alarm at this intelligence. The Cedar Spring was within a few miles of her house; the whigs were posted there, and among them were some of her own children.

Her resolution was taken at once; for there was no time to be lost. She determined to apprise them of the enemy's intention, before the blow could be struck. Bidding a hasty adieu to her husband and sons, she was upon the road as quickly as possible; rode the intervening distance of nearly sixty miles the next day, and arrived in time to bring information to her sons and friends of the impending danger. The moment they knew what was to be expected, a brief consultation was held; and measures were immediately taken for defence. The soldiers withdrew a short distance from their camp-fires, which were prepared to burn as brightly as possible. The men selected suitable positions in the surrounding woods.

Their preparations were just completed, when they heard in the distance, amid the silence of night, the cautious advance of the foe. The scene was one which imagination, far better than the pen of the chronicler, can depict. Slowly and warily, and with tread as noiseless as possible, the enemy advanced; till they were already within the glare of the blazing fires, and safely, as it seemed, on the verge of their anticipated work of destruction. No sound betrayed alarm; they supposed the intended victims wrapped in heavy slumbers; they heard but the crackling of the flames, and the hoarse murmur of the wind as it swept through the pine trees. The assailants gave the signal for the onset, and rushed towards the fires—eager for indiscriminate slaughter. Suddenly the flashes and shrill reports of rifles revealed the hidden champions of liberty. The enemy, to their consternation, found themselves assailed in the rear by the party they had expected to strike unawares. Thrown into confusion by this unexpected reception, defeat, overwhelming defeat, was the consequence to the loyalists. They were about one hundred and fifty strong, while the whigs numbered only about sixty. The victory thus easily achieved they owed to the spirit and courage of a woman! Such were the matrons of that day. . . .

UNKNOWN
NORTH CAROLINA

The following illustrative incident was communicated to the Rev. J. H. Saye, by two Revolutionary officers, one of whom lived in the vicinity where it occurred—the other being of the party concerned in the adventure.

Early in the war, the inhabitants on the frontier of Burke County, North Carolina, being apprehensive of an attack by the Indians, it was determined to seek protection in a fort in a more densely populated neighborhood in an interior settlement. A party of soldiers was sent to protect them on their retreat. The families assembled, the line of march was taken towards their place of destination, and they proceeded some miles unmolested—the soldiers marching in a hollow square, with the refugee families in the centre. The Indians, who had watched these movements, had laid a plan for their destruction. The road to be travelled lay through a dense forest in the fork of a river, where the Indians concealed themselves, and waited till the travellers were in the desired spot. Suddenly the war-whoop sounded in front, and on either side; a large body of painted warriors rushed in, filling the gap by which the whites had entered, and an appalling crash of fire-arms followed. The soldiers, however, were prepared; such as chanced to be near the trees darted behind them, and began to ply the deadly rifle; the others prostrated themselves upon the earth, among the tall grass, and

crawled to trees. The families screened themselves as best they could. The onset was long and fiercely urged; ever and anon amid the din and smoke, the warriors would rush, tomahawk in hand, towards the centre; but they were repulsed by the cool intrepidity of the back-woods riflemen. Still they fought on, determined on the destruction of the victims who offered such desperate resistance.

All at once, an appalling sound greeted the ears of the women and children in the centre; it was a cry from their defenders—a cry for powder! "Our powder is giving out," they exclaimed. "Have you any? Bring us some, or we can fight no longer!" A woman of the party had a good supply. She spread her apron on the ground, poured her powder into it, and going round from soldier to soldier as they stood behind the trees, bade each who needed powder put down his hat, and poured a quantity upon it. Thus she went round the line of defence, till her whole stock, and all she could obtain from others, was distributed. At last the savages gave way, and pressed by their foes, were driven off the ground. The victorious whites returned to those for whose safety they had ventured into the wilderness. Inquiries were made as to who had been killed, and one running up, cried, "Where is the woman that gave us the powder?" "I want to see her!" "Yes!—yes!—let us see her!" responded another and another, "without her we should have been all lost!" The soldiers ran about among the women and children, looking for her and making inquiries. Directly came in others from the pursuit, one of whom observing the commotion, asked the cause, and was told. "You are looking in the wrong place," he replied. "Is she killed? Ah, we were afraid of that!" exclaimed many voices. "Not when I saw her," answered the soldier. "When the Indians ran off, she was on her knees in prayer at the root of yonder tree—" and there, to their great joy, they found the woman safe, and still on her knees in prayer. Thinking not of herself, she received their applause without manifesting any other feeling than gratitude to Heaven for their great deliverance. . . .

ELIZABETH ZANE
VIRGINIA

The name of Elizabeth Zane is inseparably associated with the history of one of the most memorable incidents in the annals of border warfare. . . .

In May and June, 1777, a number of savage forays upon the settlements took place, and as the season advanced, these depredations became more bold and frequent. So imminent was the danger, that the people threw aside their private pursuits; the troops were constantly in service, and civil jurisdiction gave place for months to martial law throughout the country. In September it was ascertained that a large Indian force was concentrating on the Sandusky River, under the direction of the notorious white renegade and tory, Simeon Girty. This savage host, numbering, according to various estimates, from three hundred and eighty to five hundred warriors, having completed the preparations for their campaign, took up their line of march in the direction of Limestone, Kentucky; and were brought by their leader before the walls of Fort Henry, before the scouts employed by Colonel Shepherd were able to discover his real design. . . .

The Indians then advanced with loud whoops to take their position before the fort. The garrison, which had at first numbered forty-two fighting men, was now reduced to twelve, including boys. Girty, having posted his forces, appeared with a white flag, and demanded their surrender in the name of His Britannic Majesty; but Colonel Shepherd promptly replied that he should only obtain possession of the fort when there remained no longer an American soldier to defend it. The little band had a sacred charge to protect; their mothers, sisters, wives and children were assembled around them, and they resolved to fight to the last extremity, trusting in Heaven for a successful issue.

For many hours, after the opening of the siege, the firing of the Indians, eager for butchery, was met by a sure and well-directed fire from the garrison, which was composed of excellent marksmen. But the stock of gunpowder in the fort was nearly exhausted! A favorable opportunity was offered by the temporary suspension of hostilities, to procure a keg of powder known to be in the house of Ebenezer Zane, about sixty yards from the gate. The commandant explained the matter to his men, and, unwilling to order any one upon an enterprise so desperate, asked who would volunteer for the perilous service. The person going and coming would necessarily be exposed to the danger of being shot down by the Indians; yet three or four young men promptly offered to undertake it. The Colonel answered that only one man could be spared, and left it to them to decide who it should be. While they disputed —every moment of time being precious, from the

danger of a renewal of the attack before the powder could be procured—the interposition of a young girl put an end to their generous contention. Elizabeth, the sister of Ebenezer and Silas Zane, came forward, and requested that she might be permitted to go for the powder. Her proposition at first met with a peremptory refusal; but she renewed her petition with steadfast earnestness; nor would she be dissuaded from her heroic purpose by the remonstrances of the commandant and her anxious relatives. Either of the young men, it was represented, would be more likely than herself to perform the task successfully, by reason of greater familiarity with danger, and swiftness in running. Her answer was—that her knowledge of the danger attending the undertaking was her reason for offering to perform the service; her loss would not be felt, while not a single soldier could be spared from the already weakened garrison. This argument prevailed; her request was granted; and when she had divested herself of such portions of clothing as might impede her speed, the gate was opened for her to pass out.

The opening of the gate arrested the attention of several Indians straggling through the village, and it could be seen from the fort that the eyes of the savages were upon Elizabeth as she crossed the open space—walking as rapidly as possible, to reach her brother's house. But probably deeming a woman's life not worth the trouble of taking, or influenced by some sudden freak of clemency, they permitted her to pass without molestation.

In a few moments she re-appeared, carrying the powder in her arms, and walked at her utmost speed towards the gate. One account says the powder was tied in a table-cloth, and fastened around her waist. The Indians doubtless suspected, this time, the nature of her burden; they raised their firelocks, and discharged a leaden storm at her as she went on; but the balls whistled past her harmless—and the intrepid girl reached the fort in safety with her prize.

The story of this siege has been preserved in the collections of Virginia as the most important event in the history of Wheeling and is enumerated among the battles of the Revolution.

HOME SENTIMENT

Our Founding Fathers are not always credited with having the tender feelings of Christian fathers. The colonial homes, with their concern for the character of the young, are a very important factor in the beginnings of America. Editor.

PATRIOTIC
WOMEN
AND HOME
SENTIMENT

————

ELIZABETH ZANE,
VIRGINIA

CHRISTIAN
CONSTITUENT:

THE AMERICAN
CHRISTIAN HOME

*Writings of
Samuel Adams,*
Edited by
Henry Alonzo
Cushing,
Vol. 4,
New York, 1908

SAMUEL ADAMS TO HIS DAUGHTER HANNAH

Aug. 17, 1780
Philadelphia

My Dear Hannah

Nothing I assure you, but Want of Leisure has prevented my acknowledging the Receipt of your very obliging Letter of the 12th of July. You cannot imagine with how much Pleasure I received it.

I have no Reason to doubt your Sincerity when you express the warmest Affection for your Mother and me, because I have had the most convincing Proof of it in the whole Course of your Life. Be equally attentive to every Relation into which all-wise Providence may lead you, and I will venture to predict for my dear Daughter, an unfailing Source of Happiness in the Reflections of her own Mind. If you carefully fulfill the various Duties of Life, from a Principle of Obedience to your heavenly Father, you shall enjoy that Peace which the World cannot give nor take away.

In steadily pursuing the Path of Wisdom & Virtue I am sometimes inclind to think you have been influenced with a View of pleasing me. This is indeed endearing, and I owe you the Debt of Gratitude. But the pleasing an Earthly Parent, I am perswaded, has not been your principal Motive to be religious. If this has any Influence on your Mind, you know you cannot gratify me so much, as by seeking most earnestly, the Favor of Him who made & supports you—who will supply you with whatever his infinite Wisdom sees best for you in this World, and above all, who has given us his Son to purchase for us the Reward of Eternal Life—Adieu, and believe that I have. . . .

SAMUEL ADAMS TO THOMAS WELLS, HIS FUTURE SON-IN-LAW

Nov. 22, 1780
Philadelphia

My dear Mr. Wells

Although I have not yet acknowledged the obliging Letter you wrote to me some time ago, I would not have you entertain a Doubt of my sincere Respect and the Confidence I place in you. I think I gave you the strongest Proof of this when I was last in Boston. From that Moment I have considered myself particularly interested in your Wellfare. It cannot indeed be otherwise, since I then consented that you should form the most intimate Connection with the dear Girl whom I pride myself in calling my Daughter. I did this with Caution and Deliberation; and having done it, I am now led to contemplate the Relation in which I am myself to stand with you, and I can hardly forbear the same Stile in this Letter, which I should take the Liberty to use if I was writing to her. The Marriage State was designd to complete the Sum of human Happiness in this Life. It some times proves otherwise; but this is owing to the Parties themselves, who either rush into it without due Consideration, or fail in point of Discretion in their Conduct towards each other afterwards. It requires Judgment on both Sides, to conduct with exact Propriety; for though it is acknowledged, that the Superiority is & ought to be in the Man, yet as the Mannagement of a Family in many Instances necessarily devolves on the Woman, it is difficult always to determine the Line between the Authority of the one & the Subordination of the other. Perhaps the Advice of the good Bishop of St. Asaph on another Occasion, might be adopted on this, and that is, not to govern too much. When the married Couple strictly observe the great Rules of Honor & Justice towards each other, Differences, if any happen, between them, must proceed from small & trifling Circumstances. Of what Consequence is it, whether a Turkey is brought on the Table boild or roasted? And yet, how often are the Passions sufferd to interfere in such mighty Disputes, till the Tempers of both become so sowerd, that they can scarcely look upon each other with any tolerable Degree of good Humor. I am not led to this particular Mode of treating the Subject from an Apprehension of more than common Danger, that such Kind of Fricas will frequently take Place in that Connection, upon which, much of my future Comfort in Life will depend. I am too well acquainted with the Liberality of your Way of thinking, to harbour such a Jealousy; and I think I can trust to my Daughters Discretion if she will only promise to exercise it. I feel myself at this Moment so domestically disposd that I could say a thousand things to you, if I had Leisure. I could dwell on the Importance of Piety & Religion, of Industry & Frugality, of Prudence, OEconomy, Regularity & an even Government, all which are essential to the Well being of a Family. But I have not Time. I cannot however help repeating Piety, because I think it indispensible. Religion in a Family is at once its brightest Ornament & its best Security. The first Point of Justice, says a Writer I have met with, consists in *Piety;* Nothing certainly being so great a Debt

WHITEFIELD'S HYMN

From *Urania*, or a Choice Collection of Psalm Tunes,
James Lyon Collection, 1761
Hymn text from the Reverend George Whitefield's
collection. Tune: *God Save the King* (1744)

upon us, as to render to the Creator & Preserver those Acknowledgments which are due to Him for our Being, and the hourly Protection he affords us.

SAMUEL ADAMS TO HIS WIFE BETSY

Nov. 24, 1780
Philadelphia

My dear Betsy

Yesterday I wrote to Mr. Wells, and in haste because I was informd that Dr. Craigie was then instantly setting off for Boston. As he has waited another Day, I have the Opportunity of acknowledging the Receipt of your Letters of the 25th of October & the 8th of Novr which were brought to me by the Post.

You seem, my Dear, to express more Concern than I think you ought, at certain Events that have of late taken Place in the Common Wealth of Massachusetts. Do you not consider that in a free Republick, the People have an uncontroulable right of chusing whom they please, to take their Parts in the Administration of publick Affairs? No Man has a Claim on his Country, upon the Score of his having renderd publick Service. It is the Duty of every one to use his utmost Exertions in promoting the Cause of Liberty & Virtue; and having so done, if his Country thinks proper to call others to the arduous Task, he

ought chearfully to acquiesce, and to console himself with the Contemplations of an honest Man in private Life. You know, how ardently I have wishd for the Sweets of Retirement. I am like to have my Wish.—You are Witness that I have not raisd a Fortune in the Service of my Country. I glory in being what the World calls, a poor Man. If my Mind has ever been tinctured with Envy, the Rich and the Great have not been its objects. If I have been vain, Popularity, tho' I had as much of it as any Man ought to have, is not the Phantome I have pursued. He who gains the Approbation of the Virtuous Citizens, I will own, may feel himself happy; but he is in Reality much more so, *who knows he deserves it,* Such a Man, if he cannot retreat with Splendor, he may with dignity.

I will trust in that all gracious Being, who, in his own good Way, has provided us with Food and Raiment; and having spent the greatest Part of my Life in Publick Cares, like the weary Traveller, fatigud with the Journey of the Day, I can rest with you in a Cottage. If I live till the Spring, I will take my final Leave of Congress and return to Boston. I have Reasons to be fixed in this Determination which I will then explain to you. I grow more domestick as I increase in years.

Adieu my dear,
Your affectionate,

★   ★   ★   ★   ★

*The Mercy
Warren Papers,
1709–1841,*
Massachusetts
Historical
Society

MRS. MERCY WARREN TO MRS. ABIGAIL ADAMS

Plymouth January, 1774

To Mrs. A. Adams the Lady
of President Adams

It gives me no small satisfaction to find that your late visit was so agreeable to yourself, and that my friends delight in recollecting the hours spent in Plymouth. I sincerely wish them pleased in such a degree as to induce them to make a second excursion. I hope the intemperate heat of the day you left us, did not affect your health. The gentle showers of the afternoon extended to the river as you kindly wished, nor am I less pleased with the idea, that they shed their benign influences, through the hills and valleys of your neighbourhood.

You judge very right in thinking there is much pleasure in instructing the little flock committed to my care. Yet it is not without a mixture of pain when I consider the arduous work,—the importance of the charge, and frequently am I

ready to think I am unequal to the trust.

I am obliged to you for the ingenious treatise on education written by Mrs. Seamore,—you ask me if the rules I have prescribed myself in the regulation of my little family—perfectly coincide with the sentiments of this lady? I am sensible my own method will admit of much improvement, and though it has been my pleasing task for several years to cultivate the infant mind and plant the seeds of virtue in the bosom of my children, I am yet looking abroad for every foreign aid to enable me to the discharge of a duty of the highest consequence to society;—though this is for a number of years, left almost wholly to our uninstructed sex.

It is an arduous work to rear the tender plants and impress the youthful mind with such sentiments that when they go out of our hands they have only to cultivate them to become useful in their departments,—an ornament to society, and happy themselves forever, when they shall be introduced into more enlarged and glorious scenes.

I shall be happy indeed if I can acquit myself of the sacred trust by Providence delivered on every mother to the approbation of the judicious observers of life;—but far happier if my conscience, and my judge, announce that no effort has been neglected.

Yet I shall not pretend to dictate, nor to select rules or maxims of education for those who have had equal advantages with myself, and who perhaps may be better capacitated to improve them. But before I quit the subject, I would ask if you do not think *generosity*, as it is mentioned in the ninth letter of this little essay of Mrs. S—, is too comprehensive a term, to be given as the first principle to be impressed on the infant mind? This disposition doubtless includes many other virtues, yet it is not uncommon in such a world as this, to see the generous mind of youth, led into a thousand errors from that very principle.

I cannot but think the love of *truth* is of much the greatest importance; moreso than any single principle in the early culture of the mind. A careful attention to fix a sacred regard to veracity, in the bosom of youth, is the surest guard to virtue, and the most powerful barrier against the sallies of vice, through every period of life. When this principle has taken deep root, it usually produces not only generosity of mind, but very many other excellent qualities.

When I find a heart that will on no terms deviate from the laws of truth,—I do not much fear any great eccentricity from the path of rectitude, more especially, if she has obtained any degree of the childs confidence, a point at which every mother should assiduously aim.

The weakness of the human mind is apparent in every stage of present existence. The moral faculties of man are debilitated by several concurring causes. The passions are too strong and the appetites too clamourous, to be kept without deviation, in that subordination, which reason approves and which religion requires, without the work is early begun by some gentle hand.

When the youth can be brought with sincerity and ingenuity to lay open the propensities of his soul, to the eye of the parent, can anyone so effectually prune and lop off the excrescences of the mind that if neglected would often render him a monster disgraceful to humanity, as the mother who is not the dupe of her own maternal fondness?

This important subject may be resumed in the next from your sincere and affectionate friend.

M. WARREN

Plymouth February 1774

My dear Mrs. Adams:

Your last I perceive was wrote with a trembling heart, and the laudable feelings of humanity, lest your suffering country should be driven to extremities, and its innocent inhabitants be made the sacrifices to disappointed avarice and ambition. But I will yet hope a little longer for a more favourable termination of the distresses of America, though we cannot long continue in this state of suspence. It is and ever has been my opinion, that justice will finally gain a compleat victory over tyranny; but what may be the intervening sufferings of individuals, heaven only knows, and to a superintending providence we must leave the decision of the important contest of this unhappy day, and to avert the evils we fear.

I am very sensible my dear Mrs. Adams, that by our happy connection with gentlemen of distinguished zeal, integrity and virtue, (who would be marked out as early victims to successful tyranny) we should thereby be subjected to peculiar misery; but yet we shall never wish them for our sakes, to do anything repugnant to honour or conscience; yet though we may with a virtuous crook be willing to suffer pain and poverty with them rather than they should deviate from their noble principles, yet where would be our constancy and fortitude without their assistance to support the wounded heart. There are upon record many instances of female fortitude that do much honour to the sex, but the courage of a Portia or an Arria in a day of trial like theirs, I dare not boast, and pray heaven that neither you nor I may be called to such a dreadful proof of magnanimity; I do not mean to die by our own hands, rather than survive those we hold most dear and submit to live in ignominious slavery, nor do I think it would have been the case with either of those celebrated ladies, had they lived in the clearer light of Christianity. It is certainly a greater mark of an heroic soul to struggle with the calamities of life, and patiently resign to the evils we cannot avoid, than cowardly to shrink from the post allotted us by him, who knows what part in the universal drama we can best sustain, before himself sees fit to wind up the scene.

You have doubtless heard that there is a detachment from headquarters stationed in the neighbourhood of Plymouth. People here are much at a loss what can be the design of this

PATRIOTIC
WOMEN
AND HOME
SENTIMENT

SAMUEL ADAMS
TO HIS
WIFE BETSY

ridiculous movement. Probably it is with intention to provoke, till some rashness shall give a pretext, to the beginning of hostilities.

Yours of January third, begins with an instance of curiosity, which I may gratify in some future day on certain conditions, one of which is to see the whole correspondence between Mr. —— and the lady referred to in yours; for however we may fall short in some more laudable pursuits, I acknowledge we have an equal share of curiosity with the other sex, and no more, nor have they generously consigned us a larger portion for any other reason, but because they have the opportunities of gratifying their inquisitive humour to the utmost, in the great school of the world, while we are confined to the narrow circle of domestic cares. But we have one advantage peculiar to ourselves; we can conceal in the obscure retreat by our own fireside, the neglect of those mental improvements to which the more domestic animal stands in little need of, as it is not necessary for her to leave the retired roof; whereas *man* is generally called out to a full display of his abilities, and how often does he exhibit the most mortifying instances of neglected opportunities; and not withstanding the boasted advantages of a liberal education, the mind is as barren and uncultivated, and as totally devoid of every useful acquirement, as the most untutored, trifling girl. I am etc.

M. WARREN

THE AMERICAN
CHRISTIAN CHURCH

The woman, the church of Christ, has such a gift and grant from Heaven,

of this part of God's world,

for the quiet enjoyment of her liberties and privileges, civil and religious,

that no power on earth can have any right to invade,

much less to dispossess her of them.

God has, in this American quarter of the globe,

provided for the woman and her seed,

a fixed and lasting settlement and habitation,

and bestowed it upon her, to be her own property for ever.

Pastor Samuel Sherwood, A.M., Weston, Connecticut, 1776

CONGREGATIONALISM

*The Congrega-
tionalism of the
Last Three
Hundred Years,*
by Henry
Martyn Dexter,
New York, 1880

*The following three articles,"Congregational-
ism"; "The Presbyterian Church in America";
"The Protestant Episcopal Church in America"
are written by the outstanding early historians of
the denominations, i.e., Henry Martyn Dexter,
1880; Dr. Charles Hodge, 1839, and Bishop
Samuel Wilberforce, 1856, respectively.*

*These articles are excerpts of larger works and
are of importance to the reader of today in his
comprehension of the American Revolution period.
The understanding of church polity is vital to the
understanding of civil polity. The uniqueness of
the American Constitution is due, in part, to its
inclusion of aspects of the counterpart in the civil
sphere of each of these classical forms of church
government.*

*The three articles complement each other by
describing the theological situation in each colony
from their own point of view. Editor.*

UNIQUENESS OF PILGRIM CHURCH,
EARLY NEW ENGLAND CONGREGATIONALISM

The ecclesiastical beginnings of New England
were mainly of a tentative and provisional character. For eight years and seven months the
Leyden-Plymouth Church stood alone. Ten years
after the Mayflower came to her moorings inside
of the Gurnet Point, there were but five Con-

gregational churches on the continent, and twenty
years after there were but thirty-five. Brewster
and his company remained faithful to the extremely mild type of Barrowism in which Robinson had trained them, but the fact that, providentially, they had but one Elder, and, for nearly
or quite ten years, no present Pastor, thrust them
upon the practical development of a church government of the people, by the people, and for the
people, to a degree beyond their philosophy, and
beyond their original intent; and having so long
the field entirely to themselves, they were undisturbed from without in this their trend.

The company which came over to Salem in
1629 was Non-conformist, but not Separatist, in
its tastes and intentions. . . .

When Winthrop's company were leaving England, in the spring of 1630, they took the pains
to publish in London "The humble Request of
his Majesties loyall Subjects, the Governour and
the Company late gone for New England; to the
rest of their Brethren in and of the Church of
England; for the obtaining of their Prayers, and
the removal of suspicions, and misconstructions
of their Intentions;" in which they beg their
fathers and brethren to take notice:

"of the principals and body of our Company, as those
who esteem it our honour to call the *Church of England* from whence wee rise, our deare mother; and

89

cannot part from our native countrie where she specially resideth, without much sadness of heart and many tears in our eyes; ever acknowledging that such hope and part as we have obtained in the common salvation, wee have received in her bosome, and suckt it from her breasts."

They go on to say: "Wee leave it not therefore, as loathing that milk wherewith wee were nourished there;" they style themselves "a weake colony from yourselves;" and beg faithful remembrances in their prayers, "for a church springing out of your owne bowels;" reciprocally promising that their heads and hearts shall be "as fountaines of tears" for "the everlasting welfare" of the church at home, when they shall be in their "poore cottages in the wildernesse." The Rev. George Phillips was one of the signers of this "Humble Request," and he acted as a chaplain, preaching twice on Sunday and catechising on board the *Arbella* during the voyage over; and yet, within sixteen days after his landing, we find him privately telling Deacon Doctor Fuller, who had been again summoned from Plymouth to attend the sick among these new comers, that "if they will have him stand minister, by that calling which he received from the prelates in England, he will leave them;" and Winthrop— another signer—hoping that the Plymouth Church will "not be wanting in helping them" toward their necessary church organization; and four weeks later we find Fuller, who had been at Mattapan, letting blood and talking polity till he was weary, writing from Salem to Bradford and Brewster that, after counseling with Winslow, Allerton and himself, and with the Salem brethren, Winthrop's company had decided to form a church by covenant on the next Friday, and that that company do "earnestly entreat that the church at Plymouth would set apart the same day," for fraternal prayers that God would "establish and direct them in his ways." And seven days thereafter we find Fuller again writing Bradford, giving account of the formation of the church—now the First Church in Boston—and adding:

"here are divers honest christians that are desirous to see us (of Plymouth); some out of love, which they bear to us, and the good persuasion they have of us; others to see whether we be so evil, as they have heard of us. We have a name of love and holiness to God and his saints; the Lord make us answerable, and that it may be more than a name, or else it will do us no good."

Fuller, in one of these letters, adds the curious information that "one Mr. Cottington, a Boston man" (Mr. William Coddington, another signer of the "Humble Request"), told him that Mr. Cotton's charge was "that they should take advice of them at Plymouth, and should do nothing to offend them;" to which he appends his own judgment that Endecott is "a second Barrow." Rathband said, in 1644, that "Mr. W., an eminent man of the Church at Plimmoth," told him "that the rest of the Churches in New Eng. came at first to them at Plimmoth to crave their direction in Church courses, and made them their pattern." . . .

In letters from the home authorities of date some months later, we find alarm expressed at "some innovacions attempted by yo^w," with the intimation that they "vtterly disallowe any such passages," and entreat them to look back upon their "miscarriage wth repentance;" while they add that they take "leave to think that it is possible some vndigested councells haue too sodainely bin put in execucion wch may haue ill construccion wth the state heere, and make vs obnoxious to any adversary." The plain English of all which was that the patentees in England were surprised and offended that the colonists should so suddenly and so widely have departed from the church as by law established; and were apprehensive of the royal displeasure therefor, and of consequent harm to the secular interests they were seeking to promote.

In the formation of churches, for a time, each company acted its own preference, so that amid general unity there was slight variety. . . .

On the 18th-28th May, 1631, the General Court of the Massachusetts Colony adopted a regulation which came to have considerable influence upon ecclesiastical affairs, and which has been the subject of no little misconception and misrepresentation. Its terms were these:

"to the end the body of the commons may be p.serued of honest & good men, it was likewise ordered and agreed that for time to come *noe man shalbe admitted to the freedome of this body polliticke, but such as are members of some of the churches within the lymitts of the same.*"

It has been usual to assume that the Colony was then the State of Massachusetts, and this order equivalent to the declaration that no man should be a voter therein, who was not first a churchmember. The fact was that Massachusetts was then a little private trading corporation, so to speak, camping out upon land which it had received by grant; trying the experiment whether a permanent settlement could be effected, and the seeds of a plantation successfully germinated.

There was room enough outside for other people, and they simply wished to be by themselves, left in peace to work out their own experiment; . . . The corporation must fix some condition of membership. As situated, nothing seemed to them more natural or suitable than this.

Nearly four years afterward another regulation was adopted, the logical consequence of that already made—for if church membership were to be the prerequisite to membership of the Company, then surely the Company must have a vital interest in knowing the quality of the churches—to the effect that no churches were to be recognized by, and none of their members were to be admitted to the freedom of, the corporation, without they acquainted the magistrates, as well as the Elders of the churches already existing, with their intention of being organized, and gained their approbation thereto. . . .

Two considerations made it wise that as soon as possible there should be some public statement of the New England way. One, for the satisfaction of inquirers and the confutation of slanderers in England; the other for the culture of some general common agreement at home. Robinson's lamented death in Holland robbed the Plymouth Colony of the inestimable benefit of his counsels here, and the whole New England movement of the clear exposition and cogent defence of the church-method by it accepted, which he would have been so well prepared to furnish. Nor was the place left vacant by him for many years filled by any person in the Old Colony able and willing to be the exponent and champion of the New England way. So that it was left for the willing as well as able men of the Bay to do the work. As early as 1634—the year following that of his arrival—we find Mr. Cotton issuing the first of a long and valuable series of statements and discussions from his pen touching the general question of church life and order. It was entitled *Questions and Answers upon Church Government.* Its general tone is that common to all publications of the sort by the Separatists, teaching that the church is composed of congregations of faithful men, officered by Pastors, Teachers, Ruling Elders, Deacons and Widows. As to the questions at issue at Middelberg, Amsterdam and Leyden, it is made very clear that the Ruling Elders are to do the business of the church, and that one of the greatest privileges of the membership is that of "submission to all Gods Ordinances."

The order of worship as herein suggested is (1) Prayer; (2) a Psalm; (3) to "read the Worde and with all Preaching to give the sense, and applying the use, in dispensing whereof the Ministers were wont to stand above all the people in a Pulpit of wood, and the Elders on both sides, while the People hearkened to them with Reverence and Attention;" (4) if there be more prophets besides the Elders, they may then prophesy two or three, if time permit, the Elders calling to them if they have any word of exhortation to say on (and they may do this to members of other churches present); (5) any, young or old, (save only women) may ask questions "at the mouth of the Minister;" (6) the seals of Baptism and the Lord's Supper are administered; (7) they sing a Psalm; (8) collection is made for the support of the ministry, the need of poor saints, and the furthering of all outward service of the church; (9) the minister or any of the Prophets is "to dismisse the Assembly with a word of Blessing, offering Blessing unto the Lord, and puting a Blessing upon his People."

These *Questions and Answers* were issued, with additions, in 1643, which additions were mainly devoted to the statement of points touching upon the processes of church government. In these it is laid down that the royal government of the churches is in Christ, the stewardly or ministerial in the churches themselves; that Christ has committed government partly to the body of the church, but principally to the Presbytery of Ruling Elders:—to the body power to choose and call her own officers and members, to send forth any upon service, and to inquire, hear and assist in the judgment of all public scandals; to the Presbytery power (1) to call the church together, (2) to deliver the counsel of God to it with all authority, (3) to prepare matters for its hearing, (4) to propound and order the assembly, (5) to administer ordination, (6) and censure, (7) and to dismiss the people in the name of the Lord. The next question with its answer makes it very plain what kind of Congregationalism this was which John Cotton was setting up in Boston seven generations ago:

"*Qu. But hath not Christ committed some power of Government to every private Member of the Church?*
"*A.* Yes, verily, there is a power of edification which the Lord hath given to every Member of the Church, to exercise mutually one over another, to save some with compassion, others with feare, by a word of instruction, Admonition, Exhortation and Comfort."

One thing more will interest us in this, perhaps, oldest document which carries with it any

CHRISTIAN
CONSTITUENT:
───────────
THE AMERICAN
CHRISTIAN
CHURCH

authority, as shewing what the system of our fathers here was at its earliest elaboration by them, five years or more previous to the framing of the Cambridge Platform.

"*Qu. Having seen what power of Government the Church hath received and exercised within it selfe: tell me now whether any Church hath power of government over another?*

"*Ans.* No church hath power of Government over another, but each of them hath chief power within it selfe, and all of them equall power one with another, every Church hath received alike the power of binding and loosing, opening and shutting the Kingdome of heaven. But one to another, all of them are Sisters, all of them *Sarahs,* all of them Queens, none an *Hagar,* none of them Concubines, but by their own corruption or usurpation of others; finally, all of them are Candlesticks of the same precious mettall, and in the midst of them all Christ equally walketh.

"*Qu. But if one Church have no power of Government over another: what course then is there best to reform such corruptions as may arise in any Church, whether in Doctrine or practise?*

"*Ans.* The corruptions that are found in any Church do either infect part of the Church, or the whole body: if part only, then the part remaining sound may either convince and reform their Brethren themselves, if they be able, or if they be not able, they may at least prevaile so farre with them, as to send for light from some other Church, as they of *Antioch* did to the Church of *Hierusalem:* But if the corruptions found in a Church do infect the whole body, yet still there is hope in *Israel* concerning this. For though one Church hath not power of Government over another, as subordinate to them; yet every Church hath equall power one with another, as coordinate with them. And therfore look what power one Brother hath over another in the same Church, the same power hath one Church over another in Brotherly communion. As, if one Church shall heare of any offence in another, they may enquire the certainty of it, and therupon send letters and messengers to convince and admonish them of it. If the Church offending doe heare the Church admonishing, they haue gained their Brethren and their desire: if the Church heare them not, then that other Church may take one or two Churches mōe to assist them in the conviction of that sinne. If yet the Church heare them not, then upon due notice therof given, all the Churches thereabout may so meet together; and after judicious inquirie into the cause, may by the Word of God confute and condemne such errours in doctrine or practise, as are found offensive, to prevent the spreading either of the gangren of Heresie, or of the leprosie of sin. And if the Church offending shall not yet hearken to their Brethren, though the rest of the Churches have not power to deliver them to Satan, yet they have power to withdraw from them the right hand of fellowship, and no longer hold them in communion of Saints, till they approve their *repentance.*"

And now the time had come when, as Cotton Mather says, it was "convenient" that "the churches of *New England* should have a *System*

of their *Discipline,* extracted from the Word of God, and exhibited unto them, with a more effectual, acknowledged and established Recommendation: And nothing but a *Council* was proper to compose the *System.*" This convenience was manifold. The Church of England had become Presbyterian. And a little cabal of Presbyterians and others in Massachusetts—undertaking to work with the aid of the very large number who by this time were in the country resident, who were not members of the churches, and so were debarred from the privileges of freemen—had just petitioned the General Court to give them relief, and to open their way to the ballot-box and the ordinances; giving notice that, should their petition be denied, they should be "necessitated to apply our humble desires to the honorable houses of parliament, who we hope will take our sad conditions into their serious considerations." To have a Presbyterian Parliament undertake to revolutionize the ecclesiastical condition of New England would be a very serious matter indeed. Nor can it be denied that there was not a little of actual weakness consequent upon the utterly unintegrated condition of the New England churches in their absolute independence and unmitigated isolation; while large opportunity was given—in spite of all the treatises of Mr. Cotton and others—for English misconception and misrepresentation, since no even semi-authoritative statement had ever been consented to, which might stand witness and sponsor for the general faith. Under these circumstances, the Court, in May, 1646, passed an order expressing a "desire" that the churches of the Massachusetts send their Elders and Messengers to sit in Synod in Cambridge on the 1st September next ensuing, "to discusse, dispute & cleare up, by the word of God, such questions of church governm^t & discipline" in certain points before suggested, and others, "as they shall thinke needful & meete;" and requested the churches "wth in ye iurisdictions of Plimoth, Connectecott, & Newe Haven, to send their elders & messeng^rs to ye Assembly, . . . who, being so sent, shall be received as pts. & members thereof, & shall have like lib^rty & pow^r of disputing & voting therein, as shall ye messeng^rs & eld^rs of ye churches wth in ye iurisdiction of ye Massachusets."

As a matter of course, many people queried, more feared, some stoutly objected. The liberties of the churches must be looked to: would the Court undertake to rule them through a Synod?

Tuesday, the 1st-11th of September, however, found all except four of the churches of the

Massachusetts, with a few from the other colonies, assembled by representatives at Cambridge, in response to the "desire" of the Court. Concord was absent, their Elder being unable to come, and no other fit. Hingham favored Presbyterianism. Boston and Salem at first were jealous and would not send. A long time was wasted in trying to mollify Boston, but at last Mr. Norton of Ipswich was able, in a sermon on Moses and Aaron meeting in the mount and kissing each other, to soften their flinty hearts to a vote of the major part—they had to be content without being unanimous, this time—to send the Elders, and three brethren as messengers. Salem seems to have followed suit.

This Synod was a grave, learned and pious body. It had, because it deserved to have, the respectful confidence of the colonies. It sat now, however, but about a fortnight, and, appointing John Cotton, Richard Mather of Dorchester, and Ralph Partridge of Duxbury, each a committee of one to draw up the plan of a Scriptural Model of Church Government, so that the three might be compared, adjourned over till Tuesday, the 8th-18th June, 1647.

An epidemical sickness soon dispersed this re-gathering, with which Gov. Bradford was present as the messenger of the church in Plymouth; and where Ezekiel Rogers of Rowley took occasion to bear a testimony against private members making disturbing speeches in the public assemblies, long hair, and "other things amiss;" and it was not until Tuesday the 15th-25th August, 1648, that the Synod was able to begin a solid fortnight upon its real work. While Mr. Allen of Dedham on this day of re-assembling was preaching a very godly and learned discourse before the company, it fell out about the midst of his sermon that there came a snake into the seat where many of the Elders sat behind the preacher. One of the Elders of Braintree, a man of much faith, and apparently a heavy pair of shoes, trode upon the head of it, and so held it, with his foot and staff, until it was killed. They surmised that it might be the devil, and concluded that the seed of the woman had for once fulfilled prophecy concerning him. They went on comfortably, and after many "*filing* thoughts upon it," settled down substantially upon Mr. Mather's draught of a Platform; after which they broke up with singing the Song of Moses and the Lamb, in the fifteenth chapter of the Revelation, "adding another sacred Song from the nineteenth Chapter of that Book; which is to be found metrically paraphrased in the *New England* Psalm-Book."

I suppose—I may take it for granted that you are all familiar with the Cambridge Platform.

It is a terse, clear, and well-balanced summary of the general system which had been already outlined in the treatises of the New England Elders; enlarged by being carried to its logical conclusions on a few points which had never been fully developed. Portions of it strongly resemble the exact language of one or other of the books to which I have referred. I do not think it uncharitable to surmise that the Synod, while at its work, kept one eye upon Presbyterian facts, tendencies and demands, as then existing, or supposed to exist, in the mother-country; and that the strings of the harp were strained a little tighter than they might have been had the Independents controlled Parliament and the Westminster Assembly—in the view to bring them as nearly as possible up to concert pitch with the Genevan music. It would surely be a great point gained for them if, with a good conscience, matters could be so adjusted that there should be no excuse for home interference with the religious affairs of New England. . . .

It was not until the next year that the result of the Synod, having been put into print, was "presented to the Churches, and Generall Court, for their consideration and acceptance, in the Lord." In October, 1649, the Court judged:

"it meete to cōmend it to the judicyous and pious consideracōn of the seuerall churches wᵗʰin this jurisdiccōn, desiring a retourne from them at the next Gennerll Courte hou farr it is suitable to their judgments and app. bacōn, before the Courte p.ceeds any farther therein."

The churches, apparently in their majority, responded favorably to this request, while "diuerse" of them presented "some objectjons and doubts against some particculars in the sajd draught," which were commended to the Elders "to be cleared and remooved." And in October, 1651, the Court thankfully acknowledged the "learned pajnes" with which the subject had been handled, and voted "to give their testimony to the sajd booke of discipljne, that, for the substance thereof, it is that wee have practised and doe believe."

It may be worth our while to pause here long enough, in addition to what has already been said more particularly to glance, with some detail, at the working aspects of the polity thus established in New England in its earliest years.

A Church was formed—after permission had from the magistrates—by the public covenanting together, usually on a day of fasting and prayer, of such persons in any town desiring membership as satisfied each other of their mutual fitness; other churches cooperating by their delegated presence, with some formal expression of fellowship. Thus organized, it elected from its own number—if able fully to officer itself—a Pastor, whose function was intended to be practical and pastoral; a Teacher, especially to instruct in doctrine; two or more Ruling Elders, to constitute, with the Pastor and Teacher, the Presbytery of Elders, ruling the Church in the Lord; two or more Deacons, who, in addition to the care of the communion table, and the general temporalities of the body, usually were to see that the Elders had suitable support; and, to care especially for the sick, and look after the decorum of the little folks in the house of God, one or more matronly Deaconesses.

Persons wishing to join such a Church made known that desire to the Ruling Elders and were examined—sometimes in presence of members of the Church—by them as to "the worke of grace upon their soules, or how God hath beene dealing with them about their conversion." . . . Discipline proceeded on this wise. Offence arising, and personal labor failing to adjust the same, the case was taken to the Elders, and by them to the Church; which, if unsatisfied, admonished, and in the end excommunicated; but this grew to be done by silent assent to the expressed judgment of the Elders; to use Mr. Hooker's words, on the theory that "the consent of the people gives a causall vertue to the compleating of the sentence of excommunication." . . .

The order of public worship was on this wise. Sabbath morning service began about nine o'clock; in Boston and some other places, the people being called together by the "wringing of a bell," but usually by the beating of a drum, or the blowing of a shell, or horn—sometimes by the hoisting of a flag. The meeting was opened by the Pastor "with solemn prayer continuing about a quarter of an houre," after which the Teacher read and expounded a chapter of the Bible. One of the Ruling Elders next "dictated" (that is to say "lined-off") a Psalm, which was sung. The Pastor then preached, the Teacher concluded with prayer and a blessing. At afternoon worship (which in Boston was about 2 P. M., in sparser settlements the intermission being shortened so as to allow those who came long distances to remain to the second service without inconvenience), the Pastor began with prayer, and after

a Psalm the Teacher—sometimes first reading and expounding a chapter and praying—made a sermon, the Pastor concluding with prayer and the benediction.

The Lord's Supper was usually administered once a month at the close of the morning service, "all others departing save the church"; the Elders, both Teaching and Ruling, sitting at the table, and the members in their seats. . . .

Spectators desiring it, were not refused permission to be present. Members of sister churches wishing to commune, were required to make known their desire to one of the Ruling Elders, and on being personally authenticated by any member of the body, or on presentation of a "Letter testimoniall," their names were propounded to the Church "before they goe to the Sacrament." . . .

It was held that baptism might be administered wherever the Church was assembled, and the Word was preached, but it was long usually done at the close of Sabbath worship. The administrator (who might be either the Pastor or the Teacher) stood in the Deacon's seat, and made a short exhortation to the parents and the Church, and baptized by sprinkling or washing the face, praying before and after, and there were no sponsors.

Our fathers, from conscience, called their houses for worship "meeting-houses." As buildings, they were spacious but simple. The Ruling Elders occupied a seat in front of the pulpit and a little further down; the Deacons a similar seat on a still lower level—all facing the congregation. The people sat—the men on the one side and the women on the other—in an order of civil and social dignity scrupulously arranged from year to year. The children appear also to have been placed by themselves, under care of a tithing-man.

The method of supporting the gospel was different in different places. . . .

Weekly meetings for social prayer and conference, in the sense of the words now common, were unknown; although private assemblies were sometimes held for religious discussion and communion, which were opened and closed with prayer. . . .

After the churches had settled well down to their work, a weekly lecture—essentially a repetition of one Sabbath service—became a fixed institution; and there was early an annual Fast and Thanksgiving; while occasional special fasts and thanksgivings were ordered as public exigencies seemed to suggest and require. . . .

By the still unspent force of their great recoil

from Papal ways and modes of thought, marriages were made a civil contract, and solemnized by the magistrate; he offering the prayers proper to the occasion. While, of funerals, Lechford says:

> "At Burials, nothing is read, nor any Funeral Sermon made, but all the neighbourhood, or a good company of them, come together by tolling of the bell, and carry the dead solemnly to his grave, and there stand by him while he is buried. The Ministers are most commonly present." . . .

Scrupling, as did their Nonconformist contemporaries in England, the rightness of continuing the use of names of heathen origin, the Massachusetts men styled the first day of the week either the Lord's Day or the Sabbath, or First Day; and, about 1636, they carried that idea through the calendar, numbering all the days, and the months, as well. As the year then began with March, they would, for example, style the third Tuesday in May "the third third day of the third month"—and in like manner with all.

But one thing remains to put us in sufficient possession of the quality of the Congregationalism which characterized the early settlement of New England, and that is for us to look at it, as, in the judgment of that time, it stood related to the Presbyterianism which became for a short period the established religion of the Father-land.

The careful reader of the numerous volumes which discussed the relations between our fathers with their Independent brethren in England, and the Presbyterians of the Westminster Assembly, will find four subjects as to which there was decided difference between them.

The first related to the terms of membership of the Church. We have seen that it had always been fundamental with the Separatists that all who joined their churches be, in their own conviction and in the hope and belief of the body, regenerate persons; but that Cartwright and the Genevan influence leaned toward a State Church, which though governed in its congregations by an Eldership and in its entirety by Synods, should be as comprehensive as the Establishment it was intended to displace. . . .

The second touched that silent power of assent which was accorded to the brotherhood; . . .

The third divergence—and, on the whole, the chief,—had to do with the power of Synods. The New England men were clear that Synods are for advice, and for the moral power of persuasion only; the Presbyterians held that they exercise the lawful authority of Christ over the many congregations of the one Church. . . .

The fourth distinction related to the subject of toleration, as to which the Presbyterians accused the New England men of the greatest looseness. . . .

All of which goes to endorse the judgment which we have reached from other sources of evidence, that the early Congregationalism of this country was Barrowism, and not Brownism—a Congregationalized Presbyterianism, or a Presbyterianized Congregationalism—which had its roots in the one system, and its branches in the other; which was essentially Genevan within the local congregation, and essentially other outside of it. The forty or fifty churches, which, "for the substance of it," adopted the Cambridge Platform, held this general system indeed with varying degrees of strictness—from the almost Presbyterianism of Hingham and Newbury, to the large-minded and large-hearted Robinsonism of the mother Mayflower Church.

There were great expectations that this seed, thus sown two centuries and a half ago in prayer and hope, along these pine-fringed shores, would grow to a creditable and useful harvest, wherein the world, and heaven, would be glad. Not unconscious of inherent inadjustments of some main elements of their polity, our fathers yet trusted the event would prove them:

> "Not chaos-like together crush'd and bruis'd,
> But, as the world, harmoniously confus'd;
> Where order in variety we see,
> And where, though all things differ, all agree." . . .

LATER NEW-ENGLAND CONGREGATIONALISM

More than two entire generations lived and died after the adoption of the Cambridge Platform, before any important movement was made for its modification. Now and then, indeed, one may get glimpses of a considerable popular drift, which the careful investigator will note as indicating the feeling with which the churches were regarding that document, and the system which it enshrines.

That matters were not working as well as had been desired, and anticipated, became obvious within twenty years. As not all of the children of the first settlers, nor of those immigrants who with them constituted the second generation of colonists, saw their way clear to confess Christ and thus gain admission to full church privileges, it followed that many of the children who were to compose the third generation, were growing up, as Cotton Mather phrased it, "excluded from the *Baptism* of Christianity, and from the Ecclesiastical Inspection which is to accompany that Baptism." This was the greater grief to *"the Grand-fathers"* that, as he continues, "it was to leave their Offspring under the Shepherdly Government of our Lord Jesus Christ in his Ordinances, that they had brought their Lambs into this Wilderness;" and with them it was a chief concern that the religious prosperity which had blessed their beginnings, "might not be a *Res unius aetatis,* a matter of one Age alone." They labored with their sons and daughters, "sober Persons, who professed themselves desirous to renew their *Baptismal-Covenant,* and submit unto the *Church-Discipline,* and so have their Houses also marked for the Lord's;" but did not find them ready to "come up to that experimental Account of their own Regeneration, which would sufficiently embolden their Access to the other Sacrament."

It has been usual to represent the matter as further complicated by civil considerations, arising out of the law of the Massachusetts and New Haven colonies limiting the franchise to church members; making it important, as well to save the State from being enfeebled, as the church from being impoverished, that some wider door be opened into the latter. That this is an error becomes obvious, however, on careful review of the facts. Such a reason does not seem to have been mentioned at the time. I am aware of no proof that half-way covenant members of the church, by that relation did acquire any further privilege in the State. Moreover, before the action of the Synod proposing the half-way covenant had been concluded, the king's letter of 28 June-8 July, 1662, had arrived, requiring that "all the freeholders of competent estates, not vitious in conversacōn & orthodoxe in religion (though of different persuasions concerning church gouernment) may haue their votes in the election of all officers, both ciuill & military," etc.; and in Massachusetts the old law was soon formally repealed, and the order passed that "henceforth all Englishmen presenting a cirtifficat, vnder the hands of the ministers or minister of the place where they dwell, that they are orthodox in religion & not vitious in theire liues," etc., be allowed the freeman's privileges; so that any change in the constitution of the churches in this motive would hardly be natural at such a time. Which reasons are further enforced by the consideration that the controversy out of which the Council and the Synod, and the half-way covenant grew, originated in the Connecticut colony, where no such restriction of civil freedom had ever existed.

The motive, then appears to have been with most a pure and religious one. But it grew, no doubt, out of the "fermentation of that leaven of Presbyterianism which came over not with the Pilgrims in the Mayflower, but with the later Puritan emigration," and it touchingly reveals to us how tenderly the best piety of that day regarded God's covenant with His people, and how highly it estimated the practical value of "regular church watch" and discipline, as means of grace.

Connecticut, as I have said, was first to move. Unfortunate differences of opinion had for some time disturbed the church in Hartford, leading to the calling of several councils, whose results had failed to allay the excitement. There had grown up in that colony, moreover, a strong party which advocated a return to the ancient plan of admitting all persons of regular life to full communion in the churches. Obliged to contribute to the support of a minister in whose election they had no voice, and denied "the honours and privileges of church-members for themselves, and baptism for their children," because they "knew not how to comply with the rigid terms of the Congregational churches," they were uneasy and desired a change. In the hope of gaining wisdom and moral support upon a topic of common concernment, the magistrates of that colony suggested to the General Court of Massachusetts the calling of a council of some selected Elders to consider and advise in the premises. The Massachusetts Court thereon passed an order that thirteen of the Teaching Elders within its jurisdiction meet in the following summer for the purpose named, desiring the cooperation of the confederate colonies therein. Plymouth did not respond. New Haven declined to send. Connecticut delegated four of its Pastors, or Teachers. The meeting began in Boston on Thursday, 4-14 June, 1657, and after a fortnight's consideration, concluded it to be the duty of adults who had been baptized when children "tho' not yet fit for the *Lord's Supper,* to own the *Covenant* they made with their Parents by entering thereinto in their own persons;" and the correlate duty of the church to call upon them for the performance of this, and to censure them for its neglect; and further declared its judgment that in case such parents "understand the *Grounds of Religion,* and are not Scandalous, and solemnly own the *Covenant* in their own Persons," there can be no sufficient cause to deny baptism to their children.

This failed, however, to compose the strife. It indeed made matters worse. It alarmed many, as insidiously proposing a harmful innovation. And the opposition grew so formidable as "could not be encountred with any thing less than a *Synod* of *Elders* and *Messengers,* from all the Churches in the *Massachuset* Colony." Such a Synod "of above seventy," met in Boston on Tuesday, 11-21 March, 1662, and after two adjournments, reached its result in the September following. The difficulty which pressed them lay in the fact that "through their own Doubts and Fears, and partly thro' other culpable Neglects," many of the children of the first colonists "had not actually come up to the covenanting State of *Communicants* at the Table of the Lord." This excluded their children not only from baptism, but from "the Ecclesiastical Inspection" which went with it. The question was whether any way could be legitimately devised by which such persons, who had not boldness of access to the Lord's table, could yet be admitted to some relation to the church which should difference their condition from that of pagans who might happen to hear the Word of God in their assemblies. Two expedients were possible. The terms of church-membership might be so far lowered, that any baptized person not scandalous in life might be admitted to full communion, and the right to have his children baptized, without evidence of regeneration. Or a qualified and subordinate membership, allowing baptized persons of moral life and orthodox beliefs to belong to the church so far as to receive baptism for their children, and all privileges but that of the Lord's Supper for themselves, might be established. The former would have been too flagrant a backsliding from the very essentials of Puritanism, and so the latter, though involving "a grave theological error hardening and establishing itself in the form of an ecclesiastical system," received the suffrage of the Synod, by a vote of more than sixty to less than ten; the want of unanimity being emphasized by the quality of the opposition, more than by its quantity.

This "Half-way Covenant," as it has been usually and aptly called, while it made a show of meeting the difficulty, and of keeping the church pure by this fond distinction between "half-way" and full membership, was earnestly opposed by Chauncy, Davenport and others, because they had the sagacity to foresee that through the gradual effacement of all distinction in membership, it must result in filling the churches with unregenerate persons, and so poisoning at their fountain the streams of the Christian liberty and prosperity of the colonies. The contention, on the other hand, of the Synod and its apologists was, that if

something of this sort were not done, it would be impossible to prevent the churches from so lowering the terms of full communion as to admit unworthy persons to all privilege; than which evil they judged that any which might grow out of the new measure must be less. . . .

For a considerable period the controversy between the *Synodists* and the *Anti-Synodists* divided New England. As the rule in the Massachusetts colony the pastors appear to have favored the Result, while many of the more intelligent and influential laymen were "stiffly and fiercely set the other way."

Steadily, now for some years, had been coming over from Fatherland the weighty influence of the Presbyterians of the Long Parliament, the Westminster Assembly, and the Commonwealth, in favor of that larger liberty—in what Davenport stigmatized as the "parish way"—which had commended itself to them; and to which they had done their endeavor to reduce the Church of England.

When John Wilson died in 1667—following his colleague John Norton, who had rested from his labors a little more than four years before— the large majority of the First Church in Boston manifested its feeling on the subject of the half-way covenant, by inviting John Davenport, the champion of the opposing view, to come from New Haven to be Mr. Wilson's successor. His ultimate acceptance of the call was followed by the secession of twenty-eight male members; who —after much tribulation, and by the aid of the first well-marked (and perhaps the most important) *Ex-parte* council ever held in New England —were formed into what has long been honorably known as the "Old South" Church. For "two sevens of years" there was no communion between the old church and the new, and "the whole People of God throughout the Colony, were too much distinguished into such as favoured the Old Church, and such as favored the New Church; whereof the former were against the Synod, and the latter were for it."

In the New Haven Colony, where Davenport's influence was weighty, most of the churches earnestly opposed the new way, which they called "large Congregationalism." But there, as proved to be the case elsewhere, "as the aged ministers and other old men, honored and influential, who had resisted the conclusions of the Massachusetts synod, passed away, the half-way covenant came in with the new generation of pastors and church-members." As first conceived, and practiced, this might not have worked serious harm, but it was laxative rather than astringent in its nature, and its tendency was steadily downward. Originally its provisions applied only to church-members who were admitted in minority, but before many years churches which adopted it construed it as admitting those not church-members by baptism, and even men of lax personal morality who might desire baptism for their children. While thus growing less and less scrupulous as to the character of those whom it gathered in to that connection which it offered with the church; it, at the same time, broadened its view of the amount of church privilege to which such persons should be entitled. Starting with the theory that some germ of true faith, in the absence of proof to the contrary, must be assumed in one who was a child of the covenant—sufficient to transmit a right of baptism to his children, but not sufficient to entitle him to partake of the Lord's Supper; not many years passed before the inference was reached that an amount of saving faith, even in the germ, which would justify the baptism of a man's children, ought to justify his own admission to the table of the Lord. Some churches silently acted on this theory, others openly voted that "those who wish to offer their children in baptism join with the church, and have a right to all the ordinances and privileges of the church;" while "if any have doubts with regard to their preparation for the Lord's Supper, they may have the liberty to stay away from that ordinance until their doubts shall be removed." It was only necessary to add to this the theory which Solomon Stoddard of Northampton advocated in 1700, that "the Lord's Supper is instituted to be a means of Regeneration," with the inevitable corollary, that men "may and ought to come (to it) tho' they know themselves to be in a Natural Condition;" completely to efface all useful and evangelical distinction between the church and the world. Sometimes, indeed, nearly the whole body of the young people of a congregation would "own the covenant." No wonder that the decline of piety was not long in making itself painfully visible.

And so it turned out that scarcely more than half a generation had passed after this "large" way had been entered upon, before the decay of morals and manners was such as to alarm the godly; the more that heavy calamities by sea and shore, shipwrecks, droughts, conflagrations, fightings, pestilential sicknesses, and commercial disasters—which the Judaistic tendency of the piety of that day inclined to interpret strongly in the light of special divine judgments—had fallen

upon the land. So deep became the feeling among the leaders of Christian sentiment, that, in the spring of 1679, reverend Elders of the Massachusetts Colony petitioned their rulers to take action in the matter, and the Court ordered a Synod to assemble on Wednesday, the 10-20 September following, to consider:

"*Quaest.* 1. What are the euills that haue provoked the Lord to bring his judgments on New England?
"2. *Quaest.* What is to be donn that so those evills may be reformed?"

The churches of the Massachusetts Colony observed a day of general fasting and prayer for God's blessing on the movement, and the Synod itself began with a like service. Rev. John Sherman of Watertown, and Rev. Urian Oakes, who held the double office of Pastor at Cambridge, and President of Harvard College, were its moderators. It spent several days in the discussion of the two subjects submitted, "with utmost Liberty granted unto every Person, to express his Thoughts thereupon." A committee then digested these opinions into a Result which "as to the *Substance, End and Scope* thereof," was unanimously adopted, reported to the Court at its October session, and by it commended "to the serious consideration of all the churches and people." The Court further enjoined and required:

"All persons in their seuerall capacitjes concerned, to a carefull and diligent reformation of all those provoking evills mentioned therein, according to the true intent thereof, that so the anger and displeasure of God, which hath binn many wayes manifested, maybe averted from this poore people, and his favour and blessing obteyned, as in former tjmes."

The evils which the Synod particularly specified were thirteen: (1) the decay of godliness among professing Christians; (2) pride, showing itself in the unwillingness to submit to due order, and in contention, as well as in "Strange Apparel;" (3) breaches of the second commandment in the neglect of baptism and church fellowship, and that Quakers and Anabaptists have "set up an Altar against the Lord's Altar" without having been "fully testified against;" (4) the profaning of God's name by imprecations, and by irreverent behavior in the sanctuary; (5) Sabbath breaking; (6) lax government and the want of household worship in families; (7) inordinate passions, backbitings, censures, revilings, and lawsuits even between church-members; (8) intemperance, tavern-haunting, and putting the bottle to the lips of the Indians, to convert whom the first planters came into this land; heinous breaches of the seventh commandment, with wanton and seductive dress and behavior, mixed dancings, gamings and idleness; (9) promise-breaking and other untruthfulness; (10) inordinate affection for the world, showing itself in too great a desire for landed estates, leading men "to forsake Churches and Ordinances, and to live like Heathen, only that so they might have Elbow-room enough in the World," causing others to sell goods at excessive rates, still others to demand unreasonable wages, and inclining many to "strait-handedness as to Publick Concernments;" (11) opposition to the work of reformation and making excuses for sin; (12) a lamentable want of public spirit, causing schools of learning and other such common interests to languish, and raising murmurs as to philanthopic expenditures; and finally (13) sins against the Gospel in the refusal to repent, and in general unfruitfulness under the means of grace. These sins it was thought safe to assume to be the ground of the Lord's controversy with New England, because they were so common; because they had been acknowledged on days of public humiliation and yet had not been repented of; and because many of them were not punished (and some not punishable) by man, wherefore it was assumed that the Lord himself was punishing them.

Twelve prescriptions were suggested for the moral diseases thus diagnosed: (1) that the chief persons in the Church and State, "as to themselves and families become every way Exemplary;" (2) that—since a generation had passed—the Cambridge Platform be reaffirmed; (3) that care be taken to admit none to the communion in the Lord's Supper who have not made full profession of saving faith; (4) that discipline in the churches be re-invigorated and "Diligently attended, not only towards Parents, but also towards the Children of the Church, according to the Rules of Christ;" (5) that utmost endeavors be used to have the churches fully officered with pastor, as well as teacher, and with Ruling Elders; (6) that the magistrate see to it that these officers have "due encouragement and maintenance;" (7) that wholesome laws be established, and particularly that those for the regulation of public houses be rigorously enforced, and that for constables and tithing-men be chosen from among the ablest and most prudent; (8) that the churches make a solemn renewal of their covenant with God; (9) that in such renewal the sins of the times be specially "engaged against";

(10) that in such renewal "such things as are clear and indisputable be expressed, that so all the Churches may agree in Covenanting to promote the Interest of Holiness, and close walking with God;" (11) that effectual care be taken that the college, and all schools of learning in every place, be promoted and encouraged; and, finally (12)—since every expedient must be ineffectual unless divine grace attend it—that all "cry mightily unto God, both in ordinary and extraordinary manner, that He would be pleased to Rain down Righteousness" upon the land.

This action of this Synod produced a good effect. Faithful ministers were much strengthened by it in laboring with their people, and devout Christians provoked to a more earnest piety. Many churches made solemn renewal of their covenant with God. And the other colonies, particularly those of Plymouth and Connecticut, to a considerable extent followed the lead of Massachusetts.

In the estimation of the good men of the time, however, the judgments of God were not stayed in consequence. Lamentable disasters on sea and land came thick and fast. A French and Indian war; the old Charter gone; Gov. Andros come, and a Church of England service forcibly intruded into the South meeting-house; privateers infesting the coast; fires, hurricanes, very extraordinary hail-storms, floods whose violence changed the channels of rivers, ministers' houses struck with lightning; news of a tremendous earthquake swallowing two thousand victims followed by a pestilence sweeping away three thousand more, in Jamaica; the small-pox raging in New Hampshire and again in the Carolinas; great losses of cattle; a scarcity of food, bringing grain up to the highest price ever known; the coldest weather in winter since the country was settled; and the heavy cloud of the witchcraft delusion settling like a pall over some of the best places and best people of Massachusetts; who can fail to see that, to our fathers, this going out of the seventeenth century must have seemed almost like the very dawning of the day of doom? . . .

The first decade of the eighteenth century saw two endeavors made for the correction of whatever was deemed amiss in what then passed for New England Congregationalism; in 1705 in Massachusetts, and in 1708 in Connecticut. . . .

JOHN WISE

In the summer of 1652 had been born in Roxbury—the fifth child of his father, and he a serv-

ing man—John Wise. Remarkably endowed both in body and mind, he soon pushed up and on, graduating at Harvard College in 1673. In 1680 he went, under the endorsement of the General Court, to be the first minister of the Chebacco parish in Ipswich, since known as Essex; where his ordination was postponed until 12-22 Aug., 1683, by vexatious hindrances thrown in the way, under the law as it then was, by the first church. Four years after when Sir Edmund Andros's lawless order for a Province, tax came before the freemen of Ipswich for action, he opposed the measure with such effect that the town passed by the article in the warrant. For this he was arrested, deposed, fined and imprisoned. After Andros's overthrow he resumed his pastorate; in 1689 was sent to Boston by his town to help reorganize the government, and in various ways made himself patriotically helpful, until in 1690 Sir William Phips, the new Governor, led his troops to Canada, when Mr. Wise by appointment of the Legislature, accompanied the expedition as its chaplain. Thus acting, he gained confidence and renown by his great personal bravery, his fecundity of resource, and military skill; not less than by his devout and indefatigable discharge of the more appropriate duties of his sacred office. Well read in the history and literature of the past, yet never afraid of the new, fertile in original suggestion, acute in ratiocination, careless as to what direction might need to be taken in finding truth, and fearless in upholding what commended itself to him as truth when found, and by birth and conviction a man of the people; such a training had prepared John Wise to deal with these "Proposals" in a very thorough, if an unexampled manner.

For a while he seems to have tried Cotton Mather's imported plan of "generous silence, and pious contempt." But when the Connecticut Colony took up the matter and settled down upon Consociationism, as its established religion, his blood was stirred, and his solicitudes kindled, lest the churches of the Bay should in like manner go down into the Egypt of the strong governments, to escape from whom their fathers had crossed the seas. So, in 1710, there came out a little book entitled *"The Churches Quarrel Espoused: or a Reply In Satyre, to certain Proposals made, etc. By John Wise, Pastor to a Church in Ipswich,"* etc. My narrow limits—as I can best briefly handle both treatises together—compel me to advance at once to the statement that, in 1717, he published again—this time *"A Vindication of the Government of New England Churches, Drawn*

from Antiquity; the Light of Nature; Holy Scripture; its Noble Nature; and from the Dignity Divine Providence has put upon it," etc.

These two books taken together, and considered in the light of their time, and the influence which it is easy to see that they exerted, were very remarkable. Their author's mind made progress while engaged upon them; and yet, through all, he "builded better than he knew." He did not himself see, nor did his generation comprehend, either the exact bearing, or the entire force, of the principles which he enunciated. It was in his intent to justify, and bring the churches back to, the Cambridge Platform as their fundamental law; but in so doing he generated a momentum which overthrew the Platform and carried New England Congregationalism as far beyond that, as that had been beyond the Presbyterianism of the Westminster Assembly. . . .

Three things were especially intended in the first of these treatises, viz.: to alarm the churches with the thought that their inherited liberties were in danger; to stigmatize these "Proposals" as treasonable to the ancient polity; and to make the lay brethren feel that they had rights, and incite them to stand up for those rights like men. And in the conviction that in no other way so well could the laity make themselves felt, they were here urged to elect Ruling Elders in all the churches, who, "naturally Caring for your Affairs, will, like wakeful Sentinels, curiously and with Courage guard your Liberties." Seven years later, in the second treatise, Mr. Wise—still fancying that he was defending the Cambridge Platform— in the face of a prejudiced and unbelieving generation, advanced to the position that "Democracy is Christ's Government, in Church and State." I cannot ask you to dwell upon this argument here further than to note its clear conclusion, *"That the People, or Fraternity, under the Gospel, are the first Subject of Power; . . . that a Democracy in Church or State, is a very honourable and regular Government according to the Dictates of Right Reason; And therefore, That these Churches* of New England *in their ancient Constitution of Church Order; it being a Democracy, are manifestly Justified and Defended by the Law & Light of Nature."*

But if you wish to study the natural rights of man, the quality of political obligation, and the relative aspects and claims of the monarchic, the aristocratic and the democratic forms of government both for State and Church; I know of no discussion which, for density, for clearness, for largeness of vision, for conclusiveness, and for

THE BRAZEN SERPENT
BY BENJAMIN WEST (AMERICAN, 1738-1820)
OIL ON CANVAS, 148 X 115 IN. 1790.
COURTESY OF BOB JONES UNIVERSITY COLLECTION,
GREENVILLE, SOUTH CAROLINA

"And the Lord sent fiery serpents among the people, and they bit the people; and much people of Israel died. Therefore the people came to Moses, and said, We have sinned, for we have spoken against the Lord, and against thee; pray unto the Lord, that he take away the serpents from us. And Moses prayed for the people. And the Lord said unto Moses, Make thee a fiery serpent, and set it upon a pole: and it shall come to pass, that every one that is bitten, when he looketh upon it, shall live. And Moses made a serpent of brass, and put it upon a pole, and it came to pass, that if a serpent had bitten any man, when he beheld the serpent of brass, he lived." (Numbers 21:6-9)

The wilderness, through which they had passed, was all along infested with those fiery serpents, as appears, Deut. viii:15. But hitherto God had wonderfully preserved his people from receiving hurt from them, till now that they murmured; to chastise them for which, these animals, which hitherto had shunned their camp, now invaded it. Justly are those made to feel God's judgments that are not thankful for his mercies. They distrustfully concluded that they must die in the wilderness, and God took them at their word, chose their delusions, and brought their unbelieving fears upon them: many of them did die. They in their pride had lifted themselves up against God and Moses, and now God humbled and mortified them, by making these despicable animals a plague to them.

The people prayed that God would *take away the serpents from them*, but God saw fit not to do that: for he gives effectual relief in the *best* way, though not in *our* way.

Observe then a resemblance, 1. Between their *disease* and ours. Sin is the biting of this fiery serpent, it is painful to the startled conscience, and poisonous to the seared conscience. Satan's temptations are called his fiery darts. 2. Between their *remedy* and ours. It was God himself that devised and prescribed this antidote against the fiery serpents; so our salvation by Christ was the contrivance of Infinite Wisdom; God himself has found the ransom. The brazen serpent was lifted up; so was Christ—He was lifted up upon the cross. He was lifted up by the preaching of the gospel. 3. Between the *application* of their remedy and ours. They looked and lived, and we, if we believe, shall not perish; it is by faith that we look unto Jesus. The brazen serpent's being lifted up would not cure, if it was not looked upon. If they slighted this method of cure, and had recourse to natural medicines, and trusted to them, they justly perished; so, if sinners either despise Christ's righteousness, or despair of benefit by it, their wound will, without doubt, be fatal; but whoever looked up to this healing sign, though from the outmost part of the camp, though with a weak and weeping eye, was certainly healed; so whosoever believes in Christ, though as yet but weak in faith, shall not perish.

Matthew Henry, on the place

general ability and beauty of style, approaches this little 16mo tract of one hundred and five small pages from this great Ipswich father of American democracy. . . .

For the next half-century church polity was less discussed in New England than were some other subjects. The Great Awakening of 1734-1742, with the controversies in regard to Whitefield and others engendered by it, and the great declension that succeeded, were followed in turn by the war of the Revolution. Two facts, however, let us here note. One, that Samuel, son and successor in the pastoral office of Cotton Mather, ten years after his father's death (1738) published *An Apology for the Liberties of the Churches in New England,* etc., in which again and again he indicates that *he* stood essentially on the Ipswich platform; as, for example, where he says:

"Let them (the churches) never blindly resign *themselves to the Direction of their Ministers;* but consider themselves, as *Men,* as *Christians,* as *Protestants, obliged to judge and act for themselves in all the weighty Concernments of Religion,*" etc.

The other, that, early in 1772, an edition of Wise's two tracts—the third of the first, and the second of the second—was published in Boston; and so eager was the perusal of them, and so extensive the demand for their clear reasoning in favor of democracy as the best government, that another edition, of which more than one thousand copies were bespoken before its issue, was put to press in the same city in the same year. An examination of the appended names of subscribers curiously suggests the interesting fact that John Wise, now in his grave seven and forty years, was yet speaking, as a political reformer, in the ear of fellow patriots who were still eager to listen to his voice. . . .

The Great Awakening had a two-fold influence. It added from forty to fifty thousand members to the churches of New England; struck a death-blow at the half-way covenant, and its introduction of unconverted men to the communion table, if not to the pulpit; gave a mighty impulse to Christian education; reinvigorated Christian missions, and founded the Monthly Concert of Prayer for the conversion of the world. On the other hand, it thrust out to greatly increased prominence as pulpit themes the distinguishing doctrines of grace, and in so doing, and by its vigorous antagonism to Arminianism, Pelagianism, and the Socinianism which was already springing here, it began that cleavage which, by

the end of the next half-century, had fulfilled Increase Mather's prediction, and, in the "Unitarian Conflict," effected the gathering of "Churches out of Churches."

In 1760, Rev. Dr. Stiles—then of Newport, R.I., but who eighteen years after assumed, and adorned, the Presidency of Yale—preached a sermon before the Reverend Convention of the Congregational ministers of the Rhode Island Colony, in which he elaborately reviewed the ecclesiastical history of the country, commended that enfranchisement of the body of the churches which had followed John Wise's labors, and, for himself, declared:

"The exigencies of the Christian church can never be such as to legitimate, much less render it wise, to erect any body of men into a standing judicatory over the churches. If on some extraordinary occasions it may be necessary to cede up the united power into an extraordinary commission; yet when the public work designed is accomplished, let the commission end, the power revert and rest in the bosom of the churches. . . . Let them be taught to stand fast in the liberty wherewith Christ has made them free."

ECCLESIASTICAL COUNCILS

. . . Congregationalism is distinguished from Independency by adding to the principle of the self-completeness, under Christ, of the local church, the further principle that, since all local churches belong to the one family of the Lord, they necessarily owe to each other sisterly affection and activity; the normal exercise of which takes the name of the communion of the churches. Ordinarily such communion is manifested by reciprocal recognition, by exchanging members, and by laboring together, with mutual understanding, for the best promotion of the common work which Christ has laid upon his Universal Church on earth. Extraordinarily it has three functions: (1) after due warrant appears, of admitting a new candidate to the general fellowship; (2) of sisterly advice to a member of the fraternity asking it in the interest of light, or peace, or both; and (3) of the endeavor, where a sister church has been overtaken in a fault, to restore it in the spirit of meekness—in the sad case of persistence in disorderly walking, ending by formally withdrawing that fellowship which has been forfeited, as a testimony against them. Inasmuch as neighboring churches cannot wisely or conveniently assemble in a body for the discharge of these duties of extraordinary fellowship, they meet by delegation; such a meeting of the delegates of the churches being held to be the churches themselves present for consultation and action. These assemblies of the delegates of the churches for purposes of extraordinary fellowship, are called Ecclesiastical Councils. As modern Congregationalism was brought to its first full development in New England, such Councils have been more frequent here than elsewhere; and it is in the Ecclesiastical annals of New England especially that they are to be studied, their methods developed, their value estimated, and the relation which they may wisely hold to the Congregationalism of the future determined.

All Ecclesiastical Councils, as to their design, fall then naturally into these four classes; being convoked in the interest of fellowship, of light, of peace, or of purity— . . .

The whole wide record of Councils against Councils in all its variety of detail, and the philosophy alike of its causes and consequences, would repay investigation. . . .

Our fathers emphasized the *religious* side of Councils. Much prayer accompanied and interpenetrated them. Especially was this true of Councils for peace. The intent was to heighten the then practical present power of godliness in all hearts, until, under the quickening of the Holy Ghost, the glow and heat of consecration to the great Head of the Church and to His service, should lovingly conquer all discordant judgments, and, so to speak, fuse and weld together into one all divided hearts. Any falling out by the way between real Christians must be the consequence of some spiritual declension. What is needed for its satisfactory removal, is the cure of that declension. A genuine revival of religion would do the work. No hardness of feeling could stand before it. While, in the quickening of the spiritual intellection, it would carry the soul up to hights of reason and candor, to whose new fields of vision adjustments before impossible become so easy as to be inevitable. The first endeavor then of a Council for peace, should be to broaden and deepen the practical effect of the gospel in the souls of those who are parties to the quarrel. Much prayer, and a distinct aim to illuminate and invigorate the conscience, and subdue and humble the spirit, are vital to success; while such endeavor may reasonably assure itself of the loving aid of that Gracious Being who "doeth appoint meanes, not to cast out from Him, him that is expelled." Such a Council is not a "court of Jesus Christ," which, on sworn testimony and after special pleading, is to declare a judgment to which all must conform, and under which one party at the least must smart with disappoint-

ment, if not with some sense of wrong; it is the affectionate, persuasive presence of near friends, tenderly concerned to have all that is unclear clarified, and all that is selfish or exorbitant, or only mistaken and mis-done, readjusted into the harmony of absolute right. . . .

THINGS MORE CLEARLY SEEN—THE SURVEY WE HAVE TAKEN HELPS US TO DO JUSTICE TO OUR FATHERS

It has been common among us to talk penitentially of the sternness—even sourness—of the Puritans and the Pilgrims, as if it were an outgrowth of their peculiar tenets, which Congregationalism is somehow bound to explain away, to apologize for, or submit to bear the odium of. It has been alleged that they painfully kept the Mosaic rather than the Christian Sabbath; insisted that God is better pleased with a conventicle in a barn than with the most well-ordered cathedral service; prided themselves on a shabby dress; snuffled when they spake and whined when they sang; gave their children outlandish canting names, like Assurance, Tribulation and Maher-shalal-hash-baz; tricked out their commonest every-day talk with sounding phrases from the Old Testament; denounced theaters as the gates of hell; detested all amusements which generations of Englishmen had loved; and fairly kindled toward frenzy of speech when called to say anything in regard to the Church of Rome; until we have been almost driven to feel that they can hardly be seriously defended, or we avoid blushing for their narrowness while we ingenuously concede that with all their goodness of intent they probably were in reality nearly the most illiberal bigots upon whose austere lineaments the sweet sunshine ever fell.

The trouble is that we have too much judged them, and too much allowed the world to judge them, in the light of our generation instead of the light of their own; forgetting, and helping others to forget, out of what a horror of thick darkness they were scarcely more than commencing to emerge. . . .

Further, we cannot rightly estimate the subject, nor the men, without considering not only what stamp their own religious past must have impressed upon them, but also what the general social and intellectual condition of their own age must have constrained them, in common with their fellows, to be. Ordinary average life three centuries ago was so different from life now—with dissimilitudes so diverging through every department of labor and domesticity—as to make it well-nigh impossible even for the most diligent antiquary adequately to comprehend and describe that difference. . . .

While, so sluggish is the movement of men's minds in the direction of the finer elements of public justice, and so little does any faithful study of the past color the common judgments of the present; that unless we take the greatest pains to force our own imaginations back into the narrow molds of their life, and compel ourselves to realize their circumstances, we shall not thoroughly possess ourselves of their real character, nor do anything to compel a fairer estimate of them from a reluctant world. . . .

We have seen that no fewer than five underlying philosophies, so to speak, have energized and shaped the inward processes of Churches called Congregational. These were: (1) Brownism, which made Christ absolute monarch over his church, yet reigning by so imparting Himself in His wisdom and grace, and by His spirit, to its individual members,—as to leave all church power in the hands of those members—by no right inherent in them, but as His vice-gerents—making an absolute monarchy indistinguishable in its results from a pure democracy; (2) Johnsonism, or High-Church Barrowism, which lodged all church power in the hands of the presbytery of elders, leaving to the members, after they had elected those elders, the single right of implicit submission to them in the Lord; (3) Ainsworthism, or Low-Church Barrowism, which required that the elders act with the church and not in seclusion from it, and which only made the decision of the presbytery effectual after it had received the endorsement of the brethren; (4) Robinsonism, or Broad-Church Barrowism, which added to Ainsworthism the catholicizing element of the recognition of the reality—though not the regularity—of churches otherwise organized, and of guarded communion with them; and (5) the Congregationalism of today, championed by John Wise, whose fundamental principle derives all church power (as Brownism did) under God from the free consenting action of the entire covenanted body; but which justifies this right of action not so much by conceiving them to be commissioned of Christ to rule in His stead, as from the underlying endowment of God in the very constitution of nature and society, and because democracy is the fittest and best government for both Church and State. Some one of these philosophies may better meet the needs of the case than the others can. Probably *we* may all agree in preferring the latter. And yet there had been Congregational churches on both sides of the Atlantic for well nigh a hundred years, before the subtle and conclusive pleas of the Ipswich pastor for a government of the people, from the people, and for the people by natural right, began to rescue the notion of democracy from the obloquy of ages. . . .

But to be Congregational, a church *must* believe and practice these two fundamental principles:

It must be a body segregated by mutual covenant from all vital relations with other church entities; and so, under Christ, acquiring separate and complete existence, it must hold itself not merely in amicable—that it must live in toward *all* the good—but in fraternal relations with kindred organisms. When the former only is true, it is an Independent; when the latter also is true, it is a Congregational Church. It may manage its voting and its general internal affairs as it please; it is supreme over that—always provided there be no outcome thence of a nature to harm others, and impair fellowship. It may worship in a barn, a private house, a tent, or a cathedral. It may call its examining committee elders, if it like. It may elect and set apart its deacons for life, or change them with every communion season. It may order its service wholly by extempore utterance, as in the days of the ancient urgent reaction from that yoke of forms which our fathers were not able to bear; or it may use the liturgy of the Church of England, or of the Reformed Church of the United States, or that of John Calvin, or that of Richard Baxter, or that of the Rev. P. Periwinkle Piper—he happening to be its pastor with a leaning that way—as its taste and sense of need may dictate. It may devoutly praise God from whom all blessings flow by its own unanimous voice of sweet and loud acclaim; or it may be pitifully left to pay four persons to do its praising for it "as the Gentiles, and not like the Iewes," and still be a Congregational church.

Any church, holding their distinguishing principles, however its affairs be ordered in detail, so long as its neighbor Congregational churches remain willing to endorse it with their fellowship, is made, *ipso facto,* a Congregational church.

THE PRESBYTERIAN CHURCH IN AMERICA

The Constitutional History of the Presbyterian Church in the United States, by Charles Hodge, Part I, Philadelphia, 1839

It is admitted, that the early history of the Presbyterian church in the United States, is involved in great obscurity. The reason of this fact is obvious. Presbyterians did not at first emigrate in large bodies, or occupy by themselves extensive districts of country. In New England the early settlers were Congregationalists. The history of that portion of our country is, therefore, in a great measure, the history of that denomination. The same remark, to a certain extent, is applicable to the Dutch in New York, the Quakers in Pennsylvania, the Catholics in Maryland. The case was very different with regard to the presbyterians. They came, as a general rule, as individuals, or in small companies, and settled in the midst of people of other denominations. It was, therefore, in most instances, only gradually that they became sufficiently numerous in any one place to form congregations, or to associate in a presbyterial capacity. It is true their increase was very rapid; partly by the aggregation of persons of similar principles, though of different origin, and partly by constant immigration. This peculiarity in the history of American Presbyterians arose, in a great measure, from the fact, that the persecution which drove so many of the early settlers to this country, fell, in the first instance, heaviest on the Independents and Quakers; and when it came upon the Presbyterians, (at least those of Scotland,) it did not

drive them so generally from their own country, but led to a protracted struggle for liberty at home; a struggle which was eventually crowned with success.

Owing to the circumstances just referred to, we are obliged, in tracing the early history of the Presbyterian Church in this country, to review the colonial history of the several states, and gather from their records the scattered and imperfect intimations they afford of the origin of our own denomination. There is one preliminary remark, which must be constantly borne in mind. The Puritans were not all Congregationalists. The contrary impression has indeed become very general, from the fact that the Puritans settled New England, and that Congregationalism became there the prevalent form of church discipline. Hence it seems to be confidently inferred, that all emigrants from Old, or New England, bearing that designation, must have carried Congregationalism with them wherever they went. Hence too it is taken for granted, that if a minister came into our church from New England, he could not be a presbyterian. This is a great mistake. The Congregationalists or Independents were a mere handful, compared with the whole number of the Puritans. This term was applied to all who were desirous of a greater degree of purity, in ceremonies, discipline, or doctrine, than they found in the established church of England. . . .

When the arbitrary measures of Charles I. drove the nation into rebellion, the partisans of the court were of course episcopalian; the opposite party was, or became, in the main, presbyterian. It is not easy indeed to ascertain the proportion which the parties in the long parliament, opposed to the government when it first assembled, bore to each other. Of the presbyterians, there appear to have been two divisions; the one strenuous for their whole system, the other willing to admit Archbishop Usher's plan, (This plan provided for the government of the church by presbyteries and synods, under the presidency of a suffragan or bishop. A vote in favour of this plan passed the house in the summer of 1641.) either from preference, or as a compromise. A bill was brought forward by Sir Edward Dering for the utter extirpation of episcopacy, which passed its second reading by a vote of 139 to 108. Yet this gentleman afterwards advocated the plan of Usher. There is no doubt that many presbyterians would have acquiesced in this scheme which was essentially presbyterian, could it have harmonized the conflicting parties in the kingdom. When all hope, however, of a compromise was at an end, they became more strenuous in advocating their own system. When the compact came to be formed with Scotland, all the members of the commons who remained at Westminster, to the number of two hundred and twenty-eight, and between twenty and thirty peers, subscribed the solemn league and covenant. This no doubt, was done by many from motives of policy; but it is to be hoped that the strong declarations in favour of presbyterianism which that covenant contains, were not insincere on the part of the great majority. When the parliament called together the Westminster Assembly of Divines, in 1643, of the one hundred and twenty clerical and thirty lay members, of which it consisted, not more than six or seven were Independents, a few were Erastians, and the remainder, with the exception of some episcopalians, who soon retired, were presbyterians. Of these presbyterians there were the same two divisions, which were just mentioned as existing in parliament. That this Assembly was a fair representation of the state of parties among the opposers of the government, subsequent events sufficiently proved. The presbyterians became completely predominant, and their form of government was established by law, a measure to which the Independents did not object, though they insisted on freedom for themselves. That the Eng-

lish presbyterians were sufficiently decided, is evident from the fact that the Assembly asserted the *jus divinum* of presbyterianism. To this the parliament very properly demurred, and required the declaration to be put in the form in which it now stands in the Directory, viz. "that it is lawful and agreeable to the word of God, that the church be governed by congregational, classical, and synodical Assemblies." With this the English presbyterians were as little satisfied as the Scotch. Against this declaration the London ministers, as well as the mayor and common council, earnestly remonstrated.* The Independents were a small minority in parliament, among the clergy, and in the nation. Their strength was in the army. They no doubt increased greatly under Cromwell; but at his death, when the ejected members resumed their seats in parliament, the whole kingdom was in the hands of the Presbyterians. . . .

Another proof how numerous and important the presbyterians were considered, is, that it was deemed advisable in order to conciliate them, to allow Charles II. five months after his return, to issue a declaration in which so many reductions of

---

* Neal vol. iii. pp. 290, 291. One great point of difference between the Assembly and the parliament related to the power of the civil magistrates in relation to the church. The presbyterians had passed a resolution declaring that Jesus Christ had established a form of government for the church "distinct from the civil magistrate." With this the parliament were by no means satisfied. They claimed an authority in the church as extensive as that which had been exercised formerly by the king and parliament combined. The Assembly was called merely to give advice, they were expressly denied any jurisdiction, power, or authority ecclesiastical, whatsoever. Accordingly, episcopacy was abolished, the directory for worship enjoined, presbyterianism established, all by act of parliament. The church had nothing to do with it. This was in strict accordance with the English method, which has been almost completely Erastian since the time of Henry VIII. The church cannot act with authority; the form of government, the articles, the liturgy, all derive their binding force from the civil rulers. The church is the creature of the state. To assert the independence of the church has always been regarded as the height of clerical arrogance. See Hallam's remarks on Cartwright's opinions, vol. i. p. 252. The power of self-government the Church of England has never enjoyed. Every sentence of a spiritual judge is liable to be reversed by a civil tribunal. Its bishops are appointed, and their number increased or diminished at pleasure, by the government. Since the power has passed out of their own hands the high-church party begin to complain bitterly of this thraldom. See British Critic, No. 43, and various numbers of the Oxford Tracts. It was on this principle of subordination to the civil authority that presbyterianism was established by the long parliament; as provision was made for an appeal from the censures of the church to a civil tribunal. Neal vol. iii. pp. 297, 303. It is hard to see how this can be avoided in any country where ecclesiastical censures are followed by the forfeiture of civil rights.

episcopal power, and so many reforms were promised, as to make the hierarchy very little more than it would have been, had Archbishop Usher's plan been adopted. This declaration was designed, says Hallam, merely "to scatter dust in men's eyes." The motion in parliament to give it the force of law was lost by a vote of 183 to 157. Instead of compromise, the harshest measures were soon adopted. The act of uniformity was passed, which required re-ordination of those who had been presbyterially ordained; "assent and consent to all and every thing contained, and prescribed, in and by the book of common prayer," and the profession of the doctrine of passive obedience. This the presbyterians could not submit to, and were consequently ejected from the ministry of the church, to the number of about two thousand. These, of course, were only the most conscientious, or the most decided. Multitudes who had taken the covenant, comformed, and retained their stations. . . .

CONGREGATIONALISM AND PRESBYTERIANISM COMPARED

Reference is made to these familiar historical events to correct the impression that the Puritans were generally congregationalists. Every body knows, indeed, that such was not the fact, yet from our peculiar associations with the term, it is commonly taken for granted, that all who, as Puritans, emigrated to this country to avoid the persecutions which they suffered at home, were congregationalists. The truth, however, is, that as the great majority of Puritans in England were presbyterian, so no inconsiderable proportion of those who came to America, preferred the presbyterian form of church government. The question will naturally be asked, If this be so, how came congregationalism to be generally established in New England? The answer is, that the first settlers were congregationalists. They belonged to that division of the Puritans, which, departing farthest from the established church, first felt the necessity of setting up for themselves. In coming to this country, they came with the determination to carry out their principles, and thus the mould into which the additional settlers were cast, as they successively arrived, was fixed at the beginning. Again, the master-minds among the early Puritans in this country, by whom their civil and ecclesiastical polity was determined, were principally congregationalists. And, thirdly, as the Puritan presbyterians were willing, for the sake of the great ends of peace and union, to unite with the episcopalians in a modified form of epis-

copacy; so for the same important objects, they were willing to unite with the Independents in New England, in a modified form of congregationalism. Such was the intimate union between church and state, established in the New England provinces, that it was hardly possible, that different ecclesiastical organizations could exist without producing confusion and difficulty. This union between presbyterians and congregationalists was, doubtless, the more readily effected, inasmuch as with the exception of the first colony from Holland, the emigrants had not enjoyed any separate ecclesiastical organization at home. They were almost all members of the established church. The ministers were with rare exceptions, beneficed clergymen of the Church of England, who had been suspended for want of conformity, generally, in relation to matters of ceremony. Whatever, therefore, might have been their individual preferences, they had not become wedded by habit to any particular system.

It might be confidently inferred from the opinions of the English puritans, as stated above, and from the circumstances which led to their emigration, during the reigns of James I. and Charles I., that many of them would bring with them a preference for presbyterianism. It is estimated that about twenty-one thousand two hundred emigrants arrived in New England before 1640. Cotton Mather tells us that previous to that same year four thousand presbyterians had arrived. . . .

Of the two thousand presbyterian ministers cast out of the Church of England, by the act of uniformity in 1662, a considerable number, it is said, found a refuge in New England. The colony of Connecticut, in writing at an early period to the lords of trade and plantations, tell them "the people here are congregationalists, large congregationalists and moderate presbyterians, the two former being the most numerous." This form of expression evidently implies, that the latter class bore a large proportion to the former. The principal friends and patrons of this colony in England were presbyterians; particularly lord Say, an original patentee of the colony, to whom they often express their obligations, and to whose influence, and to that of the earl of Manchester, another leader of the presbyterian party, they were in a great measure indebted for the restoration of their charter. Trumbull, speaking of the Assembly which drew up the Saybrook platform, says, "Though the council were unanimous in passing the platform of discipline, yet they were not all of one opinion.

Some were for high consociational government and in their sentiments nearly presbyterians; others were much more moderate and rather verging on independency." The result of their labours proves that the former class had greatly the ascendency.

The influence of presbyterian principles in New England is, however, much more satisfactorily proved by the nature of the ecclesiastical systems which were there adopted, than by any statements of isolated facts. These systems were evidently the result of compromise between two parties, and they show that the presbyterian was much stronger than the independent element. The two leading points of difference between presbyterianism and congregationalism, particularly as the latter exists at present, relate to the mode of government within the congregation, whether it should be by elders or the brotherhood, and to the authority of synods. As to both these points the early discipline of the New England churches approached much nearer to presbyterianism than it does at present. Elders, indeed, were a regular part of the organization of the churches of the independents, even when totally disconnected with presbyterians. A tendency, however, soon manifested itself on the part of the brethren to dispense with their services, and take the keys into their own hands. ("I came from England," said one of the early inhabitants of Boston, "because I did not like the lord-bishops; but I cannot join you because I would not be under the lord brethren." -*Magnalia, vol i. p. 221.*) . . . In the Cambridge platform, which was drawn up in 1648, it is said, "The ruling elder's office is distinct from the office of pastor and teacher." He is "to join with the pastor and teacher in those acts of spiritual rule, which are distinct from the ministry of the word and sacraments committed to them," &c. In a subsequent synod, it was agreed, 1. "The power of church government belongs only to the elders of the Church." 2. "There are certain cases, wherein the elders in their management of their church government, are to take the concurrence of the fraternity;" namely, in elections, and admissions, and censures. 3. "The elders of the church are to have a negative on the votes of the brethren," &c.

As to synods, the Cambridge platform denies to them in sec. iv. ch. 16., the right to perform any act of "church authority or jurisdiction;" but adds in sec. v., "The synod's directions and determinations, so far as consonant to the word of God, are to be received with reverence and submission, not only for their agreement therewith, (which is the principal ground thereof, and without which

they bind not at all,) but also secondarily, for the power whereby they are made, as being an ordinance of God appointed thereunto in his word." This is very near the presbyterian doctrine, which teaches that the decisions of synods are binding on those voluntarily connected with them, when made in reference to things within their jurisdiction, and not contrary to the word of God, or any constitutional stipulations. The subsequent Assembly which met at Cambridge, carried the power of synods fully up to the presbyterian doctrine, if not beyond it. The second proposition on this subject, determined in that body, is in these words: "Synods duly composed of messengers chosen by them, whom they are to represent, and proceeding with a due regard to the will of God in his word, are to be reverenced as *determining* the mind of the Spirit concerning things necessary to be received and practised, in order to the edification of the churches therein represented." The third proposition is, "Synods being of apostolic example, recommended as necessary ordinance, it is but reasonable that their judgment be acknowledged as *decisive,* (in or of) the affairs for which they are ordained; and to deny them the power of such judgment is to render a necessary ordinance of none effect." Here it is evident that the presbyterial element in those churches predominated. May it not without offence be asked, whether it would not have been better, in conformity with this doctrine, to allow the church to govern itself, instead of referring so much power to the civil magistrate, as was done by the great and pious men who founded Massachusetts? Their memory deserves to be held in perpetual veneration, and their errors should be treated as the errors of a parent. Filial piety, however, permits us to learn wisdom from the mistakes of our fathers. Those excellent men ought not to be quoted, as is so often done in our days, as the advocates of the independence of each separate congregation. They had suffered so much from the tyranny of ecclesiastical rulers at home, that they went to the extreme of denying to church courts, armed with nothing but moral and spiritual censures, their legitimate authority. But feeling the necessity for some authority superior to that of a single congregation over itself, they devolved it upon the magistrate. The Cambridge platform, which denies the binding force of the decisions of a synod, declares that not only idolatry and blasphemy, but heresy and open contempt of the word preached, "are to be restrained and punished by the civil authority." And farther, "If any church, one or more, shall grow schismatical, rending itself from the communion of other churches, or shall walk incorrigibly and obstinately in any corrupt way of their own, contrary to the rule of the word; in such case the magistrate is to put forth his coercive power, as the matter shall require." The very same rules, enforced by mere ecclesiastical censures, which the presbyterian synod were so much reproached for making, and which led to the schism of 1741, were made in Connecticut by the legislature and enforced by civil penalties. The controversy, therefore, between the fathers of the New England churches and those of the American Presbyterians, would be not as to the necessity of a general authority in the Church, but as to where it should be lodged.

The churches of Connecticut appear to have had, from the beginning, more of a presbyterian influence among them than those of Massachusetts. Hooker, the patriarch of Connecticut, said with great earnestness shortly before his death, "we must settle the consociation of churches, or else we are undone." He also, it appears, laid peculiar stress on the importance of ruling elders. The Saybrook platform, accordingly, comes much nearer to the presbyterian model than that of Cambridge. . . .

In giving, therefore, the exercise of discipline to the pastor and elders, and in making the determinations of councils definitive and binding, on pain of non-communion, the Saybrook platform, unanimously approved by the Assembly which prepared it in 1708, and adopted by the legislature as the discipline of the churches established by law, comes very little short of presbyterianism. It is very evident, as this platform was a compromise between two parties, being less than the one, and more than the other wished to see adopted, that one party must have been thorough presbyterians. That they were, moreover, the stronger of the two, is evident from the platform approaching so much nearer to their system, than to that of the independents.

It is, therefore, a most unfounded assumption that the Puritans were all congregationalists, or that the emigrants from England or the New England colonies, who joined our church, as a matter of course, were disaffected to our form of government.

SPREAD OF PURITANISM

Though New England was the home of the Puritans, they did not confine themselves to that region of country. With the adventurous spirit which has always been one of their leading char-

acteristics, they extended at an early period, their settlements in various directions. Long Island, from its proximity to Connecticut, was soon occupied by emigrants from the older colonies, and by settlers direct from England. The Dutch having occupied the western end of the island, these English settlements were principally towards the central and eastern portions. Before the commencement of the last century several churches had been organized, whose ministers, in many instances, were from England. . . .

The Puritans do not appear to have made much impression upon New York before the early part of the last century, but in East Jersey their settlements were numerous and important. In 1664, a company from the western part of Long Island purchased a tract of land and laid out the town of Elizabethtown. There were, however, but four houses in the place, when Philip Carteret, in 1665, arrived as governor of the province, from England, bringing with him about thirty settlers. The first colony, therefore, must have been small. Much about the same time, Woodbridge, Middletown, and Shrewsbury were settled, in a good degree by emigrants from Long Island, and Connecticut. Newark was settled in 1667 or 1668, by about thirty families principally from Brandford in Connecticut. As the New England Puritans were some of them congregationalists and some presbyterians, it is not easy to ascertain to which class the emigrants to East Jersey belonged. It is probable that some preferred the one form of church discipline, and some the other. Those who settled at Newark were presbyterians . . .

The Puritans were not very successful in their attempts to form settlements upon the Delaware. . . .

In the southern colonies, there are here and there traces of puritan settlements, but not sufficient either in number or extent, to exert much influence on the character of the rising population. Maryland was at first a Catholic colony, but being settled upon the principles of general toleration, the number of Protestants soon greatly exceeded that of the Romanists. . . .

Virginia was so completely an episcopal province, and the laws against all non-conformists were so severe, that we can expect but few traces of the Puritans in her early history. Unity of worship was there preserved, with few exceptions, for a century after the settlement of Jamestown. There were, however, some puritan families in the colony from the beginning, and others arrived at a later period, and there were also a few settlers from Massachusetts. . . .

It was not until after the commencement of the eighteenth century, that other denominations than the episcopal, obtained permanent footing in Virginia, protected by the English toleration act. The presbyterian church in the Atlantic portion of the state was, in great measure, built up by those who had been previously episcopalians; and in the portion beyond the mountains, by the Scotch-Irish emigrants from Pennsylvania. . . .

South Carolina was settled about 1670, under the direction of the proprietors. The first colony came from England with the governor "William Sayle, who was probably a presbyterian;" the people, however, it is presumed were principally episcopalians. The country was rapidly filled up with settlers from various quarters, but no mention is made of the puritans as among the early colonists, except that a church organized in Dorchester, Massachusetts, removed in 1696 and settled on the Ashley river. . . .

I have thus endeavoured to trace the influence of the Puritans, beyond the limits of New England, in the early settlement of our country. It appears they were predominant on Long Island, numerous in East Jersey, few and scattered on the Delaware, and dotted at certain distant intervals along the southern coast.

DUTCH, GERMAN, WELSH AND FRENCH PRESBYTERIANS

The Dutch come next under consideration, for although they have been so numerous as to form by themselves, a distinct ecclesiastical organization, yet being Calvinists and Presbyterians, they have in many parts of the country entered largely into the materials of which our church is composed. . . .

The German emigrants, though never forming a distinct government, as was the case, not only with the Dutch, but even with the Swedes, were far more numerous than either, and have exerted a powerful influence on the character of our country. Gov. Hunter of New York, brought over with him in 1730, three thousand German emigrants, who had fled to England to escape the persecution which they suffered in their own country. They also formed a settlement to the west of Albany, on the German Flats. Their emigration to Pennsylvania commenced as early as 1682 or 1683, when Germantown was settled by them. In subsequent years they came in such numbers, that it was estimated in 1772, that one third of the population of the province, which was then between 200,000 and 300,000, consisted of

them and their descendents. In the year 1749, twelve thousand German emigrants arrived, and for several years nearly the same number arrived annually. From Pennsylvania they extended themselves into Virginia and Maryland. Their settlements in Carolina were also extensive. . . .

The Welsh, from their numbers, deserve particular notice. The principal settlement of them at an early period, was upon the left bank of the Schuylkill, in Pennsylvania. They there occupied three townships, and in a few years their numbers so increased that they obtained three additional townships.

The persecutions to which the French protestants were exposed during the reign of Louis XIV., consummated by the revocation of the edict of Nantes in 1685, drove hundreds of thousands of those unhappy people from their native country. They found a home in the various cities of Holland, Germany, and England, and large numbers of them came to this country. They were so numerous in Boston as to have a church by themselves in 1686. In New York, when yet under the dominion of the Dutch, they formed so large a portion of the population, that the laws were sometimes promulgated in their language as well as in that of the Hollanders. In Richmond county, they and the Dutch made up almost the entire population; and they were settled also in considerable numbers in the counties of Westchester and Ulster. Scattered emigrants fixed themselves, in greater or less numbers, in the provinces of Pennsylvania and Maryland, but their principal location was in the southern states. In 1690, king William sent "a large body" of them to Virginia, where lands were assigned them on the James river; others removed to Carolina and settled on the Santee. In 1699, and the following years, six hundred more are mentioned as settling in Virginia. Soon after the settlement of Carolina, Charles II. sent two ships with about two hundred French protestants, to introduce the culture of the productions of the south of Europe. From 1685 onward, the number of French emigrants to Carolina was very considerable; "fugitives from Languedoc on the Mediterranean, from Rochelle, and Saintange, and Bordeaux, the provinces on the bay of Biscay, from St. Quentin, Poictiers, and the beautiful valley of Tour, from St. Lo and Dieppe, men who had the virtues of the English puritans without their bigotry, came to the country to which the tolerant benevolence (?) of Shaftesbury had invited the believers of every creed." This emigration continued far into the succeeding century. In 1752, it is stated upwards

PRESBYTERIAN
CHURCH

————

DUTCH, GERMAN,
WELSH AND
FRENCH
PRESBYTERIANS

of sixteen hundred foreign protestants arrived in South Carolina. In 1764 two hundred and twelve arrived from France. The descendants of these numerous French protestants have become merged almost entirely, in the episcopal and presbyterian churches.

SCOTCH PRESBYTERIANS

"The history of American colonization is the history of the crimes of Europe." The Scotch presbyterians had not escaped their portion of the persecutions, which all opposers of prelacy, in Great Britain, experienced during the reigns of James II, and Charles I. It was not, however, until the restoration of Charles II. that the measure of their wrongs and sorrows was rendered full. . . .

Modern history hardly affords a parallel to the cruelty and oppression under which Scotland groaned for nearly thirty years. And what was all this for? It was to support episcopacy. It was done for the bishops, and, in a great measure, by them. They were the instigators and supporters of these cruel laws, and of the still more cruel execution of them. Is it any wonder, then, that the Scotch abhorred episcopacy? It was in their experience identified with despotism, superstition, and irreligion. Their love of presbyterianism was one with their love of liberty and religion. As the parliament of Scotland was never a fair representation of the people, the general assembly of their church became their great organ for resisting oppression and withstanding the encroachments of their sovereigns. The conflict therefore which in England was so long kept up between the crown and the house of commons, was in Scotland sustained between the crown and the church. This was one reason why the Scotch became so attached to presbyterianism; this too was the reason why the Stuarts hated it, and determined at all hazards to introduce prelacy as an ally to despotism.*

Considering the long-continued persecution of the Scotch presbyterians, just referred to, the wonder is that they did not universally forsake their country. The hope of regaining liberty at home, however, never entirely deserted them; and in their darkest hours there were occasional glimpses of better things to come, which led them to abandon the designs of emigration which they had formed. A company of thirty noblemen and gentlemen had contracted for a large tract of land in Carolina, as an asylum for their persecuted countrymen, when the hope of the success of the English patriots, engaged in the plot for which Russel and Sydney suffered, led them to relinquish their purpose. Still, though the emigration was not so great as might, under such sufferings, have been expected, it was very considerable. . . .

It is evident . . . that the emigrants from Scotland to East Jersey, were numerous and influential. In some places they united with the Dutch and puritan settlers in the formation of churches, in others they were sufficiently numerous

---

* (The first Confession of Faith prepared by Knox and his associates, asserted explicitly the right and duty of the people to resist the tyranny of their rulers. This was the result of the reformation being carried on by the people. In England it was carried on by the government. Hence the marked difference between the principles of the two churches as to the liberty of the subject and the power of kings. The general assembly of 1649, declared, 1st. That as magistrates and their power are ordained of God, so are they in the exercise thereof, not to walk after their own will, but according to the law of equity and righteousness. . . . A boundless and unlimited power is to be acknowledged in no king or magistrate. 2d. That there is a mutual obligation betwixt the king and his people. As both are tied to God, so each of them is tied the one to the other, for the performance of mutual and reciprocal duties. 3d. That arbitrary government and unlimited power are the fountains of all the corruptions in the church and state. Compare these sentiments with the declarations and oaths issued and enforced by the Scottish bishops. They were the principal authors of the arbitrary laws above referred to. They all voted for the famous assertory act of 1669, which declared the king's supremacy in all ecclesiastical matters, in virtue of which the ordering and disposal of the external government and polity of the church belonged to him as an inherent right of the crown; and that his orders respecting all ecclesiastical persons and matters are to be obeyed, any law, act, or custom to the contrary notwithstanding. They eagerly supported an act imposing an oath, (at first designed only for office-bearers in the church and state, but which came to be almost universally enforced,) "which no man who had not made up his mind for slavery, could swear." It declared the king to be supreme governor over all persons and in all causes, civil and ecclesiastical; that it was unlawful to consult or determine upon any subject relating to church or state without his express permission, or to form associations for redressing grievances, or to take up arms against the king, or to attempt any alteration in the political or ecclesiastical constitution of the kingdom, &c. This reference to the arbitrary principles and atrocious cruelties of the Scottish bishops, is not made with the ungenerous design of casting odium on episcopacy. The odium belongs to the men and to their principles, and not to episcopacy. Those prelates were introduced by the king, in opposition to the wishes of the people. They owed every thing to the prerogative. They could stand only so long as the power of the king should prevail over the will of the nation.

It is no wonder, therefore, that they magnified that power. Had the case been reversed, had episcopacy been abolished and presbyterianism introduced by despotic authority, we might have seen presbyterians the advocates of prerogative, and bishops the asserters of liberty.

As it was, however, prelacy and despotism in Scotland were inseparable; neither could live without the other: so they died a common death.)

to organize congregations by themselves. The church in Freehold, one of the largest in the state, was formed chiefly by them. . . .

It was, however, to Pennsylvania, that the largest emigrations of the Scotch and Irish, particularly of the latter, though at a somewhat later period, took place. Early in the last century they began to arrive in large numbers. Near six thousand Irish are reported as having come in 1729; and before the middle of the century near twelve thousand arrived annually for several years. Speaking of a later period, Proud says, "they have flowed in of late years from the north of Ireland in very large numbers." Cumberland county, he says, is settled by them, and they abound through the whole province. From Pennsylvania they spread themselves into Virginia, and thence into North Carolina. A thousand families arrived in that state from the northern colonies in the single year 1764. Their descendants occupy the western portion of the state, with a dense and homogeneous population, distinguished by the strict morals and rigid principles of their ancestors. In 1749, five or six hundred Scotch settled near Fayetteville; there was a second importation in 1754; and "there was an annual importation, from that time, of those hardy and industrious people."

A considerable number of Scotch also settled in Maryland. . . .

The Scotch and Irish were also among the early settlers of Georgia.

From this slight and imperfect view of the several classes of people by whom our country was settled, it is evident that a broad foundation for the Presbyterian Church was laid from the beginning. The English puritans were all Calvinists and many of them presbyterians. The Dutch were Calvinists and presbyterians; a moiety, at least of the Germans were of the same class. All the French protestants were Calvinists and presbyterians, and so, of course, were the Scotch and Irish. Of the several classes, the Dutch and Germans formed distinct ecclesiastical organizations, and subsist as such to the present time. In a multitude of cases, however, their descendants mingled with the descendants of other presbyterians, and have entered largely into the materials of which our church is composed. The same remark applies to the descendants of the French protestants, who have generally joined either the episcopal or presbyterian church. The early influence of the New England puritans was, as has been seen, nearly confined to Long Island and East Jersey. Of those who settled in Jersey, a portion

were, no doubt, inclined to congregationalism, others of them were presbyterians. . . .

This review accounts for the rapid increase of the presbyterian church in this country. In about a century and a quarter, it has risen from two or three ministers to between two and three thousand. This is no matter of surprise, when it is seen that so large a portion of the emigrants were presbyterians. As they merged their diversities of national character into that of American citizens, so the Scotch, Irish, French, English, Dutch, and German presbyterians became united in thousands of instances in the American Presbyterian Church. Having the same views of civil government, our population, so diversified as to its origin, forms a harmonious civil society, and agreeing in opinion on the government of the church, the various classes above specified, formed a religious society, in which the difference of their origin was as little regarded as it was in the state.

The review given above of the settlement of the country shows also, that nothing but a sectional vanity little less than insane, could lead to the assertion that congregationalism was the basis of presbyterianism in this country, and that the presbyterian church never would have had an existence, except in name, had not the congregationalists come among us from New England. The number of puritans who settled in New England, was about twenty-one thousand. If it be admitted, that three-fourths of these were congregationalists, (which is a large admission,) it gives between fifteen and sixteen thousand. The presbyterian emigrants who came to this country by the middle of the last century, were between one and two hundred thousand. Those from Ireland alone, imperfect as are the records of emigration, could not have been less than fifty thousand, and probably were far more numerous. Yet the whole Presbyterian Church owes its existence to the mere overflowings of New England! It would be much nearer the truth to say, that presbyterians have been the basis of several other denominations. Half the population of the country would now be presbyterian, had the descendants of presbyterians, in all cases, adhered to the faith of their fathers. . . .

As far then as the character of the original congregations is concerned, it would be difficult to find any church more homogeneous in its materials than our own; certainly not the church of Scotland; and certainly not the churches of New England.

The former contained, proportionably, more members inclined to episcopacy, and the latter more inclined to presbyterianism, than were to be found in our church inclined to congregationalism.

CHARACTER OF MINISTERS
AND INCREASE OF CHURCH

The next subject of inquiry is the character of the ministers of which the presbytery was at first composed. The original members, as far as can be ascertained from the minutes, were Messrs. Francis Makemie, Jedediah Andrews, George McNish, John Hampton, John Wilson, Nathaniel Taylor, and Samuel Davis. To these may be added John Boyd, who became a member by ordination in 1706. Of the original members of the presbytery, Mr. Hazard says, "It is probable that all, except Mr. Andrews, were foreigners by birth, and that they were ordained to the gospel ministry in Scotland and Ireland. (*MS History. As this statement was written perhaps thirty years ago, it must be regarded as impartial.*) . . .

The increase of the church after the organization of the presbytery, was rapid, and arose principally from the constant immigration of presbyterians, ministers as well as people, from abroad, and from the organization of those already scattered through the country. In 1707, the number of ministers was eight, all but one from Scotland or Ireland.

In 1716 the whole number was twenty-five, of whom seventeen were still living and in connexion with the presbytery. In that year it was determined to form four presbyteries; the first to consist of the following members: viz. Messrs. Andrews, Jones, Powell, Orr, Bradner, and Morgan, and to meet at Philadelphia or elsewhere; the second of Messrs. Anderson, Magill, Gillespie, Wotherspoon, Evans, and Conn, to meet at New Castle; the third to consist of Messrs. Davis, Hampton, and Henry, to meet at Snowhill; and the fourth of Messrs. McNish and Pumry, on Long Island, who were directed to endeavour to induce some of the neighbouring ministers to associate with them in forming a presbytery. The presbytery of Snowhill does not appear ever to have met. Most of its members became attached to that of Newcastle. . . .

As far as the character of the body may be inferred from that of its founders, it was a purely presbyterian church from the beginning. It was not founded upon congregationalism, nor by congregationalists. It was founded by presbyterians, and upon presbyterian principles, and those who subsequently joined it, joined it as a presbyterian body. . . .

Having taken this view of the origin of the Presbyterian Church, during its forming period, in order to ascertain its character, as far as it may be inferred from the materials of which it was composed, it is time to inquire more particularly into its doctrines and discipline, during the same period. As it regards doctrines, the point to be ascertained is, whether the Presbyterian Church was a Calvinistic body, and required adherence to that system of doctrine as a condition of ministerial communion, or whether it demanded nothing more than assent to the essential doctrines of the gospel. . . . It is admitted that the presbytery required of its members, what it considered soundness in the faith, or orthodoxy. The only question then is, what was orthodoxy, in the estimation of the founders of our church? Was it faith in the essential doctrines of the gospel? or was it faith in that system of doctrines, which, for convenience sake, has obtained the name of Calvinism? This is the only important question. The method which they adopted to decide upon the orthodoxy of a member, is of very subordinate consequence. Whether it was by personal examination; by satisfactory testimonials; or by assent to a prescribed formula of doctrines, is comparatively of but little moment. The question is, what did they require? Not, how did they satisfy themselves? It seems a matter of supererogation to prove, that men educated, towards the close of the seventeenth, or the beginning of the eighteenth century, in Scotland, Ireland, or New England, regarded Calvinism as the true doctrine of the Scriptures, and considered any essential deviation from it, as a disqualification for the work of the ministry. Is the faith of the church of Scotland at that period a matter of doubt? Was she not still reeking with the blood of her children, martyrs for her faith and discipline? Were men who had suffered so much in their own persons, or in those of their friends, for presbyterianism, likely to cast it away, the moment they got to a place of perfect security? It has never yet been made a question, what was the faith of the Puritans, who first settled New England, or what was the standard of orthodoxy among her churches. No one has ventured to assert that Christianity in the general, adherence to doctrines absolutely fundamental, was all that was there required of ministers of the gospel. And why not? Not because there is documentary evidence that every candidate for ordination was required to sign a particular formula, but because the opinions of those puritans are a matter of notoriety. Their opinions, however, were neither more pronounced, nor more notorious than those of the churches of Scotland or Ireland. Why then should it be assumed that the ministers of the latter were so latitudinarian, as soon as they reached this country, when no such assumption is made with regard to the former?

It is to be remembered that the great majority of the early ministers of our church were either ordained or licensed before they became connected with it. The very testimonials which they brought with them, if they came from Scotland or Ireland, stated explicitly that they had adopted the Westminster Confession of Faith; if they came from New England they brought evidence of their Calvinism just as unequivocal. No doubt could be entertained what was meant by 'orthodoxy' in certificates given by men, who expressed so much alarm lest 'the churches of God, should suspect that New England allowed such exorbitant aberrations' as the denial that Christ bore the penalty of the law. It was just as natural, and as much a matter of course, for the presbytery of Philadelphia to receive with confidence men coming from the Scotch and Irish presbyteries, as it is for one of our presbyteries to receive the members of another. The moment, however, it was discovered that these certificates deceived them, they began to adopt other methods to ascertain the Calvinism of those whom they admitted.

The single consideration, then, that all the early ministers of our church came from places where Calvinism not only prevailed, but where it was strenuously insisted upon, is, in the absence of all evidence to the contrary, sufficient to prove that they were not so singular, or so much in advance of the spirit of their age, as to bring down their demands to the low standard of absolutely essential doctrines. It is not, however, merely the origin, but the known opinions of these ministers, which are relied upon to prove the Calvinistic character of our church. There is not a single minister, whose sentiments are known at all, who was admitted to the church, or allowed to remain in it during the period under review, who is not known to have been not only a Calvinist, but a rigid one. This was the case with the members of the strict presbytery of Newcastle, the men who are now reproached for sectarian bigotry for their zeal for this very subject. It was the case with Jonathan Dickinson, Gilbert Tennent, and every other minister, connected with the church, before 1729, who has left any memorials of his opinions. It is contrary to all experience, and to the principles of human nature, that men, who have been accustomed to one standard of doctrines, should suddenly lower their demands, unless they themselves were disaffected towards those doctrines.

Another evidence of the Calvinistic character of our church, may be found in the circumstances attending the reception of the Rev. William Tennent in 1718. That gentleman had been episcopally ordained in Ireland; but on coming to this country, applied to be received as a member of the synod of Philadelphia. That body required him to state in writing the reasons of his dissent from the episcopal church. One of the most prominent of those reasons was, that the church of Ireland connived "at Arminian doctrines." Are we then to believe that Mr. Tennent left one church because it connived at Arminianism, to join another which tolerated Pelagianism; nay, that required nothing more than assent to the absolutely essential doctrines of the gospel! Surely the synod would have had too much selfrespect to insert in their minutes, a document charging it as a crime upon a sister church, that she connived at Arminianism, if they themselves did the same, and more.

WESTMINSTER CONFESSION OF FAITH

The Calvinistic character of our church is further evident from the fact, that as soon as some other means than personal examination, or the testimonials of ecclesiastical bodies, became necessary to ascertain the orthodoxy of its members, subscription to the Westminster Confession of Faith, was demanded and universally submitted to. As long as the church was small, and all, or a large portion of its members could be present at the admission of every new applicant, the most natural and the most effectual method to obtain a knowledge of his opinions, was personal examination. And as long as the churches with which the synod corresponded, were faithful to their own standards, their testimony was received as sufficient evidence of the soundness of the men whom they recommended. But when from the multiplication of presbyteries, the first method became impossible, and when the second was found to be unworthy of confidence, another plan was adopted. On the supposition that the church was to remain one, and that it had any zeal for its own doctrines, it was necessary that the several presbyteries should understand each other, and unite in adopting a common standard of orthodoxy. Hence arose the call for a general agreement, to make the adoption of the Westminster Confession a condition of ministerial communion. There can be no stronger evidence of the Calvinistic character of the church, than that this new test of orthodoxy was universally admitted, and that there was not a single member of the synod who objected to any one article in the confession of faith, except that which related to the power of the civil magistrates in matters of religion. That article was, by common consent, discarded; all the others were cordially adopted.

It is inconceivable that a body of men should have unanimously adopted this measure, had it been the fixing a new and higher standard of orthodoxy, and not merely a new method for ascertaining the adherence of the ministry to what had always been demanded. . . .

PRESBYTERIAN CHURCH GOVERNMENT

Presbyterianism is a mode of church government as definite and as well understood as any other form of ecclesiastical polity. Its fundamental principle is, that the government of the church rests upon the presbyteries; that is, the clerical and lay elders. It demands, therefore, congregational, classical, and provincial assemblies of such elders, i.e. sessions, presbyteries, and synods. It establishes a regular subordination of the lower of these judicatories to the higher, giving to the latter the right of review and control over the

former. And, finally, it declares the determinations and decisions of these several judicatories, relating to matters of government and discipline, to be binding upon all under their authority, when not inconsistent with the word of God, or some previous constitutional stipulation. . . .

It has already been stated that in 1716, three presbyteries were constituted, who agreed to meet annually as a synod. It is therefore necessary, in order to understand the character of American presbyterianism, to ascertain the relation which this synod sustained to the presbyteries and to the churches under their care. In order to illustrate this subject it must be stated, that the first synod not only exercised all the powers which, at the present day, are claimed by such bodies, but several others which our present synods are not in the habit of assuming. To the former class belong, first, the general power of review and control of presbyteries. This, as far as the review of records is concerned, was provided for at the time the synod was constituted. . . .

To the class of ordinary powers belongs also, the right "to take effectual care that the presbyteries observe the constitution of the church." . . .

Finally, the synod exercised a general supervision over the churches, warning them of improper or irregular preachers, receiving and answering their petitions or complaints. . . .

★   ★   ★   ★   ★

THE GREAT REVIVAL, 1740–45

The Constitutional History of the Presbyterian Church in the United States, by Charles Hodge, Part II, Philadelphia, 1840

The great revival, which about a hundred years ago, visited so extensively the American Churches, is so much implicated with the ecclesiastical history of our own denomination, that the latter cannot be understood without some knowledge of the former. The controversies connected with the revival, are identical with the disputes which resulted in the schism, which divided the Presbyterian Church in 1741. Before entering, therefore, upon the history of that event, it will be necessary to present the reader with a general survey of that great religious excitement, which arrayed in conflicting parties the friends of religion in every part of the country. This division of sentiment could hardly have occurred, had the revival been one of unmingled purity. Such a revival, however, the church has never seen. Every luminous body is sure to cause shadows in every direction and of every form. Where the Son of man sows wheat, the evil one is sure to sow tares. It must be so. For it needs be that offences come, though wo to those by whom they come.

The men, who, either from their character or circumstances, are led to take the most prominent part, during such seasons of excitement, are themselves often carried to extremes, or are so connected with the extravagant, that they are sometimes the last to perceive and the slowest to oppose the evils which so frequently mar the work of God, and burn over the fields which he had just watered with his grace. Opposition to these evils commonly comes from a different quarter; from wise and good men who have been kept out of the focus of the excitement. And it is well that there are such opposers, else the church would soon be over-run with fanaticism.

The term revival is commonly used in a very comprehensive sense. It includes all the phenomena attending a general religious excitement; as well those which spring from God, as those which owe their origin to the infirmities of men. Hence those who favour the work, for what there is divine in it, are often injuriously regarded as the patrons of its concomitant irregularities; and those who oppose what is unreasonable about it, are as improperly denounced as the enemies of religion. It

ISAIAH'S LIPS ANOINTED WITH FIRE
BY BENJAMIN WEST (AMERICAN, 1738-1820)
OIL ON CANVAS, 150 X 61 IN. 1784.
COURTESY OF BOB JONES UNIVERSITY COLLECTION,
GREENVILLE, SOUTH CAROLINA

"In the year that King Uzziah died I saw also the Lord sitting upon a throne, high and lifted up, and his train filled the temple . . . Then said I, Woe is me! for I am undone; because I am a man of unclean lips, and I dwell in the midst of a people of unclean lips: for mine eyes have seen the King, the Lord of hosts. Then flew one of the seraphims unto me, having a live coal in his hand, which he had taken with the tongs from off the altar: And he laid it upon my mouth, and said, Lo, this hath touched thy lips; and thine iniquity is taken away, and thy sin purged." (Isaiah 6:1, 5-7)

We all have reason to bewail it before the Lord; That we are of unclean lips ourselves; our lips are not consecrated to God; he has not had the *first-fruits of lips*, and therefore they are counted common and unclean, uncircumcised lips. Nay, they have been polluted with sin; we have spoken the language of an unclean heart; that evil communication corrupts good manners, and thereby many have been defiled. We are unworthy and unmeet to take God's name into our lips. The impurity of our lips ought to be the grief of our souls, for by our words we shall be condemned.

God has strong consolations ready for holy mourners: they that humble themselves in penitential shame and fear shall soon be encouraged and exalted; they that are struck down with the visions of God's glory, shall soon be raised up again with the visits of his grace; he that tears will heal. Angels are ministering spirits for the good of the saints, for their spiritual good. The blessed Spirit works as fire, (Matt. 3:11). The seraph, being himself kindled with a divine fire, put life into the prophet, to make him also zealously affected; for the way to purge the lips from the uncleanness of sin, is, to fire the soul with the love of God.

Matthew Henry, on the place

is therefore only one expression of that fanaticism which haunts the spirit of revivals, to make such a work a touchstone of character; to regard all as good who favour it, and all as bad who oppose it. That this should be done during the continuance of the excitement is an evil to be expected and pardoned; but to commit the same error in the historical review of such a period, would admit of no excuse. Hard as it was then either to see or to believe, we can now easily perceive and readily credit that some of the best and some of the worst men in the Church, were to be found on either side, in the controversy respecting the great revival of the last century. The mere geographical position of a man, in many cases, determined the part he took in that controversy. A sober and sincere Christian, within the sphere of Davenport's operations, might well be an opposer, who, had he lived in the neighbourhood of Edwards, might have approved and promoted the revival. Yet Edwards and Davenport were then regarded as leaders in the same great work.

That there had been a lamentable declension in religion both in Great Britain and in this country, is universally acknowledged by the writers of this period. The Rev. Samuel Blair, speaking of the state of religion in Pennsylvania at that time, says: "I doubt not but there were some sincerely religious persons up and down; and there were, I believe, a considerable number in several congregations pretty exact, according to their education, in the observance of the external forms of religion, not only as to attendance upon public ordinances on the Sabbath, but also as to the practice of family worship, and perhaps secret prayer too; but with those things, the most part seemed, to all appearance, to rest contented, and to satisfy their conscience with a dead formality in religion. A very lamentable ignorance of the essentials of true practical religion, and of the doctrines relating thereto, very generally prevailed. The nature and necessity of the new-birth were little known or thought of; the necessity of a conviction of sin and misery, by the Holy Spirit opening and applying the law to the conscience, in order to a saving closure with Christ, was hardly known at all to most. The necessity of being first in Christ by a vital union and in a justified state, before our religious services can be well pleasing or acceptable to God, was very little understood or thought of; but the common notion seemed to be that if people were aiming to be in the way of duty as well as they could, as they imagined, there was no reason to be much afraid." In consequence of this ignorance of the nature of practical religion, there

were, he adds, great carelessness and indifference about the things of eternity; great coldness and unconcern in public worship, a disregard of the Sabbath, and prevalence of worldly amusements and follies. (*Narrative of the late remarkable revival of religion in the congregation of New Londonderry, and in other parts of Pennsylvania. By Rev. Saml. Blair, printed in his works p. 336; and in Gillies' collections vol. ii. p. 150.*)

In 1734 the Synod of Philadelphia found it necessary to issue a serious admonition to the presbyteries to examine candidates for the ministry and for admission to the Lord's supper, "as to their experience of a work of sanctifying grace in their hearts;" and to inquire regularly into the life, conversation, and ministerial diligence of their members, especially as to whether they preached in an evangelical and fervent manner. This admonition shows that there was a defect as to all these points, on the part of at least some of the members of the Synod.

In 1740 Messrs, Gilbert Tennent and Samuel Blair presented two representations, complaining of "many defects in our ministry," that are, say the Synod, "matter of the greatest lamentation, if chargeable upon our members. The Synod do therefore solemnly admonish all the ministers within our bounds, seriously to consider the weight of their charge, and, as they will answer it at the great day of Christ, to take care to approve themselves to God, in the instances complained of. And the Synod do recommend it to the several presbyteries to take care of their several members in these particulars."

In these papers, complaint is made of the want of fidelity and zeal in preaching the Gospel, and in the discharge of other ministerial duties; and the strong conviction is expressed that many of the members of the Synod were in an unconverted state. It is true indeed that such general complaints might be uttered now, or at almost any period of the church, and that of themselves they give us but little definite information of the character of the clergy.

When or where might it not be said, that many of the preachers of the Gospel were too worldly in their conversation, too little urgent, discriminating, and faithful in their preaching? That these faults, however, prevailed at the period under consideration, to a greater extent than usual, there is little reason to doubt. . . .

It is worthy of remark that neither Mr. Tennent nor Mr. Blair, when professedly bringing forward grounds of complaint against their brethren, mentions either the denial of any of the leading doctrines of the Bible, or open immorality. It is not to be doubted, that had error or immoral conduct prevailed, or been tolerated among the clergy, it would have been prominently presented. We know, however, from other sources, that there was no prevalent defection from the truth among the ministers of our church. The complaint against the old side was, that they adhered too rigidly to the Westminster Confession; and the theology of every leading man on the new side, is known from his writings, to have been thoroughly Calvinistic. There is not a single minister of that age in connexion with our church, whose name has come down to us under the suspicion of Arminianism. False doctrine, therefore, was not the evil under which the church then suffered. It was rather a coldness, and sluggishness with regard to religion. There was, undoubtedly, before the revival, a general indifference and lukewarmness among the clergy and people; and there is too much reason to fear, that in some cases the ministers, though orthodox, knew nothing of experimental religion. These cases were indeed not so numerous as to the representations of Tennent would lead us to expect, as he himself afterwards freely acknowledged.

As far, then, as the Presbyterian church is concerned, the state of religion was very low, before the commencement of the great revival. As that work extended over the whole country, and was perhaps more general and powerful in New England than any where else, in order to have any just idea of its character, our attention must be directed to the congregational churches, as well as to those of our own denomination. After the first generation of puritans had passed away, religion seems to have declined very rapidly, so that the writings of those who had seen what the churches in New England were at the beginning, are filled with lamentations over their subsequent condition, and with gloomy prognostications as to the future. As early as 1678, Dr. Increase Mather says, "The body of the rising generation is a poor, perishing, unconverted, and (unless the Lord pour down his Spirit) an undone generation. Many are profane, drunkards, swearers, lascivious, scoffers at the power of godliness, despisers of those that are good, disobedient. Others are only civil and outwardly conformed to good order by reason of their education, but never knew what the new birth means." (*Prince's Christian History, vol. i. p. 98*) In 1721, he writes thus: "I am now in the eighty-third year of my age; and having had an opportunity to converse with the first planters of this country, and having been for sixty-five years a preacher of the Gospel, I cannot but be in the disposition of those ancient men, who had seen the foundation of the first house, and wept to see the change the work of the temple had upon it. I wish it were no other than the weakness of Horace's old man, the *laudator temporis acti,* when I complain there is a grievous decay of piety in the land, and a leaving of her first love; and that the beauties of holiness are not to be seen as once they were; a fruitful Christian grown too rare a spectacle; yea, too many are given to change, and leave that order of the Gospel to set up and uphold which, was the very design of these colonies; and the very interest of New England seems to be changed from a religious to a worldly one." (*Prince, vol. i. p. 103*) We must, however, be on our guard against drawing false conclusions from such statements. We should remember how high was the standard of piety, which such writers had in view, and how peculiarly flourishing was the original condition of those churches whose declension is here spoken of. There may have been, and doubtless was much even in that age, over which we, in these less religious days, would heartily rejoice. What was decay to them, would be revival to us. The declension, however, did not stop at this stage. The generation which succeeded that over which Increase Mather mourned, departed still further from the doctrines and spirit of their pious ancestors. "The third and fourth generations," says Trumbull, "became still more generally inattentive to their spiritual concerns, and manifested a greater declension from the purity and zeal of their ancestors. Though the preaching of the Gospel was not altogether without success, and though there were tolerable peace and order in the churches; yet there was too generally a great decay as to the life and power of godliness. There was a general ease and security in sin. Abundant were the lamentations of pious ministers and good people poured out before God on this account." (*History of Connecticut, vol. ii. p. 135*) As a single example of such lamentations, we may quote the account of the state of religion in Taunton, in 1740, as given by the Rev. Mr. Crocker. "The church was but small considering the number of inhabitants; and deadness, dulness, formality, and security prevailed among them. Any who were wise virgins (and I trust there were a few such) appeared to be slumbering and sleeping with the foolish; and sinners appeared to be at ease in Zion. In a word, it is to be feared there was but little of the life or power of godliness among them, and irreligion and immorality of one kind or another seemed awfully to increase."

The defection from sound doctrine was also very extensive at this period; and evil which the revival but partially arrested, and that only for a few years. Edwards speaks of Arminianism as making a great noise in the land in 1734, (*Dwight's Life of Edwards, p. 140*) and his biographer says, there was a prevailing tendency to that system, at that time, not only in the county of Hampshire, but throughout the province. (*Ibid. p. 434.*) This tendency was not confined to Massachusetts; it was as great, if not greater in Connecticut. President Clap, though himself a Calvinist, was elected to the presidency of Yale College in 1739, "by a board of trustees exclusively Arminian, and all his associates in office held the same tenets." (*Ibid. p. 211*) We know not on what authority this specific statement rests, but it is rendered credible by other facts. Such for example as the ordination of Mr. Whittelsey at Milford, notwithstanding the strenuous opposition of a large minority of people, founded on the belief "that he was not sound in the faith, but had imbibed the opinions of Arminius;" (*Trumbull, vol. ii. p. 335*) in which matter the ordaining council were fully sustained by the Association of New Haven.

In Scotland there had been a general decay in the power of religion from the revolution in 1688 to the time of which we are now speaking. . . .

In England the case was far worse. From the accession of Charles II. in 1660 and the exclusion of the non-conformists, true religion seems to have declined rapidly in the established church. . . .

REVIVAL IN THE PRESBYTERIAN CHURCH

Such in few words was the state of religion in England, Scotland and America, when it pleased God, contemporaneously in these several countries, remarkably to revive his work. The earliest manifestation of the presence of the Holy Spirit, in our portion of the church, during this period, was at Freehold, N.J., under the ministry of the Rev. John Tennent, who was called to that congregation in 1730, and died in 1732. . . .

The state of religion for a time in this congregation was very low. The labours of Mr. J. Tennent however, were greatly blessed. The place of public worship was generally crowded with people, who seemed to hear as for their lives. Religion became the general subject of discourse; though all did not approve of the power of it. The Holy Scriptures were searched by people on both sides of the question; and knowledge surprising increased. The terror of God fell generally on the inhabitants of the place, so that wickedness, as ashamed, in a great measure hid its head.

Mr. William Tennent, who succeeded his brother in 1733 as pastor of that church, says the effects of the labours of his predecessor were more discernible a few months after his death, than during his life. The religious excitement thus commenced continued, with various alternations, until 1744, the date of this account. . . .

The sorrows of the convinced were not alike in all, either in degree or continuance. Some did not think it possible for them to be saved, but these thoughts did not continue long. Others thought it possible, but not very probable on account of their vileness. The greatest degree of hope, which any had under a conviction which issued well, was a may-be: Peradventure, said the sinner, God will have mercy on me.

The conviction of some was instantaneous, by the Holy Spirit applying the law and revealing all the deceit of their hearts, very speedily. But that of others was more progressive. They had discovered to them one abomination after another, in their lives, and hence were led to discover the fountain of all corruption in the heart, and thus were constrained to despair of life by the law, and consequently to flee to Jesus Christ as the only refuge, and to rest entirely in his merits.

After such sorrowful exercises, such as were reconciled to God, were blessed with the spirit of adoption, enabling them to cry, "Abba, Father." Some had greater degrees of consolation than others in proportion to the clearness of the evidences of their sonship. The way in which they received consolation, was either by the application of some particular promise of Scripture; or by a soul-affecting view of the method of salvation by Christ, as free, without money and without price. With this way of salvation their souls were well pleased, and thereupon they ventured their case into his hands, expecting help from him only.

As to the effects of this work on the subjects of it, Mr. Tennent says, they were not only made to know but heartily to approve of the great doctrines of the Gospel, which they were before either ignorant of, or averse to (at least some of them); so that they sweetly agreed in exalting free, special, sovereign grace, through the Redeemer; being willing to glory only in the Lord, who loved them and gave himself for them. They approved of the law of God after the inward man, as holy, just, and good, and prized it above gold. They judged it their duty as well as privilege to wait on God in all his ordinances. A reverence for his commanding authority and gratitude for his love conspired to incite them to a willing, unfeigned, universal, unfainting obedience to his laws; yet they felt that in every thing, they came sadly short, and bitterly bewailed their defects. They loved all such as they had reason to think, from their principles, experience and practice, were truly godly, though they differed from them in sentiment as to smaller matters; and looked upon them as the excellent of the earth. They preferred others to themselves, in love; except when under temptation; and their failures they were ready to confess and bewail, generally accounting themselves that they were the meanest of the family of God.

Through God's mercy, adds Mr. Tennent, we have been quite free from enthusiasm. Our people have followed the Holy law of God, the sure word of prophecy, and not the impulses of their own minds. There have not been among us, that I know of, any visions, except such as are by faith; namely clear and affecting views of the new and living way to the Father through his dear Son Jesus Christ; nor any revelations but what have been long since written in the sacred volume. (*Letter to Rev. Mr. Prince, of Boston, by William Tennent, dated Oct. 9, 1744; published in the Christian History Nos. 90, 91, and reprinted in Gillies' Collections, vol. ii. p. 28.*)

The leading characteristics of this work were a deep conviction of sin, arising from clear apprehensions of the extent and spirituality of the divine law. This conviction consisted in an humbling sense both of guilt and corruption. It led to the acknowledgment of the justice of God, in their condemnation, and of their entire helplessness in themselves. Secondly, clear apprehensions of the mercy of God in Christ Jesus, producing a cordial acquiescence in the plan of salvation presented in the Gospel, and a believing acceptance of the offers of mercy. The soul thus returned to God through Jesus Christ, depending on his merits for the divine favour. Thirdly, this faith produced joy and peace; a sincere approbation of the doctrines of the Gospel; delight in the law of God; a constant endeavour to obey his will; love to the brethren, and a habitually low estimate of themselves and their attainments. This surely is a description of true religion. Here are faith, hope, charity, obedience and humility, and where these are, there is the Spirit of God, for these are his fruits. . . .

PHILADELPHIA

Whitefield visited Philadelphia in November, 1739. He found the Episcopal churches, for a time, freely opened to him. On one occasion, he says,

"After I had done preaching, a young gentleman, once a minister of the Church of England, but now secretary to Mr. Penn, stood up, and with a loud voice warned the people against the doctrine which I had been delivering; urging that there was no such term as imputed righteousness in Holy Scripture, and that such a doctrine put a stop to all goodness. When he had ended, I denied his first proposition, and brought a text to prove that imputed righteousness was a scriptural expression; but thinking the church an improper place for disputation, I said no more at that time. The portion of Scripture appointed to be read was Jeremiah xxiii., wherein are the words, 'The Lord our righteousness.' Upon them I discoursed in the afternoon, and showed how the Lord Jesus was to be our whole righteousness; proved how the contrary doctrine overthrew divine revelation; answered the objections that were made against the doctrine of an imputed righteousness; produced the Articles of our Church to illustrate it; and concluded with an exhortation to all, to submit to Jesus Christ, who is the end of the law for righteousness to every one that believeth. The word came with power. The church was thronged within and without; all wonderfully attentive, and many, as I was informed, convinced that the Lord Jesus Christ was our righteousness."

Whitefield's sentiments, manner of preaching, and clerical habits, were so little in accordance with those of the majority of his Episcopal brethren, that this harmonious intercourse did not long continue. Their pulpits were soon closed against him, and he commenced preaching in the open air. One of his favourite stations was the balcony of the old court-house in Market street. Here he would take his stand, while his audience arranged themselves on the declivity of the hill on which the court-house stood. (It is said that his voice was so distinct, that every word he uttered, while preaching from the court-house, could be heard by persons in a vessel at Market street wharf, a distance of more than four hundred feet. It is even stated that his voice was heard on the Jersey shore, a distance of at least a mile.—*Gillies' Life of Whitefield, p. 39*) The effects produced in Philadelphia by his preaching, "were truly astonishing. Numbers of all denominations, and many who had no connexion with any denomination, were brought to inquire, with the utmost earnestness, what they must do to be saved. Such was the eagerness of the multitude for spiritual instruction, that there was public worship regularly twice a day, for a year; and on the Lord's day, it was celebrated thrice, and frequently four times." (*Memoirs of Mrs. Hannah Hodge, Philadelphia, 1806*)

During the winter of 1739-40, Whitefield visited the South, and returned to Philadelphia by sea the following spring. His friends now erected a stage for him on what was called Society Hill, where he preached for some time to large and deeply affected audiences. When he left the city, he urged his followers to attend the ministry of the Tennents and their associates. These gentlemen, accordingly, continued to labour among the people, and thus cherished and extended the impressions produced by Whitefield's preaching. In the course of this year he collected funds for the erection of a permanent building for the use of itinerant ministers. This house afterwards became the seat of the college, and subsequently, university of Pennsylvania. Here Whitefield preached whenever he visited the city, and here his associates, especially the Tennents, and Messrs Rowland, Blair, and Finley, ministered during his absence. . . .

NEW YORK AND VIRGINIA

Mr. Whitefield preached in New York repeatedly, during his second and third visits to this country, and was kindly received by the Rev. Mr. Pemberton, pastor of the Presbyterian Church in that city, but no very remarkable results seem to have there attended his ministry.

In no part of our country was the revival more interesting, and in very few was it so pure as in Virginia. The state of religion in that province was deplorable. There was "a surprising negligence in attending public worship, and an equally surprising levity and unconcernedness in those that did attend. Family religion a rarity, and a solemn concern about eternal things a greater. Vices of various kinds triumphant, and even a form of godliness not common." (*Davies' Letter to Mr. Bellamy, Gillies' Collection, vol. ii. p. 330*) "Much the larger portion of the clergy were, at this time, deficient in the great duty of placing distinctly before the people, the fundamental truths of the gospel." (*Hawks' Contributions to the Ecclesiastical History of the United States, vol. i. p. 115*) Various circumstances had conspired to supply the established church of Virginia with ministers unfitted for their stations; and under the influence of men unqualified to be either the teachers or examples of their flocks, religion had been reduced to a very low state. There were indeed some faithful ministers, and some who were sincerely seeking the Lord in the communion of the Church of England. Still all accounts agree as to the general prevalence of irreligion among both the clergy and the laity. . . .

NEW ENGLAND AND BOSTON

While the revival was thus extending itself through almost all parts of the Presbyterian Church, it was perhaps still more general and remarkable throughout New England. In Northampton, where President Edwards had been settled since 1726, there had been a revival in 1734-35, which extended more or less through Hampshire county, and to many adjoining places in Connecticut. (*Edward's Narrative, &c., works, vol. iv. p. 25.*) In the spring of 1740, before the visit of Mr. Whitefield, there was a growing seriousness through the town, especially among the young people. When that gentleman came to the place in October, he preached four or five sermons with his usual force and influence. In about a month there was a great alteration in the town, both in the increased fervour and activity of professors of religion, and in the awakened attention of sinners. . . .

In September 1740, Mr. Whitefield first visited Boston, when multitudes were greatly affected by his ministry. Though he preached every day, the houses continued to be crowded until his departure. The December following, Mr. G. Tennent arrived, whose preaching was followed by still greater effects. Many hundreds, says Mr. Prince, were brought by his searching ministry to be deeply convinced of sin; to have clear views of the divine sovereignty, holiness, justice, and power; of the spirituality and strictness of the divine law, and of the dreadful corruption of their own hearts, and "its utter impotence either rightly to repent or believe in Christ, or change itself;" of their utter unworthiness in the sight of a righteous God, of their being "without the least degree of strength to help themselves out of this condition." On Monday March 2, 1741, Mr. Tennent preached his farewell sermon, to an extremely crowded and deeply affected audience. "And now was a time such as we never knew. Mr. Cooper was wont to say, that more came to him in one week, in deep concern about their souls, than in the whole twenty-four years of his previous ministry." In three months he had six hundred such calls, and Mr. Webb above a thousand. The very face of the town was strangely altered. There were some thousands under such religious impressions as they never knew before; and the fruits of the work, says Mr. Cooper, in 1741, as far as time had been allowed to test them, promised to be abiding. The revival in Boston seems to have been much more pure than in most other places, and it thus continued until the arrival of Mr. Davenport in June, 1742. Mr. Prince says he met with only one or two persons who talked of their impulses, that he knew of no minister who encouraged reliance on such enthusiastic impressions. "The doctrinal principles," he adds, "of those who continue in our congregations, and have been the subjects of the late revival, are the same as they all along have been instructed in, from the Westminster Shorter Catechism, which has generally been received and taught in the Churches of New England, from its first publication, for one hundred years to the present day; and which is therefore the system of doctrine most generally and clearly declarative of the faith of the New England Churches." There seems also to have been far less extravagance in Boston than attended the excitement in most other places. "We have neither had," says Dr. Colman, "those outcrys and faintings in our assemblies, which have disturbed the worship in many places, nor yet those manifestations of joy inexpressible which now fill some of our eastern parts." (*See for an account of the revival in Boston, Prince's Christian History, No. 100, &c.; or Gillies, vol. ii, p. 162.*)

When Mr. Whitefield left Boston in October, 1740, he went to Northampton, preaching at most of the intervening towns. After spending a few days with President Edwards, as already mentioned, he proceeded to New Haven, and thence to New York. Everywhere, during this journey, the churches and houses were freely opened to him, and everywhere, to a greater or less degree, his discourses were attended by the same remarkable effects as elsewhere followed his preaching. Mr. Tennent also after leaving Boston made an extended tour through New England, and was very instrumental in awakening the attention of the people. . . .

The transient impressions, however, made by a passing preacher would, in all probability, have been of little avail, had they not been followed by the laborious and continued efforts of the settled pastors. Such efforts were in most cases made, and the revival soon became general through almost the whole of Massachusetts and Connecticut, and a considerable part of Rhode Island. In Connecticut the work was probably more extensive than in any other of the colonies,

and was greatly promoted by the labours of Messrs. Pomeroy, Mills, Wheelock, and Bellamy. . . .

As this work was more extensive in Connecticut than elsewhere, so it was there attended with greater disorders, and was more violently opposed, and in many cases led to disastrous separations and lasting conflicts. Severe penal laws were enacted against itinerant preaching; several ministers were transported out of the colony; others were deprived of their salaries or fined. The act for the indulgence of sober consciences was repealed in 1743, so that there "was no relief for any persons dissenting from the established mode of worship in Connecticut, but upon application to the assembly, who were growing more rigid in enforcing the constitution." (*Trumbull's Connecticut, vol. ii. p. 173.*) The General Association on the occasion of Whitefield's second visit in 1745, declared him to be the promoter, or at least the faulty occasion of the errors and disorders which there prevailed; and voted that it was not advisable for the ministers to admit him into their pulpits, or for the people to attend his ministrations. (*Ibid. vol. ii. p. 190*)

Notwithstanding all the disorders and other evils attendant on this revival, there can be no doubt that it was a wonderful display, both of the power and grace of God. This might be confidently inferred from the judgment of those, who, as eye-witnesses of its progress, were the best qualified to form an opinion of its character. The deliberate judgment of such men as Edwards, Cooper, Colman, and Bellamy, in New England; and of the Tennents, Blair, Dickinson, and Davies, in the Presbyterian Church, must be received as of authority on such a subject. These men were not errorists or enthusiasts. They were devout and sober-minded men, well versed in the Scriptures and in the history of religion. They had their faults, and fell into mistakes; some of them very grievous; but if they are not to be regarded as competent witnesses as to the nature of any religious excitement, it will be hard to know where such witnesses are to be found. Besides the testimony of these distinguished individuals, we have that of a convention of about ninety ministers met at Boston, July 7, 1743. Similar attestations were published by several associations in Connecticut and elsewhere. (*Prince's History, No. 20, 21.*) The presbyteries of New Brunswick and New-castle, and the whole synod of New York, repeatedly and earnestly bore their testimony to the genuineness and value of this revival. (*Gillies, vol. ii. p. 319*)

We have, however, ourselves sufficient ground on which to form a judgment on this subject. We can compare the doctrines then taught, the exercises experienced, and the effects produced, with the word of God, and thus learn how far the work was in accordance with that infallible standard. The first of these points is a matter of primary importance. It would be in vain for any set of men to expect the confidence of the Christian public in the genuineness of any religious excitement, unless it could be shown that the truth of God was instrumental in its production. There have been great excitements where Pagan, Mohammedan, and Popish doctrines were preached, but no one regards such excitements with approbation, who does not regard those doctrines as true. Any revival, therefore, which claims the confidence of the people of God, must show that it is the child of the truth of God. If it cannot do this, it may safely be pronounced spurious. How will the revival under consideration abide this test? Is there any doubt as to the doctrines taught by Whitefield, the Tennents, Blair, Dickinson, and the other prominent preachers of that day? They were the doctrines of the reformation, and of the standards of the Presbyterian Church. Indeed, these men often went to a length in their statements of the peculiarities of those doctrines, that would shock the delicacy of modern ears. (*See Tennent's Sermons, especially those on original sin, regeneration, and the nature and necessity of conversion: Blair's Works, his Dissertation on Predestination and Reprobation: President Dickinson's Familiar Letters; his Dialogues, his Five Points, &c., &c. Whitefield's Theology at last was such as to satisfy even Toplady, who pronounced him a sound divine.*) These great truths were not kept under a bushel during this period. They were prominently presented, and gave to the work, as far as it was genuine, its distinctive character. "The doctrines preached," says Trumbull, "by those famous men who were owned as the principal instruments of this remarkable revival of God's work, were the doctrines of the reformers; the doctrine of original sin, of regeneration by the supernatural influences of the divine Spirit, and of the absolute necessity of it, that any man might bear good fruit, or ever be admitted into the kingdom of God; effectual calling; justification by faith, wholly on account of the imputed righteousness of Christ; repentance towards God and faith towards our Lord

Jesus Christ; the perseverance of saints; the indwelling of the Holy Spirit in them, and its divine consolations and joys." (*History, vol. ii. p. 158*)

The contemporary accounts of the doctrines inculcated by the zealous preachers of that day, fully sustain the statement just quoted. Edwards mentions that his sermon on justification by faith, though it gave offence to many, was greatly blessed, and that it was on the doctrine therein taught, the revival was founded in its beginning and during its whole progress. In the account of the revival at Plymouth, we are told that the doctrines principally insisted upon, were "the sin and apostasy of mankind in Adam; the blindness of the natural man in things of God; the enmity of the carnal mind; the evil of sin, and the ill desert of it; the utter inability of fallen man to relieve himself; the sovereignty of God, his righteousness, holiness, truth, power, eternity, and also his grace and mercy in Christ Jesus; the way of redemption by Christ; justification through his imputed righteousness received by faith, this faith being a gift of God, and a living principle that worketh by love; legal and evangelical repentance; the nature and necessity of regeneration, &c." (*Prince's Christian History, No. 92.*) . . .

The second criterion of the genuineness of any revival is the nature of the experience professed by its subjects. However varied as to degree or circumstances, the experience of all true Christians is substantially the same. There is and must be a conviction of sin, a sense of ill-desert and unholiness in the sight of God; a desire of deliverance from the dominion as well as penalty of sin; an apprehension of the mercy of God in Jesus Christ; a cordial acquiescence in the plan of redemption; a sincere return of the soul to God through Christ, depending on his merits for acceptance. These acts of faith will ever be attended with more or less of joy and peace, and with a fixed desire and purpose to live in obedience to the will of God. The distinctness and strength of these exercises, the rapidity of their succession, their modifications and combinations admit of endless diversity, yet they are all to be found in every case of genuine conversion. It is here as in the human face; all men have the same features, yet no two men are exactly alike. This uniformity of religious experience, as to all essential points, is one of the strongest collateral proofs of the truth of experimental religion. That which men of every grade of cultivation, of every period, and in every portion of the world, testify they have known and felt, cannot be a delusion. When we come to ask what was the experience of the subjects of this revival, we find, amidst much that is doubtful or objectionable, the essential characteristics of genuine conversion. This is plain from the accounts already given, which need not be here repeated. In a great multitude of cases, the same feelings were professed which we find the saints, whose spiritual life is recorded in the Bible, experienced, and which the children of God in all ages have avowed; the same sense of sin, the same apprehension of the mercy of God, the same faith in Christ, the same joy and peace in believing, the same desire for communion with God, and the same endeavour after new obedience.

Such however is the ambiguity of human language, such the deceitfulness of the human heart, and such the devices of Satan, that no mere detail of feeling, and especially no description which one man may give of the feelings of others, can afford conclusive evidence of the nature of those feelings in the sight of God. Two persons may, with equal sincerity, profess sorrow for sin, and yet their emotions be essentially different. Both may with truth declare that they believe in Christ, and yet the states of mind thereby expressed, be very dissimilar. Both may have peace, joy, and love, yet the one be a self-deceiver, and the other a true Christian. We must, therefore, look further than mere professions or detail of experiences, for evidence of the real character of this work. We must look to its effects. The only satisfactory proof of the nature of any religious excitement, in an individual or a community, is its permanent results. What then were the fruits of this revival? Mr. William Tennent says, that the subjects of this work, who had come under his observation, were brought to approve of the doctrines of the gospel, to delight in the law of God, to endeavour to do his will, to love those who bore the divine image; that the formal had become spiritual; the proud, humble; the wanton and vile, sober and temperate; the worldly, heavenly-minded; the extortioner, just; and the self-seeker, desirous to promote the glory of God. (*Gillies, vol. ii. p. 34*). This account was written in 1744.

The convention of ministers that met in Boston in 1743, state, that those who were regarded as converts, confirmed the genuineness of the change which they professed to have experienced, "by the external fruits of holiness in their lives, so that they appeared to those who had the nearest access to them, as so many epistles

of Jesus Christ, written not with ink, but by the Spirit of the living God." (*Gillies, vol. ii. p. 252. See similar testimonies in the Christian History, p. 252, 286, et passim.*) President Edwards, in his *Thoughts on the Revival*, written in 1743, says, there is a strange alteration almost all over New England among the young. Many both old and young have become serious, mortified and humble in their conversation; their thoughts and affections are now about the favour of God, an interest in Christ, and spiritual blessedness. The Bible is in much greater esteem and use than formerly. The Lord's day is more religiously observed. There has been more acknowledgment of faults and restitution within two years, than in thirty years before. The leading truths of the gospel are more generally and firmly held; and many have exhibited calmness, resignation, and joy, in the midst of the severest trials (*Edwards' Works, vol. iv. p. 105*) It is true his estimate of this work a few years later, was far less favourable, but he never ceased to regard it as a great revival of genuine religion. . . .

STATE OF RELIGION AFTER REVIVAL

If the evidence was not perfectly satisfactory, that this remarkable and extended revival was indeed the work of the Spirit of God, it would lose almost all its interest for the Christian church. It is precisely because it was in the main a work of God, that it is of so much importance to ascertain what were the human or evil elements mixed with it, which so greatly marred its beauty and curtailed its usefulness. That there were such evils cannot be a matter of doubt. The single consideration, that immediately after this excitement the state of religion rapidly declined, that errors of all kinds became more prevalent than ever, and that a lethargy gradually settled on the churches which was not broken for near half a century, is proof enough that there was a dreadful amount of evil connected with the revival. Was such, however, actually the case? Did religion thus rapidly decline? If this question must be answered in the affirmative, what were the causes of this decline, or what were the errors which rendered this revival, considered as a whole, productive of such evils? These are questions of the greatest interest to the American churches, and ought to be very seriously considered and answered.

That the state of religion did rapidly decline after the revival, we have abundant and melancholy evidence. Even as early as 1744, President Edwards says, "the present state of things in New England, is, on many accounts, very melancholy. There is a vast alteration within two years." God, he adds, was provoked at the spiritual pride and self-confidence of the people, and withdrew from them, and "the enemy has come in like a flood in various respects, until the deluge has overwhelmed the whole land. There had been from the beginning a great mixture, especially in some places, of false experiences and false religion with true; but from this time the mixture became much greater, and many were led away into sad delusions." . . .

In 1750, he writes to Mr. McCulloch in the following melancholy strain. "It is indeed now a sorrowful time on this side of the ocean. Iniquity abounds, and the love of many waxes cold. Multitudes of fair and high professors, in one place or another, have sadly backslidden, sinners are desperately hardened; experimental religion is more than ever out of credit with far the greater part; and the doctrines of grace and those principles in religion which do chiefly concern the power of godliness, are far more than ever discarded. Arminianism and Pelagianism have made a strange progress within a few years. The Church of England in New England, is, I suppose, treble what it was seven years ago. Many professors are gone off to great lengths in enthusiasm and extravagance in their notions and practices. Great contentions, separations, and confusions in our religious state prevail in many parts of the land." . . .

Somewhat later, President Clap found it necessary, on account of the increasing prevalence of error, to write a formal defence of the doctrines of the New England Churches. The leading features of the new divinity, of which he complained, were, 1. That the happiness of the creature is the great end of creation. 2. That self-love is the ultimate foundation of all moral obligation. 3. That God cannot control the acts of free agents. 4. That he cannot certainly foreknow, much less decree such acts. 5. That all sin consists in the voluntary transgression of known law; that Adam was not created in a state of holiness, but only had a power to act virtuously; and every man is now born into the world in as perfect a state of rectitude as that in which Adam was created. 6. The actions of moral agents are not free, and consequently have no moral character, unless such agents have plenary ability and full power to the contrary. Hence it is absurd to suppose that God should implant grace or holiness in any man, or keep

him from sin. 7. Christ did not die to make satisfaction for sin, and hence there is no need to suppose him to be essentially God, but only a perfect and glorious creature. No great weight ought to be laid upon men's believing Christ's divinity, or any of those speculative points which have been generally received as the peculiar and fundamental doctrines of the gospel; but we ought to have charity for all men, let their speculative principles be what they may, provided they lead moral lives. (*Brief History and vindication of the Doctrines of the Churches of New England, with a specimen of the new scheme of religion beginning to prevail. By Thomas Clap, President of Yale College. New Haven, 1755.*) These doctrines were a great advance on the Arminian or even Pelagian errors over which President Edwards lamented, and show what might indeed be expected, that the churches had gone from bad to worse.

This is certainly a gloomy picture of the state of religion so soon after a revival, regarded as the most extensive the country had ever known. It is drawn not by the enemies, but in a great measure by the best and wisest friends of religion. The preceding account, it is true, relates principally to New England. In the Presbyterian Church the same rapid decline of religion does not appear to have taken place. In 1752, President Edwards, in a letter to Mr. McCulloch, says, "As to the state of religion in America, I have little to write that is comfortable, but there seem to be better appearances in some of the other colonies than in New England." He specifies particularly New Jersey and Virginia. And we know from other sources, that while the cause of truth and piety was declining in the eastern states, the Presbyterian Church, especially that portion of it in connexion with the synod of New York, was increasing and flourishing. With regard to orthodoxy, at least, there was little cause of complaint. The only instance on record, during this whole period, of the avowal of Arminian sentiments, by a presbyterian minister, was that of the Rev. Mr. Harker, of the presbytery of New Brunswick; and he was suspended from the ministry as soon as convicted.[*]

* That there has never been any open and avowed departure from Calvinistic doctrines in the Presbyterian Church, while repeated and extended defections have occurred in New England, is a fact worthy of special consideration. The causes of this remarkable difference in the history of these two portions of the church, may be sought by different persons in different circumstances. Presbyterians may be excused if they regard their form of government as one of the most important of those causes. New England has enjoyed greater

This low state of religion, and extensive departure from the truth, in that part of the country where the revival had been most extensive, is certainly prima facie proof that there must have been something very wrong in the revival itself. It may, however, be said, that the decay of religion through the land generally, is perfectly consistent with the purity of the revival, and the flourishing state of those particular churches which had experienced its influence. The facts of the case, unfortunately, do not allow us the benefit of this assumption. It is no doubt true, that in some congregations, as in that of Hebron, mentioned by Trumbull, religion was in a very desirable state, in the midst of the general decline; but it is no less certain, that in many in-

stances, in the very places where the revival was the most remarkable, the declension was the most serious. . . .

These passages give a melancholy account of the results of the great religious excitement now under consideration. . . . If it was difficult then, it must be more so now, to detect the causes of the spurious excitement which then so extensively prevailed. Two of these causes, however, are so obvious that they can hardly fail to attract attention. These were laying too much stress on feelings excited through the imagination, and allowing, and indeed encouraging the free and loud manifestation of feeling during public or social worship.

FEELING AND IMAGINATION

It is one office of the imagination to recall and reconstruct conceptions of any object which affects the senses. It is by this faculty that we form mental images, or lively conceptions of the objects of sense. It is to this power that graphic descriptions of absent or imaginary scenes are addressed; and it is by the agency of this faculty that oratory, for the most part, exerts its power over the feelings. That a very large portion of the emotions so strongly felt, and so openly expressed during this revival, arose not from spiritual apprehensions of divine truth, but from mere imaginations or mental images, is evident from two sources; first, from the descriptions given of the exercises themselves, and secondly from the avowal of the propriety of this method of exciting feeling in connexion with religious subjects. Had we no definite information as to this point, the general account of the effects of the preaching of Whitefield and others, would satisfy us that, to a very great extent, the results were to be attributed to no supernatural influence, but to the natural power of oratory. There is no subject so universally interesting as religion, and therefore there is none which can be made the cause of such general and powerful excitement; yet it cannot be doubted that had Whitefield selected any worthy object of benevolence or patriotism, he would have produced a great commotion in the public mind. When therefore he came to address men on a subject of infinite importance, of the deepest personal concern, we need not be surprised at the effects which he produced. The man who could thaw the icy propriety of Bolingbroke; who could extort gold from Franklin, though armed with a determination to give only copper; or set Hopkinson, for

religious advantages than any other portion of our country. It was settled by educated and devoted men. Its population was homogeneous and compact. The people were almost all of the same religious persuasion. The Presbyterian Church, on the contrary, has laboured under great disadvantages. Its members were scattered here and there, in the midst of other denominations. Its congregations were widely separated, and, owing to the scattered residences of the people, often very feeble; and, moreover, not unfrequently composed of discordant materials, Irish, Scotch, German, French, and English. Yet doctrinal purity has been preserved to a far greater extent in the latter denomination than in the former. What is the reason? Is it not to be sought in the conservative influence of presbyterianism? The distinguished advantages possessed by New England, have produced their legitimate effects. It would be not less strange than lamentable, had the institutions, instructions, and example of the pious founders of New England been of no benefit to their descendants. It is to these sources that portion of our country is indebted for its general superiority. The obvious decline in the religious character of the people, and the extensive prevalence, at different periods, of fanaticism and Antinomianism, Arminianism, and Pelagianism, is, as we believe, to be mainly attributed to an unhappy, and unscriptural ecclesiastical organization. Had New England, with her compact and homogeneous population, and all her other advantages, enjoyed the benefit of a regular presbyterian government in the church, it would, in all human probability, have been the noblest ecclesiastical community in the world.

It is well known that a great majority of all the distinguished ministers whom New England has produced, have entertained the opinion here expressed, on the subject. President Edwards, for example, in a letter to Mr. Erskine, said, "I have long been out of conceit of our unsettled, independent, confused way of church government; and the presbyterian way has ever appeared to me most agreeable to the word of God, and the reason and nature of things." (*Life, p. 412*) Where the preservation of the purity of the church is committed to the mass of the people, who, as a general rule, are incompetent to judge in doctrinal matters, and who, in many cases, are little under the influence of true religion, we need not wonder that corruption should from time to time prevail. As Christ has appointed presbyters to rule in the church according to his word, on them devolve the duty and responsibility of maintaining the truth. This charge is safest in the hands of those to whom Christ has assigned it.

the time being, beside himself; might be expected to control at will the passions of the young, the ignorant, and the excitable. It is far from being denied or questioned that his preaching was, to an extraordinary degree, attended by a divine influence. That influence is needed to account for the repentance, faith, and holiness, which were in a multitude of cases, the result of his ministrations. It is not needed, however, to account for the loud outcries, faintings, and bodily agitations, which attended his course. These are sufficiently explained by his vivid descriptions of hell, of heaven, of Christ, and a future judgment, addressed to congregated thousands of excited and sympathizing hearers, accompanied by the most stirring appeals to the passions, and all delivered with consummate skill of voice and manner. It was under such preaching, the people, as he tells us, soon began to melt, to weep, to cry out, and to faint. That a large part of these results were to be attributed to natural causes, can hardly be doubted; yet who could discriminate between what was the work of the orator, and what was the work of the Spirit of God? Who could tell whether the sorrow, the joy, and the love expressed and felt, were the result of lively imaginations, or of spiritual apprehensions of the truth? The two classes of exercises were confounded; both passed for genuine, until bitter experience disclosed the mistake. It is evident that Whitefield had no opportunity of making any such discrimination; and that for the time at least, he regarded all meltings, all sorrowing, and all joy, following his fervid preaching as evidence of the divine presence. It is not however these general accounts so much as the more particular detail of the exercises of the subjects of this revival, which shows how much of the feeling then prevalent, was due to the imagination. . . .

It is not to be denied that there is a legitimate use of the imagination in religion. The Bible often addresses itself to this faculty. The descriptions which it gives of the future glory of the church, and of heaven itself, are little else than a series of images; not that we should conceive of the millennium as of a time when the lion and lamb shall feed together, or of heaven as a golden city, but that we may have a more lively impression of the absence of all destructive passions, when Christ shall reign on earth, and that we may learn to think of heaven as a state of surpassing glory. In all such cases it is the thought which the figure is meant to convey, and not the figure itself, that the mind rests upon in all truly religious exercises. When, on the other hand, the mind fixes on the image, and not upon the thought, and inflames itself with these imaginations, the result is mere spurious excitement. So far then as the imagination is used to render the thoughts which the understanding forms of spiritual things, distinct and vivid, so far may it minister to our religious improvement. But when it is made a mere chamber of imagery, in which the soul alarms or delights itself with spectres, it becomes the source of all manner of delusions. . . .

Those apprehensions of truth which arise from divine illumination, do not affect the imagination, but the moral emotions, which are very different in their nature and effects from the feelings produced by a heated fancy. This view of the subject is greatly confirmed by the consideration, that there is nothing in the Bible to lead us to regard these bodily affections as the legitimate effects of religious feeling. No such results followed the preaching of Christ, or his apostles. We hear of no general outcries, faintings, convulsions, or ravings in the assemblies which they addressed. The scriptural examples cited by the apologists of these exhibitions are so entirely inapplicable, as to be of themselves sufficient to show how little countenance is to be derived from the Bible for such irregularities. Reference is made, for example, to the case of the jailer at Philippi, who fell down at the apostles' feet; to *Acts ii. 37*, ("*Now when they heard this, they were pricked in their heart, and said, Men and brethren, what shall we do?*") and to the conversion of Paul. It is, however, too obvious to need remark, that in no one of these cases was either the effect produced, or the circumstances attending its production, analogous to the hysterical convulsions and outcries now under consideration.

The testimony of the Scriptures is not merely negative on this subject. Their authority is directly opposed to all such disorders. They direct that all things should be done decently and in order. They teach us that God is not the God of confusion, but of peace, in all the churches of the saints. These passages have particular reference to the manner of conducting public worship. They forbid every thing which is inconsistent with order, solemnity, and devout attention. It is evident that loud outcries and convulsions are inconsistent with these things, and therefore ought to be discouraged. They cannot come from God, for he is not the author of confusion. The apology made in Corinth for the disorders which Paul condemned, was precisely the same as that urged in defence of these bodily agitations.

We ought not to resist the Spirit of God, said the Corinthians; and so said all those who encouraged these convulsions. Paul's answer was, that no influence which comes from God destroys our self-control. *"The spirits of the prophets are subject to the prophets."* Even in the case of direct inspiration and revelation, the mode of communication was in harmony with our rational nature, and left our powers under the control of reason and the will. The man, therefore, who felt the divine afflatus had no right to give way to it, under circumstances which would produce noise and confusion. The prophets of God were not like the raving Pythoness of the heathen temples; nor are the saints of God converted into whirling dervishes by any influence of which he is the author. There can be little doubt that Paul would have severely reprobated such scenes as frequently occurred during the revival of which we are speaking. He would have said to the people substantially, what he said to the Corinthians. If any unbeliever or ignorant man come to your assemblies, and hears one shouting in ecstacy, another howling in anguish; if he see some falling, some jumping, some lying in convulsions, others in trances, will he not say, ye are mad? But if your exercises are free from confusion, and your discourses addressed to the reason, so as to convince and reprove, he will confess that God is among you of a truth. . . .

THE CENSORIOUS SPIRIT

The censorious spirit, which so extensively prevailed at this period, was another of those fountains of bitter waters, which destroyed the health and vigour of the church. That it should characterise such acknowledged fanatics as Davenport and his associates, is what might be expected. It was, however, the reproach and sin of far better men. Edwards stigmatises it, as the worst disease which attended the revival, "the most contrary to the spirit and rules of Christianity, and of the worst consequences." (*Works, Vol. 4, p. 238*) The evil in question consists in regarding and treating, on insufficient grounds, those who profess to be Christians, as though they were hypocrites. The only adequate ground for publicly discrediting such profession, is the denial of those doctrines which the Bible teaches us are essential to true religion, or a course of conduct incompatible with the Christian character. . . . It was by the dreadful prevalence of this habit of censorious judging during the revival, that the confidence of the people in their pastors was destroyed, their usefulness arrested, their congregations divided, and the fire-brands of jealousy and malice cast into every society, and almost into every household. It was this, more than any thing else, that produced that conflagration in which the graces, the peace, and the union of the church were consumed. Though this censorious spirit prevailed most among those who had the least reason to think themselves better than others, it was to a lamentable degree the failing of really good men.

It is impossible to open the journals of Whitefield without being painfully struck, on the one hand with the familiar confidence with which he speaks of his own religious experience, and on the other with the carelessness with which he pronounces others to be godly or graceless, on the slightest acquaintance or report. Had these journals been the private record of his feelings and opinions, this conduct would be hard to excuse; but as they were intended for the public, and actually given to the world almost as soon as written, it constitutes a far more serious offence. Thus he tells us, he called on a clergyman, (giving the initials of his name, which, under the circumstances completely identified him,) and was kindly received, but found "he had no experimental knowledge of the new birth." Such intimations are slipped off, as though they were matters of indifference. On equally slight grounds he passed judgment on whole classes of men. After his rapid journey through New England, he published to the world his apprehension "lest many, nay most that preach do not experimentally know Christ." (*New England Journal, p. 95.*) After being six days in Boston, he recorded his opinion, derived from what he heard, that the state of Cambridge college for piety and true godliness, was not better than that of the English universities, (*Ibid. p. 12*) which he elsewhere says, "were sunk into mere seminaries of paganism, Christ or Christianity being scarce so much as named among them." Of Yale he pronounces the same judgment, saying of it and Harvard, "their light is now become darkness, darkness that may be felt." A vindication of Harvard was written by the Rev. Edward Wigglesworth, a man "so conspicuous for his talents, and so exemplary for every Christian virtue," that he was unanimously appointed the first Hollis professor of divinity in the college. The president of Yale, at that time, was the Rev. Dr. Clap, an orthodox and learned man, "exemplary for piety," and zealous for the truth. Whitefield was much in the habit of speaking of ministers as being unconverted, so that the consequence was, that in a country where "the

"And Jesus, when he was baptized, went up straight-way out of the water: and, lo, the heavens were opened unto him, and he saw the Spirit of God descending like a dove, and lighting upon him: And lo a voice from heaven, saying, This is my beloved Son, in whom I am well pleased." (Matthew 3:16-17)

How solemnly Heaven was pleased to grace the baptism of Christ with a special display of glory. In and through Jesus Christ, the heavens are opened to the children of men. Sin shut up heaven, put a stop to all friendly intercourse between God and man; but now Christ has opened the kingdom of heaven to all believers. Divine light and love are darted down upon the children of men, and we have boldness to enter into the holiest. The heavens were opened when Christ was baptized, to teach us, that when we duly attend on God's ordinances, we may expect communion with him, and communications from him.

The Spirit of God descended, and lighted on him. In the beginning of the old world, the Spirit of God moved upon the face of the waters, hovered as a bird upon the nest. So here, in the beginning of this new world, Christ, as God, needed not to receive the Holy Ghost, but it was foretold that the Spirit of the Lord should rest upon him, and here he did so. The Spirit of Christ is a dove-like spirit; not like a silly dove, without heart, but like an innocent dove without gall.

The Holy Spirit manifested himself in the likeness of a dove, but God the Father by a voice; for when the law was given they saw no manner of similitude, only they heard a voice: and so this gospel came, and gospel indeed it is, the best news that ever came from heaven to earth; for it speaks plainly and fully God's favour to Christ, and us in him.

See here how God owns our Lord Jesus; This is my beloved Son. This is the sum of the whole gospel; it is a faithful saying, and worthy of all acceptation, that God has declared, by a voice from heaven, that Jesus Christ is his beloved Son, in whom he is well pleased, with which we must by faith cheerfully concur, and say, that he is our beloved Saviour, in whom we are well pleased.

Matthew Henry, on the place.

preaching and conversation of far the bigger part of the ministers were undeniably as became the gospel, such a spirit of jealousy and evil surmising was raised by the influence and example of a young foreigner, that perhaps there was not a single town," either in Massachusetts or Connecticut, in which many of the people were not so prejudiced against their pastors, as to be rendered very unlikely to be benefitted by them. (*Letter to the Rev. George Whitefield by Edward Wigglesworth, in the name of the faculty of Harvard College, 1745.*) This is the testimony of men who had received Mr. Whitefield, on his first visit, with open arms. They add, that the effect of his preaching, and of that of Mr. Tennent, was, that before he left New England, ministers were commonly spoken of as pharisees and unconverted. The fact is, Whitefield had, in England, got into the habit of taking it for granted, that every minister was unconverted, unless he had special evidence to the contrary. This is not to be wondered at, since, according to all contemporaneous accounts, the great majority of the episcopal clergy of that day, did not profess to hold the doctrines of grace, nor to believe in what Whitefield considered experimental religion. There was, therefore, no great harm in taking for granted that men had not, what they did not profess to have. When, however, he came to New England, where the great majority of the ministers still continued to profess the faith of their fathers, and laid claim to the character of experimental Christians in Whitefield's own sense of the term, it was a great injustice to proceed on the assumption that these claims were false, and take it for granted that all were graceless who had not to him exhibited evidence to the contrary.

The same excuse cannot be made for Mr. Tennent; and as his character was more impetuous, so his censures were more sweeping and his denunciations more terrible than those of Whitefield. . . . The great sinfulness of this censorious spirit, and his own offences in this respect, Mr. Tennent afterwards very penitently acknowledged. . . .

The extent to which the sin of censoriousness prevailed during this revival, may be inferred, not only from the complaints of those who were unrighteously condemned, but from the frequency with which it was testified against by the best friends of religion, and the confessions of some of those who had most grievously offended in this respect. One great evil of this spirit is, that it is contagious, and in a sense, hereditary. That

is, there always will be men disposed to rake up the sins and errors of these pious denouncers; and on the score of these deformities, to proclaim themselves the Tennents and Whitefields of their own generation. If the fruit of the Spirit of God is love, joy, peace, long-suffering, gentleness, goodness, faith, meekness, then may we be sure that a proud, arrogant, denunciatory, self-confident, and selfrighteous spirit is not of God; and that any work which claims to be a revival of religion, and is characterized by such a spirit, is so far spurious and fanatical. All attempts to account for, or excuse such a temper on the ground of uncommon manifestations, or uncommon hatred of sin, or extraordinary zeal for holiness and the salvation of souls, are but apologies for sin. . . .

RULES OF ECCLESIASTICAL ORDER

Another of the evils of this period of excitement, was the disregard shown to the common rules of ecclesiastical order, especially in the course pursued by itinerant preachers and lay exhorters. With respect to the former, no one complained of regularly ordained ministers acting the part of evangelists; that is, of their going to destitute places, and preaching the gospel to those, who would not otherwise have an opportunity of hearing it. The thing complained of was, that these itinerants came into the parishes of settled ministers, and without their knowledge, or against their wishes, insisted on preaching to the people. This was a thing of very frequent, almost daily occurrence, and was a fruitful source of heartburnings and divisions.

It is the plain doctrine of the Scriptures and the common understanding of the Christian church, that the pastoral relation is of divine appointment. Ministers are commanded to take heed to the flocks over which the Holy Ghost has made them overseers. If the Holy Ghost has made one man an overseer of a flock, what right has another man to interfere with his charge? This relation not only imposes duties, but it also confers rights. It imposes the duties of teaching and governing; of watching for souls as those who must give an account. It confers the right to claim obedience as spiritual instructors and governors. Hence the people are commanded to obey them that have the rule over them, and to submit themselves. They have indeed the right to select their pastor, but having selected him, they are bound by the authority of God, to submit to him as such. They have moreover, in extreme cases, the right to desert or discard him; as a wife has in extreme cases, the right to leave her husband, or a child to renounce the authority of a parent. But this cannot be done for slight reasons, without offending God. . . .

Mr. Tennent admitted these principles to their fullest extent; he justified his conduct and that of his associates on the ground, that the ordinary rules of ecclesiastical order cease to be obligatory in times of general declension. When the majority of ministers are unconverted men, and contentedly unsuccessful in their work, it was, he maintained, the right of any one who could, to preach the gospel to their people, and the duty of the people to forsake the ministrations of their pastors. Admitting the correctness of this principle, when can it properly be applied? When may it be lawfully taken for granted, that a minister is unconverted and unfit for his office? According to Tennent's own sober and deliberate judgment, this could be rightfully done only when he either rejected some fundamental doctrine, or was immoral in his conduct. And even when this was the case, the obviously correct course would be, to endeavour to have him removed from office by a competent authority. Not until this had been proved to be impossible, would any man be justified in trampling upon the rights of a brother minister. The conduct of Mr. Tennent and that of his associates, cannot stand the test of his own principles. They not only made no effort to have those ministers removed from office, whom they regarded as unregenerate or unfaithful, but they chose to assume them to be unconverted, and on the ground of that assumption to enter their congregations, and to exhort the people to forsake their ministry, though they admitted them to be sound in all the main articles of religion, and regular in their lives. This disorderly course was, in many cases, productive of shameful conflicts, and was in general one of the most crying evils of the times.

Whitefield far out-did Mr. Tennent, as to this point. He admitted none of the principles which Mr. Tennent believed, in ordinary times, ought to be held sacred. He assumed the right, in virtue of his ordination, to preach the gospel wherever he had an opportunity, "even though it should be in a place where officers were already settled, and the gospel was fully and faithfully preached. This, I humbly apprehend," he adds, "is every gospel minister's indisputable privilege. (*Whitefield's letter to the president, professors, &c. of Harvard College. Boston, 1745: p. 17*) It mattered not whether the pastors who thus fully

and faithfully preached the gospel, were willing to consent to the intrusion of the itinerant evangelist or not. "If pulpits should be shut," he says, "blessed be God, the fields are open, and I can go without the camp, bearing the Redeemer's reproach. This I glory in; believing if I suffer it, I suffer for righteousness' sake." (*Ibid. p. 22*) If Whitefield had the right here claimed, then of course Davenport had it, and so every fanatic and errorist has it. This doctrine is entirely inconsistent with what the Bible teaches of the nature of the pastoral relation, and with every form of ecclesiastical government, episcopal, presbyterian, or congregational. Whatever plausible pretences may be urged in its favour, it has never been acted upon without producing the greatest practical evils.

As soon as this habit of itinerant preaching within the bounds of settled congregations, began to prevail, it excited a lively opposition. The synod of Philadelphia twice unanimously resolved that no minister should preach in any congregation without the consent of the presbytery to which the congregation belonged. As soon, however, as the revival fairly commenced, Mr. Tennent and his associates refused to be bound by the rule; and, for the sake of peace, it was given up. The legislature of Connecticut made it penal for any minister to preach within the bounds of the parish of another minister, unless duly invited by the pastor and people. (*Trumbull's Connecticut, vol. ii. p. 162*) The General Association of Connecticut, in 1742, after giving thanks for the revival, bear their testimony against "ministers disorderly intruding into other ministers' parishes." (*Ibid. vol. ii. p. 173*) The convention of ministers of Massachusetts, in 1743, declared this kind of itinerant preaching, "without the knowledge, or against the leave of settled pastors," to be "a breach of order, and contrary to the Scriptures, and the sentiments of our fathers, expressed in their Platform of Church Discipline." (*Testimony of the pastors of churches in the province of Massachusetts-Bay, at their annual convention in Boston, May 25, 1743, pages 6, 7.*) And the assembly of pastors held at Boston, July 1743, in their testimony in behalf of the revival, express it as their judgment "that ministers do not invade the province of others, and, in ordinary cases, preach in another's parish, without his knowledge and consent." (*Some of the ministers present on that occasion signed this testimony and advice as to the substance merely, which Mr. Prince informs us, was owing principally to the clause above cited. Some of the pastors thought that it was not explicit enough against the practice which it condemned, while others thought it might "be perverted to the great infringement of Christian and human liberty." —Christian History, vol. i. p. 198*) Notwithstanding this general concurrence among the friends of religion, in condemning this disorderly practice, it prevailed to a great extent, and resulted in dividing congregations, unsettling ministers, and introducing endless contentions and confusion. . . .

This is a formidable array of evils. Yet as the friends of the revival testify to their existence, no conscientious historian dare either conceal or extenuate them. There was too little discrimination between true and false religious feeling. There was too much encouragement given to out-cries, faintings, and bodily agitations, as probable evidence of the presence and power of God. There was, in many, too much reliance on impulses, visions, and the pretended power of discerning spirits. There was a great deal of censoriousness, and of a sinful disregard of ecclesiastical order. The disastrous effects of these evils, the rapid spread of false religion, the dishonour and decline of true piety, the prevalence of erroneous doctrines, the division of congregations, the alienation of Christians, and the long period of subsequent deadness in the church, stand up as a solemn warning to Christians, and especially to Christian ministers in all times to come. . . .

Though this, being true, should be known and well considered, that the guilt and danger of propagating false religion and spurious excitement, may be understood, yet we are not to forget or undervalue the great good which was then accomplished. In many places there was little of these evils, especially in New Jersey and Virginia. Dickinson and Davies successfully resisted their inroads within the sphere of their influence. And in many other places the soundness of the doctrines taught, the experience detailed, and the permanent effects produced, abundantly attest the genuineness of the revival. To the Presbyterian Church particularly, it was the commencement of a new life, the vigour of which is still felt in all her veins.

SCHISM OF 1741

In 1737, an overture was introduced and approved in reference to itinerant preachers. This act forbad a licentiate to preach in any vacant congregation without the order of the presbytery to which he belonged, or of the presbytery under whose care the congregation was placed. It forbad also the congregations to invite any minister or probationer without the concurrence of their presbytery; &c. In the following year this order was so modified as to forbid any minister belonging to the synod "to preach in any congregation belonging to another presbytery," after being warned by any member of the presbytery that his so preaching would be likely to cause division. To this was added the explanation, that this prohibition by one member was to be merely temporary. If the presbytery to which the congregation belonged gave the stranger liberty to preach, he might do so. Thus explained, it was agreed to *nemine contradicente.* In 1739, it is stated that "The act made last year with respect to ministers preaching out of their own bounds being taken under a review, the synod determine that if any minister in the bounds of any of our presbyteries judge that the preaching of any minister or candidate of a neighboring presbytery has had a tendency to promote division among them, he shall complain to the Presbytery in whose bounds the said congregation is; and that the minister who is supposed to be the cause of the aforesaid division shall be obliged to appear before them, and it shall be left to them to determine whether he shall preach any more in the bounds of that congregation; and he shall be bound to stand to their determination, until they shall see cause to remove their prohibition; or the synod shall have an opportunity to take the affair under cognizance. Approved *nem. con.*" In 1740, the synod say that although this agreement had at the time it was passed met with universal acceptance, yet as some of the brethren had become dissatisfied with it, and some of their people misinterpreted it, supposing it to be intended against all itinerant preaching, they agreed to repeal it, and thus avoid all contention on the subject.

This act is not so much an illustration of the power of the synod, as it is a declaration, and enforcing the rights of presbyteries. It merely provided that no man should preach in any congregation against the will of the presbytery under whose care such congregation was placed. This is a principle fully recognised in our present constitution. If a congregation is vacant, it applies to the presbytery for supplies, or obtains permission to fill its own pulpit. That the presbytery has the right to watch over and provide for the religious instruction of its churches is one of the most familiar principles of our form of government. It very clearly shows at once the agitation existing in those days, and the moderation of synod,

art I

that they were willing to waive this principle, though twice unanimously sanctioned, for the sake of peace. The opposition to this rule seems to have proceeded principally from Mr. Tennent. No man was, under ordinary circumstances, more disposed than that gentleman to enforce the obligation of such rules, and even to push them to extremes. But when he thought they stood in the way of the interests of religion, he trampled them under his feet. To create a division in the congregation of a converted pastor, or to preach against his consent within his bounds, was, in his eyes, a high ecclesiastical offence. But to preach the gospel to the people of a graceless minister, in despite of his remonstrances, was a matter of duty; and he would have done it, in despite of all the synods in the world. In this he was clearly right, as far as the principle is concerned. There are obligations superior to those of mere ecclesiastical order; and there are times when it is a duty to disregard rules, which we admit to be legitimate both in their own nature, and in respect to the authority whence they proceed. It was on this principle that the apostles and the reformers acted. It is analogous to the right of revolution in civil communities; and consequently the cases are very rare in which it can be resorted to, with a good conscience. Because the reformers rightfully trampled on the ecclesiastical authorities to which they were subject, it does not follow that every wandering evangelist, who thinks that he is a better man or better preacher than his brethren, may properly enter into parishes, divide congregations, and unsettle pastors at pleasure. Whether Mr. Tennent was right in applying his principle in the way he did, is a very difficult question, which belongs properly to a subsequent period of our history.

It is worthy of remark that the same circumstances which called forth this act of the synod, under the different system of the Connecticut churches, led to the interference of the civil authorities. In May 1742, the General Assembly of Connecticut passed a law, in which, after a long preamble, they enacted that any settled minister, who should preach within the parish of another minister, unless invited by the latter and by the major part of the people, should be deprived of all the benefit of the law for the support of the clergy; that if any one, not a minister or licentiate, should teach or exhort in any parish, without being properly invited, he should be bound over in the penal sum of one hundred pounds; and if any stranger not an inhabitant of the colony should transgress in like manner, he

was to be sent as a vagrant from constable to constable out of the bounds of the colony.

In the year 1738, the presbytery of Lewes brought in an overture respecting the examination of candidates for the ministry. After reciting the various disadvantages under which such candidates then laboured in the prosecution of their studies, and the dangers arising from the admission of uneducated men into the ministry, it proposed that the synod should agree that all the presbyteries should require every candidate, before being taken upon trial, to be furnished with a diploma from some European or New England college; or in case he had not enjoyed the advantage of a college education, he should be examined by a committee of synod, who should give him a certificate of competent scholarship, when they found him to merit it. This overture was approved by a great majority; and Messrs. John Thompson, George Gillespie, James Anderson, Thomas Evans, Henry Hook, James Martin, and Francis Allison, were appointed the committee of examination for the presbyteries to the south of Philadelphia; and Messrs. Andrews, Robert Cross, G. Tennent, E. Pemberton, J. Dickinson, D. Cowell, and J. Pierson for the presbyteries to the north of Philadelphia.

In 1739, "the New Brunswick presbytery having brought a paper of objections against the act of last year, touching the previous examination of candidates, the synod consented to review that act, and upon deliberation agreed to the following overture, which they substitute in the place of it, viz. It being the first article in our excellent Directory for the examination of candidates for the sacred ministry, that they be inquired of what degrees they have taken in the university, &c.; and it being oftentimes impracticable for us in these remote parts of the earth, to obtain an answer to these questions of those who propose themselves for examination, many of our candidates not having enjoyed the advantage of an university education; and it being our desire to come to the nearest conformity to the incomparable prescriptions of the Directory that our circumstances will admit of; and after long deliberation of the most proper expedients to comply with the intentions of the Directory where we cannot exactly fulfill the letter of it, the synod agree and determine that every person who proposes himself for trial as a candidate for the ministry, and who has not a diploma or the usual certificate from an European or New England university, shall be examined by the whole synod, or its commission, as to those preparatory studies which are generally passed through at the college, and if they find him qualified, shall give him a certificate which shall be received by our respective presbyteries as equivalent to a diploma or certificate from the college. This, we trust, will have a happy tendency to prevent unqualified men from creeping in among us, and answer, in the best manner our present circumstances are capable of, the design which our Directory has in view, and to which by inclination and duty we are all bound to comply to our utmost ability. This was agreed to by a great majority."

Against the above act Messrs. Gilbert Tennent, William Tennent, Sen., William Tennent, Jun., Charles Tennent, Samuel Blair, and Eleazer Wales, together with four elders, protested. It is stated in the minutes of the next year, that various proposals were made with the view of reconciling these protesting brethren. As these efforts were not successful, "the synod," it is said, "still desiring that that unhappy difference may be accommodated, recommend it to any brethren of the synod to consider any further expedient to that end, to be brought in at the next *sederunt*." What these expedients were, the records do not inform us. . . . The synod then passed the following explanatory declaration: "That they do not hereby call in question the right of inferior presbyteries to ordain ministers, but only assert their own right to judge of the qualification of their own members; and though they do not deny but that such as are brought into the ministry contrary to this agreement, may be truly gospel ministers, yet, inasmuch as they cannot but think the said agreement needful to be insisted on in order to the well being of this part of the Church of Christ, they cannot admit them, when so brought into the ministry, to be members of this synod, until they submit to the said agreement, though they do consent that they be in all other respects treated and considered as ministers of the Gospel; any thing that they be otherwise construed in any of our former proceedings notwithstanding."

This act was the immediate occasion of the schism which occurred in 1741, . . . The motive therefore of Mr. Tennent's opposition to this act was not dislike of the ecclesiastical principle on which it was founded, but dislike of the object at which he thought it aimed. He believed it was adapted, and probably designed, to keep evangelical men out of the ministry, and therefore he would not submit to it. . . .

The details describing each step leading to the schism in the Presbyterian church following the revival are set forth in Dr. Hodge's book. Space does not allow more than his conclusion statements. The reader is encouraged to read the full account for its lessons are still valid. Editor

It appears . . . that the great schism was not the result of conflicting views, either as to doctrine or church government. It was the result of alienation of feeling produced by the controversies relating to the revival. In these controversies the New Brunswick brethren were certainly the aggressors. In their unrestrained zeal, they denounced brethren, whose Christian character they had no right to question. They disregarded the usual rules of ministerial intercourse, and avowed the principle that in extraordinary times and circumstances such rules ought to be suspended. Acting upon this principle, they divided the great majority of the congregations within the sphere of their operations, and by appealing to the people, succeeded in overwhelming their brethren with popular obloquy. Excited by a sense of injury, and alarmed by the disorders consequent on these new methods, the opposite party had recourse to violent measures for redress, which removed none of the evils under which they suffered, and involved them in a controversy with a large class of their brethren, with whom they had hitherto acted in concert. These facts our fathers have left on record for the instruction of their children; to teach them that in times of excitement the rules of order, instead of being suspended, are of more importance than ever to the well-being of the church; that no pretence of zeal can authorize the violation of the rules of charity and justice; and on the other hand, that it is better to suffer wrong than to have recourse to illegal methods of redress; that violence is no proper remedy for disorder, and that adherence to the constitution, is not only the most Christian, but also the most effectual means of resistance against the disturbers of the peace and order of the church.

EFFORTS IN BEHALF OF EDUCATION, DURING THE SCHISM, 1741–1776

Next to the religious instruction of their own people, and the supply of the new settlements, the duty of providing some adequate means for the education of ministers of the gospel, seems to have pressed most heavily upon the members of the synod. From an early period, probably as early as 1719, or 1720, the Rev. William Tennent, sen'r., had erected a school at Neshaminy, long known as the Log College, where some of the most distinguished and useful ministers of that generation received their education. This was a private institution, and had no immediate connexion with the synod. In 1739, Mr. John Thompson introduced an overture into the presbytery of Donegal, proposing the establishment of a school under the care of the synod. This overture was the same year referred to the synod, and "unanimously approved;" and Messrs. Pemberton, Dickinson, Cross, and Anderson, were nominated, "two of whom, if they can be prevailed upon, to be sent home to Europe to prosecute this affair, with proper directions. And in order to this, it was ordered, that the commission of synod, with correspondents from every presbytery, meet at Philadelphia, the third Wednesday of August next, and if it be necessary that Mr. Pemberton go to Boston, pursuant to this design, it is ordered, that the presbytery of New York supply his pulpit during his absence." When the commission met in accordance with this appointment, it was resolved that application should be made to every presbytery for their concurrence and assistance, and that a letter should be written to the general assembly in Scotland, soliciting their co-operation. In consequence, however, of the small number of members in attendance, it was thought best to refer the matter to the whole synod; and the commission accordingly resolved to call an extra meeting of the synod on the last Wednesday of September, enjoining "on the members present to inform their respective presbyteries of the appointment, and that the moderator send letters to the presbyteries of New Brunswick and New York, ordering their attendance at the time appointed." It was further ordered, "that a letter be remitted to Dr. Colman, to be communicated to our brethren of Boston, earnestly desiring their concurrence and assistance in this affair." It appears from the minutes of the following year, 1740, that in consequence of "war breaking out between England and Spain the calling of the synod was omitted, and the whole affair laid aside for the time." A letter from Dr. Colman, in reply to the one written to him by the commission, was read before the synod, wherein, in the name of the associated brethren of Boston, "he assures the synod of their readiness to concur with the synod in their laudable proposal of erecting a school or seminary of learning in these parts."

Nothing further was done in this business until 1744. From the minutes for that year it appears that "a committee was held at the Great Valley, November 16, 1743, by a private agreement between the presbyteries of Philadelphia, Newcastle, and Donegal, the minutes of which meeting were laid before the synod, showing that the said committee considered the necessity of speedy endeavours to educate youth for suppiying our vacancies; but as the proper method cannot be so well compassed without the synod, they refer the consideration of the affair to that reverend body; but agree, in the mean time, a school be opened for the education of youth. And this synod, it is added, now approve of that design, and take the said school under their care, and agree upon the following plan for carrying on the design:

"*First,* there shall be a school kept open, where all persons who please may send their children, and have them taught gratis, in the languages, philosophy, and divinity.

"*Second,* in order to carry on this design, it is agreed that every congregation under our care, be applied to for yearly contributions, more or less, as they can afford, and as God may incline them to contribute, until Providence open a door for our supporting the school some other way.

"*Third,* if any thing can be spared, besides what may support a master and tutor, it be applied by the trustees for buying books and other necessaries for the said school, and the benefit of it, as the trustees shall see proper. And Mr. Alison is chosen master of the said school, and has the privilege of choosing an usher under him to assist him; and he, Mr. Alison, is exempted from all public business, save only attending church judicatories, and what concerns his particular pastoral charge. And the synod agree to allow Mr. Alison £20 per annum, and the usher £15." The same day the synod appointed a board of trustees for the school, three of whom were to visit the school every quarter. "These trustees," it is added, "are to inspect into the master's diligence in, and method of teaching; consider and direct what authors are chiefly to be read in the several branches of learning; to examine the scholars from time to time as to their proficiency; to apply the money procured from our people as ordered above; and, in sum, order all affairs relating to said school, as they shall see expedient, and be accountable to the synod, making report of their proceedings and the state of the school yearly."

This it must be admitted was a very liberal plan. A school was thus established for the gratuitous instruction of the youth of all denominations, and sustained by the efforts of one of the poorest; and one of the most accomplished scholars at that time in the country, was placed at the head of it. The only record in the minutes for 1745, relating to the school, is the notice of the report of the trustees, and an order to those ministers who had not taken up a collection for its support, to attend to that duty. It appears that, by the order of the commission, Messrs. Andrews and Cross had written a letter to President Clap and the trustees of Yale College, in relation to this enterprise, as notice is taken of his reply. When President Clap's letter was presented to the synod in 1746, an answer was prepared, which is inserted on the records at length.

It may be inferred from this answer, that the commission had written to make some arrangement for the admission of the students from the synodical school into Yale College, as the president called for information as to the plan of the school, and state of the synod. This information the answer in question purports to give. It states that the synod had, some years before, endeavoured to establish a school, but were prevented by the troubles of the time, especially by the war with Spain; that in the mean time, in order to secure a learned ministry, they had agreed that those who had not a diploma from some college should obtain a certificate of competent scholarship from the synod, before being taken on trials by any presbytery. It then briefly refers to the opposition made to this agreement, and to the controversies arising out of Mr. Whitefield's preaching, and the subsequent schism in the synod. The letter then gives an account of the school, and adds, that the synod had agreed "that after the scholars had passed through the course of studies assigned to them, they shall be publicly examined by the trustees and such ministers as the synod shall see fit to appoint, and if approved, shall receive testimonials of their approbation, and without such testimonials none of the presbyteries under the care of the synod shall improve any of the scholars in the ministry." The writers further express their hope of obtaining assistance from England and Ireland as soon as the difficulties which then existed allowed of their making the necessary application. They profess their purpose to make the course of instruction in their school correspond as nearly as possible with that pursued in the British colleges. They readily agreed that their scholars in going to Yale, should be examined by the president and fellows, be required to bring recommendations, and that they should enjoy no privileges inconsistent with the good order of the college. It is not easy to understand the object of this letter, unless it be assumed that the statutes of Yale College required a certain number of years' residence before graduation, and that the synod wished their students to be allowed to enter the higher classes, when found prepared, in order to avoid the expense of a protracted absence from their own homes. In the minutes for the year 1747, there is a notice of another letter from President Clap, and of a reply on the part of the synod, but the contents of neither are given.

COLLEGE OF PHILADELPHIA

The synod continued to watch over the school with sedulous attention, as there is almost every year some record relating to it. In 1749, it was found necessary to modify the plan of gratuitous instruction. Mr. Alison's salary was increased to thirty pounds, and he was allowed to receive the usual tuition fee from all students whom the trustees did not exempt from that charge. In 1751-2, Mr. Alison removed to Philadelphia to take charge of the academy in that city, and when it was erected into a college he was appointed the vice-provost. Mr. Alexander McDowell was appointed his successor in the mastership of the synodical school. The organization of the College in Philadelphia, and the appointment of Mr. Alison, seems in a measure to have removed the necessity for a higher collegiate institution under the immediate care of the synod. That college, though principally under the control of episcopalians, was accessible to all denominations, and a large portion of its officers and trustees have ever been presbyterians.

In 1754, Mr. Matthew Wilson was appointed Mr. McDowell's assistant, and teacher of languages in the school, Mr. McDowell "from a sense of the public good continuing to teach logic, mathematics, and natural and moral philosophy." In 1755, a collection of books was received from Dublin, which were sent "for the benefit of public schools, the use of students, and the encouragement of learning in this infant church, to be disposed of by the synod in the best manner to answer these good ends." It was then agreed that these books should "be the foundation of a public library under the care of the synod." The books proper for the school were to be the property of the master, he giving security for their safe keeping and return; the others were committed to the care of the trustees of the fund for ministers' widows, who were to choose a librarian to take charge of the library for the use of members of the synod, and for the benefit of students of divinity in the college of Philadelphia. The same year an application was made to the trustees of the German schools for assistance in the support of the synodical school; the synod engaging "to teach some Dutch children the English tongue, and three or four boys Latin and Greek, if they offer themselves; and Mr. Samson Smith was directed to open the school at Chestnut Level so soon as this favour was received." These German schools were under the patronage of a general board in London, and of a subordinate board in Philadelphia. It was to the latter that the application of the synod was, in the first instance, directed. This application was the more reasonable, as the synod had for eleven years sustained the school by their own exertions, and offered its advantages gratuitiously, to the youth of all denominations. The request for assistance, therefore, was granted without much hesitation, as appears from the following extract, from the minutes of the board, communicated to the synod in answer to their petition. "June 14, 1755; met at Mr. Allen's house near Germantown the following trustees, viz: Messrs. Allen, Peters, Franklin, and Smith. And taking into their consideration the aforesaid petition of the synod of Philadelphia, were under some difficulty how to act concerning it. On the one hand they thought that to grant the petition in favour of an English synod might give offence to the Germans, who generally consider this charity as intended for their own particular benefit. The trustees were also of opinion, that it did not exactly fall under the great design of promoting the English tongue among the Germans. But they considered on the other hand, the pleas urged by the petitioners. They knew it to be a truth, that the synod of Philadelphia, at a time when ignorance, even among the ministry, was like to over-run the whole province, had begun, and with much difficulty, long supported a public school under Mr. Francis Alison; and that many able ministers, and some of them Dutch, had been educated in the said school. The trustees were also of opinion that it was no small argument in favour of the petitioners, that the mother church of Scotland had contributed so largely to this useful charity, and that if any future application to said church should be necessary, the interest and recommendation of the synod of Philadelphia might be useful in that respect, as well as in countenancing the several schools in their present infant state, and educating according to their proposal, some young men for the Dutch ministry gratis. In consideration of all which it was resolved to grant twenty-five pounds currency for one year to assist the said synod to support their

school on the following terms, viz: 1. That it shall be under the same common government with the other free schools, and be subject to the visitation of the trustees general or their deputies, appointed upon the recommendation of the synod. 2. That the master shall teach four Dutch or English scholars gratis, upon the recommendation of the trustees general, to be prepared for the ministry, and ten poor Dutch children in the English tongue gratis, if so many offer. 3. That the deputy trustees, together with the master and any of the clergy, visit the school at least once a quarter, and send down a statement thereof, to be transmitted by the general trustees to the honourable society. Agreed, that this case be transmitted to the honourable society to obtain their directions thereupon.

The synod acceded to these terms and appointed deputy trustees to visit the school every quarter. When this matter came before the society in London, they increased the annual contribution to the synod's school from twenty-five pounds currency to thirty pounds sterling. It was thus that the synod laboured diligently and successfully in promoting the cause of education. At the synodical school under Mr. Alison and Mr. McDowell, some of the most distinguished of the ministers of the next generation, were prepared for their work. This school gave rise to the Newark academy, which has since been chartered as a college. . . .

COLLEGE OF NEW JERSEY AT PRINCETON

In 1760, a proposition was made for the appointment and support of a professor of divinity, which the synod recommended to the consideration of the presbyteries, that some plan might be devised for the accomplishment of the object. The following year, though the synod agreed "to promote this good purpose, yet from the pressure of other calls, and the want of funds, they were obliged to defer it." Deeply sensible, however, "that the church suffered greatly for want of an opportunity to instruct students in the knowledge of divinity, it was agreed that every student, after he has been admitted to his first degree in college, shall read carefully, on this subject, at least one year, under the care of some minister of approved character for his skill in theology, and under his direction shall discuss difficult questions in divinity, study the sacred Scriptures, form sermons, lectures, and such other useful exercises as may be directed in the course of his studies. And it is enjoined likewise, that every preacher for the first year after his licensure, shall show all his sermons to some minister in our presbyteries on whose friendship and candour he depends, written fairly, to have them corrected and amended. And as they are but young preachers, we are persuaded that no better method can be taken in present circumstances to improve them in Christian knowledge, and render them eminently useful in their station. It is also enjoined that they preach as often as they can before stated ministers, that they may correct their gestures, pronunciation, delivery, and the like. And it is further enjoined that all our ministers and probationers forbear reading their sermons from the pulpit, if they can conveniently."

In 1768, in consequence of a request from the trustees of the college of New Jersey, that the synod would aid in the support of a professor of divinity in that institution, a general collection was ordered for that purpose, and fifty pounds were appropriated towards the salary of the Rev. John Blair, who had been elected to that office. The wants of the college at this time were so pressing, that in the following year the synod appointed a committee in every part of the church, for the purpose of raising funds for its support. In consequence of this application, the presbytery of New Brunswick addressed a memorial to the churches under their care, setting forth the condition and claims of the college. They state that its permanent funds, though once considerable, had been reduced by necessary expenditures to £1300, and must be still further reduced, as the officers could not be supported by the fees for tuition without making those fees so high as seriously to interfere with the usefulness of the institution. It was urged that the college had peculiar claims on our church. Even in 1767, there were not fewer than eighty of her sons ministers of the gospel dispersed through the several colonies, since which time there had been considerable addition to the number. "The eyes," it is said, "of by far the greater number of our vacant churches are turned to that college for a supply of ministers; especially the churches in New Jersey and the southern colonies. That from the principles there taught and received, we have reason to think that useful instruments not only have been, but from time to time will be raised up to propagate the pure evangelical doctrines of the gospel, and to make a stand against such as might be glad to abridge our liberties, and to bring us under the yoke of ecclesiastical power; instruments to plead the cause of liberty and religion, and to make our church respectable." This effort in behalf of the college

was continued for several years, with what result is not fully known, except that it is stated, that the several committees had "been very diligent and successful."

During the period now under review, viz: from 1758 to 1789, the college was under the presidency of Mr. Davies, of Dr. Samuel Finley, and of Dr. Witherspoon. Mr. Davies entered upon the duties of his office July 26, 1759, and died February 4, 1761, so that he was president little more than eighteen months. Short as was his administration, his talents, and his devotion to his duties, rendered it eminently serviceable to the institution. His successor, Dr. Samuel Finley, entered on his duties as president, July, 1761, and died July 16, 1766. He was a native of Armagh in Ireland, but removed to this country in 1734, in the nineteenth year of his age. He was licensed by the New Brunswick presbytery in 1740, and preached with great success, especially in Pennsylvania and in the lower counties of New Jersey. In 1744, he settled at Nottingham in Maryland, where he remained for seventeen years. He there instituted an academy which enjoyed a wide and deserved reputation. "He was justly famed as a scholar, and eminently qualified as a teacher." Dr. John Woodhull, who was one of his pupils, speaks of him as being always solemn and instructive, and often fervent in the pulpit, as extensively learned, and as greatly beloved and respected by his students. Under his administration the college was very flourishing, and his own reputation rapidly extending, when he was cut down in the prime of life. About a year after he entered on the presidency, there was an extensive revival of religion in the college, in which fifty of the students, about one half of the whole number then in the institution, were supposed to have become sincerely pious.

Dr. Finley died in July, 1766: the November following Dr. Witherspoon was unanimously elected president. . . . As Dr. Witherspoon, in consequence of the unwillingness of his wife to leave Scotland, had declined the presidency, the Rev. Samuel Blair was chosen president and professor of rhetoric and metaphysics. For the want of funds these appointments were conditional, and, with the exception of that of Mr. John Blair, were not to take effect for a year, and in the meantime, the college was to be conducted by Mr. Blair and three tutors. Before the expiration of the year the difficulty in the way of Dr. Witherspoon's accepting the presidency was removed, and Mr. Samuel Blair, having generously withdrawn his name, Dr. Witherspoon was re-elected, and arrived in this country August, 1768, and was inaugurated as president on the seventeenth of that month. (The above details respecting the college of New Jersey are derived from Dr. Green's history of the college.) The deficiency in the pecuniary resources of the college prevented the above plan being carried into effect. Even Mr. Blair, to relieve the funds of the institution, resigned his office as professor of divinity, and devolved the duties upon Dr. Witherspoon. Under the auspices of the latter, the college soon began to flourish, its course of instruction was enlarged, its students increased, and the funds necessary for its support were supplied. The revolutionary war, however, soon put a stop to this course of improvement. The college was, in a great measure, disbanded, and though a class graduated in each year, the number of annual graduates was often not more than four or five. When peace returned, prosperity returned to the college, and it continued to reward the labours of its pious founders, by contributing largely to the supply of educated ministers to the church. The number of clergymen educated at this college before 1789, was two hundred and twenty-nine. . . .

OPPOSITION TO INTRODUCTION
OF BISHOPS INTO AMERICA

It does not lie within the scope of the present work to enter fully, either into the history or the merits of the controversy respecting an American episcopate. It will be proper, however, to say enough on the subject to enable the reader, to form a judgment of the propriety of the course taken by the presbyterian church in so decidedly opposing the measure. After several unsuccessful attempts had been made at an earlier period, to induce the English government to send one or more bishops to America, the effort was renewed by a voluntary convention of the episcopal clergy of New York and New Jersey, who prepared a petition on the subject to be forwarded to Europe, and requested the Rev. Dr. Bradbury Chandler of Elizabethtown, to write and publish an appeal to the public in behalf of the measure. This appeal was published in 1767, and presents the claims of the episcopal church in this country to the enjoyment of a complete organization with great force and ingenuity. The appeal was answered by Dr. Charles Chauncey of Boston; and the matter soon became a subject of general controversy throughout the country; even the weekly papers were made the vehicles of vehement arguments on both sides. (*Many of these pieces are to be found in "A Collection of Tracts from the late Newspapers, containing the American Whig, A Whip for the American Whig, &c.; being controversial articles relating to protestant bishops in the American colonies: New York, 1768, 2 vols.," in the Philadelphia Library.*)

According to Dr. Chandler it was proposed, "that the bishops to be sent to America shall have no authority but purely of a spiritual and ecclesiastical nature, such as is derived altogether from the church and not from the state. That this authority shall operate only upon the clergy of the church, and not upon the laity or upon dissenters of any denomination. That the bishops shall not interfere with the property or privileges, whether civil or religious, of churchmen or dissenters. That in particular, they shall have no concern with the probate of wills, letters of guardianship and administration, or marriage licenses, nor be judges of any cases relating thereto. But that they shall only exercise the original powers of their office, i.e. ordain and govern the clergy, and administer confirmation to those who shall desire it." Against a plan so reasonable as this it is difficult to see what objection could be made. As diocesan bishops are an essential part of an episcopal church, necessary to ordain, confirm, and exercise discipline, it would seem to be a hard case that the numerous churches already formed in this country, should be deprived of this part of their system; that the clergy should be without supervision; and that candidates for orders should be obliged to make a long and expensive voyage to obtain ordination. The fact, therefore, that strenuous and united opposition was made to the introduction of American bishops, needs explanation. As far as the presbyterian church is concerned, we should be sorry that it should lie under the imputation of having resisted the reasonable wishes of another denomination to the enjoyment of their own ecclesiastical system.

It should be stated then, that there would have been no opposition to the plan as above presented, had there been any reasonable prospect of its being adhered to. Against bishops who should derive their authority "altogether from the church and not from the state," no voice was raised. The convention of the synod of New York and Philadelphia and the churches of Connecticut, say: "We would by no means have it understood as if we would endeavour to prevent an American bishop, or archbishop, or patriarch, or whatever else they might see fit to send, provided other denominations could be safe from their severity and encroachments." (Letter to the committee in London, dated Sept. 1771. Minutes of the Convention, p. 39) And Dr. Chauncy in his reply to the Appeal, says: "We desire no other liberty than to be left unrestrained in the exercise of our religious principles, in so far as we are good members of society. And we are perfectly willing that the episcopalians should enjoy this liberty to the full. If they think bishops in their appropriated sense, were constituted by Christ or his apostles, we object not a word to their having as many of them as they please, if they will be content to have them with authority altogether derived from Christ. But they both claim and desire a great deal more. They want to be distinguished by having bishops on the footing of a state establishment." And again, "Dr. Chandler quite mistakes the true ground of our dissatisfaction. It is not simply the exercise of any of their religious principles that would give us any uneasiness; nor yet the exercise of them under as many purely scriptural bishops as they could wish to have; but their having bishops under a state establishment, which would put them upon a different footing from the other denominations, and, without all doubt, sooner or later expose them to many difficulties and grievous hardships." The same sentiment is expressed by Dr. Mayhew, in his Observations on the charter and conduct of the Society for the propagation of the Gospel in foreign parts; and also by the American Whig.

The opposition, therefore, was not to bishops with purely spiritual authority, but to bishops sent by the state with powers ascertained and determined by act of Parliament. The mere fact that this opposition was so general, and that it was as strong, though not as universal, among episcopalians as among the members of other denominations, is a proof that it did not owe its origin to any ungenerous bigotry. If the Massachusetts legislature opposed it, so did the house of burgesses in Virginia. The former body, in a letter to their agent in London, dated January 12, 1768, say: "The establishment of a protestant episcopate in America, is also very zealously contended for; and it is very alarming to a people whose fathers, from the hardships which they suffered under such an establishment, were obliged to fly from their native country into a wilderness, in order peaceably to enjoy their privileges, civil and religious. Their being threatened with the loss of both at once must throw them into a very disagreeable situation. We hope in God such an establishment will never take place in America, and we desire you would strenuously oppose it."

In Virginia, when a convention was called to consider the propriety of petitioning for a bishop, only twelve out of a hundred ministers in the province attended, and of those twelve four protested against the decision to forward a petition. And soon after the house of burgesses, by an unanimous vote, thanked the protesters "for the wise and well timed opposition they had made to the pernicious project of a few mistaken clergymen for introducing an American bishop." (*Dr. Hawks' Contributions to the Ecclesiastical History of the United States, vol. i. p. 127–130*) If any thing more is necessary to show the character of this opposition, it may be found in the fact, that as soon as this country was separated from England, and thus all fear of the civil power of the bishops removed, all objection to their introduction was withdrawn.

This apprehension of danger to the religious liberty of the country was not a feverish dread of imaginary evils. It was even better founded than the apprehension of danger to our civil liberties from the claim of the British parliament to a right to tax the country. As the episcopal church was established in England, and as those who had the control of the government were members of that church, the episcopalians in America were naturally led to be constantly looking for state patronage and legal support. They claimed it as a right, that the support and extension of the episcopal church in this country should be made a national concern. Even Dr. Chandler, although his work was written to disarm prejudice and allay apprehensions, could not avoid letting this be distinctly seen. "It has been the practice of all Christian nations," he tells us, "to provide for and maintain the national religion, and to render it as respectable as possible in the most distant colonies;" and, "as some religion has ever been thought, by the wisest legislators, to be necessary for the security of civil government, and accordingly has always been interwoven into the constitution of it, so in every nation that religion which is thus distinguished, must be looked upon as, in the opinion of the legislature, the best fitted for this great purpose. Wherever, therefore, the national religion is not made in some degree a national concern, it will commonly be considered as an evidence that those who have the direction of the national affairs do not esteem their religion; or that they are negligent of the duty they owe to God, and the public, as guardians of its happiness." He then proceeds to give the reasons why "the church of England in America appears not hitherto to have been made a national concern;"

reasons which, he says, may account for, although not altogether excuse this neglect. It was this very thing, which Dr. Chandler considered so much a matter of course, that other denominations deprecated and dreaded. They denied the right of the British government thus to distinguish the episcopal church, especially in the northern provinces, where its members, even at this period, hardly constituted the thirtieth part of the population. They denied the fairness of its being made a national concern to the detriment and oppression of other denominations. The whole history of the country showed that the authorities in England acted constantly on the plan of giving the church of England, in this country, all the ascendency that could with safety be secured for it. In those colonies where the thing was possible, that church was established by law; in others, the public were taxed for its support, or national property assigned for its maintenance. . . .

The non-episcopal denominations, therefore, in this country, had abundant cause for alarm. From South Carolina to New Hampshire, they saw the power and influence of the government exerted to give ascendency to the episcopal church. This object was constantly though cautiously pursued. It was natural that it should be so. The arguments which were adduced to prove that the church of England was entitled to this ascendency, were sufficiently plausible to command the assent of those who were anxious to be convinced. And the motives of policy in behalf of the measure, were sufficiently obvious to make all see that the English government would pursue it as far as it could be done with safety. Here, as in the contest about taxation, it was not the pressure of the particular acts of injury or indignity that produced the dissatisfaction; but the power that was claimed. The assumption was the same in both cases, viz: that America was part of the nation of England, that the power of the king and parliament was here what it was there. Hence on the one hand, the inference that the British parliament could here levy what taxes they pleased; and on the other, that the king's supremacy in ecclesiastical matters, extended to the colonies; that every Englishman who came to America, did but remove from one part of the nation to another; that he stood in the same relation to the national church in this country, as he had done in England. It is readily admitted that as there were some English statesmen who denied the authority of parliament to tax America, so there were many distinguished men who denied that the ecclesiastical laws of England were in force in this country. But in both cases the interest, and bent, and general course of the government, were against the liberties of the colonies.

Another cause of irritation and uneasiness, was the conduct of the Society for the Propagation of the Gospel in foreign parts. The principal complaints urged against it were, first, that instead of sending missionaries to the heathen, according to the primary object of its institution, it devoted its resources, in a great measure, to the American colonies. The society was successfully vindicated on this point by its various advocates. It was proved that its charter contemplated the colonies as a prominent if not the chief field of its labours. And when we consider the immense extent and crying destitution of this country, we shall be more disposed to wonder and complain that the society did so little, than that it did so much for its relief. A second ground of complaint was more plausible. It was urged that instead of sending their missionaries where they were really needed, they sent them to New England where they were not wanted. At this time there were at least five hundred and fifty educated ministers in New England, and not a town, unless just settled, without a pastor, unless it was in Rhode Island. That there was ground for this complaint against the society, is admitted by its ablest and most dignified defender, who says, "In all that I have hitherto said, I am far from intending to affirm that the society hath not laid out in Massachusetts and Connecticut too large a proportion of the money put into their hands, considering the necessities of the other provinces." It is not to be wondered at that the people of New England felt irritated by having the numerous missionaries of a powerful society located among them, where their most ostensible object was not to supply the destitute, but to make proselytes from established congregations. The claims and conduct of these missionaries, in many cases, greatly increased this irritation. They spoke of all the inhabitants of the town in which they lived, as their parishioners; as bound both by the law of God and the state to be in communion with the church of England; as having no authorized ministers or valid ordinances; as belonging to churches which were mere excrescences or fungosities.

It was principally from the missionaries of this society that the demand for American bishops proceeded. It has already been stated how small a portion of the Virginia clergy concurred in the application. (*Dr. Hawks states, that the applications for a resident bishop were made "prin-*

cipally by the clergy *of the northern provinces."* *Dr. Hawks italicises the word clergy. He further says, that the convention of New York and New Jersey sent missionaries to the South to endeavour to secure the cooperation of their southern brethren in the prosecution of this object.*) The origin of the plan, therefore, was not likely to recommend it to the public. For all the legitimate purposes of a bishop, such an officer was most needed where episcopalians were the most numerous. That the request came from the provinces where they were a small minority, could not fail to produce the apprehension, that the bishop's influence was to be used to give that minority still greater ascendency. . . .

SUPPORT OF THE BISHOPS

Another ground of apprehension related to the support of these bishops. The country had abundant reason to expect that this burden would, sooner or later, be thrown upon the public. Wherever the government were able to effect the object, they had already thrown the support of the episcopal clergy upon the community. This had been done in South Carolina, Virginia, and Maryland. To a certain extent it had been done in New York; and the royal governors in other provinces, had orders to accomplish the same object as far as possible. With regard to the bishops, Dr. Chandler says, indeed, that there was no intention to tax the country for their support; yet he distinctly recognises both the right and reasonableness of such a tax. "Should," says he, "a general tax be laid upon the country, and thereby a sum be raised sufficient for the purpose; and even supposing we should have three bishops on the continent, which are the most that have been mentioned, yet I believe such a tax would not amount to more than four pence in a hundred pounds. And this would be no mighty hardship to the country. He that could think much of giving the six thousandth part of his income to any use which the legislature of his country should assign, deserves not to be considered in the light of a good subject or member of society." What mighty hardship to the country was a tax of three pence on a pound of tea? Yet how great a fire that little matter kindled. Dr. Chandler evidently assumed two things, which America never would quietly submit to. The one was, that the English parliament had a right to lay a general tax upon the country; and the other, that they had a right to tax the whole community for the support of the episcopal church. Here was the

old error, viz: that America was part of the nation of England, and consequently that the parliament had the same power here as there; and that the episcopal church was the national church in the one country as well as in the other.*

The political motives urged by Dr. Chandler in support of his plea for bishops, were not suited to conciliate special favour to the plan. "Episcopacy and monarchy," he says, "are, in their frame and constitution, best suited to each other. Episcopacy can never thrive in a republican government, nor republican principles in an episcopal church." Experience has proved this opinion to be incorrect. The episcopal church never flourished in this country so much as since the establishment of the republic. Dr. Chandler goes on to say, that as episcopacy and monarchy "are mutually adapted to each other, so they are mutually introductive of each other. He that prefers monarchy in the state, is more likely to approve of episcopacy in the church than a rigid republican. On the other hand, he that is for parity and a popular government in the church will more easily be led to approve of a similar form of government in the state, how little soever he may suspect it himself. It is not then to be wondered, if our civil rulers have always considered episcopacy as the surest friend of monarchy; and it may reasonably be expected from those in authority, that they will support and assist the church in America, if from no other motives, yet

---

* (What Dr. Chandler says in the Defense of his Appeal, in reference to the passage cited above, does not remove its objectionable character. He repeats his denial that the imposition of a tax was either probable or intended, and "Further, to show that America had no need to be terrified on that account," he adds, "I considered the matter under the most unfavourable supposition that could be made, namely, that the deficiency in the episcopal fund should be answered by a tax upon the inhabitants, and declared it as my opinion, that such a tax would be inconsiderable, and amount to no more than four pence in a hundred pounds." (p. 249.) The objection was not to the amount of the tax, but to a tax at all; and especially to a tax for such a purpose. His language in both passages clearly implies, that he recognised the power to impose such a tax, and that it would be unreasonable to complain of it. This supremacy of the imperial parliament, England never would give up. Had she been willing to adopt the theory which Franklin urged in vain upon her statesmen, and agreed to make the king and not the parliament, the bond of union between the countries, allowing every province, important enough to have a legislature, to govern itself as Scotland did before the union; had, in other words, the bonds of union been made so loose as not to be galling, the British monarch might have swayed a peaceful sceptre over near half the world. God has ordered it otherwise, and therefore, it is best it should be otherwise.)

from a regard to the state, with which it has so friendly and close an alliance." As there was at this time a rapidly increasing dread of the power of the mother country, the consideration that the introduction of bishops would tend to increase that power, and strengthen the government was not suited to allay apprehension or to conciliate favour. The long detail respecting a controversy now almost forgotten, may be excused since it relates to an important chapter in the history not only of our church but of the country. This controversy had more to do with the revolution than is generally supposed; and a knowledge of the leading facts in the case is necessary to free presbyterians, and other denominations, from the charge of unreasonable and bigotted opposition to a church fully entitled to confidence and affection. Before the revolution the episcopal church, from its connexion with the English government, and from its claim to be regarded as a branch of a great national establishment, was justly an object of apprehension. And this apprehension was confirmed and deepened by a long series of encroachments on the rights of other denominations. After the revolution, that church ceased to be the church of England, and became the protestant episcopal church in the United States. Since she has taken her stand on equal terms with sister churches, she is the object of no other feelings than respect and love, wherever she consents to acknowledge that equality.

THE CONDUCT OF THE SYNOD IN REFERENCE TO THE REVOLUTION

After reading the preceding section, no one need be at a loss to conjecture the part taken by the synod in relation to the great struggle for the liberties of America. The position in which the presbyterians and other non-episcopal denominations stood to the English government, naturally placed them in the opposition. The declaration of the English parliament, "That the king's majesty, by and with the advice and consent of the lords spiritual and temporal, and commons of Great Britain, in parliament assembled, had, hath, and of right ought to have full power and authority to make laws and statutes of sufficient force and validity to bind the colonies and people of America, subjects of the crown of Great Britain, in all cases whatsover;" (Gen. Conway's resolutions, passed by the house of commons, Feb. 1766) was quite as alarming in reference to the religious as to the civil liberties of the people. No

one doubted that the English parliament believed an established church desirable, or that the episcopal church was, in their opinion, the best and safest form of religion; and no one could doubt, as they claimed the power, they would give that church an effective establishment in every colony sufficiently under their control. In almost every province, all denominations, except the episcopal, were regarded as merely tolerated in their own country, and were subject to many unjust demands peculiar to themselves. It was impossible that the great majority of the people could be treated as inferiors; could be denied privileges which they considered their due; or that they could see a small minority of their fellow citizens regarded as standing in an alliance to the state peculiarly friendly and close, and on that account treated with special favour, without being discontented and uneasy. The declaration of independence was for all such, a declaration of religious, as well as of civil liberty. It is not surprising, therefore, that the non-episcopal clergy entered into the conflict with a decision which, in many cases, would render it more easy to prove that they did too much, than that they did too little.

If it was natural that presbyterians should side with America in that hour of trial, it was no less natural that the episcopal clergy should side with the mother country. They had no peculiar grievances to complain of, nor any fear for the liberty of their church. On the contrary, it was to England they looked for support, for patronage, for legal provision, for that property and pre-eminence which they thought due to them as a branch of the national church. Besides, many of them were born, and all had been ordained in England, and personally had taken an oath of allegiance. They were bound, therefore, by peculiar ties; ties, which, it can well be imagined good men would find it hard to break. Instead, therefore, of its being a matter of surprise that the majority of the episcopal clergy took part with England, the wonder is that so many sided with America. Those who did so, did it at a great sacrifice. They contended against their own apparent interests; and were either very enlightened patriots, or very indifferent churchmen. Considering, then, the peculiar circumstances of the episcopal clergy at that time, so far from being disposed to make it a matter of reproach that they adhered to their allegiance to the mother country, we are disposed to think that, as a general rule, they were those of most moral worth, and most entitled to respect, who took this course. This, however, must not be

THE RETURN OF THE PRODIGAL SON
BY BENJAMIN WEST (AMERICAN, 1738-1820)
OIL ON CANVAS, 54½ X 60⅛ IN. 1771.
COURTESY THE METROPOLITAN MUSEUM OF ART.
MARIA DE WITT JESUP FUND, NEW YORK, NEW YORK

"And when he came to himself, he said, How many hired servants of my father's have bread enough and to spare, and I perish with hunger! I will arise and go to my father, and will say unto him, Father, I have sinned against heaven, and before thee, And am no more worthy to be called thy son: make me as one of thy hired servants. And he arose, and came to his father. But when he was yet a great way off, his father saw him, and had compassion, and ran, and fell on his neck, and kissed him. . . . For this my son was dead, and is alive again; he was lost, and is found." (Luke 15:17-20, 24).

We have here the parable of the prodigal son; the scope of which is the same with those before, to show how pleasing to God the conversion of sinners is, of great sinners, and how ready he is to receive and entertain such, upon their repentance; . . . The parable represents God as a common Father to all mankind; It represents the children of men as of different characters, though all related to God as their common Father. The younger son is the prodigal, whose character and case are here designed to represent that of a sinner, that of every one of us in our natural state.

Now the condition of the prodigal in this ramble of his represents to us a sinful state, that miserable state, into which man is fallen. (1) A sinful state is a state of departure and distance from God. (2) A sinful state is a spending state. (3) A sinful state is a wanting state. (4) A sinful state is a vile, servile state; sinners are perfect slaves. (5) A sinful state is a state of perpetual dissatisfaction. (6) A sinful state is a state which cannot expect relief from any creature. (7) A sinful state is a state of death . . . destitute of spiritual life. (8) A sinful state is a lost state; souls that are separated from God, are lost souls. (9) A sinful state is a state of madness and frenzy.

What was the occasion of his return and repentance; it was his affliction. What was the preparative for it; it was consideration. Consideration is the first step towards conversion. He considers and turns. To consider, is to retire into ourselves, to reflect upon ourselves, and to compare one thing with another. We have here his reception and entertainment with his father. The great love and affection wherewith the father received the son. It is chiefly designed to set forth the grace and mercy of God to poor sinners that repent, and return to him, and his readiness to forgive them.

Matthew Henry, on the place.

considered as an injurious reflection on the patriot clergy. While some of them took commissions in the army, others remained faithful at once to religion and their country. The venerable Bishop White, an ornament to the church universal, was for a long time the chaplain of congress, and acted with deliberation, and well-considered principle in the course which he adopted.*

The laymen of the episcopal church did *not* feel themselves trammelled in the same manner, or to the same extent as the ministers, and hence some of the most prominent and influential of the public leaders of the day belonged to that church.

The part taken by presbyterians in the contest with the mother country, was, at the time, often made a ground of reproach; and the connexion between their efforts for the security of their religious liberty, and opposition to the oppressive measures of parliament, was then distinctly seen. Mr. Galloway, a prominent advocate of the government, ascribed, in 1774, the revolt and revolution mainly to the action of the presbyterian clergy and laity as early as 1764, when the proposition for a general synod emanated from a committee appointed for that purpose in Philadelphia. This was a great exaggeration and mistake, but it indicates the close connexion between the civil and religious part of the controversy. The same writer describes the opponents of the government, as an "united faction of congregationalists, presbyterians, and smugglers." Another writer of the same period says, "You will have discovered that I am no friend to presbyterians, and that I fix all the blame of these extraordinary American proceedings upon them." (By presbyterians this writer means non-episcopalians.) He goes on, "Believe, sir, the presbyterians have been the chief and principal instruments in all these flaming measures; and they always do and ever will act against government, from that restless and tur-

* (In a letter to Bishop Hobart, he says, "I continued, as did all of us, to pray for the king, until Sunday, (inclusively,) before the fourth of July, 1776. Within a short time after, I took the oath of allegiance to the United States, and have since remained faithful to it. My intentions were upright and most seriously weighed; and I hope they were not in contrariety to my duty." In another place he says, "Owing to the circumstances of many able and worthy ministers cherishing their allegiance to the king of Great Britain, and entertaining conscientious scruples against the use of the liturgy, with the omission of the appointed prayers for him, they ceased to officiate, and the doors of far the greater number of episcopal churches were closed for years. In this state there was a part of that time in which there was, through the whole extent, but one resident minister of the church in question: he who records the fact," —See Address, &c. by William B. Reed. Philadelphia, 1838.)

bulent anti-monarchical spirit which has always distinguished them every where when they had, or by any means could assume power, however illegally."

As the conduct of the presbyterian clergy during the revolutionary war is not a matter of dispute, all that we are called upon to do, is briefly to exhibit the action of the synod in reference to this subject. One of the first exercises of the power claimed by parliament to impose taxes on America, was the passage of the stamp-act in 1764. The opposition to this measure was so general and vehement, that the British government thought proper to repeal the act, though they accompanied the repeal with the strongest declarations of their right to tax the colonies at discretion. In the controversy relating to this subject, the synod of New York and Philadelphia publicly expressed their sympathy with their fellow citizens. As soon as the repeal was known in this country, "An overture was made by Dr. Alison, that an address be presented to our sovereign on the joyful occasion of the repeal of the stamp-act, and thereby a confirmation of our liberties; and at the same time proposing a copy of an address for examination, which was read and approved," but not recorded. (Minutes, p. 144) The synod also addressed a pastoral letter to the churches, filled with patriotic and pious sentiments. They remind the people, that after God had delivered the country from the horrors of the French and Indian war, instead of rendering to him according to the multitude of his mercies, they had become more wicked than ever. "The Almighty thus provoked, permitted counsels of the most pernicious tendency, both to Great Britain and her colonies. The imposition of unusual taxes, a severe restriction of our trade, and an almost total stagnation of business, threatened us with universal ruin. A long suspense whether we should be deprived of, or restored to a peaceable enjoyment of the inestimable privileges of English liberty, filled every breast with painful anxiety." They express their joy that government had been induced to resort to moderate measures, instead of appealing to force; and call upon the people to bless God, who, notwithstanding their sins, had saved them from the horrors of a civil war. They, finally, earnestly exhort their people not to add to the common stock of guilt, but "to be strict in observing the laws and ordinances of Jesus Christ; to pay a sacred regard to his Sabbaths; to reverence his holy name, and to adorn the doctrine of God our Saviour by good works. We pray you," say the synod, "to seek earnestly the saving knowledge of Christ, and the internal power and spirit of religion. Thus may you hope for the continued kindness of a gracious Providence; and this is the right way to express your gratitude to the Father of mercies for your late glorious deliverance. But persisting to grieve his Holy Spirit by a neglect of vital religion, and a continuance of sin, you have reason to dread that a holy God will punish you yet seven times more for your iniquities." (Minutes, p. 151)

In this letter, as in all the public documents issued before the declaration of independence, there are strong expressions of loyalty, and of the wish to preserve inviolate the union with the mother country. In the declaration of rights by the congress held at New York, in October, 1765, it is said, "The members of this congress, sincerely devoted with the warmest sentiments of affection and duty to his majesty's person and government, inviolably attached to the present happy establishment of the protestant succession, &c. &c., esteem it our indispensable duty to make the following declarations of our humble opinion respecting the most essential rights and liberties of the colonists." The first declaration is, "That his majesty's subjects in these colonies, owe the same allegiance to the crown of Great Britain, that is owing from subjects born within the realm, and all due subjection to that august body the parliament of Great Britain." And the congress held at Philadelphia, September, 1774, in their address to the people of Great Britain, say, "You have been told that we are seditious, impatient of government, and desirous of independence. Be assured that these are not facts, but calumnies. Permit us to be as free as yourselves, and we shall ever esteem an union with you to be our greatest glory and our greatest happiness; we shall ever be ready to contribute all in our power to the welfare of the empire; we consider your enemies as our enemies, and your interests as our own." There is every reason to believe that these declarations were as sincere as they were general. The American patriots regarded separation from the mother country as a great evil; and to the last moment cherished the hope that some accommodation might be made, which should secure them the enjoyment of their rights, and avoid the necessity of a violent separation.

As the indications of the coming conflict began to multiply, the synod endeavoured to prepare their people for the trial. Almost every year they appointed days for special prayer and fasting, and presented "the threatening aspect of public af-

fairs," as one of the most prominent reasons of their observance. In 1775, the record on this subject is to the following effect: "The synod considering the present alarming state of public affairs, do unanimously judge it their duty to call all the congregations under their care, to solemn fasting, humiliation, and prayer; and for this purpose appoint the last Thursday of June next to be carefully and religiously observed. But as the Continental congress are now sitting, who may probably appoint a fast for the same purpose, the synod, from respect to that august body, and for greater harmony with other denominations, and for the greater public order, if the congress shall appoint a day not above four weeks distant from the said last Thursday of June, order that the congregations belonging to this synod, do keep the day appointed by congress in obedience to this resolution; and if they appoint a day more distant, the synod order both to be observed by all our communion. The synod also earnestly recommend it to all the congregations under their care, to spend the afternoon of the last Thursday in every month, in public solemn prayer to God, during the continuance of our present troubles." (Minutes, p. 317) This recommendation of the observance of a day for prayer every month, was frequently repeated during the war.

In this memorable year also, the synod addressed a long and excellent letter to the churches. It thus begins: "The synod of New York and Philadelphia, being met at a time when public affairs wear so threatening an aspect, and when, unless God in his sovereign providence speedily prevent it, all the horrors of a civil war throughout this great continent are to be apprehended, were of opinion that they could not discharge their duty to the numerous congregations under their care, without addressing them at this important crisis. As the firm belief and habitual recollection of the power and presence of the living God, ought at all times to possess the minds of real Christians; so in seasons of public calamity, when the Lord is known by the judgments which he executeth, it would be an ignorance or indifference highly criminal, not to look up to him with reverence, to implore his mercy by humble and fervent prayer, and if possible, to prevent his vengeance, by timely repentance. We do, therefore brethren beseech you, in the most earnest manner, to look beyond the immediate authors, either of your sufferings or fears, and to acknowledge the holiness and justice of the Almighty in the present visitation." The synod then exhort the people to confession and repentance;

reminding them that their prayers should be attended with a sincere purpose and thorough endeavour after personal and family reformation. "If thou prepare thine heart and stretch out thine hand towards him, if iniquity be in thine hands put it far away, and let not wickedness dwell in thy tabernacles."

They considered it also a proper time to press on all of every rank, seriously to consider the things which belong to their eternal peace, saying, "Hostilities long feared, have now taken place; the sword has been drawn in one province; and the whole continent, with hardly any exception, seem determined to defend their rights by force of arms. If at the same time the British ministry shall continue to enforce their claims by violence, a lasting and bloody contest must be expected. Surely then it becomes those who have taken up arms, and profess a willingness to hazard their lives in the cause of liberty, to be prepared for death, which to many must be certain, and to every one is a possible or probable event.

"We have long seen with concern, the circumstances which occasioned, and the gradual increase of this unhappy difference. As ministers of the gospel of peace, we have ardently wished that it might be, and often hoped that it would have been more early accommodated. It is well known to you, otherwise it would be imprudent indeed thus publicly to profess, that we have not been instrumental in inflaming the minds of the people, or urging them to acts of violence and disorder. Perhaps no instance can be given on so interesting a subject, in which political sentiments have been so long and fully kept from the pulpit; and even malice itself has not charged us with labouring from the press. But things have now come to such a state, that as we do not wish to conceal our opinions as men and citizens, so the relation in which we stand to you, seemed to make the present improvement of it to your spiritual benefit, an indispensable duty."

Then follows an exhortation directed principally to young men, who might offer themselves as "champions of their country's cause," to cultivate piety, to reverence the name of God, and to trust his providence. "The Lord is with you while ye be with him; and if ye seek him, he will be found of you; but if ye forsake him, he will forsake you."

After this exhortation the synod offered special counsels to the churches as to their public and general conduct.

"*First:* In carrying on this important struggle, let every opportunity be taken to express your attachment and respect to our sovereign King George, and to the revolution principles by which his august family was seated on the British throne. We recommend, indeed, not only allegiance to him from principle and duty, as the first magistrate of the empire, but esteem and reverence for the person of the prince, who has merited well of his subjects on many accounts, and who has probably been misled into his late and present measures by those about him; neither have we any doubt, that they themselves have been in a great degree deceived by false representations from interested persons residing in America. It gives us the greatest pleasure to say, from our own certain knowledge of all belonging to our communion, and from the best means of information of far the greatest part of all denominations in this country, that the present opposition to the measures of administration, does not in the least arise from disaffection to the king, or a desire of separation from the parent state. We are happy in being able with truth to affirm, that no part of America would either have approved or permitted such insults as have been offered to the sovereign in Great Britain. We exhort you, therefore, to continue in the same disposition and not to suffer oppression or injury itself easily to provoke you to any thing which may seem to betray contrary sentiments. Let it ever appear that you only desire the preservation and security of those rights which belong to you as freemen and Britons, and that reconciliation upon these terms is your most ardent desire.

"*Secondly,* be careful to maintain the union which at present subsists through all the colonies. Nothing can be more manifest than that the success of every measure depends on its being inviolably preserved; and, therefore, we hope you will leave nothing undone which can promote that end. In particular, as the continental congress, now sitting at Philadelphia, consists of delegates chosen in the most free and unbiassed manner, by the body of the people, let them not only be treated with respect, and encouraged in their difficult service; not only let your prayers be offered up to God for his direction in their proceedings, but adhere firmly to their resolutions; and let it be seen that they are able to bring out the whole strength of this vast country to carry them into execution. We would also advise for the same purpose, that a spirit of candour, charity, and mutual esteem be preserved and promoted towards those of different religious denominations. Persons of probity and principle of every profession, should be united together as servants of the same Master;

and the experience of our happy concord hitherto in a state of liberty, should engage all to unite in support of the common interest; for there is no example in history in which civil liberty was destroyed, and the rights of conscience preserved entire.

"*Thirdly,* we do earnestly exhort and beseech the societies under our care to be strict and vigilant in their private government, and to watch over the morals of their several members." This duty is urged at some length, and then the letter proceeds thus:

"*Fourthly,* we cannot but recommend and urge in the warmest manner, a regard to order and the public peace; and as in many places, during the confusion that prevails, legal proceedings have become difficult, it is hoped that all persons will conscientiously pay their just debts, and to the utmost of their power serve one another, so that the evils inseparable from a civil war, may not be augmented by wantonness and irregularity.

"*Fifthly,* we think it of importance at this time, to recommend to all of every rank, but especially to those who may be called to action, a spirit of humanity and mercy. Every battle of the warrior is with confused noise and garments rolled in blood. It is impossible to appeal to the sword without being exposed to many scenes of cruelty and slaughter; but it is often observed that civil wars are carried on with a rancour and spirit of revenge much greater than those between independent states. The injuries received or supposed, in civil wars, wound more deeply than those of foreign enemies. It is, therefore, more necessary to guard against this abuse, and recommend that meekness and gentleness of spirit which is the noblest attendant on true valour. That man will fight most bravely who never begins to fight till it is necessary, and who ceases to fight as soon as the necessity is over.

"*Lastly,* we would recommend to all the societies under our care, not to content themselves with attending devoutly on general fasts, but to continue habitually in the exercise of prayer, and to have frequent occasional voluntary meetings for solemn intercession with God on this important trial. Those who are immediately exposed to danger need your sympathy; and we learn from the Scriptures, that fervency and importunity are the very characters of that prayer of the righteous man that availeth much. We conclude with our most earnest prayer, that the God of heaven may bless you in your temporal and spiritual concerns, and that the present unnatural dispute may be speedily terminated by an equitable

and lasting settlement on constitutional principles."

The Rev. Mr. Halsey, it is recorded, dissented from that paragraph of the above letter, which contains the declarations of allegiance. This gentleman, it seems, was at least a year in advance, not only of the synod, but of congress. This pastoral letter contains a decided and unanimous expression, on the part of the synod, of the side which it took in the great struggle for the liberties of America. It certainly does them and the church which they represented, great honour. They adhered to the last to the duties which they owed their sovereign; they approved of demanding no new liberties; they required only the secure possession of privileges which they were entitled to consider as their birth-right.

A month after the publication of this letter the presbyterian clergymen of Philadelphia, published an address to the ministers and presbyterian congregations of the county of ——, in North Carolina. It seems that there were some presbyterians in that province, who hesitated as to the course which they ought to take in the coming conflict. This is the more to be wondered at, as North Carolina was in advance of almost any province on the continent in its opposition to the British authorities. They had already driven away their governor, and set up a government of their own; and on the 20th of May, 1775, was issued the famous Mecklenburg declaration of independence, more than a year before congress ventured upon that step. The name of the county is left blank in the title page of this address. The Philadelphia ministers say to their North Carolina brethren: "It adds greatly to our distress to hear that you are some how led aside from the cause of liberty and freedom, by men who have given you an unfair representation of the debate between the parent country and her colonies." They make strong professions of loyalty, and appeal to the declarations of congress on the subject; and add, "We want no new privileges; let us continue connected with them as we were before the stamp act, and we demand no more." They refer also to the pastoral letter of the synod, which they beg their brethren to read. They then recount the grievances of the country, especially the claim on the part of the British parliament, of the power "to make laws to bind us in all cases whatsoever. By virtue of this power," it is added, "they have established popery in Quebec, and the arbitrary laws of France, and why may they not do the same in Pennsylvania or North Carolina?" "What shall we then do," it is asked, "in these days of trouble and distress? We must put our trust in God, who is a present help in the time of trouble; but we must depend on him in the use of means; we must unite, if possible, as one man, to maintain our just rights; not by fire and sword, or by shedding the blood of our fellow subjects, unless we are driven to it in self-defence, but by strictly observing such resolutions neither to export nor import goods, as may be recommended by our general congress." Signed July 10th, by Francis Alison, James Sproat, George Duffield, and Robert Davidson.

The presbytery of Hanover, in a memorial presented to the legislature of Virginia in 1776 expressed with earnestness their hearty adoption of their country's cause. "Your memorialists," they say, "are governed by the same sentiments which have inspired the United States of America; and are determined that nothing in our power or influence shall be wanting to give success to their common cause. We would also represent that dissenters from the church of England, in this country, have ever been desirous to conduct themselves as peaceable members of the civil government, for which reason they have hitherto submitted to several ecclesiastical burdens and restrictions, that are inconsistent with equal liberty. But now when the many and grievous oppressions of our mother country have laid this continent under the necessity of casting off the yoke of tyranny, and of forming independent governments upon equitable and liberal founda-tions, we flatter ourselves we shall be freed from all the incumbrances which a spirit of domina-tion, prejudice, or bigotry, hath interwoven with our political systems. This we are the more strongly encouraged to expect, by the declaration of rights, so universally applauded for that dignity, firmness, and precision with which it delineates and asserts the privileges of society, and the prerogatives of human nature, and which we embrace as the magna charta of our com-monwealth, that can never be violated without endangering the grand superstructure it was des-tined to sustain." (*Presbyterian Church in Vir-ginia, by Dr. J. H. Rice, p. 21*)

As at the beginning, so also at the close of the war, the synod directed a pastoral letter to their congregations expressing their sentiments in rela-tion to the contest. In the letter written in 1783, they say: "We cannot help congratulating you on the general and almost universal attachment of the presbyterian body, to the cause of liberty and the rights of mankind. This has been visible in their conduct, and has been confessed by the com-plaints and resentment of the common enemy. Such a circumstance ought not only to afford us satisfaction on the review, as bringing credit to the body in general, but to increase our gratitude to God for the happy issue of the war. Had it been unsuccessful, we must have drunk deeply of the cup of suffering. Our burnt and wasted churches, and our plundered dwellings, in such places as fell under the power of our adversaries, are but an earnest of what we must have suf-fered, had they finally prevailed.

"The synod, therefore, request you to render thanks to Almighty God, for all his mercies spir-itual and temporal; and in a particular manner for establishing the independence of the United States of America. He is the supreme disposer, and to Him belong the glory, the victory, and the majesty. We are persuaded you will easily recollect many circumstances in the course of the struggle, which point out his special and sig-nal interposition in our favour. Our most remark-able successes have generally been when things had just before worn the most unfavourable as-pect; as at Trenton and Saratoga at the begin-ning, in South Carolina and Virginia towards the end of the war." They specify among other mer-cies the assistance derived from France, and the happy selection "of a commander in chief of the armies of the United States, who, in this impor-tant and difficult charge, has given universal satis-faction, who was alike acceptable to the citizen and the soldier, to the state in which he was born, and to every other on the continent; and whose character and influence, after so long service, are not only unimpaired but augmented." . . .

The effects of the revolutionary war on the state of our church were extensively and variously disastrous. The young men were called from the seclusion of their homes to the demoralizing at-mosphere of a camp; congregations were broken up; churches were burnt, and in more than one instance pastors were murdered; the usual min-isterial intercourse and efforts for the dissemina-tion of the gospel, were in a great measure sus-pended, and public morals in various respects de-teriorated. From these effects it took the church a considerable time to recover; but she shared, through the blessing of God, in the returning health and prosperity of the country, and has since grown with the growth, and strengthened with the strength, of our highly favoured nation.

CHRISTIAN
CONSTITUENT:

THE AMERICAN
CHRISTIAN
CHURCH

*Systematic
Theology,* by
Charles Hodge,
1871

THE FOURTH COMMANDMENT

The design of the fourth commandment was, (1) To commemorate the work of creation. The people were commanded to remember the Sabbath-day and to keep it holy, because in six days God had made the heavens and the earth. (2) To preserve alive the knowledge of the only living and true God. If heaven and earth, that is, the universe, were created, they must have had a creator; and that creator must be extramundane, existing before, out of, and independently of the world. He must be almighty, and infinite in knowledge, wisdom, and goodness; for all these attributes are necessary to account for the wonders of the heavens and the earth. So long, therefore, as men believe in creation, they must believe in God. This accounts for the fact that so much stress is laid upon the right observance of the Sabbath. Far more importance is attributed to that observance than to any merely ceremonial institution. (3) This command was designed to arrest the current of the outward life of the people and to turn their thoughts to the unseen and spiritual. Men are so prone to be engrossed by the things of this world that it was, and is, of the highest importance that there should be one day of frequent recurrence on which they were forbidden to think of the things of the world, and forced to think of the things unseen and eternal. (4) It was intended to afford time for the instruction of the people, and for the public and special worship of God. (5) By the prohibition of all servile labour, whether of man or beast, it was designed to secure recuperative rest for those on whom the primeval curse had fallen: *"In the sweat of thy face shalt thou eat bread."* (6) As a day of rest and as set apart for intercourse with God, it was designed to be a type of that rest which remains for the people of God, as we learn from Psalms xcv. 11, as expounded by the Apostle in Hebrews iv. 1–10. (7) As the observance of the Sabbath had died out among the nations, it was solemnly reenacted under the Mosaic dispensation to be a sign of the covenant between God and the children of Israel. They were to be distinguished as the Sabbath-keeping people among all the nations of the earth, and as such were to be the recipients of God's special blessings. . . .

It is very common, especially for foreign-born citizens, to object to all laws made by the civil governments in this country to prevent the public violation of the Lord's Day. It is urged that as there is in the United States an entire separation of the Church and State, it is contrary to the genius of our institutions, that the observance of any religious institution should be enforced by civil laws. It is further objected that as all citizens have equal rights irrespective of their religious opinions, it is an infringement of those rights if one class of the people are required to conform their conduct to the religious opinions of another class. Why should Jews, Mohammedans, or infidels be required to respect the Christian Sabbath? Why should any man, who has no faith in the Sabbath as a divine institution, be prevented from doing on that day whatever is lawful on other days? If the State may require the people to respect Sunday as a day of rest, why may it not require the people to obey any or all other precepts of the Bible?

STATE OF THE QUESTION

It is conceded, (1) That in every free country every man has equal rights with his fellow-citizens, and stands on the same ground in the eye of the law. (2) That in the United States no form of religion can be established; that no religious test for the exercise of the elective franchise or for holding of office can be imposed; and that no preference can be given to the members of one religious denomination above those of another. (3) That no man can be forced to contribute to the support of any church, or of any religious institution. (4) That every man is at liberty to regulate his conduct and life according to his convictions or conscience, provided he does not violate the law of the land.

On the other hand it is no less true,—

1. That a nation is not a mere conglomeration of individuals. It is an organized body. It has of necessity its national life, its national organs, national principles of action, national character, and national responsibility.

2. In every free country the government must, in its organization and mode of action, be an expression of the mind and will of the people.

3. As men are rational creatures, the government cannot banish all sense and reason from their action, because there may be idiots among the people.

4. As men are moral beings, it is impossible that the government should act as though there were no distinction between right and wrong. It cannot legalize theft and murder. No matter how much it might enrich itself by rapine or by the extermination of other nations, it would deserve and receive universal condemnation and execration, should it thus set at nought the bonds of moral obligation. This necessity of obedience to the moral law on the part of civil governments, does not arise from the fact that they are instituted for the protection of the lives, rights, and property of the people. Why have our own and other Christian nations pronounced the slave-trade piracy and punishable with death? Not because it interferes with the rights or liberty of their citizens but because it is wicked. Cruelty to animals is visited with civil penalties, not on the principle of profit and loss, but because it is a violation of the moral law. As it is impossible for the individual man to disregard all moral obligations, it is no less impossible on the part of civil governments.

5. Men moreover are religious beings. They can no more ignore that element of their nature than their reason or their conscience. It is no matter what they may say, or may pretend to think, the law which binds them to allegiance to God, is just as inexorable as the law of gravitation. They can no more emancipate themselves from the one than they can from the other. Morality concerns their duty to their fellow-men; religion concerns their duty to God. The latter binds the conscience as much as the former. It attends the man everywhere. It must influence his conduct as an individual, as the head of a family, as a man of business, as a legislator, and as an executive officer. It is absurd to say that civil governments, have nothing to do with religion. That is not true even of a fire company, or of a manufactory, or of a banking-house. The religion embraced by the individuals composing these associations must influence their corporate action, as well as their individual conduct. If a man may not blaspheme, a publishing firm may not print and disseminate a blasphemous book. A civil government cannot ignore religion any more than physiology. It was not constituted to teach either the one or the other, but it must, by a like necessity, conform its action to the laws of both. Indeed it would be far safer for a government to pass an act violating the laws of health, than one violating the religious convictions of its citizens. The one would be unwise, the other would be tyrannical. Men put up with folly, with more patience than they do with injustice. It is vain for the potsherds of the earth to contend with their Maker. They must submit to the laws of their nature not only as sentient, but also as moral and religious beings. And it is time that blatant atheists, whether communists, scientists, or philosophers, should know that they are as much and as justly the objects of pity and contempt, as of indignation to all right-minded men. By right-minded men, is meant men who think, feel, and act according to the laws of their nature. Those laws are ordained, administered, and enforced by God, and there is no escape from their obligation, or from the penalties attached to their violation.

6. The people of this country being rational, moral, and religious beings, the government must be administered on the principles of reason, morality, and religion. By a like necessity of right, the people being Christians and Protestants, the government must be administered according to the principles of Protestant Christianity. By this is not meant that the government should teach Christianity, or make the profession of it a condition of citizenship, or a test for office. Nor does it mean that the government is called upon to punish every violation of Christian principle or precept. It is not called upon to punish every violation of the moral law. But as it cannot violate the moral law in its own action, or require the people to violate it, so neither can it ignore Christianity in its official action. It cannot require the people or any of its own officers to do what Christianity forbids, nor forbid their doing anything which Christianity enjoins. It has no more right to forbid that the Bible should be taught in the public schools, than it has to enjoin that the Koran should be taught in them. If Christianity requires that one day in seven should be a day of rest from all worldly avocations, the government of a Christian people cannot require any class of the community or its own officers to labour on that day, except in cases of necessity or mercy. Should it, on the ground that it had nothing to do with religion, disregard that day, and direct that the custom-houses, the courts of law, and the legislative halls should be open on the Lord's Day, and public business be transacted as on other days, it would be an act of tyranny, which would justify rebellion. It would be tantamount to enacting that no Christian should hold any office under the government, or have any share in making or administering the laws of the country. The nation would be in complete subjection to a handful of imported atheists and infidels.

PROOF THAT THIS IS A CHRISTIAN AND A PROTESTANT NATION

The proposition that the United States of America are a Christian and Protestant nation, is not so much the assertion of a principle as the statement of a fact. That fact is not simply that the great majority of the people are Christians and Protestants, but that the organic life, the institutions, laws, and official action of the government, whether that action be legislative, judicial, or executive, is, and of right should be, and in fact must be, in accordance with the principles of Protestant Christianity.

1. This is a Christian and Protestant nation in the sense stated in virtue of a universal and necessary law. If you plant an acorn, you get an oak. If you plant a cedar, you get a cedar. If a country be settled by Pagans or Mohammedans, it develops into a Pagan or Mohammedan community. By the same law, if a country be taken possession of and settled by Protestant Christians, the nation which they come to constitute must be Protestant and Christian. This country was settled by Protestants. For the first hundred years of our history they constituted almost the only element of our population. As a matter of course they were governed by their religion as individuals, in their families, and in all their associations for business, and for municipal, state, and national government. This was just as much a matter of necessity as that they should act morally in all these different relations.

2. It is a historical fact that Protestant Christianity is the law of the land, and has been from the beginning. As the great majority of the early settlers of the country were from Great Britain, they declared that the common law of England should be the law here. But Christianity is the basis of the common law of England, and is therefore of the law of this country; and so our courts have repeatedly decided. It is so not merely because of such decisions. Courts cannot reverse facts. Protestant Christianity has been, is, and must be the law of the land. Whatever Protestant Christianity forbids, the law of the land (within its sphere, i.e., within the sphere in which civil authority may appropriately act) forbids. Christianity forbids polygamy and arbitrary divorce, so does the civil law. Romanism forbids divorce even on the ground of adultery; Protestantism admits it on that ground. The laws of all the states conform in this matter to the Protestant rule. Christianity forbids all unnecessary labour, or the transaction of worldly business, on the Lord's Day; that day accordingly is a *dies non,* throughout the land. No contract is binding, made on that day. No debt can be collected on the Christian Sabbath. If a man hires himself for any service by the month or year, he cannot be required to labour on that day. All public offices are closed, and all official business is suspended. From Maine to Georgia, from ocean to ocean, one day in the week, by the law of God and by the law of the land, the people rest.

THIS CONTROLLING INFLUENCE OF CHRISTIANITY IS REASONABLE AND RIGHT

It is in accordance with analogy. If a man goes to China, he expects to find the government administered according to the religion of the country. If he goes to Turkey, he expects to find the Koran supreme and regulating all public action. If he goes to a Protestant country, he has no right to complain, should he find the Bible in the ascendancy and exerting its benign influence not only on the people, but also on the government.

The principle that the religion of a people rightfully controls the action of the government, has of course its limitations. If the religion itself be evil and require what is morally wrong, then as men cannot have the right to act wickedly, it is plain that it would be wrong for the government to conform to its requirements. If a religion should enjoin infanticide, or the murder of the aged or infirm, neither the people nor the government should conform their conduct to its laws. But where the religion of a people requires nothing unjust or cruel or in any way immoral, then those who come to live where it prevails are bound to submit quietly to its controlling the laws and institutions of the country.

The principle contended for is recognized in all other departments of life. If a number of Christian men associate themselves as a manufacturing or banking company, it would be competent for them to admit unbelievers in Christianity into their association, and to allow them their full share in its management and control. But it would be utterly unreasonable for such unbelievers to set up a cry of religious persecution, or of infringement of their rights and liberty, because all the business of the company was suspended upon the Lord's Day. These new members knew the character and principles of those with whom they sought to be associated. They knew that Christians would assert their right to act as Christians. To require them to renounce their religion would be simply preposterous.

When Protestant Christians came to this country they possessed and subdued the land. They worshipped God, and his Son Jesus Christ as the Saviour of the world, and acknowledged the Scriptures to be the rule of their faith and practice. They introduced their religion into their families, their schools, and their colleges. They abstained from all ordinary business on the Lord's Day, and devoted it to religion. They built churches, erected school-houses, and taught their children to read the Bible and to receive and obey it as the word of God. They formed themselves as Christians into municipal and state organizations. They acknowledged God in their legislative assemblies. They prescribed oaths to be taken in his name. They closed their courts, their places of business, their legislatures, and all places under the public control, on the Lord's Day. They declared Christianity to be part of the common law of the land. In the process of time thousands have come among us, who are neither Protestants nor Christians. Some are papists, some Jews, some infidels, and some atheists. All are welcomed; all are admitted to equal rights and privileges. All are allowed to acquire property, and to vote in every election, made eligible to all offices, and invested with equal influence in all public affairs. All are allowed to worship as they please, or not to worship at all, if they see fit. No man is molested for his religion or for his want of religion. No man is required to profess any form of faith, or to join any religious association. More than this cannot reasonably be demanded. More, however, is demanded. The infidel demands that the government should be conducted on the principle that Christianity is false. The atheist demands that it should be conducted on the assumption that there is no God, and the positivist on the principle that men are not free agents. The sufficient answer to all this is, that it cannot possibly be done.

THE DEMANDS OF INFIDELS ARE UNJUST

The demands of those who require that religion, and especially Christianity, should be ignored in our national, state, and municipal laws, are not only unreasonable, but they are in the highest degree unjust and tyrannical. It is a condition of service in connection with any railroad which is operated on Sundays, that the employee be not a Christian. If Christianity is not to control the action of our municipal, state, and general governments, then if elections be ordered to be held on the Lord's Day, Christians cannot vote.

If all the business of the country is to go on, on that as on other days, no Christian can hold office. We should thus have not a religious, but an anti-religious test-act. Such is the free-thinker's idea of liberty.* But still further, if Christianity is not to control the laws of the country, then as monogamy is a purely Christian institution, we can have no laws against polygamy, arbitrary divorce, or "free love." All this must be yielded to the anti-Christian party; and consistency will demand that we yield to the atheists, the oath and the decalogue; and all the rights of citizenship must be confined to blasphemers. Since the fall of Lucifer, no such tyrant has been made known to men as August Comte, the atheist. If, therefore, any man wishes to antedate perdition, he has nothing to do but to become a freethinker and join in the shout, "Civil government has nothing to do with religion; and religion has nothing to do with civil government."

CONCLUSION

We are bound, therefore, to insist upon the maintenance and faithful execution of the laws enacted for the protection of the Christian Sabbath. Christianity does not teach that men can be made religious by law; nor does it demand that men should be required by the civil-authority to profess any particular form of religious doctrine, or to attend upon religious services; but it does enjoin that men should abstain from all unnecessary worldly avocations on the Lord's Day. This civil Sabbath, this cessation from worldly business, is what the civil government in Christian countries is called upon to enforce. (1) Because it is the right of Christians to be allowed to rest on that day, which they cannot do, without forfeiting their citizenship, unless all public business be arrested on that day. (2) Because such rest is the command of God; and this command binds the conscience as much as any other command in the decalogue. So far as the point in hand is concerned, it matters not whether such be the command of God or not; so long as the people believe it, it binds their conscience; and this conscientious belief the government is bound to respect, and must act accordingly. (3) Because the civil Sabbath is necessary for the preservation of our free institutions, and of the good order of society. The indispensable condition of social order is either des-

---

* A free-thinker is a man whose understanding is emancipated from his conscience. It is therefore natural for him to wish to see civil government emancipated from religion.

CHRISTIAN
CONSTITUENT:

────────

THE AMERICAN
CHRISTIAN
CHURCH

potic power in the magistrate, or good morals among the people.

Morality without religion is impossible; religion cannot exist without knowledge; knowledge cannot be disseminated among the people, unless there be a class of teachers, and time allotted for their instruction. Christ has made all his ministers, teachers; He has commanded them to teach all nations; He has appointed one day in seven to be set apart for such instruction. It is a historical fact that since the introduction of Christianity, nine tenths of the people have derived the greater part of their religious knowledge from the services of the sanctuary.

If the Sabbath, therefore, be abolished, the fountain of life for the people will be sealed.

The Protestant Episcopal Church in America 1688 to 1775

To those who have learned to value rightly the importance of Christian unity, it will be no matter of surprise to hear, that in this divided land the Church of Christ could not flourish. So plain, in truth, had become the features of moral and religious evil in our Transatlantic colonies at the close of the seventeenth century, that the slightest observation of them at once startled good men at home, and led them to immediate action. Amongst the first of these were Sir Leoline Jenkins and the Hon. Robert Boyle; the first of whom left by will a foundation for two fellowships at Jesus College, Oxford, to be held by persons in holy orders who should be willing to take upon them the cure of souls in our foreign plantations; and the other, after undertaking to conduct a company in 1661, for the propagation of the Gospel amongst the heathen natives of New England, left an annual sum to support the lectures which to this day bear his name, that, "being dead," he might "still speak" to all succeeding generations of this great duty of converting infidels to the true faith of Christ.

VIRGINIA AND MARYLAND

From these beginnings other efforts followed. In the year 1685, the Bishop of London persuaded Dr. Blair to go as his commissary to Virginia.

For fifty-three years he held this office, and zealously discharged its duties. By him the long-neglected project of training for the ministry the English and Indian youth was happily revived, and through his unwearied labours brought at last to a successful close in the establishment of the college of "William and Mary."

The appointment of Dr. Blair was shortly followed by the nomination of Dr. Bray as commissary in Maryland.

This colony was originally founded by settlers of the Roman Catholic persuasion, but with the free allowance of all other forms of worship; and it is well worthy of remark, that at the very time when Puritan Massachusetts was persecuting to the death all who disagreed with the dominant sect, the governors of Maryland were bound by an annual oath, not "by themselves, or indirectly, to trouble, molest, or discountenance any person professing to believe in Jesus Christ, for or in respect of religion; and if any such were so molested, to protect the person molested, and punish the offender." On this basis things continued until the time of the Great Rebellion. Settlers of various views in matters of religion had been received and protected in the colony. But as soon as the government was wrested from the hands of the Lord Baltimore by the adherents of the parliament, and the Inde-

A History of the Protestant Episcopal Church in America, by Samuel Wilberforce, Lord Bishop of Oxford, London, 1853

pendents thereby made its masters, they repealed these laws of universal toleration, and proscribed entirely "popery and prelacy." It is not a little striking, that the first enactment in the statute-book of Maryland, which forbade to any one the free exercise of that which he believed to be the true form of Christian worship, should have been introduced by such fierce pretenders to religious liberty as the Independents.

So, however, it was; and such the law continued until the fall of Cromwell's party. With the Restoration, Lord Baltimore regained his rights as owner of the colony, and for a season all proceeded on its former plan. But a shock had been given to the old constitution; and the troubles which from time to time disturbed society at home, soon extended to the colony, and took there the same direction. The mass of the population were by this time Protestant; and as during the reigns of Charles and James II., fears of popery were the mainsprings of disturbances in England, Maryland, now brought anew under the rule of a Roman Catholic proprietor, was a favourable theatre for such commotions. Accordingly, the accession of William and Mary to the English throne was, after some preparatory troubles, followed by the overthrow of Lord Baltimore's authority, and the substitution in his stead of a royal governor. This change was succeeded by an act of assembly, which, in 1692, established the Church of England as the religion of the colony; divided its territory into parishes; and endowed its clergy with an income to be derived from the payment of forty pounds of tobacco by every taxable person in the province. To the operation of this law, the opponents of the Church created various hindrances. The Romanists and Quakers,—who abounded in the colony, and both looked on such a law as most injurious to themselves,—united in their opposition to it; and sometimes by colonial resistance, sometimes by misrepresentation to the government at home, they long delayed its execution.

At this critical period, the clergy, feeling their weakness, and seeing that it was in great part owing to that want of union, of which the presence of their proper head is so great a spring and safeguard, besought the Bishop of London to send them at least a commissary, clothed with such power as should "capacitate him to redress what is amiss, and supply what is wanting, in the Church." The bishop assented to their wishes; and most happy was his choice. Dr. Thomas Bray, his first commissary in Maryland, was a man of rare devotion, joined to an invincible

energy in action. He abandoned willingly the prospect of large English preferment, to nourish the infant Church in the spiritual wastes of Maryland. No sooner had he accepted the appointment than he set himself to contrive means for fulfilling all its duties. His first care was to find pious and useful ministers, whom he could persuade to settle with him on the other side of the Atlantic; and in this he so far prospered as to increase the number labouring there from three to sixteen clergymen. He began also the formation of colonial libraries; and in the course of his exertions in this work, was led on to still greater efforts. He perceived the need and the fitness of the co-operation of all ranks of Churchmen in such attempts; and having once conceived this idea, he rested not until he had laid the foundation of the Society for Promoting Christian Knowledge, and that for the Propagation of the Gospel in Foreign Parts.

In all these labours he was indefatigable. No difficulties daunted him. Finding, in the course of his preparations, that he required the personal consent of the king to some proposed arrangements, he undertook at once, and at his own expense, a voyage to Holland, where the monarch then was. In a like spirit he acted throughout; for some years he continued patiently completing his preparations in England, though his salary as commissary did not begin until he sailed for Maryland. At length, on the 12th of March, 1700, after a tedious voyage, he reached the land of his adoption. Here he soon displayed the like activity. He assembled the clergy at visitations—instructed them by charges—and enforced discipline, to the utmost of his means, against any of bad lives. . . .

What the results of such zeal might have been, if, instead of being a delegated representative of a distant prelate, Dr. Bray had himself been appointed bishop in Maryland, it is impossible to calculate. As it was, the efforts, which depended wholly on his individual zeal, instead of springing ever fresh out of the system of the Church, scarcely outlived his own stay in Maryland. This was necessarily short. The opposition made to the established rights of the colonial clergy called for his presence at headquarters, where the Quakers and Romanists were active and united; and he returned to England to maintain the cause of his afflicted community. Upon his departure religion comparatively languished, from the weakness of its imperfect planting, and the uncorrected evil lives of some among the clergy. Still, in spite of all hindrances, the Church gained some ground; and a majority of the colony, now increased to 30,000, were accounted of her communion.

NEW YORK AND NEW ENGLAND—SOCIETY FOR THE PROPAGATION OF THE GOSPEL INCORPORATED

Nor was this rising energy confined to Maryland. There was a stir also in the other provinces. New Amsterdam, or New York, as it was termed after its conquest by the English, was finally ceded by the Dutch, at the treaty of Breda, in 1667. This change of masters transferred at once the garrison-chapel to the use of the Church of England. Within these narrow walls it was limited for many years, until, in 1696, another church was built under the name of "Trinity," and endowed temporarily by Governor Fletcher, and in perpetuity by his successor the Lord Cornbury, with the freehold of a neighbouring property, known hitherto as the "King's Farm." Even in New England, in spite of penal laws, which rigidly prohibited any "ministry or Church-administration, in any town or plantation of the colony, separate from that which is openly observed and dispensed by the approved minister of the place," a movement began towards the long-despised Church of England.

In 1679 a petition, from a large body of persons in their chief town of Boston, was presented to King Charles II., praying "that a church might be allowed in that city for the exercise of religion according to the Church of England." This request was granted, and a church erected for the purpose, bearing the name of "the King's Chapel." Far more considerable matters followed the inquiry which this step occasioned. It was found, that throughout all that populous district there were but four who called themselves ministers of the Church of England; and but two of these who had been regularly sent forth to the work. This was a state of things which could not be endured; and by a happy movement, of which Dr. Bray was in great measure the suggestor, the bishops of the Church set themselves to find some means for its correction. They determined to associate themselves into a body for this purpose, with such devout members of the laity and clergy as God should incline to join them in their work of mercy. They issued their address to the community, and were joined by ready hearts on all sides; so that, having applied for and obtained a charter of incorporation, they met for despatch of business, as the Society for the Propagation of the Gospel, in June 1701, under the Archbishop of Canterbury as their president. Many great names in the English Church appear in the catalogue of their first and warmest supporters, amongst the chief of whom were Bishop Beveridge, Archbishops Wake and Sharp, and Bishops Gibson and Berkeley.

Funds soon flowed in upon them from every quarter; but the want to be relieved was greater than the worst returns had stated. England, it was found, had been indeed peopling the new world with colonies of heathens. "There is at this day," is Bishop Berkeley's declaration somewhat later, "but little sense of religion, and a most notorious corruption of manners, in the English colonies settled on the continent of America." (A "Proposal for better supplying of Churches in our Foreign Plantations," published in 1725) Nor will this language appear overstrained, if it is compared with the numerical returns which the inquiries of the day called forth. For from these it appeared that in "South Carolina there were 7000 souls, besides negroes and Indians, living without any minister of the Church . . . and above half the people living regardless of any religion. In North Carolina about 5000 souls without any minister, any administrations used; no public worship celebrated; neither the children baptised, nor the dead buried, in any Christian form. Virginia contained above 40,000 souls, divided into 40 parishes, but wanting near half the number of clergymen requisite. Maryland contained above 25,000, divided into 26 parishes, but wanting near half the number of ministers requisite. In Pennsylvania (says Col. Heathcote) there are at least 20,000 souls, of which not above 700 frequent the church, and there are not more than 250 communicants. In New York government we have 30,000 souls at least, of which about 1200 frequent the church, and we have about 450 communicants. In Connecticut there are about 30,800 souls; of which, when they have a minister among them, about 150 frequent the church, and there are 35 communicants. In Rhode Island and Narraganset there are about 10,000 souls, of which about 150 frequent the church, and there are 30 communicants. In Boston and Piscataway there are about 80,000 souls, of which about 600 frequent the church, and 120 the sacrament.

This is the true, though melancholy, state of our Church in North America." (Humphrey's History of the Society for the Propagation of the Gospel, p. 41, &c. These figures, however, it must be borne in mind, give the numbers of the Church of

England; not of the whole Christian population.)

Nor are these merely the accounts of episcopalian writers. Cotton Mather describes the state of Rhode Island colony in 1695, as "a colluvies of Antinomians, Familists, Anabaptists, Antisabbatarians, Arminians, Socinians, Quakers, Ranters, and everything but Roman Catholics and true Christians; *bona terra, mala gens.*" Such was, within little more than fifty years, the fruit of founding a people on the specious attempt of making "no man a delinquent for doctrine:" not in its true sense, of abandoning all hope of forcing men to trust in Christ by penalties and statutes, but in its most false sense, of treating them as if they were not themselves indeed responsible for their belief; of maintaining no external system of faith, but counting that as true to every man which he was pleased to gather for himself in the boundless waste of unauthorised opinion; of resting truth upon the shifting sand-bank of opinion, and not on the sure rock of revelation.

How far such a population could act as an outpost of the faith may be easily conceived. What their influence had been amongst their Indian neighbours we are told by Bishop Berkeley, when he says that these, who "formerly were in the compass of one colony many thousands, do not at present amount to one, including every age and sex; and these are all servants of the English, who have contributed more to destroy their bodies by the use of strong liquors, than by any means to improve their minds or save their souls. This slow poison, jointly operating with the small-pox and their wars (but much more destructive than both), have consumed the Indians not only in our colonies, but also far and wide upon our confines. It must be owned, our reformed planters, with respect to the natives and their slaves, might learn from those of the Church of Rome how it is their interest and duty to behave. Both the French and Spaniards . . . take care to instruct both the natives and their negroes in the Popish religion, to the reproach of those who profess a better." (*Bishop Berkeley's Sermon before the Society for the Propagation of the Gospel, 1731*)

GEORGE KEITH

To supply the spiritual necessities of these our sons and daughters, the society addressed itself with zeal. And much, under God's blessing, they accomplished in various quarters. Their choice was guided to many fit and zealous instruments for the performance of this holy work. They sent out clergy, fixed and itinerating, to all the districts except Virginia and Maryland, which were in some degree supplied already through the influence of their old endowments. Many a soul had cause to bless God for the labours of these men; who,—whether they went into the total darkness which had settled down on many districts, or preached to the "Foxian Quakers," who in their zeal for the "teaching of the inward light," were fast losing all remains of Christianity; or amongst the New Englanders, who "consisted chiefly of sectaries of many denominations . . . too many of whom had worn off a serious sense of all religion,"—alike gathered in some converts to the fold. They were indeed in labours abundant. Thus amongst the first was George Keith, who had been himself a Quaker, but was now in English holy orders, and travelled for two years, between 1702 and 1705, through all the governments of England, between North Carolina and Piscataway river in New England, preaching twice on Sundays and week-days; offering up public prayers; disputing with the Quakers; and establishing the Church. "He has done," says a letter of the day, "great service to the Church wherever he has been, by preaching and disputing publicly and from house to house; he has confuted many, especially the Anabaptists, by labour and travail night and day, by writing and printing of books, mostly at his own cost and charge, giving them out freely, which has been very expensive to him. By these means people are much awakened, and their eyes opened to see the good old way; and they are very well pleased to find the Church at last take such care of her children." Two hundred "Quakers or Quakerly-affected" converts he himself baptised with his own hand, besides "divers other dissenters also in Pennsylvania, West and East Jersey, and New York."

These successes were not gained without a sharp conflict. Bitter and grievous are the charges with which the Quakers assailed him. He who sees this sect only in the calm into which it has long since subsided can scarcely conceive the storm and fury with which its early enthusiasm raged. Yet these their old writers every where exhibit. The very index to the life of Fox thus disposes of the English clergy: "They sell the Scriptures—pray by form—are hirelings, tithe-takers, robbers of the people—not ministers of the gospel—plead for sin—dread the man in leathern breeches—are miserable comforters—reproved in the streets—one pleads for adultery—beats friends—are oppressors—persecutors—the devil's counsellors and lawyers."

THE ASCENSION OF OUR LORD
BY BENJAMIN WEST (AMERICAN, 1738-1820)
OIL ON CANVAS, 211 X 114 IN. 1781.
COURTESY OF BOB JONES UNIVERSITY COLLECTION,
GREENVILLE, SOUTH CAROLINA

"... *while they beheld, he was taken up; and a cloud received him out of their sight. And while they looked stedfastly toward heaven as he went up, behold, two men stood by them in white apparel; Which also said, Ye men of Galilee, why stand ye gazing up into heaven? this same Jesus, which is taken up from you into heaven, shall so come in like manner as ye have seen him go into heaven.*" *(Acts 1:9-11)*

He began his ascension in the sight of his disciples, even while they beheld. He vanished out of their sight, in a cloud. By the clouds there is a sort of communication kept up between the upper and lower world, in them the vapours are sent up from the earth, and the dews sent down from heaven; fitly therefore does he ascend in a cloud, who is the Mediator between God and man, by whom God's mercies come down upon us, and our prayers come up to him.

Two angels appeared to them, and delivered them a seasonable message from God. Now we are told what they said to them. To check their curiosity; to confirm their faith concerning Christ's second coming. When we stand gazing and trifling, the consideration of our Master's second coming should quicken and awaken us: and when we stand gazing and trembling, the consideration of it should comfort and encourage us.

Matthew Henry, on the place.

Men of such a temper as these extracts indicate would not easily yield up their past predominance, and there was no extremity of calumny with which they did not visit Keith. They would not hear of granting to Episcopalians the most ordinary toleration. Thus when Dr. Bray endeavored to stir up the voluntary zeal of Christians at home to make some adequate provision for religion in the colonies, his memorial was met by furious invectives from the famous Joseph Wyeth, who declares his object to be "to prevent, if I may, the setting up and establishing a power of persecuting and imposition in the colonies, which would be to the discouragement of the industrious planter," &c. Yet, in spite of all assaults, the truth steadily prevailed. "In Pennsylvania"—was his concluding report—"where there was but one Church-of-England congregation, to wit, at Pennsylvania, of few years' standing, there are now five. At Burlington, in New Jersey, a settled congregation; at Frankfort, in Pennsylvania, the Quakers' meeting is turned into a church; and within these two years thirteen ministers are planted in the northern parts of America." These, and all save the settled clergy of Virginia and Maryland, were the missionaries of the Society, then newly formed, for the Propagation of the Gospel in Foreign Parts. To the labours of that venerable body, throughout a long season of sluggish inactivity and wintry darkness, the colonies of England are indebted for all the spiritual care bestowed upon them by the mother-country. Well did its ministers deserve the honoured name of Christian Missionaries. Theirs were toils too often unrequited, carried on in the face of dangers, loss, and extreme hardships. The hardly settled country was still liable to Indian incursion. The homesteads of the settlers lay far apart from one another, severed by woods, wastes, and morasses, across which, in many places, no better roads were yet carried than an Indian path, with all its uncertainty and danger. Day by day these must be passed by those who discharged in that land the office of the ministry. "In many places also there were great rivers, from one, two, to six, twelve, and fifteen miles over, with no ferry. He that would answer the end of his mission must not only have a good horse, but a good boat and a couple of experienced watermen." . . .

MISSION IN CONNECTICUT

In New England also the Church was rooted amidst storms and opposition. Wherever the missionaries came, "the ministers and magistrates of the Independents were remarkably industrious, going from house to house persuading the people from hearing them, and threatening those who would attend with imprisonment and punishment." At one place a magistrate with officers came to the preacher's lodgings, and in the hearing of the people read a paper, declaring that "in coming among them to establish a new way of worship, he had done an illegal thing, and was now forewarned against preaching any more." Yet here too the good seed was not sown in vain; for in many spots throughout the country devout and abiding congregations of the faithful were gathered under apostolic order.

The movement began, in spite of all precautions, within the walls of Yale College, the stronghold of the Independents. So carefully had this been fenced from such attempts, that its fundamental law prescribed that no student should be allowed instruction in any other system of divinity than such as the trustees appointed; and every one was forced to learn the Assembly's Catechism, and other books of puritanical authority.

For a time the dry metaphysics of this school excluded all healthier learning. But about the year 1711, the agent of the colony in England sent over 800 volumes, amongst which were many of the standard works of the divines of the English Church. These books were eagerly devoured by the hungry students; and amongst the first whom they affected were the rector of the college, Dr. Cutler, and two of its leading tutors, Messrs. Johnson and Brown. They were amongst the most distinguished of the Puritan divines; and their humble adoption of the Church's teaching, their abandonment of their endowments in the college, laying down the ministry which without due warrant they had hitherto discharged, and setting out for England to receive ordination at the bishop's hands,—drew general attention to the subject. Brown fell a victim to the small-pox in England; Cutler suffered severely from the same disease, but recovering, was, with Johnson, ordained to the priesthood, and with him returned, in 1723, to the colony, where their influence ere long was widely felt. Cutler was settled at Boston, and, amidst unceasing persecutions, maintained to the last the standard of the faith. For fifty years of patient toil Johnson laboured earnestly at Stratford.

His answers to the queries issued by the Bishop of London will follow up this history of his ministry, amongst "a people" whom he found "low and poor in fortune, yet very serious and well minded, and ready to entertain any instructions that may forward them in the paths of virtue and truth and godliness."

"Q. How long is it since you went over to the plantations as a missionary?

"A. I arrived upon my charge November 1st, 1723.

"Q. Have you had any other church before you came to that which you now possess; and if you had, what church was it, and how long have you been removed?

"A. I was a teacher in the Presbyterian method at West Haven, about ten miles off from this town; but never was in the service of the Established Church till the honourable society admitted me into their service as missionary.

"Q. Have you been duly licensed by the Bishop of London to officiate as a missionary in the government where you now are?

"A. I was licensed by your lordship to officiate as a missionary in this colony of Connecticut.

"Q. How long have you been inducted into your living?

"A. I was admitted into the honourable society's service in the beginning of January, 1722-3.

"Q. Are you ordinarily resident in the parish to which you have been inducted?

"A. I am constantly resident at Stratford, excepting the time that I am riding about to preach in the neighbouring towns that are destitute of ministers.

"Q. Of what extent is your parish, and how many families are there in it?

"A. The town is nigh ten miles square, and has about 250 or 300 families in it, nigh 50 of which are of the Established Church. But indeed the Episcopal people of all the towns adjacent esteem themselves my parishioners; as at Fairfield about 30 families, the like number at New Town, at West Haven about 10, and sundry in other places.

"Q. Are there any infidels, bond or free, within your parish; and what means are used for their conversion?

"A. There are nigh 200 Indians in the bounds of the town, for whose conversion there are no means used, and the like in many other towns; and many negroes that are slaves in particular families, some of which go to church, but most of them to meeting.

"Q. How oft is divine service performed in your church; and what proportion of the parishioners attend it?

"A. Service is performed only on Sundays and holy-days, and many times 100 or 150 people attend it, but sometimes not half so many, and sometimes twice that number, especially upon the three great festivals; and when I preach at the neighbouring towns, especially at Fairfield and New Town, I have a very numerous audience; which places, as they very much want, so they might be readily supplied with ministers from among ourselves, and those the best that are educated here, if there was but a bishop to ordain them.

"Q. How oft is the sacrament of the Lord's supper administered? and what is the usual number of communicants?

"A. I administer the holy eucharist on the first Sunday of every month, to about thirty and sometimes forty communicants; and upon the three great festivals to about sixty. But there are nigh one hundred communicants here and in the towns adjacent, to whom I administer as often as I can attend them.

"Q. At what times do you catechise the youth of your parish?

"A. I catechise every Lord's day, immediately after evening service, and explain the catechism to them.

"Q. Are all things duly disposed and provided in the church for the decent and orderly performance of divine service?

"A. We have no church; have begun to build one; but such is the poverty of the people, that we get along but very slowly. Neither have we any furniture for the communion, save that which Narraganset people lay claim to; concerning which I have written to your lordship by my churchwarden.

"Q. Of what value is your living in sterling money? and how does it arise?

"A. I have 60 l. sterling settled on me by the honourable society, and receive but very little from my poor people, save now and then a few small presents.

"Q. Have you a house and glebe? Is your glebe in lease, or let by the year, or is it occupied by yourself?

"A. I have neither house nor glebe.

"Q. Have you more cures than one? If you have, what are they? and in what manner served?

"A. There are Fairfield, eight miles off; New Town, twenty; Repton, eight; West Haven, ten; and New London, seventy miles off; to all which places I ride, and preach, and administer the sacrament, as often as I can; but have no assistance, save that one Dr. Laborie, an ingenious gentleman, does gratis explain the catechism at Fairfield; but all these places want ministers extremely.

"Q. Have you in your parish any public school for the instruction of youth? If you have, is it endowed? and who is the master?

"A. The Independents have one or two poor schools among them, but there are no schools of the Church of England in the town nor colony; for which reason I have recommended my churchwarden to your lordship and the honourable society.

"Q. Have you a parochial library? If you have, are the books preserved, and kept in good condition? Have you any particular rules and orders for the preserving of them? Are those rules and orders duly observed?

"A. We have no library save the 10 l. worth which the honourable society gave, which I keep carefully by themselves in my study, in the same condition as I keep my own." (*July 2, 1729: Fulham MSS.*)

These inroads on their undisturbed sway were ill endured by the sturdy Congregationalists. They claimed, and endeavoured to exercise, powers rarely wielded by any established national communion. They called together synods, in which, but for the direct interposition of the civil arm, they would have enacted canons wherewith to bind men of all opinions in the colonies. They assumed the right of taxing all for the support of their ministers and meeting-houses; and, wherever they could gain over the local governor to their persuasion, proceeded to enforce their claim with signal violence. . . .

PERSECUTION AND OPPRESSION OF CHURCHMEN
BY CONGREGATIONALISTS AND PRESBYTERIANS

In the midst of these difficulties from without, the injury inflicted on the Church by its imperfect spiritual organization was felt with the greatest bitterness. "The Independents, or Congregationalists," they complain, "here in New England, especially in Massachusetts and Connecticut, without any regard to the king's supremacy, have established themselves by law, and so are pleased to consider and treat us of the Church as dissenters. . . . The Presbyterians chiefly obtain in the south-western colonies, especially in those of New York, Jersey, and Pennsylvania, where they have flourishing presbyteries and synods in full vigour; while the poor Church of England in all these colonies is in a low, depressed, and very imperfect state, for want of her pure primitive episcopal form of Church-government. We do not envy our neighbours, nor in the least desire to disquiet them in their several ways; we only desire to be at least upon as good a footing as they, and as perfect in our kind as they imagine themselves in theirs. And this we think we have a right to, both as the episcopal government was the only form at first universally established by the apostles, and is, moreover, the form established by law in our mother country. We therefore cannot but think ourselves extremely injured, and in a state little short of persecution, while our candidates are forced, at a great expense both of lives and fortunes, to go a thousand leagues for every ordination, and we are destitute of confirmation and a regular government. So that, unless we can have bishops, especially at this juncture, the Church, and with it the interest of true religion, must dwindle and greatly decay, while we suffer the contempt and triumph of our neighbours, who even plume themselves with the hopes (as from the lukewarmness and indifference of this miserably apostatizing age I doubt they have too much occasion to do) that the episcopate is more likely to be abolished at home than established abroad; and, indeed, they are vain enough to think that the civil government at home is itself really better affected to them than to the Church, and even disaffected to that; otherwise, say they, it would doubtless establish episcopacy."

Yet, in spite of all hindrances, the persecuted body grew and multiplied. Sometimes a wealthy resident would build a church upon his own estate; sometimes the movement rose amongst the mass of poorer persons. . . .

In this state things continued till the time of Mr. Whitefield's visit to New England. Here, as elsewhere, his preaching produced wonderful effects. He found the flame of piety already burning low amongst the Independent congregations; for in the institutions of no separatists from the Church has the gift of enduring spiritual vitality been found. He boldly charged them with having left "the platform" of their ancient doctrines, and reviled them in his sermons under the unwelcome titles of "hirelings and dumb dogs, half beasts and half devils."

EXCITEMENT OF WHITEFIELD'S VISIT

He endeavoured to revive the ancient spirit by a series of violent excitements. The Independent teachers betook themselves to penal inflictions, subjecting itinerants to heavy penalties, and excluding them from the protection of the laws. But the flame only burned the fiercer for this opposition. Fanaticism in its maddest forms triumphed for a while; introducing new divisions in its train, and leading many into the open profession of Antinomian tenets. These scenes are thus described in the letter of an eyewitness:—

"The duties and labours of my mission are exceedingly increased by the surprising enthusiasm, or what is worse, that rages among us; the centre of which is the place of my residence. Since Mr. Whitefield was in this country there have been a great number of vagrant preachers, the most remarkable of whom is Mr. Davenport, of Long Island, who came to New London in July, pronounced their ministers unconverted, and by his boisterous behaviour and vehement crying, 'Come to Christ,' many were *struck*, as the phrase is, and made the most terrible and affecting noise, that was heard a mile from the place. He came to this society, acted in the same manner five days, and was followed by great numbers; some could not endure the house, saying that it seemed to them more like the infernal regions than the place of worshipping the God of heaven. Many, after the amazing horror and distress that seized them, received *comfort* (as they term it); and five or six of these young men in this society are continually going about, especially in the night, converting, as they call it, their fellow-men. Two of them, as their minister and they affirm, converted above two hundred in an Irish town about twenty miles back in the country. Their meetings are almost every night in this and the neighbouring parishes; and the most astonishing effects attend them,—screechings, faintings, convulsions, visions, apparent death for twenty or thirty hours, actual

PROTESTANT
EPISCOPAL
CHURCH

PERSECUTION OF
CHURCHMEN,
1740

CHRISTIAN
CONSTITUENT:

───────────

THE AMERICAN
CHRISTIAN
CHURCH

possessions with evil spirits, as they own themselves; this spirit in all is remarkably bitter against the Church of England. Two, who were struck, and proceeded in this way of exhorting and praying, until they were actually possessed, came to me and asked the questions they all do: Are you born again? Have you the witness of the Spirit? They used the same texts of Scripture as the rest, taught the same doctrines, called me Beelzebub the prince of devils, and during their possession burnt a large amount of property. They have since both been to me, asked my forgiveness, and bless God that He has restored them to the spirit of a sound mind.

"There are at least twenty or thirty of these lay holders-forth within ten miles of my house, who hold their meetings every night in the week in some place or other, excepting Saturday night; and incredible pains are taken to seduce and draw away the members of my church; but, blessed be God, we still rather increase."

The result of this sudden excitement was by no means favourable to the ruling sect. "The Independents or Congregationalists," Mr. Johnson reports, "are miserably harassed with controversies amongst themselves, at the same time that they unite against the Church. One great cause of their quarrels is the Arminian, Calvinistic, Antinomian, and enthusiastic controversies, which run high amongst them, and create great feuds and factions; and these chiefly occasion the great increase of the Church, as they put thinking and serious persons upon coming over to it, from no other motive than the love of truth and order, and a sense of duty; at which they are much enraged, though they themselves are the chief occasion of it." "When I came here there were not a hundred adult persons of the Church in this whole colony, whereas now there are considerably more than two thousand, and at least five or six thousand young and old; and since the progress of this strange spirit of enthusiasm, it seems daily very much increasing."

From such fierce divisions many learned to value the peaceful and holy shelter of the Church; and Mr. Beach received so large an accession to his charge, that his church would not hold two-thirds of those who joined him. Not a few of these were of the first families within the colony, and a new and spacious building was soon erected for him. The same causes led to the building of eight other churches within different neighbouring towns, and to the best amongst the Independent teachers joining his communion and receiving holy orders. . . .

SECTS IN CONNECTICUT

In Connecticut her roots took a deeper hold in the soil, from the action of the storms amongst which she had grown up. In no part of America was her communion so pure and apostolical as here. Her clergy were, for the most part, natives —men of earnest piety, of settled character, and well established in Church principles; and so greatly did she flourish, that at the outbreak of the troubles which ended in the separation of the colonies and mother country, there was every reason for believing that another term of twenty years' prosperity, such as she had last enjoyed, would have brought full half the population of the state within her bosom.

A contemporary writer, professing himself "unable to recollect the names of the multifarious religious sects" then existing in Connecticut, adds the following list "of a few of the most considerable."

	Congregations
Episcopalians	73
Scotch Presbyterians	1
Sandemanians	1
Sandemanians Bastard	1
Lutherans	1
Baptists	6
Seven-day do.	1
Quakers	4
Davisonians	1
Separatists	40
Rogereens	1
Bowlists	1
Old Lights	80
New Lights	87

So greatly had the Church gained upon the sects around her, through the zeal and piety which here adorned her members.

But this is far the brightest spot in the whole picture. Here and there, indeed, throughout the continent, individual zeal imparted life and warmth to separate congregations. But altogether there are few of the marks of the Church Catholic impressed in that age upon the English branch of it settled in America. Seldom, if ever, was she zealous and full of love and holy union inwardly, and to those without "terrible as an army with banners." There was a general languor of devotion; sects and divisions multiplied and often gained upon the Church; her own sons grew careless or apostates, and scarcely any thing was done to bring the Indian tribes around her to the knowledge of her Lord. All this may be traced most easily in the history of Virginia, where from different causes it was most signally developed. A hasty sketch of such a painful subject will be all that is required.

VIRGINIA

From a contemporary writer it appears, that in the year 1722 there were in Virginia not fewer than seventy churches, with dwelling-houses and glebes for the incumbent in almost every parish. Dissent was scarcely known; since it is still a matter of dispute, whether there were in the whole country three meetings of Quakers and one of Presbyterians, or whether one of Quakers stood alone. "For one hundred and fifty years," Dr. Hawks complains, "the Church had been fixed in Virginia, and yet the state of religion was deplorably low." "Many of the clergy were unfitted for their stations;" and the laity, from "loose principles and immoral practices, were often a scandal to their country and religion." Here and there a light sprung up, as in the case of Morgan Morgan, a humble and zealous layman, through whose labours the faith was planted in the newer western settlements, amongst a population composed chiefly of Presbyterian emigrants from Ireland. It was in the year 1740 that he erected the first church on the south side of the Potomac, in the valley of Virginia. But such men were rare; while for the most part all was lethargy.

In this state Mr. Whitefield found religion in the colony. As an English clergyman he was readily received, and at the desire of Dr. Blair, then commissary for the Bishop of London, he preached at the seat of government and elsewhere. He was here far more restrained, and proportionably useful, than amidst the wild sectarian wastes of the New-England colonies. His efforts kindled some zeal amongst a lukewarm people; but his addresses, which were made too exclusively to the mere emotions of his hearers, and not sufficiently directed to the general revival of a drooping Church, laid few or no foundations for a really permanent result. The feelings of the moment passed away with the passing voice which had awakened them; and left, it must be feared, the hearts which they had ineffectually visited even colder than they were before. No lasting blessings seem to have followed from these labours. Soon after his visit, earnest but irregular attempts for the diffusion of religion were made throughout the eastern districts by a pious layman of the name of Morris. These, after a little, led to the settlement in various parts of Presbyterian teachers from New England. At first the local government objected to their entrance; but under the provisions of the act of toleration they made good their footing, and by a more apparent earnestness drew away many from the Church. With them the Anabaptists, a few of whom had come long since from England, now rose into notice. They had recently been strengthened by allies from Maryland; and they now appeared in force, ready to join with any adversary of the Church.

The time of their appearance was propitious for their purpose. The endowment of the clergy of the colony, from very early times, consisted of a certain fixed weight of tobacco, the staple produce of the land. Some years before this time, a failing harvest had so greatly raised its price, as to make this mode of payment burdensome, and a fixed money-payment had been substituted for it until the scarcity was over. To this expedient another threatened failure of the crops shortly afterwards again inclined the colonial legislature. But the act was disallowed at home, and the clergy disputed its authority by legal process. The courts of law decided in their favour; but when damages came to be assessed, the jury, predisposed by popular impression, and wrought on by a sudden burst of eloquence from the opposing counsel, awarded such as were merely nominal. The court, under the same influence, refused another trial; and the clergy lost alike their rights and the little which remained to them of the affections of the people. So rapid at this time was the progress of dissent, that a few years later it claimed, as belonging to its ranks, two-thirds of all the population. All things, indeed, were out of joint. In a country containing not less than half a million souls (all of them professing the Christian religion, and a majority of them members of the Church of England, living under British government and laws, and in general thriving, if not opulent), there was yet not a single college, and only one school with an endowment adequate to the maintenance of even a common mechanic. Two-thirds of all the little education of the colony was given by indented servants or transported felons.

The causes of this state of things are well worth examination. Some of them were evidently peculiar to Virginia, in which and in Maryland alone such questions on the rights of property could have arisen. But in other parts matters were not, on the whole, much better. No where was the Church flourishing and spreading. Every where division multiplied. Baptists, Presbyterians,

Moravians, Methodists, Tunkers, Shakers, Quakers, Socinians, and Infidels, grew daily in importance, and shed on every side of them the fruitful seed of farther sub-division. In 1729, Berkeley found at Newport, in Rhode Island, "a mixed kind of inhabitants, consisting of many sects and subdivisions of sects; four sorts of Anabaptists, besides Presbyterians, Quakers, Independents, and many of no profession at all." To the northward and the eastward of Maryland there were but eighty parochial clergymen; and all of these, except in the towns of Boston and Newport, New York and Philadelphia, were missionaries sent out from England by the Society for the Propagation of the Gospel.

THE WANT OF NATIVE CLERGY

Some general cause there must have been for such a state of things. The power of Christ's truth could not be worn out. That Church which had hitherto subdued all people, rude or polished, against whom she had gone forth, had she lost her empire over men's hearts? She who had conquered the conquerors of the great Roman empire, and gathered one and another of the hordes of Gothic and Teutonic blood, who had invaded her domin-

ion, into the faith and hope of the people whom they conquered,—she seemed in the West not only to have lost her subduing might, but to be powerless even to retain her hold upon her own.

It is not very difficult to find the cause for this great difference. Her planting in America had been after a new and unknown manner. Heretofore the great aim of her founders, in any country, had been to make her truly indigenous—to reproduce her out of the people amongst whom she had come. For this end she was sent forth complete,—a living germ, with all the powers of reproduction in herself. To this, as the greatest work of Christians, the boldest and truest hearts were summoned; and he who won and held a band of converts to her Lord, was consecrated bishop of the Church amongst them, if he went not out in that holy character. Thus he could at once ordain new pastors and evangelists from amongst his native converts. Through them he could extend his influence; at their mouths the truths he taught, coming to the hearers in the beloved tongue of their fathers' land, were listened to with new readiness. Their blood, if persecution arose, was at once the seed of new converts: the Church was perfect and complete, and she went on conquering and to conquer. Such was the equipment of

---

SPIRITUAL STATISTICS   The best calculation of the numbers of the white population, and of the various religious persuasions on the continent of North America, transmitted to the Bishop of London, in 1761, gave the following results:

North American Continent	Whites	Church People	Presbyterians and Independents	Quakers, German & Dutch of various sects, Jews, Papists, &c
Newfoundland and Nova Scotia	25,000	13,000	6,000	6,000
Four New-England Colonies:				
New Hampshire . . . 30,000				
Massachusetts 250,000	435,000	40,000	250,000	145,000
Rhode Island 35,000				
Connecticut 120,000				
New York	100,000	25,000	20,000	55,000
New Jersey	100,000	16,000	40,000	44,000
Pennsylvania	280,000	65,000*	45,000	170,000†
Maryland	60,000	36,000	6,000	18,000‡
Virginia	80,000	60,000	10,000	10,000
North Carolina	36,000	18,000	9,000	9,000
South Carolina 22,000				
Georgia 6,000	20,000	5,000	3,000
Total	1,144,000	293,000	391,000	460,000

* This includes 40,000 Swedes and German Lutherans, who reckon their service, &c. the same as that of the Church. † About a third of these are Quakers, about 10,000 Papists, the rest Germans of various sects. ‡ Chiefly Papists.

Pothinus of old, when, with Irenaeus as his deacon, he went from Asia to sow amongst the Gauls the seed of the kingdom; and the Church of Lyons was his glorious harvest. So Boniface went forth from this land of ours, to become "the apostle of Germany." But wholly unlike this was our equipment of the Church in America. We sent out individual teachers, with no common bond of visible unity, no directing head, no power of ordaining; we maintained them there like the garrison of a foreign Church; and the consequence was, what might have been foretold, the Church languished and almost passed away. To this fault the religious evils of that land may be distinctly traced. Throughout the northern colonies the scattered missionaries, whom the venerable society sent out and paid,—who had no connexion with each other, no common head, and no co-operation in their work,—were the representatives of the body of foreigners across the ocean who supported and directed them. And even in the southern colonies, where the Church was established with provincial endowments, the want of bishops produced the same effect. There was no power of obtaining ordination in America; hence any young Americans, who desired to enter the ministry, must cross the Atlantic to receive holy orders. This was both costly and perilous. One in five, it has been calculated, of all who set out returned no more. Hence in a new country, where every sort of employment abounded, few parents devoted their children to the work of the ministry. The earliest bent was given in a contrary direction. The native candidates were therefore few; whilst of those who were sent out from England, some, in spite of every care at home, would be those whose characters were most unfit for such a post,—who proposed themselves for that peculiar service because they desired to escape the vigilance of episcopal control. This brought a reproach upon the priesthood; and the proper check on clerical unfitness being thus wanting, the people began to substitute another. Upon any vacancy, the governor and commissary recommended a successor to a Virginian benefice. The vestry received the minister so sent, and he then officiated in their church. If they chose, they might present him for induction to the governor; and when inducted, he had full and legal possession of the benefice. But the common practice was to receive the minister, and give him in possession the fruits of the benefice, without presenting him for due induction; and then the vestry could dismiss him when they chose. This seems to have been meant at first to guard the people from

unworthy pastors. From the nature of the case, there could be scarcely any other check on such men. The Bishop of London, indeed, had his commissaries in America; but their limited power and derived authority could do little when their principal was on the other side of the Atlantic. Nor was the power of the Bishop of London himself over those distant provinces certain or well defined. Whence it had first sprung is exceedingly uncertain. The most probable account attributes it to the hearty concurrence of the then Bishop of London in the earliest schemes of the Virginian Company for establishing the Church amongst their settlers. This led to his being requested to find and appoint their first clergy; and from this practice there gradually grew up a notion that they were in some way in his diocese. Thus, Bishop Compton wrote, in March 1676, "As the care of your churches, with the rest of the plantations, lies upon me as your diocesan, so, to discharge that trust, I shall omit no occasions of promoting their good and interest."

BISHOP OF LONDON'S COLONIAL JURISDICTION

Such the practice continued until the appointment of Bishop Gibson to the see of London. Upon inquiring into the source of his authority, he was told, that, though no strict ecclesiastical title could be found, yet by an order in council in the reign of Charles the Second, the colonies were made a part of the see of London. For this order he, being a careful man, caused a diligent search to be made, when he discovered that none such existed. Finding, therefore, no ground whatever on which to rest his claim of jurisdiction, he declined even to appoint a commissary. Thus the colonies were separated from all episcopal control. But after a while, having obtained a special commission from the crown, committing this charge to him, and thinking it better, under all the circumstances of the case, to act under this authority than to abandon them entirely, he began to discharge it with his usual fidelity. Yet even then he felt that his hold upon those distant parts was little what it should be, if he were indeed to deem himself their bishop. Every line of his first address to them breathes this spirit.

"Being called," he tells them, "by the providence of God to the government and administration of the diocese of London, by which the care of the churches in the foreign plantations is also devolved upon me, I think it my duty to use all proper means of attaining a competent knowledge of the places, persons, and matters entrusted to my care. And as the plantations, and the constitutions of the churches there, are at a far greater distance, and much less known to me, than the affairs of my diocese here at home, so it is the more necessary for me to have recourse to the best and most effectual methods of coming to a right knowledge of the state and condition of them. Which knowledge I shall not fail, by the grace of God, faithfully to employ to the service of piety and religion, and to the maintenance of order and regularity in the Church." He then furnishes a paper of inquiries, and promises his "best advice and assistance, in order to the successful and comfortable discharge of their ministerial function."

LACK OF DISCIPLINE

This authority, shadowy as it was, expired with the life of Bishop Gibson; since the commission under which he acted was granted only to himself personally, and not to his successors. How little it sufficed to maintain any form of discipline was shown in the fearful laxity of conduct which was visible on every side. Thus, at this very time, the marriage-licenses, which, by a first stretch of principle, had been granted to any "Protestant minister," instead of the authorized clergy, were now "expounded to intend a justice of the peace, as being a *minister* of justice, and a Protestant by religion;" and they accordingly took upon them to marry all applicants at their own pleasure. No one felt this want of discipline more keenly than the Bishop of London. But it was beyond his power to remedy the evil; and, as is commonly the case where the true safeguard provided by the Church is carelessly neglected, men began to invent others for themselves. Thus, in the state of Maryland, where the scandal of ill-living clergymen had risen to a fearful height, acts were passed by the provincial assemblies subjecting the clergy to the jurisdiction of a board of laymen, or mingled laymen and clergymen. It was in vain that men of the highest character amongst the clergy exclaimed against a proposal so utterly at variance with all ecclesiastical principle. The pressing evil was keenly felt; and in the absence of the true Church-remedy, they sought another for themselves. This law they would have carried into operation, if it had not been defeated by the opposition of the governor on grounds of state-policy.

So also it was in Virginia. To secure that which lawful authority should have provided for them, the vestries at first desired to try their pastors before they confirmed their full appointment. And this, as was natural, soon grew into a great abuse.

The vestries were now the masters of the clergy. On the most paltry or unworthy grounds they changed their minister. If he testified with boldness against any prevalent iniquity, the people whom his zeal offended soon rid themselves of so disagreeable a monitor. Hence ecclesiastical appointments in the colony grew into disrepute. Few would accept such uncertain stations; and those few were led to do so by necessity. Thus the clergy declined both in numbers and character. From this sprang another evil. The lack of clergy led to a general employment of lay readers. These lay readers were naturally taken from a lower class than the ordained clergy; they were also natives. It was not difficult for them to insinuate themselves into the regard of the congregations which they served; and it happened frequently that the benefice was kept unfilled in order to prolong the more acceptable services of the unordained reader.

SLAVERY IN VIRGINIA

Thus at every hand the Church was weakened. The laity were robbed of the sacraments, and led to choose their pastors on unworthy grounds. The clergy who came out were those least fitted for a work which, far more than that of ordinary stations, required the highest gifts of holy zeal and knowledge. For in Virginia causes of moral and social corruption were at work which nothing but the holy faith in its utmost vigour could counteract. From an early time the curse of slavery had rested upon Virginian society. Conditional servitude, under covenants, had been coeval with the first settlement of the colony. The emigrant was bound to render to his master the full cost of his transportation. This led to a species of traffic in those who could be persuaded to embark. The speculation proved so lucrative that numbers soon took part in it; since men might be imported at a cost of eight pounds, who would afterwards be sold in the colony for forty pounds. So established became this evil, that white men were purchased on shipboard as horses are bought at a fair. This, under the rule of the Parliament, was the fate of the royalist prisoners of the battle of Worcester. To this was added in 1620 negro slavery, which differed from indented servitude in being perpetual instead of for a term of years, and in the degradations which the distinctive features of the race of Ham soon associated with it. Marriage was early forbidden, under ignominious penalties, between the races of the master and the slave; and the grievous social evils which follow the dishonour of humanity sprung up freely around. "All servants," was the enactment of 1670, "not being Christians, imported into this country by shipping, shall be slaves;" yet it was added, "conversion to the Christian faith doth not make free." The death of a slave from extremity of correction was not accounted felony; and it was made lawful for "persons pursuing fugitive coloured slaves to wound or even to kill them."

The evils which such laws attest and aggravate were yet more exasperated by the whole character of the first centuries of Virginian life. Whilst the New-England settlers were early gathered into villages, and even towns, the Virginian landowners dwelt apart from one another, each one a petty despot over his indented servants and his slaves. Bridle ways were their roads; bridges were unknown; and the widely scattered population met at most but once on the Lord's day for worship, and often not at all; while the remoter families could rarely find their way through the mighty forests to the distant walls of their church. Education was almost neglected. "Every man," said the governor, in 1671, "instructs his children according to his ability;" and what this instruction was, may be gathered from another of his sayings: "I thank God there are no free-schools nor printers; and I hope we shall not have them these hundred years."

WANT OF BISHOPS

In such a state of things religion could not flourish, and a ministry already depressed was sure to sink into absolute debasement. The Church was best served by those ministers, as we have seen, whom she had gained over in New England from the ranks of Congregational dissent; for these were natives of the land, trained to the work, and men of earnest zeal and self-denying love of truth. But here, too, the want of bishops and the whole Church-system was lamentably felt. The sectaries around them possessed each their own system, such as it was, in perfection: they could appoint and send out teachers; gather in the young and active to the work; hold their synods and conventions; act, in short, as a living and organized body. "It is hard," was the complaint of Churchmen at the time, "that these large and increasing dispersions of the true Protestant English Church should not be provided with bishops, when our enemies, the Roman Catholics of France and Spain, find their account in it to provide them for theirs. Even Canada, which is scarce bigger than some of our provinces, has her

bishop; not to mention the little whimsical sect of Moravians, who also have theirs." "The poor Church of America is worse off in this respect than any of her adversaries. The Presbyterians have come a great way to lay hands on one another (though, after all, they had as good stay at home, for the good they do); the Independents are called by their sovereign lord the people; the Anabaptists and Quakers pretend to the Spirit: but the poor Church has nobody upon the spot to comfort or confirm her children,—nobody to ordain such as are willing to serve; therefore they fall back into the hands of the dissenters." These complaints were but too well founded. Only that communion which clave close to the apostolic model was on all sides cramped and weakened: without the centre of visible unity—without the direction of common efforts—without the power of confirming the young, whilst it taught the young that there was a blessing in the very rite which it withheld from them—without the power of ordination, whilst it maintained that it was needful for a true succession of the priesthood,—declaring, by its own teaching, its maimed and imperfect condition, and feeling it practically at every turn.

"There is a dispute amongst our clergy," says Mr. Johnson, applying for directions from the Bishop of London, "relating to the exhortation after baptism to the godfather, to bring the child to the bishop to be confirmed. Some wholly omit this exhortation, because it is impracticable; others insert the words 'if there be opportunity,' because our adversaries object it as a mere jest to order the godfather to bring the child to the bishop when there is not one within a thousand leagues of us, which is a reproach that we cannot answer."

NEED OF THE EPISCOPATE

At any time, and under any circumstances, such a state of things must have been widely and fatally pernicious. But in this case the injury was even more than usually great. Many causes had been in operation, from the era of the Reformation, which tended to make the bishops the only external centres of vigorous and united action in the English Church. From changes in the body politic, from the weakening of her synods and councils, and from the loneliness of her condition, almost every element of outward strength and visible unity was now centred in the episcopal office. The clergy, therefore, of such a Church, when set down in the far West, without a bishop nearer than the see of London, were at once reduced to the utmost extremity of weakness. They had no other lines of strength upon which to fall back to rally and re-form their broken ranks; and they became thus single-handed combatants, instead of marching in combined phalanx against a common scattered foe. Deeply was this felt by the most earnest and spiritual amongst them; and moving, oftentimes, were their entreaties to the Church, which had thus put them forth unfitted for their charge, to send them over the succession of the apostolical episcopate.

Year after year their lamentations and entreaties crossed the Atlantic. "We beg," they write at one time to the Bishop of London, "your fatherly compassion on our truly pitiable circumstances; we are forty-four miles from the nearest Church of England to us, . . . the incumbent of which hath visited us four times a year. There have been several adults and infants baptized amongst us, . . . and a church raised, which we hope to have finished by the next fall. We have never, since our first settlement, had the Gospel of Christ, or its comfortable sacraments, regularly administered to us by any episcopal minister; whereby sundry persons bred up in the Church of England at home, others that have been baptized here and become conformists, and a greater number still strongly inclined to conformity, do labour under that last and most grievous unhappiness of being left ourselves and leaving our posterity in this wilderness, excluded, as wild uncultivated trees, from the saving benefits of a transplantation into your soundest part of the Holy Catholic Church."

Similar appeals were sent from all parts of the Continent. "The Church," they say, "is daily languishing for want of bishops." "Some that were born of the English have never heard the name of Christ, and many others who were baptized into His name have fallen away to heathenism, quakerism, and atheism, for want of confirmation." "It seems the strangest thing in the world, and it is thought history cannot parallel it, that any place which has received the Word of God so many years should still remain together in the wilderness as sheep without a shepherd." "There never was so large a tract of the earth overspread with Christians without so much as one bishop, nor ever a country wherein bishops were more wanted." (*Fulham MSS.*) "We have several countries, islands, and provinces, which have hardly an orthodox minister among them, which might have been supplied, had we been so happy as to see a bishop *apud Americanos.*" "Above all

things, we need a bishop for the confirming the baptized, and giving orders to such as are willing and well qualified to receive them; there being a considerable number of actual preachers and others of New-England education well disposed to serve in the ministry." (*1705: S.P.G. MSS.*) "We have been deprived of the advantages that might have been received of some Presbyterian and Independent ministers that formerly were, and of others that are still, willing to conform and receive the holy character, for want of a bishop to give it." "Last year (*Rev. G. Thoms. 1705: S.P.G. MSS.*) there went out, bachelors of arts, near twenty young men from the college, all or most of whom would gladly have accepted episcopal ordination, if we had been so happy as to have had a bishop of America, from whom they might have received it; but being discouraged at the trouble and charge of coming to England, they accepted of authorities from the dissenting ministers, and are all dispersed in that way." . . .

CLERGY OF SPANISH AMERICA

Letters and memorials from the colonies supply, for a whole century, a connected chain of such expostulations; yet still the mother country was deaf to their entreaties. At home they were re-echoed from many quarters. Succeeding archbishops pressed them on successive administrations; and the Society for the Propagation of the Gospel, during almost every year, made some effort in the same cause. The records of these memorials show how earnestly and with what strength of argument it pressed this great cause upon the notice of the government.

It may well seem strange that these prayers were never granted. England stood alone in not establishing her Church in all its perfectness amongst her colonies. In Spanish America, whilst the crown had carefully excluded the power of the pope, securing to itself the appointment to all benefices, and not allowing any papal bull to be published which had not first been sanctioned by the royal council of the Indies, the greatest care was taken to set up amongst the colonists that form of faith and worship which, debased as it was, the mother country believed to be alone consistent with the truth. Thus a monastery had been established in New Spain within five years from its first settlement. And in 1649, about 120 years later, Davila estimates the staff of the Spanish Church in America to have been—"1 patriarch, 6 archbishops, 32 bishops, 346 prebends, 2 abbots, 5 royal chaplains, 840 convents." Besides these, there were a vast number of inferior clergy, secular as well as regulars, who were arranged in a threefold division; "curas," or parish priests, amongst the emigrants from Spain, and their descendants; "doctrineros," to whom were entrusted the Indians who had submitted to the rule of Spain; whilst for the fiercer tribes, to whom the civil arm had not yet reached, there were bands of "missioneros," who laboured to reduce their untamed spirits to the faith.

CHARLES THE SECOND

In these institutions, as Bishop Berkeley endeavoured to enforce upon the nation, was a strong condemnation of the supineness of a people who held a purer faith, and did not in like manner exert themselves to spread it. For whatever was deemed needful for the Church's strength at home, that, as a Christian people, we are manifestly bound to give her in our colonies, where, upon the outskirts and borders of Christendom, she needed arms for every service, and defence from every enemy. Yet, even from their earliest establishment, circumstances had led to this neglect. The first episcopal colonies were settled by private adventurers; their beginnings were feeble and uncertain; they proceeded on no general and matured plan, and their continued existence was long doubtful. They had no sooner gained some strength than the king resumed the charter he had given, by which they were removed from the control of those who valued their religious interests, and fell into the hands of the courtiers of James I., who were then under Spanish influence, and therefore hostile to the extension of the English Church. Then followed the troubles of King Charles's reign, and the triumph of dissenters in the great rebellion, ending in the overthrow of throne and altar, both at home and in our colonies. After the restoration, the subject was not wholly overlooked. Lord Clarendon perceived its importance, and prevailed on Charles II. to appoint a bishop of Virginia, with a general charge over the other provinces. (*M'Vicar's Life of Hobart, pp. 177–218.*) Dr. Alexander Murray, a sharer in the royal exile, was selected for the office; and a patent was made out for his appointment by Sir Orlando Bridgeman, who was lord keeper from 1667 to 1672. But a change of ministers cut short the scheme. (*Archbishop Secker says, in his letter to Horace Walpole, it fell to the ground because the tax to support it was to be laid on the customs. Dr. Jonathan Boucher states that it was*

through the king's death.—American Revolution, p. 92.) The king, a concealed papist, could have had no warm affection for it; and the reins of government which Clarendon relinquished, fell into far different hands.

His successors set themselves against all measures planned by him, and to this the Virginian bishopric was not likely to form an exception; since of the five men who now absolutely ruled the state, two were infidels, two papists, and the fifth a presbyterian. (*The first letters of whose names formed the word Cabal. Lords Clifford and Arlington were papists, the Duke of Buckingham avowedly an atheist, Sir W. Ashley (two years afterwards Lord Shaftesbury) a deist, and Lord Lauderdale a presbyterian.*)

During the life of Charles, therefore, the scheme was dropped; and James II. certainly would not resume it. Then came the troubles of the revolution and the reign of William III., when the divisions of the Church at home, as well as the temper of those to whom the conduct of affairs was entrusted, prevented further steps being taken in the matter. Other difficulties also had now arisen. Though petitions were repeatedly sent, both from the clergy and laity of the American episcopal community, entreating this Church and nation to grant them the episcopate, yet amongst their fellow-countrymen were found some objecting to their reasonable prayer. Many of the colonies had, as we have seen, been founded by dissenters; and now they were multiplied in numbers, and grown into new sects of every name and form. The sending out of bishops would have been distasteful to them, and kindled the wrath of the upholders of dissent at home, whom William III. most sedulously courted. Our early neglect had made the line of present duty more difficult than ever; so that the scheme was for the time wholly laid aside.

QUEEN ANNE

Queen Anne's accession promised better things; and in her reign the project of an American episcopate was heartily resumed.

The Society for the Propagation of the Gospel still led the way in the efforts which were made. As early as the year 1712, a committee was appointed "to consider of proper places for the residence, of the revenues, and methods of procuring bishops and bishoprics in America." This committee sat from time to time; and agreeing that it was "a matter upon which the interests of religion, and the success of the designs of the society, do greatly depend." (*Manuscript papers of the Society for the Propagation of the Gospel*) they moved both the body at large, and the archbishops and bishops especially, to proceed in it with vigour. Several times they laid before the crown their earnest representations of the great importance of the subject.

Nor were they without the promise of immediate fruit. Queen Anne was truly minded to be a nursing mother to the Church. Preparations were made for founding at once four bishoprics—two for the islands, and two for the continent of America. The society (*February 21, 1718. MS. proceedings.*) prepared special subscription-rolls, towards raising a sum for the endowment of the sees; and from many quarters they received munificent bequests for this especial purpose. They applied to the Queen for the confiscated lands which had belonged to the popish clergy within the island of St. Kitt's, and received a most gracious answer in reply; and in 1712 they purchased Burlington House, within New Jersey, as the palace of one of the future bishops.

But just when all seemed most certainly to promise the success for which they had so long been waiting, the death of the queen again frustrated their hopes. With the accession of King George the First, and the change of the government, a blight fell upon the hopes of the friends of the colonial Church. Still the venerable society made its voice of remonstrance heard. They represented to the new monarch that, "since the time of their incorporation, in the late reign, they had used their best endeavours to answer the end of their institution, by sending over, at their very great expense, ministers for the more regular administration of God's holy word and sacraments, together with schoolmasters, pious and useful books, to the plantations and colonies in America." They recited their former arguments as to the great need of establishing colonial bishoprics, and with them the favourable answer they had met with from the queen. They entreated the king to carry out her unfulfilled intentions, and found four bishoprics, "that is to say, two for the care and superintendency of the islands, and as many for the continent."

DR. GEORGE BERKELEY

These entreaties and remonstrances were not confined to this society. Some were always found who were ready to urge this duty on the nation. Foremost amongst these stands Bishop Berkeley, whose noble devotion to this great cause deserves

more than a mere passing notice. Possessed of a most subtle understanding, he had already acquired fame and eminence, when the spiritual destitution of America attracted his attention. A finished and travelled scholar; the friend of Steele, and Swift, and Pope; and in possession of the deanery of Derry,—he was willing to renounce all, in order to redress this pressing evil. "There is a gentleman of this kingdom," writes Dr. Swift to the lord-lieutenant in 1724, "who is just gone to England; it is Dr. George Berkeley, dean of Derry, the best preferment amongst us. . . . He is an absolute philosopher with regard to money, titles, and power; and for three years past hath been struck with a notion of founding an university at Bermuda by a charter from the crown. He hath seduced several of the hopefullest young clergymen and others here, many of them well provided for, and all of them in the fairest way of preferment; but in England his conquests are greater, and I doubt will spread very far this winter. He showed me a little tract which he designs to publish; and there your excellency will see his whole scheme of a life academico-philosophical, of a college founded for Indian scholars and missionaries, where he most exorbitantly proposeth a whole hundred a year for himself, forty pounds for a fellow, and ten for a student. His heart will break if his deanery be not taken from him, and left to your excellency's disposal. I discourage him by the coldness of courts and ministers, who will interpret all this as impossible and a vision; but nothing will do. And therefore I humbly entreat your excellency either to use such persuasions as will keep one of the first men in this kingdom for learning and virtue quiet at home, or assist him by your credit to compass his romantic design, which, however, is very noble and generous, and directly proper for a great person of your excellent education to encourage." (*Life of Bishop Berkeley, pp. 17, 18*)

On this errand Berkeley went to London, and having found access by a private channel to George I., he so far interested him in the project, that the king granted a charter for the new foundation, and commanded Sir Robert Walpole to introduce and conduct through the House of Commons an address for the endowment of the college with 20,000 £. After six weeks' struggle against "an earnest opposition from different interests and motives," (*Letters of Bishop Berkeley.*) the address was "carried by an extraordinary majority, none having the confidence to speak against it, and but two giving their negatives in a low voice, as if ashamed of it." But now, when it might have seemed that "all difficulties were over," they were little more than beginning, "much opposition being raised, and that by very great men, to the design." Sir Robert Walpole was averse to the whole measure; and a year and a half after the grant of the charter, it was "with much difficulty, and the peculiar blessing of God, that it was resolved to go on with the grant, in spite of the strong opposition in the cabinet council." But Berkeley's resolution was equal to every obstacle; though he complains of having "to do with very busy people at a very busy time," he was, by May, 1727, "very near concluding the crown-grant to the college, having got over all difficulties and obstructions, which were not a few." At this moment, and before the broad seal was attached to the grant, the king died; (June, 1727) and he had all to begin again.

BERKELEY IN RHODE ISLAND

With untired energy he resumed his labours, and, "contrary to the expectations of his friends," so well succeeded, that by September, 1728, he was able to set sail with a new-married wife for the land of his choice. He went first to Rhode Island, where he intended to lay in some necessary stock for the improvement of his proposed college-farms in the Bermudas. Here he awaited the payment of the 20,000 £. endowment of his college. But a secret influence at home was thwarting his efforts. His friends in vain importuned the minister on his behalf, and equally fruitless were his own earnest representations. The promised grant was diverted to other objects. With the vigour of a healthy mind, he was labouring in his sacred calling amongst the inhabitants of Rhode Island, making provision for his future college, and serving God with thankfulness for the blessings he possessed. "I live here," he says, "upon land that I have purchased, and in a farm-house that I have built in this island; it is fit for cows and sheep, and may be of good use in supplying our college at Bermuda. Amongst my delays and disappointments, I thank God I have two domestic comforts, my wife and my little son; he is a great joy to us: we are such fools as to think him the most perfect thing in its kind that we ever saw." For three years he patiently awaited the means of accomplishing his purpose; until Bishop Gibson extracted from Sir Robert Walpole a reply, which brought him home. "If," said he, "you put this question to me as a minister, I must assure you that the money shall most undoubtedly be paid as soon as suits with public convenience; but if you

ask me as a friend, whether Dr. Berkeley should continue in America, expecting the payment of 20,000 £., I advise him by all means to return home to Europe, and to give up his present expectations." (*Chandler's Life of Johnson, pp. 53, 54.*)

Thus was this noble project, and the labour of seven years of such a life, absolutely thwarted. One consequence alone remained. The library intended for his college was left by Berkeley at Rhode Island, and sowed in after-years the seed of truth amongst that people. He himself returned to England; and until his death, 1753, repeatedly endeavoured to arouse his country to the due discharge of its duty to the western colonies.

Other great men repeated his warnings. Bishops Butler, (*See Apthorpe's Review of Mayhew's Remarks, p. 55.*) Sherlock, and Gibson, enforced in turn our clear obligations in this matter. Thus we find, in 1738, the Bishop of London "labouring much, but in vain, with the court and the ministry, and endeavoring to induce the archbishop, who had credit with both, to join him in trying what could be done to get a bishop sent into the plantations;" (*Fulham MSS.*) and in the same year there was some hope that the bishop would be "appointed archbishop of the New World, the continent of America, and the adjacent islands, and invested with authority and a fulness of power to send bishops among them."

SIR ROBERT WALPOLE

But the fears and the subtilties of worldly-wise politicians defeated all these promising appearances. Sir Robert Walpole's government was dead to all appeals founded upon moral and religious principles. The minister consented willingly to no proposal which could increase the strength of the Church at home; and whilst the sectarian opponents of the measure had put forward their objections in terms which could not be mistaken, there was no counter power to weigh against the irreligious bias of the administration. The nation knew too little of Church principles to feel much interest in the subject; while the Church herself languished beneath the benumbing influence of Hoadley, and others of his school. Still, the episcopalians in America continued their most reasonable prayer. From all parts of the continent memorials were still sent home, though the greatest earnestness upon the subject was manifested in the northern colonies, where, as we have seen, there was, from many causes, most of the life and vigour of religion. . . .

About the year 1764 a pamphlet was published on the subject in New England, by the Rev. E. Apthorpe, a missionary at Cambridge, Massachusetts, which called forth an acrimonious rejoinder from a Congregational minister at Boston, of the name of Mayhew. In this, amongst other charges against the society in whose employment Apthorpe was, he specially attacked its aim and object in desiring American bishops.

This pamphlet was answered by no less a man than Archbishop Secker. His attention had long since been drawn to the question (*In 1745 he writes from London to Dr. Johnson: "Every thing looks very discouraging here; ecclesiastical, civil, domestic, and foreign. God avert from us the judgments we have deserved. . . . We have been greatly blamable, amongst many other things, towards you, particularly in giving you no bishops."*—Life of Dr. Johnson p. 75.); and, in a letter to Horace Walpole, written in January, 1750, and published, by his order, after his decease, he had entered fully into the whole case. This letter was an answer to objections against the institution of an American episcopate, urged, in a letter to Dr. Sherlock, bishop of London, by Robert Lord Walpole, brother of the late prime minister. Lord Walpole shared his brother's apprehension of increasing the power of the Church, and into this fear all his objections resolve themselves. These the archbishop fully met, and showed, as he does again in his reply to Dr. Mayhew's angry charges, how clearly due was such an institution to our episcopalian brethren. "The Church of England," he maintained, "is in its constitution episcopal. It is in some of the plantations confessedly the established Church; in the rest are many congregations adhering to it. . . . All members of every Church are, according to the principles of liberty, entitled to every part of what they conceive to be the benefits of it entire and complete, so far as consists with the welfare of civil government. Yet the members of our Church in America do not thus enjoy its benefits, having no Protestant bishop within three thousand miles of them—a case which never had its parallel before in the Christian world. Therefore it is desired that two or more bishops may be appointed for them . . . to have no concern in the least with any persons who do not profess themselves to be of the Church of England; but to ordain ministers for such as do, to confirm their children, when brought to them at a fit age for that purpose, and take oversight of the episcopal clergy.

. . . Neither is it, nor ever was, intended to fix one in New England; but episcopal colonies have always been proposed." (*Answer to Dr. Mayhew's Observations, &c.,—Archbishop Secker's Works, vol. ix. p. 324*)

Such a plea seemed scarcely to admit of answer from the zealous advocates of religious toleration; but Dr. Mayhew still found grounds for opposition, and for the part he had taken in this matter the archbishop was maligned for years, as an overbearing violator of the rights of conscience.

VOLUNTARY CONVENTION

Though no immediate steps were taken in the matter, the archbishop did not despair of its accomplishment. "Lord Halifax," he says (in 1761), "is very earnest for bishops in America. I hope we may have a chance to succeed in that great point, when it shall please God to bless us with a peace." (*Letter of Abp. Secker,—Dr. Johnson's Life, p. 182*) Nor was the cause let to drop amongst the northern colonists. Dr. Chandler, of New Jersey, soon came forward as its advocate, and he expressed the views of all the northern clergy. Those of New York, New Jersey, and Connecticut, formed themselves into a union, under the title of "The Voluntary Convention," with a view to obtaining their desire. In May, 1771, the Connecticut clergy addressed another earnest appeal upon the subject to the Bishop of London. "Viewing," they began, "the distressed and truly pitiable state of the Church of England in America, being destitute of resident bishops, we beg leave to renew our addresses in behalf of it. . . . We apprehend it a matter of great importance, considered in every view, that the Church should be supported in America. . . . But this Church cannot be supported long in such a country as this, where it has so many and potent enemies thirsting after universal dominion, and so many difficulties to surmount, without an episcopate, which in any country is essential at least to the well-being of the Church. Must it not, then, be surprising and really unaccountable that this Church should be denied the episcopate she asks, which is so necessary to her well-being, and so harmless, that her bitterest enemies acknowledge it can injure none? While Roman Catholics in one of his majesty's colonies are allowed a bishop, and the Moravians are indulged the same favour in another; nay, and every blazing enthusiast throughout the British empire is tolerated in the full enjoyment of every peculiarity of his sect; what have the sons of the Church in America

"But Peter, standing up with the eleven, lifted up his voice, and said unto them, Ye men of Judaea and all that dwell at Jerusalem, be this known unto you, and harken to my words: For these are not drunken, as ye suppose, seeing by the prophet Joel; And it shall come to pass in the last days, saith God, I will pour out of my Spirit upon all flesh; and your sons and your daughters shall prophesy, and your young men shall see visions, and your old men shall dream dreams: And on my servants and on my handmaidens I will pour out in those days of my Spirit; and they shall prophesy." (Acts 2:14-18)

We have here the first fruits of the Spirit in the sermon which Peter preached immediately, directed, not to those of other nations in a strange language, but to the Jews in the vulgar language, even to them that mocked, for he begins with the notice of that.

His account of the miraculous effusion of the Spirit, which, is designed to awaken them all to embrace the faith of Christ, and to join themselves to his church. Two things he resolves it into—that it was the fulfilling of the scripture, and the fruit of Christ's resurrection and ascension, and consequently the proof of both.

Observe, That the Spirit should be in them a Spirit of prophecy; by the Spirit they should be enabled to foretell things to come, and to preach the gospel to every creature. This power shall be given without distinction of sex; not only your sons but your daughters shall prophesy; without distinction of age, both your young men and your old men shall see visions, and dream dreams, and in them receive divine revelations, to be communicated to the church; and without distinction of outward condition, even the servants and handmaids shall receive of the Spirit, and shall prophesy, or, in general, men and women, whom God calls his servants and his handmaids. In the beginning of the age of prophecy, in the Old Testament, there were schools of the prophets, and, before that, the Spirit of prophecy came upon the elders of Israel that were appointed to the government; but now the Spirit shall be poured out upon persons of inferior rank, and such as were not brought up in the schools of the prophets, for the kingdom of the Messiah is to be purely spiritual.

Matthew Henry, on the place

done, that they are treated with such neglect, and are overlooked by government? Must not such a disregard of the Church here be a great discouragement to her sons? Will it not prevent the growth of the Church, and thereby operate to the disadvantage of religion and loyalty? . . . We believe episcopacy to be of divine origin; and judge an American episcopate to be essential to the well-being of religion here." (*Fulham MSS.*)

The efforts of the clergy of Connecticut were not confined to sending such addresses to the powers at home. Their first endeavour was to secure the concurrent voice of episcopal America; and for this end they sent deputies (*The Rev. Dr. Cooper, president of King's College, New York, and the Rev. Mr. McKean, missionary at Amboy, New Jersey, were sent to the southern part of the continent. Seabury MSS.,—apud Dr. Hawks's Virginia, p. 126*) throughout the other states. Had such vigorous steps been taken earlier, there can be little doubt what would have been their issue. They would have called forth from all parts of that continent one general voice, which could not have been slighted here. But that season was gone by; there was now in many districts a clear indisposition to join in the attempt. Of this the convention of Connecticut avowed themselves "sadly sensible; some of the principal colonies are not desirous of bishops; and there are some persons of loose principles,—nay, some even of the clergy of those colonies where the Church is established,—who, insensible of their miserable condition, are rather averse to them. But this is so far from being a reason against it, that it is the strongest reason for sending them bishops; because they never having had any ecclesiastical government or order (which ought indeed to have obtained above seventy years ago), the cause of religion, for want of it, is sunk and sinking to the lowest ebb; while some of the clergy, as we are credibly informed (but are grieved to say it), do much neglect their duty; and some of them on the continent, and especially in the islands, are some of the worst of men: and we fear there are but too many that consider their sacred office in no other light than as a trade or means of getting a livelihood; and many of the laity, of course, consider it only as a mere craft; and deplorable ignorance, infidelity, and vice greatly obtain; so that unless ecclesiastical government can so far take place as that the clergy may be obliged to do their duty, the very appearance of the Church will in time be lost, and all kinds of sectaries will soon prevail, who are indefatigable in making their best advantage of such a sad condition of things.

It is, therefore, we humbly conceive, not only highly reasonable, but absolutely necessary, that bishops be sent, at least to some of these colonies (for we do not expect one here in New England): and we are not willing to despair but that earnest and persevering endeavours may yet bring it to pass. We humbly beg your lordship's candour with regard to the warmth our consciences oblige us to express on this melancholy occasion." (*Letter from Convention of Connecticut to the Lord Bishop of London, Oct. 1766,—Fulham MSS.*)

OPPOSITION TO THE EPISCOPATE

But these were not now the only hindrances. In many respects the time was wholly unpropitious for the effort. Discord had been long at work between the mother country and the colonies, and men's minds had become imbittered against every thing of English aspect. They associated the name of bishops with the institutions of the mother country, and were unwilling to receive them from her, even whilst they admitted and believed that their office was essential to the perfection of the Church. Other causes, too, were at work. There were some, no doubt, desirous of maintaining the union between England and America, who feared, at that moment of fierce and unnatural suspicion, to introduce any new cause of difference, or to alienate still further the sectarian population by the name of bishops. When, therefore, the Virginian clergy, who might be naturally thought most ready to unite in this appeal, were called together by their commissary, in April, 1771, for its consideration, so few appeared in council that the question was postponed. A second summons brought no more than twelve, a majority of whom, after one opposite decision, agreed to an appeal to the king in favour of an American episcopate. But against this vote, two at first, and ultimately four, out of the twelve, protested publicly; and such was the feeling of the laity, that these four received the unanimous thanks of the lower branch of the Virginian house of legislature, for "their wise and well-timed opposition to the pernicious project for introducing an American bishop." Yet of this very body the great majority would have termed themselves episcopalians; and the reasons given for the protest refer only to present expediency, whilst it professes to revere episcopacy. Three out of the four reasons on which it was grounded were, (1) the disturbances occasioned by the stamp-act; (2) a recent rebellion in North Carolina; and (3) the general clamour of the moment

181

against introducing bishops; whilst the fourth, in fact, affected only the intended form of application, which, it was contended, should be first addressed to the Bishop of London for advice, before it besought the throne for the episcopate.

SIGNS OF THE TIMES

Under these reasons the true cause of this opposition may be read. There were already signs abroad of the approaching hurricane: the whole atmosphere, political and moral, was heated and disturbed. Old men looked around them with wonder and fear at the great change in opinions as to Church and State which they saw passing upon all. They could "remember when, excepting a few inoffensive Quakers, there was not in the whole colony a single congregation of dissenters of any denomination," (*Boucher's American Revolution: a sermon preached at St. Mary's, Caroline county, Virginia, in 1771, p. 97*) and when loyalty and love for their Church was the very characteristic of the "Virginian dominion:" but now all was changed. A popular candidate applied for votes upon the profession of "low churchmanship and whiggery." (*Boucher's Sermon, p. 98*) It were as easy "to count the gnats that buzz about in a summer's evening, as the numbers of sectarian and itinerant priests; and in particular of those swarms of separatists, who had sprung up under the name of Anabaptists and New Lights within the last seven years." (*Boucher's Sermon, p. 100*)

With this increase of schismatics the Church was taunted as a proof of her remissness. It was in vain that she replied, that "itenerant preachers, with whom the colony was overrun, made their proselytes in parishes left vacant through the want of bishops to ordain successors:" (*Boucher's Sermon, p. 100*) the temper of the time was against all authority in Church or State. The party

papers of the day took up the contest. The discussion on the American Episcopate was conducted by the same organs and in the same temper as that on the recent stamp-act. Continued misrepresentation stirred up the feelings of the people into angry opposition to the plan. "It is our singular fate," boldly declared a preacher at the time, in the face of some of the warmest opposers of episcopacy, "to have lived to see a most extraordinary event in Church-history: professed churchmen fighting the battles of dissenters, and our worst enemies now literally those of our own household." "Till now, the opposition to an American episcopate has been confined chiefly to the demagogues and Independents of the New-England provinces; but it is now espoused with warmth by the people of Virginia." (*Boucher's Sermon, pp. 94. 103.*)

In such a state of things sober-minded men, who loved their country, looked onward with unfeigned alarm. "What evils," (*Boucher's Sermon, p. 79*) declared one of them almost prophetically, in 1769, "this prevalence of sectarianism, so sudden, so extraordinary, and so general, may portend to the state, I care not to think. Enthusiasts conceive it to be the commencement of a millennium: but I recollect with horror that such were the 'signs of the times' previous to the great rebellion in the last century."

In this unhappy temper of the country, unanimity of effort to secure the episcopate was manifestly hopeless. Some of the southern clergy boldly rebuked their more time-serving brethren; and an "appeal" was published "from the clergy of New York and New Jersey to the episcopalians in Virginia," full of arguments which, on their common principles, admitted of no answer. But events were hastening on to a far different end. The storm of revolution was already breaking on the land; and till its fury had swept past, the desire of every pious churchman must be unattainable.

THE ESSENTIAL RIGHTS AND LIBERTIES OF PROTESTANTS

The Essential Rights and Liberties of Protestants, by Elisha Williams, 1744

The following excerpt is from a 66-page pamphlet, the whole of which should be studied at some time by every American Christian. Alice M. Baldwin, in "The New England Clergy and The American Revolution" says of this pamphlet:

"One of the most interesting of the pleas for religious liberty was a pamphlet issued in 1744, called The Essential Rights and Liberties of Protestants, *a Seasonable Plea for Liberty of Conscience and the Right of private Judgment in matters of Religion, without any control from Human Authority. This pamphlet, signed Philalethes, is attributed by Tracy to Elisha Williams, a follower of Whitefield, and is the fullest discussion of equality and liberty since the time of John Wise. Like Wise's pamphlets it was called forth by religious and ecclesiastical difficulties, and like his* Vindication, *it deserves a careful study.*

"The author defines natural liberty as freedom from any superior earthly power, as subjection only to the law of nature, which he declares to be the law of God. He then gives the clearest and fullest explanation of the so-called natural right to property to be found among any of the clerical writings of the eighteenth century." Editor.

SIR,

I Now give you my Thoughts on the Questions you lately sent me. As you set me the Task, you must take the Performance as it is without any Apology for its Defects. I have wrote with the usual Freedom of a Friend, aiming at nothing but Truth, and to express my self so as to be understood. In order to answer your main Enquiry concerning the Extent of the civil Magistrate's Power respecting RELIGION; I suppose it needful to look back to the End, and therefore to the Original of it: By which Means I suppose a just Notion may be formed of what is properly their Business or the Object of their Power; and so without any insuperable Difficulty we may thence learn what is out of that Compass.

That the SACRED SCRIPTURES are the *alone Rule of Faith* and *Practice* to a *Christian,* all Protestants are agreed in; and must therefore inviolably maintain, that every Christian has *a Right of judging for himself* what he is to believe and practice in Religion according to that Rule: Which I think on a full Examination you will find perfectly inconsistent with any Power in the civil Magistrate to make any penal Laws in Matters of Religion. Tho' Protestants are agreed in the *Profession* of that Principle, yet too many in *Practice* have departed from it. The Evils that have been introduced thereby into the Christian Church are more than can be reckoned up. Because of the great Importance of it to the Christian and to his standing fast in that Liberty wherewith CHRIST has made him free, you will not fault me if I am the longer upon it. The more firmly this is established in our Minds; the more firm shall we be against all Attempts upon our *Christian Liberty,* and better practice that *Christian Charity* towards such as are of different Sentiments from us in Religion that is so much recommended and inculcated in those sacred Oracles, and which a just Understanding of our *Christian Rights* has a natural Tendency to influence us to. And tho' your Sentiments about some of those Points you demand my Thoughts upon may have been different from mine; yet I perswade myself, you will not think mine to be far from the Truth when you shall have throughly weighed what follows. But if I am mistaken in the Grounds I proceed upon or in any Conclusion drawn from true Premises, I shall be thankful to have the same pointed out: Truth being what I seek, to which all must bow first or last.

To proceed then as I have just hinted, I shall *First,* briefly consider the *Origin and End of Civil Government.*

First, As to the Origin—Reason teaches us that all Men are naturally equal in Respect of Jurisdiction or Dominion one over another. Altho' true it is that *Children* are not born *in* this full State of Equality, yet they are born *to* it. Their Parents have a Sort of Rule & Jurisdiction over them when they come into the World, and for some Time after: But it is but a temporary one; which arises from that Duty incumbent on them to take Care of their Offspring during the imperfect State of Childhood, to preserve, nourish and educate them (as the Workmanship of their own almighty MAKER, to whom they are to be accountable for them,) and govern the Actions of their yet ignorant Nonage, 'till *Reason* shall take its Place and ease them of that Trouble. For GOD having given *Man* an *Understanding* to direct his Actions, has given him therewith a *Freedom* of *Will* and *Liberty* of *Acting,* as properly belonging thereto, within the Bounds of *that Law* he is under: And whilst he is in a State wherein he has no Understanding of his own to direct his Will, he is not to have any Will of his own to follow: He that understands for him must will for him too.—But when he comes to such a State of *Reason* as made the *Father* free, the same must make the *Son* free too; For the *Freedom of Man* and *Liberty* of *acting* according to his own *Will* (without being subject to the Will of another) is grounded on his having *Reason,* which is able to instruct him in *that Law* he is to govern himself by, and make him know how far he is left to the Freedom of his own Will. So that we are *born Free* as we are *born Rational.* Not that we have actually the *Exercise* of either as soon as born; *Age* that brings *one,* brings the other too. *This natural Freedom* is not a Liberty for every one to do what he pleases without any Regard to any *Law;* for a *rational* Creature cannot but be made under a *Law* from its MAKER; But it consists in a *Freedom* from any *superiour Power on Earth,* and not being under the Will or legislative Authority of *Man,* and having only the *Law of Nature* (or in other Words, of its MAKER) for his Rule.

And as Reason tells us, all are born thus *naturally equal,* i.e. with an *equal Right* to their *Persons;* so also with an equal Right to their *Preservation;* and therefore to *such Things* as Nature affords for their *Subsistence.* For which Purpose God was pleased to make a Grant of *the Earth in common* to the *Children of Men,* first to *Adam* and afterwards to *Noah* and *his Sons:* as the Psalmist says, *Psal. 115.16.* And altho' no one has originally a private Dominion exclusive of the rest of Mankind in the Earth or its Products, as they are consider'd in this their natural State; yet since GOD has given *these Things* for the Use of Men and given them *Reason* also to make Use thereof to the best Advantage of Life; there must of Necessity be a *Means* to *appropriate* them some Way or other, before they can be of any Use to any particular Person. And *every Man* having a *Property* in his own *Person,* the *Labour of his body* and *the Work of his hands* are properly his own, to which no one has Right but himself; it will therefore follow that when he removes any Thing out of the State that Nature has provided and left it in, he has *mixed his Labour* with it and joined something to it that is his own, and thereby makes it his Property. He having removed it out of the *common State* Nature placed it in, it hath by *this Labour* something annexed to it that excludes the common Right of others; because *this Labour* being the unquestionable Property of the Labourer, no Man but he can have a Right to what that is once joined to, at least where there is enough and as good left in common for others. Thus *every Man* having a *natural Right* to (or being the Proprietor of) his own *Person* and his own *Actions* and *Labour* and to what he can honestly acquire by his Labour, which we call *Property;* it certainly follows, that no Man can have a Right to the *Person* or *Property* of *another:* And if every Man has a Right to his *Person* and *Property:* he has also a Right to *defend* them, and a Right to all the *necessary Means of Defence,* and so has a Right of *punishing* all Insults upon his Person and Property.

But because in *such a State of Nature,* every man must be *Judge* of the Breach of the Law of Nature and *Executioner* too, (even in his own Case) and the greater Part being no strict Observers of Equity and Justice; the *Enjoyment* of Property in this State is *not very safe. Three things* are wanting in this State (as the celebrated Lock observes) to render them safe, viz. an *established known Law* received and allowed by common Consent to be the Standard of Right and Wrong, the common Measure to decide all Controversies between them: For tho' the Law of Nature be intelligible to all rational Creatures; yet Men being biassed by their Interest as well as ignorant for Want of the Study of it, are not apt to allow of it as a Law binding to them in the Application of it to their particular Cases. There wants also a *known and indifferent Judge* with Authority to determine all Differences according to the established Law: For Men are too apt to be partial to themselves, and too much wanting in a just Concern for the Interest of others. There often wants also in a State of Nature, a *Power to back and support the Sentence* when right, and give it due Execution—Now to remedy these Inconveniencies, *Reason* teaches Men to *join in Society,* to unite together into a Commonwealth under some Form or other, to make a Body of Laws agreable to the Law of Nature, and institute one common Power to see them observed.—It is they who thus unite together, *viz.* the People, who make and alone have Right to make the Laws that are to take Place among them; or which comes to the same Thing, appoint those who shall make them, and who shall see them executed.—For every Man has an equal Right to the Preservation of his Person and Property; and so an equal Right to establish a Law, or to nominate the Makers and Executors of the Laws which are the Guardians both of Person and Property.

Hence then the Fountain and Original of all civil Power is from the People, and is certainly instituted for their Sakes; or in other Words, which was the *second Thing* proposed, *The great End of civil Government,* is *the Preservation of their Persons, their Liberties and Estates, or their Property.* Most certain it is, that it must be for their own Sakes, the rendering their Condition better than it was in what is called a State of Nature (a State without such establish'd Laws as before mentioned, or without any common

Power) that Men would willingly put themselves out of that State. It is nothing but *their own Good* can be any rational Inducement to it: and to suppose they either should or would do it on any other, is to suppose rational Creatures ought to change their State with a Design to make it worse. And *that Good* which in such a State they find a need of, is no other than a *greater Security of Enjoyment of what belonged to them.* That and that only can then be the true Reason of their uniting together in some Form or other they judge best for the obtaining that greater Security. *That greater Security* therefore of Life, Liberty, Money, Lands, Houses, Family, and the like, which may be all comprehended under that of *Person* and *Property,* is the *sole End* of all *civil Government.* I mean not that all Civil Governments (as so called) are thus constituted: (tho' the British and some few other Nations are through a merciful Providence so happy as to have such.) There are too many arbitrary Governments in the World, where the People don't make their own Laws. These are not properly speaking *Governments* but *Tyrannies;* and are absolutely against the Law of GOD and Nature. But I am considering Things as they be in their own Nature, what Reason teaches concerning them: and herein have given a *Short Sketch* of what the celebrated Mr. *Lock* in his *Treatise of Government* has largely demonstrated; and in which it is justly to be presumed all are agreed who understand the natural Rights of Mankind.

Thus having seen what the *End* of civil Government is; I suppose we see a fair Foundation laid for the Determination of the *next Thing* I propose to consider: Which is, *What Liberty or Power belonging to Man as he is a reasonable Creature does every Man give up to the civil Government whereof he is a Member.*—Some Part of their natural Liberty they do certainly give up to the Government, for the Benefit of Society and mutual Defence, (for in a political Society *every one* even an *Infant* has the whole Force of the Community to protect him) and something therefore is certainly given up to the Whole for this Purpose.—Now the Way to know what Branches of natural Liberty are *given up,* and what *remain* to us after our Admission into civil Society, is to consider *the Ends* for which Men enter into a State of Government.—For so much Liberty and no more is departed from, as is necessary to secure those Ends; the rest is certainly our own still. And here I suppose with the before-mentioned noble Assertor of the Liberties of humane Nature; *all that is given up* may be reduced to *two Heads.*—1st. The *Power* that every one has in a State of Nature *to do whatever he judgeth fit,* for the *Preservation* of his *Person* and *Property* and that of others also, within the Permission of the Law of Nature, he gives up to be regulated by Laws made by the Society, so far forth as the *Preservation* of himself (his *Person* and *Property*) and the rest of that society shall require. And, 2. The *Power of punishing* he wholly gives up, and engages his natural Force (which he might before employ in the Execution of the Law of Nature by his own single Authority as he thought fit) to assist the executive Power of the Society as the Law thereof shall require. For (he adds) being now in a *new State* wherein he is to enjoy many Conveniences, from the Labour Assistance and Society of others in the same Community, as well as Protection from its whole Strength; he is to part also with as much of his natural Liberty and providing for himself, as the Good and Safety of the Society shall require; which is not only *necessary* but *just,* since the other Members of the Society do the like. Now if the giving up these Powers be *sufficient* to answer *those Ends* for which Men enter into a State of Government, viz. the better Security of their Persons and Properties; then no more is parted with; and therefore all the rest is ours still. This I rest on as certain, that *no more natural Liberty or Power is given up than is necessary for the Preservation of Person and Property.*

I design not to mention many Particulars which according to this Rule I suppose are not parted with by entering into a State of Government; what is reducible to *one* or *two general Heads* is sufficient to our present Purpose.—Tho' as I pass I cannot forbear taking notice of *one Point of Liberty* which all Members of a free State and particularly *Englishmen* think belonging to them, and are fond of; and that is the *Right* that every one has *to speak his Sentiments openly* concerning *such Matters as affect the good of the whole.* Every Member of a Community ought to be concerned for the *whole,* as well as for *his particular Part:* His Life and all, as to this World is as it were embarked in the same Bottom, and is perpetually interested in the good or ill Success thereof: Whenever therefore he sees a *Rock* on which there is a Probability the Vessel may split, or if he sees a *Sand* that may swallow it up, or if he foresees a *Storm* that is like to arise; his own Interest is too deeply concerned not to give Notice of the Danger: And

the Right he has to his own Life and Property gives him a Right to speak his Sentiments. If the *Pilot* or *Captain* don't think fit to take any Notice of it, yet it seems to be certain they have no Right to stop the mouth of him who thinks he espys Danger to the whole Ships Crew, or to punish the well-meaning Informer. A Man would scarce deserve the Character of a *good Member of Society* who should resolve to be silent on all Occasions, and never mind, speak or guard against the Follies or Ignorance or Mistakes of those at the Helm. And Government rather encourages then takes away a Liberty, the Use of which is so needful and often very beneficial to the Whole, as Experience has abundantly shown.

But not to detain you here,

1. The Members of a civil State or Society do *retain* their natural Liberty *in all such Cases* as have *no Relation* to the *Ends* of such a Society.—In a State of Nature Men had a Right to read *Milton* or *Lock* for their Instruction or Amusement: and why they do not retain this Liberty under a Government that is instituted for the *Preservation* of their *Persons* and *Properties,* is inconceivable. From whence can such a Society derive any Right to hinder them from doing that which does not affect the *Ends* of that Society? Should a Government therefore restrain the free Use of *the Scriptures,* prohibit Men the reading of them, and make it Penal to examine and search them; it would be a manifest Usurpation upon the common Rights of Mankind, as much a Violation of natural Liberty as the Attack of a Highway man upon the Road can be upon our Civil Rights. And indeed with respect to the *Sacred Writings,* Men might not only read them if the Government did prohibit the same, but they would be bound by a higher Authority to read them, notwithstanding any humane Prohibition. The Pretence of any Authority to restrain Men from reading the same, is wicked as well as vain.—But whether in some Cases that have no Relation to the *Ends* of Government and wherein therefore Men retain their natural Liberty; if the civil Authority should attempt by a Law to restrain Men, People might not be oblig'd to submit therein, is not here at all the Question: tho' I suppose that in such Case wherein they ought to submit, the Obligation thereto would arise from some other Consideration, and not from the supposed Law; there being no binding Force in a Law where a rightful Authority to make the force is wanting.

2. The Members of a Civil State do *retain their natural Liberty or Right of judging for*

themselves *in Matters of Religion*. Every Man has an equal Right to follow the Dictates of his own *Conscience* in the Affairs of *Religion*. Every one is under an indispensible Obligation to *search the Scriptures* for himself (which contains the whole of it) and to make the best Use of it he can for his own Information in the Will of GOD, the Nature and Duties of Christianity. And as every Christian is so bound; so he has an *unalienable Right* to *judge* of the *Sense and Meaning* of it, and to follow his Judgment wherever it leads him; even an equal Right with any Rulers be they Civil or Ecclesiastical.—This I say, I take to be an original Right of the humane Nature, and so far from being given up by the Individuals of a Community that it cannot be given up by them if they should be so weak as to offer it. Man by his Constitution as he is a *reasonable* Being capable of the Knowledge of his MAKER; is a *moral & accountable* Being: and therefore as every one is accountable for himself, he must reason, judge and determine for himself. That Faith and Practice which depends on the Judgment and Choice of any other Person, and not on the Person's own Understanding Judgment and Choice, may pass for Religion in the Synagogue of *Satan,* whose Tenet is that Ignorance is the Mother of Devotion; but with no understanding Protestant will it pass for any Religion at all. No Action is a religious Action without Understanding and Choice in the Agent. Whence it follows, the Rights of Conscience are sacred and equal in all, and strictly speaking unalienable. This *Right* of *judging every one for himself in Matters of Religion* results from the Nature of Man, and is so inseperably connected therewith, that a Man can no more part with it than he can with his *Power* of *Thinking:* and it is equally reasonable, for him to attempt to strip himself of the *Power* of *Reasoning,* as to attempt the vesting of another with this Right. And whoever invades this Right of another, be he *Pope* or *Caesar,* may with equal Reason assume the other's Power of Thinking, and so level him with the Brutal Creation.—A Man may alienate some Branches of his Property and give up his Right in them to others; but he cannot transfer the *Rights* of *Conscience,* unless he could destroy his rational and moral Powers, or substitute some other to be judged for him at the Tribunal of GOD.

But what may further clear this Point and at the same Time shew the *Extent* of this *Right of private Judgment* in Matters of *Religion,* is this Truth, That the *sacred Scriptures* are the alone Rule of Faith and Practice to every individual Christian. Were it needful I might easily show, the sacred Scriptures have all the Character necessary to constitute a just and proper Rule of Faith and Practice, and that they alone have them.—It is sufficient for all such as acknowledge the divine Authority of the Scriptures, briefly to observe, that GOD the Author has therein declared he has given and designed them to be our only Rule of Faith and Practice.

Thus says the Apostle Paul, *2 Tim. 3.15,16; That they are given by Inspiration from* GOD, *and are profitable for Doctrine, for Reproof, for Correction, for Instruction in Righteousness; that the Man of* GOD *may be perfect, thoroughly furnished unto every good Work.* So the Apostle *John* in his Gospel, *Chap. 20. Ver. 31.* says: *These Things are written that ye might believe that* JESUS *is the* CHRIST, *the* SON *of* GOD, *and that believing ye might have Life through his Name.* And in his first Epistle, *Chap. 5. Ver. 13. These Things have I written, that ye may know that ye have eternal Life, and that ye may believe on the Name of the* SON *of* GOD. These Passages show that what was written was to be the standing Rule of Faith and Practice, compleat, and most sufficient for such an End, designed by infinite Wisdom in the giving them, containing every Thing needful to be known and done by Christians, or such as believe on the Name of the SON *of* GOD. Now inasmuch as the Scriptures are the only Rule of Faith and Practice to a Christian; hence every one has an unalienable Right to read, enquire into, and impartially judge of the Sense and Meaning of it for himself. For if he is to be governed and determined therein by the Opinions and Determinations of any others, the Scriptures cease to be a Rule to him, and those Opinions or Determinations of others are substituted in the Room thereof. But you will say, *The Priest's Lips should keep Knowledge, and they should seek the Law at his Mouth, Mal. 2.7.*—Yes; that is, it is their Duty to explain the Scriptures, and the People's Duty at the same Time to search the Scriptures to see whether those Things they say are so. *Acts 17.11.* The Officers CHRIST has commissioned in his Church, as *Pastors* or *Bishops,* are to teach his Laws, to explain as they are able the Mind & Will of CHRIST laid down in the Scriptures; but they have no Warrant to make any Laws for them, nor are their Sentiments the Rule to any Christian, who are *all commanded* to *prove all Things,* to *try the Spirits whether they be of* GOD. *1 Thes. 5.21. 1 Joh. 4.1. I speak as to wise Men,* says PAUL, *judge ye what I say, I Cor. 10.15.* These and many other Texts I might have alleg'd entirely answer the Objection, and establish the Point before us.

The Evidence of the Point before us arises out of the *Nature* of a *Rule of Faith and Practice.* For a Rule of Faith and Practice is certainly *that* from which we must take and rectify all our Conceptions, and by which we ought to regulate all our Actions, concerning all those Matters to which this Rule relates. As it is the *Rule* of our *Faith,* we must receive no Doctrines but what that contains: otherwise our Faith is not directed by that Rule; but other Things in that Case are taken up and believed for Truths which that Rule takes no Notice of; and therefore it is done on some other Authority, which in Reality therefore becomes our Rule, instead of that which of Right ought to be so. *A Rule,* considered as such, is a Measure or Director with which a Thing is to be compared and made to agree: And therefore a Rule of Faith and Practice is *that* which being applied to our Minds directs and regulates them, by informing the Understanding and guiding the Will, and so influencing all our Actions. That which is the *Rule* of our *Faith* must point out to us and teach us the several Doctrines and inform us of the several Facts which we are to believe: And if we have entertained any wrong Notions or erroneous Opinions, they are to be corrected and regulated, by being compared and made to agree with this Rule. So also the *Rule* of our *Practice* is *that* from which we are to learn the several Duties we are to perform, and how all our Actions are to be regulated.—'Tis the Nature of a Rule of Faith and Practice to include all this. *That* whereby Men examine into the Truth of any Thing, is to them the Rule of Truth; *that* from whence they learn what they ought to believe, is to them the Rule of Faith; *and* that to which they conform their Actions, is their Rule of Practice. If Men receive the Doctrines prescribed to them by the *Pope,* by a *Council,* by a *Convocation* or a *Parliament,* from the Writings of *Fathers,* or *any Doctors* of Learning and Reputation, and conform their Actions to the Dictates and Commands of any of these or such like Authorities; the Authority to which they give this Honour, is undoubtedly the Rule of their Faith and Practice. And so if we submit ourselves truly and impartially to the Authority of CHRIST, and search for the Truths we are to believe, and the Duties we are to perform in his *written Word;* then only do we make Him our Director and Guide,

and the Scriptures the Rule of our Faith and Practice. And it is the *sacred Scriptures alone* which have this Right to our intire Submission, as now described: and no other Authority which has yet been or ever shall be set up, has any Manner of Right at all to govern and direct our *Consciences* in *religious* Matters.

This is a Truth of too great Importance for a *Christian* ever in any Measure to give up; and is so clear and obvious a Truth, as may well pass for a self-evident Maxim, *That a Christian is to receive his Christianity from* CHRIST *alone.* For what is it which is necessarily implied and supposed in the very Notion of a Christian but this, that he is a Follower and Disciple of CHRIST, one who receives and professes to believe his Doctrines as true, and submits to his Commands? And so far only as any does this, is he a *Christian:* and so far therefore as he receives or admits any other Doctrines or Laws, is he to be denominated from that Person or Sect, from whose Authority or Instruction he receives them.

Every *Society* ought to be subject only to its own proper Legislature. The Truth of this is evident at the first View; and civil Societies readily adhere to this as an inviolable Principle. And this holds equally true with Respect to *religious* or *civil Societies;* and therefore as in the *Church* of CHRIST no other Power or Authority may be admitted but that of CHRIST alone; so no Laws may be made for, or any Doctrines be taught and enjoined upon the Church of CHRIST besides those he has made and taught and enjoined. . . . So the Doctrines of Religion of CHRIST, is only that which he has appointed and taught, and all that is contained in Scripture: every Thing else is of *Men only,* and no Part of the Christian Religion. What is taught by any established Church, and not contained in Scripture, is indeed the Doctrine of that Church, but not of CHRIST: For none can make Laws to oblige the Church of CHRIST but CHRIST himself. The Church of CHRIST as such, must receive its Laws from CHRIST only; i.e. from the *Scriptures:* for they are to be found no where else. The *Christian Religion* is that which CHRIST has taught; and therefore what he has not taught, but some other Person, is not the Christian Religion. So also the *Church* of CHRIST is that which is founded according to the Directions and Model by him laid down. *That* therefore which is not so founded, but upon Principles and Regulations laid down by Men, is so far not a Church of CHRIST, but of *Men:* And in all these Things the *Scriptures* only can be our Rule. For we cannot know what CHRIST teaches and commands, from what he does not say, and what is said only by some other Person, but it must be from what he does teach and command; and all *that* is contained in his *Word*.

Again, if CHRIST be the *Lord* of the *Conscience,* the sole King in his own Kingdom; then it will follow, that *all such* as in any Manner or Degree *assume* the Power of directing and governing the Consciences of Men, are justly chargeable with *invading* his rightful Dominion; He alone having the Right they claim. Should the King of *France* take it into his Head to prescribe Laws to the Subjects of the King of *Great Britain;* who would not say, it was an Invasion of and Insult offer'd to the *British Legislature.*

I might also add, That for any to *assume* the Power of directing the *Consciences* of Men, not leaving them to the *Scriptures* alone, is evidently a *declaring them* to be *defective* and insufficient to that Purpose; and therefore that our Lord who has left us the *Scriptures* for that Purpose, did not know what was necessary and sufficient for us, and has given us a Law, the Defects of which were to be supplied by the wisdom of some of his own wiser Disciples. How high an Impeachment this is of his infinite Wisdom, such would do well to consider, who *impose* their own Doctrines, Interpretations or Decisions upon any Men by Punishments, legal Incapacities, or any other Methods besides those used and directed to in the sacred Scriptures.

And as all *Imposers* on Men's Consciences are guilty of Rebellion against GOD and CHRIST, of manifest Disobedience to and Contempt of their Authority and Commands; so all they who submit their Consciences to any such unjust usurp'd Authority, besides the Share which such Persons necessarily have in the Guilt of the Usurpers, as countenancing and giving in to their illegal Claim and supporting their wicked Pretensions, they do likewise renounce Subjection to the Authority and Laws of CHRIST. To submit our Consciences to the Guidance of any Man or Order of Men, is not to reason and act according to our own Understanding; but to take every thing for true, that our spiritual Guide affirms to be so, and that meerly upon his Authority, without examining into, or seeing the Truth and Reasonableness of it: And in every Instance wherein we thus submit our selves to the Direction of any humane Authority, so far we set aside and renounce all other Authority, our own Light and Reason, and even the Word of GOD and CHRIST: And the Authority of the Guide we subject our selves unto is substituted in the Stead of all these. If we must be directed and governed by any humane Power, it concerns us not what any other may teach and command; this the being subject to a Power necessarily supposes and includes. An *Englishman* is subject to the Crown and Laws of *England,* and has nothing to do with the Laws and Courts of Judicature in *France* or *Spain,* or *any other State,* but disowns and renounces all Obedience thereto. This is a universal Rule: And therefore if our Consciences are under the Direction of any humane Authority as to religious Matters; they cease to be under the Direction of CHRIST. *What* CHRIST himself has told us is infallibly true, that *no Man can serve two Masters, but he must unavoidably prefer the one and neglect the other:* And consequently whoever looks upon himself to be under the Direction and Government of any humane Power in Matters of Religion, does thereby renounce the Authority of CHRIST, and withdraw Obedience from him. . . .

BENJAMIN FRANKLIN TO JOSEPH HUEY

Works of Benjamin Franklin, by Jared Sparks, Vol. VII, Boston, 1840

Philadelphia, 6 June, 1753

Sir,

I received your kind letter of the 2d instant, and am glad to hear that you increase in strength; I hope you will continue mending, till you recover your former health and firmness. Let me know whether you still use the cold bath, and what effect it has.

As to the kindness you mention, I wish it could have been of more service to you. But if it had, the only thanks I should desire is, that you would always be equally ready to serve any other person that may need your assistance, and so let good offices go round; for mankind are all of a family.

For my own part, when I am employed in serving others, I do not look upon myself as conferring favors, but as paying debts. In my travels, and since my settlement, I have received much kindness from men, to whom I shall never have any opportunity of making the least direct return; and numberless mercies from God, who is infinitely above being benefited by our services. Those kindnesses from men, I can therefore only return on their fellow men, and I can only show my gratitude for these mercies from God, by a readiness to help his other children and my brethren. For I do not think, that thanks and compliments, though repeated weekly, can discharge our real obligations to each other, and much less those to our Creator. You will see in this my notion of good works, that I am far from expecting to merit heaven by them. By heaven we understand a state of happiness, infinite in degree, and eternal in duration. I can do nothing to deserve such rewards. He that, for giving a draft of water to a thirsty person, should expect to be paid with a good plantation, would be modest in his demands, compared with those who think they deserve heaven for the little good they do on earth. Even the mixed, imperfect pleasures we enjoy in this world, are rather from God's goodness than our merit; how much more such happiness of heaven!

For my part I have not the vanity to think I deserve it, the folly to expect it, nor the ambition to desire it; but content myself in submitting to the will and disposal of that God who made me, who has hitherto preserved and blessed me, and in whose fatherly goodness I may well confide, that he will never make me miserable; and that even the afflictions I may at any time suffer shall tend to my benefit.

The faith you mention has certainly its use in the world. I do not desire to see it diminished, nor would I endeavour to lessen it in any man. But I wish it were more productive of good works, than I have generally seen it; I mean real good works; works of kindness, charity, mercy, and public spirit; not holiday-keeping, sermon-reading or hearing; performing church ceremonies, or making long prayers, filled with flatteries and compliments, despised even by wise men, and much less capable of pleasing the Deity. The worship of God is a duty; the hearing and reading of sermons may be useful; but, if men rest in hearing and praying, as too many do, it is as if a tree should value itself on being watered and putting forth leaves, though it never produced any fruit.

Your great master thought much less of these outward appearances and professions, than many of his modern disciples. He preferred the *doers* of the word, to the mere *hearers;* the son that seemingly refused to obey his father, and yet performed his commands, to him that professed his readiness, but neglected the work; the heretical but charitable Samaritan, to the uncharitable though orthodox priest and sanctified Levite; and those who gave food to the hungry, drink to the thirsty, raiment to the naked, entertainment to the stranger, and relief to the sick, though they never heard of his name, he declares shall in the last day be accepted; when those who cry Lord! Lord! who value themselves upon their faith, though great enough to perform miracles, but have neglected good works, shall be rejected. He professed, that he came not to call the righteous, but sinners to repentance; which implied his modest opinion, that there were some in his time so good, that they need not hear even him for improvement; but now-a-days we have scarce a little parson, that does not think it the duty of every man within his reach to sit under his petty ministrations; and that whoever omits them offends God.

I wish to such more humility, and to you health and happiness, being your friend and servant.

B. FRANKLIN

_____

The above letter has often been printed, and always, I believe, as having been written to Whitefield; but among the author's manuscripts I find the first draft, with the following indorsement, in Franklin's handwriting; "Letter to Joseph Huey." Jared Sparks note.

THE CLERGY OF
THE REVOLUTION

The clergy were generally consulted by the civil authorities; and not infrequently the suggestions from the pulpit, on election days and other special occasions, were enacted into laws. The statute-book, the reflex of the age, shows this influence. *The State was developed out of the Church.*

The annual "Election Sermon"—a perpetual memorial, continued down through the generations from century to century—still bears witness that our fathers ever began their civil year and its responsibilities with an appeal to Heaven, and recognized *Christian morality as the only basis of good laws.*

The origin of this anniversary is to be found in the charter of "the governor and COMPANIE of the Massachusetts Bay in New England," which provided that "one governor, one deputy-governor, and eighteen assistants, and all other officers of the said companie," not of the colony—should be chosen in their "general court, or assemblie," on "the last Wednesday in Easter Terme, yearely, for the yeare ensuing."

About the year 1633, the governor and assistants began to appoint one to preach on the day of election, and this was the first of our "Election Sermons." . . .

By the charter of William and Mary, October, 1691, the last Wednesday of May was established as election-day, and it remained so till the Revolution. The important part which this institution of the Election Sermon played at that period, and an account of its observance, are minutely and accurately presented by the Rev. William Gordon, of Roxbury, the contemporary historian of the Revolution, and in a manner so pertinent to our purpose that we give it entire.

He says that the "ministers of New England, being mostly Congregationalists, are, from that circumstance, in a professional way, more attached and habituated to the principles of liberty than if they had spiritual superiors to lord it over them, and were in hopes of possessing, in their turn, through the gift of government, the seat of power. They oppose arbitrary rule in civil concerns from the love of freedom, as well as from a desire of guarding against its introduction into religious matters. The patriots, for years back, have availed themselves greatly of their assistance. Two sermons have been preached annually for a length of time, the one on general election-day, the last Wednesday in May, when the new general court have been used to meet, according to charter, and elect counsellors for the ensuing year; the other, some little while after, on the artillery election-day, when the officers are re-elected, or new officers chosen. On these occasions political subjects are deemed very proper; but it is expected that they be treated in a decent,

The Pulpit of the American Revolution, by John Wingate Thornton, Boston, 1860

serious, and instructive manner. The general election preacher has been elected alternately by the council and House of Assembly. The sermon is styled the *Election Sermon,* and is printed. Every representative has a copy for himself, and generally one or more for the minister or ministers of his town. As the patriots have prevailed, the preachers of each sermon have been the zealous friends of liberty; and the passages most adapted to promote the spread and love of it have been selected and circulated far and wide by means of newspapers, and read with avidity and a degree of veneration on account of the preacher and his election to the service of the day. Commendations, both public and private, have not been wanting to help on the design. Thus, by their labors in the pulpit, and by furnishing the prints with occasional essays, the ministers have forwarded and strengthened, and that not a little, the opposition to the exercise of that parliamentary claim of right to bind the colonies in all cases whatever." . . .

The ministers were now to instruct the people, to reason before them and with them, to appeal

to them; and so, by their very position and relation, the people were constituted the judges. *They* were called upon to decide; *they* also reasoned; and in this way—as the conflicts *in* the church respected *polity* rather than *doctrine* —the Puritans, and especially the New Englanders, had, from the very beginning, been educated in the consideration of its elementary principles.

In this we discover how it was, as Governor Hutchinson remarked, that "men took sides in New England upon mere speculative points in government, when there was nothing in practice which could give any grounds for forming parties." This was a remarkable feature in the opening of the Revolutionary war. . . .

It is in this habitual study of political ethics, of "the liberty of the gospel,"—perhaps the principal feature in New England history,—that we discern the source of that earnestness which consciousness of right begets, and of those appeals to principle which distinguished the colonies, and which they were ever ready to vindicate with life and fortune.

★   ★   ★   ★   ★

*Military Journal
of the American
Revolution,* by
James Thatcher,
Reprint 1862

The clergymen of New England are, almost without exception, advocates of whig principles; there are a few instances only of the separation of a minister from his people, in consequence of a disagreement in political sentiment. The tories censure, in a very illiberal manner, the preacher who speaks boldly for the liberties of the people, while they lavish their praises on him who dares to teach the absurd doctrine, that magistrates have a divine right to do wrong, and are to be

implicitly obeyed. It is recommended by our Provincial Congress, that on other occasions than the sabbath, ministers of parishes adapt their discourses to the times, and explain the nature of civil and religious liberty, and the duties of magistrates and rulers.

Accordingly, we have from our pulpits the most fervent and pious effusions to the throne of Divine Grace in behalf of our bleeding, afflicted country.

★   ★   ★   ★   ★

*History of the
Siege of Boston,*
by Richard
Frothingham,
Boston, 1851

The labors of the Boston divines deserve a grateful remembrance. Some of them, distinguished by their learning and eloquence, were no less distinguished by their hearty opposition to the designs of the British administration. This opposition had been quickened into intense life by the attempts made from time to time to create a hierarchy in the colonies. The Episcopal form of worship was always disagreeable to the Congregationalists; but it was the power that endeavored to impose it on which their eyes were most steadily fixed. If Parliament could create dioceses and appoint bishops, it could introduce tithes and crush heresy. The ministry entertained the design of sending over a bishop to the colonies; and controversy, for years, ran high on this subject. So resolute, however, was the opposition to

this project, that it was abandoned. This controversy, John Adams says, contributed as much as any other cause to arouse attention to the claims of Parliament. The provisions of the Quebec act were quoted with great effect; and what had been done for Canada might be done for the other colonies. Hence, few of the Congregational clergy took sides with the government, while many were zealous Whigs; and thus the pulpit was often brought in aid of the town-meeting and the press.

Of the Boston divines, none had been more ardent and decided than Jonathan Mayhew, one of the ablest theologians of his day; but he died in 1766. Dr. Charles Chauncy, Dr. Samuel Cooper, Dr. Andrew Eliot, Dr. Ebenezer Pemberton, Reverends John Lathrop, John Bacon,

Simeon Howard, Samuel Stillman, were of those who took the popular side. They were the familiar associates and the confidential advisers of the leading patriots; but by virtue of their office, they were not less familiar or less confidential with wide circles of every calling in life, who were playing actively and well an important part, and without whose hearty cooperation the labors of even leading patriots would have been of little avail.

At a time when the pristine reverence for the ministers had hardly declined into respect, who shall undervalue the influence such men threw into the scale, in giving intensity to zeal and firmness to resolution, and thus strengthening the tone of public opinion? They gave the sanction of religion—the highest sanction that can fill the human breast—to the cause of freedom, the holiest cause that can prompt human effort. They nurtured the idea in the people that God was on their side; and that power, however great, would be arrayed in vain against them. No wonder that, in the day of Lexington, there were men who went to the field of slaughter with the same solemn sense of duty with which they entered the house of worship.

THE CLERGY
OF THE
REVOLUTION
—————
AN ARTILLERY-
ELECTION SERMON,
1773

AN ARTILLERY-ELECTION SERMON

"Stand fast therefore in the liberty wherewith Christ hath made us free." (Galations V:1)

Mankind are generally averse to innovations both in religion and government. Laws and constitutions to which they have been long used, they are fond of retaining, even though better are offered in their stead. This appeared in the Jews. Their law required a burdensome and expensive service: christianity set them free from this law. Nevertheless, many of them were desirous of continuing the observation of it, after they became christians; and of having the gentile converts also submit to it. Accordingly there were some Judaising teachers who endeavoured to persuade the Galations to this submission. The Apostle, therefore, in this epistle, particularly in the immediately foregoing chapter, asserts and proves, that christians have nothing to do with the ceremonial law of the Jews, they being freed by Christ, from this burden. And then as an inference from what he had said, and by way of admonition to the Galations, he subjoins the exhortation in the text; stand fast therefore in the liberty wherewith Christ hath made us free.

But though the words originally refer to that freedom from the Jewish law which the gospel confers on the church of God; yet the reason of the inference holds good in the case of any other real and valuable liberty which men have a right to: So that this observation is plainly deducible from the text: viz. that it is the duty of all men to stand fast in such valuable liberty, as providence has confered upon them.

This observation I shall endeavour, by the help of God, to illustrate and improve: In order to which, I shall shew:

I. What I intend by that liberty in which men ought to stand fast.

II. In what way they ought to stand fast in this liberty, or what they may and ought to do in defence of it.

III. The obligations they are under to this duty.

After which, I shall subjoin some reflections, and apply the subject to the present occasion.

I. I am to shew what is intended in this discourse by the liberty in which men ought to stand fast.

Though this word is used in various senses, I mean by it here, only that liberty which is opposed to external force and constraint, and to such force and constraint only, as we may suffer from men. Under the term liberty, taken in this sense, may naturally be comprehended all those advantages which are liable to be destroyed by the art or power of men; every thing that is opposed to temporal slavery.

This liberty has always been accounted one of the greatest natural blessings which mankind can enjoy. Accordingly, the benevolent and impartial Father of the human race, has given to all men a right, and to all naturally an equal right to this blessing.

In a state of nature, or where men are under no civil government, God has given to every one liberty to pursue his own happiness in whatever way, and by whatever means he pleases, without asking the consent or consulting the inclination of any other man, provided he keeps

Sermon
Preached to the
Ancient and
Honorable
Artillery
Company, in
Boston, June
7th, 1773,
by Simeon
Howard, A.M.
Boston, 1773

within the bounds of the law of nature. Within these bounds, he may govern his actions, and dispose of his property and person, as he thinks proper. (See Locke on Government) Nor has any man, or any number of men, a right to restrain him in the exercise of this liberty, or punish, or call him to account for using it. This however is not a state of licentiousness, for the law of nature which bounds this liberty, forbids all injustice and wickedness; allows no man to injure another in his person or property, or to destroy his own life.

But experience soon taught that, either thro' ignorance of this law, or the influence of unruly passions, some were disposed to violate it, by encroaching upon the liberty of others; so that the *weak* were liable to be greatly injured by the superior power of bad men, without any means of security or redress. This gave birth to civil society, and induced a number of individuals to combine together for mutual defence and security; to give up a part of their natural liberty for the sake of enjoying the remainder in greater safety; to agree upon certain laws among themselves to regulate the social conduct of each individual; or to intrust to one or more of their number, in whose wisdom and goodness they could confide, a power of making such laws, and putting them in execution.

In this state, the liberty which men have is all that natural liberty which has been mentioned, excepting what they have *expressly* given up for good of the whole society; a liberty of pursuing their own happiness, governing their actions, and disposing of their property and persons as they think fit, provided they transgress no law of nature, and keep those restrictions which they have consented to come under.

This liberty will be different in different communities. In every state, the members will, probably, give up so much of their natural liberty, as they think will be most for the good of the whole. But different states will judge differently upon this point; some will give up more, some less, though still with the same view, the publick good.

And every society have doubtless a right to act according to their own judgment and discretion in this matter, this being only an exercise of that natural liberty in which all are found.

When a society commits to one or a few a power to govern them, the general practice is to limit this power by certain prescribed rules and restrictions. But sometimes this is omitted, and it does not appear from any act of the people,

but that the power, with which they have intrusted their rulers, is unlimited. In this case common sense will tell us that the power granted to rulers is to be limited by the great end and design of society and government: and he must be destitute of common sense, who does not know that this is the general good, the happiness and safety of the whole society. So that though a people should, through inadvertency, neglect to prescribe any bounds to the power of their rulers, this power would nevertheless be limited, and *they* would be at liberty to refuse submission to such restraints or laws, as were plainly inconsistent with the public good.

There are some natural liberties or rights which no person can divest himself of, without transgressing the law of nature. A man cannot, for instance, give up the liberty of private judgment in matters of religion, or convey to others a right to determine of what religion he shall be, and in what way he shall worship God. A grant of this nature would destroy the foundation of all religion in the man who made it, and must therefore be a violation of the law of nature; nor would he be obliged to abide by it, if in consequence of it, he should be required to act contrary to the dictates of his conscience. Or should a man pretend to grant to others a power to order and govern all his actions, that were not of a religious nature, so that in all cases he must act agreeable to their direction; this would be inconsistent with that submission which he owes to the authority of God, and his own conscience. The grant would be in itself void, and he would, notwithstanding, be at liberty to act according to his own conscience, though contrary to the command of those to whom he had made so extravagant a donation.

Should therefore the legislature of a state make laws requiring the subjects to do things immoral, and which they knew to be so, such, for instance, as were apparently destructive of public happiness, though it was in consequence of an express grant of unlimited power, the subjects would be at liberty to refuse obedience, and not violate conscience or destroy their own happiness. So that only such laws of society as are not plainly inconsistent with the end of society, or, in any other respect, inconsistent with the law of nature, the eternal rules of morality, can restrain and limit the natural liberty of those who belong to it.

It is to be further observed here, that states or communities, as such, have naturally the same liberty which individuals have in the state of

"And Saul yet breathing out threatenings and slaughter against the disciples of the Lord, went unto the high priest. . . . And as he journeyed, he came near Damascus; and suddenly there shined round about him a light from heaven: And he fell to the earth, and heard a voice saying unto him, Saul, Saul, why persecutest thou me? And he said, Who are thou, Lord? And the Lord said, I am Jesus whom thou persecutest: it is hard for thee to kick against the pricks. And he trembling and astonished, said, Lord, what wilt thou have me to do? And the Lord said unto him, Arise, and go into the city, and it shall be told thee what thou must do." (Acts 9:1, 3-6)

How bad he was, how very bad, before his conversion; just before he was an inveterate enemy to Christianity, did his utmost to root it out, by persecuting all that embraced it. How suddenly and strangely a blessed change was wrought in him, not in the use of any ordinary means, but by miracles. The conversion of Paul is one of the wonders of the church.

He was in the way, travelling upon his journey; not in the temple, or in the synagogue. The work of conversion is not tied to the church, though ordinarily public administrations are made use of. Some are reclaimed in slumbering on the bed, (Job 33:15, 17) and some in travelling upon the road alone; thoughts are as free, and there is as good an opportunity of communing with our own hearts there, as upon the bed; and there the Spirit may set in with us; for that wind blows where it listeth.

Sometimes the grace of God works upon sinners, when they are at the worst, and hotly engaged in the most desperate sinful pursuits; which is much for the glory both of God's pity and of his power. The devil comes to the soul in darkness, by it he gets and keeps possession of it. But Christ comes to the soul in light, for he is himself the light of the world.

Those who persecute the saints, persecute Christ himself, and he takes what is done against them as done against himself, and accordingly will be the judgment in the great day. There is nothing more effectual to awaken and humble the soul than to see sin to be against Christ, an affront to him, and a contradiction to his designs. The great change in conversion is wrought upon the will, and consists in the resignation of that to the will of Christ.

Matthew Henry, on the place.

nature: but this liberty is restrained, in some measure, by what are called the laws of nations, which are certain rules, that by a tacit consent are agreed upon among all communities, at least among those who are accounted the polite and civilized part of mankind. *These,* nations are not at liberty to violate.

What has been said may be sufficient to shew what that liberty is in which men ought to stand fast. In a state of nature it is all that liberty which is consistent with the law of nature; under civil government, it is all which is consistent with the law of nature, and with such restrictions as they have consented to come under consistently with the law of nature and the end of society: and when we consider one independent state in reference to another, it is all that natural liberty which is consistent with the laws of nations.

And whatever share men enjoy of this liberty, we may properly say in the words of the text, that Christ has made them free with it: since after his resurrection and exaltation to the right hand of the Majesty on high, all power in heaven and in earth was committed to him, and he now sits, and is to continue at the head of God's providential government, till he hath put all enemies under his feet; after which, he shall deliver up the kingdom to God, even the Father—that God may be all in all.

II. I am in the next place to shew in what way men are to stand fast in their liberty, or what they may and ought to do in defence of it.

It is here supposed that some attempts are made to injure it. And it has been found in all ages and places that such attempts have been made by unreasonable and wicked men. The history of mankind is filled with instances of this; insomuch that if from the great number of historical books that have been written, we should leave out those parts that relate to their encroachments upon one another, their injuries and injustice, most of those huge volumes would shrink to a very small size. Cain began this practice very soon after the creation: and it has been continued ever since, both among kingdoms and individuals. And the same practice is still to be expected, while human nature continues what it is.

Now for men to stand fast in their liberty means, in general, resisting the attempts that are made against it, in the best and most effectual manner they can.

When any one's liberty is attacked or threatened, he is first to try gentle methods for his safety; to reason with, and persuade the adversary to desist, if there be opportunity for it; or

get out of his way, if he can; and if by such means he can prevent the injury, he is to use no other.

But the experience of all ages has shewn, that those, who are so unreasonable as to form designs of injuring others, are seldom to be diverted from their purpose by argument and persuasion alone; Notwithstanding all that can be said to shew the injustice and inhumanity of their attempt, they persist in it, till they have gratified the unruly passion which set them to work. And in this case, what is to be done by the sufferer? Is he to use no other means for his safety, but remonstrance or flight, when these will not secure him? Is he patiently to take the injury and suffer himself to be robbed of his liberty or his life, if the adversary sees fit to take it? Nature certainly forbids this tame submission, and loudly calls to a more vigorous defence. Self-preservation is one of the strongest, and a universal principle of the human mind: And this principle allows of every thing necessary to self-defence, opposing force to force, and violence to violence. This is so universally allowed that I need not attempt to prove it.

But since it has been supposed by some that christianity forbids all violent resisting of evil, or defending ourselves against injuries in such a manner as will hurt, or endanger those who attack us; it may not be amiss to enquire briefly, whether defensive war be not allowed by the gospel of Christ, the Prince of peace.

And there are, if I mistake not, several passages in the new testament, which shew, that, it was not the design of this divine institution to take away from mankind the natural right of defending their liberty, even by the sword.

I will not alledge the words of John the baptist when in answer to the demand which the soldiers made: *"What shall we do?—he said unto them, do violence to no man, neither accuse any falsely, and be content with your wages."* (*Luke 3:14*) For though they plainly imply, that, at that time, the military profession was not unlawful, and, consequently, that men might use the sword when there was occasion for it; yet it does not follow from hence, that the religion which Jesus was to institute, would allow of that profession and the use of the sword.

But there are other passages proper to be here alledged.

The first that I shall mention is our Lord's own words to Pilate, when under examination before that Governor. The chief charge bro't against Jesus was, that he was going to set up a

THE CLERGY
OF THE
REVOLUTION

AN ARTILLERY-
ELECTION SERMON,
1773

temporal kingdom inconsistent with the sovereignty of the Roman Emperor. In answer to which he declared, that his *kingdom was not of this world;* and then offered the following argument to prove the assertion: *"If my kingdom were of this world, then would my servants fight, that I should not be delivered to the Jews: But now is my kingdom not from hence."* (*John 18:36*) There is an ellipsis in the latter clause; but the sense of the whole is obviously what follows. You know that those who aim at temporal dominion, endeavour to establish their authority and defend themselves, by force of arms, when it is necessary: If this had been my aim I should have taken the same method, and ordered my servants to fight against the Jews when they came to apprehend me: Wherefore, since I have made no violent resistance; but, on the contrary, "hindred one of my disciples from fighting who fought to rescue me," it must now be evident to you, that the kingdom which I claim is not of this world. Our Lord here, plainly allows that it is fit and proper for temporal kingdoms to fight in defence of their liberty. His own kingdom is not, indeed, to be defended in this way, which being wholly spiritual, consisting in the obedience of men's wills and affections to the laws of God, is incapable of being directly either injured or defended by the sword, as the kingdoms of this world, and men's temporal interest may.

Cornelius, a centurion of the Italian band, was directed by an angel of God to send for Peter, who should tell him *"What he ought to do."* (*Acts. 10*) But we do not find that the apostle directed him to quit his military profession, or intimated that it was inconsistent with the spirit of christianity; which he certainly would have done, had the character of a soldier and a good christian been incompatible.

The apostle Paul exhorts the Romans thus: *"If it be possible, as much as lieth in you, live peaceably with all men."* (*Romans 12:18*) Which words plainly imply, that notwithstanding all their endeavours to preserve peace, it might be impossible for them to live peaceably with all men, or not to contend and be at strife with some; i.e. impossible in a moral sense, improper, unlawful; for they do not require us to do all which we have a natural power to do, for the sake of peace, but only all that we can do consistently with higher obligations, with our duty in other respects.

Once more—let me observe, that in the apocalypse of St. John, where we have a prophetic account of the future state of the church on earth,

till the consummation of all things, there are several passages which intimate, that the saints of the Most High, will fight in their defence against their enemies; and that though they shall in various instances be overcome, yet that they shall at length, by an amazing slaughter of their persecutors, obtain for themselves the peaceable enjoyment of that liberty wherewith Christ hath made them free. (Rev. XI,7; XIII, 7; XIV, 19, 20; XVII, 14; XIX, 14-21)

Now it cannot reasonably be supposed that the spirit of God would have represented his faithful servants, as thus fighting against their enemies, and being so favoured by divine providence, as finally to prevail over them, if defensive war was inconsistent with the spirit of the gospel.

It is not, however, to be denied that there are some passages in the new testament which seem to forbid all war: particularly, our Saviour's own words in his sermon on the mount. *"I say unto you that ye resist not evil—love your enemies; do good to them that hate you, &c."* (*Matthew 5:39*) And those of the apostle Paul, *"Recompence to no man evil for evil.—Avenge not yourselves:"* (*Romans 12:17, 19*) And some others of the like import. And from such passages some have supposed that christians are not allowed to defend themselves by force of arms, how violently soever they may be attacked.

Give me leave then, to offer a few remarks to take off the force of this objection.

1. When our Saviour forbids us to resist evil, he seems to have had in view only small injuries, for such are those which he mentions in the following words, as an illustration of the precept: smiting on the cheek, taking away one's coat, or compelling him to go a mile. And to such injuries it is oftentimes a point of prudence, as well as duty to submit, rather than contend. But it does not follow, that because we are forbidden to resist such slight attacks, we may not defend ourselves when the assault is of a capital kind. But,

2. Supposing our Lord's words to refer only to small injuries, they ought not to be taken in an absolute sense. Expressions of this nature frequently occur in scripture, which are universally understood with certain restrictions and limitations. For instance: *"Love not the world, nor the things that are in the world."* (*I John 2:15*) *"Lay not up for yourselves treasure on earth."* (*Matt. 6:19*) *"Give to him that asketh thee, and from him that would borrow of thee, turn not thou away."* (*Matt. 5:42*) Now, I believe, no body ever supposed, not even the honest *Quakers,* that

these precepts were to be understood so literally, as to forbid all love of the world, and all care to provide the good things of it; or to oblige us "to give to every idle fellow all he may think fit to ask, whether in charity or loan." And we have as good a right to limit the precept which forbids our resisting evil, by the nature and reason of things, as we have to limit these other indefinite expressions.

3. Defending ourselves by force of arms against injurious attacks, is a quite different thing from rendering evil for evil. The latter implies doing hurt to another, because he has done hurt to us; the former implies doing hurt to another, if he is hurt in the conflict, only because there is no other way of avoiding the mischief he endeavours to do us: the *one* proceeds from malice and revenge; the *other* merely from self-love, and a just concern for our own happiness, and argues no ill will against any man.

And therefore it is to be observed,

4. That necessary self-defence, however fatal it may prove to those who unjustly attack us, implies no principle inconsistent with that love to our enemies which Christ enjoins. For, at the same time that we are defending ourselves against their assaults, we may bear good-will towards them, wish them well, and pray God to befriend them: All which we doubtless ought to do in respect of our bitterest enemies.

Enough has been said to shew the consistency of war with the spirit of the gospel.

But it is only defensive war that can be justified in the sight of God. When no injury is offered us, we have no right to molest others. And christian meekness, patience and forbearance, are duties that ought to be practised both by kingdoms and individuals. Small injuries, that are not likely to be attended with any very pernicious consequences, are rather to be submitted to, than resisted by the sword. Both religion and humanity strongly forbid the bloody deeds of war, unless they are necessary. Even when the injury offered is great in itself, or big with fatal consequences, we should if there be opportunity, endeavour to prevent it by remonstrance, or by offering to leave the matter in dispute to indifferent judges, if they can be had. If these endeavours are unsuccessful, it then becomes proper, to use more forceable means of resistance.

A people may err by too long neglecting such means, and shamefully suffer the sword to rust in its scabberd, when it ought to be employed in defending their liberty. The most grasping and oppressive power will commonly let its neigh-

bours remain in peace, if they will submit to its unjust demands. And an incautious people may submit to these demands, one after another, till its liberty is irrecoverably gone, before they saw the danger. Injuries small in themselves, may in their consequences be fatal to those who submit to them; especially if they are persisted in. And, with respect to such injuries, we should ever act upon that ancient maxim of prudence; *obsta principiis*. The first unjust demands of an encroaching power should be firmly withstood, when there appears a disposition to repeat and encrease such demands. And oftentimes it may be both the right and duty of a people to engage in war, rather than give up to the *demands* of such a power, what they could, without any incoveniency, spare in the way of charity. War, though a great evil, is ever preferable to such concessions, as are likely to be fatal to public liberty. And when such concessions are required and insisted upon, as the conditions of peace, the only consideration to be attended to by the abused state, is that which our Saviour intimates common prudence will always suggest in such cases: *"What king going to make war against another king, sitteth not down first and consulteth whether he be able, &c."* (Luke 14:31)

An innocent people threatened with war are not always obliged to receive the first attack.— This may frequently prove fatal, or occasion an irreparable damage. When others have sufficiently manifested an injurious or hostile intention, and persist in it, notwithstanding all the admonition and remonstrance we can make, we may, in order to avoid the blow they are meditating against us, begin the assault.

After a people have been forced into a war for their own security, they ought to set reasonable bounds to their resentment, or they may become as guilty as the first aggressors. They should aim at nothing more than repelling the injury, obtaining reparation for damages sustained, and security against future injuries. If, after these ends are obtained, they continue the war, in order to distress their enemies, or reduce them under their power, they become offenders, and the war on their side is unjust.

Submitting the foregoing general observations to your candor, I go on to hint at some things proper to be attended to, by every people, in order to their being in a capacity to defend themselves against encroachments on their liberty.

1. They should endeavor to be united and at peace among themselves. The strength of a society, as well as its honour and happiness, de-

pends much upon its union. Our Saviour's maxim is founded in reason, and has been confirmed by the experience of all ages: *"Every kingdom divided against itself is brought to desolation."* (*Matt. 12:25*) When the body·politic is divided into parties, and the members make a business of opposing each other, it is in a fair way to ruin. They are not likely to unite in measures of defence against a common enemy, and will therefore lie open to the encroachments of violence and oppression, and become an easy prey to every invader. The tyrants of the earth, sensible of this, have commonly acted upon this maxim, *divide et impera:* let us first divide the people, whom we mean to enslave, into parties, and we shall then easily bring them under our power.

2. They should endeavor to maintain among themselves a general disposition to submit to government. Society cannot subsist without government; and there can be no government without laws, and a submission to laws. If a licentious spirit prevails among a people, a general disposition to trample upon laws and despise government, they will probably make but a poor figure in defending themselves against a common enemy; for, in making this defence, there must be leaders and followers, some to command and some to obey: And, other things being equal, the more a disposition to submit to rule and order prevails among a people, the more likely will they be to defend their liberty against foreign invasions. Indeed without any enemy from abroad, the general prevalence of a licentious spirit may as effectually destroy the liberty of a people, as the most despotic government; for civil "liberty is something as really different from that licentiousness which supposeth no government, as from that slavery which supposeth tyranny: it is a freedom restrained by beneficial laws, and living and dying with public happiness." (Bp. Hoadly.)

3. That people that would be in a capacity to defend themselves successfully against encroachments, should take care that their internal government be free and easy; allowing all that liberty to every one which is consistent with the necessary restraints of government; laying no burdens upon any, but what are for the good of the whole, and to which the whole society has actually or virtually consented. Though the contrary evil takes its rise from the weakness or wickedness of rulers, yet in every free state it is the right and duty of all, *subjects* as well as rulers, to use their influence against it: And where the subjects have no *constitutional* right to do any thing to prevent or remove such an evil,

they are already slaves, and it may be tho't improper to talk of their defending their liberty; though they ought, doubtless, to endeavor to recover it. However, I say, it is highly necessary that this freedom from unreasonable restraints be preserved, in order to a people's retaining a spirit of liberty, and being in a capacity to defend themselves against a common enemy. It is justly observed by that great statesman, lord Verulam, that "the blessing of Judah and Issachar will never meet, that the same people or nation should be both the lion's whelp, and the ass between two burdens: neither will it be, that a people overlaid with taxes, should ever become valiant and martial." (Bacon's Essays, p. 113.) The laying unreasonable burdens and restraints upon a people, will, if they are submitted to, debase their minds, break their spirits, enervate their courage, and sink them into cowards: if they are not submitted to, the consequence will be internal tumult, disorder, strife, and contempt of government; and in either case, the defensive power of the state is greatly diminished. Behold, then the policy, or rather the madness and folly of oppressive rulers: if they are successful in their injurious measures, they are exposing themselves and their subjects an helpless prey to the ravages of some ambitious neighbour: if they are not; they are raising up enemies against themselves at home, and, as it were setting fire to their own habitations.

4. A people who would stand fast in their liberty, should furnish themselves with weapons proper for their defence, and learn the use of them.

It is indeed an hard case, that those who are happy in the blessings of providence, and disposed to live peaceably with all men, should be obliged to keep up the idea of blood and slaughter, and expend their time and treasure to acquire the arts and instruments of death. But this is a necessity which the depravity of human nature has laid upon every state. Nor was there ever a people that continued, for any considerable time, in the enjoyment of liberty, who were not in a capacity to defend themselves against invaders, unless they were too poor and inconsiderable to tempt an enemy.

So much depends upon the military art, in the present day, that no people can reasonably expect to defend themselves successfully without it. However numerous they may be, if they are unskilled in arms, their number will tend little more to their security, than that of a flock of sheep does to preserve them from the depredations of the wolf: accordingly it is looked upon as a point of wisdom, in every state, to be furnished with this skill, though it is not to be obtained without great labor and expence.

In some nations the method has been to trust for defence and security to what is called a STANDING ARMY; a number of men paid by the public, to devote themselves wholly to the military profession; while the body of the people followed their peaceable employments, without paying any attention to the art of war.

But this has ever been thought, by the wise and prudent, a precarious defence.

Such armies are, as to the greater part of them, generally composed of men who have no real estate in the dominions which they are to defend; their pay is their living, and the main thing that attaches them to their employers; their manner of life tends to corrupt their morals, and, though they are naturally of the same temper with other men, they seldom continue long in this profession, before they become distinguished by their vices: So that neither their temporal interest, nor their regard to virtue can be supposed to attach them so strongly to the country that employs them, but that there will always be danger of their being tempted by the promise of larger pay to betray their trust, and turn their arms against it. No people therefore, can with safety trust intirely to a standing army, even for defence against foreign enemies.

But without any such enemy, a standing army may be fatal to the happiness and liberty of a community. *They* generally propagate corruption and vice where they reside, they frequently insult and abuse the unarmed and defenceless people: When there is any difference between rulers and subjects, they will generally be on the side of the former, and ready to assist them in oppressing and enslaving the latter.

For though they are really servants of the people, and paid by them; yet this is not commonly done in their name; but in the name of the supreme magistrate. The KING'S BREAD, and the KING'S SERVICE, are familiar expressions among soldiers, and tend to make them consider him as their only master, and prefer his personal interest to that of the people. So that an army may be the means, in the hands of a wicked and oppressive sovereign, of overturning the constitution of a country, and establishing the most intolerable despotism.* It would be easy to shew from history, that this measure has been fatal to the liberties of many nations. And indeed, it has seldom been approved by the body of a people.

But rulers of an arbitrary disposition, have ever endeavored to have a standing army at their command, under a pretence indeed of being for the safety of the state, though really with a view of giving efficacy to their orders. It has sometime been pretended, that this is necessary to aid and support civil government. But whoever considers, that the design of government is the good of the people, and the great improbability there is, that a people, in general, should be against measures calculated for their good, and that *such* measures only ought to be enforced, will look upon this as the idlest pretence. For rulers to use a military power, to enforce measures of a contrary tendency, is one of the wickedest and most unjustifiable kinds of offensive war; a violation not only of the common laws of justice and humanity, but of their own sacred engagements to promote the public good. The keeping up troops sufficient to guard exposed frontier posts, may be proper; but to have an army continually stationed in the midst of a people, in time of peace, is a precarious and dangerous method of security.

A safer way, and which has always been esteemed the wisest and best, by impartial men, is to have the power of defence in the body of the people, to have a well-regulated and well-disciplined militia. ("Our trained bands are the trustiest and most proper strength of a free nation." Milton's Eikon.) This is placing the sword in hands that will not be likely to betray their trust, and who will have the strongest motives to act their part well, in defence of their country, whenever they shall be called for. An army composed of men and property, who have been all their days inured to labour, will generally equal the best veteran troops, in point of strength of body and firmness of mind, and when fighting in defence of their religion, their estates, their liberty, and families, will have stronger motives to exert themselves, and may, if they have been properly disciplined, be not much inferior to them in the skill of arms. . . .

Caution however ought to be used in constituting a militia, that it may answer the end for which it is designed, and not be liable to be made an instrument of tyranny and oppression. It should be subject to discipline and order, and somewhere in the state should be lodged a power of calling

THE CLERGY
OF THE
REVOLUTION

AN ARTILLERY-
ELECTION SERMON,
1773

---

* "What are we to expect, if in a future age an ambitious Prince should arise, with a dissolute and debauched army, a *flattering Clergy,* a prostitute Ministry, a bankrupt house of L——d's, a pensioned house of C——ns, and a slavish and corrupted nation?" *Trenchard's history of standing armies in England.*

it forth to action, whenever the safety of the people requires it. But this power should be so limited and restrained, as that it cannot call it unnecessarily, or oblige it to commit violence or oppression upon any of the subjects.

5. Once more, it is necessary for a people who would preserve their liberty, to maintain the general practice of religion and virtue. This will tend to make them courageous: The truest fortitude is ever to be found where the passions and affections are in subjection to the laws of God. Religion conciliates the favor of God, upon whom success in war essentially depends; and the hope of this favour will naturally inspire a brave and undaunted resolution. Not to mention that the unity, riches, and bodily strength of a people are greatly favoured by virtue. On the other hand; vice naturally makes men timerous, and fills the breast with baseness and cowardise. What is here said is agreable to the observation of that wise King and inspired writer, who tells us, *"the wicked flee, when no man pursueth; but the righteous are bold as a lion."* (*Proverbs 28:1*).

III. Let me now offer a few considerations to shew the obligations men are under to defend that liberty which providence has conferred upon them.

This is a trust committed to us by heaven: we are accountable for the use we make of it, and ought therefore, to the best of our power to defend it. The servant, who hid his talent in a napkin, is condemned in our Lord's parable; and he who through inattention, indolence or cowardise, suffers it to be wrested from him, is little less criminal. Should a person, for instance, whose ability and circumstances enable him to do good in the world, to relieve his distressed brethren, and be an example of charity and other virtues, tamely yield up all his interest and become an absolute slave to some unjust and wicked oppressor, when he might by a manly resistance have secured his liberty, would he not be guilty of great unfaithfulness to God, and justly liable to his condemnation? This would in its consequences be really worse than hiding his talent in a napkin; it would be not only not improving it for the glory of the giver, but conveying it into hands which will, in all probability, employ it greatly to his dishonour. This reasoning is as applicable to a community as to an individual. A kingdom or common wealth, as such, is accountable for the improvement it makes of it's advantages; It is bound to preserve them, and employ them for the honour of God! so far as it can, to be an example of virtue to neighbouring communities, and

afford them relief when they are in distress: but by yielding up their possessions and liberties to an encroaching oppressive power, they become, in a great measure, incapable of their duties, and are liable to be made the ministers of sin through the compulsion of their masters. Out of faithfulness then, to God, and in order to escape the doom of slothful servants, we should endeavour to defend our rights and liberties.

Men are bound to preserve their own lives, as long as they can, consistently with their duty in other respects. Would not he, who should lose his life by neglecting to resist a wild beast, be criminal in the sight of God? And can he be innocent who loses it by neglecting to oppose the violent attacks of wicked men, oftentimes as fierce and cruel as the most savage beast?

Men are also bound, individuals and societies, to take care of their temporal happiness, and do all they lawfully can, to promote it. But what can be more inconsistent with this duty, than submitting to great encroachments upon our liberty? Such submission tends to slavery; and compleat slavery implies every evil that the malice of man and devils can inflict. Again,

The regard which we owe to the happiness of others makes this a duty.

Every man is bound both by the law of nature and revelation, to provide in the best manner he can, for the temporal happiness of his family; and he that neglects this, has, according to the declaration of an inspired apostle, *denied the faith, and is worse than an infidel.* But in what way can a man be more justly chargeable with this neglect, than by suffering himself to be deprived of his life, liberty or property, when he might lawfully have preserved them?

Reason, humanity and religion, all conspire to teach us, that we ought in the best manner we can, to provide for the happiness of posterity. We are allied to them by the common tie of nature: They are not here to act their part: A concern for them is a debt which we owe for the care which our progenitors took for us: Heaven has made us their guardians, and intrusted to our care their liberty, honour, and happiness: For when they come upon the stage, they will be deeply affected by the transactions of their fathers, especially by their public transactions. If the present inhabitants of a country submit to slavery, slavery is the inheritance which they will leave to their children. And who that has the bowels of a father, or even the common feelings of humanity, can think without horror, of being the means of subjecting unborn millions to the iron scepter of tyranny? But further: a regard to the happiness of mankind in general, makes it a duty to resist great injuries. Yielding to the unjust demands of bad men, not only lessens our power of doing good, but encourages them to repeat their injuries, and strengthens their hands to do mischief: It enables them to give fuller scope to their lusts, and more effectually to spread corruption, distress and misery.

It is therefore an act of benevolence to oppose and destroy that power which is employed in injuring others; and as much, when it is that of a tyrant, as of a wild beast.

Once more; from a regard to religion men are obliged to defend their liberty against encroachments, though the attack should not immediately affect religion. Slavery exposes to many temptations to vice, and by debasing and weakening the mind, destroying its fortitude and magnimity renders it less capable of resisting them, and creates a dependance upon, and subjection to wicked men, highly prejudicial to virtue. Hence it has been often observed, and is confirmed by experience, that the loss of liberty is soon followed by the loss of all virtue and religion.

"The conquer'd also, and inslav'd by war
Shall with their freedom lost all virtue lose
And fear of God." (Paradise Lost)

Besides; the destruction of civil liberty is generally fatal to *religion*. The latter has seldom existed long in any place without the former. Nor is it to be expected that those who are wicked enough to deprive a people of *that,* should, when they have got them under their power, suffer them long to enjoy *this;* especially as tyranny has generally made these two evils subservient to each other.

But I may not enlarge: The considerations which have been suggested shew, if I mistake not, that it is not only the right but the duty of men to defend that liberty, with which providence has made them free: And a duty of high obligation, as the neglect of it may be attended with consequences, the most prejudicial to human virtue and happiness, and greatly dishonorary to God.

All that now remains is to offer some reflections, and apply the subject to the present occasion.

1. What has been said may serve to caution all against invading the liberty of others:—Whoever does this, obliges others to resist him: he puts himself into a state of war with them, and is justly liable to all the evil which their necessary self-defence may bring upon him, And though he may think that his power is so great, and their's so little, that he can be in no danger from their resentment, the event may convince him of his mistake. Men, who have a just sense and value of liberty, will sometimes do wonders in its defence.

"They have great odds
Against the astonish'd sons of violence,
Who fight with awful justice on their side."
(Thompson.)

Oppressors may indeed for a time, be successful and overcome all opposition; yet it seldom happens that they persevere in their injurious practice, without meeting with such resistance as causes their *mischief to return upon their own heads, and their violent dealings to come down upon their own pates:* It is an old observation, that few tyrants descend in peace to the grave. If therefore, the laws of God will not, a regard to their own safety, should restrain men from invading the rights of the innocent.

2. If it be so important a duty for men to resist encroachments upon their liberty; then it cannot be improper for the christian minister, to inculcate *this* upon his hearers; to exhort them to be watchful over it, and ready to oppose all attempts against it. This is so far from being improper, that it is, I humbly conceive, his indispensible duty. Nor can I see how he could answer it to God, or his own conscience, if, when he thought his country was in danger of being enslaved, for want of a proper sense of, and opposition to the approaches of tyranny, he should neglect to point out the danger, and with

. . . "honest zeal
to rouse the watchmen of the public weal."
(Pope)

It is readily owned, that *designedly* to spread false alarms, to fill the minds of people with groundless prejudices against their rulers, or a neighbouring state, to stir up faction and encourage opposition to *good* government, are things highly criminal; and whoever does thus, whatever character he may wear among men, is in reality a minister, not of Christ, but of the devil, the father of falsehood, confusion and rebellion. But to shew people their real danger, point out the source of it, and exhort them to such exertions as are necessary to avoid it, are acts of

THE CLERGY
OF THE
REVOLUTION

AN ARTILLERY-
ELECTION SERMON,
1773

benevolence becoming every disciple, and especially every professed minister of Christ.

3. Since the preservation of public liberty depends so much upon a people's being possessed of the art of war; those who exert themselves to encourage and promote this art, act a laudable part, and are intitled to the thanks of their brethren. Upon this account, the company, which is the occasion of this solemnity, deserves to be esteemed *honorable,* though its institution were much less *ancient* than it is. And as this society has in former days furnished many brave men, who did worthily in defence of our country; so, from the spirit which at present prevails among the gentlemen who compose it, we doubt not but it will furnish others, whenever there shall be occasion for it. How far this institution, by exciting in others a spirit of imitation or emulation, has been the occasion of the present general attention to the military art among us, I pretend not to say: But whatever be the cause, it must give pleasure to every friend of public liberty, to see this people so generally engaged in military exercises. This argues a manly spirit, a sense of liberty, a just apprehension of its danger, a resolution to stand fast in it, and, as far as any thing in our power can do it, promises freedom to our country.

We are not, I hope, insensible that peace is a great blessing, and, in itself, ever to be prefered to war; nor unthankful to Him who ruleth among the nations, the God of peace, for the enjoyment we have had of this blessing for a number of years past. But we have little reason to expect, however ardently we may wish, that this country will always be the habitation of peace. Ambition, avarice, and other unruly passions have a great hand in directing the conduct of most of the kingdoms of this world. British America is already become considerable among the European nations for its numbers, and their easiness of living; and is continually rising into greater importance. I will not undertake to decypher the *signs of the times,* or to say from what quarter we are most likely to be molested. But from the course of human affairs, we have the utmost reason to expect that the time will come, when we must either submit to *slavery,* or defend our liberties by our own sword. And this perhaps may be the case sooner than some imagine. No one can doubt but there are powers on the continent of Europe, that would be glad to add North-America to their dominions, and who, if they thought the thing practicable, would soon find a pretence for attempting it. The naval power of Great-Britain

has been hitherto our chief security against invasions from that continent. But every thing belonging to the present state, is uncertain and fluctuating. Things may soon be in such a situation with Great-Britain, that it will be no longer proper for us to confide in her power, for the protection of our liberty. Our greatest security, under God, will be our being in a capacity to defend ourselves. Were we, indeed, sure that Great-Britain would always be both *able* and *willing* to protect us in our liberty, which, from present appearances, we have little reason to expect, it would be shameful for so numerous a people as this, and a people of so much natural strength and fortitude, to be, thro' inattention to the art of war, incapable of bearing a part in their own defence. Such weakness must render them contemptible to all the world.

British America, especially the northern part of it, is by its situation calculated to be a nursery of heroes. Nothing is wanting but our own care and application to make us, with the neighbouring colonies, a formidable people. And religion, honor, patriotism, and even self-love, all unite in demanding from us this application and care. This people, it may be presumed, will never of choice, keep among them a *standing army* in time of peace: Virtue, domestic peace, the insulted walls of our State-House, and even the once crimsoned *stones of the street,* all loudly *cry out* against this measure. But every well-wisher to the public, should countenance and encourage a military spirit among our militia through the province.

Our political Fathers have it in their power to do much for this end; and we have a right to expect that, out of faithfulness to God and this people, they will not neglect it. From the countenance which his Excellency and the honorable Council shew to the military transactions of this day, we would gladly hope, that, they in conjunction with the other branch of the legislature, will, in this way, as well as others, prove themselves to be God's ministers for good to the people.

It is also in the power of persons of rank and fortune, in their private capacity, greatly to promote this cause by their example and otherwise. It is highly absurd, though not uncommon, that those who have most to lose by the destruction of a state, should be least capable of bearing a part in its defence. Riches are frequently the main temptation to war. Where a people are all poor, there is little danger of their being invaded: So that there being men of affluence among a people, is often the cause of their being obliged to defend themselves by the sword. It is therefore especially *their* duty, as well as interest, to do what they can to put the people into a capacity of defence. When *they* spend their time in idleness, effeminating pleasures, or even in accumulating riches, to the total neglect of the art of war, and every measure to promote it, they act unbecoming good members of society, and set an example highly prejudicial to the community.

Whereas when gentlemen of fortune, notwithstanding the allurements of pleasure on the one hand, and the fatiguing exercise of a soldier on the other, exert themselves to acquire and promote the military art, they are an honor to their circumstances, and a blessing to the public: Their example will have great influence upon others; and, other things being equal, such men will be most likely to fight valiantly in defence of their liberty, whenever it shall be necessary. By such a conduct, they shew their regard to their country, in a way that will probably be much more beneficial to it, than merely talking, writing, or preaching in favor of liberty. And it ought to be esteemed as no inconsiderable evidence, among many others, of a public, truly patriotic spirit in the honorable gentleman (The Hon. John Hancock, Esq;) who leads his Excellency's company of Cadets, that he has so chearfully endured the fatigue of qualifying himself to be a good officer, and, by his generous exertions in conjunction with their own, rendered his company an honour to the town, to their commanders and themselves. This company in general, is indeed an example of what I was urging; of gentlemen of easy circumstances giving proper attention to the art of war, and is on that account the more respectable and important. . . . May this spirit still revive and prevail through the province, till this whole people become as considerable for their skill in arms, as they are for their natural strength and courage.

The gentlemen who are engaged in acquiring this art will remember that the true end of it is only defence; that it is to be employed, not to destroy, but to protect and secure the liberty and happiness of mankind; not to infringe the rights of others, but to defend their own. While, therefore they endeavor to resemble such men as *Alexander* and *Cæsar* in military skill and valour,

they will detest the principles from which they acted, in invading and distressing inoffensive people. For though they have been honored with the name of heroes, they were, in reality, public robbers and murderers.

They will also remember that the most desirable liberty, and which we should be ready to defend, is that of a well governed society, which is as essentially different from that licentiousness, which is without law or government, as it is from an absolute subjection to the arbitrary will of another. This is the liberty wherewith Christ has made us free; to which he has given us a right. While, therefore, these gentlemen will be always ready to stand forth in defence of true civil liberty, whenever they shall see her assaulted, and be properly called upon; they will never on any consideration be prevailed with, to employ their arms for the destruction of good government, by aiding either tyranny on the one hand, or licentiousness on the other.

But above all they will remember, that religion is the main concern of man, and a necessary qualification for a good soldier. This, beyond any thing else, inspires with the love of liberty, with fortitude and magnanimity; and this alone can enable them to meet death with a rational composure and tranquility of mind, which is an enemy before which the bravest soldier must fall at last.

To conclude: This whole assembly will bear in mind, that there is another and more valuable kind of liberty, than that to which the foregoing discourse more immediately relates, and which, at this day, so generally employs our attention and conversation; a liberty, which consists in being free from the power and dominion of sin, through the assistance of the divine spirit, concurring with our own pious, rational and persevering endeavours. Whatever our outward circumstances may be, if we are destitute of this spiritual liberty, we are in reality slaves, how much soever we may hate the name; if we possess it we are *free indeed:* And our being free in this sense, will give us the best grounds to hope for temporal freedom, through the favour of heaven; and, at length, gain us admission into the regions of perfect and uninterrupted liberty, peace and happiness.

★   ★   ★   ★   ★

CHRISTIAN
CONSTITUENT:

THE AMERICAN
CHRISTIAN
CHURCH

*Journals of the
Provincial
Congress of
Massachusetts
in 1774 and 1775,*
Boston, 1838

ASSISTANCE OF CLERGY REQUESTED

FIRST PROVINCIAL CONGRESS
MONDAY, DECEMBER 5, 1774, A.M.

Ordered, That Doct. Winthrop, Mr. Sullivan, Mr. Pickering, Mr. Bridge, and Mr. Cheever, be a committee to prepare an address to the clergy of this province, desiring them to exhort their people to carry into execution the resolves of the Continental Congress.

TUESDAY, DECEMBER 6, 1774, A.M.

The Committee appointed to prepare an address to the clergy, having amended the same, again reported; the report was read and accepted, and ordered that copies thereof be sent to all the ministers of the gospel in the province; which is as followeth:

Reverend Sirs: When we contemplate the friendship and assistance our ancestors, the first settlers of this province, (while overwhelmed with distress) received from the pious pastors of the churches of Christ, who, to enjoy the rights of conscience, fled with them into this land, then a savage wilderness, we find ourselves filled with the most grateful sensations, and we cannot but acknowledge the goodness of heaven in constantly supplying us with preachers of the gospel, whose concern has been the temporal and spiritual happiness of this people.

In a day like this, when all the friends of civil and religious liberty are exerting themselves to deliver this country from its present calamities, we cannot but place great hopes in an order of men who have ever distinguished themselves in their country's cause; and do therefore recommend to the ministers of the gospel in the several towns and other places in this colony, that they assist us in avoiding that dreadful slavery with which we are now threatened, by advising the people of their several congregations, as they wish their prosperity, to abide by, and strictly adhere to, the resolutions of the Continental Congress, as the most peaceable and probable method of preventing confusion and bloodshed, and of restoring that harmony between Great Britain and these colonies, on which we wish might be established, not only the rights and liberties of America, but the opulence and lasting happiness of the whole British empire.

Resolved, That the foregoing address be presented to all the ministers of the gospel in the province.

CHAPLAINS FOR THE ARMY

SECOND PROVINCIAL CONGRESS
THURSDAY, MAY 18, 1775, A.M.

Ordered, That Capt. Rawson, Mr. Bullen and Col. Farley, be a committee to consider the practicability of employing chaplains, for the army, out of the number of clergy of this colony.

SATURDAY, MAY 20, 1775, A.M.

The report of the committee appointed to consider the practicability of providing chaplains, was again read and accepted, and is as follows, viz:

Whereas, it is necessary that chaplains should be appointed in the Massachusetts army, under the command of the Hon. Artemus Ward, Esq., which, if appointed, on the establishment made by this Congress, will greatly enhance the colony debt; and, whereas, it has been represented to this Congress, that several ministers of the religious assemblies within this colony, have expressed their willingness to attend the army aforesaid, in the capacity of chaplains, as they may be directed by this Congress; therefore, *Resolved,* that it be, and it is hereby recommended, to the ministers of the several religious assemblies within this colony, that, with the leave of their several congregations, they attend said army in their several turns, to the number of thirteen at one time, during the time the army shall be encamped, and that they make known their resolutions, to the Congress, thereon, or to the committee of safety, as soon as may be.

THIRD PROVINCIAL CONGRESS
WEDNESDAY, MAY 31, 1775, AFTERNOON

Resolved, That a copy of the resolve of the last Congress, relative to providing the army with chaplains, be laid before the reverend gentlemen of the clergy, now in convention, at Watertown.

The order of the day (was) moved for. . . .

Ordered, That Col. Palmer, Mr. Williams and Deacon Cheever, be a committee to introduce to this Congress a committee from the reverend gentlemen of the clergy, in convention at Watertown, now at the door. The committee were accordingly introduced, and informed the Congress that the said convention would be glad of the use of the meeting house tomorrow morning, at eight o'clock. Then the said committee withdrew.

Ordered, That Col. Palmer, Mr. Williams, and Deacon Cheever, be a committee to inform the reverend gentlemen of the convention, that this Congress comply with their request, and that the committee lay before the said convention, a copy of the resolve of the last Congress, respecting chaplains.

THURSDAY, JUNE 1, 1775

Ordered, That Deacon Fisher, Mr. Spaulding, Mr. Stickney, Mr. Partridge and Major Perley, be a committee to consider the proposal of the reverend gentlemen of the clergy, now in convention at Watertown, which is as follows:

To the Hon. Joseph Warren, Esq., President of the Provincial Congress of the Colony of the Massachusetts Bay, &c.:

Sir:—We, the pastors of the congregational churches of the colony of the Massachusetts Bay, in our present annual convention, gratefully beg leave to express the sense we have of the regard shewn by the honorable Provincial Congress to us, and the encouragement they have been pleased to afford to our assembling as a body this day. Deeply impressed with sympathy for the distresses of our much injured and oppressed country, we are not a little relieved, in beholding the representatives of this people, chosen by their free and unbiassed suffrages, now met to concert measures for their relief and defence, in whose wisdom and integrity, under the smiles of Divine Providence, we cannot but express our entire confidence.

As it has been found necessary to raise an army for the common safety, and our brave countrymen have so willingly offered themselves to this hazardous service, we are not insensible of the vast burden that their necessary maintenance must devolve upon the people.

We, therefore, cannot forbear, upon this occasion, to offer our services to the public, and to signify our readiness, with the consent of our several congregations, to officiate, by rotation, as chaplains to the army.

We devoutly commend the Congress, and our

brethren in arms, to the guidance and protection of that Providence, which, from the first settlement of this country, has so remarkably appeared for the preservation of its civil and religious rights.

Samuel Langdon, *Moderator*

At the Convention of the Ministers of the Massachusetts Bay, June 1, 1775:

The convention, taking into consideration the method of furnishing the army with chaplains, agreeably to the offer they have made to the honorable Congress, think it most expedient, that a sufficient number of persons should be chosen out of their number, by the officers of the army, to officiate statedly, rather than by quick rotation, in that character; and the convention depend, that the parochial duties of those ministers who shall serve in the army, will be performed by their brethren in the vicinity.

A true copy. Test: Amos Adams, *Scribe.*

FRIDAY, JUNE 2, 1775.

The committee appointed to consider the resolve and proposals of the reverend gentlemen of the clergy, reported; the report was accepted, and is as follows, viz.:

Whereas, it is of the greatest importance that our colony army be furnished with gentlemen to act as chaplains, on whose virtue, firmness and patriotism they can safely rely; and whereas, the reverend convention of the clergy of this colony have, most nobly and without reward, tendered their services in their country's cause:

Therefore, *Resolved,* That the general and field officers be, and they hereby are empowered and directed, to choose nine gentlemen of the clergy of this colony, to act as chaplains to said army: provided that not more than two of them belong to any one county; and the general officers of said army are hereby empowered to determine the regiments to which each chaplain shall be desired to officiate; and also, the committee of supplies are hereby directed to make suitable provision for said chaplains during their continuance in camp.

★   ★   ★   ★   ★

MINISTERS OF CONNECTICUT

Considering the dark and gloomy aspect of Divine Providence over this Colony and land, and that it is the indispensible duty of every people suffering under the afflictive chastisements

of a righteous God, with deep repentance, supplication and amendment of life, to endeavour by all the ways which God has prescribed to avert his anger and incline him to become reconciled to his people:

It is therefore resolved by this Assembly, That

*Public Records
of Connecticut,
1772-5,
Hartford, 1887*

By the Great and General Court of the Colony of MASSACHUSETTS-BAY.

A PROCLAMATION.

THE Frailty of human Nature, the Wants of Individuals, and the numerous Dangers which furround them, through the Courfe of Life, have in all Ages, and in every Country, impell'd them to form Societies, and eftablifh Governments.

As the Happinefs of the People is the fole End of Government, fo the Confent of the People is the only Foundation of it, in Reafon, Morality, and the natural Fitnefs of Things : And therefore every Act of Government, every Exercife of Sovereignty, againft, or without, the Confent of the People, is Injuftice, Ufurpation, and Tyranny.

It is a Maxim, that in every Government, there muft exift fomewhere, a fupreme, fovereign, abfolute, and uncontroulable Power : But this Power refides always in the Body of the People ; and it never was, or can be delegated to one Man, or a few ; the Great Creator having never given to Men a Right to veft others with Authority over them, unlimited either in Duration or Degree.

When Kings, Minifters, Governors, or Legiflators therefore, inftead of exercifing the Powers intrufted with them, according to the Principles, Forms, and Proportions ftated by the Conftitution, and eftablifhed by the original Compact, proftitute thofe Powers to the Purpofes of Oppreffion ;—to fubvert, inftead of fupporting a free Conftitution ;—to deftroy, inftead of preferving the Lives, Liberties and Properties of the People ;—they are no longer to be deemed Magiftrates vefted with a facred Character, but become public Enemies, and ought to be refifted.

The Adminiftration of Great-Britain, defpifing equally the Juftice, Humanity and Magnanimity of their Anceftors ; and the Rights, Liberties and Courage of AMERICANS, have, for a Courfe of Years, laboured to eftablifh a Sovereignty in America, not founded in the Confent of the People, but in the mere Will of Perfons a Thoufand Leagues from Us, whom we know not, and have endeavoured to eftablifh this Sovereignty over Us, againft our Confent, in all Cafes whatfoever.

The Colonies, during this Period, have recurred to every peaceable Refource in a free Conftitution, by Petitions and Remonftrances, to obtain Juftice ; which has been not only denied to them, but they have been treated with unexampled Indignity and Contempt ; and at length, open War of the moft atrocious, cruel and fanguinary Kind, has been commenced againft them. To this, an open, manly and fuccefsful Refiftance has hitherto been made. Thirteen Colonies are now firmly united in the Conduct of this moft juft and neceffary War, under the wife Councils of their Congrefs.

It is the Will of Providence, for wife, righteous, and gracious Ends, that this Colony fhould have been fingled out, by the Enemies of America, as the firft Object both of their Envy and their Revenge ; and after having been made the Subject of feveral mercilefs and vindictive Statutes, one of which was intended to fubvert our Conftitution by Charter, is made the Seat of War.

No effectual Refiftance to the Syftem of Tyranny prepared for us, could be made without either inftant Recourfe to Arms, or a temporary Sufpenfion of the ordinary Powers of Government, and Tribunals of Juftice : To the laft of which Evils, in Hopes of a fpeedy Reconciliation with Great-Britain, upon equitable Terms, the Congrefs advifed Us to fubmit : ——And Mankind has feen a Phænomenon, without Example in the political World, a large and populous Colony, fubfifting in great Decency and Order, for more than a Year, under fuch a Sufpenfion of Government.

But as our Enemies have proceeded to fuch barbarous Extremities, commencing Hoftilities upon the good People of this Colony, and with unprecedented Malice exerting their Power to fpread the Calamities of Fire, Sword and Famine through the Land, and no reafonable Profpect remains of a fpeedy Reconciliation with Great-Britain, the Congrefs have refolved ;

" That no Obedience being due to the Act of Parliament for altering the Charter of the Colony of Maffachufetts-Bay, nor to a Go-
" vernor or Lieutenant Governor, who will not obferve the Directions of, but endeavour to fubvert that Charter ; the Governor and
" Lieutenant Governor of that Colony, are to be confidered as abfent, and their Offices vacant ; and as there is no Council there, and
" Inconveniences arifing from the Sufpenfion of the Powers of Government, are intolerable, efpecially at a Time when General Gage
" hath actually levied War, and is carrying on Hoftilities againft his Majefty's peaceable and loyal Subjects of that Colony ; that, in order
" to conform as near as may be to the Spirit and Subftance of the Charter, it be recommended to the Provincial Convention, to write
" Letters to the Inhabitants of the feveral Places which are intitled to Reprefentation in Affembly, requefting them to chufe fuch Repre-
" fentatives ; and that the Affembly when chofen, do elect Counfellors ; and that fuch Affembly and Council, exercife the Powers of Go-
" vernment, until a Governor of his Majefty's Appointment will confent to govern the Colony, according to it's Charter."

In Purfuance of which Advice, the good People of this Colony have chofen a full and free Reprefentation of themfelves, who, being

in all its branches, under the influence and controul of the People; and therefore more free and happy than was enjoyed by their Ancestors: But as a Government so popular can be supported only by universal Knowledge and Virtue, in the Body of the People, it is the Duty of all Ranks, to promote the Means of Education, for the rising Generation, as well as true Religion, Purity of Manners, and Integrity of Life, among all Orders and Degrees.

As an Army has become necessary for our Defence, and in all free States the Civil must provide for and controul the Military Power, the major Part of the Council have appointed Magistrates and Courts of Justice in every County, whose Happiness is so connected with that of the People, that it is difficult to suppose they can abuse their Trust. The Business of it is to see those Laws inforced, which are necessary for the Preservation of Peace, Virtue and good Order. And the Great and General Court expects and requires, that all necessary Support and Assistance be given, and all proper Obedience yielded to them; and will deem every Person, who shall fail of his Duty in this Respect towards them, a Disturber of the Peace of this Colony, and deserving of exemplary Punishment.

That Piety and Virtue, which alone can secure the Freedom of any People, may be encouraged, and Vice and Immorality suppressed, the Great and General Court have thought fit to issue this Proclamation, commanding and enjoining it upon the Good People of this Colony, that they lead sober, religious and peaceable Lives; avoiding all Blasphemies, Contempt of the Holy Scriptures, and of the Lord's Day, and all other Crimes and Misdemeanors, all Debauchery, Prophaneness, Corruption, Venality, all riotous and tumultuous Proceedings, and all Immoralities whatsoever: And that they decently and reverently attend the public Worship of GOD, at all Times acknowledging with Gratitude his merciful Interposition in their Behalf, devoutly confiding in Him, as the GOD of Armies, by whose Favour and Protection alone they may hope for Success, in their present Conflict.

And all Judges, Justices, Sheriffs, Grand Jurors, Tythingmen, and all other Civil Officers within this Colony, are hereby strictly enjoined and commanded that they contribute all in their Power, by their Advice, Exertions and Examples, towards a general Reformation of Manners; and that they bring to condign Punishment, every Person, who shall commit any of the Crimes or Misdemeanors aforesaid, or that shall be guilty of any Immoralities whatsoever; and that they use their utmost Endeavours, to have the Resolves of the Congress, and the good and wholsome Laws of this Colony duly carried into Execution.

And as the Ministers of the Gospel, within this Colony, have, during the late Relaxation of the Powers of Civil Government, exerted themselves for our Safety, it is hereby recommended to them, still to continue their virtuous Labours for the Good of the People, inculcating by their public Ministry, and private Example, the Necessity of Religion, Morality, and good Order.

In Council January 19, 1776.

ORDERED, That the foregoing Proclamation be read at the Opening of every Superiour Court of Judicature, &c. and Inferiour Court of Common Pleas, and Court of General Sessions for the Peace within this Colony, by their respective Clerks; and at the annual Town-Meetings in March, in each Town. And it is hereby recommended to the several Ministers of the Gospel, throughout this Colony, to read the same in their respective Assemblies on the Lord's Day next after their receiving it, immediately after Divine Service.

By Order of the General Court,

PEREZ MORTON, Dep. Sec'y.

In the House of Representatives, January 23, 1776. Read and concur'd.

WILLIAM COOPER, Speaker pro Tem.

Consented to,

WILLIAM SEVER,
WALTER SPOONER,
CALEB CUSHING,
JOHN WINTHROP,
THOMAS CUSHING,
JOHN WHETCOMB,
JEDIDIAH FOSTER,
ELDAD TAYLOR,

PEREZ MORTON, Dep'y Sec'y.

MOSES GILL,
MICHAEL FARLEY,
SAMUEL HOLTEN,
CHARLES CHAUNCY,
JOSEPH PALMER,
JOHN TAYLOR,
BENJAMIN WHITE,
JAMES PRESCOTT.

Sent down for Concurrence.

GOD Save the PEOPLE.

it be recommended to all the ministers of the gospel in this Colony, that they earnestly endeavour to dissuade their several congregations from all excess, and all diversions which may be improper in the present day of distress; and that both they and their people cry mightily to God, that he would be pleased to spare his people and be gracious unto them, and visit them with his loving kindness and tender mercies, and not give up his heritage to reproach, but preserve unto them their great and important rights and privileges, and guide and prosper the public councils of this Colony and land, and in this hour of difficulty and distress graciously manifest his power in the deliverance and salvation of his people, to the glory of his own name.

★   ★   ★   ★   ★

The New England Gazetteer, by John Hayward, Concord, N.H., 1839

SHARON, CONNECTICUT

This town took an active part in favor of the liberties of the country. The approach of a large British army from Canada, under General Burgoyne, and the expedition up the North River, under General Vaughan, in 1777, filled the whole country with terror and despondency, and created strong fears and doubts as to the issue of the controversy: the firmness and confidence of Parson Smith, however, remained unbroken, and his efforts to revive the drooping spirits of his people were unremitted.

In the month of October, he preached a sermon from these words: "Watchman, what of the night? The Watchman saith, the morning cometh." In this discourse he dwelt much upon the indications, which the dealings of Providence afforded, that a bright and glorious morning was about to dawn upon a long night of defeat and disaster. He told the congregation, that he believed they would soon hear of a signal victory crowning the arms of America; and he exhorted them to trust with an unshaken and fearless confidence in that God, who, he believed, would yet crown with success the efforts of the friends of liberty in this country. Before the congregation was dismissed, a messenger arrived, with the intelligence of the surrender of Burgoyne's army. Parson Smith read the letter, conveying the intelligence, from the pulpit, and a flood of joy and gratitude burst from the congregation.

The photographic facsimile of the Proclamation of January 23, 1776 by the General Court of Massachusetts, on the preceding pages, is illustrative of Proclamations which were issued during our colonial period. Please note particularly, paragraph eight regarding the 'Phaenomenon' of mankind. Editor.

AMERICAN
CHRISTIAN EDUCATION

Should posterity inquire why their ancestors, destitute of military education

or experience, abandoned their peaceful abodes to encounter the perils

of uncertain warfare, let them be told it was not to execute the mandates

of a tyrant in subjugating their fellow men,

but it was in defence of our most precious rights and privileges;

it was a display of that genuine patriotism and true glory

which it is ever most honorable to venerate and cherish.

While their own hearts glow with patriotic fervor, let them reflect, that true glory

consists in the love of peace and the culture of benevolence and good will to men.

Let their souls hold in detestation every species of warfare,

save that which may secure and defend the invaluable heritage

which their fathers have bequeathed them,

and for which their memories should be embalmed with the incense of gratitude.

James Thacher, M.D., Surgeon in the American Army, 1823

The Importance of
Parental Fidelity
in the Education
of Children

He established a testimony in Jacob, and appointed a law in Israel, which he commanded our fathers, that they should make them known to their children. That the generation to come might know them, even the children which should be born, who should arise and declare them to their children. That they might set their hope in God, and not forget the works of God, but keep his commandments. (*Psalm* LXXVIII, 5-7)

The importance of the rising generation, has engaged the attention of the wise and good, in all ages. Experienced old men have ardently desired the best good of posterity. Patriarchs, prophets, and apostles have laboured to promote it. The inspired writer of this Psalm, impressed deeply with the subject, calls on us to attend to the words of his mouth, even the words which had been received from the fathers which, said he, we will not hide from their children, *"shewing to the generations to come the praises of the Lord, and his strength and his wonderful works."* (*Psalm 78:4*)

The words of our text contain a summary of God's law and testimony which he appointed for his people, to be transmitted to succeeding generations; that the knowledge and practice of true religion might be preserved to the end of the world. It will not be doubted that this subject claims our most serious attention, on the present occasion. . . . The great importance of transmitting to posterity, the divine law and testimony will appear from the following considerations.

1st.   The worth of posterity.

The importance of man will deeply impress the mind which attentively considers it. The present and future existence are, both of them, highly interesting, but especially the latter. The various endowments of the mind of man, in connexion with his immortality, render his existence important, in the highest degree. Such is the worth of the human soul, that in the estimate of unerring wisdom, it is not to be exchanged for the whole world (*Matt. xvi:26*). This worth is summarily comprised in the capacity for possessing and diffusing happiness, or which issues in the same, for union to God and his kingdom. Each individual of the present and future ages will fill a place in the scale of beings, through never-ending duration: important in every period of his existence; how important then in the whole of it! The present infant of a day, is a being of immortality, and will act a part which will materially effect the felicity, not of himself only, but of the whole moral system, and that forever.

Such considerations show the importance of man, and the worth of posterity; but it is still more strongly marked in the agency of God with

The Importance of Parental Fidelity, by Levi Hart, Norwich, 1792

respect to our race. This world is evidently created to be an habitation for man, the various orders of inferior creatures, were made and appointed for his service; and the whole course of events from the first creation, is directed with reference to him. But what swallows up all other considerations on this subject, is, *the work of redemption!* to this, nothing can be added to evince the importance of man, and the worth of posterity: the whole is expressed in saying that *"in due time, Christ died for the ungodly."* (Romans *v:6*), and that, *"God so loved the world, that he gave his only begotten Son, that whosoever believeth in him should not perish, but have everlasting life."* (John *iii:16*)

2d. The felicity and usefulness of posterity depends on a becoming regulation of their principles and manners. This consists in their receiving God's testimonies, and reducing them to practice. These testimonies enjoin the several branches of that religion which is summarily contained in the love of God and man. Without which they can be neither happy nor useful. (This assertion respects only the nature and tendency of moral dispositions, and is by no means to be understood in opposition to the important truth, that God by his wise and holy agency, so over-rules the wickedness of his enemies, and counteracts its nature and tendency as to render it subservient to the purpose of his infinite wisdom and holiness, and thus, by "educing good from ill," he causes the wrath of man to praise him, and the remainder of wrath, he graciously restrains.)

That each of these depend on such dispositions will appear to be true, to whatever particular we apply the observation.

What but mutual affection constitutes that harmony of minds which is termed friendship? Such union of hearts is the source and band of domestic felicity: if this be wanting, how deplorably miserable is the nearest of human connexions even in the midst of all other earthly good. But where this is found it not only gives worth to all other enjoyments, but supplies their absence, and gives truly sublime satisfaction in the midst of calamity. All family relations, and other social connexions are found to be happy in proportion to this, and the reverse if it be wanting.

The interests of society at large are proportionably effected, and depend on the union of its members, and where this in any good measure exists, the benevolent spectator will behold it with pleasure, and exultingly cry out, *"Behold how good and how pleasant it is for brethren to dwell together in unity."* But as man is a being of im-

mortality, and a member of that vast society, comprising all intelligent beings, his felicity and usefulness are principally to be measured in relation to that. When viewed in this connexion, how interesting is the present subject! Those whose principles and manners are formed to the business and enjoyments of God's kingdom, are prepared for the noblest existence. It is by the love of God and man they are thus formed. Without this their noble endowments will be employed in a manner strongly tending to the injury of others, and with regret to themselves. This tendency will be effectual and everlasting.

The only possible method of escape from this evil is in receiving God's testimonies and reducing them to practice. And in this way only will they live in the most useful manner to others on earth, and be actively useful in heaven.

3d. That posterity may be thus useful and happy, they must be instructed in God's testimonies. It belongs indeed to God only, to form the heart to the love of divine truth. Paul may plant, and Apollos water, the best means may be applied in vain, unless attended with the blessing of God. However, it is his good pleasure to bless his own institutions. We are as totally dependent on him for the health and support of the body. Our daily bread is the gift of his bounty, no less than the food for the soul. But who will infer from thence, that we are not to apply the appointed means, to obtain food for ourselves and our families? The duty is not less evident, and is much more important in regard to the soul. A proper sense of our dependence on God, that our posterity may be formed to be useful and happy, will lead to a faithful application of the appointed means.

An acquaintance with the word of God is the great appointed medium of that felicity and usefulness which is to be sought for posterity; this is to be obtained by instruction. For many reasons it is important that this instruction should be given in youth: the mind is then most susceptible of lasting impressions; habits of ignorance and obstinacy are not formed, at most they have not attained the firmness of long indulgence; bad example has not exerted its baneful influence to strengthen them in the way of death; inveterate custom has not fixed them in the walks of vice, and rendered them callous to the truths of religion, and the remonstrances of conscience.

Sad experience evinces, that few who have spent their youth in vice and folly, are brought to repentance and reformation in advanced age. Of these few were the cases examined, it would probably be found that in most of them, the foundation was laid by early instruction. Innumerable have been the instances of its success. How many of God's people have blessed him for the instruction of their youth, and that from their childhood they have *"known the holy scriptures, which are able to make them wise to salvation, through faith in Christ Jesus."* Admitting that a few have been made wise to salvation who never enjoyed this inestimable privilege, (for we rejoice in the unlimited sovereignty of God, and that he hath mercy on whom he will have mercy:) yet how disproportioned are their means to be useful and happy, and how deeply must they lament the want of that early and pious instruction recommended in our text! and how superior the advantages of those who have enjoyed it!

But alas! how vast are the numbers of those, who live and die in extreme ignorance of God and religion; not only in the regions of unenlightened paganism, but even in the midst of those who enjoy the gospel! Their untaught childhood and youth have prepared them to despise religious knowledge in riper years. Habits of vice have induced them to add contempt to ignorance, till they have increased the number of those "fools who despise wisdom and instruction, make a mock at sin, and die for want of wisdom."

4th. The instruction of children and youth in God's testimonies, should be the great concern of parents.

If posterity are instructed at all in these things, it must be principally by their care.

This instruction cannot be supposed to be obtained by themselves, or their own unassisted exertions. If it be not the duty of parents, to whom doth it belong? and how shall it be obtained? The God of nature has established the course of society, the relations of parent and child are his appointment; he hath constituted that singleness of affection, that identity of interests and enjoyments between the two parents, which directs their joint exertions, in nursing and educating their offspring, and which nothing but the height of obstinacy in wickedness can prevent. As children in general must probably be untaught in God's testimonies, and devoted to ruin if they are neglected by their parents, so the greatest benefits may be hoped for in a compliance with this duty. The advantages in the hand of parents for success are distinguishingly great: they are much in the company of their children, and have abundant opportunity to impress the objects of religion on their minds. The earliest impressions of their offspring are highly favorable to such views. Beside

the foundation in nature for the most tender reciprocal affections between parents and children —the early dependence in one, and exertions of kindness in the other, greatly increase the nearness; the parents are strongly prompted to instruct, and the children to learn; prepossessed as they are, in favor of their parents, and inclined to adopt their sentiments and manners, will they not hang on their lips, and receive the instructions of wisdom? Allowing that the state of sin which is common to man, and in which our children are partakers, is opposed to the admission of saving knowledge, is this an objection against *parental instruction?* doth it not even shew its superior importance? Or, are all means to be neglected, because the fallen race are dull of hearing? Should we not infer just the reverse, and in imitation of the divine example, *give them "line upon line, and precept upon precept."* (*Isaiah xxviii:10*)

Moreover this important duty is committed to parents, by the wisdom of God—under the ancient dispensation such are the divine directions.

"These words, which I command thee this day, shall be in thine heart, and thou shalt teach them diligently unto thy children, and shalt talk of them when thou sittest in thine house, and when thou walkest by the way, and when thou liest down and when thou risest up. And thou shalt bind them for a sign upon thine hand, and they shall be as frontlets between thine eyes, and thou shalt write them upon the posts of thy house, and on thy gates." (*Deut. vi:6-9*) *"That your days may be multiplied, and the days of your children, in the land which the Lord sware unto your fathers to give them, as the days of heaven upon the earth."* (*Deut. xi:21*)

Among the many passages in the sacred writings inculcating this important duty, we add only this summary direction. *"Fathers provoke not your children to wrath, but bring them up in the nurture and admonition of the Lord."* (*Ephesians vi:4*)

5th. We must not omit to observe, that parental education is the great instituted mean for the good of posterity: this might be shewn from the experience of all ages, and the word of God.

It appears from particulars already mentioned, that childhood and youth are the seasons for implanting those practical sentiments in the human mind, which are to influence through life, and most essentially affect the condition of man through the whole of his existence. Experience confirms this truth, both in the happy fruits of a well directed education, and in the sad consequences where it has been neglected. Admitting that a good education has not always been attended with desired success, and that some men have become wise and good who never enjoyed it; in the former case it only proves the sad degeneracy of human nature, and the great danger of youth; and in the latter, it displays the sovereign freedom of divine grace: but in neither, counteracts the dictates of reason and common experience, founded on the stated course of events in the providence of God, and the history of man. Because the best medicines are not always successful to restore the sick, and in some instances they recover with none or with bad ones; shall we therefore not apply this stated mean of recovery, or shall we prefer the advice of Quacks and Empirics to that of the most approved practitioners?

But a truth of this importance rests not meerly or chiefly on the conclusions of fallible man. The word of God abundantly confirms it.

To set this matter in the strongest light would require long quotations from many parts of the sacred writings, and would draw out the discourse to an unreasonable length, and indeed, would be needless, as few or none have ever appeared to deny the present truth. And writers who have differed widely as to the standing of the children of faithful parents, with respect to the gracious covenant of God, and their title to its blessings, have nevertheless agreed in the divine appointment of parental education, as the great mean for the good of posterity.

Under the general term of *parental education* we mean to comprise the whole of the duty enjoined on parents in training up their children; their dedication to God in their infancy, according to his institution, perpetuated by a course of daily prayer, unreservedly devoting them to him for his blessing. A course of faithful and well directed instructions, from the first opening of their understandings, suitable to their age, capacity, and other circumstances, ultimately adapted to their last improvement in the knowledge of God and true religion, and to excite them to a life of practical holiness. Add to this, the steady and well directed exertions of parental authority and love; enforcing their instructions: and above all, the efficacious influence of wise and pious example; without which, there can be little hope from instruction and the exercise of authority.

From the combined influence of these, we are encouraged to hope for success in parental education; and not merely or chiefly from its natural tendency, however well adapted, but from divine

institution and that gracious influence which God is pleased often to bestow, in connection with the means of his own appointment. That means are divinely instituted for the best good of young children, and even *infants* cannot be questioned, after the express decision of our blessed Redeemer.

On a certain occasion, when such were brought to him, (undoubtedly by their parents,) for his blessing, some of his disciples were so remarkably blind, as to object to it; but he sweetly reproved them. The history of this event deserves our attention. It runs thus. *"And they brought young children or infants to him, that he should touch them, and lay his hands on them, and pray: and when his disciples saw it, they rebuked those who brought them. But when Jesus saw it, he was much displeased; and said, suffer the little children to come unto me, and forbid them not: for of such is the kingdom of God." "Verily I say unto you, whosoever shall not receive the kingdom of God as a little child, he shall, in no wise, enter therein. And he called them unto him, and took them up in his arms, and put his hands on them and blessed them."* (Matt. xix:13-15; Mark x:13-16; Luke xviii:15-17)

From passages, adduced in this discourse, in connection with our text; we have sufficient evidences of the divine appointment of parental education, as the great mean of the good of posterity. Would any attend more fully to the extent of the evidence, they may consult the history of God's covenant with Abraham—the history of Job's attention to the best good of his children—the inspired writings of David and Solomon—and indeed, the whole Bible.

The reflections and conduct of our divine teacher, in the case just quoted, are full of the most useful instruction. Happy parents, who brought those children to Christ for his blessing, and happy children who received it from him. For we know that those whom HE blesseth, are indeed blessed.

How much must those parents have been edified and comforted, by such condescending love of the blessed Jesus—what lasting impressions must have been made by it on the minds of the children,—and what animating encouragement is, hereby, presented to parents and children, in all ages, to go and do likewise!

From such views, we may reasonably hope for the blessing of God in common with the faithful and well directed performance of parental duty; that our children may be useful and happy on earth, and blessed forever in the kingdom of God. We proceed to observe,

6th. The education of the present generation, may be justly expected to have a happy influence on many succeeding ages.

This is a leading sentiment in the text. It was verified in the Psalmist, who had received the important truths, which it contains, in this manner through successive generations, from Moses to his own time; agreeably to the divine injunction to which he refers, which required such instructions to their children, *"that the generation to come might know them. Even the children which should be born, who should arise and declare them to their children, that they might set their hope in God, and not forget the works of God, but keep his commandments."*

Scripture history abounds with facts in confirmation of the present truth. We may reasonably conclude, it was in this way, that the knowledge and practice of true religion were preserved in the family of *Seth,* to the time of the deluge; while the pious race were distinguished by the title of *"the Sons of God."* (*Genesis vi:2*) The intercourse of these, with the wicked descendents of Cain, broke the chain of religious education, and a general apostacy brought on the destruction of mankind.

Noah was found righteous before God in that evil generation, and was saved with his family from the common ruin. His son *Ham* very soon forsook the true religion, and was the father of a degenerate and accursed race; most probably in consequence of alliance with the family of Cain. (*Genesis iv:22*) But the true religion was preserved for many years in the family of Shem. No doubt by means of the pious education which he received from his father Noah, and transmitted to his children.

When idolatry was fast spreading among his descendents, most probably as the fruit of affinity with the wicked posterity of Ham, and the consequent neglect of good parental education, it pleased God to call Abram, one of his posterity, and the ninth in descent from him, and instruct him in the religion of his pious progenitors, and also to favor him with several new and important revelations. How he improved these, in the education of his children, we learn from the divine declaration, in the following words: *"I know him, that he will command his children and his household after him, and they shall keep the way of the Lord, to do justice and judgment."* (*Genesis xviii:19*) We may have the fruits of his pious exertions in the character of his descendents,

Isaac and Jacob, *"the heirs with him of the same promise."* (*Heb. 11:9*)

As the chosen family increased, and their intercourse with their idolatrous neighbors was extended, there was a decline of religious education, and the nation became sadly degenerated. This was uniformly the case, when they married strange wives of the idolatrous nations round them, which effectually obstructed a religious education. But the good effects of it in these instances, where it did exist, are conspicuous in the history of that people from beginning to end. It is observable also, in some who were not of the chosen family—the instance of the Rachabites is instructive and memorable. The injunctions of Jonadab, their father or progenitor, were religiously observed by them for many ages (*Compare, 2d Kings x:15, with Jeremiah xxxv:1-11*). The pious Timothy was the happy subject of that *"unfeigned faith which dwelt first in his grandmother Lois, and his mother Eunice;"* (*2d Timothy 1:5*); and from a child, no doubt by the pious education of his mother, he had known the Holy Scriptures, which were able to make him *"wise to salvation through faith in Christ Jesus."* (*3d ibid:15*)

Such is the readiness of the human mind to be influenced by parental education, that, when this is opposed to the dictates of the Holy Scriptures, and the clearest reason, it often establishes youth in opposition to the truth, and fixes prejudices, which the labours of their best and wisest friends, are never after able to remove. What happy influence then may we expect from it, when wisely conducted on the principles of reason and revelation?

The influence of parental education is evident in the history of all nations. Principles and manners have descended from father to son, through successive generations—in domestic and more extended life—in laws, politics and religion. We shall be established in this truth, by attending to the past and present habits of our own country. In how many respects are those of the present generation, in business, policy and religion, to be traced back to our ancestors, through several ages? And this notwithstanding our singular convulsions and important revolution in government, so strongly tending to a similar revolution in our habits and customs.

The truth will receive confirmation, even, from ourselves and the place in which we live; as in all other things, so in particular in regard to the promotion of order, and the interests of religion. Who are the men, of the present age, among us, whose labours and example, maintain the peace and good order of society, the observation of the Lord's day, and the public institutions of religion? Are they not the descendents of those venerable ancestors who taught these things diligently to their children, and who added the pious efficacy of their examples and their prayers? and who are the people among us, that are a dead weight on society?—opposers of order, and who openly trample on the institutions of religion? and who are rarely to be seen in this house of prayer? Are they not generally, the descendents of progenitors like themselves, whose fatal examples have fixed their posterity in the path of ruin? For though instances might be named of apostates, from the good principles and examples of their ancestors, they are comparatively few, and in most cases may be accounted for, from dangerous connections, in childhood, youth, or riper years. And how few, whose unhappy lot hath been the reverse of a wise and virtuous education, have ever emerged from that degraded condition of the mind, and become useful in society; the supporters of good order and religion?

Reflections like these, must have often occurred to observers of human nature, either in the history of other ages and countries, or in attention to their own. And they must have made deep impressions of the great importance of a virtuous and well directed education. . . .

I. To the parents of the congregation. Those of you who are advanced in life, will remember that thirty years have now passed away since our first interview in this place of worship! Thirty years are usually accounted the life of a minister. I am not insensible that my life and ministry have been attended with many imperfections, for which I have cause for deep humiliation. But I am not conscious of designedly shunning to declare all the counsel of God, or of keeping back any thing which was profitable to you. "I have not fought yours but you." Sensible that the best part of my days is already past, and that the time of my departure is at hand, I would wish to be pure from the blood of all men, and especially of the people of my charge, and to be ready to give up the account of my stewardship. I am not only concerned for an admission to the joys of the redeemed for myself; but, am earnestly desirous, that you, and your children, may also be partakers. This has been a leading object, of my labours among you, from the first of my ministry. Many of you who are now advanced in life, were the youth of the congregation, at the time of my settlement. "The fathers, where are they?" The

venerable ancestors of this people, are no more on earth. The pastor with his flock, who founded this society are long since, removed to the world of spirits. Those, who were the principal actors in my settlement, are either silent in death, or struggling with the latest calamities of declining life. Many of them acted their part well, and their ever dear and honoured names are "like precious ointment" to posterity. Much is the debt of gratitude from their children. You have now succeeded to their place—to discharge that debt, you must fill it up usefully. On this condition, they will not be ashamed to own you, as their children, hereafter. That you may thus do, and be blessed, suffer the word of exhortation from him who lives if ye *"stand fast in the Lord."*

You will seriously consider, that the interests of this people and of future generations are devolved on you, and that you are to give account to God for the important betrustment. That you may do it with joy, be pleased to remember and practice the following particulars.

First of all, "Acquaint yourselves with God and be at peace with him." To this you are invited, not only by all the motives which respect yourselves, but also on account of your children and posterity: for what reasonable hope can be indulged of fidelity, in the education of your children, if you are not faithful to yourselves?

Let it be your first care then, to have just views of the religion of the bible, and reduce it to practice. True religion as exhibited in the scriptures, and existing in good men, is a beautiful and consistent whole; consisting of various parts, harmoniously uniting, and mutually illustrating each other. It is doctrinal, experimental, and practical, and in each of these, the connection and dependence, of the parts, on each other, add strength, consistence and beauty to the whole, and prove it to be every way worthy of God, and suitable to man. Let this divine religion be exemplified in your profession and your lives.

Next to your duty, as individuals, I would intreat you to do honour to christianity, as husbands and wives. This will be effected, by living in that conjugal harmony, for which there is every inducement, from personal and domestic felicity —from the interests of posterity—from this world and the world to come. Then you will *"dwell together according to knowledge, and as fellow heirs of the grace of life, and your prayers will not be hindered."* (I Peter iii:7) In this way, you may be like that excellent pair, of whom we have this honourable testimony, *"that they were both righteous before God, walking in all the commandments and ordinances of the Lord blameless."* (*Luke i:6*) Many are the branches of genuine christianity, or ways of exemplifying its excellent nature—they are correspondent to all our relations to God, and to our fellow-creatures, to society on earth, to this world and the world to come. A right apprehension, of its leading principles, will be abundantly useful in directing your judgment, and influencing your practice at all times, and in all conditions.

Our particular attention is now called to that only, which is the subject of this discourse; The education of posterity.

May I not say, in your behalf and my own, that *"we have no greater joy than to hear that our children walk in the truth."* To parents, as members of society, and as christians; their education is a leading object. We have received God's testimonies from our parents, let us commit them to our children. We are especially called to this, on account of their dangerous state, from the circumstances of the age in which they live. For though we should not *"inquire wisely in asking why the former days were better than these,"* (*Ecclesiastes vii:10*) as human nature and the world, are substantially, the same in all ages; there are, however, occasional differences, important to be regarded in the education of youth. You are not insensible, that the present age has the marks of degeneracy in several particulars, which influence the manners of the people, the order of society, and the interests of religion. The worship of God, in families, and in public, and the religious observation of the Lord's Day, were generally practised by our fathers, and with great decency. But what a sad reverse has taken place in our day! Numbers, it is to be feared, are not well grounded in the first principles of Christianity, and are in a condition to become an early prey to seducers, who would betray them into false religions, or even to none.

This may, no doubt be traced to several influencing causes. But may we not conclude, that one of the greatest, is the criminal neglect of many parents in the education of their children, and their own bad examples? The children of such families have an unhappy influence on those who are better taught, and the contagion of vice and irreligion is widely extended; for *"man is born like the wild asses colt,"* (*Job xi:12*) and human nature tends to evil.

This calamitous event of our day, adds a new and important motive to all that have been named, for parental fidelity in the education of children. Their danger is uncommonly great, and we are at least, in part accountable for it. How highly doth it concern us, to improve the remainder of our life, faithfully, for the good of our children. We wish they may grow up to be useful and happy in family connections, to be good members of society, to serve their generation, to honor their Maker and Redeemer, transmit to their children the principles of virtue and piety, and be prepared for heaven. That none of these important objects may be lost through our neglect, we should *"bring them up in the nurture and admonition of the Lord;"* (*Eph. 6:4*) that they may know and practice God's testimonies, *"and arise and declare them to their children; that they may set their hope in God, and not forget his works, but keep his commandments."* (*Ps. 78:7*) *"Let these things be in our hearts, that we may teach them diligently to our children; and talk of them when we set in our houses, and when we walk by the way, and when we lie down, and when we rise up."* (*Deut. 6:7; 11:19*) Our instructions must be adapted to their age, capacities, and other circumstances. They must be supported by the exertions of parental authority and love; but above all *by our examples and prayers.* We must devote them to God from their earliest infancy, and perpetuate the dedication by prayer, as long as we live; that the God of our pious progenitors may be their God; and we must be in all respects, as far as possible, what we would wish them to be. We must walk before them in the path of wisdom, which leads to usefulness and felicity on earth, and to glory in Heaven. Among the many inducements to this, it will be useful to recollect the instructions and example of our pious fathers; these must in some instances at least, be fresh in our minds. Such recollections must exceedingly soften the heart, and the impressions of these truths will be proportionably deep. What child or parent ever read the following address of the wise man to his children, without the tenderest emotions? *"Hear ye children the instruction of a father, and attend to know understanding. For I give you good doctrine, forsake you not my law. For I was my father's son, tender and only beloved in the sight of my mother. He taught me also and said unto me—Let thine heart retain my words, keep my commandments, and live."* (*Prov. 4:1-4*)

The happy influence of such parental education, was early displayed in his choice of wisdom, in preference to riches and long life. (*I Kings iii:1-14*) And he faithfully transmitted it to posterity, in the book of proverbs, addressed to his children. It remains, that, in our respective conditions, we go and do likewise. The remainder of our time, for parental exertions, is short; many of you like me, are in the advance of life—we shall soon be silent in death. What we do for our children and posterity, must be speedily accomplished. The leading motives to fidelity and vigor, in this honorable service have been already considered. You will recollect them. Let me hope they will ever be present to your thoughts, and influence your practice; that if our separation should be near, and I should never more address you on this subject, I may die, with the joyful prospect of your fidelity and success;—that he who sowed, and they who reap, may rejoice together.

II. To the children and youth.

A few words will comprise the substance of what I would wish to be impressed on your hearts. I have little to offer which can be called new; but it is not less weighty and interesting for being old. The text and subject are not more important to your parents, than to you. If their obligations and motives, respecting your education, are such as have been named, yours are proportionable to receive their instructions, and reduce them to practice. It is for your sakes, and because your interest is so deeply involved, that they are thus obliged. On this depends your felicity and usefulness in this and the future life.

The price in your hand to get wisdom is exceedingly precious; but its continuance is uncertain, and at best it is short. If you follow the dictates of a virtuous and truly good education, you will be useful and happy on earth, and blessed in heaven—God will be your friend and protector here, and your portion forever. But if you despise the instructions of parental piety, it is at your peril; you will be marked for wretchedness and reproach on earth, and for aggravated misery in hell. And you will *"mourn at the last, and say, how have we hated instruction, and our hearts despised reproof? And have not obeyed the voice of our teachers, nor inclined our ear to them that instructed us."* (Proverbs *v:11, 12, 13*) That this may not be your awful doom, *Remember* that you are the creatures of God—born for immortality—ruined by sin, and must partake of the gospel salvation, or be ruined forever. Your continuance on earth at most will be short, much shorter than you can, now, readily conceive. The flight of time, is exceedingly rapid. How soon have the last thirty years passed away? and are forever gone! what changes have these thirty years produced? those who were then the parents of the congregation are generally gone—we have

succeeded in their place, and you in ours. More than five hundred, of all ages, have died in the society; nearly an equal number of children, at present constitute our schools; as appears from the late visitation: They will soon fill your place—you ours, and we shall be gathered to our fathers. The following thirty years will probably be marked with changes as numerous and affecting as those which are past. Should you live during those thirty future years, which is much to be doubted, they will be but *"a vapour which appears for a little season, and then vanisheth away."*

I give you my best wishes for time and eternity, with the following short directions: *"Remember now your creator in the days of your youth, before the evil days come, and the years draw nigh, when you shall say you have no pleasure in them."* *"Fear God, and keep his commandments, for this is the whole duty of man: For God shall bring every work into judgment, with every secret thing, whether it be good, or whether it be evil."* (*Eccl. xii:1, 13, 14*) Give ear to good instruction from your parents and others—pray for a blessing—study your bibles, especially the book of Proverbs, particularly adapted for the benefit of youth—watch and pray against temptations, and the destructive influence of bad example—strive to be wise and good—a blessing to your parents, connections and society—to be useful to yourselves and others, and in readiness for death and heaven.

Let me recommend to your imitation the example of young Joseph, who rejected the allurements of guilt, with this excellent reflection, *"How can I do this great wickedness, and sin against God"* (*Gen. xxxix:9*)—and that of the pious Timothy, who attended to the religious instructions of a faithful parent, and, *"from childhood knew the holy scriptures, which were able to make him wise to salvation through faith in Christ Jesus;"* (*2 Tim. i:v & iii:15*) and whose future character marks the value of a virtuous education wisely improved.

Finally, and above all, remember and imitate the example of the blessed Jesus, who at the age of twelve years, engaged the attention, and excited the astonishment of his most learned instructors, at his understanding and answers, *"and still was subject to his parents; and as he advanced in age and stature, increased in wisdom, and in favor with God and with man."* (*Luke ii:46-52*)

May you live, and be wise, useful and happy, to a good old age—many years after your parents and minister shall be gone to their fathers. May you faithfully transmit to the children of the coming age, the pure religion of the blessed Jesus. May it be perpetuated in this place, through all generations till his second coming. May we meet in heaven, with each other, with our pious ancestors—the children of future ages, and with all the redeemed, and be to the praise of divine grace forever. Amen.

BENJAMIN FRANKLIN ON EDUCATION

To Samuel Johnson.*

*Works of
Benjamin
Franklin,*
by Jared Sparks,
Vol. VII,
Boston, 1840

Philadelphia, 23 August, 1750

Dear Sir,

We received your favor of the 16th instant. Mr. Peters will hardly have time to write to you by this post, and I must be short. Mr. Francis spent the last evening with me, and we were all glad to hear, that you seriously meditate a visit after the middle of next month, and that you will inform us by a line when to expect you. We drank your health and Mrs. Johnson's remembering your kind entertainment of us at Stratford.

I think with you, that nothing is of more importance for the public weal, than to form and train up youth in wisdom and virtue. Wise and good men are, in my opinion, the strength of a state; much more so than riches or arms, which, under the management of ignorance and wickedness, often draw on destruction, instead of providing for the safety of the people. And though the culture bestowed on *many* should be successful only with a *few,* yet the influence of those few and the service in their power may be very great. Even a single woman, that was wise, by her wisdom saved the city.

I think also, that general virtue is more probably to be expected and obtained from the education of youth, than from the exhortation of adult persons; bad habits and vices of the mind being, like diseases of the body, more easily prevented than cured. I think, moreover, that talents for the education of youth are the gift of God; and that he on whom they are bestowed, whenever a way is opened for the use of them, is as strongly *called* as if he heard a voice from heaven; nothing more surely pointing out duty in a public service, than ability and opportunity of performing it. . . .

Your tenderness of the Church's peace is truly laudable; but, methinks, to build a new church in a growing place is not properly *dividing* but *multiplying;* and will really be the means of increasing the number of those, who worship God in that way. Many, who cannot now be accommodated in the church, go to other places, or stay at home; and, if we had another church, many, who go to other places or stay at home, would go to church. I suppose the interest of the church has been far from suffering in Boston by the building of two churches there in my memory. I had for several years nailed against the wall of my house a pigeon-box, that would hold six pair; and, though they bred as fast as my neighbours' pigeons, I never had more than six pair, the old and strong driving out the young and weak, and obliging them to seek new habitations. At length I put up an additional box with apartments for entertaining twelve pair more; and it was soon filled with inhabitants, by the overflowing of my first box, and of others in the neighbourhood. This I take to be a parallel case with the building a new church here. . . .

My humble respects, if you please, to your brethren at the Commencement. I hope they will advise you to what is most for the good of the whole, and then I think they will advise you to remove hither. Please to tender my best respects and service to Mrs. Johnson and your son. I am, dear Sir, your obliged and affectionate humble servant,

B. FRANKLIN

---

* Dr. Samuel Johnson was the first President of King's (now Columbia) College, New York, the venerable father of the Episcopal Church of Connecticut, and the apostle of sound learning and elegant literature in New England. It appears to have been written at the time of the first establishment of the College of Philadelphia, the presidency of which institution had been offered to Dr. Johnson. This offer he declined, on account of a similar and more advantageous one from New York.—Jared Sparks note.

DANIEL WEBSTER ON EDUCATION

*The Works of
Daniel Webster,*
Vols. I & II,
Boston, 1851

DISCOURSE AT PLYMOUTH, DECEMBER 22, 1820

New England may be allowed to claim, I think, a merit of a peculiar character. She early adopted, and has constantly maintained the principle, that it is the undoubted right and the bounden duty of government to provide for the instruction of all youth. That which is elsewhere left to chance or to charity, we secure by law. (The first free school established by law in the Plymouth Colony was in 1670-2. One of the early teachers in Boston taught school more than seventy years—Mr. Ezekiel Cheever.) For the purpose of public instruction, we hold every man subject to taxation in proportion to his property, and we look not to the question, whether he himself have, or have not, children to be benefited by the education for which he pays. We regard it as a wise and liberal system of police, by which property, and life, and the peace of society are secured. We seek to prevent in some measure the extension of the penal code, by inspiring a salutary and conservative principle of virtue and of knowledge in an early age. We strive to excite a feeling of respectability, and a sense of character, by enlarging the capacity and increasing the sphere of intellectual enjoyment. By general instruction, we seek, as far as possible, to purify the whole moral atmosphere; to keep good sentiments uppermost, and to turn the strong current of feeling and opinion, as well as the censures of the law and the denunciations of religion, against immorality and crime. We hope for a security beyond the law, and above the law, in the prevalence of an enlightened and well-principled moral sentiment. We hope to continue and prolong the time, when, in the villages and farm-houses of New England, there may be undisturbed sleep within unbarred doors. And knowing that our government rests directly on the public will, in order that we may preserve it we endeavor to give a safe and proper direction to that public will. We do not, indeed, expect all men to be philosophers or statesmen; but we confidently trust, and our expectation of the duration of our system of government rests on that trust, that, by the diffusion of general knowledge and good and virtuous sentiments, the political fabric may be secure, as well against open violence and overthrow, as against the slow, but sure, undermining of licentiousness.

We know that, at the present time, an attempt is making in the English Parliament to provide by law for the education of the poor, and that a gentleman of distinguished character has taken the lead in presenting a plan to government for carrying that purpose into effect. And yet, although the representatives of the three kingdoms listened to him with astonishment as well as delight, we hear no principles with which we ourselves have not been familiar from youth; we see nothing in the plan but an approach towards that system which has been established in New England for more than a century and a half. It is said that in England not more than *one child in fifteen* possesses the means of being taught to read and write; in Wales, *one in twenty;* in France, until lately, when some improvement was made, not more than *one in thirty-five.* Now, it is hardly too strong to say, that in New England *every child possesses* such means. It would be difficult to find an instance to the contrary, unless where it should be owing to the negligence of the parent; and, in truth, the means are actually used and enjoyed by nearly every one. A youth of fifteen, of either sex, who cannot both read and write, is very seldom to be found. Who can make this comparison, or contemplate this spectacle, without delight and a feeling of just pride? Does any history show property more beneficently applied? Did any government ever subject the property of those who have estates to a burden, for a purpose more favorable to the poor, or more useful to the whole community?

A conviction of the importance of public instruction was one of the earliest sentiments of our ancestors. No lawgiver of ancient or modern times has expressed more just opinions, or adopted wiser measures, than the early records of the Colony of Plymouth show to have prevailed here. Assembled on this very spot, a hundred and fifty-three years ago, the legislature of this Colony declared, "Forasmuch as the maintenance of good literature doth much tend to the advancement of the weal and flourishing state of societies and republics, this Court doth therefore order, that in whatever township in this government, consisting of fifty families or upwards, any meet man shall be obtained to teach a grammar school, such township shall allow at least twelve pounds, to be raised by rate on all the inhabitants."

Having provided that all youth should be instructed in the elements of learning by the institution of free schools, our ancestors had yet another duty to perform. Men were to be educated for the professions and the public. For this purpose they founded the University, and with incredible zeal and perseverance they cherished and supported it, through all trials and discouragements. (By a law of the Colony of Massachusetts Bay, passed as early as 1647, it was ordered, that, "when any town shall increase to the number of one hundred families or householders, they shall set up a grammar school, the master thereof being able to instruct youth so far as they may be fitted for the University.") On the subject of the University, it is not possible for a son of New England to think without pleasure, or to speak without emotion. Nothing confers more honor on the State where it is established, or more utility on the country at large. A respectable university is an establishment which must be a work of time. If pecuniary means were not wanting, no new institution could possess character and respectability at once. We owe deep obligation to our ancestors, who began, almost on the moment of their arrival, the work of building up this institution.

SPEECH AT MADISON, INDIANA, JUNE I, 1837

Among the luminaries in the sky of New England, the burning lights which throw intelligence and happiness on her people, the first and most brilliant is her system of common schools. I congratulate myself that my first speech on entering public life was in their behalf. Education, to accomplish the ends of good government, should be universally diffused. Open the doors of the school-house to all the children in the land. Let no man have the excuse of poverty for not educating his own offspring. Place the means of education within his reach, and if they remain in ignorance, be it his own reproach. If one object of the expenditure of your revenue be protection against crime, you could not devise a better or cheaper means of obtaining it. Other nations spend their money in providing means for its detection and punishment, but it is the principle of our government to provide for its never occurring. The one acts by *coercion,* the other by *prevention.* On the diffusion of education among the people rest the preservation and perpetuation of our free institutions. I apprehend no danger to our country from a foreign foe. The prospect of a war with any powerful nation is too remote to be a matter of calculation. Besides, there is no nation on earth powerful enough to accomplish our overthrow. Our destruction, should it come at all, will be from another quarter. From the inattention of the people to the concerns of their government, from their carelessness and negligence, I must confess that I do apprehend some danger. I fear that they may place too implicit a confidence in their public servants, and fail properly to scrutinize their conduct; that in this way they may be made the dupes of designing men, and become the instruments of their own undoing. Make them intelligent, and they will be vigilant; give them the means of detecting the wrong, and they will apply the remedy.

REMARKS TO LADIES OF RICHMOND, VIRGINIA, OCT. 5, 1840

It is by the promulgation of sound morals in the community, and more especially by the training and instruction of the young, that woman performs her part towards the preservation of a free government. It is generally admitted that public liberty, and the perpetuity of a free constitution, rest on the virtue and intelligence of the community which enjoys it. How is that virtue to be inspired, and how is that intelligence to be communicated? Bonaparte once asked Madame de Stael in what manner he could best promote the happiness of France. Her reply is full of political wisdom. She said, "Instruct the mothers of the French people." Mothers are, indeed, the affectionate and effective teachers of the human race. The mother begins her process of training with the infant in her arms. It is she who directs, so to speak, its first mental and spiritual pulsations. She conducts it along the impressible years of childhood and youth, and hopes to deliver it to the stern conflicts and tumultuous scenes of life, armed by those good principles which her child has received from maternal care and love.

If we draw within the circle of our contemplation the mothers of a civilized nation, what do we see? We behold so many artificers working, not on frail and perishable matter, but on the immortal mind, moulding and fashioning beings who are to exist for ever. We applaud the artist whose skill and genius present the mimic man upon the canvas; we admire and celebrate the sculptor who works out that same image in enduring marble; but how insignificant are these achievements, though the highest and the fairest in all the departments of art, in comparison with the great vocation of human mothers! They work, not upon the canvas that shall perish, or the marble that shall crumble into dust, but upon mind, upon spirit, which is to last for ever, and which is to bear, for good or evil, throughout its duration, the impress of a mother's plastic hand.

I have already expressed the opinion, which all allow to be correct, that our security for the duration of the free institutions which bless our country depends upon habits of virtue and the prevalence of knowledge and of education. The attainment of knowledge does not comprise all which is contained in the larger term of education. The feelings are to be disciplined; the passions are to be restrained; true and worthy motives are to be inspired; a profound religious feeling is to be instilled, and pure morality inculcated, under all circumstances. All this is comprised in education. Mothers who are faithful to this great duty will tell their children, that

neither in political nor in any other concerns of life can man ever withdraw himself from the perpetual obligations of conscience and of duty; that in every act, whether public or private, he incurs a just responsibility and that in no condition is he warranted in trifling with important rights and obligations.

They will impress upon their children the truth, that the exercise of the elective franchise is a social duty, of as solemn a nature as man can be called to perform; that a man may not innocently trifle with his vote; that every free elector is a trustee, as well for others as himself; and that every man and every measure he supports has an important bearing on the interests of others, as well as on his own. It is in the inculcation of high and pure morals such as these, that, in a free republic, woman performs her sacred duty, and fulfills her destiny. . . .

A DISSERTATION ON THE HISTORY, ELOQUENCE, AND POETRY OF THE BIBLE

*Public
Commencement
at New Haven,*
by Timothy
Dwight, 1772

In a situation where almost every theme hath been ingeniously handled, the young speaker is left, utterly at a loss on which side to turn himself. Learning hath been panegyrized times innumerable—the particular Sciences have often received their deserved encomiums—numerous inventions have been racked in praise of Œconomy, Industry, Liberty, and *America*—the Eloquence of the Rostrum, and the Bar, hath, both in precept and example, been handsomely displayed—a most elegant parallel hath been drawn between the Ancients and the Moderns, the excellencies of each judiciously exhibited—the use and advantages of the Fine Arts have been placed in a most beautiful, striking point of view—and this day hath pleased us with many new and ingenious thoughts on Education.

What subject then is reserved for the present hour? A subject which hath, at least, novelty to recommend it—a subject, which I flatter myself will be agreeable to *some* of my audience, and I cannot but hope, disagreeable to *none*. No person hath ever attempted to entertain this assembly by displaying the excellencies of the Fountain of our Religion and Happiness—(The excellencies I mean, not of its purity and holiness, which by no

means need a panegyric; but those of fine writing, which, as they are of less importance, so we should naturally expect they would have been little attended to.) Could this proceed from dislike or inattention? Surely from inattention. For whilst we are enraptured with the fire and sublimity of *Homer,* the correctness, tenderness, and majesty of *Virgil,* the grandeur of *Demosthenes,* the art and elegance of *Cicero;* Shall we be blind to Eloquence more elegant than *Cicero,* more grand than *Demosthenes;* or to Poetry more correct and tender than *Virgil,* and infinitely more sublime than him who has long been honoured, not unjustly, with that magnificent appellation "The Father of Poetry?" Shall we be delighted with the majestic gravity, the lively, spirited relations which place *Livy* and *Robertson* on the throne of History; with the fine, enthusiastic morality which obtained *Plato* the surname of "The Divine;" and shall we, can we be insensible to History far more majestic, particular Relations far more lively and spirited than those of *Livy* and *Robertson;* and to Morality truly divine, whose glory admits of no comparison? Volumes of Criticism have been written to display the beauties of most of the above Authors, and can a few moments, spent in an attempt to illustrate the beauties of the Sacred Scriptures, be thought too many, or tedious?

The Genius of the Eastern nations, and particularly of the *Jews,* was in many respects, different from that of the *Greeks* and *Romans.* Situated in a climate nearer to the vivifying rays of the Sun, his beams acted with a more enlivening influence on the intellectual, as well as vegetable world, and lit up a more bright, glowing Genius in the human breast. Born in a region which enjoyed this advantage in the happiest degree, and fired with the glorious thoughts and images of Inspiration, can we wonder that the divine writers, though many of them illiterate, should so far transcend all others, as well in style, as in sentiment? Can we wonder that these superiour advantages should be displayed on every page, in the boldest metaphors, the most complete images, and the most lively descriptions? No writers abound so much in passionate Exclamation, in that striking way of communicating sentiments, Interrogation, or in metaphors taken from sublime objects, and from action, of all others the most animated. Unincumbered by Critical manacles, they gave their imaginations an unlimited range, called absent objects before the sight, gave life to the whole inanimate creation, and in every period, snatched the grace which is beyond the reach of art, and which, being the genuine offspring of elevated Genius, finds the shortest passage to the human soul. With all this license no writers have so few faulty passages. "But" says the Critic "they don't describe *exactly according to our rules.*" True sir; and when you can convince me that *Homer* and *Virgil,* from whom you gather those rules, were sent into the world to give Laws to all other authors; when you can convince me that every beauty of fine writing is to be found, in its highest perfection, in their works, I will allow the beauties of the divine writers to be faults. 'Till that can be demonstrated, I must continue to admire the most shining instances of Genius, unparallell'd in force, or sublimity.

In praise of *Homer,* it has been observed, that he gives *life* to every object which he attempts to describe. In the Inspired writings objects are not barely endued with life; they breathe, they think, they speak, love, hate, fear, adore, & exercise all the most extraordinary emotions of rational beings. *Homer or Virgil* can make the mountains tremble, or the sea shake, at the appearance of a God; in the *Bible* the mountains melt like wax, or flee away, the Deep utters his voice, and lifts up his hands on high, at the presence of the Lord of

the whole earth. In *other writings* rural scenes are often addressed, and receive a momentary animation; in the *Bible* the heavens and earth are called upon to hear, the winds and storms to praise; the fields rejoice, *Lebanon* shouts aloud for joy, and the neighbouring forests warmed to raptures, break forth into songs of thanksgiving.

Such a Genius must necessarily breathe an uncommon spirit, a transporting enthusiasm into every production—let us attend to its effects on History.

The great end of History is instruction. To gain the attention of mankind, something more is necessary than a bare, cold relation of distant events. The earthly part of the human soul is so disproportionate to the etherial, that every possible method must be used to extend its regard to any thing, beyond the present enjoyment. To awaken our lethargic inclinations, to put in motion the vis inertiae of our constitution, is the business of the Imagination, and the various passions. No writers understood this, as also every other part of the human frame, so well as the sacred Penmen. Perhaps, it may not be unentertaining, to trace them in some of the various arts which they have used to catch the attention of the Reader.

Sensible that the Imagination is the principal inlet to the Soul, and that it is far more easily enkindled than the Passions, they passed by no occasion for engaging its assistance. As their subject was better fitted to answer this end, than any other, they have handled it to admiration—they seize every opportunity to introduce transactions, at once new, sublime and wonderful; for this the frequent awful interpositions of the Deity, in the affairs of *Israel,* gave them the fairest chance. In every page, we are astonished by glorious and supernatural displays of the divine power. In every page, we are charmed by fanciful, yet just poetical descriptions of a great variety of scenes. By these methods their History has every advantage of Poetry for affecting the Imagination, with this happy circumstance, that it is all reality.

Added to this, though their relations are all directed, more or less, to the illustration of this great Truth "that obedience to GOD is the path to felicity" they have yet inserted an endless variety of incidents and characters. Convinced that Novelty hath a most powerful effect on the human mind, they have filled their writings with more new and uncommon events, than are to be found in those of all others united. Convinced that human manners are the most delightful, as well as the most instructive field, for readers of the human race, they have exhibited them in every point of view. Where are characters so naturally drawn? Where so strongly marked? Where so infinitely numerous and different? To what can the Legislator so advantageously apply for instructions, as to the life and laws of *Moses?* Whom can the Prince propose for examples so properly as *Solomon* and *Jehoshaphat?* In *Joshua,* and *Joab,* the General, the Hero, are magnificently displayed. In the Prophets and Patriarchs, the Gentleman, the Contemplator may find most excellent patterns, not of gaming, drinking, prophaneness, debauchery, and that unmeaning, unfriendly ceremony which poisons the lip of Hypocrisy; but of meekness, kindness to inferiors, charity, hospitality, benevolence, and every embellishment of human nature. In *Joseph,* the unwary Youth is beautifully taught to shun the gilded bait of Temptation, and is instructed that Virtue, sooner or later, will infallibly lift him to the summit of honour and felicity. Where can the Fair part of the creation find the glorious effects of beauty and virtue so finely, so tenderly, so amiably represented, as in *Ruth* and *Esther?* David's character, whether as a General, a Ruler, or a Saint, is an exhaustless fund of amusement and instruction. Whom should the Clergyman, whom should every man imitate, but the Apostles, but the glorious pattern of excellence, their great MASTER?

It is an observation of *Longinus* "that an Epic poet should put as many as possible, of his sentiments, into the mouths of his heroes." Not, as some have imagined, to dignify them—do we reverence *Ajax* more than *Homer?* but to give them the greater liveliness. How evident is it, that a man's sentiments strike much more from his own mouth, than through the medium of a second person? For this reason, and because we suppose *Ajax* to have been better acquainted with circumstances, in which he was an *actor,* than any one who, like the Poet, knew them only by *hearsay;* we choose to have his reflections in his own words, rather than in those of any relator. What *Homer* has done in Poetry, the Divine writers have done in History—Great part of their History is dramatic. By these means their characters are drawn not only in a more natural, but more striking manner. We don't barely hear of them; but we see them; we hear them speak; they become old acquaintances; and, at every appearance, we recognize them as such. Confining themselves to simple narration is what makes a principal difference between the modern and ancient Historians, entirely in favour of the latter.

But this is not all. Sensible that *General History,* though in many respects instructive, is dry and unentertaining—Sensible that *General Descriptions* leave very faint traces on the Memory; the writers of Inspiration, contented with giving a plain, concise account of every thing of that kind necessary to be known (though even this very circumstance hath made their *General Histories* more striking than those of any other nation) hurry on to events more particular, relations more minute. Perhaps not one fourth part of the Sacred History is *General.* To interest the attention, to employ the Memory, it is necessary that we should have a clear, distinct, and perfect idea of any transaction—this can only be given by an exact relation of every minute, important circumstance—and such a relation can only be made of single events.

Reasoning upon principles like these, they have every where inserted narrations of this kind; and when they have enkindled the Passions, when they have fired the Imagination to a pitch of enthusiasm, they pour into these two great passages to the Soul, truths at once instructive, moral and divine. Are not instances needless? The story of *Joseph* is too universally admired to allow a comment; I beg leave to make a few remarks on one less attended to—the subject plain and simple—the method of handling it inimitable.

Elijah would convince the *Israelites* that the God of Heaven is the only Deity. This is the subject. For this purpose, he bids the prophets of *Baal* assemble before all the congregation of *Israel,* and offer a sacrifice to *their* God, whilst he offers a similar one to *his own:* all, at the same time, agreeing that the God, whose fire consumed the oblation, should be accounted the true one. In the morning, the prophets of *Baal* erect their altar, prepare their sacrifice, and call on the imaginary Power to kindle it. From morn to noon, this was repeated—no answer was returned. Can their anguish and vexation be more finely imaged than in their leaping on the altar—cutting themselves with knives 'till the blood gushed out? Can there be severer sarcasms than those of *Elijah*—"Cry aloud—spare not—he is a God—either he is talking—or pursuing—or he is on a journey"—and particularly that cutting remark on his Godship—"peradventure he *sleepeth.*"

Having allowed them the whole day, near the sunsetting, he builds an altar, digs a trench around it, and, to put the decision beyond a possibility of contradiction, orders twelve barrels of water to be poured upon the sacrifice. The scene is now changed. From ridicule, the Prophet ascends to the highest solemnity—He calls all the people around him, invokes the DEITY in a concise, but striking and awful manner, and is answered by a flame from Heaven, which consumes the oblation, with the whole flood of water. What more solemn, affecting circumstance could have concluded this relation, than the universal voice of the people, resounding in concert, "The Lord, *he* is the GOD! The Lord, *he* is the GOD!"

I beg leave to mention a few others. The account of Creation,—of *Eliezer* and *Rebekah* (Gen. 24),—of the *Israelites'* passage thro' the Red Sea (Exod. 14),—of the Law given at *Sinai* (Exod. 19 &c.),—of *Dathan* and *Abiram* (Numb. 16),—the Histories of *Gideon* (Jud. 6 &c.), *Sampson* (Jud. 13), and *Jephthah* (Jud. 11);—the story of the Levite and his Concubine (Judges 19, 20, and 21. There is a remarkable similarity between this story and the *Trojan* war.)—of *David* and *Goliath* (I Sam. 17)—of *David* and *Jonathan* (I Sam. 18 &c.)— of *Abigail* (I Sam. 25),—of *Absalom* (2 Sam. 13)—of the dedication of the *Temple* (2 Chron. 6 and 7)—of the Queen of *Sheba* (I Kings 10)—of *Elisha* and the *Shunammite* (2 Kings 4)—of *Naaman* the *Syrian* (2 Kings 5)—of *Haman* and *Mordecai* (Esther)—of *Lazarus* (St. John 11) —of the widow of *Nain* (St. Luke 7)—the Disciples' journey to *Emmaus* (St. Luke 24)—the birth of the Saviour (St. Luke 1 &c.)—the agony in the garden—and, above all, the Crucifixion. Each of these is handled in a manner masterly and inimitable; each of these is treated with that peculiar simplicity, which is a grand characteristic of every species of inspired writing, & which affects the mind more than all the artful, studied flourishes of Rhetoric: though, as it is an object of universal attention, my remarks upon it are the less particular.

Nor are the effects of this Genius inspired, less apparent in the Eastern Eloquence, than in their History. As I have already observed, all these historical writings are chiefly dramatic and abound in a noble manly Eloquence. (See Deut. 1 &c. 28 &c., Josh. 14:6 &c., Josh. 22:15 &c., 2 Chron. 13:4, Josh. 23 and 24, Jud. 9:7 &c., I Sam. 17:44 &c., Acts 2:14 &c., Acts 3:12 &c., Acts 4:8 &c., Acts 5:35 &c., Acts 7:, Acts 13:16 &c., &c.) Almost an infinite numbers of brave striking sensible speeches well deserve particular notice: But the time will only allow me to make a few observations concerning the Eloquence of *St. Paul.*

It is universally known, that *Longinus,* a Heathen, by no means well affected to Christianity, hath placed this great Apostle on a list with *Cicero, Demosthenes, Eschines,* and others, the most eminent Orators. What his Elocution was, hath ever been vehemently disputed—to the Critics I leave it—what his Orations were, I think may be determined from those recorded in the Acts of the Apostles.

Of the vehement kind of Eloquence, which raised *Demosthenes* to so high a pitch of Glory, and which also abounds in *Cicero,* as well as of the motive he hath left us to examples; no occasion, recorded by *St. Luke* being proper for that species of speaking: And whether his having excelled them both in every other kind of Oratory, is a sufficient proof that he would also have surpassed them in those two, the most common, and the most easily attainable, I leave others to determine; and omitting conjectures, will confine my reflections to the instances of his oratorical Genius which now remain.

But what pardon can I expect from the Critic, whose life has been spent in reading the *Greeks* and *Romans;* who scarcely knows that there can be any applause, besides that which is paid to them, and who doubts whether he may eat, or breathe, unless by *Aristotle's* rules; when he hears me boldly, unconcernedly prefer *St. Paul's* address to *Agrippa,* for himself, before *Cicero's* to *Caesar,* for *Marcellus?* As our Christian Orator knew better than any other man, how to suit his addresses to time, place, and audience; we shall find that a remarkable circumstance among the excellencies of this, and the other Orations which I shall notice—a circumstance which deservedly obtains a first rank among the accomplishments of a speaker. He is now a prisoner, arraigned at the bar of *Festus,* surrounded by a numerous and splendid audience—accusers—judges—governors —princes and kings. He begins with a compliment infinitely more noble and polite, than all the thick-laid daubing, which *Cicero* has made use of, to display at once his own meanness, and *Caesar's* folly. Indeed it may be laid down as an unfailing maxim, that the most elegant compliments are ever formed upon truth. From this he proceeds to state the point, opens the case, relates his story, and adduces the reasons of his conduct, in a manner striking—majestic—convincing. Of the Power of his Eloquence, *Agrippa,* an Heathen, gave him a glorious testimony, in the observation —"Thou almost persuadest me to be Christian:" Happy, had the word, almost, been justly omitted.

But I have a mind to trespass still farther, in a declaration, that his Farewell to the *Ephesians* is much more beautiful, tender, and pathetic, than the celebrated defence of *Milo.* (*Acts 20:18 &c.*)

Never was the power of simplicity in writing so clearly, so finely demonstrated, as in this incomparable Speech. Not a shadow of art is to be found in it. Scarce a Metaphor, and not one but the most common, is used—Nothing but the natural, unstudied language of affection; and yet I flatter myself, no person can read it attentively, without a profusion of tears. Never was the precept of *Cicero* so perfectly exemplified—"To speak in such a manner, as that all should hope they could equal it, and none, upon trial, be able." But this piece will by no means allow a descant—its beauties are too frequent, in every verse, in every line, and almost in every word.

I observed that of the vehement kind of Eloquence *St. Paul* hath left no examples; but this remark can by no means be extended to the animated kind in general. What can be more animated than his speech to *Elymas* the Sorcerer (which is indeed in a few words severely invective) unless his Oration to the *Athenians?* I readily confess, I never was so much moved by any thing in *Cicero* or *Demosthenes,* as when I have figured to myself, the great Apostle standing on *Mars-hill,* in the midst of all the numerous Inhabitants of *Athens,* at that time the Capital of the universe for learning and politeness. Behold on one side, the young and gay of both sexes, on another, the aged and wise; on one side, the rich, adorned with splendour, on another, in a meaner dress, the poorer, but not less useful mechanics and husbandmen;—Here, whitened over with age, stand long rows of venerable Philosophers, here, in their robes of state, the more venerable Judges of the *Areopagus:* all in profound silence, listening to hear something of infinite importance. I can almost hear the glorious man break forth with a force and elocution which made *Felix* tremble, which converted half the world, and induced the inhabitants of *Lystra* to believe him the very Deity of Eloquence—"God who made the world, and all things that are therein, seeing he is LORD of heaven and earth, dwelleth not in temples made with hands." And whilst he proceeds in a manner more noble, philosophical, and sublime, than ever delighted any other audience, methinks I can view them, silent as the evening, leaning forward thro' attention, hanging on the words which he utters; till a clear conviction of the truth of his assertions kindles up in their faces, a smile of satisfaction and transport.

But the effects of this happy Genius, and of Inspiration, are still more conspicuous in the Poetry, than even in the History, or Eloquence of the sacred writings. As this cannot be illustrated by general remarks, I beg the patience of my audience for a few particulars.

Of Poetry the most remarkable species are, the Pastoral, Ode, Elegy, Satire, the dramatic and the Epic Poem, and a Miscellaneous kind, too various to be reduced under any general name.

Very few strokes of a satirical pen are to be found in the Bible—and even these are short, but at the same time cuttingly severe. Such, is that ironical sarcasm of *Job* to his three friends—"Doubtless ye are the people, and Wisdom shall die with you"—his description of his enemies (*Job 12:2*)—Isaiah's of an Idol (*Isaiah* 44)—*Paul's* observation concerning *Ananias,* and some others: unless it should be thought that all the reflections on the vice of man are such, which I would by no means deny.

Of Pastoral, I shall only observe, that *Solomon's* Song in beauty and tenderness, is one of the most complete that can be imagined.

The whole Collection of Prophecies is composed of poems of the miscellaneous kind.

As a most perfect example of the Ode I beg leave to mention the 104th Psalm. The Ode is defined "A short Poem, proper to be sung, written in praise of some beloved object, generally agreeable, tender, or sublime." This Ode has for its subject, the perfections of the Deity, of all themes the most sublime and agreeable. The Poet begins with his Power, the most awful and great of his Attributes, and consequently, that which first engages the attention: from this, he is led to the wonders and bounties of his Wisdom and Providence. The incidents, chosen to illustrate these Perfections of the Creator, are the most natural, beautiful, and striking. What can be more striking than the creation, the heavens, the ocean, the clouds, the winds, the flood, the thunder, the celestial Host, the glory and brightness of the DEITY? What more beautiful than the charms of Nature and prospect, illustrating infinite Wisdom and Goodness, and particularly, this great truth—That GOD is the universal Benefactor of Being?—Who, after these contemplations, can forbear crying out with the poet, in that most sublime Apostrophe—"O Lord! how manifold are thy Works! in wisdom hast thou made them all: the earth is full of thy riches!—Who can forbear concluding as he does—"Bless thou the Lord O my Soul. Praise ye the Lord."

Odes of a more tender kind, are to be found every where amongst the Psalms; but I cannot forbear observing that in the 97th, the above-mentioned 104th, & above all in the 18th, the poet's imagination rises to such a height, as *Pin-*

dar, Dryden, and *Grey* must look up to, with astonishment and despair.

In the soft, tender strain of Elegy, where are simplicity and Grief so finely united as in the Lamentations of *Jeremiah?* What can be more exquisitely pathetic than *David's* Lamentation over *Absalom?* What than his Elogium upon the death of *Saul* and *Jonathan?* His fear lest the *Philistines* should hear and rejoice, that the Beauty of *Israel* was slain upon the high places— His Apostrophe to the Mountains of Gilboa— The excellent character of his Friends, for their Heroism, in that age a man's greatest glory, and for firmly-united Friendship—His elegant address to the Fair-ones of *Israel,* to sympathize with him in his distress—His more tender address to his beloved brother *Jonathan,* upon remembrance of their Intimacy—With the repetition of that passionate exclamation—"How are the mighty fallen!"; are so many different circumstances, which all contribute to raise this piece to the highest degree of elegiac perfection.

There is no poem in the Bible, which is strictly dramatic, or heroic; but as the word Epic, commonly used for the latter poem, signifies no more than Narrative, the Book of *Job* may properly come under that denomination. The Action is one—the restoration of Job to the happiness, of which he had been deprived by Satan—The Actors, or Speakers are, the DEITY, Satan, *Elihu, Job,* his three Friends and Servants. It is almost wholly dramatic, which gives it a peculiar liveliness.

Its beauties are infinitely too numerous and various to be mentioned; but—the bold figures— the striking Interrogations—the fine description of Man's frailty (*Chap. 14*)—the Panegyric upon Wisdom (*Chap. 28*)—*Job's* contrast of his former and present circumstances—the Introduction, and above all, the Speech of the DEITY, are unequalled by any poet, ancient or modern. (*Chap. 29, 30*)

Every one is sensible of the beauty of Figures. A single instance of the Interrogation will shew its fine effect in adding liveliness to every species of writing. The Poet observes—"Man dieth and wasteth away, yea he giveth up the ghost, and where is he?"—What can be more beautiful than *Job's* description of his former, and present condition?—The Poets introduction of the CREATOR seems not to have been much attended to, and demands a few remarks.

To give a proper and awful pomp and solemnity to this part of his poem, and to the infinite Being who is now about to appear, the Poet makes *Elihu,* referring to the phenomena of nature around him, deliver himself in this manner —"Behold, GOD is great, and we know him not, neither can the number of his years be searched out. Can any understand the spreadings of his clouds or the noise of his tabernacle (i.e. the visible heavens, poetically so called.) Behold he spreadeth his light upon it; the noise thereof sheweth concerning it, the cattle also (then retiring to shelter) concerning the vapour." And as the thunder was then roaring, he cries out— "Hear attentively the noise of his voice, and the sound that goeth out of his mouth! He directeth it under the whole heaven, and his lightning to the ends of the earth. Hearken unto this, O *Job!* stand still, and consider the wondrous works of GOD. And now, *other men* see not the bright light which is in the clouds; but the wind passeth, and cleanseth them. Brightness cometh out of the north; with GOD is terrible majesty." What can be a more suitable and glorious attendance upon the CREATOR, than the winds, the rain, the horror and majesty of a storm, the splendour of the lightning, the voice of the thunder, and the brightness, or path of flame, which preceeds him as he rides in divine pomp through the north, and answers *Job* out of the whirlwind? Upon the Speech, which is undoubtedly the most sublime ever rehersed to mankind, remarks would be impertinence.

As the Epic poem is the most noble of all others, the whole force of the human Genius is exhausted in beautifying it with figures, comparisons, and descriptions.

Many Comparisons are to be found in the Bible, but few of them are extended to any length. As those penmen wrote more for Instruction than Amusement, the Comparisons which they have introduced, being made more for illustration than beauty, are always short, though pertinent and striking. If this be thought a deficiency, it is abundantly supplied by an exuberance of the finest Figures which are to be found in writing. Indeed, the Eastern Genius was so animated, that when those authors seized a Comparison, the warmth of their Imagination instantly converted it into the principal subject, and thereby formed a short, and exquisitely beautiful Allegory; than which Figure, nothing is more common in all the sacred Scriptures—An admirable instance may be seen in the 5th Chapter of *Isaiah.*

Of the other principal Figures in composition— the Metaphor, the Apostrophe, and the Personification, as well as the Antithesis, which was better understood, and more happily applied by

Isaiah, than by any other Poet, most perfect examples are to be found in his awful and sublime prophecy concerning the destruction of *Babylon* (*Isa. 13, 14*)—Particularly in the incomparable Apostrophe to that proud city—"How art thou fallen from heaven, O *Lucifer,* Son of the Morning! how art thou cast down to the ground, who didst weaken the nations!"—This undoubtedly gave *Milton* the first thought of Satan's* rebellion, and war.

Can the matchless excellence of the sacred descriptions be better illustrated, than by comparing the sublimest description of a God, in the sublimest of all the prophane writers of antiquity, with a similar one from the Bible? That from *Homer,* translated as well as I was able, and, to give it the better appearance, purposely cleared of several puerilities, runs thus—*Neptune*† emerged from the sea, and moved with indignation against *Jove,* fate and pitied the *Grecian* host yielding to the force of the *Trojans.* Suddenly, with swift steps he rushed down the broken precipice; the woods and mountains trembled beneath his immortal feet. Three times he stepped, the fourth, he reached the Aegae. There stands his glorious, incorruptible palace of shining gold—There he joined his nimble steeds, with brazen hoofs and golden manes, cloathed himself in gold, ascended his chariot, and skimmed the surface of waves. On all sides, the Whales exulted around their king; the Sea with joy parted before him; the steeds flew swiftly over it, nor moistened the brazen axle.

The other from *Habbakkuk* is thus translated —"GOD came from *Teman,* and the HOLY ONE from mount *Peran;* his Glory covered the heavens and the earth was full of his Praise. His brightness was as the light; he had horns coming out of his hand, and there was the hiding of his power. Before him went the Pestilence, and burning coals went forth at his feet. He stood, and measured the heavens; he beheld, and drove asunder the nations; the everlasting mountains were scattered, the perpetual hills did bow; his ways are everlasting. I saw the tents of *Cushan* in affliction, the

---

* See Par. lost. B.5—At length into the limits of the north/They came, and Satan took his royal seat/High on a hill, far blazing, &c.
† Ilias B. 13.

curtains of the land of *Midian,* did tremble. Thou didst cleave the earth with thy rivers. The Mountains saw thee and trembled, the over flowing of the waters passed by, the deep uttered his voice, and lift up his hands on high. The Sun and the Moon stood still in their habitation: at the light of thine arrows they went, at the shining of thy glittering spear."

Of these two passages it need only be observed, that where the circumstances are similar, the Prophet is far more lively and sublime than the Poet, and infinitely surpasses him in those which are different.

To mention a number of Descriptions in the Inspired writings, would be injustice to the rest; but how can I pass by *Ezekiel's* of the Cherubims, (*Ezek. 1*), *Daniel's,* of the Ancient of days (*Dan. 7:9*), or *St. John's,* of the Saviour amid the seven golden candlesticks? (*Rev. 1*)

Nothing gives greater weight and dignity to Poetry, than Prophecy. Sensible of this truth *Virgil* has, with great beauty, inserted something of this kind in the fourth, which is the finest of his Pastorals, and in the sixth, which is the noblest book of his Eneis. But excellent as he is, the Prophets, particularly *Isaiah* and *John,* in the beauties of this part of writing, shine without a competitor.

Instead of wild conjectures, instead of past events, instead of Generals and Heroes, instead of *Marcellus,* instead of the *Roman* City and Empire; the Prophecies are always certain, the events referred to future; Their Hero is the *Messiah,* the wonderful Counsellour, the mighty GOD, the everlasting Father, the Prince of Peace. The Empire, that of the Universe, its extension immensity, its duration eternity. The City, the new *Jerusalem,* the Heaven of Heavens, the seat of light and blessedness; its walls of gold and precious stones, its splendor that of Almighty GOD.

And this advantage attends all their writings, that every possible Reader, every one of us is infinitely more interested in the subject, than the *Romans* were in that of *Virgil;* as we are candidates for an immortal existence in that region of felicity, where the Sun doth not give light by day, nor the Moon by night, but the Lord himself is an everlasting Light, and the GOD of *Zion* her Glory.

A DIALOGUE

EUPHORMIO.

Hail glorious Day! eventful Aera hail!
Ye Moments swiftly fly, till, all reveal'd,
The deep Decrees of Providence are seen—

AMYNTOR.

What means, my Friend, that rapture speaking
    Eye?
That Joy unusual that distends thy Breast,
And brightens all thy Mien?

EUPHORMIO.

           I see, I see
The Soul-exalting Periods gayly dawn,
By the rapt Tongue of *Prophecy* foretold;
When SHILOH's heavenly Ensign, wide display'd
O'er this *new World,* shall congregate the Tribes,
"Of every Language and of every Hue,"
And beam Conviction o'r the darken'd Mind;
Till, all subdu'd and melted into Love,
The roaming *Native* seeks the peaceful Shade
Of social Life, and bends at Wisdom's Shrine!
For lo! in this blest Spot, where nought was seen,
But Woods umbrageous o'er the lonesome Wild;
Where late the *Savage,* grim, tremendous, fierce,
And bloody from the butcher'd Victim, stalk'd;
Fair *Science* now hath rear'd this sacred Dome,
"To pour Instruction o'er th' untutor'd Mind!

AMYNTOR.

Hail to the Day that sees this glorious Change!
When the fell *Indian,* long to Blood inur'd,
Himself the *evangelic Strain* shall catch,
That strung th' adoring Seraph's golden Lyre,
While Hills and Vales, responsive to his Song,
Eccho *Hosannas* to the GOD OF LOVE:
And sacred Science, o'er the western World,
Pours her best Gifts; like yonder radiant Sun,
That, in Profusion, from the Carr of Day,
Sheds his unbounded Glories all around!
Witness, ye conscious Woods, how blest the
    Change!
Witness majestic *Delaware;* and thou
Hoarse *Brandywine,* as headlong thro' thy Cliffs
Ragged, from Steep to Steep, thou thunder'st
    down
And heard'st the dismal Yell, nor ought beheld'st
On all your Banks, but Haunts of savage Beasts
And savage Men—Witness, how chang'd the
    Scene!

EUPHORMIO.

Hail Blissful Change! see now fair Cities rise;

Where once the dreary Wilderness appear'd!
And Arts and Commerce, Equity and Laws,
And Freedom fair, the Glory of Mankind,
The polar Star, by which each Patriot firm
Directs the Helm of State—have fix'd their Reign.
Here too, the youthful Breast is taught to pant
For Glory, and to raise its generous Aim
To each diviner Deed; aspiring still
To gain the Summit of unfading Praise,
Sweet Peace of Mind and Heaven's applauding
    Smile!
Here too the Bard is taught to mount sublime
Upon Imagination's airy Carr—
And here the grave Philosopher to scan
The Ways of Providence, and joyous rise
Through *Nature's Works* to *Nature's gracious*
    GOD!
Here too the searchful mathematic Eye,
Above this lowly Earth's contracted Span,
Above the Chambers of the northern Blast,
And all yon rolling Orbs, is taught to stray
Thro' Fields of Light, and number all the Stars,
And trace the great Creator's wondrous Law,
That binds each Sun and Planet to its Sphere,
And bids the Whole, in chastest mystic Dance,
Roll round his Throne, who launch'd them thro'
    the Deep!

AMYNTOR.

Hail happy Land! the last and best Retreat
Of all that can exalt or bless Mankind!
New LOCKES shall here the complex Thought un-
    fold,
New MILTONS soar on Fancy's ardent Wing,
And future NEWTONS to astonish'd Worlds
Great Nature's deepest Secrets shall reveal.
Even other HANDELLS shall exalt the Soul
With Music's Charms above the starry Skies!
And other TULLIES fill the ravish'd Ear
Of listening Senates, with their patriot Strains!

EUPHORMIO.

What owe we then to you, whose gen'rous Toils
And lib'ral Aid, have rais'd this goodly Dome,
And consecrated it to Youths unborn,
A Nursery of *Science* and of *Truth!*—
Oh! may your Names, to Ages far remote,
From Sire to Son, be borne in Tides of Praise!
And chiefly thine, O PENN! sprung from a Race
Of Worthies, by whose charter'd Powers we meet
And dedicate this Day to festive Joy!

Spoken at
Opening of the
Public Grammar
School at
Wilmington,
October 26, 1773

231

LETTERS ON THE EDUCATION
OF CHILDREN

*Letters on the
Education of
Children,*
by Rev. John
Witherspoon,
1797

LETTER I

After so long a delay, I now set myself to fulfil my promise of writing to you a few thoughts on the education of children. Though I cannot wholly acquit myself of the crimes of laziness and procrastination, yet I do assure you, what contributed not a little to its being hitherto not done, was, that I considered it not as an ordinary letter, but what deserved to be carefully meditated on, and thoroughly digested. The concern you show on this subject, is highly commendable: for there is no part of your duty, as a Christian, or a citizen, which will be of greater service to the public, or a source of greater comfort to yourself.

The consequence of my thinking so long upon it, before committing my thoughts to paper, will probably be the taking the thing in a greater compass than either of us at first intended, and writing a series of letters, instead of one. With this view I begin with a preliminary to the successful education of children, viz. that husband and wife ought to be entirely one upon this subject, not only agreed as to the end, but as to the means to be used, and the plan to be followed, in order to attain it. . . . However, I content myself with repeating, that certainly husband and wife ought to conspire and cooperate in every thing relating to the education of their children; and if their opinions happen, in any particular, to be different, they ought to examine and settle the matter privately by themselves, that not the least opposition may appear either to children or servants. When this is the case, every thing is enforced by a double authority, and recommended by a double example: but when it is otherwise, the pains taken are commonly more than lost, not being able to do any good, and certainly producing very much evil.

Be pleased to remember, that this is by no means intended against those unhappy couples, who, being essentially different in principles and character, live in a state of continual war. It is of little advantage to speak either to, or of such persons. But even differences incomparably smaller, are of very bad consequence: when one, for example, thinks a child may be carried out, and the other thinks it is wrong; when one thinks a way of speaking is dangerous, and the other is

positive there is nothing in it. The things themselves may indeed be of little moment; but the want of concurrence in the parents, or the want of mutual esteem and deference, easily observed even by very young children, is of the greatest importance.

As you and I have chiefly in view the religious education of children, I take it to be an excellent preliminary that parental affection should be purified by the principles and controled or directed by the precepts of religion. A parent should rejoice in his children, as they are the gift of a gracious God; should put his trust in the care of an indulgent Providence for the preservation of his offspring, as well as himself; should be supremely desirous that they may be, in due time, the heirs of eternal life; and, as he knows the absolute dependence of every creature upon the will of God, should be ready to resign them at what time his Creator shall see proper to demand them. This happy qualification of parental tenderness, will have a powerful influence in preventing mistakes in the conduct of education. It will be the most powerful of all incitements to duty, and at the same time a restraint upon that natural fondness and indulgence, which, by a sort of fascination of fatality, make parents often do or permit what their judgment condemns, and then excuse themselves by saying that no doubt it is wrong, but truly they cannot help it.

BENEFIT OF PROPER EDUCATION

Another preliminary to the proper education of children, is a firm persuasion of the benefit of it, and the probable, at least, if not certain success of it, when faithfully and prudently conducted. This puts an edge upon the spirit, and enables the christian not only to make some attempts, but to persevere with patience and diligence. I know not a common saying either more false or pernicious, than "that the children of good men are as bad as others." This saying carries in it a supposition, that whereas the force of education is confessed with respect to every other human character and accomplishment, it is of no consequence at all as to religion. This, I think, is contrary to daily experience. Where do we expect to find young persons piously disposed but in pious families? The exceptions, or rather appearances to the contrary, are easily accounted for, in more ways than one. Many persons appear to be religious, while they are not so in reality, but are chiefly governed by the applause of men. Hence their visible conduct may be specious, or their public performances applauded, and yet their families be neglected.

It must also be acknowledged that some truly well disposed persons are extremely defective or imprudent in this part of their duty, and therefore it is no wonder that it should not succeed. This was plainly the case with Eli, whose sons we are told, made themselves vile, and he restrained them not. However, I must observe, if we allow such to be truly good men, we must at the same time confess that this was a great drawback upon their character; and that they differed very much from the father of the faithful, who had this honorable testimony given him by God, *"I know him, that he will command his children and his household after him, that they serve me."* (*Gen. 18:19*) To this we may add, that the child of a good man, who is seen to follow dissolute courses, draws the attention of mankind more upon him, and is much more talked of, than any other person of the same character. Upon the whole, it is certainly of moment, that one who desires to educate his children in the fear of God, should do it in a humble persuasion, that if he is not defective in his own duty, he will not be denied the blessing of success. I could tell you some remarkable instances of parents who seemed to labor in vain for a long time, and yet were so happy as to see a change at last; and of some children in whom even after the death of the parents, the seed which was early sown, and seemed to have been entirely smothered, has at last produced fruit. And indeed no less seems to follow from the promise, annexed to the command, *Train up a child in the way he should go, and when he is old he will not depart from it.* (*Prov. 22:6*) . . .

LETTER II
ENTIRE AND ABSOLUTE AUTHORITY

The next thing I shall mention as necessary, in order to the education of children, is, to establish as soon as possible, an entire and absolute authority over them. This is a part of the subject which requires to be treated with great judgment and delicacy. I wish I may be able to do so. Opinions, like modes and fashions, change continually upon every point; neither is it easy to keep the

just middle, without verging to one or other of the extremes. On this, in particular, we have gone in this nation in general, from one extreme to the very utmost limits of the other. In the former age, both public and private, learned and religious education was carried on by mere dint of authority. This, to be sure, was a savage and barbarous method, and was in many instances terrible and disgusting to the youth. Now, on the other hand, not only severity, but authority, is often decried; persuasion, and every soft and gentle method, are recommended, on such terms as plainly lead to a relaxation. I hope you will be convinced that the middle way is best, when you find it recommended by the spirit of God in his word, *Prov. xix.18.* *"Chasten thy son while there is hope, and let not thy soul spare for his crying."* You will also find a caution against excess in this matter, *Col. iii.21.* *"Fathers, provoke not your children to anger, lest they be discouraged."*

I have said above, that you should "establish as soon as possible an entire and absolute authority." I would have it early, that it may be absolute, and absolute that it may not be severe. If parents are too long in beginning to exert their authority, they will find the task very difficult. Children, habituated to indulgence for a few of their first years, are exceedingly impatient of restraint, and if they happen to be of stiff or obstinate tempers, can hardly be brought to an entire, at least to a quiet and placid submission; whereas, if they are taken in time, there is hardly any temper but what may be made to yield, and by early habit the subjection becomes quite easy to themselves.

The authority ought also to be absolute, that it may not be severe. The more complete and uniform a parent's authority is, the offences will be more rare, punishment will be less needed, and the more gentle kind of correction will be abundantly sufficient. We see every where about us examples of this. A parent that has once obtained, and knows how to preserve authority, will do more by a look of displeasure, than another by the most passionate words and even blows. It holds universally in families and schools, and even the greater bodies of men, the army and navy, that those who keep the strictest discipline, give the fewest strokes. I have frequently remarked that parents, even of the softest tempers, and who are famed for the greatest indulgence to their children, do, notwithstanding, correct them more frequently, and even more severely, though to very little purpose, than those who keep up their authority. The reason is plain. Children, by foolish indulgence, become often so froward and petulant in their tempers, and they provoke their easy parents past endurance; so that they are obliged, if not to strike, at least to scold them, in a manner as little to their own credit, as their children's profit.

There is not a more disgusting sight than the impotent rage of a parent who has no authority. Among the lower ranks of people, who are under no restraint from decency, you may sometimes see a father or mother running out into the street after a child who is fled from them, with looks of fury and words of execration; and they are often stupid enough to imagine that neighbors or passengers will approve them in this conduct, though in fact it fills every beholder with horror. There is a degree of the same fault to be seen in persons of better rank, though expressing itself somewhat differently. Ill words and altercations will often fall out between parents and children before company; a sure sign that there is defect of government at home or in private. The parent stung with shame at the misbehaviour or indiscretion of the child, desires to persuade the observers that it is not his fault, and thereby effectually convinces every person of reflection that it *is*.

I would therefore recommend to every parent to begin the establishment of authority much more early than is commonly supposed to be possible: that is to say, from about the age of eight or nine months. You will perhaps smile at this: but I do assure you from experience, that by setting about it with prudence, deliberation, and attention, it may be in a manner completed by the age of twelve or fourteen months. Do not imagine I mean to bid you use the rod at that age; on the contrary, I mean to prevent the use of it in a great measure, and to point out a way by which children of sweet and easy tempers may be brought to such a habit of compliance, as never to need correction at all; and whatever their temper may be, to need much less than upon any other supposition. This is one of my favourite schemes; let me try to explain and recommend it.

Habits in general may be very early formed in children. An association of ideas is, as it were, the parent of habit. If then, you can accustom your children to perceive that your will must always prevail over theirs, when they are opposed, the thing is done, and they will submit to it without difficulty or regret. To bring this about, as soon as they begin to show their inclination by desire or aversion, let single instances be chosen now and then (not too frequently) to contradict them. For example, if a child shows a desire to have any

thing in his hand that he sees, or has any thing in his hand with which he is delighted, let the parent take it from him, and when he does so, let no consideration whatever make him restore it at that time. Then at a considerable interval, perhaps a whole day is little enough, especially at first, let the same thing be repeated. In the mean time, it must be carefully observed, that no attempt should be made to contradict the child in the intervals. Not the least appearance of opposition, if possible, should be found between the will of the parent and that of the child, except in those chosen cases when the parent must always prevail.

I think it necessary that those attempts should always be made and repeated at proper intervals by the same person. It is also better it should be by the father than the mother or any female attendant, because they will be necessarily obliged, in many cases, to do things displeasing to the child, as in dressing, washing, &c. which spoil the operation; neither is it necessary that they should interpose, for when once a full authority is established in one person, it can easily be communicated to others, as far as is proper. Remember, however, that mother or nurse should never presume to condole with the child, or show any signs of displeasure at his being crossed; but on the contrary, give every mark of approbation, and of their own submission, to the same person.

This experiment frequently repeated will in a little time so perfectly habituate the child to yield to the parent whenever he interposes, that he will make no opposition. I can assure you from experience, having literally practised this method myself, that I never had a child of twelve months old, but who would suffer me to take any thing from him or her, without the least mark of anger or dissatisfaction; while they would not suffer any other to do so without the bitterest complaints. You will easily perceive how this is to be extended gradually and universally, from one thing to another, from contradicting to commanding them. But this, and several other remarks upon establishing and preserving authority, must be referred to another letter.

LETTER III
DIVERSITY IN TEMPER AND DISPOSITION OF CHILDREN

The theory laid down in my last letter, for establishing an early and absolute authority over children, is of much greater moment than, perhaps, you will immediately apprehend. There is a great diversity in the temper and disposition of children; and no less in the penetration, prudence and resolution of parents. From all these circumstances, difficulties arise, which increase very fast as the work is delayed. Some children have naturally very stiff and obstinate tempers, and some have a certain pride, or if you please, greatness of mind, which makes them think it a mean thing to yield. This disposition is often greatly strengthened in those of high birth, by the ideas of their own dignity and importance, instilled into them from their mother's milk. I have known a boy not six years of age, who made it a point of honor not to cry when he was beat, even by his parents. Other children have so strong passions, or so great sensibility, that if they receive correction, they will cry immediately, and either be, or seem to be, affected to such a degree, as to endanger their health or life. Neither is it uncommon for the parents in such a case to give up the point, and if they do not ask pardon, at least they give very genuine marks of repentance and sorrow for what they have done.

I have said this is not uncommon, but I may rather ask you whether you know any parents at all, who have so much prudence and firmness as not to be discouraged in the one case, or to relent in the other? At the same time it must always be remembered, that the correction is wholly lost which does not produce absolute submission. Perhaps I may say it is more than lost, because it will irritate instead of reforming them, and will instruct or perfect them in the art of overcoming their parents, which they will not fail to manifest on a future opportunity. It is surprising to think how early children will discover the weak side of their parents, and what ingenuity they will show in obtaining their favor or avoiding their displeasure. I think I have observed a child in treaty or expostulation with a parent, discover more consummate policy at seven years of age, than the parent himself, even when attempting to cajole him with artful evasions and specious promises. On all these accounts, it must be a vast advantage that a habit of submission should be brought on so early, that even memory itself shall not be able to reach back to its beginning. Unless this is done, there are many cases in which, after the best management, the authority will be imperfect; and some in which any thing that deserves that name will be impossible. There are some families, not contemptible either in station or character, in which the parents are literally and properly obedient to their children, are forced to do things against their will, and chidden if

they discover the least backwardness to comply. If you know none such, I am sure I do.

Let us now proceed to the best means of preserving authority, and the way in which it ought to be daily exercised. I will trace this to its very source. Whatever authority you exercise over either children or servants, or as a magistrate over other citizens, it ought to be dictated by conscience, and directed by a sense of duty. Passion or resentment ought to have as little place as possible; or rather, to speak properly, though few can boast of having arrived at full perfection, it ought to have no place at all. Reproof or correction given in a rage, is always considered by him to whom it is administered, as the effect of weakness in you, and therefore the demerit of the offence will be either wholly denied or soon forgotten. I have heard some parents often say, that they cannot correct their children unless they are angry; to whom I have usually answered, then you ought not to correct them at all. Every one would be sensible, that for a magistrate to discover an intemperate rage in pronouncing sentence against a criminal, would be highly indecent. Ought not parents to punish their children in the same dispassionate manner? Ought they not to be at least equally concerned to discharge their duty in the best manner, in the one case as in the other?

PARENTS OWN CONDUCT

He who would preserve his authority over his children, should be particularly watchful of his own conduct. You may as well pretend to force people to love what is not amiable, as to reverence what is not respectable. A decency of conduct, therefore, and dignity of deportment, are highly serviceable for the purpose we have now in view. Lest this, however, should be mistaken, I must put in a caution, that I do not mean to recommend keeping children at too great a distance by a uniform sternness and severity of carriage. This, I think, is not necessary, even when they are young; and it may, to children of some tempers, be very hurtful when they are old. By and by you shall receive from me a quite contrary direction. But by dignity of carriage, I mean parents showing themselves always cool and reasonable in their own conduct; prudent and cautious in their conversation with regard to the rest of mankind; not fretful or impatient, or passionately fond of their own peculiarities; and though gentle and affectionate to their children, yet avoiding levity in their presence. This probably is the

LETTERS
ON THE
EDUCATION OF
CHILDREN,
1797

PARENTS
OWN CONDUCT

meaning of the precept of the ancients, *maxima debetur pueris reverentia*.* I would have them cheerful, yet serene. In short, I would have their familiarity to be evidently an act of condescension. Believe it, my dear sir, that which begets esteem, will not fail to produce subjection.

That this may not be carried too far, I would recommend every expression of affection and kindness to children when it is safe, that is to say, when their behaviour is such as to deserve it. There is no opposition at all between parental tenderness and parental authority. They are the best supports to each other. It is not only lawful, but will be of service, that parents should discover the greatest fondness for children in infancy, and make them perceive distinctly with how much pleasure they gratify all their innocent inclinations. This, however, must always be done when they are quiet, gentle, and submissive in their carriage. Some have found fault with giving them, for doing well, little rewards of sweet meats and play-things, as tending to make them mercenary, and leading them to look upon the indulgence of appetite as the chief good. This I apprehend, is rather refining too much: the great point is, that they be rewarded for doing good, and not for doing evil. When they are cross and froward, I would never buy peace, but force it. Nothing can be more weak and foolish, or more destructive of authority, than when children are noisy and in an ill humor, to give them or promise them something to appease them. When the Roman emperors began to give pensions and subsidies to the Northern nations to keep them quiet, a man might have foreseen without the spirit of prophecy, who would be master in a little time. The case is exactly the same with children. They will soon avail themselves of this easiness in their parents, command favours instead of begging them, and be insolent when they should be grateful.

The same conduct ought to be uniformly preserved as children advance in years and understanding. Let parents try to convince them how much they have their real interest at heart. Sometimes children will make a request, and receive a hasty or froward denial: yet upon reflection the thing appears not to be unreasonable, and finally it is granted; and whether it be right or wrong, sometimes by the force of importunity, it is extorted. If parents expect either gratitude or submission for favors so ungraciously bestowed, they

will find themselves egregiously mistaken. It is their duty to prosecute, and it ought to be their comfort to see, the happiness of their children; and therefore they ought to lay it down as a rule, never to give a sudden or hasty refusal; but when any thing is proposed to them, consider deliberately and fully whether it is proper—and after that, either grant it cheerfully, or deny it firmly.

USE AUTHORITY FOR GOD

It is a noble support of authority, when it is really and visibly directed to the most important end. My meaning in this, I hope, is not obscure. The end I consider as most important is, the glory of God in the eternal happiness and salvation of children. Whoever believes in a future state, whoever has a just sense of the importance of eternity to himself, cannot fail to have a like concern for his offspring. This should be his end both in instruction and government; and when it visibly appears that he is under the constraint of conscience, and that either reproof or correction are the fruit of sanctified love, it will give them irresistible force. I will tell you here, with all the simplicity necessary in such a situation, what I have often said in my course of pastoral visitation in families, where there is in many cases, through want of judgment, as well as want of principle, a great neglect of authority. "Use your authority for God, and he will support it. Let it always be seen that you are more displeased at sin than at folly. What a shame is it, that if a child shall, through the inattention and levity of youth, break a dish or a pane of the window, by which you may lose the value of a few pence, you should storm and rage at him with the utmost fury, or perhaps beat him with unmerciful severity; but if he tells a lie, or takes the name of God in vain, or quarrels with his neighbors, he shall easily obtain pardon: or perhaps, if he is reproved by others, you will justify him, and take his part."

You cannot easily believe the weight that it gives to family authority, when it appears visibly to proceed from a sense of duty, and to be itself an act of obedience to God. This will produce coolness and composure in the manner, it will direct and enable a parent to mix every expression of heart-felt tenderness, with the most severe and needful reproofs. It will make it quite consistent to affirm, that the rod itself is an evidence of love, and that it is true of every pious parent on earth, what is said of our Father in heaven:—"*Whom the Lord loveth, he chasteneth, and scourgeth every son whom he receiveth. If ye endure chas-*

* We should be particularly careful of our conduct in the presence of children.

REVEREND JOHN WITHERSPOON
BY CHARLES WILLSON PEALE, (AMERICAN, 1741-1827)
OIL ON CANVAS, 22½ X 19 IN. C. 1783
COURTESY INDEPENDENCE NATIONAL
HISTORICAL PARK COLLECTION.
PHILADELPHIA, PENNSYLVANIA

tening, God dealeth with you as with sons: for what son is he whom the Father chasteneth not? But if ye are without chastisement, whereof all are partakers, then are ye bastards and not sons." (*Heb. 12:6–8*) With this maxim in your eye, I would recommend, that solemnity take the place of, and be substituted for severity. When a child for example, discovers a very depraved disposition, instead of multiplying stripes in proportion to the reiterated provocations, every circumstance should be introduced, whether in reproof or punishment, that can either discover the seriousness of your mind, or make an impression of awe and reverence upon his. The time may be fixed before hand, at some distance—on the Lord's day—his own birth day—with many other circumstances that may be so special that it is impossible to enumerate them. I shall just repeat what you have heard often from me in conversation, that several pious persons made it an invariable custom, as soon as their children could read, never to correct them, till after they had read over all the passages of scripture which command it, and generally accompanied it with prayer to God for his blessing. I know well with what ridicule this would be treated by many, if publicly mentioned; but that does not shake my judgment in the least, being fully convinced it is a most excellent method, and that it is impossible to blot from the minds of children, while they live upon earth, the impressions that are made by these means, or to abate the veneration they will retain for the parents who acted such a part.

Suffer me here to observe to you, that such a plan as the above requires judgment, reflection, and great attention in your whole conduct. Take heed that there be nothing admitted in the intervals that may counteract it. Nothing is more destructive of authority, than frequent disputes and chiding upon small matters. This is often more irksome to children than parents are aware of. It weakens their influence insensibly, and in time makes their opinion and judgment of little weight, if not wholly contemptible. As before I recommended dignity in your general conduct, so in a particular manner, let the utmost care be taken not to render authority cheap, by too often interposing it. There is really too great a risk to be run in every such instance. If parents will be deciding directly, and censuring every moment, it is to be supposed they will be sometimes wrong, and when this evidently appears, it will take away from the credit of their opinion, and weaken their influence, even where it ought to prevail.

Upon the whole, to encourage you to choose a wise plan, and to adhere to it with firmness, I can venture to assure you, that there is no doubt of your success. To subdue a youth after he has been long accustomed to indulgence, I take to be in all cases difficult, and in many impossible; but while the body is tender, to bring the mind to submission, to train up a child *in the nurture and admonition of the Lord,* I know is not impossible: and He who hath given the command, can scarcely fail to follow it with his blessing.

LETTER IV
EXAMPLE OF PARTICULARS

Having now finished what I proposed to say on the means of establishing and preserving authority, I shall proceed to another very important branch of the subject, and beg your very particular attention to it, viz. example. Do not, however, suppose that I mean to enter on that most beaten of all topics, the influence of example in general, or to write a dissertation on the common saying, that "example teaches better than precept." And able writer, doubtless, might set even this in some new lights, and make it a strong argument with every good man to pay the strictest attention to his visible conduct. What we see every day has a constant and powerful influence on our temper and carriage. Hence arise national characters, and national manners, and every characteristic distinction of age and place. But of this I have already said enough.

Neither is it my purpose to put you in mind of the importance of example to enforce instruction, or of the shamefulness of a man's pretending to teach others what he despises himself. This ought in the strongest manner to be laid before pastors and other public persons, who often defeat habitually by their lives, what they attempt to do occasionally in the execution of their office. If there remains the least suspicion of your being of that character, these letters would have been quite in another strain. I believe there are some persons of very irregular lives, who have so much natural light in their consciences, that they would be grieved or perhaps offended, if their children should tread exactly in their own steps: but even these, and much less others, who are more hardened, can never be expected to undertake or carry on the system of education, we are now endeavouring to illustrate. Suffer me, however, before I proceed, to make one remark; when I have heard of parents who have been watched by their own children, when drunk, and taken care of, lest they should meet with injury or hurtful accidents—or whose intemperate rage and horrid blasphemies, have, without scruple, been exposed both to children and servants—or who, as has been sometimes the case, were scarcely at the pains to conceal their criminal amours, even from their own offspring—I have often reflected on the degree of impiety in principle, or searedness of conscience, or both united, necessary to support them in such circumstances. Let us leave all such with a mixture of pity and disdain.

By mentioning example, therefore, as an important and necessary branch of the education of children, I have chiefly in view a great number of particulars, which, separately taken, are, or at least are supposed to be, of little moment; yet by their union or frequent repetition, produce important and lasting effects. I have also in view to include all that class of actions, in which there is, or may be, a coincidence between the duties of piety and politeness, and by means of which, the one is incorporated with the other. These are to be introduced under the head of example, because they will appear there to best advantage, and because many of them can hardly be taught or understood in any other way.

PIETY AND POLITENESS

This, I apprehend, you will readily approve of, because, though you justly consider religion as the most essential qualification, you mean at the same time that your children should be fitted for an appearance becoming their station in the world. It is also the more necessary, as many are apt to disjoin wholly the ideas of piety and politeness, and to suppose them not only distinct, but incompatible. This is a dangerous snare to many parents, who think there is no medium between the grossest rusticity, and giving away to all the vanity and extravagance of a dissipated life. Persons truly pious have often by their conduct given countenance to this mistake. By a certain narrowness of sentiment and behavior they have become themselves, and rendered their children, unfit for a general intercourse with mankind, or the public duties of an active life.

You know, sir, as much as any man, how contrary my opinion and conduct have been upon this subject. I cannot help thinking that true religion is not only consistent with, but necessary to the perfection of true politeness. There is a noble sentiment to this purpose illustrated at considerable length in the Port-royal essays, viz. "That worldly politeness is no more than an imitation or imperfect copy of christian charity, be-

ing the pretence or outward appearance, of that deference to the judgment, and attention to the interest of others, which a true Christian has as the rule of his life, and the disposition of his heart." I have at present in my mind the idea of certain persons, whom you will easily guess at, of the first quality; one or two of the male, and twice that number, at least, of the female sex, in whom piety and high station are united. What a sweetness and complacency of countenance, what a condescension and gentleness of manners, arising from the humility of the gospel being joined to the refined elegance inseparable from their circumstances in life!

Be pleased to follow me to the other extreme of human society. Let us go to the remotest cottage of the wildest country, and visit the family that inhabits it. If they are pious, there is a certain humanity and good will attending their simplicity, which makes it highly agreeable. There is also a decency in their sentiments, which, flowing from the dictates of conscience, is as pleasing in all respects as the restraints imposed by the rules of good breeding, with which the persons here in view have little opportunity of being acquainted. On the contrary, unbred country people, when without principle, have generally a savageness and brutality in their carriage, as contrary to good manners as to piety itself. No one has a better opportunity of making observations of this kind, than I have from my office and situation, and I can assure you, that religion is the great polisher of the common people. It even enlarges their understanding as to other things. Having been accustomed to exercise their judgment and reflection on religious subjects, they are capable of talking more sensibly on agriculture, politics, or any common topic of indifferent conversation.

Let me not forget to speak of the middle ranks of life. Here, also, I scruple not to affirm, that whatever sphere a man has been bred in, or attained to, religion is not an injury, but an addition to the politeness of his carriage. They seem indeed to confess their relation to one another, by their reciprocal influence. In promiscuous conversation, as true religion contributes to make men decent or courteous, so true politeness guards them effectually from any outrage against piety or purity. If I were unhappily thrown into mixed or dangerous company, I should not apprehend any thing improper for me to hear from the most wicked man, but from the greatest clown. I have known gentlemen who were infidels in principle, and whose lives, I had reason to believe, were privately very bad, yet in conversation they were guarded, decent and improving; whereas if there come into company a rough, unpolished country gentleman, no man can promise that he will not break out into some profane exclamation or obscene allusion, which it would be wrong to attribute to impiety, so much as to rudeness and want of reflection.

I have been already too long in the introduction, and in giving the reasons for what I propose shall make a part of this branch of the subject, and yet I must make another preliminary remark: there is the greater necessity for uniting piety and politeness in the system of family example, that as piety is by that means inculcated with the greatest advantage, so politeness can scarcely be attained in other way. It is very rare that persons reach a higher degree of politeness, than what they have been formed to in the families of their parents and other near relations. True politeness does not consist in dress, or a few motions of the body, but in a habit of sentiment and conversation: the first may be learned from a master, and in a little time; the last only by a long and constant intercourse with those who possess, and are therefore able to impart it. As the difficulty is certainly greatest with the female sex, because they have fewer opportunities of being abroad in the world, I shall take an example from among them.

Suppose a man of low birth living in the country, by industry and parsimony has become wealthy, and has a daughter to whom he desires to give a genteel education. He sends her to your city to a boarding school, for the other which is nearer me, you are pleased not to think sufficient for that purpose. She will speedily learn to buy expensive and fashionable clothes, and most probably be in the very height of extravagance of fashion, one of the surest signs of a vulgar taste. She may also, if her capacity is tolerable, get rid of her rustic air and carriage; and if it be better than ordinary, learn to discourse upon whatever topic is then in vogue, and comes in immediately after the weather, which is the beginning of all conversation. But as her residence is only for a time, she returns home; where she can see or hear nothing but as before. Must she not relapse speedily in the same vulgarity of sentiment, and perhaps the same provincial dialect, to which she had been accustomed from her youth? Neither is it impossible that she may just retain as much of the city ceremonial, as by the incongruous mixture, will render her ridiculous. There is but one single way of escape, which we have seen some young women of merit and capacity take, which

is to contract an intimacy with persons of liberal sentiments and higher breeding, and be as little among their relations as possible. I have given this description to convince you that it is in their father's house and by the conversation and manners, to which they are there accustomed, that children must be formed to politeness, as well as to virtue. I carry this matter so far, that I think it a disadvantage to be bred too high, as well as too low. I do not desire, and have always declined any opportunities given me of having my children reside long in families of high rank. I was afraid they would contract an air and manner unsuitable to what was to be their condition the remainder of their lives. I would wish to give my children as just, as noble, and as elegant sentiments as possible, to fit them for rational conversation; but a dress and carriage suited to their station, and not inconsistent with the meekness of the gospel.

Though the length of this digression, or explanatory introduction, has made it impossible to say much in this letter on forming children's character and manners by example, before I conclude I will give one direction which is pretty comprehensive. Give the utmost attention to the manner of receiving and entertaining strangers in your family, as well as to your sentiments and expressions with regard to them when they are gone. I am fully persuaded that the plainest and shortest road to real politeness of carriage, and the most amiable sort of hospitality, is to think of others just as a Christian ought, and to express these thoughts with modesty and candor. This will keep you at an equal distance from a surly and morose carriage on the one hand, and a fawning, cringing obsequiousness, or unnecessary compliment and ceremony on the other. As these are circumstances to which children in early life are very attentive, and which occur constantly in their presence, it is of much moment what sentiments they imbibe from the behaviour of their parents. I do not mean only their learning from them an ease and dignity of carriage, or the contrary; but also, some moral or immoral habits of the last consequence. If they perceive you happy and lifted up with the visit or countenance of persons of high rank, solicitous to entertain them properly, submissive and flattering in your manner of speaking to them, vain and apt to boast of your connexion with them: and if, on the contrary, they perceive you hardly civil to persons of inferior stations, or narrow circumstances, impatient of their company, and immediately seizing the opportunity of their departure to despise or expose them; will not this naturally lead the

LETTERS
ON THE
EDUCATION OF
CHILDREN,
1797

PIETY AND
POLITENESS

young mind to consider riches and high station as the great sources of earthly happiness? Will it not give a strong bias to their whole desires and studies, as well as visibly affect their behaviour to others in social life? Do not think that this is too nice and refined: the first impressions upon young persons, though inconsiderable in themselves, have often a great as well as lasting effect.

I remember to have read many years ago, in the archbishop of Cambray's education of a daughter, an advice to parents to let their children perceive that they esteem others, not according to their station or outward splendor, but their virtue and real worth. It must be acknowledged that there are some marks of respect due to men, according to their place in civil life, which a good man would not fail to give them, even for conscience sake. But it is an easy matter, in perfect consistency with this, by more frequent voluntary intercourse, as well as by our usual manner of speaking, to pay that homage which is due to piety, to express our contempt or indignation at vice, or meanness of every kind. I think it no inconsiderable addition to this remark, that we should be as cautious of estimating *happiness* as *virtue* by outward station; and keep at the same distance from envying as from flattering the great.

But what I must particularly recommend to you, is, to avoid that common but detestable custom of receiving persons with courtesy, and all the marks of real friendship in your house; and the moment they are gone, falling upon their character and conduct with unmerciful severity. I am sensible there are some cases, though they are not numerous, in which it may be lawful to say of others behind their back, what it would be at least imprudent or unsafe to say in their own presence. Neither would I exclude parents from the advantage of pointing out to their children the mistakes and vices of others, as a warning or lesson of instruction to themselves. Yet as detraction in general is to be avoided at all times; so of all others the most improper season to speak to any man's prejudice, is, after you have just received and treated him in an hospitable manner, as a friend. There is something mean in it, and something so nearly allied to hypocrisy and disingenuousness, that I would not choose to act such a part, even to those whom I would take another opportunity of pointing out to my children, as persons whose conversation they should avoid, and whose conduct they should abhor.

In every station, and among all ranks, this rule is often transgressed; but there is one point in which it is more frequently and more universally

transgressed than in any other, and that is by turning the absent into ridicule, for any thing odd or awkward in their behaviour. I am sorry to say that this is an indecorum that prevails in several families of high rank. A man of inferior station, for some particular reason is admitted to their company. He is perhaps not well acquainted with the rules of politeness, and the presence of his superiors, to which he is unaccustomed, increases his embarrassment. Immediately on his departure, a petulant boy or giddy girl will set about mimicking his motions and repeating his phrases, to the great entertainment of the company, who apparently derive much self-satisfaction from a circumstance, in which there is no merit at all. If any person renders himself justly ridiculous, by affecting a character which he is unable to sustain, let him be treated with the contempt he deserves. But there is something very ungenerous in people's treating their inferiors with disdain, merely because the same Providence that made their ancestors great, left the others in a lower sphere.

It has often given me great indignation to see a gentleman or his wife, of real worth, good understanding, but simple manners, despised and ridiculed for a defect which they could not remedy, and that often by persons the most insignificant and frivolous, who never uttered a sentence in their lives that deserved to be remembered or repeated. But if this conduct is ungenerous in the great, how diverting is it to see the same disposition carried down through all the inferior ranks, and showing itself in a silly triumph of every class over those who are supposed to be below them. I have known many persons, whose station was not superior to mine, take great pleasure in expressing their contempt of *vulgar ideas* and *low life;* and even a tradesman's wife in a city, glorying over the unpolished manners of her country acquaintance.

Upon the whole, as there is no disposition to which young persons are more prone than derision, and few that parents are more apt to cherish —under the idea of its being a sign of sprightliness and vivacity—there is none which a pious and prudent parent should take greater care to restrain by admonition, and destroy by a contrary example.

LETTER V
RELIGION NECESSARY, RESPECTABLE, AMIABLE, PROFITABLE, AND DELIGHTFUL

Let us now proceed to consider more fully what it is to form children to piety by example. This is a subject of great extent, and, perhaps, of difficulty. The difficulty, however, does not consist either in the abstruseness of the arguments, or uncertainty of the facts upon which they are founded, but in the minuteness or trifling nature of the circumstances, taken separately, which makes them often either wholly unnoticed or greatly undervalued. It is a subject, which, if I mistake not, is much more easily conceived than explained. If you have it constantly in your mind, that your whole visible deportment will powerfully, though insensibly, influence the opinions and future conduct of your children, it will give a form or color, if I may speak so, to every thing you say or do. There are numberless and nameless instances in which this reflection will make you speak, or refrain from speaking, add, or abstain from, some circumstances of action, in what you are engaged in; nor will this be accompanied with any reluctance in the one case, or constraint in the other.

But I must not content myself with this. My profession gives me many opportunities of observing, that the impression made by general truths, however justly stated or fully proved, is seldom strong or lasting. Let me, therefore descend to practice, and illustrate what I have said by examples. Here again a difficulty occurs. If I give a particular instance it will perhaps operate no farther than recommending a like conduct in circumstances the same, or perhaps perfectly similar. For example, I might say, in speaking to the disadvantage of absent persons, I beseech you never fail to add the reason why you take such liberty, and indeed never take that liberty at all, but when it can be justified upon the principles of prudence, candor and charity. A thing may be right in itself, but children should be made to see why it is right. This is one instance of exemplary caution, but if I were to add a dozen more to it, they would only be detached precepts; whereas I am anxious to take in the whole extent of edifying example. In order to this, let me range or divide what I have to say under distinct heads.

A parent who wishes that his example should be a speaking lesson to his children, should order it so as to convince them, that he considers religion as *necessary, respectable, amiable, profitable,* and *delightful.* I am sensible that some of these characters may seem so nearly allied, as scarcely to admit of a distinction. Many parts of a virtuous conduct fall under more than one of these denominations. Some actions perhaps deserve all the epithets here mentioned, without exception

and without prejudice one of another. But the distinctions seem to me very useful, for there is certainly a class of actions which may be said to belong peculiarly, or at least eminently to each of these different heads. Taking them separately, therefore, will serve to point out more fully the extent of your duty, and to suggest it when it would not otherwise occur, as well as to set the obligation to it in the stronger light.

1. You should in your general deportment, make your children perceive that you look upon religion as absolutely *necessary.* I place this first, because it appears to me first both in point of order and force. I am far from being against taking all pains to show that religion is rational and honorable in itself, and vice the contrary; but I despise the foolish refinement of those, who, through fear of making children mercenary, are for being very sparing of the mention of heaven or hell. Such conduct is apt to make them conceive, that a neglect of their duty is only falling short of a degree of honor and advantage, which, for the gratification of their passions, they are very willing to relinquish. Many parents are much more ready to tell their children such or such a thing is mean, and not like a gentleman, than to warn them that they will thereby incur the displeasure of their Maker. But when the practices are really and deeply criminal, as in swearing and lying, it is quite improper to rest the matter there. I admit that they are both mean, and that justice ought to be done to them in this respect; but I contend that it should only be a secondary consideration.

Let not human reasonings be put in the balance with divine wisdom. The care of our souls is represented in scripture as the one thing needful. *He* makes a miserable bargain, who gains *the whole world and loses his own soul.* It is not the native beauty of virtue, or the outward credit of it, or the inward satisfaction arising from it, or even all these combined together, that will be sufficient to change our natures and govern our conduct; but a deep conviction, that unless we are reconciled to God, we shall without doubt perish everlastingly.

You will say, this is very true and very fit for a pulpit—but what is that class of actions that should impress it habitually on the minds of children? perhaps you will even say, what one action will any good man be guilty of—much more habitual conduct—that can tend to weaken their belief of it! This is the very point which I mean to explain. It is certainly possible that a man may at stated times give out that he looks upon religion

LETTERS
ON THE
EDUCATION OF
CHILDREN,
1797

———

RELIGIOUS
EDUCATION
NECESSARY

to be absolutely necessary, and yet his conduct in many particulars may have no tendency to impress this on the minds of his children. If he suffers particular religious duties to be easily displaced, to be shortened, postponed or omitted, upon the most trifling accounts, depend upon it, this will make religion in general seem less necessary, to those who observe it. If an unpleasant day will keep a man from public worship, when perhaps a hurricane will not keep him from an election meeting—if he chooses to take physic, or give it to his children on the Lord's day, when it could be done with equal ease on the day before or after —if he will more readily allow his servants to pay a visit to their friends on that day than any other, though he has reason to believe they will spend it in feasting and idleness—it will not be easy to avoid suspecting that worldly advantage is what determines his choice.

Take an example or two more on this head. Supposing a man usually to worship God in his family; if he sometimes omits it—if he allows every little business to interfere with it—if company will make him dispense with it, or shift it from its proper season—believe me, the idea of religion being every man's first and great concern is in a good measure weakened, if not wholly lost. It is a very nice thing in religion to know the real connexion between spirit and form, and how far the latter may be dispensed with without losing the former. The form without the spirit is good for nothing; but on the other hand, the spirit without the form, never yet existed. I am of opinion, that punctual and even scrupulous regularity, in all those duties that occur periodically, is the way to make them easy and pleasant to those who attend them. They also become, like all other habits, in some degree necessary; so that those who have been long accustomed to them, feel an uneasiness in families where they are generally or frequently neglected. I cannot help also mentioning to you, the great danger of paying and receiving visits on the Lord's day, unless when it is absolutely necessary. It is a matter not merely difficult, but wholly impracticable, in such cases, to guard effectually against improper subjects of conversation. Nor is this all, for let the conversation be what it will, I contend that the duties of the family and the closet are fully sufficient to employ the whole time; which must therefore be wasted or misapplied by the intercourse of strangers. . . .

2. You ought to live so as to make religion appear *respectable*. Religion is a venerable thing in itself, and it spreads an air of dignity over a person's whole deportment. I have seen a common tradesman, merely because he was a man of true piety and undeniable worth, treated by his children, apprentices and servants, with a much greater degree of deference and submission, than is commonly given to men of superior station, without that character. Many of the same meannesses are avoided, by a gentleman from a principle of honor, and by a good man from a principle of conscience. The first keeps out of the company of common people, because they are below him— the last is cautious of mixing with them, because of that levity and profanity that is to be expected from them. If, then, religion is really venerable when sincere, a respectable conduct ought to be maintained, as a proof of your own integrity, as well as to recommend it to your children. To this add, if you please, that as reverence is the peculiar duty of children to their parents, any thing that tends to lessen it is more deeply felt by them than by others who observe it. When I have seen a parent, in the presence of his child, meanly wrangling with his servant, telling extravagant stories, or otherwise exposing his vanity, credulity or folly, I have felt just the same proportion of sympathy and tenderness for the one, that I did of contempt or indignation at the other.

What has been said, will, in part, explain the errors which a parent ought to shun, and what circumstances he ought to attend to, that religion may appear respectable. All meannesses, whether of sentiment, conversation, dress, manners, or employment, are carefully to be avoided. You will apply this properly to yourself. I may, however, just mention, that there is a considerable difference in all these particulars, according to men's different stations. The same actions are mean in one station, that are not so in another. The thing itself, however, still remains; as there is an order and cleanliness at the table of tradesmen, that is different from the elegance of a gentleman's, or the sumptuousness of a prince's or nobleman's. But to make the matter still plainer by particular examples. I look upon talkativeness and vanity to be among the greatest enemies to dignity. It is needless to say how much vanity is contrary to true religion; and as to the other, which may seem rather an infirmity than a sin, we are expressly cautioned against it, and commanded to be swift to hear, and slow to speak. Sudden anger, too, and loud, clamorous scolding, are at once contrary to piety and dignity. Parents should, therefore, acquire as much as possible, a composure of spirit, and meekness of language; nor are there many circumstances that will more recommend religion to children, when they see that this self command is the effect of principle and a sense of duty.

There is a weakness I have observed in many parents, to show a partial fondness for some of their children, to the neglect, and in many cases approaching to a jealousy or hatred of others. Sometimes we see a mother discover an excessive partiality to a handsome daughter, in comparison of those that are more homely in their figure. This is a barbarity, which would be truly incredible, did not experience prove that it really exists. One would think they should rather be excited by natural affection, to give all possible encouragement to those who labour under a disadvantage and bestow every attainable accomplishment to balance the defects of outward form. At other times we see a partiality which cannot be accounted for at all, where the most ugly, peevish, froward child of the whole family, is the favourite of both parents. Reason ought to counteract these errors; but piety ought to extirpate them entirely. I do not stay to mention the bad effects that flow from them, my purpose being only to show the excellence of that character which is exempted from them. . . .

I shall have done with this particular, when I have observed, that those who are engaged in public, or what I may call political life, have an excellent opportunity of making religion appear truly respectable. What I mean is, by showing themselves firm and incorruptible, in supporting those measures that appear best calculated for promoting the interest of religion, and the good of mankind. In all these cases, I admire that man who has principles, whose principles are known, and whom every body despairs of being able to seduce, or bring over to the opposite interest. I do not commend furious and intemperate zeal. Steadiness is a much better, and quite a different thing. I would contend with any man who should speak most calmly, but I would also contend with him who should act most firmly. As for your placebo's, your prudent, courtly, compliant gentlemen, whose vote in assembly will tell you where they dined the day before, I hold them very cheap indeed, as you very well know. I do not enter further into this argument, but conclude at this time, by observing, that public measures are always embraced under pretence of principle; and therefore a uniform uncorrupted public character is one of the best evidences of real principle. The free thinking gentry tell us, upon this subject, that "every man has his price." It lies out of my way to attempt refuting them at present, but it is to be hoped there are many whose price is far above their reach.

LETTERS
ON THE
EDUCATION OF
CHILDREN,
1797

LIVE TO
MAKE RELIGION
RESPECTABLE

OBSERVATIONS ON THE AMERICAN REVOLUTION

Published According to a Resolution of Congress, Philadelphia, 1779

The efforts of Great-Britain to reduce these United States being now almost brought to a period; it is proper that the citizens of America should look over the ground they have trodden. This becomes necessary in order that the present generation may fully comprehend those two points which posterity indeed will perceive at a single glance, but which it is of importance to the consciences of men to be well informed of now. For certainly it becomes us to know that the contest which hath emancipated our country, originated with our enemies, and hath been by them urged on for the purposes of domination; while on our part every step hath been taken consistent with possible safety to deprecate their vengeance and avert the calamities of war.

For the better understanding this important subject, we must take a cursory view of the British colonies before the revolution, previous to which it may be necessary to make some few remarks on the circumstance of colonization. This tho' it introduced new incidents not to be met with in the antient histories of human affairs, neither did or could introduce any new reason or new maxims of justice.

The great principle therefore is and ever will remain in force, that MEN ARE BY NATURE FREE. As accountable to Him that made them, they must be so; and so long as we have any idea of divine justice, we must associate that of human freedom. Whether men can part with their liberty is among the questions which have exercised the ablest writers; but it is conceded on all hands, that the right to be free can never be alienated. Still less is it practicable for one generation to mortgage the privileges of another. The right of a state over its own members hath also been brought into question; and there are not wanting authorities to shew, that citizens who renounce allegiance and protection may fly from the territories of the state, and erect new independent governments in new countries. Be this as it may, the point is clear that when the consent of government is obtained, the individuals are again in a state of nature; alike free either to submit to a society existing or to establish one, as their interest or their inclination may prompt.

Here then is the situation of those who wearied with the contentions and oppressions of the old world, boldly threw themselves upon the protection of Providence to explore the new, and traversed the ocean to inhabit a wilderness amid nations of barbarous foes. These first adventurers, inspired by freedom, supported by industry, and protected by Heaven, became inured to toil, to hardship, and to war. In spite therefore of every obstacle they obtained a settlement; and then turned their attention to the security of those equal rights for which they had encountered so many perils and inconveniencies. For this purpose they framed independent constitutions; and these however different in form, were all inspired by the same spirit, and all founded on that eternal maxim of free governments, that no man can be bound by laws to which he does not consent. These little republics soon began to flourish with a vigor and beauty adequate to the radical energy of their first principle. Of consequence they became a desirable object to that genius of enterprize which had animated the monarchies of Europe. On the other hand, their weakness required some antient trunk to support them for a while in the storm of ambition. Our ancestors therefore, stimulated by their necessities, and seduced by ancient habits, and the remembrance of former friendships and connections, were easily prevailed on to subject themselves to the king of England, in consequence of his solemn promise to afford them protection in common with all his other subjects against foreign force and internal violence.

The British colonies then, under that name, were in fact so many independent states, whose only political connection with each other and with the several parts of the British empire, was by means of a common sovereign. It followed from their natural and political situation that this connection could not be permanent, and indeed the fabric must have crumbled to pieces at a much earlier period if it had not been cemented by the sameness of manners and language, a striking similarity of civil institutions, a continued intercourse for the purposes of commerce and other circumstances of the like kind. For the interests of Great-Britain and America were diametrically opposite, whether we consider them either in a political or commercial view. It was for instance the interest of Great-Britain, that needy dependents there should rebuild their shattered fortunes, here, and the wealthy citizens of this country expend their property at the metropolis. That we should be obliged to take part in all their wars whether for defence or conquest. That our trade should be confined to their ports; and finally, that they should have a power by laws passed in their parliament to bind us in all cases whatsoever; and not only did the difference of interest work to this end, but nature had so widely separated the two countries, that it was impossible they could long have been joined together upon terms even of despotism.

From what hath already been said it must appear, that as a free people we could not be bound by arbitrary edicts of the prince, that by still stronger reasons we could not be bound by the more arbitrary edicts of our fellow subjects; and of consequence, that altho' the prince and our fellow subjects should join against us whatever force they might acquire, they could acquire no right by the union. But it will appear also, that we had on every principle a right to become independent, particularly if the crown should violate those contracts which formed the basis of an union. For let us suppose that when our ancestors quitted Europe, they went on the general principle of disclaiming allegiance to and protection from the several states of which they were subjects, or that they came hither with the permission of those states, and even under a contract with the king of England. And when they arrived here, let us suppose either that they established independent governments which afterwards became subject by agreement, or that a conditional subjection was interwoven in their frame;—still the existence of the contract remains unimpeached; or even on a supposition that they had actually bargained for unconditional submission, still that bargain would have been from its very nature void as to them; or if not to them, at least to their offspring; and of consequence from the principle of all free societies, the contract will still result. And it being evident that the two countries not only had not, but really could not have (on free principles) any political connection but thro' the prince—so that right exercised in the revolution of England demonstrated since, and generally admitted, must necessarily draw with it the right to independence, which is above stated.

Previous to the last war a few acts were passed in England infringing on the liberties of America; and but a few for the two following reasons, 1st. Because America was at that time an object of very little national attention. 2dly. Because the possessions of the French enabled them to give such effectual aid in case of rupture, that it was imprudent to tempt us too far. These acts however were obeyed, because the restraints were of no great consequence; and because we were too sensible of our weakness to be fully sensible of our rights, or at least to vindicate them. But during the course of the war, the weight and magnitude of America became visible; and at the peace, this great object was (or at least seemed to be) inseparably annexed to the crown of Britain. On the other hand, we had felt our own force, and were relieved from a neighbour whose views at that time cramped our growth and repressed our efforts. The consequence of this change was instantly perceived. Great-Britain claimed revenue and dominion. We refused the one, and disputed the other. . . .

This Report of the Committee of Congress, specially appointed, for "the consideration of those who are desirous of comparing the conduct of the opposed Parties and the several consequences which have flowed from it" continues with an account of the events since 1765, and gives the various letters, petitions and reports issued by the Congress in an endeavor to obtain proper reconciliation with Great Britain. The Report was printed and sent to all Colonies. Only the introduction and conclusion are given here. Editor.

Considering our present situation and connections, we cannot but be sensible that the independence of America is fully secured, and nothing left to guard against but the ravages of a cruel foe, and the derangement of our finances. To effect the former, we must hold ourselves ready to repel force by force wherever assailed, and firmly retort every infringement of the law of nations with unfeeling perseverance. To remedy the latter, economy in the expenditure of money, and taxation, are the natural means, and, in addition to these, private economy, founded on a conviction that the monies wantonly expended in the present moment of depreciation, will soon be deeply regretted when it hath recovered its full

value. By such steps we shall frustrate the designs of our enemies, and hasten that moment when the United States of North-America, rising from distress to glory, shall dispense to their citizens the blessings of that peace, liberty and safety for which we have virtuously and vigorously contended.

The portals of the temple we have raised to freedom, shall then be thrown wide, as an asylum to mankind. America shall receive to her bosom and comfort and cheer the oppressed, the miserable and the poor of every nation and of every clime. The enterprise of extending commerce shall wave her friendly flag over the billows of the remotest regions. Industry shall collect and bear to her shores all the various productions of the earth, and all by which human life and human manners are polished and adorned. In becoming acquainted with the religions, the customs and the laws, the wisdom, virtues and follies and prejudices of different countries, we shall be taught to cherish the principles of general benevolence. We shall learn to consider all men as our brethren, being equally children of the Universal Parent—that God of the heavens and of the earth, whose infinite majesty, for providential favor during the late revolution, almighty power in our preservation from impending ruin, and gracious mercy in our redemption from the iron shackles of despotism, we cannot cease with gratitude and with deep humility to praise, to reverence and adore.

JOHN QUINCY ADAMS
ON THE AMERICAN REVOLUTION

*The Lives of
James Madison
and James
Monroe,*
by John Quincy
Adams, 1850

AMERICAN REVOLUTION PRECEDED
BY PERVADING MIND

There are three stages in the history of the North American Revolution—the first of which may be considered as commencing with the order of the British Council for enforcing the acts of trade in 1760, and as having reached its crisis at the meeting of the first Congress fourteen years after at Philadelphia. It was a struggle for the preservation and recovery of the rights and liberties of the British Colonies. It terminated in a civil war, the character and object of which was

changed by the Declaration of Independence.

The second stage is that of the War of Independence, usually so called—but it began fifteen months before the Declaration, and was itself the immediate cause and not the effect of that event. It closed by the preliminary Treaty of Peace concluded at Paris on the 30th of November, 1782.

The third is the formation of the Anglo-American People and Nation of North America. This event was completed by the meeting of the first Congress of the United States under their present Constitution, on the 4th of March, 1789. Thirty years is the usual computation for the duration of one generation of the human race. The space of time from 1760 to 1790 includes the generation with which the North American Revolution began, passed through all its stages, and ended.

The attention of the civilized European world, and perhaps an undue proportion of our own, has been drawn to the second of these three stages—to the contest with Great Britain for Independence. It was an arduous and apparently a very unequal conflict. But it was not without example in the annals of mankind. It has often been remarked that the distinction between rebellion and revolution consists only in the event, and is marked only by difference of success. But to a just estimate of human affairs there are other elementary materials of estimation. A revolution of government, to the leading minds by which it is undertaken, is an object to be accomplished. William Tell, Gustavus Vasa, William of Orange, had been the leaders of revolutions, the object of which had been the establishment or the recovery of popular liberties. But in neither of those cases had the part performed by those individuals been the result of deliberation or design.

The sphere of action in all those cases was incomparably more limited and confined—the geographical dimensions of the scene narrow and contracted—the political principles brought into collision of small compass—no foundation of the social compact to be laid—no people to be formed —the popular government of the American Revolution had been preceded by a foreseeing and directing mind. I mean not to say by one mind; but by a pervading mind, which in a preceding age had inspired the prophetic verses of Berkley, and which may be traced back to the first Puritan settlers of Plymouth and of Massachusetts Bay. "From the first institution of the Company of Massachusetts Bay," says Dr. Robertson, "its members seem to have been animated with a spirit of innovation in civil policy as well as in religion; and by the habit of rejecting established usages in the one, they were prepared for deviating from them in the other.

"They had applied for a royal charter, in order to give legal effect to their operations in England, as acts of a body politic; but the persons whom they sent out to America, as soon as they landed there, considered themselves as individuals, united together by voluntary association, possessing the natural right of men who form a society to adopt what mode of government and to enact what laws they deemed most conducive to general felicity."

And such had continued to be the prevailing spirit of the people of New England from the period of their settlement to that of the revolution. The people of Virginia, too notwithstanding their primitive loyalty, had been trained to revolutionary doctrines and to warlike habits; by their frequent collision with Indian wars; by the convulsions of Bacon's rebellion, and by the wars with France, of which their own borders were the theatre, down to the close of the war which immediately preceded that of the revolution. The contemplation and the defiance of danger, a qualification for all great enterprise and achievement upon earth, was from the very condition of their existence, a property almost universal to the British Colonists in North America; and hardihood of body, unfettered energy of intellect and intrepidity of spirit, fitted them for trials, which the feeble and enervated races of other ages and climes could never have gone through.

CONTEST OF PRINCIPLE

For the three several stages of this new Epocha in the earthly condition of man, a superintending Providence had ordained that there should arise from the native population of the soil, individuals with minds organized and with spirits trained to the exigencies of the times, and to the successive aspects of the social state. In the contest of principle which originated with the attempt of the British Government to burden their Colonies with taxation by act of Parliament, the natural rights of mankind found efficient defenders in James Otis, Patrick Henry, John Dickinson, Josiah Quincy, Benjamin Franklin, Arthur Lee and numerous other writers of inferior note. As the contest changed its character, Samuel and John Adams and Thomas Jefferson were among the first who raised the standard of Independence and prepared the people for the conflict through which they were to pass. For the contest of physical force by arms, Washington, Charles Lee, Putnam, Green, Gates, and a graduation of others of inferior ranks had been prepared by the preceding wars—by the conquest of Canada and by the previous capture of Louisburg. From the beginning of the war, every action was disputed with the perseverance and tenacity of veteran combatants, and the minute men of Lexington and Bunker's Hill were as little prepared for flight at the onset as the Macedonian phalanx of Alexander or the tenth legion of Julius Caesar.

But the great work of the North American revolution was not in the maintenance of the rights of the British Colonies by argument, nor in the conflict of physical force by war. The Declaration of Independence annulled the national character of the American people. That character had been common to them all as subjects of one and the same sovereign, and that sovereign was a king. The dissolution of that tie was pronounced by one act common to them all, and it left them as members of distinct communities in the relations towards each other, bound only by the obligations of the law of nature and of the Union, by which they had renounced their connexion with the mother country.

NEW ERA IN SCIENCE OF GOVERNMENT

But what was to be the condition of their national existence? This was the problem of difficult solution for them; and this was the opening of the new era in the science of government and in the history of mankind.

Their municipal governments were founded upon the common law of England, modified by their respective charters; by the Parliamentary law of England so far as it had been adopted by their usages, and by the enactments of their own Legislative assemblies. This was a complicated system of law, and has formed a subject of much internal perplexity to many of the States of the Union, and in several of them continues unadjusted to this day. By the common consent of all, however, this was reserved for the separate and exclusive regulation of each state within itself.

As a member of the community of nations, it was also agreed that they should constitute one body—"E Pluribus Unum" was the device which they assumed as the motto for their common standard. And there was one great change from their former condition, which they adopted with an unanimity so absolute, that no proposition of a different character was ever made before them. It was that all their governments should be republican.

They were determined not only to be separately republics, but to tolerate no other form of government as constituting a part of their community.

IMPORTANCE OF AMERICAN ARCHIVES

*American
Archives:
Fourth Series,*
by Peter Force,
Vol. I,
Washington,
1837

A complete collection of the materials for a history of this country would not only be a proud monument to the memory of our ancestors, whose deeds they commemorate and whose opinions they embody, but would serve as an invaluable guide to us and to our posterity, by exhibiting the vital spirit which has pervaded the past, the true foundations upon which our institutions rest, and the essential principles upon which their existence and perpetuity depend. It would furnish an ample vindication of those who had preceded us upon this stage, from the imputations which ignorance and prejudice have laboured to cast upon their motives and their acts; and our free institutions, by having their foundations laid open to the world, and the whole plan of their structure exhibited, will recommend themselves, more and more, to the philosophical inquirer, and to the affection and imitation of mankind.

If history be philosophy teaching by example, how infinitely instructive must be the history of such a country as this. The example which it presents is the purity of principle, the singleness of effort, the stern adherence to constitutional right, the manly subordination to law, the indig-

nant hostility to usurpation, which are manifested in every page of our past history; the philosophy it inculcates is—that the same purity of motive, the same respect for lawful authority, the same opposition to tyranny, the same vigilance in detecting the first insidious approaches of despotism, the same stern resolution in resisting its progress, which made us a Nation, are equally essential, as the means of preserving those liberties our fathers bequeathed to us, and those institutions which they framed.

Even to this day much ignorance and much misapprehension prevail as to the principles of the American Revolution, and the true character and tendency of our institutions. Nor is this ignorance altogether confined to foreigners, it exists, to a great extent, among ourselves. By many superficial persons, it is supposed that the American Revolution began with the battle of Lexington, and terminated with the evacuation by the British Troops of these United States. It seems to be the opinion of such, that the whole history of that Revolution is to be found in the narrative of the campaigns of that War. Widely different from this is the truth, as developed by history;

widely different was the opinion of those who mainly aided in severing the connexion with Great Britain. "What do we mean by the American Revolution?" asks one of the most prominent actors in those days: "Do we mean the American War? The Revolution was effected before the War commenced. The Revolution was in the mind and heart of the people. The radical change in the principles, opinions, sentiments, and affections of the people was the real American Revolution."

Even this language may, without due reflection, be understood in a sense not contemplated by its illustrious author. A full and careful examination of the history of the times will abundantly show, that so far as regards the nature and extent of their rights, and the foundations upon which they were claimed, there was, substantially, no revolution or change in the principles of the American People. The first emigrants to these shores brought with them, in their full vigour, in their original purity, and in their complete development, the principles of the American Revolution. They abandoned their native homes, they crossed the ocean, braved the horrours of an inhospitable clime, encountered the perils of the tempest, of war, and of famine, to escape the burthen of governmental oppression. They braved all, and encountered all, in the same cause for which their sons subsequently fought and bled. From the moment they placed their feet upon the soil of this Western Hemisphere, they asserted and maintained their independency of the Parliamentary power of taxation, and denied, to that extent, the authority of a Legislature in which they were not, themselves, represented. Although the Colonies were, originally, settled by individual enterprise, and by insulated rather than combined efforts, yet the Colonists, at a very early period, perceived the advantages of union in repelling or resisting a common foe. . . . Nor did the principles for which the Colonists contended originate on this side of the Atlantick. The doctrine that representation and taxation were essentially and indissolubly connected, was claimed as a portion of English Liberty, as interwoven in the very structure of the English Constitution, and as recognized among the most ancient and firmly established principles of the Common Law. It was no innovation, serving as a cloak for rebellion and revolution. It was drawn from the most ancient and pure fountains of Liberty, and sanctioned by the authority of the most eminent judicial characters in the British Parliament.

It is a source of honest pride, in reverting to the contemporaneous history of England, to contrast the characters of the individuals who, at times, it is true, with some modifications, yet concurring in the great and essential principles upon which our ancestors placed themselves, sustained the doctrines which were designated as American, with those who originated and defended those measures of the Ministry which drove the Colonists first to resistance, and, finally, to a dissolution of the political connexion by which they had so long been bound to the Mother Country. Such an examination will conduct to the conclusion, that had the questions upon which the controversy turned, assumed a judicial instead of a political character, and been carried for decision before the English Courts, the same eminent Judge, who first decided against the legality of general warrants, would have pronounced it to be the law of the land that these Colonists were not subject to the taxing power of Parliament.

The Work, of which the present volume is a specimen, will clearly unfold and develop the whole foundation of American principles, and will exhibit to the world the most conclusive evidence that they were, without exception, grounded in strict right, based upon constitutional Law, and upon the well settled doctrines of the English Government: that there was no taint or tinge of anarchy, of insubordination to all authority, no novelty, no innovation. The important, practical truth will be clearly deducible from these premises, that if such be the foundations they must ever constitute the support of our institutions. Their beautiful simplicity, their fair proportions, their majestick symmetry, and their stable grandeur, will equally recommend them to our love and veneration, and to the respect and imitation of others. . . .

It was urged on more than one occasion and by high authority in England, that the American contest originated in, and was sustained by, the selfish or ambitious designs of a few leading individuals. That personal interest gave it birth, and sustenance and support. This was only one of the palpable misrepresentations and gross delusions of the times. The present Work will show, beyond the possibility of future rational doubt, that the roots of American freedom had penetrated into every corner of our land and drew their active and living nourishment from every family fountain. Every reader of this compilation will perceive as one of the most distinctly marked facts which it establishes, that the American Revolution was the act of the whole American People, and that all our institutions are the work of the same creator. This we esteem as one of the most precisely taught lessons of our history, and if properly appreciated and applied, the most valuable which it inculcates. We shall learn that unless the People, as such, had worked out their own rescue from the oppression, which was rather seen in perspective than actually endured, all the personal influence and intellect of the great men of the day would have failed to accomplish this result. Happy will it be for our beloved country, if, drawing the obvious inference from this history of the past, every American citizen shall be impressed with the conviction that as he is individually interested, in the blessings which freedom confers, so there is imposed upon him the personal duty and sacred trust of vigilantly watching and manfully sustaining that liberty which has been transmitted to him. . . .

WASHINGTON, December, 1837

★   ★   ★   ★   ★

It is impossible for one to make a close study of the printed acts and works of these various governing bodies, whether in Committee, Legislature, or Congress, and not be impressed by the high principles and lofty spirit which animated the writers. They are not written in the heat of passion, but are evidently the work of calm, clear-headed, high thinking men, who moved deliberately, weighed the consequences of each act, and after determining a line of conduct pursued it unflinchingly to the end. In the rapid growth of the Colonies from their small beginnings to their flourishing state in wealth and population, which the British government eyed only as a source of revenue for them to squander through a weak king, they saw the distinguishing hand of Heaven, and it impressed them with the belief that no design formed against them could prosper. Their whole aim, at first, was to obtain their object by peaceful retaliatory measures, and to prevent bloodshed; to oppose British pretensions on British principles; and they were prepared to thresh the questions at issue out in the public forum of political discussion.

The same fatality which led the British ministry to pass the Stamp-Act, led them to the passage of the Act for blocking up the harbor of Boston —an Act which knit the Colonies together into a closer bond than any previous event in their history. . . . Heretofore they had been Colonies with separate interests, now they saw in the action of the British ministry only a revengeful measure which, unless resisted, might befall every seaport town in the Colonies, and they made the cause of Boston their own. This common feeling being well expressed in Virginia by an act, unprecedented in her history, setting apart the first of June, 1774, the date of the enactment of the Boston Port-Bill, as a day of public fasting, humiliation and prayer.

While the other Colonies were wondering what new form of ministerial arrogance was being prepared to force them into submission, New England, stunned by the blow which threatened to destroy its chief city and the centre of its learning, wealth and population during its development, reviewed their course during the one hundred and fifty years of colonization, and asked themselves the question, in what way had they changed that they should now be regarded by Great Britain as a conquered people upon whom tribute should be laid; and could not find in their Charters any provision which allowed them to be taxed without their consent, and none which treated of them as serfs upon a kingly estate. As the only episode in her history equal to the arbitrary action of the ministry. They reprinted Increase Mather's *Narrative of the miseries of New-England,* during the arbitrary government of Sir Edmund Andros, and recalled how this had been quickly ended by their petition to the good King George. Reprinted *Elijah's mantle,* in which the great end and interest New England should strive for was declared by four of its greatest ministers: Jonathan Mitchel, John Higginson, William Stroughton, and Increase Mather, in apostolic succession; and saw that, as a people, they had not wavered in their faith. Twice reprinted Thomas Prince's *The Providences of God in 1746,* which recalled the time when the best blood, and the treasure, of New England had been freely given to uphold the power of Great Britain in the French and Indian War; and which now did double duty in encouraging and animating the people to put their trust in God under the distresses of the rigorous execution of the Boston Port-Bill. They asked these questions of themselves and could find no answering reasons for the changed policy of the British government toward them. And, at this late day, one may still wonder in what way had the people of New England wandered from the straight, if narrow way, their leaders had marked out for them to follow from the first. When we compare the earliest printed document, The Oath of a free man, with another Oath taken by the freemen of New Hampshire in 1776, we find the same true ring in both: the same steadfastness in the truth as they saw the light; the same trust in God; the same personal honor and honesty with man.

THE AMERICAN REVOLUTION
A WAR OF PRINCIPLE

The WAR of the AMERICAN REVOLUTION was emphatically a war of Principle; a conflict of Opinion and for Power, between Despotism and Freedom; a struggle of the patrician few with the plebeian many for the mastery. Under the banner of the former, were marshalled the bold assumption of the divine right of kings—of sovereignty vested in one man, *Dei Gratia;* the feudal pretensions and asserted prerogatives of titled aristocracy, and the blind and almost unconquerable bigotry of the governed, voluntarily chained by their prejudices to the car of monarchy, and led captive with ease.

Under the banner of the latter, were marshalled the sublime jurisprudential theories of bygone reformers; freedom of thought, opinion and action; faith in the capacity of man for self-government; a just appreciation of the true dignity of humanity, and the fearless assertion of the glorious principles of equality of birth, and equality in the exercise of inalienable rights, conferred impartially by our Creator. These were the moral antagonisms, whose attrition produced the flame of the American Revolution.

The physical forces which these discordant principles drew up in battle array, were equally antipodal, viewed as subjects for patient endurance of hardships, and indomitable energy in the accomplishment of declared purposes.

The armies sent by monarchy to conquer the Colonies, were officered by men who had been reared in the halls of nobility, or the mansions of opulence; men, who made war a profession whereby to obtain the bauble GLORY,—military glory—that brilliant lie that for so many ages has led mankind astray—and not as an instrumentality for developing or maintaining principles that form the basis of human happiness. The troops which they led were mostly veteran warriors. They came from the continental battle fields; they came from the easy conquests of the Indian Peninsula; and the discipline of the camp was to them an easy restraint. Officers and men, all came fully panoplied for the conflict. Their "military chest" commanded the ready service of the exchequer of a wealthy and powerful people. Their superior numbers and discipline, coupled with a feeling of utter contempt for the *"rebels"* they came to subdue and humble, gave them such confidence of certain and speedy success, that the thoughts of hardships to be endured, difficulties to encounter, a disastrous overthrow, never interposed between their vision and the glittering prize of glory to be won; and hence no misgivings weakened their courage; no doubts made them falter. The dynasties of the Old World wished them success; they were confident and firm.

The colonial army was composed of men unused to the arts of war. Its ranks were filled by farmers and artizans; men, who had seldom heard the bray of the trumpet, or the roll of the drum, awakened into action by the behests of war. Their officers were men of comparatively small military renown. They were nurtured amid the quiet scenes of a peaceful people; and they were called to the command of battalions, not specially because of their excellence as military tacticians, but because of their possession of a combination of excellence as patriots; as men of prudence and sound judgment; men to be relied on. Officers and soldiers well knew the hardships to be endured, and the obstacles to be overcome. They well knew how limited were the resources of the country; how few the men, how scanty the supplies to be obtained. They well knew the power and the resources of the enemy from abroad, and they had carefully numbered the inimical phalanx of royalists and "faint-hearts" in their midst. They went into the conflict fully prepared to suffer much; yet, relying upon the justice of their cause, they felt as confident of final success as did their haughty foes. Such were the physical elements engaged in the War of the Revolution.

*Seventeen
Hundred
and Seventy-Six,*
by Benson
J. Lossing,
New York, 1847

253

A thirst for glory; a blind devotion to royalty, and a mercenary spirit on one side; and aspirations for freedom, devotion to, and faith in, Republican doctrines, and the faithful guardianship of *home* from the unhallowed foot-prints of tyranny on the other, were the impulses that brought the *heroes* of Britain, and the *patriots* of America, upon the field of personal combat. The struggle was long and desperate, and year after year, the balance of destiny was equipoised. Victory at length gave her palm to Republicanism, and Royalty discomfited, retired from the arena. The ways of a mysterious Providence were made plain; a mighty problem was solved; a brighter morning than earth ever saw, save when angels proclaimed, "Peace on earth, good will to men," dawned upon humanity, and the car of progress, so long inert, started upon its wondrous course.

The pæan of victory, chanted by the great chorus of American freemen, was echoed back from Europe by thousands upon thousands of hearts attuned in unison; yet in that response were heard the trembling notes of fear and doubt. Prayer was fervent; hope lifted high her oriflamme; yet fear interposed its cautious counsels, and doubt whispered its dangerous suggestions in the ear of hope. Enlightened statesmen and philanthropists turned to the chronicles of the past for a parallel or a prototype on which to build a confident hope of success; and despotism and its abettors also delved therein for examples of failure and destruction, incident to such a presumptuous begetting of a nation. Both read the same lesson; one with despondency, the other with exultation. The democracy of the Greeks, and the republicanism of the Romans, appeared, as in truth they were, misnomers; the shadows of unknown substances. Liberty, at first pure and chaste, became speedily arrayed in meretricious garb, and changed to libertinism; and the tyranny of republican majorities speedily assumed the most hateful features of despotism. In a word, the ever-tangible discordance and speedy overthrow of ancient republics, and the more recently recorded destiny of Venice and Genoa, taken as criterions for judgment, furnished philanthropy with scanty hope for the success of the disenthralled Colonies; while royalty, certain of their speedy downfall, like their predecessors, made the birth of this Republic a standing jest, and its early demise a scoffing prophecy.

But there was an element of vitality in the constitution of the new Republic, unknown to its predecessors, and all important for its perpetuity. It was the element of personal equality, in the possession and enjoyment of social and political rights. No privileged class was recognized, no demarkation lines of caste defaced the charter of our prerogatives. The fountain of knowledge was freely unsealed to all; the road to wealth and honor was freely opened to all. The prize of distinction was the incentive to learn and to educate; and general intelligence was (and is now) the main pillar of the State, growing with the growth, and strengthening with the strength, of the Republic. This was wanting in all past republics, and hence their speedy decadence and annihilation.

The war of the American Revolution taught monarchs and statesmen a great moral lesson, universal in its application, and valuable beyond estimate. It taught them to respect the inalienable rights of the governed, and to regard political freedom as the firmest pillar of the throne. It taught them to abandon the dangerous policy of coercing men into submission to the ministrations of palpable error, and of quieting the rebellion of intellect and sentiment by physical power. It taught them to regard as futile and impious, any attempt to stay the progress of truth, for its power is almighty; it is the throne of the Eternal. It opened their understanding to the fact, that the legitimate source of power is the people; and that *vox populi vox Dei,* cannot be denied when that voice utters the wise lessons of truth. It taught them to respect opinion; to eschew intolerance; to receive with caution, and view with scrutiny, the pharisaical teachings of creeds, whether religious or political; and to regard the race as a unity; children of one father; co-heirs in the inheritance of those prerogatives which God alone can bestow, and which God alone can withhold. These were hard and almost incomprehensible lessons for bigots to learn. Their minds, long clouded with the gross error of kingcraft and priest-craft, were almost impervious to the light of political and religious truth, which the war of the Revolution unveiled; and it was long after the judgment was convinced, and the intellect acknowledged the truth of the lesson, ere the heart, at whose portal stood human pride mailed in the panoply of hoary precedent, would yield its assent, and allow the spirit of human progress to enter and assume control. . . .

Our experiment in self-government has been fairly tried. It is no longer an experiment, but a grand demonstration. May we not in sober truth, and not in a boastful spirit, claim for our Republic the meed of superiority? Is it not to jurisprudence, what the Venus de' Medici is to art, a model of classic grace, disfigured, it is true, by impurities cast upon it by the careless and unwise, but in form and features, as perfect as human judgment can fashion it? Will it not be a study for all time; and will not the transatlantic republics yet to be chiselled from the rough stones of old systems, look to the beauteous child of the American Revolution, as a model *par excellence?* These are questions which the honest pride of every American citizen answers in the affirmative.

But another question forces itself upon the mind and heart of the enlightened patriot—Shall this rich inheritance be long perpetuated, and how? The answer is at hand. *Educate every child —educate every emigrant,* for "education is the cheap defence of nations" (Burke). Educate *all,* physically, intellectually and morally. Instruct, not only the *head,* but the *heart;* enlighten the mind, and, by cultivation, enlarge and multiply the affections.

Above all, let our youth be instructed in all that appertains to the vital principles of our Republic. To appreciate the blessings they enjoy, and to create in them those patriotic emotions, which shall constitute them ardent defenders in the hour of trial, it is necessary for them to

be taught the price of their goodly heritage; the fearful cost of blood and treasure, suffering and woe, at which it was obtained. They should be led by the hand of history into every patriotic council; upon every battle field; through every scene of trial and hardship, of hope and despondency, of triumph and defeat, where our fathers acted and endured, so that when we

"Go ring the bells and fire the guns,
And fling the starry banner out—
Cry FREEDOM! till our little ones
Send back their tiny shout;"

Whittier.

our children may not, in their ignorance, ask, *"What mean ye by this service?"* (*Exodus 12:26*).

The duty of the historian of the Revolution, as one of the national teachers, is a difficult one, and if he truly feels the weight of the responsibility resting upon him, he will instinctively shrink from the task, or approach it with trembling misgivings, relying solely upon Omnipotent Wisdom, in the exercise of his judgment and the guidance of his pen.

ADVICE TO THE YOUNG

Almost all the civil liberty now enjoyed in the world owes its origin to the principles of the Christian religion. Men began to understand their natural rights, as soon as the reformation from popery began to dawn in the sixteenth century; and civil liberty has been gradually advancing and improving as genuine Christianity has prevailed. By the principles of the Christian religion we are not to understand the decisions of ecclesiastical councils, for these are the opinions of mere men; nor are we to suppose that religion to be any particular church established by law, with numerous dignitaries, living in stately palaces, arrayed in gorgeous attire, and rioting in luxury and wealth, squeezed from the scanty earnings of the laboring poor; nor is it a religion which consists in a round of forms, and in pompous rites and ceremonies. No; the religion which has introduced civil liberty, is the religion of Christ and his apostles, which enjoins humility, piety, and benevolence; which acknowledges in

every person a brother, or a sister, and a citizen with equal rights. This is genuine Christianity, and to this we owe our free constitutions of government. . . .

For a knowledge of the human heart, and the characters of men, it is customary to resort to the writings of Shakspeare, and of other dramatic authors, and to biography, novels, tales, and fictitious narratives. But whatever amusement may be derived from such writings, they are not the best authorities for a knowledge of mankind. The most perfect maxims and examples for regulating your social conduct and domestic economy, as well as the best rules of morality and religion, are to be found in the Bible. The history of the Jews presents the true character of man in all its forms. All the traits of human character, good and bad; all the passions of the human heart; all the principles which guide and misguide men in society, are depicted in that short history, with an artless simplicity that has no parallel in modern writings.

History of the United States, by Noah Webster, New Haven, 1833

255

As to maxims of wisdom or prudence, the Proverbs of Solomon furnish a complete system, and sufficient, if carefully observed, to make any man wise, prosperous, and happy. The observation, that "a soft answer turneth away wrath," if strictly observed by men, would prevent half the broils and contentions that inflict wretchedness on society and families.

Let your first care through life, be directed to support and extend the influence of the Christian religion, and the observance of the sabbath. This is the only system of religion which has ever been offered to the consideration and acceptance of men, which has even probable evidence of a divine original; it is the only religion that honors the character and moral government of the Supreme Being; it is the only religion which gives even a probable account of the origin of the world, and of the dispensations of God towards mankind; it is the only religion which teaches the character and laws of God, with our relations and our duties to him; it is the only religion which assures us of an immortal existence; which offers the means of everlasting salvation, and consoles mankind under the inevitable calamities of the present life.

But were we assured that there is to be no future life, and that men are to perish at death like the beasts of the field; the moral principles and precepts contained in the scriptures ought to form the basis of all our civil constitutions and laws. These principles and precepts have truth, immutable truth, for their foundation; and they are adapted to the wants of men in every condition of life. They are the best principles and precepts, because they are exactly adapted to secure the practice of universal justice and kindness among men; and of course to prevent crimes, war, and disorders in society. No human laws dictated by different principles from those in the gospel, can ever secure these objects. All the miseries and evils which men suffer from vice, crime, ambition, injustice, oppression, slavery, and war, proceed from their despising or neglecting the precepts contained in the Bible.

As the means of temporal happiness then the Christian religion ought to be received, and maintained with firm and cordial support. It is the real source of all genuine republican principles. It teaches the equality of men as to rights and duties; and while it forbids all oppression, it commands due subordination to law and rulers. It requires the young to yield obedience to their parents, and enjoins upon men the duty of selecting their rulers from their fellow citizens of mature age, sound wisdom, and real religion—"men who fear God and hate covetousness." The ecclesiastical establishments of Europe, which serve to support tyrannical governments, are not the Christian religion, but abuses and corruptions of it. The religion of Christ and his apostles, in its primitive simplicity and purity, unencumbered with the trappings of power and the pomp of ceremonies, is the surest basis of a republican government.

Never cease then to give to religion, to its institutions, and to its ministers, your strenuous support. The clergy in this country are not possessed of rank and wealth; they depend for their influence on their talents and learning, on their private virtues and public services. They are the firm supporters of law and good order, the friends of peace, the expounders and teachers of Christian doctrines, the instructors of youth, the promoters of benevolence, of charity, and of all useful improvements. During the war of the revolution, the clergy were generally friendly to the cause of the country. The present generation can hardly have a tolerable idea of the influence of the New-England clergy, in sustaining the patriotic exertions of the people, under the appalling discouragements of the war. The writer remembers their good offices with gratitude. Those men therefore who attempt to impair the influence of that respectable order, in this country, attempt to undermine the best supports of religion; and those who destroy the influence and authority of the christian religion, sap the foundations of public order, of liberty, and of republican government.

For instruction then in social, religious, and civil duties, resort to the scriptures for the best precepts and most excellent examples for imitation. The example of unhesitating faith and obedience in Abraham, when he promptly prepared to offer his son Isaac, as a burnt offering, at the command of God, is a perfect model of that trust in God which becomes dependent beings. The history of Joseph furnishes one of the most charming examples of fraternal affection, and of filial duty and respect for a venerable father, ever exhibited in human life.

Christ and his apostles presented, in their lives, the most perfect example of disinterested benevolence, unaffected kindness, humility, patience in adversity, forgiveness of injuries, love to God, and to all mankind.

If men would universally cultivate these religious affections and virtuous dispositions, with as much diligence as they cultivate human science and refinement of manners, the world would soon become a terrestrial paradise.

CHRISTIAN LIBERTY "READY TO PASS TO THE AMERICAN STRAND"

And why should man organize resistance to the grand design of Providence?

George Bancroft

CHRONOLOGICAL ANNALS

OF ENGLISH HISTORY

CHRISTIAN
LIBERTY
"READY TO
PASS TO THE
AMERICAN
STRAND"

Battle of Newbury, Oct.
1645. Self-renouncing Ordinance, April.
New Model raised.
Battle of Naseby, June 14.
Battle of Philiphaugh, Sept.
1646. Charles surrenders to the Scots, May.
1647. Scots surrender Charles to the Houses, Feb.
Army elects Adjutators, April.
The King seized at Holmby House, June.
"Humble Representation" of the Army, June.
Expulsion of the Eleven Members.
Army occupies London, Aug.
Flight of the King, Nov.
Secret Treaty of Charles with the Scots, Dec.
1648. Outbreak of the Royalist Revolt, Feb.
Revolt of the Fleet, and of Kent, May.
Fairfax and Cromwell in Essex and Wales, June-July.
Battle of Preston, Aug. 18.
Surrender of Colchester, Aug. 27.
Pride's Purge, Dec.
Royal Society begins at Oxford.
1649. Execution of Charles I., Jan. 30.
Scotland proclaims Charles II.
England proclaims itself a Commonwealth.
Cromwell storms Drogheda, Aug.
1650. Cromwell enters Scotland, May.
Battle of Dunbar, Sept. 3.
1651. Battle of Worcester, Sept. 3.
Union with Scotland and Ireland.
Hobbes's *"Leviathan."*
1652. Outbreak of Dutch War, May.
Victory of Van Tromp, Nov.
1653. Victory of Blake, Feb.
Cromwell drives out the Parliament, April 19.
Constituent Convention (Barebones Parliament), July.
Convention dissolves, Dec.
1654. The Instrument of Government.
Oliver Cromwell, Lord Protector, died 1658.
Peace concluded with Holland.
First Protectorate Parliament, Sept.
1655. Dissolution of the Parliament, Jan.
The Major-Generals.
Settlement of Scotland and Ireland.
Settlement of the Church.
1656. Blake in the Mediterranean.
War with Spain and Conquest of Jamaica.
Second Protectorate Parliament, Sept.

1657. Blake's victory at Santa Cruz.
Cromwell refuses title of King.
Act of Government.
1658. Parliament dissolved, Feb.
Battle of the Dunes.
Capture of Dunkirk.
Death of Cromwell, Sept. 3.
Richard Cromwell, Lord Protector, died 1712.
1659. Third Protectorate Parliament.
Parliament dissolved.
Long Parliament recalled.
Long Parliament again driven out.
1660. Monk enters London.
The "Convention" Parliament.
Charles the Second, lands at Dover, May, died 1685.
Union of Scotland and Ireland undone.
1661. Cavalier Parliament begins.
Act of Uniformity re-enacted.
1662. Puritan clergy driven out.
Royal Society at London.
1663. Dispensing Bill fails.
1664. Conventicle Act.
Dutch War begins.
1665. Five-Mile Act.
Plague and Fire of London.
Newton's Theory of Fluxions.
1667. The Dutch in the Medway.
Dismissal of Clarendon.
Peace of Breda.
Lewis attacks Flanders.
Milton's *"Paradise Lost."*
1668. The Triple Alliance.
Peace of Aix-la-Chapelle.
1669. Ashley shrinks back from toleration to Catholics.
1670. Treaty of Dover.
Bunyan's *"Pilgrim's Progress"* written.
1671. Milton's *"Paradise Regained"* and *"Samson Agonistes."*
Newton's Theory of Light.
Closing of the Exchequer.
1672. Declaration of Indulgence.
War begins with Holland.
Ashley made Chancellor.
Declaration of Indulgence withdrawn.
1673. The Test Act.
Shaftesbury dismissed.
Shaftesbury takes the lead of the Country Party.
1674. Bill of Protestant Securities fails.
Charles makes peace with Holland.
Danby Lord Treasurer.

1675. Treaty of mutual aid between Charles and Lewis.

1676. Shaftesbury sent to the Tower.

1677. Bill for Security of the Church fails.
Address of the Commons for War with France.
Prince of Orange marries Mary.

1678. Peace of Nimeguen.
Oates invents the Popish Plot.
Fall of Danby.
New Ministry with Shaftesbury at its head.
Temple's plan for a new Council.

1679. New Parliament meets.
Habeas Corpus Act passed.
Exclusion Bill introduced.
Parliament dissolved.
Shaftesbury dismissed.

1680. Committee for agitation formed.
Monmouth pretends to the throne.
Petitioners and Abhorrers.
Exclusion Bill thrown out by the Lords.
Trial of Lord Stafford.

1681. Parliament at Oxford.
Limitation Bill rejected.
Monmouth and Shaftesbury arrested.

1682. Conspiracy and flight of Shaftesbury.
Rye-house Plot.

1683. Death of Shaftesbury.
Lord Russell and Algernon Sidney executed.

1684. Town charters quashed.
Army increased.

1685. *James the Second,* died 1701.
Insurrection of Argyle and Monmouth.
Battle of Sedgemoor, July 6.
The Bloody Circuit.
Army raised to 20,000 men.
Revocation of Edict of Nantes.

1686. Parliament refuses to repeal Test Act.
Test Act dispensed with by Royal authority.
Ecclesiastical Commission set up.

1687. Newton's *"Principia."*
Expulsion of the Fellows of Magdalen.
Dismissal of Lords Rochester and Clarendon.
Declaration of Indulgence.
The boroughs regulated.
William of Orange protests against the Declaration.
Tyrconnell made Lord Deputy in Ireland.

1688. Clergy refuse to read Declaration of Indulgence.
Threat of the Seven Bishops.

Irish troops brought over to England.
Lewis attacks Germany.
William of Orange lands at Torbay.
Flight of James.

1689. Convention Parliament.
Declaration of Rights.
William and Mary made King and Queen.
William forms the Grand Alliance against Lewis.
Battle of Killicrankie, July 27.
Siege of Londonderry.
Mutiny Bill.
Toleration Bill.
Bill of Rights.
Secession of the Nonjurors.

1690. Abjuration Bill and Act of Grace.
Battle of Beachy Head, June 29.
Battle of the Boyne, July 6.
William repulsed from Limerick.

1691. Battle of Aughrim, July.
Capitulation and Treaty of Limerick.

1692. Massacre of Glencoe.
Battle of La Hogue, May 19.

1693. Sunderland's plan of a Ministry.

1694. Bank of England set up.
Death of *Mary.*

1696. Currency restored.

1697. Peace of Ryswick.

1698. First Partition Treaty.

EIGHTEENTH CENTURY

1700. Second Partition Treaty.

1701. Duke of Anjou becomes King of Spain.
Death of *James the Second.*
Act of Settlement passed.

1702. *Anne,* died 1714.

1704. Battle of Blenheim, August 13.
Harley and St. John take office.

1705. Victories of Peterborough in Spain.

1706. Battle of Ramillies, May 23.

1707. Act of Union with Scotland.

1708. Battle of Oudenarde.
Dismissal of Harley and St. John.

1709. Battle of Malplaquet.

1710. Trial of Sacheverel.
Tory Ministry of Harley and St. John.

1712. Dismissal of Marlborough.

1713. Treaty of Utrecht.

1714. *George the First,* died 1727.
Ministry of Townshend and Walpole.

1715. Jacobite Revolt under Lord Mar.

1716. Ministry of Lord Stanhope.
The Septennial Bill.

CHRISTIAN
LIBERTY
"READY TO
PASS TO THE
AMERICAN
STRAND"

1717. The Triple Alliance.
1718. The Quadruple Alliance.
1720. Failure of the Peerage Bill.
The South Sea Company.
1721. Ministry of Sir Robert Walpole.
1722. Exile of Bishop Atterbury.
1727. War with Austria and Spain.
George the Second, died 1760.
1729. Treaty of Seville.
1730. Free exportation of American rice
allowed.
1731. Treaty of Vienna.
1733. Walpole's Excise Bill.
War of the Polish Succession.
Family Compact between France and
Spain.
1737. Death of Queen Caroline.
1738. The Methodists appear in London.
1739. War declared with Spain.
1740. War of the Austrian Succession.
1742. Resignation of Walpole.
1743. Ministry of Henry Pelham.
Battle of Dettingen, June 27.
1745. Battle of Fontenoy, May 31.
Charles Edward lands in Scotland.
Battle of Prestonpans, Sept. 21.
Charles Edward reaches Derby, Dec. 4.
1746. Battle of Falkirk, Jan. 23.
Battle of Culloden, April 16.
1748. Peace of Aix-la-Chapelle.
1751. Clive's surprise of Arcot.
1754. Death of Henry Pelham.
Ministry of Duke of Newcastle.
1755. The Seven-Years' War.
Defeat of General Braddock.
1756. Loss of Port Mahon.
Retreat of Admiral Byng.
1757. Convention of Closter-Seven.
Ministry of William Pitt.
Battle of Plassey, June 23.
1758. Capture of Louisburg and Cape Breton.
Capture of Fort Duquesne.
1759. Battle of Minden, Aug. 1.
Battle of Quiberon Bay, Nov. 20.

Capture of Fort Niagara and
Ticonderoga.
Wolfe's victory on Heights of Abraham.
1760. *George the Third,* died 1820.
Battle of Wandewash.
1761. Ministry of Lord Bute.
Brindley's Canal over the Irwell.
1762. Peace of Paris.
1763. Wedgwood establishes Potteries.
1764. Hargreaves invents Spinning-Jenny.
1765. Stamp Act passed.
Ministry of Lord Rockingham.
Meeting and Protest of American
Congress.
Watt invents Steam-engine.
1766. Repeal of the Stamp Act.
Ministry of Lord Chatham.
1768. Ministry of the Duke of Grafton.
Wilkes expelled from House of
Commons.
Arkwright invents Spinning-machine.
1769. Wilkes three times elected for Middlesex.
House of Comomns seats Col. Luttrell.
Occupation of Boston by British troops.
Letters of *Junius.*
1770. Ministry of Lord North.
Chatham proposes Parliamentary Reform.
1771. Last attempt to prevent Parliamentary
reporting.
Beginning of the great English Journals.
1773. Hastings appointed Governor-General.
Boston tea-ships.
1774. Military occupation of Boston. Port
closed.
Massachusetts Charter altered.
Congress assembles at Philadelphia.
1775. Rejection of Chatham's plan of
conciliation.
Skirmish at Lexington.
Americans, under Washington, besiege
Boston.
Battle of Bunker's Hill.
Southern Colonies expel their Governors.

God Rules
in the Affairs of Men

The revolution, which, in 1660, came to its end, had been in its origin a democratic revolution, and had apparently succeeded in none of its ultimate purposes. The power of the feudal aristocracy had been gradually broken by the increased authority of the monarch; and the people, beginning to claim the lead in the progress of humanity, prepared to contend for equality against privilege, as well as for freedom against prerogative. The contest failed, because too much was attempted. Immediate emancipation from the past was impossible; hereditary inequalities were themselves endeared to the nation, through the beneficent institutions with which they were connected; the mass of the people was still buried in listless ignorance; even for the strongest minds, public experience had not yet generated the principles by which a reconstruction of the government on a popular basis could have been safely undertaken; and thus the democratic revolution in England was a failure, alike from the events and passions of the fierce struggle which rendered moderation impossible, and from the unripeness of the age, which had not as yet acquired the political knowledge that time alone could generate or gather up.

Charles I. (1629-1640), inheriting his father's belief in the unlimited rights of the king of England, conspired against the national constitution, which he, as the most favored among the natives of England, was the most solemnly bound to protect; and he resolved to govern without the aid of a parliament. To convene one was therefore, in itself, an acknowledgment of defeat. The house of commons, which assembled in April, 1640, was filled with men not less loyal to the monarch than faithful to the people; yet the king, offended by its firmness, disregarded the wishes of his more prudent friends, and capriciously dissolved a parliament more favorable to the crown than any which he could again hope for.

The exercise of absolute power became more and more difficult. There were those who refused to take the oath never to consent to alterations in the church of England, "Send for the chief leaders," wrote Strafford, "and lay them by the heels; no other satisfaction is to be thought of." But Strafford was not without his enemies among the royalists. During the suspension of parliament, two parties in the cabinet had disputed with each other for the emoluments of despotism. The ministers and the council of state were envied by the queen and the courtiers; and Strafford and Laud had as bitter rivals in the palace as they had enemies in the nation. There was no unity among the upholders of absolutism.

The expedient of a council of peers, convened in 1640 at York, could not satisfy a people that

History of the United States of America, by George Bancroft, Vol. I, New York, 1886

CHRISTIAN
LIBERTY
"READY TO
PASS TO THE
AMERICAN
STRAND"

venerated representative government as the most valuable bequest of its ancestors; and a few weeks showed clearly that concession was necessary. The advisers of Charles hesitated from rivalries and the want of plan; while the popular leaders were full of energy and united in the distinct purpose of limiting the royal authority. The summons of a new parliament was, on the part of the monarch, a surrender at discretion. But, by the English constitution, the royal prerogative was in some cases the bulwark of popular liberty; the subversion of the royal authority made a way for the despotism of parliament.

THE LONG PARLIAMENT

The Long Parliament, which met on the third of November, 1640, was not originally homogeneous. The usurpations of the monarch threatened the privileges of the nobility not less than the liberties of the people. The movement in the public mind, though it derived its vigor as well as its origin from the influence of the Puritans, aimed only at raising an impassable barrier against the encroachments of royalty. This object met with favor from a majority of the peerage, and from royalists among the commons; and the past arbitrary measures of the court found opponents in Hyde, the faithful counsellor of the Stuarts; in the more scrupulous Falkland, who inclined to the popular side, till he began to dread innovations from its leaders more than from the king; and even in Capel, afterward one of the bravest of the cavaliers, and a martyr on the scaffold for his obstinate fidelity. When the highest authority in England began to belong to the majority in parliament, no republican party as yet existed; the first division ensued between the ultra royalists and the undivided friends of constitutional monarchy; and, though the house was in a great measure filled with members of the aristocracy, the moderate royalists united with the friends of the people. On the choice of speaker, an immense majority appeared in favor of the constitution.

PROGRESS OF REFORMS,
WRIT OF HABEAS CORPUS INTRODUCED

The Earl of Strafford anticipated danger, and he desired to remain in Ireland. "As I am king of England," said Charles, "the parliament shall not touch one hair of your head;" and the reiterated urgency of the king compelled his attendance. His arraignment, within eight days of the commencement of the session, marks the spirit of the commons; his attainder was the sign of their ascendency. "On the honor of a king," wrote Charles, in April, 1641, to the prisoner, "you shall not be harmed in life, fortune, or honor;" and, the fourth day after the passage of the bill of attainder, the king sent his adhesion to the commons, adding: "If Strafford must die, it were charity to reprieve him till Saturday." Men dreaded the service of a sovereign whose love was so worthless, and whose prerogative was so weak; and the parliament proceeded without control to its work of reform. Its earliest acts were worthy of all praise. The liberties of the people were recovered and strengthened by appropriate safeguards; the arbitrary courts of high commission and the court of wards were broken up; the star-chamber, doubly hated by the aristocracy, as "ever a great eclipse to the whole nobility," was with one voice abolished; the administration of justice was rescued from the paramount influence of the crown; and taxation, except by consent, was forbidden. The principle of the writ of habeas corpus was introduced; and the kingdom of England was lifted out of the bondage of feudalism by a series of reforms, which were afterward renewed, and which, when successfully embodied among the statutes, the commentator on English law esteemed above Magna Charta itself. These measures were adopted almost without opposition, and received the nearly unanimous assent of the nation. They were truly English measures, directed in part against abuses introduced at the Norman conquest, in part against the encroachments of the sovereign. They wiped away the traces that England had been governed as a conquered country; they were in harmony with the intelligence and the pride, the prejudices and the wants, of England. Public opinion was the ally of the parliament.

LONG PARLIAMENT BECOMES A TYRANT

But an act declaring that the parliament should neither be prorogued nor dissolved, unless with its own consent, had been urged with pertinacity, till it received the royal concurrence. Parliament, in its turn, set aside the constitution, by establishing its own paramount authority, and making itself virtually irresponsible to its constituents. The usurpation forboded the overthrow of the throne and the subjection of the people.

As the demands of the commons advanced, stormy debates ensued. In November, 1641, the remonstrance on the state of the kingdom, an uncompromising manifesto against the arbitrary measures of Charles, proposed no specific reform, but was rather a general and passionate appeal to popular opinion. The English mind was as restless as the waves of the ocean by which the isle is environed; the remonstrance was designed to increase that restlessness; in a house of more than five hundred members, it was adopted by the meagre majority of eleven. "Had it not been carried," said Cromwell to Falkland, "I should have sold all I possess, and left the kingdom; many honest men were of the same resolution." From the contest for "English liberties," men advanced to the discussion of natural rights; with the expansion of their views, their purposes ceased to be definite; reform was changing into a revolution; and it was observable that religious faith was on the side of innovation, while incredulity abounded among the supporters of the established church and the divine right.

The king had yielded where he should have been firm; moderation and sincerity would have restored his influence. But when, in January, 1642, attended by armed men, he repaired in person to the house of commons, with the intent of seizing six of the leaders of the patriot party, the attempt, so bloody in its purpose and so illegal in its course, could only justify for the time every diminution of his prerogative, and drive the leaders of the popular party to a gloomy inflexibility. A change of dynasty was not then proposed; and England languished of a disease for which no cure had been discovered. It was evident that force must decide the struggle. The parliament demanded the control of the national militia with the possession of the fortified towns; to Charles no alternative remained but resistance or the surrender of all power; and, unfurling the royal standard, he began a civil war.

CIVIL WAR—PRESBYTERIANS & THE INDEPENDENTS

The contest was between a permanent parliament and an arbitrary king. The people had no mode of intervention except by serving in the armies; they could not act as mediators or as masters. The parliament was become a body, of which the duration depended on its own will, unchecked by a supreme executive or by an independent co-ordinate branch of legislation; and, therefore, of necessity, a multitudinous despot, unbalanced and irresponsible; levying taxes, enlisting soldiers, commanding the navy and the army, enacting laws, and changing at its will the forms of the English constitution. The issue was certain. Every representative assembly is swayed by the public interests, the pretensions of its own body, and the personal interests of its respective members; and never was the successive predominance of each of these sets of motives more clear than in the Long Parliament. Its first acts were mainly for its constituents, whose rights it vindicated and whose liberties it increased; its corporate ambition next asserted itself against the throne and the peerage, both of which it was hurried forward to subvert; individual selfishness at last prevailed.

In 1644, after one hundred and eighteen royalist members, obeying the summons of the king, repaired to Oxford, the friends of royalty and of the church of England were unrepresented in the national legislature. The commons at once divided into two imposing parties—the Presbyterians and the Independents; the friends of a revolution which should yet preserve a nobility, a limited monarchy, and a national church, and the friends of a revolution on the principle of equality.

The Presbyterians represented a powerful branch of the aristocracy of England; they had a majority in the commons; the exclusive possession of what remained of the house of lords; the command of the army; and numerous and active adherents among the clergy. The English people favored them; Scotland was devoted to them; and they were at all times prepared to make peace with the king, if he would but accept Presbyterianism as the religion of the state.

The Independents could hope for superior influence only by rising above the commons, the peers, the commanders of the army, all Scotland, and the mass of the English people. They had no omen of success but the tendency of revolutions to go forward, the enthusiasm of converts for the newly accepted ideas, the inclination of the human mind to push principles to their remoter consequences. They gradually became the advocates of religious liberty and the power of the people; and the glorious vision of emancipating the commons of England from feudal oppression, from intellectual servitude, and from royalty itself, kindled a zeal which would not be rebuked by the inconsistency of their schemes with the opinions, habits, and institutions of the nation.

The Presbyterian nobility were unwilling that innovation should go so far as to impair their rank or diminish their grandeur; the Independents, as new men, who had their fortunes to make, were ready not only to subvert the throne, but to con-

CHRISTIAN
LIBERTY
"READY TO
PASS TO THE
AMERICAN
STRAND"

tend for equality against privilege. "The Presbyterian earl of Manchester," said Cromwell, "shall be content with being no more than plain Montague." The men who broke away from the forms of society, and venerated nothing but truth; others who, in the folly of their pride, claimed for their opinions the sanctity and the rights of truth; they who longed for a more equal diffusion of social benefits; the friends of entire liberty of conscience; the friends of a reform in the law and a diminution of the profits of the lawyers; the men, like Milton and Sidney, whose imagination delighted in pictures of Roman liberty; the less educated, who indulged in visions of a restoration of that happy Anglo-Saxon system which had been invented in the woods in days of Anglo-Saxon simplicity; the republicans, the levellers, the fanatics—all ranged themselves on the side of the new ideas.

VANE & CROMWELL—TRIUMPH OF THE INDEPENDENTS

The true representative of the better principles of the Independents was Henry Vane; their acknowledged leader was Oliver Cromwell. Was he sincere? It is difficult to disbelieve that he was imbued with the principles of Puritan reforms, and may have always thought himself faithful to the interest of England; as in his foreign policy he most certainly was. All great men incline to fatalism, for their success is a mystery to themselves; and it was not entirely with hypocrisy that Cromwell professed himself the servant of Providence, borne along by irresistible necessity.

Had peace never been broken, the Independents would have remained a powerless minority; the civil war gave them a rallying point in the army. In the season of great public excitement, fanatics crowded to the camp; an ardor for popular liberty mingled with the fervors of religious excitement. Cromwell had early perceived that the pride and valor of the cavaliers could never be overthrown by ordinary hirelings; he therefore sought to fill the ranks of his army with enthusiasts. His officers were alike ready to preach and pray, and to take the lead in the field of battle. With much hypocrisy, his camp was the scene of much real piety; and long afterward, when his army was disbanded, its members, who for the most part were farmers and yeomen and their sons, resumed their places in the industrious classes, while the soldiers of the royalists were often found among vagabonds and beggars. It was the troops of Cromwell that first, in the

open field, broke the ranks of the royal squadrons; and the decisive victory of Marston Moor was won by their iron energy and valor.

The final overthrow of the prospects of Charles in the field, in 1647, marks the crisis of the struggle for the ascendent between the Presbyterians and Independents. The former had their organ in the parliament, the latter in the army, in which the Presbyterian commander had been surprised into a resignation by the self-denying ordinance and the intrigues of Cromwell. As the duration of the parliament depended on its own will, the army refused to be disbanded, claiming to represent the interests of the people, and actually constituting the only balance to the otherwise unlimited power of the parliament. The army could call the parliament a usurper, and the parliament could arraign the army as a branch of the public service, whose duty was obedience, and not counsel. On the other hand, if the parliament pleaded its office as the grand council of the nation, the army could urge its merits as the active and successful antagonist to royal despotism.

HOUSE OF COMMONS INVADED

The Presbyterians broke forth into menaces against the army. "These men," whispered Cromwell to Ludlow, "will never leave till the army pull them out by the ears." The Presbyterian majority appeared to possess paramount power, and did not possess it. Could they gain the person of the king, and succeed in pacific negotiations, their influence would be renewed by the natural love of order in the minds of the English people. A conflict with the Independents was unavoidable; for the Independents could in no event negotiate with the king. In every negotiation, a free parliament must have been a condition; and a free parliament would have been their doom. Self-preservation, uniting with ambition and wild enthusiasm, urged them to uncompromising hostility with Charles I. He or they must perish. "If my head or the king's must fall," argued Cromwell, "can I hesitate which to choose?" By an act of violence the Independents seized on the king, and held him in their special custody. "Now," said the exulting Cromwell, "now that I have the king in my hands, I have the parliament in my pocket."

At length the Presbyterian majority, sustained by the eloquence of Prynne, attempted to dispense with the army, and, by a decided vote, resolved to make peace with the king. To save its party from an entire defeat, in December, 1648, the army interposed, and "purged" the house of commons. "Hear us," said the excluded members to Colonel Pride, who expelled them. "I cannot spare the time," replied the soldier. "By what right are we arrested?" demanded they of the extravagant Hugh Peter. "By the right of the sword," answered the late envoy from Massachusetts. "You are called," said he, as he preached to the decimated parliament, "to lead the people out of Egyptian bondage; this army must root up monarchy, not only here, but in France and other kingdoms round about." Cromwell, the night after "the interruption," reiterated: "I knew nothing of these late proceedings; but, since the work has been done, I am glad of it and will endeavor to maintain it."

CHARLES I. EXECUTED

When the winnowing of the house of commons was finished, there remained few beside republicans; and it was resolved to bring the unhappy monarch to trial before a special commission. "Providence and necessity," said Cromwell, affecting indecision, "have cast the house upon this deliberation. I shall pray God to bless our counsels." The young and sincere Algernon Sidney opposed, and saw the danger of a counter-revolution. "No one will stir," cried Cromwell impatiently: "I tell you, we will cut off his head with the crown on it." Sidney withdrew; and Charles was abandoned to the sanguinary severity of a sect. To sign the death-warrant was a solemn deed, from which some of his judges were inclined to shrink; Cromwell concealed the magnitude of the act under an air of buffoonery; the chamber rung with gayety; he daubed the cheek of one of the judges that sat next him with ink, and, amidst shouts of laughter, compelled another, the wavering Ingoldsby, to sign the paper as a jest. The ambassadors of foreign princes presented no remonstrance; and, when the admirable collections of the unhappy king were sold at auction, they purchased his favorite works of art with rival eagerness. Holland alone negotiated. The English people were overawed. . . .

Tried by the standard of his own intentions and his own actions, Charles I., it may be, had little right to complain. Yet, when history gives its impartial verdict on the execution, it remembers that the king was delivered, by a decimated parliament, which had prejudged his case, to a commission composed of his bitterest enemies, and erected in defiance of the wishes of the people.

His judges were but a military tribunal; and the judgment, which assumed to be a solemn exercise of justice on the worst of criminals, arraigned by a great nation and tried by its representatives, was, in truth, an act of tyranny. His accusers could have rightfully proceeded only as the agents of the popular sovereignty; and the people disclaimed the deed. An appeal to them would have reversed the decision. The churchmen, the Presbyterians, the lawyers, the opulent landowners, the merchants, and the great majority of the English nation, preferred the continuance of a limited monarchy. There could be no republic. Not sufficient advancement had been made in political knowledge. Milton believed himself a friend of popular liberty; and defended the revocable nature of all conceded civil power; yet his scheme of government, which proposed to subject England to the executive authority of a self-perpetuating council, is ruinous to equal freedom. Not one of the proposed methods of government was practicable.

If the execution of Charles, on the thirtieth of January, 1649, be considered by the rule of utility, its effects will be found to have been entirely bad. A free parliament would have saved the king, and reformed church and state; in aiming at the immediate enjoyment of democratic liberty, the Independents of that day delayed popular enfranchisements. Nations change their institutions but slowly: to attempt to pass abruptly from feudalism and monarchy to democratic equality was the thought of enthusiasts, who understood neither the history, the character, nor the condition of the country. It was like laying out into new streets a city already crowded with massive structures. The death of the king was the policy of Cromwell, and not the policy of the nation.

The remaining members of the commons were now by their own act constituted the sole legislature and sovereign of England. The peerage was abolished with monarchy; the connection between state and church rent asunder; but there was no republic. Selfish ambition forbade it; the state of society and the distribution and tenure of property forbade it. The commons usurped not only all powers of ordinary legislation, but even the right of remoulding the constitution. They were a sort of collective, self-constituted, perpetual dictatorship. Like Rome under its decemviri, England was enslaved by its legislators; English liberty had become the patrimony and estate of the commons; the forms of government, the courts of justice, peace and

GOD RULES IN
THE AFFAIRS
OF MEN

CHARLES I
EXECUTED,
JANUARY 30,
1649

CHRISTIAN
LIBERTY
"READY TO
PASS TO THE
AMERICAN
STRAND"

war, all executive, all legislative power, rested with them. They were irresponsible, absolute, and apparently never to be dissolved but at their own pleasure.

But the commons were not sustained by public opinion. They were resisted by the royalists and the Catholics, by the Presbyterians and the fanatics, by the honest republicans and the army. In Ireland, the Catholics dreaded from them the worst cruelties that Protestant bigotry could inflict. Scotland, almost unanimous in its adhesion to Presbyterianism, regarded with horror the rise of democracy and the triumph of the Independents; the fall of the Stuarts foreboded the overthrow of its independence; it loved liberty, but it loved its nationality. It feared the sovereignty of an English parliament, and desired the restoration of monarchy as a guarantee against the danger of being treated as a conquered province. In England, the opulent landholders, who swayed their ignorant dependants, rendered popular institutions impossible; and too little intelligence had as yet been diffused through the mass of the people to make them capable of taking the lead in the progress of civilization. The schemes of social and civil equality found no support but in the enthusiasm of the few who fostered them; and clouds of discontent gathered sullenly over the nation.

THE COUNTER-REVOLUTION

The attempt at a counter-revolution followed. But the parties by which it was made, though they formed a vast majority of the three nations, were filled with mutual antipathies; the Catholics of Ireland had no faith in the Scottish Presbyterians; and these in their turn were full of distrust of the English cavaliers. They feared each other as much as they feared the commons. There could, therefore, be no concert of opposition; the insurrections, which, had they been made unitedly, would probably have been successful, were not simultaneous. The strength of the Independents lay in a small but well-disciplined army; the celerity and military genius of Cromwell ensured to them unity of counsels and promptness of action; they conquered their adversaries in detail; and the massacre of Drogheda, the field of Dunbar, and the victory of Worcester, destroyed the present hopes of the friends of monarchy.

The lustre of Cromwell's victories ennobled the crimes of his ambition. When the forces of the insurgents had been beaten down, there re-

mained but two powers in the state—the Long Parliament and the army. To submit to a military despotism was inconsistent with the genius of the people of England; and yet the Long Parliament, now containing but a fraction of its original members, could not be recognized as the rightful sovereign of the country, and possessed only the shadow of executive power. Public confidence rested on Cromwell alone. The few true republicans had no party in the nation; a dissolution of the parliament would have led to anarchy; a reconciliation with Charles II., whose father had just been executed, was impossible; a standing army, it was argued, required to be balanced by a standing parliament; and the house of commons, the mother of the commonwealth, insisted on nursing the institutions which it had established. But the public mind reasoned differently; the virtual power rested with the army; men dreaded confusion, and yearned for peace; and they were pleased with the retributive justice that the parliament, which had destroyed the English king, should itself be subverted by one of its members.

Thus the effort at absolute monarchy on the part of Charles I. yielded to a constitutional, true English parliament; the control of parliament passed from the constitutional royalists to the Presbyterians, or representatives of a part of the aristocracy opposed to Episcopacy; from the Presbyterians to the Independents, the enthusiasts for popular liberty; and, when the course of the revolution had outstripped public opinion, a powerful reaction gave the supreme authority to Cromwell. Sovereignty had escaped from the king to the parliament, from the parliament to the commons, from the commons to the army, and from the army to its successful commander. Each revolution was a natural and necessary consequence of its predecessor.

CHARACTER OF CROMWELL

Cromwell was one whom even his enemies cannot name without acknowledging his greatness. The farmer of Huntingdon, accustomed only to rural occupations, unnoticed till he was more than forty years old, engaged in no higher plots than how to improve the returns of his land and fill his orchard with choice fruit, of a sudden became the best officer in the British army, and the greatest statesman of his time; overturned the English constitution, which had been the work of centuries; held in his own grasp the liberties which formed a part of the nature of the English people, and cast the kingdoms into a new mould.

Religious peace, such as England till now has never again seen, flourished under his calm mediation; justice found its way even among the remotest Highlands of Scotland; commerce filled the English marts with prosperous activity; his fleets rode triumphant in the West Indies; Nova Scotia submitted to his orders without a struggle; the Dutch begged of him for peace as for a boon; Louis XIV. was humiliated; the Protestants of Piedmont breathed their prayers in security. His squadron made sure of Jamaica; he had strong thoughts of Hispaniola and Cuba; and, to use his own words, resolved "to strive with the Spaniard for the mastery of all those seas." The glory of the English was spread throughout the world: "Under the tropic was their language spoke."

And yet his career was but an attempt to conciliate a union between his power and permanent public order; and the attempt was always unavailing, from the inherent impossibility growing out of the origin of his power. It was derived from the submission, not from the will, of the people; it came by the sword, not from the nation, nor from national usages. Cromwell saw the impracticability of a republic, and offered no excuse for his usurpations but the right of the strongest to restore tranquility—the plea of tyrants and oppressors from the beginning of the world. He had made use of the enthusiasm of liberty for his advancement; he sought to sustain himself by conciliating the most opposite sects.

DEATH OF CROMWELL

The question of a sovereign for England seemed but to relate to the Protector Cromwell and the army, or King Cromwell and the army; and, for the last time, Cromwell hoped, through a parliament, to reconcile his dominion to the English people, and to take a place in the line of English kings. For a season, the majority was not unwilling; the scruples of the more honest among the timid he overcame by levity. Our oath, he would say, is not against the three letters that make the word REX. "Royalty is but a feather in a man's cap; let children enjoy their rattle." But here his ambition was destined to a disappointment; the Presbyterians, ever his opponents, found on this point allies in many officers of the army; and Owen, afterward elected president of Harvard College, drafted for them an effectual remonstrance. In view of his own elevation, Cromwell had established an upper house, its future members to be nominated by the protector, in concurrence with the peers. But the wealth of

the ancient hereditary nobility continued; its splendor was not yet forgotten; the new peerage, exposed to the contrast, excited ridicule without imparting strength; the house of commons continually spurned at their power, and controverted their title. This parliament, of 1658, was dissolved. Unless Cromwell could exterminate the Catholics, convert the inflexible Presbyterians, chill the loyalty of the royalists, and corrupt the judgment of the republicans, he never could hope the cheerful consent of the British nation to the permanence of his government, which was well understood to be coextensive only with his life. He did not connect himself with the revolution, for he put himself above it, and controlled it; nor with the monarchy, for he was an active promoter of the execution of Charles; nor with the church, for he overpowered it; nor with the Presbyterians, for he barely tolerated their worship without gratifying their ambition. He rested on himself; his own genius and his own personal resources were the basis of his power. Having subdued the revolution, there was no firm obstacle but himself to the restoration of the Stuarts, of which his death was necessarily the signal.

The accession of Richard Cromwell, in September, 1658, met with no instant opposition. Like his father, he had no party in the nation; unlike his father, he had no capacity for public affairs. He met a parliament in January, 1659, but only to dissolve it; he could not control the army, and he could not govern England without the army. Involved in perplexities, he resigned. His accession had changed nothing; his abdication changed nothing; content to be the scoff of the proud, he acted upon the consciousness of his own incompetency, and, in the bosom of private life, remote from wars, from ambition, from power, he lived to extreme old age in the serene enjoyment of a gentle and modest temper. English politics went forward in their course. . . .

THE RESTORATION OF MONARCHY—CHARLES II

All classes demanded the restoration of monarchy, as the only effectual guarantee of peace. The Presbyterians, hoping to gain favor by an early and effectual union with the royalists, contented themselves with a vague belief that the martyrdoms of Dunbar would never be forgotten; misfortunes and the fate of Charles I. were taken as sureties that Charles II. had learned moderation in the school of exile; and his return could have nothing humiliating, for it was the nation itself that recalled its sovereign. Every

CHRISTIAN
LIBERTY
"READY TO
PASS TO THE
AMERICAN
STRAND"

party that had opposed the dynasty of the Stuarts had failed in the attempt to give England a government; the constitutional royalists, the Presbyterians, the Independents, the Long Parliament, the army, had all in their turn been unsuccessful; the English, preserving a latent zeal for their ancient liberties, were at the time carried away with a passionate enthusiasm for their hereditary king. The Long Parliament is reassembled; the Presbyterians, expelled before the trial of Charles, resume their seats; and the parliament is dissolved, to be succeeded by a new assembly. The king's return is at hand. They who had been its tardiest advocates endeavor to throw oblivion on their hesitancy by the excess of loyalty; men vie with one another in eagerness for the restoration; no one of them is disposed to gain the certain ill-will of the monarch by proposing conditions which might not be seconded; they forget their country in their zeal for the king; they forget liberty in their eagerness to advance their fortunes; a vague proclamation on the part of Charles II., promising a general amnesty, fidelity to the Protestant religion, regard for tender consciences, and respect for the English laws, was the only pledge from the sovereign. And now that peace dawns, after twenty years of storms, all England was in ecstasy. Groups of men gathered round buckets of wine in the streets, and drank the king's health on their knees. The bells in every steeple rung merry peals; the bonfires round London were so numerous and brilliant that the city seemed encircled with a halo; and under a clear sky, with a favoring wind, the path of the exiled monarch homeward to the kingdom of his fathers was serene. As he landed on the soil of England, he was received by infinite crowds with all imaginable love. The shouting and general joy were past imagination. On the journey from Dover to London, the hillocks all the way were covered with people; the trees were filled; and such was the prodigality of flowers from maidens, such the acclamations from throngs of men, the whole kingdom seemed gathered along the roadsides. The companies of the city welcomed the king with loud thanks to God for his presence. . . .

THE REVOLUTION OF 1688

On the restoration of Charles II., the Puritan or republican element lost all hope of dominion in England; and its history from 1660 to 1688 is but the history of the struggle for a compromise between the republic and absolute monarchy. The contest was continued, yet within limits so narrow as never to endanger the existence, or even question the right, of monarchy itself. The people had attempted a democratic revolution, and had failed; they awaited the movements of the aristocracy. . . .

Liberty, which at the restoration insane loyalty repressed in the public thought and purpose, glided between rakes and the king's mistress into the royal councils. Driven from the palace, it appealed to parliament and the people, and won power through the frenzied antipathy to Roman Catholics. Dismissed from parliament by its dissolution, from the people by the ebb of excitement, it concealed itself in an aristocratic association and a secret aristocratic council. Chased from its hiding-place by disclosures and executions, and having no hope from parliament, people, the press, the courts of justice, or the king, it left the soil of England, and fled for refuge to the prince of Orange.

On the death of Charles II., in 1685, his brother ascended the throne without opposition, continued taxes by his prerogative, easily suppressed the insurrection of Monmouth, and under the new system of charters convened a parliament so subservient that it bowed its back to royal chastisement. The "Presbyterian rascals," the troublesome Calvinists, who, from the days of Edward VI., had kept English liberty alive, were consigned to the courts of law. . . .

THE TORY PARTY,—THE WHIG PARTY,—
THE THIRD PARTY

To understand fully the revolution which followed, it must be borne in mind that the great mass of dissenters were struggling for liberty; but, checked by the memory of the disastrous issue of the previous revolution, they ranged themselves, with deliberate moderation, under the more liberal party of the aristocracy. Of Cromwell's army, the officers had been, "for the most part, the meanest sort of men, even brewers, cobblers, and other mechanics;" recruits for the camp of William of Orange were led by bishops and the high nobility. There was a vast popular movement, but it was subordinate; the proclamation of the prince took notice of the people only as "followers" of the gentry. Yet the revolution of 1688 is due to the dissenters quite as much as to the whig aristocracy; to Baxter hardly less than to Shaftesbury. It is the consummation of the collision which, in the days of Henry VIII. and Edward, began between the churchmen and the Puritans, between those who invoked religion on the side of passive obedience, and those who held resistance to tyranny a Christian duty. If the whig aristocracy looked to the stadholder of aristocratic Holland as the protector of their liberties, Baxter and the Presbyterians saw in William the Calvinist their tolerant avenger.

Of the two great aristocratic parties of England, both respected the established British constitution. But the tory defended his privileges against the encroachments of advancing civilization, and asserted the indefeasible rights of the bishops, of the aristocracy, and of the king, against dissenters, republicans, and whigs.

The whigs were bent on the preservation of their privileges against the encroachments of the monarch. In an age that demanded liberty, they gathered up every liberty, feudal or popular, known to English law, and sanctioned by the fictitious compact of prescription. In a period of progress in the enfranchisement of classes, they extended political influence to the merchants and bankers; in an age of religious sects, they embraced the more moderate and liberal of the church of England, and those of the dissenters whose dissent was the least glaring; in an age of speculative inquiry, they favored freedom of the press. How vast was the party is evident, since it cherished among its numbers men so opposite as Shaftesbury and Sidney, as Locke and Baxter.

These two parties embraced almost all the wealth and learning of England. But there was a third party of those who were pledged to "seek and love and chuse the best things." They insisted that all penal statutes and tests should be abolished; that, for all classes of non-conformists, whether Roman Catholics or dissenters, for the plebian sects, "the less noble and more clownish sort of people," "the unclean kind," room should equally be made in the English ark; that the church of England, satisfied with its estates, should give up jails, whips, halters, and gibbets, and cease to plough the deep furrows of persecution; that the concession of equal freedom would give strength to the state, security to the prince, content to the multitude, wealth to the country, and would fit England for its office of asserting European liberty against the ambition of France; that reason, natural right, and public interest demanded a glorious magna charta for intellectual freedom, even though the grant should be followed by "a dissolution of the great corporation of conscience." These were the views which were advocated by William Penn against what he calls "the prejudices of his times;" and which overwhelmed his name with obloquy as a friend to tyranny and a Jesuit priest in disguise.

MONARCHICAL PARTY DIVIDES

But the easy issue of the contest grew out of a division in the monarchical party itself. James II. (1685-1689) could not comprehend the value of freedom or the obligation of law. The writ of habeas corpus he esteemed inconsistent with monarchy, and "a great misfortune to the people." A standing army, and the terrors of corrupt tribunals, were his dependence; he delighted in military parades; swayed by his confessor, he dispensed with the laws, multiplied Catholic chapels, rejoiced in the revocation of the edict of Nantes, and sought to intrust civil and military power to Roman Catholics.

The bishops had unanimously voted against his exclusion; and, as the badge of the church of England was obedience, he for a season courted the alliance of "the fairest of the spotted kind." To win her favor for Roman Catholics, he was willing to persecute Protestant dissenters. This is the period of the influence of Rochester.

The church of England refused the alliance. The king, from 1687, would put no confidence in any zealous Protestant; he applauded the bigotry of Louis XIV., from whom he solicited money. "I hope," said he, "the king of France will aid me, and that we together shall do great things for religion;" and the established church became the object of his implacable hatred. "Her day of grace was past." The royal favor was withheld, that she might silently waste and dissolve like snows in spring. To diminish her numbers, and apparently from no other motive, he granted—what Sunderland might have done from indifference, and Penn from love of justice—equal franchises to every sect; to the powerful Calvinist and to the "puny" Quaker, to Anabaptists and Independents, and "all the wild increase" which unsatisfied inquiry could generate. The declaration of indulgence was esteemed a death-blow to the church, and a forerunner of the reconciliation of England to Rome. . . .

WILLIAM AND MARY,—NOVEMBER 5, 1688

The party of prerogative was trampled under foot; and, in their despair, they looked abroad for the liberty which they themselves had assisted to exile. The obedient church of England set the example of rebellion. Thus are the divine counsels perfected. "What think you now of predesti-

CHRISTIAN
LIBERTY
"READY TO
PASS TO THE
AMERICAN
STRAND"

nation?" demanded William, as he landed in England. Tories took the lead in inviting the prince of Orange to save the English church; the whigs joined to rescue the privileges of the nobility; the Presbyterians rushed eagerly into the only safe avenue to toleration; the people quietly acquiesced. On the fifth of November, 1688, William of Orange landed in England. King James was left alone in his palace. His terrified priests escaped to the continent; Sunderland was always false; his confidential friends betrayed him; his daughter Anne, pleading conscience, proved herself one of his worst enemies. "God help me," exclaimed the disconsolate father, bursting into tears, "my very children have forsaken me;" and his grief was increased by losing a piece of the true wood of the cross, that had belonged to Edward the Confessor. Paralyzed by the imbecility of doubt, and destitute of counsellors, he fled beyond the sea. Aided by falsehoods, the prince of Orange, without striking a blow, ascended the throne of his father-in-law; and Mary, by whose letters James was lulled into security, came over to occupy the throne, the palace, and the bed of her father, and sequester the inheritance of her brother.

The great news of the invasion of England and the declaration of the prince of Orange reached Boston on the fourth day of April, 1689. The messenger was immediately imprisoned, but his message could not be suppressed; and "the preachers had already matured the evil design" of a revolution.

NEWS OF REVOLUTION REACHES AMERICA

From Massachusetts "the amazing news did soon fly like lightning;" and the people of Connecticut spurned the government which Andros had appointed, and which they had always feared it was a sin to obey. The charter was resumed; an assembly was convened; and, in spite of the FINIS of Andros, on the ninth of May, 1689, new chapters were begun in the records of freedom. Suffolk county, on Long Island, rejoined Connecticut.

New York shared the impulse, but with less unanimity. . . .

In New Jersey there was no insurrection. The inhabitants were unwilling to invoke the interference of the proprietaries. . . .

This New England revolution, beginning at Boston, extended to the Chesapeake and to the wilderness, and "made a great noise in the world." Its object was Protestant liberty; William and

Mary, the Protestant sovereigns, were proclaimed with rejoicings such as America had never before known in its intercourse with England.

Could it be that America was deceived in her confidence; that she had but substituted the absolute sovereignty of parliament, which to her would prove the double despotism of a commercial as well as a landed aristocracy, for the rule of the Stuarts? Boston was the centre of the revolution which now spread to the Chesapeake; in less than a century it will begin a revolution for humanity, and rouse a spirit of power to emancipate the world.

THEORY OF THE REVOLUTION

The revolution of 1688, though narrow in its principle, imperfect in its details, ungrateful toward Puritans, intolerant toward Catholics, formed an auspicious era in the history of England and of mankind. Henceforward the title of the king to the crown was bound up with the title of the aristocracy to their privileges, of the people to their liberties: it sprung from law, and it accepted an accountability to the nation. The revolution respected existing possessions, yet made conquests for freedom, preserved the ascendency of the aristocracy, yet increased the weight of the middling class, the security of personal liberty, opinion, and the press. England became the star of constitutional government, shining as a beacon on the horizon of Europe, compelling the eulogies of Montesquieu and the joy of Voltaire. Never had so large a state been blessed with institutions so favorable to public happiness, to the arts of peace, to the development of its natural resources; and its colonies were to participate in the benefit of the change.

The domestic and colonial system of the Stuarts rested on the simple idea that implicit obedience is due from every member of the British dominions to the sacred prerogative of the crown. In like manner the convention parliament and the ministers of King William and Mary applied the principles of the English revolution of 1688 to the reconstruction of America. The revolution restored to Great Britain its free legislature; and it permitted the reassumption of legislative rights by every colony in which they had been suppressed. The revolution vindicated chartered rights in England; in like manner it respected colonial charters. The revolution recovered for the British parliament the sole right of taxing England; and the analogous right was reclaimed

GOD RULES IN
THE AFFAIRS
OF MEN

———

THE AMERICAN
REVOLUTION—
ITS NECESSITY,
ITS PRINCIPLE

by the legislatures of America. But when, in the course of events, the government at home found that it did not hold the colonies within its control, inferior and irresponsible boards were the first to revive the bad precedents of a wrongful use of the prerogative; or insinuate that parliament should add the sanction of law to royal instructions; or revoke the charters that protected self-government; or legislate directly for the colonies in all cases of a difference between them and the crown; or by its own authority establish a new and complete system of colonial administration. . . .

Indeed, that revolution loved not liberty, but privilege, and respected popular liberty only where it had the sanction of a vested right. . . .

FRANCE, ENGLAND, AND THE NEW ENGLISH NATION

Vol. I

The relations of the rising colonies, the representatives of democratic freedom, are chiefly with France and England; with the monarchy of France, which was the representative of absolute despotism having subjected the three estates of the realm, the clergy by a treaty with the pope, feudalism by standing armies, the communal institutions by executive patronage and a vigorous police; with the parliament of England, which was the representative of aristocratic liberties, and had ratified royalty, primogeniture, corporate charters, the peerage, tithes, prelates, prescriptive franchises, and every established immunity and privilege. The three nations and the three systems were, by the revolution of 1688, brought into direct contrast with one another. . . . God rules in the affairs of men.

THE AMERICAN REVOLUTION. ITS NECESSITY, ITS PRINCIPLE

Vol. II

The hour of the American revolution was come. The people of the continent obeyed one general impulse, as the earth in spring listens to the command of nature and without the appearance of effort bursts into life. The movement was quickened, even when it was most resisted; and its fiercest adversaries worked with the most effect for its fulfillment. Standing in manifold relations with the governments, the culture, and the experience of the past, the Americans seized as their peculiar inheritance the traditions of liberty. Beyond any other nation they had made trial of the possible forms of popular representation, and respected individual conscience and thought. The

resources of the country in agriculture and commerce, forests and fisheries, mines and materials for manufactures, were so diversified and complete that their development could neither be guided nor circumscribed by a government beyond the ocean. The numbers, purity, culture, industry, and daring of its inhabitants proclaimed the existence of a people rich in creative energy, and ripe for institutions of their own.

They refused to acknowledge even to themselves the hope that was swelling within them, and yet in their political aspirations they deduced from universal principles a bill of rights, as old as creation and as wide as humanity. The idea of freedom had always revealed itself at least to a few of the wise whose prophetic instincts were quickened by love of their kind, and its growth can be traced in the tendency of the ages. In America, it was the breath of life to the people. For the first time it found a region and a race where it could be professed with the earnestness of an indwelling conviction, and be defended with the enthusiasm that had marked no wars but those for religion. When all Europe slumbered over questions of liberty, a band of exiles, keeping watch by night, heard the glad tidings which promised the political regeneration of the world.

THE GRAND DESIGN OF PROVIDENCE

A revolution, unexpected in the moment of its coming, but prepared by glorious forerunners, grew naturally and necessarily out of the series of past events by the formative principle of a living belief. And why should man organize resistance to the grand design of Providence? Why should not the consent of the ancestral land and the gratulations of every other call the young nation to its place among the powers of the earth? Britain was the mighty mother who bred men capable of laying the foundation of so noble an empire, and she alone could have trained them up. She had excelled all the world as the founder of colonies. The condition which entitled them to independence was now fulfilled. Their vigorous vitality refused conformity to foreign laws and external rule. They could take no other way to perfection than by the unconstrained development of that which was within them. They were not only able to govern themselves, they alone were able to do so; subordination visibly repressed their energies. Only by self-direction could they at all times employ their collective and individual faculties in the fullest extent of their ever-increasing intelligence. Could not the illus-

CHRISTIAN
LIBERTY
"READY TO
PASS TO THE
AMERICAN
STRAND"

trious nation, which had gained no distinction in war, in literature, or in science, comparable to that of having wisely founded distant settlements on a system of liberty, willingly perfect its beneficent work, now when no more was required than the acknowledgment that its offspring was come of age? Why must the ripening of lineal virtue be struck at, as rebellion in the lawful sons? Why is their unwavering attachment to the essential principle of their existence to be persecuted as treason, rather than viewed with delight as the crowning glory of the country from which they sprung? If the institutions of Britain were so deeply fixed in its usages and opinions that their deviations from justice could not as yet be rectified; if the old continent was pining under systems of authority not fit to be borne, and not ripe for amendment, why should not a people be heartened to build a commonwealth in the wilderness, where alone it was offered a home?

EUROPE AND ENGLAND IN 1763

The successes of the Seven Years' War were the triumphs of Protestantism. For the first time since the breach made in the church by Luther, the great Catholic powers, attracted by a secret consciousness of the decay of old institutions, banded themselves together to arrest the progress of change. In vain did the descendants of the feudal aristocracies lead to the field superior numbers; in vain did the Pope bless their banners as though uplifted against unbelievers; no God of battles breathed life into their hosts, and the resistless heroism of the earlier chivalry was no more. A wide-spread suspicion of insincerity weakened the influence of priestcraft, which relapsed from confident menace into a decorous compromise with scepticism. The Catholic monarchies, in their struggle against innovations, had encountered overwhelming defeat; and the cultivated world stood ready to welcome a new era. The forms of religion, government, military service, and industry, which lent to the social organisation of the Middle Ages a compacted unity, were undermined; and the venerable fabric, clinging to the past, hung over the future as

A mighty rock,
Which has, from unimaginable years,
Sustained itself with terror and with toil
Over a gulf; and with the agony
With which it clings, seems slowly coming down.

The dynasties which received their consecration from the Roman Church, would cease to array themselves in arms against the offspring of the Reformers; in the long tumultuous strife, Protestantism had fulfilled its political ends, and was never again to convulse the world.

REFORMATION FOLLOWED BY SCEPTICISM

But from Protestantism there came forth a principle of all-pervading energy, the common possession of civilised man, and the harbinger of new changes in the state. The life-giving truth of the Reformation was the right of private judgment. This personal liberty in affairs of conscience had, by the illustrious teachings of Descartes, been diffused through the nations which adhered to the old faith, under the more comprehensive form of philosophical freedom. Everywhere throughout intelligent Europe and America, the separate man was growing aware of the inhering right to the unfettered culture and enjoyment of his whole moral and intellectual being. Individuality was the groundwork of new theories in politics, ethics, and industry.

In Europe, where the human mind groped its way through heavy clouds of tradition, inquisitive activity assumed universally the form of doubt. From discussions on religion, it turned to

History of the American Revolution, by George Bancroft, Vol. II, London, 1852

CHRISTIAN
LIBERTY
"READY TO
PASS TO THE
AMERICAN
STRAND"

the analysis of institutions and opinions. Having, in the days of Luther and Calvin, pleaded the Bible against popes and prelates and the one indivisible church, it now invoked the authority of reason, and applied it to every object of human thought; to science, speculative philosophy, and art; to the place of our planet in the order of the heavens, and the nature and destiny of the race that dwells on it; to every belief and every polity inherited from the past; to the priestly altar which the veneration of centuries had glorified; to the royal throne which the Catholic Church had hallowed, and which the social hierarchy of feudalism had required as its head. Scepticism was the method of the new reform; its tendency, revolution. Sad era for European humanity! which was to advance towards light and liberty only through universal distrust; and, before faith could be inspired by genial love to construct new governments, was doomed to gaze helplessly as its received institutions crumbled away. The Catholic system embraced all society in its religious unity; Protestantism broke that religious unity into sects and fragments; philosophy carried analysis through the entire range of human thought and action, and appointed each individual the arbiter of his own belief and the director of his own powers. Society would be organised again; but not till after the recognition of the rights of the individual. Unity would once more be restored, but not through the canon and feudal law; for the new Catholic element was the people.

PRUSSIA AND ITS KING

Yet Protestantism, albeit the reform in religion was the seed-plot of democratic revolutions, had at first been attended by the triumph of absolute monarchy throughout continental Europe; where even the Catholic powers themselves grew impatient of the authority of the Pope over their temporal affairs. The Protestant king, who had just been the ally of our fathers in the Seven Years' War, presented the first great example of the passage of feudal sovereignty into unlimited monarchy, resting on a standing military force. Still surrounded by danger, his inflexible and uncontrolled will stamped the impress of harshness even on his necessary policy, of tyranny on his errors of judgment, and of rapine and violence on his measures for aggrandisement. Yet Prussia, which was the favourite disciple of Luther and the child of the Reformation, while it held the sword upright, bore with every creed, and set reason free. It offered a shelter to Rousseau, and called in

D'Alembert and Voltaire as its guests; it set Semler to hold the Bible itself under the light of criticism; it breathed into the boldly thoughtful Lessing widest hopes for the education of the race to a universal brotherhood on earth; it gave its youth to the teachings of Immanuel Kant, who, for power of analysis and universality, was inferior to none since Aristotle. "An army and a treasure do not constitute a power," said Vergennes; but Prussia had also philosophic liberty. All freedom of mind in Germany hailed the peace of Hubertsburg as its own victory. In every question of public law, Frederic, though full of respect for the rights of possession, continuing to noble birth its prescriptive posts and almost leaving his people divided into castes, made the welfare of the kingdom paramount to privilege. He challenged justice under the law for the humblest against the highest. He among Protestants set the bright pattern of the equality of Catholics in worship and in civil condition. To heal the conflict of franchises in the several provinces of his realm, he planned a general code, of which the faults are chiefly due to the narrowness of the lawyers of his day. His ear was open to the sorrows of the poor and the complaint of the crushed; and as in time of war he shared peril and want with the common soldier, in peace the peasant that knocked at his palace gate was welcome to a hearing. "I love the lineage of heroes," he would say, "but I love merit more." "Patents of nobility are but phantoms; true worth is within." As he studied the history of the human race, the distinctions of rank vanished before his eyes; so that he would say, "Kings are nothing but men, and all men are equal." Thus he arraigned the haughtiness of hereditary station, yet without forming purposes or clear conceptions of useful change. Not forfeiting the affection of his people, and not exciting their restless impatience, he yet made no effort to soften the glaring contrast between his philosophy and the political constitution of his kingdom. In the age of doubt he was its hero. Full of hope for the people, yet distrusting them for their blind superstitions; scoffing at the arrogance of the nobility and the bigoted pride of legitimate kings, yet never devising their overthrow; rejecting atheism as an absurdity, yet never achieving the serene repose of an unwavering faith; passionate against those who held that human thought and the human soul are but forms of matter, yet never inspired with the sense of immortality; confiding neither in the capacity of the great multitude, nor the wisdom of philosophers, nor the power of religion, nor the disposition of kings, nor the promise of the coming age, he moved through the world as the colossal genius of scepticism, questioning the past, which he knew not how to reform. Holding no colonies, he could calmly watch their growth to independence; indulging an antipathy against the king of England, he might welcome the experiment of the widely-extending American commonwealth, but not with confidence in its happy course.

RUSSIA

If the number of active minds in cultivated Prussia was not yet large enough to give to forming opinion a popular aspect, in Russia, the immense empire which was extending itself along the Baltic and the Euxine, and had even crossed the Pacific to set up its banners in North-western America, free inquiry had something of solitary dignity as the almost exclusive guest of the Empress. First of the great powers of Europe in population, and exceeding all of them together in extent of European lands, the great Slavonic State was not proportionably strong and opulent. More than two-thirds of its inhabitants were bondsmen and slaves, thinly scattered over vast domains. The slave held the plough; the slave bent over the anvil, or threw the shuttle; the slave wrought the mines. The nobles, who directed the labour on their estates, in manufactures, or the search for ores, read no books from abroad, and as yet had no native literature. The little science that faintly gleamed on the interior was diffused through the priests of the Greek Church, themselves bred up in superstition; so that the Slavonic race, which was neither Protestant nor Catholic—which had neither been ravaged by the wars of religion, nor educated by the discussions of creeds—a new and rising power in the world, standing on the confines of Europe and Asia, not wholly Oriental, and still less of the West, displayed the hardy but torpid vigour of a people not yet vivified by intelligence, still benumbed by blind belief, ignorance, and servitude. Its political unity existed in the strength of its monarchy, which organised its armies, and commanded them without control; made laws, and provided for their execution; appointed all officers, and displaced them at will; directed the internal administration and the relations with foreign powers. The sovereign who held these absolute prerogatives was Cathcrine, a princess of a German Protestant house. Her ambition had secured the throne by adopting her husband's religion, conniving at his deposition, and not avenging his murder. Her love of pleasure solicited a licentiousness of moral opinion; her passion for praise sought to conciliate the good will of men of letters; so that she blended the adoption of the new philosophy with the grandeur, the crimes, and the voluptuousness of Asiatic despotism. If she invaded Poland, it would be under the pretext of protecting religious freedom; if she moved towards the Bosphorus, she would surround herself with the delusive halo of some imaginary restoration of the liberties of ancient Greece. At home respecting the property of the nobles, yet seeking to diminish the number of slaves, an apparent devotee to the faith of the Greek Church, yet giving religious freedom to the Catholic and the Protestant, and even printing the Koran for the Mussulmans of her dominions; abroad, she bent neither to France nor to England. Her policy was thoroughly true to the empire that adopted her, and yet imbued with the philosophy of western Europe. With deserts near at hand to colonise, with the Mediterranean inviting her flag, she formed no wish of conquering Spanish colonies on the Pacific; and we shall find her conduct towards England, in its relations with America, held in balance between the impulse from the liberal systems of thought which she made it her glory to cherish, and the principle of monarchy which flattered her love of praise and was the basis of her power.

AUSTRIA

Soon after the peace of Hubertsburg, the youthful heir to the Austrian dominions, which, with Prussia and Russia, shaped the politics of eastern and northern Europe, was elected the successor to the imperial crown of Germany. As an Austrian prince, it was the passion of Joseph II. to rival Frederic of Prussia. His mother, Maria Theresa, was a devotee in her attachment to the church. The son, hating the bigotry in which he was nurtured, inclined to scepticism and unbelief. The mother venerated with an absurd intensity of deference the prerogatives of an unmixed aristocratic descent; the son affected to deride all distinctions of birth, and asserted the right to freedom of mind with such integrity, that he refused to impair it when afterwards it came to be exercised against himself. But, in the conflict which he provoked with the past, he mixed philanthropy with selfishness, and his hasty zeal to abolish ancient abuses was subordinate to a passion for sequestering political immunities, and concentrating all power in his own hands. As a

CHRISTIAN
LIBERTY
"READY TO
PASS TO THE
AMERICAN
STRAND"

reformer, he therefore failed in every part of his dominions; and as he brought no enduring good to Hungary, but rather an example of violating its constitution, so we shall find the Austrian court the only great European power which, both as an ally of England and an enemy to republics, remained inflexibly opposed to America. Yet the efforts of Joseph II., ill-judged and vain as they were, illustrate the universality of the new influence.

THE GERMAN EMPIRE

The German empire, of which he was so soon to be the head, was the creature and the symbol of the Middle Ages. Its life was gone. The forms of liberty were there, but the substance had perished under the baleful excess of aristocracy. The Emperor was an elective officer, but his constituents were only princes. Of the nine electors, three were Roman Catholic archbishops, owing their rank to the choice of others; but their constituents were of the unmixed nobility, to whom entrance into the electoral chapters was exclusively reserved. The sovereignty of the empire resided, not in the Emperor, but in the great representative body of the whole country, or Diet, as it was called, which was composed of the Emperor himself, of about one hundred independent prelates and princes, and of delegates from nine and forty independent towns. These last, besides the free cities of Bremen and Hamburg, had internally not only municipal liberties, but self-government, and were so many little republics, dotted throughout the land, from the Rhine to the Danube. But in the Diet, their votes counted as nothing. As the people on the one side were not heard, so the dignity of the imperial crown on the other brought no substantial power; and as the hundred princes were never disposed to diminish their separate independence, it followed that the German empire was but a vain shadow. The princes and nobles parcelled out the land, and ruled it in severalty with an authority which there was none to dispute, to guide, or to restrain.

Nobility throughout Germany was strictly a caste. The younger son of a subordinate and impoverished noble family would not have wedded with the wealthiest plebeian heiress. Various chapters and ecclesiastical preferments were accessible to those only who were of unmixed aristocratic ancestry. It followed, that, in the breast of the educated commoner, no political passion was so strong as the hatred of nobility; for nowhere in the world was the pride of birth so great as in the

petty German principalities. The numerous little princes—absolute within their own narrow limits over a hopeless people, whose fortunes they taxed at will, whose lives and services they not only claimed for the service of the state and of themselves, but as merchantable property which might be transferred to others—made up for the small extent of their dominions by an excess of self-adulation; though, after all, as was said of them by one of the greatest German poets, who was ready to praise merit wherever found, they were but "demi-men, who, in perfectly serious stupidity, thought themselves beings of a higher nature than we." But their pride was a pride which licked the dust, for "almost all of them were venal and pensionary."

THE NETHERLANDS

The United Provinces of the Netherlands, the forerunner of nations in religious tolerance, were, from the origin of their confederacy, the natural friends of intellectual freedom. Here thought ranged through the wide domain of speculative reason. Here the literary fugitive found an asylum, and the boldest writings, which in other countries circulated by stealth, were openly published to the world. But in their European relations, the Netherlands were no more a great maritime power. They had opulent free ports in the West Indies, colonies in South America, Southern Africa, and the East Indies, with the best harbour in the Indian Ocean: their paths, as of old, were on the deep, and their footsteps in many waters. They knew they could be opulent only through commerce, and their system of mercantile policy was liberal beyond that of every nation in Europe. Even their colonial ports were less closely shut against the traffic with other countries. This freedom bore its fruits: they became wealthy beyond compare, reduced their debt, and were able so to improve their finances, that their funds, bearing only two per cent interest, rose considerably above par. Ever the champions of the freedom of the seas, at the time of their greatest naval power, they had in their treaty of 1674 with England, embodied the safety of neutrals in time of war, limiting contraband articles of trade, and making goods on shipboard as safe as the ships that bore them. But the accession of the Stadtholder, William of Orange, to the throne of England was fatal to the political weight of the Netherlands. From the rival of England they became her ally, and almost her subordinate; and guided by her policy, they exhausted their means in land forces and barriers against France, leaving their navy to decline, and their fleets to disappear from the ocean. Hence arose the factions by which their councils were distracted and their strength paralysed. The friends of the Stadtholder, who in 1763 was a boy of fifteen, sided with England, desired the increase of the army, were averse to expenditures for the navy, and forfeiting the popular favour which they once enjoyed, inclined more and more towards monarchical interests.

The patriots saw in their weakness at sea a state of dependence on Great Britain; they cherished a deep sense of the wrongs unatoned for and unavenged, which England, in the pride of strength, and unmindful of treaties, had in the last war inflicted on their carrying trade and their flag; they grew less jealous of France; they opposed the increase of the army—longed to restore the maritime greatness of their country; and including much of the old aristocratic party among the merchants, they were fervid lovers of their country and almost republicans.

SPAIN

The kingdom from which the United Provinces had separated, which Philip II. had made the citadel of Catholicism—in which Loyola had organised his "Society of Jesus" as a spiritual army against Protestantism and modern philosophy, might seem to have been inaccessible to the ameliorating influence of a more enlightened public reason. The territory was compact and almost insulated; and since the Cortes had ceased to be assembled, the government was that of absolute monarchy, controlled by no national representation, or independent judiciary, or political institution. "The royal power," says its apologist and admirer, "moved majestically in the orbit of its unlimited faculties." The individual to whom these prerogatives were confided, was the bigoted, ignorant, kindly Charles III. A fond husband, a gentle master, really wishing well to his subjects, he had never read a book, not even in his boyhood with his teachers. He indulged systematically his passion for the chase, crossing half his kingdom to hunt a wolf: and chronicling his achievements as a sportsman. He kept near his person the prayer-book and playthings of his childhood as amulets; and yielding his mind to his confessors, he never strayed beyond the established paths in politics and religion. Yet the light that shone in his time penetrated even his palace: externally he followed the direction of France; at home, the mildness of

his nature, and some good sense, and even his timidity, made him listen to the counsels of the most liberal of his ministers; so that in Spain also criminal law was softened, the use of torture discountenanced, and the papal power and patronage more and more restrained. The fires of the Inquisition were extinguished, though its ferocity was not subdued; and even the Jesuits, as reputed apologists of resistance and regicide when kings are unjust, were on the point of being driven from the most Catholic country of Europe.

Spain ranked as the fourth European power in extent of territory, the fifth in revenue, while its colonies exceeded all others of the world beside; embracing nearly all South America, except Brazil and the Guianas; all Mexico and Central America; California, which had no bounds on the north; Louisiana, which came to the Mississippi, and near its mouth beyond it; Cuba, Porto Rico, and part of Hayti; and midway between the Pacific and the Indian Ocean, the Marianna and Philippine groups of isles; in a word, the countries richest in soil, natural products, and mines, and having a submissive population of nearly twenty millions of souls.

In the midst of this unexampled grandeur of possession, Spain, which with Charles V. and Philip II. had introduced the mercantile system of restrictions, was weak, and poor, and wretched. It had no canals, no good roads, no manufactures. There was so little industry, or opportunity of employing capital, that though money was very scarce, the rate of interest was as low at Madrid as in Holland. Almost all the lands were entailed in perpetuity, and were included in the immense domains of the grandees. These estates, never seen by their owners, were poorly cultivated and ill managed; so that almost nothing fell to the share of the masses. Except in Barcelona and Cadiz, the nation everywhere presented the most touching picture of misery and poverty.

And Spain, which by its laws of navigation reserved to itself all traffic with its colonies, and desired to make the Gulf of Mexico and the Caribbean its own close seas, allowed but four and thirty vessels, some of them small ones, to engage in voyages between itself and the continent of America on the Atlantic side, and all along the Pacific; while but four others plied to and fro between Spain and the West India Isles. Having admirable harbours on every side, and a people on the coasts, especially in Biscay and Catalonia, suited to life at sea, all its fisheries, its coasting trade, its imports and exports; and all its colonies, scarcely employed sixteen thousand sailors. Such

CHRISTIAN
LIBERTY
"READY TO
PASS TO THE
AMERICAN
STRAND"

were the fruits of commercial monopoly, as illustrated by its greatest example.

The political relations of Spain were analogous. From a consciousness of weakness it leaned on the alliance with France; and the deep veneration of the Catholic king for the blood of the Bourbons confirmed his attachment to the Family Compact. Besides, like France—and more than France—he had griefs against England. The English in holding the rock of Gibraltar, hurled at him a perpetual insult; England encroached on Central America; England encouraged Portugal to extend the bounds of Brazil; England demanded a ransom for the Manillas; England was always in the way, defying, subduing, overawing; sending its ships into forbidden waters; protecting its smugglers; ever ready to seize the Spanish colonies themselves. The court of Spain was so wrapt up in veneration of the kingly power, that by its creed such a monarch of such an empire ought to be invincible; it dreamed of a new and more successful Armada, and hid its unceasing fears under gigantic propositions of daring; but the King, chastened by experience, had all the while an unconfessed misgiving; and slily timid, delighted in intrigue and menace, affected to be angry at the peace, and was perpetually stimulating France to undertake a new war, of which it yet carefully avoided the outbreak.

FRANCE

France, the "beautiful kingdom" of central Europe, was occupied by a most ingenious people, formed of blended elements, and still bearing traces not only of the Celtic, but of the German race; of the culture of Rome, and the hardihood of the Northmen. In the habit of analysis it excelled all nations: its delight in logical exactness and in precision of outline, and expression of thought, gave the style alike to its highest efforts and to its ordinary manufactures; to its poetry and its prose; to the tragedies of Racine and the pictures of Poussin, as well as to its products of taste for daily use, and the adornment of its public squares with a careful regard to fitness and proportion. Its severe method in the pursuit of mathematical science corresponded to its nicety of workmanship in the structure of its ships of war, its canals, its bridges, its fortifications, and its public buildings. Lighthearted, frivolous and vain, no people were more ready to seize a new idea, and to pursue it with rigid dialectics to all its consequences; none were so eager to fill, and as it were to burden, the fleeting moment with pleas-

ure; and none so ready to renounce pleasure, and risk life for a caprice, or sacrifice it for glory. Self-indulgent, they abounded in offices of charity. Often exhibiting the most heartless egotism, they were also easily inflamed with a most generous enthusiasm. Seemingly lost in profligate sensuality, they were yet capable of contemplative asceticism. To the superficial observer, they were a nation of atheists; and yet they preserved the traditions of their own Bossuet and Calvin, of Descartes and Fénélon.

In this most polished and cultivated land,—whose government had just been driven out from North America, whose remaining colonies collectively had but about seventy thousand white persons, whose commerce with the New World could only be a consequence of American Independence,—two opposite powers competed for supremacy; on the one side monarchy, claiming to be absolute; on the other, free thought, which was becoming the mistress of the world.

CHECKS ON THE ROYAL POWER—
MAGISTRATES AND FREE OPINION

Absolute power met barriers on every side. The arbitrary central will was circumscribed by the customs and privileges of the provinces, and the independence of its own agents.—Many places near the King were held by patent; the officers of his army were poorly paid, and often possessed of large private fortunes; the clergy, though named by him, held office irrevocably, and their vast revenues, of a hundred and thirty millions of livres annually, were their own property. His treasury was always in need of money, not by taxes only, but by loans, which require the credit that rests on an assured respect for law. Former kings had in their poverty made a permanent sale of the power of civil and criminal justice; so that the magistrates were triply independent, being themselves wealthy, holding their office of judges as a property, and being irremovable. The high courts of justice, or parliaments as they were called, were also connected with the power of legislation; for as they enforced only those laws which they themselves had registered, so they assumed the right of refusing to register laws; and if the King came in person to command their registry, they would still remonstrate, even while they obeyed.

But the great impairment of royal power was the decay of the faith on which it had rested. France was no more the France of the Middle Ages. The caste of the nobility, numbering, of both sexes and all ages, not much more than one hundred thousand souls, was overtopt in importance by the many millions of an industrious people; and its young men, trained by the study of antiquity, sometimes imbibed republican principles from the patriot writings of Greece and Rome. Authority, in its feeble conflict with free opinion, did but provoke licentiousness, and was braved with the invincible weapons of ridicule. Freedom was the vogue, and it had more credit than the King. Scepticism found its refuge in the social circles of the capital; and infusing itself into every department of literature and science, blended with the living intelligence of the nation. Almost every considerable house in Paris had pretensions as a school of philosophy. Derision of the established church was the fashion of the world; many waged warfare against every form of religion, and against religion itself, while some were aiming also at the extermination of the throne. The new ideas got abroad in remonstrances and sermons, comedies and songs, books and epigrams.

VOLTAIRE

On the side of modern life, pushing free inquiry to the utmost contempt of restraint, though not to total unbelief, Voltaire employed his peerless wit and activity. The Puritans of New England changed their hemisphere to escape from bishops, and hated prelacy with the rancour of faction; Voltaire waged the same warfare with widely different weapons, and, writing history as a partisan, made the annals of his race a continuous sarcasm against the hierarchy of the Roman Catholic Church. His power reached through Europe; he spoke to the free-thinkers throughout the cultivated world. In the age of scepticism he was the prince of scoffers; when philosophy hovered round saloons, he excelled in reflecting the brilliantly licentious mind of the intelligent aristocracy. His great works were written in retirement, but he was himself the spoiled child of society. He sunned himself in its light, and dazzled it by concentrating its rays. He was its idol, and he courted its idolatry. Far from breaking with authority, he loved the people as little as he loved the Sorbonne. The complaisant courtier of sovereigns and ministers, he could even stand and wait for smiles at the toilet of the French King's mistress, or prostrate himself in flattery before the Semiramis of the north; willing to shut his eyes on the sorrows of the masses, if the great would but favour men of letters. He it was, and not an English poet, that

praised George I. of England as a sage and a hero who ruled the universe by his virtues; he could address Louis XV. as a Trajan; and when the French King took a prostitute for his associate, it was the aged Voltaire who extolled the monarch's mistress as an adorable Egeria. "The populace which has its hands to live by," such are the words, and such the sentiments of Voltaire, and as he believed of every landholder, "the people has neither time nor capacity for self-instruction; they would die of hunger before becoming philosophers. It seems to me essential that there should be ignorant poor. Preach virtue to the lower classes; when the populace meddles with reasoning all is lost."

The school of Voltaire did not so much seek the total overthrow of despotism as desire to make his philosophy its counsellor; and shielded the vices of a libidinous oligarchy by proposing love of self as the cornerstone of morality. The great view which pervades his writings is the humanising influence of letters, and not the regenerating power of truth. He welcomed, therefore, every thing which softened barbarism, refined society, and stayed the cruelties of superstition; but he could not see the hopeful coming of popular power, nor hear the footsteps of Providence along the line of centuries, so that he classed the changes in the government of France among accidents and anecdotes. Least of all did he understand the tendency of his own untiring labours. He would have hated the thought of hastening a democratic revolution; and, in mocking the follies and vices of French institutions, he harboured no purpose of destroying them. "Spare them," he would say, "though they are not all of gold and diamonds. Take the world as it goes; if all is not good, all is passable."

Thus scepticism proceeded unconsciously in the work of destruction, invalidating the past, yet unable to construct the future. For good government is not the creation of scepticism. Her garments are red with blood, and ruins are her delight; her despair may stimulate to voluptuousness and revenge; she never kindled with the disinterested love of man.

MONTESQUIEU

The age could have learnt, from the school of Voltaire, to scoff at its past; but the studious and observing Montesquieu discovered "the title-deeds of humanity," as they lay buried under the rubbish of privileges, conventional charters, and statutes. His was a generous nature that disdained

CHRISTIAN
LIBERTY
"READY TO
PASS TO THE
AMERICAN
STRAND"

the impotence of epicureanism, and found no rest-ing-place in doubt. He saw that society, notwith-standing all its revolutions, must repose on prin-ciples that do not change; that Christianity, which seems to aim only at the happiness of another life, also constitutes man's blessedness in this. He ques-tioned the laws of every nation to unfold to him the truth that had inspired them; and behind the confused masses of positive rules, he recognised the anterior existence and reality of justice. Full of the inquiring spirit of his time, he demanded tolerance for every opinion; and to him belongs the peaceful and brilliant glory of leading the way to a milder and more effective penal code. Shun-ning speculative conjecture, he limited his rea-sonings to the facts in European political life, and though he failed to discover, theoretically, the true foundation of government, he revived and quickened faith in the principles of political lib-erty, and showed to the people of France how monarchy may be tempered by a division of its power, and how republics, more happy than those of Italy, may save themselves from the passionate tyranny of a single senate. That free commerce would benefit every nation, is a truth which Montesquieu is thought to have but imperfectly perceived. The moment was come when the languishing agriculture of his country would in-voke science to rescue it from oppression by en-treating the liberty of industry and trade. The great employment of France was the tillage of land, than which no method of gain is more grate-ful in itself, or more worthy of free-men, or more happy in rendering service to the whole human race. No occupation is nearer heaven.

PHYSIOCRATS

But authority had invaded this chosen domain of labour; as if protection of manufactures needed restrictions on the exchanges of the products of the earth, the withering prohibition of the export of grain had doomed large tracts of land to lie desolately fallow. Indirect taxes, to the number of at least ten thousand, bringing with them custom-houses between provinces, and cus-tom-houses on the frontier, and a hundred thou-sand tax-gatherers, left little "to the peasant but eyes to weep with." The treasury was poor, for the realm was poor; and the realm was poor, be-cause the husbandman was poor. While every one, from the palace to the hovel, looked about for a remedy to this system of merciless and improvi-dent spoliation, there arose a school of upright and disinterested men, who sought a remedy for

the servitude of labour by looking beyond the precedents of the statute-book, or forms of gov-ernment, to universal principles and the laws of social life; beyond the power of the people or the power of princes, to the power of nature. They found that man in society renounces no natural right, but remains the master of his person and his faculties, with the right to labour and to en-joy or exchange the fruits of his labour. Expor-tation has no danger, for demand summons sup-plies: dearness need not appal, for high prices, quickening production, as manure does the soil, are their own certain, as well as only cure. So there should be no restriction on commerce and industry, internal or external; competition should supersede monopoly, and private freedom displace the regulating supervision of the state.

Such was "the liberal and generous" system of the political economists who grouped themselves round the calm and unpretending Quesnai, star-tling the world by their axioms and tables of rustic economy, as though a discovery had been made like that of the alphabet or of metallic coin.

TURGOT

The new ideas fell, in France, on the fruitful genius of Turgot, who came forward in the virgin purity of philosophy to take part in active life. He was well-informed and virtuous, most ami-able, and of a taste the most delicate and sure; a disinterested man, austere, yet holding it to be every man's business to solace those who suffer; wishing the effective accomplishment of good, not his own glory in performing it. For him the hu-man race was one great whole, composed, as the Christian religion first taught, of members of one family under a common Father; always, through calm and through "agitations," through good and through ill, through sorrow and through joy, on the march, though at a "slow step," towards a greater perfection.

To further this improvement of the race, opin-ion, he insisted, must be free, and liberty conceded to industry in all its branches and in all its con-nexions. "Do not govern the world too much," he repeated, in the words of an earlier statesman. Corporations had usurped the several branches of domestic trade and manufactures; Turgot vindi-cated the poor man's right to the free employ-ment of his powers. Statesmen, from the days of Philip II. of Spain, had fondly hoped to promote national industry and wealth by a system of pro-hibitions and restrictions, and had only succeeded in deceiving nations into mutual antipathies, which did but represent the hatreds and envy of avarice: Turgot would solve questions of trade abstractedly from countries as well as from provinces, and make it free between man and man, and between nation and nation; for commerce is neither a captive to be ransomed, nor an infant to be held in leading-strings. Thus he followed the teachings of nature, living as one born not for himself, but for the service of truth, and the welfare of mankind.

JEAN JACQUES ROUSSEAU

In those days the people toiled and suffered, with scarce a hope of a better futurity even for their posterity. In life Turgot employed his powers and his fortune as a trust, to relieve the sorrows of the poor; but, under the system of uncontrolled individual freedom, the labourer, from the pressure of competition, might underbid his fellow-labourer till his wages should be reduced to a bare support. Thus the sceptical philosopher, the erudite magistrate, the philanthropic founder of the science of political economy, proposed what they could for human progress. From the discipleship of Calvin, from the republic of Geneva, from the abodes of poverty, there sprung up a writer, through whom the "ignorant poor" breathed out their wrongs, and a new class gained a voice in the world of published thought. With Jean Jacques Rousseau truth was no more to employ the discreet insinuations of academicians; nor seek a hearing by the felicities of wit; nor compromise itself by exchanging flattery for the favour of the great; nor appeal to the interests of the industrial classes. Full of weaknesses and jealousies, shallow and inconsiderate, betrayed by poverty into shameful deeds, yet driven by remorse to make atonement for his vices, and possessing a deep and real feeling for humanity, in an age of scepticism and in the agony of want, tossed from faith to faith, as from country to country, he read the signs of death on the features of the past civilisation; and in tones of sadness, but not of despair—clinging always to faith in man's spiritual nature, and solacing the ills of life by trust in God—he breathed the spirit of revolution into words of flame. Fearlessly questioning all the grandeurs of the world—despots and prelates, and philosophers and aristocrats, and men of letters; the manners, the systems of education, the creeds, the political institutions, the superstitions of his time;—he aroused Europe to the inquiry, if there did not exist a people. What though the church cursed his writings with its ban, and

parliaments burned them at the gibbet by the hangman's hand? What though France drove him from her soil, and the republic of his birth disowned her son? What though the men of letters hooted at his wildness, and the humane Voltaire himself led the cry against this "savage charlatan," "this beggar," who sought "fraternal union among men" by setting "the poor to plunder all the rich." Without learning or deep philosophy, from the woes of the world in which he had suffered, from the wrongs of the down-trodden which he had shared, he derived an eloquence which went to the heart of Europe. He lit up the darkness of his times with flashes of sagacity; and spoke out the hidden truth, that the old social world was smitten with inevitable decay; that if there is life still on earth, "it is the masses alone that live."

At the very time when Bedford and Choiseul were concluding the peace that was ratified in 1763, Rousseau, in a little essay on the social compact, published to the millions, that while true legislation has its source in divinity, the right to exercise sovereignty belongs inalienably to the people; but rushing eagerly to the doctrine which was to renew the world, he lost out of sight the personal and individual freedom of mind. The race as it goes forward, does not let fall one truth, but husbands the fruits of past wisdom for the greater welfare of the ages to come. Before government could grow out of the consenting mind of all, there was need of all the teachers who had asserted freedom for the reason of each separate man. Rousseau claimed power for the public mind over the mind of each member of the state, which would make of democracy a homicidal tyranny. He did not teach that the freedom, and therefore the power, of the general mind, rests on the freedom of each individual mind; that the right of private judgment must be confirmed before the power of the collective public judgment can be justified; that the sovereignty of the people presupposes the entire personal freedom of each citizen. He demanded for his commonwealth the right of making its power a religion, its opinions a creed, and of punishing every dissenter with exile or death; so that his precepts were at once enfranchising and despotic, involving revolution, and constituting revolution and exterminating despotism. This logical result of his lessons was at first less observed. His fiery eloquence, and the concerted efforts of men of letters who fashioned anew the whole circle of human knowledge, overwhelmed the priesthood and the throne. The ancient forms of the state and the church were still

EUROPE AND
ENGLAND IN
1763

PHYSIOCRATS,
TURGOT,
AND ROUSSEAU

CHRISTIAN
LIBERTY
"READY TO
PASS TO THE
AMERICAN
STRAND"

standing; but monarchy and the hierarchy were as insulated columns, from which the building they once belonged to had crumbled away; where statues, formerly worshipped, lay mutilated and overthrown, among ruins that now sheltered the viper and the destroyer.

ENGLAND—AN ARISTOCRATIC REPUBLIC

North of the channel that bounded France, liberty was enjoyed by a wise and happy people, whose domestic character was marked by moderation, and, like its climate, knew but little of extremes. The opinions on religion and on government which speculative men on the continent of Europe were rashly developing without qualification or reserve, were derived from England. She rose before the philosophers as the asylum of independent thought, and upon the nations as the home of revolution, where liberty emanated from discord and sedition. There free opinion had carried analysis boldly to every question of faith as well as of science. English free-thinkers had led the way in the reaction of Protestant Europe against the blind adoration of the letter of the Bible. English Deists, tracing Christianity to reason and teaching that it was as old as creation, were the forerunners of the German Rationalists. English treatises on the human understanding were the sources of the materialism of France. In the atmosphere of England Voltaire ripened the speculative views which he published as English Letters; there Montesquieu sketched a government which should make liberty its end; and from English writings and example Rousseau derived the idea of a social compact. Every Englishman discussed public affairs; busy politicians thronged the coffee-houses; petitions were sent to Parliament from popular assemblies; cities, boroughs, and counties framed addresses to the King: and yet, such was the stability of the institutions of England amidst the factious conflicts of parties, such her loyalty to law even in her change of dynasties, such her self-control while resisting power, such the fixedness of purpose lying beneath the restless enterprise of her intelligence, that the ideas which were preparing radical changes in the social system of other monarchies, held their course harmlessly within her borders, as winds playing capriciously round some ancient structure whose massive buttresses tranquilly bear up its roof, and towers, and pinnacles, and spires.

The great Catholic kingdoms sanctified the kingly power by connecting it with the Church

and deriving its title-deed directly from heaven. Prussia was as yet the only great modern instance of a warlike state resting on an army; England limited its monarchy by law. Its constitution was venerable from its antiquity. Some traced it to Magna Charta, some to the Norman Conquest, and some to the forests of Germany, where acts of legislation were debated and assented to by the people and by the nobles; but it was at the revolution of 1688, that the legislature definitively assumed the sovereignty by dismissing a monarch from the kingdom, as a landlord might dismiss a farmer from his holding. In England, monarchy, in the Catholic sense, had gone off; the dynasty on its throne had abdicated the dignity of hereditary right and the sanctity of divine right, and wore the crown in conformity to a statute, so that its title was safe only with the constitution. The framework of government had for its direct end, not the power of its chief, but personal liberty and the security of property. The restrictions, which had been followed by such happy results, had been established under the lead of the aristocracy, to whom the people in its gratitude for security against arbitrary power and its sense of inability itself to reform the administration, had likewise capitulated; so that England was become an aristocratic republic with the King as the emblem of a permanent executive.

CHURCH OF ENGLAND

In the Catholic world, the Church, as the independent interpreter of the Divine will, placed itself above the State, and might interpose to protect itself and the people against feudal tyranny by appeals to that absolute truth which it claimed and was acknowledged to represent. In England, the Church had no independent power; and its connection with the State was purchased by its subordination. None but conformists could hold office; but in return, the Church, in so far as it is a civil establishment, was the creature of Parliament; a statute enacted the articles of its creed, as well as its Book of Prayer; it was not even entrusted with a co-ordinate power to reform its own abuses; any attempt to have done so would have been treated as a usurpation; amendment could proceed only from Parliament. The Convocations of the Church were infrequent, and if laymen were not called to them, it was because the assembly was merely formal. Through Parliament the laity ruled the Church. It seemed, indeed, as if the bishops were still elected; but it was only in appearance; the crown, which gave

KING GEORGE III
BY ALLAN RAMSAY (SCOTTISH, 1713-1784)
OIL ON CANVAS, 95 X 61¼ IN. 1761
COURTESY NATIONAL PORTRAIT GALLERY.
LONDON, ENGLAND

King George in his coronation robes when twenty-two
years of age.

leave to elect, named also the person to be chosen, and obedience to its nomination was enforced by the penalties of a premunire.

The laity, too, had destroyed the convents and monasteries, which, under other social forms, had been the schools, the poor-houses, and the hostelries of the land; and all the way from Netley Abbey to the rocky shores of Northumberland and even to the remote loneliness of Iona, had filled the country with the ruins of buildings, which once rose in such numbers and such beauty of architecture that they seemed like a concert of voices engaged in a hymn of praise. And the property of the Church, which had been enjoyed by the monasteries that undertook the performance of the parochial offices, had now fallen into the hands of impropriators; so that the fund set apart for charity, instruction, and worship, often became the plunder of laymen, who took the great tithes and left a remaining pittance to their vicars.

The lustre of spiritual influence was tarnished by this strict subordination to the temporal power. The clergy had never slept so soundly over the traditions of the Church; and the dean and chapter, at their cathedral stalls, seemed like strangers encamped among the shrines, or lost in the groined aisles which the fervid genius of men of a different age and a heartier faith had fashioned; filling the choir with religious light from the blended colours of storied windows, imitating the graceful curving of the lambent flame in the adornment of the tracery, and carving in stone every flower and leaf of the garden to embellish the light column, whose shafts soared upwards, as if to reach the sky.

The clergy were Protestant, and married. Their great dignitaries dwelt in palaces, and used their vast revenues not to renew cathedrals, or beautify chapels, or build new churches, or endow schools; the record of their wealth was written in the rolls of the landed gentry, into which the fortunes they accumulated introduced their children; so that the Church, though it was represented among the barons, never came in conflict with the landed aristocracy with which its interests were identified.

HOUSE OF LORDS

The hereditary right of the other members of the House of Lords was such a privilege as must, in itself, always be hateful to a free people; and yet, in England, it was not so. In France, the burgesses were preparing to overthrow the peerage; but in England there was no incessant struggle to be rid of it. The reverence for its antiquity was enhanced by pleasing historical associations. But for the aid of the barons, Magna Charta would not have been attained; and but for the nobility and gentry, the revolution of 1688 would not have succeeded. A sentiment of gratitude was, therefore, blended in the popular mind with submission to rank.

Besides, nobility was not a caste, but rather an office, personal and transmissible to but one. The right of primogeniture made its chief victims in the bosom of the families which it kept up, and which themselves set the leading example of resignation to its injustice. Not younger sons only, who might find employment in public office, or at the bar, or in the church, the army, or navy, or in mercantile adventures and pursuits; the daughters of the great landed proprietors, from a delicate sense of self-sacrifice, characteristic of the sex, applauded the rule by which they were disinherited, and placed their pride in upholding a system which left them dependent or destitute. In the splendid houses of their parents they were bred to a sense of their own poverty, and were bred to endure that poverty cheerfully. They would not murmur against the system, for their sighs might have been taunted as the repinings of selfishness. They all revered the head of the family, and by their own submission taught the people to do so. Even the mother who might survive her husband, after following him to his tomb in the old manorial church, returned no more to the ancestral mansion, but vacated it for the heir; and the dowager must be content with her jointure, which might often be paid grudgingly as to one

Long wintering on a young man's revenue.

As the daughters of the nobility were left poor, and most of them necessarily remained unmarried, or wedded persons of inferior birth, so the younger sons became commoners; and though they were in some measure objects of jealousy, because they so much engrossed the public patronage, yet, as they really were commoners, and entered the body of the people, they kept up between classes a sympathy unknown in any other country. Besides, the road to the honours of the peerage, as all knew, lay open to all. It was a body, constantly invigorated by recruits from some among the greatest men of England. Had it been left to itself, it would have perished long before. Once, having the gentle Addison for a supporter of the

287

CHRISTIAN
LIBERTY
"READY TO
PASS TO THE
AMERICAN
STRAND"

measure, it voted itself to be a close order, but was saved by the House of Commons from consummating its selfish purpose, where success would have prepared its ruin; and it remained that the son of a coal-heaver, the poorest man who ever struggled upwards in the rude competition of the law, might come to preside in the House of Lords. So the peerage was doubly connected with the people; the larger part of its sons and daughters descended to the station of commoners, and commoners were at all times making their way to the peerage. In no country was rank so privileged or classes so blended.

The peers, too, were, like all others, amenable to the law; and though the system of finance bore evidence of their controlling influence in legislation, yet the houses, lands, and property of the peers were not exempt from taxation. The law, most unequal as it certainly was, yet, such as it was, applied equally to all.

HOUSE OF COMMONS

One branch of the legislature was reserved to the hereditary aristocracy of land-holders; the House of Commons partook of the same character: it represented every blade of grass in the kingdom, but not every labourer; the land of England, but not her men. No one but a landholder was qualified to be elected into that body; and most of those who were chosen were scions of the great families—sons of peers, even the oldest son, while his father lived, could sit in the House of Commons; and there might be, and usually were, many members of one name.

Nor was the condition of the elective franchise uniform. It was a privilege; and the various rights of election depended on capricious charters or immemorial custom rather than on reason.

Of the five hundred and fifty-eight members, of whom the House of Commons then consisted, the counties of England, Wales, and Scotland elected one hundred and thirty-one as knights of the shires. These owed their election to the goodwill of the owners of great estates in the respective counties; for it was a usage that the tenant should vote as his landlord directed, and his compliance was certain, for the ballot was unknown, and the vote was given by word of mouth or a show of hands. The representatives of the counties were, therefore, as a class, country gentlemen, independent of the court. They were comparatively free from corruption, and some of them fervidly devoted to English liberty.

The remaining four hundred and twenty-seven

members, "citizens and burgesses," were arbitrarily distributed among cities, towns, and boroughs, with little regard to the wealth or to the actual numbers of the inhabitants. The bare name of Old Sarum, where there was not so much as the ruins of a town, and scarce so much housing as a sheep-cot, or more inhabitants than a shepherd, sent as many representatives to the grand assembly of law-makers as the whole county of Yorkshire, so numerous in people and powerful in riches. The lord of the borough of Newport, in the Isle of Wight, in like manner, named two members, while Bristol elected no more; the populous capital of Scotland but one; and Manchester none. Two hundred and fifty-four members had such small constituencies, that about five thousand seven hundred and twenty-three votes sufficed to choose them. Fifty-six were elected by so few that, had the districts been equally divided, six and a half votes would have sufficed for each member. In an island counting more than seven and a half millions of people, and at least a million and a half of mature men, no one could pretend that it required more than ten thousand voters to elect the majority of the House of Commons. But, in fact, it required the consent of a far less number.

London, and Bristol, and perhaps a few more of the larger places, made independent selections; but they were so few, independence seemed to belong to London alone. The boroughs were nearly all dependent on some great proprietor, or on the crown. The burgage tenures belonged to men of fortune; and as the elective power attached to borough houses, the owner of those houses could compel their inhabitants to elect whom he pleased. The majority of the members were able to command their own election, sat in parliament for life as undisturbed as the peers, and bequeathed to their children the property and influence which secured their seats. The same names occur in the rolls of parliament, at the same places, from one generation to another.

The exclusive character of the representative body was completed by the prohibition of the publication of the debates, and by the rule of conducting all important negotiations with closed doors. Power was with the few. The people was swallowed up in the lords and commons.

Such was the Parliament whose favour conferred a secure tenure of office, whose judgment was the oracle of British statesmen. In those days they never indulged in abstract reasoning, and cared little for general ideas. Theories and philosophy from their lips would have been ridiculed or neglected; for them the applause at St. Stephen's weighed more than the approval of posterity, more than the voice of God in the soul. That hall was their arena of glory, their battlefield for power. They pleaded before that tribunal, and not in the forum of humanity. They studied its majorities, to know on which side was "the best of the lay" in the contest of factions for office. How to meet Parliament was the Minister's chief solicitude; and sometimes, like the spendthrift at a gaming-table, he would hazard all his political fortunes on its one decision. He valued its approval more than the affections of mankind, and could boast that this servitude, like obedience to the Divine Law, was perfect freedom.

INADEQUATE REPRESENTATION IN PARLIAMENT

The *representation in Parliament* was manifestly *inadequate,* and might seem to introduce that unmixed aristocracy which is the worst government under the sun. But the English system was so tempered with popular franchises that faithful history must place it among the very best which the world had seen. If no considerable class desired to introduce open and avowed republicanism, no British statesman of that century had as yet been suspected of deliberately planning how to narrow practical liberty, by substituting the letter of the constitution for its vital principle. It was the custom of Parliament to listen with deference to the representations of the opulent industrial classes, and the House of Commons was sympathetic with the people.

Hence the inconsistency involved in the English electoral system, which was altogether a domestic question and not likely to be reformed by any influence from within, was less considered than the fact, that the country, alone among monarchies, really possessed a legislative constitution. In the pride of comparison with France and Spain, it was a part of the Englishman's nationality to maintain the perfection of British institutions, and to look down with scorn on all the kingdoms of the Continent, as lands of slaves. Every Englishman, in the comparison, esteemed himself as his own master and lord, having no fear of oppression, obeying no laws but such as he seemed to have assisted in making, and reasoning on politics with that free inquiry which, in a despotism, leads to revolution. The idea of the perfection of representative government veiled the inconsistencies of practice. It was received as yet without much question, that every independent man had, or might have, a vote; that every man was governed by himself; and that the people of England, as a corporate body, exercised legislative power.

ADMINISTRATIVE SYSTEM

Men considered, too, the functions of Parliament, and especially of the House of Commons. It protected the property of every man by taking from the executive the power of taxation, and establishing the ideal principle, that taxes could be levied only with the consent of the people. It maintained the supremacy of the civil power by making the grants for the army and navy annual, limiting the number of troops that might be kept up, and keeping the control over their discipline by leaving even the Mutiny Bill to expire once a year. Thus it guarded against danger from a standing army, of which it always stood in dread. All appropriations, except the civil list for maintaining the dignity of the crown, it made specific and only for the year. As the great inquest of the nation, it examined how the laws were executed, and was armed with the power of impeachment. By its control of the revenue, it was so interwoven with the administration, that it could force the King to accept, as advisers, even men who had most offended him; so that it might seem doubtful if he named, or if Parliament designated, the ministers.

The same character of aristocracy was imprinted on the administration. The King reigned, but, by the theory of the constitution was not to govern. He appeared in the Privy Council on occasions of state; but Queen Anne was the last of the English Monarchs to attend the debates in the House of Lords, or to preside at a meeting of her ministers. In the Cabinet, according to the rule of aristocracy, every question was put to vote, and after the vote the dissentients must hush their individual opinions, and present the appearance of unanimity. The King himself must be able to change his council, or must yield. Add to this, that the public offices were engrossed by a small group of families, that favour dictated appointments of bishops in the church, of officers in the navy, and still more in the army, in which even boys at school held commissions, and we shall find that the aristocracy of England absorbed all the functions of administration.

Yet, even here, the spirit of aristocracy was reined in. Every man claimed a right to sit in judgment on the administration; and the mighty power of public opinion, embodied in a free press,

CHRISTIAN
LIBERTY
"READY TO
PASS TO THE
AMERICAN
STRAND"

pervaded, checked, and, in the last resort, nearly governed the whole.

LITERATURE

Nor must he who will understand the English institutions leave out of view the character of the enduring works which had sprung from the salient energy of the English mind. Literature had been left to develope itself. William of Orange was foreign to it; Anne cared not for it; the first George knew no English; the second, not much. Devotedness to the monarch is not impressed on English literature; but it willingly bore the mark of its own aristocracy,

Envy must own I live among the great,

was the boast of the most finished English poet of the eighteenth century.

Neither the earlier nor the later literature put itself at war with the country or its classes. The philosophy of *Bacon,* brilliant with the richest lustre of a creative imagination and extensive learning, is marked by moderation as well as grandeur; and, like that principle of English institutions which consults precedents and facts rather than theories, it prepared the advancement of science by the method of observation. *Newton* was a contented member of a university, and never thought to rebel against the limits that nature has set to the human powers in the pursuit of science.

The inmost character of the English mind, in the various epochs of its history, was imprinted on its poetry. *Chaucer* recalled the joyous heroism, and serious thought, and mirth, and sadness, that beguiled the pious pilgrimages, or lent a charm to the hospitality of Catholic England. *Spenser* threw the dim halo of allegory round the monotonous caprices of departing chivalry. *Shakespeare,* "great heir of fame," rising at the proud moment of the victory of English nationality and Protestant liberty over all their enemies, seeming to be master of every chord that vibrates in the human soul, and knowing all that can become the cottage or the palace, the town or the fields and forests, the camp or the banqueting hall, unfolded the panorama of English history, and embodied in "easy numbers" all that is wise, and lovely, and observable in English manners and social life, proud of his countrymen and his country, to him

This land of such dear souls, this dear, dear land,
Dear for her reputation through the world.

WRITERS OF ENGLISH REPUBLICANISM

Milton, with his heroic greatness of mind, was the stately representative of English republicanism, eager to quell the oppressor, but sternly detesting libertinism and disorder, and exhorting to "patience," even in the days of the later Stuarts. *Dryden,* living through the whole era of revolutions, yielded to the social influences of his time, and reproduced in his verse the wayward wavering of the English Court between Protestantism and the Roman Catholic religion, between voluptuousness and faith; least read, because least proudly national. And *Pope* was the cherished poet of English aristocratic life, as it existed in the time of Bolingbroke and Walpole; flattering the great with sarcasms against kings; an optimist, proclaiming order as the first law of Heaven. None of all these, not even Milton, provoked to the overthrow of the institutions of England.

SCEPTICISM

Nor had the scepticism of modern philosophy penetrated the mass of the nation, or raised vague desires of revolution. It kept, rather, what was held to be the best company. It entered the palace during the licentiousness of the two former reigns; and though the court was now become decorous and devout, still the nobility, and those who, in that day, were called "the great," affected free-thinking as a mark of high breeding, and laughed at the evidence of piety in any one of their order. But the spirit of the people rebelled against materialism; if worship, as conducted in the parish church, had no attractive warmth, they gathered round the preacher in the fields, eager to be assured that they had within themselves a spiritual nature and a warrant for their belief in immortality; yet, under the moderating influence of Wesley, giving the world the unknown spectacle of a fervid reform in religion, combined with unquestioning deference to authority in the state.

English metaphysical philosophy itself bore a character of moderation analogous to English institutions. In open disregard of the traditions of the Catholic Church, Locke had denied that thought implies an immaterial substance; and Hartley and the chillingly repulsive Priestley asserted that the soul was but of flesh and blood; but the more genial Berkeley, armed with "every virtue," insisted rather on the certain existence of the intellectual world alone; while from the bench of English bishops the inimitable Butler pressed the analogies of the material creation itself into the service of spiritual life, and, with the authority of reason, taught the supremacy of conscience. If Hume embodied the logical consequences of the sensuous philosophy in the most skilfully constructed system of idealism which the world had ever known, his own countryman, Reid, in works worthy to teach the youth of a republic, illustrated the active powers of man and the reality of right; Adam Smith found a criterion of morality in the universal sentiment of mankind; and the English Dissenter, Price, enforced the eternal, necessary, and unchanging distinctions of morality. So philosophic freedom in England rebuked its own excesses, and self-balanced and self-restrained, never sought to throw down the august fabric which had for so many centuries stood before Europe as the citadel of liberty.

COURTS OF LAW

The blended respect for aristocracy and for popular rights was impressed upon the courts of law. They were charged with the protection of every individual without distinction, securing to the accused a trial by sworn men, who were taken from among his peers, and held their office for but one short term of service. And especially the judges watched over the personal liberty of every Englishman, with power on the instant to set free any one illegally imprisoned, even though in custody by the King's express command.

At the same time the judiciary, with a reputation for impartiality, in the main well deserved, was by its nature conservative, and by its constitution the associate and the support of the House of Lords. Westminster Hall, which had stood through many revolutions and many dynasties, and was become venerable from an unchanged existence of five hundred years, sent the first officer in one of its courts, from however humble an origin he might have sprung, to take precedence of the nobility of the realm, and act as President of the Chamber of Peers. That branch of the legislature derived an increase of its dignity from the great lawyers whom the crown, from time to time, was accustomed to ennoble; and moreover, it formed, of itself, a part of the judicial system. The House of Commons, whose members, from their frequent elections, best knew the temper of the people, possessed exclusively the right to originate votes of supply; but the final judgment on all questions of law respecting property rested with the House of Lords.

The same cast of aristocracy, intermingled with popularity, pervaded the systems of education. From climate, compact population, and sober national character, England was capable beyond any other country in the world of a system of popular education. Nevertheless it had none. The mass of its people was left ignorant how to write or read.

But the benevolence of Catholic ages, emulated also in later times, had benefited science by endowments, which in their conception were charity schools; founded by piety for the education of poor men's sons; where a place might sometimes be awarded to favour, but advancement could be obtained only by merit, and the sons of the aristocracy, having no seminaries of their own, grouped themselves as at Eton, or Westminster, or Harrow, or Winchester, round the body of the scholars on the foundation; submitting like them to the accustomed discipline, even to the use of the rod, at which none rebelled, since it fell alike on all.

The same constitution marked the universities. The best scholars on the foundation were elected from the public schools to the scholarships in the several colleges, and formed the continuing line of succession to their appointments as well as the central influence of industry, order, and ambition, round which the sons of the opulent clustered. Thus the genius of the past claimed the right to linger in the streets of Mediaeval Oxford; and the sentiment of loyalty, as in earlier days, still hovered over the meadows of Christ Church and the walks of Maudlin: but if the two universities were both loyal to the throne and devoted to the church, it was from their own free choice, and not from deference to authority or command. They had proved their independence and had resisted kings. If they were swayed on the surface by ministerial influences, they were at heart intractable and self-determined. The King could neither appoint their officers, nor prescribe their studies, nor control their government, nor administer their funds. The endowments of the colleges, which, in their origin, were the gifts of piety and charity, were held as property, independent of the state; and were as sacred as the estates of any one of the landed gentry. The sons of the aristocracy might sometimes be prize-men at Oxford or wranglers at Cambridge; but if they won collegiate honours, it was done fairly by merit alone. In the pursuit, the eldest sons of peers stood on no vantage ground over the humblest commoner; so that the universities in their whole organization, at once upheld

CHRISTIAN
LIBERTY
"READY TO
PASS TO THE
AMERICAN
STRAND"

the institutions of England, and found in them the security of their own privileges.

LIFE IN TOWNS

It might be supposed that the gates of the cities would have been barred against the influence of the aristocracy. But it was not so. The influence was interwoven with the prosperity of the towns. Entails were not perpetual; but land was always in the market; estates were often encumbered; and the national debt, which was intimately connected with all private credit and commercial transactions, was also in fact a mortgage upon all the soil of the kingdom. The swelling expenses of the government increased its dependence on the moneyed class; and the leading minister needed the confidence of the city as well as of the country and the court. Besides, it was not uncommon to see a wealthy citizen toiling to amass yet greater wealth, that he might purchase land and found a family, or giving his richly-dowered daughter in marriage to a peer.

Every body formed a part of the aristocratic organisation; a few desired to enter the higher class; the rest sought fortune in serving it.

Moreover, the interests of the trade of the nation had precedence of the political interests of the princes. The members of the legislature watched popular excitements, and listened readily to the petitions of the merchants; and these in their turn did not desire to see one of their own number charged with the conduct of the finances as chancellor of the exchequer; but wished rather for some member of the aristocracy, friendly to their interests. They preferred to speak through such an one, and rebelled against the necessity of doing so, as little as they did at the employment of a barrister to plead their cause in the halls of justice.

LIFE IN THE COUNTRY

But if aristocracy was not excluded from towns, still more did it pervade the rural life of England. The climate not only enjoyed the softer atmosphere that belongs to the western side of masses of land, but was further modified by the proximity of every part of it to the sea. It knew neither long-continuing heat nor cold; and was more friendly to daily employment throughout the whole year, within doors or without, than any in Europe. The island was "a little world" of its own; with a "happy breed of men" for its inhabitants, in whom the hardihood of the Nor-

man was intermixed with the gentler qualities of the Celt and the Saxon, just as nails are rubbed into steel to temper and harden the Damascus blade. They loved country life, of which the mildness of the clime increased the attractions; since every grass and flower and tree that had its home between the remote north and the neighbourhood of the tropics would live abroad, and such only excepted as needed a hot sun to unfold their bloom, or perfect their aroma, or ripen their fruit, would thrive in perfection: so that no region could show such a varied wood. The moisture of the sky favoured a soil not naturally very rich; and so fructified the earth, that it was clad in perpetual verdure. Nature had its attractions even in winter. The ancient trees were stripped indeed of their foliage, but showed more clearly their fine proportions, and the undisturbed nests of the noisy rooks among their boughs; the air was so mild, that the flocks and herds still grazed on the freshly-springing herbage; and the deer found shelter enough by crouching amongst the fern; the smoothly-shaven grassy walk was soft and yielding under the foot; nor was there a month in the year in which the plough was idle. The large landed proprietors dwelt often in houses which had descended to them from the times when England was gemmed all over with the most delicate and most solid structures of Gothic art. The very lanes were memorials of early days, and ran as they had been laid out before the Conquest; and in mills for grinding corn, water-wheels revolved at their work just where they had been doing so for at least eight hundred years. Hospitality also had its traditions; and, for untold centuries, Christmas had been the most joyous of the seasons.

The system was so completely the ruling element in English history and English life, especially in the country, that it seemed the most natural organisation of society, and was even endeared to the dependent people. Hence the manners of the aristocracy, without haughtiness or arrogance, implied rather than expressed the consciousness of undisputed rank; and female beauty added to its loveliness the blended graces of dignity and humility—most winning, where acquaintance with sorrow had softened the feeling of superiority, and increased the sentiment of compassion.

Yet the privileged class defended its rural pleasures and its agricultural interests with impassioned vigilance. The game laws parcelling out among the large proprietors the exclusive right of hunting, which had been wrested from the King

EUROPE AND
ENGLAND IN
1763

LIFE IN
ENGLISH TOWNS
AND COUNTRY,
MANUFACTURES

as too grievous a prerogative, were maintained with relentless severity; and to steal, or even to hamstring a sheep, was as much punished by death as murder or treason. During the reign of George II, sixty-three new capital offences had been added to the criminal laws, and five new ones, on the average, continued to be discovered annually; so that the criminal code of England, formed under the influence of the rural gentry, seemed written in blood, and owed its mitigation only to executive clemency.

But this cruelty, while it encouraged and hardened offenders, did not revolt the instinct of submission in the rural population. The tenantry, for the most part without permanent leases, holding lands at a moderate rent, transmitting the occupation of them from father to son through many generations,

With calm desires that asked but little room,

clung to the lord of the manor as ivy to massive old walls. They loved to live in his light, to lean on his support, to gather round him with affectionate deference, rather than base cowering; and, by their faithful attachment, to win his sympathy and care; happy when he was such an one as merited their love. They caught refinement of their superiors, so that their cottages were carefully neat, with roses and honeysuckles clambering to their roofs. They cultivated the soil in sight of the towers of the church, near which reposed the ashes of their ancestors for almost a thousand years. The whole island was mapped out into territorial parishes, as well as into counties, and the affairs of local interest, the assessment of rates, the care of the poor and of the roads, were settled by elected vestries or magistrates, with little interference from the central government. The resident magistrates were unpaid, being taken from among the landed gentry; and the local affairs of the county, and all criminal affairs of no uncommon importance, were settled by them in a body at their quarterly sessions, where a kind-hearted landlord often presided, to appal the convicted offender by the solemn earnestness of his rebuke, and then to show him mercy by a lenient sentence.

Thus the local institutions of England shared the common character; they were at once the evidence of aristocracy, and the badges of liberty.

MANUFACTURES

The climate, so inviting to rural life, was benign also to industry of all sorts. Nowhere could labour apply itself so steadily, or in the same time achieve so much; and it might seem that the population engaged in manufactures would have constituted a separate element not included within the aristocratic system; but the great manufacture of the material not produced at home was still in its infancy. The weaver toiled in his own cottage, and the thread which he used was with difficulty supplied to him sufficiently by the spinners at the wheel of his own family and among his neighbours. Men had not as yet learned by machinery to produce, continuously and uniformly, from the down of cotton, the porous cords of parallel filaments; to attenuate them by gently drawing them out; to twist and extend the threads as they are formed; and to wind them regularly on pins of wood, as fast as they are spun. At that time the inconsiderable cotton manufactures of Great Britain, transported from place to place on packhorses, did not form one two-hundredth part of the present production, and were, politically, of no importance. Not yet had art done more than begin the construction of channels for still-water navigation. Not yet had Wedgwood fully succeeded in changing, annually, tens of thousands of tons of clay and flint into brilliantly-glazed and durable ware, capable of sustaining heat, cheap in price, and beautiful and convenient in form. Not yet had the mechanics of England, after using up its forests, learned familiarly to smelt iron with pit-coal, or perfected the steam-engines that were to do the heavy work in mining coal, and to drive machinery in workshops.

Let the great artificers of England, who work in iron or clay, adopt science as their patron; let the cotton-spinners, deriving their raw material from abroad, perfect their manufacture by inventive plebian genius, and so prosper as to gather around their mills a crowded population; and there will then exist a powerful, and opulent, and numerous class, emancipated from aristocratic influence, thriving independently outside of the old society of England.

But, in 1763, the great manufactures of the realm were those of wool, and the various preparations from sheepskins and hides, far exceeding in value all others of all kinds put together; and for these the land-owner furnished all the raw material; so that his prosperity was bound up in that of the manufacturer. The manufacture of wool was cherished as the most valuable of all. It had grown with the growth and wealth of England, and flourished in every part of the island: at Kidderminster, and Wilton, and Norwich, not less than in the West Riding of Yorkshire. It had

CHRISTIAN
LIBERTY
"READY TO
PASS TO THE
AMERICAN
STRAND"

been privileged by King Stephen, and regulated by the iron-hearted Richard. Its protection was as much a part of the statute-book as the game-laws, and was older than Magna Charta itself. To foster it was an ancient custom of the country, coeval with the English constitution; and it was so interwoven with the condition of life in England, that it seemed to form an intimate dependency of the aristocracy. The land-owner, whose rich lawns produced the fleece, sympathised with the industry that wrought it into beautiful fabrics. Mutual confidence was established between the classes of society; no chasm divided its orders.

NATIONALITY

Thus, unity of character marked the constitution and the social life of England. The sum of the whole was an intense nationality in its people. They were happy in their form of government, and were justly proud of it; for they enjoyed more perfect freedom than the world up to that time had known. In spite of all the glaring defects of this system, Greece, in the days of Pericles or Phocion, had not been blessed with such liberty. Italy, in the fairest days of her ill-starred republics, had not possessed such security of property and person, so pure an administration of justice, such unlicensed expression of mind.

These benefits were held by a firm tenure; safe against revolutions and sudden changes in the state; the laws reigned, and not men; and the laws had been the growth of centuries; yielding to amendment only by the gradual method of nature, when opinions exercising less instant influence should slowly infuse themselves through the public mind into legislation; so that the English constitution, though like all things else perpetually changing, changed like the style of architecture along the aisles of its own cathedrals, where the ponderous severity of the Norman age melts in the next, almost imperceptibly, into the more genial pointed arch, and the seemingly lighter sheaf of columns, yet without sacrificing the stately majesty of the proportions, or the massive durability of the pile.

The English knew this, and were boastfully conscious of it. As a people, they cared not to hear of the defects in the form of their constitution. They looked out upon other states, and compared their own condition with that of the peoples on the continent, abjectly exposed to the sway of despots; they seemed to enjoy liberty in its perfection, and lost sight of the actual inadequacy of their system in their joy at its ideal purity. They

felt that they were great, not by restraining laws, not by monopoly, but by liberty and labour. Liberty was the cry of the whole nation; and every opposition, from whatever selfish origin it might spring, took this type, always demanding more than even a liberal government would concede. Liberty and industry gave England its nationality and greatness. As a consequence, they thought themselves superior to every other nation. The Frenchman loved France, and when away from it, longed to return to it, as the only country where life could be thoroughly enjoyed. The German, in whom the sentiment of his native land was enfeebled by its divisions into so many states and sovereignties, gained enlargement in his sphere of vision, and at home had a curiosity for all learning; away from home, had eyes for everything. The Englishman, wherever he went, was environed by an English atmosphere. He saw the world abroad as if to perceive how inferior it was to his birth-place. The English statesmen, going from the classical schools to the universities—brought up in a narrow circle of classical and mathematical learning, with no philosophical training or acquaintance with general principles, travelled as Englishmen. They went young to the House of Commons: and were so blinded by admiration of their own country, they seemed to think nothing harmful that promoted its glory, its power, or its welfare. They looked out upon the surrounding sea as their wall of defence

Against the envy of less happier lands.

The great deep seemed to them their inheritance, inviting them everywhere to enter upon possession of it as their rightful domain. They looked beyond the Atlantic, and not content with their own colonies, they counted themselves defrauded of their due as the sole representatives of liberty, so long as Spain should hold exclusively such boundless empires. Especially to them the House of Bourbon was an adder, that might at any time be struck at, whenever it should rear its head. To promote British interests, and command the applause of the British Senate, they were ready to infringe on the rights of other countries, and even on those of the outlying dominions of the crown.

BRITISH DOMINION IN THE EAST INDIES

So England was one united nation. The landed aristocracy was the sovereign, was the legislature, was the people, was the state. The separate influence of each of the great component parts of English society may be observed in the British dominions outside of Great Britain.

From the wrecks of the empire of the Great Mogul, a monopolising company of English merchants had gained dominion in the East; with factories, subject provinces, and territorial revenues on the coast of Malabar, in the Carnatic, and on the Ganges. They despised the rivalry of France, whose East India Company was hopelessly ruined, and whose feeble factories were in a state of confessed inferiority;—and with eager zeal they pushed forward their victories, openly avowing gain as the sole end of their alliances and their trade, of their warfare and their civil rule.

In America, the middling class, chiefly rural people, with a few from the towns of England, had founded colonies in the forms of liberty; and themselves owned and cultivated the soil.

IRELAND

Ireland, whose government was proposed as a model for the British colonies, and whose history is from this time intimately connected with the course of events in America, had been seized by the English oligarchy.

The island was half as large as England, with a still milder climate, and a more fertile soil. From the midst of its wild mountain scenery in the west gushed numerous rivers, fed by the rains which the sea breeze made frequent. These, now forming bogs and morasses, now expanding into beautiful lakes, now rushing with copious volume and swift descent, offered, along their courses, water-power without limit, and near the sea formed deep and safe harbours. The rich limestone plains under the cloudy sky were thickly covered with luxuriant grasses, whose unequalled verdure vied in colour with the emerald.

Centuries before the Christian era, the beautiful region had been occupied by men of one of the Celtic tribes, who had also colonised the Highlands of Scotland. The Normans, who, in the eighth century, planted commercial towns on its sea coast, were too few to maintain separate municipalities. The old inhabitants had been converted to Christianity by apostles of the purest fame, and abounded in churches and cathedrals, in a learned, liberal and numerous clergy. Their civil government was an aristocratic confederacy of septs or families and their respective chiefs; and the remote land seemed set apart by nature as the safe abode of an opulent, united, and happy

people. In the reign of Henry II. of England, and in his name, English barons and adventurers invaded Ireland; and, before the end of the thirteenth century, its soil was parcelled out among ten English families.

IRISH PARLIAMENT—
NO IRISHMAN COULD HOLD A SEAT

As the occupation became confirmed, the English system of laws was continued to the English colonists living within the pale which comprised the four counties of Dublin, Louth, Meath, and Kildare. In the Irish Parliament, framed ostensibly after the model of the English constitution, no Irishman could hold a seat: it represented the intruders only, who had come to possess themselves of the land of the natives, now quarrelling among themselves about the spoils, now rebelling against England, but always united against the Irish.

When Magna Charta was granted at Runnymede, it became also the possession and birthright of the Norman inhabitants of Ireland; but to the "mere Irish" its benefits were not extended, except by special charters of enfranchisement or denisation, of which the sale furnished a ready means of exaction.

The oligarchy of conquerors in the process of time began to amalgamate with the Irish; they had the same religion; they inclined to adopt their language, dress, and manners; and to speak for the rights of Ireland more warmly than the Irish themselves. To counteract this tendency of "the degenerate English," laws were enacted so that the Anglo-Irish could not intermarry with the Celts, nor permit them to graze their lands, nor present them to benefices, nor receive them into religious houses, nor entertain their bards. The mere Irish were considered as out of the King's allegiance; in war, they were accounted rebels; in peace, the statute-book called them Irish enemies; and to kill one of them was adjudged no felony.

During the long civil wars in England, English power declined in Ireland. To recover its subordination, in the year 1495, the tenth after the union of the Roses, the famous statute of Drogheda, known as Poyning's Law, from the name of the Lord Deputy who obtained its enactment, reserved the initiative in legislation to the crown of England. No Parliament could, from that time, "be holden in Ireland till the King's lieutenant should certify to the King, under the great seal of the land, the causes and considerations, and all such acts as it seems to them ought to be passed thereon, and such be affirmed by the King and his

CHRISTIAN
LIBERTY
"READY TO
PASS TO THE
AMERICAN
STRAND"

council, and his license to summon a Parliament be obtained." Such remained the rule of Irish Parliaments, and began to be regarded as a good precedent for America.

THE CHURCH

The change in the relations of England to the See of Rome, at the time of the reform, served to amalgamate the Celtic, Irish, and the Anglo-Norman Irish; for the Catholic lords within the pale, as well as Catholic Ireland, adhered to their ancient religion.

The Irish resisted the Act of Supremacy; and the accession of Queen Elizabeth brought the struggle to a crisis. She established the Protestant Episcopal Church by an act of what was called an Irish Parliament, in which the Celtic Irish had no part, and English retainers, chosen from select counties and boroughs, and new boroughs made for the occasion, held the ascendant over the Anglo-Norman Irish. The laws of supremacy and uniformity were adopted, in the words of the English statutes; the common prayer was appointed instead of mass, and was to be read in the English language, or, where that was not known, in the Latin.

The Anglican prelates and priests, divided from the Irish by the insuperable barrier of language, were quartered upon the land—shepherds without sheep—pastors without people,—strangers to the inhabitants, wanting not them but theirs. The churches went to ruin; the benefices fell to men who were held as foreigners and heretics, and who had no care for the Irish, but to compel them to pay tithes. The inferior clergy were men of no parts or erudition, and were as immoral as they were illiterate. No pains were taken to make converts, except by penal laws; and the Norman-Irish and Celtic-Irish now became nearer to one another, drawn by common sorrows, as well as by a common faith; for "the people of that country's birth, of all degrees, were papists, body and soul."

The Anglican church in Ireland represented the English interest. Wild and incoherent attempts at self-defence against relentless oppression were followed by the desolation of large tracts of country, new confiscations of land; and a new colonial garrison in the train of the English army. Even the use of Parliaments was suspended for seven and twenty years.

The accession of James I., with the counsels of Bacon, seemed to promise Ireland some alleviation of its woes; for the pale was broken down; and when the King, after a long interval, convened a

Parliament, it stood for the whole island. But, in the first place, the law tolerated only the Protestant worship; and, when colonies were planted on lands of six counties in Ulster escheated to the crown, the planters were chiefly Presbyterians from Scotland, than whom none more deeply hated the Catholic religion. And next, the war of chicane succeeded to the war of arms and hostile statutes. Ecclesiastical courts wronged conscience; soldiers practised extortions; the civil courts took away lands. Instead of adventurers despoiling the old inhabitants by the sword, there came up discoverers, who made a scandalous traffic of pleading the King's title against the possessors of estates, to force them to grievous compositions, or to effect the total extinction of the interests of the natives in their own soil.

This species of subtle ravage continued with systematic iniquity in the next reign, and carried to the last excess of perfidy, oppression, and insolence, inspired a dread of extirpation, and kindled the flames of the rising of 1641.

To suppress this rebellion, when it had assumed the form of organised resistance, large forfeitures of lands were promised to those who should aid in reducing the island. The Catholics had successively against them, the party of the King, the Puritan Parliament of England, the Scotch Presbyterians among themselves, the fierce, relentless energy of Cromwell, a unanimity of hatred, quickened by religious bigotry; greediness after confiscated estates, and the pride of power in the Protestant interest. Modern history has no parallel for the sufferings of the Irish nation from 1641 to 1660.

At the restoration of Charles II., a declaration of settlement confirmed even the escheats of land, decreed by the republican party, for the loyalty of their owners to the crown. It is the opinion of an English historian, that "upon the whole result the Irish Catholics, having previously held about two-thirds of the kingdom, lost more than one-half of their possessions by forfeitures on account of their rebellion. . . . They were diminished, also, by much more than one-third through the calamities of that period."

Even the favour of James II. wrought the Catholic Irish nothing but evil, for they shared his defeat; and after their vain attempt to make of Ireland his independent place of refuge, and a gallant resistance, extending through a war of three years, the Irish, at Limerick, capitulated to the new dynasty, obtaining the royal promise of security of worship to the Roman Catholics, and the continued possession of their estates, free from all outlawries or forfeitures. Of these articles, the first was totally disregarded; the second was evaded. New forfeitures followed to the extent of more than a million of acres: and, at the close of the seventeenth century, the native Irish, with the Anglo-Irish Catholics, possessed not more than a seventh of their own island.

AFTER THE REVOLUTION OF 1688

The maxims on which the government of Ireland was administered by Protestant England after the revolution of 1688 brought about the relations by which that country and our own reciprocally affected each other's destiny: Ireland assisting to people America, and America to redeem Ireland.

The inhabitants of Ireland were four parts in five, certainly more than two parts in three, Roman Catholics. Religion established three separate nationalities; the Anglican Churchmen, constituting nearly a tenth of the population; the Presbyterians, chiefly Scotch-Irish; and the Catholic population, which was a mixture of the old Celtic race, the untraceable remains of the few Danish settlers, and the Normans and first colonies of the English.

In settling the government, England entrusted it exclusively to those of "the English colony," who were members of its own church; so that the little minority ruled the island. To facilitate this, new boroughs were created; and wretched tenants, where not disfranchised, were so coerced in their votes at elections, that two-thirds of the Irish House of Commons were the nominees of the large Protestant proprietors of the land.

DISFRANCHISEMENT OF THE CATHOLICS

In addition to this, an act of the English Parliament rehearsed the dangers to be apprehended from the presence of popish recusants in the Irish Parliament, and required of every member the new oaths of allegiance and supremacy, and the declaration against transubstantiation. But not only were Roman Catholics excluded from seats in both branches of the legislature; a series of enactments, the fruit of relentless perseverance, gradually excluded "papists," from having any votes in the election of members to serve in Parliament.

The Catholic Irish being disfranchised, one enactment pursued them after another, till they suffered under a universal, unmitigated, indispensable, exceptionless disqualification. In the courts of law, they could not gain a place on the bench, nor act as a barrister, or attorney, or solicitor, nor be employed even as a hired clerk, nor sit on a grand jury, nor serve as a sheriff or a justice of the peace, nor hold even the lowest civil office of trust and profit, nor have any privilege in a town corporate, nor be a freeman of such corporation, nor vote at a vestry. If papists would trade and work, they must do it, even in their native towns, as aliens. They were expressly forbidden to take more than two apprentices in whatever employment, except in the linen manufacture only. A Catholic might not marry a Protestant—the priest who should celebrate such a marriage was to be hanged; nor be a guardian to any child, nor educate his own child, if the mother declared herself a Protestant; or even if his own child, however young, should profess to be a Protestant.

PROHIBITION OF EDUCATION AND WORSHIP

None but those who conformed to the established church were admitted to study at the universities, nor could degrees be obtained but by those who had taken all the tests, oaths, and declarations. No Protestant in Ireland might instruct a papist. Papists could not supply their want by academies and schools of their own; for a Catholic to teach, even in a private family, or as usher to a Protestant, was a felony, punishable by imprisonment, exile, or death. Thus, "papists" were excluded from all opportunity of education at home, except by stealth, and in violation of law. It might be thought that schools abroad were open to them; but, by a statute of King William, to be educated in any foreign Catholic school was an "unalterable and perpetual outlawry." The child sent abroad for education, no matter of how tender an age, or himself how innocent, could never after sue in law or equity, or be guardian, executor, or administrator, or receive any legacy or deed of gift; he forfeited all his goods and chattels, and forfeited for his life all his lands. Whoever sent him abroad, or maintained him there, or assisted him with money or otherwise, incurred the same liabilities and penalties. The crown divided the forfeiture with the informer; and when a person was proved to have sent abroad a bill of exchange or money, on him rested the burden of proving that the remittance was innocent, and he must do so before justices without the benefit of a jury.

The Irish Catholics were not only deprived of their liberties, but even of the opportunity of worship, except by connivance. Their clergy, taken

CHRISTIAN
LIBERTY
"READY TO
PASS TO THE
AMERICAN
STRAND"

from the humbler classes of the people, could not be taught at home, nor be sent for education beyond seas, nor be recruited by learned ecclesiastics from abroad. Such priests as were permitted to reside in Ireland were required to be registered, and were kept like prisoners at large within prescribed limits. All "papists" exercising ecclesiastical jurisdiction, all monks, friars, and regular priests, and all priests not then actually in parishes, and to be registered, were banished from Ireland under pain of transportation, and, on a return, of being hanged, drawn, and quartered. Avarice was stimulated to apprehend them by the promise of a reward; he that should harbour or conceal them was to be stripped of all his property. When the registered priests were dead, the law, which was made perpetual, applied to every popish priest.. By the laws of William and of Anne, St. Patrick, in Ireland, in the eighteenth century, would have been a felon. Any two justices of the peace might call before them any Catholic, and make inquisition as to when he heard mass, who were present, and what Catholic schoolmaster or priest he knew of; and the penalty for refusal to answer was a fine or a year's imprisonment. The Catholic priest abjuring his religion received a pension of thirty, and afterwards of forty, pounds. And, in spite of these laws, there were, it is said, four thousand Catholic clergymen in Ireland; and the Catholic worship gained upon the Protestant, so attractive is sincerity when ennobled by persecution, even though "the laws did not presume a papist to exist there, and did not allow them to breathe but by the connivance of the Government."

PROHIBITION OF LAND OWNERSHIP

The Catholic Irish had been plundered of six-sevenths of the land by iniquitous confiscations; every acre of the remaining seventh was grudged them by the Protestants. No non-conforming Catholic could buy land, or receive it by descent, devise, or settlement; or lend money on it, as the security; or hold an interest in it through a Protestant trustee: or take a lease of ground for more than thirty-one years. If, under such a lease, he brought his farm to produce more than one-third beyond the rent, the first Protestant discoverer might sue for the lease before known Protestants, making the defendant answer all interrogatories on oath; so that the Catholic farmer dared not drain his fields, nor inclose them, nor build solid houses on them. If in any way he improved their productiveness, his lease was forfeited. It was his

interest rather to deteriorate the country, lest envy should prompt some one to turn him out of doors. In all these cases the forfeitures were in favour of Protestants. Even if a Catholic owned a horse worth more than five pounds, any Protestant might take it away. Nor was natural affection or parental authority respected. The son of a Catholic landholder, however dissolute or however young, if he would but join the English church, could revolt against his father, and turn his father's estate in fee-simple into a tenancy for life, becoming himself the owner, and annulling every agreement made by the father, even before his son's conversion.

The dominion of the child over the property of the Popish parent was universal. The Catholic father could not in any degree disinherit his apostatising son; but the child, in declaring himself a Protestant, might compel his father to confess upon oath the value of his substance, real and personal, in which the Protestant court might out of it award the son immediate maintenance, and after the father's death, any establishment it pleased. A new bill might at any time be brought by one or all of the children, for a further discovery. If the parent, by his industry, improved his property, the son might compel a new account of the value of the estate, in order to a new disposition. The father had no security against the persecution of his children but by abandoning all acquisition or improvement.

Ireland, of which by far the greater part had been confiscated since the reign of Henry VIII., and much of it more than once, passed away from the ancient Irish. The proprietors in fee were probably fewer than in an equal area in any part of Western Europe, Spain only excepted. The consequence was, an unexampled complication of titles. The landlord in chief was often known only as having dominion over the estate; leases of large tracts had been granted for very long terms of years; these were again subdivided to those who subdivided them once more, and so on indefinitely. Mortgages brought a new and numerous class of claimants. Thus humane connection between the tenant and landlord was not provided for. Leases were in the last resort most frequently given at will; and then what defence had the Irish Catholic against his Protestant superior? Hence the thatched mud cabin, without window or chimney; the cheap fences; the morass undrained; idleness in winter; the tenant's concealment of good returns: for to spend his savings in improving his farm would have been giving them to his immediate landlord.

To the native Irish the English oligarchy appeared not in the attitude of kind proprietors, whom residence and a common faith, long possession, and hereditary affection united with the tenantry, but as men of a different race and creed, who had acquired the island by force of arms, rapine, and chicane, and derived revenues from it by the employment of extortionate underlings or overseers.

This state of society, as a whole, was what ought not to be endured, and the English were conscious of it. The common law respects the right of self-defence; yet the Irish Catholics, or Popish recusants as they were called, were, by one universal prohibition, forbidden using or keeping any kind of weapons whatsoever, under penalties which the crown could not remit. Any two justices might enter a house and search for arms, or summon any person whomsoever, and tender him an oath, of which the repeated refusal was punishable as treason.

Such was the Ireland of the Irish;—a conquered people, whom the victors delighted to trample upon, and did not fear to provoke. Their industry within the kingdom was prohibited or repressed by law, and then they were calumniated as naturally idle. Their savings could not be invested on equal terms in trade, manufactures, or real property; and they were called improvident. The gates of learning were shut on them, and they were derided as ignorant. In the midst of privations they were cheerful. Suffering for generations under acts which offered bribes to treachery, their integrity was not debauched; no son rose against his father, no friend betrayed his friend. Fidelity to their religion, to which afflictions made them cling more closely, chastity, and respect for the ties of family, remained characteristics of the down-trodden race. America as yet offered it no inviting asylum, though her influence was soon to mitigate its sorrows and relax its bonds.

Relief was to come through the conflicts of the North American colonies with Great Britain. Ireland and America, in so far as both were oppressed by the commercial monopoly of England, had a common cause; and while the penal laws against the Catholics did not affect the Anglo-Irish, they suffered equally with the native Irish from the mercantile system. The restrictions of the acts of trade extended not to America only, but to the sister kingdom. It had harbours, but it could not send a sail across the Atlantic, nor ship directly to the colonies, even in English vessels, anything but "servants and horses, and victuals," and at last linens; nor receive sugar, or coffee, or

other colonial produce, but from England. Its great staple was wool; its most important natural manufacture was the woollen. "I shall do all that lies in my power to discourage the woollen manufactures of Ireland," said William of Orange. The exportation of Irish woollens to the colonies and to foreign countries was prohibited; and restrictive laws so interfered with the manufacture, that it seemed probable Irishmen would not be able to wear a coat of their own fabric.

In the course of years the "English colonists" themselves began to be domiciliated in Ireland; and with the feeling that the country in which they dwelt was their home, there grew up discontent that it continued to be treated as a conquered country. Proceeding by insensible degrees, they at length maintained openly the legislative equality of the two kingdoms. In 1692, the Irish House of Commons claimed "the sole and undoubted right to prepare and resolve the means of raising money." In 1698, Molyneux, an Irish Protestant, and member for the University of Dublin, asserted, through the press, the perfect and reciprocal independence of the Irish and English Parliaments; that Ireland was not bound by the acts of a legislative body in which it was not represented. Two replies were written to the tract, which was also formally condemned by the English House of Commons. When, in 1719, the Irish House of Lords denied for Ireland the judicial power of the House of Lords of Great Britain, the British Parliament, making a precedent for all its outlying dominions, enacted, that "the King, with the consent of the Parliament of Great Britain, had, hath, and of right ought to have full power and authority to make laws and statutes of force to bind the people and the kingdom of Ireland!"

But the opposite opinion was confirmed among the Anglo-Irish statesmen. The Irish people set the example of resisting English laws by voluntary agreements to abstain from using English manufactures, and the patriot party had already acquired strength and skill, just at the time when the British Parliament, by its purpose of taxing the American colonies, provoked their united population to raise the same questions, and in their turn to deny its power.

SCOTCH-IRISH PRESBYTERIANS

But besides the conforming Protestant population, there was in Ireland another class of Protestants who shared in some degree the disqualifications of the Catholics. To Queen Anne's Bill for

EUROPE AND
ENGLAND IN
1763

LAND OWNERSHIP
PROHIBITED
IRISH CATHOLICS

CHRISTIAN
LIBERTY
"READY TO
PASS TO THE
AMERICAN
STRAND"

preventing the further growth of Popery, a clause was added in England, and ratified by the Irish Parliament, that none should be capable of any public employment, or of being in the magistracy of any city, who did not receive the sacrament according to the English Test Act, thus disfranchising the whole body of Presbyterians. At home, where the Scottish nation enjoyed its own religion, the people were loyal: in Ireland, the disfranchised Scotch Presbyterians, who still drew their ideas of Christian government from the Westminster Confession, began to believe that they were under no religious obligation to render obedience to the British Government. They could not enter the Irish Parliament to strengthen the hands of the patriot party; nor were they taught by their faith to submit in patience, like the Catholic Irish. Had all Ireland resembled them, it could not have been kept in subjection. But what could be done by unorganised men, constituting only about a tenth of the people, in the land in which they were but sojourners? They were willing to quit a soil which was endeared to them by no traditions; and the American colonies opened their arms to receive them. They began to change their abode as soon as they felt oppression; and every successive period of discontent swelled the tide of emigrants. Just after the peace of Paris, "the Heart of Oak" Protestants of Ulster, weary of strife with their landlords, came over in great numbers; and settlements on the Catawba, in South Carolina, dated from that epoch. At different times in the eighteenth century, some had found homes in New England, but they were most numerous south of New York, from New Jersey to Georgia. In Pennsylvania they peopled many counties, till, in public life, they already balanced the influence of the Quakers. In Virginia, they went up the valley of the Shenandoah; and they extended themselves along the tributaries of the Catawba, in the beautiful upland region of North Carolina. Their training in Ireland had kept the spirit of liberty and the readiness to resist unjust government as fresh in their hearts, as though they had just been listening to the preachings of Knox, or musing over the political creed of the Westminster Assembly. They brought to America no submissive love for England; and their experience and their religion alike bade them meet oppression with prompt resistance. We shall find the first voice publicly raised in America to dissolve all connection with Great Britain came, not from the Puritans of New England, or the Dutch of New York, or the planters of Virginia, but from Scotch-Irish Presbyterians.

TOWNSHEND CONTEMPLATES CHANGING CHARTERS

At the peace of 1763 the fame of England was exalted throughout Europe above that of all other nations. She had triumphed over those whom she called her hereditary enemies, and retained half a continent as the monument of her victories. Her American dominions stretched without dispute from the Atlantic to the Mississippi, from the Gulf of Mexico to Hudson's Bay; and in her older possessions that dominion was rooted as firmly in the affections of the colonists as in their institutions and laws. The ambition of British statesmen might well be inflamed with the desire of connecting the mother country and her transatlantic empire by indissoluble bonds of mutual interest and common liberties.

But the Board of Trade had long been angry with provincial assemblies for claiming the right of free deliberation. For several years it had looked forward to peace as the moment when the colonies were to feel the superiority of the parent land. Now that the appointed time had come, the Earl of Bute, with the full concurrence of the King, making the change which had long been expected, assigned to Charles Townshend the office of First Lord of Trade, with the administration of the colonies. Assuming larger powers than had ever been exercised by any of his predecessors except Halifax, called also to a seat in the cabinet, and enjoying direct access to the King on the affairs of his department, he, on the 23rd of February, became Secretary of State for the colonies in all but the name.

COLLEAGUES OF TOWNSHEND

In the council, in which Townshend took a place, there was Bute, its chief, having the entire confidence of his sovereign; the proud restorer of peace, fully impressed with the necessity of bringing the colonies into order, and ready to give his support to the highest system of authority of Great Britain over America. Being at the head of the Treasury, he was, in a special manner, responsible for every measure connected with the finances; and though he was himself a feeble man of business, yet his defects were in a measure supplied by Jenkinson, his able, indefatigable and confidential private secretary.—There was Mansfield, the illustrious jurist, who had boasted publicly of his early determination never to engage in public life "but upon Whig principles"; and, in conformity to them, had asserted that an act of

Parliament in Great Britain could alone prescribe rules for the reduction of refractory colonial assemblies.—There was George Grenville, then First Lord of the Admiralty, bred to the law; and ever anxious to demonstrate that all the measures which he advocated reposed on the British Constitution, and the precedents of 1688; eager to make every part of the British empire tributary to the prosperity of Great Britain, and making the plenary authority of the British Legislature the first article of his political creed.—There was the place as Keeper of the Privy Seal for Bedford, the head of the house of Russell, and the great representative of the landed aristocracy of Great Britain, absent from England at the moment, but, through his friends, ready to applaud the new colonial system, to which he had long ago become a convert. There was the weak and not unamiable Halifax, so long the chief of the American administration, heretofore baffled by the colonies, and held in check by Pitt; willing himself to be the instrument to carry his long cherished opinions of British omnipotence into effect. There was the self-willed, hot-tempered Egremont, using the patronage of his office to enrich his family and friends; the same who had menaced Maryland, Pennsylvania and North Carolina—obstinate and impatient of contradiction, ignorant of business, passionate, and capable of cruelty in defence of authority; at variance with Bute, and speaking of his colleague, the Duke of Bedford, "as a headstrong, silly wretch."

To these was now added the fearless, eloquent and impetuous Charles Townshend, trained to public life, first in the Board of Trade, and then as Secretary at War—a statesman who entered upon the gravest affairs with all the courage of eager levity, and with a daring purpose of carrying difficult measures with unscrupulous speed. No man in the House of Commons was thought to know America so well; no one was so resolved on making a thorough change in its constitutions and government. "What schemes he will form," said the proprietary of Pennsylvania, "we shall soon see." But there was no disguise about his schemes. He was always for making thorough work of it with the colonies.

HIS POLICY

James II., in attempting the introduction of what was called order into the New World, had employed the prerogative. Halifax and Townshend, in 1753, had tried to accomplish the same ends by the royal power, and had signally failed.

It was now settled that no tax could be imposed on the inhabitants of a British plantation but by their own assembly, or by an act of Parliament; and though the ministers readily employed the name and authority of the King, yet, in the main, the new system was to be enforced by the transcendental power of the British Parliament.

On his advancement, Townshend became at once the most important man in the House of Commons; for Fox commanded no respect, and was preparing to retire to the House of Lords; and Grenville, offended at having been postponed, kept himself sullenly in reserve. Besides; America, which had been the occasion of the war, became the great subject of consideration at the peace; and the minister who was charged with its government took the lead in public business.

Townshend carried with him into the cabinet and the House of Commons the experience, the asperities, and the prejudices of the Board of Trade; and his plan for the interference of the supreme legislature derived its character from the selfish influences under which it had been formed, and which aimed at obtaining an unlimited, lucrative, and secure patronage.

The primary object was, therefore, a revenue, to be disposed of by the British ministry, under the sign manual of the King. The ministry would tolerate no further "the disobedience of long time to royal instructions," nor bear with the claim of "the lower houses of assemblies" in the colonies to the right of deliberating on their votes of supply, like the Parliament of Great Britain. It was announced "by authority" that there were to be "no more requisitions from the King," but instead of such requisitions an immediate taxation of the colonies by the British legislature.

The first charge upon that revenue was to be the civil list, that all the royal officers in America, the judges in every court not less than the executive, might be wholly superior to the assemblies, and dependent on the King's pleasure alone for their appointment to office, their continuance in it, and the amount and payment of their emoluments; so that the corps of persons in the public employ might be a civil garrison, set to keep the colonies in dependence, and to sustain the authority of Great Britain.

The charters were obstacles, and, in the opinion of Charles Townshend, the charters should fall, and one uniform system of government be substituted in their stead. The little republics of Connecticut and Rhode Island, which Clarendon had cherished, and every ministry of Charles II. had spared, were no longer safe. A new territorial

CHRISTIAN
LIBERTY
"READY TO
PASS TO THE
AMERICAN
STRAND"

arrangement of provinces was in contemplation; Massachusetts itself was to be restrained in its boundaries, as well as made more dependent on the King.

This arbitrary policy required an American standing army, and that army was to be maintained by those whom it was to oppress. To complete the system, the navigation acts were to be strictly enforced. It would seem that the execution of so momentous a design must have engaged the attention of the whole people of England, and of the civilised world. But so entirely was the British Government of that day in the hands of the few, and so much was their curiosity engrossed by what would give influence at court, or secure votes in the House of Commons, that the most eventful measures ever adopted in that country were entered upon without any observation on the part of the historians and writers of memoirs at the time. The ministry itself was not aware of what it was doing. And had some seer risen up to foretell that the charter of Rhode Island derived from its popular character a vitality that would outlast the unreformed House of Commons, the faithful prophet would have been scoffed at as a visionary madman. . . .

The peace, too, the favourite measure of the Ministry and the King, had been gratefully welcomed in the New World. "We in America," said Otis to the people of Boston, on being chosen moderator at their first town meeting in 1763, "have abundant reason to rejoice. The heathen are driven out and the Canadians conquered. The British dominion now extends from sea to sea, and from the great rivers to the ends of the earth. Liberty and knowledge, civil and religious, will be co-extended, improved and preserved to the latest posterity. No constitution of government has appeared in the world so admirably adapted to these great purposes as that of Great Britain. Every British subject in America is, of common right, by act of Parliament, and by the laws of God and nature, entitled to all the essential privileges of Britons. By particular charters, particular privileges are justly granted, in consideration of undertaking to begin so glorious an empire as British America. Some weak and wicked minds have endeavoured to infuse jealousies with regard to the colonies; the true interests of Great Britain and her plantations are mutual; and what God in His providence has united, let no man dare attempt to pull asunder." Such was the unanimous voice of the colonies.

Fervent attachment to England was joined with love for the English constitution, as it had been imitated in America, at the very time when the ministry of Bute was planning the thorough overthrow of colonial liberty.

BRITISH WESTERN POLICY

In the seventh decade of the eighteenth century a newspaper contributor in Great Britain wrote the following concerning the rapid succession of ministries that had attempted the government of the country during the early years of the reign of George III:

"The variety of persons, who within a very short compass of years, have been produced to the public in the first employments of the state, hath diverted our attention from a more important object; from the measures they have pursued or meant to pursue. Amused and deluded by a succession of illustrious names, we have hardly had time to consider their different systems of administration, and have been more anxious to know by whom employments were filled, than how they were executed." (Almon, *A New and Impartial Collection of Interesting Letters from the Public Papers*—Sept., 1760 to May, 1767)

To the present-day student of the period, the same difficulty presents itself under a similar guise; for the kaleidoscopic changes in the British ministry during the middle of the eighteenth century renders the tracing of the ministerial development interesting, while it has made difficult the discovery of the principles of policy. Instead of several distinct parties with definite platforms, such as is characteristic of the present politics of Great Britain, there were in the middle of the eighteenth century many groups of men around

their several leaders, whose chief object was office-holding. To accomplish this end the various groups were willing to make combinations with almost no consideration of conflicting policies. In fact, one of the prevailing theories of government justified such non-partisan ministries, by preaching the need of harmony between king and parliament, which could never be maintained by the predominance of either, as had been the case in former years.

Arbitrary absolutism under the Stuarts, and party government under the supremacy of the Old Whig nobility, had both been tried. Harmony could be obtained, it was thought, by a ministry composed of all factions working in union with the king. This theory made acceptable to many politicians of that period the hybrid ministry, composed of opposing groups, which the Earl of Chatham brought together in 1766, and that not less curious combination of 1768 under the Duke of Grafton.

It would be a hopeless task to seek for ministerial policies in such a jumble of factions, were the groups and sub-groups of politicians, with their personal biases, not easily distinguishable; and if the hostility of certain groups to each other did not render combination difficult, if not impossible. Thus among the various factions, such as George Grenville's, the Duke of Bedford's, the

The British Ministry and the Treaty of Fort Stanwix, by Clarence Walworth Alvord, 1909

303

CHRISTIAN
LIBERTY
"READY TO
PASS TO THE
AMERICAN
STRAND"

Duke of Newcastle's, the Earl of Bute's, the Marquis of Rockingham's, and William Pitt's, with the sub-groups led by Lord Shelburne and Conway, we find that certain of these would not act with others. In spite of attempts at reconciliation, the Rockinghams would not join with the Grenvilles, and the Bedfords always objected to Conway and Shelburne. It is out of such slight indications that we must draw an interpretation of the policy favored by any given ministry. This is the purpose of the present paper, wherein it is attempted to trace the Western policy of the ministry from the autumn of 1763 to the autumn of 1768.

THREE PERIODS OF POLICY MAKING

The period which has been selected begins with a definite act on the part of the ministry; namely, the proclamation of 1763, wherein is formulated for the first time the policy proposed to be followed towards the West. The intermediate time is one of constantly changing or inchoate ministries, when the West as such received very slight attention, so that it is most difficult to determine what was the attitude of the ministerial party at any given time. The period ends with the treaty of Fort Stanwix, in 1768, which is the first definitive action taken after the proclamation. Our subject narrows itself down, therefore, to tracing the relation between these two acts, the Proclamation of 1763 and the Treaty of Fort Stanwix. The management of Indian affairs during the previous years had been so badly conducted by the several colonies, that the natives were being continually exasperated, until they broke out in the uprising known in history as Pontiac's War.

PURPOSE OF THE PROCLAMATION

The particular grievances of the Indians were, the irregular practices of the traders, and the illegal encroachments on their lands by the colonists. After a careful examination of the conditions, the British ministry determined that the only means of maintaining justice in their relation with the native tribes, was to centralize the management directly under the imperial government. This was the purpose of the proclamation. The policy formulated at that time, as far as it interests the argument of this paper, may be divided under the following headings:

First. There should be established a boundary between the lands that may be settled by white men and those reserved for the Indians.

Second. The land reserved for the Indians should be opened up for future colonization only through purchase by the crown.

Third. Regulations for the Indian trade should be made in the future.

Two of these subjects require some further notice. On account of the outbreak of Pontiac's War, the ministry felt the necessity of determining immediately a temporary boundary line in order to reassure the Indians. Therefore, the line of the Appalachian divide was chosen; but this was to be replaced, as soon as peace with the Indians was secured, by a line farther to the westward, which should include the already partially-settled lands of the upper Ohio region. The neglect to do this, was the cause of many disturbances on the frontier, caused by speculators and settlers pushing westward in anticipation of the ministerial action.

The ministerial policy in regard to future settlements beyond this Indian boundary line, is not so easy to determine. Lord Shelburne was responsible for the wording of these passages concerning Indian affairs, and there can be no doubt but that he, like his friend Benjamin Franklin, anticipated a time when colonies would be planted as far west as the Mississippi. As far as our scanty evidence shows, his colleagues agreed with him in this; but this subject became, in the period under consideration, the one concerning which there was the greatest disagreement among the ministers. Should the policy of westward expansion be decided upon, it would be necessary to establish western boundaries for several colonies, such as Virginia, the Carolinas, and Georgia, which claimed the West on account of their sea-to-sea charters, and any action directed to that end was likely to arouse protests from the Americans. This policy was frequently contemplated, and at times apparently adopted, by the ministry; but positive and final action was deferred till the outbreak of the Revolutionary War, which brought all negotiations to an end.

BOARD OF TRADE

After the resignation of Lord Shelburne from the presidency of the Board of Trade, in early September, 1763, his place was filled by Lord Hillsborough, who enjoyed the favor of the Bedford faction. The new president had had no experience in colonial affairs, and, since the situation on the frontiers was critical, he adopted the proclamation already partially written by Lord Shelburne; and this was issued on October 7,

1763. The policy announced at this time remained, practically unchanged, as the ministerial policy for over four years.*

Before 1768, Lord Hillsborough did not, except in minor details, oppose the plan for the West formulated by his predecessor. This is true also of those who succeeded him as president of the Board of Trade, and of those who held the more important position of secretary of state for the Southern department, the office that had general charge of colonial affairs.

The principal duty in regard to Western affairs that remained for Lord Hillsborough, was to carry out two lines of policy that had already been determined. These were to draw up the regulations for the Indian trade, and to establish by treaty with the Indians the boundary line west of the Alleghanies. On account of the unsettled condition of the Indians due to the war, Lord Hillsborough was unable, before he was superseded, to take up this latter subject, although he kept it constantly in mind. The new president of the Board of Trade undertook, however, to work out the regulations of trade. In this he was ably assisted by the Indian agent, Sir William Johnson, and others, who kept up a continuous correspondence with him concerning the subject.

REGULATION OF INDIAN TRADE

The result of these efforts, was a plan for the future management of the Indian trade, that was submitted to Johnson and others for criticism on July 10, 1764. The plan contemplated the complete centralization of Indian affairs. The representatives of the British government were to be two superintendents, one for the Northern department and one for the Southern, under each of whom were deputy agents, commissaries, and other minor officials. All relations with the Indians were to be conducted through these officers.

* The administration of colonial affairs was complicated by the exercise of power by both the secretary of state for the Southern department and the Board of Trade, who were not always in agreement concerning policies. During the period under discussion three methods of unifying the administration were tried. From 1757 to 1766, the president of the Board of Trade was generally given a seat in the ministry, where he could defend the recommendations of himself and his colleagues. In July, 1766, at the coming into power of the Chatham ministry, the Board of Trade gave up all its executive functions to the secretary of state for the Southern department, so that one man became responsible for all colonial policies. In January, 1768, another step was taken toward unification, when the new secretaryship of state for the colonies was created. Shortly after that, this secretary became president of the Board of Trade also.

For the maintenance of justice among the traders and Indians, the deputy agents and commissaries were, in civil and criminal cases, to be granted the judicial power of justices of the peace; and the right of appeal to the superintendents, in major cases, was reserved to all pleaders in the courts. Trade was to be permitted only at designated posts, where commissaries were to be stationed. That the Lords of Trade had in mind the prevention of some of the evils from which the Indian trade had suffered under the previous management of the colonies, is shown by the articles prohibiting the sale of liquors to the Indians and the one fixing the price of goods. The last articles dealt with the boundary which was still to be established, and prove that the Board of Trade intended to follow the policy of Shelburne in this matter.

This plan for the management of trade was, in the course of time, submitted to many persons for criticism. Sir William Johnson approved the spirit of the plan, and criticised only a few articles. His acceptance of the plan as a whole might have been anticipated, as the Board of Trade had followed almost exclusively the recommendations which he had made during the past years. The criticisms of Lieutenant Governor Colden of New York and those of Colonel Bradstreet were also distinctly favorable. A few years later Lord Shelburne asked Benjamin Franklin for his opinion. He answered: "The regulations in this plan seem to me in general very good." He then proceeded to make a few criticisms of several details, such as fixing prices and the prohibition of the sale of liquor.

The Grenville ministry adopted the plan, but since the maintenance of the proposed establishment would be expensive, and the principle of the ministry was economy, it was proposed by the Lords of Trade to lay a tax on the Indian trade for the support of the Indian government. This required an act of parliament, but the subject was never pushed; and later the outcry of the colonists against the stamp act made such action appear inexpedient.

ROCKINGHAM MINISTRY

In July, 1765, the Grenvilles yielded to the Rockingham ministry. This was the only true party ministry of the period. It was composed of representatives of the old line Whigs, who were distinctly favorable to the American colonies. The attention of the ministry during its year of life was so occupied with undoing the acts of its pred-

CHRISTIAN
LIBERTY
"READY TO
PASS TO THE
AMERICAN
STRAND"

ecessor, such as the stamp act, the cider act, etc., that the question of the West never became a live issue. That the ministry was in favor of a liberal policy, is proved by the offer of the presidency of the Board of Trade to Lord Shelburne, but this he refused. Conway became secretary of state for the Southern department; after Shelburne's refusal, the presidency of the Board of Trade was given to Lord Dartmouth; and the personnel of the board was taken over from the previous ministry almost without change. Although there is no act of these men during this year to indicate their attitude toward the West, their later acts and letters show that they were ready to accept the policy that had been so ably formulated by Lord Shelburne in the Proclamation of 1763. This is as much as can be said concerning the Western policy of the Rockingham ministry.

EARL OF CHATHAM

In July, 1766, the newly-created Earl of Chatham came into office again and formed his "broad bottom ministry," which included representatives from as many factions as was possible. Chatham brought into the ministry only four of his immediate followers, among whom was Shelburne. He was made secretary of state for the Southern department, and was granted liberty to carry out his American policy.

It is surprising to find Lord Hillsborough accepting the position of president of the Board of Trade under Shelburne. In a letter to George Grenville, Hillsborough explained that the position as it was offered to him by the minister carried with it a seat in the cabinet; but that he refused the presidency unless the board was made a committee for report only, and was relieved of all the executive functions that had been acquired during the last decade. The letter contains many insinuations against an unnamed person, who can only be Lord Shelburne; but the fact remains that Shelburne made the offer, and Hillsborough accepted the post on condition that Shelburne assume all executive duties, and thus have a free hand to carry out his American policy. Hillsborough did this in the year 1766—Hillsborough, who has been regarded as a constant opponent of the expansion of the colonies westward.

The explanation is to be found in the fact that since the year 1763, the question of the West had not been a live issue, and that while Hillsborough was president of the Board of Trade, he had shown his willingness to carry out Shelburne's policy, as far as action was needed at the time.

In 1766, therefore, there was no means for either to know that they would differ radically when the West should again enter the horizon of ministerial policy. As far as the trouble in the seaboard colonies was concerned, it is apparent that Hillsborough was willing to give Shelburne every opportunity. Within two years the two men were to discover that they differed on many questions; but before that time, Hillsborough had resigned his subordinate position in order to enter upon other duties. This occurred in December, 1766. Lord Clare accepted his place on the Board of Trade, and he also appears to have been ready to follow rather than to lead.

Never was there a weaker ministry than this one of the Earl of Chatham's. Before the end of the year, Chatham himself withdrew, on account of illness, from active participation in affairs, and left to Grafton and Conway the guidance of the ministry. But his deputies constantly feared to assume responsibility for action without consulting their chief, who almost as constantly denied them access to his presence. Shelburne was not on friendly terms with his colleagues, was frequently absent from meetings, and would have willingly resigned had he not regarded himself as Chatham's personal representative. It was hardly to be expected that definitive action would come from such a jellyfish body; yet it was this ministry that was to take the first step toward the completion of the policy of 1763.

You will recall that I grouped this policy under three headings: first, the establishment of an Indian boundary line west of the Alleghanies; second, the purchase of territory west of this line for the purpose of colonization; and third, the announcement of regulations for the Indian trade. Nothing had been done towards carrying out any of these provisions. It is not surprising, therefore, that the father of the policy, Lord Shelburne, should urge the ministry to action.

AFFAIRS IN AMERICA

Before following Shelburne's career, it will be necessary to take a hasty glance at affairs in America, so that we may follow the sequence of events. Since 1763 settlers had been crowding across the mountains, which were still the boundary line, and settling in the upper Ohio valley. The settlement at Pittsburg was already called a town, and pioneers were finding their way down the river in the search of fertile fields, thus invading territory where the Indian titles had not yet been purchased by the crown. Although the ministry had fully intended that this territory should be opened for settlement, the delay in establishing the proposed boundary line made the action of the frontiersmen distinctly illegal, and contrary to solemn pledges given to the Indians. In spite of the exertions of Sir William Johnson, and because of the failure to proclaim the needed regulations of the trade, the Indians were as systematically and regularly cheated as under the former rule of the colonies. For both these causes Indian outbreaks occurred, settlers and traders were killed, and a general Indian war was imminent, so that it was time that the ministry should act.

At the same time pressure was being brought by Americans upon the ministry, to fulfill the implied policy of the famous proclamation and to open up to colonization wide stretches of land west of the proposed boundary. As early as 1762, General Amherst urged the erection of a colony around Detroit. In the spring of 1763 some Virginians, among whom the Washingtons and Lees were conspicuous, formed the Mississippi Company for the purpose of establishing a settlement on that great Western river. George Croghan wrote from London, in 1764, that there was talk of a colony in the Illinois country, and that he was recommending to the ministry such an undertaking. At about the same time General Lyman went to London to promote his scheme of a settlement on the lower Mississippi. In 1766 some Philadelphia merchants, having learned of the possibility of a colony in the Illinois, associated with themselves Governor Franklin and Sir William Johnson in a company to take up a large tract of land in that region. Benjamin Franklin was made a member of the company, and was appointed its representative in London, where it might be expected that his friendship with Lord Shelburne would give him an advantage over his competitors for ministerial favors.

SHELBURNE'S WESTERN POLICY

Moved by the petitions and letters of these interested parties, Lord Shelburne began in the fall of 1767 to put into execution his comprehensive plan for the West. The first subject to receive his attention was that of the boundary line, concerning which he had received letters from General Gage, Sir William Johnson, and others. How unimportant this whole subject had been deemed by the ministry during the last few years, is shown by the fact that the letters from the Indian superintendents, announcing that arrangements

were already made with the Indians to cede the required territory, had been mislaid; and it was only after diligent search that they were found.

The actual urgency of the case, for an Indian war was threatening, compelled the Board of Trade, on December 23, 1767, to agree with Shelburne in recommending that the line should immediately be established; and orders were sent to America to that effect. By a series of treaties —the one at Fort Stanwix with the Iroquois, and that of Lochabar, in 1770, with the Southern Indians, being the most important—a continuous boundary line was run from the Great Lakes, back of the Appalachians, around the coast of Florida, and through the southern part of the East and West Floridas, almost to the Mississippi River. Thus, in accordance with the policy intended at the time of the Proclamation of 1763, a large extent of territory was opened up to immediate settlement, the most important part of which lay south of the Ohio and extended westward to the Great Kanawha.

To understand Shelburne's plans for Indian management and the erection of colonies within the Indian reservation, the financial situation in England must be kept in mind. The ministry had been greatly embarrassed by the success of the opposition in cutting down the British land tax from four to three shillings in the pound. The consequence of this was, a demand upon all departments for economy, and a desire to find revenue from other sources. Charles Townshend, the chancellor of the exchequer, proposed to the ministry his famous duties on imports into the American colonies, in order to compensate somewhat for this loss of income.

This proposal called from Shelburne a letter to Chatham, dated February 1, 1767, in which he briefly outlined his plans for raising a revenue in America. "I have always thought," he wrote, "the quit rents may be so managed, without having too great a retrospect, as to produce a certain sum; and I have likewise had reason to think that such a new method of granting lands might be devised, under the direction of my Lord President, as might give infinite satisfaction to America, contribute to the ascertaining property, preventing future suits at law, and in great measure prevent the Indian disturbances, and besides all, incidentally produce a certain revenue, without its being the object." During the summer, these ideas assumed more concrete form, and led to direct proposals. His plan and reasons are set forth in the following quotable words in a letter to General Gage on November 14, 1767:

CHRISTIAN
LIBERTY
"READY TO
PASS TO THE
AMERICAN
STRAND"

"The enormous expence attending the present method of employing the Troops cantoned in the back settlements and frontier posts of North America with the heavy contingent charges arising from the transportation of Stores, and the danger to which the discipline of the army is exposed to by the regiments being broken into small detachments, have all been very often and very justly represented in your letters. To remedy these evils no measure seems to bid fairer than one, which by establishing Governments where provisions and necessaries may be furnished on the spot, will render half the posts now kept up unnecessary, while the remainder may be partly transferred to the care of the several Provinces, and partly maintained at a much less expence. The illicit Trade with the French and Spaniards will be intercepted by our Traders in their passage; the Indians will be prevented from incursions into the back settlements, precise and definite boundaries will be put to the old Colonies; the Trade and Manufactures of Great Britain will be extended into the remotest Indian Nations; and such posts only will require to be garrisoned as command the different Indian communications or the intercourse between His Majesty's different Colonies by the great Rivers and Lakes."

These were the ideas that inspired Shelburne's communication of October 5, 1767, to the Board of Trade, wherein he outlined the scope of his Western policy. He pointed out that the present method of managing Indian affairs was very expensive, and that, if the plan proposed by Lord Hillsborough in 1764 were now put into execution, this expense would be increased; and he intimated that the colonials were better able to manage these delicate matters than a ministry unfamiliar with the nature of the Indians. He recommended, therefore, that the British Government renounce the attempt to centralize the management of the Indian trade, and place it in the control of the colonies, as was the case a decade before.

His other recommendation reminds us of Franklin's plan to cut up the whole West into colonies. Shelburne desired that three new colonies be formed at this time: one at the mouth of the Ohio, one at Detroit, and the third at the Illinois. This plan proposed the immediate purchase from the Indians of territory west of the boundary line, which was according to Shelburne's plan to be made the western boundary of the Eastern colonies. The policy received the support of Secretary Conway, and it was expected that the members of the Board of Trade could be persuaded to recommend it. Before the Board of Trade could make any recommendation concerning these proposals, changes in the ministry occurred, which withdrew the management of colonial affairs from Shelburne's hands.

For many months negotiations had been conducted by the Duke of Grafton, who was selected as head of the proposed new combination, although the Earl of Chatham still retained his position in the ministry. After the failure to secure the cooperation of other factions, Grafton determined to unite with the Bedfords, in spite of their known hostility to the American colonies. For two reasons it was determined to divide the secretaryship of state for the Southern department: first, because the duties were too many to be properly performed by one man, particularly since colonial affairs had become so important; and secondly, in order to create a new position in the cabinet for a friend of the Bedfords. The division of the secretaryship into that of the Southern department and that of the American colonies was not a new proposal, for it had been discussed by the two previous ministries.

This decision affected Shelburne's department, and the negotiations throw some light on the attitude of his colleagues toward his colonial policy. The Bedfords, who believed in coercive measures towards the colonies, desired that Shelburne should retain the Southern department and leave to them the American affairs. But this did not please the Duke of Grafton, who urged Shelburne to take charge of the new department; because, he said, "the Bedfords cannot be trusted with it, on account of different principles" and because he (Grafton) was well pleased with Shelburne's administration. Shelburne, however, preferred to retain charge of European affairs, unless he received from the Earl of Chatham an order to the contrary. On account of ill health, Chatham made no sign. The negotiations ended, therefore, according to the wish of Shelburne and the Bedfords; and Lord Hillsborough was appointed secretary of state for the colonies. The policies pursued toward the West for the next few years, may be regarded as his.

LORD HILLSBOROUGH, SECRETARY OF STATE

Little is known as to what Hillsborough's exact attitude was, at the time of his appointment, towards the various American problems. We have already seen that he had twice held the presidency of the Board of Trade, but on neither occasion had developed any decided policy. As far as the West was concerned, he had been ready to carry out Lord Shelburne's plans. So far were his ideas unknown, that there was talk of making Benjamin

Franklin his under-secretary, to assist him in building up the new department. Although Franklin put no faith in the ministerial talk, he was very uncertain in regard to Hillsborough's plans and did not regard him "in general an enemy to America." It is probable that the choice of Hillsborough was made because he was not pledged to violent measures toward the American colonies, as were the intimate friends of the Duke of Bedford.

Lord Shelburne's letter of October 5th to the Board of Trade had forced the issue of the West upon the ministry. The object of Shelburne's plan had been so concealed in the proclamation of 1763 that few had understood it; but now its full scope was disclosed, and a careful consideration and a decision thereon was expected from the ministry.

The question of the management of the trade was financial in character and, since economy was the talk of all ministers, the recommendation to transfer the burden of this department of Indian affairs to the colonies met with no opposition. The utility of erecting colonies in the far West was, however, open to dispute, at least it so appeared to many men of that time. To them such a course seemed of little commercial value to the mother country, since the new colonies would be situated so far from the sea-coast; it would be likely to arouse another Indian war, at a time that it was expected the boundary lines would satisfy the Indians; it did not appear necessary, so long as the colonies remained uncrowded; it would destroy the fur-trade, which had not proved as valuable as was anticipated in 1763; finally, the expense of such enterprises would be great.

The answer of the Board of Trade to Lord Shelburne's recommendations, dated March 7, 1768, was undoubtedly inspired by Lord Hillsborough. There was substantial agreement with the recommendation concerning the transference of the management of the trade to the colonies; but the lords of trade did not think it wise to abolish altogether the offices of superintendents of the Indians, since there were several functions that could best be executed by the British government—such as the purchase of land, the making of treaties, and general oversight over the interests of the Indians. It was, therefore, determined to continue these offices.

The Board of Trade did not misunderstand the significance of Shelburne's policy concerning colonies in the far West. They wrote:

"The Proposition of forming inland Colonies in America is, we humbly conceive, entirely new; it adopts principles in respect to American Settlement different from what has hitherto been the policy of this Kingdom; and leads to a system which if pursued through all its consequences, is in the present state of this Country of the greatest importance."

The scope of this new policy was revealed to them by the arguments advanced "by the authors of the proposals themselves," to be nothing less than "the entire possession and peopling of all the Country which has Communication with the Rivers Mississippi and St. Lawrence." This was the issue before the Board of Trade and the new secretary of the colonies. After setting forth the reasons, which have already been indicated, the report opposed the recommendation of Lord Shelburne, and his broad-gauged policy was rejected.

It would be a mistake to interpret this action as indicating a final purpose on the part of the ministry to maintain a large Indian reservation in the heart of America. Two years later, Lord Hillsborough was still in doubt in regard to the final disposition of this vast West. In a most illuminating letter to General Gage, in which the secretary exposes his most secret thoughts, he writes:

"The commercial advantages which may be derived from these possessions and the near relation they bear to the safety and security of His Majesty's North American Dominions in general under them are an object deserving the most serious attention but the great difficulty lies in suggesting a proper plan for the improvement of them to these ends that will not either be attended with an Expense too heavy for the State to bear, or otherwise liable to very great objections."

After stating the arguments for and against posts and colonies west of the Indian boundary line, he sums up his own state of mind in these words:

"In the meantime from what I have said you will see, that though I am fully aware of the propriety of some possession on the Mississippi that should have the effect to secure the Commerce and mark the Dominion of the Country which belongs to his Majesty on the East side of it; yet nevertheless the only two methods of obtaining this object are each of them accompanied with such objections as leave my judgement in a state of perplexity I am not able to get over."

In closing it is necessary to call attention to the difficulties confronting the ministry over the disposal of the land on the south of the Ohio and outside of Pennsylvania, that had been opened up for colonization by the establishment of the Indian

CHRISTIAN
LIBERTY
"READY TO
PASS TO THE
AMERICAN
STRAND"

boundary line. According to the opinion of the Board of Trade, this belonged to Virginia by her charter rights; and already surveys had been made there for the Virginia soldiers of the French and Indian War. There were, however, other possible means of disposing of it. The old Ohio Company began immediately to put forth its claims. The merchants, who had suffered during the Pontiac War, and had been reimbursed by a concession of land by the Indians at the treaty of Fort Stanwix, also set forth their claims. The Mississippi Company, of Virginia, having failed to obtain territory for the establishment of a colony on the Mississippi, applied for territory in this region. The Philadelphia merchants associated with Benjamin Franklin, Governor Franklin, and Sir William Johnson, immediately formed a new company, known by the name of the Walpole Company, and desired permission to establish a colony there also.

Here were, indeed, a plenty of claimants. But among them all, Lord Hillsborough and his colleagues favored the Philadelphians and gave them every encouragement. Several reasons for the establishment of a new colony in this corner of the West appealed to the ministry. It would promote law and order among the disorderly crowd of the frontier; it would prevent encroachments on the Indian lands; it would settle once for all the question of the western boundaries of the seaboard colonies. Therefore the ministry, under the influence of Hillsborough, were ready to promote such an establishment.

In the next few years, the disposal of this land on the upper Ohio became one of the paramount issues in the Western policy of the ministry. Conditions then arose that made Hillsborough change his mind; and he wrote his famous report opposing all colonies west of the Alleghanies, which has misled so many into believing that he and all ministries of which he was a member were at all times opposed to westward expansion.

THE IROQUOIS IN THE REVOLUTION

*George H.
Harris,*
Rochester
Historical
Society, Vol.
VIII, 1929

When the white man first entered the present State of New York, a Confederacy of Indian Nations occupied the greater part of its territory.

For mutual convenience and protection they lived in communities, the members of a clan occupying one house; each family had, perhaps, its own apartment and fire, but when a new family desired a habitation, one end of the common building was extended for its use. These structures varied in length from forty to two hundred and fifty feet and contained from four to twenty fires. This form of dwelling was called Ga-no'-sote, or Longhouse, in contradistinction to the smaller dwellings or huts used by surrounding tribes; the peoples of these nations called themselves Ho-de'-no-sau-nee, or "People of the Longhouse."

The Confederacy consisted of Five Nations bearing the following descriptive titles: Gä-ne-ä'-ga-o-no' or, People Possessors of the Flint; O-nun'-dä-ga-o-no', or People on the Hills; Nun-da'-wä-o-no', or Great Hill People; O-na'-yote-kä-o-no', or Granite People; Gwe-u'-gweh-o-no', or People at the Mucky Land.

In 1680, they were called by the French Goyogouens, Onnontagués, Onneiouts, Agniés,

Sonnontouans. The modern English names are Cayugas, Onondagas, Oneidas, Mohawks, and Senecas. They spoke dialects of the ancient Huron language, and were united by ties of blood and governed by a council of Sachems chosen by the several nations, yet each nation had distinct geographical bounds, and an independent existence. The Mohawks lived between the Mohawk and Hudson Rivers; the Oneidas, west of the Mohawks; the Onondagas, beyond the Oneidas, the Cayugas, westward to Seneca Lake, while the Senecas claimed the national territory west of the Cayugas.

The Mohawk River and Lakes Oneida, Onondaga, Cayuga and Seneca were included within the limits of the respective nations bearing those names.

These nations likened their domains to a Long House covering its outmost limits; its eastern door at the Hudson, its western at the Genesee. Each nation was sheltered within its boundaries, even as were the families within its clan dwelling; hence they called their country Ho-de'-no-sau-nee-ga, or "Territory of the People of the Long House."

The French termed these people Iroquois; the

Baronial home of Sir William Johnson (1715-1774),
British superintendent of Indian affairs in New York.

In the year 1762, Sir William began the building of
Johnson Hall at Johnstown. This was the beginning of
the first settlement of importance in this area. Johnson
was born in Ireland and came to America in 1738 to
be superintendent of an estate on the south side of the
Mohawk River east of the present city of Amsterdam,
which had been purchased as a speculation by his
uncle, Sir Peter Warren. In 1742, Johnson moved
across the river to go into business for himself and
built Fort Johnson in 1749, still standing. From here he
marched with Indian troops to Lake George to engage
the French where he won the battle of that name,
September 8, 1755. As a result of this victory, the
crown made him a baronet of the hereditary class and
he was henceforth known as Sir William. In addition
to his title, he was given five thousand pounds and an
annual salary of six hundred pounds as Superintendent
of Indian Affairs in North America. Being cramped
for room and expansion in his desire to become a
landed proprietor, he decided to make his future home
on the Kingsborough Patent and the site of Johnstown,
the center of his large estate.

Dutch, Maguas; and the English, the Five Nations.

The Iroquois extended their territory by conquest until they claimed the country from the Hudson, west to Lake Huron, and from Lake Ontario to the Tennessee.

About 1715, the Dus-ga′-o-weh-o-no′, or Shirt Wearing People, known as Tuscaroras, were driven out of North Carolina, and were permitted by the Iroquois to settle between the Onondagas and Oneidas, on Oneida territory. Thereafter the Confederacy was known as the "Six Nations of the Iroquois."

England and France long disputed the right to govern the Iroquois territory. England pushed slowly from the Atlantic seaboard westward, and France, firmly seated in Canada, struggled to extend its domain to the Gulf of Mexico. Each tried to frustrate the other in occupation by erecting forts upon the Great Lakes and principal streams. The Iroquois, east of Canandaigua Lake, were the allies of the English; while those west inclined to the French.

The French and Indian War continued ten years until, in 1763, France, at the Treaty of Paris, relinquished her claim to Iroquois soil, and England assumed the right of jurisdiction.

During a treaty held at Johnson Hall in April, 1764, the English recognized the title of the Iroquois to all lands claimed by them in the Colony of New York, excepting a strip six miles wide along the Niagara reserved for government uses, with possession and control of the St. Lawrence and Niagara Rivers, the Great Lakes, and the continued occupation of Forts Oswego and Niagara.

November 5, 1768, a definite line of separation between the white and red men was fixed by formal agreement between the British Crown and Colonies, and the Sachems of the Six Nations. This boundary was intended to be permanent, and was known as, "The Line of Property."

Guy Johnson's map of 1771 located the line of property, according to the treaty of 1768, and shows the principal Indian Trails of that day, though minor trails followed the lesser streams affording communication to the main trails from the Great Lakes to the Susquehanna, and the Ocean.

A later continuation carried the Line of Property to the northward along the eastern border of the Oneida lands to the present village of Clayton, on the St. Lawrence. Although the French and English had long navigated the Great Lakes and built a line of military forts and trading posts from Quebec to the Mississippi, the interior of the Iroquois country west of the Line of Property, at the opening of the Revolution, had never been surveyed and thoroughly explored by the white man.

About 1735, William Johnson came from Ireland to the Mohawk Valley as agent for his uncle, Admiral Sir Peter Warren. In 1740, he built a residence three miles above the present city of Amsterdam, but later, settled at Johnstown. Through the influence of his uncle he became British Agent of Indian Affairs. He associated familiarly with the Mohawks, assumed their dress and customs, took for his second wife an Indian girl, Molly Brant, and through force of will and official position acquired a powerful influence over the Six Nations. He accumulated a large estate, was commissioned Major-General, and in 1757, was made a Baron, thereafter being known as Sir William Johnson. After his death in 1774, he was succeeded in his title and estate by his son, Sir John Johnson.

The department of British Indian Affairs was organized with Guy Johnson, a nephew and son-in-law; Daniel Claus, also son-in-law of Sir William. John Butler, as Deputy Superintendent; and Joseph Chew, Secretary. These men were influential citizens of the Mohawk division of Tryon County, a tract in which were included the settlements west and south of Schenectady.

At the beginning of the Revolution, these men adhered to the English Crown and employed every means at their command to secure the Indians within the reach of their influence in the interest of the King. They were aided in their efforts by Thayendanegea, Joseph Brant, a brother of Molly Brant. By the generosity of Sir William Johnson he had been sent to England and educated, and at the time of Sir William's death, had an important standing among his own people, the Canajoharie Mohawks.

The Indians did not respond to the English as they desired. Congress tried to induce them to remain neutral during the impending conflict. With few exceptions the Brothertowns, Tuscaroras, and scattering members of the other tribes, through the influence of Rev. Samson Occum, an educated Indian, and the Rev. Samuel Kirkland, Oneida missionary, continued friendly to the Americans. Little Abraham, Chief of the Lower Castle, of the Mohawks, refused to join the English, and the Johnson faction recognized Joseph Brant as the War Chief of the nation.

313

CHRISTIAN
LIBERTY
"READY TO
PASS TO THE
AMERICAN
STRAND"

The loyalists of the Mohawk Valley, becoming convinced of the strength and unity of the American Colonies, Guy Johnson sent messages to the Six Nations calling a council at Oswego. He left Johnstown in May, 1775, with a body of armed white men and a band of Mohawks under Brant, and reached Ontario, June 17. A few days later, he held a conference with some fourteen hundred Indians, who, according to his official report, agreed to enter the service of the King; the Indians themselves reported that Johnson simply requested them not to take part in the coming war. From Oswego, Johnson went to Montreal and established his Mohawks in camp on the Island.

Sir Guy Carlton, commanding the British forces, pledged his word to Joseph Brant that if the Mohawks would abandon their homes and join the forces of the King, at the close of the war, they should be restored to their former condition. His pledge was accepted, the Mohawks became wanderers, and soon after, Brant led his followers against his former friends in New York.

Sir John Johnson continued to reside at Johnstown, and on December 9, 1775, Congress advised the Tryon County Committee not to molest him as long as he remained inactive, but Sir John was then secretly organizing a band of royalists and Indians for the King's service; he gathered about him a large number of loyalists, and in other ways manifested his intention to defeat the plans of Congress; therefore, in January, 1776, General Schuyler placed him under arrest.

A MEMORIAL CONCERNING THE IROQUOIS, &C

*The
Documentary
History of the
State of New
York*, Vol. IV,
Albany, 1851

TO THE READER

In the year 1770, the Rev. Charles Inglis, then assistant minister of Trinity Church, New-York, paid a visit to Sir Wm. Johnson. His interest in the spiritual and moral wants of the Six Nations was, it would seem, then awakened, and the result was, the present "Memorial concerning the Iroquois," which having been "copied out fair in a good Hand, and in a quarto size, and having a Marble cover, with Col. Johnson's accurate and neat Map prefixed, made a handsome looking Pamphlet," (*Ante,* 468.) and was sent in 1771, to Lord Hillsborough, then Secretary of State, with recommendations from Gov. Tryon and Sir Wm. Johnson. . . .

My Lord,

The Iroquois, or Five Confederate Nations of Indians distinguished and known by that name, are settled on the frontier of the Province of New-York. From the first reduction of this Province by the British arms, they entered into a strict alliance with the English, which they have always inviolably observed. . . .

Those Nations, ever since their union in a league of confederacy, were greatly superior in courage and military skill to the other savages of North America. From that period, which commenced before we had any knowledge of this Province, they have been the terror of all the neighboring tribes, most of which they have subdued; some they have entirely extirpated. The spirit of conquest carried them far beyond the limits of their own native districts. They have extended their empire over a tract of country twelve hundred miles in length, from north to south, and six hundred in breadth, from east to west.

Their alliance with the English naturally led them to take part with us when at war with France. The French have often severely felt the power of their arms. The Iroquois have more than once defeated the united forces of the French, and their confederate Indians, and have carried fire and sword into the very heart of their settlements, threatening them with utter ruin. They formed a barrier along our frontiers against the French and the savages in their interest; and by this protection, and the lucrative trade we carried on with them, they greatly contributed to raise this Province to its present flourishing state.

THE MOHAWKS OF THE FIVE CONFEDERATE
NATIONS BROUGHT TO CHRISTIANITY

The Five Confederate Nations are the Mohawks, the Oneidas, the Onondagas, the Cayugas and the Senekas. To these may be added the Tuscaroras, who moved some years ago from the south, were taken into the confederacy, and in-

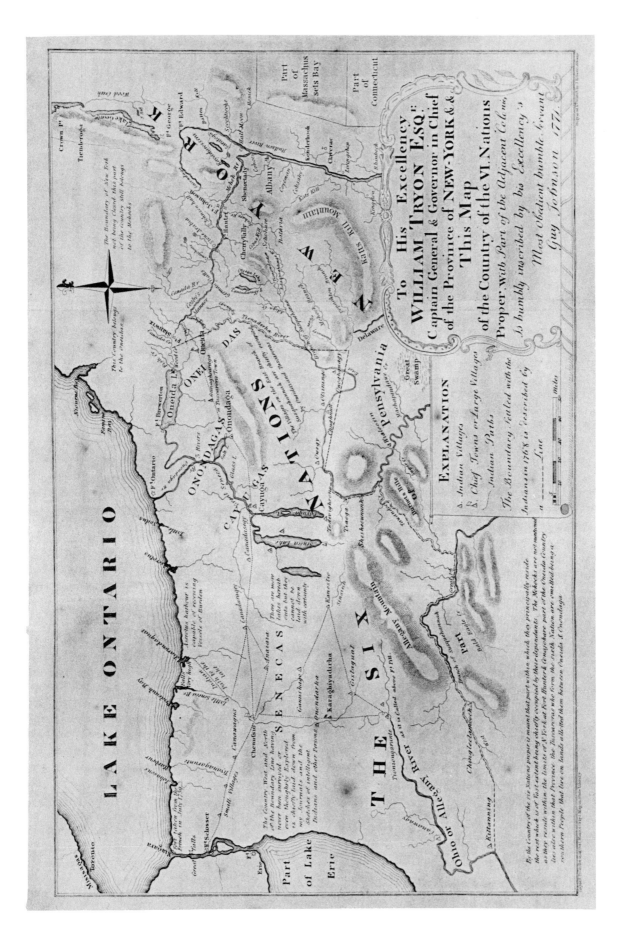

AREA MAP OF THE STATE OF NEW YORK, 1771

SHOWING THE EXTENSIVE TERRITORY HELD BY THE IROQUOIS CONFEDERACY UP TO THE TIME OF THE REVOLUTIONARY WAR.

From *Documentary History of New York*, Vol. I, 1849

CHRISTIAN
LIBERTY
"READY TO
PASS TO THE
AMERICAN
STRAND"

corporated with the Five Nations. The continual wars in which the Iroquois have been engaged, have considerably reduced their number from what it was formerly. This is particularly the case of the Mohawks. They, by their wisdom in council and bravery in the field, had gained an ascendancy over the other tribes which they preserve to this day. In all deliberations which relate to the common interest of the confederacy, and in the execution of every enterprise, the Mohawks generally take the lead. Being situated the most easterly, and consequently the nearest to our first settlements, of any of the Five Nations, the missionaries sent by the Society for the Propagation of the Gospel in foreign Parts, to convert the Indians of this Province, resided among them. The labors of those missionaries were attended with such success, that in time the whole nation was brought over to christianity.

This attached the Mohawks more firmly to us. They always stood forth our faithful allies, especially in the late war, though in the course of it, the greater part of their bravest warriors perished. Our victories were often purchased at the expense of their blood, for they were among the first in almost every danger.

The Mohawks have three villages—Schoare, Fort Hunter, and Canajohare. These are all within the English settlements, and contain four hundred and twenty souls. Fort Hunter, the central village, where a missionary from the Society now resides, is distant from Albany forty miles. The Oneidas are situated eighty miles west from the Mohawks, somewhat beyond our settlements, and have two villages containing six hundred souls. Many of the Oneidas profess christianity, being instructed partly by French Jesuits, partly by a dissenting teacher, lately sent among them, but chiefly by the Society's missionaries to the Mohawks. Next to the Oneidas are the Onondagas, at the distance of forty miles westerly; their number is eight hundred. The Cayugas, amounting to one thousand and forty, are forty miles southwest of the Onondagas. The Senekas, forty miles northwest of the Cayugas, are in number four thousand, dispersed in several villages; and the Tuscaroras amount to one thousand. Very few of the four tribes last mentioned have any impressions of christianity.

The extensive country, inhabited by all these Indians, is open, healthy, and in general extremely fertile. It is watered by several rivers navigable for battoes, which are very advantageous to commerce, as there are only a few miles of land carriage from Albany to Oswego on Lake Ontario. These Nations are able to bring two thousand fighting men, at least, into the field.

Such a multitude of people, if reduced to order and civil life, and attached to us by ties of religion, would evidently be a great acquisition to the community. To effect this must therefore be the wish of every Friend to the State; and I flatter myself with your Lordship's indulgence whilst attempting to point out a method by which it may be accomplished, especially as I conceive it to be a duty owing to His Majesty and to the public.

CIVIL EFFECTS OF CHRISTIANITY

Manners are the result of principles. The former naturally flow from, and are regulated by, the latter. Hence we find that Barbarity and brutal vices, such as are pernicious to mankind, have always been the portion of ignorant nations; and that Virtue and the polished manners of social life, have distinguished those who were enlightened with knowledge. In order to civilise the Iroquois, it is necessary to begin with instructing them, especially in the principles of Religion. Christianity is well adapted to this purpose. Whilst it has a more immediate and important end in view, which equally concerns all; it insensibly forms moral habits, corrects irregularities, and disposes the mind to submit to the restraints of government and laws; without giving any alarm to the Savages, who are extremely jealous of their liberty, and wedded to their present mode of life.

I shall not consider this subject in a religious view, nor adduce theological arguments for undertaking the Conversion of the Savages. I shall confine myself to such as are merely political; and only mention their conversion as being subservient to the purpose of civilising them, and riveting them more firmly to our interest. It may not, however, be improper to observe here, that if we believe there is a God, and a future state of rewards and punishments, if our future happiness or misery depends on our conduct here, if christianity gives the justest notions of the Deity, teaches that worship which is most worthy of Him, as well as the purest morals, and promotes the happiness of States and Individuals— if, I say, we believe all this, certainly humanity should induce us to diffuse the light of Christianity among those poor Savages who have been so faithful and serviceable to us. . . .

A Memorial
Concerning
the Iroquois

MOHAWKS
BROUGHT TO
CHRISTIANITY

The friendship of the Iroquois should be gained and settled on the firmest basis, as it will be of the utmost consequence to us in case of any future attempt by the French on Canada, or any of the other adjoining provinces. Those Indians who have been christianised by the French, are as much attached to them as our converts are to us. This is true even of such of the Iroquois as have been converted to Popery by French priests. . . . It should be further observed, that there are now many French missionaries among the Indians—perhaps as many as ever, and their success, already great, will increase still in proportion to our neglect. They are very careful to preserve their influence over the Indians, by keeping their converts steady in the faith they were taught, and gaining new proselytes. They are busy in sowing the seeds of discontent among the Savages, which they will continue to do as long as they have an intercourse with any part of the Continent, notwithstanding our utmost vigilance to prevent it. The residence of a Popish Bishop in Canada will greatly favour those proceedings. . . .

These reflections will receive additional weight by considering that the Iroquois themselves have often requested Missionaries might be sent to them, and are much dissatisfied at being neglected in matters of religion by the government. They frequently express their dissatisfaction and uneasiness on this head. They are surprised that when the present government supports two Popish Missionaries among Indians who are of another religion, and fought against us during the last war; they who were our friends, who shed their blood in our cause, and profess the same religion, should be passed over and quite neglected. Their surprise is not at all abated by reflecting, as they often do, that the clamorous demands of those popish Indians, accompanied with menaces, proved successful in obtaining Missionaries, whilst their mild and equitable requests to the same purpose have been always rejected. They proceed further to make a comparison between our conduct and that of the French in this respect, which is always to the advantage of the latter, who constantly paid the closest attention to the conversion of the Indians. These things they have sagacity enough to observe. Even those who care little about religion will mention them with warmth, considering all this as the effect of disregard to them, and our neglect of them besides in these matters, gives them a mean opinion of our principles and wisdom. It were needless to say that this disposition will afford great ad-

vantages to the French priests, and procure them a more favorable reception, which they will not fail to improve. Under these circumstances the affection of the Indians will be alienated from us more and more, to which the pomp and ceremonies of the Romish religion, with which the Savages are much captivated, will not a little contribute. The only method that is left to counteract this and prevent the bad consequences that must evidently attend it, is to send Protestant Missionaries among the Iroquois. Establishments of this kind, if properly supported, will be a counterpoise to the advantages those Popish Missionaries possess, and to the assiduity of their endeavors. Hereby those Savages who are yet in the bosom of heathenism, may be brought to the knowledge of Christianity, and preserved from their influence; those more perfectly instructed, who have received some impressions of religion, and the false prejudices they have embibed from Romish priests entirely removed. . . .

Our frontier settlements are extended to a great length; they are defenceless, and open to the incursions of an enemy. Christianising those Indians would not only secure a lasting peace with them, but they would by this means form a barrier to our frontiers against any Indians that are more remote, and might be at war with us. The security of our frontiers would contribute to the quick population of this Province, and among several advantages of which this would be productive, the following is one—that as the lands are held of the crown, and pay quit rents, this branch of his majesty's revenue would be proportionably increased. Our commerce with the Indians would also gain by their conversion. For although it has been alledged by some who knew little of Indian affairs, or thought superficially on the subject, that were the Indians converted to Christianity, and civilized, it would injure our trade with them; yet the reverse of this is evidently true. Indolence, idleness, and intemperance are inseparable concomitants of a savage life. A Savage life also obstructs population. A civilised state, on the contrary, naturally promotes industry, and the increase of mankind. Of course our trade with the Indians would be benefited in proportion as they became more numerous and industrious—the consequence of their being civilised, and brought over to christianity. This reasoning is obvious and just, and supported by experience, which is our surest guide in such matters. The Mohawks, to mention no other instance, are in some measure civilised. They cultivate land, several of them have learned

CHRISTIAN
LIBERTY
"READY TO
PASS TO THE
AMERICAN
STRAND"

trades; all have fixed habitations; they have also cattle of various kinds, many of the conveniences of polished life; are professors of Christianity, and as regular and virtuous in their conduct as the generality of white people. Yet the Mohawks are still alert in hunting, like the other tribes, but surpass them far in point of industry in other respects, and have increased much more in proportion to their number since the late war. . . .

Perhaps it may be thought, that as we are now masters of Canada, and the Indians dependent on us for Ammunition, Arms and Clothing, there is little danger to be apprehended from them, and that this should remove any anxiety for their Conversion or reduction to a civilised State.

I answer, that this opinion seems to be ill-founded from what has been said already; and the Inference made from it, is repugnant to the plain dictates of humanity and good policy. For surely we should not leave those Savages a Prey to Intemperance and the other miseries of their present state, when it is in our power to alter their condition so much for the better. Especially if it be considered that we have been instrumental in multiplying their miseries by teaching them Vices they knew not before, and that the near approach of the English Settlers administers to those Vices, by supplying more readily what will surely instigate the Indians to the perpetration of them. Justice, at least, demands that we should apply an antidote against the Evils we have brought upon them, nor can this be done otherwise than by inculcating Principles which will restrain those Enormities. . . .

PLAN PROPOSED

To ensure success in the execution of any design, much depends on pursuing proper measures. If these are ill-concerted, or not adapted to the end in view, a failure of the whole will probably follow. In attempting to convert and civilise Savages, great attention should be paid to their Situation, Prejudices, Temper, Disposition, and other circumstances. These should be minutely considered, and made as subservient as possible to the general design. Should Government, influenced by the above motives, think fit to engage in this Undertaking with respect to the Iroquois, the following Plan is humbly proposed; in which I shall keep within the strict Bounds of what is practicable, and promises success on the one hand; and avoid any unnecessary expense, as well as what would tend to give Umbrage to the Indians,

on the other. For sake of Order and Perspicuity, I shall range under distinct heads the several parts of this Plan, in which I would propose—

I. That two Missionaries, men of good character, abilities, and prudence, and in the orders of the established Church of England, be sent to the Iroquois, one to reside at Conajohare, the other at the old Oneida Town. Most of the Indians at both these villages have been baptised, and even profess Christianity; all are willing to be further instructed. Each of these Missionaries should have a Salary of £150 sterling a year at least, to enable them to shew some marks of favor to the more deserving Indians, by making small Presents to them from time to time. This will be expected from them, and if judiciously managed, will have a good effect in conciliating the affections of the Indians. If these Missionaries had some knowledge of Physic, so as to be able to assist the Indians in sickness, it would also increase their influence, and make their Spiritual Labors more successful.

II. That a Schoolmaster be fixed at each of those villages, viz: Conajohare, and the old Oneida Town; another at Onondaga; one at the principal village of the Cayugas, and two among the Senekas. These Schoolmasters, for whom admission and protection may be easily procured, should be prudent, and virtuous young men, and such as have had a liberal education. Their business will be to teach the Indians to read and write. They ought also to apply themselves diligently to learn the Indian Language, by which they will be better qualified to act as Missionaries afterwards, should their behaviour and merit entitle them to that office. Schools, if properly conducted, will be of infinite service. The Indians are all willing that their Children should be taught to read and write; and Youth is the properest season to instill principles of Morality and Religion, which the Schoolmasters will have constant opportunities of doing. Of these they ought to avail themselves; and gradually unfold the Principles of the Christian Systems to their pupils. Each of those Schoolmasters ought to have a salary of £40 Sterl. a year, which might be increased according to their industry and success. They also, as well as the Missionaries, should be furnished with Prayer-books, and such other Tracts in the Indian language as can be procured; which will be necessary to teach the Indians to read, and instruct them in the principles of Religion.

III. That Smiths be placed at some of the most convenient Indian Villages. These would be of great service to the Indians, and therefore very acceptable; and probably some of the Indians, from a sense of their utility might be induced to learn their Trade. Their Wives might also be engaged to teach such of the Indian women as are willing to learn Spinning, Sewing and other Branches of female Industry. The Government formerly allowed Smiths at several of the Indian Villages, with a competent salary. These Mechanics would now be of much service in promoting the general design, and might be had at a trifling expense. The Spaniards have employed mechanics, and do still, for the same purpose to great advantage.

IV. That the Missionaries and Schoolmasters employed in this Scheme be appointed, or at least approved, by the Society for the Propagation of the Gospel in Foreign Parts. The Superintendency of those matters naturally belongs to that Venerable Body, not only by reason that they coincide with the design of their Incorporation, and with their connections on this Continent, but also because the Society have with great fidelity discharged the important trust reposed in them, and have already done much towards Converting and Civilising the Iroquois. . . .

V. That a set of Rules and Instructions be prepared by the Society for the Regulation of the Missionaries and Schoolmasters in the Discharge of their Respective Duties, which Rules and Instructions however shall, for the reasons already mentioned be inspected and approved by His Majesty's Superintendant of Indian Affairs, previous to their Establishment. . . .

VI. The last Article I shall mention as necessary to compleat this Plan, and make it more extensively useful, is the erecting a College or Seminary in the old Oneida Town, where the Young Indians who are distinguished for their Genius, may repair for a more enlarged Education, and be fitted for the Ministry. . . .

After much Reflection on the State and Disposition of the Indians, and receiving the best Information from those who had an intimate intercourse with them for many years, I am persuaded that this Plan is well adapted to their Circumstances, and would, if duly executed, produce the desired Effect in converting them to Christianity. If that can once be Accomplished, their firm Attachment to us will naturally follow, and their Reduction to a civilised State will be gradually and insensibly promoted at the same Time. Too much should not be attempted at first; especially in civilising them. It would probably alarm them, and thereby defeat the whole

Design. The more westerly Tribes have yet received few Impressions of Christianity, and are least civilised. . . .

These particulars might be enlarged, were it necessary, and others added to them which would evince this point further. But enough has been said, in my humble opinion, to remove any Apprehension of a Failure in the Success of the Scheme now laid down; or that the Expence and Trouble attending it would be fruitless. . . .

OBJECTIONS RAISED

But altho I am fully satisfied on this Head; yet I am sensible that Objections have been raised concerning it. . . .

Among other Things it has been suggested— "That the Iroquois are such an ignorant, barbarous People, that they are incapable of being civilised or brought over to Christianity."

But this Language is manifestly dictated by Prejudice, I grant the Iroquois are ignorant, when compared with civilised Nations; but certainly we should distinguish between Ignorance and Dulness—between the Want of Knowledge and the Want of Capacity to receive it. Whoever has any Acquaintance with the Iroquois, must know they are not deficient in Point of Understanding. No People have more Sagacity to discern their Interest, according to their prevailing Notions, or can reason better on it; none can project Schemes with more Subtilty to promote it, or have more Spirit and Resolution to carry those Schemes into Execution. Their Speeches at Treaties, their Conversation and Conduct are incontestable Proofs of this. Besides it is well known that such of them as will learn to read and write, generally make a more rapid Progress than Persons of the same Age among us. It may then with Truth be affirmed, that the Indians are not inferior in their Intellectual Faculties to other Nations, or less capable of Improvement. Their Knowledge indeed, for Want of Culture, is confined within a narrow Circle; but notwithstanding, they shew a Discernment, and a Force of Understanding, which place them on a Level with the Best of Mankind.

It is further granted that the Iroquois are barbarous; but this by no means proves that they are incapable of being civilised. We know of very few Nations which were not originally as barbarous as they. No ancient People surpassed the Greeks in Knowledge, Policy and Refinement of Manners; or left to the World such Monuments of exalted genius. Yet History testifies that the

CHRISTIAN
LIBERTY
"READY TO
PASS TO THE
AMERICAN
STRAND"

Greeks were once extremely rude and savage—much more so than the Iroquois at present. Without Letters, Laws, or Policy, or even Food proper for Men, they wandered in Fields and Woods, having no Places of Shelter, but Dens and Caverns. Their own Writers, and those of best Note, confirm this Account; and that many Ages had elapsed before they emerged out of this brutal State. It was by very slow steps, by repeated Efforts of wise and great Men, that they rose to that Eminence which afterwards so much distinguished them. About the Commencement of the Christian Era, the Germans and Britons were as barbarous as the Indians of this Continent, whom they greatly resembled in many Particulars. Yet experience hath evinced that those Nations were as capable of Improvement as any upon Earth. . . .

These Reflections might be carried much further. But I shall only observe, that the Iroquois resemble other barbarous Nations, seem to have much the same Vices, and are equally attached to their own Manners. They also possess the same Faculties, with as great a share of Reason and understanding, as others of the human Species in general. Experience hath demonstrated that the most ignorant and barbarous People may be civilised; and why not here as well as elsewhere? I am persuaded that no solid Reason can be assigned why the Iroquois should be an Exception to the general Rule. Human Nature is much the same in every Clime and Age. Culture, with other external Circumstances, constitute the principal Difference between the various Parts of Mankind. For we find the same Nation, at different Periods, differ from itself, in Point of Manners, as much as the most distant Nations, can differ from each other.

It is certain that the Mohawks, from the Impressions of Religion they have received, and their Intercourse with the English, have already made considerable Progress towards civilised Life. Were proper Measures taken for the Purpose, there can be no Doubt, but much more might be done this Way. Nothing but the Want of those Measures, and their Connections with the Nations of their Confederacy, still buried in Darkness and Barbarity, at the Head of which they are ambitious to figure, prevent it. If the Mohawks were intirely to adopt our Manners, their Influence over the other Tribes would be at an End. But if these Tribes were instructed as They are, the Case would be very different.

As to the Notion that the Iroquois cannot be converted to Christianity, it is utterly groundless.

Not to mention the great Number of Converts made by the French among Nations bordering on the Iroquois, and equally barbarous; the Success of the few Missionaries we sent among them, is a sufficient Refutation of it. In the year 1745 Dr. Barclay, the Society's Missionary to the Mohawks, was obliged in Consequence of the French War, and Practices of Popish Emissaries, to abandon Fort Hunter. He had resided in that Mission 8 years only: during which Time the Iroquois were often engaged in War. This worthy Missionary had no Interpreter; his Life was frequently in Danger; besides numberless other Difficulties he had to struggle with. Yet his Congregation consisted at his Departure, of no less than 500 Indian Converts, of whom more than 80 were regular communicants; which was more than Double the number he found there at his first coming. If so great a Progress could be made in christianising the Indians amidst so many Obstructions; Reason will tell us that much greater Progress might be made in it at present, when those Embarrassments are removed.

An ignorant, Savage People, accustomed to a Life free from Care or Restraint, and possessed of an high Sense of Liberty, cannot without the utmost Difficulty be brought to submit to Labour or the Controll of Laws. The Pleasure or Benefits resulting from Knowledge, Arts or refined Manners, have no Charms for them. They are outweighed by their Love of Liberty and Ease, which they hold in much greater Estimation. This hath been true of rude, uncivilised Nations in every part of the World; and hence we find that Legislators in general, when attempting to civilise barbarous People, did not content themselves with merely displaying the temporal Advantages arising from a civilised State. Sensible that some Motives more powerful were necessary to counteract inveterate Habits and Prejudices, they called in Religion to their aid. Accordingly they availed themselves of the Belief of a Supream Being, which they found People everywhere possessed of, and made it subservient to their Purpose. The first Thing they did was to confirm this Belief, institute a Ceremonial of Religious Worship, and inculcate the Doctrine of a future Life. This Expedient had the desired Effect; and accomplished what had been otherwise attempted in vain. To this Purpose we have the Testimony of some of the most judicious Writers of Antiquity, that the Eleusinian Mysteries (in which were probably taught the Belief of a Supream Being, a Providence and future Life, with the Necessity of a Rectitude of Moral

Conduct) contributed more than any other Means to soften the Savage Manners of the first Inhabitants of Europe. . . .

The Iroquois, and other Indian Tribes of North America, believe in a God, in a Providence and future State of Existence, and what is very remarkable, even those who have yet had no Tincture of Christianity, discover the most reverential Awe of the Supream Being, and pay uncommon Defference to the Ministers of Religion. They are hereby prepared in some Degree for receiving the Truths of Christianity, which will naturally dispose them to Change their Manners, and admit the Arts of civil Life; and they would certainly Spurn at any Proposal for introducing the latter without the former. My opinion therefore is that our Endeavours to civilise the Iroquois, and Convert them to Christianity, should be joined together, as is specified in the preceding Plan. They will mutually promote and assist each other; and thus the End in View will be more speedily and effectually accomplished. . . .

Another Circumstance which is worthy of particular Notice on this Head is, That the Indians discover a much greater Inclination to be Instructed in the Principles of Christianity by Clergymen of the Church of England, than by dissenting Ministers. The Solemnity of our Worship is more pleasing to them. The Savages are incapable of entering into the spirit of our Religious Disputes and Divisions, or of forming a Proper Judgment concerning them. As we are all under one King and worship one God, they think we ought to have but one Religion; and they suppose that which is professed by the King is best. Hence proceeds the dislike shewn by the Indians to some dissenting Teachers who have lately attempted their Conversion; for on hearing their Religion was not the same with the King's they were much disgusted. Besides, the gloomy Cast of those Teachers, and their Mode of Worship, are forbidding and disagreable to the Indians. But the present Plan, which proposes that they should be proselyted by Clergymen of the National Church, would be clear of those Embarrassments; and as Supreme Head of the Church of England, it should be carried on in his Majesty's Name. Or even supposing that the Dissenters should at least prove successful in their endeavours among the Indians; yet it deserves serious Consideration, whether it would not be more eligible and safe that the Iroquois were Converted to the National Faith, and in such a Manner, as would indubitably secure their Fidelity to the Crown. I shall not enlarge on so delicate a Point. Your Lordship can reflect on this Hint. . . .

I shall only add; that Nothing would reflect greater Lustre on, or be more worthy of, our present gracious Sovereign, who is Himself an illustrious Example of every Virtue, than to deliver those poor Savages from their present wretched State of Darkness, Error and Barbarity, and diffuse the Blessings of Religion and social Life among them; thereby securing many Benefits to the Community, particularly to His Subjects in this Part of the World, who have in numberless Instances already experienced the Effects of His Royal Munificence and Paternal goodness.

The whole is submitted, with all Defference, to your Lordships Judgement and Wisdom.

New-York, Octob. 1, 1771.

THE SPARK

American Archives: Fourth Series, Vol. I, by Peter Force, Washington, 1837

KING PROHIBITS EXPORTATION OF ARMS AND AMMUNITION TO AMERICA

THE EARL OF DARTMOUTH
TO THE GOVERNOURS OF THE COLONIES

(Circular)   Whitehall, October 19, 1774

SIR: His Majesty having thought fit by his Order in Council this day to prohibit the exportation from Great Britain of Gunpowder, or any sort of Arms or Ammunition, I herewith enclose to you a copy of the Order; and it is his Majesty's command that you do take the most effectual measures for arresting, detaining, and securing any Gunpowder, or any sort of Arms or Ammunition which may be attempted to be imported into the Province under your Government, unless the master of the ship having such Military Stores on board shall produce a license from his Majesty or the Privy Council for the exportation of the same from some of the Ports of this Kingdom.

I am, sir,

your most obedient humble servant,

DARTMOUTH.

ORDER IN COUNCIL

At the Court of St. James's, the 19th day of October, 1774: Present, the King's most Excellent Majesty in Council, Earl of Rockford, Earl of Dartmouth, Earl of Suffolk, Lord Viscount Townshend, Lord Mansfield, Lord North.

Whereas an Act of Parliament was passed in the twenty-ninth year of the reign of his Majesty King George the Second, entitled, "An Act to empower his Majesty to prohibit the importation of Saltpetre, and to enforce the law for empowering his Majesty to prohibit the exportation of Gunpowder, or any sort of Arms and Ammunition; and also to empower his Majesty to restrain the carrying coastwise of Saltpetre, Gunpowder, or any sort of Arms or Ammunition:" And his Majesty judging, it neccessary to prohibit the exportation of Gunpowder, or any sort of Arms or Ammunition out of this Kingdom, or carrying the same coastwise for some time, doth therefore, with the advice of his Privy Council, hereby order, require, prohibit, and command, that no person or persons whatsoever (except the Master General of the Ordnance for his Majesty's service,) do at any time during the space of six months from the date of this Order in Council, presume to transport into any parts out of this Kingdom, or carry coastwise any Gunpowder, or any sort of Arms or Ammunition, or ship or lade any Gunpowder, or any sort of Arms or Ammunition on board any ship or vessel, in order to transport the same into any parts beyond the seas, or carrying the same coastwise, without leave or permission in that behalf, first obtained from his Majesty or his Privy Council, upon pain of incurring and suffering the respective forfeitures and penalties inflicted by the aforementioned Act. And the Lords Commissioners of his Majesty's Treasury, the Commissioners for executing the office of Lord High Admiral of Great Britain, the Lord Warden of the Cinque Ports, the Master General of the Ordnance, and his Majesty's Secretary at War, are to give the necessary directions herein, as to them may respectively appertain.

G. CHETWYND.

★   ★   ★   ★   ★

AMERICA LEARNS OF ARMS PROHIBITION

Monday, December 12, 1774

We learn from undoubted authority, that Lord Dartmouth, Secretary of State, has wrote a Circular Letter to the Governors upon this Continent, informing them that his Majesty has thought fit by his Order in Council, dated the 19th of October, to prohibit the Exportation from Great Britain of Gun-Powder or any sort of Arms and Ammunition; and has signified to them his Majesty's Command that they do take the most effectual Measures for arresting, detaining and securing any Gun Powder, or any sort of Arms or Ammunition, which may be attempted to be imported into the Province over which they respectively preside, unless the Master of the Ship having such Military Stores on board, shall produce a License from his Majesty or the Privy Council for the Exportation of the same from some of the Ports of Great-Britain.

Boston Evening Post, 1774

★   ★   ★   ★   ★

GOVERNOUR WENTWORTH TO
GOVERNOUR GAGE

Portsmouth, New Hampshire,
December 14, 1774

SIR: I have the honour to receive your Excellency's letter of the 9th instant, with the letter from the Secretary of State, which were both delivered to me on Monday evening last by Mr. Whiting.

It is with the utmost concern I am called upon by my duty to the King, to communicate to your Excellency a most unhappy affair perpetrated here this day.

Yesterday in the afternoon, Paul Revere arrived in this Town, express from a Committee in Boston to another Committee in this Town, and delivered his despatch to Mr. Samuel Cutts, a Merchant of this Town, who immediately convened the Committee, of which he is one, and as I learn, laid it before them. This day, about noon, before any suspicions could be had of their intentions, about four hundred men were collected together, and immediately proceeded to his Majesty's Castle, *William* and *Mary,* at the entrance of this Harbour, and forcibly took possession thereof, notwithstanding the best defence that could be made by Captain Cochran, (whose conduct has been extremely laudable, as your Excellency will see by the enclosed letter from him,) and by violence, carried off upwards of one hundred barrels of Powder, belonging to the King, deposited in the Castle. I am informed that expresses have been circulated through the neighbouring Towns, to collect a number of people tomorrow, or as soon as possible, to carry away all the Cannon and Arms belonging to the Castle, which they will undoubtedly effect, unless some assistance should arrive from Boston in time to prevent it. This event too plainly proves the imbecility of this Government to carry into execution his Majesty's Order in Council, for seizing and detaining Arms and Ammunition imported into this Province, without some strong Ships-of-War in this Harbour: neither is this Province or Custom House Treasury in any degree safe, if it should come into the mind of the popular leaders to seize upon them.

The principal persons who took lead in this enormity are well known. Upon the best information I can obtain this mischief originates from the publishing the Secretary of State's letter, and the King's Order in Council, at Rhode Island, prohibiting the exportation of Military Stores from Great Britain, and the proceedings in that Colony in consequence of it, which have been published here by the forementioned Mr. Revere, and the despatch brought, before which all was perfectly quiet and peaceable here.

J. WENTWORTH

American Archives: Fourth Series, Vol. I, II, by Peter Force, Washington, 1837

To the PUBLIC.

City of New-York, ss. PERSONALLY appeared before me, Benjamin Blagge, Esq; one of his Majesty's justices of the peace for the city and county of New-York, Thomas Mesnard, master of the ship Lady Gage, who being duly sworn on the Holy Evangelists of Almighty God, deposeth and saith, that ten cases of merchandize marked TC, which he supposes were fire-arms, and 3 cases and one cask marked IC, shipped by Mess. Haley and Co. merchants in London, and addressed to Walter Franklin, of this city, were included in the manifest of the said ship's cargo, which he delivered at the custom-house; and this deponent further says, that two officers of his Majesty's customs, for the port of London, were on board the ship, at the time the said goods were received; and further this deponent saith not.

THOMAS MESNARD.

Sworn this 30th of December, 1774, before me,

Bn. BLAGGE.

It is material to inform the public, that the ship Lady Gage, cleared at the custom-house, London, the 15th day of October, and took her papers from the office at Gravesend, the 18th of that month. The King's proclamation prohibiting the exportation of arms, bears date the 19th of October, so that the ship was clear of all the offices a day before the date of the proclamation. It is said the arms seized, were cleared at London and entred here as hardware, under which denomination arms have generally been cleared for, and entered into North-America. For the truth of this, we appeal to every merchant who has imported arms from England to America.—It is no less material to observe, that the arms in question, were suffered to be landed, and remained in the store of Mr. Walter Franklin, for several days.—From all which there is great reason to suspect that the arms were not seized for want of the usual formalities of law, but to prevent their falling into the hands of the owner, and thereby to deprive the country of the use of them, at this important crisis.

A Number of Citizens.

At the Court of St. James's, the 5th day of April, 1775: Present the King's Most Excellent Majesty in Council.

Whereas, the time limited by His Majesty's Order in Council of the 19th of October last, for the prohibiting the exporting out of this Kingdom, or carrying coastwise, Gunpowder or any sorts of Arms or Ammunition, will expire upon the 19th of April: And whereas, it is judged expedient that the said prohibition should be continued for some time longer, His Majesty doth therefore, by and with the advice of his Privy Council, hereby command, that no person or persons whatsoever, (except the Master-General, Lieutenant-General, or principal officers of the Ordnance for His Majesty's service) do, at any time during six months, to commence from the said 19th instant, presume to transport into any parts out of this Kingdom, or carry coastwise, any Gunpowder, or any sort of Arms or Ammunition, or ship or lade any Gunpowder, or any sort of Arms or Ammunition on board any Ship or Vessel, in order to transport the same into any parts beyond the Seas, or carrying the same coastwise, without leave or permission first obtained from His Majesty, or his Privy Council, upon pain of incurring and suffering the respective forfeitures and penalties inflicted by an Act passed in the 29th year of His late Majesty's reign, entitled "An Act to empower His Majesty to prohibit the exportation of Saltpetre, &c.,

JOHN POWNALL TO THE GOVERNOURS OF THE SEVERAL COLONIES.

Whitehall, April 5, 1775

Sir: As it may be of use that His Majesty's subjects in America should be informed of the Proclamation issued by the order of the States General, prohibiting the exportation of Arms and Ammunition from their Dominions, in British Ships, or in their own Ships, without leave of their College of Admiralty, I am directed by Lord Dartmouth to transmit to you the enclosed Gazette, containing the said Proclamation, which you will cause to be printed and published in such manner as you shall think fit.

JOHN POWNALL.

Hague, March 20, 1775

Their High Mightinesses the States General have this day issued a Proclamation, of which the following is a translation:

Be it known, that we, for particular reasons thereunto moving, have thought fit absolutely to prohibit, and we hereby absolutely do prohibit all exportation of Ammunition, Gunpowder, Guns, and Shot, by Ships belonging to the Dominions of Great Britain, provisionally, for the term of six months, upon pain not only of confiscation of the Arms and Ammunition which shall be found there on board, but also of a fine of a Thousand Guilders over and above, at the charge of the Commander, whose Ship shall be answerable and liable to execution for the same.

That we have further thought fit to enact, and we do hereby enact, that during the above-said term of six months, no Gunpowder, Guns, Shot, or other Instruments of War, shall be embarked on board any other Ships, whether foreign or belonging to this Country, to be transported abroad, without consent or permission of the College of Admiralty, under whose jurisdiction the embarkation shall be made, upon pain of confiscation of the Arms, Gunpowder, Guns, Shot, or other Ammunition, which shall have been embarked without permission, and of the Commander incurring a fine of a Thousand Guilders, on board of whose Ship the said Arms and Ammunition shall have been embarked, and his Ship be answerable and liable to execution for the said fine.

And that no one may pretend ignorance hereof, we call upon and require the States, the Hereditary Stadtholder, the Committee of Council, and the deputations of the States of the respective Provinces, and all other Officers and Justices of these Countries, to cause this our Proclamation to be forthwith promulgated, published, and affixed, in all places where such publication is wont to be made. And we do further charge and command the Counsellors of the Admiralty, the Advocates General, together with all Admirals, Vice-Admirals, Captains, Officers, and Commanders, to pay obedience to this our Proclamation, proceeding and causing to be proceeded against the transgressors thereof, without favour, connivance, dissimulation, or composition. For such have we found meet.

Given at the Hague, under the seal of the States, signature of the President of our Assembly, and the counter signature of our Greffier, the 20th day of March, 1775.

G. VAN HARDENBROEK.

By order of the States General:

H. FAGEL   325

CHRISTIAN
LIBERTY
"READY TO
PASS TO THE
AMERICAN
STRAND"

MONEY AND MONEY UNITS
IN THE AMERICAN COLONIES

Simon L. Adler,
Rochester
Historical
Society
Publication,
Vol. VIII, 1929

During our entire colonial period and practically until the adoption of our present system of money, each colony had a unit of money value of its own. The English colonists brought with them some English money and naturally adopted the English table of money values wherever they settled. Very early in the colonial history, however, a pound in the colonies began to take on a different meaning from the pound sterling of England; and in every colony the valuation placed on the local pound was less than that of the English pound. The amount of this depreciation was not uniform in the different colonies. In each colony, too, the local pound varied in intrinsic value at different periods. At about the middle of the eighteenth century the colonial pounds had all ceased fluctuating and had obtained the several values which were standard until our present monetary system went into operation.

Though the colonists reckoned in pounds, shillings and pence, yet their money had, in intrinsic value, no identity with the pounds, shillings and pence of Great Britain. They had the same name, it is true, and the colonial pound was derived directly from the English pound; but the pound of the colonies had become, from its change in value, so distinct a unit of money from the pound sterling, that it might as well have been called by another name. When the value of the pound of New York had become fixed by the people of that colony at 966¾ grains of pure silver, they created for themselves a new unit of money. The colonial pound, then, must not be confounded with the English pound.

While it is said that the colonial pound was a different amount of money, a different weight of silver, than the pound of England, it must be remembered that there were no coins corresponding to the colonial pounds or their subdivisions; that there was no mintage of money to correspond to colonial money values. If a contract was made to pay a sum amounting to one hundred pounds in New York money, the payment would not be made in coins representing New York pounds. There were no such pieces. The debt must be liquidated in pieces of foreign gold or silver which had a fixed value placed on them in each colony; in the paper money of the colony; or in some form of barter. The colonial money was simply a money of account. In their business transactions among themselves the colonists bought and sold in terms of their local currency. It often happened that a sale was made for so many Spanish dollars, which had a recognized value the world over, or in so many pounds of tobacco; but most contracts, sales and values were reckoned in the pounds, shillings and pence of the several colonies though there were no coins to represent these values, and usually very little money of any kind changed hands. The colonists ignored the English pound, except when they were buying goods of the English merchants or satisfying English bills of exchange.

COLONIAL POUND AND SPANISH DOLLAR

When the different colonial pounds had become definitely determined in value the colonies were divided into four groups according to the value of their respective units of money. Thomas Jefferson in his notes on the establishment of a money unit for the United States says that in Georgia the local pound contained 1,547 grains of pure silver; in Virginia, Connecticut, Rhode Island, Massachusetts and New Hampshire, 1,289 grains; in Maryland, Delaware, Pennsylvania and New Jersey, 1,031¼ grains, and in New York and North Carolina, 966¾ grains. The pound sterling of England contained 1,718¾ grains. But, perhaps, it would be clearer, as it is more common, to rate the different colonial currencies in terms of the piece of eight, or Spanish dollar, probably the only piece of money which was common to all of the colonies and in general use in all of them. A piece of eight, or dollar, was equivalent to the following:

4s. 6d. in English sterling money.
6s. 0d. in New Hampshire, Massachusetts, Rhode Island, Connecticut and Virginia money.
8s. 0d. in New York and North Carolina money.
7s. 6d. in New Jersey, Pennsylvania, Maryland and Delaware money.
4s. 8d. in South Carolina and Georgia money.

The Spanish dollar was a coin common to all of the colonies and when it came to be valued in terms of the local currency it was found, that while it took eight shillings of the New York and North Carolina money to make a dollar, it took only six shillings of the New England and Virginia money. A shilling in New York was a fixed and invariable sum equal to one-eighth of a Spanish dollar; and the shilling of New England was just as fixed and invariable, but equal to one-sixth of a Spanish dollar. So the Spanish dollar was worth only four shillings and six pence in English sterling money; and in Georgia and South Carolina, before the introduction of paper money in the latter colony, where the local currency was very nearly of the same value as sterling, the dollar was worth four shillings and eight pence. The relative values of the colonial currencies and sterling money may be expressed:

- 100 represents the value of the English pound sterling.
- 90 will then represent the value of the Georgia and South Carolina pound.
- 75 the New England and Virginia pound.
- 60 the Pennsylvania, Maryland, New Jersey and Delaware pound.
- 56¼ the New York and North Carolina pound.

This difference in the standards of value of the different colonies was the cause of infinite inconvenience. In the colonial days people had a more difficult experience, from a monetary point of view, when they went from one colony to another, than we have now when we travel from one nation to another. Their troubles were aggravated by the fact that when they got into a neighboring colony the price of an article would be quoted to them in terms which were familiar to them, so many shillings and pence; but whose real value could not be appreciated until those shillings and pence had been turned into the kind of shillings and pence that they used at home. If a New Jersey farmer asked a New York merchant ten shillings and six pence a bushel for his wheat, the merchant would have to go through the not very simple computation of changing New Jersey money into New York money; or else be perfectly familiar with both standards. All money transactions between the colonies were frequently difficult and always annoying. They were inevitable, however, so that up to the adoption of our present system of money the inhabitant of New York was expected to be able to convert with facility the money of his own colony into that of Massachusetts or Pennsylvania or Georgia. These different values were taught to the children in the schools and the early arithmetics contain many pages of rules which, committed to memory, would enable the pupil easily to translate the money of one colony into that of another. Most of

these rules were of the nature of empirical formulae; and to the children of that time the study of the money must have been a subject not exceeded in difficulty by the proverbial Greek verbs.

MERCHANTS DIFFICULTIES

The merchants, too, of both England and America, who traded in the different colonies, were obliged to be well up in the different rates of exchange, and constantly on their guard against loss, through ignorance or dishonesty, from the conversion of one set of values into another. The trade between England and the colonies was very large and the numerous merchants, ship owners and navigators had to keep posted on the different rates of exchange between the colonies and with England. A book published in London in 1765 entitled *The American Negotiator or the Various Currencies of the British Colonies in America,* passed through several editions and had over five thousand subscribers. It contains several hundred pages of tables; and a glance at its pages gives some idea of the monetary difficulties of the time. If the problem was to determine the value of 550 pounds New York money in Boston money, the merchant would, by using one table, find that 550 pounds in New York, where the dollar was worth 8s. was equivalent to 1,375 dollars. Then from another table he would reach his result by finding that the value of 1,375 dollars at 6s. each was 412 pounds, 10 shillings. This was the simplest method by which the currency of one place could be reduced to that of another, the value of the dollar being known in both. If he did not own a table he would still find it comparatively easy to change New York money into Boston money because the New York pound was just three-fourths as large as the Massachusetts pound; and by multiplying 550 by three and dividing by four the same result would be reached. The difficulty is much increased in the exchanges between colonies when the ratio of the money standards is not a simple one, and when you have to deal besides with shillings and pence.

GENERAL WASHINGTON'S PROBLEMS

Instances of the difficulty and annoyances met with at this time in all transactions involving the use of money might be multiplied indefinitely. Washington began keeping the account of his expenses during the Revolutionary war in June, 1775, and ended in June, 1783. From June, 1775, until April 1, 1776, he kept the record of receipts

THE
AMERICAN NEGOTIATOR,
OR THE
VARIOUS CURRENCIES
OF THE
BRITISH COLONIES
IN
AMERICA;

As well the ISLANDS, as the CONTINENT.

The CURRENCIES of

NOVA SCOTIA,	EAST JERSEY,	VIRGINIA,
CANADA,	PENSYLVANIA,	NORTHCAROLINA,
NEW ENGLAND,	WEST JERSEY,	SOUTHCAROLINA,
NEW YORK,	MARYLAND,	GEORGIA, &c.

And of the ISLANDS of

BARBADOES,	St. CHRISTOPHERS,	NEVIS,
JAMAICA,	ANTIGUA,	MONTSERRAT,&c.

Reduced into ENGLISH MONEY.

By a Series of TABLES suited to the several Exchanges between the COLONIES and BRITAIN, adapted to all the Variations that from Time to Time have, or may happen. With TABLES reducing the current Money of the Kingdom of IRELAND into Sterling, and the contrary, at all the Variations of Exchange.

ALSO

A Chain of TABLES for the interchangeable Reduction of the Currencies of the Colonies into each other.

And many other useful TABLES relating to the Trade in AMERICA.

By J. WRIGHT, Accomptant.
The THIRD EDITION.

LONDON:

Printed for DAVID STEEL, at the Bible and Crown, King-Street, Little Tower-Hill, and ROBINSON and ROBERTS, No. 25, Pater-noster-row. 1767.
[Price Bound Seven Shillings.

---

as Philadelphia, New York, Virginia and Maryland. Therefore, to render the present Impression of this Book more perfect, I have, from Page 42 to Page 112, inserted 48 Pages of new calculated Tables, rising one Pound a Step, and have at the same Time, and in the said Chain of Tables, retained the Tables that rise and fall 2½; and to give Room for so material an Improvement of this Edition, I have taken away all the Tables of Exchanges that were in the former Impression from 200 to 500, as being at this Day intirely out of Use. The Tables from 500 to 1000 stand the same as in the former Edition in regard to the Variations that may happen to the Currency of South Carolina.

The Use of the Tables of Interchangeable Reduction.

These Tables extend from Page 181 to Page 257, and perform what their general Title sets forth. They are founded on the same Principles as the universal Rule for the arbitrating Exchanges throughout the commercial World, and on which the Pars of all trading Nations are founded, that is, to receive so much intrinsic Value in real Money, in one Country, as is paid in another, if the Way of accounting, or Difference of the Specie, vary ever so much.

EXAMPLE I.

What is 550l. *New York* Money in the lawful Money of *Boston*, the Dollar passing for 8s. in the former, and 6s. in the latter Places.

Find how many Dollars are contained in 550l. at 8s. each, by Page 242, you will have,   Then find the Value of 1375 Dollars at 6s. Page 218.

N. York Money, l. s. d.	Specie, Dol. rs. 10.	Specie, Dol. rs. 10.	Boston Money, l. s. d.
500 0 0	1250 0 0	1000 0 0	300 0 0
50 0 0	125 0 0	300 0 0	90 0 0
		70 0 0	21 0 0
		5 0 0	1 10 0
550 0 0	1375 0 0	1375 0 0	412 10 0

By using two Tables as above it appears, that 550l. *New York* Money is equal to 412l. 10s. od *Boston* Money. In like Manner, and with the same Ease, the Currency of any two Places may be reduced into each other, the Value of the Dollar in both being known.

Sterling

DOLLARS contained in Plantation Currency.
The Value of each Dollar, as under.

Curr.	at 6s. 0d. Specie			at 6s. 1d. Specie			Shillings	6s. 0d. Specie			6s. 1d. Specie		
1.	dol.	ryals	10th	dol.	ryals	10th	Pence	d.	r.	10t.	d.	r.	10t.
1	3	3	3	3	3	3	1	0	1	3	0	1	3
2	6	6	7	6	2	6	2	0	2	7	0	2	7
3	10	2	3	9	4	0	3	0	4	0	0	4	0
4	13	5	7	13	5	3	4	0	5	2	0	5	2
5	16	1	3	16	3	5	5	0	6	6	0	6	6
6	20	5	0	19	5	7	6	1	0	9	1	0	9
7	23	0	7	23	0	3	7	1	2	2	1	2	2
8	26	4	3	26	2	6	8	1	3	6	1	3	8
9	30	0	0	29	4	0	9	1	5	0	1	5	1
10	33	3	7	32	6	3	10	1	6	5	1	5	8
20	66	0	3	65	5	6	11	1	7	8	1	7	1
30	100	0	0	98	4	2	12	2	0	4	2	0	5
40	133	3	3	131	3	1	13	2	1	7	2	2	4
50	166	2	5	164	2	0	14	2	3	0	2	4	7
60	200	0	0	197	1	2	15	2	4	3	2	5	0
70	233	5	7	230	0	7	16	2	5	6	2	6	1
80	266	5	3	263	0	2	17	2	7	7	2	7	2
90	300	0	0	295	5	1	18	3	1	8	2	7	0
100	333	2	7	328	3	0	19	3	1	9	3	0	0
200	666	5	3	657	4	3							
300	1000	0	0	986	2	4	1	0	0	1	0	0	1
400	1333	2	7	1315	6	2	2	0	0	2	0	0	2
500	1666	5	3	1643	0	6	3	0	0	3	0	0	3
600	2000	0	0	1972	4	4	4	0	0	5	0	0	5
700	2333	2	7	2301	2	1	5	0	0	6	0	0	6
800	2666	5	3	2630	5	7	6	0	0	7	0	0	7
900	3000	0	0	2958	7	2	7	0	0	8	0	0	8
1000	3333	2	4	3287	6	4	8	0	0	9	0	0	9
2000	6666	5	7	6575	5	7	9	0	1	0	0	1	0
3000	10000	0	5	9863	4	5	10	0	1	1	0	1	1
4000	13333	2	5	13150	2	9	11	0	1	2	0	1	2
5000	16666	5	2	16438	1	6		0	0	0	0	0	0
6000	20000	0	6	19726	0	8		0	0	0	0	0	0
7000	23333	2	7	23013	5	0		0	0	0	0	0	0
8000	26666	5	3	26301	3	1		0	0	0	0	0	0
9000	30000	0	0	29589	0	2		0	0	0	0	0	0
10000	33333	2	7	32876	5	7	Value						

DOLLARS contained in Plantation Currency.
The Value of each Dollar, as under.

Curr.	at 8s. 0d. Specie			at 8s. 1d. Specie			Shillings	8s. 0d. Specie			8s. 1d. Specie		
1.	dol.	ryals	10th	dol.	ryals	10th	Pence	d.	r.	10t.	d.	r.	10t.
1	2	2	0	2	3	8	1	0	1	0	0	1	0
2	5	4	0	4	7	6	2	0	2	1	0	2	1
3	7	7	0	7	3	4	3	0	3	2	0	3	2
4	10	9	0	9	7	0	4	0	4	3	0	4	3
5	12	2	0	12	6	8	5	0	5	5	0	5	5
6	15	4	0	14	2	6	6	0	6	6	0	6	6
7	17	7	0	17	6	4	7	0	7	0	0	7	0
8	20	9	0	19	2	2	8	1	0	1	0	7	0
9	22	2	0	22	6	9	9	1	1	2	1	0	1
10	25	4	0	24	2	3	10	1	3	3	1	1	2
20	50	0	0	49	4	9	11	1	4	4	1	3	3
30	75	0	0	74	3	8	12	1	5	5	1	4	4
40	100	0	0	98	7	8	13	1	6	6	1	5	5
50	125	0	0	123	5	7	14	1	7	0	1	6	6
60	150	0	0	148	1	6	15	2	0	1	1	7	7
70	175	0	0	173	3	5	16	2	1	2	2	0	8
80	200	0	0	197	7	5	17	2	2	2	2	1	8
90	225	0	0	222	5	3	18	2	3	2	2	2	8
100	250	0	0	247	3	4	19	2	3	2			
200	500	0	0	494	6	8							
300	750	0	0	742	0	5	1	0	0	1	0	0	1
400	1000	0	0	989	5	5	2	0	0	2	0	0	2
500	1250	0	0	1237	0	9	3	0	0	3	0	0	3
600	1500	0	0	1484	4	7	4	0	0	4	0	0	4
700	1750	0	0	1731	7	7	5	0	0	5	0	0	5
800	2000	0	0	1979	3	0	6	0	0	6	0	0	6
900	2250	0	0	2226	6	4	7	0	0	7	0	0	7
1000	2500	0	0	2474	1	6	8	0	0	8	0	0	8
2000	5000	0	0	4948	3	0	9	0	0	9	0	0	9
3000	7500	0	0	7422	4	4	10	0	1	0	0	1	0
4000	10000	0	0	9896	7	3	11	0	1	1	0	1	1
5000	12500	0	0	12371	1	1		0	0	0	0	0	0
6000	15000	0	0	14845	2	9		0	0	0	0	0	0
7000	17500	0	0	17319	4	7		0	0	0	0	0	0
8000	20000	0	0	19793	6	5		0	0	0	0	0	0
9000	22500	0	0	22268	0	3		0	0	0	0	0	0
10000	25000	0	0	24742	2	1	Value						

Sterling and *Irish* Money may in this Manner be readily reduced into any of the Plantation Currencies, and the Contrary; by first finding the Number of Dollars that are contained in the Sterling Money; at the Price Silver passes for in *England*; and then find the Value in Plantation Money of the said Dollars, at the Current Price they go for in any Province. *Irish* Money is reduced interchangeably just the same Way, by valuing the Dollar at 5s. *Irish* Money, which I think an equitabe Valuation, as may be seen by the first Line in the Table of Pars.

EXAMPLE II.

A Merchant in Philadelphia consigns a Cargo of Flour to his Factor in *South Carolina*, amounting as per Invoice to 1579l. 10s. 0d. Pensilvania Money, how much is the Amount thereof in Carolina Money at prime Cost, the Dollar being valued at 7s. 6d. in Philadelphia, and at 32s. in *South Carolina*?

As before the Number of Dollars in 1579l. 10s. 0d. at 7s. 6d. each will by Page 236 found to be viz.

l.	s.	d.		doll.	rs.	10.
1000	0	0		2666	5	3
500	0	0		1333	2	7
70	0	0		186	5	3
9	0	0		24	0	6
0	10	0		1	2	6
1579	10	0		4211	7	9

The Value of 4211 Dollars, at 7 Ryals, 9 10ths. at 32s. each will by Table Page 255 found to be viz.

doll.	rs.	10th.		l.	s.	d.
4000	0	0		6400	0	0
200	0	0		320	0	0
10	0	0		16	0	0
1	0	0		1	12	0
0	7	0		0	8	0
0	0	9		0	3	7
4211	7	9		6739	3	7

Which shews that 1579l. 10s. Pensilvania Money is equal to 6739l. 3s. 7d. South Carolina Money, at the Rates of the Dollar above mentioned. And suppose the said Cargo of Flour cost 12s. per Hundred Weight, all Charges concluded, in Pensilvania, what must it be valued at in *South Carolina* to make equal Money. By the Tables used as above 12s. will be found to contain in Pensilvania 1 doll. 4 rs. 8 10ths. and the Value of the same Number of Dollars, Ryals, &c. in *South Carolina*, at the above Rate of 32s. each, will be found to be 2l. 11s. *South Carolina* Money. The reasonable Expectations of Profit at 20, 30, 40, or 50 P. C. &c. may be easily computed of at Hand by any Merchant, Factor, Clerk, &c.

EXAMPLE

Value in Currency of DOLLARS.

The Value of each in Currency, as under.

Dollars	at 6s. 0d. Currency — l.	s.	d.	q.	at 6s. 1d. Currency — l.	s.	d.	q.
1	0	6	0	0	0	6	1	0
2	0	12	0	0	0	12	2	0
3	0	18	0	0	0	18	3	0
4	1	4	0	0	1	4	4	0
5	1	10	0	0	1	10	5	0
6	1	16	0	0	1	16	6	0
7	2	2	0	0	2	2	7	0
8	2	8	0	0	2	8	8	0
9	2	14	0	0	2	14	9	0
10	3	0	0	0	3	0	10	0
20	6	0	0	0	6	1	8	0
30	9	0	0	0	9	2	6	0
40	12	0	0	0	12	3	4	0
50	15	0	0	0	15	4	2	0
60	18	0	0	0	18	5	0	0
70	21	0	0	0	21	5	10	0
80	24	0	0	0	24	6	8	0
90	27	0	0	0	27	7	6	0
100	30	0	0	0	30	8	4	0
200	60	0	0	0	60	16	8	0
300	90	0	0	0	91	5	0	0
400	120	0	0	0	121	13	4	0
500	150	0	0	0	152	1	8	0
600	180	0	0	0	182	10	0	0
700	210	0	0	0	212	18	4	0
800	240	0	0	0	243	6	8	0
900	270	0	0	0	273	15	0	0
1000	300	0	0	0	304	3	4	0
2000	600	0	0	0	608	6	8	0
3000	900	0	0	0	912	10	0	0
4000	1200	0	0	0	1216	13	4	0
5000	1500	0	0	0	1520	16	8	0
6000	1800	0	0	0	1825	0	0	0
7000	2100	0	0	0	2129	3	4	0
8000	2400	0	0	0	2433	6	8	0
9000	2700	0	0	0	2737	10	0	0
10000	3000	0	0	0	3041	13	4	0

Ryals & 10th	at 6s. 1d. Currency — s.	d.	q.	at 6s. 0d. Currency — s.	d.	q.
1	0	9	1	0	9	0
2	1	6	2	1	6	0
3	2	3	3	2	3	0
4	3	1	0	3	0	0
5	3	10	1	3	9	0
6	4	7	2	4	6	0
7	5	4	3	5	3	0

DOLLARS

Value in Currency of DOLLARS.

The Value of each in Currency, as under.

Dollars.	at 32s. od. Currency. l.	s.	d.	q.	at 32s. 6d. Currency. l.	s.	d.	q.
1	1	12	0	0	1	12	6	0
2	3	4	0	0	3	5	0	0
3	4	16	0	0	4	17	6	0
4	6	8	0	0	6	10	0	0
5	8	0	0	0	8	2	6	0
6	9	12	0	0	9	15	0	0
7	11	4	0	0	11	7	6	0
8	12	16	0	0	13	0	0	0
9	14	8	0	0	14	12	6	0
10	16	0	0	0	16	5	0	0
20	32	0	0	0	32	10	0	0
30	48	0	0	0	48	15	0	0
40	64	0	0	0	65	0	0	0
50	80	0	0	0	81	5	0	0
60	96	0	0	0	97	10	0	0
70	112	0	0	0	113	15	0	0
80	128	0	0	0	130	0	0	0
90	144	0	0	0	146	5	0	0
100	160	0	0	0	162	10	0	0
200	320	0	0	0	325	0	0	0
300	480	0	0	0	487	10	0	0
400	640	0	0	0	650	0	0	0
500	800	0	0	0	812	10	0	0
600	960	0	0	0	975	0	0	0
700	1120	0	0	0	1137	10	0	0
800	1280	0	0	0	1300	0	0	0
900	1440	0	0	0	1462	10	0	0
1000	1600	0	0	0	1625	0	0	0
2000	3200	0	0	0	3250	0	0	0
3000	4800	0	0	0	4875	0	0	0
4000	6400	0	0	0	6500	0	0	0
5000	8000	0	0	0	8125	0	0	0
6000	9600	0	0	0	9750	0	0	0
7000	11200	0	0	0	11375	0	0	0
8000	12800	0	0	0	13000	0	0	0
9000	14400	0	0	0	14625	0	0	0
10000	16000	0	0	0	16250	0	0	0

Ryals & 10th	at 32s. od. Currency l.	s.	d.	q.	at 32s. 6d. Currency l.	s.	d.	q.
1	0	4	0	0	0	4	0	3
2	0	8	0	0	0	8	1	2
3	0	12	0	0	0	12	2	1
4	0	16	0	0	0	16	3	0
5	1	0	0	0	1	0	3	3
6	1	4	0	0	1	4	4	2
7	1	8	0	0	1	8	5	1

Ryals (10th)	at 32s. od. Currency l.	s.	d.	q.	at 32s. 6d. Currency l.	s.	d.	q.
1	0	0	4	3	0	0	4	3
2	0	0	9	2	0	0	9	3
3	0	1	2	1	0	1	2	2
4	0	1	7	0	0	1	7	2
5	0	2	0	0	0	2	0	1
6	0	2	4	3	0	2	5	1
7	0	2	9	2	0	2	10	0
8	0	3	2	1	0	3	3	0
9	0	3	7	0	0	3	7	3
								Dollars

DOLLARS contained in Plantation Currency.

The Value of each Dollar, as under.

Curr. l.	at 7s. 6d. Specie dol.	ryals	10th	at 7s. 7d. Specie dol.	ryals	10th
1	2	5	3	2	5	1
2	5	2	7	5	2	2
3	8	0	0	7	7	3
4	10	5	3	10	4	4
5	13	2	7	13	1	5
6	16	0	0	15	6	6
7	18	5	3	18	3	7
8	21	2	7	21	0	8
9	24	0	0	23	5	9
10	26	5	3	26	3	0
20	53	2	7	52	6	0
30	80	0	0	79	1	0
40	106	5	3	105	4	0
50	133	2	7	131	6	9
60	160	0	0	158	1	9
70	186	5	3	184	4	9
80	213	2	7	210	7	9
90	240	0	0	237	2	9
100	266	5	3	263	5	9
200	533	2	7	527	3	8
300	800	0	0	791	1	7
400	1066	5	3	1054	7	6
500	1333	2	7	1318	5	5
600	1600	0	0	1582	3	3
700	1866	5	3	1846	1	2
800	2133	2	7	2109	7	1
900	2400	0	0	2373	5	0
1000	2666	5	3	2637	2	9
2000	5333	2	7	5274	5	8
3000	8000	0	0	7912	0	7
4000	10666	5	3	10549	3	6
5000	13333	2	7	13186	6	5
6000	16000	0	0	15824	1	4
7000	18666	5	3	18461	4	3
8000	21333	2	7	21098	7	2
9000	24000	0	0	23736	2	1
10000	26666	5	3	26373	5	0

Shillings	at 7s. 6d. Specie d.	r.	10th	at 7s. 7d. Specie d.	r.	10th
1	0	1	1	0	1	1
2	0	2	1	0	2	1
3	0	3	2	0	3	2
4	0	4	3	0	4	2
5	0	5	3	0	5	3
6	0	6	4	0	6	3
7	0	7	5	0	7	4
8	1	0	5	1	0	4
9	1	1	6	1	1	5
10	1	2	7	1	2	5
11	1	3	7	1	3	6
12	1	4	8	1	4	7
13	1	5	9	1	5	7
14	1	6	9	1	6	8
15	2	0	0	1	7	8
16	2	1	1	2	0	9
17	2	2	1	2	1	9
18	2	3	2	2	3	0
19	2	4	3	2	4	0

Pence	at 7s. 6d. Specie d.	r.	10th	at 7s. 7d. Specie d.	r.	10th
1	0	0	1	0	0	1
2	0	0	2	0	0	2
3	0	0	3	0	0	3
4	0	0	4	0	0	4
5	0	0	4	0	0	4
6	0	0	5	0	0	5
7	0	0	6	0	0	6
8	0	0	7	0	0	7
9	0	0	8	0	0	8
10	0	0	9	0	0	9
11	0	1	0	0	1	0
						Value

CHRISTIAN
LIBERTY
"READY TO
PASS TO THE
AMERICAN
STRAND"

and expenditures in Pennsylvania money and in what he designated lawful currency which was in terms of pounds, shillings and pence of six shillings to the dollar. From April, 1776, until January, 1777, he used New York and lawful currency. From 1777 until 1783 he used continental dollars and lawful currency. In every case, on the balancing up of the accounts, the Pennsylvania or New York money, or the dollars, are translated into lawful currency for final presentation to Congress. The different items were entered into the account book in the money of the section in which he was principally staying and afterward all is carefully and laboriously balanced up in terms of lawful money.

SCARCITY OF REAL MONEY

One of the chief annoyances of the people was a scarcity of real money of any kind, and this led to numerous devices for keeping with them what little of it they had. There was, in the first place very little English money in the colonies. There was a great scarcity of money in England itself during our colonial period, and extreme penalties were imposed for any exportation of the current coin of the realm. What English money the colonists saw was only what was smuggled out of England and this was comparatively little. Even in England the Spanish piece of eight was a more familiar and a more desirable coin than any of their own. What money did come to the colonies was mainly Spanish and Portuguese, and this it was impossible to keep. The colonists imported much and exported comparatively little. They had the balance of trade always against them, and their gold and silver of whatever kind had to make up this deficiency. Nearly all the good coin was thus drained out of the colonies by the foreign trade, leaving only the clipped, plugged and counterfeit pieces on their hands. It is estimated that the richest colonies together, in their most flourishing circumstances never had, at most, more than £80,000 to £100,000 in money, and that in 1767 there was not one-third of that amount. Many of the estimates of the amount of currency in the colonies were made at the time of the discussions over the Stamp Act, and it was then said with some bitterness that "if you would have collected sterling cash from them (the colonists) it should have been in England where all they have is generally found."

Edmund Burke said: "It may be easily judged that the balance of trade with Great Britain is very much against the colonists, and, therefore, whatever gold or silver they may receive from the other branches of their commerce makes but a short stay in America. Very little money is seen among them, notwithstanding the vast increase of their trade."

BARTER

Driven to get along without a staple currency on even a sufficiency of money of any kind, and forbidden to coin money of their own, the colonists wherever possible conducted their exchanges by means of barter. Originally, as in most newly settled districts, this bartering was in the simplest form, but as the settlements grew and commercial relations extended, it became necessary, on account of lack of a medium of exchange, to make more certain this primitive substitute for money. Consequently, in many of the colonies, what was known as "barter currency" or "country pay" was legalized. It was enacted that the cereals and other products of the farm, and animals and fowls as well, be taken in payment for all debts at a certain price to be set upon them. Everything was carefully appraised and became a legal tender in payment of debts and taxes. This was, of course, a crude and unsatisfactory expedient and a poor substitute for real money, but it was the best that could be done.

It can well be understood that the use of this barter currency worked infinite annoyance and confusion. Possibly the debt would be paid with a lean cow or with poor grain; but the value had been placed on the article by law and it had to be received. So great was the aversion of the colonists themselves to barter currency that large discounts were made if payment would be in money. The colony of Massachusetts at one time abated 25 per cent of all taxes payable in grain to all who would advance cash.

Virginia and Maryland, more fortunate than their sister colonies, found an admirable substitute for money in tobacco, and it served as their principal medium of exchange throughout the entire colonial period. Even as late as Revolutionary times it was legally receivable for officers' fees and for taxes.

Like the other colonies, they utilized all commodities—corn (meaning all cereals), hens, pigs, beef, cheese and even powder and shot in their domestic trade; but tobacco soon came to be considered a staple in which most kinds of money indebtedness was liquidated. It was in tobacco that the early colonists paid for their wives, and it was a controversy over the value of tobacco, in which the Virginia parsons received their salaries, that first brought to general notice the oratorical powers and ability of Patrick Henry. Previous to 1633 all accounts were almost universally kept in terms of tobacco and not in money, but in that year the Legislature enacted that "All contracts, bargains, pleas and judgments to be set down in lawful money of England and in no other commodity." From this time the colonial statutes of Virginia are filled with enactments respecting the price of tobacco and its use as a principal medium of exchange in the colony. . . .

PAPER MONEY

By far the largest amount of the currency of the country consisted of paper money. This was issued by each of the colonies and later by the Continental Congress. In the main, these issues were excessive, and many times involved the colonies in financial ruin. The first were put out by Massachusetts in 1690; the other colonies quickly followed suit, and soon the whole country was flooded with paper currency. In Massachusetts eleven hundred pounds currency would exchange at one time for but one hundred pounds of silver, and in 1758 Edmund Burke wrote: "There are parts of New England wherein, if the whole stock and the people along with it were sold, they would not bring money enough to take in all the bills which they have emitted." Massachusetts, however, redeemed her paper currency in 1750 with pieces of eight which had been sent from England as reimbursement for her expense in the reduction of Cape Breton.

The depreciation of the continental money caused Washington much trouble in the settling up of his accounts, and he appended this note to his ledger: "104,364 of the above dollars were received after 1780, and altho' credited at 40 for 1, many of them did not fetch 1 for a hundred—while 27,775 of them were returned without deducting anything from the above account." In Rhode Island 2,300 pounds currency passed for only 100 pounds sterling and a similar tale might be told of South Carolina and some of the other colonies. Pennsylvania and New York were especially careful in the issue of their paper money and proved themselves fairly able to control its value.

The scarcity of a medium of exchange of any kind prompted the issue of this paper currency. The colonists were obliged to go to extremes in order to obtain money, and in most cases the issuing of bills of credit was a last resort. Even in

the straits in which the people found themselves, the first proposals for the adoption of paper currency met with much resistance, and we are told that in Pennsylvania a convincing pamphlet of Benjamin Franklin's did much to turn the scale in favor of its issue. The conditions which called for it were pressing, and it is a question if it was not the best as well as the only means of meeting the necessity for a medium of exchange. In many cases, however, the people abused their privilege, and the result was disastrous. In a few of the colonies their paper currency had some effect on the value of the unit of the money of account, and it must be taken into consideration when the value of the different colonial pounds is considered.

There were several attempts made in the colonies to set up a mint for the issue of silver coins, but with one exception they were unsuccessful. The only native colonial silver money of any importance was that issued in Massachusetts between the years 1652 and 1686. This was the famous pine tree coinage. . . . During its existence the mint was a great boon to the Massachusetts people; and as soon as it had to be abandoned they were obliged to resort again to all kinds of expedients for making what money they had suffice for the purposes of their trade. These were generally unsuccessful and they soon began the issue of their paper currency.

The establishment of a mint was one of the boldest and most important acts of the early settlers of America. It illustrated their capacity for business, their determination to found permanent institutions, and their ability to govern themselves. It may be said to be one of the earliest of those exhibitions of self-reliance and assertions of the right of self-government which culminated in the American Revolution. . . .

SPANISH DOLLAR

Certainly the most substantial money of the time consisted of gold and silver coins of foreign mintage which were brought to the colonies through the foreign trade. For many years they comprised all the real money of the colonies and they always represented the best part of it. The Spanish dollar or piece of eight was the most numerous of the foreign coins. It was practically a standard of value in all of the colonies and even in England; and was probably the only piece of money common to them all. It did not receive the name dollar until about the middle of the eighteenth century; and before that time it was known as the piece of eight reals, rials, ryalls or royalls, or

MONEY AND
MONEY UNITS
IN THE
AMERICAN
COLONIES

SCARCITY OF
REAL MONEY

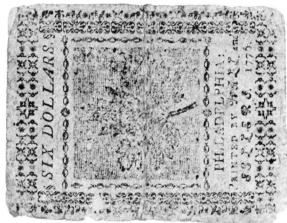

SAMPLES OF COLONIAL CURRENCY *Opposite page:* [1] Two Dollars, Philadelphia, May 10, 1775. "Trubulatio ditat", Affliction enriches. (Hand and flail) Grain threshed by a flail. Nature print, Raspberry and two filbert. [2] One Third of a Dollar, Philadelphia, February, 1776. Sundial rebus and linked colony device created by Benjamin Franklin. "Fugio", I fly (therefore) mind your business. [3] 6s New Jersey, March 25, 1776. Small coat of Arms. Leaf printed back. [4] Four Dollars, Philadelphia, July 22, 1776. "Aut mors aut vita decora", Either death or an honorable life. Wild boar charging spear. Nature print, Skeletonized maple fruit. *Above:* [1] Six Dollars, Philadelphia, July 22, 1776. "Perseverando", By perseverance. Beaver gnawing down tree. Nature print, Buttercup. [2] Thirty Dollars, Philadelphia, September 26, 1778. "Si Recte Facies", If you have lived righteously. Nature print, Three Willow. [3] Five Dollars, Philadelphia, January 4, 1779. "Sustine Vel Abstine", Either sustain yourself or abstain. Hand gathering food bleeding because of thorn pricks. Nature print, Feverfew. *Early Paper Money of America*, by Eric P. Newman, 1967.

CHRISTIAN
LIBERTY
"READY TO
PASS TO THE
AMERICAN
STRAND"

simply the piece of eight. This was the most popular coin of the time and it has, perhaps, played a larger part in the history of the world than any other piece of money. From the time of the discovery of America to the present day this coin in its various mintages has been a familiar and important assistant to the commerce of the nations. During this long period it has passed through various changes in weight and has been known by numerous names. Sir Isaac Newton's assay of 1717 values the Seville piece of eight at 387 grains of pure silver; the Mexico piece of eight at 385½ grains; the Pillar piece of eight at 385¾ grains, and the new Seville piece of eight at 308⁷⁄₁₀ grains. The weight of this coin varied greatly; the average being a trifle less than seventeen and one-half penny weights. When the legislatures of the colonies valued the foreign coin within their jurisdiction they found it necessary not only to specify the mintage of the dollar, whether Mexico, Pillar or Seville; but also to give the weight of the different pieces that were in circulation among them. This celebrated coin, which practically regulated the colonial trade, is the unit on which our present coinage is based.*

OTHER COINS USED IN COLONIES

As the Spanish piece of eight was the most celebrated silver coin known to the world of trade, so the Portuguese, johannes or "joe" was the most celebrated of gold coins; and the most frequently met with in the trade of the colonies. The rich gold mines of Brazil furnished the Portuguese with large quantities of the precious metal; and the numerous Portuguese traders distributed it, in the form of "joes," "half joes" and moidores throughout the world. The unit of Portuguese money was the rei, of which one thousand were equivalent to about one and one-quarter Spanish dollars. The coinage of the famous johannes series was begun in 1722. . . .

Other foreign coins frequently met with during the colonial period are the subdivisions of the Spanish dollar, its half, quarter, eighth, sixteenth and even thirty-second; the pistareen, worth about twenty cents; its double, half and quarter; the Spanish gold doubloon worth from fifteen to sixteen dollars; and the Spanish pistole of about three and two thirds dollars. The double and half pistole were also in circulation. Of French coins there were principally the crown and the guinea; the former being about one and one-fourth dollars and the latter from four and one-half to four and five-ninths dollars. The English crown was valued the same as the French crown, but the English guinea went for about four and two-thirds dollars, a little more than the French guinea. Besides these there were some Dutch and German coins in some of the colonies at different times and a few other pieces of French and English coinage.

Four other Spanish silver coins were more or less common. These were the double pistareen, the pistareen, the half-pistareen or Spanish bit and the quarter pistareen or half-bit. The pistareen is most commonly valued at about one-fifth of a dollar and subsequent to the Revolution it quite universally passed at twenty cents. Mr. Jefferson in his notes on a money unit says: "The tenth (of the dollar) will be precisely the Spanish bit or half pistareen in some of the states, and in others will differ from it but a very small fraction. This is a coin perfectly familiar to us all." And in another place he says: "Perhaps it would not be amiss to coin three more pieces of silver, one of the value of five-tenths or half a dollar, one of the value of two-tenths which would be equal to the Spanish pistareen, and one of the value of

---

* Author's note: Alexander Del Mar, in his *History of the Precious Metals* (London: Geo. Bell & Sons, 1880, p. 50) says: "The origin of the dollar is obscure. The etymology of the word appears to be German, though some have deducted it from the dobla, one of the first silver pieces coined in America. The synonyms are thaler, daller, aslani, etc. The piece of silver now known in the United States by the name of dollar appears to have been derived, so far as weight is concerned, from the Spanish ounce, and in Spain and her colonies it has passed at various times by the names onza de plata; piastre, piece of eight (8 reals); pillar piece of eight; Seville piece of eight; peso; peso duro; duro; onxa; dollar," etc.

Its weight in Troy grains of pure silver, so far as can be ascertained from Newton, Irving, Hamilton and Kelly has been at various times as follows:

Period	Weight	Authority
Ferdinand & Isabella	439.984	Irving's Columbus, Appendix, 18.
1497	(?)	Edict of Medina.
1641	(?)	Date of change of ratio to 1461
16—	386.75	Hamilton's Rep., Jan. 28, 1791
1704	388.5	Postlethwayte, art. "Currency."
1717	388.5	Sir Isaac Newton's Rep. of Sept. 21, 1717.
1730	382.897	Kelly's Cambist.
1761	377.	Hamilton.
1772	374.875	Kelly I, 320.
1786	374.875	Kelly.
1790	386.	Hamilton.

The real is the unit of Spanish money. Reals are of three kinds: The Mexican or Spanish real, of which eight make a dollar; the real of new plate of which ten make a dollar; and the real vellon, of which twenty make a dollar. In Spain proper the real vellon is in general use.

In the American colonies during the seventeenth and eighteenth centuries the real of eight to the dollar was the one commonly met with.

MONEY AND
MONEY UNITS
IN THE
AMERICAN
COLONIES

VALUES OF COINS

five coppers, which would be equal to the Spanish half bit." This fixes the value of the pistareen very definitely; but the fact is that the pistareen was valued differently in the different states. Even in the same state or colony its valuation was different at different times. So in New York in 1775 the pistareen passed for one shilling, seven pence, colonial currency; and in 1793 it went for only one shilling, four and one-half pence. At both times the dollar, its half and quarter remained constant in value in the colonial currency. This variation in the value of the pistareen when the other Spanish coins remained constant in value is probably because the pistareen was of a coarser alloy than the other standard Spanish silver pieces, the piece of eight reals, its half, quarter, etc.; and was not therefore universally accepted in trade. The *American Negotiator,* published in 1765, has this note respecting them: "All Spanish moneys, great or small, either of gold or silver, if full Spanish standard weight, are fit to remit to Europe, except a particular sort which circulates in great quantities in the British Sugar Islands which are called Pistareens, whose current value is two ryals. Those pieces of money, if full weight, are not fit to remit to Europe, as they are coarse silver at least 6d. sterling the ounce under standard silver. The blackness of their color is a sufficient mark to distinguish them by." . . .

MUTILATED MONEY

Mutilated money played nearly as great havoc with the colonial trade as did depreciated paper. Nearly all the good gold and silver was sent to England to pay for the excess of imports over exports; and much of what remained at home was counterfeit or underweight. The foreign coins, then, while they had certain values placed on them by the different colonies at different times were not always taken at their tale value. They passed according to the gold or silver there was in them, and were usually weighed when taken in exchange. Consequently, every one who handled any amount of coin was obliged to own a pair of scales; and many persons carried them around in their pockets. The devices for reducing the weight of the coins were numerous and ingenious. Clip, sweat, round, waste, wash and grind are some of the terms used to designate the methods employed in reducing the coins. . . .

The penalties for altering the coin were, corresponding to the other punishments of the time, very severe. In South Carolina the offense of clipping or counterfeiting any foreign coin cur-

rent in the colony was deemed felony without benefit of clergy. In Maryland the same offense was also adjudged felony "and every offender thereof convicted according to the law of this province shall suffer pain of death and forfeit his or her lands, goods and chattels." In Pennsylvania too in 1767 the penalty of counterfeiting was death without benefit of clergy, and any person convicted of paying or tendering any such counterfeit coin was "sentenced to the pillory for the space of one hour, and to have both his or her ears cut off, and nailed to the pillory, and be publickly whipped, on his or her bare back, with twenty-one lashes, well laid on, and, moreover, every such offender shall forfeit the sum of one hundred pounds, lawful money of the province." Most of the paper money, too, issued by the colonies, bore the device: "To counterfeit is death." Despite the severity of the penalties the counterfeiters and clippers continued to be very numerous, and plied their vocations industriously. At the beginning of the Revolution there were in the colonies very few if any coins of full weight. . . .

VALUE OF CURRENCY RELATED
TO LEGISLATIVE POLICY

The change in value of the units of account of the different colonies was gradual, and the transitions are not generally clearly defined. Even the times when the values became finally fixed were at widely different periods and are not in all cases certain. The depreciation was taking place in one colony or another during a large part of the colonial period and numerous forces were acting, every one of which probably influenced this depreciation to a greater or less extent.

In an endeavor to determine what these forces were and the manner of their action, the history of the currency in a single colony may be traced in connection with the history of the colony; and the different fluctuations at the different periods carefully noted. . . .

Every time a colonial Legislature placed a value on the foreign coins and made them current in its jurisdiction, whether from a desire to retain certain coins amongst them, or to render a certain amount of money adequate to meet the demands of the domestic trade, or to draw the coins from other colonies or countries, it had the effect of changing the unit of account of that colony. The financial policies of the different colonies were by no means uniform and the units of the different colonies were not of equal value. Other forces, however, were instrumental in

CHRISTIAN
LIBERTY
"READY TO
PASS TO THE
AMERICAN
STRAND"

bringing about the depreciations. In Virginia the piece of eight was early recognized as worth from five to six shillings, and in 1654 its value was definitely fixed at five shillings. It remained at this value until it was found that the "country was almost drained of it by exportation to places where it passed for more than it did in Virginia." Then an attempt was made to raise its value. This one idea, the regulation of money values with reference to the value of the same coins in neighboring provinces, was at the bottom of much of the legislation respecting this subject in Virginia. The Virginians were not eminently practical and they were influenced by the more energetic colonies to the north. One reason is given by Virginia for changing the value of the silver coins which is not found in the acts of other legislatures. It is "in order to bring the silver currency to a nearer proportion to the gold." Although this may have been considered in other places it probably had but little effect in changing values, and no mention of it is elsewhere made.

In Virginia, too, we see the effect of the paper currency on the money of account. Paper money was first issued in 1755 and evidently on the basis of the value placed on the foreign coin. The paper soon began to depreciate and it was found before long that a piece of eight worth but five shillings, ten pence by proclamation would buy as much as six shillings in paper. But the paper was the legal money of the colony and the Legislature ordered that a piece of eight should pass legally at six shillings. The policy of legalizing the depreciated value of the paper did not continue and the piece of eight remained of the value of six shillings to the end. Two pence in a piece of eight of the increased value of the Virginia currency over sterling was due to the depreciation of the Virginia paper money. The colonies had cut entirely loose from the money system of England, and regulated their local currency according to their local needs. When the Virginia Legislature decreed that the piece of eight pass for six shillings, they ignored the value of the silver in it as measured by the standard of English sterling money, and they placed a value on it by which they created for themselves an entirely new unit of money. . . .

Much of the colonial legislation respecting money was very erratic and the result of mistaken policy; but it was usually actuated by a desire to keep gold and silver coins of every kind in the country at all hazards, and to make them as nearly as possible sufficient for the domestic trade.

AMERICAN MANUFACTURERS

*Principles and
Acts of the
Revolution in
America,* by
Hezekiah Niles,
1876 Reprint

PROVINCIAL CONGRESS OF MASSACHUSETTS
CAMBRIDGE
THURSDAY, DECEMBER 8, 1774

As the happiness of particular families arises, in a great degree, from their being more or less dependent upon others; and as the less occasion they have for any article belonging to others, the more independent; and consequently the happier they are: So the happiness of every political body of men upon earth is to be estimated, in a great measure, upon their greater or less dependence upon any other political bodies; and from hence arises a forcible argument, why every state ought to regulate their internal policy in such a manner as to furnish themselves, within their own body, with every necessary article for subsistence and defence: Otherwise their political existence will depend upon others who may take advantage of such weakness and reduce them to the lowest state of vassalage and slavery. For preventing so great an evil, more to be dreaded than death itself, it must be the wisdom of this colony at all times, more especially at this time, when the hand of power is lashing us with the scorpions of despotism, to encourage agriculture, manufactures and economy, so as to render this state as independent of every other state as the nature of our country will admit. From the consideration thereof, and trusting that the virtue of the people of this colony is such, that the following resolutions of this congress, which must be productive of the greatest good, will by them be effectually carried into execution. And it is therefore resolved—

1. That we do recommend to the people the improvement of their breed of sheep, and the greatest possible increase of the same; and also the preferable use of our own woolen manufactures; and to the manufacturers, that they ask

only reasonable prices for their goods; and especially a very careful sorting of the wool, so that it may be manufactured to the greatest advantage, and as much as may be, into the best goods.

2. We do also recommend to the people the raising of hemp and flax; and as large quantities of flax-seed, more than may be wanted for sowing, may be produced, we would also further recommend the manufacturing the same into oil.

3. We do likewise recommend the making of nails; which we do apprehend must meet with the strongest encouragement from the public, and be of lasting benefit both to the manufacturer and the public.

4. The making of steel, and the preferable use of the same, we do also recommend to the inhabitants of this colony.

5. We do in like manner recommend the making tin-plates, as an article well worth the attention of this people.

6. As fire-arms have been manufactured in several parts of this colony, we do recommend the use of such, in preference to any imported. And we do recommend the making of gun-locks, and furniture and other locks, with other articles in the iron way.

7. We do also earnestly recommend the making of salt-petre, as an article of vast importance to be encouraged, as may be directed hereafter.

8. That gun-powder is also an article of such importance, that every man amongst us who loves his country, must wish the establishment of manufactories for that purpose, and, as there are the ruins of several powder mills, and sundry persons among us who are acquainted with that business, we do heartily recommend its encouragement, by repairing one or more of said mills, or erecting others, and renewing said business as soon as possible.

9. That as several paper mills are now usefully employed, we do likewise recommend a preferable use of our own manufactures in this way; and a careful saving and collecting rags, etc., and also that the manufacturers give a generous price for such rags, etc.

10. That it will be the interest, as well as the duty of this body, or of such as may succeed us, to make such effectual provision for the further manufacturing of the several sorts of glass, as that the same may be carried on to the mutual benefit of the undertaker and the public, and firmly established in this colony.

11. That whereas buttons of excellent qualities and of various sorts are manufactured among us, we do earnestly recommend the general use of the same; so that the manufactories may be extended to the advantage of the people and manufacturers.

12. That whereas salt is an article of vast consumption within this colony, and in its fisheries, we do heartily recommend the making the same, in the several ways wherein it is made in the several parts of Europe; especially in the method used in that part of France where they make bay salt.

13. We do likewise recommend an encouragement of horn-smiths in all their various branches, as what will be of public utility.

14. We do likewise recommend the establishment of one or more manufactories for making wool comber's combs, as an article necessary in our woolen manufactures.

15. We do in like manner heartily recommend the preferable use of the stocking and other hosiery wove among ourselves, so as to enlarge the manufactories thereof, in such a manner as to encourage the manufacturer and serve the country.

16. As madder is an article of great importance in the dyer's business, and which may be easily raised and cured among ourselves, we do therefore earnestly recommend the raising and curing the same.

17. In order the more effectually to carry these resolutions into effect, we do earnestly recommend, That a society or societies be established for the purpose of introducing and establishing such arts and manufactures as may be useful to this people, and are not yet introduced, and the more effectually establishing such as we have already among us.

18. We do recommend to the inhabitants of this province to make use of our manufactures, and those of our sister colonies, in preference to all other manufactures.

Signed by order of the Provincial Congress,

JOHN HANCOCK, President

A true extract from the minutes,

BENJAMIN LINCOLN, Secretary

Philadelphia, March 27, 1775

A speech delivered in CARPENTER'S HALL, *March 16th, before the subscribers towards a fund for establishing manufactories of woolen, cotton and linen, in the city of Philadelphia. Published at the request of the company.*

GENTLEMEN. . . . I cannot help laying a good deal of stress upon the public spirit of my country-

CHRISTIAN
LIBERTY
"READY TO
PASS TO THE
AMERICAN
STRAND"

men, which removes the success of these manufactories beyond a bare possibility, and seems to render it in some measure certain. The resolves of the congress have been executed with a fidelity hardly known to laws in any country, and that too without the assistance of fire and sword, or even of the civil magistrate, and in some places, in direct opposition to them all. . . .

By establishing the woolen, cotton and linen manufactories in this country, we shall invite manufacturers from every part of Europe, particularly from Britain and Ireland, to come and settle among us. . . . But there are higher motives which should lead us to invite strangers to settle in this country. Poverty, with its other evils, has joined with it in every part of Europe, all the miseries of slavery. America is now the only asylum for liberty in the whole world. The present contest with Great Britain was perhaps intended by the Supreme Being, among other wise and benevolent purposes, to show the world this asylum, which, from its remote and uncon-

nected situation with the rest of the globe, might have remained a secret for ages. . . .

By establishing manufactories among us, we erect an additional barrier against the encroachments of tyranny. A people, who are *entirely* dependent upon foreigners for food or clothes, must always be subject to them. I need not detain you in setting forth the misery of holding property, liberty and life upon the precarious will of our fellow subjects in Britain. I beg leave to add a thought in this place which has been but little attended to by the writers upon this subject, and that, is that poverty, confinement and death are trifling evils, when compared with that *total* depravity of heart which is connected with slavery. By becoming slaves, we shall lose every principle of virtue. We shall transfer unlimited obedience from our Maker, to a corrupted majority in the British house of commons, and shall esteem their crimes, the certificates of their divine commission to govern us. . . . We shall hug our chains. We shall cease to be men. We shall be SLAVES.

★   ★   ★   ★   ★

*American
Archives:
Fourth Series,*
Vol. III,
by Peter Force,
Washington,
1839

Philadelphia, August 9, 1775
To the Spinners in this City, the Suburbs, and County:

Your services are now wanted to promote the American Manufactory, at the corner of Market and Ninth-streets, where cotton, wool, flax, &c., are delivered out. Strangers who apply are desired to bring a few lines, by way of recommendation, from some respectable person in their neighbourhood.

One distinguishing characteristick of an excellent woman, as given by the wisest of men is, (Proverbs 31:13, 19) *"That she seeketh wool and flax, and worketh willingly with her hands; she layeth her hands to the spindle, and her hands holdeth the distaff."* In this time of publick distress you have now, each of you, an opportunity not only to help sustain your families, but likewise to cast your mite into the treasury of the publick good. The most feeble effort to help to save the State from ruin, when it is all you can do, is, as the widow's mite, entitled to the same reward as they who of their abundant abilities have cast in much.

JAMES STEWART TO THE PEOPLE OF VIRGINIA

Williamsburgh, Sept. 15, 1775
The subscriber, who is an inhabitant of Virginia, and just returned from England (where he

has been for these eighteen months past, on purpose to make himself acquainted with the culture and preparation of several dyes) has brought in with him the seeds and roots of madder, woad, and welde, (commonly called dyer's weed,) which are the fundamental dyes of all colours, either in the linen, cotton, or woollen manufactures, with a view to propagate them, and makes no doubt of being able to afford them full as cheap as they are sold in England. He has likewise brought in the seeds and roots of the aranatto, which dyes yellow and pompadour colours; also, the genuine rhubarb and licorice plants, with some thriving olive trees, &c, &c. But as the cultivation of them all is too much for him to undertake, he offers to supply any gentleman, or company of gentlemen, in Virginia, with seeds and roots, and to instruct them how to prepare them for the manufacturers; and as the utensils for preparing the different articles for market are to be had in the Country, at a small expense, nothing else is required but the labour of one hand for every five acres.

Madder sells in England, according to the quality, from ten pence to two shillings and five shillings per pound; woad from eighteen pounds to twenty pounds a ton, four or five crops of which may be made yearly in Virginia; and welde is worth five shillings a sheaf, but, for the convenience of exportation, it is intended to manufacture it as they do indigo.

He also offers to instruct one or two ingenious spinning wheel makers, that may be appointed by any County Committee, to make a machine, or wheel, for spinning cotton, with which one hand may spin from fifteen to thirty threads at a time; and he expects no further recompense than as the merit of the machine may appear to deserve.

All persons who intend applying to him must be expeditious, as the land for the cultivation of the above articles ought to be prepared this fall. He may be spoke with at Mrs. Vobe's, for these eight or ten days; afterwards at Winchester, in Frederick County; and all letters for him may be left at the constitutional post-office in this City, directed to the care of Mr. Alexander Wodrow, merchant in Falmouth.

ADDRESS OF THE MANAGERS OF THE UNITED COMPANY OF PHILADELPHIA FOR PROMOTING AMERICAN MANUFACTURES

To the Inhabitants of this Province:

The great reason that there was to apprehend that, through the infatuation and obstinacy of the British Parliament, the Non-Importation and Non-Exportation Agreement of these Colonies would continue for a considerable time, and the great distress that might consequently ensue, unless some means were devised to give employment to the necessitous, together with the advantage that would arise to the publick if manufactories could be established amongst us, were considerations which induced us to make the experiment; and although at first we met with difficulties, owing chiefly to our inexperience, we have now the pleasure to inform you, that we are thoroughly convinced of the utility of this institution; that it is practicable, and may be profitable, not only to the persons who are actually employed in labour, but to the contributors themselves; and, in order to render it still more extensively useful, we are extremely desirous that the company may be enlarged, and that every person who can conveniently spare the small sum of ten Pounds would become a proprietor. There are now upwards of four hundred persons in employment, which numbers are daily increasing; and nothing is now wanting but capital stock, to carry on a very extensive trade.

As the inhabitants of this Province are distinguished for humanity, if there was no other motive but the employment of the poor, it must be a strong incitement to join the company; but when private interest, charity to the poor, and the publick good, unitedly urge us thereto, who that has ability can refuse? Persons of experience in the linen branch assure us that our climate is much more favourable than either England or Ireland, and that nothing is wanting to carry on manufactories very extensively, but experienced workmen, and a disposition in the people to promote the design.

As the bleaching of linen is a material part of the manufacture, we may inform the publick that there is a gentleman now in this City, who has been bred to the business, a man of character and abilities, who, if sufficient encouragement should be given, will soon establish a bleachfield.

Such as incline to become subscribers to the manufactory are desired to call at the Factory House, in Market Street, at the corner of Ninth Street or at the London Coffee House, where articles will be left for them to sign.

SALT PETRE

Journals of the Continental Congress, Vol. II, Washington, 1905

CONTINENTAL CONGRESS
SATURDAY, JUNE 10, 1775

Several letters, from Massachusetts Bay, Ticonderoga, Crown Point, &c. were laid before the Congress, and read;

Upon motion the Congress came to the following resolutions:

Resolved: That it be, and is hereby earnestly recommended to the several Colonies of New Hampshire, Rhode Island, Connecticut and the interior towns of Massachusetts bay, that they immediately furnish the American army before Boston with as much powder out of their town, and other publick stocks as they can possibly spare; keeping an exact account of the quantities supplied, that it may be again replaced, or paid for by the Continent; this to be effected with the utmost secrecy and despatch.

That it be recommended to the committees of

CHRISTIAN
LIBERTY
"READY TO
PASS TO THE
AMERICAN
STRAND"

the several towns and districts in the colonies of the Massachusetts bay, New Hampshire, Rhode Island, and Providence Plantations, Connecticut, New York, and the eastern division of New Jersey, to collect all the salt petre and brimstone in their several towns and districts, and transmit the same, with all possible despatch, to the provincial Convention at New York.

That it be recommended to the provincial Congress of the colony of New York, to have the powder Mills, in that colony, put into such a condition as immediately to manufacture, into gun powder, for the use of the Continent, whatever materials may be procured in the manner above directed.

That it be recommended to the committees of the western division of New Jersey, the colonies of Pensylvania, lower counties on Delaware and Maryland, that they, without delay, collect the salt petre and sulphur in their respective Colonies, and transmit the same to the committee for the city and liberties of Philadelphia; to the end, that those articles may be immediately manufactured into gun powder, for the use of the continent.

That it be recommended to the conventions and committees of the colonies of Virginia, North Carolina and South Carolina, that they, without delay, collect the salt petre and sulphur in their respective colonies, and procure these articles to be manufactured, as soon as possible, into gun powder, for the use of the Continent.

That it be recommended to the several inhabitants of the united colonies, who are possessed of salt petre and sulphur, for their own use, to dispose of them for the purpose of manufacturing gun powder.

That the salt petre and sulphur, collected in consequence of the resolves of Congress for that purpose, be paid for out of the continental fund.

Resolved, that Mr. Robert Treat Paine, Mr. Richard Henry Lee, Mr. Benjamin Franklin, Mr. Philip Schuyler and Mr. Thomas Johnson, be a committee to devise ways and means to introduce the manufacture of salt petre in these colonies.

MONDAY, JUNE 26, 1775

The Congress met according to adjournment.

A letter from Governor Trumbull was read, and referred to the committee appointed to devise ways and means for introducing the manufacture of salt petre into these colonies.

★ ★ ★ ★ ★

American Archives: Fourth Series, Vol. II, by Peter Force, Washington, 1839

GOVERNOUR TRUMBULL TO CONTINENTAL CONGRESS

Lebanon June 20, 1775

Sir: This acknowledges the receipt of your letter of the 10th instant, and enclosed resolves. Am happy in being able to inform you, that by advice of my Council, appointed to act in the recess of the Assembly, convened on the 7th instant, I had ordered fifty barrels of powder from this Colony, containing one hundred and ten pounds each, to be sent with all despatch and secrecy to the American Army before Boston, which reached them about Friday last; and since the receipt of yours have ordered ten barrels more, of the same quantity each, which moved the 19th, and to proceed night and day; and wish it was in our power to supply much more for the necessity of the Army, and in compliance with the request of your wise, firm and patriotick assembly, on whom, under God, the salvation of America greatly depends. It is an unhappy truth, that no supplies of that article are to be obtained in this Colony. We have taken all care in our power to procure much larger quantities than we have yet received, but daily hope to expect the arrival of some, yet fear it may be intercepted by the vigilant malice of our enemies.

The New York Congress informs us they have sent six hundred and fifty-five pounds for the same purpose, which I find has been detained at Stamford, for General Wooster's Regiment, but the same quantity is to be immediately furnished from the eastern part of the Colony, in addition to what is already sent. Only eight hundred and forty pounds have been imported into this Colony since our Delegates left it.

I am not at present able to procure any accurate estimate of powder, arms and ammunition. By the standing law, every Town ought to have fifty pounds to every sixty militia men, four pounds of bullets, and twelve flints; and by an act of last October, a double quantity of powder is ordered; but, I suppose, take one with another, we are more than half deficient of a single supply. If they were full, it would be about forty-four thousand seven hundred pound. As to lead and flints, perhaps we have a tolerable supply.

Have not yet been able to carry into execution your resolve of collecting saltpetre and brimstone, and forwarding to the Provincial Congress of New-York, but shall pay the greatest attention to it as fast as possible, but expect no great quantity can be obtained.

The General Assembly of this Colony, at their last session, offered very large premiums on saltpetre manufactured in and of materials found within the same, for one year; and on sulphur manufactured in this Colony from materials found in any of them, viz: twenty pounds per hundred weight of the first, and five for the second. Proposals have been made to me by Mr. DeWitt of Norwich, with two of his friends near New-York, for speedily making very large quantities of the saltpetre, if they could be assisted with the loan of a sum sufficient to erect necessary buildings, &c., for which they will give ample security. This Colony having given such bounty, and the Assembly not sitting, nothing can be done here in that way. Your wisdom will direct what might be proper for you to do, if application should be made; and your patriotism will certainly incline you to every thing your wisdom shall dictate for the common good. If it is possible for Philadelphia or any Southern Colony to spare any manufactured, or other powder, to the Cambridge Army, it is an would be a most neces-

sary and acceptable thing. I fear for their supply, where there is most important occasion.

You are doubtless possessed of every intelligence that is attainable, and can better judge whether, notwithstanding every shew and appearance to the contrary, the whole force of the enemy will not be collected, and their utmost exertions made to cut off the head of the snake; if so, although our men are ever so resolute or numerous, they can do nothing without powder; and there must be a vast consumption of it. A very great proportion must have been expended in the several engagements which have already happened, and we have just received the important (but very imperfect) news of a vigorous attack on our Army, on Friday night or Saturday morning last, in consequence of their attempting to take possession of the important posts at Bunker's Hill in Charlestown. Our forces have been obliged to retreat, but on the whole suppose they have suffered far less than their enemies.

I am, with great truth and regard, Sir, your most obedient humble servant,

JONATHAN TRUMBULL

★   ★   ★   ★   ★

FRIDAY, JULY 28, 1775

Whereas the safety and freedom of every community depends greatly upon having the means of defence in its own power, and that the United Colonies may not, during the continuance of their present important contest for Liberty, nor in any future time, be under the expensive, uncertain and dangerous necessity of relying on foreign importations for Gun Powder: And it being very certain from observation and experiment, that Salt Petre is to be obtained in great abundance from most parts of this Northern Continent; that the surface of the earth, in long used tobacco warehouses and their yards, or of common tobacco houses, is particularly and strongly impregnated with Nitre.

Resolved, That it be recommended to the Provincial Conventions of the tobacco Colonies, that as quickly as may be, they appoint one or more manufactories on each river, contiguous to the great inspections, and under the direction of persons qualified by their skill and diligence to bring this important business to a speedy and successful issue.

To the Assemblies and Conventions of the other Colonies, it is recommended immediately to put in practice such other mode of making

Salt Petre, as may be found best adapted to their respective circumstances.

That all persons may be encouraged to apply themselves to the manufacture of Salt Petre, it is recommended to the several Assemblies and Conventions, to buy up, on account of the United Colonies, all the good and merchantable Salt Petre at *half a dollar* for each pound, that is, or shall be made in their respective Colonies before the first day of October, 1776.

It is recommended that the collecting Sulphur be encouraged:—And it is recommended to the several Provincial Conventions, to grant such premiums, for the refining of Sulphur in their respective Provinces, as may be judged proper.

And it is further recommended to the several Assemblies and Conventions, that they cause mills to be erected, and skilful persons to be procured and employed for making Gun Powder.

As Salt Petre is an article so necessary for defence, and in other respects, so extensively useful, it is an object that not only requires the public patronage, but demands the attention of individuals:—The following systems or methods of making Salt-Petre, suited to different circumstances and different materials, is recommended to the attention of the good people of these United Colonies.

CHRISTIAN
LIBERTY
"READY TO
PASS TO THE
AMERICAN
STRAND"

*American
Archives:
Fourth Series,*
Vol. III,
by Peter Force,
Washington,
1839

★　　　★　　　★　　　★　　　★

MASSACHUSETTS HOUSE OF REPRESENTATIVES
AUGUST 24, 1775

The Report of the Committee appointed to consider the Resolves of the Continental Congress relative to Saltpetre being amended, was read and accepted, and is as follows, viz:

Whereas the honourable Continental Congress have strongly recommended to the Assemblies and Conventions of the United Colonies, to appoint one or more person or persons, in each Colony, to put in practice the making Saltpetre, according to such mode as shall be best adapted to their particular circumstances and to buy up, on account of the United Colonies, all the good merchantable Saltpetre that shall be made in said Colonies by the first day of October, 1776: Therefore, in compliance with said recommendation, and for the carrying so valuable a purpose into execution,

It is Resolved, That Dr. Whiting, Deacon Baker, of Boston, and Captain John Peck, be a Committee, whose business it shall be faithfully and diligently to apply themselves to the manufacturing of Saltpetre, for the space of three months from the first day of September, 1775, jointly or severally, in such places in this Colony as they shall judge most suitable for that purpose; and they are hereby directed to use all diligence to discover the most eligible and successful method of manufacturing that important commodity, and to communicate all the useful knowledge they shall acquire in said business to all such as request it of them, and that they from time to time publish, in the newspapers or otherwise, all the useful discoveries they may make in the progress of said business; and each of the said Committee shall be allowed and paid out of the publick Treasury of this Colony, for the said term of three months, four Shillings per day for every day they shall be employed in said service, as a reward for the aforesaid service.

And it is further Resolved, That said Committee are hereby empowered to buy up all the good and merchantable Saltpetre that shall be made within this Colony by the first day of said October, 1776, at half a dollar a pound; and the said Committee are also directed to buy up all the good and merchantable Sulphur that shall be refined in this Colony by the first day of said October, at nine Pence per pound, the sellers of Sulphur producing a certificate from a major part of the Selectmen either of the Towns to which he or they belong or the Town where such Sulphur was refined, certifying that the same was produced and refined from mines and ores within this Colony; and the said Committee shall deliver such Saltpetre and Sulphur to such person or persons as shall be appointed by the General Court to receive the same, and shall receive out of the Colony Treasury from time to time such sums of money as upon the presentation made to them by said Committee, they shall judge necessary for buying up said Saltpetre and Sulphur.

And it is further Resolved, That it be strongly recommended to the inhabitants of the several Towns in this Colony that they exert themselves in promoting this important manufacture, as the surest means of preserving their own lives, liberties and estates; of insuring the salvation of their Country and its future prosperity, by erecting one or more Saltpetre works, in each Town where it may be done with probable success; and that they not only thoroughly attend to the working of those materials from which Saltpetre may be speedily procured without any previous management, but that they also take especial care to collect together under proper sheds those materials (the knowledge of which may be easily obtained from publications) which, by fermenting and putrefying together, will in due time afford Saltpetre with ease and in great plenty.

And it is further Resolved, That the several methods of making Saltpetre recommended by the honourable Continental Congress to the United Colonies be immediately reprinted, together with the foregoing Resolves, and that there be added thereto, by way of appendix, the method of making Saltpetre practised by Doctor Graham, and that one of the pamphlets be sent to the Selectmen of each Town within this Colony; and that Dr. Whiting procure the reprinting the several methods recommended by the honourable Continental Congress for making Saltpetre, together with the foregoing Resolves, and distribute them agreeable thereto.

In Council, August 24, 1775: Read and concurred.

REPORT OF COMMITTEE APPOINTED TO OBTAIN KNOWLEDGE IN MANUFACTORY OF SALTPETRE

The Committee who were appointed by this honourable Assembly to carry on the manufacture of saltpetre, for three months from the first day of September, 1775, having been ordered by this honourable House, on the 30th day of September ultimo, to repair to Windsor, in Connecticut, in order to acquire further knowledge in that important manufacture, the subscriber, as Chairman of that Committee, begs leave to report the following state of facts, viz: That as Captain Bowman, one of said Committee, was at Newburyport, did not think it expedient to wait until he could be sent for from so great a distance, but immediately set out for Windsor, by the way of Bolton, in order to consult Deacon Baker, another of said Committee, who refused to accompany me, alleging that one could do the business effectually, and that his going would only put the Colony to unnecessary charge. From thence I proceeded on my way with all expedition for Windsor; but, luckily, in passing through Enfield, a Town adjoining to Windsor, I lit on a saltpetre work, where the business had been carried on with success by Messrs. Blakerlige and Wilson. They had erected a house for that purpose, about thirty by twenty feet square. They had three vats, containing about forty-five bushels each. They had also two potash kettles, conveniently set in brick, for boiling. They had just finished a very successful process, and showed me a vessel of very fine saltpetre crystals, containing twenty-seven pounds weight, which they had obtained at one boiling. They appeared like gentlemen truly patriotick; and their late success inspired them with such generosity that they immediately told me they would freely communicate to me all the knowledge they had acquired in this art; which they did, as follows, viz: They told me that they had been endeavouring to make saltpetre, by different processes, for more than a month, with very ordinary success, not having been able, from a great number of processes, to obtain but about twenty weight in the whole; and after entirely failing of success, without knowing the cause, were about to give over; but hearing that one Mr. Kibbe, of Windsor, Goshen, had discovered a successful method of making saltpetre, they immediately applied to him for instructions, who acquainted them that he had, by repeated experiments, found out a method by which he could make fifteen or sixteen weight of saltpetre in a day, but utterly refused to give them any information until they had given him a fee of four Pounds, lawful money. Upon which he told them as follows, viz: That saltpetre, he found, might be extracted from almost any earth in some quantity. He had tried common earth, taken up directly from the ground, which had never been

under any cover, and from his vat full, (containing between fifty and sixty bushels) he had made six pounds of good saltpetre; but the best earth he could find was from under old buildings, standing on pretty high land, of a light, sandy, or loamy nature. In using this earth, he found the light loose dirt on the surface contained the largest proportion of nitre; but when he got below this, the lower he dug the better it yielded, as he had gone, which was about three feet deep. With this earth he filled his vat, as he had but one, leaving it hollow on the top. He then sprinkled on the earth, in the vat, lie, drawn from common ashes, in the proportion of about a pint to a bushel of earth. He then poured on water, sufficient to wet the earth, about milk-warm. He then poured on cold water until he had added about as much as there was of the earth, letting it run through the earth as soon as it would; if the first running was foul, he returned it on to the earth until it came through perfectly clear. He continued to save the lie, for boiling, as long as it came through clear; but as soon as it began to change to a yellow or brown colour, he put all that came through after that into his next vat of earth, alleging, very justly, that the nitre, being easily dissolved by water, came through first, and that when the colour changed, the unctuous, bituminous parts of the earth were coming through, which, though they contained some nitre, yet would so clog and entangle the nitrous salts, as to prevent their freely shooting into crystals. When he had collected a sufficient quantity of lie to fill his two kettles, he began to boil; and as the lie consumed in the kettles, he constantly filled the kettle he intended to boil off in with hot liquor, out of the other kettle, and filled that other kettle with cold lie from the vats, observing carefully, through the whole boiling, to skim off what arose to the top of the boiling liquor; which scum he saved to put into his next vat of earth. When he had got all the liquor he designed for one boiling, into one kettle, and had reduced it to about double or treble the quantity he expected to reduce it to for crystallizing, he poured it into a tub, previously fixed for the purpose, by being let nearly on a level, being perforated, and a tap fixed within about an inch of the bottom. After letting it stand in this tub a sufficient time for all the gross matter to settle to the bottom, he drew it off by the abovementioned tap, which left the sediment in the bottom of the tub, below the tap. He then returned it into his kettle, and boiled it gently, throwing in at this time a small quantity of alum, viz: about

CHRISTIAN
LIBERTY
"READY TO
PASS TO THE
AMERICAN
STRAND"

two spoonfuls into a quantity of liquor, from which he expected fifteen pounds of nitre. This would occasion it to throw up the impurities, plentifully, to the surface of the boiling liquor, which he carefully skimmed off, until by setting a little of the liquor in a cool place, in a spoon, he found it begin to shoot into crystals. He then dipped it out of the kettle into the abovementioned perforated tub, being clean washed. Here he let it stand long enough for the gross matter again to subside, taking care, however, to draw it off into his coolers before it grew so cold as to crystallize in the tub. For crystallizing vessels, he preferred wooden trays to any other, into which he now drew his liquor, and set it in a cool place, where, in about twelve hours, it would be sufficiently crystallized. He then carefully drained off the liquor from the crystals, and boiled it again, until he found it would again crystallize. He then poured it into his tub, in order for the sediment to subside as before, and then drew it off and set it to crystallize. This he repeated twice after the first crystallizing, and the remaining liquor he put into his next vat of earth. His method of refining was exactly similar to that recommended from Virginia, published in the pamphlet ordered by the Continental Congress.

By exactly following these directions, these gentlemen informed me they had produced the fine crop of crystals I there saw; and by computing from the success they had there had, and even making some allowance, they should be able (in that works, consisting of three vats, holding about forty-five bushels each, and two potash kettles to boil in) to make fifty weight a week.

Having got this intelligence from these gentlemen, I went to visit Mr. Kibbe, who appeared very reserved on the subject; but he told me that he had honestly told these gentlemen all he knew at that time, and that the knowledge I had got in the business was sufficient to carry it on with success; but that he had, in the course of his experiments, since he informed them, made some very useful, advantageous discoveries; but as he had obtained his knowledge by great expense of time, and painful assiduity, he did not think it his duty to give it away; but as their Assembly was to sit soon, he intended to make them an offer of his skill, on reasonable terms, which, if they complied with, no doubt the whole would be soon published. He told me, positively, that he could make fifteen pounds a day, and confirmed the above accounts those gentlemen had given me, respecting the nitrous qualities of the earth, from his own experience.

WILLIAM WHITING.

GOD PREPARES A CHRISTIAN PEOPLE TO ESTABLISH THE AMERICAN NATION

When we contemplate the coincidence of circumstances

and wonderful combination of causes,

which gradually prepared the people of this country for independence;

when we contemplate the rise, progress and termination of the late war,

which gave them a name among the nations of the earth,

we are, with you, unavoidably led to acknowledge and adore

the great arbiter of the universe, by whom empires rise and fall.

A review of the many signal instances of divine interposition

in favor of this country claims our most pious gratitude:—

From Answer to President Washington's Speech to Senate, May 7, 1789

William S. Johnson, Conn.; William Paterson, N.J.; Charles Carroll, Md., Committee

CHRONOLOGY OF IMPORTANT EVENTS, 1761 TO 1775

1761

JAN. 27. Hutchinson chief justice of Mass. John Adams considered that the American Revolution began at this date.

1761-2

Discussion over the "Writs of Assistance" in Mass.

1762

JAN. 1. England declares war with Spain; takes Martinique, St. Lucia, and St. Vincent; AUG. 13, takes Havana.

The question of either restoring to France Guadaloupe with its sugar trade, or Canada with its fur trade, under discussion in England.

AUTUMN. Pontiac planning his conspiracy.

NOV. 3. Louis XV by a secret treaty cedes to Spain Louisiana west of the Mississippi, with the island of New Orleans east of it.

1763

JAN. The English government orders Connecticut to cease colonizing the Wyoming country. Mason and Dixon's line.

Bigot's trial in Paris.

FEB. 10. Treaty of Paris, by which Spain cedes Florida to England; the islands of St. Pierre and Miquelon are confirmed to France; Acadia is confirmed to England.

APR. 16. Bute ceases to be prime minister of England.

MAY-NOV. Pontiac's conspiracy; siege of Detroit.

MAY-JUNE. Various western forts yield to the Pontiac forces.

Geo. Grenville prime minister of England.

The English ministry determines to raise a revenue from the Colonies, and the reports reach America in the winter of 1764.

AUG. 5 AND 6. Battle of Bushy Run.

OCT. 7. The proclamation of George III, defining the boundaries respectively of Quebec, East Florida, West Florida, and Grenada; but the regions north of the great Lakes and west of the Alleghanies to the Mississippi remain crown lands.

Proclamation of George III to induce settlers in Canada.

OCT. 15. Connecticut settlers attacked in the Susquehanna country (Pennsylvania).

NOV. Gen Gage succeeds Amherst as commander-in-chief of the English forces in N. America.

NOV. 3. Treaty of Fontainebleau between England and Spain.

DEC. Patrick Henry argues the Parsons case and

Narrative and Critical History of America, Edited by Justin Winsor, Vol. VIII, Boston, 1889

God Prepares
a Christian
People
to Establish
the American
Nation

questions the king's prerogative.
Dec. 14-27. The Paxton boys massacre the Conestogoes.
Jona. Mayhew's controversy with Apthorpe.

1764

Apr. 6. Grenville's act to take effect Sept. 30, modifying the sugar act of 1733.
May 24. Boston organizes action against taxation by parliament.
Courts of vice-admiralty for Brit. America.
"Wilkes and Liberty".
June. Col Bradstreet's campaign along the great Lakes.
Maj. Loftus with English troops ascends the Mississippi from New Orleans.
Oct. Nov. Bouquet marches into the Muskingum Valley.
Sir William Johnson's treaties with the Indians.
Fontleroy sent by the French government to observe the American colonies.
Publication of Hutchinson's *Massachusetts Bay* begins.

1765

Feb. 6. Barré applies the words "Sons of Liberty" to the Amer. patriots.
Mar. 22. Stamp Act.
Apr. The Mutiny Act extended to the English colonies.
July 13. The Rockingham ministry in England comes in, and lasts till Aug. 2 of the next year.
Andrew Oliver hanged in effigy in Boston.
Non-importation movements in the English colonies.
Aug. 26. Hutchinson's house in Boston sacked.
Oct. 7-25. The Stamp Act Congress in N. York.
Oct. 10. Fort Chartres turned over to English troops, and English troops for the first time occupy the Illinois country.
The right of taxation by Parliament much discussed.
John Adams combating the monarchical and Anglican system.
Croghan sent by Gage toward the Illinois country.
Nov. 7. Dennis Deberdt the London agent of Massachusetts.
Samuel Holland surveyor-general of the northern district of the English colonies during this and succeeding years.

1766

Jan. 28. Franklin examined before Parliament as to the Stamp Act.
Mar. Ulloa takes possession of New Orleans for Spain.
Mar. 7. The Declaratory Act passed by the English Parliament.
Mar. 18. Stamp Act repealed.
July 30. Pitt becomes Earl of Chatham.
Oct. The Daniel Malcolm riot in Boston.
Royal artillery arrive in Boston.
The Chatham-Grafton ministry in England for three years.
Capt. Harry Gordon on the Ohio.

1767

Expulsion of the Jesuits from Spain and South America.
June 29. The act of the Eng. Parliament proposing duties on tea to go into effect Nov. 20.
Dec. Shelburne in the English ministry succeeded by Hillsborough.
John Dickinson's *Farmer's Letters*, a discussion of colonial rights.

1768

Feb. 11. The circular letter to the other colonies written by Samuel Adams of Mass.
June 10. John Hancock's sloop "Liberty" seized.
July 4. Dickinson's Liberty Song published.
Sept. British troops arrive in Boston harbor.
Sept. 24. The treaty at Fort Stanwix, defining a line between the English colonies and the Indians, later known as the "property line".
Sept. 27-29. Convention of the Mass. towns on the coming of the troops.
Oct. Chatham resigns and Grafton becomes the head of the English ministry.
Baron DeKalb sent by Choiseul to observe the spirit of the American colonies of England.
The proprietaries of Pennsylvania secure by an Indian deed the territory which Connecticut, as the contest went on, claimed to be under her charter, and built there, Jan. 1769, a blockhouse, while the Connecticut people in Feb. contested their occupancy on the ground. The warfare lasted till 1771.
War of the Regulators in No. Carolina, lasting for three years.
Jesuits expelled from Paraguay, and their rule ceases.
Temporary French republic in Louisiana.

Frequent political publications in England.

1769

Hearne's explorations in the Arctic regions for three years.
AUG. Bernard sails for England; Lieut. gov. Hutchinson in authority in Mass.
Virginia non-importation agreement.
Daniel Boone explores the Kentucky region.
Watauga Association settlements (Tennessee).
Dartmouth College founded.
The American Philosophical Society begins its publications.
Spanish occupation of California.
Monterey (California) founded.
San Francisco Bay discovered.

1770

Lord North begins to be premier of England.
Many political tracts on the relations of England to her colonies.
MAR. 5. Boston Massacre.
APR. The Townshend Act repealed, except the duty on tea.
Washington visits the Ohio region to select land for the soldiers.
The Zane family settle on the Ohio near the mouth of Wheeling creek.
William Gordon comes to America.
Edmund Burke agent for New York, holding the office five years.
Walpole Grant, in the Ohio country (Colony of Vandalia) secured and ratified; and finally abandoned.
Samuel Hearne traces the Coppermine River.

1771

MAR. Hutchinson becomes gov. of Mass.
The Mohegan case, begun by Dudley, settled.
The right of the press to publish reports of Parliamentary debates conceded.

1772

Map of Behring's Straits.
Vaugondy's map of the Arctic regions.
Sam. Adams forms a local committee of correspondence in Boston.
JUNE. The burning of the "Gaspee" at Providence.
AUG. 4. Hillsborough succeeded by Dartmouth in the English ministry.

AUG. 8. Gage warns white settlers not to pass the line established in 1768.
The Moravians and their converts remove from Pennsylvania to the Muskingum.
Rufus Putnam on the lower Mississippi.

1773

Matthew Phelps in the Ohio country during this and succeeding years.
Controversy of Va. and Penna. over their respective rights in the country beyond the Alleghanies begins.
Presidios created in Upper California.
Celtic settlers in Nova Scotia.
The Hutchinson letters, written to England in 1768-69, sent to the Speaker of the Mass. House of Representatives.
JAN., FEB. Hutchinson's controversy with the General Court in Massachusetts.
MARCH. Intercolonial committees of correspondence established by Virginia.
The tea importations, and the opposition in Boston and elsewhere.
DEC. 16. Boston Tea Party.
Franklin before the Privy Council.

1774

JAN. 31. Franklin removed from the office of deputy postmaster-general for the colonies.
MAR. 31. Boston Port Bill, to take effect June 1st.
APR. George Rogers Clark in the Kentucky country.
Cresap, or the Dunmore war on the western frontiers of the English colonies in N. America.
Immigrants reach Kentucky.
The first log cabin in Kentucky built at Harrodsburg.
APR. 19. Edmund Burke's speech on American taxation.
The Quebec Bill.
Letter of Congress to the people of Canada.
John Wilkes's commotions begin in London.
MAY 13. Gen. Gage arrives in Boston.
MAY 17. Rhode Island proposes a General Congress.
JUNE. Solemn League and Covenant in Mass.
JUNE 1. Hutchinson leaves Boston.
JULY. Sir William Johnson dies. Col. Guy Johnson succeeds him as Indian superintendent.
SEPT. Lewis's march against the Ohio Indians.
SEPT. 5. First Continental Congress in Philadelphia.

GOD PREPARES
A CHRISTIAN
PEOPLE
TO ESTABLISH
THE AMERICAN
NATION
———————

SEPT. 9. The "Suffolk Resolves" in Mass.

OCT. Articles of Association adopted by the Congress.

OCT. 5. The legislative assembly of Massachusetts resolves itself into a Provincial Congress.

OCT. 10. Battle of Point Pleasant on the Ohio.

DEC. 12. John Adams and Daniel Leonard, as "Novanglus" and "Massachusettensis" continue their controversy till April.

DEC. 14. Fort William and Mary at Portsmouth robbed.

The Westchester Farmer letters.

Connecticut votes to issue paper money,—the first of the Revolution.

Newspapers divided for and against the government.

Constantine Phipps's attempt to reach the North Pole.

Louis XVI on the throne of France; Maurepas prime minister; Turgot head of the Treasury.

1775.

Parliament occupied with American affairs.

Speeches of Camden, Mansfield and Fox in Parliament.

Jan. Gage sends troops to Marshfield from Boston.

Jan. 20. Chatham's motion for conciliation with America.

Feb. 1. The second Provincial Congress of Massachusetts assembles.

Feb. 26. Leslie's troops at Salem, Mass.

Feb. Franklin in London conferring with the Howes.

Mar. Franklin leaving London.

Apr. 18. Paul Revere's ride.

Apr. 19. Lexington and Concord fights.

May. Conflicts in Boston harbor.

Sir John Johnson flies from the Mohawk Valley to Canada.

May 5. Naval skirmish at Martha's Vineyard.

May 10. Arnold and Allen capture Ticonderoga. The Second Continental Congress assembles.

May 20. Mecklenburg County (N.C.) Resolves. Artemas Ward commander-in-chief at Cambridge, Mass.

May 25. Burgoyne, Clinton, and Howe arrive in Boston.

May, June. Col. Guy Johnson watched.

June. Boone builds his fort in Kentucky.

First Continental money.

June 7. Massachusetts considering the creation of a naval force.

June 15. Almon's *Remembrancer* begins in London.

Massachusetts privateers.

June 12. The "Margaretta" seized at Machias, Me.

Rhode Island commissions two cruisers.

Rhode Island sends Abraham Whipple to Bermuda to seize powder.

June 12. GENERAL GAGE PROCLAIMS MARTIAL LAW IN MASSACHUSETTS.

June 12. CONTINENTIAL CONGRESS PROCLAIMS JULY 20 AS CONTINENTAL FAST DAY.

June 17. Washington chosen commander-in-chief.

June 17. Battle of Bunker Hill.

July 3. Washington takes command, with instruction to keep the forces already in the field, and these included Indians which the Massachusetts government had enlisted before April.

July. Col. Guy Johnson holds a conference with the Indians at Montreal.

July 20. OBSERVANCE OF CONTINENTAL FAST DAY.

MERCY OTIS WARREN

NEW ENGLAND HISTORIAN COTEMPORARY WITH THE AMERICAN REVOLUTION

"The sudden rotations in human affairs are wisely permitted by Providence,
to remind mankind of their natural equality, to check the pride of wealth,
to restrain the insolence of rank and family distinctions,
which too frequently oppress the various classes in society."

PRELUDE TO THE AMERICAN REVOLUTION, 1765 TO 1775

AN ADDRESS TO THE INHABITANTS OF THE UNITED STATES OF AMERICA

At a period when every manly arm was occupied, and every trait of talent or activity engaged, either in the cabinet or the field, apprehensive, that amidst the sudden convulsions, crowded scenes, and rapid changes, that flowed in quick succession, many circumstances might escape the more busy and active members of society, I have been induced to improve the leisure Providence had lent, to record as they passed, in the following pages, the new and unexperienced events exhibited in a land previously blessed with peace, liberty, simplicity, and virtue. . . .

Connected by nature, friendship, and every social tie, with many of the first patriots, and most influential characters on the continent; in the habits of confidential and epistolary intercourse with several gentlemen employed abroad in the most distinguished stations, and with others since elevated to the highest grades of rank and distinction, I had the best means of information, through a long period that the colonies were in suspense, waiting the operation of foreign courts, and the success of their own enterprising spirit. The solemnity that covered every countenance,

when contemplating the sword uplifted, and the horrors of civil war rushing to habitations not inured to scenes of rapine and misery; even to the quiet cottage, where only concord and affection had reigned; stimulated to observation a mind that had not yielded to the assertion, that all political attentions lay out of the road of female life. It is true there are certain appropriate duties assigned to each sex; and doubtless it is the more peculiar province of masculine strength, not only to repel the bold invader of the rights of his country and of mankind, but in the nervous style of manly eloquence, to describe the blood-stained field, and relate the story of slaughtered armies.

Sensible of this, the trembling heart has recoiled at the magnitude of the undertaking, and the hand often shrunk back from the task; yet, recollecting that every domestic enjoyment depends on the unimpaired possession of civil and religious liberty, that a concern for the welfare of society ought equally to glow in every human breast, the work was not relinquished. The most interesting circumstances were collected, active characters portrayed, the principles of the times developed, and the changes marked; nor need it cause a blush to acknowledge, a detail was preserved with a view of transmitting it to the rising youth of my country, some of them in infancy, others in the European world, while the most in-

History of the Rise, Progress and Termination of the American Revolution, by Mercy Warren, Vol. I, Boston, 1805

357

GOD PREPARES
A CHRISTIAN
PEOPLE
TO ESTABLISH
THE AMERICAN
NATION

teresting events lowered over their native land.

Conscious that truth has been the guide of my pen, and candor, as well as justice, the accompaniment of my wishes through every page, I can say, with an ingenious writer, "I have used my pen with the liberty of one, who neither hopes nor fears, nor has any interest in the success or failure of any party, and who speaks to posterity —perhaps very far remote."

The sympathizing heart has looked abroad and wept the many victims of affliction, inevitably such in consequence of civil feuds and the concomitant miseries of war, either foreign or domestic. The reverses of life, and the instability of the world, have been viewed on the point of both extremes. Their delusory nature and character have been contemplated as becomes the philosopher and the christian: the one teaches us from the analogies of nature, the necessity of changes, decay, and death; the other strengthens the mind to meet them with the rational hope of revival and renovation. . . . Providence has clearly pointed out the duties of the present generation, particularly the paths which Americans ought to tread. The United States form a young republic, a confederacy which ought ever to be cemented by a union of interests and affection, under the influence of those principles which obtained their independence. . . .

The state of the public mind, appears at present to be prepared to weigh these reflections with solemnity, and to receive with pleasure an effort to trace the origin of the American revolution, to review the characters that effected it, and to justify the principles of the defection and final separation from the parent state. With an expanded heart, beating with high hopes of the continued freedom and prosperity of America, the writer indulges a modest expectation, that the following pages will be perused with kindness and candor: this she claims, both in consideration of her sex, the uprightness of her intentions, and the fervency of her wishes for the happiness of all the human race.

Mercy Warren.
Plymouth, Mass.
March, 1805

INTRODUCTORY OBSERVATIONS

History, the deposite of crimes, and the record of every thing disgraceful or honorary to mankind, requires a just knowledge of character, to investigate the sources of action; a clear comprehension, to review the combination of causes; and

precision of language, to detail the events that have produced the most remarkable revolutions.

To analyze the secret springs that have effected the progressive changes in society; to trace the origin of the various modes of government, the consequent improvements in science, in morality, or the national tincture that marks the manners of the people under despotic or more liberal forms, is a bold and adventurous work.

The study of the human character opens at once a beautiful and a deformed picture of the soul. We there find a noble principle implanted in the nature of man, that pants for distinction. This principle operates in every bosom, and when kept under the control of reason, and the influence of humanity, it produces the most benevolent effects. But when the checks of conscience are thrown aside, or the moral sense weakened by the sudden acquisition of wealth or power, humanity is obscured, and if a favorable coincidence of circumstances permits, this love of distinction often exhibits the most mortifying instances of profligacy, tyranny, and the wanton exercise of arbitrary sway. Thus when we look over the theatre of human action, scrutinize the windings of the heart, and survey the transactions of man from the earliest to the present period, it must be acknowledged that ambition and avarice are the leading springs which generally actuate the restless mind. From these primary sources of corruption have arisen all the rapine and confusion, the depredation and ruin, that have spread distress over the face of the earth from the days of Nimrod to Cesar, and from Cesar to an arbitrary prince of the house of Brunswick.

The indulgence of these turbulent passions has depopulated cities, laid waste the finest territories, and turned the beauty and harmony of the lower creation into an aceldama. Yet candor must bear honorable testimony to many signal instances of disinterested merit among the children of men; thus it is not possible to pronounce decidedly on the character of the politician or the statesman till the winding up of the drama. To evince the truth of this remark, it is needless to adduce innumerable instances of deception both in ancient and modern story. It is enough to observe, that the specious Augustus established himself in empire by the appearance of justice, clemency, and moderation, while the savage Nero shamelessly weltered in the blood of the citizens; but the sole object of each was to become the sovereign of life and property, and to govern the Roman world with a despotic hand.

Time may unlock the cabinets of princes, unfold the secret negotiations of statesmen, and hand down the immortal characters of dignified worth, or the blackened traits of finished villany in exaggerated colours. But truth is most likely to be exhibited by the general sense of contemporaries, when the feelings of the heart can be expressed without suffering itself to be disguised by the prejudices of the man. Yet it is not easy to convey to posterity, a just idea of the embarrassed situation of the western world, previous to the rupture with Britain; the dismemberment of the empire, and the loss of the most industrious, flourishing, and perhaps virtuous colonies, ever planted by the hand of man. . . .

The love of domination and an uncontrolled lust of arbitrary power have prevailed among all nations, and perhaps in proportion to the degrees of civilization. They have been equally conspicuous in the decline of Roman virtue, and in the dark pages of British story. It was these principles that overturned that ancient republic. It was these principles that frequently involved England in civil feuds. It was the resistance to them that brought one of their monarchs to the block, and struck another from his throne. It was the prevalence of them that drove the first settlers of America from elegant habitations and affluent circumstances, to seek an asylum in the cold and uncultivated regions of the western world. Oppressed in Britain by despotic kings, and persecuted by prelatic fury, they fled to a distant country, where the desires of men were bounded by the wants of nature; where civilization had not created those artificial cravings which too frequently break over every moral and religious tie for their gratification.

The tyranny of the Stuart race has long been proverbial in English story: their efforts to establish an arbitrary system of government began with the weak and bigoted reign of James the first, and were continued until the excision of his son Charles. The contest between the British parliament and this unfortunate monarch arose to such an height, as to augur an alarming defection of many of the best subjects in England. Great was their uneasiness at the state of public affairs, the arbitrary stretch of power, and the obstinacy of king Charles, who pursued his own despotic measures in spite of the opposition of a number of gentlemen in parliament attached to the liberties and privileges of Englishmen. Thus a spirit of emigration adopted in the preceding reign began to spread with great rapidity through the nation. Some gentlemen endowed with talents to defend their rights by the most cogent and resistless arguments, were among the number who had taken the alarming resolution of seeking an asylum far from their natal soil, where they might enjoy the rights and privileges they claimed, and which they considered on the eve of annihilation at home. Among these were Oliver Cromwell, afterwards protector, and a number of other gentlemen of distinguished name, who had actually engaged to embark for New-England. This was a circumstance so alarming to the court, that they were stopped by an order of government, and by royal edict all further emigration was forbidden. The spirit of colonization was not however much impeded, nor the growth of the young plantations prevented, by the arbitrary resolutions of the court. It was but a short time after this effort to check them, before numerous English emigrants were spread along the borders of the Atlantic from Plymouth to Virginia.

The independency with which these colonists acted; the high promise of future advantage from the beauty and fertility of the country; and, as was observed soon after, "the prosperous state of their settlements, made it to be considered by the heads of the puritan party in England, many of whom were men of the first rank, fortune and abilities, as the sanctuary of liberty." The order above alluded to, indeed prevented the embarkation of the Lords Say and Brook, the Earl of Warwick, of Hampden, Pym, and many others, who, despairing of recovering their civil and religious liberty on their native shore, had determined to secure it by a retreat to the New World, as it was then called. Patents were purchased by others, within a short period after the present, who planted the thirteen American colonies with a successful hand. Many circumstances concurred to awaken the spirit of adventure, and to draw out men, inured to softer habits, to encounter the difficulties and dangers of planting themselves and families in the wilderness.

The spirit of party had thrown accumulated advantages into the hands of Charles the second, after his restoration. The divisions and animosities at court rendered it more easy for him to pursue the same system which his father had adopted. Amidst the rage for pleasure, and the licentious manners that prevailed in his court, the complaisance of one party, the fears of another, and the weariness of all, of the dissensions and difficulties that had arisen under the protectorship of Cromwell, facilitated the measures of the high monarchists, who continually im-

God Prepares
a Christian
People
to Establish
the American
Nation

proved their advantages to enhance the prerogatives of the crown. The weak and bigoted conduct of his brother James increased the general uneasiness of the nation, until his abdication. Thus, through every successive reign of this line of the Stuarts, the colonies gained additional strength by continual emigrations to the young American settlements. . . .

But unhappily both for Great Britain and America, the encroachments of the crown had gathered strength by time; and after the successes, the glory, and the demise of George the second, the sceptre descended to a prince, bred under the auspices of a Scotch nobleman of the house of Stuart. Nurtured in all the inflated ideas of kingly prerogative, surrounded by flatterers and dependants, who always swarm in the purlieus of a palace, this misguided sovereign, dazzled with the acquisition of empire, in the morning of youth, and in the zenith of national prosperity; more obstinate than cruel, rather weak than remarkably wicked, considered an opposition to the mandates of his ministers, as a crime of too daring a nature to hope for the pardon of royalty.

Lord Bute, who from the preceptor of the prince in the years of pupilage, had become the director of the monarch on the throne of Britain, found it not difficult, by that secret influence ever exercised by a favorite minister, to bring over a majority of the house of commons to co-operate with the designs of the crown. Thus the parliament of England became the mere creature of administration, and appeared ready to leap the boundaries of justice, and to undermine the pillars of their own constitution, by adhering stedfastly for several years to a complicated system of tyranny, that threatened the new world with a yoke unknown to their fathers.

It had ever been deemed essential to the preservation of the boasted liberties of Englishmen, that no grants of monies should be made, by tolls, talliage, excise, or any other way, without the consent of the people by their representative voice. Innovation in a point so interesting might well be expected to create a general ferment through the American provinces. Numberless restrictions had been laid on the trade of the colonies previous to this period, and every method had been taken to check their enterprising spirit, and to prevent the growth of their manufactures. Nor is it surprising, that loud complaints should be made when heavy exactions were laid on the subject, who had not, and whose local situation rendered it impracticable that he should have, an

equal representation in parliament. What still heightened the resentment of the Americans, in the beginning of the great contest, was the reflection, that they had not only always supported their own internal government with little expense to Great Britain; but while a friendly union existed, they had, on all occasions, exerted their utmost ability to comply with every constitutional requisition from the parent state.

We need not here revert further back than the beginning of the reign of George the third, to prove this, though earlier instances might be adduced.

The extraordinary exertions of the colonies, in co-operation with British measures, against the French, in the late war, were acknowledged by the British parliament to be more than adequate to their ability. After the successful expedition to Louisburg, in one thousand seven hundred and forty-five, the sum of two hundred thousand pounds sterling was voted by the commons, as a compensation to some of the colonies for their vigorous efforts, which were carried beyond their proportional strength, to aid the expedition.

Not contented with the voluntary aids they had from time to time received from the colonies, and grown giddy with the lustre of their own power, in the plenitude of human grandeur, to which the nation had arrived in the long and successful reign of George the second, such weak, impolitic and unjust measures were pursued, on the accession of his grandson, as soon threw the whole empire into the most violent convulsions.

THE STAMP ACT, 1765

The project of an American taxation might have been longer meditated, but the memorable era of the stamp-act, in one thousand seven hundred and sixty-four, was the first innovation that gave a general alarm throughout the continent. By this extraordinary act, a certain duty was to be levied on all bonds, 1764
bills of lading, public papers, and writings of every kind, for the express purpose of raising a revenue to the crown. As soon as this intelligence was transmitted to America, an universal murmur succeeded; and while the judicious and penetrating thought it time to make a resolute stand against the encroachments of power, the resentment of the lower classes broke out into such excesses of riot and tumult, as prevented the operation of the favorite project.

Multitudes assembled in the principal towns and cities, and the popular torrent bore down all before it. The houses of some, who were the avowed abettors of the measure, and of others, who were only suspected as inimical to the liberties of America, in Boston, in Newport, Connecticut, and many other places, were rased to the ground. The commissioners of the stamp-office were every where compelled to renounce their employments, and to enter into the most solemn engagements to make no further attempts to act in this obnoxious business. At New York the act was printed, and cried about the streets, under the title of *"The folly of England, and the ruin of America."* In Philadelphia the cannon were spiked up, and the bells of the city, muffled, tolled from morning to evening, and every testimony of sincere mourning was displayed, on the arrival of the stamp papers. Nor were any of the more southern colonies less opposed to the operation of this act; and the house of Burgesses, in Virginia, was the first who formally resolved against the encroachments of power, and the unwarrantable designs of the British parliament.

The novelty of their procedure, and the boldness of spirit that marked the resolutions of that assembly, at once astonished and disconcerted the officers of the crown, and the supporters of the measures of administration. These resolves were ushered into the house, on the thirtieth of May, one thousand, seven hundred and sixty five, by Patrick Henry, esq. a young gentleman of the law, till then unknown in political life. He was a man, possessed of strong powers, much professional knowledge, and of such abilities as qualified him for the exigencies of the day. Fearless of the cry of *'treason,'* echoed against him from several quarters, he justified the measure, and supported the resolves, in a speech, that did honor both to his understanding, and his patriotism. The governor, to check the progress of such daring principles, immediately dissolved the assembly.

May 30, 1765

But the disposition of the people was discovered, when, on a new election, those gentlemen were everywhere re-chosen, who had shewn the most firmness and zeal, in opposition to the stamp act. Indeed, from New Hampshire to the Carolinas, a general aversion appeared against this experiment of administration. Nor was the flame confined to the continent; it had spread to the insular regions, whose inhabitants, constitutionally more sanguine than those born in colder climates, discovered stronger marks of resentment, and prouder tokens of disobedience to ministerial authority. Thus several of the West India islands shewed equal violence, in the destruction of the stamp papers, disgust at the act, and indignation towards the officers who were bold enough to attempt its execution. Nor did they at this period appear less determined to resist the operation of all unconstitutional mandates, than the generous planters of the southern, or the independent spirits of the northern colonies.

When the general assembly of the Massachusetts met this year, it appeared that most of the members of the house of representatives had instructions from their constituents to make every legal and spirited opposition to the distribution of the stamped papers, to the execution of the act in any form, and to very other parliamentary infringement on the rights of the people of the colonies. A specimen of the spirit of the times may be seen in a single instance of those instructions, which were given to the representative of the town of Plymouth, the capital of the old colony.

PLYMOUTH TOWN MEETING

On the twenty-first of October, the freeholders and other inhabitants of the town of Plymouth had a meeting, and unanimously agreed on instructions to Thomas Foster, Esq., their representative in the general assembly of Massachusetts Bay. In which, after expressing the highest esteem for the British constitution, shewing how far the people of America have exerted themselves in support thereof, and detailing their grievances, they proceed as follows:

October 21, 1764

"You, sir, represent a people who are not only descended from the first settlers of this country, but inhabit the very spot they first possessed. Here was first laid the foundation of the British empire in this part of America; which from a very small beginning, has increased and spread in a manner very surprising, and almost incredible; especially when we consider, that all this has been effected without the aid or assistance of any power on earth; that we have *defended, protected,* and *secured* ourselves, against the invasions and cruelty of savages, and the subtlety and inhumanity of our inveterate and natural enemies the French: and all this without the appropriation of any tax by stamps, or stamp-acts laid upon our fellow-subjects in any part of the king's dominions, for defraying the expenses thereof. This place, sir, was at first the asylum of liberty, and we hope will ever be preserved sacred to it; though it was then no more than a forlorn wilderness, inhabited only by savage men and beasts. To this place our fathers, (whose memories be revered!) possessed of the principles of liberty in their purity, disdaining slavery, fled, to enjoy those privileges which they had an undoubted right to, but were deprived of by the hands of violence and

GOD PREPARES
A CHRISTIAN
PEOPLE
TO ESTABLISH
THE AMERICAN
NATION

oppression in their native country. We, sir, their posterity, the freeholders and other inhabitants of this town, legally assembled for that purpose, possessed of the same sentiments, and retaining the same ardor for liberty, think it our indispensable duty on this occasion, to express to you these our sentiments of the stamp-act, and its fatal consequences to this country, and to enjoin upon you, as you regard not only the welfare, but the very being of this people, that you, (consistent with our allegiance to the king, and relation to the government of Great Britain,) disregarding all proposals for that purpose, exert all your power and influence in relation to the stamp-act, at least until we hear the success of our petitions for relief. We likewise, to avoid disgracing the memories of our ancestors, as well as the reproaches of our own consciences, and the curses of posterity, recommend it to you to obtain, if possible, in the honorable house of representatives of this province, a full and explicit assertion of our rights, and to have the same entered on their public records—that all generations yet to come may be convinced, that we have not only a just sense of our rights and liberties, but that we never (with submission to Divine Providence) will be slaves to any power on earth. And as we have at all times an abhorrence of tumults and disorders, we think ourselves happy in being at present under no apprehensions of any, and in having good and wholesome laws, sufficient to preserve the peace of the province in all future times, unless provoked by some imprudent measure; so we think it by no means adviseable, for you to interest yourself in the protection of stamp papers or stamp-officers.

"The only thing we have further to recommend to you at this time is, to observe on all occasions, a suitable frugality and economy in the public expenses; and that you consent to no unnecessary or unusual grant at this time of distress, when the people are groaning under the burthen of heavy taxes; and that you use your endeavours to inquire into, and bear testimony against, any past, and to prevent any future, unconstitutional draughts on the public treasury."

Similar measures were adopted in most of the other provinces. In consequence of which, petitions from the respective assemblies, replete with the strongest expressions of loyalty and affection to the king, and a regard to the British nation, were presented to his majesty, through the hands of the colonial agents.

The ferment was however too general, and the spirits of the people too much agitated, to wait patiently the result of their own applications. So universal was the resentment and discontent of the people, that the more judicious and discreet characters were exceedingly apprehensive that the general clamor might terminate in the extremes of anarchy. Heavy duties had been laid on all goods imported from such of the West India islands as did not belong to Great Britain. These duties were to be paid into the exchequer, and all penalties incurred, were to be recovered in the courts of vice-admiralty, by the determination of a single judge, without trial by jury, and the judge's salary was to be paid out of the fruits of the forfeiture.

A CONGRESS CONVENED AT NEW YORK

All remonstrances against this innovating system had hitherto been without effect; and in this period of suspense, apprehension and anxiety, a general congress of delegates from the several provinces was proposed by the honorable James Otis, of Barnstable, in the Massachusetts. He was a gentleman of great probity, experience, and parliamentary abilities, whose religious adherence to the rights of his country had distinguished him through a long course of years, in which he had sustained some of the first offices in government. This proposal, from a man of his acknowledged judgment, discretion and firmness, was universally pleasing. The measure was communicated to some of the principal members of the two houses of assembly, and immediately adopted, not only by the Massachusetts, but very soon after by most of the other colonies. Thus originated the first congress ever convened in America by the united voice of the people, in order to justify their claims to the rights of Englishmen, and the privileges of the British constitution.

It has been observed that Virginia and the Massachusetts made the first opposition to parliamentary measures, on different grounds. The Virginians, in their resolves, came forward, conscious of their own independence, and at once asserted their rights as men. The Massachusetts generally founded their claims on the rights of British subjects, and the privileges of their English ancestors; but the era was not far distant, when the united colonies took the same ground, the claim of native independence, regardless of charters or foreign restrictions.

At a period when the taste and opinions of Americans were comparatively pure and simple, while they possessed that independence and dignity of mind, which is lost only by a multiplicity of wants and interests, new scenes were opening, beyond the reach of human calculation. At this important crisis, the delegates appointed from several of the colonies, to deliberate on the lowering aspect of political affairs, met at New York, on the first Tuesday of October, one thousand seven hundred and sixty-five.

October 7, 1765

The moderate demands of this body, and the short period of its existence, discovered at once the affectionate attachment of its members to the parent state and their dread of a general rupture, which at that time universally prevailed. They stated their claims as subjects to the crown of Great Britain; appointed agents to enforce them in the national councils; and agreed on petitions for the repeal of the stamp act, which had sown the seeds of discord throughout the colonies. The prayer of their constituents was, in a spirited, yet respectful manner, offered through them to the king, lords, and commons of Great Britain: they then separated, to wait the event.

STAMP ACT REPEALED, 1766

A majority of the principal merchants of the city of London, the opulent West India proprietors who resided in England, and most of the manufacturing towns through the kingdom, accompanied with similar petitions, those offered by the congress convened at New York. In consequence of the general aversion to the stamp act, the British ministry were changed in appearance, though the same men who had fabricated the American system, still retained their influence on the mind of the king, and in the councils of the nation. The parliamentary debates of the winter of one thousand seven hundred and sixty-six, evinced the important consequences expected from the decision of the question, relative to an American taxation. Warm and spirited arguments in favor of the measure, energetic reasonings against it, with many sarcastic strokes on administration, from some of the prime orators in parliament, interested the hearers of every rank and description. Finally, in order to quiet the public mind, the execution of the stamp-act was pronounced inexpedient by a majority of the house of commons, and a bill passed for its repeal on March the eighteenth, one thousand seven hundred and sixty-six. But a clause was inserted therein, holding up a parliamentary right to make laws binding on the colonies in all cases whatsoever: and a kind of condition was tacked to the repeal, that compensation should be made to all who had suffered, either in person or property, by the late riotous proceedings.

A short-lived joy was diffused throughout America, even by this delusive appearance of lenity: the people of every description manifested the strongest desire, that harmony might be re-established between Great Britain and the colonies. Bonfires, illuminations, and all the usual expressions of popular satisfaction, were displayed on the joyful occasion: yet, amidst the demonstrations of this lively gratitude, there were some who had sagacity enough to see, that the British ministry was not so much instigated by principles of equity, as impelled by necessity. These deemed any relaxation in parliament an act of justice, rather than favor; and felt more resentment for the manner, than obligation for the design, of this partial repeal. Their opinion was fully justified by the subsequent conduct of administration.

When the assembly of Massachusetts met the succeeding winter, there seemed to prevail a general disposition for peace: the sense of injury was checked; and such a spirit of affection and loyalty appeared, that the two houses agreed to a bill for compensation to all sufferers, in the late times of confusion and riot. But they were careful not to recognize a *right* in parliament to make such a requisition: they ordered it to be entered on the journals of the house, that "for the sake of internal peace, they waved all debate and controversy, though persuaded, the delinquent sufferers had no just claim on the province: that, influenced by a loyal regard to his majesty's recommendation, (not considering it as a requisition;) and that, from a deference to the opinions of some illustrious patrons of America, in the house of commons, who had urged them to a compliance: They therefore acceded to the proposal; though, at the same time, they considered it a very reprehensible step in those who had suffered, to apply for relief to the parliament of Britain, instead of submitting to the justice and clemency of their own legislature."

They made several other just and severe observations on the high-toned speech of the governor, who had said, "that the requisition of the ministry was founded on so much justice and humanity, that it could not be controverted." They inquired, if the authority with which he introduced the ministerial demand, precluded all disputation about complying with it, what freedom of choice they had left in the case? They said, "With regard to the rest of your excellency's speech, we are constrained to observe, that the general air and style of it favors much more of an act of free grace and pardon, than of a parliamentary address to the two houses of assembly: and we most sincerely wish your excellency had been pleased to reserve it, if needful, for a proclamation."

In the bill for compensation by the assembly of Massachusetts, was added a very offensive clause. A general pardon and oblivion was granted to all offenders in the late confusion,

1767

March 18, 1766

AT a Meeting of the Freeholders and other Inhabitants of the Town of Boston, legally qualified and warned, in Publick Town-Meeting, assembled at Faneuil-Hall on Monday the 21st Day of *April*, Anno Domini, 1766.

VOTED, That the Selectmen be desir'd, when they shall have a certain Account of the Repeal of the Stamp-Act, to notify the Inhabitants of the Time they shall fix upon for the general Rejoicings, and to publish the following Vote, viz.

" UNDER the deepest Sense of Duty and Loyalty to our Most Gracious SOVEREIGN King GEORGE, and in Respect and Gratitude to the present Patriotic Ministry, Mr. PITT, and the glorious Majority of both Houses of Parliament, by whose Influence, under Divine Providence, against a most strenuous Opposition, a happy Repeal of the Stamp-Act, so unconstitutional as well as grievous to His Majesty's good Subjects of AMERICA, is attained ; whereby our incontestible Right of Internal Taxation still remains to us inviolate :

" VOTED, That at the Time the Selectmen shall appoint, every Inhabitant be desired to illuminate his Dwelling-House ; and that it is the Sense of the Town, that the Houses of the Poor, as well as those where there are sick Persons, and all such Parts of Houses as are used for Stores, together with the Houses of those (if there are any) who from certain religious Scruples cannot conform to this Vote, ought to be protected from all Injury ; and that all Abuses and Disorders on the Evening for Rejoicing, by breaking Windows or otherwise, if any should happen, be prosecuted by the Town.

A true Copy, Attest. WILLIAM COOPER, *Town-Clerk.*

THE *Selectmen having received certain Intelligence, that the Act repealing the Stamp-Act, has passed all the requisite Formalities, congratulate the Inhabitants of the Town on the joyful News, and appoint Monday next, the 19th Instant, for the Day of General Rejoicing, in Compliance with the foregoing Votes, recommending to all Persons a due and punctual Observance of the salutary Regulations enjoined therein.*

By Order of the Selectmen,

William Cooper, *Town-Clerk.*

Boston, May 16. 1766.

tumults and riots. An exact detail of these proceedings was transmitted to England. The king and council disallowed the act, as comprising in it a bill of indemnity to the Boston rioters; and ordered compensation made to the late sufferers, without any supplementary conditions. No notice was taken of this order, nor any alteration made in the act. The money was drawn from the treasury of the province to satisfy the claimants for compensation; and no farther inquiries were made relative to the authors of the late tumultuary proceedings of the times, when the minds of men had been wrought up to a ferment, beyond the reach of all legal restraint.

The year one thousand seven hundred and sixty-six had passed over without any other remarkable political events. All colonial measures agitated in England, were regularly transmitted by the minister for the American department to the several plantation governors; who, on every communication, endeavoured to enforce the operation of parliamentary authority, by the most sanguine injunctions of their own, and a magnificent display of royal resentment, on the smallest token of disobedience to ministerial requisitions. But it will appear, that through a long series of resolves and messages, letters and petitions, which passed between the parties, previous to the commencement of hostilities, the watchful guardians of American freedom never lost sight of the intrigues of their enemies, or the mischievous designs of such as were under the influence of the crown, on either side the Atlantic.

It may be observed, that the tranquillity of the provinces had for some time been interrupted by the innovating spirit of the British ministry, instigated by a few prostitutes of power, nurtured in the lap of America, and bound by every tie of honor and gratitude, to be faithful to the interests of their country. The social enjoyments of life had long been disturbed, the mind fretted, and the people rendered suspicious, when they saw some of their fellow-citizens, who did not hesitate at a junction with the accumulated swarms of hirelings, sent from Great Britain to ravish from the colonies the rights they claimed both by nature and by compact. That the hard-hearted judges of admiralty, and the crowd of revenue officers that hovered about the custom houses, should seldom be actuated by the principles of justice, is not strange. Peculation was generally the prime object of this class; and the oaths they administered, and the habits they encouraged, were favorable to every species of bribery and corruption. The rapacity which instigated these

descriptions of men had little check, while they saw themselves upheld even by some governors of provinces. In this grade, which ought ever to be the protectors of the rights of the people, there were some who were total strangers to all ideas of equity, freedom, or urbanity. It was observed at this time, in a speech before the house of commons, by colonel Barre, that "to his certain knowledge, some were promoted to the highest seats of honor in America, who were glad to fly to a foreign country, to escape being brought to the bar of justice in their own."

NEW GRIEVANCES

However injudicious the appointments to American departments might be, the darling point of an American revenue was an object too consequential to be relinquished, either by the court at St. James's, the plantation governors, or their mercenary adherents dispersed through the continent. Besides these, there were several classes in America, who were at first exceedingly opposed to measures that militated with the designs of administration. Some, impressed by long connexion, were intimidated by her power, and attached by affection to Britain: others, the true disciples of passive obedience, had real scruples of conscience with regard to any resistance to the powers that be: these, whether actuated by affection or fear, by principle or interest, formed a close combination with the colonial governors, custom house officers, and all in subordinate departments, who hung on the court for subsistence. By the tenor of the writings of some of these, and the insolent behaviour of others, they became equally obnoxious in the eyes of the people, with the officers of the crown and the danglers for place; who, disappointed of their prey by the repeal of the stamp-act, and restless for some new project that might enable them to rise into importance on the spoils of America, were continually whispering malicious insinuations into the ears of the financiers and ministers of colonial departments.

They represented the mercantile body in America as a set of smugglers, forever breaking over the laws of trade and of society; the people in general as factious, turbulent, and aiming at independence; the legislatures in the several provinces as marked with the same spirit; and government every where in so lax a state, that the civil authority was insufficient to prevent the fatal effects of popular discontent.

It is indeed true, that resentment had in sev-

GOD PREPARES
A CHRISTIAN
PEOPLE
TO ESTABLISH
THE AMERICAN
NATION

eral instances arisen to outrage; and that the most unwarrantable excesses had been committed on some occasions, which gave grounds for unfavorable representations. Yet it must be acknowledged, that the voice of the people seldom breathes universal murmur, but when the insolence or the oppression of their rulers extorts the bitter complaint. On the contrary, there is a certain supineness which generally overspreads the multitude, and disposes mankind to submit quietly to any form of government, rather than to be at the expense and hazard of resistance. They become attached to ancient modes by habits of obedience, though the reins of authority are sometimes held by the most rigorous hand. Thus we have seen in all ages, the many become the slaves of the few: preferring the wretched tranquillity of inglorious ease, they patiently yield to despotic masters, until awakened by multiplied wrongs to the feelings of human nature; which, when once aroused to a consciousness of the native freedom and equal rights of man, ever revolts at the idea of servitude.

Perhaps the story of political revolution never exhibited a more general enthusiasm in the cause of liberty, than that which for several years pervaded all ranks in America, and brought forward events little expected by the most sanguine spirits in the beginning of the controversy. A contest now pushed with so much vigour, that the intelligent yeomanry of the country, as well as those educated in the higher walks, became convinced that nothing less than a systematical plan of slavery was designed against them. They viewed the chains as already forged to manacle the unborn millions; and though every one seemed to dread any new interruption of public tranquillity, the impetuosity of some led them into excesses which could not be restrained by those of more cool and discreet deportment. To the most moderate and judicious it soon became apparent, that unless a timely and bold resistance prevented, the colonists must in a few years sink into the same wretched thraldom, that marks the miserable Asiatic.

Few of the executive officers employed by the king of Great Britain, and fewer of their adherents, were qualified either by education, principle, or inclination, to allay the ferment of the times, or to eradicate the suspicions of men, who, from an hereditary love of freedom, were tenderly touched by the smallest attempt, to undermine the invaluable possession. Yet, perhaps few of the colonies, at this period, suffered equal embarrassments with the Massachusetts. The inhabitants of that province were considered as the

prime leaders of faction, the disturbers of public tranquillity, and Boston the seat of sedition. Vengeance was continually denounced against that capital, and indeed the whole province, through the letters, messages, and speeches of their first magistrate.

Unhappily for both parties, governor Bernard was very illy calculated to promote the interest of the people, or support the honor of his master. He was a man of little genius, but some learning. He was by education strongly impressed with high ideas of canon and feudal law, and fond of a system of government that had been long obsolete in England, and had never had an existence in America. His disposition was choleric and sanguine, obstinate and designing, yet too open and frank to disguise his intrigues, and too precipitant to bring them to maturity. A revision of colony charters, a resumption of former privileges, and an American revenue, were the constant topics of his letters to administration. To prove the necessity of these measures, the most trivial disturbance was magnified to a riot; and to give a pretext to these wicked insinuations, it was thought by many, that tumults were frequently excited by the indiscretion or malignancy of his own partizans.

The declaratory bill still hung suspended over the heads of the Americans, nor was it suffered to remain long without trying its operative effects. The clause holding up a right to tax America at pleasure, and "to bind them in all cases whatsoever," was comprehensive and alarming. Yet it was not generally expected, that the ministry would soon endeavour to avail themselves of the dangerous experiment; but, in this, the public were mistaken.

It has already been observed, that the arbitrary disposition of George the third; the absurd system of policy adopted in conformity to his principles, and a parliamentary majority at the command of the ministry, rendered it not difficult to enforce any measures that might tend to an accession to the powers of the crown. It was a just sentiment of an elegant writer, that "almost all the vices of royalty have been principally occasioned by a slavish adulation in the language of their subjects; and to the shame of the English it must be said, that none of the enslaved nations in the world have addressed the throne in a more fulsome and hyperbolical style." (*Mrs. Macauley's letter to earl Stanhope.*)

The dignity of the crown, the supremacy of parliament, and the disloyalty of the colonies, were the theme of the court, the echo of its crea-

MERCY
WARREN:
PRELUDE TO
THE AMERICAN
REVOLUTION,
1765–1775

TOWNSHEND ACTS,
JAMES OTIS, ESQ.

tures, and of the British nation in general; nor was it thought good policy to let the high claims of government lie long in a dormant state. Accordingly not many months after the repeal of the stamp act, the chancellor of the exchequer, Charles Townshend, Esq. came forward and pawned his character on the success of a new attempt to tax the American colonies. He was a gentleman of conspicuous abilities, and much professional knowledge; endowed with more boldness than discretion; he had "the talent of bringing together at once all that was necessary to establish, to illustrate, and to decorate the side of the question he was on."

He introduced several bills in support of his sanguinary designs, which without much difficulty obtained the sanction of parliament, and the royal assent. The purport of the new project for revenue was to levy certain duties on paper, glass, painters' colors, and several other articles usually imported into America. It was also directed that the duties on India teas, which had been a productive source of revenue in England, should be taken off there, and three pence per pound levied on all kinds that should in future be purchased in the colonies.

This inconsiderable duty on teas finally became an object of high importance and altercation; it was not the sum, but the principle that was contested; it manifestly appeared that this was only a financiering expedient to raise a revenue from the colonies by imperceptible taxes. The defenders of the privileges and the freedom of the colonies, denied all parliamentary right to tax them in any way whatever. They asserted that if the collection of this duty was permitted, it would establish a precedent, and strengthen the claim parliament had assumed, to tax them at pleasure. To do it by the secret modes of imposts and excises would ruin their trade, corrupt the morals of the people, and was more abhorrent in their eyes than a direct demand. The most judicious and intelligent Americans at this time considered all *imperceptible* taxes fraught with evils, that tended to enslave any country plunged in the boundless chaos of fiscal demands that this practice introduces.

In consequence of the new system, a board of customs was instituted and commissioners appointed to set in Boston to collect the duties; which were besides other purposes to supply a fund for the payment of the large salaries annexed to their office. A civil list was soon after established, and the governors of the Massachusets, judges of the superior court, and such other officers as had heretofore depended on the free grants of the representative body, were to be paid out of the revenue chest.

Thus rendered wholly independent of the general assembly, there was no check left on the wanton exercise of power in the crown officers, however disposed they might be to abuse their trust. The distance from the throne, it was said, must delay, if not wholly prevent, all relief under any oppressions the people might suffer from the servants of government; and to crown the long list of grievances, specified by the patriots of the day, the extension of the courts of vice-admiralty was none of the least. They were vested with certain powers that dispensed with the mode of trial by jury, annihilated the privileges of Englishmen, and placed the liberty of every man in the hand of a petty officer of the customs. By warrant of a writ of assistance from the governor or lieutenant governor, any officer of the revenue was authorized to enter the dwelling of the most respectable inhabitant on the smallest suspicion of a concealment of contraband goods, and to insult, search, or seize, with impunity.

An attorney* at law, of some professional abilities and ingenuity but without either property or principle, was, by the instigation of Mr. Bernard, appointed sole judge of admiralty in the Massachusetts. The dangerous aspect of this court, particularly when aided by writs of assistance, was opposed with peculiar energy and strength of argument, by James Otis, Esq. of Boston, who, by the exertion of his talents and the sacrifice of interest, may justly claim the honor of laying the foundation of a revolution, which has been productive of the happiest effects to the civil and political interests of mankind.

He was the first champion of American freedom, who had the courage to put his signature to the contest between Great Britain and the colonies. He had in a clear, concise, and nervous manner, stated and vindicated the rights of the American colonies, and published his observations in Boston, while the stamp act hung suspended. This tract was written with such a spirit of liberality, loyalty, and impartiality, that though at the time some were ready to pronounce it *treasonable,* yet, when opposition run higher, many of the most judicious partizans of the crown were willing to

---

* Jonathan Sewall, a native of the province, whose pen had been employed to vindicate the measures of administration and the conduct of governor Bernard, under the signature of Philalethes, Massachusettensis, &c. &c.

GOD PREPARES
A CHRISTIAN
PEOPLE
TO ESTABLISH
THE AMERICAN
NATION

admit it as a just criterion of political truth. But the author was abused and vilified by the scribblers of the court, and threatened with an arrest from the crown, for the boldness of his opinions. Yet he continued to advocate the rights of the people, and in the course of his argument against the iniquitous consequences of writs of assistance, he observed, that "his engaging in this cause had raised the resentment of its abettors; but that he argued it from principle, and with peculiar pleasure, as it was in favor of *British liberty,* and in opposition to the exercise of a power, that in former periods of English history, had cost one king of England his head, and another his crown." He added, "I can sincerely declare, that I submit myself to every opprobrious name for conscience sake, and despise all those, whom guilt, folly or malice have made my foes."

It was on this occasion, that Mr. Otis resigned the office of judge advocate, and renounced all employment under so corrupt an administration, boldly declaring in the face of the supreme court, at this dangerous crisis, that "the only principle of public conduct, worthy a gentleman or a man, was the sacrifice of health, ease, applause, estate, or even life, to the sacred calls of his country; that these manly sentiments in private life made the good citizen, in public, the patriot and the hero." Thus was verified in his conduct the observation of a writer* of merit and celebrity, that "it was as difficult for Great Britain to frighten as to cheat Americans into servitude; that she ought to leave them in the peaceable possession of that liberty which they received at their birth, and were resolved to retain to their death."

When the new parliamentary regulations reached America, all the colonies in their several departments petitioned in the most strenuous manner against any American taxation, and all other recent innovations relative to the government of the British provinces. These petitions were, when received by the ministry, treated by them with the utmost contempt. But they were supported by a respectable party in the parliament of Britain, who did not neglect to warn the administration of the danger of precipitating measures, that might require before the termination of a contest thus hurried on, "more virtue and abilities than the ministry possessed."

By some steps taken by administration previous to the present period, there was reason to suppose that they were themselves apprehensive, that their system for governing the colonies in a more arbitrary manner would give great offence, and create disturbances of so alarming a nature, that perhaps the aid of military power might become necessary to enforce the completion of their designs. Doubtless it was with a view of facilitating the new projects, that an extraordinary bill had been passed in parliament, making it lawful for the officers of the British army to quarter their troops in private houses throughout the colonies. Thus while mixed in every family, it might become more easy to awe the people into submission, and compel them by military terrors to the basest compliances. But the colony agents residing in London, and the merchants concerned in the American trade, remonstrated so warmly against the injustice and cruelty of such a procedure, that a part of the bill was dropped. Yet it was too important a point wholly to relinquish; of consequence a clause was left, obliging the several legislative assemblies to provide quarters for the king's marching regiments, and to furnish a number of specified articles at the expense of the province, wherever they might be stationed.

May 15, 1765

This act continued in full force after the stampact was repealed, though it equally militated with that part of the British constitution which provides that no monies should be raised on the subject without his consent. Yet rather than enter on a new dispute, the colonists in general chose to evade it for the present, and without many observations thereon had occasionally made some voluntary provisions for the support of the king's troops. It was hoped the act might be only a temporary expedient to hold up the authority of parliament, and that in a short time the claim might die of itself without any attempt to revive such an unreasonable demand. But New York, more explicit in her refusal to *obey,* was suspended from all powers of legislation until the quartering act should be complied with in the fullest extent. By this unprecedented treatment of one of the colonies, and the innumerable exactions and restrictions on all, a general apprehension prevailed, that nothing but a firm, vigorous and united resistance could shield from the attacks that threatened the total extinction of civil liberty through the continent.

June 15, 1767

CURSORY OBSERVATIONS

The British colonies at this period through the American continent contained, exclusive of Can-

---

* John Dickinson, author of the much admired *Farmer's Letters.*

ada and Nova Scotia, the provinces of New Hampshire, and Massachusetts Bay, of Rhode Island, Connecticut, New York, New Jersey, Pennsylvania, the Delaware counties, Virginia, Maryland, the two Carolinas, and Georgia, besides the Floridas, and an unbounded tract of wilderness not yet explored. These several provinces had been always governed by their own distinct legislatures. It is true there was some variety in their religious opinions, but a striking similarity in their political institutions, except in the proprietary governments. At the same time the colonies, afterwards the thirteen states, were equally marked with that manly spirit of freedom, characteristic of Americans from New Hampshire to Georgia.

Aroused by the same injuries from the parent state, threatened in the same manner by the common enemies to the rights of society among themselves, their petitions to the throne had been suppressed without even a reading, their remonstrances were ridiculed and their supplications rejected. They determined no longer to submit. All stood ready to unite in the same measures to obtain that redress of grievances they had so long requested, and that relief from burdens they had so long complained of, to so little purpose. Yet there was no bond of connexion by which a similarity of sentiment and concord in action might appear, whether they were again disposed to revert to the hitherto fruitless mode of petition and remonstrance, or to leave that humiliating path for a line of conduct more cogent and influential in the contests of nations.

MASSACHUSETTS CIRCULAR LETTER

A circular letter dated February the eleventh, one thousand seven hundred and sixty-eight, by the legislature of Massachusetts, directed to the representatives and burgesses of the people through the continent, was

February 11, 1768   a measure well calculated for this salutary purpose. This letter painted in the strongest colors the difficulties they apprehended, the embarrassments they felt, and the steps already taken to obtain relief. It contained the full opinion of that assembly relative to the late acts of parliament; while at the same time they expatiated on their duty and attachment to the king, and detailed in terms of respect the representations that had been made to his ministers, they expressed the boldest determination to continue a free but a loyal people. Indeed there were few, if any, who in-

dulged an idea of a final separation from Britain at so early a period; or that even wished for more than an equal participation of the privileges of the British constitution.

INDEPENDENCE was a plant of a later growth. Though the soil might be congenial, and the boundaries of nature pointed out the event, yet every one chose to view it at a distance, rather than wished to witness the convulsions that such a dismemberment of the empire must necessarily occasion.

After the circulation of this alarming letter, wherever any of the governors had permitted the legislative bodies to meet, an answer was returned by the assemblies replete with encomiums on the exertion and the zeal of the Massachusetts. They observed that the spirit that dictated that letter was but a transcript of their own feelings; and that though equally impressed with every sentiment of respect to the prince on the throne of Britain, and feeling the strongest attachment to the house of Hanover, they could not but reject with disdain the late measures, so repugnant to the dignity of the crown and the true interest of the realm; and that at every hazard they were determined to resist all acts of parliament for the injurious purpose of raising a revenue in America. They also added, that they had respectively offered the most humble supplications to the king; that they had remonstrated to both houses of parliament, and had directed their agents at the British court to leave no effort untried to obtain relief, without being compelled to what might be deemed by royalty an illegal mode of opposition.

Copy of the circular letter which was sent from the house of representatives of the province of Massachusetts Bay, to the speakers of the respective houses of representatives and burgesses on the continent of North America.

"Province of the Massachusetts Bay,
Feb. 11, 1768
"Sir,
"The house of representatives of this province have taken into their serious consideration, the great difficulties that must accrue to themselves and their constituents, by the operation of the several acts of parliament imposing duties and taxes on the American colonies.
"As it is a subject in which every colony is deeply interested, they have no reason to doubt but your house is duly impressed with its importance; and that such constitutional measures will be come into as are proper. It seems to be necessary, that all possible care should be taken that the representations of the several assemblies, upon so delicate a point, should harmonize with each other: the house therefore hope

GOD PREPARES
A CHRISTIAN
PEOPLE
TO ESTABLISH
THE AMERICAN
NATION

that this letter will be candidly considered, in no other light than as expressing a disposition freely to communicate their mind to a sister colony, upon a common concern, in the same manner as they would be glad to receive the sentiments of your, or any other house of assembly on the continent.

"The house have humbly represented to the ministry their own sentiments; that his majesty's high court of parliament is the supreme legislative power over the whole empire; that in all free states the constitution is fixed; and as the supreme legislative derives its power and authority from the constitution, it cannot overleap the bounds of it, without destroying its foundation. That the constitution ascertains and limits both sovereignty and allegiance; and therefore his majesty's American subjects, who acknowledge themselves bound by the ties of allegiance, have an equitable claim to the full enjoyment of the fundamental rules of the British constitution. That it it an essential, unalterable right in nature, engrafted into the British constitution as a fundamental law, and ever held sacred and irrevocable by the subjects within the realm, that what a man hath honestly acquired, is absolutely his own, which he may freely give, but cannot be taken from him without his consent. That the American subjects may therefore, exclusive of any consideration of charter rights, with a decent firmness, adapted to the character of freemen and subjects, assert this natural, constitutional right.

"It is moreover their humble opinion, which they express with the greatest deference to the wisdom of the parliament, that the acts made there, imposing duties on the people of this province for the sole and express purpose of raising a revenue, are infringements of their natural and constitutional rights. Because as they are not represented in the British parliament, his majesty's commons in Britain, by those acts grant their property without their consent.

"The house further are of opinion that their constituents, considering their local circumstances, cannot by any possibility be represented in the parliament; and that it will forever be impracticable that they should be equally represented there, and consequently not at all, being separated by an ocean of a thousand leagues. That his majesty's royal predecessors for this reason were graciously pleased to form a subordinate legislative here, that their subjects might enjoy the unalienable right of a representation. Also that considering the utter impracticability of their ever being fully and equally represented in parliament, and the great expense that must unavoidably attend even a partial representation there, this house think that a taxation of their constituents, even without their consent, grievous as it is, would be preferable to any representation that could be admitted for them there.

"Upon these principles, and also considering that were the right in the parliament ever so clear, yet for obvious reasons it would be beyond the rule of equity, that their constituents should be taxed on the manufactures of Great Britain here, in addition to the duties they pay for them in England, and other advantages arising to Great Britain from the acts of trade; this house have preferred a humble, dutiful, and loyal petition to our most gracious sovereign, and made such representations to his majesty's ministers, as they apprehend would tend to obtain redress.

"They have also submitted to consideration, whether any people can be said to enjoy any degree of freedom, if the crown in addition to its undoubted authority of constituting a governor, should appoint him such a stipend as it should judge proper, without the consent of the people, and at their expense: and whether while the judges of the land and other civil officers, hold not their commissions during good behaviour, their having salaries appointed for them by the crown, independent of the people, hath not a tendency to subvert the principles of equity, and endanger the happiness and security of the subject.

"In addition to these measures, the house have wrote a letter to their agent, Mr. De Berdt, the sentiments of which he is directed to lay before the ministry; wherein they take notice of the hardship of the act for preventing mutiny and desertion, which requires the governor and council to provide enumerated articles for the king's marching troops, and the people to pay the expense; and also the commission of the gentlemen appointed commissioners of the customs, to reside in America, which authorizes them to make as many appointments as they think fit, and to pay the appointees what sums they please, for whose malconduct they are not accountable. From whence it may happen that officers of the crown may be multiplied to such a degree, as to become dangerous to the liberty of the people, by virtue of a commission which doth not appear to this house to derive any such advantages to trade as many have been led to expect.

"These are the sentiments and proceedings of this house; and as they have too much reason to believe that the enemies of the colonies have represented them to his majesty's ministers, and the parliament, as factious, disloyal, and having a disposition to make themselves independent of the mother country, they have taken occasion in the most humble terms, to assure his majesty and his ministers, that with regard to the people of this province, and as they doubt not of all the colonies, that the charge is unjust.

"The house is fully satisfied that your assembly is too generous, and enlarged in sentiment, to believe that this letter proceeds from an ambition of taking the lead, or dictating to the other assemblies; they freely submit their opinion to the judgment of others, and shall take it kind in your house to point out to them any thing further that may be thought necessary.

"This house cannot conclude without expressing their firm confidence in the king, our common head and father, that the united and dutiful supplications of his distressed American subjects will meet with his royal and favorable acceptance."

(Signed by the Speaker.)

A NEW HOUSE OF REPRESENTATIVES CALLED

In consequence of the spirited proceedings of the house of representatives, the general assembly of Massachusetts was dissolved, nor were they suffered to meet again until a new election. These transactions were carefully transmitted to administration by several of the plantation gover-

March 4, 1768

nors, and particularly Mr. Bernard, with inflammatory observations of his own, interlarded with the most illiberal abuse of the principal leaders of the late measures in the assembly of Massachusetts.

Their charter, which still provided for the election of the legislature, obliged the governor to summon a new assembly to meet May the twenty-fourth, one thousand seven hundred and sixty-eight. The first communication laid before the house by the governor contained a haughty requisition from the British minister of state, directing in his majesty's name that the present house should immediately *rescind* the resolutions of a former one, which had produced the celebrated circular letter. Governor Bernard also intimated, that it was his majesty's pleasure, that on a non-compliance with this extraordinary mandate, the present assembly should be dissolved without delay.

What heightened the resentment to the manner of this singular order, signed by Lord Hillsborough, secretary of state for the American department, was, that he therein intimated to the governor that he need not fear the most *unqualified obedience* on his part to the high measures of administration, assuring him that it would not operate to his disadvantage, as care would be taken in future to provide for his interest, and to support the dignity of government, without the interpositions or existence of a provincial legislature.

These messages were received by the representative body with a steadiness and resolution becoming the defenders of the rights of a free people. After appointing a committee to consider and prepare an answer to them, they proceeded with great coolness to the usual business of the session, without further notice of what had passed.

Within a day or two, they received a second message from the governor, purporting that he expected an immediate and an explicit answer to the authoritative requisition; and that if they longer postponed their resolutions, he should consider their delay as an *"oppugnation to his majesty's authority, and a negative to the command, by an expiring faction."* On this, the house desired time to consult their constituents on such an extraordinary question. This being peremptorily and petulantly refused, the house ordered the board of council to be informed, that they were entering on a debate of importance, that they should give them notice when it was over, and directed the door-keeper to call no member out, on any pretence whatever.

The committee appointed to answer the governor's several messages, were gentlemen of known attachment to the cause of their country, who on every occasion had rejected all servile compliances with ministerial requisitions. They were not long on the business. When they returned to the house, the galleries were immediately cleared, and they reported an answer, bold and determined, yet decent and loyal. In the course of their reply, they observed that it was not an *"expiring faction,"* that the governor had charged with *"oppugnation to his majesty's authority,"* that it was the best blood of the colony who opposed the ministerial measures, men of reputation, fortune and rank, equal to any who enjoyed the smiles of government; that their exertions were from a conscious sense of duty to their God, to their king, to their country, and to posterity.*

This committee at the same time reported a very spirited letter to Lord Hillsborough, which they had prepared to lay before the house. In this they remonstrated on the injustice as well as absurdity of a requisition, when a compliance was impracticable, even had they the inclination to rescind the doings of a former house. This letter was approved by the house, and on a division on the question of rescinding the vote of a former assembly, it was negatived by a majority of ninety-two to seventeen.

GOVERNOR BERNARD IMPEACHED

The same committee was immediately nominated to prepare a petition to the king to remove Mr. Bernard from the government of Massachusetts. They drew up a petition for this purpose without leaving the house, and immediately reported it. They alleged a long list of accusations against the governor, and requested his majesty that one more worthy to represent so *great* and *good* a *king,* might be sent to preside in the province. Thus impeached by the house, the same minority that had appeared ready to rescind the circular letter, declared themselves against the impeachment of governor Bernard. Their servility was marked with peculiar odium: they were stigmatized by the appellation of the *infamous seventeen,* until their names were lost in a succession of great events and more important characters.

When the doors of the house were opened, the

* The principal members of this committee, were Major Joseph Hawley, of Northampton, James Otis, Esq. of Boston, Samuel Adams, James Warren, of Plymouth, John Hancock, and Thomas Cushing, Esqrs.

GOD PREPARES
A CHRISTIAN
PEOPLE
TO ESTABLISH
THE AMERICAN
NATION

secretary who had been long in waiting for admission, informed the house that the governor was in the chair, and desired their attendance in the council chamber. They complied without hesitation, but were received in a most ungracious manner. With much ill humor the governor reprimanded them in the language of an angry pedagogue, instead of the manner becoming the first magistrate when addressing the representatives of a free people: he concluded his harangue by proroguing the assembly, which within a few days he dissolved by proclamation.

July 1, 1768

In the meantime by warm and virulent letters from this indiscreet governor; by others full of invective from the commissioners of the customs, and by the *secret influence* of some, who yet concealed themselves within the visard of moderation, "who held the language of patriotism, but trod in the footsteps of tyranny," leave was obtained from administration to apply to the commander in chief of the king's troops, then at New York, to send several regiments to Boston, as a necessary aid to civil government, which they represented as too weak to suppress the disorders of the times. It was urged that this step was absolutely necessary, to enable the officers of the crown to carry into execution the laws of the supreme legislature.

A RIOT ON THE SEIZURE OF A VESSEL

A new pretext had been recently given to the malignant party, to urge with a shew of plausibility, the immediate necessity of the military arm, to quell the riotous proceedings of the town of Boston, to strengthen the hands of government, and restore order and tranquillity to the province. The seizure of a vessel belonging to a popular gentleman, (John Hancock, Esq.) under suspicion of a breach of the acts of trade, raised a sudden resentment among the citizens of Boston. The conduct of the owner was indeed reprehensible, in permitting a part of the cargo to be unladen in a clandestine manner; but the mode of the seizure appeared like a design to raise a sudden ferment, that might be improved to corroborate the arguments for the necessity of standing troops to be stationed within the town.

June 10, 1768

On a certain signal, a number of boats, manned and armed, rowed up to the wharf, cut the fasts of the suspected vessel, carried her off, and placed her under the stern of a ship of war, as if apprehensive of a rescue. This was executed in the edge of the evening, when apprentices and the younger classes were usually in the streets. It had what was thought to be the desired effect; the inconsiderate rabble, unapprehensive of the snare, and thoughtless of consequences, pelted some of the customhouse officers with brick-bats, broke their windows, drew one of their boats before the door of the gentleman they thought injured, and set it on fire; after which they dispersed without further mischief.

This trivial disturbance was exaggerated until it wore the complexion of a riot of the first magnitude. By the insinuations of the party, and their malignant conduct, it was not strange that in England it was considered as a *London mob* collected in the streets of Boston, with some formidable desperado at their head. After this *fracas,* the custom-house officers repaired immediately to Castle William, as did the board of commissioners. This fortress was about a league from the town. From thence they expressed their apprehensions of personal danger, in strong language. Fresh applications were made to general Gage, to hasten on his forces from New York, assuring him that the lives of the officers of the crown were insecure, unless placed beyond the reach of popular resentment, by an immediate military aid. In consequence of these representations, several detachments from Halifax, and two regiments lately from Ireland, were directed to repair to Boston, with all possible dispatch.

The experience of all ages, and the observations both of the historian and the philosopher agree, that a standing army is the most ready engine in the hand of despotism, to debase the powers of the human mind, and eradicate the manly spirit of freedom. The people have certainly every thing to fear from a government, when the springs of its authority are fortified only by a standing military force. Wherever an army is established, it introduces a revolution in manners, corrupts the morals, propagates every species of vice, and degrades the human character. Threatened with the immediate introduction of this dread calamity, deprived by the dissolution of their legislature of all power to make any legal opposition; neglected by their sovereign, and insulted by the governor he had set over them, much the largest part of the community was convinced, that they had no resource but in the strength of their virtues, the energy of their resolutions, and the justice of their cause.

In this state of general apprehension, confusion, and suspense, the inhabitants of Boston again requested governor Bernard to convoke an assembly, and suffer the representatives of the whole people to consult and advise at this critical conjuncture. He rejected this application with an air of insult, and no time was to be lost. Letters were instantly forwarded from the capital, requesting a delegation of suitable persons to meet in convention from every town in the province before the arrival of the troops, and if possible to take some steps to prevent the fatal effects of these dangerous and unprecedented measures.

A CONVENTION AT BOSTON

The whole country felt themselves interested, and readily complied with the proposal. The most respectable persons from an hundred and ninety-six towns were chosen delegates to assemble at Boston, on the twenty-second of September. They accordingly met at that time and place; as soon as they were convened the governor sent them an angry message, admonishing them immediately to disperse, assuring them "the king was determined to maintain his entire sovereignty over the province,—that their present meeting might be in consequence of their ignorance,—but that if after this admonition, they continued their *usurpation,* they might repent their temerity, as he was determined to assert the authority of the crown in a more public manner, if they continued to disregard this authoritative warning."

He however found he had not men to deal with, either ignorant of law, regardless of its sanctions, or terrified by the frowns of power. The convention made him a spirited but decent answer, containing the reasons of their assembling, and the line of conduct they were determined to pursue in spite of every menace. The governor refused to receive their reply; he urged the illegality of the assembly, and made use of every subterfuge to interrupt their proceedings.

Their situation was indeed truly delicate, as well as dangerous. The convention was a body not known in the constitution of their government, and in the strict sense of law it might be styled a treasonable meeting. They still professed fealty to the crown of Britain; and though the principle had been shaken by injuries, that might have justified a more sudden renunciation of loyalty, yet their's was cherished by a degree of religious scruple, amidst every species of insult. Thus while they wished to support this temper, and to cherish their former affection, they felt with poignancy the invasion of their rights, and hourly expected the arrival of an armed force, to back the

threatenings of their first magistrate. Great prudence and moderation however marked the transactions of an assembly of men thus circumstanced; they could in their present situation only recapitulate their sufferings, felt and feared.

This they did in a pointed and nervous style, in a letter addressed to Mr. De Berdt, the agent of the province, residing in London. They stated the circumstances that occasioned their meeting, and a full detail of their proceedings. They inclosed him a petition to the king, and ordered their agent to deliver it with his own hand. The convention then separated, and returned to their respective towns, where they impressed on their constituents the same perseverance, forbearance and magnanimity that had marked their own resolutions.

TROOPS ARRIVE

Within a few days after their separation, the troops arrived from Halifax. This was indeed a painful era. The American war may be dated from the hostile parade of this day; a day which marks with infamy the councils of Britain. At this period, the inhabitants of the colonies almost universally breathed an unshaken loyalty to the king of England, and the strongest attachment to a country whence they derived their origin. Thus was the astonishment of the whole province excited, when to the grief and consternation of the town of Boston several regiments were landed, and marched sword in hand through the principal streets of their city, then in profound peace.

The disembarkation of the king's troops, which took place on the first of October, one thousand seven hundred and sixty-eight, was viewed by a vast crowd of spectators, who beheld the solemn prelude to devastation and bloodshed with a kind of sullen silence, that denoted the deepest resentment. Yet whatever might be the feelings of the citizens, not one among the gazing multitude discovered any disposition to resist by arms the power and authority of the king of Great Britain. This appearance of decent submission and order was very unexpected to some, whose guilty fears had led them to expect a violent and tumultuous resistance to the landing of a large body of armed soldiers in the town. The peaceable demeanor of the people was construed, by the party who had brought this evil on the city, as a mark of abject submission.

September 22, 1768

September 28, 1768

October 1, 1768

373

God Prepares
a Christian
People
to Establish
the American
Nation

As they supposed from the present acquiescent deportment, that the spirit of the inhabitants was totally subdued on the first appearance of military power, they consequently rose in their demands.

General Gage arrived from New York soon after the king's troops reached Boston. With the aid of the governor, the chief justice of the province, and the sheriff of the county of Suffolk, he forced quarters for his soldiers in all the unoccupied houses in the town. The council convened on this occasion opposed the measure; but to such a height was the insolence of power pushed, by their passionate, vindictive and wrongheaded governor, that in spite of the remonstrances of several magistrates, and the importunities of the people, he suffered the state house, where the archives of the province were deposited, to be improved as barracks for the king's troops. Thus the members of council, the magistrates of the town and the courts of justice were daily interrupted, and frequently challenged in their way to their several departments in business, by military centinels posted at the doors.

October 12, 1768

A standing army thus placed in their capital, their commerce fettered, their characters traduced, their representative body prevented meeting, the united petitions of all ranks that they might be convened at this critical conjuncture rejected by the governor; and still threatened with a further augmentation of troops to enforce measures in every view repugnant to the principles of the British constitution; little hope remained of a peaceful accommodation.

The most rational arguments had been urged by the legislative assemblies, by corporate bodies, associations, and individual characters of eminence, to shake the arbitrary system that augured evils to both countries. But their addresses were disdainfully rejected; the king and the court of Great Britain appeared equally deaf to the cry of millions, who only asked a restoration of their rights. At the same time every worthless incendiary, who, taking advantage of these miserable times, crossed the Atlantic with a tale of accusation against his country, was listened to with attention, and rewarded with some token of royal favor.

A COMBINATION AGAINST ALL COMMERCE WITH GREAT BRITAIN

In this situation, no remedy appeared to be left short of an appeal to the sword, unless an entire suspension of that commercial intercourse, which had contributed so much to the glory and grandeur of Britain, could be effected throughout the colonies. As all the American continent was involved in one common danger, it was not found difficult to obtain a general combination against all further importations from England, a few articles only excepted. The mercantile body through all the provinces entered into solemn engagements, and plighted their faith and honor to each other, and to their country, that no orders should be forwarded by them for British or India goods within a limited term, except for certain specified articles of necessary use. These engagements originated in Boston, and were for a time strictly adhered to through all the colonies. Great encouragement was given to American manufactures, and if pride of apparel was at all indulged, it was in wearing the stuffs fabricated in their own looms. Harmony and union, prudence and economy, industry and virtue, were inculcated in their publications, and enforced by the example of the most respectable characters.

In consequence of these determinations, the clamors of the British manufacturers arose to tumult in many parts of the kingdom; but no artifice was neglected to quiet the trading part of the nation. There were some Americans, who by letters encouraged administration to persevere in their measures relative to the colonies, assuring them in the strongest terms, that the interruption of commerce was but a temporary struggle, or rather an effort of despair. No one in the country urged his opinion with more indiscreet zeal than Andrew Oliver, Esq. then secretary in the Massachusetts. He suggested, "that government should stipulate with the merchants in England to purchase large quantities of goods proper for the American market; agreeing beforehand to allow them a premium equal to the advance of their stock in trade, if the price of their goods was not sufficiently enhanced by a tenfold demand in future, even though the goods might lay on hand, till this temporary stagnation of business should cease." He concluded his political rhapsody with this inhuman boast to his correspondent;* *"By such a step the game will be up with my countrymen."*

The prediction on both sides the Atlantic, that this combination, which depended wholly on the commercial part of the community, could not be of long duration, proved indeed too true. A re-

---

* See the original letters of Mr. Oliver to Mr. Whately and others, which were afterwards published in a pamphlet; also, in the British Remembrancer, 1773.

GIII.   R.

By His EXCELLENCY

FRANCIS BERNARD, Esq;

Captain-General and Governor in Chief, in and over His Majesty's Province of the *Massachusetts-Bay*, in *New England*, and Vice-Admiral of the same.

A PROCLAMATION

For a General Fast.

AS the Time is now approaching wherein it has been usual, according the laudable Custom of this Country, for the People on a Day appointed to humble themselves before Almighty GOD, and implore his Blessing upon the Business of the ensuing Year:

I HAVE thought fit to appoint, and I do, by and with the Advice and Consent of His Majesty's Council, appoint Thursday the Sixth Day of *April* next ensuing, to be a Day of Fasting and Prayer throughout this Province, that the Ministers of God's holy Word, with their several Congregations, may thereon prostrate themselves before the Throne of Grace, meekly confessing their Sins, and beseeching Almighty GOD, that notwithstanding our Unworthiness He would be pleased to continue his gracious Providence over us: And especially that He would be pleased to bless our most Gracious Sovereign the KING, in the Maintenance of his Health, Wealth, Peace and Honor, in the Preservation of his Royal Consort, their Issue, and all the Royal Family, and in the Prosperity of the whole British Empire, and all its Members and Dependencies ; that He would be pleased to regard the People of this Province with the Eye of his Mercy, to prosper them in their Husbandry, Fishery and Trade, and to bless the Works of their Hands, and that they may reap the Fruits of the Earth in due Season and a sufficient Plenty ; and above all, that He would be pleased to give us true Repentance, to forgive us all our Sins, and endue us with his Grace that we may amend our Lives according to his Word, and finally be accepted by him through the Merits and Mediation of his Son *JESUS CHRIST.*
And I command and enjoin all Magistrates and Civil Officers to see that the said Day be observed, as a Day set apart for Religious Worship, and that no servile Labour nor Recreation be permitted thereon.

GIVEN at the Council-Chamber in Boston, *the Eighth Day of* March, *in the Ninth Year of the Reign of our Sovereign Lord* GEORGE *the* Third, *by the Grace of GOD, of* GREAT-BRITAIN, FRANCE, *and* IRELAND, KING, *Defender of Faith, &c. and in the Year of our Lord* 1769.

By His Excellency's Command,
   A. OLIVER, Secr'y.   *Fra. Bernard.*

GOD Save the KING.

BOSTON: Printed by RICHARD DRAPER, Printer to His Excellency the Governor, and the Honourable His Majesty's Council, 1769.

GOD PREPARES
A CHRISTIAN
PEOPLE
TO ESTABLISH
THE AMERICAN
NATION

gard to private interest ever operates more forcibly on the bulk of mankind than the ties of honor, or the principles of patriotism; and when the latter are incompatible with the former, the balance seldom hangs long in equilibrio. Thus it is not uncommon to see virtue, liberty, love of country, and regard to character, sacrificed at the shrine of wealth.

The winter following this salutary combination, a partial repeal of the act imposing duties on certain articles of British manufacture took place. On this it immediately appeared that some in New York had previously given conditional orders to their correspondents, that if the measures of parliament should in any degree be relaxed, that without farther application they should furnish them with large quantities of goods. Several in the other colonies had discovered as much avidity for an early importation as the Yorkers. They had given similar orders, and both received larger supplies than usual, of British merchandize, early in the spring one thousand seven hundred and sixty nine. The people of course considered the agreement nullified by the conduct of the merchants, and the intercourse with England for a time went on as usual, without any check. Thus, by breaking through the agreement within the limited time of restriction, a measure was defeated, which, had it been religiously observed, might have prevented the tragical consequences which ensued.

1769

After this event, a series of altercations and abuse, of recrimination and suspense, was kept up on both sides the Atlantic, without much appearance of lenity on the one side, or decision on the other. There appeared little disposition in parliament to relax the reins of government, and less in the Americans to yield implicit obedience. But whether from an opinion that they had taken the lead in opposition, or whether from their having a greater proportion of British sycophants among themselves, whose artful insinuations operated against their country, or from other concurring circumstances, the Massachusetts was still the principal butt of ministerial resentment. It is therefore necessary yet to continue a more particular detail of the situation of that province.

As their charter was not yet annihilated, governor Bernard found himself under a necessity, as the period of annual election approached, to issue writs to convene a general assembly. Accordingly a new house of representatives met at Boston as usual on the thirty-first of May, one thousand seven hundred and sixty-nine. They immediately

May 31, 1769

petitioned the governor to remove the military parade that surrounded the state-house, urging, that such a hostile appearance might over-awe their proceedings, and prevent the freedom of election and debate.

A unanimous resolve passed, "that it was the opinion of the house, that placing an armed force in the metropolis while the general assembly is there convened, is a breach of privilege, and totally inconsistent with the dignity and freedom with which they ought to deliberate and determine;"—adding, "that they meant ever to support their constitutional rights, that they should never voluntarily recede from their just claims, contained both in the letter and spirit of the constitution."

After several messages both from the council and house of representatives, the governor, ever obstinate in error, declared he had no authority over the king's troops, nor should he use any influence to have them removed. Thus by express acknowledgment of the first magistrate, it appeared that the military was set so far above the civil authority, that the last was totally unable to check the wanton exercise of this newly established power in the province. But the assembly peremptorily determined to do no business while thus insulted by the planting of cannon at the doors of the state house, and interrupted in their solemn deliberations by the noisy evolutions of military discipline.

A GENERAL ASSEMBLY CONVENED AT BOSTON— REMOVED TO CAMBRIDGE

The royal charter required that they should proceed to the choice of a speaker, and the election of a council, the first day of the meeting of the assembly. They had conformed to this as usual, but protested against its being considered as a precedent on any future emergency. Thus amidst the warmest expressions of resentment from all classes, for the indignity offered a free people by this haughty treatment to their legislature, the governor suffered them to sit several weeks without doing business; and at last compelled them to give way to an armed force, by adjourning the general assembly to Cambridge.

The internal state of the province required the attention of the house at this critical exigence of affairs. They therefore on their first meeting at Cambridge, resolved, "That it was their opinion that the British constitution admits no armed force within the realm, but for the purpose of offensive or defensive *war*. That placing troops in the

376

colony in the midst of profound peace was a breach of privilege, an infraction on the natural rights of the people, and manifestly subversive of that happy form of government they had hitherto enjoyed. That the honor, dignity, and service of the sovereign should be attended to by that assembly, so far as was consistent with the just rights of the people, their own dignity, and the freedom of debate; but that proceeding to business while an armed force was quartered in the province, was not a dereliction of the privileges legally claimed by the colony, but from necessity, and that no undue advantage should be taken from their compliance."

After this, they had not time to do any other business, before two messages of a very extraordinary nature, in their opinion, were laid before them. The first was an order under the sign-manual of the king, that Mr. Bernard should repair to England to lay the state of the province before him. To this message was tacked a request from the governor, that as he attended his majesty's pleasure as commander in chief of the province, his salary might be continued, though absent. The substance of the other message was an account of general Gage's expenditures in quartering his troops in the town of Boston; accompanied by an unqualified demand for the establishment of funds for the discharge thereof. The governor added, that he was requested by general Gage to make requisition for future provision for quartering his troops within the town.

The subsequent resolves of the house on these messages were conformable to the usual spirit of that assembly. They warmly censured both governor Bernard and general Gage for wantonly acting against the constitution; charged them with making false and injurious representations against his majesty's faithful subjects, and discovering on all occasions a most inimical disposition towards the colonies. They observed that general Gage had rashly and impertinently intermeddled with affairs altogether out of his line, and that he had betrayed a degree of ignorance equal to his malice, when he presumed to touch on the civil police of the province. They complained heavily of the arbitrary designs of government, the introduction of a standing army, and the encroachments on civil liberty; and concluded with a declaration replete with sentiments of men conscious of their own freedom and integrity, and deeply affected with the injuries offered their country. They observed, that to the utmost of their power they should vindicate the rights of human nature and the privileges of Englishmen, and explicitly declared that

duty to their constituents forbade a compliance with either of these messages. This clear, decided answer being delivered, the governor summoned the house to attend, and after a short, angry, and threatening speech, he prorogued the assembly to January, one thousand seven hundred and seventy.

GOVERNOR BERNARD
AFTER HIS IMPEACHMENT
REPAIRS TO ENGLAND

Governor Bernard immediately embarked for Europe, from whence he never more returned to a country, he had, by his arbitrary disposition and indiscreet conduct inflamed to a degree, that required both judgment and prudence to cool, perhaps beyond the abilities, and certainly incompatible with the views, of the administration in being.

The province had little reason to suppose, that considerations of the interest of the people had any part in the recall or detention of this mischievous emissary. His reception at court, the summary proceedings with regard to his impeachment and trial, and the character of the man appointed to succeed him, strongly counteracted such a flattering opinion. Notwithstanding the high charges that had been alleged against governor Bernard, he was acquitted by the king and council, without allowing time to the assembly to support their accusations, honored with a title, and rewarded with a pension of one thousand pounds sterling per annum on the Irish establishment.

Governor Bernard had reason to be perfectly satisfied with the success of his appointment to the government of Massachusetts, as it related to his personal interest. His conduct there procured him the smiles of the British court, an honorary title, and a pension for life. Besides this, the legislature of that province had in the early part of his administration, in a moment of complacency, or perhaps from digested policy, with a hope of bribing him to his duty and stimulating him to defend their invaded rights, made him a grant of a very large tract of land, the whole of the island of Mount Desert. This was afterwards reclaimed by a Madame Gregoire, in right of her ancestors, who had obtained a patent of some part of that country in the early days of European emigration. But as governor Bernard's property in America had never been confiscated, the general assembly of Massachusetts afterwards granted to his son, Sir John Bernard, who still possesses this territory, two townships of land near the river Kennebeck, in lieu of the valuable isle recovered by Madame Gregoire.

GOD PREPARES
A CHRISTIAN
PEOPLE
TO ESTABLISH
THE AMERICAN
NATION

CHARACTER OF MR. HUTCHINSON

It is ever painful to a candid mind to exhibit the deformed features of its own species; yet truth requires a just portrait of the public delinquent, though he may possess such a share of private virtue as would lead us to esteem the man in his domestic character, while we detest his political, and execrate his public transactions.

The barriers of the British constitution broken over, and the ministry encouraged by their sovereign, to pursue the iniquitous system against the colonies to the most alarming extremities, they probably judged it a prudent expedient, in order to curb the refractory spirit of the Massachusetts, perhaps bolder in sentiment and earlier in opposition than some of the other colonies, to appoint a man to preside over them who had renounced the *quondam* ideas of public virtue, and sacrificed all principle of that nature on the altar of ambition.

APPOINTED GOVERNOR OF MASSACHUSETTS

Soon after the recall of Mr. Bernard, Thomas Hutchinson, Esq. a native of Boston, was appointed to the government of Massachusetts. All who yet remember his pernicious administration and the fatal consequences that ensued, agree, that few ages have produced a more fit instrument for the purposes of a corrupt court. He was dark, intriguing, insinuating, haughty and ambitious, while the extreme of avarice marked each feature of his character. His abilities were little elevated above the line of mediocrity; yet by dint of industry, exact temperance, and indefatigable labor, he became master of the accomplishments necessary to acquire popular fame. Though bred a merchant, he had looked into the origin and the principles of the British constitution, and made himself acquainted with the several forms of government established in the colonies; he had acquired some knowledge of the *common law* of England, diligently studied the intricacies of *Machiavelian policy,* and never failed to recommend the Italian master as a model to his adherents.

Raised and distinguished by every honor the people could bestow, he supported for several years the reputation of integrity, and generally decided with equity in his judicial capacity; (Judge of probate for the county of Suffolk, and chief justice of the supreme court) and by the appearance of a tenacious regard to the religious institutions of his country, he courted the public *eclat* with the most profound dissimulation, while he engaged the affections of the lower classes by

an amiable civility and condescension, without departing from a certain gravity of deportment mistaken by the vulgar for *sanctity.*

The inhabitants of the Massachusetts were the lineal descendants of the *puritans,* who had struggled in England for liberty as early as the reign of Edward the sixth; and though obscured in the subsequent bloody persecutions, even Mr. Hume has acknowledged that to them England is indebted for the liberty she enjoys. Attached to the religious forms of their ancestors, equally disgusted with the hierarchy of the church of England, and prejudiced by the severities their fathers had experienced before their emigration, they had, both by education and principle, been always led to consider the religious as well as the political characters of those they deputed to the highest trust. Thus a profession of their own religious mode of worship, and sometimes a tincture of superstition, was with many a higher recommendation than brilliant talents. This accounts in some measure for the unlimited confidence long placed in the specious accomplishments of Mr. Hutchinson, whose character was not thoroughly investigated until some time after governor Bernard left the province.

But it was known at St. James's, that in proportion as Mr. Hutchinson gained the confidence of administration, he lost the esteem of the best of his countrymen; for this reason, his advancement to the chair of government was for a time postponed or concealed, lest the people should consider themselves insulted by such an appointment, and become too suddenly irritated. Appearances had for several years been strong against him, though it was not then fully known that he had seized the opportunity to undermine the happiness of the people, while he had their fullest confidence, and to barter the liberties of his country by the most shameless duplicity. This was soon after displayed beyond all contradiction, by the recovery of sundry letters to administration under his signature.

Mr. Hutchinson was one of the first in America who felt the full weight of popular resentment. His furniture was destroyed, and his house levelled to the ground, in the tumults occasioned by the news of the stamp-act. Ample compensation was indeed afterwards made him for the loss of property, but the strong prejudices against his political character were never eradicated.

All pretences to moderation on the part of the British government now laid aside, the full appointment of Mr. Hutchinson to the government of the Massachusetts was publickly announced at the close of the year one thousand seven hundred and sixty-nine. On his promotion the new governor uniformly observed a more highhanded and haughty tone than his predecessor. He immediately, by an explicit declaration, avowed 1770 his independence on the people, and informed the legislative that his majesty had made ample provision for his support without their aid or suffrages. The vigilant guardians of the rights of the people directly called upon him to relinquish the unconstitutional stipend, and to accept the free grants of the general assembly for his subsistence, as usually practiced. He replied that an acceptance of this offer would be a breach of his instructions from the king. This was his constant apology for every arbitrary step.

Secure of the favor of his sovereign, and now regardless of the popularity he had formerly courted with such avidity, he decidedly rejected the idea of responsibility to, or dependence on, the people. With equal inflexibility he disregarded all arguments used for the removal of the troops from the capital, and permission to the council and house of representatives to return to the usual seat of government. He silently heard their solicitations for this purpose, and as if with a design to pour contempt on their supplications and complaints, he within a few days after withdrew a garrison, in the pay of the province, from a strong fortress in the harbour of Boston; placed two regiments of the king's troops in their stead, and delivered the keys of the castle to colonel Dalrymple, who then commanded the king's troops through the province.

These steps, which seemed to bid defiance to complaint, created new fears in the minds of the people. It required the utmost vigilance to quiet the murmurs and prevent the fatal consequences apprehended from the ebullitions of popular resentment. But cool, deliberate and persevering, the two houses continued to resolve, remonstrate, and protest, against the infractions on their charter, and every dangerous innovation on their rights and privileges. Indeed the intrepid and spirited conduct of those, who stood forth undaunted at this early crisis of hazard, will dignify their names so long as the public records shall remain to witness their patriotic firmness.

Many circumstances rendered it evident that the ministerial party wished a spirit of opposition to the designs of the court might break out into violence, even at the expense of blood. This they thought would in some degree have sanctioned a measure suggested by one of the faction in America, devoted to the arbitrary system, "That some

method must be devised, to take off the original *incendiaries** whose writings instilled the poison of sedition through the vehicle of the Boston Gazette." Had this advice been followed, and a few gentlemen of integrity and ability, who had spirit sufficient to make an effort in favor of their country in each colony, have been seized at the same moment, and immolated early in the contest on the bloody altar of power, perhaps Great Britain might have held the continent in subjection a few years longer.

THE ATTEMPTED ASSASSINATION OF MR. OTIS

That they had measures of this nature in contemplation there is not a doubt. Several instances of a less atrocious nature confirmed this opinion, and the turpitude of design which at this period actuated the court party was clearly evinced by the attempted assassination of the celebrated Mr. Otis, justly deemed the first martyr to American freedom; and truth will enroll his name among the most distinguished patriots who have expired on the "bloodstained theatre of human action."

This gentleman, whose birth and education was equal to any in the province, possessed an easy fortune, independent principles, a comprehensive genius, strong mind, retentive memory, and great penetration. To these endowments may be added that extensive professional knowledge, which at once forms the character of the complete civilian and the able statesman.

In his public speeches, the fire of eloquence, the acumen of argument, and the lively sallies of wit, at once warmed the bosom of the stoic and commanded the admiration of his enemies. To his probity and generosity in the public walks were added the charms of affability and improving converse in private life. His humanity was conspicuous, his sincerity acknowledged, his integrity unimpeached, his honor unblemished, and his patriotism marked with the disinterestedness of the Spartan. Yet he was susceptible of quick feelings and warm passions, which in the ebullitions of zeal for the interest of his country sometimes betrayed him into unguarded epithets that gave his foes an advantage, without benefit to the cause that lay nearest his heart.

He had been affronted by the partizans of the crown, vilified in the public papers, and treated (after his resignation of office of judge advocate in governor Bernard's administration) in a man-

---

* See Andrew Oliver's letter to one of the ministry, dated February 13, 1769.

GOD PREPARES
A CHRISTIAN
PEOPLE
TO ESTABLISH
THE AMERICAN
NATION

ner too gross for a man of his spirit to pass over with impunity. Fearless of consequences, he had always given the world his opinions both in his writings and his conversation, and had recently published some severe strictures on the conduct of the commissioners of the customs and others of the ministerial party, and bidding defiance to resentment, he supported his allegations by the signature of his name.

A few days after this publication appeared, Mr. Otis with only one gentleman in company was suddenly assaulted in a public room, by a band of ruffians armed with swords and bludgeons. They were headed by John Robinson, one of the commissioners of the customs. The lights were immediately extinguished, and Mr. Otis covered with wounds was left for dead, while the assassins made their way through the crowd which began to assemble; and before their crime was discovered, fortunately for themselves, they escaped soon enough to take refuge on board one of the king's ships which then lay in the harbor.

In a state of nature, the savage may throw his poisoned arrow at the man, whose soul exhibits a transcript of benevolence that upbraids his own ferocity, and may boast his blood-thirsty deed among the hordes of the forest without disgrace; but in a high state of civilization, where humanity is cherished, and politeness is become a science, for the dark assassin then to level his blow at superior merit, and screen himself in the arms of power, reflects an odium on the government that permits it, and puts human nature to the blush.

The party had a complete triumph in this guilty deed; for though the wounds did not prove mortal, the consequences were tenfold worse than death. The future usefulness of this distinguished *friend* of his country was destroyed, reason was shaken from its throne, genius obscured, and the great man in ruins lived several years for his friends to weep over, and his country to lament the deprivation of talents admirably adapted to promote the highest interests of society.

This catastrophe shocked the feelings of the virtuous not less than it raised the indignation of the brave. Yet a remarkable spirit of forbearance continued for a time, owing to the respect still paid to the opinions of this unfortunate gentleman, whose voice though always opposed to the strides of despotism was ever loud against all tumultuous and illegal proceedings. He was after a partial recovery sensible himself of his incapacity for the exercise of talents that had shone with peculiar lustre, and often invoked the messenger of death to give him a sudden release from a life

become burdensome in every view but when the calm interval of a moment permitted him the recollection of his own integrity. In one of those intervals of beclouded reason he forgave the murderous band, after the principal ruffian had asked pardon in a court of justice;* and at the intercession of the gentleman whom he had so grossly abused, the people forebore inflicting that summary vengeance which was generally thought due to so black a crime.

Mr. Otis lived to see the independence of America, though in a state of mind incapable of enjoying fully the glorious event which his own exertions had precipitated. After several years of mental derangement, as if in consequence of his own prayers, his great soul was instantly set free by a flash of lightning, from the evils in which the love of his country had involved him. His death took place in May, one thousand seven hundred and eighty three, the same year the peace was concluded between Great Britain and America.†

Though the parliamentary system of colonial regulations was in many instances similar, and equally aimed to curtail the privileges of each province, yet no military force had been expressly called in aid of civil authority in any of them, except the Massachusetts. From this circumstance

---

* On a civil process commenced against him, John Robinson was adjudged to pay five thousand pounds sterling damages; but Mr. Otis despising all pecuniary compensation, relinquished it on the culprit's asking pardon and setting his signature to a very humble acknowledgement.

† A sister touched by the tenderest feelings, while she has thought it her duty to do justice to a character neglected by some, and misrepresented by other historians, can exculpate herself from all suspicion of partiality by the testimony of many of his countrymen who witnessed his private merit and public exertions. But she will however only subjoin a paragraph of a letter written to the author of these annals, on the news of Mr. Otis's death, by John Adams, Esq. then minister plenipotentiary from the United States to the court of France.

"Paris, September 10th, 1783

"It was, Madam, with very afflicting sentiments I learned the death of Mr. Otis, my worthy master. Extraordinary in death as in life, he has left a character that will never die while the memory of the American revolution remains; whose foundation he laid with an energy, and with those masterly abilities, which no other man possessed."

The reader also may not be displeased at an extemporary exclamation of a gentleman of poetic talents, on hearing of the death of Mr. Otis.

"When God in anger saw the spot,
   On earth to Otis given,
In thunder as from Sinai's mount,
   He snatch'd him back to heaven."

some began to flatter themselves that more lenient dispositions were operating in the mind of the king of Great Britain, as well as in the parliament and the people towards America in general.

They had grounded these hopes on the strong assurances of several of the plantation governors, particularly Lord Botetourt, who then presided in Virginia. He had in a speech to the assembly of the colony, in the winter of one thousand seven hundred and sixty-nine, declared himself so confident that full satisfaction would be given to the provinces in the future conduct of administration, that he pledged his faith to support to the last hour of his life the interest of America. He observed, that he grounded his own opinions and his assurances to them, on the intimations of the confidential servants of the king which authorized him to promise redress. He added, that to his certain knowledge his sovereign had rather part with his crown, than preserve it by deception.

The credulity of this gentleman was undoubtedly imposed upon; however, the Virginians, ever steady and systematic in opposition to tyranny, were for a time highly gratified by those assurances from their first magistrate. But their vigilance was soon called into exercise by the maladministration of a succeeding governor, though the fortitude of this patriotic colony was never shaken by the frown of any despotic master or masters. Some of the other colonies had listened to the soothing language of moderation used by their chief executive officers, and were for a short time influenced by that, and the flattering hopes held up by the governor of Virginia.

But before the period to which we have arrived in the narration of events, these flattering appearances had evaporated with the breath of the courtier. The subsequent conduct of administration baffled the expectations of the credulous. The hand of government was more heavily felt through the continent; and from South Carolina to Virginia, and from Virginia to New Hampshire, the mandate of a minister was the signal for the dissolution of their assemblies. The people were compelled to resort to conventions and committees to transact all public business, to unite in petitions for relief, or to take the necessary preparatory steps if finally obliged to resist by arms.

In the meantime the inhabitants of the town of Boston had suffered almost every species of insult from the British soldiery; who, countenanced by the royal party, had generally found means to screen themselves from the hand of the civil officers. Thus all authority rested on the point of the sword, and the partizans of the crown triumphed

for a time in the plenitude of military power. Yet the measure and the manner of posting troops in the capital of the province, had roused such jealousy and disgust, as could not be subdued by the scourge that hung over their heads. Continual bickerings took place in the streets between the soldiers and the citizens; the insolence of the first, which had been carried so far as to excite the African slaves to murder their masters, with the promise of impunity,* and the indiscretion of the last, was often productive of tumults and disorder that led the most cool and temperate to be apprehensive of consequences of the most serious nature.

TRANSACTIONS ON THE FIFTH OF MARCH, ONE THOUSAND SEVEN HUNDRED AND SEVENTY

No previous outrage had given such a general alarm, as the commotion on the fifth of March, one thousand seven hundred and seventy. Yet the accident that created a resentment which emboldened the timid, determined the wavering, and awakened an energy and decision that neither the artifices of the courtier, nor the terror of the sword could easily overcome, arose from a trivial circumstance; a circumstance which but from the consideration that these minute accidents frequently lead to most important events, would be beneath the dignity of history to record.

A centinel posted at the door of the custom-house had seized and abused a boy, for casting some opprobrious reflections on an officer of rank; his cries collected a number of other lads, who took the childish revenge of pelting the soldier with snow-balls. The main-guard stationed in the neighborhood of the custom-house, was informed by some persons from thence, of the rising tumult. They immediately turned out under the command of a captain Preston, and beat to arms. Several *fracas* of little moment had taken place between the soldiery and some of the lower class of inhabitants, and probably both were in a temper to avenge their own private wrongs.

The cry of fire was raised in all parts of the town, the mob collected, and the soldiery from all quarters ran through the streets sword in hand, threatening and wounding the people, and with

___

* Capt. Wilson of the 29th regiment was detected in the infamous practice; and it was proved beyond a doubt by the testimony of some respectable citizens, who declared on oath, that they had accidentally witnessed the offer of reward to the blacks, by some subaltern officers, if they would rob and murder their masters.

God Prepares
a Christian
People
to Establish
the American
Nation

every appearance of hostility, they rushed furiously to the centre of the town.

The soldiers thus ready for execution, and the populace grown outrageous, the whole town was justly terrified by the unusual alarm. This naturally drew out persons of higher condition, and more peaceably disposed, to inquire the cause. Their consternation can scarcely be described, when they found orders were given to fire promiscuously among the unarmed multitude. Five or six persons fell at the first fire, and several more were dangerously wounded at their own doors. These sudden popular commotions are seldom to be justified, and their consequences are ever to be dreaded. It is needless to make any observations on the assumed rights of royalty, in a time of peace to disperse by military murder the disorderly and riotous assemblage of a thoughtless multitude. The question has frequently been canvassed; and was on this occasion thoroughly discussed, by gentlemen of the first professional abilities.

The remains of loyalty to the sovereign of Britain were not yet extinguished in American bosoms, neither were the feelings of compassion, which shrunk at the idea of human carnage, obliterated. Yet this outrage enkindled a general resentment that could not be disguised; but every method that prudence could dictate, was used by a number of influential gentlemen to cool the sudden ferment, to prevent the populace from attempting immediate vengeance, and to prevail on the multitude to retire quietly to their own houses, and wait the decisions of law and equity. They effected their humane purposes; the people dispersed; and captain Preston and his party were taken into custody of the civil magistrate. A judicial inquiry was afterwards made into their conduct; and so far from being actuated by any partial or undue bias, some of the first counsellors at law engaged in their defence; and after a fair and legal trial they were acquitted of premeditated murder, by a jury of the county of Suffolk.

The people, not dismayed by the blood of their neighbors thus wantonly shed, determined no longer to submit to the insolence of military power. Colonel Dalrymple, who commanded in Boston, was informed the day after the riot in King Street, "that he must withdraw his troops from the town within a limited term, or hazard the consequences."

The inhabitants of the town assembled in Faneuil Hall, where the subject was discussed with becoming spirit, and the people unanimously resolved, that no armed force should be suffered longer to reside in the capital; that if the king's troops were not immediately withdrawn by their own officers, the governor should be requested to give orders for their removal, and thereby prevent the necessity of more rigorous steps. A committee from the body was deputed to wait on the governor, and request him to exert that authority which the exigencies of the times required from the supreme magistrate. Mr. Samuel Adams, the chairman of the committee, with a pathos and address peculiar to himself, exposed the illegality of quartering troops in the town in the midst of peace; he urged the apprehensions of the people, and the fatal consequences that might ensue if their removal was delayed.

But no arguments could prevail on Mr. Hutchinson; who either from timidity, or some more censurable cause, evaded acting at all in the business, and grounded his refusal on a pretended want of authority. After which, colonel Dalrymple, wishing to compromise the matter, consented that the twenty-ninth regiment, more culpable than any other in the late tumult, should be sent to Castle Island. This concession was by no means satisfactory; the people, inflexible in their demands, insisted that not one British soldier should be left within the town; their requisition was reluctantly complied with, and within four days the whole army decamped. It is not to be supposed, that this compliance of British veterans originated in their fears of an injured and incensed people, who were not yet prepared to resist by arms. They were undoubtedly sensible they had exceeded their orders, and anticipated the designs of their master; they had rashly begun the slaughter of Americans, and enkindled the flames of civil war in a country, where allegiance had not yet been renounced.

After the hasty retreat of the king's troops, Boston enjoyed for a time, a degree of tranquillity to which they had been strangers for many months. The commissioners of the customs and several other obnoxious characters retired with the army to Castle William, and their governor affected much moderation and tenderness to his country; at the same time he neglected no opportunity to ripen the present measures of administration, or to secure his own interest, closely interwoven therewith. The duplicity of Mr. Hutchinson was soon after laid open by the discovery of a number of letters under his signature, written to some individuals in the British cabinet. These letters detected by the vigilance of some friends in England, were procured and sent on to America.*

MERCY
WARREN:
PRELUDE TO
THE AMERICAN
REVOLUTION,
1765–1775

ORIGIN OF
GOVERNMENT
DISCUSSED

Previous to this event there were many persons in the province who could not be fully convinced, that at the same period when he had put on the guise of compassion to his country, when he had promised all his influence to obtain some relaxation of the coercive system, that at that moment Mr. Hutchinson should be so lost to the ideas of sincerity, as to be artfully plotting new embarrassments to the colonies in general, and the most mischievous projects against the province he was entrusted to govern. Thus convicted as the grand incendiary who had sown the seeds of discord, and cherished the dispute between Great Britain and the colonies, his friends blushed at the discovery, his enemies triumphed, and his partizans were confounded. In these letters, he had expressed his doubt of the propriety of suffering the colonies to enjoy all the privileges of the parent state: he observed, that "there must be an *abridgment of English liberties,* in colonial administration," and urged with malignant art the necessity of the resumption of the charter of Massachusetts.

Through this and the succeeding year the British nation were much divided in opinion relative to public measures, both at home and abroad. Debates and animosities ran high in both houses of parliament. Many of their best orators

1771 had come forward in defence of America, with that eloquence and precision which proved their ancestry, and marked the spirit of a nation that had long boasted their own freedom. But reason and argument are feeble barriers against the will of a monarch, or the determinations of potent aristocratical bodies. Thus the system was fixed, the measures were ripening, and a minister had the boldness to declare publickly, that "America should be brought to the footstool of parliament," and humbled beneath the pedestal of majesty. (Lord North's speech in the house of commons.)

The inhabitants of the whole American continent, appeared even at this period nearly ready for the last appeal, rather than longer to submit to the mandates of an overbearing minister of state, or the execution of his corrupt designs. The masterly writers of this enlightened age, had so clearly defined the nature and origin of government, the equal claims and natural rights of man, the principles of the British constitution, and the freedom the subject had a right to enjoy thereby; that it had become a prevailing opinion, that government and legislation were instituted for the benefit of society at large, and not for the emolument of a few; and that whenever prerogative began to stretch its rapacious arm beyond certain bounds, it was an indispensable duty to resist.

Strongly attached to Great Britain, not only by the impression of ancient forms, and the habits of submission to government, but by religion, manners, language, and consanguinity, the colonies still stood suspended in the pacific hope, that a change of ministry or a new parliament, might operate in their favor, and restore tranquillity, by the removal of the causes and the instruments of their sufferings.

Not yet conscious of her own strength, and scarcely ambitious of taking an independent rank among the nations, America still cherished the flattering ideas of reconciliation. But these expectations were finally dissipated, by the repeated attempts to reduce the colonies to unlimited submission to the supreme jurisdiction of parliament, and the illegal exactions of the crown, until by degrees all parliamentary decisions became as indifferent to an American ear, as the rescripts of a Turkish divan.

The tame acquiescence of the colonies, would doubtless have given great advantage to the corrupt party on one side of the Atlantic, while their assiduous agents on the other, did not revolt at the meanest and most wicked compliances to facilitate the designs of their employers, or to gratify their own inordinate passion for power and wealth. Thus for a considerable time, a struggle was kept up between the power of one country, and the perseverance of the other, without a possibility of calculating consequences.

A particular detail of the altercations between the representatives, the burgesses, and the provincial governors, the remonstrances of the people, the resolves of their legislative bodies, and the dissolution of their assemblies by   1773 the *fiat* of a governor, the prayers of corporate and occupational societies, or the petitions of more public and respectable bodies; the provocations on the side of government, and the

---

* The original letters which detected his treachery were procured by Dr. Franklin, and published in a pamphlet at Boston. They may also be seen in the British Annual Register, and in a large collection of historical papers printed in London, entitled the Remembrancer. The agitation into which many were thrown by the transmission of these letters, produced important consequences. Dr. Franklin was shamefully vilified and abused in an outrageous *philippic* pronounced by Mr. Wedderburne, afterwards Lord Loughborough. Threats, challenges, and duels took place, but it was not discovered by what means these letters fell into the hands of Dr. Franklin, who soon after repaired to America, where he was eminently serviceable in aid of the public cause of his native country.

GOD PREPARES
A CHRISTIAN
PEOPLE
TO ESTABLISH
THE AMERICAN
NATION

riotous, and in some degree, unjustifiable proceedings of the populace, in almost every town on the continent, would be rather tedious than entertaining, in a compendious narrative of the times. It may therefore, be well to pass over a year or two, that produced nothing but a sameness of complaint, and a similarity of opposition, on the one side; and on the other, a systematic effort, to push the darling measure of an American taxation, while neither party had much reason to promise themselves a speedy decision.

BOSTON TEA PARTY, DECEMBER 16, 1773

It has already been observed, that the revenue acts which had occasioned a general murmur, had been repealed, except a small duty on all India teas, by which a claim was kept up to tax the colonies at pleasure, whenever it should be thought expedient. This was an article used by all ranks in America; a luxury of such universal consumption, that administration was led to believe, that a monopoly of the sales of tea, might be so managed, as to become a productive source of revenue.

It was generally believed that governor Hutchinson had stipulated for the agency for his sons, as they were the first in commission; and that he had solicited for them, and obtained this odious employment, by a promise, that if they were appointed sole agents to the East India company, the sales should be so executed as to give perfect satisfaction, both to them and to administration. All communities furnish examples of men sufficiently base, to share in the spoils of their country; nor was it difficult to find such in every colony, who were ready enough to execute this ministerial job.

Thus in consequence of the insinuations of those interested in the success of the measure, a number of ships were employed by government, to transport a large quantity of teas into each of the American colonies. The people throughout the continent, apprized of the design, and considering at that time, all teas a pernicious article of commerce, summoned meetings in all the capital towns, and unanimously resolved to resist the dangerous project by every legal opposition, before they proceeded to any extremities.

The first step taken in Boston, was to request the consignees to refuse the commission. The inhabitants warmly remonstrated against the teas being landed in any of their ports, and urged the return of the ships, without permitting them to break bulk. The commissioners at New York,

Philadelphia, and in several other colonies, were applied to with similar requests; most of them complied. In some places the teas were stored on proper conditions, in others, sent back without injury. But, in Massachusetts, their difficulties were accumulated by the restless ambition of some of her own degenerate sons. Not the smallest impression was made on the feelings of their governor, by the united supplications of the inhabitants of Boston and its environs. Mr. Hutchinson, who very well knew that virtue is seldom a sufficient restraint to the passions, but that, in spite of patriotism, reason, or religion, the scale too frequently preponderates in favor of interest or appetite, persisted in the execution of his favorite project. As by force of habit, this drug had become almost a necessary article of diet, the demand for teas in America was astonishingly great, and the agents in Boston, sure of finding purchasers, if once the weed was deposited in their stores, haughtily declined a resignation of office, and determined when the ships arrived, to receive and dispose of their cargoes at every hazard.

Before either time or discretion had cooled the general disgust, at the interested and supercilious behaviour of these young pupils of intrigue, the long expected ships arrived, which were to establish a precedent, thought dangerously consequential. Resolved not to yield to the smallest vestige of parliamentary taxation, however disguised, a numerous assembly of the most respectable people of Boston and its neighborhood, repaired to the public hall, and drew up a remonstrance to the governor, urging the necessity of his order, to send back the ships without suffering any part of their cargoes to be landed. His answer confirmed the opinion, that he was the instigator of the measure; it irritated the spirits of the people, and tended more to increase, than allay the rising ferment.

A few days after this the factors had the precaution to apply to the governor and council for protection, to enable them to receive and dispose of their consignments. As the council refused to act in the affair, the governor called on colonel Hancock, who commanded a company of cadets, to hold himself in readiness to assist the civil magistrate, if any tumult should arise in consequence of any attempt to land the teas. This gentleman, though professedly in opposition to the court, had oscillated between the parties until neither of them at that time, had much confidence in his exertions. It did not however appear, that he had any inclination to obey the summons; neither did he explicitly refuse; but he soon after resigned his commission, and continued in future, unequivocally opposed to the ministerial system. On the appearance of this persevering spirit among the people, governor Hutchinson again resorted to his usual arts of chicanery and deception; he affected a mildness of deportment, and by many equivocal delays detained the ships, and endeavoured to disarm his countrymen of that manly resolution which was their principal *fort*.

The storage or detention of a few cargoes of teas is not an object in itself sufficient to justify a detail of several pages; but as the subsequent severities towards the Massachusetts were grounded on what the ministry termed their *refractory behaviour* on this occasion; and as those measures were followed by consequences of the highest magnitude both to Great Britain and the colonies, a particular narration of the transactions of the town of Boston is indispensable. There the sword of civil discord was first drawn, which was not re-sheathed until the emancipation of the thirteen colonies from the yoke of foreign domination was acknowledged by the diplomatic seals of the first powers in Europe. This may apologize, if necessary, for the appearance of locality in the preceding pages, and for its farther continuance in regard to a colony, on which the bitterest cup of ministerial wrath was poured for a time, and where the energies of the human mind were earlier called forth, than in several of the sister states.

Not intimidated by the frowns of greatness, nor allured by the smiles of intrigue, the vigilance of the people was equal to the importance of the event. Though expectation was equally awake in both parties, yet three or four weeks elapsed in a kind of *inertia;* the one side flattered themselves with hopes, that as the ships were suffered to be so long unmolested, with their cargoes entire, the point might yet be obtained; the other thought it possible, that some impression might yet be made on the governor, by the strong voice of the people.

Amidst this suspense a rumour was circulated, that admiral Montague was about to seize the ships, and dispose of their cargoes at public auction, within twenty-four hours. This step would as effectually have secured the duties, as if sold at the shops of the consignees, and was judged to be only a *finesse,* to place them there on their own terms. On this report, convinced of the necessity of preventing so bold an attempt, a vast body of people convened suddenly and repaired to one of the largest and most commodious churches in Boston; where, previous to any other steps, many fruitless messages were sent both to

the governor and the consignees, whose timidity had prompted them to a seclusion from the public eye. Yet they continued to refuse any satisfactory answer; and while the assembled multitude were in quiet consultation on the safest mode to prevent the sale and consumption of an herb, noxious at least to the political constitution, the debates were interrupted by the entrance of the sheriff with an order from the governor, styling them an illegal assembly, and directing their immediate dispersion.

This authoritative mandate was treated with great contempt, and the sheriff instantly hissed out of the house. A confused murmur ensued, both within and without the walls; but in a few moments all was again quiet, and the leaders of the people returned calmly to the point in question. Yet every expedient seemed fraught with insurmountable difficulties, and evening approaching without any decided resolutions, the meeting was adjourned without delay.

Within an hour after this was known abroad, there appeared a great number of persons, clad like the aborigines of the wilderness, with tomahawks in their hands, and clubs on their shoulders, who without the least molestation marched through the streets with silent solemnity, and amidst innumerable spectators, proceeded to the wharves, boarded the ships, demanded the keys, and with much deliberation knocked open the chests, and emptied several thousand weight of the finest teas into the ocean. No opposition was made, though surrounded by the king's ships; all was silence and dismay.

This done, the procession returned through the town in the same order and solemnity as observed in the outset of their attempt. No other disorder took place, and it was observed, the stillest night ensued that Boston had enjoyed for many months. This unexpected event struck the ministerial party with rage and astonishment; while, as it seemed to be an attack upon private property, many who wished well to the public cause could not fully approve of the measure. Yet perhaps the laws of self-preservation might justify the deed, as the exigencies of the times required extraordinary exertions, and every other method had been tried in vain, to avoid this disagreeable alternative. Besides it was alleged, and doubtless it was true, the people were ready to make ample compensation for all damages sustained, whenever the unconstitutional duty should be taken off, and other grievances radically redressed. But there appeared little prospect that any conciliatory advances would soon be made. The officers of government

God Prepares
a Christian
People
to Establish
the American
Nation

discovered themselves more vindictive than ever; animosities daily increased and the spirits of the people were irritated to a degree of alienation, even from their tenderest connexions, when they happened to differ in political opinion.

COMMITTEES OF CORRESPONDENCE

By the frequent dissolution of the general assemblies, all public debate had been precluded, and the usual regular intercourse between the colonies cut off. The modes of legislative communication thus obstructed, at a period when the necessity of harmony and concert was obvious to every eye, no systematical opposition to gubernatorial intrigues, supported by the king and parliament of Great Britain, was to be expected without the utmost concord, confidence, and union of all the colonies. Perhaps no single step contributed so much to cement the union of the colonies, and the final acquisition of independence, as the establishment of committees of correspondence. This supported a chain of communication from New Hampshire to Georgia, that produced unanimity and energy throughout the continent.

1772

As in these annals there has yet been no particular mention made of this institution, it is but justice to name at once the author, the origin, and the importance of the measure.

At an early period of the contest, when the public mind was agitated by unexpected events, and remarkably pervaded with perplexity and anxiety, James Warren, Esq. of Plymouth first proposed this institution to a private friend, on a visit at his own house (Samuel Adams, Esq. of Boston). Mr. Warren had been an active and influential member of the general assembly from the beginning of the troubles in America, which commenced soon after the demise of George the second. The principles and firmness of this gentleman were well known, and the uprightness of his character had sufficient weight to recommend the measure. As soon as the proposal was communicated to a number of gentlemen in Boston, it was adopted with zeal, and spread with the rapidity of enthusiasm, from town to town, and from province to province.* Thus an intercourse was established, by which a similarity of opinion, a connexion of interest, and a union of action

appeared, that set opposition at defiance, and defeated the machinations of their enemies through all the colonies.

The plan suggested was clear and methodical; it proposed that a public meeting should be called in every town; that a number of persons should be selected by a plurality of voices; that they should be men of respectable characters, whose attachment to the great cause of America had been uniform; that they should be vested by a majority of suffrages with power to take cognizance of the state of commerce, of the intrigues of *toryism,* of litigious ruptures that might create disturbances, and every thing else that might be thought to militate with the rights of the people, and to promote every thing that tended to general utility.

The business was not tardily executed. Committees were every where chosen, who were directed to keep up a regular correspondence with each other, and to give information of all intelligence received, relative to the proceedings of administration, so far as they affected the interest of the British colonies throughout America. The trust was faithfully and diligently discharged, and when afterwards all legislative authority was suspended, the courts of justice shut up, and the last traits of British government annihilated in the colonies, this new institution became a kind of juridical tribunal. Its injunctions were influential beyond the hopes of its most sanguine friends, and the recommendations of committees of correspondence had the force of law. Thus, as despotism frequently springs from anarchy, a regular democracy sometimes arises from the severe encroachments of despotism.

This institution had given such a general alarm to the adherents of administration, and had been replete with such important consequences through the union, that it was justly dreaded by those who opposed it, and considered by them as the most important bulwark of freedom. A representation of this establishment, and its effects, had been transmitted to England, and laid before the king and parliament, and Mr. Hutchinson had received his majesty's disapprobation of the measure. With the hope of impeding its farther operation, by announcing the frown and the censure of royalty, and for the discussion of some other important questions, the governor had thought proper to convene the council and house of representatives, to meet in January one thousand seven hundred and seventy-three.

The assembly of the preceding year had passed a number of very severe resolves, when the origi-

---

* The general impulse at this time seemed to operate by sympathy, before consultation could be had; thus it appeared afterwards that the vigilant inhabitants of Virginia had concerted a similar plan about the same period.

nal letters mentioned above, written by governor Hutchinson and lieutenant-governor Oliver were detected, sent back to the Massachusetts, and laid before the house. They had observed that "the letters contained wicked and injurious misrepresentations, designed to influence the ministry and the nation, and to excite jealousies in the breast of the king, against his faithful subjects." (11th resolve, 1772) They had proceeded to an impeachment, and unanimously requested, that his majesty would be pleased to remove both Mr. Thomas Hutchinson and Mr. Andrew Oliver from their public functions in the province, forever. But before they had time to complete their spirited measures, the governor had as usual dissolved the assembly. This was a stretch of power, and a manifestation of resentment, that had been so frequently exercised both by Mr. Hutchinson and his predecessor, that it was never unexpected, and now totally disregarded. This mode of conduct was not confined to the Massachusetts; it was indeed the common signal of resentment exhibited by most of the colonial governors: they immediately dissolved the legislative assemblies on the discovery of energy, enterprise, or patriotism, among the members.

When the new house of assembly met at Boston the present year, it appeared to be composed of the principal gentlemen and landholders in the province; men of education and ability, of fortune and family, of integrity and honor; jealous of the infringements of their rights, and the faithful guardians of a free people.

THE RIGHT OF PARLIAMENTARY TAXATION WITHOUT REPRESENTATION URGED BY MR. HUTCHINSON

Their independency of mind was soon put to the test. On the opening of the new session, the first communication from the governor was, that he had received his majesty's express disapprobation of all *committees* of *correspondence;* and to enforce the displeasure of the *monarch,* he very indiscreetly ventured himself to censure with much warmth this institution, and every other stand that the colonies had unitedly made to ministerial and parliamentary invasions. To complete the climax of his own presumption, he in a long and labored speech imprudently agitated the grand question of a parliamentary right of taxation without representation; he endeavoured to justify, both by law and precedent, every arbitrary step that had been taken for ten years past to reduce the colonies to a disgraceful subjugation.

This gave a fair opening to the friends of their country which they did not neglect, to discuss the illegality, injustice, and impolicy of the late innovations. They entered on the debate with freedom of inquiry, stated their claims with clearness and precision, and supported them with such reasoning and perspicuity, that a man of less hardiness than Mr. Hutchinson would not have made a second attempt to justify so odious a cause, or to gain such an unpopular point by dint of argument. But whether owing to his own intemperate zeal, or whether instigated by his superiors on the other side the Atlantic, to bring on the dispute previous to the disclosure of some extraordinary measures then in agitation, is uncertain. However this was, he supported his opinions with industry and ingenuity, and not discouraged by strong opposition, he spun out the debate to a tedious and ridiculous length. Far from terminating to the honor of the governor, his officious defence of administration served only to indicate the necessity of the most guarded watchfulness against the machinations of powerful and designing men; and fanned, rather than checked the *amor patriae* characteristic of the times.

Soon after this altercation ended, the representative body took cognizance of an affair that had given great disgust, and created much uneasiness through the province. By the royal charter granted by William and Mary, the governor, lieutenant-governor and secretary were appointed by the king; the council were chosen by the representatives of the people, the governor being allowed a negative voice; the judges, justices, and all other officers, civil and military, were left to his nomination, and appointed by him, with the advice and consent of a board of counsellors. But as it is always necessary in a free government, that the people should retain some means in their own hands, to check any unwarrantable exercise of power in the executive, the legislature of Massachusetts had always enjoyed the reasonable privilege of paying their own officers according to their ability, and the services rendered to the public.

It was at this time well known that Mr. Hutchinson had so far ingratiated himself as to entitle him to peculiar favor from the crown; and by a handsome salary from the king, he was rendered entirely independent of the people. His brother-in-law also, the lieutenant-governor, had obtained by misrepresentations, thought by some to have been little short of perjury, a pension which he had long solicited; but chagrin at the detection of his letters, and the discovery of his duplicity, soon put a period to a life that might

GOD PREPARES
A CHRISTIAN
PEOPLE
TO ESTABLISH
THE AMERICAN
NATION

have been useful and exemplary, had he confined his pursuits only to the domestic walks of life.

A strong family as well as political connexion, had for some time been forming among those who had been writing in favor of colonial regulations, and urging the creation of a *patrician rank,* from which all officers of government should in future be selected. Intermarriages among their children in the near degree of consanguinity before the parties were of age for maturity of choice, had strengthened the union of interests among the candidates for preferment. Thus by a kind of compact, almost every department of high trust as it became vacant by resignation, suspension or death, was filled by some relation or dependent of governor Hutchinson; and no other qualification was required except a suppleness of opinion and principle that could readily bend to the measures of the court.

But it was more recently discovered that the judges of the superior court, the near relations or coadjutors of Mr. Hutchinson, and few of them more scrupulously delicate with regard to the violation of the rights of their country than himself, had taken advantage of the times, and successfully insinuated that the dignity of their offices must be supported by an allowance from the crown sufficient to enable them to execute the designs of government, exclusively of any dependence on the general assembly. In consequence of these representations, the judges were appointed to hold their places during the king's pleasure, and a yearly stipend was granted them to be paid out of the new revenue to be raised in America.

The general court had not been convened after the full disclosure of this system before the present period; of course no constitutional opposition could be made on the infraction of their charter, until a legal assembly had an opportunity to meet and deliberate. Uncertain how long the intriguing spirit of the governor would permit them to continue in existence, the sitting assembly judged it necessary early in the session to proceed to a parliamentary inquiry into the conduct of their judiciary officers. Accordingly the judges of the supreme court were called upon to receive the grants for their services as usual from the treasury of the province; to renounce all unconstitutional salaries, and to engage to receive no pay, pension or emolument in reward of services as justices of the court of judicature, but from the free grants of the legislative assembly.

Two of the judges, Trowbridge and Ropes, readily complied with the demand, and relin-

quished the offensive stipend. A third was William Cushing, Esq. a gentleman rendered respectable in the eyes of all parties by his professional abilities and general integrity. He was a sensible, modest man, well acquainted with law, but remarkable for the secrecy of his opinions: this kept up his reputation through all the ebullitions of discordant parties. He readily resigned the royal stipend without any observations of his own; yet it was thought at the time that it was with a reluctance that his taciturnity could not conceal. By this silent address he retained the confidence of the court faction, nor was he less a favorite among the republicans. He was immediately placed on the bench of justice after the assumption of government in the Massachusetts.

The next that was called forward was Foster Hutchinson, a brother of the governor's, a man of much less understanding, and as little public virtue; in short, remarkable for nothing but the malignancy of his heart. He, after much altercation and abuse of the general assembly, complied with a very ill grace with the requisitions of the house.

CHIEF JUSTICE OF THE PROVINCE IMPEACHED

But the chief seat of justice in this extraordinary administration was occupied by a man (Peter Oliver, Esq. a brother-in-law of the governor's) unacquainted with law, and ignorant of the first principles of government. He possessed a certain credulity of mind that easily seduced him into erroneous opinions; at the same time a frigid obstinacy of temper that rendered him incapable of conviction. His insinuating manners, his superficial abilities, and his implicit devotion to the governor, rendered him a fit instrument to give sanction by the forms of law to the most atrocious acts of arbitrary power. Equally deaf to the dictates of patriotism and to the united voice of the people, he peremptorily refused to listen to the demands of their representatives; and boldly declared his resolution to receive an annual grant from the crown of England in spite of the opinions or resentment of his country: he urged as an excuse, the depreciation of his private fortune by his judicial attentions. His station was important and influential, and his temerity was considered as holding a bribe to execute the corrupt measures of the British court.

The house of representatives not interrupted in their system, nor intimidated by the presumption of the delinquent, proceeded directly to exhibit articles of impeachment against Peter

Oliver, Esq. accusing him of high crimes and misdemeanors, and laid their complaints before the governor and council. On a division of the house there appeared ninety-two members in favour of the measure, and only eight against it. The governor, as was expected, both from personal attachment and a full approbation of Mr. Oliver's conduct, refused to act or sit on the business; of course all proceedings were for a time suspended.

BOSTON PORT BILL, JUNE I, 1774

When a detail of these spirited measures reached England, exaggerated by the colorings of the officers of the crown, it threw the nation, more especially the trading part, into a temporary fever. The ministry rose in their resentment, and entered on the most severe steps against the Massachusetts, and more particularly the town of Boston. It was at this period that lord North ushered into the house of commons the memorable bill for shutting up the port of Boston, also the bill for better regulating the government of the Massachusetts.

The port-bill enacted that after the first of June one thousand seven hundred and seventy-four, "Every vessel within the points Alderton and Nahant, (the boundaries of the harbor of Boston,) should depart within six hours, unless laden with food or fuel." That no merchandize should be taken in or discharged at any of the stores, wharves, or quays, within those limits; and that any ship, barge or boat, attempting to convey from other parts of America, either stores, goods or merchandize to Boston, (one of the largest maritime towns on the continent) should be deemed a legal forfeiture to the crown.

This act was opposed with becoming zeal by several in both houses of parliament, who still inherited the generous spirit of their ancestors, and dared to stand forth the defenders of English liberty, in the most perilous seasons. Though the cruelty and injustice of this step was warmly criminated, the minister and his party urged the necessity of strong measures; nor was it difficult to obtain a large majority to enforce them. An abstract of an act for the more impartial administration of justice in the province of Massachusetts, accompanied the port-bill. Thus by one of those severe and arbitrary acts, many thousands of the best and most loyal subjects of the house of Brunswick were at once cut off from the means of subsistence; poverty stared in the face of affluence, and a long train of evils threatened every

June 1, 1774

rank. No discriminations were made; the innocent were equally involved with the real or imputed guilty, and reduced to such distresses afterwards, that, but from the charitable donations of the other colonies, multitudes must have inevitably perished.

The other bill directed, that on an indictment for riot, resistance of the magistrate, or impeding the laws of revenue in the smallest degree, any person, at the option of the governor, or in his absence, the lieutenant-governor, might be transported to Great Britain for trial, and there be ordered to wait amidst his foes, the decisions of strangers unacquainted with the character of the prisoner, or the turpitude of a crime, that should subject him to be transported a thousand leagues from his own vicinity, for a final decision on the charges exhibited against him. Several of the southern colonies remonstrated warmly against those novel proceedings towards the Massachusetts, and considered it as a common cause. The house of burgesses in Virginia vigorously opposed this measure, and passed resolutions expressing "their exclusive right to tax their constituents, and their right to petition their sovereign for redress of grievances, and the lawfulness of procuring the concurrence of the other colonies in praying for the royal interposition in favour of the violated rights of America: and that all trials for treasons, or for any crime whatsoever, committed in that colony, ought to be before his majesty's courts within the said colony; and that the seizing any person residing in the said colony, suspected of any crime whatsoever committed therein, and sending such person to places beyond the sea to be tried, was highly derogatory of the rights of British subjects."

These acts were to continue in full force until satisfaction should be made to the East India company for the loss of their teas; nor were any assurances given, that in case of submission and compliance, they should be repealed. The indignation which naturally arose in the minds of the people on these unexpected and accumulated grievances, was truly inexpressible. It was frequently observed, that the only melioration of the present evils was, that the recall of Mr. Hutchinson accompanied the bills, and his leaving the province at the same period the port-bill was to be put in operation, seemed to impress a dawn of hope from time, if not from his immediate successor.

Every historical record will doubtless witness that he was the principal author of the sufferings of the unhappy Bostonians, previous to the con-

God Prepares
a Christian
People
to Establish
the American
Nation

vulsions which produced the revolution. So deeply riveted was this opinion among his enraged countrymen, that many apprehended the summary vengeance of an incensed populace would not suffer so notorious a parricide to repair quietly to England. Yet such were the generous and compassionate feelings of a people too virtuous to punish without a legal process, that he escaped the blow he had reason to fear would overtake him, when stripped of authority, and no longer acting as the representative of *majesty*.

GOVERNOR HUTCHINSON LEAVES
THE PROVINCE

Chagrined by the loss of place, mortified by the neglect of some, and apprehensive from the resentment of others, he retired to a small village in the neighborhood of Boston, and secluded himself from observation until he embarked for London. This he did on the same memorable day when, by act of parliament, the blockade of Boston took place. Before his departure, the few partizans that still adhered to the man and his principles, procured by much assiduity a complimentary address, thanking him for past *services,* and held up to him the idea, that by his *talents* he might obtain a redress of grievances, which they well knew had been drawn on their country by the agency of Mr. Hutchinson. Much derision fell on the character of this group of flatterers, who were long distinguished only by the appellation of *Hutchinson's addressers.*

Mr. Hutchinson furnished with these pitiful credentials, left his native country forever. On his arrival in England, he was justified and caressed by his employers; and notwithstanding the criminality of his political conduct had been so fully evinced by the detection and recovery of his original letters, his impeachment, which was laid before the lords of the privy-council, was considered by them in a very frivolous light. A professional character, by some thought to have been hired for the purpose, was permitted to abuse the petitioners and their agent in the grossest terms scurrility could invent; and the lords reported, that "the petition was groundless, vexatious, and scandalous, and calculated only for the seditious purposes of keeping up a spirit of discontent and clamour in the province; that nothing had been laid before them which did or could, in their opinion, in any manner or in any degree impeach the honour, integrity, or conduct of the governor or lieutenant-governor;" who had been at the same time impeached.

But the operation of his measures, while governor of the Massachusetts, was so productive of misfortune to Great Britain, as well as to the united colonies, that Mr. Hutchinson soon became the object of disgust to all parties. He did not live to see the independence of America established, but he lived long enough to repent in bitterness of soul, the part he had acted against a country once disposed to respect his character. After his mind had been involved many months in a state of chagrin, disappointment and despair, he died on the day the riots in London, excited by lord George Gordon, were at the height, in the year one thousand seven hundred and eighty. Those of the family who survived their unhappy father remained in obscurity in England.

It must however be acknowledged that governor Hutchinson was uniform in his political conduct. He was educated in reverential ideas of monarchic government, and considered himself the servant of a king who had entrusted him with very high authority. As a true disciple of passive obedience, he might think himself bound to promote the designs of his master, and thus he might probably release his conscience from the obligation to aid his countrymen in their opposition to the encroachments of the crown. In the eye of candor, he may therefore be much more excusable, than any who may deviate from their principles and professions of republicanism, who have not been biassed by the patronage of kings, nor influenced in favor of monarchy by their early prejudices of education or employment.

GENERAL GAGE APPOINTED GOVERNOR
OF MASSACHUSETTS

The speculatist and the philosopher frequently observe a casual subordination of circumstances independent of political decision, which fixes the character and manners of nations. This thought may be piously improved till it leads the mind to view those casualties, directed by a secret hand which points the revolutions of time, and decides the fate of empires. The occasional instruments for the completion of the grand system of Providence, have seldom any other stimulus but the bubble of *fame,* the lust of *wealth,* or some contemptible passion that centres in *self.* Even the bosom of virtue warmed by higher principles, and the man actuated by nobler motives, walks in a narrow sphere of comprehension. The scale by which the ideas of mortals are circumscribed generally limits his wishes to a certain point without consideration, or a just calculation of extensive consequences. Thus while the king of Great Britain was contending with the colonies for a three-penny duty on *tea,* and the Americans with the bold spirit of patriotism resisting an encroachment on their rights, the one thought they only asked a moderate and reasonable indulgence from their sovereign, which they had a right to demand if withheld; on the other side, the most severe and strong measures were adopted and exercised towards the *colonies,* which parliament considered as only the proper and necessary chastisement of *rebellious subjects.* Thus on the eve of one of the most remarkable revolutions recorded in the page of history, a revolution which Great Britain precipitated by her indiscretion, and which the hardiest sons of America viewed in the beginning of opposition as a work reserved for the enterprising hand of posterity, few on either side comprehended the magnitude of the contest, and fewer still had the courage to name the independence of the American colonies as the *ultimatum* of their *designs.*

After the spirits of men had been wrought up to a high tone of resentment, by repeated injuries on the one hand, and an open resistance on the other, there was little reason to expect a ready compliance with regulations, repugnant to the feelings, the principles, and the interest of Americans. The parliament of Britain therefore thought it expedient to enforce obedience by the sword, and determined to send out an armament sufficient for the purpose, early in the spring one thousand seven hundred and seventy-four. The subjugation of the colonies by arms, was yet considered in England by some as a work of such facility, that four or five regiments, with a few ships of the line, were equal to the business, provided they were commanded by officers who had not sagacity enough to judge of the impropriety of the measures of administration, nor humanity to feel for the miseries of the people, or liberality to endeavour to mitigate the rigors of government.

In consequence of this opinion, admiral Montague was recalled from Boston, and admiral Graves appointed to succeed, whose character was known to be more avaricious, severe and vigilant than his predecessor, and in all respects a more fit instrument to execute the weak, indigested and irritating system.

General Gage, unhappily for himself, as will appear in the sequel, was selected as a proper person to take the command of all his majesty's forces in North America, and reduce the country to submission. He had married a lady of re-

spectable connexions in New York, and had held with considerable reputation for several years a military employment in the colonies. He was at this time appointed governor and commander in chief of the province of Massachusetts Bay; directed to repair immediately there, and on his arrival to remove the seat of government from Boston, and to convene the general assembly to meet at Salem, a smaller town, situated about twenty miles from the capital. The governor, the lieutenant-governor, the secretary, the board of commissioners, and all crown officers were ordered by special mandate to leave Boston, and make the town of Salem the place of their future residence.

A few days before the annual election for May, one thousand seven hundred and seventy-four, the new governor of Massachusetts arrived. He was received by the inhabitants of Boston with the same respect that had been usually shewn to those, who were dignified by the title of the king's representative. An elegant entertainment was provided at Faneuil Hall, to which he was escorted by a company of cadets, and attended with great civility by the magistrates and principal gentlemen of the town; and though jealousy, disgust, and resentment burnt in the bosom of one party, and the most unwarrantable designs occupied the thoughts of the other, yet the appearance of politeness and good humor was kept up through the *etiquette* of the day.

The week following was the anniversary of the general election, agreeable to charter. The day was ushered in with the usual parade, and the house of representatives proceeded to business in the common form: but a specimen of the measures to be expected from the new administration appeared in the first act of authority recorded of governor Gage. A list of counsellors was presented for his approbation, from which he erased the names of thirteen gentlemen out of twenty-eight, unanimously chosen by the free voice of the representatives of the people, leaving only a quorum as established by charter, or it was apprehended, in the exercise of his new prerogative he might have annihilated the whole. Most of the gentlemen on the negative list had been distinguished for their attachment to the ancient constitution, and their decided opposition to the present ministerial measures. Among them was James Bowdoin, Esq. whose understanding, discernment, and conscientious deportment, rendered him a very unfit instrument for the views of the court, at this extraordinary period. John

May, 1774

God Prepares
a Christian
People
to Establish
the American
Nation

Winthrop, Hollisian professor of mathematics and natural philosophy at Cambridge; his public conduct was but the emanation of superior genius, united with an excellent heart, as much distinguished for every private virtue as for his attachment to the liberties of a country that may glory in giving birth to a man of his exalted character. Colonel Otis of Barnstable, whose name has already been mentioned; and John Adams, a barrister at law of rising abilities; his appearance on the theatre of politics commenced at this period; we shall meet him again in still more dignified stations. These gentlemen had been undoubtedly pointed out as obnoxious to administration by the predecessor of governor Gage, as he had not been long enough in the province to discriminate characters.

GENERAL ASSEMBLY MEET AT SALEM

The house of representatives did not think proper to replace the members of council by a new choice; they silently bore this indiscreet exercise of authority, sensible it was but a prelude to the impending storm. The assembly was the next day adjourned for a week; at the expiration of that time, they were directed to meet at Salem. In the interim the governor removed himself, and the whole band of revenue and crown officers deserted the town of Boston at once, as a place devoted to destruction.

Every external appearance of respect was still kept up towards the new governor. The council, the house, the judiciary officers, the mercantile and other bodies, prepared and offered congratulatory addresses as usual, on the recent arrival of the commander in chief at the seat of government. The incense was received both at Boston and Salem with the usual satisfaction, except the address from the remaining board of counsellors; this was checked with asperity, and the reading it through forbidden, as the composition contained some strictures on administration, and censured rather too freely, for the delicate ear of an infant magistrate, the conduct of some of his predecessors. But this was the last compliment of the kind, ever offered by either branch of the legislature of the Massachusetts to a governor appointed by the king of Great Britain. No marks of ministerial resentment had either humbled or intimidated the spirits, nor shook the intrepidity of mind necessary for the times; and though it was first called into action in the Massachusetts it breathed its influence through all the colonies. They all seemed equally prepared to suffer, and

equally determined to resist in unison, if no mean but that of absolute submission was to be the test of loyalty.

The first day of June, one thousand seven hundred and seventy-four, the day when the Boston port-bill began to operate, was observed in most of the colonies with uncommon solemnity as a day of fasting and prayer. In all of them, sympathy and indignation, compassion and resentment, alternately arose in every bosom. A zeal to relieve, and an alacrity to support the distressed *Bostonians,* seemed to pervade the whole continent, except the dependents on the crown, and their partizans, allured by interest to adhere to the royal cause. There were indeed a few others in every colony led to unite with, and to think favorably of the measures of administration, from their attachment to monarchy, in which they had been educated; and some there were who justified all things done by the hand of power, either from fear, ignorance, or imbecility.

The session at Salem was of short duration, but it was a busy and an important period. The leading characters in the house of representatives contemplated the present moment, replete with consequences of the utmost magnitude; they judged it a crisis that required measures bold and decisive, though hazardous, and that the extrication of their country from the designs of their enemies, depended much on the conduct of the present assembly. Their charter was on the point of annihilation; a military governor had just arrived, with troops on the spot, to support the arbitrary systems of the court of St. James.

These appearances had a disagreeable effect on some who had before cooperated with the patriots; they began to tremble at the power and the severity of Britain, at a time when firmness was most required, zeal indispensable, and secrecy necessary. Yet those who possessed the energies of mind requisite for the completion or the defeat of great designs, had not their ardor or resolution shaken in the smallest degree, by either dangers, threats or caresses. It was a prime object to select a few members of the house, that might be trusted most confidentially on any emergence. This task fell on Mr. Samuel Adams of Boston, and Mr. Warren of Plymouth. They drew off a few chosen spirits, who met at a place appointed for a secret conference; several others were introduced the ensuing evening, when a discussion of circumstances took place. Immediate decision, and effectual modes of action were urged, and such caution, energy and dispatch were observed by this daring and dauntless secret *council,* that on the third evening of their conference their business was ripe for execution.

A PROPOSAL FOR A CONGRESS FROM ALL THE COLONIES, TO BE CONVENED AT PHILADELPHIA

This committee had digested a plan for a general congress from all the colonies, to consult on the common safety of America;* named their own delegates; and as all present were convinced of the necessity and expediency of such a convention, they estimated the expense, and provided funds for the liquidation, prepared letters to the other colonies, enforcing the reasons for their strong confederacy, and disclosed their proceedings to the house, before the governmental party had the least suspicion of their designs. Before the full disclosure of the business they were upon, the doors of the house were locked, and a vote passed, that no one should be suffered to enter or retire, until a final determination took place on the important questions before them. When these designs were opened, the partizans of administration then in the house, were thunderstruck with measures so replete with ability and vigour, and that wore such an aspect of high and dangerous consequences. These transactions might have been legally styled *treasonable,* but loyalty had lost its influence, and power its terrors. Firm and disinterested, intrepid and united, they stood ready to submit to the chances of war, and to sacrifice their devoted lives to preserve inviolate, and to transmit to posterity, the inherent rights of men, conferred on all by the God of nature, and the privileges of Englishmen, claimed by Americans from the sacred sanctions of compact.

When the measures agitated in the secret conference were laid before the house of representatives, one of the members a devotee to all governors, pretended a sudden indisposition, and requested leave to withdraw; he pleaded the necessities of nature, was released from his uneasy confinement, and ran immediately to governor

June 17, 1774

Gage with information of the bold and high-handed proceedings of the lower house. The governor not less alarmed than the sycophant, at these unexpected manoeuvres, instantly directed the secretary to dissolve the assembly by proclamation.

Finding the doors of the house closed, and no prospect of admittance for him, the secretary desired the door-keeper to acquaint the house he had a message from the governor, and requested leave to deliver it. The speaker replied, that it was the order of the house, that no one should be permitted to enter on any pretence whatever, before the business they were upon was fully completed. Agitated and embarrassed, the secretary then read on the stairs a proclamation for the immediate dissolution of the general assembly.

The main point gained, the delegates for a congress chosen, supplies for their support voted, and letters to the other colonies requesting them to accord in these measures, signed by the speaker, the members cheerfully dispersed, and returned to their constituents, satisfied, that notwithstanding the precipitant dissolution of the assembly, they had done all that the circumstances of the times would admit, to remedy the present, and guard against future evils.

This early step to promote the general interest of the colonies, and lay the foundation of union and concord in all their subsequent transactions, will ever reflect lustre on the characters of those who conducted it with such firmness and decision. It was indeed a very critical era: nor were those gentlemen insensible of the truth of the observation, that "whoever has a standing army at command, has, or may have the state." Nor were they less sensible, that in the present circumstances, while they acknowledged themselves the subjects of the king of England, their conduct must be styled *rebellion,* and that death must be the inevitable consequence of defeat. Yet life was then considered a trivial stake in competition with liberty.

All the old colonies except Georgia, readily acceded to the proposal of calling a general congress; they made immediate exertions that there might be no discord in the councils of the several provinces, and that their opposition should be consistent, spirited and systematical. Most of them had previously laid aside many of their local prejudices, and by public resolves and various other modes, had expressed their disgust at the summary proceedings of parliament against the Massachusetts. They reprobated the port-bill in

---

* Such a remarkable coincidence of opinion, energy and zeal, existed between the provinces of Virginia and the Massachusetts, that their measures and resolutions were often similar, previous to the opportunity for conference. Thus the propriety of a general congress had been discussed and agreed upon by the Virginians, before they were informed of the resolutions of Massachusetts. Some of the other colonies had contemplated the same measure, without any previous consultation.

God Prepares
a Christian
People
to Establish
the American
Nation

terms of detestation, raised liberal contributions for the suffering inhabitants of Boston, and continued their determination to support that province at every hazard, through the conflict in which they were involved.

In conformity to the coercive system, the governors of all the colonies frowned on the sympathetic part the several legislative bodies had been disposed to take with the turbulent descendants, as they were pleased to style the Massachusetts, of *puritans, republicans* and *regicides.* Thus most of the colonial assemblies had been petulantly dissolved, nor could any applications from the people prevail on the supreme magistrate, to suffer the representatives and burgesses to meet, and in a legal capacity deliberate on measures most consistent with loyalty and freedom. But this persevering obstinacy of the governors did not retard the resolutions of the people; they met in parishes, and selected persons from almost every town, to meet in provincial conventions, and there to make choice of suitable delegates to meet in general congress.

The beginning of autumn, one thousand seven hundred and seventy-four, was the time appointed, and the city of Philadelphia chosen, as the most central and convenient place, for this body to meet and deliberate, at so critical a conjuncture. Yet such was the attachment to Britain, the strength of habit, and the influence of ancient forms; such the reluctant dread of spilling human blood, which at that period was universally felt in America, that there were few, who did not ardently wish some friendly intervention might yet prevent a rupture, which probably might shake the empire of Britain, and waste the inhabitants on both sides the Atlantic.

At this early period, there were some who viewed the step of their summoning a general congress, under existing circumstances of peculiar embarrassment, as a *prelude* to a *revolution* which appeared pregnant with events, that might affect not only the political systems, but the character and manners of a considerable part of the habitable globe.

America was then little known, her character, ability, and police, less understood abroad; but she soon became the object of attention among the potentates of Europe, the admiration of both the philosophic and the brave, and her fields the theatre of fame throughout the civilized world. Her principles were disseminated: the seeds sown in America ripened in the more cultivated grounds of Europe, and inspired ideas among the enslaved nations that have long trembled at the name of the *bastile* and the *bastinado.* This may finally lead to the completion of prophetic predictions, and spread universal liberty and peace, as far at least as is compatible with the present state of human nature.

The wild vagaries of the *perfectibility* of man, so long as the passions to which the species are liable play about the hearts of all, may be left to the dreaming *sciolist,* who wanders in search of impracticable theories. He may remain entangled in his own web, while that rational liberty, to which all have a right, may be exhibited and defended by men of principle and heroism, who better understand the laws of social order.

Through the summer previous to the meeting of congress, no expressions of loyalty to the sovereign, or affection to the parent state, were neglected in their public declarations. Yet the colonies seemed to be animated as it were by one soul, to train their youth to arms, to withhold all commercial connexion with Great Britain, and to cultivate that unanimity necessary to bind society when ancient forms are relaxed or broken, and the common safety required the assumption of new modes of government. But while attentive to the regulations of their internal economy and police, each colony beheld with a friendly and compassionate eye, the severe struggles of the Massachusetts, where the arm of power was principally levelled, and the ebullitions of ministerial resentment poured forth, as if to terrify the sister provinces into submission.

Not long after the dissolution of the last assembly ever convened in that province on the principles of their former charter, admiral Graves arrived in Boston, with several ships of the line and a number of transports laden with troops, military stores, and all warlike accoutrements. The troops landed peaceably, took possession of the open grounds, and formed several encampments within the town.

MANDAMUS COUNSELLORS URGED TO RESIGN

At the same time arrived the bill for new modelling the government of the Massachusetts. By this bill their former charter was entirely vacated: a council of thirty-six members was appointed by *mandamus,* to hold their places during the king's pleasure; all judges, justices, sheriffs, &c. were to be appointed by the governor, without the advice of council, and to be removed at his sole option. Jurors in future were to be named by the sheriff, instead of the usual and more impartial mode of drawing them by lot. All town-meetings without express leave from the governor were forbidden, except those annually held in the spring for the choice of representatives and town-officers. Several other violations of the former compact completed the system.

This new mode of government, though it had been for some time expected, occasioned such loud complaints, such universal murmurs, that several of the newly appointed counsellors had not the courage to accept places which they were sensible would reflect disgrace on their memory. Two of them seemed really to decline from principle, and publickly declared they would have no hand in the dereliction of the rights of their country. These were James Russell, Esq. of Charlestown, and William Vassal, Esq. of Boston. Several others relinquished their seats for fear of offending their countrymen; but most of them, selected by Mr. Hutchinson as proper instruments for the purpose, were destitute of all ideas of public virtue. They readily took the qualifying oaths, and engaged to lend their hand to erase the last vestige of freedom in that devoted province.

The people still firm and undaunted, assembled in multitudes and repaired to the houses of the obnoxious counsellors. They demanded an immediate resignation of their unconstitutional appointments, and a solemn assurance that they would never accept any office incompatible with the former privileges enjoyed by their country. Some of them terrified by the resolution of the people complied, and remained afterwards quiet and unmolested in their own houses. Others, who had prostrated all principle in the hope of preferment, and were hardy enough to go every length to secure it, conscious of the guilty part they had acted, made their escape into Boston where they were sure of the protection of the king's troops. Indeed that unhappy town soon became the receptacle of all the devotees to ministerial measures from every part of the province: they there consoled themselves with the barbarous hope, that parliament would take the severest measures to enforce their own acts; nor were these hopes unfounded.

It has been observed that by the late edict for the *better administration* of *justice* in the Massachusetts, any man was liable on the slightest *suspicion* of *treason,* or *misprision* of *treason,* to be dragged from his own family or vicinity, to any part of the king of England's dominions for trial. It was now reported that general Gage had orders to arrest the leading characters in opposition, and transport them beyond sea, and that a reinforcement of troops might be hourly expected sufficient to enable him to execute all the mad projects of a rash and unprincipled ministry.

Though the operation of this system in its utmost latitude was daily threatened and expected, it made little impression on a people determined to withhold even a tacit consent to any infractions on their charter. They considered the present measures as a breach of a solemn covenant, which at the same time that it subjected them to the authority of the king of England, stipulated to them the equal enjoyment of all the rights and privileges of free and natural born subjects. They chose to hazard the consequences of returning back to a state of nature, rather than quietly submit to unjust and arbitrary measures continually accumulating. This was a dangerous experiment, though they were sensible that the necessities of man will soon restore order and subordination, even from confusion and anarchy: on the contrary, the yoke of despotism once rivetted, no human sagacity can justly calculate its termination.

While matters hung in this suspense, the people in all the shire towns collected in prodigious numbers to prevent the sitting of the courts of common law; forbidding the justices to meet, or the jurors to empannel, and obliging all civil magistrates to bind themselves by oath, not to conform to the late acts of parliament in any judiciary proceedings; and all military officers were called upon to resign their commissions. Thus were the bands of society relaxed, law set at defiance, and government unhinged throughout the province. Perhaps this may be marked in the annals of time, as one of the most extraordinary eras in the history of man: the exertions of spirit awakened by the severe hand of power had led to that most alarming experiment of levelling all ranks, and destroying all subordination.

It cannot be denied that nothing is more difficult than to restrain the provoked multitude, when once aroused by a sense of wrong, from that supineness which generally overspreads the common class of mankind. Ignorant and fierce, they know not in the first ebullitions of resentment, how to repel with safety the arm of the oppressor. It is a work of time to establish a regular opposition to long established tyranny. A celebrated writer has observed, that "men bear with the defects in their police, as they do with their inconveniences and hardships in living:" and perhaps the facility of the human mind in adapting itself to its circumstances, was never more remarkably exemplified, than it was at this time in America.

GOD PREPARES
A CHRISTIAN
PEOPLE
TO ESTABLISH
THE AMERICAN
NATION

Trade had long been embarrassed throughout the colonies by the restraints of parliament and the rapacity of revenue officers; the shutting up the port of Boston was felt in every villa of the New England colonies; the bill for altering the constitution of Massachusetts, prevented all legislative proceedings; the executive officers were rendered incapable of acting in their several departments, and the courts of justice shut up. It must be ascribed to the virtue of the people, however reluctant some may be to acknowledge this truth, that they did not feel the effects of anarchy in the extreme.

But a general forbearance and complacency seemed for a time almost to preclude the necessity of legal restraint; and except in a few instances, when the indiscretion of individuals provoked abuse, there was less violence and personal insult than perhaps ever was known in the same period of time, when all political union was broken down, and private affection weakened, by the virulence of party prejudice, which generally cuts in sunder the bands of social and friendly connexion. The people irritated in the highest degree, the sword seemed to be half drawn from the scabbard, while the trembling hand appeared unwilling to display its whetted point; and all America, as well as the Massachusetts, suspended all partial opposition, and waited in anxious hope and expectation the decisions of a continental congress.

RESOLUTIONS OF THE GENERAL CONGRESS

This respected assembly, the *Amphyctions* of the western world, convened by the free suffrages of twelve colonies, met at the time proposed, on the fourth of September, one thousand seven hundred and seventy-four. They entered on business with hearts warmed with the love of their country, a sense of the common and equal rights of man, and the dignity of human nature. Peyton Randolph, Esq. a gentleman from Virginia, whose sobriety, integrity, and political abilities, qualified him for the important station, was unanimously chosen to preside in this grand council of American peers.

September 4, 1774

Though this body was sensibly affected by the many injuries received from the parent state, their first wish was a reconciliation on terms of reciprocity, justice and honor. In consequence of these sentiments they cautiously avoided, as far as was consistent with the duty due to their constituents, every thing that might tend to widen the breach between Great-Britain and the colonies. Yet they were determined, if parliament continued deaf to the calls of justice, not to submit to the yoke of tyranny, but to take the preparatory steps necessary for a vigorous resistance.

After a thorough discussion of the civil, political, and commercial interests of both countries, the natural ties, and the mutual benefits resulting from the strictest amity, and the unhappy consequences that must ensue, if driven to the last appeal, they resolved on a dutiful and loyal petition to the king, recapitulating their grievances, and imploring redress; they modestly remonstrated, and obliquely censured the authors of those mischiefs, which filled all America with complaint.

They drew up an affectionate, but spirited memorial to the people of England, reminding them that they held their own boasted liberties on a precarious tenure, if government, under the sanction of parliamentary authority, might enforce by the terrors of the sword their unconstitutional edicts. They informed them, that they determined, from a sense of justice to posterity, and for the honor of human nature, to resist all infringements on the natural rights of men; that, if neither the dictates of equity, nor the suggestions of humanity, were powerful enough to restrain a *wanton* administration from shedding blood in a cause so derogatory to the principles of *justice,* not all the exertions of superior strength should lead them to submit servilely to the impositions of a foreign power. They forwarded a well-adapted address to the French inhabitants of Canada, to which they subjoined a detail of their rights, with observations on the alarming aspect of the late Quebec bill, and invited them to join in the common cause of America.

Energy and precision, political ability, and the genuine *amor patriae,* marked the measures of the short session of this congress. They concluded their proceedings with an address to the several American colonies, exhorting them to union and perseverance in the modes of opposition they had pointed out. Among the most important of these was a strong recommendation to discontinue all commerce with Great Britain, and encourage the improvement of arts and manufactures among themselves. They exhorted all ranks and orders of men to a strict adherence to industry, frugality, and sobriety of manners; and to look primarily to the supreme Ruler of the universe, who is able to defeat the crafty designs of the most potent enemy. They agreed on a declaration of rights, and entered into an association, to which the signature of every member of congress was affixed; in which they bound themselves to suspend all farther intercourse with Great Britain, to import no merchandize from that hostile country, to abstain from the use of all India teas; and that after a limited time, if a radical redress of grievances was not obtained, no American produce should be exported either to England or the West India islands under the jurisdiction of Britain.

To these recommendations were added several sumptuary resolves; after which they advised their constituents to a new choice of delegates, to meet in congress on the tenth of May, one thousand seven hundred and seventy-five: they judged it probable that, by that time, they should hear the success of their petitions to the throne. They then prudently dissolved themselves, and returned to their private occupations in their several provinces, there to wait the operation of their resolutions and addresses.

OCCASIONAL OBSERVATIONS

It is scarcely possible to describe the influence of the transactions and resolves of congress on the generality of the people throughout the wide extended continent of America. History records no injunctions of men, that were ever more religiously observed; or any human laws more readily and universally obeyed, than were the recommendations of this revered body. It is indeed a singular phenomenon in the story of human conduct, that when all legal institutions were abolished, and long established governments at once annihilated in so many distinct states, that the recommendations of committees and conventions, not enforced by penal sanctions, should be equally influential and binding with the severest code of law, backed by royal authority, and strengthened by the murdering sword of despotism. Doubtless the fear of popular resentment operated on some, with a force equal to the rod of the magistrate: the singular punishments, (such as tarring and feathering, &c.) inflicted in some instances by an inflamed rabble, on a few who endeavored to counteract the public measures, deterred others from openly violating the public resolves, and acting against the general consent of the people.

Not the bitterest foe to American freedom, whatever might be his wishes, presumed to counteract the general voice by an avowed importation of a single article of British merchandize, after the first day of February, one thousand seven hundred and seventy-five. The cargoes of all ves-

sels that happened to arrive after this limited period were punctually delivered to the committees of correspondence, in the first port of their arrival, and sold at public auction. The prime cost and charges, and the half of one per cent was paid to the owners, and the surplus of the profits was appropriated to the relief of the distressed inhabitants of Boston, agreeable to the seventh article in the association of the continental congress.

The voice of the multitude is as the rushing down of a torrent, nor is it strange that some outrages were committed against a few obstinate and imprudent partizans of the court, by persons of as little consideration as themselves. It is true that in the course of the arduous struggle, there were many irregularities that could not be justified, and some violences in consequence of the general discontent, that will not stand the test, when examined at the bar of equity; yet perhaps fewer than ever took place in any country under similar circumstances. Witness the convulsions of Rome on the demolition of her first race of kings; the insurrections and commotions of her colonies before the downfall of the commonwealth; and to come nearer home, the confusions, the mobs, the cruelties in Britain in their civil convulsions, from William the conqueror to the days of the Stuarts, and from the arbitrary Stuarts to the riots of London and Liverpool, even in the reign of George the third.

Many other instances of the dread effects of popular commotion, when wrought up to resistance by the oppressive hand of power, might be adduced from the history of nations,* and the ferocity of human nature, when not governed by interest or fear. Considering the right of personal liberty, which every one justly claims, the

---

* France might have been mentioned, as a remarkable instance of the truth of these observations, had they not been written several years before the extraordinary revolutions and cruel convulsions, that have since agitated that unhappy country. Every one will observe the astonishing difference in the conduct of the people of America and of France, in the two revolutions which took place within a few years of each other. In the one, all was horror, robbery, assassination, murder, devastation and massacre; in the other, a general sense of rectitude checked the commission of those crimes, and the dread of spilling human blood withheld for a time the hand of party, even when the passions were irritated to the extreme. This must be attributed to the different religion, government, laws and manners of the two countries, previous to these great events; not to any difference in the nature of man; in similar circumstances, revenge, cruelty, confusion, and every evil work, operate equally on the ungoverned passions of men in all nations.

GOD PREPARES
A CHRISTIAN
PEOPLE
TO ESTABLISH
THE AMERICAN
NATION

tenacious regard to property, and the pride of opinion, which sometimes operates to the dissolution of the tenderest ties of nature, it is wonderful, when the mind was elevated by these powerful springs, and the passions whetted by opposition or insult, that riot and confusion, desolation and bloodshed, was not the fatal consequence of the long interregnum of law and government throughout the colonies. Yet not a life was lost till the trump of war summoned all parties to the field.

Valor is an instinct that appears even among savages, as a dictate of nature planted for self-defence; but patriotism on the diffusive principles of general benevolence, is the child of society. This virtue with the fair accomplishments of science, gradually grows and increases with civilization, until refinement is wrought to a height that poisons and corrupts the mind. This appears when the accumulation of wealth is rapid, and the gratifications of luxurious appetite become easy; the seeds of benevolence are then often destroyed, and the *man* reverts back to selfish barbarism, and feels no check to his rapacity and boundless ambition, though his passions may be frequently veiled under various alluring and deceptive appearances.

America was now a fair field for a transcript of all the virtues and vices that have illumined or darkened, disgraced and reigned triumphant in their turn over all the other quarters of the habitable globe. The progress of every thing had there been remarkably rapid, from the first settlement of the country. Learning was cultivated, knowledge disseminated, politeness and morals improved, and valor and patriotism cherished, in proportion to the rapidity of her population. This extraordinary cultivation of arts and manners may be accounted for, from the stage of society and improvement in which the first planters of America were educated before they left their native clime. The first emigrations to North America were not composed of a strolling banditti of rude nations, like the first people of most other colonies in the history of the world. The early settlers in the newly discovered continent were as far advanced in civilization, policy, and manners; in their ideas of government, the nature of compacts, and the bands of civil union, as any of their neighbors at that period among the most polished nations of Europe. Thus they soon grew to maturity, and became able to vie with their European ancestors in arts, in arms, in perspicuity in the cabinet, courage in the field, and ability for foreign negociations, in the same space of time

that most other colonies have required to pare off the ruggedness of their native ferocity, establish the rudiments of civil society, and begin the fabric of government and jurisprudence. Yet as they were not fully sensible of their own strength and abilities, they wished still to hang upon the arm, and look up for protection to their original parent.

The united voice of millions still acknowledged the sceptre of Brunswick; firmly attached to the house of Hanover, educated in the principles of monarchy, and fond of that mode of government under certain limitations, they were still petitioning the king of England only to be restored to the same footing of privilege claimed by his other subjects, and wished ardently to keep the way open to a reunion, consistent with their ideas of honor and freedom.

Thus the grand council of the union were disposed to wait the operations of time, without hurrying to momentous decisions that might in a degree have sanctioned severities in the parent state that would have shut up every avenue to reconciliation. While the representatives of all the provinces had thus been deliberating, the individual colonies were far from being idle. Provincial congresses and conventions had in almost every province taken place of the old forms of legislation and government, and they were all equally industrious and united in the same modes to combat the intrigues of the governmental faction, which equally infested the whole, though the eastern borders of the continent more immediately suffered. But their institutions in infancy, commerce suspended, and their property seized; threatened by the national orators, by the proud chieftains of military departments, and by the British fleet and army daily augmenting, hostilities of the most serious nature lowered on all sides; the artillery of war and the fire of rhetoric seemed to combine for the destruction of America.

The minds of the people at this period, though not dismayed, were generally solemnized, in expectation of events, decisive both to political and private happiness, and every brow appeared expressive of sober anxiety. The people trembled for their liberties, the merchant for his interest, the tories for their places, the whigs for their country, and the virtuous for the manners of society.

THE MASSACHUSETTS ATTENTIVE TO THE
MILITARY DISCIPLINE OF THEIR YOUTH

It must be allowed that the genius of America was bold, resolute and enterprising; tenacious of the rights their fathers had endured such hardships to purchase, they determined to defend to the last breath the invaluable possession. To check this ardent characteristic it had, previous to the time we are upon, been considered, as if by common consent among the plantation governors, a stroke of policy to depress the militia of the country. All military discipline had for several years been totally neglected; thus untrained to arms, whenever there had been an occasional call in aid of British operations in America, the militia were considered as a rustic set of auxiliaries, and employed not only in the least honorable, but the most menial services. Though this indignity was felt, it was never properly resented; they had borne the burthen of fatigue and subordination without much complaint: but the martial spirit of the country now became conspicuous, and the inclination of the youth of every class was universally cherished, and military evolutions were the interludes that most delighted even children in the intermission of their sedentary exercises at school.

Among the manoeuvres of this period of expectation, a certain quota of hardy youth were drawn from the train-bands in every town, who were styled *minute men*. They voluntarily devoted a daily portion of their time to improve themselves in the military art, under officers of their own choice. Thus when hostilities commenced, every district could furnish a number of soldiers, who wanted nothing but experience in the operations of war, to make them a match for any troops the sovereign of Britain could boast.

This military ardor wore an unpleasant aspect in the eyes of administration. By a letter from lord Dartmouth to general Gage, soon after he was appointed governor of the Massachusetts, it appeared that a project for disarming certain provinces was seriously contemplated in the cabinet. General Gage in his reply to the minister upon the above suggestion, observes, "Your lordship's idea of disarming certain provinces, would doubtless be consistent with prudence and safety; but it neither is, nor has been practicable, without having recourse to *force:* we must first become masters of the country."

The parliament actually prohibited the exportation of arms, ammunition and military stores to any part of America, except for their own fleets and armies employed in the colonies; and the king's troops were frequently sent out in small parties to dismantle the forts, and seize the powder magazines or other military stores wherever they could be found. The people throughout the colonies with better success, took similar measures to secure to themselves whatever warlike stores were already in the country. Thus a kind of predatory struggle almost universally took place; every appearance of hostilities was discoverable in the occasional rencontres, except the drawing of blood, which was for a time suspended; delayed on one side from an apprehension that they were not quite ripe for the conflict; on the other, from an expectation of reinforcements that might ensure victory on the easiest terms; and perhaps by both, from the recollection of former connexion and attachment.

A disunion of the colonies had long been zealously wished for, and vainly attempted by administration; as that could not be effected, it was deemed a wise and politic measure, to make an example of one they judged the most refractory. Thus resentment seemed particularly levelled at the Massachusetts; consequently they obliged that colony first to measure the sword with the hardy veterans of Britain.

SUFFOLK RESOLVES, SEPTEMBER 9, 1774

The spirited proceedings of the county of Suffolk, soon after the arrival of governor Gage, and his hasty dissolution of the general assembly, in some measure damped the expectation of the ministry, who had flattered themselves that the depression and ruin of the Massachusetts would strike terror through the other provinces, and render the work of conquest more easy. But the decision and energy of this convention, composed of members from the principal towns in the county, discovered that the spirit of Americans at that time was not to be coerced by dragoons; and that if one colony, under the immediate frowns of government, with an army in their capital, were thus bold and determined, new calculations must be made for the subjugation of all.

The convention met in Suffolk, at once unanimously renounced the authority of the new legislature, and engaged to bear harmless all officers who should refuse to act under it. They pronounced all those, who had accepted seats at the board of council by mandamus, the incorrigible enemies of their country. They recommended to the people to perfect themselves in the art of war, and to prepare to resist by force of arms, every hostile invasion. They resolved, that if any person should be apprehended for his exertions in the public cause, reprisals should be made, by seizing and holding in custody the principal officers of the crown, wherever they could be found, until

God Prepares
a Christian
People
to Establish
the American
Nation

ample justice should be done. They advised the collectors and receivers of all public monies to hold it in their hands, till appropriations should be directed by authority of a provincial congress. They earnestly urged an immediate choice of delegates for that purpose, and recommended their convening at Salem.

These and several other resolves in the same style and manner, were considered by government as the most overt acts of *treason* that had yet taken place; but their doings were but a specimen of the spirit which actuated the whole province. Every town, with the utmost alacrity, chose one or more of the most respectable gentlemen, to meet in provincial congress, agreeable to the recommendation on the fifteenth of October, one thousand seven hundred and seventy-four. They were requested by their constituents, to take into consideration the distressed state of the country, and to devise the most practicable measures to extricate the people from their present perplexed situation.

In the meantime, to preclude the appearance of necessity for such a convention, governor Gage issued precepts, summoning a new general assembly to meet at Salem, the week preceding the time appointed for the meeting of the convention. The people obeyed the order of the governor, and every where chose their representatives; but they all chose the same persons they had recently delegated to meet in convention. Whether the governor was apprehensive that it would not be safe for his mandamus council to venture out of the capital, or whether conscious that it would not be a constitutional assembly, or from the imbecility of his own mind, in a situation altogether new to him, is uncertain; but from whatever cause it arose, he discovered his embarrassment by a proclamation, dated the day before he was to meet them at Salem, to dissolve the new house of representatives. This extraordinary dissolution only precipitated the predetermination of the delegates; they had taken their line of conduct, and their determinations were not easily shaken.

The council chosen by the house on the day of their last election had also, as requested, repaired to Salem. The design was, to proceed to business as usual, without any notice of the annihilation of their charter. Their determination was, if the governor refused to meet with or countenance them, to consider him as absent from the province. It had been usual under the old charter, when the governor's signature could not be obtained, by reason of death or absence, that by the names of fifteen counsellors affixed thereto, all

the acts of assembly were equally valid, as when signed by the governor. But by the extraordinary conduct of the chief magistrate, the general assembly was left at liberty to complete measures in any mode or form that appeared most expedient; accordingly they adjourned to Concord, a town situated about thirty miles from Salem, and there prosecuted the business of their constituents.

MASSACHUSETTS PROVINCIAL CONGRESS,
OCTOBER 5, 1774

As it was not yet thought prudent to assume all the powers of an organized government, they chose a president, and acted as a provincial congress, as previously proposed. They recommended to the militia to choose their own officers, and submit to regular discipline at least thrice a week, and that a fourth part of them should be draughted, and hold themselves in readiness to march at a moment's warning to any part of the province. They recommended to the several counties to adhere to their own resolves, and to keep the courts of common law shut till some future period, when justice could be legally administered. They appointed a committee of supplies to provide ammunition, provisions, and warlike stores, and to deposite them in some place of safety, ready for use, if they should be obliged to take up arms in defence of their rights.

This business required talents and energy to make arrangements for exigencies, new and untried. Fortunately Elbridge Gerry, Esq. was placed at the head of this commission, who executed it with his usual punctuality and indefatigable industry. This gentleman entered from principle, early in the opposition to British encroachments, and continued one of the most uniform republicans to the end of the contest. He was the next year chosen a delegate to the continental congress. Firm, exact, perspicuous, and tenacious of public and private honor, he rendered essential service to the union for many years that he continued a member of that honorable body.

The provincial congress appointed a committee of safety, consisting of nine members, and vested them with powers to act as they should see fit for the public service, in the recess, and to call them together again, on any extraordinary emergence; and before they separated, they chose a new set of delegates, to meet in general congress the ensuing spring. After this they held a conference with the committees of donation and correspondence, and the selectmen of the town of Boston, on the expediency of an effort to remove the inhabitants from a town blockaded on all sides. They then separated for a few weeks, to exert their influence in aid to the resolutions of the people; to strengthen their fortitude, and prepare them for the approaching storm, which they were sensible could be at no great distance.

Though the inhabitants of Boston were shut up in garrison, insulted by the troops, and in many respects felt the evils of a severe military government; yet the difficulty of removing thousands from their residence in the capital, to seek an asylum in the country on the eve of winter, appeared fraught with inconveniencies too great to be attempted, they were of consequence, the most of them obliged to continue amidst the outrages of a licentious army, and wait patiently the events of the ensuing spring.

The principal inhabitants of the town, though more immediately under the eye of their oppressors, lost no part of their determined spirit, but still acted in unison with their friends more at liberty without the city. A bold instance of this appeared, when Mr. Oliver, the chief justice, regardless of the impeachment that lay against him, attempted with his associates to open the superior court, and transact business according to the new regulations. Advertisements were posted in several public places, forbidding on their peril, the attornies and barristers at law, to carry any cause up to the bar. Both the grand and petit-jurors refused attendance, and finally the court was obliged to adjourn without day.

These circumstances greatly alarmed the party, more especially those natives of the country who had taken sanctuary under the banners of an officer, who had orders to enforce the acts of administration, even at the point of the bayonet. Apprehensive they might be dragged from their asylum within the gates, they were continually urging general Gage to more vigorous measures without. They assured him, that it would be easy for him to execute the designs of government, provided he would by law-martial seize, try, or transport to England, such persons as were most particularly obnoxious; and that if the people once saw him thus determined, they would sacrifice their leaders and submit quietly.

They associated, and bound themselves by covenant, to go all lengths in support of the projects of administration against their country; but the general, assured of reinforcements in the spring, sufficient to enable him to open a bloody campaign, and not remarkable for resolution or activity, had not the courage, and perhaps not the inclination, to try the dangerous experiment, till he felt himself stronger. He was also sensible of the striking similarity of genius, manners, and conduct of the colonies in union. It was observable to every one, that local prejudices, either in religion or government, taste or politics, were suspended, and that every distinction was sunk, in the consideration of the necessity of connexion and vigor in one general system of defence. He therefore proceeded no farther, during the winter, than publishing proclamations against congresses, committees, and conventions, styling all associations of the kind unlawful and treasonable combinations, and forbidding all persons to pay the smallest regard to their recommendations, on penalty of his majesty's severest displeasure.

These feeble exertions only confirmed the people in their adherence to the modes pointed out by those, to whom they had intrusted the safety of the commonwealth. The only active movement of the season was that of a party commanded by colonel Leslie, who departed from Castle William on the evening of Saturday, February twenty-seventh, one thousand seven hundred and seventy-five, on a secret expedition to Salem. The design was principally to seize a few cannon on the ensuing morning. The people apprized of his approach, drew up a bridge over which his troops were to pass. Leslie, finding his passage would be disputed, and having no orders to proceed to blows, after much expostulation engaged, that if he might be permitted to go on the ground, he would molest neither public nor private property. The bridge was immediately let down, and through a line of armed inhabitants, ready to take vengeance on a forfeiture of his word, he only marched to the extreme part of the town, and then returned to Boston, to the mortification of himself and of his friends, that an officer of colonel Leslie's acknowledged bravery should be sent out on so frivolous an errand. This incident discovered the determination of the Americans, carefully to avoid every thing that had the appearance of beginning hostilities on their part; an imputation that might have been attended with great inconvenience; nor indeed were they prepared to precipitate a conflict, the consequences and the termination of which no human calculation could reach. This manoeuver also discovered that the people of the country were not deficient in point of courage, but that they stood charged for a resistance, that might smite the sceptred hand, whenever it should be stretched forth to arrest by force the inheritance purchased by the blood of ancestors, whose self-denying virtues had rivalled the admired heroes of antiquity.

In *Provincial Congress*,

Cambridge, *December* 6, 1774.

THE Operation of the cruel and iniquitous *Boston*-Port-Bill, that Instrument of ministerial Vengeance, having reduced our once happy Capital and the neighbouring Town of *Charlestown*, from Affluence and Ease, to extreme Distress ; many of their Inhabitants being deprived of even the Means of procuring the Necessaries of Life : From all which they have most nobly refused to purchase an Exemption, by surrendering the Rights of Americans. And although the charitable Donations from the other Colonies, and several Towns in this Province, have in good Measure relieved their immediate Necessities, while their Approbation has animated them to persevere in patient Suffering for the public Good ; yet as the Severity of Winter is now approaching, which must add greatly to their Misery ; and there has been no general Collection for them in this Colony, we hold ourselves obliged in Justice to contribute to their Support, while they under such a Weight of Oppression are supporting our Rights and Privileges.

It is therefore RESOLVED, That it be recommended to our Constituents the Inhabitants of the other Towns, Districts and Parishes within this Province, that they farther contribute liberally to alleviate the Burden of those Persons who are the more immediate Objects of ministerial Resentment, and are suffering in the common Cause of their Country : Seriously considering how much the Liberty, and consequently the Happiness of Ourselves, and Posterity, depend, under GOD, on the Firmness and Resolution of those worthy Patriots.

And it is *Ordered*, That Doctor *Foster*, Mr. *Devens*, and Mr. *Cheever*, be a Committee to transmit printed Copies of the above RESOLVE to the Ministers of the Gospel in the several Towns, Districts and Parishes in this Province, who are desired to read the same to their several Congregations, in Order that their Contributions of such Necessaries of Life as they can spare, may be forwarded as soon as possible.

Signed by Order of the Provincial Congress,

JOHN HANCOCK, President.

A true Extract from the Minutes.

BENJAMIN LINCOLN, Secretary.

MERCY
WARREN:
PRELUDE TO
THE AMERICAN
REVOLUTION,
1765–1775

SYSTEM OF
COERCION
IN BRITAIN

PARLIAMENTARY DIVISIONS ON
AMERICAN AFFAIRS

We have seen several years pass off in doubtful anxiety, in repression and repulsion, while many yet indulged the pleasing hope, that some able genius might arise, that would devise measures to heal the breach, to revive the languishing commerce of both countries, and restore the blessings of peace, by removing the causes of complaint. But these hopes evanished, and all expectations of that kind were soon cut off, by the determined system of coercion in Britain, and the actual commencement of *war* in *America*.

The earliest accounts from England, after the beginning of the year one thousand seven hundred and seventy-five, announced the ferments of the British nation, principally on account of American measures, the perseverance of the ministry, and the obstinacy of the king, in support of the system;—the sudden dissolution of one parliament, and the immediate election of another, composed of the same members, or men of the same principles as the former.

Administration had triumphed through the late parliament over reason, justice, the humanity of individuals, and the interest of the nation. Notwithstanding the noble and spirited opposition of several distinguished characters in both houses, it soon appeared that the influence of the ministry over the old parliament was not depreciated, or that more lenient principles pervaded the councils of the new one. Nor did more judicious and favorable decisions lead to the prospect of an equitable adjustment of a dispute that had interested the feelings of the whole empire, and excited the attention of neighboring nations, not as an object of curiosity, but with views and expectations that might give a new face to the political and commercial systems of a considerable part of the European world.

The petition of the continental congress to the king, their address to the people of England, with general Gage's letters, and all papers relative to America, were introduced early in the session of the new parliament. Warm debates ensued, and the cause of the colonies was advocated with ability and energy by the most admired orators among the commons, and by several very illustrious names in the house of lords. They descanted largely on the injustice and impolicy of the present system, and the impracticability of its execution. They urged that the immediate repeal of the revenue acts, the recall of the troops, and the opening the port of Boston, were necessary,

preliminary steps to any hope of reconciliation; and that these measures only would preserve the empire from consequences that would be fatal to her interests, as well as disgraceful to her councils. But, pre-determined in the cabinet, a large majority in parliament appeared in favor of strong measures. The ministerial party insisted that coercion only could ensure obedience, restore tranquillity to the colonies, repair the insulted dignity, and re-establish the supremacy of parliament.

An act was immediately passed, prohibiting New Hampshire, Massachusetts, Rhode Island, and Connecticut from carrying on the fishing business on the banks of Newfoundland. By this arbitrary step, thousands of miserable families were suddenly cut off from all means of subsistence. But, as if determined the rigors of power should know no bounds, before parliament had time to cool, after the animosities occasioned by the bill just mentioned, another was introduced by the minister, whereby the trade of the southern colonies was restrained, and in future confined entirely to Great Britain. The minority still persevered in the most decided opposition both against the former and the present modes of severity towards the colonies. Very sensible and spirited protests were entered against the new bills, signed by some of the first nobility. A young nobleman of high rank and reputation predicted, that "measures commenced in iniquity, and pursued in resentment, must end in blood, and involve the nation in immediate civil war." It was replied, that the colonies were already in a state of rebellion; that the supremacy of parliament must not even be questioned; and that compulsory measures must be pursued from absolute necessity. Neither reason nor argument, humanity or policy, made the smallest impression on those determined to support all despotic proceedings. Thus after much altercation, a majority of two hundred and eighty-two appeared in favor of augmenting the forces in America, both by sea and land, against only seventy in the house of commons, who opposed the measure.

All ideas of courage or ability in the colonists to face the dragoons and resist the power of Britain, were treated with the greatest derision, and particularly ridiculed by a general officer, General Burgoyne, then in the house, who soon after delivered his standards, and saw the surrender of a capital army under his command, to those undisciplined Americans he had affected to hold in so much contempt. The first lord of the admiralty also declared, "the Americans were neither disciplined, nor capable of discipline."

GOD PREPARES
A CHRISTIAN
PEOPLE
TO ESTABLISH
THE AMERICAN
NATION

Several ships of the line and a number of frigates were immediately ordered to join the squadron at Boston. Ten thousand men were ordered for the land service, in addition to those already there. A regiment of light-horse, and a body of troops from Ireland, to complete the number, were directed to embark with all possible dispatch to reinforce general Gage.

The speech from the throne, approving the sanguinary conduct of the minister and the parliament, blasted all the hopes of the more moderate and humane part of the nation. Several gallant officers of the first rank, disgusted with the policy, and revolting at the idea of butchering their American brethren, resigned their commissions. The earl of Effingham was among the first, who, with a frankness that his enemies styled a degree of insanity, assured his majesty, "that though he loved the profession of a soldier, and would with the utmost cheerfulness sacrifice his fortune and his life for the safety of his majesty's person, and the dignity of his crown; yet the same principles which inspired him with those unalterable sentiments of duty and affection, would not suffer him to be instrumental in depriving any part of the people of their liberties, which to him appeared the best security of their fidelity and obedience; therefore without the severest reproaches of conscience he could not consent to bear arms against the Americans."

But there is no age which bears a testimony so honorable to human nature; as shews mankind at so sublime a pitch of virtue, that there are not always enough to be found ready to aid the arm of the oppressor, provided they may share in the spoils of the oppressed. Thus many officers of ability and experience courted the American service as the readiest road to preferment.

Administration not satisfied with their own severe restrictions, set on foot a treaty with the Dutch and several other nations, to prevent their aiding the colonies by supplying them with any kind of warlike stores. Every thing within and without wore the most hostile appearance, even while the commercial interest of Great Britain was closely interwoven with that of America; and the treasures of the colonies, which had been continually pouring into the lap of the mother country, in exchange for her manufactures, were still held ready for her use, in any advance to harmony.

The boundaries of the king of England's continental domains were almost immeasurable, and the inhabitants were governed by a strong predilection in favor of the nation from whom they

derived their origin: hence it is difficult to account on any principles of human policy, for the infatuation that instigated to the absurd project of conquering a country, already their's on the most advantageous terms. But the seeds of separation were sown, and the *ball* of empire rolled westward with such astonishing rapidity, that the pious mind is naturally excited to acknowledge a superintending Providence, that led to the period of independence, even before America was conscious of her maturity. Precipitated into a war, dreadful even in contemplation, humanity recoiled at the idea of civil feuds, and their concomitant evils.

When the news arrived in the colonies that the British army in Boston was to be reinforced, that the coercive system was at all hazards to be prosecuted, though astonished at the persevering severity of a nation still beloved and revered by Americans, deeply affected with the calamities that threatened the whole empire, and shocked at the prospect of the convulsions and the cruelties ever attendant on civil war, yet few balanced on the part they were to act. The alternative held up was a bold and vigorous resistance, or an abject submission to the ignoble terms demanded by administration. Armed with resolution and magnanimity, united by affection, and a remarkable conformity of opinion, the whole people through the wide extended continent seemed determined to resist in blood, rather than become the slaves of arbitrary power.

Happily for America, the inhabitants in general possessed not only the virtues of native courage and a spirit of enterprise, but minds generally devoted to the best affections. Many of them retained this character to the end of the conflict by the dereliction of interest, and the costly sacrifices of health, fortune and life. Perhaps the truth of the observation, that "a national force is best formed where numbers of men are used to equality, and where the meanest citizen may consider himself destined to command as well as to obey," was never more conspicuous, than in the brave resistance of Americans to the potent and conquering arm of Great Britain, who, in conjunction with her colonies, had long taught the nations to tremble at her strength.

But the painful period hastened on, when the connexion which nature and interest had long maintained between Great Britain and the colonies, must be broken off; the sword drawn, and the scabbard thrown down the gulf of time. We must now pursue the progress of a war enkindled by avarice, whetted by ambition, and blown up into a thirst for revenge by repeated disappointment. Not the splendor of a diadem, the purple of princes, or the pride of power, can ever sanction the deeds of cruelty perpetrated on the western side of the Atlantic, and not unfrequently by men, whose crimes emblazoned by title, will enhance the infamy of their injustice and barbarism, when the tragic tale is faithfully related.

We have already observed on the supplicatory addresses every where offered to the old government, the rebuffs attending them, the obstruction to legal debate, and the best possible regulations made by the colonies in their circumstances, under the new modes established by themselves.

The authority of congresses and committees of correspondence, and the spirit which pervaded the united colonies in their preparations for war, during the last six months previous to the commencement of hostilities, bore such a resemblance, that the detail of the transactions of one province is an epitome of the story of all.

MEASURES FOR RAISING AN ARMY OF OBSERVATION BY THE FOUR NEW ENGLAND GOVERNMENTS

The particular resentment of Great Britain levelled at the Massachusetts, made it necessary for that province to act a more decided part, that they might be in some readiness to repel the storm which it appeared probable would first burst upon them. Their provincial congress was sitting when the news first arrived, that all hope of reconciliation was precluded by the hostile resolutions of parliament. This rather quickened than retarded the important step, which was then the subject of their deliberations. Persuaded that the unhappy contest could not terminate without bloodshed, they were consulting on the expediency of raising an army of observation, from the four New England governments, that they might be prepared for defence in case of an attack, before the continental congress could again meet, and make proper arrangements for farther operations. They proceeded to name their own commanding officers, and appointed delegates to confer with New Hampshire, Connecticut, and Rhode Island, on the proportion of men they would furnish, and their quota of expense for the equipment of such an armament.

Connecticut and New Hampshire readily acceded to the proposal, but in Rhode Island several embarrassments were thrown in the way, though the people in that colony were in general as ready to enter warmly into measures for the common

safety as any of the others; nor had they less reason. They had long been exasperated by the insolence and rapacity of the officers of a part of the navy stationed there to watch their trade. These had, without color of right, frequently robbed Newport, and plundered the adjacent islands. They had seized the little skiffs, in which a number of poor people had gained a scanty subsistence; and insulted, embarrassed and abused the inhabitants in various ways through the preceding year.

It is the nature of man, when he despairs of legal reparation for injuries received, to seek satisfaction by avenging his own wrongs. Thus, some time before this period, a number of men in disguise, had riotously assembled, and set fire to a sloop of war in the harbour. When they had thus discovered their resentment by this illegal proceeding, they dispersed without farther violence. For this imputed crime the whole colony had been deemed guilty, and interdicted as accessary.

A court of inquiry was appointed by his majesty, vested with the power of seizing any person on suspicion, confining him on board a king's ship, and sending him to England for trial. But some of the gentlemen named for this inquisitorial business, had not the temerity to execute it in the latitude designed; and after sitting a few days, examining a few persons, and threatening many, they adjourned to a distant day.

The extraordinary precedent of erecting such a court among them was not forgotten; but there was a considerable party in Newport, strongly attached to the royal cause. These, headed by their governor, Mr. Wanton, a man of weak capacity, and little political knowledge, endeavoured to impede all measures of opposition, and to prevent even a discussion on the propriety of raising a defensive army. The gentlemen who composed this court, were Wanton, governor of Rhode Island, Horsemanden, chief justice of New York, Smith, chief justice of New Jersey, Oliver, chief justice of Massachusetts, and Auchmuty, judge of admirality.

BATTLE OF LEXINGTON, APRIL 19, 1775

The news of an action at Lexington on the nineteenth of April, between a party of the king's troops and some Americans hastily collected, reached Providence on the same evening, a few hours after the gentlemen entrusted with the mission for conference with the colony had arrived there; they had not entered on business,

GOD PREPARES
A CHRISTIAN
PEOPLE
TO ESTABLISH
THE AMERICAN
NATION

having been in town but an hour or two before this intelligence was received by a special messenger.

On this important information, James Warren, Esq., the head of the delegation, was of opinion, that this event not only opened new prospects and expectations, but that it entirely changed the object of negociation, and that new ground must be taken. Their mission was by the Massachusetts designed merely as a defensive movement, but he observed to the principal inhabitants collected to consult on the alarming aspect of present affairs, that there now appeared a necessity, not only for defensive but for offensive operations; he urged his reasons with such ability and address, that an immediate convention of the assembly was obtained. They met at Providence the ensuing day, where, by the trifling of the governor and the indiscretion of his partizans, the business labored in the upper house for several days. But the representative branch, impatient of delay, determined to act without any consideration of their governor, if he continued thus to impede their designs, and to unite, by authority of their own body, in vigorous measures with their sister colonies. A majority of the council however, at last impelled the governor to agree to the determination of the lower house, who had voted a number of men to be raised with the utmost dispatch; accordingly a large detachment was sent forward to the Massachusetts within three days.

When the gentlemen left congress for the purpose of combining and organizing an army in the eastern states, a short adjournment was made. Before they separated they selected a standing committee to reside at Concord, where a provincial magazine was kept, and vested them with power to summon congress to meet again at a moment's warning, if any extraordinary emergence should arise.

In the course of the preceding winter, a single regiment at a time had frequently made excursions from the army at Boston, and reconnoitred the environs of the town without committing any hostilities in the country, except picking up cannon, powder, and warlike stores, wherever they could find and seize them with impunity. In the spring, as they daily expected fresh auxiliaries, they grew more insolent; from their deportment, there was the highest reason to expect they would extend their researches, and endeavour to seize and secure, as they termed them, the *factious leaders* of *rebellion*. Yet this was attempted rather sooner than was generally expected.

On the evening of the eighteenth of April, the grenadiers and light infantry of the army stationed at Boston, embarked under the command of lieutenant colonel Smith, and were ordered to land at Cambridge before the dawn of the ensuing day. This order was executed with such secrecy and dispatch, that the troops reached Lexington, a small village nine miles beyond Cambridge, and began the tragedy of the day just as the sun rose.

An advanced guard of officers had been sent out by land, to seize and secure all travellers who might be suspected as going forward with intelligence of the hostile aspect of the king's troops. But notwithstanding this vigilance to prevent notice, a report reached the neighboring towns very early, that a large body of troops, accompanied by some of the most virulent individuals among the *tories,* who had taken refuge in Boston, were moving with design to destroy the provincial magazine at Concord, and take into custody the principal persons belonging to the committee of safety. Few suspected there was a real intention to attack the defenceless peasants of Lexington, or to try the bravery of the surrounding villages. But it being reduced to a certainty, that a number of persons had, the evening before, in the environs of Cambridge, been insulted, abused, and stripped, by officers in British uniform; and that a considerable armament might be immediately expected in the vicinity, captain Parker, who commanded a company of militia, ordered them to appear at beat of drum on the parade at Lexington, on the nineteenth. They accordingly obeyed, and were embodied before sunrise.

Colonel Smith, who commanded about eight hundred men, came suddenly upon them within a few minutes after, and, accosting them in language very unbecoming an officer of his rank, he ordered them to lay down their arms, and disperse immediately. He illiberally branded them with the epithets of *rebel* and *traitor;* and before the little party had time, either to resist or to obey, he, with wanton precipitation, ordered his troops to fire. Eight men were killed on the spot; and, without any concern for his rashness, or little molestation from the inhabitants, Smith proceeded on his rout.

By the time he reached Concord, and had destroyed a part of the stores deposited there, the country contiguous appeared in arms, as if determined not to be the tame spectators of the outrages committed against the persons, property, and lives of their fellow-citizens. Two or three

By the HONORABLE

JONATHAN TRUMBULL, Esquire,

Governor of the English Colony of *Connecticut*, in *New-England*, in
AMERICA;

A PROCLAMATION.

*A*LTHOUGH we have great Reason to adore the Divine Goodness, for the Plenty, and general
Health, we have enjoyed in the past Year ; yet we ought, with humble Reverence, to take Notice
of the Frowns of GOD, in visiting divers Towns and Places, with Sickness and Mortality,
especially amongst the Children :---And also, in still holding his Rod of Correction over us,
threatning the Loss of our Privileges and Liberty ; and considering that we see not a spirit
of Repentance and general Reformation, under his awful Threatnings,---and, that all our
Salvation, and the supply of all our Wants, depend on his Pleasure ;---to whom we are to
seek for all Good.

HAVE therefore thought fit, by and with the Advice of the Council, to appoint,
and do hereby appoint, *Wednesday*, the *nineteenth* Day of *April* next, to be observed
as a Day of publick Fasting and Prayer, throughout this Colony, by all Christian
Churches and Societies in it ;---hereby exhorting both Ministers and People to humble
themselves sincerely before GOD,---and mourn for all our Sins, which are the procuring Cause of all the Tokens of Divine Displeasure that we are under ;---and deprecate the awful
Judgments we are threatened with, in the loss of our inestimable Privileges. Particularly, to
lament that carelessness and unteachableness of Spirit which appears amongst us ;---that we are no
more awakened, humbled and reformed, when the awful Judgments of GOD are threatened to punish
us :---Earnestly to beg the pardon of our Sins,---and that GOD would graciously pour out his
HOLY SPIRIT on us, to bring us to a thorough Repentance and effectual Reformation, that our
Iniquities may not be our Ruin :---That He would restore, preserve and secure the Liberties of
this, and all the other *British American* Colonies, and make this Land a mountain of Holiness, and
habitation of Righteousness forever.---That GOD would preserve and confirm the Union of the
Colonies in the pursuit and practice of that Religion and Virtue which will honour Him,---and be
our greatest Honour and Security.

And to offer up fervent Prayers to Almighty GOD for his Blessing on our rightful Sovereign, King
GEORGE the Third, that He may have the Divine Direction in all his Administrations ; and his
Government be just, benign, gracious and happy to the Nation, and these Colonies :---That He
would bless our gracious Queen CHARLOTTE, the Prince of WALES, and the rest of the Royal
Family :---That He would bless, guide and assist the Rulers of this Colony ; give them Wisdom and
Firmness, in this dark and difficult Day ; lead them into right Measures, in all the administrations
of Government, and succeed them :---Unite the Hearts of the People to live in all Godliness and
Honesty ; and preserve all our just Rights and Liberties :---That He would bless and succeed the
Gospel Ministry, and make it the Power of GOD to the Salvation of many Souls ; and build up
the Churches in Faith and Holiness :---Bless and smile on the College and means of Education, that
our Children may be trained up in the love of GOD and their Country, and in all useful Knowledge ;---and succeed the Endeavours used to civilize and christianize the Heathen :---That it would
please GOD to bring forward the springing of the Year, and give suitable Seasons ;---cause the Earth
to yield its Fruits and Increase ;---smile upon the Labours of his People ;---dispose them to Industry
and Frugality ;---give them Opportunity quietly to attend their Business ;---and crown the Year
with his Blessing ;---cause Glory to dwell in our Land, and give Peace to Israel.

And all servile Labour is forbidden on said Day.

GIVEN *under my Hand in* Lebanon, *the twenty-second Day of March, in the fifteenth Year
of the Reign of Our Sovereign Lord* GEORGE *the Third, by the Grace of* GOD *of Great-
Britain, France and Ireland,* KING, *Defender of the Faith, &c.* Annoque Domini, 1775.

Jonath. Trumbull.

GOD save the KING.

NEW-LONDON : *Printed by* Timothy Green, *Printer to the* GOVERNOR *and* COMPANY.

GOD PREPARES
A CHRISTIAN
PEOPLE
TO ESTABLISH
THE AMERICAN
NATION

hundred men assembled under the command of colonel Barrett. He ordered them to begin no onset against the troops of their sovereign, till farther provocation; this order was punctually obeyed. Colonel Smith had ordered a bridge beyond the town to be taken up, to prevent the people on the other side from coming to their assistance. Barrett advanced to take possession before the party reached it, and a smart skirmish ensued; several were killed, and a number wounded on both sides. Not dismayed or daunted, the small body of yeomanry, armed in the cause of justice, and struggling for every thing they held dear, maintained their stand until the British troops, though far superior in numbers, and in all the advantages of military skill, discipline, and equipment, gave ground and retreated, without half executing the purpose designed, by this forced march to Concord.

The adjacent villagers collected, and prepared to cut off their retreat; but a dispatch had been sent by colonel Smith to inform general Gage, that the country was arming, and his troops in danger. A battalion under the command of lord Percy was sent to succour him, and arrived in time to save Smith's corps. A son of the duke of Northumberland,* previous to this day's work, was viewed by Americans with a favorable eye; though more from a partiality to the father, than from any remarkable personal qualities discoverable in the son. Lord Percy came up with the routed corps near the fields of Menotomy; where barbarities were committed by the king's army, which might have been expected only from a tribe of savages. They entered, rifled, plundered, and burnt several houses; and in some instances, the aged and infirm fell under the sword of the ruffian; women, with their new-born infants, were obliged to fly naked, to escape the fury of the flames in which their houses were enwrapped.

The footsteps of the most remorseless nations have seldom been marked with more rancorous and ferocious rage, than may be traced in the transactions of this day; a day never to be forgotten by Americans. A scene like this had never before been exhibited on her peaceful plains; and the manner in which it was executed, will leave an indelible stain on a nation, long famed for their courage, humanity, and honor. But they appeared at this period so lost to a sense of dignity, as to be engaged in a cause that required perfidy and meanness to support it. Yet the impression

of justice is so strongly stamped on the bosom of man, that when conscious the sword is lifted against the rights of equity, it often disarms the firmest heart, and unnerves the most valiant arm, when impelled to little subterfuges and private cruelties to execute their guilty designs.

The affair of Lexington, and the precipitant retreat after the ravages at Menotomy, are testimonies of the truth of this observation. For, notwithstanding their superiority in every respect, several regiments of the best troops in the royal army, were seen, to the surprise and joy of every lover of his country, flying before the raw, inexperienced peasantry, who had ran hastily together in defence of their lives and liberties. Had the militia of Salem and Marblehead have come on, as it was thought they might have done, they would undoubtedly have prevented this routed, disappointed army, from reaching the advantageous post of Charlestown. But the tardiness of colonel Pickering, who commanded the Salem regiment, gave them an opportunity to make good their retreat. Whether Mr. Pickering's delay was owing to timidity, or to a predilection in favor of Britain, remains uncertain; however it was, censure at the time fell very heavily on his character.

Other parts of the country were in motion; but the retreat of the British army was so rapid, that they got under cover of their own ships, and many of them made their escape into Boston. Others, too much exhausted by a quick march and unremitting exercise, without time for refreshment from sunrise to sunset, were unable, both from wounds and fatigue, to cross the river. These were obliged to rest the night, nor were they mistaken in the confidence they placed in the hospitality of the inhabitants of Charlestown; this they reasonably enough expected, both from motives of compassion and fear.

Intimidated by the appearance of such a formidable body of troops within their town, and touched with humanity on seeing the famished condition of the king's officers and soldiers, several of whom, from their wounds and their sufferings, expired before the next morning; the people every where opened their doors, received the distressed Britons, dressed their wounds, and contributed every relief: nothing was neglected that could assist, refresh, or comfort the defeated.

The victorious party, sensible they could gain little advantage by a farther pursuit, as the British were within reach of their own ships, and at the same time under the protection of the town of Charlestown; they therefore retreated a few

---

* The duke of Northumberland, father of earl Percy, had been uniformly opposed to the late measures of administration, in their American system.

miles to take care of their own wounded men, and to refresh themselves.

The action at Lexington, detached from its consequences, was but a trivial manoeuvre when compared with the records of war and slaughter, that have disgraced the page of history through all generations of men: but a circumstantial detail of lesser events, when antecedent to the convulsions of empire, and national revolution, are not only excusable, but necessary. The provincials lost in this memorable action, including those who fell, who were not in arms, upwards of fourscore persons. It was not easy to ascertain how many of their opponents were lost, as they endeavoured by all possible means to conceal the number, and the disgrace of the day. By the best information, it was judged, including those who died soon after of wounds and fatigue, that their loss was very much greater than that of the Americans. Thus resentment stimulated by recent provocation, the colonies, under all the disadvantages of an infant country, without discipline, without allies, and without resources, except what they derived from their own valor and virtue, were compelled to resort to the last appeal, the precarious decision of the sword, against the mighty power of Britain.

The four New England governments now thought proper to make this last appeal, and resolved to stand or fall together. It was a bold and adventurous enterprise; but conscious of the equal privileges bestowed by Heaven, on all its intelligent creatures on this habitable ball, they did not hesitate on the part they had to act, to retain them. They cheerfully engaged, sure of the support of the other colonies, as soon as congress should have time to meet, deliberate, and resolve. They were very sensible, the middle and southern colonies were generally preparing themselves, with equal industry and ability, for a decision by arms, whenever hostilities should seriously commence in any part of the continent.

RESPONSE OF COUNTRY

As soon as intelligence was spread that the first blow was struck, and that the shrill clarion of war actually resounded in the capital of the eastern states, the whole country rose in arms. Thousands collected within twenty-four hours, in the vicinity of Boston; and the colonies of Connecticut, Rhode Island, and New Hampshire seemed all to be in motion. Such was the resentment of the people, and the ardor of enterprise, that it was with difficulty they were restrained from rushing into Boston, and rashly involving their friends in common with their enemies, in all the calamities of a town taken by storm.

The day after the battle of Lexington, the congress of Massachusetts met at Watertown. They immediately determined on the number of men necessary to be kept on the ground, appointed and made establishments for the officers of each regiment, agreed on regulations for all military movements, and struck off a currency of paper for the payment of the soldiers, making the bills a tender for the payment of debts, to prevent depreciation. They drew up a set of judicious rules and orders for the army, to be observed by both officers and soldiers, until they should be embodied on a larger scale, under the general direction of the continental congress.

In the mean time, the consternation of general Gage was equalled by nothing but the rage of his troops, and the dismay of the *refugees* under his protection. He had known little of the country, and less of the disposition and bravery of its inhabitants. He had formed his opinions entirely on the misrepresentations of men, who, judging from their own feelings more than from the general conduct of mankind, had themselves no idea that the valor of their countrymen could be roused to hazard life and property for the sake of the common weal. Struck with astonishment at the intrepidity of a people he had been led to despise, and stung with vexation at the defeat of some of his best troops, he ordered the gates of the town to be shut, and every avenue guarded, to prevent the inhabitants, whom he now considered as his best security, from making their escape into the country. He had before caused entrenchments to be thrown up across a narrow isthmus, then the only entrance by land: still apprehensive of an attempt to storm the town, he now ordered the environs fortified; and soon made an entrance impracticable, but at too great an expense of blood.

The Bostonians thus unexpectedly made prisoners, and all intercourse with the country, from whence they usually received their daily supplies, cut off; famine stared them in the face on one side, and on the other they beheld the lawless rapine of an enraged enemy, with the sword of vengeance stretched over their heads. Yet, with a firmness worthy of more generous treatment, the principal citizens assembled, and after consultation, determined on a bold and free remonstrance to their military governor. They reminded him of his repeated assurances of personal liberty, safety, and protection, if they would not

In *Provincial Congrefs, Watertown, June* 16th, 1775.

AS it has pleafed Almighty GOD in his Providence to fuffer the Calamities of an unnatural War to take Place among us, in Confequence of our finful Declenfions from Him, and our great Abufe of thofe ineftimable Bleffings beftowed upon us.

And as we have Reafon to fear, that unlefs we become a penitent and reformed People, we fhall feel ftill feverer Tokens of his Difpleafure.

And as the moft effectual Way to efcape thofe defolating Judgments, which fo evidently hang over us, and if it may be, obtain the Reftoration of our former Tranquility, will be— That we repent and return every one from his Iniquities, unto him that correcteth us, which if we do in Sincerity and Truth, we have no Reafon to doubt but he will remove his Judgments---caufe our Enemies to be at Peace with us---and profper the Work of our Hands.

And as among the prevailing Sins of this Day, which threaten the Deftruction of this Land, we have Reafon to lament the frequent Prophanation of the Lord's-Day, or Chriftian Sabbath; many fpending their Time in Idlenefs and Sloth, others in Diverfions, and others in Journeying or Bufinefs, which is not neceffary on faid Day:

And as we earneftly defire that a Stop might be put to this great and prevailing Evil:

It is therefore RESOLVED, That it be recommended by this Congrefs, to the People of all Ranks and Denominations throughout this Colony, that they not only pay a religious Regard to that Day, and to the public Worfhip of God thereon; but that they alfo ufe their Influence to difcountenance and fupprefs any Prophanations thereof in others.

And it is further RESOLVED, That it be recommended to the Minifters of the Gofpel to read this Refolve to their feveral Congregations, accompanied with fuch Exhortations as they fhall think proper.

And whereas there is great Danger that the Prophanation of the Lord's-Day will prevail in the Camp:

We earneftly recommend to all the Officers, not only to fet good Examples; but that they ftrictly require of their Soldiers to keep up a religious Regard to that Day, and attend upon the public Worfhip of God thereon, fo far as may be confiftent with other Duties.

A true Copy from the Minutes,

Atteft.   SAMUEL FREEMAN, Secr'y.

. *By Order of the Congrefs,*

JAMES WARREN, Prefident.

evacuate the town, as they had long been solicited to do by their friends in the country. Had this been seasonably done, the Americans would have reduced the garrison by withholding provisions. The inhabitants of the town now earnestly requested, that the gates might be opened, that none who chose to retire with their wives, families, and property, might be impeded.

Whether moved by feelings of compassion, of which he did not seem to be wholly destitute, or whether it was a premeditated deception, yet remains uncertain; however, general Gage plighted his faith in the strongest terms, that if the inhabitants would deliver up their arms, and suffer them to be deposited in the city hall, they should depart at pleasure, and be assisted by the king's troops in removing their property. His shameful violation of faith in this instance, will leave a stain on the memory of the governor, so long as the obligations of truth are held sacred among mankind.

The insulted people of Boston, after performing the hard conditions of the contract, were not permitted to depart, until after several months of anxiety had elapsed, when the scarcity and badness of provisions had brought on a pestilential disorder, both among the inhabitants and the soldiers. Thus, from a reluctance to dip their hands in human blood, and from the dread of insult to which their feebler connexions were exposed, this unfortunate town, which contained near twenty thousand inhabitants, was betrayed into a disgraceful resignation of their arms, which the natural love of liberty should have inspired them to have held for their own defence, while subjected to the caprice of an arbitrary master. After their arms were delivered up and secured, general Gage denied the contract, and forbade their retreat; though afterwards obliged to a partial compliance, by the difficulty of obtaining food for the subsistence of his own army. On certain stipulated gratuities to some of his officers, a permit was granted them, to leave their elegant houses, their furniture, and goods, and to depart naked from the capital, to seek an asylum and support from the hospitality of their friends in the country.

The islands within the harbour of Boston were so plentifully stocked with sheep, cattle, and poultry, that they would have afforded an ample supply to the British army for a long time, had they been suffered quietly to possess them. General Putnam, an officer of courage and experience, defeated this expectation by taking off every thing from one of the principal islands, under the fire of the British ships; at the same time, he was so fortunate as to burn several of their tenders, without losing a man. His example was followed; and from Chelsea to Point Alderton, the islands were stripped of wheat and other grain, of cattle and forage; and whatever they could not carry off, the Americans destroyed by fire. They burnt the light-house at the entrance of the harbour, and the buildings on all the islands, to prevent the British availing themselves of such convenient appendages for encampments so near the town.

CHARACTER OF GOVERNORS

While these transactions were passing in the eastern provinces, the other colonies were equally animated by the spirit of resistance, and equally busy in preparation. Their public bodies were undismayed; their temper, their conduct, and their operations, both in the civil and military line, were a fair and uniform transcript of the conduct of the Massachusetts; and some of them equally experienced thus early, the rigorous proceedings of their unrelenting governors.

NEW YORK was alarmed soon after the commencement of hostilities near Boston, by a rumor, that a part of the armament expected from Great Britain, was to be stationed there to awe the country, and for the protection of the numerous loyalists in the city. In some instances, the province of New York had not yet fully acceded to the doings of the general congress; but they now applied to them for advice, and shewed themselves equally ready to renounce their allegiance to the king of Great Britain, and to unite in the common cause in all respects, as any of the other colonies. Agreeable to the recommendation of congress, they sent off their women, children, and effects, and ordered a number of men to be embodied, and hold themselves in readiness for immediate service.

Tryon was the last governor who presided at New York under the crown of England. This gentleman had formerly been governor of North Carolina, where his severities had rendered him very obnoxious. It is true, this disposition was principally exercised towards a set of disorderly, ignorant people, who had felt themselves oppressed, had embodied, and styling themselves *regulators,* opposed the authority of the laws. After they had been subdued, and several of the ringleaders executed, governor Tryon returned to England, but was again sent out as governor of the province of New York. He was received

GOD PREPARES
A CHRISTIAN
PEOPLE
TO ESTABLISH
THE AMERICAN
NATION

with cordiality, treated with great respect, and was for a time much esteemed, by many of the inhabitants of the city, and the neighbouring country. Very soon after the contest became warm between Great Britain and the inhabitants of America, he, like all the other governors in the American colonies, tenacious of supporting the prerogatives of the crown, laid aside that spirit of lenity he had previously affected to feel.

Governor Tryon entered with great zeal into all the measures of administration; and endeavoured with art, influence, and intrigue, of which he was perfectly master, to induce the city of New York, and the inhabitants under his government, to submit quietly, and to decline a union of opinion and action with the other colonies, in their opposition to the new regulations of the British parliament. But he soon found he could not avail himself sufficiently of the interest he possessed among some of the first characters in the city, to carry the point, and subdue the spirit of liberty, which was every day appreciating in that colony.

On the determination of the provincial congress to arrest the crown officers, and disarm the persons of those who were denominated *tories,* governor Tryon began to be apprehensive for his own safety. The congress of New York had resolved, "that it be recommended to the several provincial assemblies, or conventions, and councils, or committees of safety, to arrest and secure every person in their respective colonies, whose going at large may, in their opinion, endanger the safety of the colony, or the liberties of America."

Though governor Tryon was not particularly named, he apprehended himself a principal person pointed at in this resolve. This awakened his fears to such a degree, that he left the seat of government, and went on board the Halifax packet; from whence he wrote the mayor of the city, that he was there ready to execute any such business, as the circumstances of the times would permit. But the indifference as to the residence, or even the conduct of a plantation governor, was now become so general among the inhabitants of America, that he soon found his command in New York was at an end. After this he put himself at the head of a body of loyalists, and annoyed the inhabitants of New York and New Jersey, and wherever else he could penetrate, with the assistance of some British troops that occasionally joined them.

The governors of the several colonies, as if hurried by a consciousness of their own guilt, flying like fugitives to screen themselves from the resentment of the people, on board the king's ships, appear as if they had been composed of similar characters to those described by a writer of the history of such as were appointed to office in the more early settlement of the American colonies. He said, "it unfortunately happened for our American provinces, that a government in any of our colonies in those parts, was scarcely looked upon in any other light than that of a hospital, where the favorites of the ministry might lie, till they had recovered their broken fortunes, and oftentimes they served as an asylum from their creditors." (*Modern Universal History, vol. xxxix. p. 357*)

The neighbouring government of NEW JERSEY was for some time equally embarrassed with that of New York. They felt the effects of the impressions made by governor Franklin, in favor of the measures of administration; but not so generally as to preclude many of the inhabitants from uniting with the other colonies, in vigorous steps to preserve their civil freedom. Governor Franklin had, among many other expressions which discovered his opinions, observed in a letter to Mr. secretary Conway, "it gives me great pleasure, that I have been able through all the late disturbances, to preserve the tranquillity of this province, notwithstanding the endeavours of some to stimulate the populace to such acts as have disgraced the colonies." He kept up this tone of reproach, until he also was deprived by the people of his command; and New Jersey, by the authority of committees, seized all the money in the public treasury, and appropriated it to the pay of the troops raising for the common defence. They took every other prudent measure in their power, to place themselves in readiness for the critical moment.

PENNSYLVANIA, though immediately under the eye of congress, had some peculiar difficulties to struggle with, from a proprietary government, from the partizans of the crown, and the great body of the quakers, most of them opposed to the American cause. But the people in general were guarded and vigilant, and far from neglecting the most necessary steps for general defence.

In VIRGINIA, MARYLAND, AND THE CAROLINAS, where they had the greatest number of African slaves, their embarrassments were accumulated, and the dangers which hung over them, peculiarly aggravated. From their long habit of filling their country with foreign slaves, they were threatened with a host of domestic enemies, from which the other colonies had nothing to fear. The Virginians had been disposed in general to treat their governor, lord Dunmore, and his family, with every mark of respect; and had not his intemperate zeal in the service of his master given universal disgust, he might have remained longer among them, and finally have left them in a much less disgraceful manner.

However qualified this gentleman might have been to preside in any of the colonies, in more pacific seasons, he was little calculated for the times, when ability and moderation, energy and condescension, coolness in decision, and delicacy in execution, were highly requisite to govern a people struggling with the poniard at their throat and the sword in their hand, against the potent invaders of their privileges and claims.

He had the inhumanity early to intimate his designs if opposition ran high, to declare freedom to the blacks, and on any appearance of hostile resistance to the king's authority, to arm them against their masters. Neither the house of burgesses, nor the people at large, were disposed to recede from their determinations in consequence of his threats, nor to submit to any authority that demanded implicit obedience, on pain of devastation and ruin. Irritated by opposition, too rash for consideration, too haughty for condescension, and fond of distinguishing himself in support of the parliamentary system, lord Dunmore dismantled the fort in Williamsburg, plundered the magazines, threatened to lay the city in ashes, and depopulate the country: As far as he was able, he executed his nefarious purposes.

When his lordship found the resolution of the house of burgesses, of committees and conventions, was no where to be shaken, he immediately proclaimed emancipation to the blacks, and put arms into their hands. He excited disturbances in the back settlements, and encouraged the natives bordering on the southern colonies, to rush from the wilderness, and make inroads on the frontiers. For this business, he employed as his agent one *Connolly,* a Scotch renegado, who travelled from Virginia to the Ohio, and from the Ohio to general Gage at Boston, with an account of his success, and a detail of his negociations. From general Gage he received a colonel's commission, and was by him ordered to return to the savages, and encourage them, with the aid of some British settlers on the river Ohio, to penetrate the back country, and distress the borders of Virginia. But fortunately, Connolly was arrested in his career, and with his accomplices taken and imprisoned on his advance through Maryland; his papers were seized, and a full disclosure of the cruel designs of his employers sent forward to congress.

By the indiscreet conduct of lord Dunmore, the ferments in Virginia daily increased. All respect towards the governor. was lost, and his lady terrified by continual tumult left the palace, and took sanctuary on board one of the king's ships. After much altercation and dispute, with every thing irritating on the one side, and no marks of submission on the other, his lordship left his seat, and with his family and a few loyalists retired on board the Fowey man of war, where his lady in great anxiety had resided many days. There he found some of the most criminal of his partizans had resorted before he quitted the government; with these and some banditti that had taken shelter in a considerable number of vessels under his lordship's command, and the assistance of a few run-away negroes, he carried on a kind of predatory war on the colony for several months. The burning of Norfolk, the best town in the territory of Virginia, completed his disgraceful campaign.

The administration of lord William Campbell, and Mr. Martin, the governors of the two CAROLINAS, had no distinguished trait from that of most of the other colonial governors. They held up the supreme authority of parliament in the same high style of dignity, and announced the resentment of affronted majesty, and the severe punishment that would be inflicted on congresses, conventions and committees, and the miserable situation to which the people of America would be reduced, if they continued to adhere to the *factious demagogues* of party. With the same spirit and cruel policy that instigated lord Dunmore, they carried on their negociations with the Indians, and encouraged the insurrections of the negroes, until all harmony and confidence were totally destroyed between themselves and the people, who supported their own measures for defence in the highest tone of freedom and independence. Both the governors of North and South Carolina soon began to be apprehensive of the effects of public resentment, and about this time thought it necessary for their own safety to repair on board the king's ships, though their language and manners had not been equally rash and abusive with that of the governor of Virginia.

Henry Laurens, Esq. was president of the provincial congress of South Carolina at this period; whose uniform virtue and independence of spirit, we shall see conspicuously displayed hereafter on many other trying occasions. It was not long after the present period, when he wrote to a friend and observed, that "he meant to finish his peregrinations in this world, by a journey through the

GOD PREPARES
A CHRISTIAN
PEOPLE
TO ESTABLISH
THE AMERICAN
NATION

United States; then to retire and learn to die." But he had this important lesson to learn in the ordeal of affliction and disappointment, that he severely experienced in his public life and domestic sorrows, which he bore with that firmness and equanimity, which ever dignifies great and good characters.

Sir Robert Eden, governor of MARYLAND, a man of social manners, jovial temper, and humane disposition, had been more disposed to lenity and forbearance, than any of the great officers in the American department. But so high wrought was the opposition to British authority, and the jealousies entertained of all magistrates appointed by the crown, that it was not long after the departure of the neighbouring governors, before he was ordered by congress to quit his government, and repair to England. He was obliged to comply, though with much reluctance. He had been in danger of very rough usage before his departure, from general Lee, who had intercepted a confidential letter from lord George Germaine to governor Eden. Lee threatened to seize and confine him, but by the interference of the committee of safety, and some military officers at Annapolis, the order was not executed. They thought it wrong to consider him as responsible for the sentiments contained in the letters of his correspondents; and only desired Mr. Eden to give his word of honor, that he would not leave the province before the meeting of a general congress of that state; nor did they suffer him to be farther molested. He was permitted quietly to take leave of his friends and his province, after he had received the order of the continental congress for his departure; and in hopes of returning in more tranquil times, he left his property behind him, and sailed for England in the summer, one thousand seven hundred and seventy-six.

The influence of sir James Wright the governor of GEORGIA, prevented that state from acceding to the measure of a general congress, in one thousand seven hundred and seventy-four. Yet the people at large were equally disaffected, and soon after, in an address to his excellency, acknowledged themselves the only link in the great American chain, that had not publicly united with the other colonies in their opposition to the claims of parliament. They called a provincial congress, who resolved in the name of their constituents, that they would receive no merchandize whatever from Great Britain or Ireland after the seventh day of July, one thousand, seven hundred and seventy-five; that they fully approved and adopted the American declaration and bill of rights, published by the late continental congress; that they should now join with the other colonies, choose delegates to meet in general congress; and that they meant invariably to adhere to the public cause, and that they would no longer lie under the suspicion of being unconcerned for the rights and freedom of America.

TICONDEROGA TAKEN

Indeed the torch of war seemed already to have reached the most distant corner of the continent, the flame had spread and penetrated to the last province in America held by Great Britain, and a way opened to the gates of Quebec, before administration had dreamed of the smallest danger in that quarter. Soon after the action at Lexington, a number of enterprising young men, principally from Connecticut, proposed to each other a sudden march towards the lakes, and a bold attempt to surprize Ticonderoga, garrisoned by the $\qquad$ May 10, 1775 king's troops. These young adventurers applied to governor Trumbull, and obtained leave of the assembly of Connecticut to pursue their project; and so secretly, judiciously, and rapidly was the expedition conducted, that they entered the garrison, and saluted the principal officer as their prisoner, before he had any reason to apprehend an enemy was near. This enterprise was conducted by the colonels Easton, Arnold, and Allen; the invaders possessed themselves of a considerable number of brass and iron cannon, and many warlike stores, without suffering any loss of life.

It had been proved beyond a doubt that the British government had spared no pains to encourage the inroads of the savages; of consequence this *coup de main* was deemed a very meritorious and important step. Ticonderoga commanded all the passes between Canada and the other provinces. The possession of this important fortress on the lake Champlain, in a great measure secured the frontiers from the incursions of the savages, who had been excited by the cruel policy of Britain to war, which, by these ferocious nations, is ever carried on by modes at which humanity shudders, and civilization blushes to avow.

Thus was the sword brandished through the land, and hung suspended from cruel execution of all the evils attendant on a state of civil convulsion, only by the faint hope, that the sovereign of Britain might yet be softened to hold out the olive-branch in one hand, and a redress of grievances in the other. But every pacific hope was reversed, and all prospect of the restoration of harmony annihilated early in the summer, by the arrival of a large reinforcement at Boston, commanded by three general officers of high consideration. All former delusive expectations now extinguished, both the statesman and the peasant, actuated by the feelings of the man and the patriot, discovered a most unconquerable magnanimity of spirit. Undismayed by the necessity of an appeal to the sword, though unprovided with sufficient resources for so arduous a conflict, they animated each other to sustain it, if necessary, until they should leave their foes only a depopulated soil, if victory should declare in their favor. Nature revolts at the idea, when the poniard is pushed by despair; yet preferring death to thraldom, the Americans were everywhere decisive in council, and determined in action. There appeared that kind of enthusiasm, which sets danger at defiance, and impels the manly arm to resist, till the warm current that plays round the heart, is poured out as a libation at the shrine of freedom.

ARRIVAL OF REINFORCEMENTS

On the other hand, the fears of the dependents on the crown were dissipated by the augmentation of the British army, their hopes invigorated, and every artifice used, to spread terror and dismay among the people. The turpitude of *rebellion,* and the dread consequences of defeat, were painted in the most gloomy colours; the merits and the abilities of the principal officers extolled, their distinguished names and characters enhanced, and every thing circulated that might tend to weaken the resolution of the people. It was said, general Burgoyne commanded a squadron of light-horse, which was to scour the country, and pick up the leading insurgents in every quarter. The capacity, bravery, and virtues of general Clinton were every where announced by the votaries of administration; and the name of *Howe* was at that time, at once revered, beloved, and dreaded in America. A monumental tribute of applause had been reared in honor of one brother, who had fallen in that country in the late war between Great Britain and France; and the gratitude of the people had excited a predilection in favor of the other, and indeed of every branch of that family. But this partiality was soon succeeded by an universal disgust towards the two surviving brothers, lord and general Howe, who undertook the conquest of America; a project held reproachful, and which would have reflected dishonor on the perpetrators, even had it been crowned with success.

GENERAL GAGE PROCLAIMS MARTIAL LAW

In the beginning of June, one thousand seven hundred and seventy-five, general Gage thought proper to act a more decided part than he had hitherto done. He published a proclamation, denouncing *martial* law in all its rigors against any one who should supply, conceal, or correspond with, any of those he was pleased to stigmatize by the epithets of *traitors, rebels,* or *insurgents.* But as an act of grace, he offered pardon in the king's name to all who should lay down their arms and submit to mercy, only excluding by name, Samuel Adams and John Hancock; he alleged that their crimes were of too flagitious a nature to hope for pardon. This proscription discovered the little knowledge which general Gage then possessed of the temper of the times, the disposition of the people at large, or the character of individuals. His discrimination, rather accidental than judicious, set these two gentlemen in the most conspicuous point of view, and drew the particular attention of the whole continent to their names, distinguished from many of their compeers, more by this single circumstance, than by superior ability or exertion. By this they became at once the favorites of popularity, and the objects of general applause, which at that time would have been the fortune of any one, honored by such a mark of disapprobation of the British commander in chief.

SAMUEL ADAMS AND JOHN HANCOCK IN PHILADELPHIA

Mr. Adams was a gentleman of a good education, a decent family, but no fortune. Early nurtured in the principles of civil and religious liberty, he possessed a quick understanding, a cool head, stern manners, a smooth address, and a Roman-like firmness, united with that sagacity and penetration that would have made a figure in a conclave. He was at the same time liberal in opinion, and uniformly devout; social with men of all denominations, grave in deportment; placid, yet severe; sober and indefatigable; calm in seasons of difficulty, tranquil and unruffled in the vortex of political altercation; too firm to be intimidated, too haughty for condescension, his mind was replete with resources that dissipated fear, and extricated in the greatest emergencies. Thus qualified, he stood forth early, and continued firm, through the great struggle, and may justly claim a large share of honor, due to that spirit of energy which opposed the measures of administration, and produced the independence of

GOD PREPARES
A CHRISTIAN
PEOPLE
TO ESTABLISH
THE AMERICAN
NATION

America. Through a long life he exhibited on all occasions, an example of patriotism, religion, and virtue honorary to the human character.

Mr. Hancock was a young gentleman of fortune, of more external accomplishments than real abilities. He was polite in manners, easy in address, affable, civil, and liberal. With these accomplishments, he was capricious, sanguine, and implacable: naturally generous, he was profuse in expense; he scattered largesses without discretion, and purchased favors by the waste of wealth, until he reached the ultimatum of his wishes, which centered in the focus of popular applause. He enlisted early in the cause of his country, at the instigation of some gentlemen of penetration, who thought his ample fortune might give consideration, while his fickleness could not injure, so long as he was under the influence of men of superior judgment. They complimented him by nominations to committees of importance, till he plunged too far to recede; and flattered by ideas of his own consequence, he had taken a decided part before the battle of Lexington, and was president of the provincial congress, when that event took place.

By the appearance of zeal, added to a certain alacrity of engaging in any public department, Mr. Hancock was influential in keeping up the tide of opposition; and by a concurrence of fortuitous circumstances, among which this proscription was the most capital, he reached the summit of popularity, which raised him afterwards to the most elevated stations, and very fortunately he had the honor of affixing his signature as president, to many of the subsequent proceedings of the continental congress, which will ever hold an illustrious rank in the page of history.

Mr. Hancock had repaired to Philadelphia, to take his seat in congress, immediately after he made his escape from Lexington. Part of the object of the excursion of the eighteenth of April, was the capture of him and Mr. Adams; they were both particularly inquired for, and the house in which they lodged surrounded by the king's troops, the moment after these gentlemen had retreated half-naked. Had they been found, they would undoubtedly have been shut up in Boston, if nothing more fatal had been inflicted, instead of being left at liberty to pursue a political career that will transmit their names with applause to posterity.

The absence of the late worthy president of congress, Mr. Randolph, and the arrival of Mr. Hancock at Philadelphia, at the fortunate moment when the enthusiasm inspired by Gage's proclamation was at the height, both concurred to promote his elevation. He was chosen to preside in the respectable assembly of delegates, avowedly on the sole principle of his having been proscribed by general Gage. It was uncouthly said, by a member of congress, that "they would shew *mother Britain* how little they cared for her, by choosing a Massachusetts man for their president, who had been recently excluded from pardon by public proclamation." The choice was suddenly made, and with rather too much levity for the times, or for the dignity of the office. Mr. Hancock's modesty prompted him for a moment to hesitate on the unexpected event, as if diffident of his own qualifications; when one of the members,* of a more robust constitution, and less delicacy of manners, took him in his arms, and placed him in the presidential chair.

This sudden elevation might place the fortunate candidate in a similar situation with the celebrated pope Ganganelli, who observed of himself, that after putting on the triple crown, he often felt his own pulse, to see if he was the same identical person he was a few years before. Mr. Hancock continued in the presidential chair until October, one thousand seven hundred and seventy-nine, when he took a formal leave of congress, and never again rejoined that respectable body. His time however was fully occupied in his own state in the various employments, to which he was called by a majority of voices in the Massachusetts, where his popular talents had a commanding influence, during the residue of his life. But in the progress of the revolution, several men of less consequence than Mr. Hancock, and far inferior claims to patriotism, were raised to the same dignified station.

In the effervescence of popular commotions, it is not uncommon to see the favorites of fortune elevated to the pinnacle of rank by trivial circumstances, that appear the result of accident.

Those who mark the changes and the progress of events through all revolutions, will frequently see distinctions bestowed, where there are no commanding talents, and honors retained, more from the strong influence of popular enthusiasm, than from the guidance of reason, which operates too little on the generality of mankind.

It may be observed, that public commotions in human affairs, like the shocks of nature, convulse the whole system, and level the lofty mountains, which have arisen for ages above the clouds, be-

---

* A Mr. Harrison, from Virginia, the same who made the above speech. These circumstances were verbally detailed to the author of these annals by a respectable member of congress then present.

neath the vallies; while the hillock, unnoticed before, is raised to a pitch of elevation, that renders it a land-mark for the eye of the weary seaman to rest upon.

All revolutions evince the truth of the observation of a writer, that "Many men great in title, have the spirit of slaves, many low in fortune, have great spirits, many a Cicero has kept sheep, many a Caesar followed the plough, many a Virgil folded cattle." (*Sir Francis Osborne's Memoirs*)

The sudden rotations in human affairs are wisely permitted by Providence, to remind mankind of their natural equality, to check the pride of wealth, to restrain the insolence of rank and family distinctions, which too frequently oppress the various classes in society.

BATTLE OF BUNKER HILL, JUNE 17, 1775

The late proclamation of general Gage was considered as a prelude to immediate action, and from all intelligence that could be obtained from the town, there appeared the strongest reason to expect a second sally from the troops lying in Boston. Uncertain on which side the storm would begin, the provincials thought it necessary to guard against surprise, by fortifying on both sides of the town, in the best manner they were able. They threw up some slight entrenchments at Roxbury, and several other places on the south side of Boston; at the same time, on the night of the sixteenth of June, they began some works at the extreme part of a peninsula at the north, running from Charlestown to the river, which separates that town from Boston. They executed this business with such secrecy and dispatch, that the officers of a ship of war then in the river, expressed their astonishment in the morning, when they saw some considerable works reared and fortified in the compass of a few hours, where, from the contiguous situation,* they least expected the Americans would look them in the face.

The alarm was immediately given, and orders issued, that a continual fire should be kept playing upon the unfinished works, from the ships, the floating batteries in the river, and a fortified

hill on the other side; but with unparralleled perseverance, the Americans continued to strengthen their entrenchments, without returning a shot until near noon, when the British army, consisting of ten companies of grenadiers, four battalions of infantry, and a heavy train of artillery, advanced under the command of general Pigot and major general Howe. A severe engagement ensued: many men and several brave officers of the royal army fell on the first fire of the Americans. This unexpected salute threw them into some confusion; but by the firmness of general Howe, and the timely assistance of general Clinton, who, with a fresh detachment arrived in season, the troops were immediately rallied, and brought to the charge with redoubled fury. They mounted the ramparts with fixed bayonets, and notwithstanding the most heroic resistance, they soon made themselves masters of the disputed hill.

Overpowered by numbers, and exhausted by the fatigue of the preceding night, and all hope of reinforcement cut off by the incessant fire of the ships across a neck of land that separated them from the country, the provincials were obliged to retreat, and leave the ground to the British troops. Many of their most experienced officers acknowledged the valor of their opponents; and that in proportion to the forces engaged, there had been few actions in which the military renown of British troops had been more severely tried. Their chagrin was manifest, that the bravery of British soldiers, which had been often signalized in the noblest feats of valor, should be thus resisted; that they should be galled, wounded, and slaughtered, by an *handful* of *cottagers,* as they termed them, under officers of little military skill, and less experience, whom they had affected to hold in ineffable contempt.

There is a certain point of military honor, that often urges against the feelings of humanity, to dip the sword in blood. Thus, from the early maxims of implicit obedience, the first principle of military education, many men of real merit hazarded fortune, life, and reputation, in the inglorious work of devastation and ruin, through the fields and villages of America. Yet such was the reluctance shewn by some to engage with spirit in the disagreeable enterprise of this day, that their officers were obliged to use the utmost severity towards them, to stimulate others to persevere. The town of Charlestown was reduced to ashes by the fire of the shipping, while the land forces were storming the hills. Thus, in concert, was this flourishing and compact town destroyed,

---

* These works were erected on Breed's hill. This was the spot that cost the British army so dear through the glorious action of that day, generally styled the battle of Bunker hill. After the Americans retreated, the British left Breed's hill, took their stand, and strongly fortified Bunker hill, about a fourth of a mile distant. Thus has the name of the place of action been frequently confounded.

God Prepares
a Christian
People
to Establish
the American
Nation

in the most wanton display of power. There were about four hundred dwelling-houses in the centre of Charlestown, which, with the out-houses adjacent, and many buildings in the suburbs, were also sunk in the conflagration. The fate of this unfortunate town was beheld with solemnity and regret, by many even of those who were not favorably disposed to the liberties of the western world. The ingratitude which marked the transaction aggravated the guilty deed. We have recently seen the inhabitants of that place, prompted by humanity, opening their doors for the relief, and pouring balm into the wounds, of the routed corps on the nineteenth of April: This in the eye of justice must enhance the atrocity, and forever stigmatize the ingratitude, which so soon after wrapped the town in flames, and sent out the naked inhabitants, the prey of poverty and despair.

There are few things which place the pride of man in a more conspicuous point of view, than the advantages claimed in all military rencontres that are not decisive. Thus, though at the expense of many lives, and the loss of some of their bravest officers, the British army exulted much in becoming masters of an unfinished entrenchment, and driving the Americans from their advanced post. Upwards of one thousand men, including the wounded, fell in this action on the royal side. Among the slain was lieutenant colonel Abercrombie, an officer much esteemed by his friends and his country, and a major Pitcairn, a gentleman of so much merit, that his fall was lamented even by his enemies. His valor on this occasion would have reflected glory on his memory, had it been signalized in a more honorable cause.

While this tragedy was acting on the other side of the Charles river, the terror and consternation of the town of Boston are scarcely describable. In the utmost anxiety, they beheld the scene from the eminences. Apprehensive for themselves, and trembling for their friends engaged in the bloody conflict, they were not less affected by the hideous shrieks of the women and children connected with the king's troops, who beheld their husbands, their friends, and relations, wounded, mangled, and slain, ferried over the river in boat-loads, from the field of carnage.

On the other side, though the Americans were obliged to quit the field with very considerable loss, yet they gloried in the honor they had this day acquired by arms. They retired only one mile from the scene of action, where they took possession of an advantageous height, and threw up

new works on Prospect hill, with the enthusiasm of men determined to be free. They soon environed the town of Boston on all sides with military parade, and though they wept the fall of many brave men, they bade a daily challenge to their enemies.

DEATH OF JOSEPH WARREN

But a cloud was cast over every face by the death of the intrepid major general Joseph Warren, who, to the inexpressible grief of his countrymen, lost his life in the memorable action usually styled the battle of Bunker hill. He fell covered with laurels, choosing rather to die in the field, than to grace the victory of his foes by the triumph they would have enjoyed in his imprisonment. He had been chosen president of the provincial congress, when Mr. Hancock repaired to Philadelphia, and was an active volunteer in several skirmishes that had taken place since the commencement of hostilities, which in the minds of his enemies would have sanctioned the severest indignities their resentment might have dictated, had he fallen into their hands at this early period of the war.

This gentleman had been appointed a major general only four days previous to the late action: he was educated in the medical line, and was much respected for his professional as well as his political abilities. He possessed a clear understanding, a strong mind, a disposition humane and generous, with manners easy, affable, and engaging; but zealous, active, and sanguine, in the cause of his oppressed country, it is to be lamented, that he rather incautiously courted the post of danger, and rushed precipitately on his fate, while more important occasions required his paying some regard to personal safety. Yet, if the *love* of *fame* is the strongest passion of the mind, and human nature pants for distinction in the flowery field, perhaps there was never a moment of more unfading glory, offered to the wishes of the brave, than that which marked the *exit* of this heroic officer. He was the first victim of rank that fell by the sword in the contest between Great Britain and America: and the conflagration of Charlestown, enkindled by the wanton barbarity of his enemies, lighted his *manes* to the grave. These circumstances ensure a record in every historical annal, while his memory will be revered by every lover of his country, and the name of *Warren* will be enrolled at the head of that band of patriots and heroes, who sacrificed their lives to purchase the independence of America.

After the late action, the British troops appeared to be in no condition for further operations; weakened by the severe engagement near Bunker hill, sickly in the camp, and disheartened by unexpected bravery, where they had feared no resistance; straitened for provisions, and destitute of forage, except what was piratically plundered from the neighbouring shores, they kept themselves shut up in Boston the remainder of the summer. Here they continued in so quiet a manner, that had they not sometimes for their own amusement saluted the country with the sound of a useless cannonade, or the bursting of a shell, the people might have forgotten, that the monarch of Britain had several thousand soldiers cooped up within the walls of a city that still acknowledged him as their sovereign. The inhabitants of the town were held in duress, but their military masters did not presume to enlarge their own quarters.

MASSACHUSETTS RESUMES REGULAR GOVERNMENT UNDER ARTICLES OF CONFEDERATION

While this interesting scene had been acting in the field, the congress of the Massachusetts had sent on to Philadelphia for the opinion of the united delegates relative to their assumption of a regular form of government. Articles of confederation had been agreed to in general congress, in which a recapitulation of grievances, and the reasons for taking up arms were subjoined in terms little short of a declaration of war. These had been published in May, one thousand seven hundred and seventy-five; but their ratification by legislative bodies, or provincial congresses, had not yet generally taken place. But as the independence of America was not yet formally declared, it was in contemplation with many members of congress, as well as others of equal judgment, that when all should be convinced, that the breach between the two countries was totally irreconcileable, that the same modes of legislation and government should be adopted in all the colonies. It was then thought that a similarity of manners, police, and government, throughout the continent, would cement the union, and might support the sovereignty of each individual state, while yet, for general purposes, all should be in subordination to the congressional head.

An elegant writer has observed, that it is no easy matter to render the union of independent states perfect and entire, unless the genius and forms of their respective governments are in some degree similar. The judicious body assembled at Philadelphia were fully convinced of this; they were not insensible that a number of states, under different constitutions, and various modes of government and civil police, each regulated by their own municipal laws, would soon be swayed by local interests that might create irreconcileable feuds tending to disjoint the whole.* It was therefore judged best, to recommend to the Massachusetts, the resumption of a regular form of government in the present exigence, on the plan of the old charter of William and Mary, which gave authority to the majority of counsellors, chosen by an house of representatives, to exercise all governmental acts, as if the governor was really absent or dead.

On this recommendation, James Warren, Esq. president of the provincial congress, by their authority, issued writs in his own name, requiring the freeholders in every town to convene, and elect their representatives, to meet at Watertown on the twentieth of July, one thousand seven hundred and seventy-five. This summons was readily obeyed, and a full house appeared at the time and place appointed; the late president of the provincial congress was unanimously chosen speaker of the new house. Regardless of the vacant chair, they selected a council, and the two branches proceeded to legislation and the internal police of the province, as usually had been the practice in the absence of the governor and lieutenant governor.

Thus, after living for more than twelve months without any legal government, without law, and without any regular administration of justice, but what arose from the internal sense of moral obligation, which is seldom a sufficient restraint on the people at large, the Massachusetts returned peaceably to the regular and necessary subordination of civil society. Reduced nearly to a state of nature with regard to all civil or authoritative ties, it is almost incredible, that the principles of rectitude and common justice should have been so generally influential. For, such is the restless and hostile disposition of man, that it will not suffer him to remain long in a state of repose, whether on the summit of human glory,

* Congress had about this time adopted the resolution to advise each of the colonies explicitly to renounce the government of Great Britain, and to form constitutions of government for themselves, adequate to their exigencies, and agreeable to their own modes of thinking, where any variation of sentiment prevailed. This was acted upon, and a representative government, consisting of one or more branches, was adopted in each colony.

GOD PREPARES
A CHRISTIAN
PEOPLE
TO ESTABLISH
THE AMERICAN
NATION

or reclined on his own native turf, when probable contingencies promise him the acquisition of either wealth or fame. From the wants, the weakness, and the ferocity of human nature, mankind cannot subsist long in society, without some stable system of coercive power. Yet amidst the complicated difficulties with which they were surrounded, the horrors of anarchy were far from prevailing in the province: vice seemed to be abashed by the examples of moderation, disinterestedness, and generosity, exhibited by many of the patriotic leaders of present measures.

It has been observed already, that not a drop of blood had ever been spilt by the people in any of the commotions preceding the commencement of war, and that the fear of popular resentment was undoubtedly a guard on the conduct of some individuals. Others, checked by the frowns of public virtue, crimes of an atrocious nature had seldom been perpetrated: all classes seemed to be awed by the magnitude of the objects before them; private disputes were amicably adjusted or postponed, until time and events should give the opportunity of legal decision, or render the claims of individuals of little consequence, by their being ingulfed in the torrent of despotism, generally poured out by the conqueror, who fights for the establishment of uncontrolled power.

A CONTINENTAL ARMY

Freedom, long hunted round the globe by a succession of tyrants, appeared at this period, as if about to erect her standard in America; the scimitar was drawn from principles, that held life and property as a feather in the balance against the chains of servitude that clanked in her disgusted ear. The blood of innocence had already crimsoned over the fields which had teemed for the nourishment of Britain, who, instead of listening to the groans of an oppressed country, had recently wrung out the tears of anguish, until the inhabitants of the plundered towns were ready to quit the elegancies of life, and take refuge in the forest, to secure the unimpaired possession of those privileges which they considered as a grant from heaven, that no earthly potentate had a right to seize with impunity.

The bulk of mankind have indeed, in all countries in their turn, been made the prey of ambition. It is a truth that no one will contest, though all may regret, that in proportion to the increase of wealth, the improvement in arts, and the refinements in society, the great body of the people have either by force or fraud, become the slaves of the few, who by chance, violence, or accident, have destroyed the natural equality of their associates. Sanctioned by time and habit, an indefeasible right has been claimed, that sets so mischievous a creature as man above all law, and subjects the lives of millions, to the rapacious will of an individual, who, by the intoxicating nature of power, soon forgets that there are any obligations due to the subject, a reptile in his opinion, made only for the drudgery necessary to maintain the splendor of government, and the support of prerogative. Every step taken by the British government, relative to the colonies, confirmed this truth, taught them their danger, and evinced to the Americans the necessity of guarding at all points, against the assumed jurisdiction of an assembly of men, disposed to innovate continually on the rights of their fellow subjects who had no voice in parliament, and whose petitions did not reach, or had no influence on the ear of the sovereign.

The success of the last supplicatory address offered to the parliament of Britain by the United States, still hung in suspense; yet the crisis appeared so alarming, that it was thought necessary by many, to attend immediately to the establishment of a continental army on some stable and respectable footing. But there were some influential members in congress, who dreaded the consequence of a step so replete with the appearance of hostility, if not with the avowed design of independence; they observed, that such a measure would be an inevitable bar to the restoration of harmony.

Some, who had warmly opposed the measures of administration, and ably advocated the rights of the colonies, were of this opinion. The idea of dissevering the empire, shocked their feelings; they still ardently wished, both from the principles of humanity, and what they judged the soundest policy, to continue if possible, the natural connexion with Britain. Others of a more timid complexion, readily united with these gentlemen, and urged, notwithstanding the contempt poured on all former supplications, that even, if their late petition should be rejected, they should yet make one effort more for conciliation and relief, by the hitherto fruitless mode of prayer and remonstrance. Men of more enlarged and comprehensive views, considered this proposal as the *finesse* of shallow politicians, designed only to prevent the organization of a continental army.

The celebrated Machiavel, pronounced by some the prince of politicians, has observed, "that every state is in danger of dissolution, whose government is not frequently reduced to its original principles." The conduct of the British administration towards the colonies, the corruption of the government in every department, their deviations from first principles, and the enormous public debt of the nation, evinced not only the necessity of a reform in parliament, but appeared to require such a renovation of the British constitution, as was not likely soon to take place. Thus circumstanced, many thought it the interest of America, to dissolve the connexion with such a government, and were utterly opposed to delay, or any further application to the British king or parliament, by petition or concession.

After a long debate on the subject, the last description of persons were obliged reluctantly to accede to a measure which they thought promised nothing but delay or disgrace. By a kind of necessary compromise, a most humble and loyal petition directly to the king of Great Britain, was again agreed to by the delegated powers of the United States. At the same time, it was stipulated by all parties, that military preparations should be made, and an army raised without farther hesitation. A decided majority in congress, voted, that twenty thousand men should be immediately equipped and supported at the expense of the United States of America. The honorable William Penn, late governor of Pennsylvania, was chosen agent to the court of Britain, and directed to deliver the petition to the king himself, and to endeavor by his personal influence, to procure a favorable reception to this last address.

GEORGE WASHINGTON AT CAMBRIDGE

The command of the army, by the unanimous voice of congress, was vested in George Washington, Esq. then a delegate from the State of Virginia. He received this mark of confidence, from his country, with becoming modesty, and declined all compensation for his services, more than should be sufficient to defray his expenditures, for which he would regularly account.

Mr. Washington was a gentleman of family and fortune, of a polite, but not a learned education; he appeared to possess a coolness of temper, and a degree of moderation and judgment, that qualified him for the elevated station in which he was now placed; with some considerable knowledge of mankind, he supported the reserve of the statesman, with the occasional affability of the courtier. In his character was blended a certain dignity, united with the appearance of good

humour; he possessed courage without rashness, patriotism and zeal without acrimony, and retained with universal applause the first military command, until the establishment of independence. Through the various changes of fortune in the subsequent conflict, though the slowness of his movements was censured by some, his character suffered little diminution to the conclusion of a war, that from the extraordinary exigencies of an infant republic, required at times, the caution of Fabius, the energy of Caesar, and the happy facility of expedient in distress, so remarkable in the military operations of the illustrious Frederick. With the first of these qualities, he was endowed by nature; the second was awakened by necessity; and the third he acquired by experience in the field of glory and danger, which extended his fame through half the globe.

In the late war between England and France, Mr. Washington had been in several military encounters, and had particularly signalized himself in the unfortunate expedition under general Braddock, in the wilderness on the borders of the Ohio, in the year one thousand seven hundred and fifty-five. His conduct on that occasion raised an *eclat* of his valor and prudence; in consequence of which many young gentlemen from all parts of the continent, allured by the name of major Washington, voluntarily entered the service, proud of being enrolled in the list of officers under one esteemed so gallant a commander.

General Washington arrived at the camp at Cambridge in the neighbourhood of Boston, the beginning of July, one thousand, seven hundred and seventy-five. He was accompanied by several officers of distinction from the southern states, and by Charles Lee and Horatio Gates, both natives of Great Britain, appointed now to high rank in the American army. There appeared much expectation from his abilities, and a general satisfaction in the appointment of Mr. Washington to the chief command. A congratulatory address, expressive of their esteem, with the strongest assurances of their aid and support, to enable him to discharge the duties of his arduous and exalted station, was presented him from the provincial congress of Massachusetts, through the hand of their president, James Warren. To this gentleman, general Washington brought letters of importance, and to him he was referred for advice by the delegates of the Massachusetts, as "a judicious, confidential friend, who would never deceive him."

In his reply to this address, general Washing-

July 3, 1775

God Prepares
a Christian
People
to Establish
the American
Nation

ton observed, "That in leaving the enjoyments of domestic life, he had only emulated the virtue and public spirit of the whole province of Massachusetts Bay; who with a firmness and patriotism without example in history, had sacrificed the comforts of social and private felicity, in support of the rights of mankind, and the welfare of their country." Indeed all ranks were emulous to manifest their respect to the commander of the army. Multitudes flocked from every quarter to the American standard, and within a few weeks the environs of Boston exhibited a brave and high spirited army, which formed to order, discipline, and subordination, more rapidly than could have been expected from their former habits. Fired with an enthusiasm arising from a sense of the justice of their cause; ardent, healthy, and vigorous; they were eager for action, and impatient to be led to an attack on the town of Boston, where the British army was encamped. But they were still ignorant that both private and political adventurers, had been so negligent of their own and the public safety, as to pay little attention to the importation of powder, arms, and other warlike stores, previous to the prohibition of Britain, restricting the shipment of those articles to America, but for the immediate use of the king's troops.

RELIANCE ON PROVIDENCE

Thus when hostilities commenced, and a war was denounced against the colonies, they had innumerable difficulties to surmount. Several of the most formidable powers of Europe had been invited by Britain to aid the cruel purposes of administration, either by the loan of auxiliaries, or by a refusal of supplies to the infant states, now struggling alone against a foe, whose power, pride and success, had often made the nations tremble. On a retrospect of the critical situation of America, it is astonishing she did not fall at the threshold; she had new governments to erect in the several states, her legislatures to form, and her civil police to regulate on untrodden ground. She had her armies to establish, and funds to provide for their payment: she had her alliances to negociate, new sources of trade to strike out, and a navy to begin, while the thunder of Britain was alarming her coasts, the savages threatening her borders, and the troops of George the third, with the sword uplifted, pushing their execrable purpose to exterminate the last vestige of freedom.

But as Providence had led to the period of independence, the powers of industry and invention were called forth. Not discouraged by the magnitude of the work, or the numberless obstacles to the completion of their design, no difficulties damped the ardor and unanimity of their exertions, though for a time it appeared, as if their magazines must be furnished by the nitre from heaven, and the ore dug by their own hands from the bowels of the earth. The manufacture of salt-petre, at first considered as the ideal project of some enthusiast for freedom, was not only attempted, but became the easy occupation of women and children. Large quantities were furnished from many parts of America, and powder-mills were erected, which worked it with success. Sulphur, lead, and iron ore, are the natural productions of the country, and mountains of flint had recently been discovered and wrought for use. As nature had thus furnished the materials, every hand that was not engaged in arms was employed in arts, with an alacrity and cheerfulness that discovered a determination to be free.

DAVID RAMSAY

SOUTHERN HISTORIAN COTEMPORARY WITH THE AMERICAN REVOLUTION

"They looked up to Heaven, as the source of their rights,
and claimed, not from the promises of kings,
but from the Parent of the universe."

DAVID RAMSAY
BY REMBRANDT PEALE (AMERICAN, 1778-1860)
OIL ON CANVAS, 24 X 20 IN. C. 1795-1797.
COURTESY INDEPENDENCE NATIONAL HISTORICAL PARK
PHILADELPHIA, PENNSYLVANIA

Prelude to the American Revolution, 1765 to 1775

History of the United States, by David Ramsay, Vol. I, II, Philadelphia, 1816

For several centuries after the subversion of the Roman empire, the world was benighted in deep ignorance, and held in bondage. The baleful influence of despotism in Asia, of savage manners in Africa, of canon and feudal law in Europe, had, for ages, kept the mass of mankind, in a state of miserable degradation. When these evils were at their height, the discovery of the art of printing, and the reformation of religion, laid a foundation in Europe, for improving the condition of its inhabitants. About the same time, a new hemisphere was found, which afforded a fair opportunity for trying what might be done for the advancement of human happiness. To it, the poor and the distressed of the old world repaired, in great numbers. In it, many circumstances encouraged, and nothing hindered the establishment of government, on new principles, highly favourable to the rights of man, and the happiness of the people. How far this has been done, is an interesting subject of inquiry. The investigation of it gives high importance to the history of the New World; particularly of that part of its northern continent, which, being first released from the dominion of Europe, claims the merit of having contributed largely to the melioration of the state of man. . . .

In the space of seventy-four years, part of the seventeenth century, the North American continent, from New Hampshire to Georgia, was parcelled out into distinct governments. Little did the wisdom of these early periods of American history foresee of the consequences, both good and evil, that were to result to the old world, from discovering and colonizing the new. When we consider the immense floods of gold and silver, which have flowed from it into Europe, the subsequent increase of industry and population, the prodigious extension of commerce, manufactures, and navigation, and the influence of the whole on manners and arts; we see such an accumulation of goods, as leads us to rank Columbus among the greatest benefactors of the human race: but when we view the injustice done the natives; the extirpation of many of their numerous nations, whose names are no more heard; the havoc made among the first settlers; the slavery of the Africans, to which America has furnished the temptation, and the many long and bloody wars which it has occasioned; we behold such a crowd of woes, as excites an apprehension, that the evil has outweighed the good.

SLAVE TRADE AND PIRATES

The slave trade, or bringing negroes from Africa, to be sold as slaves, grew out of the discovery of America, and commenced seventy-one

God Prepares
a Christian
People
to Establish
the American
Nation

years after that event. Captain Hawkins, who was the first to engage in this branch of commerce, brought three hundred negroes from Africa, in 1563, and sold them for slaves, to the Spaniards in Hispaniola. It commenced in British America, thirteen years after the settlement of James Town. The first importers of slaves into America were Englishmen. The first importers into the country, now called the United States, were Dutchmen. In about seventeen years after the first settlement of New England, negroes were imported into it, in the course of trade, from the West Indies. The trade was never brisk, in the northern colonies; for, in them, labour could be advantageously performed by white men: but in the warmer southern states, especially near the sea coast, the capacity of white men to labour in the swamps, and under higher degrees of solar heat, was very little. In these states, the introduction of slaves was carried to so great an extent, that their aggregate number, inclusive of their issue, born in the country, at the commencement of the revolution, was about half a million. The evil did not terminate with the revolution; for the most southern states continued the importation, till it was prohibited, in 1808.

The discovery of America was also the occasion of a great increase of piracy. Hordes of lawless men associated, and took their station in some of the uninhabited spots of the new world, where they gave themselves up to all manner of licentiousness. They lived by hunting swine and cattle, which abounded in the mountains, and acquired the name of Buccaneers, from the practice of preserving their beef and pork, called in French *boucane*. After living in this manner, some became cultivators; but others betook themselves to piracy. They fortified themselves in Tortuga, and, sallying forth, in small companies, sought for booty. This was divided with the most scrupulous justice. Though they violated that virtue with others, they observed it among themselves. After their plunder was expended, they went in quest of more. To these enemies of the human race, frequent accessions were made from the outcasts of all nations. They became formidable, and attacked several Spanish towns. In 1697, they took Carthagena, and property to the value of seven or eight millions of dollars. They also extended their depredations along the American coast, from Main to Carolina, especially in the southern extreme. Landing in several places, they buried their ill-gotten wealth, in spots known only to themselves. To dig for this hidden treasure, was the amusement of several credulous inhabitants, for a considerable part of the eighteenth century. The pirates, at one time, had the command of the gulf of Florida, and in it made many valuable prizes. They almost ruined the trade to the West Indies, and, for a short time, nearly blocked up the port of Charleston, in South Carolina. They had two contiguous harbours, one in cape Fear river, North Carolina, and another at New Providence, from which they sallied forth, and made many prizes. Their rendezvous, in the latter place, was broke up by captain Rogers; in the former, in the year 1718, by governor Johnson and colonel Rhett, of South Carolina. Many years passed away, and the strong arm of government was vigorously exerted, before the American seas were cleared of freebooters.

UNIQUENESS OF ENGLISH COLONIES

In vain do we look among ancient nations, for examples of colonies, established on principles of policy, similar to those of the colonies of Great Britain. England did not, like the republics of Greece, oblige her sons to form distant communities, in the wilds of the earth. Like Rome, she did not give lands as a gratuity to soldiers, who became a military force, for the defence of her frontiers: she did not, like Carthage, subdue the neighbouring states, in order to acquire an exclusive right to their commerce. No conquest was ever attempted over the aborigines of America. Their right to the soil was disregarded, and their country looked upon as a waste, open to the occupancy and use of other nations. It was considered that settlements might be there formed, for the advantage of those who should migrate thither, as well as of the mother country. The rights and interests of the native proprietors were, all this time, deemed of no account.

What was the extent of obligations, by which colonies, planted under these circumstances, were bound to the mother country, is a subject of nice discussion. Whether these arose from nature and the constitution, or from compact, is a question necessarily connected with many others. While the friends of union contended, that the king of England had a property in the soil of America, by virtue of a right derived from prior discovery, and that his subjects, by migrating from one part of his dominions to another, did not lessen their obligations, to obey the supreme power of the nation, it was inferred, that the emigrants to English America continued to owe the same obedience to the king and parliament, as if they had never quitted the land of their nativity. But if, as others contended, the Indians were the only lawful proprietors of the country, in which their Creator had placed them, and they sold their right to emigrants, who, as men, had a right to leave their native country, and as subjects, had obtained chartered permission to do so, it follows, that the obligations of the colonists, to their parent state, must have resulted more from compact, and the prospect of reciprocal advantage, than from natural obligation. The latter opinions seem to have been adopted by several of the colonists, particularly in New England. Sundry persons of influence in that country always held, that birth was no necessary cause of subjection; for that the subject of any prince or state had a natural right to remove to any other state or quarter of the globe; especially if deprived of liberty of conscience; and that, upon such removal, his subjection ceased.

CHARTERS

The validity of charters, about which the emigrants to America were universally anxious, rests upon the same foundation. If the right of the sovereigns of England, to the soil of America, were ideal, and contrary to natural justice, and if no one can give what is not his own, their charters were on several accounts a nullity. In the eye of reason and philosophy, they could give no right to American territory. The only validity, which such grants could have, was, that the grantees had from their sovereign, a permission to depart from their native country, and negotiate with the proprietors for the purchase of the soil, and thereupon to acquire a power of jurisdiction subject to his crown. These were the opinions of many of the settlers in New England. They looked upon their charters as a voluntary compact, between their sovereign and themselves, by which they were bound neither to be subject to, nor seek protection from any other prince; nor to make any laws repugnant to those of England: but did not consider them as inferring an obligation of obedience to a parliament, in which they were unrepresented. The prospects of advantage, which the emigrants to America expected from the protection of their native sovereign, and the prospect of aggrandizement, which their native sovereign expected from the extension of his empire, made the former very solicitous for charters, and the latter very ready to grant them. Neither reasoned clearly on their nature, nor well understood their extent. In less

than eighty years, fifteen hundred miles of the sea coast were granted away; and so little did they who gave, or they who accepted of charters, understand their own transactions, that in several cases the same ground was covered by contradictory grants; and with an absurdity that can only be palliated by the ignorance of the parties, some of the grants extended to the South Sea, over a country whose breadth is yet unknown, and which to this day is unexplored.

Ideal as these charters were, they answered a temporary purpose. The colonists reposed confidence in them, and were excited to industry on their credit. They also deterred foreign European powers from disturbing them, because, agreeably to the late law of nations, relative to the appropriation of newly-discovered heathen countries, they inferred the protection of the sovereign who gave them. They also opposed a barrier to open and gross encroachments of the mother country on the rights of the colonists. A particular detail of these is not now necessary. Some general remarks may, nevertheless, be made on the early periods of colonial history, as they cast light on the late revolution. Long before the declaration of independence, several of the colonies, on different occasions, declared, that they ought not to be taxed, but by their own provincial assemblies; and that they considered subjection to acts of a British parliament, in which they had no representation, as a grievance. It is also worthy of being noted, that of the thirteen colonies, which have been lately formed into states, no one, Georgia excepted, was settled at the expense of government. Towards the settlement of that southern frontier, considerable sums have at different times been granted by parliament; but the twelve more northern Atlantic provinces have been wholly settled by private adventurers, without any advances from the national treasury. It does not appear, from existing records, that any compensation for their lands was ever made to the aborigines of America, by the crown or parliament of England; but policy, as well as justice, led the colonists to purchase and pay for what they occupied. This was done in almost every settlement; and they prospered most, who, by justice and kindness, took the greatest pains to conciliate the good will of the natives.

It is in vain to look for well-balanced constitutions, in the early periods of colonial history. Till the revolution, in the year 1688, a period subsequent to the settlement of the colonies, England herself can scarcely be said to have had a fixed constitution. At that eventful era, the line

GOD PREPARES
A CHRISTIAN
PEOPLE
TO ESTABLISH
THE AMERICAN
NATION

was first drawn, between the privileges of subjects and the prerogatives of sovereigns. It is sufficient in general to observe, that in less than eighty years from the first permanent English settlement in North America, the two original patents, granted to the Plymouth and London companies, were divided, and subdivided, into twelve distinct and unconnected provinces; and in fifty years more a thirteenth, by the name of Georgia, was added to the southern extreme of previous establishments.

COLONIAL CIVIL HISTORY

To each of these, after various changes, there was ultimately granted a form of government, resembling, in its most essential parts, as far as local circumstances would permit, that which was established in the parent state. A minute description of constitutions, which no longer exist, would be both tedious and unprofitable. In general, it may be observed, that agreeably to the spirit of the British constitution, considerable provision was made for the liberties of the inhabitants. The prerogatives of royalty, and dependence on the mother country, were but feebly impressed, on the colonial forms of government. In some of the provinces, the inhabitants chose their governors, and all other public officers; and their legislatures were under little or no control. In others, the crown delegated most of its power to particular persons, who were also invested with the property of the soil. In those which were most immediately dependent on the king, he exercised no higher prerogatives over the colonists, than over their fellow-subjects, in England; and his power over the provincial legislative assemblies was not greater, than what he was constitutionally vested with, over the house of commons, in the mother country. From the acquiescence of the parent state, the spirit of her constitution, and daily experience, the colonists grew up in a belief, that their local assemblies stood in the same relation to them, as the parliament of Great Britain to the inhabitants of that island. The benefits of legislation were confered on both, only through these constitutional channels.

It is remarkable, that though the English possessions in America were far inferior in natural riches to those which fell to the lot of other Europeans, yet the security of property and of liberty, derived from the English constitution, gave them a consequence to which the colonies of other powers, though settled at an earlier day, have not yet attained. The wise and liberal policy of

England towards her colonies, during the first hundred and fifty years after their settlement, had a considerable influence in exalting them to this pre-eminence. She, for the most part, gave them full liberty to govern themselves, by such laws as their local legislatures thought necessary, and left their trade open to every individual in her dominions. She generally gave them permission to pursue their respective interests, in such manner as they thought proper, and reserved little for herself, but the benefit of their trade, and that of a political union, under the same head. The colonies, founded by other powers, experienced no such indulgences. Portugal and Spain burdened theirs with many vexatious regulations; gave encouragement only to what was for their own interest; and punished whatever had a contrary tendency. France and Holland did not adopt such oppressive maxims; but were, in fact, not much less rigorous and coercive. They assigned their colonies to mercantile associations, which sold to colonists the commodities of Europe, at an enormous advance, and took the produce of their lands, at a low price; and, at the same time, discouraged the growth of any more than they could dispose of, at excessive profits. These oppressive regulations were followed with their natural consequences. The settlements, thus restricted, advanced but slowly in population and in wealth.

The English colonies participated in that excellent form of government, with which their parent isle was blessed, and which had raised it to an admirable height of agriculture, commerce, and manufactures. After many struggles, it had been acknowledged to be essential to the constitution of Great Britain, that the people could not be compelled to pay any taxes, nor be bound by any laws, but such as had been granted, or enacted, with the consent of themselves, or of their representatives. It was also one of their privileges, that they could not be affected, either in their property, their liberties or their persons, but by the unanimous consent of twelve of their peers.

AMAZING GROWTH

From the operation of these general principles of liberty, and the wise policy of Great Britain, her American settlements increased in number, wealth, and resources, with a rapidity which surpassed all previous calculations. Neither ancient nor modern history can produce an example of colonies governed with equal wisdom, or flourishing with equal rapidity. In the short space of a hundred and fifty years, their numbers increased to three millions, and their commerce to such a degree, as to be more than a third of that of Great Britain. They also extended their settlements fifteen hundred miles on the sea coast, and three hundred miles to the westward. Their rapid population, though partly accelerated by the influx of strangers, was principally owing to internal causes. In consequence of the equality of fortune and simplicity of manners, which prevailed among them, their inhabitants multiplied far beyond the proportion of old nations, corrupted and weakened by the vices of wealth, and above all, of vanity; than which, perhaps, there is no greater enemy to the increase of the human species.

NEW ENGLAND PROVINCES

The good effects of a wise policy, and equal government, were not only discernible, in raising the colonies of England, to a pre-eminence over those of other European powers, but in raising some among themselves to greater importance than others. Their relative population and wealth were by no means correspondent to their respective advantages of soil and climate. From the common disproportion between the natural and artificial wealth of different countries, it seems to be a general rule, that the more nature does for any body of men, the less they are disposed to do for themselves.

The New England provinces, though possessed of a comparatively barren country, were improved much faster than others, which were blessed with a superior soil and milder climate. Their first settlers were animated with a high degree of that religious fervour, which excites to great undertakings. They also settled their vacant lands on principles of the wisest policy. Instead of granting large tracts to individuals, they sold the soil in small farms, to those who personally cultivated the same. Instead of disseminating their inhabitants over an extensive country, they formed successive settlements, in townships of six miles square. They also made such arrangements, in these townships, as co-extended the blessings of education, and of religious instruction, with their settlements. By these means, industry and morality were propagated, and knowledge was generally diffused.

In proportion to their respective numbers, it is probable that no other country in the world contained more sober, orderly citizens, and fewer who were profligate and abandoned. Those high crimes, which are usually punished with death, were so rare in New England, that many years have elapsed, in large populous settlements, without a single execution. Their less fertile soil disposed them to a spirit of adventure, and their victorious industry rose superior to every obstacle. In carrying on the whale fishery, they not only penetrated the deepest frozen recesses of Hudson's Bay, and Davis's Straits, but pierced into the opposite regions of polar cold. While some of them were striking the harpoon, on the coast of Africa, others pursued their gigantic game, near the shores of Brazil. While they were yet in their infancy, as a political society, they carried on this perilous business to an extent exceeding all that the perseverance of Holland, the activity of France, or the vigour of English enterprise, had ever accomplished. A spirit of liberty prompted their industry, and a free constitution guarded their civil rights. The country was settled with yeomanry, who were both proprietors and cultivators of the soil. Luxury was estranged from their borders. Enervating wealth and pinching poverty were both equally rare. Early marriages and a numerous offspring were common; thence population was rapid, and the inhabitants generally possessed that happy state of mediocrity, which favours the improvement, both of mind and body.

NEW YORK AND PENNSYLVANIA

New York adjoined New England, but did not increase with equal rapidity. A few, by monopolizing large tracts of land, reduced many to the necessity of being tenants, or of removing to other provinces, where land could be obtained on more favourable terms. The increase of population, in this province, was nevertheless great, when compared with that of old countries. This appears from the following statement of their numbers, at different periods. In 1756, the province of New York contained 83,233 whites and in 1771, 148,124; an increase of nearly two for one, in the space of fifteen years.

Pennsylvania was at first settled by industrious inhabitants, chiefly of the sect of Quakers. The population of this country advanced equally, with that of the New England provinces. Among the inducements operating on foreigners to settle in Pennsylvania, was a most excellent form of provincial government, which secured the religious, as well as the civil rights of its inhabitants. While the mother country laboured under an

GOD PREPARES
A CHRISTIAN
PEOPLE
TO ESTABLISH
THE AMERICAN
NATION

oppressive ecclesiastical establishment, and while partialities of the same kind were sanctioned by law, in some of the American provinces; perfect liberty of conscience, and an exact equality of all sects, were, in every period, a part of the constitution of Pennsylvania.

Quaker simplicity, industry, and frugality, contributed, in like manner, to the flourishing of that province. The habits of that plain people correspond, admirably, with a new country, and with republican constitutions. Opposed to idleness and extravagance, they combined the whole force of religion, with customs and laws, to exile these vices from their society. The first Quaker settlers were followed by Germans, whose industry was not inferior to their own. The emigrants from other countries, who settled in Pennsylvania, followed these good examples; and industry and frugality became predominant virtues, over the whole province.

The policy of a loan-office was also eminently beneficial. The proprietaries of Pennsylvania sold their lands, in small tracts, and on long credit. The purchasers were indulged with the liberty of borrowing, on interest, paper bills of credit, out of the loan-office, on the mortgage of their lands. Perhaps there never was an institution which contributed more to the happiness of the people, or to the flourishing of a new country, than this land loan-office scheme. The province, being enriched by the clear interest of its loaned paper, was thereby enabled to defray the expenses of government, with moderate taxes. The industrious farmer was furnished with the means of cultivating and stocking his farm. These improvements, by increasing the value of the land, not only established the credit of the paper, but enabled the borrower, in a few years, to pay off the original loan, with the productions of the soil. The progressive improvement of Pennsylvania may be estimated, from the increase of its trade. In the year 1704, that province imported goods from the mother country, amounting in value only to 11,499£ sterling; but in 1772, to the value of 507,909£ an increase of nearly fifty for one, in little more than half a century.

MARYLAND AND VIRGINIA

In Maryland and Virginia, a policy less favourable to population, and somewhat different from that of Pennsylvania, took place. The church of England was incorporated, simultaneously, with the first settlement of Virginia; and, in the lapse of time, it also became the established religion of Maryland. In both these provinces, long before the American revolution, that church possessed a legal pre-eminence, and was maintained at the expense, not only of its own members, but of all other denominations. This deterred great numbers, especially of the Presbyterian denomination, who had emigrated from Ireland, from settling within the limits of these governments, and fomented a spirit of discord, between those who belonged to, and those who dissented from the established church.

SOUTHERN COLONIES AND SLAVERY

In these and the other southern provinces, domestic slavery was common. Though it was not by law forbidden any where, yet there were comparatively few slaves any where to the northward of Maryland. The peaceable and benevolent religion of the Quakers induced their united opposition to all traffic in the human race. Many individuals of other denominations, in like manner, discountenanced it; but the principal ground of difference on this head, between the northern and southern provinces, arose, less from religious principles, than from climate, and local circumstances. In the former, they found it to be their interest to cultivate their lands with white men, in the latter, with those of an opposite colour. The stagnant waters, and low lands, so frequent on the shores of Maryland and Virginia, and on the coasts, and near the rivers in the southern provinces, generate diseases, which are more fatal to whites than blacks.

It is certain, that a great part of the low country, in several of the provinces, must have remained without cultivation, if it had not been cultivated by black men. From the natural state of the country, domestic slavery seemed to be forced on the southern provinces. It favoured cultivation, but produced many baneful consequences. It was particularly hostile to the proper education of youth. Industry, temperance, and abstinence, virtues essential to the health and vigour of both mind and body, were with difficulty practised, where the labour of slaves procured an abundance, not only of the necessaries, but of the delicacies of life, and where daily opportunities and facilities were offered, for early, excessive, and enervating indulgences. Slavery also led to the monopoly of land, in the hands of a few. It impeded the introduction of labouring freemen, and of course diminished the capacity of the country for active defence; and at the same time endangered internal tranquility, by multiplying a species of inhabitants, who had no interest in the soil. Where it is common, a few grow rich, and live in ease and luxury; but the community is deprived of many of its resources for independent happiness, and depressed to a low station on the scale of national greatness. The aggregate industry of a country, in which slaves and freemen are intermixed, will always be less than where there is a number of freemen equal to both. Nothing stimulates to industry so much as interest. The man who works for another will contrive many artifices, to make that work as little as possible: but he who has an immediate profit from his labour, will disregard tasks, times, and seasons. In settlements where the soil is cultivated by slaves, it soon becomes unfashionable for freemen to labour; than which no greater curse can befall a country. The individuals, who, by the industry of their slaves, are released from the necessity of personal exertions, will be strongly tempted to many practices, injurious to themselves and others. Idleness is the parent of every vice; while labour of all kinds favours and facilitates the practice of virtue. Unhappy is that country, where necessity compels the use of slaves; and unhappy are the people, where the original decree of heaven, "that man should eat his bread in the sweat of his face," is by any means whatever generally eluded.

The influence of these causes was so extensive, that, though the southern provinces possessed the most fruitful soil, the most valuable staples, and the mildest climate, yet they were far inferior to their neighbours in strength, population, industry, and aggregate wealth. This inferiority increased or diminished, with the number of slaves in each province, contrasted with the number of freemen. The same observation held good between different parts of the same province. The sea coast, which, from necessity, could be cultivated only by black men, was deficient in many of the enjoyments of life, and lay at the mercy of every bold invader; while the western country, where cultivation was more generally carried on by freemen, though settled at a later period; sooner attained the means of self defence, and, relatively, a greater proportion of those comforts, with which a cultivated country rewards its industrious inhabitants.

FUNDAMENTAL ENGLISH PRINCIPLES

In the southern provinces, the long credit, given by British merchants, was a principal source of their flourishing. The immense capitals of the merchants, trading to the North American continent, enabled them to extend credit to the term of several years. They received a profit on their goods, and an annual interest of five per cent, on the sums for which they were sold. This enabled the American merchant to extend credit to the planter, from whom he received a higher interest than he paid in Great Britain. The planters, being furnished on credit, with every thing necessary for the cultivation of their lands, when careful and industrious, cleared so much more than the legal interest, with which they were charged, that in a few years of successful planting, the difference enabled them to pay their debts, and clear their capital. By the help of credit, a beneficial intercourse was established, redounding to the benefit of both parties. These causes eminently contributed to the prosperity of the English provinces. Others, besides co-operating to the same end, produced a warm love for liberty, a high sense of the rights of human nature, and a predilection for independence.

The first emigrants from England, for colonizing America, left the mother country at a time when the dread of arbitrary power was the predominant passion of the nation. Except the very modern charter of Georgia, in the year 1732, all the English colonies obtained their charters, and their greatest number of European settlers, between the years 1603 and 1688. In this period a remarkable struggle between prerogative and privilege commenced, and was carried on till it terminated in a revolution, highly favourable to the liberties of the people. In the year 1621, when the English House of Commons claimed freedom of speech, "as their ancient and undoubted right, and an inheritance transmitted to them from their ancestors;" King James replied, "that he could not allow of their style, in mentioning their ancient and undoubted rights; but would rather have wished they had said, that their privileges were derived from the grace and permission of their sovereign." This was the opening of a dispute which occupied the tongues, pens and swords, of the most active men in the nation, for a period of seventy years. It is remarkable that the same period is exactly co-incident with the settlement of the English colonies. James, educated in the arbitrary sentiments of the divine right of kings, conceived his subjects to be his property, and that their privileges were matters of grace and favour, flowing from his generosity. This high claim of prerogative excited opposition in support of the rights of the people.

In the progress of the dispute, Charles, son

GOD PREPARES
A CHRISTIAN
PEOPLE
TO ESTABLISH
THE AMERICAN
NATION

of King James, in attempting to levy ship-money, and other revenues, without consent of parliament, involved himself in a war with his subjects; in which, after various conflicts, he was brought to the block, and suffered death as an enemy to the constitution of his country. Though the monarchy was restored under Charles the second, and transmitted to James the second, yet, the same arbitrary maxims being pursued, the nation, tenacious of its rights, invited the prince of Orange to the sovereignty of the island, and expelled the reigning family from the throne. While these spirited exertions were made, in support of the liberties of the parent isle, the English colonies were settled, and chiefly with inhabitants of that class of people, which was most hostile to the claims of prerogative. Every transaction, in that period of English history, supported the position, that the people have a right to resist their sovereign, when he invades their liberties, and to transfer the crown from one to another, when the good of the community requires it.

The English colonists were, from their first settlement in America, devoted to liberty, on English ideas, and English principles. They not only conceived themselves to inherit the privileges of Englishmen, but, though in a colonial situation, actually possessed them.

After a long war between king and parliament, and a revolution, these were settled on the following fundamental principles: "that it was the undoubted right of English subjects, being freemen or freeholders, to give their property only by their own consent; that the house of commons exercised the sole right of granting the money of the people of England, because that house alone represented them; that taxes were the free gifts of the people to their rulers; that the authority of sovereigns was to be exercised only for the good of their subjects; that it was the right of the people to meet together, and peaceably to consider of their grievances; to petition for a redress of them; and finally, when intolerable grievances were unredressed, to seek relief, on the failure of petitions and remonstrances, by forcible means."

Opinions of this kind, generally prevailing, produced, among the colonists, a more determined spirit of opposition to all encroachments on their rights, than would probably have taken place, had they emigrated from the mother country, in the preceding century, when the doctrines of passive obedience, non resistance, and the divine right of kings, were generally received.

That attachment to their sovereign, which was

diminished in the first emigrants to America, by being removed to a great distance from his influence, was still farther diminished, in their descendants. When the American revolution commenced, the inhabitants of the colonies were, for the most part, the third and fourth, and sometimes, the fifth or sixth generation, from the original emigrants. In the same degree as they were removed from the parent stock, they were weaned from that partial attachment, which bound their forefathers to the place of their nativity. The affection for the mother country, as far as it was a natural passion, wore away in successive generations, till at last it had scarcely any existence.

That mercantile intercourse, which connects different countries, was, in the early periods of the English colonies, far short of that degree, which is necessary to perpetuate a friendly union. The eastern provinces were the first, which were thickly settled: and as they did not for a long time cultivate an extensive trade with England, their descendants speedily lost the fond attachment, which their forefathers felt to their parent state. The majority of the people in New England knew little of the mother country, having only heard of her as a distant kingdom, the rulers of which had, in the seventeenth century, persecuted and banished their ancestors to the woods of America.

The distance of America from Great Britain generated ideas, in the minds of the colonists, favourable to liberty. Three thousand miles of ocean separated them from the mother country. Seas rolled, and months passed, between orders, and their execution. In large governments, the circulation of power is enfeebled at the extremities. This results from the nature of things, and is the eternal law of extensive or detached empire. Colonists, growing up to maturity, at such an immense distance from the seat of government, perceived the obligation of dependence much more feebly, than the inhabitants of the parent isle, who not only saw, but daily felt, the fangs of power. The wide extent and nature of the country contributed to the same effect. The natural seat of freedom is among high mountains, and pathless deserts, such as abound in the wilds of America.

RELIGION OF THE COLONISTS

The religion of the colonists also nurtured a love for liberty. They were chiefly protestants; and all protestantism is founded on a strong claim to natural liberty, and the right of private judgment. A majority of them were of that class of men, who, in England, are called Dissenters. Their tenets, being the protestantism of the protestant religion, are hostile to all interference of authority, in matters of opinion, and predispose to a jealousy for civil liberty. They who belonged to the Church of England were, for the most part, independents, as far as church government and hierarchy were concerned. They used the liturgy of that church, but were without bishops, and were strangers to those systems, which make religion an engine of state. That policy, which unites the lowest curate with the greatest metropolitan, and connects both with the sovereign, was unknown among the colonists. Their religion was their own, and neither imposed by authority, nor made subservient to political purposes. Though there was a variety of sects, they all agreed in the communion of liberty; and all reprobated the courtly doctrines of passive obedience, and non-resistance. The same dispositions were fostered by the usual modes of education in the colonies. The study of law was common and fashionable. The infinity of disputes, in a new and free country, made it lucrative, and multiplied its followers. No order of men has, in all ages, been more favourable to liberty, than lawyers. Where they are not won over to the service of government, they are formidable adversaries to it. Professionally taught the rights of human nature, they keenly and quickly perceive every attack made on them. While others judge of bad principles, by the actual grievances they occasion, lawyers discover them at a distance, and trace future mischiefs from gilded innovations.

READING OF THE COLONISTS

The reading of those colonists, who were inclined to books, generally favoured the cause of liberty. Large libraries were uncommon in the New World. Disquisitions on abstruse subjects, and curious researches into antiquity, did not accord with the genius of a people, settled in an uncultivated country, where every surrounding object impelled to action, and little leisure was left for speculation. Their books were generally small in size, and few in number: a great part of them consisted of those fashionable writers, who have defended the cause of liberty. Sydney and Locke were their standard authors in politics. Cato's letters, the Independent Whig, and such productions, were common in one extreme of the colonies; while in the other, histories of the Puri-

tans kept alive the remembrance of the sufferings of their forefathers, and inspired a warm attachment, both to the civil and the religious rights of human nature.

In the southern colonies, slavery nurtured a spirit of liberty, among the free inhabitants. All masters of slaves, who enjoy personal liberty, will be both proud and jealous of their freedom. It is, in their opinion, not only an enjoyment, but a kind of rank and privilege. In them, the haughtiness of domination combines with the spirit of liberty. Nothing could more effectually animate the opposition of a planter to the claims of Great Britain, than a conviction that those claims, in their extent, degraded him to a degree of dependence on his fellow-subjects, equally humiliating with that which existed between his slaves and himself.

"THEY LOOKED UP TO HEAVEN, AS THE SOURCE OF THEIR RIGHTS"

The state of society in the colonies favoured a spirit of liberty and independence. Their inhabitants were all of one rank. Kings, nobles, and bishops, were unknown among them. From their first settlement, the English provinces received impressions favourable to democratic forms of government. Their dependent situation forbade any inordinate ambition among their native sons, and the humility of their society, abstracted as they were from the splendor and amusements of the Old World, held forth few allurements to invite the residence of such from the mother country, as aspired to hereditary honours. In modern Europe, the remains of the feudal system have occasioned an order of men superior to that of the commonalty; but, as few of that class migrated to the colonies, they were settled with the yeomanry. Their inhabitants, unaccustomed to that distinction of ranks, which the policy of Europe has established, were strongly impressed with an opinion, that all men are by nature equal. They could not easily be persuaded, that their grants of land, or their civil rights, flowed from the munificence of princes. Many of them had never heard of magna charta, and those who knew the circumstances of the remarkable period of English history, when that was obtained, did not rest their claims to liberty and property on the transactions of that important day. They looked up to Heaven, as the source of their rights, and claimed, not from the promises of kings, but from the Parent of the universe.

435

GOD PREPARES
A CHRISTIAN
PEOPLE
TO ESTABLISH
THE AMERICAN
NATION

POLITICAL CREED OF AN AMERICAN

The political creed of an American colonist was short, but substantial. He believed that God made all mankind originally equal; that he endowed them with the rights of life, property, and as much liberty, as was consistent with the rights of others; that he had bestowed on his vast family of the human race, the earth for their support; and that all government was a political institution between men naturally equal, not for the aggrandizement of one, or a few, but for the general happiness of the whole community. Impressed with sentiments of this kind, they grew up, from their earliest infancy, with that confidence which is well calculated to inspire a love for liberty, and a prepossession in favour of independence.

COLONIES WERE COMMUNITIES
OF SEPARATE INDEPENDENT INDIVIDUALS

In consequence of the vast extent of vacant country, every colonist was, or easily might be, a freeholder. Settled on lands of his own, he was both a farmer and landlord. Producing all the necessaries of life from his own grounds, he felt himself both free and independent. Each individual might hunt, fish, or fowl, without injury to his neighbours. These immunities, which, in old countries, are guarded by the sanction of penal laws, and monopolized by a few, are the common privileges of all, in America. Colonists, growing up in the enjoyment of such rights, felt the restraint of law more feebly than they, who are educated in countries, where long habits have made submission familiar. The mind of man naturally relishes liberty; where, from the extent of a new and unsettled country, some abridgments thereof are useless, and others impracticable, the natural desire of freedom is strengthened, and the independent mind revolts at the idea of subjection.

The colonists were preserved from the contagion of ministerial influence, by their distance from the metropolis. Remote from the seat of power and corruption, they were not overawed by the one, nor debauched by the other. Few were the means of detaching individuals from the interest of the public. High offices were neither sufficiently numerous, nor lucrative, to purchase many adherents; and the most valuable of these were conferred on natives of Britain. Every man occupied that rank only, which his own industry, or that of his near ancestors, had procured him.

Each individual being cut off from all means of rising to importance, but by his personal talents, was encouraged to make the most of those, with which he was endowed. Prospects of this kind excited emulation, and produced an enterprising, laborious set of men, not easily overcome by difficulties, and full of projects for bettering their condition.

The enervating opulence of Europe had not yet reached the colonists. They were destitute of gold and silver, but abounded in the riches of nature. A sameness of circumstances and occupations created a great sense of equality, and disposed them to union in any common cause, from the success of which, they might expect to partake of equal advantages.

The colonies were communities of separate independent individuals, under no general influence, but that of their personal feelings and opinions. They were not led by powerful families, nor by great officers, in church or state. Residing chiefly on lands of their own, and employed in the wholesome labours of the field, they were, in a great measure, strangers to luxury. Their wants were few, and, among the great bulk of the people, for the most part, supplied from their own grounds. Their enjoyments were neither far-fetched, nor dearly purchased; and were so moderate in their kind, as to leave both mind and body unimpaired. Inured, from their early years, to the toils of a country life, they dwelt in the midst of rural plenty. Unacquainted with ideal wants, they delighted in personal independence. Removed from the pressures of indigence, and the indulgence of affluence, their bodies were strong, and their minds vigorous.

FARMERS

The great majority of the British colonists were farmers, or planters, who were also proprietors of the soil. The merchants, mechanics, and manufacturers, taken collectively, did not amount to one-fifteenth of the whole number of inhabitants. While the cultivators of the soil depend on nothing but heaven and their own industry, other classes of men contract more or less of servility, from depending on the caprice of their customers. The excess of the farmers, over the collective numbers of all the other inhabitants, gave a cast of independence to the manners of the people, and diffused the exalting sentiments, which have always predominated among those, who are cultivators of their own grounds. These were further promoted by their moderate

436

circumstances, which deprived them of all super-fluity for idleness, or effeminate indulgence.

PROVINCIAL CONSTITUTIONS

The provincial constitutions of the English colonies nurtured a spirit of liberty. The king and government of Great Britain held no patron-age in America, which could create a portion of attachment and influence, sufficient to counteract that spirit in popular assemblies, which, when left to itself, can ill brook any authority that inter-feres with its own.

The inhabitants of the colonies, from the be-ginning, especially in New England, enjoyed a government, which was but little short of being independent. They had not only the image, but the substance of the English constitution. They chose most of their magistrates, and paid them all. They had, in effect, the sole direction of their internal government. The chief mark of their subordination consisted, in making no laws re-pugnant to the laws of their mother country; their submitting such laws as they made, to be repealed by the king; and their obeying such re-strictions, as were laid on their trade, by parlia-ment. The latter were often evaded, and with impunity. The other small checks were scarcely felt, and, for a long time, were in no respect injurious to their interests.

Under these favorable circumstances, colonies in the New World had advanced nearly to the magnitude of a nation, while the greatest part of Europe was almost wholly ignorant of their progress. Some arbitrary proceedings of gover-nors, proprietary partialities, or democratical jealousies, now and then interrupted the political calm, which generally prevailed among them; but these, and other occasional disputes, soon sub-sided, without any other effect, than a more gen-eral diffusion of political knowledge, and a keener sense of the rights of man. The circumstances of the country afforded but little scope for the in-trigues of politicians, or the turbulence of dema-gogues. The colonists, being but remotely affected by the bustlings of the Old World, and having but a few objects of ambition or contention among themselves, were absorbed in the ordinary cares of domestic life, and, for a long time, ex-empted from a great proportion of those evils, which the governed too often experience, from the passions and follies of statesmen: but all this time they were rising higher, and, though not sensible of it, growing to a greater degree of political consequence.

The colonies, which now form the United States, may be considered as Europe transplanted. Ireland, England, Scotland, France, Germany, Holland, Switzerland, Sweden, Poland, and Italy, furnished the original stock of the present population, and are supposed to have contributed to it, in the order they are enumerated. The first settlers of the two first colonies, Virginia and Massachusetts, were chiefly from England. Their posterity are now of the seventh, eighth, or ninth generation. For the last seventy or eighty years, no nation has contributed so much to the popu-lation of America as Ireland. From it, there has been an annual stream of emigrants, directed to the country, now called the United States. The Hollanders settled New York and New Jersey, in the first half of the seventeenth century. The French Protestant refugees fled to America, in great numbers, from and after the revocation of the edict of Nantz, in 1685. The Germans, since 1730. The Swedes were among the most early settlers, near the river Delaware; but their num-ber was not great. The emigrants from Poland and Italy were inconsiderable. From the other European nations, which are not mentioned, there were few or none. The descendants of these respective nations have coalesced into one. They have generally dropped the language of their original countries; and in the second, or at the most the third generation, are divested of the peculiarities of the parent nation, and all par-tial attachments to it. Where whole settlements consisted of one species of emigrants, the dialect of their descendants, and some national peculiari-ties, have been more permanent. These original settlers were generally of the Reformed or Prot-estant religion. Maryland was first planted by Roman Catholics, and Virginia by members of the Church of England; but the other provinces, chiefly by Dissenters, or foreign Protestants. In Rhode Island, Pennsylvania, Delaware, and New Jersey, there never was any established religion. Roger Williams and William Penn, the found-ers of three of these colonies, had, in this early period, unusually correct ideas of religious lib-erty. Taught in the school of persecution, they appreciated the rights of private judgment. They discarded the word toleration, as a term, which, in its common acceptance, has no meaning among equal freemen: but having suffered, from the intolerance of others, without appearing to grant as a favour what was a matter of common right, they left the settlers, in the colonies which they

DAVID
RAMSAY:
PRELUDE TO
THE AMERICAN
REVOLUTION,
1765–1775

POLITICAL CREED
OF AN AMERICAN

437

GOD PREPARES
A CHRISTIAN
PEOPLE
TO ESTABLISH
THE AMERICAN
NATION

established, at full liberty to pursue their own ideas of religion, without any diminution of their natural or civil rights. In some of the provinces, legal provision was made for the support of the clergy, but on so limited a scale, as to be scarcely felt. The government of all the churches was little more than advisory; for it inflicted no civil penalties. Spiritual courts were harmless.

The civil government of all the provinces was so far republican, that, in every one of them, the assent of the people was indispensably necessary to acts of legislation. Neither royal nor proprietary governors, nor councils, could constitutionally pass any law, without their concurrence. The prerogatives of juries were the same, on the English and American sides of the Atlantic. The rights of British subjects, and the common law of England, were equally respected in both.

FISCAL HISTORY

The fiscal history of the provinces was very different from that of the parent state. In every period of time, and in every one of the colonies, there was a deficiency of gold and silver, for the necessary purposes of exchange. This resulted, in some degree, from their state of dependence, and the monopoly of their trade by Great Britain. The manufactures of the mother country were so much wanted in the colonies, that payments for the native commodities of the latter were seldom made in gold or silver; and the balance of trade was always against America. In addition to this natural necessity for bills of credit, there was superadded one that was artificial or political. In the various wars, between 1690 and 1763, in which Great Britain was engaged, the colonies, in general, took an active part. Their military operations would have been crippled, without paper credit; for all the real money, within their grasp, was far short of a sufficiency, for raising, paying, and supporting the armies they brought forward, in aid of the cause, which was common to the parent state and her colonies. On both accounts, there was an incessant call for paper money, or some domestic medium of circulation. Bills of credit were first authorized by Massachusetts, in the year 1690, to defray the expenses of an unsuccessful expedition, for the conquest of Canada; but they were issued, more or less, at successive periods, in several provinces; nor were they wholly discontinued, till about the year 1789, when the constitution of the United States prohibited all further emissions. The long experience the colonists had, of the possibility of

substituting paper for money, encouraged them to urge this expedient, in the revolutionary war, to a great extent. While paper money was the principal currency of America, its value was frequently varying. Where the quantity was small, and that punctually called in by taxes, very little depreciation took place. Under other circumstances, the paper bills lost much of their nominal value. Being made a legal tender, in payment of debts, they furnished opportunities for defrauding creditors. As the country was improving, and capital much wanted, paper bills of credit were, in many respects, useful; but when they were not well supported, or emitted in too great quantities, they proved a source of great injustice. A fondness for them kept up increasing contentions, between the governors and the assemblies; for the former were generally inimical to paper money, and the latter friendly to it. . . .

COLONIAL EDUCATION

Massachusetts, though not the first settled, was the first which made legislative provision for the education of youth. This was so effectually done, that, for the most part, on the death of the first literary emigrants, natives of the province were qualified to fill their places. After the lapse of sixty years, subsequent to the first settlement of Massachusetts, few men rose to any considerable distinction, either in church or state, but those who had been educated in New England. The first settlers were excited to foster literature, from their eager desire to furnish the means of fitting young men for the service of the church. Among their first settlers, were several who had been educated at the English universities, and who were possessed of all the learning of the times. Several of their early emigrant clergymen were men of considerable erudition. (One of them, president Chauncey, before his arrival in America, had been professor of Greek, in the university of Cambridge, in England.) A multitude of this description came over nearly together, in consequence of the act of uniformity, passed in 1662, when upwards of two thousand Puritan ministers were, in one day, ejected from their livings, in England. The learning, piety, and personal character of these, and the other clergymen in New England, gave them an ascendency over the minds of the laity. Their advice was frequently asked, by the ruling powers of the country: and few great changes in its policy were decided upon, before they were consulted. In the formation of new settlements, a minister and a meeting-house, or church, were essential appendages. Scarcely had the venerable founders of New England felled the trees of the forest, when they began to provide means to insure the stability of their colony. They wisely judged learning and religion to be the firmest pillars of the church and commonwealth. The legislature of Massachusetts, having previously founded a public school or college, in 1637, ordered that it be at Newtown, and appointed a committee, to carry the order into effect. The liberality of an individual contributed to the speedy completion of this wise and pious design. John Harvard, a worthy minister, left a legacy of nearly 800 £. to this infant seminary. In honour of him, it was named Harvard College: and Newtown, in compliment to the college, and in memory of the place, where many of the first settlers of New England received their education, was called Cambridge. In 1642, this first American college began to confer degrees.

In 1691, the general assembly of Virginia solicited, and obtained a charter from the crown, for the establishment of a college, in that colony. The king and queen gave, at the same time, nearly two thousand pounds towards the building, and endowed the seminary with twenty thousand acres of the best land, together with the perpetual revenue, arising from the duty of one penny per pound, on all tobacco transported from Virginia and Maryland, to the other English plantations. In grateful acknowledgment of the royal patronage and benefaction, the college was called William and Mary. The instruction of Indians was one of the objects of this institution. Before the establishment of William and Mary college, the learning of Virginia had been in a state of retrogradation. In the eighty-four years of settlement, which had preceded that establishment, most of the original emigrants, educated in England, had died. Their places were supplied by later emigrants, or a new race, born in a new country, in which the means of education had not been generally planted. Indeed, the ruling powers seem to have been averse to the encouragement of learning. . . .

The next college was established in Connecticut, and obtained its charter and endowments, in 1701. It was called Yale College, in honour of one of its principal benefactors. The principal motive that led to this establishment, was a desire of training up young men, for the ministry of the gospel.

A college, which began at Newark, New Jersey, was finally established at Princeton, in the

same state, and began to confer degrees, in 1748. The trustees proposed to call it Belcher Hall, in compliment to governor Belcher, who had been its friend and benefactor; but he declined the honour, and suggested the propriety of calling it Nassau Hall, commemorative of king William, prince of Orange and Nassau, the revolutionary deliverer of England from arbitrary power. To train up young men, for the service of the church, was a primary object of the founders of this institution. A charter, and permission to draw lotteries, were all the favours conferred on this college, by the province of New Jersey. It depended, for support, on private donations, and the ardent zeal of its founders, who were uncommonly active, in promoting its interests, as connected with the cause of religion, learning, and liberty.

Soon after the year 1750, two colleges were established, one in New York, and the other in Philadelphia.

A college was established at Rhode Island, in 1764, and, in five years after its foundation, it began to confer the higher degrees in the arts.

A college was established in New Hampshire, in 1769, which, in ten years, began to confer degrees. To this institution was given the name of Dartmouth College, in honour of lord Dartmouth, who had been its friend and benefactor. The instruction of Indians was one of the principal objects contemplated by the first patrons of this institution. English youths were educated with the Indians, that the latter might, by the example of the former, be allured to love learning and agriculture. Indians labour under a strong prejudice, that it is beneath the dignity of man to delve in the earth.

In addition to the colleges, founded prior to the revolution, there were grammar schools in every town of New England, and free schools established in the counties of Maryland, and parishes of South Carolina, by their respective legislatures; in all of which public aid was given to the contributions of private inhabitants, in support of literature.

Besides these literary institutions, fostered by government, there were several founded at different periods, either by religious societies, private donations, or by enterprising individuals. Of the first kind, one of the most useful, and which continues to this day, with undiminished reputation, was the Friends' school, in Philadelphia. This began in 1689, in the eighth year after the settlement of Pennsylvania. Its funds were furnished by Quakers, and its overseers were of that profession. Poor children were taught gratis;

DAVID
RAMSAY:
PRELUDE TO
THE AMERICAN
REVOLUTION,
1765–1775

COLONIAL
EDUCATION

GOD PREPARES
A CHRISTIAN
PEOPLE
TO ESTABLISH
THE AMERICAN
NATION

but others paid a moderate sum for instruction. The first master was George Keith. . . .

COLONIAL LITERATURE

Some of the early settlers of Virginia were learned men: but, with the exception of their Historians, Smith, Stith, Beverley, and Keith, either they have not published any literary works, or, if published, they are not generally known. The pens of Virginians were used much to the benefit of their fellow-colonists, in the twelve years of paper war, that preceded the revolution. Their memorials, remonstrances, and other public acts, in vindication of their rights, were executed in a masterly manner. In addition to these official papers, there were sundry valuable pamphlets published, on the great question of American taxation, particularly "An Enquiry into the Rights of the British Colonies," by Richard Bland, in 1776; "The Monitor's Letters," by Dr. Arthur Lee, in 1769; "A Summary View of the Rights of British America," by Thomas Jefferson, in 1774; "Considerations, &c." by Robert Carter Nicholas, about the same time.

The controversy was, in like manner, ably supported by the New England writers, both in and out of the legislature. They had a much more subtle opponent, in governor Hutchinson, to contend with, than the shallow minions, who represented king George, in most of the other provinces. Theology boasts of her Edwards, and Philosophy of her Franklin, about the middle of the eighteenth century. The first volume of the transactions of the American Philosophical Society, held at Philadelphia, is the only work of general literature, produced in the colonies, prior to their revolution. Anterior to that event, the few philosophers in English America, published their ordinary lucubrations, in the newspapers of the country; and, such as were of a higher grade, through the medium of the Royal Society of London. Fourteen Americans, namely, four of the name of Winthrop, Paul Dudley, President Leverett, Thomas Brattle, Cotton Mather, Benjamin Franklin, doctors Boylston, Mitchel, Morgan, Garden, and Rittenhouse, were admitted members of that society, in the colonial state of their country. These, with Morton, of Plymouth, Clayton, of Virginia, Bartram and Logan, of Pennsylvania, Colden, of New York, Brownrigg, of North Carolina, and Lining, of South Carolina, transmitted papers on philosophical subjects, which were read and published by that society, before the revolution. For more than a century after the first settlement of the colonies, such of their inhabitants, as were devoted to literature, gave an undue proportion of their time to the study of languages. Several of the early settlers of New England were well skilled in Latin, Greek, and Hebrew; and a few in the oriental languages. Their ministers excelled in knowledge of the Holy Scriptures, and all branches of Biblical learning, and wrote well on theological subjects.

In most of the middle and southern colonies, the lawyers and planters took the lead, as writers; but in New England, the clergy were their principal historians and public writers. To particularize them all, at the distance of Charleston, S.C. with all the assistance which public and private libraries afford, would be impossible. . . .

NEW ENGLAND CLERGY

The indelibility of the clerical character was, at no time, the creed of New England men. The versatility of the talents of these enterprising people, in all cases remarkable, has been particularly so, in the case of clergymen, who, from particular reasons, laid aside their clerical character. Several such attained to high eminence, as statesmen. One instance deserves particular notice. Elisha Williams, who had been a preacher, and a publisher of theological works, and president of Yale college for several years, after resigning these offices, became colonel of a regiment of regular troops, raised for the reduction of Canada; speaker of the house of representatives; and a provincial agent, at the court of Great Britain. He discharged his duty, in all these capacities, with credit to himself, and greatly to the satisfaction and advantage of his country.

In New England, from its first settlement, public business was generally introduced with a sermon. Their frequent fast and thanksgiving days, their ordinations, elections, the meetings of their general courts, and other public occasions, gave birth to an infinity of discourses, which were afterwards printed. These frequent calls for popular addresses made the art of composition, to meet both the public eye and ear, a common study, and diffused a taste for literature. At the same time, their regular devotional exercises on Sundays kept their minds under the constant influence of religious impressions. The New Englanders entered upon the revolution, with tongues and pens prepared to justify their measures, as well as with swords, to defend them. The popular leaders, in consequence of this general illumination, were enabled to carry along with them the people, fully convinced of the rectitude of the measures adopted by their common councils. . . .

FRANCE OR ENGLAND IN NEW WORLD

Till the year 1758, or rather 1759, it seemed doubtful whether France or England should have the ascendency in the New World; and, in particular, whether the British should not be confined to a narrow slip of land, on the shores of the Atlantic. The superior population and wealth of the English colonies, and the immense superiority of the British navy over that of France, and particularly the energy of Pitt's administration, turned the scales in favour of England. Great joy was diffused throughout the British dominions: but in no place was it felt, in a higher degree, or with greater reason, than in America. For one hundred and fifty years, France and England had been contending for American territory, and for the last half of that period, almost incessantly. Neither knew the precise extent of their boundaries; but both were willing to enlarge them. They possessed much, but coveted more. Neither was backward to make encroachments on the other; and both were prompt to repel them, when made, or supposed to be made, on themselves. Throughout this period, especially the last half of it, in addition to the unavoidable calamities of war, indiscriminate massacres had been so frequently and extensively committed, on numerous settlers, dispersed over many hundred miles of exposed frontier, that it has been supposed, that the British colonies lost not less than twenty thousand inhabitants. War assumed a most terrific aspect among the colonists. Not confined to men in arms, as is common in Europe, aged persons, women, and children were frequently its victims. The Tomahawk and scalping knife, carried to the fire sides of peaceable helpless families, were applied promiscuously to every age and sex. It was hoped, that the reduction of Canada would close these horrid scenes forever, with respect to the northern and middle colonies. As the Indians could in future derive supplies from none but the English, and as they would no longer be exposed to the seduction of French influence; it was confidently expected, that they would desist from their depredations, and leave the colonists to pursue their own happiness. This was in a great measure the case, for about twelve years after the peace of Paris, in 1763. At the end of that period, a new war, on new principles, commenced, in which,

the same ground was fought over, and the same posts were contended for, by new parties. The Indians were again called in as auxiliaries, and encouraged to the same horrid scenes of devastation and murder, from which, the colonists had fondly hoped, that the conquest of Canada had forever delivered them. . . .

One hundred and fifty-six years had passed away, between the first permanent British establishment, in North America, and the conquest of Canada. In a considerable portion of that period, the three greatest naval powers of Europe, England, France, and Spain, had been incessantly contending for the same American Territory. The boundaries of the colonies, which now form the United States, were subjects of controversy, on every side, except where nature's highway, the ocean, precluded all ideas of appropriation. Ignorance of American geography laid the foundation for disputes, respecting the boundaries of adjoining provinces, though granted by the same sovereign; and, still more so, respecting the extent of territory, claimed by different nations. The former might be adjusted in civil courts; but the latter, where there was no common umpire, to whom an appeal could be made, were generally referred to the decision of the sword. For seventy years, wars had succeeded wars, without settling any of the points in controversy. At length a great and decisive effort took place, in which a complete trial of strength was made, by the naval powers. The law of war decided differently, from the new law of nations, in favour of prior occupants: the sword settled all claims of territory, in such a manner, that the English, who were the last occupiers of a part, became the sole possessors of almost the whole North American continent, to the exclusion of their vanquished rivals, who had a prior possession of its northern and southern extremities.

PROVINCES INSTRUMENTS OF COMMERCE

From the first settlement of English America till the close of the war of 1755, the general conduct of Great Britain towards her colonies affords an useful lesson to those who are disposed to colonization. From that era, it is equally worthy of the attention of those who wish for the reduction of great empires to small ones. In the first period, Great Britain regarded the provinces as instruments of commerce. Without charging herself with the care of their internal police, or seeking a revenue from them, she contented herself with a monopoly of their trade.

DAVID
RAMSAY:
PRELUDE TO
THE AMERICAN
REVOLUTION,
1765–1775

NEW ENGLAND
CLERGY

GOD PREPARES
A CHRISTIAN
PEOPLE
TO ESTABLISH
THE AMERICAN
NATION

She treated them as a judicious mother does her dutiful children. They shared in every privilege belonging to her native sons, and but slightly felt the inconveniences of subordination. Small was the catalogue of grievances, with which even democratical jealousy charged the parent state, antecedent to the period before mentioned.

Till the year 1764, the colonial regulations seemed to have no other object, but the common good of the whole empire. Exceptions, to the contrary, were few, and had no appearance of system. When the approach of the colonies to manhood made them more capable of resisting impositions, Great Britain changed the ancient system, under which her colonies had long flourished. When policy would rather have dictated a relaxation of authority, she rose in her demands, and multiplied her restraints.

From the conquest of Canada, in 1760, some have supposed, that France began secretly to lay schemes, for wrestling those colonies from Great Britain, which she was not able to conquer. Others allege, that from that period, the colonists, released from all fears of dangerous neighbours, fixed their eyes on independence, and took sundry steps, preparatory to the adoption of that measure. Without recurring to either of these opinions, the known selfishness of human nature is sufficient to account for that demand on the one side, and that refusal on the other, which occasioned the revolution. It was natural for Great Britain, to wish for an extension of her authority over the colonies, and equally so for them, on their approach to maturity, to be more impatient of subordination, and to resist every innovation, for increasing the degree of their dependence.

COLONIAL OPPRESSION COMMENCED BY SUBJECTING THEM TO TAXATION

The sad story of colonial oppression commenced in the year 1764. Great Britain, then, adopted new regulations, respecting her colonies, which, after disturbing the ancient harmony of the two countries, for about twelve years, terminated in a dismemberment of the empire.

These consisted in restricting their former commerce, but more especially in subjecting them to taxation, by the British parliament. By adhering to the spirit of her navigation act, in the course of a century, the trade of Great Britain had increased far beyond the expectation of her most sanguine sons; but by rigidly enforcing the strict letter of the same, in a different situation

of public affairs, effects, directly the reverse, were produced. From the enterprising commercial spirit of the colonists, the trade of America, after filling all its proper channels to the brim, swelled out on every side, and overflowed its proper banks, with a rich redundance.

In the cure of evils, which are closely connected with the causes of national prosperity, vulgar precaution ought not to be employed. In severely checking a contraband trade, which was only the overflowing of an extensive fair trade, the remedy was worse than the disease.

For some time before and after the termination of the war of 1755, a considerable intercourse had been carried on between the British and Spanish colonies, consisting of the manufactures of Great Britain, imported by the former, and sold to the latter, by which the British colonies acquired gold and silver, and were enabled to make remittances to the mother country. This trade, though it did not clash with the spirit of the British navigation laws, was forbidden by their letter. On account of the advantages, which all parties, and particularly Great Britain, reaped from this intercourse, it had long been winked at, by persons in power; but, at the period before mentioned, some new regulations were adopted, by which it was almost destroyed. This was effected by armed cutters, whose commanders were enjoined to take the usual customhouse oaths, and to act in the capacity of revenue officers. So sudden a stoppage of an accustomed and beneficial commerce, by an unusually rigid execution of old laws, was a serious blow to the northern colonies. It was their misfortune, that, though they stood in need of vast quantities of British manufactures, their country produced very little, that afforded a direct remittance, to pay for them. They were, therefore, under a necessity of seeking, elsewhere, a market for their produce, and, by a circuitous route, acquiring the means of supporting their credit, with the mother country. This they found, by trading with the Spanish and French colonies, in their neighbourhood. From them they acquired gold, silver, and valuable commodities, the ultimate profits of which centered in Great Britain. This intercourse gave life to business of every denomination, and established a reciprocal circulation of money and merchandise, to the benefit of all parties concerned. Why a trade, essential to the colonies, and which, so far from being detrimental, was indirectly advantageous to Great Britain, should be so narrowly watched, and so severely restrained, was not obvious to the Americans.

Instead of viewing the parent state, as formerly, in the light of an affectionate mother, they conceived her, as beginning to be influenced by the narrow views of an illiberal stepdame.

FIRST ACT OF REVENUE

In 1764, the trade between the British, and the French and Spanish colonies, was in some degree legalized, but under circumstances, that brought no relief to the colonists; for it was loaded with such enormous duties, as were equivalent to a prohibition. It was also enacted, that the monies, arising from these duties, should be paid into the receipt of his majesty's exchequer, there to be entered separately, and reserved, to be disposed of by parliament, towards defraying the necessary expenses of defending, protecting, and securing America. Till that act passed, no act avowedly for the purpose of revenue, and with the ordinary title and recital of such, was to be found in the parliamentary statute book. The wording of it made the colonists fear, that the parliament would go on, in charging them with such taxes, as they pleased, and for the support of such military force, as they should think proper. The act was the more disgusting, because the monies, arising from it, were ordered to be paid in specie, and regulations were adopted against colonial paper money. To obstruct the avenues of acquiring gold and silver, and, at the same time, to interdict the use of paper money, appeared to the colonists as a further evidence, that their interests were either misunderstood, or disregarded. The imposition of duties, for the purpose of raising a revenue, in America, was considered as a dangerous innovation; but the methods adopted, for securing their collection, were resented as arbitrary and unconstitutional. It was enacted by parliament, that, whenever offences should be committed against the acts, which imposed them, the prosecutor might bring his action for the penalty, in the courts of admiralty; by which means the defendant lost the advantage of being tried by a jury, and was subjected to the necessity of having his case decided upon, by a single man, a creature of the crown, whose salary was to be paid out of forfeitures, adjudged by himself; and, also, according to a course of law, which exempted the prosecutor from the trouble of proving his accusation, and obliged the defendant, either to evince his innocence, or to suffer. By these regulations, the guards, which the constitution had placed round property, and the fences, which the ancestors of both countries had erected, against arbitrary power, were thrown down, as far as they concerned the colonists, charged with violating the laws for raising a revenue in America.

They who directed public affairs in Great Britain feared, that, if the collection of these duties were enforced, only in the customary way, payment would be often eluded. To obviate that disposition which the colonists discovered to screen one another, in disobeying offensive acts of parliament, regulations were adopted, bearing hard on their constitutional rights. Unwilling as the colonists were to be excluded, by the imposition of enormous duties, from an accustomed and beneficial line of business, it is not wonderful that they were disposed to represent these innovations of the mother country, in the most unfavourable point of view. The heavy losses, to which many individuals were subjected, and the general distress of the mercantile interest, in several of the oldest colonies, soured the minds of many. That the mother country should infringe her own constitution, to cramp the commerce of her colonies, was a fruitful subject of declamation: but these murmurings would have evaporated in words, had Great Britain proceeded to no further innovations. Instead of this, she adopted the novel idea of raising from the colonies, an efficient revenue, by direct internal taxes, laid by authority of her parliament.

Though all the colonies disrelished, and many, from the pressure of actual sufferings, complained of the British restrictions on their manufactures and commerce, yet a great majority was disposed to submit to both. Most of them acknowledged, that the exercise of these powers was incident to the sovereignty of the mother country; especially when guarded by an implied contract, that they were to be only used for the common benefit of the empire. It was generally allowed, that, as the planting of colonies was not designed to erect an independent government, but to extend an old one, the parent state had a right to restrain their trade in every way, which conduced to the common emolument.

They, for the most part, considered the mother country authorized to name ports and nations, to which alone their merchandise should be carried, and with which alone they should trade: but the novel claim, of taxing them without their consent, was universally reprobated, as contrary to their natural, chartered, and constitutional rights. In opposition to it, they not only alleged the general principles of liberty, but ancient usage. During the first hundred and fifty years of their existence,

GOD PREPARES
A CHRISTIAN
PEOPLE
TO ESTABLISH
THE AMERICAN
NATION

they had been left to tax themselves, and in their own way. If there were any exceptions to this general rule, they were too inconsiderable to merit notice. In the war of 1755, the events of which were fresh in the recollection of every one, the parliament had in no instance attempted to raise either men or money in the colonies, by its own authority. As the claim of taxation on one side, and the refusal of it on the other, were the very hinges on which the revolution turned, they merit a particular discussion.

Colonies were formerly planted by warlike nations, to keep their enemies in awe, to give vent to a surplus of inhabitants, or to discharge a number of discontented and troublesome citizens: but in modern ages, the spirit of violence being in some measure sheathed in commerce, colonies have been settled, by the nations of Europe, for the purposes of trade. These were to be attained by their raising, for the mother country, such commodities as she did not produce, and supply themselves from her with such things as they wanted. In subserviency to these views, Great Britain planted colonies, and made laws, obliging them to carry to her, all their products which she wanted, and all their raw materials which she chose to work up. Besides this restriction, she forbade them to procure manufactures from any other part of the globe, or even the products of European countries, which could rival her, without being first brought to her ports. By a variety of ways, she regulated their trade, in such a manner, as was thought most conducive to their mutual advantage, and her own particular welfare.

This principle of commercial monopoly ran through no less than twenty-nine acts of parliament, from 1660, to 1764. In all these acts, the system of commerce was established, as that from which, alone, their contributions to the strength of the empire were expected. During this whole period, a parliamentary revenue was no part of the object of colonization. Accordingly, in all the laws which regarded them, the technical words of revenue laws were avoided. Such have usually a title, purporting their being "grants," and the words, "give and grant," usually precede their enacting clauses. Although duties were imposed on America, by previous acts of parliament, no one title of "giving an aid to his majesty," or any other of the usual titles to revenue acts, was to be found in any of them. They were intended as regulations of trade, and not as sources of national supplies.

Till the year 1764, all stood on commercial regulation and restraint.

VALUE OF AMERICAN TRADE

While Great Britain attended to this first system of colonization, her American settlements, though exposed in unknown climates, and unexplored wildernesses, grew and flourished; and in the same proportion the trade and riches of the mother country increased. Some estimate may be made of this increase, from the following statement. The whole export trade of England, including that to the colonies, in the year 1704, amounted to 6,509,000£ sterling: but so immensely had the colonies increased, that the exports to them alone, in the year 1772, amounted to 6,022,132£ sterling, and they were yearly increasing. In the short space of sixty-eight years, the colonies added nearly as much to the export commerce of Great Britain, as she had grown to, by a progressive increase of improvement, in seventeen hundred years. And this increase of colonial trade was not at the expense of the general trade of the kingdom; for that increased, in the same time, from six millions to sixteen. . . .

RIGHT OF SUBJECTS TO GRANT
OR WITHHOLD TAXES

Immediately after the peace of Paris, 1763, a new scene was opened. The national debt of Great Britain then amounted to one hundred and forty-eight millions, for which an interest of nearly five millions was annually paid. While the British minister was digesting plans, for diminishing this amazing load of debt, he conceived the idea of raising a substantial revenue in the British colonies, from taxes laid by the parliament of the parent state. On the one hand it was urged, that the late war originated on account of the colonies; and that it was reasonable, more especially as it had terminated in a manner so favourable to their interest, that they should contribute to defraying the expenses it had occasioned. Thus far both parties were agreed; but Great Britain contended, that her parliament, as the supreme power, was constitutionally vested with an authority to lay them on every part of the empire. This doctrine, plausible in itself, and conformable to the letter of the British constitution, when the whole dominions were represented in one assembly, was reprobated in the colonies, as contrary to the spirit of the same government, when the empire became so far extended, as to have many distinct representative assemblies. The colonists believed, that the chief excellence of the British constitution consisted in the right of the subjects to grant, or withhold taxes; and in their having a share in enacting the laws, by which they were to be bound.

They conceived, that the superiority of the British constitution, to other forms of government, was, not that their supreme council was called parliament, but that the people had a share in it, by appointing members, who constituted one of its constituent branches, and without whose concurrence, no law, binding on them, could be enacted. In the mother country, it was asserted to be essential to the unity of the empire, that the British parliament should have a right of taxation, over every part of the royal dominions. In the colonies, it was believed, that taxation and representation were inseparable; and that they could neither be free nor happy, if their property could be taken from them, without their consent.

The common people in America reasoned on this subject, in a summary way: "If a British parliament," said they, "in which we are unrepresented, and over which we have no control, can take from us any part of our property, by direct taxation, they may take as much as they please; and we have no security for any thing that remains, but a forbearance on their part, less likely to be exercised in our favour, as they lighten themselves of the burdens of government, in the same proportion that they impose them on us." They well knew, that communities of mankind, as well as individuals, have a strong propensity to impose on others, when they can do it with impunity; and especially when there is a prospect, that the imposition will be attended with advantage to themselves. The Americans, from that jealousy of their liberties, which their local situation nurtured, and which they inherited from their forefathers, viewed the exclusive right of laying taxes on themselves, free from extraneous influence, in the same light, as the British parliament views its peculiar privilege of raising money, independent of the crown. The parent state appeared, to the colonists, to stand in the same relation to their local legislatures, as the monarch of Great Britain to the British parliament. His prerogative is limited by that palladium of the people's liberty, the exclusive privilege of granting their own money. While this right rests in the hands of the people, their liberties are secured. In the same manner reasoned the colonists: "In order to be styled freemen, our local assemblies, elected by ourselves, must enjoy the exclusive privilege of imposing taxes upon us." They contended, that

men settled in foreign parts, to better their condition, not to submit their liberties; to continue the equals, not to become the slaves of their less adventurous fellow-citizens; and that, by the novel doctrine of parliamentary power, they were degraded from being the subjects of a king, to the low condition of being subjects of subjects. They argued, that it was essentially involved in the idea of property, that the possessor had such a right therein, that it was a contradiction to suppose any other man, or body of men, possessed a right to take it from him, without his consent. Precedents in the history of England justified this mode of reasoning. The love of property strengthened it; and it had a peculiar force on the minds of colonists, three thousand miles removed from the seat of government, and growing up to maturity, in a New World, where, from the extent of country, and the state of society, even the necessary restraints of civil government were impatiently borne.

ATTITUDE OF PEOPLE OF GREAT BRITAIN

On the other hand, the people of Great Britain revolted against the claims of the colonists. Educated in habits of submission to parliamentary taxation, they conceived it to be the height of contumacy, for the colonists to refuse obedience to the power, which they had been taught to revere. Not adverting to the common interest, which existed between the people of Great Britain and their representatives, they believed, that the said community of interests was wanting. The pride of an opulent, conquering nation, aided this mode of reasoning. "What!" said they, "shall we, who have so lately humbled France and Spain, be dictated to by our own colonists? Shall our subjects, educated by our care, and defended by our arms, presume to question the rights of parliament, to which we are obliged to submit?" Reflections of this kind, congenial to the natural vanity of the human heart, operated so extensively, that the people of Great Britain spoke of their colonies and of their colonists, as of a kind of possession annexed to their persons. The love of power, and of property, on the one side of the Atlantic, were opposed by the same powerful passions on the other.

The disposition to tax the colonies was also strengthened, by exaggerated accounts of their wealth. It was said, "that the American planters lived in affluence, and with inconsiderable taxes; while the inhabitants of Great Britain were borne down, by such oppressive burdens, as to make a

GOD PREPARES
A CHRISTIAN
PEOPLE
TO ESTABLISH
THE AMERICAN
NATION

bare subsistence, a matter of extreme difficulty." The officers who had served in America, during the late war, contributed to this delusion. Their observations were founded on what they had seen in cities, and at a time, when large sums were spent by government, in support of fleets and armies, and when American commodities were in great demand. To treat with attention those, who came to fight for them, and also to gratify their own pride, the colonists had made a parade of their riches, by frequently and sumptuously entertaining the gentlemen of the British army. These, judging from what they saw, without considering the general state of the country, concurred in representing the colonists, as very able to contribute, largely, towards defraying the common expenses of the empire.

A GREAT CONSTITUTIONAL QUESTION

The charters, which were supposed to contain the principles on which the colonies were founded, became the subject of serious investigation on both sides. One clause was found to run through the whole of them, except that which had been granted to Mr. Penn. This was a declaration, "that the emigrants to America should enjoy the same privileges, as if they had remained, or had been born within the realm;" but such was the subtilty of disputants, that both parties construed this general principle, so as to favour their respective opinions. The American patriots contended, that as English freeholders could not be taxed, but by representatives, in choosing whom, they had a vote, neither could the colonists: but it was replied, that, if the colonists had remained in England, they must have been bound to pay the taxes, imposed by parliament. It was therefore inferred, that, though taxed by that authority, they lost none of the rights of native Englishmen, residing at home. The partizans of the mother country could see nothing in charters, but security against taxes, by royal authority. The Americans, adhering to the spirit more than to the letter, viewed their charters as a shield against all taxes, not imposed by representatives of their own choice. This construction they contended to be expressly recognised by the charter of Maryland. In that, king Charles bound both himself and his successors, not to assent to any bill, subjecting the inhabitants to internal taxation, by external legislation.

The nature and extent of the connection between Great Britain and America, was a great constitutional question, involving many interests, and the general principles of civil liberty. To decide this, recourse was, in vain, had to parchment authorities, made at a distant time; when neither the grantor, nor grantees, of American territory, had in contemplation, any thing like the present state of the two countries.

Great and flourishing colonies, daily increasing in numbers, and already grown to the magnitude of a nation, planted at an immense distance, and governed by constitutions, resembling that of the country from which they sprung, were novelties in the history of the world. To combine colonies, so circumstanced, in one uniform system of government, with the parent state, required a great knowledge of mankind, and an extensive comprehension of things. It was an arduous business, far beyond the grasp of ordinary statesmen, whose minds were narrowed by the formalities of law, or the trammels of office. An original genius, unfettered with precedents, and exalted with just ideas of the rights of human nature, and the obligations of universal benevolence, might have struck out a middle line, which would have secured as much liberty to the colonies, and as great a degree of supremacy to the parent state, as their common good required: but the helm of Great Britain was not in such hands. The spirit of the British constitution, on the one hand, revolted at the idea, that the British parliament should exercise the same unlimited authority over the unrepresented colonies, which it exercised over the inhabitants of Great Britain. The colonists, on the other hand, did not claim a total exemption from its authority. They in general allowed the mother country a certain undefined prerogative over them, and acquiesced in the right of parliament, to make many acts, binding them in many subjects of internal policy, and regulating their trade. Where parliamentary supremacy ended, and at what point colonial independency began, was not ascertained. Happy would it have been, had the question never been agitated; but much more so, had it been compromised by an amicable compact, without the horrors of a civil war.

The English colonies were originally established on the principles of a commercial monopoly. While England pursued trade, her commerce increased at least four fold. The colonies took the manufactures of Great Britain, and paid for them with provisions, or raw materials. They united their arms in war, their commerce and their councils in peace, without nicely investigating the terms on which the connection of the two countries depended.

A perfect calm in the political world is not

long to be expected. The reciprocal happiness, both of Great Britain and of the colonies, was too great to be of long duration. The calamities of the war, of 1755, had scarcely ended, when the germ of another war was planted, which soon grew up and produced deadly fruit.

At that time, sundry resolutions passed the British parliament, relative to the imposition of a stamp duty in America, which gave a general alarm. By them the right, the equity, the policy, and even the necessity of taxing the colonies, was formally avowed. These resolutions being considered as the preface of a system of American revenue, were deemed an introduction to evils of much greater magnitude. They opened a prospect of oppression, boundless in extent, and endless in duration. They were nevertheless not immediately followed by any legislative act. Time, and an invitation, were given to the Americans, to suggest any other mode of taxation, that might be equivalent in its produce to the stamp act: but they objected, not only to the mode, but the principle; and several of their assemblies, though in vain, petitioned against it. An American revenue was, in England, a very popular measure. The cry in favour of it was so strong, as to silence the voice of petitions to the contrary. The equity of compelling the Americans, to contribute to the common expenses of the empire, satisfied many, who, without inquiring into the policy or justice of taxing their unrepresented fellow-subjects, readily assented to the measures adopted by the parliament, for this purpose. The prospect of easing their own burdens, at the expense of the colonists, dazzled the eyes of gentlemen of landed interest, so as to keep out of their view the probable consequences of the innovation.

STAMP ACT, 1765,
THE REACTION OF AMERICA

The omnipotence of parliament was so familiar a phrase, on both sides of the Atlantic, that few in America, and still fewer in Great Britain, were impressed, in the first instance, with any idea of the illegality of taxing the colonists.

Illumination on that subject was gradual. The resolutions in favour of an American stamp act, which passed in March, 1764, met with no opposition. In the course of the year, which intervened between these resolutions, and the passing of a law grounded upon them, the subject was better understood, and constitutional objections against the measure, were urged by several, both in Great Britain and America. This astonished

and chagrined the British ministry: but as the principle of taxing America had been, for some time, determined upon, they were unwilling to give it up.

Impelled by partiality for a long cherished idea, Mr. Grenville, in March 1765, brought into the house of commons his long-expected bill, for laying a stamp duty in America. By this, after passing through the useful forms, it was enacted, that the instruments of writing, in daily use among a commercial people, should be null and void, unless they were executed on stamped paper or parchment, charged with a duty imposed by the British parliament. . . .

The bill met with no opposition in the house of Lords; and, on the 22nd of March, 1765, it received the royal assent. The
night after it passed, Dr.   March 22, 1765
Franklin wrote to Mr. Charles
Thomson; "The sun of liberty is set; you must light up the candles of industry and economy." Mr. Thomson answered: "I was apprehensive, that other lights would be the consequence;" and he foretold the opposition which shortly took place. On its being suggested from authority, that the stamp officers would not be sent from Great Britain, but selected from among the Americans, the colony agents were desired to point out proper persons for the purpose. They generally nominated their friends, which affords a presumptive proof, that they supposed the act would have gone down. In this opinion, they were far from being singular. That the colonists would be, ultimately, obliged to submit to the stamp act, was at first commonly believed, both in England and America. The framers of it, in particular, flattered themselves, that the confusion, which would arise upon the disuse of writings, and the insecurity of property, which would result from using any other than that required by law, would compel the colonies, however reluctant, to use the stamp paper, and consequently to pay the taxes imposed thereon. They, therefore, boasted that it was a law, which would execute itself. By the term of the stamp act, it was not to take effect till the first day of November; a period of more than seven months after its passing. This gave the colonists an opportunity for leisurely canvassing the new subject, and examining it fully on every side. In the first part of this interval, struck with astonishment, they lay
in silent consternation, and could   May 29, 1765
not determine what course to
pursue. By degrees, they recovered their recollection. Virginia led the way in opposition to the

GOD PREPARES
A CHRISTIAN
PEOPLE
TO ESTABLISH
THE AMERICAN
NATION

stamp act. Mr. Patrick Henry, on the 29th of May, 1765, brought into the house of burgesses of that colony, . . . resolutions, which were substantially adopted. . . .

The countenance of so respectable a colony, as Virginia, confirmed the wavering, and emboldened the timid. Opposition to the stamp act, from that period, assumed a bolder face. The fire of liberty blazed forth from the press. Some well-judged publications set the rights of the colonists, in a plain, but strong point of view. The tongues and the pens of the well-informed citizens laboured in kindling the latent sparks of patriotism. The flame spread from breast to breast, till the conflagration became general. In this business, New England had a principal share. . . .

NEWSPAPERS

It was fortunate for the liberties of America, that newspapers were the subject of a heavy stamp duty. Printers, when uninfluenced by government, have generally arranged themselves on the side of liberty, nor are they less remarkable for attention to the profits of their profession. A stamp duty, which openly invaded the first, and threatened a diminution of the last, provoked their united zealous opposition. They daily presented to the public, original dissertations, tending to prove, that, if the stamp act were suffered to operate, the liberties of America were at an end, and their property virtually transferred, to their trans-Atlantic fellow-subjects. The writers among the Americans, seriously alarmed for the fate of their country, came forward with essays, to prove, that, agreeably to the British constitution, taxation and representation were inseparable; that the only constitutional mode of raising money, from the colonists, was by acts of their own legislatures; that the crown possessed no further power, than that of requisition; and that the parliamentary right of taxation was confined to the mother country, where it originated from the natural right of man, to do what he pleased with his own, transferred by consent from the electors of Great Britain, to those whom they chose to represent them in parliament. They also insisted much on the misapplication of public money, by the British ministry. Great pains were taken, to inform the colonists, of the large sums, annually bestowed on pensioned favourites, and for the various purposes of bribery. Their passions were inflamed, by high coloured representations of the hardship of being obliged to pay the earnings of their industry, into a British treasury,

well known to be a fund for corruption. The writers on the American side were opposed by arguments, drawn from the unity of the empire; the necessity of one supreme head; the unlimited power of parliament; and the great numbers in the mother country, who, though legally disqualified from voting at elections, were nevertheless bound to pay the taxes, imposed by the representatives of the nation. To these objections it was replied, that the very idea of subordination of parts excluded the notion of simple undivided unity; that, as England was the head, she could not be the head and the members too; that, in all extensive empires, where the dead uniformity of servitude did not prevent, the subordinate parts had many local privileges and immunities; that, between these privileges and the supreme common authority, the line was extremely nice; and that, nevertheless, the supremacy of the head had an ample field of exercise, without arrogating to itself the disposal of the property of the unrepresented subordinate parts.

To the assertion, that the power of parliament was unlimited, the colonists replied, that before it could constitutionally exercise that power, it must be constitutionally formed; and that, therefore, it must at least, in one of its branches, be constituted by the people, over whom it exercised unlimited power; that, with respect to Great Britain, it was so constituted; and with respect to America, it was not. They therefore inferred, that its power ought not to be the same over both countries. They argued also, that the delegation of the people was the source of power, in regard to taxation; and, as that delegation was wanting in America, they concluded the right of parliament, to grant away their property, could not exist; and that the defective representation in Great Britain, should be urged as an argument for taxing the Americans, without any representation at all, proved the encroaching nature of power. Instead of convincing the colonists of the propriety of their submission, it demonstrated the wisdom of their resistance; for, said they, "one invasion of natural right is made the justification of another, much more injurious and oppressive."

The advocates for parliamentary taxation, laid great stress on the rights supposed to have accrued to Great Britain, on the score of her having reared up and protected the English settlements, in America, at great expense. It was, on the other hand, contended by the colonists, that, in all the wars which were common to both countries, they had taken their full share; but in all their own dangers, in all the difficulties belonging separately to their situation, which did not immediately concern Great Britain, they were left to themselves, and had to struggle through a hard infancy; and, in particular, to defend themselves, without any aid from the parent state, against the numerous savages in their vicinity; that, when France had made war upon them, it was not on their own account, but as appendages to Great Britain; that, confining their trade for the exclusive benefit of the parent state, was an ample compensation for her protection, and a sufficient equivalent for their exemption from parliamentary taxation; and that the taxes imposed on the inhabitants of Great Britain, were incorporated with their manufactures, and ultimately fell on the colonists, who were the consumers.

The advocates, for the stamp act, also contended, that, as the parliament was charged with the defence of the colonies, it ought to possess the means of defraying the expenses incurred thereby. The same argument had been used by king Charles the first, in support of ship-money; and it was now answered in the same manner, as it was by the patriots of that day; "that the people, who were defended or protected, were the fittest to judge of and to provide the means of defraying the expenses incurred on that account." In the mean time, the minds of the Americans underwent a total transformation. Instead of their late peaceable and steady attachment to the British nation, they were daily advancing to the opposite extreme. The people, especially in the large cities, became riotous, insulted the persons, and destroyed the property of such as were known or supposed to be friendly to the stamp act. The mob were the visible agents, in these disorderly proceedings; but they were encouraged by persons of rank and character.

As opportunities offered, the assemblies generally passed resolutions, asserting their exclusive right, to lay taxes on their constituents. The people, in their town meetings, instructed their representatives to oppose the stamp act. . . .

STAMP ACT CONGRESS, OCTOBER 1765

The expediency of calling a continental congress, to be composed of deputies from each of the provinces, had early occurred to the people of Massachusetts. The assembly of that province passed a resolution in favour of that measure, and fixed on New York as the place, and the second Tuesday of October, 1765, as the time, for holding the same. They sent circular letters to the speakers of the several assemblies, requesting

their concurrence. This first advance towards continental union was seconded in South Carolina, before it had been agreed to by any colony to the southward of New England. The example of this province had a considerable influence, in recommending the measure to others, divided in their opinions, as to its propriety.

The assemblies of Virginia, North Carolina, and Georgia, were prevented, by their governors, from sending a deputation to this congress. Twenty-eight deputies from Massachusetts, Rhode Island, Connecticut, New York, New Jersey, Pennsylvania, Delaware, Maryland, and South Carolina, met at New York; and, after mature deliberation, agreed on a declaration of their rights, and on a statement of their grievances. They asserted, in strong terms, their exemption from all taxes, not imposed by their own representatives. They also concurred in a petition to the king, a memorial to the house of lords, and a petition to the house of commons. The colonies, prevented from sending their representatives to this congress, forwarded petitions similar to those adopted by the deputies who attended. . . .

REPEAL OF STAMP ACT, MARCH 1766

From the decided opposition to the stamp act, which had been adopted by the colonies, it became necessary for Great Britain to enforce, or to repeal it. Both methods of proceeding had supporters. The opposers of a repeal urged arguments, drawn from the dignity of the nation, the danger of giving way to the clamours of the Americans, and the consequences of weakening parliamentary authority over the colonies. On the other hand, it was evident, from the determined opposition of the colonies, that it could not be enforced without a civil war, by which, in every event, the nation must be a loser. In the course of these discussions, Dr. Franklin was examined at the bar of the house of commons, and gave extensive information on the state of American affairs, and the impolicy of the stamp act, which contributed much to remove prejudices, and to produce a disposition that was friendly to a repeal. . . .

After much debating, two protests in the house of lords, and passing an act, "for securing the dependence of America on Great Britain," the repeal of the stamp act was carried, in March, 1766. This event gave great joy in London. Ships in the river Thames displayed their colours; and houses were illuminated, all over the city. It was no sooner known in America, than the colonists

DAVID RAMSAY: PRELUDE TO THE AMERICAN REVOLUTION, 1765–1775

NEWSPAPERS, STAMP ACT CONGRESS, 1765

GOD PREPARES
A CHRISTIAN
PEOPLE
TO ESTABLISH
THE AMERICAN
NATION

rescinded their resolutions, and recommenced their mercantile intercourse with the mother country. They presented their homespun clothes to the poor; and imported more largely than ever. The churches resounded with thanksgivings; and their public and private rejoicings knew no bounds. By letters, addresses, and other means, almost all the colonies showed unequivocal marks of acknowledgment and gratitude. So sudden a calm, after so violent a storm, is without a parallel in history. By the judicious sacrifice of one law, the parliament of Great Britain procured an acquiescence, in all that remained.

There were enlightened patriots, fully impressed with an idea, that the immoderate joy of the colonists was disproportioned to the advantage they had gained.

The stamp act, though repealed, was not repealed on American principles. . . .

DECLARATORY ACT

At the same time that the stamp act was repealed, the absolute, unlimited supremacy of parliament was, in words, asserted. The opposers of the repeal contended for this as essential. The friends of that measure acquiesced in it, to strengthen their party, and make sure of their object. Many of both sides thought, that the dignity of Great Britain required something of the kind, to counter-balance the loss of authority, that might result from her yielding to the clamours of the colonists. The act for this purpose was called the declaratory act; and was, in principle, more hostile to American rights, than the stamp act; for it annulled those resolutions and acts of the provincial assemblies, in which they had asserted their right to exemption from all taxes, not imposed by their own representatives; and also enacted, "that the parliament had, and of right ought to have, power to bind the colonies, in all cases whatsoever." . . .

The repeal of the stamp act, in a relative connection with all its circumstances and consequences, was the first direct step to American independence. The claims of the two countries were not only left undecided; but a foundation was laid for their extending, at a future period, to the impossibility of a compromise. Though, for the present, Great Britain receded from enforcing her claim of American revenue, a numerous party, adhering to that system, reserved themselves for more favourable circumstances to enforce it; and, at the same time, the colonists, more enlightened on the subject, and more fully

convinced of the rectitude of their claims, were encouraged to oppose it, under whatsoever form it should appear, or under whatsoever disguise it should cover itself. . . .

TOWNSEND BILL, 1767

Mr. Charles Townsend, afterwards chancellor of the exchequer, pawned his credit to accomplish what many so earnestly desired. He accordingly, in 1767, brought into parliament a bill, for granting duties in the British colonies on glass, paper, painters' colours, and tea, which was afterwards enacted into a law. If the small duties, imposed on these articles, had preceded the stamp act, they might have passed unobserved: but the late discussions, occasioned by that act, had produced among the colonists, not only an animated conviction of their exemption from parliamentary taxation, but a jealousy of the designs of Great Britain. . . .

The colonists contended that there was no real difference, between the principle of these new duties and the stamp act. They were both designed to raise a revenue in America, and in the same manner. The payment of the duties, imposed by the stamp act, might have been eluded by the total disuse of stamped paper; and so might the payment of these duties, by the total disuse of those articles on which they were laid: but in neither case, without great difficulty. The colonists were, therefore, reduced to the hard alternative of being obliged, totally, to disuse articles of great utility in human life, or to pay a tax without their consent. The fire of opposition, which had been smothered by the repeal of the stamp act, burned afresh against the same principle of taxation, exhibited in its new form. Mr. Dickinson, of Pennsylvania, on this occasion, presented to the public a series of letters, signed a Farmer, proving the extreme danger which threatened the liberties of America, from their acquiescence in a precedent, which might establish the claim of parliamentary taxation. . . . It was now demonstrated by several writers, especially by the Pennsylvania Farmer, that a small tax, though more specious, was equally dangerous; as it established a precedent, which eventually annihilated American property. The declaratory act, which at first was the subject of but few comments, was now dilated upon, as a foundation for every species of oppression; and the small duties, lately imposed, were considered as the beginning of a train of much greater evils. . . .

The revenue acts of 1767, produced resolves, petitions, addresses, and remonstrances, similar to those, with which the colonists opposed the stamp act. It also gave rise to a second association, for suspending further importations of British manufactures, till these offensive duties should be taken off. Uniformity, in these measures, was promoted by a circular letter from the assembly of Massachusetts, to the speakers of the other assemblies. . . . Most of the provincial assemblies, as they had opportunities of deliberating on the subject, approved the proceedings of the Massachusetts assembly, and harmonised with them in the measures, which they had adopted. . . .

Lord Hillsborough, who had lately been appointed secretary of state, for the American department, wrote letters to the governors of the respective provinces, urging them to exert their influence, to prevent the assemblies from taking any notice of it; and he called on the Massachusetts assembly, to rescind their proceedings on that subject. This measure was both injudicious and irritating. To require a public body to rescind a resolution, for sending a letter, which was already sent, answered, and acted upon, was a bad specimen of the wisdom of the new minister. To call a vote, for sending a circular letter, to invite the assemblies of the neighbouring colonies to communicate together, in the pursuit of legal measures, to obtain a redress of grievances, "a flagitious attempt to disturb the public peace," appeared to the colonists a very injudicious application of harsh epithets, to their constitutional right of petitioning. To threaten a new house of assembly with dissolution, in case of their not agreeing to rescind an act of a former assembly, which was not executory, but executed, clashed no less with the dictates of common sense, than the constitutional rights of British colonists. The proposition for rescinding was negatived, by a majority of ninety-two to seventeen. The assembly was immediately dissolved, as had been threatened. This procedure of the new secretary was considered, by the colonists, as an attempt to suppress all communication of sentiments between them; and to prevent their united supplications from reaching the royal ear.

The bad humour, which, from successive irritation, already too much prevailed, was about this time wrought up to a high pitch of resentment and violence, on occasion of the seizure of Mr. Hancock's sloop Liberty, June 10th, 1768, for not having entered all the wines she had brought from Madeira. The popularity of her owner, the name of the sloop, and the general aversion to the board of commissioners, and parliamentary taxation, concurred to inflame the minds of the people. They used every means in their power to interrupt the officers, in the execution of their business; and numbers swore that they would be revenged. Mr. Harrison, the collector, Mr. Hallowell, the comptroller, and Mr. Irwine, the inspector of imports and exports, were so roughly handled, as to bring their lives in danger. The windows of some of their houses were broken; and the boat of the collector was dragged through the town, and burned on the common. Such was the temper and disposition of many of the inhabitants, that the commissioners of the customs thought proper to retire on board the Romney man of war; and afterwards to Castle William. . . .

MILITARY ENFORCEMENT

The declaratory act of 1766, the revenue act of 1767, together with the pomp and expense of this board, so disproportionate to the small income of the present duties, conspired to convince not only the few who were benefitted by smuggling, but the great body of enlightened freemen, that further and greater impositions of parliamentary taxes were intended. In proportion as this opinion gained ground, the inhabitants became more disrespectful to the executive officers of the revenue, and more disposed, in the frenzy of patriotism, to commit outrages on their persons and property. The constant bickering, that existed between them and the inhabitants, together with the steady opposition given by the latter, to the discharge of the official duties of the former, induced the commissioners and friends of an American revenue, to solicit the protection of a regular force, to be stationed at Boston. In compliance with their wishes, his majesty ordered two regiments and some armed vessels to repair thither, for supporting and assisting the officers of the customs, in the execution of their duty. This restrained the active exertion of that turbulent spirit, which, since the passing of the late revenue laws, had revived; but it added to its pre-existing causes.

THE WAR OF WORDS

When it was reported in Boston, that one or more regiments were ordered there, a meeting of the inhabitants was called, and a committee appointed, to request the governor to issue precepts, for convening a general assembly. He replied, "that he could not comply with this request, till

DAVID
RAMSAY:
PRELUDE TO
THE AMERICAN
REVOLUTION,
1765–1775

WAR OF WORDS

GOD PREPARES
A CHRISTIAN
PEOPLE
TO ESTABLISH
THE AMERICAN
NATION

he had received his majesty's commands for that purpose." This answer being reported, it was voted, that the select men of Boston should write to the select men of other towns, to propose, that a convention of deputies from each, be held, to meet at Faneuil hall, in Boston.

Ninety-six towns, and eight districts, agreed to the proposal made by the inhabitants of Boston, and appointed deputies, to attend a convention; but the town of Hatfield refused its concurrence. When the deputies met, they conducted with moderation; disclaimed all legislative authority; advised the people to pay the greatest deference to government; and to wait patiently for a redress of their grievances, from his majesty's wisdom and moderation. After stating to the world the causes of their meeting, and an account of their proceedings, they dissolved themselves, after a short session, and went home.

Within a day after the convention broke up, the expected regiments arrived, and were peaceably received. Hints had been thrown out by some, that they should not be permitted to come on shore. Preparations were made, by the captains of the men of war in the harbour, to fire on the town, in case opposition had been made to their landing; but the crisis for an appeal to arms was not yet arrived. It was hoped by some, that the folly and rage of the Bostonians would have led them to this rash measure, and thereby have afforded an opportunity for giving them some naval and military correction; but both prudence and policy induced them to adopt a more temperate line of conduct.

While the contention was kept alive, by the successive irritations, which have been mentioned, there was, particularly in Massachusetts, a species of warfare carried on between the royal governors, and the provincial assemblies. Each watched the other with all the jealousy, which strong distrust could inspire. The latter regarded the former as instruments of power, wishing to pay their court to the mother country, by curbing the spirit of American freedom; and the former kept a strict eye on the latter, lest they might smooth the way to independence, at which they were charged with aiming. Lieutenant governor Hutchinson, of Massachusetts, virtually challenged the assembly to a dispute, on the ground of the controversy between the two countries. This was accepted by the latter; and the subject discussed with all the subtilty of argument which the ingenuity of either party could suggest.

The war of words was not confined to the colonies. While the American assemblies passed reso-

lutions, asserting their exclusive right to tax their constituents, the parliament, by resolves, asserted their unlimited supremacy in and over the colonies. While the former, in their public acts, disclaimed all views of independence, they were successively represented in parliamentary resolves, royal speeches, and addresses from lords and commons, as being in a state of disobedience to law and government; as having proceeded to measures subversive of the constitution; and manifesting a disposition to throw off all subordination to Great Britain.

TRIALS IN ENGLAND, 1769

In February, 1769, both houses of parliament went one step beyond all that had preceded. They concurred in a joint address to his majesty, in which they expressed their satisfaction in the measures his majesty had pursued; gave the strongest assurances, that they would effectually support him in such further measures, as might be found necessary, to maintain the civil magistrates in a due execution of the laws, in Massachusetts Bay; beseeched him, "to direct the governor to take the most effectual methods for procuring the fullest information, touching all treasons or misprisions of treason, committed within the government, since the 30th day of December, 1767; and to transmit the same, together with the names of the persons, who were most active in the commission of such offences, to one of the secretaries of state, in order that his majesty might issue a special commission for inquiring of, hearing, and determining, the said offences, within the realm of Great Britain, pursuant to the provision of the statute of the thirty-fifth of King Henry the eighth." The latter part of this address which proposed the bringing of delinquents from Massachusetts, to be tried at a tribunal in Great Britain, for crimes committed in America, underwent many severe animadversions. . . .

REPEAL ALL DUTIES—EXCEPT TEA, 1770

In consequence of the American non-importation agreement, founded in opposition to the duties of 1767, the manufacturers of Great Britain experienced a renewal of the distresses, which followed the adoption of similar resolutions, in the year 1765. The repeal of these duties was therefore solicited by the same influence, which had procured the repeal of the stamp act. The rulers of Great Britain acted without decision. Instead of persevering in their own system of coercion, or, indeed, in any one uniform system, they struck out a middle line, embarrassed with the consequences, both of severity and of lenity, and without the complete benefits of either. Soon after the spirited address to his majesty, last mentioned, had passed both houses of parliament, assurances were given for repealing all the duties, imposed in 1767, excepting that of three pence per pound on tea.

Anxious on the one hand to establish parliamentary supremacy, and on the other afraid to stem the torrent of opposition, they conceded enough to weaken the former, and yet not enough to satisfy the latter. Had Great Britain generously repealed the whole, and for ever relinquished all claim to the right, or even the exercise of the right of taxation, the union of the two countries might have lasted for ages. Had she seriously determined to compel the submission of the colonies, nothing could have been more unfriendly to this design, than her repeated concessions to their reiterated associations. The declaratory act, and the reservation of the duty on tea, left the cause of contention between the two countries, in full force; but the former was only a claim on paper, and the latter might be evaded, by refusing to purchase any tea, on which the parliamentary tax was imposed. The colonists, therefore, conceiving that their commerce might be renewed, without establishing any precedent, injurious to their liberties, relaxed in their associations, in every particular, except tea, and immediately recommended the importation of all other articles of merchandise. A political calm once more took place. The parent state might now have closed the dispute for ever, and honourably receded, without a formal relinquishment of her claims. Neither the reservation of the duty on tea, by the British parliament, nor the exceptions made by the colonists, of importing no tea, on which a duty was imposed, would, if they had been left to their own operation, have disturbed the returning harmony of the two countries. Without fresh irritation, their wounds might have healed, and not a scar been left behind.

Unfortunately for the friends of union, so paltry a sum as three pence per pound on so insignificant an article as tea, in consequence of a combination between the British ministry and East India company, revived the dispute to the rending of the empire.

These two abortive attempts, to raise a parliamentary revenue in America, caused a fermentation in the minds of the colonists, and gave birth to many inquiries respecting their natural rights.

Reflections and reasonings on this subject produced a high sense of liberty, and a general conviction, that there could be no security for their property, if they were to be taxed at the discretion of a British parliament, in which they were unrepresented, and over which they had no control. A determination not only to oppose this new claim of taxation, but to keep a strict watch, lest it might be established in some disguised form, took possession of their minds.

It commonly happens, in the discussion of doubtful claims between states, that the ground of the original dispute insensibly changes. When the mind is employed in investigating one subject, others, associated with it, naturally present themselves. In the course of inquiries on the subject of parliamentary taxation, the restriction on the trade of the colonists, and the necessity that was imposed on them, to purchase British and other manufactures, loaded with their full proportion of all taxes, paid by those who made or sold them, became more generally known. While American writers were vindicating their country from the charge of contributing nothing to the common expenses of the empire, they were led to set off, to their credit, the disadvantage of their being confined exclusively to purchase manufactures in Britain. They instituted calculations, by which they demonstrated, that the monopoly of their trade drew from them greater sums, for the support of government, than were usually paid by an equal number of their fellow-citizens of Great Britain; and that taxation, superadded to such a monopoly, would leave them in a state of perfect uncompensated slavery. The investigation of these subjects brought matters into view, which the friends of union ought to have kept out of sight. These circumstances, together with the extensive population of the eastern states, and their adventurous spirit of commerce, suggested to some bold spirits, that not only British taxation, but British navigation laws, were unfriendly to the interests of America. Speculations of this magnitude suited well with the extensive views of some capital merchants; but never would have roused the bulk of the people, had not new matter brought the dispute between the two countries to a point, in which every individual was interested.

On reviewing the conduct of the British ministry, respecting the colonies, much weakness as well as folly appears. For on succession of years, there was a steady pursuit of American revenue; but great inconsistency in the projects for obtaining it. In one moment, the parliament was for enforcing their laws; the next, for repealing

GOD PREPARES
A CHRISTIAN
PEOPLE
TO ESTABLISH
THE AMERICAN
NATION

them. Doing and undoing, menacing and submitting, straining and relaxing followed each other, in alternate succession. The object of administration, though twice relinquished, as to any present efficiency, was invariably pursued; but without any unity of system.

On the 9th of May, 1769, the king, in his speech to parliament, highly applauded their hearty concurrence, in maintaining the execution of the laws, in every part of his dominions. Five days after this speech, Lord Hillsborough, secretary of state for the colonies, wrote to lord Botetourt, governor of Virginia: "I can take upon me to assure you, notwithstanding information to the contrary, from men, with factious and seditious views, that his majesty's present administration have at no time entertained a design to propose to parliament, to lay any further taxes upon America, for the purpose of raising a revenue; and that it is, at present, their intention to propose, the next session of parliament, to take off the duties upon glass, paper, and colours, upon consideration of such duties having been laid contrary to the true principles of commerce." The governor was also informed, that "his majesty relied upon his prudence and fidelity, to make such an explanation of his majesty's measures, as would tend to remove prejudices, and to re-establish mutual confidence and affection, between the mother country and the colonies." In the exact spirit of his instructions, lord Botetourt addressed the Virginia assembly as follows: "It may possibly be objected, that, as his majesty's present administration are not immortal, their successors may be inclined to attempt to undo, what the present ministers shall have attempted to perform; and to that objection I can give but this answer: that it is my firm opinion, that the plan, I have stated to you, will certainly take place, and that it will never be departed from; and so determined am I forever to abide by it, that I will be content to be declared infamous, if I do not to the last hour of my life, at all times, in all places, and upon all occasions, exert every power, with which I either am, or ever shall be, legally invested, in order to obtain and maintain for the continent of America, that satisfaction, which I have been authorized to promise this day, by the confidential servants of our gracious sovereign, who, to my certain knowledge, rates his honour so high, that he would rather part with his crown, than preserve it by deceit."

These assurances were received, with transports of joy, by the Virginians. They viewed

May 9, 1769

them as pledging his majesty for security, that the late design for raising a revenue in America was abandoned, and never more to be resumed. The assembly of Virginia, in answer to lord Botetourt, expressed themselves thus: "We are sure our most gracious sovereign, under whatever changes may happen in his confidential servants, will remain immutable in the ways of truth and justice, and that he is incapable of deceiving his faithful subjects; and we esteem your lordship's information not only as warranted, but even sanctified by the royal word."

How far these solemn engagements, with the Americans, were observed, subsequent events will demonstrate. In a perfect reliance on them, most of the colonists returned to their ancient habits of good humour, and flattered themselves that no future parliament would undertake to give, or grant away their property.

From the royal and ministerial assurances given in favour of America, in the year 1769, and the subsequent repeal in 1770, of five-sixths of the duties which had been imposed in 1767; together with the consequent renewal of the mercantile intercourse between Great Britain and the colonies, many hoped, that the contention between the two countries was finally closed. In all the provinces, excepting Massachusetts, appearances seemed to favour that opinion. Many incidents operated there to the prejudice of that harmony, which had begun, elsewhere, to return. Stationing a military force among them was a fruitful source of uneasiness. The royal army had been brought thither, with the avowed design of enforcing submission to the mother country. Speeches from the throne, and addresses from both houses of parliament, had taught them to look upon the inhabitants as a factious, turbulent people, who aimed at throwing off all subordination to Great Britain. They, on the other hand were accustomed to look upon the soldiery as instruments of tyranny, sent on purpose to dragoon them out of their liberties. . . .

BOSTON MASSACRE, MARCH 5, 1770

On the second of March, 1770, a fray took place near Mr. Gray's ropewalk, between a private soldier of the twenty-ninth regiment, and an inhabitant. The former was supported by his comrades, the latter by the rope-makers, till several on both sides were involved in the consequences. On the 5th, a more dreadful scene was presented. The soldiers, when under arms, were pressed upon, insulted and pelted by a mob, armed with clubs, sticks, and snowballs covering stones. They were also dared to fire. In this situation, one of the soldiers who had received a blow, in resentment fired at the supposed aggressor. This was followed by a single discharge from six others. Three of the inhabitants were killed, and five were dangerously wounded. The town was immediately in commotion. Such were the temper, force, and number of the inhabitants, that nothing but an engagement to remove the troops out of the town, together with the advice of the moderate men, prevented the townsmen from falling on the soldiers. Preston, the captain who commanded, and the party, who fired on the inhabitants, were committed to jail, and afterwards tried. The captain and six of the men were acquitted. Two were brought in guilty of manslaughter. It appeared on the trial, that the soldiers were abused, insulted, threatened, and pelted, before they fired. It was also proved, that only seven guns were fired by the eight prisoners. These circumstances induced the jury to give a favourable verdict. The result of the trial reflected great honour on John Adams, and Josiah Quincy, the counsel for the prisoners; and, also, on the integrity of the jury, who ventured to give an upright verdict, in defiance of popular opinions. . . .

The obstacles to returning harmony, which have already been mentioned, were increased, by making the governor and judges in Massachusetts, independent of the province. Formerly they had been paid by yearly grants from the assembly; but about this time provision was made for paying their salaries by the crown. This was resented as a dangerous innovation; as an infraction of their charter; and as destroying that balance of power, essential to free governments. That the crown should pay the salary of the chief justice, was represented by the assembly as a species of bribery, tending to bias his judicial determination. They made it the foundation for impeaching Mr. Justice Oliver, before the governor; but he excepted to their proceedings, as unconstitutional. The assembly, nevertheless, gained two points. They rendered the governor more odius to the inhabitants, and increased the public respect for themselves, as the counterpart of the British house of commons, and as guardians of the rights of the people.

A personal animosity, between lieutenant governor Hutchinson, and some distinguished patriots, in Massachusetts, contributed to perpetuate a flame of discontent in that province, after it had elsewhere visibly abated. This was worked up, in the year, 1773, to a high pitch, by a singular combination of circumstances. Some letters had been written, in the course of the dispute, by governor Hutchinson, lieutenant governor Oliver, and other royal servants in Boston, to persons of power in England, which contained a very unfavourable representation, of the state of public affairs, and tended to show the necessity of coercive measures, and of changing the chartered system of government, to secure the obedience of the province. These letters fell into the hands of Dr. Franklin, agent of the province, who transmitted them to Boston. The indignation and animosity, which was excited on the receipt of them, had no bounds. The house of assembly agreed on a petition and remonstrance to his majesty, in which they charged their governor, and lieutenant governor, with being betrayers of the people they governed, and of giving private, partial, and false information. They also declared them enemies to the colonies, and prayed for justice against them, and for their speedy removal from their places. These charges were carried through by a majority of eighty-two to twelve.

The petition and remonstrance being transmitted to England, their merits were discussed before his majesty's privy council. After an hearing before that board, in which Dr. Franklin represented the province of Massachusetts, the governor and lieutenant governor were acquitted. Mr. Wedderburne, who defended the accused royal servants, in the course of his pleadings, inveighed against Dr. Franklin, in the severest language, as the fomenter of the disputes between the two countries. It was no protection to this venerable sage, that, being the agent of Massachusetts, he conceived it his duty to inform his constituents, of letters, written on public affairs, calculated to overturn their chartered constitution. The age, respectability, and high literary character, of the subject of Mr. Wedderburne's philippic, turned the attention of the public, on the transaction. The insult offered to one of their public agents, and especially to one, who was both the pride and ornament of his native country, sunk deep in the minds of the Americans. That a faithful servant, whom they loved, should be insulted, for discharging his official duty, rankled in their hearts. Dr. Franklin was immediately dismissed from the office of deputy postmaster general, which he held under the crown. It was not only by his transmission of these letters, that he had given offence to the British ministry, but by his popular writings, in

DAVID
RAMSAY:
PRELUDE TO
THE AMERICAN
REVOLUTION,
1765–1775

BOSTON
MASSACRE,
MARCH 5, 1770

GOD PREPARES
A CHRISTIAN
PEOPLE
TO ESTABLISH
THE AMERICAN
NATION

favour of America. Two pieces of his, in particular, had lately attracted a large share of public attention, and had an extensive influence on both sides of the Atlantic. The one purported to be an edict from the king of Prussia, for taxing the inhabitants of Great Britain, as descendants of emigrants from his dominions. The other was entitled: "Rules for reducing a great empire to a small one." In both of which he had exposed the claims of the mother country, and the proceedings of the British ministry, with the severity of poignant satire.

For ten years there had now been little intermission to the disputes, between Great Britain and her colonies. Their respective claims had never been compromised on middle ground. The calm, which followed the repeal of the stamp act, was in a few months disturbed, by the revenue act of the year 1767. The tranquility, which followed the repeal of five-sixths of that act, in the year 1770, was nothing more than a truce. The reservation of the duty on tea, as an avowed evidence of the claims of Great Britain to tax her colonies, kept alive the jealousy of the colonists; while, at the same time, the stationing of an army in Massachusetts, the continuance of a board of commissioners in Boston, the constituting the governors and judges of that province independent of the people, were constant sources of irritation. The altercations which, at this period, were common between the royal governors and the provincial assemblies, together with numerous vindications of the claims of America, made the subject familiar to the colonists. The ground of the controversy was canvassed in every company. The more the Americans read, reasoned, and conversed on the subject, the more were they convinced on their right to the exclusive disposal of their property. This was followed by a determination to resist all encroachments on that palladium of liberty. They were as strongly convinced on their right, to refuse and resist parliamentary taxation, as the ruling powers of Great Britain of their right, to demand and enforce their submission to it.

The claims of the two countries, being thus irreconcileably opposed to each other, the partial calm, which followed the concession of parliament, in 1770, was liable to disturbance, from every incident. Under such circumstances, nothing less than the most guarded conduct on both sides could prevent a renewal of the controversy. Instead of following those prudential measures, which would have kept the ground of the dispute out of sight, an impolitic scheme was con-

certed, between the British ministry and the East India company, that placed the claims of Great Britain and of her colonies in hostile array against each other.

1773—NEW ERA IN AMERICAN CONTROVERSY

In the year 1773, commenced an new era of the American controversy.

To understand this in its origin, it is necessary to recur to the period, when the solitary duty on tea was excepted from the partial repeal of the revenue act of 1767. When the duties which had been laid on glass, paper, and painters' colours, were taken off, a respectable minority in parliament contended, that the duty on tea should also be removed. To this it was replied; "that as the Americans denied the legality of taxing them, a total repeal would be a virtual acquiescence in their claims; and that in order to preserve the rights of the mother country, it was necessary to retain the preamble, and at least one of the taxed articles." It was rejoined, that a partial repeal would be a source of endless discontent; and that the tax on tea would not defray the expenses of collecting it. The motion in favour of a total repeal was rejected by a great majority. As the parliament thought fit to retain the tax on tea, for an evidence of their right of taxation, the Americans, in like manner, to be consistent with themselves in denying that right, discontinued the importation of that commodity. While there was no attempt to introduce tea into the colonies, against this declared sense of the inhabitants, these opposing claims were in no danger of collision. In that case, the mother country might have solaced herself, with her ideal rights, and the colonies, with their favourite opinion of a total exemption from parliamentary taxes, without disturbing the public peace. This mode of compromising the dispute, which seemed at first designed as a salvo for the honour and consistency of both parties, was, by the interference of the East India company, in combination with the British ministry, completely overset.

The expected revenue from tea failed, in consequence of the American association to import none on which a duty was charged. This proceeded as much from the spirit of gain, as of patriotism. The merchants found means of supplying their countrymen with tea, smuggled from countries to which the power of Britain did not extend. . . .

The love of gain was not peculiar to the American merchants. From the diminished ex-

GENTLEMEN,   *Boston, September 21, 1773.*

THE State of publick Affairs undoubtedly still demands the greatest Wisdom, Vigilance and Fortitude. Our Enemies who are alarmed at the Union which they see is already established in this Province, and the Confederacy into which they expect the whole Continent of America, will soon be drawn, for the Recovery of their violated RIGHTS, are now aiming to perswade us of their earnest Desire that our Grievances should be redress'd, and are insinuating that if we will wave our Claim of Rights, Relief will be readily granted to us.

We well remember how greatly the British Ministry were alarmed at the Combination of the Americans against the Importation of British Manufactures :——Their Artifice was then to pretend to meet us half Way ; and by this Shew of Candor and Integrity, to spread Divisions among us.— Upon this Principle, the Duties on Painter's Colors, Oil and Glass were repealed. The Merchants were thereby disunited in Sentiments,—the Councils of the Americans confused, and the Non-Importation Agreement (which had it been a little longer continued, wou'd have brought our Oppressors to Terms of Reason) was entirely broken up.—The Moment this was known, the Necessity of attending to our Complaints vanished.

When it is considered, how much that rich and powerful Body the East-India Company resent the Act that was passed in the last Session of Parliament, by which their sacred Charter Rights were arbitrarily taken from them ; and how much the City of London, and other great Corporations, are alarmed thereby, it would not seem strange if Administration should at this Time be desirous of silencing every Opposition to their Measures in general ; and especially such an Opposition as this extensive Continent, when united, is able to make.

Ought we not also to bear in our Minds, that the Time for a new Election of the House of Commons in Great-Britain is drawing near ? And, will it not be highly pleasing to our Enemies, if by a strange Kind of Policy recommended by some, we should lead our Friends in England to think, that we are at Length brought to place a Confidence in the good Intentions of Administration, although the most ruinous Measures are still continued against repeated Petitions, and thereby should become ourselves instrumental in giving them the Aid of our Friends, for the obtaining an Election of such Members as will be agreeable to their Wishes ? And if, which Heaven avert ! a House of Commons determined to subvert the Liberties of America, should be elected, what Oppressions may we not expect, in another seven Years, if through a weak Credulity, while the most arbitrary Measures are still persisted in, we should be prevail'd upon to submit our Rights, as the patriotic Farmer expresses it, " to the tender Mercies of the *Ministry*."

We mean not to agitate the Minds of our Brethren with groundless Apprehensions : But to excite in them that Watchfulness which alone will be a Guard against a false Security, forever dangerous to our Rights and Liberties ; and to entreat, that the Eye of Jealousy may be still attentively fixed on the Movements of our Enemies, in Britain and America. We trust you will always communicate to us any Discoveries or just Suspicions of their sinister Designs ; and also, that you will never be wanting in encouraging that Unity and Harmony in Councils, so essentially necessary to the obtaining the great End we have in View, *the Salvation of Ourselves and Posterity from Tyranny & Bondage.*

And we have still an animating Confidence in the Supreme Disposer of Events, that he will never suffer a sensible, brave and virtuous People to be enslaved.

We are,

Your Friends and humble Servants,

Signed by the Direction of the Committee of Correspondence for the Town of *Boston*,

                                    William Cooper } Clerk.

To the Committee of Correspondence for the Town of

Sr. There being no Committee of Correspondence in the Town of Barnstable I am directed to transmitt the foregoing to you tobe communicated to such of your Friends as you shall think proper

Your humble Servant
William Cooper. Clerk

God Prepares
a Christian
People
to Establish
the American
Nation

portation to the colonies, the ware-houses of the British East India company had in them seventeen millions of pounds of tea, for which a market could not be procured. The ministry and East India company, unwilling to lose, the one, the expected revenue from the sale of the tea in America, the other, their usual commercial profits, agreed on a measure by which they supposed both would be secured.

The East India company was, by law, authorized to export their tea free of duties, to all places whatsoever. By this regulation, tea, though loaded with an exceptionable duty, would come cheaper to the colonies, than before it had been made a source of revenue: for the duty taken off it, when exported from Great Britain, was greater than that to be paid on its importation into the colonies.

Confident of success, in finding a market for their tea, thus reduced in its price, and also of collecting a duty on its importation and sale in the colonies, the East India company freighted several ships, with teas, for the different colonies, and appointed agents for its disposal. . . . The cry of endangered liberty once more excited an alarm, from New Hampshire to Georgia.

COLONISTS REFUSE TEA

The first opposition to the execution of the scheme, adopted by the East India company, began with the American merchants. They saw a profitable branch of their trade likely to be lost, and the benefits of it to be transferred to people in Great Britain. They felt for the wound, that would be inflicted on their country's claim of exemption from parliamentary taxation; but they felt, with equal sensibility, for the losses they would sustain, by the diversion of the streams of commerce, into unusual channels. Though the opposition originated in the selfishness of the merchants, it did not end there. The great body of the people, from principles of the purest patriotism, were brought over to second their wishes. They considered the whole scheme as calculated to seduce them into an acquiescence with the views of parliament, for raising an American revenue. Much pains were taken to enlighten the colonists on this subject, and to convince them of the eminent hazard to which their liberties were exposed.

The provincial patriots insisted largely on the persevering determination of the parent state, to establish her claim of taxation, by compelling the sale of tea in the colonies, against the solemn resolutions and declared sense of the inhabitants; and that, at a time, when the commercial intercourse of the two countries was renewed, and their ancient harmony fast returning. The proposed venders of the tea were represented as revenue officers, employed in the collection of an unconstitutional tax, imposed by Great Britain. The colonists contended, that, as the duty and the price of the commodity were inseparably blended, if the tea were sold, every purchaser would pay a tax imposed by the British parliament, as part of the purchase money. To obviate this evil, and to prevent the liberties of a great country from being sacrificed by inconsiderate purchasers, sundry town meetings were held in the capitals of the different provinces, and combinations were formed to obstruct the sales of the tea, sent by the East India company.

The resolutions adopted, by the inhabitants of Philadelphia, on the 18th of October, 1773, afford a good specimen of the whole. These were as follow: October 18, 1773

"1. That the disposal of their own property is the inherent right of freemen; that there can be no property in that which another can, of right, take from us without our consent; that the claim of parliament to tax America, is, in other words, a claim of right to levy contributions on us at pleasure.

"2. That the duty, imposed by parliament upon tea landed in America, is a tax on the Americans, or levying contributions on them, without their consent.

"3. That the express purpose, for which the tax is levied on the Americans, namely, for the support of government, administration of justice, and defence of his majesty's dominions in America, has a direct tendency to render assemblies useless, and to introduce arbitrary government and slavery.

"4. That a virtuous and steady opposition, to this ministerial plan of governing America, is absolutely necessary, to preserve even the shadow of liberty; and is a duty which every freeman in America owes to his country, to himself, and to his posterity.

"5. That the resolution, lately entered into by the East India company, to send out their tea to America, subject to the payment of duties on its being landed here, is an open attempt to enforce this ministerial plan, and a violent attack upon the liberties of America.

"6. That it is the duty of every American to oppose this attempt.

"7. That whoever shall, directly or indirectly, countenance this attempt, or, in any wise, aid or abet in unloading, receiving, or vending the tea sent, or to be sent out by the East India company, while it remains subject to the payment of a duty here, is an enemy to his country.

"8. That a committee be immediately chosen, to wait on those gentlemen, who, it is reported, are appointed by the East India company, to receive and sell said tea, and request them, from a regard to their own character and the peace and good order of the city and province, immediately to resign their appointment."

As the time approached, when the arrival of the tea ships might be soon expected, such measures were adopted, as seemed most likely to prevent the landing of their cargoes. . . .

The event of this business was very different from what had been expected in England. The colonists acted with so much union and system, that there was not a single chest, of any of the cargoes sent out by the East India company, sold for their benefit.

PROCEEDINGS OF THE BRITISH PARLIAMENT, IN CONSEQUENCE OF THE DESTRUCTION OF THE TEA, BY THE BOSTONIANS

Intelligence of the events, which have been stated in the last chapter, was, on the 7th of March, 1774, communicated, in a message from the throne, to both houses of parliament. In this communication, the conduct of the colonists was represented, as not only obstructing the commerce of Great Britain, but as subversive of its constitution. The message was accompanied with a number of papers, containing copies and extracts of letters, from the several royal governors and others; from which it appeared, that the opposition to the sale of tea was not peculiar to Massachusetts; but common to all the colonies. These papers were accompanied with declarations, that nothing short of parliamentary interference could re-establish order, among the turbulent colonists; and that, therefore, decisive measures should be immediately adopted. If the right of levying taxes on the Americans were vested in the parent state, these inferences were well-founded; but if it were not, their conduct, in resisting an invasion of their rights, was justified, not only by many examples in the history of Britain, but by the spirit of the constitution of that country, which they were opposing.

By the destruction of the tea, the people of

Boston had incurred the sanction of penal laws. Those in Great Britain, who wished for an opportunity to take vengeance on that town, commonly supposed by them to be the mother of sedition and rebellion, rejoiced, that her inhabitants had laid themselves open to castigation.

It was well known, that the throwing of the tea into the river did not originate with the persons, who were the immediate instruments of that act of violence; and that the whole had been concerted, at a public meeting, and was, in a qualified sense, the act of the town. The universal indignation, which was excited in Great Britain, against the people of Boston, pointed out to the ministry the suitableness of the present moment for humbling them. Though the ostensible ground of complaint was nothing more than a trespass, on private property, committed by private persons; yet it was well known to be part of a long digested plan of resistance, to parliamentary taxation. Every measure, that might be pursued on the occasion, seemed to be big with the fate of the empire. To proceed in the usual forms of law, appeared to the rulers, in Great Britain, to be a departure from their dignity. It was urged by the ministry, that parliament, and parliament only, was capable of re-establishing tranquility, among these turbulent people, and of bringing order out of confusion. To stifle all opposition from the merchants, the public papers were filled with writings, which stated the impossibility of carrying on a future trade to America, if this flagrant outrage on commerce should go unpunished.

It was in vain urged, by the minority, that no good could arise from coercion, unless the minds of the Americans were made easy on the subject of taxation. Equally vain was a motion for a retrospect into the conduct of the ministry, which had provoked their resistance.

The parliament confined themselves solely to the late misbehaviour of the Americans, without any inquiry into its provoking causes.

The violence of the Bostonians, in destroying an article of commerce, was largely insisted upon, without any indulgence for the jealous spirit of liberty, in the descendants of Englishmen. The connection between the tea, and the unconstitutional duty imposed thereon, was overlooked, and the public mind of Great Britain solely fixed on the obstruction given to commerce, by the turbulent colonists. The spirit raised against the Americans became as high, and as strong, as their most inveterate enemies desired. This was not confined to the common people; but took posses-

March 7, 1774

459

GOD PREPARES
A CHRISTIAN
PEOPLE
TO ESTABLISH
THE AMERICAN
NATION

sion of legislators, whose unclouded minds ought to be exalted above the mists of prejudice or partiality. Such, when they consult on public affairs, should be free from the impulses of passion; for it rarely happens, that resolutions, adopted in anger, are founded in wisdom. The parliament of Great Britain, transported with indignation against the people of Boston, in a fit of rage resolved to take legislative vengeance on that devoted town.

A COMPLETE SYSTEM OF TYRANNY

I. BOSTON PORT BILL, MARCH 31, 1774

Disregarding the forms of her own constitution, by which none are to be condemned unheard, or punished without a trial, a bill was finally passed, by which the port of Boston was virtually blocked up; for it was legally precluded from the privilege of landing and discharging, or of lading and shipping of goods, wares, and merchandise. The minister, who proposed this measure, stated, in support of it, that the opposition, to the authority of parliament, had always originated in that colony, and had always been instigated by the seditious proceedings of the town of Boston; that it was therefore necessary to make an example of that town, which, by an unparalleled outrage, had violated the freedom of commerce; and that Great Britain would be wanting in the protection she owed to her peaceable subjects, if she did not punish such an insult, in an exemplary manner. He therefore proposed, that the town of Boston should be obliged to pay for the tea, which had been destroyed. He was further of opinion, that making a pecuniary satisfaction, for the injury committed, would not alone be sufficient; but that, in addition thereto, security must be given in future, that trade might be safely carried on; property protected; laws obeyed; and duties paid. He urged, therefore, that it would be proper to take away, from Boston, the privileges of a port, until his majesty should be satisfied, in these particulars, and publicly declare in council, on a proper certificate of the good behaviour of the town, that he was so satisfied. Until this should happen, he proposed that the custom-house officers should be removed to Salem. The minister hoped, that this act would execute itself; or at most, that a few frigates would secure its execution. He also hoped, that the prospect of advantage to the town of Salem, from its being made the seat of the custom-house, and from the occlusion of the port of Boston,

would detach them from the interest of the latter, and dispose them to support a measure, from which they had so much to expect. It was also presumed, that the other colonies would leave Boston to suffer the punishment due to her demerits. The abettors of parliamentary supremacy flattered themselves, that this decided conduct of Great Britain would, forever, extinguish all opposition of the refractory colonists to the claims of the mother country; and the apparent equity of obliging a delinquent town to make reparation, for an injury occasioned by the factious spirit of its inhabitants, silenced many of the friends of America. The consequences, resulting from this measure, were the reverse of what were wished by the first, and dreaded by the last.

By the operation of the Boston port act, the preceding situation of its inhabitants, and that of the East India company, was reversed. The former had more reason to complain of the disproportionate penalty, to which they were indiscriminately subjected, than the latter of that outrage on their property, for which punishment had been inflicted. Hitherto, the East India company were the injured party; but, from the passing of this act, the balance of injury was on the opposite side. If wrongs received entitled the former to reparation, the latter had a much stronger title on the same ground. For the act of seventeen or eighteen individuals, as many thousands were involved in one general calamity.

Both parties viewed the case on a much larger scale than that of municipal law. The people of Boston alleged, in vindication of their conduct, that the tea was a weapon aimed at their liberties; and that the same principles of self-preservation, which justify the breaking of the assassin's sword, uplifted for destruction, equally authorized the destruction of that tea, which was the vehicle of an unconstitutional tax, subversive of their liberties. The parliament of Great Britain considered the act of the people of Boston, in destroying the tea, as an open defiance of that country. The demerit of the action, as an offence against property, was lost, in the supposed superior demerit of treasonable intention, to emancipate themselves from a state of colonial dependence. The Americans conceived the case to be intimately connected with their liberties: the inhabitants of Great Britain with their supremacy. The former considered it as a duty they owed their country, to make a common cause with the people of Boston; the latter thought themselves under equal obligations, to support the privileges of parliament.

On the third reading of the Boston port Bill, a petition was presented by the lord mayor, in the name of several natives and inhabitants of North America, then residing in London. It was drawn with great force of language, and states that, "the proceedings of parliament against Boston were repugnant to every principle of law and justice, and established a precedent, by which no man in America could enjoy a moment's security." The friends of parliamentary supremacy had long regretted the democratic constitutions of the provinces, as adverse to their schemes. They saw, with concern, the steady opposition that was given to their measures, by the American legislatures. These constitutions were planned, when Great Britain neither feared nor cared for her colonies. Not suspecting that she was laying the foundation of future states, she granted charters that gave to the people so much of the powers of government, as enabled them to make, not only a formidable, but a regular, constitutional opposition, to the country from which they sprung.

Long had her rulers wished for an opportunity to revoke these charters, and to new model these governments. (The three last kings of the Stuart line laboured hard, to annihilate the charters of the English colonies in America; and nothing but the revolution of 1688, in England, prevented the accomplishment of their designs. The four first sub-revolutionary sovereigns of England discontinued the attempt; but it was revived, in the reign of the fifth. This abrogation of the charter of Massachusetts was the entering wedge, and, if successful, would doubtless have been followed, by a prostration of the charters of the other provinces, to make room for a more courtly system, less dependent on the people. The American revolution saved the colonies, in the last case, as the English revolution had in the first. So necessary are occasional revolutions, to bring governments back to first principles, and to teach rulers, that the people are the fountain of all legitimate power, and their happiness the object of all its delegations.)

The present moment seemed favourable to this design. The temper of the nation was high; and the resentment against the province of Massachusetts general and violent. The late outrages in Boston furnished a pretence for the attempt. An act of the British parliament speedily followed the one for shutting up the port of Boston, entitled, an act for the better regulating the government of Massachusetts. The object of this was to alter the charter of the province, in the following particulars.

2. ACT TO CHANGE THE CONSTITUTION OF MASSACHUSETTS, MAY 20, 1774

The council, or second branch of the legislature, heretofore elected by the general court, was to be, from the first of August, 1774, appointed by the crown. The royal governor was, also, by the same act, invested with the power of appointing and removing all judges of the inferior courts of common pleas, commissioners of oyer and terminer, the attorney general, provost marshal, justices, sheriffs, &c. The town meetings, which were sanctioned by the charter, were with a few exceptions expressly forbidden to be held, without the leave of the governor or lieutenant governor in writing, expressing the special business of said meeting, first had and obtained; and with a further restriction, that no matter should be treated of at these meetings, except the election of public officers, and the business expressed in the leave given by the governor or lieutenant governor. Jurymen, who had been before elected by the freeholders and inhabitants of the several towns, were to be, by this new act, all summoned and returned, by the sheriffs of the respective counties. The whole executive government was taken out of the hands of the people; and the nomination of all important officers vested in the king or his governor.

This act excited a greater alarm than the port act. The one affected only the metropolis; the other the whole province. The one had the appearance of being merited; as it was well known, that an act of violence had been committed by its inhabitants, under the sanction of a town meeting: but the other had no stronger justifying reason than that the proposed alterations were, in the opinion of the parliament absolutely necessary, in order to the preservation of the peace and good order of the said province. In support of this bill, the minister who brought it in alleged, that an executive power was wanting in the country. The very people, said he, who commit the riots are the posse comitatus, in which the force of the civil power consists. He further urged the futility of making laws, the execution of which, under the present form of government in Massachusetts, might be so easily evaded; and therefore contended for a necessity to alter the whole frame of their constitution, as far as related to its executive and judicial powers. In opposition it was urged, that the taking away the civil constitution of a whole people, secured by a solemn charter, upon general charges of delinquencies and defects, was a stretch of power, of

God Prepares
a Christian
People
to Establish
the American
Nation

the most arbitrary and dangerous nature. By the English constitution, charters were sacred, revocable only by a due course of law, and on a conviction of misconduct. They were solemn compacts between the prince and the people, and without the constitutional power of either party.

The abettors of the British schemes reasoned in a summary way. Said they, "the colonies, particularly Massachusetts, by their circular letters, associations, and town meetings, have, for years past, thwarted all the measures of government, and are meditating independency. This turbulent spirit of theirs is fostered by their constitution, which invests them with too much power, to be consistent with their state of subordination. Let us therefore lay the axe at the root; new model their charter; and lop off those privileges which they have abused."

When the human mind is agitated with passion, it rarely discerns its own interest, and but faintly foresees consequences. Had the parliament stopped short with the Boston port act, the motives to union, and to make a common cause with that metropolis, would have been feeble, perhaps ineffectual to have roused the other provinces; but the arbitrary mutilation of the important privileges contained in a solemn charter, without a trial, and without a hearing, by the will of parliament, convinced the most moderate, that the cause of Massachusetts was the cause of all the provinces.

3. ACT FOR TRIAL IN ENGLAND, MAY 20, 1774

It readily occurred to those who guided the helm of Great Britain, that riots would probably take place, in attempting the execution of the acts just mentioned. They also discerned, that such was the temper of the people, that trials for murders, committed in suppressing riots, if held in Massachusetts, would seldom terminate in favour of the parties, who were engaged on the side of government. To make their system complete, it was necessary to go one step further, and to screen their active friends from the apprehended partiality of such trials. It was therefore provided by law, that if any person was indicted for murder, or for any capital offence, committed in aiding magistracy, that the government might send the person, so indicted, to another colony, or to Great Britain, to be tried. This law was the subject of severe comments. It was considered as an act of indemnity to those, who should embrue their hands in the blood of their fellow-citizens.

It was asked, how the relations of a murdered man could effectually prosecute, if they must go three thousand miles to attend that business. It was contended, that the act, by stopping the usual course of justice, would give rise to assassinations, and dark revenge among individuals; and encourage all kinds of lawless violence. The charge of partiality was retorted. For said they, "if a party spirit, against the authority of Great Britain, would condemn an active officer, in Massachusetts, as a murderer, the same party spirit, for preserving the authority of Great Britain, would, in that country, acquit a murderer as a spirited performer of his duty." The case of captain Preston was also quoted, as a proof of the impartial administration of justice in Massachusetts.

The same natives of America, who had petitioned against the Boston port bill, presented a second one against these two bills. With uncommon energy of language, they pointed out many constitutional objections against them; and concluded with fervently beseeching, "that the parliament would not, by passing them, reduce their countrymen to an abject state of misery and humiliation, or drive them to the last resource of despair." The lords of the minority entered also a protest against the passing of each of these bills.

It was fortunate for the people of Boston, and those who wished to promote a combination of the colonies against Great Britain, that these three several laws passed nearly at the same time. They were presented in quick succession: either in the form of bills, or of acts, to the consideration of the inflamed Americans, and produced effects on their minds, infinitely greater than could have been expected from either, especially from the Boston port act alone.

When the fire of indignation, excited by the first, was burning, intelligence of these other acts, operated like fuel, and made it flame out with increasing vehemence. The three laws were considered as forming a complete system of tyranny, from the operation of which, there was no chance of making a peaceable escape.

"By the first," said they, "the property of unoffending thousands is arbitrarily taken away, for the act of a few individuals. By the second, our chartered liberties are annihilated: and by the third, our lives may be destroyed with impunity. Property, liberty, and life, are all sacrificed on the altar of ministerial vengeance." This mode of reasoning was not peculiar to Massachusetts. These three acts of parliament, contrary to the expectation of those who planned them, became the cement of a firm union among the colonies, from New Hampshire to Georgia. They now openly said, "Our charters and other rights and immunities, must depend on the pleasure of parliament." They were sensible that they had all concurred, more or less, in the same line of opposition, which had provoked these severe statutes against Massachusetts; and they believed, that vengeance, though delayed, was not remitted; and that the only favour, the least culpable could expect, was to be the last that would be devoured. The friends of the colonies contended, that these laws were in direct contradiction to the letter and the spirit of the British constitution. Their opposers could support them on no stronger grounds than those of political necessity and expedience. They acknowledged them to be contrary to the established mode of proceeding; but defended them, as tending ultimately to preserve the constitution, from the meditated independency of the colonies.

Such was the temper of the people in England, that the acts hitherto passed were popular. A general opinion had gone forth in the mother country, that the people of Massachusetts, by their violent opposition to government, had drawn on themselves merited correction.

4. QUEBEC ACT, JUNE 22, 1774

The parliament did not stop here; but proceeded one step further, which inflamed their enemies in America, and lost them friends in Great Britain. The general clamour in the provinces was, that the proceedings in the parliament were arbitrary and unconstitutional. Before they completed their memorable session, in the beginning of the year 1774, they passed an act respecting the government of Quebec, which, in the opinion of their friends, merited these appelations. By this act, the government of that province was made to extend southward to the Ohio, and westward to the banks of the Mississippi, and northward to the boundary of the Hudson's Bay company. The principal objects of the act were to form a legislative council, for all the affairs of the province, except taxation, which council should be appointed by the crown; the office to be held during pleasure; his majesty's Roman Catholic subjects to be entitled to a place therein; to establish the French laws, and a trial without jury, in civil cases; and the English laws, with a trial by jury, in criminal; and to secure, to the Roman Catholic clergy, except the regulars, the legal enjoyment of their estates, and their tythes,

from all who were of their own religion. Not only the spirit, but the letter of this act were so contrary to the English constitution, that it diminished the popularity of the measures, which had been formed against the Americans.

Among the more southern colonists, it was conceived, that its evident object was to make the inhabitants of Canada fit instruments, in the hands of power, to reduce them to a state of slavery.

They well remembered the embarrassments occasioned to them, in the late war between France and England, by the French inhabitants of Canada. They supposed, that the British administration meant, at this time, to use these people in the same line of attack, for their subjugation. As Great Britain had new modelled the chartered government of Massachusetts, and claimed an authority so to do in every province, the colonists were apprehensive, that, in the plenitude of her power, she would impose on each of them, in their turn, a constitution, similar to the one projected for the province of Canada.

They foresaw, or thought they foresaw, the annihilation of their ancient assemblies, and their whole legislative business transferred to creatures of the crown. The legal parliamentary right to a maintenance, conferred on the clergy of the Roman Catholic religion, gave great offence to many in England; but the political consequences, expected to result from it, were most dreaded by the colonists.

They viewed the whole act as an evidence, that hostilities were intended against them, and as calculated to make Roman Catholics subservient to the purposes of military coercion.

The session of parliament, which passed these memorable acts, had stretched far into summer. As it drew near a close, the most sanguine expectations were indulged, that, from the resolution and great unanimity of parliament, on all American questions, the submission of the colonists would be immediate, and their future obedience and tranquillity effectually secured. The triumphs and congratulations of the friends of the ministry, were unusually great.

In passing the acts, which have been just mentioned, dissentients, in favour of America, were unusually few. The ministerial majority, believing that the refractory colonists depended chiefly on the countenance of their English abettors, were of opinion, that as soon as they received intelligence of the decrease of their friends, and of the decisive conduct of parliament, they would

463

God Prepares
a Christian
People
to Establish
the American
Nation

acquiesce in the will of Great Britain. The fame and grandeur of the nation was such, that it was never imagined, they would seriously dare to contend with so formidable a people. The late triumphs of Great Britain had made such an impression on her rulers, that they believed the Americans, on seeing the ancient spirit of the nation revive, would not risk a trial of prowess with those fleets and armies, which the combined forces of France and Spain, were unable to resist. By an impious confidence in their superior strength, they precipitated the nation into rash measures, from the dire effects of which, the world may learn a useful lesson.

PROCEEDINGS OF THE COLONIES, IN 1774,
IN CONSEQUENCE OF THE BOSTON PORT ACT

The winter which followed the destruction of the tea in Boston, was fraught with anxiety to those of the colonists, who were given to reflection. Many conjectures were formed about the line of conduct Great Britain would probably adopt, for the support of her dignity. The fears of the most timid were more than realized, by the news of the Boston port bill. This arrived on the 10th of May, 1774; and its operation was to commence the 1st of the next month. Various town meetings were called, to deliberate on the state of public affairs. On the 13th of May, the town of Boston passed the following vote:

May 10, 1774
May 13, 1774

"That it is the opinion of this town, that, if the other colonies come to a joint resolution, to stop all importation from Great Britain and the West Indies, till the act, for blocking up this harbour, be repealed, the same will prove the salvation of North America, and her liberties. On the other hand, if they continue their exports and imports, there is high reason to fear that fraud, power, and the most odious oppression, will rise triumphant over justice, right, social happiness, and freedom. And, moreover, that this vote be transmitted by the moderator, to all our sister colonies, in the name and behalf of this town."

Copies of this vote were transmitted to each of the colonies. The opposition to Great Britain had hitherto called forth the pens of the ingenious, and, in some instances, imposed the self-denial of non-importation agreements: but the bulk of the people had little to do with the dispute. The spirited conduct of the people of Boston, in destroying the tea, and the alarming precedents set by Great Britain, in consequence thereof, brought subjects into discussion, with which every peasant and day labourer was concerned.

The patriots, who had hitherto guided the helm, knew well, that, if the other colonies did not support the people of Boston, they must be crushed; and it was equally obvious, that in their coercion a precedent, injurious to liberty, would be established. It was therefore the interest of Boston, to draw in the other colonies. It was also the interest of the patriots, in all the colonies, to bring over the mass of the people, to adopt such efficient measures as were likely to extricate the inhabitants of Boston, from the unhappy situation in which they were involved. To effect these purposes, much prudence as well as patriotism was necessary. The other provinces were but remotely affected by the fate of Massachusetts. They had no particular cause, on their own account, to oppose the government of Great Britain. That a people so circumstanced, should take part with a distressed neighbour, at the risk of incurring the resentment of the mother country, did not accord with the selfish maxims by which states, as well as individuals, are usually governed. The ruled are, for the most part, prone to suffer as long as evils are tolerable: and, in general, they must feel before they are roused to contend with their oppressors: but the Americans acted on a contrary principle.

They commenced an opposition to Great Britain, and ultimately engaged in a defensive war, on speculation. They were not so much moved by oppression, actually felt, as, by a conviction, that a foundation was laid, and a precedent about to be established for future oppressions. To convince the bulk of the people, that they had an interest in foregoing a present good, and submitting to a present evil, in order to obtain a future greater good, and to avoid a future greater evil, was the task assigned to the colonial patriots. It called for the exertion of their utmost abilities. They effected it in a great measure, by means of the press. Pamphlets, essays, addresses, and newspaper dissertations, were daily presented to the public, proving that Massachusetts was suffering in the common cause; and that interest and policy required the united exertions of all the colonies, in support of that much injured province. It was inculcated on the people, that, if the ministerial schemes were suffered to take effect, in Massachusetts, the other colonies must expect the loss of their charters, and that a new government would be imposed upon them, like that projected

VOTES and PROCEEDINGS of

the Town of

BOSTON,

JUNE 17, 1774.

AT a legal and very full meeting of the freeholders and other inhabitants of the town of Boston, by adjournment at Faneuil-hall, June 17, 1774.

The Hon. JOHN ADAMS, Esq; Moderator.

UPON a motion made, the town again entered into the consideration of that article in the warrant, Viz. " To consider and determine what measures are proper to be taken upon the present exigency of our public affairs, more especially relative to the late edict of a British parliament for blocking up the harbour of Boston, and annihilating the trade of this town," and after very serious debates thereon,

VOTED, (With only one dissentient) 'That the committee of correspondence be enjoined forthwith to write to all the other colonies, acquainting them that we are not idle, that we are deliberating upon the steps to be taken on the present exigencies of our public affairs; that our brethren the landed interest of this province, with an unexampled spirit and unanimity, are entering into a non-consumption agreement; and that we are waiting with anxious expectation for the result of a continental congress, whose meeting we impatiently desire, in whose wisdom and firmness we can confide, and in whose determinations we shall chearfully acquiesce.

Agreable to order, the committee of correspondence laid before the town such letters, as they had received in answer to the circular letters, wrote by them to the several colonies and also the sea port towns in this province since the reception of the Boston port bill; and the same being publicly read,

VOTED, unanimously, That our warmest thanks be transmitted to our brethren on the continent, for that humanity, sympathy and affection with which they have been inspired, and which they have expressed towards this distressed town at this important season.

VOTED, unanimously, That the thanks of this town be, and hereby are, given to the committee of correspondence, for their faithfulness, in the discharge of their trust, and that they be desired to continue their vigilance and activity in that service.

Whereas the Overseers of the poor in the town of Boston are a body politic, by law constituted for the reception and distribution of all charitable donations for the use of the poor of said town,

VOTED, That all grants and donations to this town and the poor thereof at this distressing season, be paid and delivered into the hands of said Overseers, and by them appropriated and distributed in concert with the committee lately appointed by this town for the consideration of ways and means of employing the poor.

VOTED, That the townclerk be directed to publish the proceedings of this meeting in the several news papers.

The meeting was then adjourned to Monday the 27th of June, instant.

Attest,

WILLIAM COOPER, Town Clerk.

GOD PREPARES
A CHRISTIAN
PEOPLE
TO ESTABLISH
THE AMERICAN
NATION

for Quebec. The king and parliament held no patronage in America, sufficient to oppose this torrent. The few, who ventured to write in their favour, found a difficulty in communicating their sentiments to the public. No pensions or preferments awaited their exertions. Neglect and contempt were their usual portion; but popularity, consequence, and fame, were the rewards of those who stepped forward in the cause of liberty. In order to interest the great body of people, the few, who were at the helm, disclaimed any thing more decisive, than convening the inhabitants, and taking their sense on what was proper to be done. In the mean time, great pains were taken to prepare them for the adoption of vigorous measures.

WHIGS AND TORIES,
NEW YORK AND PENNSYLVANIA

The words whigs and tories, for want of better, were now introduced, as the distinguishing names of parties. By the former, were meant those who were for making a common cause with Boston, and supporting the colonies in their opposition to the claims of parliament. By the latter, those who were, at least, so far favourers of Great Britain, that they wished, either that no measures, or only palliative measures, should be adopted in opposition to her schemes.

These parties were so nearly balanced in New York, that nothing more was agreed to, at the first meeting of the inhabitants, than a recommendation to call a congress.

At Philadelphia, the patriots had a delicate part to act. The government of the colony being proprietary, a multitude of officers, connected with that interest, had much to fear from convulsions, and nothing to expect from a revolution. A still greater body of people, called Quakers, denied the lawfulness of war; and therefore could not adopt such measures, for the support of Boston, as naturally tended to produce an event so adverse to their system of religion.

The citizens of Boston not only sent forward their public letter, to the citizens of Philadelphia, but accompanied it with private communications, to individuals of known patriotism and influence, in which they stated the impossibility of their standing alone, against the torrent of ministerial vengeance, and the indispensable necessity, that the leading colony of Pennsylvania, should afford them its support and countenance. The advocates in Philadelphia, for making a common cause with Boston, were fully sensible of the state of parties in Pennsylvania. They saw the dispute with Great Britain brought to a crisis, and a new scene opening, which required exertions different from any heretofore made. The success of these, they well knew, depended on the wisdom, with which they were planned, and the union of the whole people, in carrying them into execution. They saw the propriety of proceeding with the greatest circumspection; and, therefore, resolved, at their first meeting, on nothing more than to call a general meeting of the inhabitants, on the next evening. At this second meeting, the patriots had so much moderation and policy, as to urge nothing decisive, contenting themselves with taking the sense of the inhabitants, simply on the propriety of sending an answer to the public letter from Boston. This was universally approved. The letter agreed upon was firm but temperate. They acknowledged the difficulty of offering advice on the present occasion; sympathized with the people of Boston in their distress; and observed, that all lenient measures, for their relief, should be first tried. They said, that, if the making restitution for the tea destroyed, would put an end to the unhappy controversy, and leave the people of Boston upon their ancient footing of constitutional liberty, it could not admit of a doubt what part they should act; but that it was not the value of the tea; it was the indefeasible right of giving and granting their own money, which was the matter in consideration; that it was the common cause of America; and, therefore, necessary, in their opinion, that a congress of deputies from the several colonies should be convened, to devise means for restoring harmony between Great Britain and the colonies, and preventing matters from coming to extremities. Till this could be brought about, they recommended firmness, prudence, and moderation to the immediate sufferers; assuring them, that the people of Pennsylvania would continue to evince a firm adherence to the cause of American liberty.

In order to awaken the attention of the people, a series of letters was published, well calculated to rouse them to a sense of their danger, and point out the fatal consequences of the late acts of Parliament. Every newspaper teemed with dissertations in favour of liberty; and with debates of the members of parliament, especially with the speeches of the favourers of America, and the protests of the dissenting lords. The latter had a particular effect on the colonists, and were considered by them as proofs, that the late acts against Massachusetts were unconstitutional and arbitrary.

The minds of the people being thus prepared, the friends of liberty promoted a petition to the governor, for convening the assembly. This they knew would not be granted, and that the refusal of it, would smooth the way for calling the inhabitants together.

June 18, 1774

The governor having refused to call the assembly, a general meeting of the inhabitants was requested. About eight thousand met, on the 18th of June, 1774, and adopted sundry spirited resolutions. In these they declared, that the Boston port act was unconstitutional; that it was expedient to convene a continental congress; to appoint a committee for the city and county of Philadelphia, to correspond with their sister colonies and the several counties of Pennsylvania; and to invest that committee with power to determine on the best mode for collecting the sense of the province, and appointing deputies to attend a general congress. Under the sanction of this last resolve, the committee appointed for that purpose, wrote a circular letter to all the counties of the province, requesting them to appoint deputies to a general meeting, proposed to be held on the 15th of July. Part of this letter was in the following words:

July 15, 1774

"We would not offer such an affront to the well-known public spirit of Pennsylvanians, as to question your zeal on the present occasion. Our very existence in the rank of freemen, and the security of all that ought to be dear to us, evidently depends on our conducting this great cause to its proper issue, by firmness, wisdom, and magnanimity. It is with pleasure we assure you, that all the colonies, from South Carolina to New Hampshire, are animated with one spirit, in the common cause, and consider this as the proper crisis, for having our differences, with the mother country, brought to some certain issue, and our liberties fixed upon a permanent foundation. This desirable end can only be accomplished by a free communication of sentiments, and a sincere and fervent regard for the interests of our common country."

CONVENTION OF PENNSYLVANIA

The several counties readily complied with the request of the inhabitants of Philadelphia, and appointed deputies; who met at the time appointed, and passed sundry resolves, in which they reprobated the late acts of parliament; expressed their sympathy with Boston, as suffering in the common cause; approved of holding a con-

gress; and declared their willingness to make any sacrifices, that might be recommended by a congress, for securing their liberties.

Thus, without tumult, disorder, or divided counsels, the whole province of Pennsylvania was, by prudent management and temperate proceedings, brought into the opposition, with its whole weight and influence. This is the more remarkable, as it is probable, that, if the sentiments of individuals had been separately taken, there would have been a majority against involving themselves in the consequences of taking part, with the destroyers of the tea, at Boston.

While these proceedings were carrying on in Pennsylvania, three of the most distinguished patriots of Philadelphia, under colour of an excursion of pleasure, made a tour throughout the province, in order to discover the real sentiments of the common people. They were well apprized of the consequences of taking the lead in a dispute, which every day became more serious, unless they could depend on being supported by the yeomanry of the country. By freely associating and conversing with many of every class and denomination, they found them unanimous in that fundamental principle of the American controversy, "that the parliament of Great Britain had no right to tax them." From their general determination on this subject, a favourable prognostic was formed, of a successful opposition to the claims of Great Britain.

VIRGINIA

In Virginia, the house of burgesses, on the 26th of May, 1774, resolved, that the first of June, the day on which the operation of the Boston port bill was to commence, should be set apart by the members, as a day of fasting, humiliation and prayer;

May 26, 1774

"devoutly to implore the divine interposition, for averting the heavy calamities which threatened destruction to their civil rights, and the evils of a civil war; and to give them one heart and one mind, to oppose, by all just and proper means, every injury to American rights." On the publication of this resolution, the royal governor, the earl of Dunmore, dissolved them. The members, notwithstanding their dissolution, met in their private capacities, and signed an agreement, in which, among other things, they declared, "that an attack made on one of their sister colonies, to compel submission to arbitrary taxes, was an attack made on all British America, and threatened ruin to the

God Prepares
a Christian
People
to Establish
the American
Nation

rights of all, unless the united wisdom of the whole be applied."

SOUTH CAROLINA

In South Carolina the vote of the town of Boston, of the 13th of May, being presented to a number of the leading citizens in Charleston, it was unanimously agreed to call a meeting of the inhabitants.

That this might be as general as possible, letters were sent to every parish and district in the province, and the people were invited to attend, either personally, or by their representatives at a general meeting of the inhabitants. A large number assembled, in which were some, from almost every part of the province. The proceedings of the parliament against the province of Massachusetts were distinctly related to this convention. Without one dissenting voice, they passed sundry resolutions, expressive of their rights, and of their sympathy with the people of Boston. They also chose five delegates to represent them in a continental congress, and invested them, "with full powers, and authority, in behalf of them and their constituents, to concert, agree to, and effectually to prosecute such legal measures as, in their opinion, and the opinion of the other members, would be most likely to obtain a redress of American grievances."

May 13, 1774

The events of this time may be transmitted to posterity; but the agitation of the public mind can never be fully comprehended, by those who were not witnesses of it.

In the counties and town of the several provinces, as well as in the cities, the people assembled and passed resolutions, expressive of their rights, and of their detestation of the late acts of parliament. These had an instantaneous effect on the minds of thousands. Not only the young and impetuous, but the aged and temperate, joined in pronouncing them to be unconstitutional and oppressive. They viewed them as deadly weapons aimed at the vitals of that liberty, which they adored; and as rendering abortive the generous pains taken by their forefathers, to procure for them in a new world, the quiet enjoyment of their rights. They were the subjects of their meditation when alone, and of their conversation when in company.

Within little more than a month, after the news of the Boston port bill reached America, it was communicated from state to state; and a flame was kindled, in almost every breast, through the widely extended provinces. In order to understand the mode by which this flame was spread, with such rapidity, over so great an extent of country, it is necessary to observe, that the several colonies were divided into counties, and these again sub-divided into districts, distinguished by the names of towns, townships, precincts, hundreds of parishes. In New England the subdivisions, which are called towns, were, by law, bodies corporate; had their regular meetings; and might be occasionally convened by their proper officers. The advantages derived from these meetings, by uniting the whole body of the people, in the measures taken to oppose the stamp act, induced other provinces to follow the example. Accordingly, under the association which was formed to oppose the revenue act of 1767, committees were established, not only in the capitals of every province, but in most of the subordinate districts. Great Britain, without designing it, had, by her two preceding attempts at American revenue, taught her colonies, not only the advantages, but the means of union.

The system of committees, which prevailed, in 1765, and also in 1767, was revived in 1774. By them there was a quick transmission of intelligence, from the capital towns, through the subordinate districts, to the whole body of the people, and an union of counsels and measures was effected, among widely disseminated inhabitants.

It is perhaps impossible for human wisdom, to contrive any system more subservient to these purposes, than such a reciprocal exchange of intelligence, by committees. From the want of such a communication with each other, and consequently of union among themselves, many states have lost their liberties, and more have been unsuccessful in their attempts to regain them, after they were lost.

What the eloquence and talents of Demosthenes could not effect, among the states of Greece, might have been effected by the simple device of committees of correspondence. The few have been enabled to keep the many in subjection, in every age, from the want of union among the latter. Several of the provinces of Spain complained of oppression, under Charles the fifth, and in transports of rage took arms against him; but they never consulted or communicated with each other. They resisted separately, and were therefore separately subdued.

The colonists, sympathizing with their distressed brethren in Massachusetts, felt themselves called upon, to do something for their relief; but to determine what was most proper, did not so obviously occur. It was a natural idea, that, for harmonising their measures, a congress of deputies from each province should be convened. This early occurred to all; and, being agreed to, was the means of producing union and concert among inhabitants, removed several hundred miles from each other. In times less animated, various questions about the place and legality of their meeting, and about the extent of their power, would have produced a great diversity of sentiments; but on this occasion, by the special agency of Providence, there was the same universal bent of inclination, in the great body of the people. A sense of common danger extinguished selfish passions. The public attention was fixed on the great cause of liberty. Local attachments and partialities were sacrificed on the altar of patriotism.

There were not wanting moderate men, who would have been willing to pay for the tea destroyed, if that would have put an end to the controversy; for, it was not for the value of the tea, nor of the tax, but the right of giving and granting their money, that the colonists contended. The act of parliament was so cautiously worded, as to prevent the opening of the port of Boston, even though the East India company had been reimbursed for all damages, "until it was made appear to his majesty in council, that peace and obedience to the laws were so far restored, in the town of Boston, that the trade of Great Britain might be safely carried on there, and his majesty's customs duly collected." The latter part of this limitation, "the due collection of his majesty's customs," was understood to comprehend submission to the late revenue laws. It was therefore inferred, that payment, for the tea destroyed, would produce no certain relief, unless they were willing to give operation to the law, for raising a revenue on future importations of that commodity, and also to acquiesce in the late mutilation of their charter. As it was deliberately resolved, never to submit to either, the most lukewarm of well-informed patriots, possessing the public confidence, neither advised nor wished for the adoption of that measure. A few in Boston, who were known to be in the royal interest, proposed a resolution for that purpose; but they met with no support. Of the many, who joined the British in the course of the war, there was scarcely an individual to be found in this early state of the controversy, who advocated the right of parliamentary taxation. There were doubtless many timid persons, who, fearing the power of Britain, would rather have submitted to her en-

croachments, than risked the vengeance of her arms; but such, for the most part, suppressed their sentiments. Zeal for liberty being immediately rewarded with applause, the patriots had every inducement to come forward, and avow their principles; but there was something so unpopular in appearing to be influenced by timidity, interest, or excessive caution, when essential interests were attacked, that such persons shunned public notice, and sought the shade of retirement.

In the three first months, which followed the shutting up of the port of Boston, the inhabitants of the colonies in hundreds of small circles, as well as in their provincial assemblies and congresses, expressed their abhorrence of the late proceedings of the British parliament against Massachusetts; their concurrence in the proposed measure of appointing deputies for a general congress; and their willingness to do and suffer whatever should be judged conducive to the establishment of their liberties.

A patriotic flame, created and diffused by sympathy, was communicated to so many breasts, and reflected from such a variety of objects, as to become too intense to be resisted.

While the combination of the other colonies, to support Boston, was gaining strength, new matter of dissention daily took place in Massachusetts. The resolution, for shutting the port of Boston, was no sooner taken, than it was determined to order a military force to that town. General Gage, the commander in chief of the royal forces in North America, was also sent thither, in the additional capacity of governor of Massachusetts. He arrived in Boston, on the third day after the inhabitants received the first intelligence of the Boston port bill. Though the people were irritated by that measure, and though their republican jealousy was hurt by the combination of the civil and military character in one person, yet the general was received with all the honours which had been usually paid to his predecessors. Soon after his arrival, two regiments of foot, with a detachment of artillery, and some cannon, were landed in Boston. These troops were by degrees reinforced with others from Ireland, New York, Halifax and Quebec.

The governor announced that he had the king's particular command, for holding the general court at Salem, after the first of June. When that eventful day arrived, the act for shutting up the port of Bos- June 1, 1774 ton commenced its operation. It was devoutly kept at Williamsburg, as a day of fasting and humiliation. In Philadelphia, it was

GOD PREPARES
A CHRISTIAN
PEOPLE
TO ESTABLISH
THE AMERICAN
NATION

solemnized with every manifestation of public calamity and grief. The inhabitants shut up their houses. After divine service, a stillness reigned over the city, which exhibited an appearance of the deepest distress.

In Boston, a new scene opened on the inhabitants. Hitherto, that town had been the seat of commerce and of plenty. The immense business, transacted therein, afforded a comfortable subsistence to many thousands. The necessary, the useful, and even some of the elegant arts were cultivated among them. The citizens were polite and hospitable. In this happy state, they were sentenced, on the short notice of twenty-one days, to a total deprivation of all means of subsisting. The blow reached every person. The rents of the landholders either ceased, or were greatly diminished. The immense property, in stores and wharves, was rendered comparatively useless. Labourers, artificers, and others, employed in the numerous occupations created by an extensive trade, partook of the general calamity. They who depended on a regular income, flowing from previous acquisitions of property, as well as they, who, with the sweat of their brow, earned their daily subsistence, were equally deprived of the means of support; and the chief difference between them was, that the distresses of the former were rendered more intolerable, by the recollection of past enjoyments. All these inconveniencies and hardships were borne with a passive, but inflexible fortitude. Their determination to persist in the same line of conduct, which had been the occasion of their suffering, was unabated.

The authors and advisers of the resolution, for destroying the tea, were in the town, and still retained their popularity and influence. The execrations of the inhabitants fell not on them, but on the British parliament. Their countrymen acquitted them of all selfish designs, and believed that, in their opposition to the measures of Great Britain, they were actuated by an honest zeal for constitutional liberty. The sufferers, in Boston, had the consolation of sympathy from the other colonists. Contributions were raised, in all quarters, for their relief. Letters and addresses came to them from corporate bodies, town meetings, and provincial conventions, applauding their conduct, and exhorting them to perseverance.

The people of Marblehead, who, by their proximity, were likely to reap advantage from the distresses of Boston, generously offered the merchants thereof, the use of their harbour, wharves, ware-houses, and also their personal attendance on the lading or unlading of their goods, free of

all expense. The inhabitants of Salem, in an address to governor Gage, concluded with these remarkable words: "By shutting up the port of Boston, some imagine that the course of trade might be turned hither, and to our benefit: but nature, in the formation of our harbour, forbids our becoming rivals in commerce, of that convenient mart; and, were it otherwise, we must be dead to every idea of justice, and lost to all feelings of humanity, could we indulge one thought to seize on wealth, and raise our fortunes, on the ruins of our suffering neighbours."

The Massachusetts general court met at Salem, according to adjournment, on the 7th of June. Several of the popular leaders took, in a private way, the sense of the members, on what was proper to be done. Finding they were able to carry such measures,   June 7, 1774 as the public exigencies required, they prepared resolves, and moved for their adoption: but before they went on the latter business, their door was shut.

One member, nevertheless, contrived means of sending information to governor Gage of what was doing. His secretary was sent off, to dissolve the general court; but was refused admission. As he could obtain no entrance, he read the proclamation at the door, and immediately afterwards in council; and thus dissolved the general court. The house, while sitting with their doors shut, appointed five of the most repectable inhabitants as their committee, to meet committees from other provinces, that might be convened the 1st of September at Philadelphia; voted them seventy-five pounds sterling each; and recommended, to the several towns and districts, to raise the said sum by equitable proportions. By these means, the designs of the governor were disappointed. His situation in every respect was truly disagreeable. It was his duty to forward the execution of laws, which were universally execrated. Zeal for his master's service prompted him to endeavour, that they should be carried into full effect; but his progress was retarded by obstacles from every quarter. He had to transact his official business with a people, who possessed a high sense of liberty, and were   August 1, 1774 uncommonly ingenious in evading disagreeable acts of parliament. It was a part of his duty, to prevent the calling of the town meetings, after the 1st of August, 1774. These meetings were nevertheless held. On his proposing to exert authority, for the dispersion of the people, he was told by the selectmen, that they had not offended against the act of parliament; for that only prohibited the calling of town meetings; and no such call had been made: a former constitutional meeting, before the 1st of August, having only adjourned themselves from time to time. Other evasions, equally founded on the letter of even the late obnoxious laws, were practised.

As the summer advanced, the people of Massachusetts received stronger proofs of support, from the neighbouring provinces. They were, therefore, encouraged to further opposition. The inhabitants of the colonies, at this time, with regard to political opinions, might be divided into three classes. Of these, one was for rushing precipitately into extremities. They were for immediately stopping all trade, and could not even brook the delay of waiting, till the proposed continental congress should meet. Another party, equally respectable, both as to character, property, and patriotism, was more moderate; but not less firm. These were averse to the adoption of any violent resolutions, till all others were ineffectually tried. They wished that a clear statement of their rights, claims, and grievances, should precede every other measure. A third class disapproved of what was generally going on: a few from principle, and a persuasion that they ought to submit to the mother country; some from the love of ease; others from self-interest; but the bulk from fear of the mischievous consequences likely to follow.

All these latter classes, for the most part, lay still, while the friends of liberty acted with spirit. If they, or any of them, ventured to oppose popular measures, they were not supported, and therefore declined further efforts. The resentment of the people was so strong against them, that they sought for peace by remaining quiet. The same indecision, that made them willing to submit to Great Britain, made them apparently acquiesce in popular measures which they disapproved. The spirited part of the community, being on the side of liberty, the patriots had the appearance of unanimity; though many either kept at a distance from public meetings, or voted against their own opinion, to secure themselves from resentment, and promote their present ease and interest.

Under the influence of those who were for the immediate adoption of efficacious measures, an agreement, by the name of the solemn league and covenant, was adopted by numbers. The subscribers of this bound themselves, to suspend all commercial intercourse with Great Britain, until the late obnoxious laws were repealed, and the colony of Massachusetts restored to its chartered rights. General Gage published a proclamation, in

which he styled this solemn league and covenant, "an unlawful, hostile, and traitorous combination." And all magistrates were charged to apprehend, and secure for trial, such as should have any agency in publishing or subscribing the same, or any similar covenant.

This proclamation had no other effect, than to exercise the pens of the lawyers, in showing that the association did not come within the description of legal treason; and that, therefore, the governor's proclamation was not warranted by the principles of the constitution.

LAW FOR REGULATING GOVERNMENT OF PROVINCES

The late law, for regulating the government of the provinces, arrived near the beginning of August, and was accompanied with a list of thirty-six new counsellors, appointed by the crown, and in a mode variant from that prescribed by the charter. Several of these, in the first instance, declined an acceptance of the appointment. Those, who accepted of it, were every where declared to be enemies to their country. The new judges were rendered incapable of proceeding in their official duty. Upon opening the courts, the juries refused to be sworn, or to act in any manner, either under them, or in conformity to the late regulations. In some places, the people assembled, and filled the court-houses, and avenues to them, in such a manner, that neither the judges, nor their officers, could obtain entrance: and, upon the sheriff's commanding them, to make way for the court, they answered, "that they knew no court independent of the ancient laws of their country, and to none other would they submit."

In imitation of his royal master, governor Gage issued a proclamation, "for the encouragement of piety and virtue, and for the prevention and punishing vice, prophaneness, and immorality."

In this proclamation, hypocrisy was inserted as one of the immoralities, against which the people were warned. This was considered by the inhabitants, who had often been ridiculed for their strict attention to the forms of religion, to be a studied insult, and as such was more resented than an actual injury.

The proceedings and apparent dispositions of the people, together with the military preparations, which were daily made through the province, induced general Gage to fortify that neck of land, which joins Boston to the continent.

God Prepares
a Christian
People
to Establish
the American
Nation

He also seized upon the powder lodged in the arsenal at Charlestown.

This excited a most violent and universal ferment. Several thousand of the people assembled at Cambridge; and it was with difficulty, they were restrained from marching directly to Boston, to demand a delivery of the powder, with a resolution, in case of refusal, to attack the troops.

The people, thus assembled, proceeded to lieutenant governor Oliver's house, and to the houses of several of the new counsellors, and obliged them to resign, and to declare, that they would no more act under the laws lately enacted. In the confusion of these transactions, a rumour went abroad, that the royal fleet and troops were firing upon the town of Boston. This was probably designed by the popular leaders, on purpose to ascertain what aid they might expect from the country, in case of extremities. The result exceeded their most sanguine expectations. In less than twenty-four hours, there were upwards of thirty thousand men in arms marching towards the capital. Other risings of the people took place in different parts of the colony; and their violence was such, that in a short time the new counsellors, the commissioners of the customs, and all who had taken an active part in favour of Great Britain, were obliged to screen themselves in Boston. The new seat of government at Salem was abandoned: and all the officers connected with the revenue were obliged to consult their safety, by taking up their residence in a place, which an act of parliament had proscribed from all trade.

About this time, delegates from every town and district, in the county of Suffolk, of which Boston is the county town, had a meeting; at which they prefaced a number of spirited resolutions, containing a detail of the particulars of their intended opposition to the late acts of parliament, with a general declaration, "that no obedience was due from the province to either, or any part of the said acts; but that they should be rejected as the attempts of a wicked administration to enslave America." The resolves of this meeting were sent on to Philadelphia, for the information and opinion of the congress, which, as shall be hereafter related, had met there about this time.

The people of Massachusetts rightly judged, that from the decision of congress on these resolutions, they would be enabled to determine what support they might expect. Notwithstanding present appearances, they feared that the other colonies, who were no more than remotely concerned,

would not hazard the consequences of making a common cause with them, should subsequent events make it necessary to repel force by force. The decision of congress exceeded their exceptions. They "most thoroughly approved the wisdom and fortitude, with which opposition to wicked ministerial measures had been hitherto conducted in Massachusetts; and recommended to them perseverance in the same firm and temperate conduct, as expressed in the resolutions of the delegates, from the county of Suffolk." By this approbation and advice, the people of Massachusetts were encouraged to resistance, and the other colonies became bound to support them. The former, more in need of a bridle than a spur, proceeded as they had begun; but with additional confidence.

MASSACHUSETTS PROVINCIAL CONGRESS

Governor Gage had issued writs for holding a general assembly at Salem; but subsequent events, and the heat and violence which every where prevailed, made him think it expedient to counteract the writs, by a proclamation for suspending the meeting of the members. The legality of a proclamation for that purpose was denied; and, in defiance thereof, ninety of the newly elected members met, at the time and place appointed. They soon afterwards resolved themselves into a provincial Congress, and adjourned to Concord, about twenty miles from Charlestown. On their meeting there, they chose Mr. Hancock president, and proceeded to business. One of their

October 11, 1774

first acts was to appoint a committee, to wait on the governor, with a remonstrance, in which they apologized for their meeting, from the distressed state of the colony; complained of their grievances; and, after stating their apprehensions, from the hostile preparations on Boston neck, concluded with an earnest request, "that he would desist from the construction of the fortress, at the entrance into Boston, and restore that pass to its natural state."

The governor found some difficulty in giving them an answer, as they were not, in his opinion, a legal body; but the necessity of the time overruled his scruples. He replied by expressing his indignation at the supposition, "that the lives, liberties, or property of any people, except enemies, could be in danger, from English troops." He reminded them, that, while they complained of alterations, made in their charter, by acts of parliament, they were by their own acts subverting it altogether. He, therefore, warned them of the rocks they were upon, and to desist from such illegal and unconstitutional proceedings. The governor's admonitions were unavailing. The provincial congress appointed a committee, to draw up a plan for the immediate defence of the province. It was resolved to inlist a number of the inhabitants, under the name of minute men, who were to be under obligations to turn out at a minute's warning. Jedediah Prebble, Artemas Ward, and Seth Pomeroy, were elected general officers to command these minute men and the militia, in case they should be called out to action. A committee of safety, and a committee of supplies were appointed. These consisted of different persons, and were intended for different purposes. The first were invested with an authority to assemble the militia, when they thought proper, and were to recommend to the committee of supplies the purchase of such articles, as the public exigencies required. The last were limited to the small sum of 15,627 *l*. 15s. sterling, which was all the money at first voted, to oppose the power and riches of Great Britain. Under this authority, and with these means, the committees of safety and of supplies, acting in concert, laid in a quantity of stores, partly at Worcester, and partly at Concord. The same congress met again, and soon afterwards resolved, to get in readiness twelve thousand men, to act on any given emergency; and that a fourth part of the militia should be enlisted as minute men, and receive pay. John Thomas and William Heath were appointed general officers. They also sent persons to New Hampshire, Rhode Island, and Connecticut, to inform them of the steps they had taken, and to request their co-operation in making up an army of twenty thousand men. Committees, from these several colonies, met a committee from the provincial congress of Massachusetts, and settled their plans.

The proper period, for commencing opposition to general Gage's troops, was determined to be, whenever they marched out with their baggage, ammunition, and artillery. The aid of the clergy was called in upon this occasion; and a circular letter was addressed to each of the several ministers in the province, requesting their assistance, "in avoiding the dreadful slavery with which they were threatened."

As the winter approached, general Gage ordered barracks for his troops to be erected; but such was the superior influence of the popular leaders, that, on their recommendation, the workmen desisted from fulfilling the general's wishes, though the money for their labour would have been paid by the crown. An application to New York was equally unsuccessful; and it was with difficulty, that the troops could be furnished with winter lodgings. Similar obstructions were thrown in the way, of getting winter covering for the soldiery. The merchants of New York, on being applied to, answered, "that they would never supply any article for the benefit of men, who were sent as enemies to the country." The inhabitants of Massachusetts encouraged the desertion of the soldiers; and acted systematically in preventing their obtaining any other supplies, but necessary provisions. The farmers were discouraged from selling them straw, timber, boards, and such like articles of convenience. Straw, when purchased for their service, was frequently burnt. Vessels, with bricks intended for their use, were sunk; carts with wood were overturned; and the king's property was daily destroyed.

A proclamation had been issued by the king, prohibiting the exportation of military stores from Britain, which reached America, in the latter end of the year 1774. On receiving intelligence thereof,   December 13, 1774 in Rhode Island, the people seized upon, and removed from the public battery, about forty pieces of cannon; and the assembly passed resolutions for obtaining arms and military stores by every means, and also for raising and arming the inhabitants. About this time, December 13th, a company of volunteers, headed by John Sullivan and John Langdon, beset his majesty's castle at Portsmouth. They stormed the fort, and secured and confined the garrison, till they broke open the powder-house, and took the powder away. The powder being secured, the garrison was released from confinement.

Throughout this whole season, civil government, legislation, judicial proceedings, and commercial regulations were in Massachusetts, to all appearance, annihilated. The provincial congress exercised all the semblance of government which existed. From their coincidence, with the prevailing disposition of the people, their resolutions had the weight and efficacy of laws. Under the simple style of recommendation, they organized the militia, and made ordinances respecting public monies, and such further regulations as were necessary for preserving order, and for defending themselves against the British troops.

In this crisis, it seemed to be the sense of the inhabitants of Massachusetts to wait events. They dreaded every evil, that could flow from resistance, less than the operation of the late acts of

In *Provincial Congress*,

Cambridge, December 6, 1774.

RESOLVED, That the following Addreſs be preſented to the ſeveral Miniſters of the Goſpel in this Province.

REVEREND SIR,

WHEN we contemplate the Friendſhip and Aſſiſtance, our Anceſtors the firſt Settlers of this Province (while over-whelmed with Diſtreſs) received from the pious Paſtors of the Churches of CHRIST, who, to enjoy the Rights of Conſcience, fled with them into this Land, then a ſavage Wilderneſs, we find ourſelves fill'd with the moſt grateful Senſations.---And we cannot but acknowledge the Goodneſs of Heaven, in conſtantly ſupplying us with Preachers of the Goſpel, whoſe Concern has been the temporal and ſpiritual Happineſs of this People.

In a Day like this, when all the Friends of civil and religious Liberty are exerting themſelves to deliver this Country from its preſent Calamities, we cannot but place great Hopes in an Order of Men, who have ever diſtinguiſhed themſelves in their Country's Cauſe ; and do therefore recommend to the Miniſters of the Goſpel, in the ſeveral Towns and other Places in this Colony, that they aſſiſt us, in avoiding that dreadful Slavery with which we are now threatened, by adviſing the People of their ſeveral Congregations, as they wiſh their Proſperity, to abide by and ſtrictly adhere to the *Reſolutions* of the *Continental Congreſs*, as the moſt peaceable and probable Method of preventing Confuſion and Bloodſhed, and of reſtoring that Harmony between Great-Britain and theſe Colonies, on which we wiſh might be eſtabliſhed not only the Rights and Liberties of America, but the Opulence and laſting Happineſs of the whole Britiſh Empire.

Sign'd by Order of the Provincial Congreſs,

JOHN HANCOCK, Preſident.

A true Extract from the Minutes.

BENJAMIN LINCOLN, Secretary.

parliament; but, at the same time, were averse to be the aggressors, in bringing on a civil war. They chose to submit to a suspension of regular government, in preference to permitting the streams of justice to flow in the channel, prescribed by the late acts of parliament, or to conducting them forcibly in the old one, sanctioned by their charter. From the extinction of the old, and the rejection of the new constitution, all regular government was, for several months abolished. Some hundred thousands of people were in a state of nature, without legislation, magistrates, or executive officers. There was, nevertheless, a surprising degree of order. Men of the purest morals were among the most active opposers of Great Britain. While municipal laws ceased to operate, the laws of reason, morality, and religion, bound the people to each other as a social band, and preserved as great a degree of decorum, as had at any time prevailed. Even those who were opposed to the proceedings of the populace, when they were prudent and moderate, for the most part enjoyed safety, both at home and abroad.

Though there were no civil, there was an abundance of military officers. These were chosen by the people; but exercised more authority, than any who had been honoured with commissions, from the governor. The inhabitants in every place devoted themselves to arms. Handling the musket, and training, were the fashionable amusements of the men; while the women, by their presence, encouraged them to proceed. The sound of drums and fifes was to be heard in all directions. The young and the old were fired with a martial spirit. On experiment, it was found, that to force on the inhabitants, a form of government, to which they were totally averse, was not within the fancied omnipotence of parliament.

FIRST CONTINENTAL CONGRESS—1774

During these transactions in Massachusetts, effectual measures, had been taken, by the colonies, for convening a continental congress. Though there was no one entitled to lead in this business, yet, in consequence of the general impulse on the public mind, from a sense of common danger, not only the measure itself, but the time and place of meeting were, September 5, 1774 with surprising unanimity, agreed upon. The colonies, though formerly agitated with local prejudices, jealousies, and aversions, were led to assemble together in a general diet, and to feel their weight and importance in a common union. Within four months from the day, on which the first intelligence of the Boston port bill reached America, the deputies of eleven provinces had convened in Philadelphia; and in four days more, by the arrival of delegates from North Carolina, there was a complete representation of twelve colonies, containing three millions of people, disseminated over two hundred and sixty thousand square miles of territory. Some of the delegates were appointed by the constitutional assemblies. In other provinces, where they were embarrassed by royal governors, the appointments were made in voluntary meetings of the people. Perhaps there never was a body of delegates, more faithful to the interest of their constituents, than the congress of 1774. The public voice elevated none to a seat in that august assembly, but such as, in addition to considerable abilities, possessed that ascendency over the minds of their fellow-citizens, which can neither be acquired by birth, nor purchased by wealth. The instructions given to these deputies were various; but, in general, they contained strong professions of loyalty, and of constitutional dependence on the mother country. The framers of them acknowledged the prerogatives of the crown, and disclaimed every wish of separation from the parent state. On the other hand, they were firm in declaring, that they were entitled to all the rights of British born subjects, and that the late acts respecting Massachusetts were unconstitutional and oppressive.

They particularly stated their grievances, and for the most part concurred, in authorizing their deputies to concert and agree to such measures, in behalf of their constituents, as, in their joint opinion, would be most likely to obtain a redress of American grievances, ascertain American rights, on constitutional principles, and establish union and harmony between Great Britain and the colonies. Of the various instructions on this occasion, those which were drawn up, by a convention of delegates, from every county in the province of Pennsylvania, and presented by them, in a body, to the constitutional assembly, were the most precise and determinate. By these it appears, that the Pennsylvanians were disposed to submit to the acts of navigation, as they then stood, and, also, to settle a certain annual revenue on his majesty, his heirs, and successors, subject to the control of parliament; and to satisfy all damages, done to the East India company, provided their grievances were redressed, and an amicable compact was settled, which, by establishing American rights, in the manner of a new

GOD PREPARES
A CHRISTIAN
PEOPLE
TO ESTABLISH
THE AMERICAN
NATION

magna charta, would have precluded future disputes.

Of the whole number of deputies, which formed the continental congress, of 1774, one half were lawyers. Gentlemen of that profession had acquired the confidence of the inhabitants, by their exertions in the common cause. The previous measures, in the respective provinces, had been planned and carried into effect, more by lawyers than by any other order of men. Professionally taught the rights of the people, they were among the foremost, to descry every attack made on their liberties. Bred in the habits of public speaking, they made a distinguished figure in the meetings of the people, and were particularly able to explain to them the tendency of the late acts of parliament. Exerting their abilities and influence, in the cause of their country, they were rewarded with its confidence.

On the meeting of congress, they chose Peyton Randolph their president, and Charles Thomson their secretary. They agreed, as one of the rules of their doing business, that no entry should be made on their journals of any propositions discussed before them, to which they did not finally assent.

DECLARATION OF THEIR RIGHTS

This august body, to which all the colonies looked up for wisdom and direction, had scarcely convened, when a dispute arose about the mode of conducting business, which alarmed the friends of union. It was contended by some, that the votes of the small provinces should not count as much as those of the larger ones. This was argued with some warmth; and invidious comparisons were made between the extensive dominion of Virginia, and the small colonies of Delaware and Rhode Island. The impossibility of fixing the comparative weight of each province, from the want of proper materials, induced congress to resolve, that each should have one equal vote. The mode of conducting business being settled, two committees were appointed: one, to state the rights of the colonies; the several instances in which these rights had been violated; and the means most proper to be pursued for obtaining a restoration of them; the other, to examine and report the several statutes which affected the trade and manufactures of the colonies. The first committee were further instructed, to confine themselves to the consideration of such rights, as had been infringed since the year 1763.

Congress, soon after their meeting, agreed upon a declaration of their rights, by which it was, among other things, declared, that the inhabitants of the English colonies, in North America, by the immutable laws of nature, the principles of the English constitution, and the several charters or compacts, were entitled to life, liberty, and property; and that they had never ceded, to any sovereign power whatever, a right to dispose of either, without their consent. That their ancestors, who first settled the colonies, were entitled to all the rights, liberties, and immunities of free and natural born subjects, within the realm of England, and, by their migrating to America, they by no means forfeited, surrendered, or lost any of those rights; that the foundation of English liberty, and of all free government, was a right, in the people, to participate in their legislative council; and that, as the English colonists were not, and could not be properly represented in the British parliament, they were entitled to a free and exclusive power of legislation, in their several provincial legislatures, in all cases of taxation and internal polity, subject only to the negative of their sovereign. They then ran the line, between the supremacy of parliament, and the independency of the colonial legislatures, by provisos and restrictions, expressed in the following words: "But, from the necessity of the case, and a regard to the mutual interests of both countries, we cheerfully consent to the operation of such acts of the British parliament, as are, *bona fide,* restrained to the regulation of our external commerce, for the purpose of securing the commercial advantages of the whole empire to the mother country, and the commercial benefits of its respective members, excluding every idea of taxation, internal and external, for raising a revenue on the subjects in America without their consent."

This was the very hinge of the controversy. The absolute unlimited supremacy of the British parliament, both in legislation and taxation, was contended for on one side; while, on the other, no further authority was conceded, than such a limited legislation, with regard to external commerce, as would combine the interest of the whole empire. In government, as well as in religion, there are mysteries, from the close investigation of which little advantage can be expected. From the unity of the empire, it was necessary that some acts should extend over the whole. From the local situation of the colonies, it was equally reasonable, that their legislatures should, at least, in some matters be independent. Where the supremacy of the first ended, and the independency of the last began, was to the best informed a puzzling question. A different state of things would exist at this day, had the discussion of this doubtful point never been attempted.

Congress also resolved, that the colonists were entitled to the common law of England, and more especially to the privilege of being tried by their peers of the vicinage; that they were entitled to the benefit of such of the English statutes, as existed at the time of their colonization, and which they had found to be applicable to their local circumstances, and also to the immunities and privileges, granted and confirmed to them by royal charters, or secured by provincial laws; that they had a right peaceably to assemble, consider of their grievances, and petition the king; that the keeping a standing army in the colonies, without the consent of the legislature of the colony where the army was kept, was against law; that it was indispensably necessary to good government, and rendered essential, by the English constitution, that the constituent branches of the legislature be independent of each other; and that, therefore, the exercise of legislative power, in several colonies, by a council, appointed during pleasure by the crown, was unconstitutional, dangerous, and destructive to the freedom of American legislation. All of these liberties, congress, in behalf of themselves, and their constituents, claimed, demanded, and insisted upon, as their indubitable rights, which could not be legally taken from them, altered, or abridged, by any power whatever, without their consent.

Congress then resolved, that sundry acts, which had been passed in the reign of George the third, were infringements and violations of the rights of the colonists; and that the repeal of them was essentially necessary in order to restore harmony between Great Britain and the colonies. . . .

Congress declared, that they could not submit to these grievous acts and measures. In hopes that their fellow-subjects in Great Britain would restore the colonies to that state, in which both countries found happiness and prosperity, they resolved, for the present, only to pursue the following peaceable measures:

1. To enter into a non-importation, non-consumption, and non-exportation agreement or association.

2. To prepare an address to the people of Great Britain, and a memorial to the inhabitants of British America.

3. To prepare a loyal address to his majesty. . . .

All these addresses were written with uncommon ability. Coming from the heart, they were calculated to move it. Inspired by a love of liberty, and roused by a sense of common danger, the patriots of that day spoke, wrote, and acted, with an animation unknown in times of public tranquility; but it was not so much, on the probable effect of these addresses, that congress founded their hopes of obtaining a redress of their grievances, as on the consequences which they expected, from the operation of their non-importation, and non-exportation agreement. The success that had followed the adoption of a measure, similar to the former, in two preceding instances, had encouraged the colonists to expect much from a repetition of it. They indulged in extravagant opinions of the importance of their trade to Great Britain. The measure of a non-exportation of their commodities was a new expedient; and, from that, even more was expected, than from the non-importation agreement. They supposed, that it would produce such extensive distress among the merchants and manufacturers of Great Britain, and, especially, among the inhabitants of the British West India islands, as would induce their general co-operation, in procuring a redress of American grievances. Events proved that young nations, like young people, are prone to overrate their own importance.

Congress having finished all this important business, in less than eight weeks, dissolved themselves, on the 26th of October, after giving their opinion, "that another congress should be held on the 10th of May next ensuing, at Philadelphia, unless the redress of their grievances should be previously obtained," and recommending "to all the colonies to choose deputies as soon as possible, to be ready to attend at that time and place, should events make their meeting necessary."

On the publication of the proceedings of congress, the people obtained that information which they desired. Zealous to do something for their country, they patiently waited for the decision of that body, to whose direction they had resigned themselves. Their determinations were no sooner known, than cheerfully obeyed. Though their power was only advisory, yet their recommendations were more generally and more effectually carried into execution, than the laws of the best-regulated states. Every individual felt his liberties endangered, and was impressed with an idea, that his safety consisted in union. A common interest in warding off a common danger, proved a powerful incentive to the most implicit submission. Pro-

October 26, 1774

GOD PREPARES
A CHRISTIAN
PEOPLE
TO ESTABLISH
THE AMERICAN
NATION

vincial congresses and subordinate committees were every where instituted. The resolutions of the continental congress were sanctioned, with the universal approbation of these new representative bodies; and institutions were formed under their directions to carry them into effect.

The regular constitutional assemblies, also, gave their assent to the measures recommended. The assembly of New York was the only legislature, which withheld its approbation. Their metropolis had long been the head-quarters of the British army in the colonies; and many of their best families were connected with people of influence in Great Britain. The unequal distribution of their land fostered an aristocratic spirit. From the operation of these and other causes, the party for royal government was both more numerous and respectable in New York, than in the other colonies.

The assembly of Pennsylvania, though composed of a majority of Quakers, or of those who were friendly to their interest, was the first legal body of representatives, that ratified, unanimously, the acts of the general congress. They not only voted their approbation of what that body had done, but appointed members to represent them in the new congress, proposed to be held on the 10th day of May next ensuing; and took sundry steps to put the province in a posture of defence.

To relieve the distresses of the people of Boston, liberal collections were made, throughout the colonies, and forwarded for the supply of their immediate necessities. Domestic manufactures were encouraged, that the wants of the inhabitants, from the non-importation agreement, might be diminished; and the greatest zeal was discovered, by a large majority of the people, to comply with the determinations of these new-made representative bodies. In this manner, while the forms of the old government subsisted, a new and independent authority was virtually established. It was so universally the sense of the people, that the public good required a compliance with the recommendations of congress, that any man, who discovered an anxiety about the continuance of trade and business, was considered as a selfish individual; preferring private interest to the good of his country. Under the influence of these principles, the intemperate zeal of the populace transported them, frequently, so far beyond the limits of moderation, as to apply singular punishments to particular persons, who contravened the general sense of the community.

One of these was forcibly subjecting the ob-noxious persons to a stream of cold water, discharged on them from the spout of a pump. Another and more serious one was, after smearing their bodies with tar, to roll them in feathers, and expose them, thus covered with tar and feathers, to the ridicule of spectators. A more common mode was to treat them with contempt and scorn, arising, in particular cases, to such a height, as to abstain from all social intercourse with them. Frequently their names were stuck up in public places, with the appellation of tories, traitors, cowards, enemies to the country, &c.

"THE TIME TO PART BEING COME"

The British ministry were not less disappointed than mortified, at this unexpected combination of the colonies. They had flattered themselves with a belief, that the malcontents in Boston were a small party, headed by a few factious men, and that the majority of the inhabitants would arrange themselves on the side of government, as soon as they found Great Britain determined to support her authority; and, should even Massachusetts take part with its offending capital, they could not believe that the other colonies would make a common cause, in supporting so intemperate a colony: but, should even that expectation fail, they conceived that their association must be founded on principles so adverse to the interests and feelings of individuals, that it could not be of long duration. They were encouraged in these ill-founded opinions, by the recollection, that the colonies were frequently quarrelling about boundaries, clashing in interest, differing in policy, manners, customs, forms of government, and religion, and under the influence of a variety of local prejudices, jealousies, and aversions. They also remembered the obstacles, which prevented the colonies from acting together, in the execution of schemes, planned for their own defence, in the late war against the French and Indians. The failure of the expected co-operation of the colonies, in one uniform system, at that time, was not only urged by the British ministry, as a reason for parliamentary control over the whole, but flattered them with a delusive hope, that they never could be brought to combine their counsels and their arms. Perhaps the colonists apprehended more danger from British encroachments, on their liberties, than from French encroachment, on Indian territories, in their neighbourhood: or more probably, the time to part being come, the Governor of the Universe, by a secret influence on their minds, disposed them to union. From whatever cause it proceeded, it is certain, that a disposition to do, to suffer, and to accommodate, spread from breast to breast, and from colony to colony, beyond the reach of human calculation. It seemed as though one mind inspired the whole. The merchants put far behind them the gains of trade, and cheerfully submitted to a total stoppage of business, in obedience to the recommendations of men, invested with no legislative powers. The cultivators of the soil, with great unanimity, assented to the determination, that the hard-earned produce of their farms should remain unshipped, although, in case of a free exportation, many would have been eager to have purchased it from them, at advanced prices. The sons and daughters of ease renounced imported conveniences; and voluntarily engaged to eat, drink, and wear, only such articles as their country afforded. These sacrifices were made, not from the pressure of present distress, but on the generous principle of sympathy, with an invaded sister colony, and the prudent policy of guarding against a precedent which might, in a future day, operate against their liberties.

This season of universal distress exhibited a striking proof, how practicable it is for mankind to sacrifice ease, pleasure, and interest, when the mind is strongly excited by its passions. In the midst of their sufferings, cheerfulness appeared in the face of all the people. They counted every thing cheap in comparison with liberty, and readily gave up whatever tended to endanger it. A noble strain of generosity and mutual support was generally excited. A great and powerful diffusion of public spirit took place. The animation of the times raised the actors in these scenes above themselves, and excited them to deeds of self-denial, which the interested prudence of calmer seasons can scarcely credit.

TRANSACTIONS IN GREAT BRITAIN, IN CONSEQUENCE OF THE PROCEEDINGS OF CONGRESS, IN 1774

Some time before the proceedings of congress reached England, it was justly apprehended, that a non-importation agreement would be one of the measures they would adopt. The ministry, apprehending that this event, by distressing the trading and manufacturing towns, might influence votes against the court, in the election of a new parliament, which was of course to come on in the succeeding year, suddenly dissolved the parliament, and immediately ordered a new one to be chosen. It was their design to have the whole business of elections over, before the inconveniences of a non-importation agreement could be felt. The nation was thus surprised into an election, without knowing that the late American acts had driven the colonies into a firm combination, to support, and make a common cause with, the people of Massachusetts. A new parliament was returned; which met in thirty-four days after the proceedings of congress were first published in Philadelphia, and before they were known in Great Britain. This, for the most part, consisted, either of the former members, or of those who held similar sentiments.

On the 30th of November, the king, in his speech to his new parliament, informed them "that a most daring spirit of resistance and disobedience to the laws, unhappily prevailed in the province of Massachusetts, and had broken forth in fresh violences of a very criminal nature; that these proceedings had been countenanced and encouraged in his other colonies; that unwarrantable attempts had been made to obstruct the commerce of his kingdoms, by unlawful combinations; and that he had taken such measures, and given such orders, as he judged most proper and effectual, for carrying into execution the laws, which were passed in the last session of the late parliament, relative to the province of Massachusetts."

November 30, 1774

An address, proposed in the house of commons, in answer to this speech, produced a warm debate. The minister was reminded of the great effects, he had predicted from the late American acts. "They were to humble that whole continent, without further trouble; and the punishment of Boston was to strike so universal a panic on all the colonies, that it would be totally abandoned, and, instead of obtaining relief, a dread of the same fate would awe the other provinces, to a most respectful submission." An address re-echoing the royal speech was, nevertheless, carried by a great majority. A similar address was carried, after a spirited debate, in the upper house: but the lords Richmond, Portland, Rockingham, Stamford, Stanhope, Torrington, Ponsonby, Wycombe, and Camden entered a protest against it, which concluded with these remarkable words: "Whatever may be the mischievous designs, or the inconsiderate temerity which leads others to this desperate course, we wish to be known as persons, who have disapproved of measures so injurious in their past effects, and future tendency, and who are not in haste, without inquiry or information, to commit ourselves in declarations,

GOD PREPARES
A CHRISTIAN
PEOPLE
TO ESTABLISH
THE AMERICAN
NATION

which may precipitate our country into all the calamities of a civil war."

Soon after the meeting of the new parliament, the proceedings of the congress reached Great Britain. The first impression, made by them, was in favour of America. Administration seemed to be staggered; and their opposers triumphed, in the eventual truth of their prediction, that an universal confederacy, to resist Great Britain, would be the consequence of the late American acts. The secretary of state, after a day's perusal, during which a council was held, said that the petition of congress, to the King, was a decent and proper one. He also cheerfully undertook to present it; and afterwards reported, that his majesty was pleased very graciously to receive it, and to promise to lay it before his two houses of parliament. From these favourable circumstances, the sanguine friends of America concluded, that it was intended to make the petition a foundation of a change of measures: but these hopes were of short duration.

The partisans of administration placed so much confidence in the efficacy of the measures, they had lately taken, to bring the Americans to obedience, that they regarded the boldest resolutions of congress, as the idle clamours of an unruly multitude, which proper exertions on the part of Great Britain would speedily silence. So much had been asserted and contradicted by both parties, that the bulk of the people could form no certain opinion on the subject.

The parliament adjourned for the Christmas holidays, without coming to any decision on American affairs. As soon as they met, in January, 1775, a number of papers, containing information, were laid before them.

January, 1775 These were mostly letters from governors, and other servants of his majesty, which detailed the opposition of the colonists, in language calculated to give a bad impression of their past conduct, and an alarming one of their future intentions.

It was a circumstance unfavourable to the lovers of peace, that the rulers of Great Britain received almost the whole of their American intelligence from those, who had an interest in deceiving them. Governors, judges, revenue officers, and other royal servants, being both appointed and paid by Great Britain, fancied that zeal, for the interest of that country, would be the most likely way to ensure their further promotion. They were therefore, in their official dispatches to government, often tempted to abuse the colonists, with a view of magnifying their own watch-

fulness, and recommending themselves to Great Britain. The plain, simple language of truth was not acceptable to courtly ears. Ministers received and caressed those, and those only, whose representations coincided with their own views and wishes. They, who contended that, by the spirit of the English constitution, British subjects, residing on one side of the Atlantic, were entitled to equal privileges, with those who resided on the other, were unnoticed; while the abettors of ministerial measures were heard with attention.

In this hour of national infatuation, lord Chatham, after a long retirement, resumed his seat in the house of lords, and exerted his unrivalled eloquence, in sundry attempts to dissuade his countrymen from attempting to subdue the Americans, by force of arms. The native dignity of his superior genius, and the recollection of his important services, entitled him to distinguished notice. His language, voice, and gesture, were calculated to force conviction on his hearers. Though venerable for his age, he spoke with the fire of youth. He introduced himself with some general observations on the importance of the American quarrel. He enlarged on the dangerous events that were coming on the nation, in consequence of the present dispute. He arraigned the conduct of ministers, with great severity; reprobated their whole system of American politics; and moved, that an humble address be presented to his majesty, most humbly to advise and beseech him, to dispatch orders to general Gage, to remove his majesty's forces from the town of Boston. His lordship supported this motion in a pathetic animated speech; but it was rejected by a great majority. From this and other circumstances, it soon became evident, that the Americans could expect no more favour from the new parliament, than they had experienced from the late one. A majority in both houses were against them, and resolved to compel them to obedience: but a respectable minority in their favour was strongly seconded by petitions, from the merchants and manufacturers, throughout the kingdom, and particularly by those of London and Bristol. As these were well apprised of the consequences, that must follow from a prosecution of coercive measures, and deeply interested in the event, they made uncommon exertions to prevent their adoption. They pointed out the various evils, that would result from them, and warned their countrymen of the danger, to which their commercial interests were exposed.

When the petition from the merchants of London was read in the house of commons, it was moved to refer it to the committee appointed to take into consideration the American papers; but it was moved by way of amendment, on the ministerial side, that it should be referred to a separate committee, to meet on the 27th, the day succeeding that appointed for the consideration of American papers. This, though a dishonourable evasion, was carried by a majority of more than two to one.

A similar fate attended the petitions from Bristol, Glasgow, Norwich, Liverpool, Manchester, Birmingham, Woolverhampton, Dudley, and some other places. These, on their being presented, were in like manner consigned to, what the opposition humourously termed, the committee of oblivion.

About the same time, a petition was offered from Mr. Bollan, Dr. Franklin, and Mr. Lee, stating that they were authorized by congress to present their petition to the king, which his majesty had referred to that house; that they were enabled to throw great light on the subject; and praying to be heard, at the bar, in support of the said petition. The friends of the ministry alleged, that as congress was not a legal body, nothing could be received from them. It was in vain replied, that the congress, however illegal as to other purposes, was sufficiently legal for presenting a petition; that, as it was signed by the individual members of congress, it might be received as a petition from individuals; that the signers of it were persons of great influence in America; and it was the right of all subjects to have their petitions heard.

LORD CHATHAM'S BILL

In the course of the debate on lord Chatham's motion, for addressing his majesty, to withdraw his troops from Boston, it had been observed, by some lords in administration, that it was common and easy to censure their measures; but those who did so proposed nothing better. Lord Chatham answered, that he should not be one of those idle censurers; that he had thought long and closely upon the subject; and purposed soon to lay before their lordships the result of his meditations, in a plan for healing the differences between Great Britain and the colonies, and for restoring peace to the empire. When he had matured his plan, he introduced it into the house, in the form of a bill, for settling the troubles in America. In this he proposed, that the colonists should make a full acknowledgment of the supremacy of the legislature, and the superintending power of the British

parliament. The bill did not absolutely decide on the right of taxation; but, partly as a matter of grace, and partly as a compromise, declared and enacted, "that no tax, or other charge, should be levied in America, except by common consent in their provincial assemblies." It asserted the right of the king, to send a legal army to any part of his dominions at all times; but declared, "that no military force could ever be lawfully employed, to violate or destroy the just rights of the people." It also legalized the holding a congress, in the ensuing May, for the double purpose, "of recognizing the supreme legislative authority, and superintending power of parliament over the colonies; and for making a free grant to the king, his heirs, and successors, of a certain and perpetual revenue, subject to the disposition of parliament, and applicable to the alleviation of the national debt." On these conditions the bill proposed, "to restrain the powers of the admiralty courts to their ancient limits, and suspended, for a limited time, those acts, which had been complained of by congress." It proposed to place the judges, in America, on the same footing, as to the holding of their salaries and offices, with those in England; and secured to the colonies all the privileges, franchises, and immunities, granted by their several charters and constitutions. His lordship introduced this plan with a speech, in which he explained, and supported every part of it. When he sat down, lord Dartmouth rose, and said, "it contained matter of such magnitude as to require consideration; and therefore hoped, that the noble earl did not expect their lordships to decide upon it, by an immediate vote; but would be willing it should lie on the table for consideration." Lord Chatham answered, "that he expected no more:" but lord Sandwich rose, and, in a petulant speech, opposed its being received at all, and gave his opinion, "that it ought immediately to be rejected, with the contempt it deserved; that he could not believe it to be the production of any British peer; that it appeared to him rather the work of some American;" and, turning his face towards Dr. Franklin, who was leaning on the bar, said, "he fancied he had in his eye the person, who drew it up; one of the bitterest and most mischievous enemies this country had ever known." This turned the eyes of many lords on the insulted American, who, with that self-command, which is peculiar to great minds, kept his countenance unmoved. Several other lords of the administration gave their sentiments, also, for rejecting lord Chatham's conciliatory bill; urging that it not only gave a sanction to the traitorous proceedings

GOD PREPARES
A CHRISTIAN
PEOPLE
TO ESTABLISH
THE AMERICAN
NATION

of the congress already held, but legalized their future meeting. They enlarged on the rebellious temper, and hostile disposition of the Americans; and said, "that, though the duty on tea was the pretence, the restrictions on their commerce, and the hopes of throwing them off, were the real motives of their disobedience; and that to concede now, would be, to give up the point forever."

The dukes of Richmond and Manchester, lord Camden, lord Lyttleton, and others, were for receiving lord Chatham's conciliatory bill; some from approbation of its principles; but others only from a regard to the character and dignity of the house.

Lord Dartmouth, who, from indecision, rarely had any will or judgment of his own, and who, with dispositions for the best measures, could be easily prevailed upon to join in support of the worst, finding the opposition from his coadjutors in administration unexpectedly strong, turned round, and gave his voice with them for immediately rejecting the plan. Lord Chatham, in reply to lord Sandwich, declared, "the bill proposed by him to be entirely his own; but he made no scruple to declare, that, if he were the first minister of the country, and had the care of settling this momentous business, he should not be ashamed of publicly calling to his assistance a person, so perfectly acquainted with the whole of the American affairs, as the gentleman alluded to, and so injuriously reflected upon (Dr. Franklin): one whom all Europe held in high estimation for his knowledge and wisdom, and ranked with the Boyles and Newtons; who was an honour, not only to the English nation, but to human nature."

The plan proposed by lord Chatham was rejected, by a majority of sixty-four to thirty-two; and without being admitted to lie on the table. That a bill on so important a subject, offered by one of the first men of the age, and who, as prime minister of the nation, had, but a few years before, taken up Great Britain, when in a low despondency, and conducted her to victory and glory, through a war with two of the most powerful kingdoms of Europe, should be rejected without any consideration, or even a second reading, was not only a breach of decency, but a departure from that propriety of conduct, which should mark the proceedings of a branch of the national legislature. It could not but strike every thinking American, that such legislators, influenced by passion, prejudice, and party spirit, many of whom were totally ignorant of the subject, and who would not give themselves an opportunity, by a second reading, or further consideration, to inform

themselves better, were very unfit to exercise unlimited supremacy over three millions of virtuous, sensible people, inhabiting the other side of the globe.

PETITION OF SUGAR PLANTERS AND MERCHANTS

On the day after the rejection of lord Chatham's bill, a petition was presented to the house of commons, from the planters of the sugar colonies, residing in Great Britain, and the merchants of London, trading to the colonies. In this they stated, that the British property in the West India islands amounted to upwards of thirty millions; that a further property of many millions was employed in the commerce, created by the said islands; and that the profits and produce of these immense capitals, which ultimately centered in Great Britain, would be deranged and endangered, by the continuance of the American troubles. The petitioners were admitted to a hearing; when Mr. Glover, as their agent, ably demonstrated the folly and danger of persevering in the contest; but without any effect. The immediate coercion of the colonies was resolved upon; and the ministry would not suffer themselves to be diverted from its execution. They were confident of success, if they could once bring the controversy to the decision of arms. They expected more from conquest, than they could promise themselves by negociation or compromise. The free constitutions of the colonies, and their rapid progress in population, were beheld with a jealous eye, as the natural means of independence. They conceived the most effectual method, of retaining them long, would be to reduce them soon. They hoped to be able to extinguish remonstrance and debate, by such a speedy and decisive conquest, as would give them an opportunity to new-model the colonial constitutions, on such principles as would prevent future altercations, on the subject of their chartered rights. Every representation, that tended to retard or obstruct the coercion of the colonies, was therefore considered as tending only to prolong the controversy. Confident of victory, and believing that nothing short of it would restore the peace of the empire, the ministry turned a deaf ear to all petitions and representations. They even presumed, that the petitioners, when they found Great Britain determined on war, would assist in carrying it on with vigour, in order to expedite the settlement of the dispute. They took it for granted, that, when the petitioning towns were convinced, that a renewal of the commercial intercourse, between the two countries, would be sooner obtained by going on, than turning back, the same interest, which led them at first to petition, would lead them afterwards to support coercive measures, as the most effectual and shortest way of securing commerce from all future interruptions.

DETERMINATION OF MINISTERS

The determination of ministers, to persevere, was also forwarded by hopes of the defection of New York from her sister colonies. They flattered themselves, that, when one link of the continental chain gave way, it would be easy to make an impression on the disjointed extremities.

Every attempt to close the breach, which had been opened by the former parliament, having failed, and the ministry having made up their minds, on the mode of proceeding with the colonists, their proposed plan was briefly unfolded. This was to send a greater force to America, and to bring in a temporary act, to put a stop to all the foreign trade of the New England colonies, till they should make proper submissions and acknowledgments. An address to his majesty was, at the same time, moved to "beseech him to take the most effectual measures, to enforce due obedience to the laws and authority of the supreme legislature."

Truly critical was the moment to the union of the empire. A new parliament might, without the charge of inconsistency, have repealed acts, passed by a former one, which had been found inconvenient on experiment; but pride and passion, under the specious names of national dignity, and zeal for the supremacy of parliament, induced the adoption of measures, for immediately compelling the submission of the colonies.

The repeal of a few acts of parliament would, at this time, have satisfied America. Though she had been extending her claims, yet she was still willing that Great Britain should monopolize her trade, and that the parliament should regulate it for the common benefit of the empire. Nor was she disposed to abridge his majesty of any of his usual prerogatives. This authority was sufficient for the mother country, to retain the colonists, in a profitable state of subordination, and yet not so much as to be inconsistent with their claims, or the security of their most important interests. Britain viewed the matter in a different light. To recede, at this time, would be to acknowledge, that the ministry had hitherto been in the wrong; a concession rarely made by private persons, and more rarely by men in public sta-

tions. The leading members in parliament, not distinguishing the opposition of freemen to unconstitutional innovation, from the turbulence of licentious mobs breaking over the bounds of law and constitution, supposed that to redress grievances was to renounce sovereignty. This inference, in some degree, resulted from the broad basis, which they had assigned to the claims of the mother country. If, as was contended, on the part of Great Britain, they had a right to bind the colonies, in all cases whatsoever, and the power of parliament over them were absolute and unlimited, they were precluded from rescinding any act of theirs, however oppressive, when demanded as a matter of right. They were too highly impressed with the ideas of their unlimited authority, to repeal any of their laws, on the principle, that they had not a constitutional power to enact them, and too unwise to adopt the same measure on the ground of political expediency. Unfortunately for both countries, two opinions were generally held, neither of which was, perhaps, true in its utmost extent, and one of which was most assuredly false. The ministry and parliament of England proceeded on the idea, that the claims of the colonists amounted to absolute independence, and that a fixed resolution to renounce the sovereignty of Great Britain was concealed, under the specious pretext of a redress of grievances. The Americans, on the other hand, were equally confident, that the mother country not only harboured designs unfriendly to their interests, but seriously intended to introduce arbitrary government. Jealousies of each other were reciprocally indulged, to the destruction of all confidence, and to the final dismemberment of the empire.

In discussing the measures proposed by the minister, for the coercion of the colonies, the whole ground of the American controversy was traversed. The comparative merits of concession and coercion were placed in every point of view. Some of the minority, in both houses of parliament, pointed out the dangers that would attend a war with America; the likelihood of the interference of other powers; and the probability of losing, and the impossibility of gaining any thing more than was already possessed. On the other hand, the friends of the ministry asserted, that the Americans had been long aiming at independence; that they were magnifying pretended grievances, to cover a premeditated revolt; that it was the business and duty of Englishmen, at every hazard, to prevent its completion, and to bring them back to a remembrance that their present

GOD PREPARES
A CHRISTIAN
PEOPLE
TO ESTABLISH
THE AMERICAN
NATION

greatness was owing to the mother country; and that even their existence had been purchased at an immense expense of British blood and treasure. They acknowledged the danger to be great; but said "it must be encountered; that every day's delay increased the evil; and that it would be base and cowardly to shift off, for the present, an unavoidable contest, which must fall with accumulated weight on the heads of their posterity." The danger of foreign interference was denied. It was contended, that an appearance of vigorous measures, with a further reinforcement of troops at Boston, would be sufficient to quell the disturbances. It was also urged, that the friends of government were both strong and numerous, and only waited for proper support, and favourable circumstances, to declare themselves.

JOINT ADDRESS OF FEBRUARY 9, 1775— RUBICON PASSED

After long and warm debates, and one or two protests, the ministerial plans were carried by great majorities. In consequence thereof, on the 9th of February, 1775, a joint address, from both lords and commons, was presented to his majesty, in which, "they returned thanks for the communication of the papers, relative to the state of the British colonies in America; gave it as their opinion, that a rebellion actually existed in the province of Massachusetts; besought his majesty, that he would take the most effectual measures, to enforce due obedience to the laws and authority of the supreme legislature, and begged, in the most solemn manner, to assure his majesty, that it was their fixed resolution, at the hazard of their lives and properties, to stand by his majesty against all rebellious attempts, in the maintenance of the just rights of his majesty, and of the two houses of parliament."

The lords, Richmond, Craven, Archer, Abergavenny, Rockingham, Wycombe, Courtenay, Torrington, Ponsonby, Cholmondely, Abingdon, Rutland, Camden, Effingham, Stanhope, Scarborough, Fitzwilliam, and Tankerville, protested against this address, "as founded on no proper parliamentary information, being introduced by refusing to suffer the presentation of petitions against it; as following the rejection of every mode of conciliation; as holding out no substantial offer of redress of grievances; and as promising support to those ministers, who had inflamed America, and grossly misconducted the affairs of Great Britain."

By the address, against which this protest was

entered, the parliament of Great Britain passed the Rubicon. In former periods, it might be alleged, that the claims of the colonies were undefined, and that their unanimous resolution to defend them, was unknown: but after a free representation from twelve provinces had stated their rights, and pledged themselves to each other to support them, and their determinations were known, a resolution that a rebellion actually existed, and that, at the hazard of their lives and properties, they would stand by his majesty, against all rebellious attempts, was a virtual declaration of war. Both parties were now bound, in consequence of their own acts, to submit their controversy to a decision of arms. Issue was joined, by the approbation congress had given to the Suffolk resolves, and by this subsequent joint address of both houses of parliament to his majesty. It is probable, that neither party, in the beginning, intended to go thus far; but by the inscrutable operations of Providence, each was permitted to adopt such measures as not only rent the empire, but involved them both, with their own consent, in all the calamities of a long and bloody war. The answer from the throne, to the joint address of parliament, contained assurances of taking the most speedy and effectual measures, for enforcing due obedience to the laws, and authority of the supreme legislature. This answer was accompanied with a message to the commons, in which they were informed, that some augmentation to the forces by sea and land would be necessary. An augmentation of four thousand three hundred and eighty-three men to the land forces, and of two thousand seamen, to be employed for the ensuing year, was accordingly asked for and carried without difficulty. With the first, it was stated, that the force at Boston would be ten thousand men, a number supposed to be sufficient for enforcing the laws. Other schemes, in addition to a military force, were thought advisable for promoting the projected coercion of the colonies. With this view a punishment was proposed, so universal in its operation, that it was expected the inhabitants of the New England colonies, to obtain a riddance of its heavy pressure, would interest themselves in procuring a general submission to parliament. Lord North moved for leave to bring in a bill "to restrain the trade and commerce of the provinces of Massachusetts Bay and New Hampshire, the colonies of Connecticut and Rhode Island, and Providence Plantations in North America, to Great Britain, Ireland, and the British islands in the West Indies, and to prohibit such provinces and colonies from carrying on any fishery on the banks of Newfoundland, or other places therein to be mentioned, under certain conditions, and for a limited time." The motion for this bill was supported, by declaring, that, as the Americans had refused to trade with the mother country, they ought not to be permitted to trade with any other. It was known that the New England colonies carried on a circuitous trade and fishery, on the banks of Newfoundland, to a great extent. To cut them off from this resource, they were legislatively forbidden to fish, or to carry on foreign trade. It was presumed, that the wants of a large body of people, deprived of employment, would create a clamour in favour of reconciliation.

TRADE RESTRAINT BILL AND PROHIBITION OF NEWFOUNDLAND FISHING, MARCH 21, 1775

The British ministry expected to excite the same temper in the unemployed New England men, that congress meant to raise by the non-importation agreement, among the British merchants and manufacturers. The motion, for this bill brought into view the whole of the American controversy. The opposers of it said, that its cruelty exceeded the examples of hostile rigour with avowed enemies; for that, in the most dangerous wars, the fishing craft was universally spared. They desired the proposer of the bill to recollect, that he had often spoken of the multitude of friends he had in those provinces, and that now he confounded the innocent with the guilty; friends with enemies; and involved his own partizans in one common ruin with his opposers. They alleged further, that the bill would operate against the people of Great Britain; as the people of New England were in debt to them, and had no other means of paying that debt, but through the fishery, and the circuitous trade dependent on it. It was observed, that the fishermen, being cut off from employment, must turn soldiers; and that, therefore, while they were provoking the Americans to resistance, by one set of acts, they were furnishing them with the means of recruiting an army by another.

The favourers of the bill denied the charge of severity, alleging that the colonists could not complain of any distress the bill might bring on them, as they not only deserved it, but had set the example; and that they had entered into unlawful combinations to ruin the merchants and manufacturers of Great Britain. It was said, that, if any foreign power had offered a similar insult or injury, the whole nation would have demanded satisfaction. They contended that it was a bill of humanity and mercy; for, said they, the colonists have incurred all the penalties of rebellion, and are liable to the severest military execution. Instead of inflicting the extent of what they deserved, the bill only proposes to bring them to their senses, by restricting their trade. They urged further, that the measure was necessary; for, said they, "the Americans have frequently imposed on us, by threatening to withdraw their trade, hoping through mercantile influence to bend the legislature to their demands; that this was the third time, they had thrown the commerce of Great Britain into a state of confusion; and that both colonies and commerce were better lost, than preserved on such terms. They added further, that they must either relinquish their connection with America, or fix it on such a basis, as would prevent a return of these evils. They admitted the bill to be coercive; but said, "that the coercion, which put the speediest end to the dispute, was eventually the most merciful."

In the progress of the bill, a petition from the merchants and traders of London, who were interested in the American commerce, was presented against it. They were heard by their agent, Mr. David Barclay; and a variety of witnesses were examined before the house. In the course of their evidence it appeared, that, in the year 1764, the four provinces of New England employed, in their several fisheries, no less than forty-five thousand eight hundred and eighty ton of shipping, and six thousand and two men; and that the produce of their fisheries that year, in foreign markets, amounted to 322,220 *l.* 16s. sterling. It also appeared, that the fisheries had very much increased since that time; that all the materials used in them, except salt, and the timber of which the vessels were built, were purchased from Great Britain; and that the net proceeds of the whole were remitted thither. All this information was disregarded. After much opposition in both houses, and a protest in the house of lords, the bill was, by a great majority, finally ratified. So intent were the ministry and parliament on the coercion of the colonists, that every other interest was sacrificed to its accomplishment. They conceived the question between the two countries to be, simply, whether they should abandon their claims, and at once give up all the advantages arising from sovereignty and commerce, or resort to violent measures for their security.

GOD PREPARES
A CHRISTIAN
PEOPLE
TO ESTABLISH
THE AMERICAN
NATION

Since the year 1769, when a secretary of state officially disclaimed all views of an American revenue, little mention had been made of that subject; but the decided majority, who voted with the ministry on this occasion, emboldened lord North once more to present it to the view of his countrymen. He, therefore, brought into parliament a scheme, which, had the double recommendation of holding forth the semblance of conciliation, and the prospect of an easement of British taxes, by a productive revenue from the colonies. This resolution passed on the 20th of February, and was as follows:

"Resolved, that, when the governor, council, and assembly, or general court, of any of his majesty's provinces or colonies in America, shall propose to make provision according to the condition, circumstances, and situations of such province or colony, for contributing their proportion for the common defence, such proportion to be raised under the authority of the general court or general assembly of such province or colony, and disposable by parliament, and shall engage to make provision, also, for the support of the civil government, and the administration of justice in such province or colony, it will be proper, if such proposal shall be approved by his majesty, and the two houses of parliament, and for so long as such provision shall be made accordingly, to forbear, in respect of such province or colony, to levy any duty, tax, or assessment, except only such duties as it may be expedient to continue to levy or to impose for the regulation of commerce; the net produce of the duties last mentioned, to be carried to the account of such province or colony respectively."

This was introduced by the minister, in a long speech, in which he asserted, that it would be an infallible touch-stone to try the Americans. "If," said he, "their opposition be only founded on the principles which they pretend, they must agree with this proposition; but if they have designs in contemplation, different from those they avow, their refusal will convict them of duplicity." The opposition to the minister's motion originated among those who had supported him in previous questions. They objected to the proposal, that, in effect, it was an acknowledgment of something grievous in the idea of taxing America by parliament; and that it was, therefore, a departure from their own principles. They contended, that it was improper to make concessions to rebels, with arms in their hands; or to enter into any measures for a settlement with the Americans, in which they did not, as a preliminary, acknowledge the supremacy of parliament. The minister was likely to be deserted by some of his partizans,

till others explained the consistency of the scheme with their former declarations. It was said, "what shall parliament lose by acceding to this resolution? Not the right of taxing America; for this is most expressly reserved. Not the profitable exercise of this right; for it proposed to enforce the only essential part of taxation, by compelling the Americans to raise not only what they, but what we, think reasonable. We are not going to war for trifles, and a vain point of honour; but for substantial revenue." The minister further declared, that he did not expect his proposition to be generally relished by the Americans. But, said he, if it do no good in the colonies, it will do good here. It will unite the people of England, by holding out to them a distinct object of revenue. He added further, as it tends to unite England, it is likely to disunite America: for if only one province accept the offer, their confederacy, which only makes them formidable, will be broken.

The opposers of ministry attacked the proposition, with the combined force of wit and argument. They animadverted on the inconsistency of holding forth the same resolution as a measure of concession, and as an assertion of authority. They remarked, that, hitherto, it had been constantly denied, that they had any contest about an American revenue; and that the whole had been a dispute about obedience to trade-laws, and the general legislative authority of parliament: but now ministers suddenly changed their language, and proposed to interest the nation; and console the manufacturers, and animate the soldiery, by persuading them, that it is not a contest for empty honour, but for the acquisition of a substantial revenue. It was said, that the Americans would be as effectually taxed, without their consent, by being compelled to pay a gross sum, as by an aggregate of small duties to the same amount; and that this scheme of taxation exceeded, in oppression, any that the rapacity of mankind had hitherto devised. In other cases, a specific sum was demanded; and the people might reasonably presume that the remainder was their own: but here they were wholly in the dark, as to the extent of the demand.

This proposition, however, for conciliation, though disrelished by many of the friends of ministry, was carried, on a division of two hundred and seventy-four to eighty-eight. On its transmission to the colonies, it did not produce the effects of disunion expected from it. It was unanimously rejected.

Other plans for conciliation with the colonies,

founded on principles very different from those which were the basis of lord North's conciliatory motion, were brought forward, in the house of commons; but without receiving its approbation.

EDMUND BURKE'S PLAN

The most remarkable of these was proposed by Mr. Edmund Burke, in a speech which, for strength of argument, extent of information, and sublimity of language, would bear a comparison with the most finished performance that ancient or modern times have produced. In his introduction to this admirable speech, he examined and explained the natural and accidental circumstances of the colonies, with respect to situation, resources, number, population, commerce, fisheries, and agriculture; and from these considerations showed their importance. He then inquired into their unconquerable spirit of freedom; which he traced to its original sources. From these circumstances, he inferred the line of policy which should be pursued with regard to America. He showed that all proper plans of government must be adapted to the feelings, established habits, and received opinions of the people. On these principles, he reprobated all plans of governing the colonies by force; and proposed, as the groundwork of his plan, that the colonists should be admitted to an interest in the constitution. He then went into an historical detail of the manner, in which British privileges had been extended to Ireland, Wales, and the counties palatine of Chester and Durham; the state of confusion before that event; and the happy consequences which followed it. He contended, that a communication, to the members, of an interest in the constitution, was the great ruling principle of British government. He, therefore, proposed to go back to the old policy for governing the colonies. He was for a parliamentary acknowledgment of the legal competency of the colonial assemblies, for the support of their government in peace, and for public aids in the time of war. He maintained the futility of parliamentary taxation, as a method of supply. He stated, that much had been given in the old way of colonial grant; that, from the year 1748 to 1763, the journals of the house of commons repeatedly acknowledged, that the colonies not only gave, but gave to satiety; and that, from the time, in which parliamentary imposition had superseded the free gifts of the provinces, there was much discontent, and little revenue. He, therefore, moved six resolutions, affirmatory of these facts; and grounded on them

resolutions, for repealing the acts complained of by the Americans, trusting to the liberality of their future voluntary contributions. This plan of conciliation, which promised immediate peace to the whole empire, and a lasting obedience of the colonies, though recommended by the charms of the most persuasive eloquence, and supported by the most convincing arguments, was by a great majority rejected.

Mr. D. Hartley, not discouraged by the negative, which had been given to Mr. Burke's scheme, came forward with another for the same purpose. This proposed, that a letter of requisition should be sent to the colonies, by the secretary of state, on a motion from the house, for a contribution to the expenses of the whole empire. He meant to leave, to the provincial assemblies, the right to judge of the expedience, amount, and application of the grant. In confidence that the colonies would give freely, when called on, in this constitutional way, he moved, to suspend the acts complained of by the Americans. This was also rejected.

Another plan was digested in private by Dr. Franklin, on the part of the Americans, and Dr. Fothergill and David Barclay, on behalf of the British ministry. There appeared a disposition to concede something considerable on both sides; but the whole came to nothing, in consequence of an inflexible determination to refuse a repeal of the act of parliament for altering the chartered government of Massachusetts. Dr. Franklin agreed, that the tea destroyed should be paid for; the British ministers, that the Boston port act should be repealed: but the latter contended, "that the late Massachusetts acts, being real amendments of their constitution, must, for that reason, be continued, as well as to be a standing example of the power of parliament." On the other hand, it was declared by Dr. Franklin, "that, while the parliament claimed and exercised a power of internal legislation for the colonies, and of altering American constitutions at pleasure, there could be no agreement; as that would render the Americans unsafe in every privilege they enjoyed, and would leave them nothing in which they could be secure."

THE FATAL ROCK

This obstinate adherence to support parliament, in a power of altering the laws and charters of the provinces, particularly to enforce their late laws for new-modelling the chartered constitution of Massachusetts, was the fatal rock, by

GOD PREPARES
A CHRISTIAN
PEOPLE
TO ESTABLISH
THE AMERICAN
NATION

dashing on which the empire broke in twain; for every other point, in dispute between the two countries, seemed in a fair way for an amicable compromise.

SOUTHERN FISHERY BILL—EXEMPTING NEW YORK, DELAWARE, NORTH CAROLINA— ATTEMPT TO DIVIDE AND CONQUER

The fishery bill was speedily followed by another, for restraining the trade and commerce of the colonies and provinces of New Jersey, Pennsylvania, Maryland, Virginia, and South Carolina. The reasons assigned for this were the same with those offered for the other. These provinces had adopted the continental association. The British minister thought it proper, that, as they had voluntarily interdicted themselves from trade with Great Britain, Ireland, and the West Indies, they should be restrained from it with all other parts of the world. He contended, that the inhabitants of the colonies might render this act a dead letter, by relinquishing their own resolutions, as then they would meet with no restraint in carrying on trade in its ancient legal channel. It is remarkable, that three of the associated colonies, viz. New York, Delaware, and North Carolina, were omitted in this restraining bill. Whatever might be the view of the British ministry for this discrimination, it was considered in the colonies as calculated to promote disunion among them. It is certain, that the colonies, exempted from its operation, might have reaped a golden harvest from the exemption in their favour, had they been disposed to avail themselves of it: but such was the temper of the times, that a renunciation of immediate advantage in favour of the public was fashionable. The selfish passions, which, in seasons of peace, are too often the cause of quarrels, were hushed by the pressure of common danger.

The exempted colonies spurned the proffered favour, and submitted to the restraints imposed on their less favoured neighbours, so as to be equal sharers of their fate. The indulgence granted to New York, in being kept out of this restraining bill, was considered by some as a premium for her superior loyalty. Her assembly had refused to approve the proceedings of the congress, and had, in some other instances, discovered less warmth than the neighbouring legislatures. Much was expected from her moderation. At the very time the British parliament was framing the restraining acts just mentioned, the constitutional assembly of New York petitioned for a redress of their grievances. Great stress had been laid on the circumstance, that congress was not a legal assembly; and the want of constitutional sanction had been assigned as a reason for the neglect, with which their petition had been treated. Much praise had been lavished on the colony of New York, for its moderation; and occasion had been taken, from their refusing to approve the proceedings of the congress, to represent the resolutions and claims of that body to be more the ebullitions of incendiaries, than the sober sentiments of the temperate citizens. It was both unexpected and confounding to those who supported these opinions, that the representation and remonstrance of the very loyal assembly of New York stated, "that an exemption from internal taxation, and the exclusive right of providing for their own civil government, and the administration of justice in the colony, were esteemed by them as their undoubted and unalienable rights."

A motion being made, in the house of commons, for bringing up this representation and remonstrance of the assembly of New York, it was amended, on the suggestion of lord North, by adding, "in which the assembly claim to themselves rights derogatory to, and inconsistent with, the legislative authority of parliament, as declared by the declaratory act." The question, so amended, being put, passed in the negative. The fate of this representation extinguished the hopes of those moderate persons, both in the parent state and the colonies, who flattered themselves, that the disputes, subsisting between the two countries, might be accommodated by the mediation of the constitutional assemblies. Two conclusions were drawn from this transaction; both of which were unfriendly to a reconciliation. The decided language, with which the loyal assembly of New York claimed exemption from parliamentary taxation, proved to the people of Great Britain, that the colonists, however they might differ in modes of opposition, or in degrees of warmth, were, nevertheless, united in that fundamental principle. The rejection of their representation proved, that nothing more was to be expected from proceeding in the constitutional channel of the legal assemblies, than from the new system of a continental congress. Solid revenue and unlimited supremacy were the objects of Great Britain; and exemption from parliamentary taxation, that of the most moderate of the colonies. So wide were the claims of the two countries from each other, that to reconcile them on any middle ground seemed to be impossible.

CONSEQUENCES IN AMERICA, RESULTING
FROM PARLIAMENT'S TRANSACTIONS

DAVID
RAMSAY:
PRELUDE TO
THE AMERICAN
REVOLUTION,
1765–1775

JEALOUSY OF
LIBERTY
VS. DESIRE OF
SUPREMACY

The year 1774 terminated with an expectation in America, that a few months would bring them a redress of their grievances. But the probability of that event daily diminished. The colonists had indulged themselves in an expectation that the people of Great Britain, from a consideration of the dangers and difficulties of a war with their colonies, would, in their elections, have preferred those who were friends to peace and a reconciliation. But when they were convinced of the fallacy of these hopes, they turned their attention to the means of self-defence. It had been the resolution of many never to submit to the operation of the late acts of parliament. Their number daily increased; and in the same proportion that Great Britain determined to enforce, did they determine to oppose. Intelligence of the rejection of lord Chatham's bill, of the address of both houses of parliament to the king on the 9th of February, and of the fishery bill, arrived among the colonists, about the same time, and diminished what remained of their first hopes of a speedy accommodation. The fishery bill excited a variety of emotions. The obvious tendency of it was to starve thousands. The severity of it did not strike an Englishman, for he viewed it as a merited correction for great provincial offences. But it appeared in the blackest colours to an American, who felt no consciousness of guilt, and who fancied that heaven approved his zeal in defence of liberty. It alienated the affections of the colonists, and produced in the breasts of thousands, a hatred of Great Britain.

JEALOUSY OF LIBERTY VS. DESIRE OF SUPREMACY

The penal acts of parliament in 1774, were all levelled against Massachusetts; but the fishery bill extended to New Hampshire, Connecticut and Rhode Island. The reasons assigned for this by lord North were, that they had aided and abetted their offending neighbours, and were so near to them that the intentions of parliament would be frustrated, unless they were in like manner comprehended in the proposed restraints. The extension of this penal statute to three additional provinces, operated powerfully in favour of union, and convinced the most moderate, of the increasing necessity for all the provinces to make a common cause in their opposition. Whatever might be the designs of parliament, their

acts had a natural tendency to enlarge the demands of the Americans, and to cement their confederacy, by firm principles of union. At first they only claimed exemption from internal taxation; but by the combination of the East Indian company and the British ministry, an external tax was made to answer all the purposes of a direct internal tax. They, therefore, in consistence with their own principles, were constrained to deny the right of taxing in any form for a supply. Nothing could contribute more to make the colonists deny the parliamentary claim of internal legislation, than the manner in which it was exercised, in depriving them of their charters, and passing an act relative to trials, which promised indemnity to murderers. This convinced them that an opposition to so injurious a claim was essentially necessary to their security. But they still admitted the power of parliament to bind their trade. This was conceded by congress only a few months before an act passed, that they should have no foreign trade, nor be allowed to fish on their own coasts. The British ministry by their successive acts, impelled the colonists to believe, that while the mother country retained any authority over them, that authority would, in some shape or other, be exerted so as to answer all the purposes of a power to tax. While Great Britain stretched that portion of controling supremacy which the colonists were disposed to allow her, to such an extent as covered oppression equally grievous with that which they would not allow, the way was fast opening for a total renunciation of her sovereignty. The coercive measures adopted by the parent state, produced a disposition in the colonies to extend their claims: and the extension of their claims produced an increasing disposition in Great Britain to coerce them still more. The jealousy of liberty on one side, and the desire of supremacy on the other, were reciprocally cause and effect; and urged both parties, the one to rise in their demands, and the other to enforce submission. In the contest between Great Britain and her colonies, there had been a fatal progression from small to greater grounds of dissention. The trifling tax of 3d. per pound on tea, roused the jealous inhabitants of Boston to throw 340 chests of it into the ocean. This provoked the British parliament to shut up their port, and to new-model their charter. Statutes so unconstitutional and alarming, excited a combination in twelve of the colonies, to stop all trade with Great Britain, Ireland, and the West Indies. Their combination gave birth to the restraining acts of parliament, by which nine of the colonies were

AT a meeting of the freeholders and other inhabitants of the town of Boston, duly qualified and legally warned, in public town meeting, assembled at Faneuil-hall, on Tuesday the 26th day of July, Anno Domini 1774, at 10 o'clock forenoon.

VOTED, THAT a printed copy of the following letter to our brethren in the several towns and districts in the province be forthwith signed by the Town-Clerk, and transmitted by the Committee of Correspondence in the name and behalf of this town.

Attest. *William Cooper Town Clerk*

FRIENDS and BRETHREN,

OUR public calamities have for a series of years been increasing both in number and weight. We have endeavoured under all our public misfortunes to conduct as good citizens in a COMMON CAUSE. Being stationed by providence in the front rank of the conflict, it hath been our aim to behave with vigilance, activity and firmness. To warn our brethren of approaching danger, to encounter with becoming spirit the trials of our patience, hath been our aim and our duty. Our friends and generous countrymen have given us reason to think we have not altogether failed in our honest endeavors in the way of this duty.

Two acts of parliament, altering the course of justice, and annihilating our once free constitution of government, are every day expected.

When we consider the conduct of our late worthy house of representatives, relative to our superior court Judges, and their impeachment of the Honorable Peter Oliver, Esq; for his accepting a salary from the crown in his office of Chief Justice; and when we consider the uniform spirit and conduct of the several Grand Jurors through the province, touching the same grievance, since that impeachment ; we cannot but suppose the aforementioned acts will bring on a most important and decisive trial.

You, gentlemen, our friends, countrymen and benefactors, may possibly look towards us at this great crisis. We trust that we shall not be left of Heaven to do any thing derogatory to our common liberties, unworthy the fame of our ancestors, or inconsistent with our former professions and conduct.

Though surrounded with a large body of armed men (who, having the sword, have also our blood in their hands) we are yet undaunted ; we trust in the GOD of our fathers, and we feel the animating support of a good cause ; but while suffering, a DOUBLE weight of oppression, and exasperated by a military camp in the very bowels of our town, our minds are not more in a temper to DELIBERATE, than our bodies in a situation to MOVE, as the perils and exigencies of the times may probably demand.

To you, gentlemen, our brethren and dear companions *in the cause of GOD and our country,* we apply ; from you we have *received that countenance and aid,* which have strengthened our hands, *and that bounty which hath* occasioned *smiles on the face of distress :* To you, therefore, we look for that *wisdom, advice* and EXAMPLE, which, giving strength to our understanding, and vigor to our actions, shall, with the blessing of GOD, save us from destruction.

Looking up to Heaven, and, under divine direction, to our brethren in the country and on the continent, for aid and support, and with earnest prayers for a happy issue out of our great troubles, We are, Your

FRIENDS and BRETHREN,

The INHABITANTS of BOSTON.

By order of the Town,

William Cooper Town Clerk

interdicted all other trade but that from which they had voluntarily excluded themselves; and four of these nine were further devoted to famine, by being forbidden to fish on their coasts. Each new resolution on the one side, and new act on the other, reciprocally gave birth to something from the opposing parties, that was more irritating or oppressive, than what had preceded.

BEGINNING OF STRIFE LIKE THE LETTING OUT OF WATERS

The beginning of strife between the parent state and her colonies, was like the letting out of waters. From inconsiderable causes love was changed into suspicion, which gradually ripened into ill-will, and soon ended in hostility. Prudence, policy, and reciprocal interest, urged the expediency of concession: but pride, false honour, and misconceived dignity, drew in an opposite direction. Undecided claims and doubtful rights, which under the influence of wisdom and humility might have been easily compromised, imperceptibly widened into an irreconcileable breach. Hatred at length took the place of kind affections, and the calamities of war were substituted, in lieu of the benefits of commerce. . . .

NEW ENGLAND'S PROVIDENTIAL PREPARATION

It was a fortunate circumstance for the colonies that the royal army was posted in New England. The people of that northern country have their passions more under the command of reason and interest, than in the southern latitudes, where a warmer sun excites a greater degree of irascibility. One rash offensive action against the royal forces at this early period, though successful, might have done great mischief to the cause of America. It would have lost them European friends, and weakened the disposition of the other colonies to assist them. The patient and the politic New England men, fully sensible of their situation, submitted to many insults, and bridled their resentment. In civil wars or revolutions it is a matter of much consequence who strikes the first blow. The compassion of the world is in favour of the attacked, and the displeasure of good men on those who are the first to imbrue their hands in human blood. For the space of nine months after the arrival of general Gage, the behaviour of the people of Boston is particularly worthy of imitation, by those who wish to overturn established governments. They conducted their opposition with exquisite address. They avoided every kind of outrage and violence, preserved peace and good order among themselves, successfully engaged the other colonies to make a common cause with them, and counteracted general Gage so effectually as to prevent his doing any thing for his royal master, while by patience and moderation they skreened themselves from censure. Though resolved to bear as long as prudence and policy dictated, they were all the time preparing for the last extremity. They were furnishing themselves with arms and ammunition, and training their militia.

Provisions were also collected and stored in different places, particularly at Concord, about 20 miles from Boston. General Gage, though zealous for his royal master's interest, discovered a prevailing desire after a peaceable accommodation. He wished to prevent hostilities by depriving the inhabitants of the means necessary for carrying them on. With this view he determined to destroy the stores which he knew were collected for the support of a provincial army. Wishing to accomplish this without bloodshed, he took every precaution to effect it by surprise, and without alarming the country.

BATTLE OF LEXINGTON, APRIL 19, 1775

At eleven o'clock at night, April 18th, 1775, 800 grenadiers and light infantry, the flower of the royal army, embarked at the Common, landed at Phipps's farm, and marched for Concord, under the command of lieutenant colonel Smith. Neither the secrecy with which this expedition was planned, the privacy with which the troops marched out, nor an order that no one inhabitant should leave Boston, were sufficient to prevent intelligence from being sent to the country militia, of what was going forward. About two in the morning, 130 of the Lexington militia had assembled to oppose them, but intelligence respecting the regulars being uncertain, they were dismissed, with orders to appear again at beat of drum. They collected a second time to the number of 70, between four and five o'clock in the morning of the 19th, and the British regulars soon after made their appearance. Major Pitcairn, who led the advanced corps, rode up to them and called out: "Disperse, you rebels; throw down your arms, and disperse." They still continued in a body; on which he advanced nearer, discharged his pistol, and ordered his soldiers to fire. This was done with a huzza. A dispersion of the militia was the consequence; but the firing of the regulars was nevertheless continued. Individuals finding they

GOD PREPARES
A CHRISTIAN
PEOPLE
TO ESTABLISH
THE AMERICAN
NATION

were fired upon, though dispersing, returned the fire. Three or four of the militia were killed on the green. A few more were shot after they had begun to disperse. The royal detachment proceeded to Concord, and executed their commission. They disabled two 24 pounders, threw 500 lb. of ball into wells, and broke in pieces about 60 barrels of flour. Mr. John Butterick, of Concord, major of a minute regiment, not knowing what had passed at Lexington, ordered his men not to give the first fire, that they might not be the aggressors. Upon his approaching near the regulars, they fired, and killed captain Isaac Davis, and one private of the provincial minute men. The fire was returned, and a skirmish ensued. The king's troops having done their business, began their retreat towards Boston. This was conducted with expedition, for the adjacent inhabitants had assembled in arms, and began to attack them in every direction. In their return to Lexington they were exceedingly annoyed, both by those who pressed on their rear, and others who pouring in from all sides, fired from behind stone walls, and such like coverts, which supplied the place of lines and redoubts. At Lexington the regulars were joined by a detachment of 900 men, under lord Piercy, which had been sent out by general Gage to support lieutenant colonel Smith. This reinforcement, having two pieces of cannon, awed the provincials, and kept them at a greater distance: but they continued a constant, though irregular and scattering fire, which did great execution. The close firing from behind the walls by good marksmen, put the regular troops in no small confusion, but they nevertheless kept up a brisk retreating fire on the militia and minute men. A little after sunset the regulars reached Bunker's-hill, worn down with excessive fatigue, having marched that day between thirty and forty miles. On the next day, they crossed Charlestown ferry, and returned to Boston.

There never were more than 400 provincials engaged at one time, and often not so many. As some tired and gave out, others came up and took their places. There was scarcely any discipline observed among them. Officers and privates fired when they were ready, or saw a royal uniform, without waiting for the word of command. Their knowledge of the country enabled them to gain opportunities by crossing fields and fences, and to act as flanking parties against the king's troops, who kept to the main road.

The regulars had 65 killed, 180 wounded, and 28 made prisoners. Of the provincials 50 were killed, and 38 wounded and missing.

As arms were to decide the controversy, it was fortunate for the Americans that the first blood was drawn in New England. The inhabitants of that country are so connected with each other by descent, manners, religion, politics, and a general equality, that the killing of a single individual interested the whole, and made them consider it as a common cause. The blood of those who were killed at Lexington and Concord proved the firm cement of an extensive union. . . .

Intelligence that the British troops had marched out of Boston into the country on some hostile purpose, being forwarded by expresses from one committee to another, great bodies of the militia, not only from Massachusetts but the adjacent colonies, grasped their arms and marched to oppose them. The colonies were in such a state of irritability, that the least shock in any part was, by a powerful and sympathetic affection, instantaneously felt throughout the whole. The Americans who fell were revered by their countrymen, as martyrs who had died in the cause of liberty. Resentment against the British burned more strongly than ever. Martial rage took possession of the breasts of thousands. Combinations were formed, and associations subscribed, binding the inhabitants to one another by the sacred ties of honour, religion, and love of country, to do whatever their public bodies directed for the preservation of their liberties. Hitherto the Americans had no regular army. From principles of policy they cautiously avoided that measure, lest they might subject themselves to the charge of being aggressors. All their military regulations were carried on by their militia, and under the old established laws of the land. For the defence of the colonies, the inhabitants had been, from their early years, enrolled in companies, and taught the use of arms. The laws for this purpose had never been better observed than for some months previous to the Lexington battle. These military arrangements, which had been previously adopted for defending the colonies from hostile French and Indians, were on this occasion turned against the troops of the parent state. Forts, magazines, and arsenals, by the constitution of the country, were in the keeping of his majesty. Immediately after the Lexington battle, these were for the most part taken possession of throughout the colonies, by parties of the provincial militia. Ticonderoga, in which was a small royal garrison, was surprised and taken by adventurers from different states. Public money which had been collected in consequence of previous grants, was also seized for common services. Before the commencement of hostilities, these

DAVID
RAMSAY:
PRELUDE TO
THE AMERICAN
REVOLUTION,
1765–1775

CONTRAST OF
AMERICANS
WITH EUROPEANS

measures would have been condemned by the moderate even among the Americans: but that event justified a bolder line of opposition than had been adopted. Sundry citizens having been put to death by British troops, self preservation dictated measures which, if adopted under other circumstances, would have disunited the colonists. One of the most important of this kind was the raising an army. Men of warm tempers, whose courage exceeded their prudence, had for months urged the necessity of raising troops; but they were restrained by the more moderate, who wished that the colonies might avoid extremities, or at least that they might not lead in bringing them on. The provincial congress of Massachusetts being in session at the time the battle of Lexington was fought, voted that "an army of 30,000 men be immediately raised; that 13,600 be of their own province; and that a letter and delegate be sent to the several colonies of New Hampshire, Connecticut and Rhode Island." In consequence of this vote, the business of recruiting was begun: and in a short time a provisional army was paraded in the vicinity of Boston, which, though far below what had been voted by the provincial congress, was much superior in numbers to the royal army. The command of this force was given to general Ward.

Had the British troops confined themselves to Boston, as before the 18th of April, the assembling an American army, though only for the purpose of observation and defence, would have appeared in the nature of a challenge; and would have made many less willing to support the people of Massachusetts: but after the British had commenced hostilities, the same measure was adopted without subjecting the authors of it to censure, and without giving offence or hazarding the union. The Lexington battle not only furnished the Americans with a justifying apology for raising an army, but inspired them with ideas of their own prowess. Amidst the most animated declarations of sacrificing fortune, and risking life itself for the security of American rights, a secret sigh would frequently escape from the breasts of her most determined friends, for fear that they could not stand before the bravery and discipline of British troops. Hoary sages would shake their heads, and say: "Your cause is good, and I wish you success; but I fear that your undisciplined valour must be overcome, in the unequal contest. After a few thousands of you have fallen, the provinces must ultimately bow to that power which has so repeatedly humbled France and Spain." So confident were the British of their superiority in arms,

that they seemed desirous that the contest might be brought to a military decision. Some of the distinguished speakers in parliament had publicly asserted that the natives of America had nothing of the soldier in them, and that they were in no respect qualified to face a British army. European philosophers had published theories, setting forth that not only vegetables and beasts, but that even men degenerated in the western hemisphere. Departing from the spirit of true philosophy, they overlooked the state of society in a new world, and charged a comparative inferiority, on every production that was American. The colonists themselves had imbibed opinions from their forefathers, that no people on earth were equal to those with whom they were about to contend. Impressed with high ideas of British superiority, and diffident of themselves, their best informed citizens, though willing to run all risks, feared the consequence of an appeal to arms. The success that attended their first military enterprize, in some degree banished these suggestions. Perhaps in no subsequent battle did the Americans appear to greater advantage than in their first essay at Lexington. It is almost without parallel in military history, for the yeomanry of a country to come forward in a single disjointed manner, without order, and for the most part without officers, and by an irregular fire, to put to flight troops equal in discipline to any in the world. In opposition to the bold assertions of some, and the desponding fears of others, experience proved that Americans might effectually resist British troops. The diffident grew bold in their country's cause, and indulged in cheerful hopes that heaven would finally crown their labours with success.

CONTRAST OF AMERICANS WITH EUROPEANS

From a variety of circumstances the Americans had good reason to conclude that hostilities would soon be carried on vigorously in Massachusetts, and also to apprehend that, sooner or later, each province would be the theatre of war. . . . They were fully apprized of the power of Britain; they knew that her fleets covered the ocean, and that her flag waved in triumph through the four quarters of the globe; but the animated language of the time was, "It is better to die freemen, than to live slaves." Though the justice of their cause, and the inspiration of liberty gave, in the opinion of disinterested judges, a superiority to the writings of Americans, yet in the latter mode of conducting their opposition, the candid among themselves acknowledged an inferiority. Their form

GOD PREPARES
A CHRISTIAN
PEOPLE
TO ESTABLISH
THE AMERICAN
NATION

of government was deficient in that decision, despatch, and coercion, which are necessary to military operations.

Europeans, from their being generally unacquainted with fire arms, are less easily taught the use of them than Americans, who are from their youth familiar with these instruments of war; yet on other accounts they are more susceptible of military habits. The proportion of necessitous men in the new world is small compared with that in the old.

To procure subsistence is a powerful motive with an European to enlist: and the prospect of losing it makes him afraid to neglect his duty; but these incitements to the punctual discharge of military services, are wanting in America. In old countries the distinction of ranks and the submission of inferiors to superiors, generally takes place: but in the new world, an extreme sense of liberty and equality indisposes to that implicit obedience which is the soul of an army. The same causes which nurtured a spirit of independence in the colonies, were hostile to their military arrangements. It was not only from the different state of society in the two countries, but from a variety of local causes, that the Americans were not able to contend in arms, on equal terms, with their parent state. From the first settlement of the British colonies, agriculture and commerce, but especially the former, had been the favorite pursuits of their inhabitants. War was a business abhorrent from their usual habits of life. They had never engaged in it from their own motion, nor in any other mode than as appendages to British troops, and under British establishments. By these means the military spirit of the colonies had had no opportunity of expanding itself. At the commencement of hostilities, the British troops possessed a knowledge of the science and discipline of war, which could be acquired only by a long series of application, and substantial establishments. Their equipments, their artillery, and every other part of their apparatus for war approached perfection. To these important circumstances was added a high national spirit of pride, which had been greatly augmented by their successes in their last contest with France and Spain. On the other hand the Americans were undisciplined, without experienced officers, and without the shadow of military establishments. In the wars which had been previously carried on, in or near the colonies, the provincials had been, by their respective legislatures, frequently added to the British troops: but the pride of the latter would not consider the former, who were with-

out uniformity of dress, or the pertness of military airs, to be their equals. The provincial troops were therefore for the most part, assigned to services which, though laborious, were not honorable.

The ignorance of British generals commanding in the woods of America, sometimes involved them in difficulties from which they had been more than once relieved by the superior local knowledge of the colonial troops. These services were soon forgotten: and the moment the troops who performed them could be spared, they were disbanded. Such like obstacles had hitherto depressed military talents in America; but they were now overcome by the ardour of the people.

In the year 1775, a martial spirit pervaded all ranks of men in the colonies. They believed their liberties to be in danger, and were generally disposed to risk their lives for their establishment. Their ignorance of the military art, prevented their weighing the chances of war with that exactness of calculation, which, if indulged, might have damped their hopes. They conceived that there was little more to do than fight manfully for their country. They consoled themselves with the idea, that though their first attempt might be unsuccessful; their numbers would admit of a repetition of the experiment, till the invaders were finally exterminated. Not considering that in modern wars the longest purse decides oftener than the longest sword, they feared not the wealth of Britain. They both expected and wished that the whole dispute would be speedily settled in a few decisive engagements. Elevated with the love of liberty, and buoyed above the fear of consequences, by an ardent military enthusiasm, unabated by calculations above the extent, duration, or probable issue of the war, the people of America seconded the voice of their rulers, in an appeal to heaven for the vindication of their rights. At the time the colonies adopted these spirited resolutions, they possessed not a single ship of war, nor so much as an armed vessel of any kind. It had often been suggested that their seaport towns lay at the mercy of the navy of Great Britain; this was both known and believed, but disregarded. The love of property was absorbed in the love of liberty. The animated votaries of the equal rights of human nature, consoled themselves with the idea that though their whole sea coast should be laid in ashes, they could retire to the western wilderness, and enjoy the luxury of being free; on this occasion it was observed in congress, by Christopher Gadsden, one of the South Carolina delegates: "Our houses being constructed of

By the HONORABLE

JONATHAN TRUMBULL, Esquire,

Governor of the Englifh Colony of *Connecticut*, in *New-England*, in
AMERICA;

A PROCLAMATION

For a Day of Fafting and Prayer.

CONSIDERING the prefent unhappy and increafing Difference between Great-Britain, and the
Englifh Colonies in America, will be a Subject of the wife Deliberation and Counfel of the Britifh
Parliament, in the prefent Seffion ;---and confidering the awful Frowns of Divine Providence, in
threatening thefe Colonies with the lofs of their Liberties,---and of that Harmony, which hath fo
long fubfifted between the Parent-State and them, fo neceffary for the mutual Interefts of both
Countries ;---we are loudly called upon, with true Humility, Sincerity and Fervency to look up
to Almighty GOD, the Fountain of all Wifdom and Goodnefs,---to give Wifdom,---to forgive our
Sins,---to avert the Tokens of His Anger,---and to remember Mercy for His People.

 HAVE therefore, by and with the Advice of the Council, thought fit to appoint,
and do hereby appoint WEDNESDAY THE FIRST DAY OF FEBRUARY NEXT, to be obferved
as a Day of FASTING and PRAYER throughout this Colony :---Hereby exhorting both
Minifters and People of all Denominations, to humble themfelves before GOD,---
confeffing our Sins, and entreating His Grace and Favour.
Particularly, to confefs and lament our paft neglects, and mifimprovement of the ineftimable
Privileges of the Gofpel, and trifling with the Liberties wherewith CHRIST hath made us free ;---
mourn for our Pride, Senfuality, Worldlinefs, Security, and infenfibility of the Obligations we
are under to the Divine Author of all our Bleffings :---To confider how far we have abufed our
Civil Liberties, and made them the occafion and means of Vanity, Luxury and Diffipation.
To offer up fervent Supplications to GOD, for His gracious Prefence with us---to give us true
Repentance and Reformation---to make us fully fenfible that our Dependence muft be on His
Power and Grace alone, to deliver us from all the Evils we feel or fear ;---that He would not leave
us to truft in an Arm of Flefh ;---that He would preferve us from a Spirit of Licentioufnefs, and from
all unlawful and unjuftifiable Means to obtain Redrefs ;---that GOD would dwell in and blefs this
Colony,---preferve all our Rights and Privileges,---blefs and guide the Civil Rulers, in this, and
the other Colonies,---difpofe them to exert their Authority and Influence to fupprefs Vice, and every
Thing offenfive to GOD,---to promote Virtue, and ftedfaftly purfue the beft Means to reftore
Tranquility to the Colonies,---Harmony between the Mother-Country and them,---and to preferve,
fecure and eftablifh their Liberties.
And likewife to offer up fervent Prayers, for His Majefty King *GEORGE* the Third, for our
gracious Queen *CHARLOTTE*, the Prince of WALES, and the reft of the Royal Family :---That
GOD would direct and incline the Heart of the King, and Britifh Parliament, to fuch wife, equitable
and righteous Meafures as may preferve and fecure the juft Rights and Liberties---the Profperity and
Tranquility of the whole *Britifh Empire*.
In our prefent dark and diftreffed State, I do heartily recommend to the feveral Churches, and
Societies of Chriftians in this Colony, as frequently as their Circumftances will permit, Seafons
of Prayer to Him, who has gracioufly ftiled Himfelf *a GOD hearing Prayer*. And do further
exhort all, on the Day of our Humiliation, to pray fervently for the effufion of the HOLY SPIRIT,
the revival of Religion and Virtue, in this and all the Colonies, in our Nation, and through the
Chriftian World ;---and that all Nations may be given to CHRIST, and be made free in Him.

And all fervile Labour is forbidden on faid Day.

GIVEN under my Hand in the Council-Chamber in Hartford, *the fifth Day of* January, *in the
fifteenth Year of the Reign of Our Sovereign Lord* GEORGE *the Third, by the Grace of GOD
of* Great-Britain, France *and* Ireland, *KING, Defender of the Faith, &c. Annoque Domini,*
1775.

Jonath. Trumbull.

GOD fave the KING.

NEW-LONDON : Printed by Timothy Green, Printer to the GOVERNOR and COMPANY.

COURTESY CONNECTICUT HISTORICAL SOCIETY, HARTFORD, CONNECTICUT

God Prepares
a Christian
People
to Establish
the American
Nation

brick, stone, and wood, though destroyed may be rebuilt: but liberty once gone is lost forever."

The sober discretion of the present age will more readily censure than admire, but can more easily admire than imitate the fervid zeal of the patriots of 1775 and 1776, who in idea sacrificed property in the cause of liberty, with the ease that they now sacrifice almost every other consideration for the acquisition of property.

CONTRAST OF BRITISH AND AMERICAN FINANCES

The revenues of Britain were immense; and her people were habituated to the payment of large sums in every form which contributions to government have assumed. But the American colonies possessed neither money nor funds; nor were their people accustomed to taxes equal to the exigencies of war. The contest having begun about taxation, to have raised money by taxes for carrying it on, would have been impolitic. The temper of the times precluded the necessity of attempting the dangerous expedient; for such was the enthusiasm of the day, that the colonists gave up both their personal services and their property to the public, on the vague promises that they should at a future time be reimbursed. Without enquiring into the solidity of funds, or the precise period of payment, the resources of the country were commanded on general assurances, that all expenses of the war should ultimately be equalized. The parent state abounded with experienced statesmen and officers: but the dependent form of government exercised in the colonies, precluded their citizens from gaining that practical knowledge which is acquired from being at the head of public departments. There were very few in the colonies who understood the business of providing for an army, and still fewer who had experience and knowledge to direct its operations. The disposition of the finances of the country, and the most effectual mode of drawing forth its resources, were subjects with which scarce any of the inhabitants were acquainted. Arms and ammunition were almost wholly deficient; and though the country abounded with the materials of which they are manufactured, yet there was neither time nor artists enough to supply an army with the means of defence. The country was destitute both of fortifications and engineers. Amidst so many discouragements, there were some flattering circumstances. The war could not be carried on by Great Britain, but at a great disadvantage, and at an immense ex-

pense. It was easy for ministers, at St. James's, to plan campaigns: but hard was the fate of the officer, from whom the execution of them, in the woods of America, was expected. The country was so extensive, and abounded so much with defiles, that, by evacuating and retreating, the Americans, though they could not conquer, yet might save themselves from being conquered. The authors of the acts of parliament, for restraining the trade of the colonies, were most excellent recruiting officers for congress. They imposed a necessity on thousands to become soldiers. All other business being suspended, the whole resources of the country were applied in supporting an army. Though the colonists were without discipline, they possessed native valour. Though they had neither gold nor silver, they possessed a mine, in the enthusiasm of their people. Paper, for upwards of two years, produced to them more solid advantages, than Spain derived from her superabounding precious metals. Though they had no ships to protect their trade or their towns, they had simplicity enough to live without the former, and enthusiasm enough to risk the latter; rather than submit to the power of Britain. They believed their cause to be just, and that heaven approved their exertions in defence of their rights. Zeal originating from such motives, supplied the place of discipline; and inspired a confidence and military ardour, which overleaped all difficulties. . . .

BATTLE OF BUNKER HILL, JUNE 17, 1775

The forces which had been collected in Massachusetts, were stationed in convenient places, for guarding the country, from further excursions of the regulars from Boston. Breast-works were also erected in different places, for the same purpose. While both parties were attempting to carry off stock from the several islands, with which the bay of Boston is agreeably diversified, sundry skirmishes took place. These were of real service to the Americans. They habituated them to danger; and, perhaps, much of the courage of old soldiers, is derived from an experimental conviction, that the chance of escaping unhurt from engagements, is much greater than young recruits suppose.

About the latter end of May, a great part of the reinforcements ordered from Great Britain, arrived at Boston. Three British generals, Howe, Burgoyne and Clinton, whose behaviour in the preceding war, had gained them great reputation, arrived about the same time. General Gage, thus reinforced, prepared for acting with more decision: but, before he proceeded to extremities, he conceived it due to ancient forms, to issue a proclamation, holding forth to the inhabitants the alternative of peace or war. He therefore offered pardon, in the king's name, to all who should forthwith lay down their arms, and return to their respective occupations and peaceable duties: excepting only from the benefit of that pardon, "Samuel Adams, and John Hancock, whose offences were said to be of too flagitious a nature, to admit of any other consideration, than that of condign punishment." He also proclaimed, that not only the persons above-named and excepted, but, also, all their adherents, associates, and correspondents, should be deemed guilty of treason and rebellion; and treated accordingly. By this proclamation, it was also declared, "that as the courts of judicature were shut, martial law should take place, till a due course of justice should be re-established." (June 12, 1775.)

It was supposed that this proclamation was a prelude to hostilities; and preparations were accordingly made by the Americans. A considerable height, by the name of Bunker's hill, just at the entrance of the peninsula of Charlestown, was so situated as to make the possession of it, a matter of great consequence, to either of the contending parties. Orders were therefore issued, by the provincial commanders, that a detachment of a thousand men should intrench upon this height. By some mistake, Breed's hill, high and large like the other, but situated nearer Boston, was marked out for the intrenchments, instead of Bunker's hill. The provincials proceeded to Breed's hill; and worked with so much diligence, that between midnight and the dawn of the morning, they had thrown up a small redoubt about eight rods square. They kept such a profound silence, that they were not heard by the British, on board their vessels, though very near. These having derived their first information of what was going on, from the sight of the works, nearly completed, began an incessant firing upon them. The provincials bore this with firmness; and, though they were only young soldiers, continued to labour till they had thrown up a small breast-work, extending from the east side of the redoubt to the bottom of the hill. As this eminence overlooked Boston, general Gage thought it necessary to drive the provincials from it. About noon, therefore, he detached major general Howe and brig. general Pigot, with the flower of his army, consisting of four battalions, ten companies of the grenadiers and ten of light infantry, with a proportion of field artillery, to effect this business. These troops landed at Moreton's point, and formed after landing; but remained in that position, till they were reinforced by a second detachment of light infantry and grenadier companies, a battalion of land forces, and a battalion of marines, making in the whole, nearly 3000 men. While the troops, who first landed, were waiting for this reinforcement, the provincials for their further security, pulled up some adjoining post and rail fences, and set them down in two parallel lines, at a small distance from each other; and filled the space between with hay, which, having been lately mowed, remained on the adjacent ground.

The king's troops formed in two lines, and advanced slowly, to give their artillery time to demolish the American works. While the British were advancing to the attack, they received orders to burn Charlestown. These were not given, because they were fired upon from the houses in that town: but, from the military policy, of depriving enemies of a cover in their approaches. In a short time, this ancient town, consisting of about 500 buildings, chiefly of wood, was in one great blaze. The lofty steeple of the meeting house formed a pyramid of fire above the rest, and struck the astonished eyes of numerous beholders, with a magnificent but awful spectacle. In Boston, the heights of every kind were covered with the citizens, and such of the king's troops, as were not on duty. The hills around the adjacent country, which afforded a safe and distinct view, were occupied by the inhabitants of the country.

Thousands, both within and without Boston, were anxious spectators of the bloody scene. The honour of British troops, beat high in the breasts of many; while others, with a keener sensibility, felt for the liberties of a great and growing country. The British moved on slowly; which gave the provincials a better opportunity for taking aim. The latter, in general, reserved themselves, till their adversaries were within ten or twelve rods: but then began a furious discharge of small arms. The stream of the American fire was so incessant, and did so great execution, that the king's troops retreated in disorder and precipitation. Their officers rallied them, and pushed them forward with their swords: but they returned to the attack with great reluctance. The Americans again reserved their fire, till their adversaries were near; and then put them a second time to flight. General Howe and the officers redoubled

497

GOD PREPARES
A CHRISTIAN
PEOPLE
TO ESTABLISH
THE AMERICAN
NATION

their exertions, and were again successful; though the soldiers discovered a great aversion to going on. By this time, the powder of the Americans began so far to fail, that they were not able to keep up the same brisk fire. The British then brought some cannon to bear, which raked the inside of the breast-works from end to end. The fire from the ships, batteries, and field artillery was redoubled; the soldiers in the rear were goaded on by their officers. The redoubt was attacked on three sides at once. Under these circumstances, a retreat from it was ordered: but the provincials delayed, and made resistance with their discharged muskets, as if they had been clubs, so long, that the king's troops, who easily mounted the works, had half filled the redoubt, before it was given up to them.

While these operations were going on at the breast-work and redoubt, the British light infantry were attempting to force the left point of the former, that they might take the American line in flank. Though they exhibited the most undaunted courage, they met with an opposition which called for its greatest exertions. The provincials reserved their fire, till their adversaries were near; and then poured it upon the light infantry, with such an incessant stream, and in a direction so true, as mowed down their ranks. The engagement was kept up on both sides with great resolution. The persevering exertions of the king's troops could not compel the Americans to retreat, till they observed that their main body had left the hill. This, when begun, exposed them to new danger; for, it could not be effected, but by marching over Charlestown neck; every part of which was raked by the shot of the Glasgow man of war, and of two floating batteries. The incessant fire, kept up across this neck, prevented any considerable reinforcement, from joining their countrymen who were engaged: but the few, who fell on their retreat, over the same ground, proved that the apprehensions of those provincial officers, who declined passing over to succour their companions, were without any solid foundation.

The number of Americans engaged, amounted only to 1500. It was apprehended that the conquerors would push the advantage they had gained, and march immediately to American head quarters at Cambridge; but they advanced no further than Bunker's hill. There, they threw up works, for their own security. The provincials did the same, on Prospect hill, in front of them. Both were guarding against an attack; and both were in a bad condition to receive one. The loss

of the peninsula depressed the spirits of the Americans; and the great loss of men produced the same effect on the British. There have been few battles in modern wars, in which, all circumstances considered, there was a greater destruction of men, than in this short engagement. The loss of the British, as acknowledged by general Gage, amounted to 1054. Nineteen commissioned officers were killed, and 70 more were wounded. The battle of Quebec, in 1759, which gave Great Britain the province of Canada, was not so destructive to British officers, as this affair of a slight intrenchment, the work only of a few hours. That the officers suffered so much, must be imputed to their being aimed at. None of the provincials in this engagement were riflemen: but, they were all good marksmen. The whole of their previous military knowledge had been derived from hunting, and the ordinary amusements of sportsmen. The dexterity which, by long habit, they had acquired in hitting beasts, birds, and marks, was fatally applied to the destruction of British officers. From their fall, much confusion was expected. They were therefore particularly singled out. Most of those, who were near the person of general Howe, were either killed or wounded: but the general, though he greatly exposed himself, was unhurt. The light infantry and grenadiers lost three-fourths of their men. Of one company, not more than five, and of another, not more than fourteen escaped. The unexpected resistance of the Americans was such, as wiped away the reproach of cowardice, which had been cast on them, by their enemies in Britain. The spirited conduct of the British officers, merited and obtained great applause: but, the provincials were justly entitled to a large portion of the fame, for having made the utmost exertions of their adversaries necessary, to dislodge them from lines, which were the work only of a single night.

The Americans lost five pieces of cannon. Their killed amounted to 139: their wounded and missing to 314. Thirty of the former fell into the hands of the conquerors. They particularly regretted the death of general Warren. To the purest patriotism and most undaunted bravery, he added the virtues of domestic life, the eloquence of an accomplished orator, and the wisdom of an able statesman. A regard to the liberty of his country only, induced him to oppose the measures of government. He aimed not at a separation from, but a coalition with the mother country. He took an active part in defence of his country; not that he might be applauded, and rewarded for a patriotic spirit: but, because he was, in the best sense of the word, a real patriot. Having no interested or personal views to answer, the friends of liberty confided in his integrity. The soundness of his judgment, and his abilities as a public speaker, enabled him to make a distinguished figure in public councils: but, his intrepidity and active zeal, induced his countrymen to place him in the military line. Within four days after he was appointed a major general, he fell a noble sacrifice to a cause, which he had espoused from the purest principles. Like Hambden he lived, and like Hambden he died; universally beloved, and universally regretted. His many virtues were celebrated in an elegant eulogium, written by Dr. Rush, in language equal to the illustrious subject.

The burning of Charlestown, though a place of great trade, did not discourage the provincials. It excited resentment and execration: but not any disposition to submit. Such was the high toned state of the public mind, and so great the indifference for property, when put in competition with liberty, that military conflagrations, though they distressed and impoverished, had no tendency to subdue the colonists. They might answer in the old world: but were not calculated for the new, where the war was undertaken, not for a change of masters, but for securing essential rights. The action at Breed's-hill, or Bunker's-hill, as it has been commonly called, produced many and very important consequences. It taught the British so much respect for Americans, intrenched behind works, that their subsequent operations were retarded with a caution, that wasted away a whole campaign, to very little purpose. It added to the confidence the Americans began to have in their own abilities; but inferences, very injurious to the future interests of America, were drawn from the good conduct of the new troops, on that memorable day. It inspired some of the leading members of congress, with such high ideas of what might be done by militia, or men engaged for a short term of enlistment, that it was long before they assented to the establishment of a permanent army. Not distinguishing the continued exertions of an army, through a series of years, from the gallant efforts of the yeomanry of the country, led directly to action, they were slow in admitting the necessity of permanent troops. They conceived the country might be defended, by the occasional exertions of her sons, without the expense and danger of an army, engaged for the war. In the progress of hostilities, as will appear in the sequel, the militia lost much

of their first ardour; while leading men in the councils of America, trusting to its continuance, neglected the proper time of recruiting, for a series of years. From the want of perseverance in the militia, and the want of a disciplined standing army, the cause for which arms were at first taken up, was more than once brought to the brink of destruction.

THE SECOND CONGRESS MEETS

The time of the meeting of this second congress, was fixed at so distant a day, that an opportunity might be afforded for obtaining information of the plans adopted by the British parliament, in the winter of 1774, 1775. Had these been favourable, the delegates would either not have met, or dispersed after a short session: but as the resolution was then fixed, to compel the submission of the colonies, and hostilities had   May 10, 1775 already commenced, the meeting of congress, on the tenth of May, which was at first eventual, became fixed.

On their meeting, they chose Peyton Randolph, for their president, and Charles Thompson, for their secretary. On the next day, Mr. Hancock laid before them a variety of depositions, proving that the king's troops were the aggressors, in the late battle at Lexington, together with sundry papers relative to the great events, which had lately taken place in Massachusetts. Whereupon, congress resolved itself into a committee of the whole, to take into consideration the state of America. They proceeded in the same line of moderation and firmness, which marked the acts of their predecessors in the past year.

The city and county of New York, having applied to congress, for advice how they should conduct themselves with regard to the troops they expected to land there; they were advised, "to act on the defensive, so long as might be consistent with their safety; to permit the troops to remain in the barracks, so long as they behaved peaceably: but not to suffer fortifications to be erected, or any steps to be taken for cutting off the communication between the town and country." Congress also resolved: "That exportation to all parts of British America, which had not adopted their association, should immediately cease;" and that, "no provision of any kind, or other necessaries, be furnished to the British fisheries, on the American coasts;" and, "that no bill of exchange, draft, or order, of any officer in the British army or navy, their agents or con-

499

God Prepares
a Christian
People
to Establish
the American
Nation

tractors, be received or negociated, or any money supplied them, by any person in America; that no provisions or necessaries of any kind, be furnished or supplied, to or for the use of the British army or navy, in the colony of Massachusetts Bay; that no vessel employed in transporting British troops to America, or from one part of North America, to another, or warlike stores or provisions for said troops, be freighted or furnished with provisions or any necessaries." These resolutions may be considered as the counterpart of the British acts for restraining the commerce, and prohibiting the fisheries of the colonies. They were calculated to bring distress on the British islands, in the West Indies; whose chief dependence for subsistence, was on the importation of provision, from the American continent. They also occasioned new difficulties in the support of the British army and fisheries. The colonists were so much indebted to Great Britain, that government bills for the most part found among them a ready market. A war in the colonies was therefore made subservient to commerce, by increasing the sources of remittance. This enabled the mother country, in a great degree, to supply her troops without shipping money out of the kingdom. From the operation of these resolutions, advantages of this nature were not only cut off, but the supply of the British army, was rendered both precarious and expensive. In consequence of the interdiction of the American fisheries, great profits were expected, by British adventurers, in that line. Such frequently found it most convenient to obtain supplies in America, for carrying on their fisheries: but, as Great Britain had deprived the colonists of all benefits from that quarter, they now, in their turn, interdicted all supplies from being furnished to British fishermen. To obviate this unexpected embarrassment, several of the vessels, employed in this business, were obliged to return home, to bring out provisions, for their associates. These restrictive resolutions, were not so much the effect of resentment, as of policy. The colonists conceived, that by distressing the British commerce, they would increase the number of those, who would interest themselves in their behalf.

JOHN HANCOCK SUCCEEDS PEYTON RANDOLPH

The new congress had convened but a few days, when their venerable president, Peyton Randolph, was under the necessity of returning home. On his departure, John Hancock, who had lately been proscribed, by general Gage, was

unanimously chosen his successor. The objects of deliberation, presented to this new congress, were, if possible, more important than those which, in the preceding year, had engaged the attention of their predecessors. The colonists had now experienced the inefficacy of those measures, from which relief had been formerly obtained. They found a new parliament disposed to run all risks in compelling their submission. They also understood, that administration was united against them, and its members firmly established in their places. Hostilities were commenced. Reinforcements had arrived; and more were daily expected. Added to this, they had information, that their adversaries had taken measures to secure the friendship and cooperation of the Indians and Canadians.

The coercion of the colonies being resolved upon, and their conquest supposed to be inevitable, the British ministry judged, that it would be for the interest of both countries, to proceed in that vigorous course, which promised the speediest attainment of their object. They hoped, by pressing the colonists on all quarters, to intimidate opposition, and ultimately to lessen the effusion of human blood.

DIFFICULTIES FACING CONGRESS

In this awful crisis, congress had only a choice of difficulties. The New England states had already organized an army, and blockaded general Gage. To desert them, would have been contrary to plighted faith, and to sound policy. To support them, would make the war general, and involve all the provinces, in one general promiscuous state of hostility. The resolution of the people in favour of the latter was fixed; and only wanted public sanction for its operation. Congress therefore resolved: "that for the express purpose of defending and securing the colonies, and preserving them in safety, against all attempts to carry the late acts of parliament into execution, by force of arms, they be immediately put in a state of defence: but, as they wished for a restoration of the harmony, formerly subsisting between the mother country and the colonies, to the promotion of this most desirable reconciliation, an humble and dutiful petition be presented to his majesty." To resist, and to petition, were coeval resolutions. As freemen, they could not tamely submit: but as loyal subjects, wishing for peace, as far as was compatible with their rights, they once more, in the character of petitioners, humbly stated their grievances, to the common father of the empire. To dissuade the Canadians from co-operating with the British, they again addressed them; representing the pernicious tendency of the Quebec act, and apologizing for their taking Ticonderoga, and Crown-Point, as measures which were dictated by the great law of self-preservation. About the same time, congress took measures for warding off the danger, that threatened their frontier inhabitants from the Indians. Commissioners to treat with them, were appointed; and a supply of goods for their use was ordered. A talk was also prepared by congress, and transmitted to them, in which the controversy between Great Britain and her colonies was explained in a familiar Indian style. They were told, that they had no concern in the family quarrel; and were urged by the ties of ancient friendship, and a common birth place, to remain at home; keep their hatchet buried deep; and to join neither side.

The novel situation of Massachusetts, made it necessary for the ruling powers of that province, to ask the advice of congress, on a very interesting subject: "the taking up and exercising the powers of civil government." For many months, they had been kept together, in tolerable peace and order, by the force of ancient habits; under the simple style of recommendation and advice from popular bodies, invested with no legislative authority. But, as war now raged in their borders, and a numerous army was actually raised, some more efficient form of government became necessary. At this early day, it neither comported with the wishes, nor the designs of the colonists, to erect forms of government independent of Great Britain. Congress, therefore, recommended only such regulations, as were immediately necessary; and these were conformed, as near as possible, to the spirit and substance of the charter; and were only to last, till a governor, of his majesty's appointment, would consent to govern the colony according to its charter.

POST OFFICE ESTABLISHED

On the same principles of necessity, another assumption of new powers became unavoidable. The great intercourse that daily took place throughout the colonies, pointed out the propriety of establishing a general post-office. This was accordingly done; and Dr. Franklin, who had, by royal authority, been dismissed from a similar employment, about three years before, was appointed by his country, the head of the new department.

PUBLISHING TO WORLD OUR REASONS FOR TAKING UP ARMS

While congress was making arrangements for their proposed continental army, it was thought expedient, once more to address the inhabitants of Great Britain, and to publish to the world a declaration setting forth their reasons, for taking up arms; to address the speaker and gentlemen of the assembly of Jamaica, and the inhabitants of Ireland; and also to prefer a second humble petition to the king. In their address to the inhabitants of Great Britain, they again vindicated themselves, from the charge of aiming at independency; professed their willingness to submit to the several acts of trade and navigation, which were passed before the year 1763; recapitulated their reasons for rejecting lord North's conciliatory motion; stated the hardships they suffered, from the operations of the royal army in Boston; and insinuated the danger that the inhabitants of Britain would be in, of losing their freedom, in case their American brethren were subdued.

In their delaration, setting forth the causes and necessity of their taking up arms, they enumerated the injuries they had received, and the methods taken by the British ministry to compel their submission; and then said: "we are reduced to the alternative of choosing an unconditional submission to the tyranny of irritated ministers, or resistance by force. The latter is our choice. We have counted the cost of this contest, and find nothing so dreadful as voluntary slavery." They asserted, "that foreign assistance was undoubtedly attainable." This was not founded on any private information, but was an opinion derived from their knowledge of the principles of policy, by which states usually regulate their conduct towards each other.

In their address to the speaker and gentlemen of the assembly of Jamaica, they dilated on the arbitrary systems of the British ministry; and informed them, that, in order to obtain a redress of their grievances, they had appealed to the justice, humanity, and interest, of Great Britain. They stated, that to make their schemes of non-importation and non-exportation, produce the desired effects, they were obliged to extend them to the islands. "From that necessity, and from that alone, said they, our conduct has proceeded." They concluded with saying: "the peculiar situation of your island forbids your assistance; but we have your good wishes. From the good wishes of the friends of liberty and mankind, we shall always derive consolation."

God Prepares
a Christian
People
to Establish
the American
Nation

In their address to the people of Ireland, they recapitulated their grievances; stated their humble petitions, and the neglect with which they had been treated. "In defence of our persons and properties under actual violations, said they, we have taken up arms. When that violence shall be removed, and hostilities cease on the part of the aggressors, they shall cease on our part also."

These several addresses were executed in a masterly manner, and were well calculated to make friends to the colonies. But their petition to the king, which was drawn up at the same time, produced more solid advantages in favour of the American cause, than any other of their productions. This was in a great measure carried through congress by Mr. Dickinson. Several members, judging from the violence with which parliament proceeded against the colonies, were of opinion, that further petitions were nugatory: but, this worthy citizen, a friend to both countries, and devoted to a reconciliation on constitutional principles, urged the expediency and policy of trying, once more, the effect of an humble, decent, and firm petition, to the common head of the empire. The high opinion that was conceived of his patriotism and abilities, induced the members to assent to the measure, though they generally conceived it to be labour lost. The petition agreed upon, was the work of Mr. Dickinson's pen. In this, among other things, it was stated: "That, notwithstanding their sufferings, they had retained too high a regard for the kingdom, from which they derived their origin, to request such a reconciliation, as might, in any manner, be inconsistent with her dignity and welfare. Attached to his majesty's person, family, and government, with all the devotion that principle and affection can inspire; connected with Great Britain by the strongest ties, that can unite society; and deploring every event that tended, in any degree, to weaken them, they not only most fervently desired the former harmony, between her and the colonies, to be restored, but that a concord might be established between them, upon so firm a basis, as to perpetuate its blessings, uninterrupted by any future dissentions, to succeeding generations, in both countries. They, therefore, beseeched, that his majesty would be pleased to direct some mode, by which the united applications of his faithful colonists to the throne, in pursuance of their common councils, might be improved into a happy and permanent reconciliation."

By this last clause, congress meant, that the mother country should propose a plan, for establishing by compact, something like Magna Charta, for the colonies. They did not aim at a total exemption from the controul of parliament; nor were they unwilling to contribute in their own way, to the expenses of government: but, they feared the horrors of war less than submission to unlimited parliamentary supremacy. They desired an amicable compact, in which doubtful, undefined points, should be ascertained, so as to secure that proportion of authority and liberty, which would be for the general good of the whole empire. They fancied themselves in the condition of the barons at Runnymede; with this difference, that, in addition to opposing the king, they had also to oppose the parliament. This difference was more nominal than real; for, in the latter case, the king and parliament stood precisely in the same relation to the people of America, which subsisted in the former, between the king and people of England. In both, popular leaders were contending with the sovereign, for the privileges of subjects. This well-meant petition was presented on September 1st, 1775, by Mr. Penn, and Mr. Lee; and, on the 4th, lord Dartmouth informed them, "that to it, no answer would be given."

KING REFUSES TO ANSWER SECOND PETITION

This slight contributed, not a little, to the union and perseverance of the colonists. When pressed by the calamities of war, a doubt would sometimes arise, in the minds of scrupulous persons, that they had been too hasty, in their opposition to the protecting, parent state. To such, it was usual to present the second petition of congress to the king; observing thereon, that all the blood, and all the guilt of the war, must be charged on British, and not on American counsels. Though the colonists were accused, in a speech from the throne, as meaning only "to amuse, by vague expressions of attachment to the parent state, and the strongest protestations of loyalty to their king, while they were preparing for a general revolt; and that their rebellious war was manifestly carried on, for the purpose of establishing an independent empire:" yet, at that time, and for months after, a redress of grievances was their ultimate aim. Conscious of this intention, and assenting, in the sincerity of their souls, to the submissive language of their petition, they illy brooked the contempt, with which their joint supplication was treated; and, still worse, that they should be charged from the throne, with studied duplicity.

Nothing contributes more to the success of revolutions, than moderation. Intemperate zealots overshoot their object, and soon spend their force; while the calm and dispassionate persevere to the end. The bulk of the people, in civil commotions, are influenced to a choice of sides, by the general complexion of the measures adopted by the respective parties. When these appear to be dictated by justice and prudence, and to be uninfluenced by passion, ambition or avarice, they are disposed to favour them. Such was the effect of this second petition, through a long and trying war, in which, men of serious reflection were often called upon to examine the rectitude of their conduct.

Though the refusal of an answer, to this renewed application of congress to the king, was censured by numbers in Great Britain, as well as in the colonies; yet, the partisans of ministry varnished the measure, as proper and expedient. They contended, that the petition, as it contained no offers of submission, was unavailing, as a ground work of negociation. Nothing was further from the thoughts of congress, than such concessions, as were expected in Great Britain. They conceived themselves to be more sinned against than sinning. They claimed a redress of grievances, as a matter of right: but were persuaded, that concessions, for this purpose, were acts of justice, and not of humiliation; and, therefore, could not be disgraceful to those by whom they were made. To prevent future altercations, they wished for an amicable compact, to ascertain the extent of parliamentary supremacy. The mother country wished for absolute submission to her authority; the colonists, for a repeal of every act, that imposed taxes, or that interfered in their internal legislation. The ministry of England, being determined not to repeal these acts, and the congress equally determined not to submit to them; the claims of the two countries were so wide from each other, as to afford no reasonable ground to expect a compromise. It was, therefore, concluded, that any notice taken of the petition would only afford an opportunity for the colonies to prepare themselves for the last extremity.

GEORGE WASHINGTON APPOINTED COMMANDER IN CHIEF

A military opposition to the armies of Great Britain, being resolved upon by the colonies, it became an object of consequence to fix on a proper person, to conduct that opposition. Many of the colonists had titles of high rank in the militia, and several had seen something of real service, in the late war between France and England: but there was no individual of such superior military experience, as to entitle him to a decided pre-eminence; or even to qualify him, on that ground, to contend, on equal terms, with the British masters of the art of war. In elevating one man, by the free voice of an invaded country, to the command of thousands of his equal fellow citizens, no consideration was regarded but the interest of the community. To bind the uninvaded provinces more closely to the common cause, policy directed the views of congress to the south.

Among the southern colonies, Virginia, for numbers, wealth, and influence, stood pre-eminent. To attach so respectable a colony to the aid of Massachusetts, by selecting from it a commander in chief, was not less warranted by the great military genius of one of its distinguished citizens, than dictated by sound policy. George Washington was, by an unanimous vote, appointed commander in chief of all the forces raised, or to be raised, for the defence of the colonies. It was a fortunate circumstance attending his election, that it was accompanied with no competition, and followed by no envy. That same general impulse on the public mind, which led the colonists to agree in many other particulars, pointed to him, as the most proper person for presiding over the military arrangements of America. Not only congress, but the inhabitants, in the east and the west, in the north and the south, as well before as at the time of embodying a continental army, were in a great degree unanimous in his favour.

General Washington was born on the 22d of February, 1732. His education favoured the production of a solid mind, and a vigorous body. Mountain air, abundant exercise in the open country, the wholesome toils of the chase, and the delightful scenes of rural life, expanded his limbs to an unusual, graceful, and well proportioned size. His youth was spent in the acquisition of useful knowledge, and in pursuits, tending to the improvement of his fortune, or the benefit of his country. Fitted more for active, than for speculative life, he devoted the greater proportion of his time to the former: but this was amply compensated by his being frequently in such situations, as called forth the powers of his mind, and strengthened them by repeated exercise. Early in life, in obedience to his country's call, he entered the military line, and began his

God Prepares
a Christian
People
to Establish
the American
Nation

career of fame, in opposing that power, in concert with whose troops, he acquired his last and most distinguished honours. He was aid-de-camp to general Braddock in 1755; when that unfortunate officer was killed. He was eminently serviceable in covering the retreat, and saving the remains of the routed army. For three years after the defeat of Braddock, George Washington was commander in chief of the forces of Virginia, against the incursions of the French and Indians, from the Ohio. He continued in service till the reduction of Fort Duquesne, in 1758, gave peace to the frontiers of his native colony, Virginia. Soon after that event, he retired to his estate, Mount Vernon, on the banks of the Potomac, and with great industry and success, pursued the arts of peaceful life. When the proceedings of the British parliament alarmed the colonists with apprehensions, that a blow was levelled at their liberties, he again came forward into public view, and was appointed a delegate to the congress, which met in September, 1774. Possessed of a large proportion of common sense, and directed by a sound judgment, he was better fitted for the exalted station to which he was called, than many others who, to a greater brilliancy of parts, frequently add the excentricity of original genius. Engaged in the busy scenes of life, he knew human nature, and the most proper method of accomplishing proposed objects. His passions were subdued and kept in subjection to reason. His soul, superior to party spirit, to prejudice, and illiberal views, moved according to the impulses it received from an honest heart, a good understanding, common sense, and a sound judgment. He was habituated to view things on every side, to consider them in all relations, and to trace the possible and probable consequences of proposed measures. Much addicted to close thinking, his mind was constantly employed. By frequent exercise, his understanding and judgment expanded, so as to be able to discern truth, and to know what was proper to be done, in the most difficult conjunctures.

Coeval with the resolution for raising an army, was another for emitting a sum, not exceeding two millions of dollars, in bills of credit, for the defence of America; and the colonies were pledged for their redemption. This sum was increased from time to time by further emissions. The colonies, having neither money nor revenue at their command, were forced to adopt this expedient; the only one which was in their power for supporting an army. No one delegate opposed the measure. So great had been the credit of the

former emissions of paper, in the greater part of the colonies, that very few at that time foresaw or apprehended the consequences of unfunded paper emissions: but had all the consequences which resulted from this measure, in the course of the war, been foreseen, it must, notwithstanding, have been adopted: for it was a less evil, that there should be a general wreck of property, than that the essential rights and liberties of a growing country should be lost. A happy ignorance of future events, combined with the ardour of the times, prevented many reflections on this subject, and gave credit and circulation to these bills of credit.

General Washington, soon after his appointment to the command of the American army, set out for the camp, at Cambridge. On his way thither, he was treated with the highest honours, in every place through which he passed. Large detachments of volunteers, composed of private gentlemen, turned out to escort him.

On his arrival at Cambridge, July 3d, 1775, he was received with the joyful acclamations of the American army. At the head of his troops, he published a declara- July 3, 1775 tion, previously drawn up by congress, in the nature of a manifesto, setting forth the reasons for taking up arms. . . . When general Washington joined the American army, he found the British intrenched on Bunker's hill, having also three floating batteries in Mystic river, and a twenty gun ship below the ferry, between Boston and Charlestown. They had also a battery on Copse's hill, and were strongly fortified on the neck. The Americans were intrenched at Winter-hill, Prospect-hill, and Roxbury, communicating with one another by small posts, over a distance of ten miles. There were also parties stationed in several towns, along the sea coast. They had neither engineers to plan suitable works, nor sufficient tools for their erection.

THE AMERICAN CAMP

In the American camp, was collected a large body of men: but without those conveniences, which ancient establishments have introduced for the comfort of regular armies. Instead of tents, sails, now rendered useless by the obstructions of commerce, were applied for their covering: but, even of them, there was not a sufficiency. The American soldiers, having joined the camp, in all that variety of clothing, which they used in their daily labour, were without uniformity of dress. To abolish provincial distinctions, the hunting

DAVID
RAMSAY:
PRELUDE TO
THE AMERICAN
REVOLUTION,
1765–1775

CONTINENTAL
FAST DAY,
JULY 20, 1775

shirt was introduced. They were also without those heads of departments, in the line of commissaries, or quarter masters, which are necessary for the regular and economical supply of armies. Individuals, brought to camp their own provisions, on their own horses. In some parts, committees of supplies were appointed, who purchased necessaries at public expense, sent them on to camp, and distributed them to such as were in want, without any regularity or system. The country afforded provisions; and nothing more was wanting, than proper systems for their collection, and distribution. Other articles, though equally necessary, were almost wholly deficient; and could not be procured, but with difficulty. On the 4th of August, the whole stock of powder in the American camp, and in the public magazines, of the four New England provinces, would make little more than nine rounds a man. The continental army remained in this destitute condition, for a fortnight or more. This was generally known among themselves, and was also communicated to the British, by a deserter: but they, suspecting a plot, would not believe it. A supply of a few tons was sent on to them from the committee of Elizabethtown: but this was done privately, lest the adjacent inhabitants, who were equally destitute, should stop it for their own use. The public rulers in Massachusetts issued a recommendation to the inhabitants, not to fire a gun at beast, bird or mark; in order that they might husband their little stock, for the more necessary purpose of shooting men. A supply of several thousand pounds weight of powder, was soon after obtained from Africa, in exchange for New England rum. This was managed with so much address, that every ounce for sale in the British forts on the African coasts, was purchased up, and brought off for the use of the Americans.

Embarrassments, from various quarters, occurred in the formation of a continental army. The appointment of general officers, made by congress, was not satisfactory. Enterprising leaders had come forward, with their followers, on the commencement of hostilities, without scrupulous attention to rank. When these were all blended together, it was impossible to assign to every officer the station which his services merited, or his vanity demanded. Materials for a good army were collected. The husbandmen who flew to arms, were active, zealous, and of unquestionable courage: but to introduce discipline and subordination, among free men who were habituated to think for themselves, was an arduous labour.

The want of system, and of union under proper heads, pervaded every department. From the circumstance, that the persons employed in providing necessaries for the army were unconnected with each other, much waste and unnecessary delays were occasioned. The troops of the different colonies came into service, under variant establishments. Some were enlisted with the express condition of choosing their officers. The rations promised by the local legislatures, varied both as to quantity, quality and price. To form one uniform mass of these discordant materials, and to subject the licentiousness of independent freemen to the control of military discipline, was a delicate and difficult business.

The continental army, put under the command of general Washington, amounted to 14,500 men. These had been so judiciously stationed round Boston, as to confine the British to the town, and to exclude them from the forage and provisions, which the adjacent country and islands in Boston-bay afforded. This force was thrown into three grand divisions. General Ward commanded the right wing, at Roxbury. General Lee, the left, at Prospect-hill; and the centre was commanded by General Washington. In arranging the army, the military skill of adjutant-general Gates, was of great service. Method and punctuality were introduced. The officers and privates were taught to know their respective places, and to have the mechanism and movements, as well as the name of an army.

CONTINENTAL FAST DAY,
JULY 20, 1775

Resistance being resolved upon by the Americans, the pulpit, the press, the bench and the bar, severally laboured to unite and encourage them. The clergy of New England were a numerous, learned and respectable body, who had a great ascendancy over the minds of their hearers. They connected religion and patriotism; and in their sermons and prayers, represented the cause of America, as the cause of heaven. The synod of New York and Philadelphia also sent forth a pastoral letter, which was publicly read in their churches. This earnestly recommended such sentiments and conduct, as were suitable to their situation. Writers and printers followed in the rear of the preachers; and, next to them, had the greatest hand in animating their countrymen. Gentlemen, of the bench and of the bar, denied the charge of rebellion, and justified the resistance of the colonists. A distinction founded on law, be-

GOD PREPARES
A CHRISTIAN
PEOPLE
TO ESTABLISH
THE AMERICAN
NATION

tween the king and his ministry, was introduced. The former, it was contended, could do no wrong. The crime of treason was charged on the latter; for using the royal name, to varnish their own unconstitutional measures. The phrase of a ministerial war became common; and was used, as a medium for reconciling resistance with allegiance.

Coeval with the resolutions for organizing an army, was one appointing the 20th day of July, 1775, a day of public humiliation, fasting and prayer to Almighty God; (June 12, 1775) "to bless their rightful sovereign king George; and to inspire him with wisdom to discern and pursue the true interest of his subjects; that the British nation might be influenced, to regard the things that belonged to her peace, before they were hid from her eyes; that the colonies might be ever under the care and protection of a kind providence, and be prospered in all their interests; that America might soon behold a gracious interposition of heaven, for the redress of her many griev-

ances, the restoration of her invaded rights, a reconciliation with the parent state, on terms constitutional and honourable to both."

Since the fast of the Ninevites, recorded in sacred writ, perhaps there has not been one, which was more generally kept, with suitable dispositions, than that of July 20th, 1775. It was no formal service. The whole body of the people felt the importance, the weight and the danger of the unequal contest, in which they were about to engage; that every thing dear to them was at stake; and that a divine blessing only could carry them through it successfully. This blessing they implored with their whole souls, poured forth in ardent supplications, issuing from hearts deeply penetrated with a sense of their unworthiness, their dependence and danger; and at the same time, impressed with an humble confidence, in the mercies and goodness of that Being, who had planted and preserved them hitherto, amid many dangers, in the wilderness of a new world.

Arm of Flesh or Arm of the Lord

We have heard with our ears, O God,

our fathers have told us what work thou didst in their days, in the times of old.

How thou didst drive out the heathen with thy hand, and plantedst them;

how thou didst afflict the people, and cast them out.

For they got not the land in possession by their own sword,

neither did their own arm save them:

but thy right hand, and thine arm, and the light of thy countenance,

because thou hadst a favour unto them. (Psalm 44:1-3)

G R

BY HIS EXCELLENCY

The Hon. *Thomas Gage*, Efq;

Governor, and Commander in Chief in and over his Majefty's Province of Maffachufetts-Bay, and
Vice Admiral of the fame.

A PROCLAMATION.

WHEREAS the infatuated multitudes, who have long fuffered
themfelves to be conducted by certain well known Incendiaries and Traitors, in a fatal progreffion of crimes, againft
the conftitutional authority of the ftate, have at length pro-

in his Majefty's name, offer and promife, his moft gracious pardon to all perfons
who fhall forthwith lay down their arms, and return to the duties of peaceable
fubjects, excepting only from the benefit of fuch pardon, Samuel Adams and John.
Hancock, whofe offences are of too flagitious a nature to admit of any other con-

pical ignorance of the consequences of . . . . only the persons above-named and excepted, but also all their adherents, associates, and abettors, meaning to comprehend in those terms, all and every person, and persons of what class, denomination or description soever, who have appeared in arms against the King's government, and shall not lay down the same as afore-mentioned; and likewise all such as shall so take arms after the date hereof, or who shall in any-wise protect or conceal such offenders, or assist them with money, provision, cattle, arms, ammunition, carriages, or any other necessary for subsistence or offence; or shall hold secret correspondence with them by letter, message, signal, or otherwise, to be rebels and traitors, and as such to be treated.

And whereas, during the continuance of the present unnatural rebellion, justice cannot be administered by the common law of the land, the course whereof has, for a long time past, been violently impeded, and wholly interrupted, from whence results a necessity for using, and exercising the law martial, I have therefore thought fit, by the authority vested in me, by the Royal Charter to this province, to publish, and I do hereby publish, proclaim, and order the use and exercise of the law martial, within and throughout this province, for so long time as the present unhappy occasion shall necessarily require; whereof all persons are hereby required to take notice, and govern themselves, as well to maintain order and regularity among the peaceable inhabitants of the province, as to resist, encounter, and subdue the Rebels and Traitors above-described by such as shall be called upon for those purposes.

To these inevitable, but I trust salutary measures, it is a far more pleasing part of my duty, to add the assurances of protection and support, to all who in so trying a Crisis, shall manifest their allegiance to the King, and affection to the parent state. So that such persons as may have been intimidated to quit their habitations in the course of this alarm, may return to their respective callings and professions; and stand distinct and seperate from the parricides of the constitution, till God in his mercy shall restore to his creatures, in this distracted land, that system of happiness from which they have been seduced, the religion of peace, and liberty founded upon law.

GIVEN at BOSTON, this Twelfth Day of June, in the Fifteenth Year of the Reign of his Majesty GEORGE the Third, by the Grace of GOD, of Great-Britain, France and Ireland, KING, Defender of the Faith, &c. Annoque Domini, 1775.

By His Excellency's Command,
Tho's Flucker, Secr'y.

Tho's Gage.

GOD SAVE THE KING.

---

the same evil counsels, it only remains for those who are outrushed with lu- preme rule, as well for the punishment of the guilty, as the protection of the well-affected, to prove they do not bear the sword in vain.

The infringements which have been committed upon the most sacred rights of the crown and people of Great-Britain, are too many to enumerate on one side, and are all too atrocious to be palliated on the other. All unprejudiced people who have been witnesses of the late transactions, in this and the neighbouring provinces, will find upon a transient review, marks of premeditation and conspiracy that would justify the fulness of chastisement: And even those who are least acquainted with facts, cannot fail to receive a just impression of their enormity, in proportion as they discover the arts and affiduity by which they have been falsified or concealed. The authors of the present unnatural revolt never daring to trust their cause or their actions to the judgment of an impartial public, or even to the dispassionate reflection of their followers, have uniformly placed their chief confidence in the suppression of truth: And while indefatigable and shameless pains have been taken to obstruct every appeal to the real interest of the people of America; the grossest forgeries, calumnies and absurdities that ever insulted human understanding, have been impored upon their credulity. The press, that distinguished appendage of public liberty, and when fairly and impartially employed its best support, has been invariably prostituted to the most contrary purposes: The animated language of ancient and virtuous times, calculated to vindicate and promote the just rights and interest of mankind, have been applied to countenance the most abandoned violation of those sacred blessings; and not only from the flagitious prints, but from the popular harrangues of the times, men have been taught to depend upon activity in treason, for the security of their persons and properties; till to compleat the horrid profanation of terms, and of ideas, the name of God has been introduced in the pulpits to excite and justify devastation and massacre.

The minds of men have been thus gradually prepared for the worst extremities; a number of armed persons, to the amount of many thousands, assembled on the 19th of April last, and from behind walls, and lurking holes, attacked a detachment of the King's troops, who not expecting so consummate an act of phrenzy, unprepared for vengeance, and willing to decline it, made use of their arms only in their own defence. Since that period, have rebels, deriving confidence from impunity, have added insult to outrage; have repeatedly fired upon the King's ships and subjects, with cannon and small arms, have possessed the roads, and other communications by which the town of Boston was supplied with provisions; and with a preposterous parade of military arrangement, they affect to hold the army besieged; while part of their body make daily and indiscriminate invasions upon private property, and with a wantonness of cruelty ever incident to lawless tumult, carry depredation and distress wherever they turn their steps. The actions of the 19th of April are of such notoriety, as must baffle all attempts to contradict them; and the flames of buildings and other property from the islands, and adjacent country, for some weeks past, spread a melancholy confirmation of the subsequent assertions.

In this exigency of complicated calamities, I avail myself of the last effort within the bounds of my duty, to spare the effusion of blood; to offer, and I do hereby

In Congress,

MONDAY, JUNE 12, 1775.

AS the GREAT GOVERNOR OF THE WORLD, by his supreme and universal Providence, not only conducts the course of nature with unerring wisdom and rectitude, but frequently influences the minds of men to serve the wise and gracious purposes of His providencial Government; and it being, at all times, our indispensible duty, devoutly to acknowledge His superintending Providence, especially in times of impending danger, and public calamity, to reverence and adore his immutable Justice, as well as to implore his merciful Interposition for our deliverance.

THIS CONGRESS, therefore, considering the present critical, alarming and calamitous state of these Colonies, do earnestly recommend, that THURSDAY, the *Twentieth* day of *July* next, be observed by the INHABITANTS of all the English Colonies on this Continent, as a day of public HUMILIATION, FASTING, and PRAYER, that we may, with united hearts and voices, unfeignedly confess and deplore our many sins, and offer up our joint supplications to the All-wise, Omnipotent and Merciful Disposer of all Events, humbly beseeching Him, to forgive our iniquities, to remove our present calamities, to avert those desolating judgments with which we are threatened, and to bless our rightful Sovereign King GEORGE the IIId. and inspire him with wisdom to discern and pursue the true interest of all his subjects,---that a speedy end may be put to the civil discord between Great-Britain and the American Colonies, without further effusion of blood,---and that the British nation may be influenced to regard *the things that belong to her peace, before they are hid from her eyes,*---that these Colonies may be ever under the care and protection of a kind Providence, and be prospered in all their interests,---that the divine Blessing may descend and rest upon all our civil Rulers, and upon the Representatives of the people in their several Assemblies and Conventions, that they may be directed to wise and effectual measures for preserving the Union and securing the just Rights and Privileges of the Colonies,---that virtue and true religion may revive and flourish throughout our land,---and that America may soon behold a gracious interposition of Heaven for the redress of her many grievances, the restoration of her invaded Rights, a reconciliation with the parent State, on terms constitutional and honourable to both,---and that her civil and religious Privileges may be secured to the latest posterity. And it is recommended to Christians of all nominations to assemble for public Worship, and to abstain from servile Labour and Recreations on said day.

By Order of the Congress,

JOHN HANCOCK, PRESIDENT.

(A true Copy.)

CHARLES THOMSON, SECRETARY.

PHILADELPHIA : Printed by WILLIAM & THOMAS BRADFORD

81

Georgia Completes the "American Chain" Continental Fast Day July 20, 1775

Jonathan Trumbull, July 13,1775, Lebanon, Connecticut, to George Washington:

The Honorable Congress have proclaimed a Fast to be observed

by the inhabitants of all the English Colonies on this continent,

to stand before the Lord in one day, with public humiliation, fasting, and prayer,

to deplore our many sins, to offer up our joint supplications to God, for forgiveness,

and for his merciful interposition for us in this day of unnatural darkness and distress.

They have, with one united voice, appointed you to the high station you possess.

The Supreme Director of all events

hath caused a wonderful union of hearts and counsels to subsist among us.

Now, therefore, be strong and very courageous.

May the God of the armies of Israel shower down the blessings

of his Divine Providence on you, give you wisdom and fortitude,

cover your head in the day of battle and danger, add success, convince our enemies

of their mistaken measures, and that all their attempts to deprive these Colonies

of their inestimable constitutional rights and liberties are injurious and vain.

THE LAW OF LIBERTY

PROVINCIAL CONGRESS
OF GEORGIA
JULY 4, 1775

At a Provincial Congress held agreeable to appointment, at *Tondee's* Long Room, at *Savannah,*
on the 4th day of July, 1775, and continued from
day to day. . . .

Archibald Bullock, Esq., being proposed as
President, was unanimously elected; and *George
Walton,* Esq. being proposed as Secretary, was
also unanimously elected.

The Congress then adjourned to the Meeting
House of the Reverend Doctor *Zubly,* where he
preached a sermon on the alarming state of
American affairs.

A SERMON ON AMERICAN AFFAIRS
BY JOHN J. ZUBLY, D.D.

*So speak ye, and so do, as they that shall be judged
by the Law of Liberty. James ii:12*

There was a time when there was no king in
Israel, and every man did what was good in his
own eyes. The consequence was a civil war in the
nation, issuing in the ruin of one of the tribes, and
a considerable loss to all the rest.

And there was a time when there was a king in
Israel, and he also did what was right in his own
eyes, a foolish son of a wise father; his own im-
prudence, the rashness of his young counsellors,
his unwillingness to redress the grievances of the
nation, and the harsh treatment he gave to those
who applied for relief, also brought on a civil war,
and issued in the separation of the ten tribes from
the house of David. He sent his treasurer to
gather an odious duty or tribute, but the children
of Israel stoned him that he died; and when he
gathered one hundred and four score thousand
men, that he might bring again the kingdom unto
Roboam, God sent them a message, *"ye shall not
go up, nor fight against your brethren, return
every man to his house, for this thing is done of
me."* God disapproved of the oppressive measures
and ministry of Roboam, and that king's army appears more ready to obey the command of their
God, than slay their brethren by orders of a
tyrant. *"They obeyed the voice of the Lord, and
returned from going against Jeroboam."* (2
Chron. x:18, xi:4).

The things that happened before are written
for our learning. By comparing past times and
proceedings with these that are present, prudence
will point out many salutary and religious lessons.
The conduct of Roboam verifies the lamentation
of his father, *"Woe to thee, O land, when thy*

*American
Archives:
Fourth Series,*
Vol. II,
by Peter Force,
Washington,
1839

king is a child." (*Eccl. x:16*). A very small degree of justice and moderation might have preserved his kingdom, but he thought weapons of war better than wisdom; he hearkened not, neither to the people, nor to some of his more faithful counsellors, and the consequence was that, instead of enslaving the ten tribes who stood up for their liberty, God gave Judah to be servants to the king of Egypt, that they might learn the difference between his service and the service of the kingdoms of the nations. A people that claim no more than their natural rights, in so doing, do nothing displeasing unto God; and the most powerful monarch that would deprive his subjects of the liberties of man, whatever may be his success, he must not expect the approbation of God, and in due time will be the abhorrence of all men.

In a time of public and general uneasiness it behoves both superiors and inferiors to consider. It is easy to extinguish a spark, it is folly to blow up discontent into a blaze; the beginning of strife is like the letting out of waters, and no man may know where it will end. There is a rule given to magistrates and subjects; which, if carefully attended to, would secure the dignity and safety of both; which, if not duly regarded, is usually attended with the worst consequences. The present, my hearers, will easily be allowed is a day of trouble, and surely in this day of adversity we ought to consider.

When a people think themselves oppressed, and in danger, nothing can be more natural than that they should enquire into the real state of things, trace their grievances to their source, and endeavour to apply the remedies which are most likely to procure relief: This I take to be the design of the present meeting of persons deputed from every part of the country; and as they have thought proper to open and begin their deliberations with a solemn address unto God, and the consideration of his holy word, I most chearfully comply with their request to officiate on this occasion, and shall endeavour, as I may be enabled, to point out such directions from the holy scriptures as may make us wise in the knowledge of time, and direct us how to carry ourselves worthy of the character of good subjects and Christians: Whatever may be necessary for this purpose, I take to be comprehended in the apostolical rule, which I have laid down as the subject of this discourse, *"So speak, and so do, as they that shall be judged by the law of liberty."*

There are two things which properly come before us, viz.

I. That we are to be judged by the law of liberty; and

II. The exhortation to act worthy, and under the influence, of this important truth on every occasion.

A law is a rule of behaviour, made under proper authority, and with penalties annexed, suitable to deter the transgressions. As all laws suppose man to be in a social state, so all laws ought to be made for the good of man: A law that is not made by such as have authority for so doing, is of no force; and if authority makes laws destructive in themselves, no authority can prevent things from finally taking their natural course.

Wherever there is society, there must also be law; it is impossible that society should subsist without it. The will, minds, tempers, dispositions, views and interests of men are so very different, and sometimes so opposite, that without law, which cements and binds all, every thing would be in endless disorder and confusion. All laws usually wear the complexion of those by whom they were made, but it cannot be denied that some bad men, from a sense of necessity, have made good laws, and that some good men, from mistake, or other weaknesses, have enacted laws bad in themselves, and pernicious in their consequences.

All human laws partake of human imperfection; it is not so with the laws of God. He is perfect, and so are all his works and ways. *"The law of the Lord is perfect, converting the soul. The testimony of the Lord is sure, making wise the simple. The statutes of the Lord are right, rejoicing the heart. The commandment of the Lord is pure, enlightening the eyes. All his judgments are truth, and righteousness altogether."* (*Psalm xix*)

Among men every society and country has its own laws and form of government, which may be very different, and cannot operate beyond their limits; but those laws and that form of government is undoubtedly best which has the greatest tendency to make all those that live under it secure and happy. As soon as we consider man as formed into society, it is evident that the *safety of the whole must be the grand law which must influence and direct every other: Men did not pass from a state of nature into a state of society, to render their situation more miserable, and their rights more precarious. That government and tyranny is the hereditary right of some, and that slavery and oppression is the original doom of others, is a doctrine that would reflect

---

* Salus populi suprema lex.

dishonour upon God; it is treason against all mankind, it is indeed an enormous faith that millions were made for one; transubstantiation is but a harmless absurdity, compared with the notion of a divine right to govern wrong, or of making laws which are contrary to every idea of liberty, property and justice.

The law which the apostle speaks of in our text, is not a law of man, but of Him who is the only lawgiver, that can save and condemn, to whom all owe obedience, and whose laws none can transgress with impunity.

Though all the laws that God ever gave unto man are worthy of God, and tend to promote the happiness of those to whom they were given, yet we may observe a very striking variety in the different laws which he gave at different times and to different people. *"He shewed his word unto Jacob, his statutes and his judgments unto Israel; he has not dealt so with any other nation."* (*Psalm cxlvii:19, 20.*)

To the generality of mankind he gave no written law, but yet left not himself without a witness among them; the words of the law were written in their hearts, their conscience also bearing witness, and their thoughts the mean while excusing or else accusing one another: It cannot be said they were without law, whilst what they were to do, and what they were to forbear, was written in their hearts.

To Israel God came with a fiery law in his hands, it was given with the most awful solemnity upon mount Sinai; and as the sum and substance of all their ceremonial, political and moral law centered in the ten commandments, so the sum and substance of these is comprehended in love to God and love to man, which, as our Lord himself informs us, contains all the law and all the prophets.

All manifestations of the will of God have been gradual, and it is probable the means of knowing God will be progressive through different ages, till eternity gives the good man a full sight of God in his immediate presence. During the dispensation of the old testament and the ceremonial law, a spirit of bondage obtained unto fear, the law was a schoolmaster to bring us unto CHRIST; neither did the law make any thing perfect, but the bringing in of a better hope: Grace and truth was brought to light by JESUS CHRIST, and hence the dispensation of the gospel, under which we live, is called the law of LIBERTY.

Though there is a manifest distinction between law and gospel, and sometimes these two things are even opposed to one another, yet the doctrine of the gospel is also called *"the law of faith;"* (*Rom. 3:27.*) partly because it was usual with the Jewish writers to call every doctrine a law, and partly also because the doctrine of the gospel presents us with a rule of life, which all its professors are bound to obey; hence they are said to be *"not without law, but under the law of CHRIST;"* (*1 Cor. 9:21*) and hence our apostle speaks of a royal law, which, though we cannot obey in perfection, nor derive any merit from our imperfect obedience, we cannot neglect without danger, nor disobey without shewing our disregard to the doctrine of the gospel in general.

It deserves very particular attention that the doctrine of the gospel is called a law of LIBERTY. Liberty and law are perfectly consistent; liberty does not consist in living without all restraint; for were all men to live without restraint, as they please, there would soon be no liberty at all; the strongest would be master, the weakest go to the wall; right, justice and property must give way to power, and, instead of its being a blessing, a more unhappy situation could not easily be devised unto mankind than that every man should have it in his power to do what is right in his own eyes: well regulated liberty of individuals is the natural offspring of laws, which prudently regulate the rights of whole communities; and as laws which take away the natural rights of men, are unjust and oppressive, so all liberty which is not regulated by law, is a delusive phantom, and unworthy of the glorious name.

The gospel is called a law of liberty, because it bears a most friendly aspect to the liberty of man; it is a known rule, *Evangelium non tollit politias,* the gospel makes no alteration in the civil state; it by no means renders man's natural and social condition worse than it would be without the knowledge of the gospel. When the Jews boasted of their freedom, and that they never were in bondage, our Lord does not reprove them for it, but only observes, that national freedom still admits of improvement: *"If the Son shall make you free, then are you free indeed."* (*John viii:36*). This leads me to observe that the gospel is a law of liberty in a much higher sense: By whomsoever a man is overcome, of the same he is brought into bondage; but no external enemy can so completely tyrannize over a conquered enemy, as sin does over all those who yield themselves its servants; vicious habits, when once they have gained the ascendant in the soul, bring man to that unhappy pass that he knows better things and does worse; sin, like a torrent, carries him away against knowledge and conviction, while conscience fully convinceth him that he travels the road of death, and must expect, if he so continues, to take up his abode in hell; though his decaying body clearly tells him sin breaks his constitution, as well as wastes his substance, though he feels the loss of credit and wealth, still sin has too strong a hold of him to be forsaken, though he faintly resolves to break off, yet, till the grace of God brings salvation, when he would do good, evil is present with him; in short, instead of being under a law of liberty, he is under the law of sin and death, but whenever he feels the happy influence of the grace of the gospel, then this *"law of liberty makes him free from the law of sin and death;" (Rom. viii:2)* it furnisheth him not only with motives to resist but with power also to subdue sin; sin reigns no longer in his mortal body, because he is not under the law, but under grace. By this law of liberty he is made free from sin, and has his fruit unto holiness, and the end of it eternal life. There is another reason why the gospel is called a law of liberty, which is to distinguish it from the ceremonial law under the Mosaic dispensation; a yoke, of which an apostle saith, neither they nor their fathers were able to bear; it was superadded on account of their transgressions, and suited to the character of a gross and stubborn nation, to whom it was originally given; they were so prone to idolatry, and so apt to forget their God, their notions were so gross and carnal, that a number of external rites and ceremonies became necessary, to put them in mind of him, and to attach them to some degree of his worship and service. This, however necessary, was a heavy burden; it bid them "touch not, taste not, handle not;" it required of them expensive sacrifices, and a costly and painful service; it was attended with the most fearful threatenings, if any man brake Moses law, he died under two or three witnesses; and the very spirit they then received, was a spirit of bondage unto fear: Whereas the gospel dispensation breatheth a spirit of confidence, and under the law of liberty we call upon God as Abba Father. By this law of liberty the professors of the gospel will be judged.

Every man is a rational, and therefore accountable, creature. As a creature he must needs depend on his Creator, and as a rational creature he must certainly be accountable for all his actions. Nothing is more evident than that man is not of himself; and if once we admit that he holds his existence, his faculties and favours from God, that made him, it becomes a very obvious conclusion, that his Maker must have had some view in giving him existence, and more understanding than to the beasts of the field, neither can it be a matter of indifference to him whether man acts agreeably or contrary to his designs. The Creator of the natural world, is also its moral ruler; and if he is now the proprietor and ruler of intelligent beings, at some time or other he must also be their judge.

If God had not made his will known unto man, there could have been neither transgression nor judgement. If it should be said that God has not manifested himself alike unto all men, and that some have much smaller opportunities to know his will and their duty than others, it is enough to observe, that no man will be judged by a rule of which it was impossible he should have any knowledge. Every work and every man will be brought into judgment, and the judgment of God will never be otherwise than according to truth; but those that never had the law of liberty, will not be judged by that law, and those that have been favoured with the revelation of the gospel will be more inexcusable than any others, if they neglect the day of their visitation. *"As many as have sinned without law, shall also perish without law, and as many as have sinned in the law, shall be judged by the law." (Rom. ii:12.)* All men are under some law, they feel, they are conscious, that they are so; the thoughts which already excuse or condemn one another, are an anticipation of a final and decisive judgment, when every man's reward will be according to his works.

That all those who heard and professed to believe the gospel, will be finally judged by that, we have the fullest assurance. God will judge the secrets of men by JESUS CHRIST according to his gospel. *"The word that I have spoken,"* saith CHRIST, *"the same will judge them that heard it, on the last day." (John xii:48)*. It greatly interests us clearly to know what is the import and consequence of being judged by the gospel as a law of liberty; and it contains the following things,

The general character, all the thoughts, words and actions, together with the general conduct of all those who professed the gospel, will be brought to the test, and tried by this rule. Man's own opinion of himself, the good opinion of others, will here stand him in no stead; his character will not be determined by his external appearance, but by his inward reality. *"Man looketh on the outward appearance, but the Lord looketh on the heart." (I Sam. xvi:7)*. The self-righteous pharisee will be rejected, notwithstanding his fair appearance and boasting; the penitent publican will be received, though he has nothing to plead but Lord have mercy on me a sinner. The law is spiritual, and no law more so than the law of the gospel; it requires not merely an external obedience, but an internal conformity to the will of God; it demands truth in the inward part, it looks not only to the actions that are done, but to the principle from which they flow; we must judge of man's inward disposition by his visible action, but God judges of the actions of men according to their invisible spring; thoughts are out of the reach of human cognizance, but they are the first object of divine notice; there is not a word that drops from our tongue but what our judge hears, whatever we do, or whatever we neglect, is all under his immediate eye, and he not only attends to our general character, but also to every thought, word or action, and the prevailing complexion of all these taken together form our true and real character.

In the judgment, according to this law, our character, words, thoughts and actions will be brought to the test of this rule, our conduct will be compared with these precepts, this is the balance of the sanctuary, in which the professors of the gospel shall be weighed, and as they shall be found approved or deficient, their case must be determined. Those whose temper and actions shall be found conformable to the law of liberty, will be acquitted, graciously accepted, and made ever happy, and those who turned the grace of God into wantonness, and made the liberty of the gospel a cloak for their sins, will be finally rejected. The gospel informs us, that a day is already appointed for that purpose; it acquaints us with the person of our judge, and every circumstance, as well as the rule according to which he will proceed in judgment. Perhaps on that day when all nations shall appear before the judge, and he will divide them as a shepherd divideth the sheep from the goats, distinct places will also be allotted to those who are to be judged by natural conscience and the law of nature, and those who have been favoured with a divine revelation, and especially with the light of the gospel: The people of Niniveh will arise against empty professors of the gospel, and will condemn them. Those who have been exalted above others in means and privileges, will sit proportionably lower than those who have made a better improvement of lesser means; and notwithstanding the fondest hope and finest profession, it is a determined rule of the law of liberty, that *"except our righteousness shall exceed that of the scribes and pharisees, we shall in no case enter into the kingdom of heaven."*

It deserves our peculiar attention, that the apostle considers the gospel as a law of liberty, at the same time when he sets it before us as the rule by which we are to be judged. We are not to imagine because the gospel is a law of liberty, therefore men will not be judged; on the contrary judgment will be the more severe against all who have heard and professed the gospel, and yet walked contrary to its precepts and doctrine. As the transgression of a law of liberty must be more inexcusable, than the transgression of a law unjust or oppressive in itself, or even the ceremonial law, which was given only for a certain period, and to answer temporary purposes, so their judgment and doom must be proportionably heavier, who have sinned against love and liberty, as well as against power and justice.

According to this law the fate of men will not only be determined, but sentence will also be put into execution. God sitteth on the throne of judgment every day, and judgeth righteously, but he hath moreover appointed a particular day when he will manifest his power and justice before the whole creation; when the dead both small and great will stand before God; when those that acted agreeable to the law of liberty, will attain the fulness of glory of the freedom of the sons of God, and when he will also take vengeance on all that have not known God, and have not obeyed his holy gospel. This naturally leads to the second thing proposed, to take a nearer view of the importance of the exhortation, *"So speak, and so do, as they that shall be judged by the law of liberty."*

It seems as though the apostle had an eye to some particular branch of the law of liberty, i.e. the love which we owe unto our neighbour, and that his design is to obviate the mistake as though men might be considered as fulfilling the law of CHRIST, in paying respect to some of its commands and prohibitions, at the same time that they were entirely regardless of the rest. He assures them, that *"whosoever shall keep the whole law, but shall transgress in one point"* (e.g. having respect of persons) *"is guilty of all."* On this principle the apostle builds the general exhortation, *"So speak, and so do, as they that shall be judged by the law of liberty."* This implies:

1. Be thoroughly convinced of the certainty of a judgment to come, and that it extends to you, to all your thoughts, words and actions. There is not any truth of greater moment, nor perhaps more easily forgotten. The belief or unbelief of this important doctrine must have the most sensible effects. All the apostles frequently put their hearers in mind of a judgment to come; and there is not any truth more necessary to be frequently

inculcated and daily thought on, and wherever this truth is really believed and felt, it will have a constant and natural influence on the behaviour of those who truly believe it.

2. See to it that in judgment you may stand. All men will be brought into judgment, but few will be able to stand; none will be excused, or be able to withdraw, and only those who have acted worthily, will meet with the divine acceptance. The difference will be amazing and beyond all conception: An eternity of happiness, which eye has not seen, ear has not heard, and which never entered into the heart of any man, lies on the one side, and despair, misery and torment on the other. Those that are able to stand, will meet with the smiles and approbation of their judge, and to all the rest the king will say, *"These mine enemies that would not have me to bear rule over them, bring them here, and slay them before mine eyes."* Those that believe and are convinced of this awful alternative, should certainly make it their care that they may be able to stand in judgment; neither should the persuasion of this only influence their conduct in general, but these words ought to be considered as a rule, which we ought to have constantly before our eyes in all our discourses and every undertaking; we should ever *"so speak, and so act, as they that shall be judged by the law of liberty."*

I shall draw a few inferences, before I conclude with a more particular address to the worthy Gentlemen at whose request I preach on this occasion.

1. The gospel is a law of Liberty.

A late writer *asserts, "Every religion countenances despotism, but none so much as the Christian." This is a very heavy charge against religion in general, but bears hardest on the Christian. Whether it proceeds from malice, ignorance, or misapprehension, it is needless to determine; but if christianity be a law of liberty, it must be obvious how ill-grounded is such a charge against it. It cannot be denied but some Christian writers have wrote against the rights of mankind. All those who stand up for unlimited passive obedience and non-resistance, may have given but too much cause for such surmises and suspicions; but the truth is, that both those which make this charge, and those who gave occasion for it, were alike ignorant of the spirit and temper of Christianity; and it may well be doubted whether the venders of such odious doctrines, who foisted tenets, so abominable and injurious to mankind,

into the system of Christian religion, have not done that holy religion greater hurt under the pretence of friendship and defence than its most barefaced enemies by all their most violent attacks. Some Christian divines have taught the enormous faith, that millions were made for one, they have ascribed a divine right to kings to govern wrong; but what then? Are such abominable doctrines any part of christianity, because these men say so? does the gospel cease to be a law of liberty, because some of its professors pervert it into an engine of tyranny, oppression and injustice.

The assertion, that all religion countenances despotism, and christianity more than any other, is diametrically opposite to fact. Survey the globe, and you will find that liberty has taken its seat only in Christendom, and that the highest degree of freedom is pleaded for and enjoyed by such as make profession of the gospel.

There are but two religions, which are concerned in this charge; the Jewish and the Christian. Natural religion writers of this kind I suppose would not include in their charge; if they do, they set all religion at variance with the rights of mankind, contrary to the sense of all nations, who are generally agreed, that, abstractly of a world to come, religion is of real service and necessity to mankind, for their better government and order.

As to the Jewish religion, it seems really strange that any should charge it with favouring despotism, when by one of its express rites at certain times it proclaimed *"liberty throughout the land, to the inhabitants thereof."* (*Levit. xxv:10.*) It required their kings *"not to be lifted up in their hearts above their brethren."* (*Deut. xvii:20*) And the whole system of that religion is so replete with laws against injustice and oppression, it pays such an extraordinary regard to property, and gives such strict a charge to rule in justice and the fear of God, and to consider those, over whom they judge, as their brethren, even when dispensing punishments, and forbids all excess in them, that it is really surprizing any one acquainted with its precepts, should declare it favourable to despotism or oppression.

The Christian religion, while it commands due respect and obedience to superiors, no where requires a blind and unlimited obedience on the part of the subjects; nor does it vest any absolute and arbitrary power in the rulers. It is an institution for the benefit, and not for the distress, of mankind. It preacheth not only *"glory to God on high,"* but also *"peace on earth, and good will among men."*

---

* *See a tract, entitled, "Chains of slavery." Printed London. 1775*

The gospel gives no higher authority to magistrates than to be *"the ministers of God, for the good of the subject." Rom. xiii.* From whence it must surely follow, that their power is to edify, and not to destroy: When they abuse their authority, to distress and destroy their subjects, they deserve not to be thought ministers of God for good; nor is it to be supposed, when they act so contrary to the nature of their office, that they act agreeable to the will of God, or in conformity to the doctrine of the gospel.

The gospel recommends unto masters to forbear threatnings, and to remember that they also have a master in heaven; it assures them that the eye of God is equally upon the servant and the master, and that with God there is no respect of persons: It commands masters, from the most solemn considerations, to give unto servants that which is just and equal; it saith to the meanest slave: *"Art thou called being a servant, care not for it, but if thou mayest be made free, use it rather." (I Cor. vii:21.)*

The doctrine of the gospel has that regard to property, that it commands even soldiers, *"Do violence to no man, and be content with your wages:" (Luke iii:14.)*—that a Paul sent back a run-away slave, though now converted, and belonging to his intimate friend, and at a time when he seems to have stood in real need of his service, from a delicacy that he would do nothing without the owner's mind, less his benefit should appear as if it were of necessity, and not willingly. (*Philem. 14.*) From the same spirit of justice a Zacheus, after his conversion, restored fourfold what before he had taken from any by false accusation: Surely then the spirit of the gospel is very friendly to the rights and property of men.

The gospel sets conscience above all human authority in matters of faith, and bids us to *"stand fast in that liberty wherewith the Son of God has made us free." (Gal. v:1)* Freedom is the very spirit and temper of the gospel: *"He that is called in the Lord being a servant, is the Lord's freeman. Ye are bought with a price, be ye not the servants of men." (I Cor. vii:22, 23)* At the same time that it commands us to submit to every ordinance of men, it also directs us to act *"as free, and not using liberty as a cloke of maliciousness, but as the servants of God." (I. Pet. ii:13–18)*,

Those therefore that would support arbitrary power, and require an unlimited obedience, in vain look for precedents or precepts for such things in the gospel, an institution equally tending to make men just, free and happy here, and perfectly holy and happy hereafter.

2. The main design of the gospel is not to direct us in our external and civil affairs, but how we may at last stand with comfort before God, the judge of all.

Human prudence is to be our guide in the concerns of time; the gospel makes us wise unto salvation, and points out the means to be pursued that it may be well with us in the world to come. As rational creatures we are to make use of our reason; as Christians we are to repent and believe the gospel. Motives of a worldly nature may very properly influence us in our worldly concern, we are created not only for eternity, but also for time: It is not at all improper for us to have a due regard for both. The gospel will regulate our desires and restrain our passions as to earthly things, and will raise us at the same time above time and sense, to objects of a nature more worthy of ourselves. A due regard for, and frequent meditation on, a judgment to come, will greatly assist us in all our concerns; and this very consideration the gospel holds out to us in the clearest manner. It not only affirms as a truth, what reason and conscience might consider only as probable, but it takes away as it were the veil from between us and things to come; it gives us a present view of the future bliss of saints, and the terrors and despair of sinners; —rather a historical account than a prophetic description of all the proceedings of the dreadful pleasing day; it clearly points out the road to destruction, and the way to escape; it affords us a plain and general rule to obtain safety and comfort, when it bids us, *"So speak, and so do, as they that shall be judged by the law of liberty."*

This general rule may also be of considerable service in extraordinary and particular cases. It is impossible to provide express directions for every particular case, and in the course of things circumstances may happen when a good man may be at a loss to know his duty, and find it difficult so to act as to obtain his own approbation. There may be danger of going beyond, and danger in not coming up to, the mark. To act worthy of God, who has called us, is the general rule of the Christian at all times, and upon every occasion, and did we but always follow this rule, what manner of persons should we then be! But in cases of intricacy we may still be in doubt what may be most for the glory of God, and most consistent with our duty. Sometimes also our relative duties may seem to come in competition with one another, and we may hesitate in our own mind which for the present has the strongest call. We would fain obey our superiors, and yet we cannot think of giving up our natural, our civil and religious rights, nor acquiesce in or contribute to render our fellow-creatures or fellow-citizens slaves and miserable. We would willingly follow peace with all men, and yet would be very unwilling that others should take the advantage of a pacific disposition, to injure us in hopes of impunity. We would express duty, respect and obedience to the king, as supreme, and yet we would not wish to strengthen the hands of tyranny, nor call oppression lawful: In such a delicate situation it is a golden rule, *"So to speak, and so to do, as they that shall be judged by the law of liberty."* Nothing has a greater tendency to make men act wrong than the disbelief of a future judgment, and nothing will more effectually restrain and direct them than the full persuasion that such an event will certainly take place; nothing would have a happier tendency to make us act with prudence, justice and moderation than the firm persuasion that God will bring every work into judgment, and every secret thing, whether it be good or bad.

Neither could I think on any direction more applicable to the design of our present meeting, or which I might more properly recommend to the respectable Gentlemen, now met together to consult on the recovery and preservation of the liberties of America, and who chose to begin their deliberations with a solemn act of worship to almighty God who has established government as his ordinance, and equally abhors licentiousness and oppression; whose singular blessing it is if subjects enjoy a righteous government, and under such a government lead a quiet and peaceable life in all godliness and honesty.

You are met, Gentlemen, in a most critical time, and on a most alarming occasion, not in a legislative capacity, but (while the sitting of the usual representation is not thought for the king's service, or necessary for the good of this province) you are chosen by the general voice of this province to meet on their behalf, to consult on such measures as in our local circumstances may be most to the real advantage and tend to the honour of our gracious sovereign, as well as the good and safety of this province and of all this great continent. For the sake of the auditory, I shall briefly state the immediate causes that have given rise to this Provincial and a general American Congress, and then offer such humble advice as appears to me most suitable to our circumstances.

To enforce some Acts for laying on a duty to raise a perpetual revenue in America, which the Americans think unjust and unconstitutional, which all America complains of, and some prov-

inces have in some measure opposed.* A fleet and army has been sent to New England, and after a long series of hardships by that province patiently endured, it is now out of all question that hostilities have been commenced against them; blood has been shed, and many lives have been taken away; thousands, never as much as suspected of having any hand in the action which is made the pretence of all the severity now used against that province, have been and still are reduced to the greatest distress. From this other provinces have taken the alarm; an apprehension of nearer foes, not unlikely to appear as auxiliaries in an unjust cause, has thrown our neighbours into arms; how far and wide the flame so wantonly kindled may be permitted to spread, none can tell; but in these alarming circumstances the liberty of this continent, of which we are a part, the safety and domestic peace of this province will naturally become a subject of your deliberations; and here I may well adapt the language of old, *"There was no such deed done nor seen from the day that America was first settled unto this day; consider of it, take advice, and speak your minds."* (*Judges xix:30*). I mean not to anticipate and direct your counsels, but from your desire I should speak on this occasion; I take it for granted you will permit me to offer such hints as may appear suitable to the place and design of our present meeting.

In the first place, as there is no evil in a city in which the hand of God may not be seen, so in vain is salvation looked for from the hills and from the mountains, but can come from him only who has made heaven and earth. This undoubtedly is a day of trouble, but God saith to his people, *"Call upon me in a day of trouble, and I will deliver thee."* (*Ps. 50:15*). *What nation has God so nigh unto them, as the Lord our God is in all things that we call upon him for."* (*Deut. iv:7*) If this be our first step, if first of all we look unto him from whom our help cometh, we may hope all will be well at last. Let us be thoroughly convinced of this, we must stand well with God, else it can never be well with us at all; without him and his help we can never prosper. The Lord is with you, if you are with him; *"if you seek him, you will find him, but if you forsake him, you will be forsaken by him."* (*2 Chron. xv:2*). If God be for us, who can be against us?

---

*This opposition in some provinces consisted in sending the tea on which this duty was to be paid, back to England, not suffering it to be sold or landed in others, and in Boston, when they were prevented from sending it back, it was entirely destroyed, but no person hurt, nor any blood shed.

if he be against us, who can be for us? Before we think on, or look any where else, may our eyes be unto God, that he may be gracious unto us. Let us humbly confess and speedily turn from our sins, deprecate his judgment, and secure his favour. *"Rent your hearts, and not your garments, and turn unto the Lord your God, for he is gracious and merciful, slow to anger and of great kindness, and repenteth him of the evil, who knoweth if he will return and repent, and leave a blessing behind him, even a meat-offering and a drink-offering unto the Lord your God."* (*Joel ii:13.14*)

Let it be a standing rule with every one that is to sit in council upon this occasion, *"so to speak, and so to do, as one that is to be judged by the law of liberty."* Let us most carefully avoid every thing that might make us incur the displeasure of God, and wound our own consciences. The effects of your deliberation may become very serious and extensive, and the consequences extremely important: Think therefore before you speak, deliberate before you execute, and let the law of liberty, by which you are hereafter to be judged, be the constant rule of all your words and actions: Far be it from us to be reduced under laws inconsistent with liberty, and as far to wish for liberty without law; let the one be so tempered with the other that when we come to give our account to the supreme lawgiver, who is the great judge of all, it may appear we had a due regard to both, and may meet with his approbation.

Such always hath been, and such is still, the attachment of America to the illustrious house of Hanover, that I need not put you in mind of our duty to the king as supreme. By our law the king can do no wrong; but of his present Majesty, who is universally known to be adorned with many social virtues, may we not justly conclude that he would not do any wrong, even though he could.

May we not hope that to the greatness of a monarch, he will super-add the feelings of the man, the tenderness of a father. May we not hope that when the truth of things, the tears of his suffering subjects, the distresses caused by Acts extremely ill advised, once reach his notice, a generous pity will force his heart, and that pity, when he feels it, will command redress. *"The heart of the king is in the hand of the Lord, as the rivers of water, and he turneth it as he pleaseth;"* (*Prov. xxi:1*) most earnestly therefore let us pray that in this great and most important matter also God may give unto the king an understanding heart, that power may be governed by

wisdom, and the wheels of government roll on with justice and moderation. Should you think that all our present distress is owing to evil counsellors, nothing need to hinder you from praying that God would turn their counsels into foolishness; you may make it your earnest request both in public and in private, that the wicked being removed from before the king, his throne may be established in righteousness, that the rod of the oppressor may be broke, and justice and equity take place of tyranny and oppression.

It may be owing to nothing but the firm attachment to the reigning family that so many Americans look upon the present measures as a deep laid plan to bring in the Pretender. Perhaps this jealousy may be very groundless, but so much is certain, that none but Great-Britain's enemies can be gainers in this unnatural contest.*

Never let us loose out of sight that our interest lies in a perpetual connection with our mother country. Notwithstanding the present unwise and harsh measures, there are thousands in Great-Britain that think with us, and wish well to the American cause, and make it their own; let us convince our enemies that the struggles of America have not their rise in a desire of independency, but from a warm regard to our common constitution; that we esteem the name of Britons, as being the same with freemen; let every step we take afford proof how greatly we esteem our mother country, and that, to the wish of a perpetual connexion, we prefer this only consideration, that we may be virtuous and free.†

Let me intreat you, Gentlemen, think coolly, and act deliberately; rash counsels are seldom good ones: ministerial rashness and American

---

* Were it designed to give the Pretender an opportunity; to raise divisions in Great-Britain, starve the manufacturers, send away troops from Ireland and Scotland, and breed civil war in America, must all be circumstances too favourable, and I may say, very tempting to promote such a project.

† The idea of a separation between America and Great-Britain is big with so many and such horrid evils, that every friend to both must shudder at the thought. Every man that gives the most distant hint of such a wish, ought instantly to be suspected as a common enemy; nothing would more effectually serve the cause of our enemies, than any proposal of this kind; all wise men and all good men would immediately speak, write and act against it; such a proposal, whenever it should be made, would be an inlet to greater evils than any we have yet suffered: But what America detests as the greatest evil, a British ministry has taken the greatest pains to effect: has wasted British blood and treasure to alienate America and Great Britain; the breach is growing wider and wider, it is become great like a sea, every moment is a loss that is not improved towards bringing about a reconciliation.

rashness can only be productive of untoward compounds; inconsiderate measures, framed on the other side of the atlantic, are the cause of all our mischiefs, and it is not in the least probable that inconsiderate measures in America can be productive of any good.

Let nothing be done through strive and vain glory; let no private resentment or party zeal disgrace your honest warmth for your country's welfare: Measures determined on by integrity and prudence, are most likely to be carried into execution by steadiness and moderation.

Let neither the frowns of tyranny, nor pleasure of popularity, sway you from what you clearly apprehend just and right, and to be your duty.

Consider how much lies at stake, how greatly your religion, your liberty, your property, your posterity, is interested.

Endeavour to act like freemen, like loyal subjects, like real Christians, and you will *"so speak, and so act, as they that shall be judged by the law of liberty."*

Act conscientiously, and with a view to God, then commit your ways to him, leave the event with God, and you will have great reason to hope that the event will be just, honourable and happy.

And now, Gentlemen, you have the wishes and prayers of every thoughtful person, that your deliberations may be carried on with candour, unanimity and prudence, may be blessed to preserve the quietness of this province, and co-operate in restoring the rights and tranquillity of all America, as well as promote the prosperity of the whole British empire. This will afford you a heartfelt satisfaction, and transmit your name to posterity with honour, when all those who had opposite views, and sought their greatness in the ruins of others, will be held in abhorrence and detestation.

I have but a few hints to give to my hearers in general.

The times are evil; this is a day of adversity, and in a time of adversity we ought to consider. It may perhaps soon become impossible, even to the most indolent, to continue unconcerned, and those that wish no more than to hide themselves in quiet obscurity, may not always have it in their power to remain neuter: To know the signs of the time, is a considerable part of human prudence, and it is a still greater to walk circumspectly, and redeem the time, because the days are evil. Whatever part you may think yourselves obliged to take, *"So speak, and so do, as they that shall be judged hereafter, and judged by the law of liberty."* In these times of confusion I would

press on my hearers a most conscientious regard to the common laws of the land. Let our conduct shew that we are not lawless; by well-doing let us put to silence the reproaches of our adversaries. Let us convince them that we do not complain of law, but of oppression; that we do not abhor these acts because we are impatient to be under government, but being destructive of liberty and property, we think them destructive also of all law. Let us act *"as free, and yet not make liberty a cloke of maliciousness, but as the servants of God."*

While it is yet peace and quietness with us, let us not think ourselves inaccessible to the evils which are already come upon others; there are some evils which we would rather deprecate in private than speak of in public, against which being forewarned, we should be forearmed; every trifling report should not alarm us, but it would be folly still greater not to be on our guard against sudden dangers.

Remember them that suffer adversity, as being yourselves also in the body. Think on those who are driven from their habitations and all their conveniencies of life, or confined in their own houses by an enraged soldiery, to starve in their own country, in the midst of property and plenty, not permitted to enjoy their own, and distressed in every connexion, and this without any cause alleged against numbers of them, without complaint, suspicion or a legal trial: The like was never heard since the cruel siege of Londonderry, and is a species of cruelty at which even that hard-hearted bigot James II relented.

Above all, let every one earnestly pray that He that is higher than the highest would soon make a righteous end of all their confusion; that he would incline the king to hear the cries of his subjects, and that no more innocent blood may be shed in America.

One thing more: Consider the extreme absurdity of struggling for civil liberty, and yet to continue slaves to sin and lust. *"Know ye not to whom ye yield yourselves servants to obey, his servants ye are, to whom ye obey, whether of sin unto death, or of obedience unto righteousness."* (*Rom. vi:16.*) Cease from evil, and do good, seek peace, and pursue it, who will hurt you while you follow that which is good; become the willing servants of the Lord JESUS CHRIST, harken to and obey the voice of his gospel; for *"where the spirit of the Lord is, there is liberty;"* and *"if the Son makes you free,"* THEN, and not till then, *"*SHALL YOU BE FREE INDEED."

PROVINCIAL CONGRESS OF GEORGIA

JULY 4, 1775

The Congress being returned, a motion was made and seconded, that the thanks of this Congress be given to the Rev. Doctor *Zubly,* for the excellent Sermon he preached this day to the Members; which being unanimously agreed to, it was *Ordered,* That *Basil Cowper, Joseph Clay, John Houstoun, John Glen,* and *George Houstoun,* Esqrs., be a Committee for that purpose.

WEDNESDAY, JULY 5, 1775

A motion was made and seconded, that this Congress apply to his Excellency the Governour, by message, requesting him to appoint a day of Fasting and Prayer throughout this Province, on account of the disputes subsisting between *America* and the Parent State; which being unanimously passed in the affirmative, it was

Ordered, That Doctor *Zubly, William Young, Joseph Clay, Stephen Drayton,* and *William Maxwell,* be a Committee for that purpose.

Copy of the Message.

MAY IT PLEASE YOUR EXCELLENCY: The Provincial Congress, deeply concerned at the present alarming state of affairs, and the distresses of *America,* humbly request that your Excellency would appoint a day of Fasting and Prayer, to be observed throughout this Province, that a happy reconciliation may soon take place between America and the Parent State, and that, under the auspicious reign of His Majesty and his descendants, both Countries may remain united, virtuous, free, and happy, till time shall be no more.

By order of the Congress:

ARCHIBALD BULLOCK, *President*

The President being informed by the Messenger, that *John Jamieson* and *John Simpson,* Esquires, were in waiting, and desired to be admitted; which being agreed to, they were desired to walk in. They then produced and delivered in to the President a Paper containing several Resolutions entered into by a number of persons, inhabitants of the Town of *Savannah;* which was ordered to be read, and is as follows, viz:

"At a meeting of several of the Inhabitants of the Town of *Savannah,* at Mrs. *Cuyler's,* on

Friday, the 13th of *June,* 1775, *John Mullryne,* Esq., in the chair; *Joseph Clay, James Mossman,* Rev. *J. J. Zubly, John Simpson, Noble Wimberly Jones, John Jamieson, William Moss, John Glen, Josiah Tattnall, John Graham, Lewis Johnston, William Young, Richard Wylly, Andrew McLean, Basil Cowper, Philip Moore, George Houstoun, Joseph Butler, James Read, Thomas Ried, William Panton, James Edward Powell, William Struthers, Alexander McGowen, John C. Lucena, Thomas Sherman, J. N. Faming, Levi Sheftall, Charles Hamilton, George Spencer, William Brown,* Junior, *Francis Courvoizie, James Anderson.*

"Whereas, publick confusions and grievances are much increased by private dissensions and animosities:

"*Resolved, therefore, nem. con.,* That we will use our utmost endeavours to preserve the peace and good order of this Province; and that no person behaving himself peaceably and inoffensively, shall be molested in his person or property, or even in his private sentiments, while he expresses them with decency, and without any illiberal reflections upon others.

"Whereas, the acts for raising a perpetual revenue in *America,* and all the measures used to enforce these acts, are not partial but general grievances, and it is more likely that redress will be obtained by the joint endeavours of all who may think these acts unconstitutional or oppressive, than by any measure that might be taken singly by individuals; therefore,

"*Resolved,* That it is the opinion of this meeting, (as a proper measure to be pursued, because the General Assembly is not now sitting, from whom an application to the Throne must be very proper, and as no time should be lost,) that a humble, dutiful, and decent Petition be addressed to His Majesty, expressive of the sense, apprehensions, and feelings of all such as may choose to subscribe such a Petition, which it is hoped will be done by every man in the Province; and it is therefore the wish of this meeting, that such a measure be adopted by the Provincial Congress, intended to be held on *Tuesday* next, the fourth of *July.*

"*Resolved,* That the interest of this Province is inseparable from the Mother Country, and all the sister Colonies; and that to separate themselves from the latter would only be throwing difficulties in the way of its own relief, and that of the other Colonies, and justly incurring the resentment of all those to whose distress our disunion might cause an addition.

"*Resolved,* That this Province ought, and it is hoped will forthwith join the other Provinces in every just and legal measure to secure and restore the liberties of all *America,* and for healing the unhappy divisions now subsisting between *Great Britain* and her Colonies.

"*Resolved,* That the proceedings of this meeting be laid before the Provincial Congress on *Tuesday,* the fourth day of *July* next, and that Mr. *Jamieson* and Mr. *Simpson* do wait upon them with the same, as recommended to them by this meeting. By order of the meeting:

JOHN MULLRYNE."

A motion was made and seconded, that the Paper above mentioned do lie upon the table for the perusal of the members; which being carried, the same was ordered to lie upon the table accordingly.

A motion was made and seconded, that this Congress do put this Province upon the same footing with our sister Colonies; which being put, it was ordered that it be taken into consideration to-morrow morning.

THURSDAY, JULY 6, 1775

The Order of the Day being read, the same was taken into consideration, and, after some deliberation, it was unanimously

1. *Resolved,* That this Province will adopt and carry into execution all and singular the measures and recommendations of the late Continental Congress.

2. *Resolved,* In particular, that we, in behalf of ourselves and our constituents, do adopt and approve of the *American* Declaration or Bill of Rights, published by the late Continental Congress, and also of their several resolves made in consequence of some infractions thereof.

3. That from and after this day we will not receive into this Province any Goods, Wares, or Merchandise, shipped from *Great Britain* or *Ireland;* or from any other place, any such Goods, Wares, or Merchandises as shall have been exported from *Great Britain* or *Ireland;* nor will we import any *East-India* Tea from any part of the world, nor any Molasses, Syrups, Paneles, Coffee, or Pimento, from the *British Plantations,* or from *Dominica;* nor Wines from *Madeira* or the *Western Islands,* nor foreign Indigo.

4. That we will neither import or purchase any Slave imported from *Africa,* or elsewhere, after this day.

5. As a Non-Consumption Agreement, strictly adhered to, will be an effectual security for the observation of the Non-Importation, we, as above, solemnly agree and associate, that, from this day, we will not purchase or use any Tea imported on account of the *East-India* Company, or any on which a duty hath or shall be paid; and we will not purchase or use any *East-India* Tea whatever, nor will we, nor shall any person for or under us, purchase any of these Goods, Wares, or Merchandises we have agreed not to import, which we shall know, or have cause to suspect were imported after this day.

6. The earnest desire we have not to injure our fellow-subjects in *Great Britain* and *Ireland,* and the *West-Indies,* induces us to suspend a Non-Exportation until the tenth day of *September,* 1775, at which time, if the acts and parts of acts of the *British* Parliament hereinafter mentioned are not repealed, we will not, directly or indirectly, export any Merchandise or commodity whatsoever to *Great Britain* or *Ireland,* or the *West-Indies,* except Rice to *Europe.*

7. Such as are merchants, and use the *British* and *Irish* trade, will give orders as soon as possible to their factors, agents, and correspondents in *Great Britain* and *Ireland,* not to ship any Goods to them, on any pretence whatever, as they cannot be received in this Province; and if any merchant residing in *Great Britain* or *Ireland* shall, directly or indirectly, ship any Goods, Wares, or Merchandise for *America,* in order to break the said Non-Importation Agreement, or in any manner contravene the same, on such unworthy conduct being well attested, it ought to be made publick, and on the same being so done, we will not, from thenceforth, have any commercial connexions with such merchant.

8. That such as are owners of vessels will give positive orders to their Captains or masters not to receive on board their vessels any Goods prohibited by the said Non-Importation Agreement, on pain of immediate dismission from their service.

9. We will use our utmost endeavours to improve the breed of Sheep, and increase their numbers to the greatest extent; and to that end we will kill them as sparingly as may be, especially those of the most profitable kind, nor will export any to the *West-Indies* or elsewhere; and those of us who are or may become overstocked with, or can conveniently spare any Sheep, will dispose of them to our neighbours, especially to the poorer sort, on moderate terms.

10. That we will, in our several stations, encourage frugality, economy, and industry, and

promote agriculture, arts, and the manufactures of *British America,* especially that of Wool; and will discountenance and discourage every species of extravagance and dissipation, especially horse-racing, and every kind of gaming, cock-fighting, exhibition of shows, plays, and other expensive diversions and entertainments; and on the death of any relation or friend, none of us, or any of our families, will go into any farther mourning dress than a black crape or ribbon on the arm or hat for gentlemen, and a black ribbon and neck-lace for ladies; and we will discontinue the giving of gloves and scarfs at funerals.

11. That such as are venders of Goods or Merchandise will not take advantage of the scarcity of Goods that may be occasioned by this Association, but will sell the same at the rates we have been respectively accustomed to do for twelve months last past; and if any vender of Goods or Merchandise shall sell any such Goods or Merchandise on higher terms, or shall in any manner, or by any device whatsoever, violate or depart from this agreement, no person ought, nor will any of us deal with any such person, or his or her factor or agent, at any time thereafter for any commodity whatever.

12. In case any merchant, trader, or other persons shall attempt to import any Goods or Merchandise into this Province after this day, the same shall be forthwith sent back again, without breaking any of the packages thereof.

13. That a Committee be chosen in every Town, District, and Parish within this Province, by those who pay towards the general tax, whose business it shall be attentively to observe the conduct of all persons touching this Association; and when it shall be made appear, to the satisfaction of a majority of any such Committee, that any person within the limits of their appointment has violated this Association, that such majority do forthwith cause the truth of the case to be published in the *Gazette,* to the end that all such foes to the rights of *British America* may be publickly known and universally contemned as the enemies of *American* liberty, and thenceforth we will break off all connexion with him or her.

14. That a Committee of Correspondence to this Province do frequently inspect the entries of the Custom-House, and inform the Committees of the other Colonies which have acceded to the Continental Association, from time to time of the true state thereof, and of every other material circumstance that may occur relative to this Association.

15. That all manufactures of this Province be sold at reasonable prices, so that no undue advantage be taken of a future scarcity of Goods.

16. And we do further agree and resolve, that we will have no trade, commerce, dealings, or intercourse whatsoever with any Colony or Province in *North America* which shall not accede to, or which shall hereafter violate this Association, but will hold them as unworthy of the rights of freemen, and as inimical to the liberties of their Country.

And we do solemnly bind ourselves and our constituents, under the ties of virtue, honour, and love of our Country, to adhere to this Association, until such parts of the several acts of Parliament, passed since the close of the last war, as impose or continue duties upon Tea, Wines, Molasses, Syrups, Paneles, Coffee, Sugar, Pimento, Indigo, foreign Paper, Glass, and Painters' Colours, imported into *America;* and extend the powers of the Admiralty Courts beyond their ancient limits, deprive American subjects of trial by Jury, authorize the Judge's certificate to indemnify the prosecutor from damages that he might otherwise be liable to from a trial by his peers, require oppressive security from claimants of Ships or Goods seized before he is allowed to defend his property, are repealed; and until that part of the Act of 12 *George* 3, ch. 24, entitled "An Act for the better securing His Majesty's Dock-Yards, Magazines, Ships, Ammunition, and Stores," by which any person charged with committing any of the offences therein described in *America* may be tried within any Shire or County within the Realm, is repealed; and until the four acts passed in the last session of Parliament, viz: that for stopping the Port and blocking up the Harbour of *Boston,* that for altering the Charter and Government of the *Massachusetts-Bay,* and that which is entitled "An Act for the better administration, &c." and that for extending the limits of *Quebeck,* &c., are repealed; and until the two acts passed in the present session of Parliament, the one entitled "A Bill to restrain the Trade and Commerce of the Colonies of *New-Jersey, Pennsylvania, Maryland, Virginia,* and *South-Carolina,* to *Great Britain, Ireland,* and the *British Islands* in the *West-Indies,* under certain conditions and limitations;" and the other, "An Act commonly called the Fishery Bill."

FRIDAY, JULY 7, 1775

The following is his Excellency's Answer to the Message of this Congress:

Savannah, July 7, 1775

GENTLEMEN: I have taken the opinion of His Majesty's Council relative to the request made by the gentlemen who have assembled together by the name of a Provincial Congress, and must premise, that I cannot consider that meeting as constitutional; but as the request is expressed in such loyal and dutiful terms, and the ends proposed being such as every good man must most ardently wish for, I will certainly appoint a day of Fasting and Prayer to be observed throughout this Province.

JAS. WRIGHT.

A motion was made and seconded, that the thanks of this Congress be given to his Excellency the Governour, for his Answer to the Message of this Congress, and his ready compliance with their request; which, being put, unanimously passed in the affirmative.

Ordered, That Dr. *Zubly, John Smith,* and *Joseph Clay* be a Committee for that purpose.

A motion was made and seconded, that five persons be chosen to represent this Province in the Continental Congress appointed to be held at the City of *Philadelphia* on the 10th of *May* last; and the question being put, it passed unanimously in the affirmative.

The Congress then proceeded to the choice, when *John Houstoun* and *Archibald Bullock,* Esquires, the Rev. Dr. *Zubly, Noble Wimberly Jones,* and *Lyman Hall,* Esq's, were duly elected.

Dr. *Zubly* expressed his surprise at being chosen, and said that he thought himself, for many reasons, a very improper person; but the choice was insisted upon, and the Doctor declared he would by no means go unless he had the approbation of his congregation; whereupon, *Noble Wimberly Jones* and *John Houstoun,* Esquires, were appointed to request their consent.

A motion was made and seconded, that a Secret Committee be appointed, which being agreed to, it was

Resolved, That the President do nominate seven persons to be that Committee, whose business it shall be to be vigilant and active in the discovery of all matters which may affect the publick; and that they shall have right to lay all such intelligence and information before the President of this Congress while sitting, and in its recess before the President of the Council of Safety, in order that the evil designs of wicked men may be early frustrated.

A motion was made and seconded, that the Congress do petition the King upon the present unhappy situation of affairs; which being agreed to, it was ordered that Dr. *Zubly* do prepare and bring in the same.

A motion was made and seconded, that a Letter be forthwith wrote to the President of the Continental Congress, giving him an account of the proceedings of this Congress; which being agreed to, it was ordered that Dr. *Zubly, John Smith, William Young, William Le Conte,* and *William Gibbons,* Esquires, be a Committee for that purpose.

A motion was made and seconded, that an Address be presented to his Excellency the Governour by this Congress; which being agreed to, it was ordered that Dr. *Zubly, Basil Cowper, John Walton, Joseph Clay,* and *Edward Telfair,* be a Committee to draw up the same.

SATURDAY, JULY 8, 1775

Resolved, That this Congress are of opinion that the Paper delivered into this Congress on the second day of its meeting, ought not to have been entitled or dressed in the form of Resolves, but rather as recommendations, or in nature of a Petition or Address to this Congress.

Resolved, nevertheless, from the desire this Congress hath to promote union and concord among ourselves, and as it does not appear that the said Paper was intended to be considered as coming from a distinct or independent body, that therefore the matter contained in the same (being such as is in the general agreeable to us) shall be duly considered and attended to.

A motion was made and seconded, that a sum, not exceeding Ten Thousand Pounds, sterling, be provided to defray the necessary services of this Province in the present alarming and distracted state of affairs, which passed unanimously in the affirmative.

A motion was then made and seconded, that the Congress resolve itself into a Committee of the Whole, to consider ways and means for raising and sinking the said sum of Ten Thousand Pounds sterling; which being agreed to, the Congress resolved itself into a Committee accordingly.

The President having resumed the Chair, Mr. *Clay,* from the Committee of the Whole Congress, reported, that they had entered upon the consideration of ways and means, had made some progress therein, and desired leave to sit again.

The President reported to the Congress that he had, in obedience to the resolution of yesterday, nominated seven persons to be a Secret Committee.

Doctor *Zubly,* who was ordered to prepare and bring in a Petition to His Majesty, reported that he had done so, and produced a Paper containing the same, which he delivered in to the President; and the said Paper being read, and approved of, it was *Resolved* that the President do sign the same.

A motion was made and seconded, that a Committee of Intelligence be appointed; which being agreed to, it was

Ordered, That *William Young, David Zubly, Stephen Drayton, Daniel Roberts, John Glen, Edward Telfair, William Ewen, Joseph Clay,* and *George Walton,* Esquires, be that Committee.

William Young, Esquire, of the Committee appointed to write a Letter to the President of the Continental Congress, reported, that they had done so, and delivered a Paper in to the President containing the same; which being read, and approved of, it was

Resolved, That the President do sign the same, and that it be forthwith sent.

MONDAY, JULY 10, 1775

The following Resolves were unanimously entered into:

Whereas, by the unrelenting fury of a despotick Ministry, with a view to enforce the most oppressive Acts of a venal and corrupted Parliament, an army of mercenaries, under an unfeeling commander, has actually begun a civil war in *America:* and whereas, the apparent iniquity and cruelty of these destructive measures have, however, had this good effect, to unite men of all ranks in the common cause: and whereas, to consult on means of safety, and the method of obtaining redress, the good people of this Province of *Georgia* have thought proper to appoint a Provincial Congress, the Delegates met at the said Congress, now assembled from every part of the Province, besides adopting the Resolutions of the late Continental Congress, find it prudent to enter into such other Resolutions as may best express their own sense and the sense of their constituents, on the present unhappy situation of things, and therefore thought fit and necessary to resolve as follows, viz:

Resolved, That we were born free, have all the feelings of men, and are entitled to all the natural rights of mankind.

Resolved, That by birth or incorporation we are all Britons, and whatever *Britons* may claim as their birthrights is also ours.

Resolved, That in the *British* Empire, to which we belong, the Constitution is superiour to every man or set of men whatever, and that it is a crime of the deepest dye, in any instance, to impair or take it away, or deprive the meanest subject of its benefits.

Resolved, That that part of the *American* Continent which we inhabit was originally granted by the Crown, and the Charter from *Charles* the Second expressly makes its constitutional dependance on the Crown only.

Resolved, That those who would now subject all *America,* or this Province, to dependancy on the Crown and Parliament, are guilty of a very dangerous innovation, which in time will appear as injurious to the Crown as it is inconsistent with the liberty of the American subject.

Resolved, That by the law of nature, and the *British* Constitution, no man can legally be deprived of his property without his consent, given by himself or his representatives.

Resolved, That the Acts of the *British* Parliament for raising a perpetual revenue on the *Americans,* by laying a tax on them without their consent, and contrary to their protestations, are diametrically opposite to every idea of property, to the spirit of the Constitution, and at one stroke deprive this vast Continent of all liberty and property, and as such, must be detested by every well-wisher to *Great Britain* and *America.*

Resolved, That the subsequent laws, made with a view to enforce these Acts, viz: The *Boston* Port Bill; the alteration of their Charter; the Act to carry beyond sea for trial; and (what refines upon every species of cruelty) the Fishery Bill; are of such a complexion that we can say nothing about them for want of words to express our abhorrence and detestation.

Resolved, That the loyalty, patience, and prudence of the inhabitants of *New-England,* under their unparalleled pressures, having been construed into a timidity and a dread of Regular Troops, a civil war, in support of acts extremely oppressive in themselves, hath actually been begun, and that there is too much reason to believe that plans have been in agitation big with every thing horrible to other Provinces; plans as rash, barbarous, and destructive, as the cause which they were intended to serve.

Resolved, That in these times of extreme danger, our Assembly not being permitted to sit, we must either have been a people without all thought or counsel, or have assembled as we now are in Provincial Congress, to consult upon measures which, under GOD, may prove the means of a perpetual union with the Mother Country, and tend to the honour, freedom, and safety of both.

Resolved, That the Province bears all true allegiance to our own rightful Sovereign, King *George* the Third, and always will, and ought to bear it, agreeable to the Constitution of *Great Britain,* by virtue of which only the King is now our Sovereign, and which equally binds Majesty and Subjects.

Resolved, That we are truly sensible how much our safety and happiness depend on a constitutional connection with *Great Britain;* and that nothing but the being deprived of the privileges and natural rights of *Britons* could ever make the thought of a separation otherwise than intolerable.

Resolved, That in case His Majesty, or his successors, shall, at any time hereafter, make any requisition to the good people of this Province, by his representative, it will be just and right that such sums should be granted as the nature of the service may require, and the ability and situation of this Province will admit of.

Resolved, That this Province join with all the Provinces in *America,* now met by Delegates in Continental Congress, and that *John Houstoun* and *Archibald Bullock,* Esquires, the Rev. Dr. *Zubly, Lyman Hall,* and *Noble Wimberly Jones,* Esquires, be the Delegates from this Province, and that any three constitute a quorum for that purpose.

Resolved, That a Committee be appointed, whose duty it shall be to see that the Resolutions of the Continental and Provincial Congresses be duly observed, and that every person who shall act in opposition thereto, have his name transmitted to the Continental Congress, and his misdeeds be published in every *American* paper.

Resolved, That with all such persons, except the indispensable duties that we owe all mankind, (bad men and enemies are not excepted,) we will have no dealings nor connection; and we extend this our Resolution also to all such persons or corporations in *Great Britain* who have shown themselves enemies to *America.*

Resolved, That we will do what in us lies to preserve and promote the peace and good order of this Province; and should any person become an innocent sufferer on account of these grievances, we will do whatever we justly may for his relief and assistance.

Resolved, That in such calamitous times as the present every possible indulgence ought to be given to honest debtors; that it would be un-

generous, unless there appear intention of fraud, in any gentleman of the law to sue without previous notice; and any person so sued may apply to the Committee, and should it appear to them that the creditor is in no danger of losing his money, or can be properly secured, they shall interpose their friendly offices to persuade him to drop the prosecution; and every prosecutor that shall appear to take advantage of the confusion of the times to distress his debtor, ought to be publickly pointed out and held in abhorrence.

Resolved, That notwithstanding, in a late bill for restraining the trade of several Provinces in *America,* this Province is excepted, we declare that we look upon this exception rather as an insult than a favour; as being meant to break the union of the Provinces, and as being grounded on the supposition that the inhabitants of such excepted Province can be base enough to turn the oppression of *America* into a mean advantage.

TUESDAY, JULY 11, 1775

John Houstoun and *Noble Wimberly Jones,* Esquires, appointed to request the consent of Doctor *Zubly's* congregation for their permission for him to go to *Philadelphia,* reported, that they had done so, and that the said congregation had voted that they were willing to spare their Minister for a time for the good of the common cause. Doctor *Zubly* then declared that he was willing to go, and thanked the Congress for so signal a mark of honour and confidence.

Mr. *Clay,* from the Committee appointed to draw up an Address to his Excellency the Governour, from this Congress, reported, that they had done so, and delivered it in to the President; which was ordered to be read, and is as follows, viz:

To His Excellency, Sir James Wright, *Baronet, Captain-General and Governour-in-Chief in and over His Majesty's Province of Geor-gia, Chancellor and Vice-Admiral of the same:*

May it please your Excellency:
We, his Majesty's dutiful and loyal subjects, the Delegates of this Province, in Provincial Congress met, beg leave to address your Excellency.

In these very critical and alarming times the good people of this Province find themselves under an absolute necessity to take some measures for the security and preservation of their liberties, and every thing that is near and dear to them; and they have accordingly chosen a large number of persons to meet together at *Savannah*, to consult on the means to obtain redress under our many and very heavy grievances. These being accordingly met, (to be distinguished from the usual representation,) have styled themselves a Provincial Congress; and from the number and character of the names, which your Excellency may see in our last *Gazette*, your Excellency will be convinced the Province was never more fully represented in any Assembly; though possibly this measure never would have taken place, had we not, from several successive prorogations or adjournments, but too much reason to fear your Excellency had received very strong instructions not to suffer the Assembly to enter into any measures to secure the rights of *America*, or even to petition for relief, unless in terms which would have been giving up the rights, and fixing lasting disgrace on the petitioners.

Although there is no doubt but a great majority of the inhabitants of this Province always looked upon the claim of Parliament to take away the property of *Americans* as illegal and oppressive, yet, from a variety of causes, not unknown to your Excellency, this Province, in the AMERICAN CHAIN,* has hitherto been the defaulting link. We have now joined with the other Provinces in the Continental Congress, and have sent a Petition to His Majesty, appointed Delegates to the *American* Congress, and entered into such Resolutions, which we mean inviolably to adhere to, as will convince the friends and foes of *America* that we would not live unworthy of the name of *Britons*, or labour under the suspicion of being unconcerned for the rights and freedom of *America*.

Extracts of some letters which are inserted in Parliamentary proceedings, widely differ from what must appear to every unprejudiced person the real state of this Province. We are not acquainted with an individual in *Georgia* that looks upon the claims of Parliament as just; and all men speak with abhorrence of the measures made use of to enforce them. Our fellow-subjects who formerly entered a dissent, which we find was transmitted to the Minister in terms that bespeak the great pleasure it gave the transmitter, now generally say, they never differed with *America* as to the reality of grievances, but only in the mode of obtaining redress.

Though candour may allow these mutilated extracts, laid before Parliament, were probably

* Editor's emphasis.

rather designed by the Minister to screen himself, and justify his own measures, than to give a just and true account of what information he might have received, yet we cannot help observing the general purport of these letters seem to have a much greater regard to the designs of the Minister, than to give an impartial account of the real state of things. Other Provinces, no doubt, if they find themselves mentioned in any part of them, will view them in what light they may think fit; but as to any prejudicial informations they may contain against many persons in this Province, while it is not to be expected they will give up their feelings as private men, your Excellency may be assured we shall always pay due respect to His Majesty's representative, and shall with great pleasure acknowledge every service your Excellency may hereafter render to *Great Britain* and *America*, whose interest we know, and whose connection we wish to be forever inseparable.

Your Excellency may be assured these are objects which we have greatly at heart, and shall ever do what in us lies towards a reconciliation with our Parent State on constitutional principles, as well as endeavour to preserve the peace and good order of this Province.

Resolved, That the foregoing Address be signed by the President, and be presented to his Excellency the Governour; and that *Stephen Drayton, Edward Telfair, William Le Conte, John Walton, George Houstoun,* and *Philip Box,* be a Committee to present the same.

WEDNESDAY, JULY 12, 1775

The Congress resolved itself into a Committee of the Whole, to take into consideration ways and means to raise and sink Ten Thousand Pounds sterling; and, after some time spent therein, the President resumed the Chair.

Resolved, That the Congress being a full representation of the whole Province, the members of the same, their constituents, and all others resident or holding property within the same, are bound to contribute, by an equal and general tax, towards the sinking the Ten Thousand Pounds sterling.

Resolved, That the Congress while sitting, and the Council of Safety in its recess, have power to issue Certificates from time to time, as occasion shall require, to the amount of Ten Thousand Pounds sterling, and that all such Certificates shall be signed by the Treasurers, and at least three of the Members of the Council of Safety.

Resolved, That any person who shall not receive any such Certificate in payment will be guilty of a breach of the publick faith, and ought to be considered as an enemy to the Province, and treated accordingly.

Resolved, That the said Certificate be sunk in three years after a reconciliation shall take place between *Great Britain* and the Colonies.

THURSDAY, JULY 13, 1775

Resolved, That this Congress do approve of, and adopt the Association entered into at *Savannah,* on the fifth day of *June* last past, viz:

Association unanimously entered into by the Provincial Congress, at SAVANNAH, *in* GEORGIA, *on* THURSDAY, *the thirteenth of* JULY, *1775.*

GEORGIA

Being persuaded that the salvation of the rights and liberties of *America* depend, *under God,* on the firm union of the inhabitants in its vigorous prosecution of the measures necessary for its safety; and convinced of the necessity of preventing the anarchy and confusion which attend the dissolution of the powers of Government, we, the freemen, freeholders, and inhabitants of the Province of *Georgia,* being greatly alarmed at the avowed design of the Ministry to raise a revenue in *America,* and shocked by the bloody scene now acting in the *Massachusetts-Bay,* do, in the most solemn manner, resolve never to become slaves; and do associate, under all the ties of religion, honour, and love to our Country, to adopt, and endeavour to carry into execution, whatever may be recommended by the Continental Congress, or resolved upon by our Provincial Convention, appointed for the purpose of preserving our Constitution, and opposing the execution of the several arbitrary and oppressive Acts of the *British* Parliament, until a reconciliation between *Great Britain* and *America,* on constitutional principles, which we most ardently desire, can be obtained; and that we will in all things follow the advice of our General Committee, appointed respecting the purposes aforesaid, the preservation of peace and good order, and the safety of individuals and private property.

Resolved, That *John Smith, Basil Cowper, George Houstoun, Joseph Clay, William Young, Philip Box, Seth John Cuthbert, William O'Bryan, George Walton, William Le Conte,*

William Gibbons, Samuel Elbert, Edward Telfair, and *Oliver Bowen,* be a Committee to present the Association to all the inhabitants of the Town and District of *Savannah,* to be signed; in doing which, expedition is particularly recommended, and an account of all who decline signing shall be returned to the General Committee.

FRIDAY, JULY 14, 1775

A motion was made and seconded, that a Committee be appointed, to report their opinion who shall be qualified to vote for Delegates to sit in future Congresses, and the most equal method of representation; and the same being agreed to, a Committee was appointed accordingly.

Committee: *Stephen Drayton, John Glen,* and *Joseph Clay,* Esquires.

Resolved, That in every case where a summons shall be applied for, the Magistrate to whom such application shall be made, do in the first place, and before the issuing of such summons, give notice thereof, either by personal information, message, or letter, to the party defendant, and also use his best endeavour to compromise and settle the matter, and, unless the defendant has discovered circumstances of fraud or delay, and is ready and willing to give security for the debt, and shall actually offer to do so, payable in a reasonable time, no such summons ought to be issued. And in case a warrant in a civil case shall be applied for, the same ought not to be granted, unless there appears to the satisfaction of the Magistrate, that there are good and sufficient grounds, besides the plaintiff's oath, to apprehend the defendant means to abscond; but the same method ought to be observed as is recommended respecting summonses.

Mr. *Drayton,* from the Committee appointed to report their opinion who shall be qualified to vote for Delegates to sit in future Congresses, &c., reported, as the opinion of that Committee, that every man contributing towards the general tax shall be qualified to vote for Delegates to sit in future Congresses, and that the following proportion will be the most equal representation, viz: the Town and District of *Savannah* shall have seventeen members; District of *Little Ogechee,* three; *Vernonburgh,* two; *Acton,* two; *Sea Islands,* three; *Goshen and Abercorn,* two; *Parish of St. Matthew,* seven; *St. George,* nine; *St. Paul,* nine; *St. Philip,* seven; *St. John,* twelve; *St. Andrew,* nine; *St. David,* three; *St. Patrick,* two; *St. Thomas,* two; *St. Mary,* two; *St. James,* two; *Ceded Lands,* three: and that the

President and thirty-four members do constitute a Congress to proceed upon business.

Resolved, That the foregoing Report be approved of, and that Delegates be elected by the persons, and in the proportion therein mentioned.

Resolved, That the following form of Delegation be recommended to the inhabitants of the several Parishes and Districts throughout the Provinces, to prevent clashing and unequal powers being given by different Parishes and Districts, viz:

GEORGIA

The affairs of the Continent of *America* being now brought to a truly alarming and critical situation, and there being no other method left but that the whole body of the people unite as one, in opposing such acts as tend utterly to destroy the liberty, property, and birthright of America; and it having been thought necessary and convenient, in order to consult on proper ways and means for our mutual security, to assemble and convene the people in each Colony and Province, by their representatives, into one body or Council, styled a Provincial Congress, who shall act in all cases whatsoever for the good of the common cause. Now, therefore, be it known, that we, the inhabitants of . . . . . Parish, (or District,) being met together in order to choose such men as are capable of the important trust, do choose A,B,C,D, &c., being the number determined on in the Provincial Congress, held at *Savannah,* 4th *July,* 1775, to represent us in the Provincial Congress to be held at said Town of Savannah on the fourth *December* next. And we do require you, the said A,B,&c., to do, transact, join, and concur with the other Delegates of this Province, so sitting as above recited, in all things as shall appear eligible and fit at this alarming time, for the preservation and defence of our rights and liberties; and we further empower you to choose other Delegates, if in your wisdom you think proper, or if any requisition in that case should be made by the Grand Continental Congress, in order to join or succeed the Delegates in that Congress, now chosen by the people of this Province. And we do bind ourselves solemnly, under the sacred ties of religion, virtue, honour, and love of our Country, to abide by, enforce, and carry into execution, or endeavour so to do, at the risk and peril of our lives and fortunes, whatsoever you, with the other Delegates, shall resolve and agree upon to be necessary for the well-doing and preservation

of the violated rights of this Province, and the Continent in general.

Signed by us this . . . day of . . . . , 1775.

The following are copies of a Petition from the Inhabitants of *Georgia,* which was presented to the King on *Friday, October* twenty-eighth, by Governour *Johnstone,* and of Letters which accompanied it:

Savannah, July 14, 1775

To GEORGE JOHNSTONE, *Esquire:*

SIR: It is with a singular pleasure I am desired to transmit the accompanying papers to you, sensible that in a cause where the essential rights of so many millions are concerned, no endeavours on your part will be wanting to give them their full effect.

The many proofs which the people of this Province had of your magnanimity, justice and disinterested integrity, in establishing the neighbouring Colony of *West-Florida,* have rendered your name respected throughout *America;* and your subsequent conduct has endeared you still further to every lover of mankind in the eastern and western world. These motives have determined the Congress in the application they now make.

I am sensible if the same Councils prevail, the task of conveying such disagreeable truths to the Throne must prove very painful; but we believe there is no person who would undertake the office with less reluctance, or execute it with more becoming duty and respect to His Majesty.

I am, &c.

Savannah, Georgia, July 14, 1775

SIR: When turbulent and wicked minds are employed solely to raise commotions in the State, and disturb the tranquillity of the subject; when, by their baneful influence, life, property, and freedom, are inhumanly invaded, and the innocence and loyalty of thousands are unjustly questioned; we, the inhabitants of *Georgia,* by a just delegation from the different Parishes, being now convened in Congress in this Town, have resolved to address His Majesty in a dutiful petition, setting forth our grievances, and the bad tendency of the many wicked and treacherous proceedings against this Continent, that have passed since the year 1763.

Although we know the fate of all other petitions on this head, and cannot flatter ourselves that we should meet with one different; yet, as the right of petitioning is the subject's, we beg leave to enclose this our prayer and remonstrance to you, hoping and trusting on the noble sentiments you entertain and support, in favour of us much injured *Americans,* that, countenanced by one of your great abilities, it may approach the Throne.

We assure you, Sir, we are, and always were, firmly attached to His Majesty's family; nor can any thing shake our integrity. But when, by evil and wicked Ministers, our birthright as *Englishmen* shall be violated, that integrity must urge us to hand down to our children a right so invaluable.

We conceive our immediate dependance on the Crown can by no means hinder our doing that indispensable duty in joining with the rest of America against acts that tend to enslave a people whose loyalty and faith were never even suspected, until the actions of the times wanted an excuse.

We have the honour to be, Sir, your most obedient and very humble servants,

WILLIAM YOUNG,	EDW. TELFAIR,
JOHN GLEN,	DANIEL ROBERTS,
DAVID ZUBLY, JUN.,	WILLIAM IRVEN,
STEP. DRAYTON,	

A Committee of Intelligence.
To *George Johnstone,* Esquire.

To the King's Most Excellent Majesty:
The humble Address and Representation of his loyal subjects, the Delegates of the Inhabitants of GEORGIA, *now met in Provincial Congress:*

MAY IT PLEASE YOUR MAJESTY: Though we bring up the rear of *American* petitioners, and, from the fate of so many petitions presented to your Majesty from *America,* your great City of *London,* and others of your European subjects, have a most melancholy prospect, we still hope He, by whom Kings rule, and to whom Monarchs are accountable, will incline you to pay some regard to our most humble and faithful representation.

In times like these, when the edge of present feelings is blunted by the expectation of calamities still greater, we must take the liberty to speak before we die. We would acquaint our Sovereign with things which greatly affect his interest; we would endeavour to awaken the feeling and pity of our common father.

Your Majesty is the rightful sovereign of the most important empire in the universe. The blessings of Providence on your arms has put a country in *America* under you of greater importance and extent than several kingdoms in *Europe.* In this large extent of territory, by some late acts, Popery is not only tolerated, (which we conceive would have been but an act of justice,) but an indulgence has been granted, little short of a full establishment, to a religion which is equally injurious to the rights of sovereigns and of mankind. *French* and arbitrary laws have there, by authority, taken place of the just and mild *British* Constitution; and all this has been done with a professed and avowed design to overawe your Majesty's ancient Protestant and loyal subjects, some of whom had no small share in the merit of that conquest. Acts to raise a perpetual revenue on the *Americans,* without their consent, have been enacted, which at one stroke turn all your American subjects into slaves, and deprive them of that right which the most oppressive taskmaster does not deny to the servant bought with his money. Experience must now have shown, as it will clearer, should these acts be enforced, that instead of increasing the revenue, or lessening the burden of your *European* subjects, they can only serve to increase their taxation.

Laws which we conceive fraught with so much injustice, have been attempted to be enforced by equal cruelty; and whenever we thought ourselves at the height of our troubles, your Majesty's Ministers have stretched their unhappy ingenuity to find out new methods of distress; and it is believed methods have been more than thought of, too shocking to human nature to be even named in the list of grievances suffered under a *British* King.

The goodness of *God* hath made your Majesty the father of a very numerous issue, on whom we place the pleasing hopes of a Protestant succession; but your Majesty's arms in *America* now every day make mothers childless, and children fatherless. The blood of your subjects has been shed with pleasure, rather than with pity. For an act which amounted to no more, even under the worst construction, than an irregular zeal for constitutional liberty, and without any step taken to find out the supposed guilty persons, the capital of your *American* Dominions has been blocked up, deprived of its trade, and its poor of subsistence. Thousands, confessedly innocent, have been starved, ruined, driven from, or kept like prisoners in their own habitations; their cries and blood, innocently shed, have undoubtedly, and daily do reach His ears who hateth injustice and oppression.

Believe us, great Sir, *America* is not divided:

THE LAW
OF LIBERTY

GEORGIA NO MORE
THE DEFAULTING
LINK IN THE
AMERICAN CHAIN

all men (Crown officers not excepted) speak of these acts and measures with disapprobation; and if there has been some difference of opinion as to the mode of relief, the rigorous experiments which your Ministry thought fit to try on the *Americans,* have been the most effectual means to convince these of the iniquitous designs of your Ministry, and to unite them all as in a common cause.

Your Majesty's Ministers, after introducing the demon of discord into your Empire, and driving *America* to the brink of despair, place all their dignity in measures obstinately pursued, because they were once wantonly taken. They hearkened to no information, but what represented *Americans* as rebels or cowards. Time will every day make it clearer how much they were infatuated and mistaken.

Too long, we must lament, have these men imposed on your paternal affection. Deign now, most gracious Prince, in their room, to hearken to the cries of your loyal and affectionate subjects of this extensive Continent; let the goodness of your own heart interpose between weak or wicked Ministers and millions of loyal and affectionate subjects; no longer let the sword be stained with the blood of your own children; recall your troops and fleets; and if any misunderstanding remains, let the *Americans* be heard, and justice and equity take place; let us be ruled according to the known principles of our excellent Constitution, and command the last shilling of our property, and the last drop of our blood in your service.

Uncertain as to the event of this our humble representation, it affords us a relief that we may, unrestrained, apply to the great and merciful Sovereign of the whole earth, who will not despise the prayer of the oppressed; and to him we most ardently pray, that the wicked being removed from before the King, the King's Throne may be established in righteousness.

By order of the Congress at *Savannah,* this 14th day of July.

ARCH. BULLOCK, *President.*

GEORGIA NO MORE
THE DEFAULTING LINK
IN THE AMERICAN CHAIN

SATURDAY, JULY 15, 1775

A motion was made and seconded, that a Committee be appointed to report their opinion with respect to the better governing the Militia of this Province; which being agreed to, a Committee was appointed accordingly, to wit: *Stephen Drayton, Samuel Elbert, Dr. Brownson, and Peter Tarlin.* A motion was made and seconded, that a Committee be appointed to communicate to the inhabitants of this Province, an account of the disputes subsisting between *Great Britain* and the Colonies, and also the proceedings of this Congress; and the same being agreed to, it was

Ordered, That the Rev. Dr. *Zubly, Noble Wimberly Jones, William Young,* and *George Walton,* be a Committee for that purpose.

Resolved, That the Congress shall expire on the twentieth day of *August* next; that a new election be made at such times between the said twentieth day of *August* and first of *September,* as the inhabitants of the several Parishes and Districts (except the Town and District of *Savannah*) shall think fit, respectively, and that the members so elected, with those who shall afterwards be chosen for the Town and District of *Savannah,* do meet in General Congress at *Savannah,* on the fourth day of *December* next, or sooner, if the Council of Safety shall think it expedient to summon them.

Resolved, That the Members of this Congress use every endeavour to give as publick notice of elections as possible; and that each Parish and District shall, at the time of such elections, likewise choose a sufficient number as a Parochial or District Committee, to enforce the different Resolves of the Continental and Provincial Congresses.

Resolved, That the inhabitants of the Town and District of *Savannah* do meet at *Savannah* on *Friday,* the fifteenth day of *September* next, to choose seventeen Delegates to represent them in Provincial Congress.

Resolved, That the several Delegates for the Town and District of *Savannah,* or a majority of them, together with all other Delegates who shall happen to be in Town, shall be a General Committee for the Province; that they shall have power to superintend, direct, and advise all the Parochial or District Committees, and, in case of difficulty, to inform them of their duty. And any person who shall apprehend himself aggrieved by the decision of any of the Parochial or District Committees, may appeal to the said General Committee, who shall hear his case, and do justice according to the spirit and intention of this Congress. And in case such appellant shall still be dissatisfied, he may lay his case before the next Congress, provided there be no delay occasioned by any such appeal, but the sentence of each Committee shall take effect immediately after being pronounced.

MONDAY, JULY 17, 1775

Resolved, That the Reverend Mr. *Haddon Smith,* by twice refusing to comply with the request of this Congress, and to join on a day of Fasting and Prayer, appointed by the Continental Congress to be observed throughout all *America,* besides the day appointed by his Excellency the Governour, at the request of this Congress, has given too much reason to believe he does not wish that the happy event, mentioned in the *American* Proclamation, may take place, and that the said Mr. *Haddon Smith* has thereby incurred the censure of this Congress, and ought to be considered as unfriendly to *America.*

Resolved nemine contradicente, That the Delegates appointed by this Congress to go to *Philadelphia,* do apply to the Continental Congress to incorporate this Province with the other united Provinces of *North America,* and that they pledge the faith of us and our constituents, to contribute an adequate part of the expenses which have or may accrue, in the defence of the violated rights of *America.*

Resolved, That the Council of Safety have full power, upon every emergency, during the recess of Congress, to give such information and propose such measures, by way of advice to our Continental Delegates, as the circumstances of the case may require, and they shall think conducive to the publick good.

Resolved, That it be strongly recommended to the friends of America in this Province, that they use their utmost endeavours to preserve peace and good order, and to cultivate harmony with one another, and always to avoid national reflections, which can only tend to produce divisions and jealousies among the inhabitants.

Resolved, That this Congress do adjourn to the nineteenth day of *August* next, and that the General Committee have power to call it to sit at *Savannah* sooner, if they, upon any emergency, shall deem it expedient for the good of the Province. By order of the Congress.

A true copy from the Minutes:

GEORGE WALTON, *Secretary.*

Savannah, July 25, 1775

To the Inhabitants of the Province of GEORGIA:

FELLOW-COUNTRYMEN: We are directed to transmit to you an account of the present state of *American* affairs, as well as the proceedings of the late Provincial Congress.

It is with great sorrow we are to acquaint you,

that what our fears suggested, but our reason thought impossible, is actually come to pass. A civil war in *America* is begun. Several engagements have already happened. The friends and foes of *America* have been equally disappointed. The friends of *America* were in hopes British Troops could never be induced to slay their brethren. It is, however, done, and the circumstances are such as must be an everlasting blot on their character for humanity and generosity. An unfeeling commander has found means to inspire his troops with the same evil spirit that possesseth himself. After the starving, helpless, innocent inhabitants of *Boston* delivered up their arms, and received his promise that they might leave that virtuous devoted Town, he is said to have broke his word, and the wretched inhabitants are still kept, to fall a prey to disease, famine, and confinement. If there are powers that abhor injustice and oppression, it may be hoped such perfidy cannot go long unpunished. But the enemies of *America* have been no less disappointed. Nothing so contemptible in their eyes like the rabble of an *American* Militia, nothing more improbable than that they would dare to look Regulars in the face, or stand a single fire. By this time they must have felt how much they were mistaken. In every engagement the *Americans* appeared with a bravery worthy of men that fight for the liberties of their oppressed Country; their success has been remarkable; the number of the slain and wounded on every occasion vastly exceeds theirs; and the advantages they gained are the more honourable, because, with a patience that scarce has an example, they bore every act of injustice and insult till their lives were attacked, and then gave the fullest proof that the man of calmness and moderation in council, is usually also the most intrepid and courageous in battle.

You will doubtless lament with us the hundreds that died in their Country's cause; but does it not call for greater sorrow that thousands of *British* soldiers fought and found their deaths, when they were active to enslave their brethren and their Country?

However irritating all those proceedings, yet so unnatural is this quarrel, that every good man must wish and pray that it may soon cease, that the injured rights of *America* may be vindicated by milder means, and that no more blood may be shed, unless it be of those who fomented, and mean to make an advantage of those unhappy divisions.

From the proceedings of the Congress, a copy of which accompanies the present, you will be convinced that a reconciliation, on honourable principles, is an object which your Delegates never lost sight of. We have sent an humble and manly Petition to His Majesty; addressed his representative, our Governour; provided, as far as in our power, for internal quiet and safety; and Delegates will soon attend the General Congress, to assist and cooperate in every measure that shall be thought necessary for the saving of *America*.

His Excellency, at our request, having appointed the nineteenth instant as a day of humiliation, and news being afterwards received that the Continental Congress had recommended the twentieth instant to be observed as such, both days have been observed with a becoming solemnity, and we humbly hope many earnest prayers have been presented to the Father of Mercies on that day, through this extensive Continent, and that he has heard the cries of the destitute, and will not despise their prayers.

You will permit us most earnestly to recommend to you a steady perseverance in the cause of liberty, and that you will use all possible caution not to say or do any thing unworthy of so glorious a cause; to promote frugality, peace, and good order; and, in the practice of every social and religious duty, patiently to wait for the return of that happy day when we may sit quietly under our vine and fig-tree, and no man make us afraid.

J. J. ZUBLY,

N. W. JONES,

GEORGE WALTON

★   ★   ★   ★   ★

CONTINENTAL CONGRESS

THURSDAY, JULY 20, 1775

An Express arriving with dispatches from Genl Schuyler, the same were read.

A letter was likewise received from the Convention of Georgia, and read, setting forth, that that Colony had acceded to the general Association, and appointed delegates to attend this Congress.

Adjourned till one o'Clock, P.M.

SR. As we appear so late in the American Cause, We must introduce ourselves with Expressions of Regret, that our Province has been so long divided, A Number of Incidents have Contributed thereto, which we think the less necessary to particularize as we hope they are pretty well got over.—

It gives us therefore pleasure to inform You, That a Provincial Congress being appointed to be held at Savannah, was accordingly opened on Tuesday the 4th Instant, to which every Parish has sent Delegates, except the two Small Parishes of St. James and St. Patrick,—These Parishes are Scarcely inhabited and we do not Suppose Contain a Score of Freeholders Inhabitants. Some Parishes that upon former Occasions seemed rather reluctant and even Protested against our Proceedings have manifested a very Laudable Zeal upon this Occasion. Several Gentlemn in this Place that have been hitherto neuter or declared against America, now Speak of the Proceedings of Parliament, as Illegal and Oppressive. We flatter ourselves for the future You may look upon Us as an United People.

The Congress addressed our Governor, that he would appoint a Day of Fasting and Prayer to obtain a Happy Reconciliation with the Parent State, To which he Sent a very Civil answer in writing, importing, that he could not look upon the Congress as a Constitutional Meeting, but would certainly comply with their request and issue his Proclamation accordingly—

We have also proceeded to the Choice of Delegates to represent Us in Continental Congress, when John Houstoun, Archd Bullock Esqrs The Revd Dr. Zubly, Lyman Hall and Noble Wimberly Jones Esqrs were duly Elected, One of these Gentlemen is with you, and three others have agreed to attend the Congress with all convenient Speed, And we doubt not will be received as their great Zeal for the Common Cause deserves.

We have already Resolved strictly to adhere to the Continental Association, and are heartily disposed Zealously to Enter into every measure that your Congress may deem necessary for the Saving of America,

We subjoin a Copy of the Resolve Entered into at the time of Electing our Delegates, And have the Honor to be Sir

Yr most Obedt Servants

By Order of the Congress

ARCH :D BULLOCK president

The Continental Congress adjourned to Christ Church, Philadelphia, where they heard a sermon preached by Rev. Jacob Duche, M.A. entitled "The American Vine" from the text "Return, we beseech thee, O God of Hosts! Look down from Heaven, and behold and visit this Vine! (Ps. lxxx:xiv). Editor

Journals of the Continental Congress, Vol. II, Washington, 1905

CONTINENTAL FAST DAY
JULY 20, 1775

*A Sermon
Preached on
the Day of the
Continental
Fast, at
Tredyffryn, in
Chester County,*
by The Rev.
David Jones,
A.M.,
Philadelphia,
1775

DEFENSIVE WAR IN A JUST CAUSE SINLESS

And I looked and rose up, and said unto the nobles, and to the rulers, and to the rest of the people, Be not ye afraid of them: Remember the Lord, which is great and terrible, and fight for your brethren, your sons and your daughters, your wives and your houses. Nehemiah iv:14.

When a people become voluntary slaves to sin; when it is esteemed a reproach to reverence and serve God; when profaneness and dissolute morals become fashionable; when pride and luxury predominate, we cannot expect such a nation to be long happy.

ISRAEL, when first planted in the land of Canaan, were a brave, heroic and virtuous people, being firmly attached to the true worship of God. They were both formidable and invincible: when their armies went forth to battle, thousands and tens of thousands fell before them: thus being cloathed with the majesty of virtue and true religion, a panic seized the hearts of all their enemies around them. But when vice and immorality became prevalent; when they forsook and rebelled against their God, they lost their martial spirit, and were soon enslaved by the king of Babylon. Yet, as God is gracious and merciful, when seventy years were expired in this furnace of affliction, he remembered their low estate, and stirred up Cyrus, king of Persia, to proclaim liberty for the Jews to return and build their temple at Jerusalem. Nevertheless some of the people still remained in Persia, of which Nehemiah was one. He was a favourite in the days of Artaxerxes the king, therefore he obtained leave to go and build the walls of that antient city Jerusalem. But when Sanballat the Horonite, Tobiah the Ammonite, and Geshem the Arabian heard that there were men come to seek the welfare of the Jews, they were filled with indignation: therefore, in scornful language, they bring a state-accusation against them, saying: *"What is this thing that ye do? will you rebel against the king*?"* However, though they treated the Jews with scorn and insult, yet their labour became a subject of conversation. Sanballat once speaking on the occasion, Tobiah makes a reply to this effect, viz. "Tush, Sanballat, it is not worth your notice, nor should you give yourself the least concern about these feeble wretches, they build indeed, but if a fox in his meanders was to ascend their stone wall, and

---

* These three gentlemen were governors, and consequently pensioners. It is common for such to profess great loyalty to kings, when in reality it is their pension they love, and not their king. They speak in court language, "Will ye rebel against the king?"

only give a few scratches, it would fall down." These scornful insults were spoken that the Jews might hear them, and be discouraged; but when they saw that the work went on with rapidity, they were filled with the highest indignation, and resolved, if bitter taunts, these swords of their mouths, would not discourage them, their swords of steel should compel them to cease from their work: therefore Sanballat, Tobiah, the Arabians, the Ammonites and Ashdodites all conspire together, to come with their united force against Jerusalem. Their design was made known to Nehemiah; and, as all should do, especially in distress, he lifts up his eyes to heaven, and makes his supplication to the Lord of host; nor does he think his preservation shall be effected in neglect of the use of means; therefore he sets a watch against them day and night, and addresses himself to all ranks of people in these spirited and excellent words, viz. *Be not ye afraid of them: Remember the* LORD, *which is great and terrible, and fight for your brethren, your sons and your daughters, your wives and your houses.*

In the words observe,

1. A caution against cowardice, or fear of an enemy unjustly enraged. *Be not ye afraid of them.*

It is of great importance in war to be delivered from fear of the enemy; for soldiers in a panic generally fall a victim in the dispute.

2. We have an argument to excite fortitude and firmness of mind in martial engagements. *Remember the* LORD, *which is great and terrible.*

3. A fervent call to present duty in times of distress. *And fight for your brethren, your sons, your daughters, your wives and your houses.*

To improve the words suitable to the occasion of the present solemnity, the following order shall be attempted,

I. An endeavour shall be made to prove, that in some cases, when a people are oppressed, insulted and abused, and can have no other redress, it then becomes our duty as men, with our eyes to GOD, to fight for our liberties and properties; or in other words, that a defensive war is sinless before GOD, consequently to engage therein, is consistent with the purest religion. Here some texts in the New Testament, which prevent some good men from engaging in the present dispute, shall be considered.

II. Some particulars shall be presented to our consideration, to demonstrate the alarming call, which we now have to take up arms in our own defence.

III. A few arguments shall be advanced to excite fortitude in martial engagements.

And lastly, Some inferences shall be drawn.

The subject before us is of great importance. It is to be lamented that we have the present occasion to consider it. It is very copious, and as it is new to me, brevity and great accuracy can scarcely be expected. If GOD shall enable us to consider each proposition consistent with his honour, and worthy of his majesty, we may rest satisfied. Your attention, my Brethren and Countrymen is begged, while an endeavour is made.

I. To prove, that in some cases, when a people are oppressed, insulted and abused, and can have no other redress, it then becomes our duty as men, with our eyes to GOD, to fight for our liberties and properties; or in other words, that *a defensive war is sinless* before GOD; consequently to engage therein, is consistent with the purest religion.

If antiquity, if the united voice of all kingdoms, that now or ever have existed, could be admitted as a proof, the point would easily be determined; for there has been no kingdom, whether composed of Jews or Gentiles, Barbarians or Christians, but have embraced it as their common creed, that a defensive war is innocent. But though this is a presumptive argument, yet it must be confessed, that it is not a decisive proof: for antient mistakes are mistakes, and a multitude may be wrong.

But if this proposition can be made appear from the holy scriptures, as we profess them to be our only rule of faith and practice, then it must be acknowledged that a defensive war is sinless, and consistent with the purest religion. To them let us repair with attentive ears, to hear what the lively oracles of GOD will say on this point.

Among all the antient servants of GOD none is more famous for true piety and pure religion than the patriarch Abraham—to him the highest epithets are given—he is more than once called the friend of GOD—in his steps the righteous are to walk—to him were many great and precious promises made, and yet we find this great, this holy man firmly of the faith that a defensive war is sinless. He makes a bright display of his faith, when the four kings took Lot, his brother's son, captive. Doth his religion prevent his pursuit of the enemy? No, verily. With a heart depending on the most high GOD, he collects his servants and some confederates; with martial weapons in his hands, he pursues the foes, and utterly discomfits the four kings, and triumphantly brings back the captives, with all the spoil. This was the very time that Melchizedeck, the priest of the most high GOD, met him. And did he reprove or curse him? No, says the text, "he brought forth bread and wine," giving him the highest expressions of approbation, he thus addressed him, viz. *"Blessed be Abraham of the most high GOD, possessor of heaven and earth, and blessed be the most high GOD, which hath delivered thine enemies into thine hand." Gen. xiv:18. 19. 20.* This passage proves not only that this was Abram's belief, but also that Melchizedek, priest of the most high GOD, Melchizedek, the brightest type of CHRIST, was fully of the same opinion, and therefore may be admitted as an evidence in favour of a defensive war. For any of us to presume that we have a better conscience than Melchizedeck, would argue either pride or ignorance.

If we trace the sacred history, and descend to succeeding ages, we shall find that Moses is of the same faith. Among all the children of men none was more meek, and admitted to greater familiarity with GOD, than Moses. He is often called, by way of eminence, "Moses, the servant of GOD." By his hands we received the lively oracles of God, and the apostle bears him witness, that "he was faithful in all things;" yet we find him often engaged in bloody battles. One instance may suffice at present, out of many that might be produced, and that is, when, on the most reasonable terms, he requests to pass through the land of Sihon, king of the Amorites, pledging his honour that no damage should be done; *Num. xxi:22.* but Sihon, instead of granting the small privilege of passing along the highway, advances with all his armies against Israel. Doth Moses think it his duty to make no defence? Let us view his conduct. Israel advances with sword in hand, and utterly discomfits the Amorites. If we read the book of Joshuah, his immediate successor, we shall find him of the same mind. Israel are called the peculiar people of GOD, to whom his mind was revealed, and this is the faith of the whole house of Israel. If it was a sin to engage in a defensive war, can we suppose that Israel should be ignorant of it? Seeing therefore that it is sinless, it is meet that we should tread in the footsteps of this flock, which is gone before us. And were we further to attend to the sacred history, we shall find, that after the death of Joshuah and the elders, which saw the mighty works of GOD, that Israel first being enslaved by sin, were oppressed by various nations; but when they cried unto the Lord, he raised up deliverers, among whom were Othniel, Ehud, Barak, Gideon, Jephtha, and many others, which performed

glorious exploits, and were blessed instruments under GOD to deliver Israel from oppression and bondage. Some of these, you know, are spoken of as the worthies of Israel, and have much recorded in their praise; and yet all these died in the faith, that a defensive war is sinless before GOD. Still were we to descend and pursue the chain of history, we shall find all the kings of Israel of the same faith. Among many that might be mentioned, we shall at present take notice only of one. David, a man eminent for pure religion, the sweet psalmist of Israel, David, a man after GOD's own heart, yet all his life is a scene of war. When he was even a youth, he began his martial exploits, and delivered Israel by slaying great Goliath of Gath, the champion of the Philistines. And what shall I say more? The time would fail me to enumerate all who were avouchers of this proposition: It is therefore a clear point, that a defensive war is sinless, and consistent with the purest religion.

This indeed is generally acknowledged, when our dispute is with a foreign enemy, but at present it seems like a house divided against itself; our dispute is with administration. This is cause of great sorrow, that such a heavy judgment has befallen the kingdom; and yet we are not without some instances in scripture of people refusing obedience to kings, when they became arbitrary and oppressive. When Rehoboam threatened Israel with nothing but tyranny, they did not long hesitate till they gave the king this answer, *"What portion have we in David? Neither have we inheritance in the son of Jesse: To your tents, oh Israel! Now see to thine own house David." I Kings xii:16.*

And this certainly has been the faith of Great-Britain, as might be made appear by many instances, one of which I shall at present just mention. When king James II. departed from the constitution, and became arbitrary, by dispensing with acts of Parliament by proclamation, issuing *quo warrantos* against charters, and endeavouring to introduce popery, the people esteemed it no sin to invite William, the prince of Orange, to invade England, and obliged James to abdicate a kingdom he had forfeited his right to govern.

But there are some texts of scripture urged on this occasion, which were to be considered. The following are thought to enjoin non-resistance in the strongest terms, viz. *Let every soul be subject to the higher powers: For there is no power but of GOD; the powers that be, are ordained of GOD. Whosoever therefore resisteth the power, resisteth the ordinance of GOD: and they that re-*

CONTINENTAL
FAST DAY,
JULY 20, 1775

——————

DEFENSIVE WAR
IN A JUST CAUSE
SINLESS

sist, shall receive to themselves condemnation. Rom. xiii:1. 2, etc. The apostle is no friend to anarchy, for he well knew the corruption and depravity of man would oppress the innocent, if there were no legal restraints. But, in order rightly to understand these words, it is of great importance to determine first, what is meant by the higher powers: For this is what every soul is to be subject unto. We shall find no exposition liable to less exception, than to understand by the higher powers the just, the good, the wholesome and constitutional laws of a land, merely respecting civil government. The very design of these higher powers is to secure the property and promote the happiness of the whole community. These higher powers therefore appear as binding on princes as people. And as GOD has ordained these powers for the good of the whole, whosoever resisteth the same, resisteth the ordinance of GOD, and receiveth finally condemnation, and that justly; for anarchy and tyranny are essentially the same, and equally to be dreaded, as each resists the higher powers. We cannot suppose, either that this text enjoins absolute submission to all laws, which may be made in a land; for some are so wicked, oppressive and unjust in their nature and tendency, that the best of men have thought it their indispensable duty to disobey them. You may well remember, that Nebuchadnezzar made it a certain law, that all nations in his empire should, on pain of death, worship his golden image. Was it the duty of his subjects to obey or not? The conduct of Shadrach, Meshach and Abednego will determine the point, who, refusing to comply, were cast into a fiery furnace. Remember also, when Darius, king of Persia, made a statute, that no man should petition either GOD or man, save himself, for thirty days, Daniel refused obedience unto the decree, because it was unrighteous. Call to mind also, that in the days of Pharaoh, king of Egypt, he enjoined it as a law to all the midwives, that they should kill all the male-children of the Jews. Did they obey or not? The text informs us that the fear of GOD prevented them, believing that no law can make that just, which in its own nature is unrighteous. The higher powers, of which Paul speaks, are ordained of GOD, and if ordained of him, they must be like unto him, who is a GOD of unspotted justice and truth.

Certain it is, that the people must be the judges whether the laws are good or not;—and I think it must be acknowledged by all, that laws are not good, except they secure every man's liberty and property, and defend the subject against the arbi-

trary power of kings, or any body of men whatsoever.

Again, another text, used to enforce the doctrine of nonresistance in the present dispute, is, *Submit yourselves to every ordinance of man, for the Lord's sake, whether unto the king as supreme, or unto governors as unto them that are sent by him, for the punishment of evil-doers, and for the praise of them that do well. I Pet. ii:13. 14.* This text is to be understood in a restricted and limited sense as above. We cannot suppose, that the apostle meant obedience to all despotic ordinances of tyrants; for this would condemn the conduct of the midwives, Daniel, Shadrach, Meshach and Abednego. The ordinances here can be none other than such as are good, and ordained of GOD, for whose sake we are to submit unto them; for these higher powers, or ordinances, are the provision of GOD, which he has ordained for the Safety of the people, to defend them against oppression and arbitrary power. There is none, but GOD, suitably qualified to rule according to his own will and pleasure, so that when man assumes to rule arbitrarily, he sets himself in the temple of GOD, shewing himself that he is GOD; for none is qualified for that seat, but him that is infinitly wise, just and holy. We see, when these words are taken in a limited sense, there is no evil consequence follows, but if we understand them to bind us to obey all that taskmasters require, then it is plain that we condemn king Henry VIII. for refusing obedience to the pope of Rome. Many *bulls* were thundered out against him, but he and the parliament resolved that they were a complete legislative body in themselves, paying no regard to the threats of Rome. If we were to embrace any other exposition of these passages of scripture, we should absolutely condemn the Reformation; nay, we would condemn all England, who refused obedience to king James II. because he would not be subject to the higher powers, but endeavoured to subvert the constitution, and to reign arbitrarily. Such a sentiment, if pursued, would lead back to all the horrors of popery and despotism; nay, it would even condemn the blessed martyrs, who refused obedience to arbitrary and wicked laws.

Some will object, that these laws respected religion, which makes an essential difference; for when religion is affected, one may withstand a kingdom. Calvin and Luther were of this faith. It is granted, that there is great difference between state affairs and religion; for Christ says, *"his kingdom is not of this world;"* none dare impose laws in matters of religion on his subjects, without being guilty of a daring insult: but the instances above do not all respect religion, therefore are suitable on the present occasion; and those that do respect religion, were brought to prove that the words are to be taken in a restricted sense. I have met with none, but acknowledge these texts must be so understood, as to justify opposition to popish tyranny. And pray, my countrymen, what better is protestant tyranny than popish? Is there any essential difference between being robbed by a *protestant* or a papist? Is it not the very same thing? Tyranny is tyranny, slavery is slavery, by whomsoever it is imposed. Names change not the nature of things. If despotism is bad in a papist, it cannot be good in a *protestant*. If it may be resisted in one, it ought to be in the other.

But to proceed: There is another objection, which good people make against war of any kind, viz. "That war is not agreeable to the disposition of souls newly converted to the knowledge of CHRIST: Then we long for the salvation of souls, and have a tender regard for all men: Surely martial engagements do not suit a meek and loving disciple of JESUS." I confess, no objection to me is of equal importance to this. It is a solemn consideration:—Alas! alas! that ever there was occasion of even a defensive war: but occasion there has been, and occasion there now is. The reason why a defensive war seems so awful to good people, is, they esteem it to be some kind of murder: but this is a very great mistake; for it is no more murder than a legal process against a criminal. The end is the same, the mode is different. In some cases it is the only mode left to obtain justice. And surely that religion is not from heaven, which is against justice on earth. Remember all men are not converted; if they were, there could be no necessity of war in any sense. For, says the scripture, *"they shall not hurt nor destroy."* But remember, this is when the earth shall be filled with the knowledge of the LORD. Alas! this is not the case now; for darkness, gloomy darkness, prevails throughout the kingdoms of this world. Oh! that the kingdom of JESUS was come, when we should have occasion to learn war no more. But to give a more particular answer to the objection, consider that the design of laws is to punish evil-doers, —to bring to justice offenders, and to secure the innocent in the peaceable possession of their properties: for this end GOD has ordained these higher powers; but it some times has been the case, that those, in whose hands these powers are entrusted, become tyrannical, and the greatest

offenders, and shall they live with impunity? GOD forbid! how shall justice be obtained? every mode is evaded. The case is similar with a foreign enemy, we cannot have redress any other way, no other method is left to obtain justice; and though the mode is different, the issue is the same as when we execute a criminal condemned by a jury. Suppose, a villain was to rob you of a valuable sum of money, and thereby expose you and your family to distress and poverty, would you not think it your duty to prosecute such a public offender? yes, without doubt, or else you could not be a friend to the innocent part of mankind. But suppose, he not only robs you, but in a daring manner, in your presence, murders your only son, will you not think that blood calls aloud for punishment? Surely both reason and revelation will justify you in seeking for justice in that mode by which it can be obtained. The present case is only too similar:—by an arbitrary act all the families that depended on the Newfoundland fishery are abandoned to distress and poverty, and the blood of numbers spilt already without a cause. Surely it is consistent with the purest religion to seek for justice. Consider the case in this point of view, and he that is not clear in conscience to gird on his sword, if he would act consistently, must never sit on a jury to condemn a criminal.

II. This brings me to the second thing proposed, which was to present a few particulars to your consideration, which will demonstrate the alarming call, which we now have, to take up arms, and fight in our own defence.

We have no choice left to us, but to submit to absolute slavery and despotism, or as free-men to stand in our own defence, and endeavour a noble resistance. Matters are at last brought to this deplorable extremity;—every reasonable method of reconciliation has been tried in vain;—our addresses to our king have been treated with neglect or contempt. It is true that a plan of accommodation has been proposed by administration; but they are men of more sense than to think it could be accepted. It could be proposed for no other purpose than to deceive England into an opinion, that we did not desire reconciliation. What was the substance of this pretended plan? In short this, that we should give them as much money as they were pleased to ask, and we might raise it in our own mode. Slaves therefore we must be, only we shall be indulged to put on our fetters, to suit ourselves. This plan is no better than that clause, which says, "That

CONTINENTAL
FAST DAY,
JULY 20, 1775

DEFENSIVE WAR
IN A JUST CAUSE
SINLESS

the parliament have a right to make laws to bind us in all cases whatsoever." For if they may fix the sum, and we must raise it, the case is the same, we having nothing left, but what they have no use for;—all is at their disposal, and we shall have no voice in the application of our own money. They may apply it to raise forces in Canada, to cut our throats. The call therefore is alarming—we cannot submit to be slaves—we were born free, and we can die free. Only attend to the voice of parliament, viz. "That they have a right to make laws to bind us in all cases whatsoever." Even our religion is not excepted —they assume a right to bind us in all cases. Agreeable to this proposition, they may oblige us to support popish priests, on pain of death:— they have already given us a specimen of the good effects of their assumed power, in establishing popery in near one half of North America. Is not this the loudest call to arms? All is at stake— we can appeal to GOD, that we believe our cause is just and good. But to attend to our text, "and fight for your brethren," our brethren in the Massachusetts are already declared *rebels;* —they are treated as such, and we as abettors are involved in the same circumstances;—nothing can be more unjust than such a proclamation. Rebels are men disaffected with their sovereign in favour of some other person. This is not the case of America; for if Jacobites were not more common in England than with us, we should not have had occasion of the present dispute. We very well know what follows this proclamation, all our estates are confiscated, and were we even to submit, we should be hanged as dogs. Now therefore let us join, and fight for our brethren. Remember our Congress is in eminent danger. It is composed of men of equal characters and fortunes of most, if not superior to any in North America. These worthy gentlemen have ventured all in the cause of liberty for our sakes;—if we were to forsake them, they must be abandoned to the rage of a relentless ministry. Some of them are already proscribed, and no doubt this would be the fate of the rest:—How could we bear to see these worthy patriots hanged as criminals of the deepest dye? their families plundered of all that they possess, and abandoned to distress and poverty? This, my countrymen, must be the case, if you will not now as men fight for your brethren: Therefore if we do not stand by them, even unto death, we should be guilty of the basest ingratitude, and entail on ourselves everlasting infamy. But if the case of our brethren is not so near as suitably to affect us, let us consider the condition of our sons and daughters. Your sons are engaged in the present dispute, and therefore subject to all the consequences: Oh! remember if you submit to arbitrary measures, you will entail on your sons despotic power. Your sons and your daughters must be strangers to the comforts of liberty;—they will be considered like beasts of burden, only made for their *masters use.* If the groans and cries of posterity in oppression can be any argument, come now, my noble countrymen, fight for your sons and your daughters. But if this will not alarm you, consider what will be the case of your wives, if a noble resistance is not made: all your estates confiscated, and distributed to the favourites of arbitrary power, your wives must be left to distress and poverty. This might be the better endured, only the most worthy and flower of all the land shall be hanged, and widowhood and poverty both come in one day. The call to arms is therefore alarming, especially when we consider the tender mercies of the wicked are cruel, we can expect no favour from administration. They seem to be callous, so as to have no feeling of human distress. What can be a greater demonstration than to excite the barbarous savages against us? * These, instead of coming against our armed men, will beset our defenceless frontiers, and barbarously murder with savage cruelty poor helpless women and children. Oh, did ever mortal hear of such inhuman barbarity! † Come then, my countrymen, we have no other remedy, but, under GOD, to fight for our brethren, our sons and our daughters, our wives and our houses.

III. It is probable that the most will acknowledge, that the call to arms is alarming, but we are comparatively weak to Great Britain; an answer to this will bring us to the third thing under consideration, which was, to advance a few arguments to excite fortitude in martial engagements. And no argument is greater than our text, viz. *"Remember the* LORD *is great and terrible."* All human aid is subject to disappointment, but when our dependance is on the almighty God, we may hope for success, *for the eyes of the Lord run to and fro throughout the whole earth, to shew himself strong in behalf of them whose heart is perfect towards him. 2 Chron. xvi:9.* He gives

---

* It is beyond dispute, that Guy Johnson is using his influence with the Mohawks against us, as well as the Superintendant of South Carolina. These must be bribed by Administration, whose tools and pensioners they are.

† It is a received maxim, that he that employs an assassin is as bad as himself.

us a glorious display of his assistance in the case of Abraham, who lifted up his hand to the most high GOD, and pursued the four kings with their numerous armies, and GOD delivered them into his hand, for he is great, and doth great and marvellous things in behalf of them that trust in him. Remember what the LORD has done in ages past: Israel were in the days of Saul sorely beset by the Philistines,—their hearts trembled at the formidable aspect of great Goliath of Gath; but GOD sends forth a youth, even a stripling, against this man of war, and soon we see the insulting foe lie prostrate at the feet of David. Call to mind what he did to the Assyrian host in the days of Hezekiah: with bitter taunts Rabshakeh reproaches Israel, threatening, that if they did not soon surrender, that he would oblige them to eat their own excrements and drink their own urine. But behold the hand of the LORD is with Israel, therefore an angel of death is sent, who smote the Assyrian camp, so that an hundred four score and five thousand were dead corps in the morning light. Kings and captains may boast great things, but GOD alone is truly great, and greatly to be feared; he doth his pleasure in the heavens above, and among the inhabitants of the earth, and all nations are as nothing in his sight. GOD is not only great, but terrible in his judgments; an instance we have in Pharaoh, king of Egypt, who was resolved to keep Israel in bondage, but was fatally disappointed in the red sea. His judgments are both great and various; how easy is it for GOD to baffle all the counsels of our enemies? how easily can he divide them, or raise up enemies that shall give them employment enough at home? So he delivered David in the wilderness of Maon. Our GOD is able to give us pity in the eyes of the nations around us, so that they will afford their aid, if required. If GOD be for us, who can be against us? We have great reason to bewail the sins of the land, yet the LORD has a people in it reserved for himself, and if this had been the case with Sodom, it would have been saved. Our present dispute is just, our cause is good. We have been as loyal subjects as any on earth;—at all times, when occasion called, we have contributed towards the expence of war, with liberal hands, beyond our power, even in their estimation. When we have been called to venture our lives in defence of our king and country, have we refused? No, verily; we have been willing to spill our precious blood. We have been charged with designs of independency: This possibly may be the event, but surely against our wills; the decent addresses to his Majesty, as well as all other prudential measures, are arguments in our favour. But all our measures are disregarded, the terms offered us are but a few degrees milder than what the Ammonites offered to Jabesh-Gilead. These poor men offered more than reason could ask, but nothing would serve, only for each to have his right eye put out—the terms were bad—tears flowed from every eye—wailing reached the ears of Saul, and the spirit of the LORD came on him. *1 Sam. xi:6.* By the spirit of GOD here we may understand a martial spirit stirred up in Saul. He assembles all Israel, and makes a noble resistance, attended with a glorious victory over the enemy. The spirit of GOD coming on him was a presage of success. And has not the same spirit come on us? A martial spirit from GOD has spread throughout the land. Surely, if this is not a heavy judgment, it is a presage of success. We are fully persuaded, that this spirit is not a judgment, because our cause is good, even in the sight of other States. To the Most High we can appeal, and submit the event to his pleasure. It is more than probable that we may meet with some defeats, and have much blood shed; but even if this should be the case, let us not be discouraged; for so it was with Israel in their first battles with Benjamin, but in the third battle the whole tribe of Benjamin is cut off, save six hundred men.

There is only one consideration that is very discouraging, and that is the great and many sins that prevail in our land. "Unfeignedly to confess and deplore our many sins," is recommended by our Congress as one duty of this day. And, alas! we have many great sins abounding in our land, for which we may justly bewail our case before GOD, some of which, it may not be amiss to mention here:—but where shall I begin? There is one heaven daring and GOD provoking sin, which prevails even among many who otherwise are gentlemen, that is profaneness of language, in taking the tremendous name of GOD in vain. This is a sin of the first magnitude—men have the least excuse for it—no sense is gratified—it is attended with no profit—yet how common is it in almost every town and province! Remember that it is him, who is great and terrible, that says, he will not hold him guiltless that taketh his name in vain. Add to this, the dissolute debauchery, drunkenness, pride and excess which prevails in our land, and we shall not wonder that the LORD has a controversy with the kingdom. These and many other sins we have reason to bewail before GOD, and are the only discouragements in the present dispute. And if we are successful in our present struggle for liberty, we cannot expect to enjoy any lasting happiness without a reformation, and a life worthy of the glorious gospel. Was the fear of GOD suitably in our hearts, we should be invincible; for if GOD be for us, who can be against us? But, alas! there seems but little concern about forsaking sin and a saving acquaintance with GOD, though our present state is so alarming: All the horrors of a war is at hand—death is ready to triumph over his thousands, and are we still asleep in sin? We are called to fight for our brethren, our sons and our daughters, our wives and our houses; and if GOD forsakes us, our slavery is sure. Many trust too much on the arm of flesh; but let us place all our confidence in GOD, and use every prudential step. Nehemiah prays, but omits not the use of means, he sets a watch night and day to guard against the enemy, and every man is equipped for battle.

Thus, my hearers, I have considered every point which demanded our present attention. I hope that it has been made evident, that a defensive war is sinless, and consistent with the purest religion. This I can say, these arguments have removed all difficulties from my own breast. Seeing therefore, that it is sinless, and we are called to take the bloody weapons of death in hand, let not the expence of war discourage us. This indeed must be very great, but be it so; we fight not for present profit, no, our noble struggle is for

liberty itself, without which even life would be miserable—what though the half, nay the three parts, of our estates be lost, we shall have the fourth remaining;—our land is good, we can live. Providence can easily compensate our loss. And remember the LORD is great, matters may have a speedy issue; he can raise the spirit of the inhabitants of Great-Britain in our favour; —their voice shall reach the throne;—he is able to open the eyes of administration, or remove our enemies from about his Majesty, so that there may yet be a happy reconciliation with Great-Britain. We have considered the alarming call, which we have to take up arms;—let us unite as men possessed of a true sense of liberty. If any are not clear in conscience, let us not despise them. I confess some are provoking, but mildness is our duty; that with well-doing we may silence the obstinacy of evil men. On the whole, we are come to the unhappy state of a civil war, and I remember Bishop Burnet makes a remark to this effect, viz. "Of all calamities it is the greatest, for though we know where it begins, we know not where it shall end." If ever there was one time that called for more religion than another, this is the very time. And yet, alas! alas! how few are seeking GOD! how few are seeking their salvation, when death is even at the door, and all at stake! Let me therefore entreat you seriously to lay to heart the present state, and *"remember the* LORD, *which is great and terrible." Amen.*

★   ★   ★   ★   ★

A SERMON PREACHED AT YORK-TOWN, BEFORE CAPTAIN MORGAN'S AND CAPTAIN PRICE'S COMPANIES OF RIFLE-MEN

THURSDAY, JULY 20, 1775

Being the Day recommended by the Honorable Continental Congress for a General Fast throughout the Twelve United Colonies of North-America.

A PRAYER

O Most Mighty God, terrible in thy judgments, and wonderful in thy doings towards the children of men! We thy sinful servants here assembled before thee, confess, and adore the mysterious strokes of thy supreme Providence.

Long has the land rejoiced in the abundant emanation of thy tender mercies. Not our merit but thy goodness, has turned the wilderness into

fruitful fields, and the lonesome solitude into the cheerful dwellings of men. From year to year, almost from day to day, new habitations have sprung up, which ought to resound with the praise of thy holy name, of thy eternal and uncreated son, and of thy most blessed spirit.

But alas with grief and shame we acknowledge, that we have not always made a right use of thy continued favours. Not according to thy benefits have been our improvements, not according to thy bounty has been our gratitude. Our hearts smite us when we reflect on the many instances of our neglect of heavenly, and our attachment to earthly things. Creation and all its blessings, redemption and all its graces have but too frequently elapsed from our memories; and whilst we have been anxiously attentive to the life that now is, we have been foolishly inattentive to the promise of the life to come. We see, we feel, we own ourselves unworthy of the least of thy gracious vouchsafements; whereby as a state we have been gradually led from weakness to strength, as individuals from lonely helplessness to all the numerous comforts of society.

Hence doubtless it is; so it becomes us to believe, and so confess, that thou hast permitted the brightness of our prospect to be overclouded, hence, for without thy sovereign will nothing can take effect, the dreadful flame of discord has been kindled, and the devouring sword of war unsheathed: Hence, we are wounded in the tenderest part, are at variance with those whom hitherto we have revered as fathers, honoured as teachers, loved as brethren, and dealt with as friends. For it is not an open enemy that has done us this dishonour, neither is it an adversary that has magnified himself against us; but it is even our brother, our guide, and familiar friend, with whom we took sweet council, and in the most amicable intercourse, walked together in the house of God.

In this severe distress whither shall we fly but to thy presence? As a religious society, prayer is our only weapon: O may it prove the prayer of the humble, may it pierce through the clouds, reach the footsteps of thy Almighty throne, and not turn away till thou, O most high, regardest it! St. Paul, the chosen vessel of thy son, our saviour Jesus Christ, has taught us to make prayer and supplication for all men—for Kings, and for all that are in eminent place; that they, exercising their authority with righteousness and justice, we may lead a peaceable life in all godliness and honesty, urged therefore alike by our duty, our inclination, and our necessity, we meekly and devoutly implore thee in behalf of George thy servant, our King, and Governor, that wisdom descending from above may inform his soul, and regulate his thoughts, words, and actions; that looking upon himself as the common father and protector of all his subjects, he may cherish them all without distinction, watch over them for their good, and endeavour to preserve them in wealth, peace and happiness: and more particularly because it is our more immediate concern; that he may extend his care and regard to the inhabitants of this land and province—may know, and accept, and rejoice in their loyalty and dutiful affection—may be always ready to hear their complaints, and redress their sufferings, that so, happy in the felicity of his people, and distinguished by a life of goodness here, he may reign over us honoured and beloved, till it shall be thy pleasure to remove him to a life of glory hereafter. We also pray thee for the rulers of this our country, that thou would'st give them righteous and understanding hearts, that wisdom and gentleness, for-

544

titude and moderation may equally animate their councils and actions, that in the present dangerous crisis of affairs, they may leave nothing undone that appertains to our safety and welfare, nor do any thing from a principle of ambition, vain-glory, or self interest, that in the midst of war they may remember peace, and in the very moment of opposition, wish, long, pant, for a safe, happy, and honourable accommodation.

O Gracious God who alone makest men to be of one mind in a house, a city, a kingdom, a continent, and even a whole world, suffer not, in the sincerity of our hearts, and bitterness of our souls we beseech thee, suffer not those to remain long divided, whom the same language, the same descent, the same manners, the same constitution, the same religion, have so intimately united. We confess that we are severed for our mutual sins, but do thou most gracious father, re-unite us for thy mercy's sake. A terrible misconception is gone forth, remove it, O remove it, thou, whose conceptions are clearer than light, and who alone can'st regulate the wills and affections of sinful men. We humble ourselves under thy correcting hand, and confess the justice of all thy judgments, but we pray, we are allowed to pray, that the duration of our punishment may be shortened, and our tribulations come to an end. We pray for millions now under affliction, and for millions yet unborn in both countries, who without thy interposing favour, will hereafter be affected by the consequence of the present calamities, yet not on ourselves but on thee do we rely for our deliverance, not on our merits, but on our Saviour's merits do we depend for mercy: Hear us therefore, O Lord, hear thy people who call upon thee, that all the world may know, that thou art our saviour and mighty deliverer, through Jesus Christ our Lord.

A SERMON

That they may fear thee all the days that they live in the land which thou gavest to our fathers. I Kings, viii. 40

By the covenant which Almighty God was pleased to enter into with his people the Jews, an immediate intercourse was established between heaven and earth. Each deviation from the divine law was followed by sure pains and penalties; each return to holiness was a certain return to peace and prosperity. The sin of individuals never failed to bring upon them the curse, their repentance always restored them to the blessing.

Whensoever the state fell from its allegiance to Jehovah, then straightway came the great, the terrible day of vengeance: No sooner was the trumpet blown in Zion, the fast sanctified, and the solemn assembly called, no sooner did the Priests and Ministers weep between the porch and the alter, and say spare thy people, O Lord, and give not thine heritage to reproach; no sooner was the act of public humiliation performed, than public redress ensued—the Lord was jealous for his land, and pitied his people, and removed far off them the northern army.

On this foundation of God's unchangeable promise it is, that King Solomon at the dedication of the temple frames his petition in the verses preceding the text. His claim, the sacred historian goes on to inform us, was allowed; and the most high by fire from Heaven ratified afresh the covenant.

The process is most plain and most awful. Israel offended, the God of Israel punished with the famine, the pestilence, or the sword: The people conscious of their sins, made solemn prayer and supplication; the Lord saw the sincerity of their repentance, and heard from heaven his dwelling place and forgave them. What was the consequence? Man by correction learned to fear his God, and that holy fear insuring the divine protection, he continued to dwell in safety in the land of his fathers.

Happy will it be for us, happy will it be for every nation under the sun, if due attention is given to this important lesson. Were we but all convinced that *righteousness exalteth a kingdom, whilst sin is a reproach to any people,* and did we sanctify this conviction by practice, what a glorious, what a delightful scene of things would immediately present itself to our view! The nations would be bound in a golden chain of amity: None would groan under oppression, for no one would dare to oppress: The haughty invader, the cruel spoiler, the relentless destroyer, would be terms no more made use of: And each man sitting in safety under his own vine, and under his own fig tree would rapturously exclaim, —Lo this is the true, the genuine reign of Christ upon earth! Behold, the kingdoms of this world are become, not in name, but in deed, not in appearance, but in reality, the kingdoms of our Lord and of his Christ.

But the multiplied provocations of the sons of men forbid us to indulge the least expectation of so pleasing a prospect. The beautious vision shifts away from before our eyes, and in a moment we return to the real unhappy state of things, a world of discord and lamentation, of violence and woe, where the long forbearance of the Almighty is much more conspicuous than his judgments. Where it is more reasonable to ask, why cities and states are permitted to stand, than why they are destroyed—where the abominations of Canaan, and even of Sodom and Gomorrah, are frequent in some communities—and where in the best and most virtuous congregations, the preacher has still to cry aloud with solemn and unceasing voice,—except ye repent ye must inevitably perish.

Blessed forever be the hallowed lips of our most gracious redeemer, who foreseeing that faith would decay, and love wax cold among his disciples, has so affectionately called us to repentance, who delivering us from sin, and well knowing that we should lead ourselves therewith a fresh, has softened all the difficulties of this essential duty, and rendered it easy for us to perform; who kindly himself receives our intercessions, presents them to the throne of grace, and from thence procures us indubitable and authentic pardon! and blessed be the influence of that divine comforter, who has this day removed the stony from our hearts, and melted them into the sincerest contrition, all humbly to bewail our manifold transgressions, all devoutly to acknowledge the divine dispensations, all piously to pray for the removal of them from ourselves and our brethren, and all, I trust to depart in peace and comfort, full of good hopes and good resolutions, unburthened of our sins, our consciences appeased, and the love of the Father, of the Son, and of the Holy Ghost, beaming upon our souls with unclouded splendor.

Religious discomposure tends ultimately to our composure and tranquility, *When the judgments of God are abroad, the inhabitants of the earth learn righteousness.* Did we ever expect to see the day, when all the various communions of this wide-extended continent should be bowed as the heart of one man to deprecate the wrath, and to entreat the protection of heaven, in one and the same hour, in one and the same cause? O it is a goodly sight, and all the angelick host will applaud our humiliation! it is to begin at the right end; for being once secure of defence from above, what is it that can possibly confound us. Lovest thou, and art thou beloved of thy maker? His friendship *shall deliver thee in six troubles, yea, in seven shall no evil touch thee; in famine he shall redeem thee from death, and in war from the power of the sword, thou shalt not be afraid of the scourge of the tongue, nor of destruction when it cometh, yea though thou walkest through the valley of the shadow of death thou shalt fear no evil, for he is with thee his rod and his staff shall comfort thee.*

The present situation is the most distressful that could have happened to beings endued with humanity. It is more replete with anguish, than even with danger. I have heard, and can well believe, that the opposing armies respect and pity each other in the very instant that their weapons are uplifted to destroy. Can we avoid praying that hearts so framed might be permitted to meet in equal and honourable union; neither conquering nor conquered, but as free citizens of the same realm, intitled to the same rights and privileges. Much, too much, does our case resemble that recorded in scripture where King Rehoboam assembled the house of Judah, with the tribe of Benjamin to fight against the house of Israel: But alas! alas! there is no Prophet, no Shemiah the man of God, to speak unto *Rehoboam and to all the house of Judah and Benjamin, saying, ye shall not go up, nor fight against your brethren the house of Israel; return ye every man to his house.*

But my duty in this sacred place leads me no farther than to bewail the miseries brought upon this country by those fatal misconceptions that have gone forth on the other side of the atlantick, and to exhort my little flock, so to prepare themselves by unfeigned faith, by holy prayer, and by genuine repentance to deserve (if man can be said to deserve) the temporal blessings of the Almighty, which I trust, nor trust in vain, will be poured out upon us, if we patiently and manfully abide the appointed trial. There is who reigns on high, and at his pleasure *breaketh the bow and knappeth the spear in sunder, and burneth the chariots in the fire;* for his good time let us wait with calmness and submission, and let us endeavour to shorten the period by the integrity of our behaviour, and by the fervour of our devotions. That good time will come; let us not doubt it for we have a gracious master in heaven; when the labour of some of our fellow citizens, and the sorrows of others shall cease—when our darkness shall be turned into light, and our mourning into joy—when our loyalty shall stand confirmed, and our liberty established by sufferings—and when we shall meet again in the Lord's house, to celebrate his returning mercies, whose wrath we now deprecate, and to whose judgments we now bend with submissive addoration.

For in revolving the days of old, and considering the manner in which it has pleased the al-

mighty ruler to exercise his moral government, there is no reason to think, that any state legitimately constituted, will be destroyed by his supreme fiat, till that state has rendered itself unworthy of continuance, by acts that defile its purity, and corrupt its very essence. I say legitimately constituted, meaning where the natural rights of mankind have been respected in its constitution, because with domination founded in tyranny the allwise, and alljust ruler has no connection: That is not his work, but rather the work of that malignant being, who delights in human wretchedness. Now the means by which the rulers of a state may shamefully deviate, and thereby provoke the fulness of divine anger, are chiefly idolatry, persecution for religious opinions, wanton invasion of their neighbours, mean pilfering and stealing of adjacent lands, and laws made on purpose to oppress, or corrupt the people. When enormities such as these prevail, it is neither to be wondered or murmured at, if the storm descends from above, and sweeps away such a perverted government from the face of the earth. But from enormities such as these, blacker than the blackest night, more savage than the howlings of the wild beasts of the forest, disgraceful to reason, to truth, to justice, and to human nature, this land of our hopes, and desires is most notoriously, and remarkably free. No man can dwell therein who believes in more than one God, the Creator of the universe, and none who profess themselves the servants of that all-glorious being, can be molested for their religious principles. It is not upon the records of history, nor in the memory of man, that this government has ever in any shape, much less in wantonness, invaded the property of others: From the poor untutored Indian it has uniformly disdained to borrow, and abhorred to steal: Fair and open purchases have preceded every settlement: Its laws—but why should I praise its laws to those who live under them, when their good report is spread far and near, when I have heard it a thousand times acknowledged in Europe, that they are the mildest and most equitable now in force on the terrestrial globe? Can we entertain a suspicion that such a state is obnoxious to the supreme legislator? No, we may rather comfort ourselves with the assurance, that however greatly we have sinned as individuals, yet that the judge of all the earth will not suffer the benevolent work of one immortal man to be defaced or demolished.

With respect to the present unnatural disputes, it would ill become my place and station to say any thing with the tone of decisive authority: My master's kingdom is not of this world, nor am I appointed a Ruler, a Judge, or a Divider: But if nothing more is designed, than what is professed; if to preserve our rights and privileges be the sole aim of the Continental Congress, and of those who assemble at their biddings; if no sparks of disloyalty, no desire of change, no intentions of removing the ancient land marks, lie concealed beneath the fair outside of public good; I say, if this be the case, and according to the best of my observation it really is so, then we have a good cause, and may expect the blessing of Heaven upon our endeavours. For the blessing of legal, and equal Liberty we pray; and tho' our prayers are sincere, yet because of our tender attachment to our parent state, grief mixes with our devotions: For the same liberty our fellow citizens are to fight; and they will surely do it, with steady tho' reluctant courage—with hearts that wish to save, in the same moment that they are obliged to destroy.

It happens, that many defenders of this land are now before me. Summoned to immediate service, they have arrived here at this solemn season, and have joined in our act of humiliation. These I will exhort to go on to their appointed destination, in the fear of God, in the sentiments of true honor, in the love of Liberty and of their Country. Descended from ancestors who in the old world often proved, they preferred freedom to life, I trust you have not degenerated from their nobleness of soul, but will even strive to exceed your forefathers in deeds of valour, generosity and humanity. Remember that a glorious cause is put into your hands; beware of disgracing it by any unworthy proceeding: Remember, that the Congress, where resides the collected wisdom and the general voice of the people, breathes a firm and manly, but yet a moderate and reconciling spirit: Remember that they mean to hazard every thing dear for the recovery of our rights, and the moment those are recovered to sheathe the sword. I have a commission, and it is written in the most luminous characters of truth; to bid you honour the King—yet I trust you want not the admonition: But I have no commission to bid you honour those, who wickedly stand between the throne and the subject; and

yet I believe, you will begin to respect them, when they learn to respect themselves, and the common rights of humanity. Go, Brethren, and may the Lord of Hosts be with you: Go, and fill up the measure of your fame, more by generous behaviour, than even by feats of arms: Go, and defend our franchises, our wives, our children, and possessions: Go, and bring us back a speedy and honourable peace: And having done so, may you long enjoy in the bosom of that peace, the illustrious title you will have acquired of Protectors and Preservers of your Country.

For us, Brethren, beloved in the Lord, let us, as I have already admonished you, proceed as we have this day begun, and strive to deserve in some sort, the Benediction of the Almighty. Nor only now with united hearts and voices, but also singly and separately in the closet, unfeignedly confess and deplore our many sins, and offer up our supplications to the allwise, omnipotent, and merciful Disposer of all events, to forgive our iniquities, remove our calamities, and avert those dessolating judgments with which we are threatened: That he will bless our rightful Sovereign King George the Third, and inspire him with wisdom to discern and pursue the true interest of all his subjects: That a speedy end may be put to the discord between Great-Britain and the American Colonies without further effusion of blood; and that the British nation may be influenced to regard the things that belong to her peace before they are hid from her eyes: That these Colonies may be ever under the care and protection of a kind Providence; and be prospered in all their interests: That the divine blessing may descend upon all our civil rulers, and upon the Representatives of the People in their several Assemblies and Conventions; that they may be directed to wise and effectual measures for preserving the Union, and securing the just Rights and Privileges of the Colonies: That virtue and true religion may revive and flourish throughout our land: That America may soon behold a gracious interposition of Heaven, for the redress of her many grievances, the restoration of her invaded rights, a reconciliation with the parent state on terms constitutional and honourable to both: And that her civil and religious Liberties may be secured to the latest posterity.

THE SPIRITUAL WARFARE

The New England Clergy and the American Revolution, by Alice Baldwin, New York, 1858

The New England clergy of the eighteenth century occupied a position of peculiar influence and power in the life of their own communities and of the several colonies. . . . The sources from which the New England ministers developed their theories may be learned partly from the quotations and foot-notes which frequently are to be found in sermons and pamphlets, partly from diaries, letters, and other documents. . . .

The most common source was the Bible. The Old Testament furnished many illustrations of covenant relations, of the limitations placed upon rulers and people, of natural rights, of the divine constitution, etc. The New Testament gave authority for the liberties of Christians, for the relation of Christians to those in authority over them, and for the right of resistance. Indeed, there was never a principle derived from more

secular reading that was not strengthened and sanctified by the Scriptures. . . . The next great source was the works of John Locke, his essays on religious toleration and human understanding as well as those on government. He was quoted by name as early as 1738. . . .

Another source of political theory was the commentaries and annotations on the Bible. Those most frequently mentioned were Whitby, Henry, and Pool. (Daniel Whitby, *A Paraphrase and Commentary on the New Testament,* 2 vols., 1700, many editions; also sermons, treatises, and other works; Matthew Henry, *An Exposition of the Old and New Testament,* 5 vols., 1st collective ed. 1710 (many later editions); *Miscellaneous Works,* 1st ed. 1726; Matthew Pool, *Synopsis Criticorum aliorumque S. Scripturae Interpretum,* 5 vol., 1669-76;).

★　　　★　　　★　　　★　　　★

Matthew Henry's Commentary on the Whole Bible, Vol. VI, Reprint, New York

EPHESIANS *6: 10-18*

10 Finally, my brethren, be strong in the Lord, and in the power of his might. 11 Put on the whole armour of God, that ye may be able to stand against the wiles of the devil. 12 For we wrestle not against flesh and blood, but against principalities, against powers, against the rulers of the darkness of this world, against spiritual wickedness in high places. 13 Wherefore take

unto you the whole armour of God, that ye may be able to withstand in the evil day, and having done all, to stand. 14 Stand therefore, having your loins girt about with truth, and having on the breastplate of righteousness; 15 And your feet shod with the preparation of the gospel of peace; 16 Above all, taking the shield of faith, wherewith ye shall be able to quench all the fiery darts of the wicked. 17 And take the helmet of salvation, and the sword of the Spirit, which is

548

the word of God: 18 Praying always with all prayer and supplication in the Spirit, and watching thereunto with all perseverance and supplication for all saints.

Here is a general exhortation to constancy in our Christian course, and to courage in our Christian warfare. Is not our life a warfare? It is so; for we struggle with the common calamities of human life. Is not our religion much more a warfare? It is so; for we struggle with the opposition of the powers of darkness, and with many enemies who would keep us from God and heaven. We have enemies to fight against, a captain to fight for, a banner to fight under, and certain rules of war by which we are to govern ourselves. *"Finally, my brethren (v. 10), it yet remains that you apply yourselves to your work and duty as Christian soldiers."* Now it is requisite that a soldier be both stout-hearted and well armed. If Christians be soldiers of Jesus Christ,

I. They must see that they be stout-hearted. This is prescribed here: *Be strong in the Lord,* &c. Those who have so many battles to fight, and who, in their way to heaven, must dispute every pass, with dint of sword, have need of a great deal of courage. *Be strong therefore,* strong for service, strong for suffering, strong for fighting. Let a soldier be ever so well armed without, if he have not within a good heart, his armour will stand him in little stead. Note, Spiritual strength and courage are very necessary for our spiritual warfare. Be strong in the Lord, either in his cause and for his sake, or rather in his strength. We have no sufficient strength of our own. Our natural courage is as perfect cowardice, and our natural strength as perfect weakness; but all our sufficiency is of God. In his strength we must go forth and go on. By the actings of faith, we must fetch in grace and help from heaven to enable us to do that which of ourselves we cannot do, in our Christian work and warfare. We should stir up ourselves to resist temptations in a reliance upon God's all-sufficiency and the omnipotence of his might.

II. They must be well armed: *"Put on the whole armour of God (v. 11),* make use of all the proper defensives and weapons for repelling the temptations and stratagems of Satan—get and exercise all the Christian graces, the whole armour, that no part be naked and exposed to the enemy."* Observe, Those who would approve themselves to have true grace must aim at all grace, the whole armour. It is called the armour of God, because he both prepares and bestows it.

We have no armour of our own that will be armour of proof in a trying time. Nothing will stand us in stead but the armour of God. This armour is prepared for us, but we must put it on; that is, we must pray for grace, we must use the grace given us, and draw it out into act and exercise as there is occasion. The reason assigned why the Christian should be completely armed is *that he may be able to stand against the wiles of the devil*—that he may be able to hold out, and to overcome, notwithstanding all the devil's assaults, both of force and fraud, all the deceits he puts upon us, all the snares he lays for us, and all his machinations against us. This the apostle enlarges upon here, and shows,

1. What our danger is, and what need we have to put on this whole armour, considering what sort of enemies we have to deal with—the devil and all the powers of darkness: *For we wrestle not against flesh and blood,* &c., v. 12. The combat for which we are to be prepared is not against ordinary human enemies, nor barely against men compounded of *flesh and blood,* nor against our own corrupt natures singly considered, but against the several ranks of devils, who have a government which they exercise in this world. (1) We have to do with a subtle enemy, an enemy who uses wiles and stratagems, as v. 11. He has a thousand ways of beguiling unstable souls: hence he is called a serpent for subtlety, an old serpent, experienced in the art and trade of tempting. (2) He is a powerful enemy: *Principalities,* and *powers,* and *rulers.* They are numerous, they are vigorous; and rule in those heathen nations which are yet in darkness. The dark parts of the world are the seat of Satan's empire. Yea, they are usurping princes over all men who are yet in a state of sin and ignorance. Satan's is a kingdom of darkness; whereas Christ's is a kingdom of light. (3) They are spiritual enemies: *Spiritual wickedness in high places,* or wicked spirits, as some translate it. The devil is a spirit, a wicked spirit; and our danger is the greater from our enemies because they are unseen, and assault us ere we are aware of them. The devils are wicked spirits, and they chiefly annoy the saints with, and provoke them to, spiritual wickednesses, pride, envy, malice, &c. These enemies are said to be *in high places,* or in heavenly places, so the word is, taking heaven (as one says) for the whole *expansum,* or spreading out of the air between the earth and the stars, the air being the place from which the devils assault us. Or the meaning may be, *"We wrestle* about heavenly places or heavenly things;"* so some of the ancients inter-

pret it. Our enemies strive to prevent our ascent to heaven, to deprive us of heavenly blessings and to obstruct our communion with heaven. They assault us in the things that belong to our souls, and labour to deface the heavenly image in our hearts; and therefore we have need to be upon our guard against them. We have need of faith in our Christian warfare, because we have spiritual enemies to grapple with, as well as of faith in our Christian work, because we have spiritual strength to fetch in. Thus you see your danger.

2. What our duty is: to take and put on the whole armour of God, and then to stand our ground, and withstand our enemies.

(1) We must *withstand, v. 13.* We must not yield to the devil's allurements and assaults, but oppose them. Satan is said to *stand up against us,* 1 Chron. xxi. 1. If he stand up against us, we must stand against him; set up, and keep up, an interest in opposition to the devil. Satan is the wicked one, and his kingdom is the kingdom of sin: to stand against Satan is to strive against sin. *That you may be able to withstand in the evil day,* in the day of temptation, or of any sore affliction.

(2) We must stand our ground: *And, having done all, to stand.* We must resolve, by God's grace, not to yield to Satan. Resist him, and he will flee. If we give back, he will get ground. If we distrust our cause, or our leader, or our armour, we give him advantage. Our present business is to withstand the assaults of the devil, and to stand it out; and then, having done all that is incumbent on the good soldiers of Jesus Christ, our warfare will be accomplished, and we shall be finally victorious.

(3) We must stand armed; and this is here most enlarged upon. Here is a Christian in complete armour: and the armour is divine: *Armour of God, armour of light,* Rom. xiii. 12. *Armour of righteousness,* 2 Cor. vi. 7. The apostle specifies the particulars of this armour, both offensive and defensive. The military girdle or belt, the breastplate, the greaves (or soldier's shoes), the shield, the helmet, and the sword. It is observable that, among them all, there is none for the back; if we turn our back upon the enemy, we lie exposed.

[1] Truth or sincerity is our girdle, v. 14. It was prophesied of Christ (Isa. xi:5) that *righteousness should be the girdle of his loins and faithfulness the girdle of his reins.* That which Christ was girded with all Christians must be girded with. God desires truth, that is, sincerity, in the inward parts. This is the strength of our loins;

and it girds on all other pieces of our armour, and therefore is first mentioned. I know no religion without sincerity. Some understand it of the doctrine of the truths of the gospel: they should cleave to us as the girdle does to the loins, Jer. xiii. 11. This will restrain from libertinism and licentiousness, as a girdle retrains and keeps in the body. This is the Christian soldier's belt: ungirded with this, he is unblessed.

[2] Righteousness must be our breast-plate. The breast-plate secures the vitals, shelters the heart. The righteousness of Christ imputed to us is our breast-plate against the arrows of divine wrath. The righteousness of Christ implanted in us is our breast-plate to fortify the heart against the attacks which Satan makes against us. The apostle explains this in 1 Thess. v. 8, *Putting on the breast-plate of faith and love.* Faith and love include all Christian graces; for by faith we are united to Christ and by love to our brethren. These will infer a diligent observance of our duty to God, and a righteous deportment towards men, in all the offices of justice, truth, and charity.

[3] Resolution must be as the greaves to our legs: *And their feet shod with the preparation of the gospel of peace,* v. 15. Shoes, or greaves of brass, or the like, were formerly part of the military armour (1 Sam. xvii. 6): the use of them was to defend the feet against the gall-traps, and sharp sticks, which were wont to be laid privily in the way, to obstruct the marching of the enemy, those who fell upon them being unfit to march. *The preparation of the gospel of peace* signifies a prepared and resolved frame of heart, to adhere to the gospel and abide by it, which will enable us to walk with a steady pace in the way of religion, notwithstanding the difficulties and dangers that may be in it. It is styled the *gospel of peace* because it brings all sorts of peace, peace with God, with ourselves, and with one another. It may also be meant of that which prepares for the entertainment of the gospel, namely, repentance. With this our feet must be shod: for by living a life of repentance we are armed against temptations to sin, and the designs of our great enemy. Dr. Whitby thinks this may be the sense of the words: "That you may be ready for the combat, be shod with the gospel of peace, endeavour after that peaceable and quiet mind which the gospel calls for. Be not easily provoked, nor prone to quarrel: but show all gentleness and all long-suffering to all men, and this will certainly preserve you from many great temptations and persecutions, as did those shoes of brass the soldiers from those gall-traps," &c.

[4] Faith must be our shield: *Above all,* or chiefly, *taking the shield of faith,* v. 16. This is more necessary than any of them. Faith is all in all to us in an hour of temptation. The breastplate secures the vitals; but with the shield we turn every way. *This is the victory over the world, even our faith.* We are to be fully persuaded of the truth of all God's promises and threatenings, such a faith being of great use against temptations. Consider faith as it *is the evidence of things not seen and the substance of things hoped for,* and it will appear to be of admirable use for this purpose. Faith, as receiving Christ and the benefits of redemption, so deriving grace from him, is like a shield, a sort of universal defence. Our enemy the devil is here called *the wicked one.* He is wicked himself, and he endeavours to make us wicked. His temptations are called *darts,* because of their swift and undiscerned flight, and the deep wounds that they give to the soul; *fiery darts,* by way of allusion to the poisonous darts which were wont to inflame the parts which were wounded with them, and therefore were so called, as the serpents with poisonous stings are called fiery serpents. Violent temptations, by which the soul is set on fire of hell, are the darts which Satan shoots at us. Faith is the shield with which we must quench these fiery darts, wherein we should receive them, and so render them ineffectual, that they may not hit us, or at least that they may not hurt us. Observe, Faith, acted upon the word of God and applying that, acted upon the grace of Christ and improving that, quenches the darts of temptation.

[5] Salvation must be our helmet (v. 17); that is, *hope,* which has salvation for its object; so 1 Thess. v. 8. The helmet secures the head. A good hope of salvation, well founded and well built, will both purify the soul and keep it from being defiled by Satan, and it will comfort the soul and keep it from being troubled and tormented by Satan. He would tempt us to despair; but good hope keeps us trusting in God, and rejoicing in him.

[6] The word of God is the sword of the Spirit. The sword is a very necessary and useful part of a soldier's furniture. The word of God is very necessary, and of great use to the Christian, in order to his maintaining the spiritual warfare and succeeding in it. It is called *the sword of the Spirit,* because it is of the Spirit's inditing and he renders it efficacious and powerful, and *sharper than a two-edged sword.* Like Goliath's sword, none like that; with this we

assault the assailants. Scripture-arguments are the most powerful arguments to repel temptation with. Christ himself resisted Satan's temptations with, *It is written,* Matt. iv. 4, 6, 7, 10. This, being hid in the heart, will preserve from sin (Ps. cxix. 11), and will mortify and kill those lusts and corruptions that are latent there.

[7] Prayer must buckle on all the other parts of our Christian armour, v. 18. We must join prayer with all these graces, for our defence against these spiritual enemies, imploring help and assistance of God, as the case requires: and we must pray always. Not as though we were to do nothing else but pray, for there are other duties of religion and of our respective stations in the world that are to be done in their place and season; but we should keep up constant times of prayer, and be constant to them. We must pray upon all occasions, and as often as our own and others' necessities call us to it. We must always keep up a disposition to prayer, and should intermix ejaculatory prayers with other duties, and with common business. Though set and solemn prayer may sometimes be unseasonable (as when other duties are to be done), yet pious ejaculations *can* never be so. We must pray *with all prayer and supplication,* with all kinds of prayer: public, private, and secret, social and solitary, solemn and sudden; with all the parts of prayer: confession of sin, petition for mercy, and thanksgivings for favours received. We must pray *in the Spirit;* our spirits must be employed in the duty and we must do it by the grace of God's good Spirit. We must *watch thereunto,* endeavouring to keep our hearts in a praying frame, and taking all occasions, and improving all opportunities, for the duty: we must watch to all the motions of our own hearts towards the duty. When God says, *Seek my face,* our hearts must comply, Ps. xxvii. 8. This we must do *with all perseverance.* We must abide by the duty of prayer, whatever change there may be in our outward circumstances; and we must continue in it as long as we live in the world. We must persevere in a particular prayer; not cutting it short, when our hearts are disposed to enlarge, and there is time for it, and our occasions call for it. We must likewise persevere in particular requests, notwithstanding some present discouragements and repulses. And we must pray *with supplication,* not for ourselves only, but *for all saints;* for we are members one of another. Observe, None are so much saints, and in so good a condition in this world, but they need our prayers, and they ought to have them.

APPENDIX

BIBLIOGRAPHY

ADAMS, JOHN QUINCY. *The Lives of James Madison and James Monroe.* Buffalo, 1850.

ADAMS, SAMUEL. *The Writings of Samuel Adams.* Edited by Harry Alonzo Cushing. Volume 4. New York: G. P. Putnam's Sons, 1908.

ADLER, SIMON L. *Money and Money Units in the American Colonies.* The Rochester Historical Society Publication Fund Series, Vol. VIII, 1929.

ALVORD, CLARENCE WALWORTH. *The British Ministry and the Treaty of Fort Stanwix.* Proceedings of the State Historical Society of Wisconsin. Madison: 1909.

BALDWIN, ALICE M. *The New England Clergy and the American Revolution.* Frederick Ungar Publishing Co. New York, 1958.

BANCROFT, GEORGE. *History of the American Revolution.* Volume II. London, 1852.
History of the United States of America. Volume I. New York, 1886.

BATWELL, DANIEL. *A Sermon Preached at York-town, Before Captain Morgan's and Captain Price's Companies of Rifle-Men.* July 20, 1775. Philadelphia: 1775.

BOUDINOT, ELIAS. *The Life Public Services, Addresses and Letters of Elias Boudinot, LL.D.* Volume II. Houghton, Mifflin And Company, Boston and New York, 1896.

BROADSIDE. *A Dialogue spoken at opening the Public Grammar-School at Wilmington,* on Tuesday, October 26, 1773. Library Company of Philadelphia.

BROWN, HENRY ARMITT. *The Valley Forge Oration, June 19, 1878.* Philadelphia: 1895. Historical Society of Pennsylvania.

BURNET, GILBERT. *The History of the Reformation of The Church Of England.* Volume I. Oxford, 1889.

CONNECTICUT. *The Public Records of the Colony of Connecticut, October, 1772, to April, 1775, Inclusive.* Edited by Charles J. Hoadly. Hartford: 1887.

DEXTER, HENRY MARTYN. *The Congregationalism of the last Three Hundred Years, As Seen in its Literature.* New York: Harper & Brothers, 1880.

DWIGHT, TIMOTHY. *A Dissertation on the History, Eloquence, and Poetry of the Bible.* Delivered at the Public Commencement at New Haven, 1772.

ELLET, ELIZABETH F. *The Women of the American Revolution.* 2 Volumes. New York: 1849.

ELLICOTT, JOHN, Ed., *A New Testament Commentary for English Readers.* London: 1884. Vol. I, III.

EVANS, CHARLES. *American Bibliography,* Volume 5. 1903.

FOLJAMBE, REV. S. W. *The Hand of God in American History.* A Sermon . . . at the Annual Election, January 5, 1876. Boston: 1876.

FORD, WORTHINGTON C., Ed., *The Journals of the Continental Congress, 1774–1789,* Vol. II. Washington: 1905.

FORCE, PETER, Ed., *American Archives,* 4th Series, Volumes I, II, III. Washington, 1837–46.

FRANKLIN, BENJAMIN. *The Works of Benjamin Franklin.* Edited by Jared Sparks, Volume VII. Boston: 1840.

FRENCH, REV. JONATHAN. *A Sermon delivered on the Anniversary Thanksgiving November 29, 1798.* Andover: 1799.

FROTHINGHAM, RICHARD JR. *History of the Siege of Boston, and of the Battles of Lexington, Concord, and Bunker Hill.* Boston: Little and Brown, 1851.

GREEN, J. R. *A Short History of the English People.* New York: 1879.

GREEN, HARRY CLINTON and MARY WOLCOTT. *The Pioneer Mothers of America.* New York: G. P. Putnam's Sons, 1912.

HARRIS, GEORGE H. *The Iroquois in the Revolution.* The Rochester Historical Society Publication Fund Series, Vol. VIII. 1929.

HART, REV. LEVI. *The Importance of Parental Fidelity*

in the Education of Children Illustrated. February 28, 1792. Norwich: 1792.

HENRY, MATTHEW. *Commentary on the Whole Bible.* Volume VI.

HITCHCOCK, REV. GAD. *A Sermon Preached at Plymouth, December 22, 1774.* Boston: 1775.

HODGE, PROF. CHARLES. *The Constitutional History of the Presbyterian Church in the United States of America.* Part I and II. Philadelphia: 1839, 1840.
Systematic Theology, Volume III. 1871–3. Reprinted by Wm. B. Eerdmans Publishing Company, Grand Rapids, Michigan.

HOWARD, REV. SIMEON. *A Sermon preached to the Ancient and Honorable Artillery Company, in Boston,* June 7, 1773. Boston: 1773.

INGLIS, REV. CHARLES. *A Memorial Concerning the Iroquois . . . 1775.* The Documentary History of the State of New York, edited by E. B. O'Callaghan. Volume IV. Albany: 1851.

JONES, REV. DAVID. *Defensive War in a Just Cause Sinless.* A Sermon preached on the day of the Continental Fast, at Tredyffryn, in Chester County, July 20, 1775. Philadelphia: 1775.

LOSSING, BENSON J. *Seventeen Hundred and Seventy-Six.* New York: 1847.

MASSACHUSETTS. *The Journals of the Provincial Congress of Massachusetts in 1774 and 1775.* Boston: 1838.

NARRATIVE OF THE PLANTING OF THE MASSACHUSETTS COLONY, Anno. 1628. *Collections* of the Massachusetts Historical Society, 4th series, IV, 1858.

NEANDER, DR. AUGUSTUS. *General History of the Christian Religion and Church.* Boston: Houghton, Mifflin & Co., 1871.

NEW ENGLAND GAZETTEER. John Hayward. Concord, N.H.: 1839.

NILES, HEZEKIAH, Ed., *Principles and Acts of the Revolution in America.* Republication by A. S. Barnes & Co.: 1876.

OBSERVATIONS ON THE AMERICAN REVOLUTION. Published according to a Resolution of Congress, by their Committee. Philadelphia: 1779.

RAMSAY, DAVID. *History of the United States from their First Settlement as English Colonies, in 1607 to 1808.* Vol. I, II. Philadelphia: 1816.

THACHER, JAMES, M.D. *Military Journal of the American Revolution.* Reprinted, 1862.

THORNTON, JOHN WINGATE. *The Pulpit of the American Revolution.* Boston: 1860.

TURNER, REV. CHARLES. *A Sermon preached at Plymouth, December 22d, 1773.* Boston: 1774.

WARREN, MERCY, PAPERS, 1709–1841. Massachusetts Historical Society. Boston.

WARREN, MERCY. *History of the Rise, Progress and Termination of the American Revolution.* Vol. I. Boston: 1805.

WEBSTER, DANIEL. *The Works of Daniel Webster.* Vol. I & II. Boston: Little, Brown & Co., 1851.

WEBSTER, NOAH. *History of the United States.* New Haven: 1833.

WILBERFORCE, BISHOP SAMUEL. *A History of the Protestant Episcopal Church in America.* London: 1856.

WILLIAMS, ELISHA. *A Seasonable Plea for the Liberty of Conscience and the Right of Private Judgment.* Boston: 1744.

WINSOR, JUSTIN, Ed., *Narrative and Critical History of America.* Vol. VIII. Boston: 1889.

WINTHROP, ROBERT C. *Addresses and Speeches on Various Occasions.* Vol. I, II. Boston: Little, Brown & Co., 1852.

WITHERSPOON, JOHN. *Letters on the Education of Children and on Marriage.* New York: 1797.

BIOGRAPHIES OF THE WRITERS

SIMON L. ADLER
1867–1934

Born at Seneca Falls, N.Y., this eminent jurist received a Bachelor of Law degree from Cornell University in 1889. He was admitted to the bar in 1892 and started his law practice in Rochester. Between 1900 and 1907, he practiced law in New York City.

Adler became active in politics while living in New York. In 1910, he was elected to the State Assembly. During his service there he became chairman of the committee on banks whose work resulted in a "complete revision" of the state's banking laws. In 1927, he became U.S. District Court judge and, in 1931, senior judge of the Western New York District.

Judge Adler was greatly interested in American history and wrote several historical monographs, including *Sullivan's Campaign 1779* and *Money and Money Units in the American Colonies*, which were republished by the Rochester Historical Society.

CLARENCE WALWORTH ALVORD
1868–1928

Born in Greenfield, Massachusetts, he was descended of a long line of New Englanders and was educated in New England, graduating from Williams College in 1891 after having attended schools in Northampton and Phillips Academy, Andover. In 1897 he joined the faculty of the University of Illinois where he taught for nineteen years and where he received his PhD in 1900.

Alvord's appointment as general editor of the *Illinois Historical Collections*, published by the state Historical Library, was the result of his discovery in 1905 of the long-lost historical records of two old French settlements in Illinois: Cahokia and Kaskaskia. This appointment was followed in 1909 by another as director of the University's research bureau (The Illinois Historical Survey). In 1920, he wrote the first volume of the five-volume *Centennial History of Illinois*.

In addition to his many distinguished contributions to regional American history he was very knowledgeable in regard to the broad canvas of American history. His *Mississippi Valley in British Politics*, published in 1917, won the Loubat prize as the most outstanding work in the field of American history to appear over a five-year period. This two-volume history of the years between 1763 and 1774 is a brilliant study which throws new light on both English and American Colonial history. Its many merits won the admira-

Prepared by
Mary Elaine
Adams Swanson

557

tion of European as well as American scholars.

In 1925, Alvord was invited to give the Raleigh lecture at the British Academy. The following year, he was the first American to give the Creighton lecture at the University of London. In the years before these honors, he organized the Mississippi Valley Historical Association (1907) and started its magazine (1914), the *Mississippi Valley Historical Review*, later known as the *Journal of American History*, which he edited until 1923. From 1920 until his retirement in 1923, he was on the faculty of the University of Minnesota as professor of history. After retiring, he spent his last years in Europe writing, studying, and lecturing.

HENRY ARMITT BROWN
1844–1878

"Politics did not lower in him the standard of high morality and honor. His ambition was founded upon his patriotism . . . How safe would be the Republic and how glorious its destiny were all its sons like him." So runs a eulogy for Henry Armitt Brown, the brilliant young orator who died at the age of 33. He was born at Philadelphia, Pa., December 1, 1844 and entered Yale in 1861 where he was soon extremely active. Here his talent for oratory first came to the surface and soon he was much in demand as a speaker at various University events. Brown read widely, particularly the Latin classics, but he also read deeply on philosophy, history, and political economy. After his graduation from Yale, he entered Columbia Law School, New York City. He was admitted to the bar in 1869.

On December 19, 1872, he was asked to speak at a complimentary dinner honoring former Chief Justice Thompson. As a representative of "the Juniors of the Bar," his was the eighth and last "toast" of the evening, but it created a sensation. From then on he was often asked to speak in the political arena. He had the happy faculty of bringing to the surface with his hearers their own dormant sense of patriotism and idealism, making their heritage come to life before them. *The Philadelphia Press*, commenting on the audience's reaction to his address on the 100th anniversary of the meeting of Congress in 1774, said: "Those there seated were no longer men of business, but sons of liberty, who had suddenly realized the grandeur of their birthright." Perhaps the most famous of his orations was that on the anniversary of the evacuation of Valley Forge. Delivered on June 19, 1878, this was his last and most

brilliant address. On his return home he came down with a fever and died on August 21, 1878. It was one biographer's hope that his brief, but outstanding, career might be an inspiration to other young people. "The young men in our American colleges, we think, ever look forward to becoming public men, the recognized servants of the Republic; and they should act upon the principle that, from the very talents entrusted to them, they are expected to become the strong stays and helpers of the commonwealth."

HENRY MARTYN DEXTER
1821–1890

He was the son of a distinguished Massachusetts clergyman, Elijah Dexter, who was minister of the Congregational Church at Plympton, Plymouth County, for some forty-two years. Henry was born at Plympton and enrolled at Yale when he was fifteen. Family finances made it necessary for him to earn part of his tuition, which he did by teaching during the summer.

After his graduation in 1840, he became principal of a school at Rochester, Massachusetts. He held this position for a year when he then enrolled in Andover Theological Seminary. In the year of his graduation from Andover (1844) he was ordained minister of a new church in Manchester, New Hampshire. From this post, he was called to Boston in 1849 to serve as minister of the Pine Street Church where he remained for eighteen years.

Not long after moving to Boston, he began contributing articles to the *Congregationalist* and also became a special correspondent for the *New York Independent*. By 1851, he was invited to become an editor of the *Congregationalist*. He was to remain with this periodical until his death, becoming its editor-in-chief in 1856. Later, in 1867, he became part owner and editor of the combined *Congregationalist and Boston Recorder*, and resigned his ministry at the Pine Street Church in order to accept this full-time activity.

He was always intensely devoted to the concepts embodied in the Congregational Church and was keenly interested in New England's history. A fine scholar, he wrote many books and was often called upon to preach and to lecture on Congregational history.

Among his works are: *Congregationalism* (1865); *The Church Polity of The Pilgrims* (1870); *As to Roger William* (1876); *The Congregationalism of the Last 300 Years* (1880); and *A Handbook of Congregationalism* (1880).

TIMOTHY DWIGHT
1752–1817

This grandson of Jonathan Edwards gained distinction in three fields: theology, literature, and education. He showed early signs of intellectual brilliance, and his mother undertook to educate him at home. By the time he was thirteen, he was ready to enter Yale, where he graduated in 1769. He then became principal of the Hopkins Grammar School in New Haven, Connecticut and remained there until 1771 when he returned to Yale as a tutor.

Deeply religious, he became a born-again Christian at the age of fifteen. In 1776, the Congregational Church gave him a license to preach and a year later he left Yale to become a Chaplain in the Continental Army. He was strongly patriotic and while with the Army, he became well known as the author of several patriotic songs. In 1779, he resigned his chaplaincy and went to live at Northampton, Massachusetts, the town of his birth. Soon he was involved in several activities. He opened a school, ran two farms, and in 1783, he became minister of the Church at Greenfield Hill, Connecticut. There he remained until 1795. In the midst of many other activities including opening another school, he yet found time to write prolifically: numerous epic poems as well as many sermons were published during this period.

But all this, which would have been success enough for many men, was only the beginning for Timothy Dwight. In 1795, he was offered, and accepted, the presidency of Yale University, which post he held until his death. He was also professor of theology at Yale and was a staunch supporter of revivalism. He had strong leadership qualities, and, in the view of many of his associates, seemed unable to delegate authority, preferring to take upon himself as many responsibilities as he could possibly shoulder. His detractors dubbed him "Pope Dwight," but his students greatly admired him. His versatility and exceptional abilities over a wide range of activities were impressive, and posterity has judged him to be "one of the most important men of his time."

He was married to Mary Wolsey in 1777 and of their large family, two sons became active in the ministry and in education, and his grandson Timothy followed in his footsteps becoming, in his turn, president of Yale (1886–1899).

Among his best known poems are: *The Conquest of Canaan*, written in 1785, and *Greenfield Hill*, which appeared in 1794. His *Dissertation on the History, Eloquence, and Poetry of the Bible* combines his Biblical erudition with his literary sensitivity.

ELIZABETH FRIES (LUMMIS) ELLET
1818–1877

Author of books on the contribution of women to American life, and translator of literary works from the French, German, and Italian, this versatile writer was born at Sodus Point, Lake Ontario, N.Y., the daughter of Dr. William and Sarah Lummis. She received the typical education of a young lady of means, attending a "female seminary" in Aurora, N.Y. The result, however, was not typical. In addition to learning the usual graces (dancing, playing the piano, drawing, and singing) she developed an intense interest in literature and languages. At the age of sixteen, her translation of Silvio Pellico's tragedy, *Euphemio of Messina*, was published. The following year saw publication of a poem of her own composition: *Teresa Contarini*.

After her marriage to Dr. William Ellet, a research chemist, she lived for a time in the South where her husband was a professor at South Carolina College. The couple returned to New York, however, in 1849. Here Mrs. Ellet lived until her death in 1877. Although she was at first better known for her work as a translator and adapter of the writings of foreign authors, she became deeply interested in the neglected history of American women and soon was engaged in writing the books for which she is remembered today. Strongly patriotic, she wanted to show the contribution made by women to the founding and development of the new nation. Although gifted with a lively imagination, she was scrupulously honest and factual in these works. Her *Women of The American Revolution* is considered one of the most comprehensive accounts published. She is also known for *Pioneer Women of The West* and *Queens of American Society*.

CHARLES JOHN ELLICOTT
1819–1905

This Church of England clergyman, who was Bishop of Gloucester and Bristol, served for eleven years as chairman of the group of scholars who were responsible for the translation of the Revised Version of the New Testament. He was a well-known Bible Commentator throughout his life and, in 1859, was Hulsean lecturer at Cambridge University. His lectures there appeared later under the title: *On the Life of Our Lord, Jesus Christ*. Among his numerous publications were his critical and grammatical commentaries on most of the Epistles of St. Paul. He was Bishop of Gloucester and Bristol between 1863 and 1897 and Bishop of Gloucester alone from 1897 until his death in 1905.

CHARLES EVANS
1850–1935

His reputation rests on his *American Bibliography*, twelve volumes published between 1903 and 1934, which lists some 38,000 pamphlets and books and other publications that appeared in early America between 1639 and 1799. (The work was continued after his death by C. K. Shipton who, in Volume 13, brought these listings up to 1800.) Evans was a librarian who studied at the Boston Athenaeum and held posts at the Indianapolis public library and the Enoch Pratt Free Library of Baltimore.

SAMUEL W. FOLJAMBE
1827–1890

Dr. Foljambe was a Baptist minister who held pastorates in Pittsburgh, Pa.; Dayton, Ohio; Framingham, Massachusetts, East Boston; Albany, N.Y.; Harvard-street Church, Boston; and Malden, Massachusetts. At the time of his death at age 63, he was pastor of the Woonsocket, Rhode Island, Baptist Church. His sermon, *The Hand of God in American History*, was published in Boston in 1876.

PETER FORCE
1790–1868

Although better known today as a historian and archivist, he began his professional life as a printer and went on to become a newspaper publisher and politician. He was born near Passaic Falls, New Jersey, but was brought up in New York; it was in New York City that he learned the printer's trade. After service with the Army during the War of 1812, he went to live in Washington, D.C. where his employer had moved in order to fulfill various printing contracts with the government. Here Force's interest in politics developed and, in 1822, he was elected councilman and served as president of the council. Later, as an elected alderman, he became president of that board.

He was a strong supporter of John Quincy

Adams, starting a semi-weekly newspaper *The National Journal* in 1823 in order to support Adams in his candidacy. During 1824, the year of the campaign, Force turned his paper into a daily. As an Adams supporter, he naturally joined the new Whig Party as soon as it was formed and, running on the Whig platform, he was elected Mayor of Washington in 1836 and in 1838 was re-elected. Although a staunch Whig, Force did not yield to the temptation to indulge in political muck-raking or harshly partisan attacks on the opposition which then (as now) were often popular tactics with politicians. By nature he was a quiet, courteous gentleman who conducted his newspaper in a dignified, fair-minded manner.

Force's major work as an archivist began in 1820, when he first printed *The National Calendar*, a statistical and historical annual. With the exception of a three-year period when his political activities were too demanding, he published this annual until 1836. (It became known as *The National Calendar and Annals of the United States*.) This was followed by publication of a collection of reprints of rare pamphlets dating from colonial days. Published as *Tracts and Other Papers, Relating Principally to the Origin, Settlement, and Progress of the Colonies in North America*, its four volumes appeared between 1836 and 1846. His father, who had been a soldier in the Revolution, inspired Force with a keen interest in American history, and he spent the better part of his life from his middle years in collecting all the historical data he could find on the Revolution and on pre-revolutionary days. His greatest achievement was his *American Archives* which, in nine volumes, documents colonial history from 1765 to 1776. The series appeared between 1837 and 1853.

Force had intended it should be comprised of some twenty folio volumes which would span the period from the seventeenth century through 1789. The volumes were being financed through a contract with the State Department, which had been authorized by an Act of Congress to go ahead with the project. In 1853, however, Secretary of State Marcy refused to continue the project and it was terminated. This was a great disappointment to Force who, on the basis of his contract with the government, had gone deeply into debt to purchase the historical materials to be used in the work. It was suggested that he sue the government for reparation or else petition Congress for redress, but he refused both of these alternatives. At age sixty, he suddenly found himself facing grave financial problems. He realized, however, that the material he had collected so laboriously, records of legislative proceedings, various kinds of official documents, and personal correspondence—formed a very valuable and rare collection. This large library, consisting of 30,000 pamphlets and some 20,000 volumes of Americana, he finally sold to the Library of Congress in 1867 for $100,000.

In addition to his monumental achievement in the *American Archives* and the collection of so much valuable historical material, Force also published another important paper in the field of American history, *The Declaration of Independence, or Notes on Lord Mahon's History of the American Declaration of Independence* (1855). He was also keenly interested in Arctic research and in 1852 published a paper entitled *Grinnell Land: Remarks on the English Maps of Arctic Discoveries in 1850 and 1851*, and, in 1856, a *Record of Auroral Phenomena observed in the Higher Northern Latitudes* (see *Smithsonian Contributions to Knowledge*, Vol. III). In 1840, Force became first president of the National Institute for the Promotion of Science.

JONATHAN FRENCH
1740–1809

He was born the son of a Massachusetts farmer and until he was seventeen, this son of Moses and Esther French worked on the family farm at Braintree where he had been born. In 1757, he enlisted in the army during the war against the French and Indians. After only a few months' service, he contracted small pox, followed by an attack of fever and ague, and was discharged from service. He went home to recover—but not to stay. As soon as he was well, he rejoined the army and served at Castle William as a sergeant. While in the army, he became interested in possibly becoming a physician and studied under several physicians. But at the end of his army service, he decided he should go to college first before making a final decision. He entered Harvard in 1767 and graduated in 1771. He remained at Cambridge, however, to study theology. After finishing his theological studies, he was soon summoned to the pastorate of the South Parish of Andover. Here he remained from 1772 until his death in 1809 at the age of seventy. Among his published sermons are: *A Sermon against Extortion*, (1777); *A Sermon at the General Election*, (1796); and *A Sermon at the Anniversary Thanksgiving*, (1798).

LEVI HART
1738–1808

He was born in Southampton, Connecticut and graduated from Yale in 1760. Both of his parents were deeply religious and as a boy, Levi appears to have had strong Christian convictions. As a young man, however, he became indifferent to religion for a time. Then, during his second year at Yale, when he was age twenty-one, he felt himself convicted of sin and keenly felt his need of the Lord whom he publicly professed at that time. From that moment on, a biographer relates, "his Christian character shone with a constantly increasing lustre."

Immediately after graduating from Yale, young Hart began theological studies with Dr. Bellamy of Bethlehem, completing his course in 1761. He was then licensed to preach in June of that year, and his first sermon was given in his teacher's pulpit at Bethlehem. He preached at a number of churches and then was called to be the pastor of the church at Preston, Connecticut in 1763 where he was ordained in November. Many felt the blessing of his preaching in a time when there was an intense religious revival.

During the Revolutionary War, Rev. Hart was a staunch defender of the Independence cause. Although he was deeply distressed by the bloodshed this cost the new nation, he never wavered from his conviction that the war for independence was "a righteous cause." He visited the army camp at Roxbury in 1775, preaching to Colonel Parsons' regiment. Later he delivered a stirring address at Fort Griswold, Gorton, during a meeting to commemorate those who had died there defending their country. The title of this address was *The Causes, the Origin, and Progress of War, with its Dreadful Effects*. It has been said that this talk "breathed a spirit of patriotism, sympathy, and piety."

Rev. Hart was instrumental in the founding of the Connecticut Missionary Society, as he was deeply committed to missionary activity. Years before the founding of the Society, he had journeyed to Maine to work among the destitute, and in 1795 he went North between the Oxbow and Canada line to do missionary work.

In 1800, he was honored by the degree of Doctor of Divinity from the College of New Jersey. Between 1784 and 1788, he was a member of the Plymouth College Corporation and also served in this capacity for Yale from 1791 to the year before his death. He was an important link in the formation of union between the General Association of Connecticut and the General Assembly of the Presbyterian Church. In 1801, he attended the General Assembly as a delegate from the Connecticut General Association. Among his published sermons were an Election Sermon in 1786 and a sermon on the death of General Washington in 1799. He died in 1808 at age seventy. After his death, the Reverend Samuel Nott, D.D., of Franklin, Connecticut, said that "Few ministers in New England, previous to the establishment of theological seminaries, had so much to do as he, in training young men for the ministry." Dr. Nott, along with other contemporaries, remarked on his wisdom, coupled with compassion, and on his abilities as a wise judge and peacemaker in regard to the differences that arose in church councils. Dr. Nott said: "I have scarcely ever known a person so much distinguished as he for self-government. Nothing seemed ever to take him by surprise. No provocation could throw him off guard . . . He lived as seeing Him who is invisible; and therefore he was never moved."

With regard to his practical Christianity, Dr. Nott commented that "he was always devising some plan for doing good. To be instrumental of glorifying God's grace in saving the souls of men was the great object for which he lived."

MATTHEW HENRY
1662–1714

Although this well-known Biblical commentator only lived to the age of fifty-two, he made a distinguished contribution to the vast literature concerning the Bible. He was born at Broad Oak, Flintshire, Wales, and was the son of an enlightened non-conformist minister, Philip Henry, whose diaries were published in 1882. Matthew Henry is best known for his *Exposition of the Old and New Testaments* (1708–10). But he is also known for *A Method for Prayer*, and his *Commentary on the Whole Bible*. He died at Norwich, England. He was widely read and quoted by the colonial clergy.

GAD HITCHCOCK
1718–1803

This Congregational minister was born in Springfield, Connecticut of Captain Ebenezer Hitchcock and Mary Sheldon Hitchcock. It is believed that his parish minister, Robert Buck, prepared him for entrance into Harvard College, where it was necessary for him to wait on tables until he won a scholarship. While preparing for the ministry, Hitchcock preached at various churches. He was then called by the people of Tunk (part of Pembroke, Mass.) to become pastor of the church they were organizing. He became their minister in October of 1748. His ordination was accompanied by lively controversy, however, since Hitchcock (like the pastor who had taught him) was a theological liberal—i.e., he could not accept all the tenets of Calvinism. Despite the controversy over his religious beliefs, Hitchcock was finally ordained, and the people of Tunk apparently never regretted their choice. Hitchcock earned a high reputation as one of the most distinguished clergymen of his day. It was said of him that he had every quality that could be desired in a minister—except frugality (which was apparently supplied by a wise and loving wife, Dorothy Angier Hitchcock, of Cambridge, whom he married in December of 1748).

Hitchcock's parish was originally extremely small; although it grew quickly because of his presence as minister, it always remained a modest parish. Fellow clergymen often remarked it was a pity that "such a great light should be hid under such a small bushel. Pastor Hitchcock, however, would not consider leaving his beloved church for a larger parish. Hitchcock was an eloquent preacher and was often called to preach at ordinations and to deliver sermons to the general public on important occasions, e.g., his *Artillery Sermon of 1765*, and the *Election Sermon of 1774*; the *Convention Sermon of 1787*; and the *Dudleian Lecture of 1799*. In the many ordination sermons he preached, he always reminded the candidates for the ministry that no one had the right to add "one jot or one tittle" to the gospel that Jesus Christ had delivered, and that dogmas and creeds often needlessly confuse and perplex the mind because they are human additions to divine truth which, as such, should never be given unthinking obedience. In one ordination sermon preached in 1786, he said: "Be not servilely dictated to by any man, as to the certain sense and meaning of particular passages of sacred writ, or what scheme of doctrine you ought to adopt, but make use of your own understanding—employ your best abilities, and judge even of yourself what is right, what is truth, and what truths you are to preach." Views like these resulted in Hitchcock being accused of "High Arianism"; yet even the most orthodox could not help liking him; so kindly was his nature, that they found it very difficult to quarrel with him. He had the unusual faculty of being able to acknowledge, even in the midst of controversy, that it was always possible he was wrong and the other person right.

A genial man with a great sense of humor, Hitchcock evidently never took himself too seriously. As a speaker at ministerial conventions in Boston, his wit often reduced the audience to helpless laughter. But his wit was only the adornment of a mind that looked deeply into things and was not afraid to speak out against "everything illiberal", as one contemporary expressed it. When he walked to and from Boston on weekdays, he often met sailors with whom he became friendly. By getting to know these men and others of various backgrounds, he gained valuable insights. In political matters, as in religious, his views were independent. He was firmly convinced that men could not progress as God intended they should without political as well as religious liberty.

Perhaps the most dramatic moment of his life came in 1774 when he was asked to deliver the *Election Sermon of 1774*. At that time it was not anticipated that General Gage would be Governor, still less that he could appear personally at the ceremonies. When it was discovered that Gage did in fact plan to attend, Hitchcock was urged to speak with the utmost discretion. When the day came, however, he spoke out as fearlessly as if the General in all his royal authority had not been facing him.

"The people are the only source of civil authority on earth," he declared. As if in warning to General Gage, he went on to say: "Civil authority is the production of combined society—not born with, but delegated to certain individuals for the advancement of the common benefit." Employing Lockean terms, he said that when the power of the government was abused, it was the people's duty to give it into other hands. He also boldly asserted: "If I am mistaken in supposing plans are formed, and executing, subversive of our natural and charter rights . . . and incompatible with every idea of liberty, all America is mistaken with me."

Hitchcock spoke with the boldness of a prophet and Gage heard him with mounting anger. Hitchcock insisted that the danger of the colonists was "not visionary, but real . . . Our contention is not about trifles, but about liberty and property; and not ours only, but those of posterity, to the latest generation . . ." He was evidently aware that there were also colonists there who, like Gage, did not agree with what he was saying. Nevertheless, he went on without hesitation: "For however some few, even from among ourselves, appear sufficiently disposed to ridicule the rights of America, and the liberties of subjects, 'tis plain St. Paul, who was a good judge, had a very different sense of them—He was on all occasions for standing fast not only in the liberties with which Christ had made him free . . . but also in that liberty, with which the laws of nature, and the Roman state, had made him free from oppression and tyranny." (With his habitual wit, Hitchcock later remarked that it must have been a very moving sermon, because so many people got up and left while he was preaching.)

When the Revolution was declared, Hitchcock served as a chaplain and in 1779, the town of Pembroke sent him to the Massachusetts Constitutional Convention, where he was a member of the committee to draw up the Constitution. After the discussion there on slavery, Hitchcock freed his own slaves who were so devoted to him, however, that they refused to leave him. In 1787, Harvard bestowed a D.D. degree on him. He died on August 8, 1803 leaving instructions that his funeral service should consist of a prayer only. Many of his sermons were published, including a sermon preached on Forefather's Day at Plymouth, December 22, 1774 (Boston, 1775); the *Election Sermon of 1774* (Boston, 1774); and *Natural Religion*, a sermon given in the Chapel of the University, September 1, 1779 (Boston, 1779); and numerous ordination sermons.

CHARLES HODGE
1797–1878

He was the son of a well-known Philadelphia physician who had served as a surgeon in the Revolutionary Army. When Charles was six months old, his father died leaving his mother, Mary Blanchard Hodge of Boston, with two sons to support on very slender financial means. By careful management of her limited resources, she was able to send both boys to Princeton where Charles graduated in 1815.

After graduating from Princeton, Charles attended Princeton Theological Seminary, graduating in 1819. He then became a professor of Oriental and Biblical literature at the Seminary and later (1840) a professor of theology. Hodge exercised great influence on the Presbyterian Church and his distinguished reputation as a scholar extended through his writings to Scotland where he was admired by many Scottish theologians. A kindly, gentle person, it was said of him that although he was a staunch Calvinist, he loved little children "so well that he made a special chink in his logic to save them from the general damnation."

In 1825, he founded the publication known then as *Biblical Repertory*, later re-named *Biblical Reportery and Princeton Review*. In 1835, his *Commentary on the Epistle to the Romans* was published and by 1880, nineteen editions of the work had appeared. Another work which became well known was his *Constitutional History of the Presbyterian Church in the United States of America* published in 1839–40. He is best known, however, for his *Systematic Theology*, which has been reprinted by Wm. B. Eerdmans Publishing Company, Grand Rapids, Michigan and which, even in his own time, was considered to be the outstanding exposition of Calvinism. He spent fifty-eight years as a teacher of divinity students and more students (both Presbyterian and others) are said to have been prepared by him for the ministry than by any other teacher during the nineteenth century. Through his writings and his teaching, he had a profound influence on American religious life.

SIMEON HOWARD
1733–1804

This clergyman was born in Bridgewater, Maine and graduated from Harvard in 1758. After completing his theological studies, he became the minister of a church in Cumberland, Nova Scotia. He returned to Harvard, however, to become a resident graduate student in 1765 and a tutor in 1766. The following year he was appointed minister of the West Church, Boston, where he was pastor for the rest of his life, with the exception of a year and a half when he and others among his congregation sought refuge in Nova Scotia during the Revolution. In 1785 Edinburgh University bestowed upon him a Doctor of Divinity degree. Among other positions of note which he held were: Overseer and fellow of Harvard, member of the Academy of Arts and Sciences, and of the Society for the Propagation of the Gospel, and vice-president of the Humane Society.

Simeon Howard was an earnest promoter of the American Revolution and delivered a number of memorable election sermons: *Artillery Election Sermon*, 1773; *Election Sermon*, 1780. Other published sermons include his *Dudleian Lecture*, 1787; *Convention Sermon*, 1790. His portrait in oil hangs in the First Church in Lancaster a reminder of the character and conviction of our early Congregational clergy.

CHARLES INGLIS
1734–1816

This Anglican Bishop, who was born in Ireland in 1734, was sent by the Society for the Propagation of the Gospel to be a missionary at Dover, Delaware. In 1765 he moved to New York City to become assistant minister at Trinity Church. He was in New York in 1775 when he wrote a pamphlet replying to Thomas Paine's *Common Sense*. It so incensed the Sons of Liberty that they publicly burned it. Even so, two more editions of the pamphlet were published at Philadelphia. So strong and outspoken were his royalist sympathies that in 1776, he closed his church and left for the royalist territory of Flushing, Rhode Island. In 1783 he emigrated to Halifax, Nova Scotia, Canada. In 1787 he went to England and was appointed bishop of Nova Scotia. On his return, he remained in Nova Scotia until his death. A number of his sermons were published and his *Memorial Concerning the Iroquois . . . 1775* appears in *The Documentary History of the State of New York*.

DAVID JONES
1736–1820

Because of the zeal with which he championed the Colonial cause during the American Revolution, the Reverend David Jones once had a price put on his head. His eloquence was so extraordinarily persuasive of public opinion in the Philadelphia area that it proved irksome to General Howe who promised a reward for his capture.

This eloquent preacher and writer was born at White Clay Creek Hundred, New Castle County, Delaware. He was of Welsh stock, his father, Morgan Jones, having been born in Wales, his mother, Eleanor Evans Jones, was also of Welsh descent through her father who emigrated to Philadelphia from Radnorshire, Wales, in 1695.

David grew up in a simple Welsh family community. He joined the Welsh Tract Baptist Church when he was twenty-one. Although raised as a farmer, he had a strong scholarly bent and soon after his twenty-first birthday, he moved to New Jersey to study Latin and Greek under Rev. Isaac Eaton at the Hopewell Academy, Hunterdon County. In 1761, the Welsh Tract Baptist Church gave him a license to preach, and he also began studies under his cousin, Abel Morgan, who was minister of the church in Middletown, New Jersey. He was ordained a minister in December of 1766 and was called to the pastorate of the church in Freehold, Monmouth County, New Jersey.

He was an early—and outspoken—advocate of the Colonial cause. By 1774, this was a dangerous position to take in the town of Freehold, which was strongly Royalist in sentiment, and his life was threatened. The following year, he fortunately received an invitation (which he accepted) from the Great Valley Baptist Church in Chester County, Pennsylvania, to become its pastor. Here he was to remain for the rest of his life (except for service with the Army and a period as the pastor of Southampton Church, Buck County, Pennsylvania, between 1786–92).

Like so many men of his time, David excelled in several fields. While his duties as a pastor were naturally of paramount importance to him, he threw his abundant energies into farming, as well as into his labors as a scholar and a writer. (In 1774, he was honored with a Master of Arts degree from Rhode Island College—now Brown University—in recognition of his scholarship.) At one time, he was also a missionary to the Indians in Ohio, and he served three terms in the Army as a chaplain.

In addition to his service with the Third and Fourth Pennsylvania Battalions in 1776, where his patriotism attracted the attention of General Wayne, he also served again between 1794 and 1796 at the request of the General who was sent into Ohio to protect the settlers from Indian attacks. Then, when the War of 1812 was declared, he thought nothing of his age (he was seventy-six) but promptly volunteered once again and served as a chaplain for the duration of that war.

On his return home, he took up his pastoral duties once more and also found time to write many newspaper articles. Among his published works is the famous sermon which he preached in 1775 to the Pennsylvania troops, *A Defensive War in a Just Cause Sinless*, in which he stirringly defended the case for independence. It was published in that same year and was of far-reaching influence.

BENSON JOHN LOSSING
1813–1891

This historian, newspaper editor, and wood-engraver was born in Beekman, Dutchess County, N.Y. He was a farmer's son and was descended from Pietre Pieterse Lassinghe, a native of Holland who emigrated to Albany, N.Y. in 1658.

Both Benson's Father and Mother died when he was still a child, and he received a sketchy education attending a public school for only three years. Despite this handicap, he devised his own courses in history during the years that he was apprenticed to a watchmaker. When he was only twenty-two, he became the editor of the official Democratic journal for Dutchess County—the Poughkeepsie Telegraph. Later, as the joint editor of the *Poughkeepsie Casket*, a literary magazine, he began to study engraving with one of the paper's illustrators. In 1839, after moving to New York, he became editor and illustrator for the *Family Magazine*. Meanwhile, in his spare time, he wrote and illustrated an *Outline History of the Fine Arts* which Harper's published in 1840 as one of the Family Library series.

Lossing's outstanding achievement was his *Pictorial Field Book of the American Revolution*, which was published between 1850 and 1852 and which took him five years and eight thousand miles of travel in the United States and Canada just to accomplish the preparatory labor for the work. As he traveled, he would take notes and make sketches which he afterward used in making final block drawings for engraving. Harper and Brothers made the book possible by advancing Lossing the money he needed to travel and collect the needed information. The *Pictorial Field Book* made Lossing's reputation and he wrote continuously and successfully for the next thirty-five years in both the historical and biographical fields. He produced more than fifty works including two more pictorial series, one on the War of 1812, published in 1868, and one on the Civil War, published in three volumes between 1866 and 1868. Other works in the biographical field include: *The Life and Times of Philip Schuyler* (2 vols., 1860–73); a biography of James A. Garfield (1882). His works on the American scene include *The Hudson from the Wilderness to the Sea* (1866); *Our Country* (2 vols., 1876–78); *History of New York City* (1884); and *The Empire State* (1887).

JOHANN AUGUST WILHELM NEANDER
1789–1850

"The idea of the state was the highest idea of ethics (in the ancient world), and within that was included all actual realization of the highest good . . . Thus the religious element also was subordinated to the political . . . It was first and only Christianity that could overcome this principle of antiquity, release men from the bondage of the world . . . by the idea of the kingdom of God, as the highest good, comprehending all other good in itself . . ." (Neander's *General History of the Christian Religion and Church*. See pp. 61–62) One of the best-known and often-quoted ecclesiastical historians, Neander was born at Gottingen, June 17, 1789, of Jewish parents. On February 15, 1806, he "publicly renounced Judaism" and was baptized a Christian in St. Catharine's Church, Hamburg. He then changed his name from David Mendel to Neander (which in the Greek means "new man"). His Christian names he took from various Christian friends. He studied Christian theology extensively, concluding his academic courses in his home town of Gottingen. In 1812 he became professor of Church History at the new University of Berlin. He accepted the post and here he remained until his death on July 14, 1850, having become a legend in his own lifetime. Students from all over the Protestant world flocked to Berlin to attend his courses, so great was his renown. His *General History of the Christian Religion and Church* (trans. by Joseph Torry, 5 vols., Boston, 1882) remains a definitive text on the history of Christianity. He was also the author of other important works: *History of the Planting and Training of the Christian Church by the Apostles* (1842), *Memorials of Christian Life in the Early Middle Ages* (1832), *Life of Jesus Christ* (1848) and commentaries on Philippians, James and First John.

Hezekiah Niles
1777–1839

This prominent Baltimore Journalist whose newspaper is still consulted by historians because of its unbiased reporting, was born at Jefferis Ford, Chester County, Pennsylvania. He was the son of a plane maker from Wilmington, Delaware and would have been born there, rather than in Pennsylvania, except for the Battle of Brandywine. His parents, Hezekiah and Mary Niles, had gone to Chester County just before the battle so that the child could be born in relative peace. Later, they returned to Wilmington. Little is known about young Hezekiah's childhood, but it is believed that he received his schooling at the Friends' School in Delaware. When he was seventeen, he was apprenticed to a Philadelphia printer whose financial reverses compelled him to release the boy after three years. Later, however, young Niles succeeded in becoming a job printer and, in 1815, the editor of a Baltimore

newspaper, the *Evening Post*, which was known for its strong Jeffersonian views. Six years later, when the paper was sold, Niles struck out on his own and started his own paper, which at first was known simply as the *Weekly Register*. He was to edit and publish this paper, which came to be known as *Niles Weekly Register*, for the next twenty-five years. His only other published writing, apart from those in his newspaper and in a few pamphlets, was his *Principles and Acts of The Revolution in America*, to which he brought the same scrupulous factual objectivity. The work was republished in 1876.

His capable editing of his newspaper resulted in its becoming the most widely read American newspaper of its time, both here and abroad. Today it is often consulted by the historian for its reliable coverage of the historical events of the day, reprints appearing in 1947.

Dr. David Ramsay
1749–1815

"By the novel doctrine of parliamentary power, they (the colonists) were degraded from being the subjects of a king, to the low condition of being subjects of subjects. They argued that it was essentially involved in the idea of property, that the possessor had such a right therein, that it was a contradiction to suppose any other man, or body of men, possessed a right to take it from him, without his consent." So wrote Dr. David Ramsay in his *History of the United States* (1816). Born in Lancaster County, Pennsylvania, April 2, 1749, Dr. Ramsay's career was threefold: physician, legislator, and historian. He studied medicine at the University of Pennsylvania, but began practice in Charleston, S.C., in 1773, and during the Revolution he served as a field surgeon for the Continental Army. From 1776 to 1783 he was a member of the South Carolina Legislature, and he was a member of the Council of Safety of Charleston. He was taken prisoner by the British at St. Augustine, Florida and was held between 1780–81. The views quoted above were undoubtedly his own convictions, as he was a member of the Continental Congress, acting as its president in 1785–86. After the war, he again was a member of the South Carolina Legislature, from 1801 to 1815. He also was president of the State Senate. He died on May 8, 1815 at Charleston, shot by a lunatic. Among his many historical works, Dr. Ramsay wrote: *History of the American Revolution* (1789); *Life of George Washington*

(1807), *History of South Carolina* (1809) and *History of the United States: 1607–1808* (1816–17).

JOHN WINGATE THORNTON
1818–1878

A lawyer and historian, he was born in Saco, Maine. The son of a shipping merchant who was strongly interested in promoting the development of water power and of railroads, he came of a long line of New Englanders dating back to the Thomas Thornton who left England for the New England in 1663.

Although he became a lawyer after graduating from Harvard Law School. Thornton's deepest interest lay in American history. While practicing law in Boston, he began to write on historical subjects and, in 1844, was a founder of the New England Historic Genealogical Society. He was an indefatigable collector of Americana, collecting many letters by famous people, and rare historical documents of various kinds. Among his numerous works are: *The Landing at Cape Anne* (1854); *Peter Oliver's "Puritan Commonwealth" Reviewed* (1857); *The First Records of Anglo-American Colonization* (1859); *The Pulpit of The American Revolution, or the Political Sermons of the Period of 1776* (1860); and *The Historical Relation of New England to the English Commonwealth* (1874). He played a prominent part in the rediscovery of Governor Bradford's history *Of Plimouth Plantation*, which was then in the Fulham Library.

Thornton is described as having a generous, kind nature. He was deeply loyal and strongly religious, with a mind "evenly poised and well regulated."

JAMES THACHER
1754–1844

A physician by profession, his service with the Revolutionary Army resulted in his becoming an author. His diary, *A Military Journal During The American Revolutionary War*, relates his experiences as an Army physician between 1775 and 1783 and is an important source for the historian. He was born in Barnstaple, Massachusetts, the son of a farmer of modest means. His mother, born Content Norton, was a granddaughter of William Coddington, who served as governor of Rhode Island.

At age sixteen, young Thacher began his medical apprenticeship, and when the Revolution broke out, the Army accepted him as a "surgeon's mate" at Cambridge Military Hospital. Later, he served as surgeon in several other hospitals and also for a light-infantry corps. After the war, he set up practice in Plymouth and soon became a highly respected physician. He died at the advanced age of ninety. In addition to his diary, he also produced several medical works including the first *American Medical Biography*, which related the lives of prominent medical men of the period and was considered to be both accurate and exhaustive. He received an honorary M.A. from Harvard in 1808 and their M.D. degree in 1810.

CHARLES TURNER
1732–1818

Minister and legislator, Turner was born in Scituate, Maine. His parents, Charles and Eunice James Turner, attended the Second Church (Congregational) of Scituate and there Charles was baptized. He early felt a strong calling to the ministry. As an undergraduate at Harvard, he sometimes preached in the Church at Truro, Massachusetts, which he joined in 1752. Although he received a unanimous call from that church in 1753 to be its minister as soon as he should be ordained, he declined the offer because of the "dissenting" views of his parents and his own "bodily infirmities." Instead, he accepted a Hopkins Fellowship for graduate theological studies at Cambridge. In 1754, the town of Duxbury, Massachusetts, in concurrence with its church, gave him a unanimous call to its ministry. William Rand preached the ordination sermon and later, in 1757, Turner married Rand's daughter, Mary.

Turner became a highly-respected minister, well-known for his Biblical Christianity. While he strongly supported liberty of conscience, he recognized, as he said, that "people who settle a minister, have a just claim to reasonable satisfaction, as to the candidate being a real Christian: and so as to the purity of his mind in searching after the important truths of Christianity." But he cautioned that we should "guard against our judgments being perverted by any prejudice, while we inquire into the meaning of God's words." Nor should one yield an implicit, unenquiring assent to the instructions, nor tamely submit to what one judges to be the . . . unscriptural dictates of the most dignified, and sacred stations, and characters."

As the pastor of the Duxbury church, Turner

took a great interest in the Pilgrims; the more he learned about them, the more he tended to take the separatist viewpoint in regard to the political situation of his own time. Because his political views were well-known, Governor Hutchinson was very perturbed when Turner was chosen to preach the *Election Sermon of 1773*. While some urged Turner to use all "prudence" in his sermon, James Otis said he was sure Turner would not fail to "speak a word in season." This he did. He told the General Court unequivocally that the great issue before them was whether the people should be at the "*absolute* disposal of a distant Legislature." He also asserted in Lockean terms that it was the people who "may, by a constitution, make an office hereditary in a family." Hence, it is the people who "have an unalienable right to alter such constitution at pleasure and to interpose *immediately* in the election of their officers, whenever they judge it proper." These were fearless—and dangerous—words. They filled Governor Hutchinson with dismay and indignation, so much so that he failed to follow custom and invite Turner to occupy the place of honor at the public dinner following the sermon. Later he evidently realized this was a mistake because such an omission was likely to deeply offend the Whigs. When he tardily summoned Turner, however, no one could find him, some ardent Whigs having already repaired the Governor's omission by taking Turner to dinner.

Because Turner was so closely connected with both John and Sam Adams and the Committees of Correspondence, he became (as he wrote later) "obnoxious to the British and Tories." Finally, his church was surrounded during a service by a group of armed men who threatened him with bodily harm as they hurled verbal abuse at him. Friends then advised him to "withdraw to a place of more security," and in 1775 he left his beloved parish and "the people with whom he had passed twenty years in the utmost friendship and cordiality" and returned to his home town of Scituate.

In 1780, the town sent him to the House of Representatives, and in 1783 to the State Senate where he served until 1788. When the Federal Constitution was first proposed, Turner was against it. As a member of the convention called to consider ratification, his cautionary voice was often heard in the debates. His main fear was of the power of government. He felt that all government tended to become corrupt, and he warned particularly against the people themselves allowing the love of luxury to weaken them and, hence,

to be reflected in a corrupt government. "As people become more luxurious, they become more incapacitated for governing themselves . . . Alike people, alike prince." But, at last, because of the proposed amendments to the Constitution, which he felt afforded greater protection to liberty, he swallowed his doubts and voted for ratification. At the time of the Jay Treaty, Turner was a staunch supporter of the Federalists. But as a presidential elector in 1804, his vote went to Jefferson.

During his activity as a State senator, Turner still continued to preach from time to time. At the conclusion of his term of office, he started to look for a ministerial post and, in 1789, was made chaplain of a fort on Castle Island which was then a prison. When his old friend, Gad Hitchcock, heard him say he didn't know if he had the ability to convert these men, he replied puckishly that the task should be easy because Turner would have a congregation that was already under "conviction." In fact, Turner was chaplain there for four years, during which time he often visited the former Sylvester Plantation in Maine which, in 1786, was renamed "Turner" in his honor. Before the Revolution, he had taken an active role in urging its settlement and in preaching to the settlers. By 1791, his brother and son living there, Turner also took up residence in the town named for him. The town of Turner wanted him to be pastor of the church there, but the church itself chose John Strickland, a Presbyterian. Turner joined the church at Turner, however, and through his influence, it later returned to the Congregational fold.

A number of Turner's sermons were published; among them are: *General Directions* (1762); *Gospel Ministers* (1770); the fateful *Election Sermon* preached before Governor Hutchinson (1773); a sermon at Plymouth commemorating the landing of the Pilgrims (1774); and *Due Glory is to be given to God* preached at Cambridge (1783).

In *Due Glory* he addressed the students in these terms: "Extremely happy should I be, to be furnished with satisfactory evidence that the young Gentlemen of the University were captivated with the spirit, which I have endeavoured, my present discourse should breathe. We do not censure their inclination to excel, in various arts and sciences, which are embellishing and in a more moderate degree, useful to society; but our grand wish is, to see their ambition chiefly engaged about those things, which are the most worthy, important and glorious; to see them emulous for excelling in divine science; in love to God and their Country; in truly Christian and republican sobriety and oeconomy."

ELISHA WILLIAMS
1694–1755

This clergyman's son, born in Hatfield, Hampshire County, Massachusetts, filled many roles in his lifetime. While perhaps best known today as the fourth president (or rector) of Yale University, he also served at different periods of his life as clergyman, teacher, lawmaker, and judge.

In 1711, he graduated from Harvard and, upon completing his law studies, he became Clerk of the Connecticut Assembly. Later, in 1716, he was a tutor of fourteen delinquent youths in a school in Wethersfield, Connecticut, where he was so successful that he remained in this work until 1719. He studied for the ministry, meanwhile, and in 1721 was ordained pastor of the Newington Church, near Hartford. In 1725, however, he left this ministry to become rector of Yale which, it is said, "he reformed very much." He remained rector until 1739 when the college had become firmly established.

After leaving Yale, he often served in the Connecticut Assembly and also became a judge of the Superior Court. Then, in 1744, he wrote and published a widely-read pamphlet which expressed his deep concern for the cause of religious liberty: *A Seasonable Plea for the Liberty of Conscience and the Right of Private Judgment*. Its enlightened views on Christian liberty served to educate the people of Connecticut.

In the expedition on Louisburg in 1745, he served in the Army as Chaplain and the next year found him a colonel of a regiment. Later, in 1749, because of difficulties in getting back pay owing his men, he had to go to England to lodge their claim. While there, he made the acquaintance of many of the most distinguished English dissenters with whom he formed several close friendships. Here, too, he met his future wife, the English hymn writer, Elizabeth Scott, whom he married in 1751. One English gentleman, who knew him at this time and introduced him to Elizabeth, described him as having "solid learning . . . great candor and sweetness of temper, and a certain nobleness of soul." In 1752, Williams returned to America, and was employed in several public services for his country, and maintained an active correspondence with his transatlantic friends.

He died at Wethersfield in 1755.

JUSTIN WINSOR
1831–1897

This prolific author—he wrote history, criticism, poetry, and fiction—was born in Boston, and his roots in Massachusetts date back to Samuel Winsor, who was born in Duxbury in 1725. Winsor was educated at Boston Latin School and Harvard College and became interested in history at a very early age. When just a lad, he started attending the new England Historic Genealogical Society's meetings and got the idea of writing a history of Duxbury. During his freshman year at Harvard (1849) his book, *History of the Town of Duxbury*, was published.

Despite his lively interest in historical writing, Winsor also dreamed of becoming a poet. Although he was a close student of any subject that really interested him, he found many of his studies at Harvard irksome duties and he finally left the college in his senior year without graduating. (Harvard gave him a degree fifteen years later, however.)

After leaving college, he went abroad to study languages—spending two years in Paris and Heidelberg learning French and German. (Later, he also became proficient in Dutch, Italian, Spanish, and Portuguese.) He returned to Boston in 1854, determined to become a writer; from 1854 to 1868, he wrote steadily—not only poetry, but also criticism and fiction. In 1868, after having served for two years as a trustee of the Boston Public Library, he accepted what was to have been a temporary appointment as superintendent of the library. His ideas for library reform, however, had already become known through a report he had written while trustee, and resulted in his remaining superintendent for nine years. He left this post in 1877 in order to accept appointment as librarian of Harvard College. Throughout his life, he gave active support to the development of libraries in the United States and was a founder of the American Library Association and the *Library Journal*. Between 1876 and 1885, he served as the first president of the Association and was elected again in 1897 to represent it at a meeting in England.

Meanwhile, during all these activities, he still pursued historical research and, in 1880, his *Reader's Handbook of the American Revolution* appeared. As a result of this work, he was asked to produce a full-scale history of the City of Boston—to be completed in two years. Nothing daunted, he planned the work carefully, employing some seventy writers as contributors to the project, and completed it a month ahead of schedule. This four-volume *Memorial History of Boston* received critical acclaim from scholars and encouraged him to produce *The Narrative and Critical History of America* (8 volumes) which was published between 1884 and 1889. This work also was made up largely of contributions by other authors, although it also included his own critical bibliographical studies. After this much-praised work, Winsor published in quick succession four works of his own: *Christopher Columbus* (1891); *Cartier to Frontenac* (1894); *The Mississippi Basin* (1895); and *The Westward Movement* (1897). Cartography is an important element in all of Winsor's books. In the beginning, he used maps mainly as auxiliaries to the narrative, but soon they played a more prominent role until he became known as the foremost cartographer of his day.

SAMUEL WILBERFORCE
1805–1873

An Episcopal bishop and church historian, he was a son of William Wilberforce, a prominent politician and philanthropist well known for his crusade against African slavery. Samuel was sent to Oriel College, Oxford, where he took his B.A. degree in 1826 and his M.A. in 1829, and where he was awarded his Doctor of Divinity degree in 1845. After entering orders, he became rector of Brightstone (or Brixton) on the Isle of Wight in 1830, becoming rural dean of the northern division of the Isle in 1836. In 1839, he became archdeacon of Surrey and, in 1840, canon of the Cathedral of Westminster. The following year saw him become chaplain to Prince Albert and in 1843 sub-almoner to Queen Victoria. He became dean of Westminster in 1845, and that same year saw his elevation to the bishopric of Oxford. Here he remained until 1869, when he became Bishop of Winchester. At Oxford he introduced many reforms resulting in an improved organization of the diocese. After becoming Bishop of Winchester, he presided over a revision of the New Testament. He was the author of a number of books, the best known being his *History of the Protestant Episcopal Church in America*, published in 1844.

ROBERT CHARLES WINTHROP
1809–1894

Writer, orator, and legislator, he was born in Boston, Massachusetts, in the house of his great-uncle, James Bowdoin. He was the son of the Massachusetts lieutenant governor, Thomas Lindall Winthrop, who was descended from John Winthrop. He graduated from Harvard in 1828 and, after completing his law studies under Daniel Webster, he began legal practice in 1831. In 1834, he was elected to the General Court, where he served for six years; for three of these, he was speaker of the Court and soon won a reputation for eloquence. In November 1840, he was elected to Congress, where he served until his resignation in May of 1842 owing to the serious illness of his wife. After her death, he was re-elected and served from November 1842 to July 1850. He was speaker of the Thirtieth Congress between 1847 and 1849. He was appointed to the Senate in 1850 to fill Webster's unexpired term upon the latter's resignation.

He continued to be known as an outstanding orator with a vivid grasp of history, and his *Oration on the Hundredth Anniversary of the Surrender of Cornwallis*, which was given before Congress in 1881 at the invitation of both houses, is one of the outstanding examples of the orator's art. He was a member of the Massachusetts Historical Society from 1839 to 1894 and was its president for thirty of those years.

JOHN WITHERSPOON
1722–1794

During the great debates at the Continental Congress in 1776, one of the strongest voices in favor of independence was that of Dr. Witherspoon, who was to represent the State of New Jersey at the Congress for the ensuing six years. On July 2, 1776, he told the Congress that the country "was not only ripe for the measure, but in danger of rotting for the want of it."

Dr. Witherspoon was a distinguished Presbyterian minister—the only clergyman to sign the Declaration of Independence—and was President of the College of New Jersey.

Of sturdy build, with bushy eyebrows, and a soft Scots "burr," he was an eloquent preacher and public speaker, gifted with a naturally commanding presence, vigorous intellect, and penetrating wit.

Born in South Yester, near Edinburgh, Scotland, he was the son of that town's pastor, the Reverend James Witherspoon; on his mother's side, it is said he could trace his ancestry back to John Knox. He attended grammar school at Haddington where his intellectual precocity soon became apparent. At age 13, he was admitted to the University of Edinburgh where he received his M.A. in 1739 and his B.D. in 1743. In 1743, he was licensed to preach and by 1745 was an ordained minister at Beith in Ayrshire. Marriage followed in 1748 to Elizabeth Montgomery by whom he had 10 children, five of whom died in early childhood. In 1757, the Low Church of Paisley called him to be its pastor and (1759) he was called to be moderator of the Synod of Glasgow and Ayr. In 1764, he was given a D.D. degree from the University of St. Andrews. In this same year, he visited London where a three-volume edition of essays from his pen was published. Through this work, his reputation as a theologian spread throughout England, to the continent, and even to far-off America. He received pastoral invitations from congregations in Dublin, Rotterdam, and Dundee, all of which he declined.

Early in his ministry at Paisley, he had allied himself with the Church's Popular Party, becoming one of its most influential leaders. A major plank of the Party was "the right of personal conscience," which Dr. Witherspoon heartily supported. Although the General Assembly of the Presbyterian Church insisted that the ecclesiastical authorities had the final word in regard to the appointment of ministers, Dr. Witherspoon defended the right of congregations to choose their own ministers.

Full as it was of activity and accomplishment, this first half of Dr. Witherspoon's life was only the preparation for the great events that were to claim his talents during the latter half of his life. For him, these events began when he accepted the second invitation proferred to him by the Trustees of the College of New Jersey to become its President. The first request had come in 1766, but Dr. Witherspoon had reluctantly declined because his wife did not wish to leave their native land. She yielded when the second invitation came, feeling that it must be God's plan for them.

After a long and fatiguing voyage, Dr. Witherspoon and his family were warmly welcomed in the New World. The evening they arrived in Princeton, they were astonished and touched to see the college buildings brilliantly illuminated in honor of the new President. Dr. Witherspoon was inaugurated on August 17, 1768 and delivered a memorable address in Latin entitled *The Union of Piety and Science*. He introduced many improvements in the college curriculum, including new teaching methods. Teaching by lecture was one. This method apparently was unknown in the Colonies prior to Dr. Witherspoon's

introduction of it at Princeton. He broadened the curriculum to include philosophy, Hebrew (which he taught), French, history, and oratory. He himself lectured on four subjects: Eloquence and Comparative Taste and Criticism; Moral Philosophy; Chronology and History; and Divinity. Dr. Witherspoon was an accomplished linguist and is reported to have spoken French with "almost as much ease and elegance as his own tongue." He believed in the necessity of a thorough mastery of the English language as he felt he was preparing his students for a life of public service.

Learning as a mere adornment of the gentleman did not appeal to him. He felt that scholarship should have a practical value to the living of life. Learning should therefore be fully rounded. He was very critical of over-specialization. He felt that any one who confined himself to any one branch of knowledge "cannot be a man of extensive knowledge; and it is but seldom that he can be a man of a liberal or noble turn of mind; because his time is consumed by the particularities and his mind narrowed by attending to one particular art." Pedants who accumulated useless knowledge received sharp criticism from him as, despite their learning, such persons were "greatly inferior to more ignorant persons in clear, sound common sense." Dr. Witherspoon became known as the founder of a new philosophy, the philosophy of "common sense," which permeated American educational thought for a long period.

When Dr. Witherspoon became President of the College of New Jersey, it was in sad financial straits; the Trustees could not even pay his salary. But Dr. Witherspoon was not only a distinguished theologian and scholar; he also turned out to be an expert fund-raiser. He journeyed throughout New England soliciting contributions and, by his efforts, the College raised several thousand pounds. At his instigation, a subscription fund also was started in Virginia and South Carolina which served to bring in additional funds. As a result of all this fund-raising activity, the college debts soon were paid off and a small surplus remained.

This intellectual and practical activity of Dr. Witherspoon's he viewed as underpinning to the all-important part of his College program. As a dedicated Minister of Christ's Gospel, he viewed the spiritual life of his students as of paramount importance. Under his aegis, there was a remarkable revival of religion at the College of New Jersey.

As an ardent Churchman, Dr. Witherspoon soon became a leader of the Presbyterian Church in America. When he arrived in the Colonies, the Church was divided by various factions and, as a result, was in a stagnant state. Under his leadership, these factional differences were healed, the church institution became better organized, and—best of all—ties of friendship were formed with the Congregational Church. Thus revitalized, the Church began to grow and soon spread to the frontiers.

It was not until 1774 that Dr. Witherspoon was called to bring his intellectual abilities to bear on still another field—politics. Prior to 1774, he had been averse to the idea of ministers engaging in politics. In the beginning of the controversy between the Colonies and the Mother Country, he held himself aloof; but, in 1774, he joined with his neighbors as a county delegate to a provincial convention. He also served on the Committees of Correspondence that were rapidly springing up. He was chairman of his county delegation by the winter of 1775-6 and was ardently working to bring New Jersey into accord with the other Colonies. He was a leader of the movement to remove the royalist governor, William Franklin, from his post.

When the Congress declared May 17 as a day of fasting, Dr. Witherspoon preached a sermon (later published with a dedication to John Hancock). Titled *The Dominion of Providence over the Passions of Men*, it was a full discussion of the great political crisis lying before the country, its causes and its cure. While it was received with enthusiasm in the Colonies, it shocked his friends in England when they read it, and some labeled him a traitor.

On June 22, 1776, Dr. Witherspoon, together with five others, was elected to represent New Jersey in the Continental Congress. They were empowered to speak for independence if, in their opinion, this was the right course.

Dr. Witherspoon arrived at Philadelphia just as Congress was debating the resolution for independence. When some suggested it was too soon to take the fateful step, Dr. Witherspoon urged the delegates not to hang back but to declare independence with no further delay. He said that the whole country "had been for some time past loud in its demand for the proposed declaration." Dr. Witherspoon's conviction that independence was the only answer to the dispute with England was not a new one adopted in the heat of the moment. At least two years earlier, he had seen its inevitability. He had written an essay in 1774 outlining the course of action which now, in 1776, the Congress was to follow: "To profess loyalty to the King and our 'backwardness' to break connection with Great Britain unless forced thereto; To declare the firm resolve never to submit to the claims of Great Britain, but deliberately to prefer war with all its horrors, and even extermination, to slavery; To resolve union and to pursue the same measures until American liberty is settled on a solid basis . . ."

During Dr. Witherspoon's service at the Congress (1776–1782), he served on more than 100 committees, two of which were of great importance: the committee on Foreign Affairs and the Board of War. He actively debated on the Articles of Confederation, was active in the organization of the executive department, and worked on forming alliances useful to the new government. He also participated prominently in the drawing up of instructions to the Peace Commissions. Many of the most important state papers, such as those concerned with the paper money crisis, were written by Dr. Witherspoon. He was much opposed to paper money and to issuing bonds with no amortization. "No business can be done, some say, because money is scarce," he wrote. "It may be said, with more truth, money is scarce, because little business is done."

Dr. Witherspoon viewed his work at the Congress, not as a departure from his role as minister, but as an opportunity to act there as one of the Church's ambassadors. He frequently preached in Philadelphia on Sundays and at the Congress he would never consent to changing his clerical dress (as did some other clerical members of Congress).

After the war, he set about rebuilding the College of New Jersey which had been closed during most of that time. He also was twice elected to serve in the State Legislature—in 1783 and 1789. During part of this time, he was also actively engaged in work on a plan to organize a national body of the Presbyterian Church. He was chosen as moderator of the Church's first General Assembly held in 1789.

In his last years he was plagued with many financial worries owing to the College's acute money problems and the depleted state of his own finances which he had generously applied to the aid of the college in its difficult post-war years. He died at his farm two miles out of Princeton at the age of seventy-one.

An edition of his works in four volumes was published in America in 1800–01, and a nine-volume edition was brought out in Edinburgh in 1815. (It was Witherspoon who, in an article on the differences between English and American idiom, created the word "Americanism.")

JOHN JOACHIM ZUBLY
1724–1781

Rev. Zubly was born in St. Gall, Switzerland in 1724. He was ordained to the Gospel ministry in the German Reformed Church, London, England, arriving the same year in Savannah, Georgia, the chief scene of his labors. He was pastor from 1760 of the Independent Presbyterian Church of Savannah where he preached in English. But to one neighboring congregation he preached in German, and to another in French. The degree of Doctor of Divinity was conferred upon him from the College of New Jersey (Princeton) in 1770.

Such was the confidence of the people of Georgia in the intelligence and patriotism of Dr. Zubly, that he was appointed a delegate to the Continental Congress, of which he was a member from 1775–76. But, like many of the colonists who favored the rights of the Colonies against the unjust exactions of the British Crown, when the question of actual separation from, and independence of, the mother country came up for action, he was found opposed to extreme measures, and suddenly quitting his post at Philadelphia, he returned to Georgia.

He took sides against the Colonies, and in consequence was banished from Georgia. But, from his correspondence, it appears that he was in Savannah during the siege of that place by French and American armies in 1779 and that his losses of property, books, etc. were considerable.

Dr. Zubly did not live to see the conclusion of the war and the achievement of American Independence. He possessed a confiding and contented spirit and died in Savannah in 1781. Despite his conduct in opposing the cause of American Independence he was not uncharitably judged by those who knew him best. Two of the streets of Savannah are named for him *Joachim* and *Zubly*.

Among his published works Dr. Zubly left a small volume entitled *The Real Christian's Hope in Death*, 1756; a Sermon on the value of faith, 1772; a Sermon on the death of the Rev. John Osgood of Midway, 1773; and his famous sermon *The Law of Liberty*: a Sermon on American Affairs at the opening of the Provincial Congress of Georgia, with an Appendix, giving an account of the struggle of Switzerland to recover liberty, 1775.

BIOGRAPHIES OF THE ARTISTS

Prepared by
John Grossman

[American
artists are
arranged in
chronological
order]

"And so at last these old Painters became to me venerable personages—men whose names made me think of Plymouth Rock, which always brought back the wild vision of the Mayflower rocking in Massachusetts Bay, her icy deck covered with old men, and females, and young children, all kneeling in solemn covenant with God. Indeed, there was something more to me in these painters, than Pilgrims—they were mysterious men, for they seemed to have a kind of incomprehensible relation with the old Heroes of Revolutionary Senates and Battle-fields. This impression was not done away with even after Trumbull and Stuart were guests at our house, and I sat on their knee. I am quite willing that portion of the world which knows no better, should simper a little to hear me talk so about Pilgrims and Painters,—but the day is coming as surely as another eclipse of the sun, when the men of this country will pile up everlasting bronze to our early Painters, as they have already piled up everlasting granite to the Pilgrims, and God will give us a Webster to speak when the foundation is laid."
—C. Edwards Lester, *Artists of America*, 1846

"Perhaps the strangest development in all Colonial America was the development of a school of great painters. Some spent parts of their lives in England and competed successfully with Reyn-

olds and Gainsborough, Raeburn and Lawrence; the first famous painters born on our continent enjoyed a greater European acclaim than came to any other American artists for at least a century. And they were not the only competent workmen of the American school; others such as Charles Willson Peale, painting almost entirely on this side of the water, produced canvases much admired today. This amazing story has been largely neglected by the historians of our national life . . ."—James Thomas Flexner, *America's Old Masters*, 1967.

BENJAMIN WEST
1738–1820

At twelve a professional painter, at twenty famous in the provinces of New York and Pennsylvania, the plain Quaker, Benjamin West, went on to achieve perhaps the most successful career of any American artist. He was regarded all over the world as the leading exponent of the "grand style" of painting. West's life was a true American success story, beginning in a Pennsylvania farm house and ending amid fame and wealth in London.

When his mother was far advanced in her pregnancy, an English evangelist came to Chester County, whom Mrs. West, despite her condition, went to hear. In his sermon he preached against the wickedness of the Old World and urged the congregation to turn their eyes to America, where "the forests shall be seen fading away, cities rising along the shores, and the terrified nations of Europe flying out of the smoke of the burning to find refuge here." Mrs. West was so moved that she was seized by labor pains, causing the meeting to break up. Although they subsided, Benjamin was born thirteen days later. His father was deeply impressed by his wife's seizure in the meeting house, and the possibility that the Lord had manifested Himself by signs to the most humble, showing He had selected his son for a Divine mission.

When six years old, left to watch over his sister's baby, he spontaneously drew the infant's picture. His mother was delighted. "I do declare," she cried, "he has made a likeness of Sally!" And she kissed him. "That kiss," West often said later, "made me a painter." His father was impressed and encouraged him to continue to draw, as did most of the other Friends even though it could have been considered contrary to their strict tenets against graven images. Accordingly, there were few if any pictures in the Quaker community for him to emulate. His first colors were red and yellow earths provided by Indian friends, and a piece of indigo from his mother. For brushes, he removed fur from the tail of the family cat, then patches elsewhere, until it was thought it had the mange; West confessed and was forgiven.

A Philadelphia Friend gave him a box of paints, several prepared canvases, and six engravings when he was eight years old. Up to that point West had never seen any drawings but his own and did not know that engravings existed. Playing hooky from school to complete his first canvas by combining elements from the engravings, his mother found the truant painting in the attic. Her anger turned to joy when she saw the picture; clasping him in her arms, she exclaimed, "Oh, thou wonderful child!" The picture convinced his parents and many of his neighbors that he had been chosen by God to be a painter.

He met the artist William Williams (active in America 1747–1770) during a visit to Philadelphia, whose paintings were the first by another artist he had ever seen. They impressed him greatly. In his twelfth year he sold several canvases to local gentlemen; by the time he was eighteen, he was doing a flourishing business in portraits of his neighbors, and gaining a wide-

spread reputation. It was at this time that he produced a neo-classic picture, *The Death of Socrates* (1756), well in advance of a coming movement in European art.

The painting attracted the attention of the Reverend Dr. William Smith, provost of the College of Philadelphia, who felt that West's education was being neglected. He offered to direct his studies if his father would agree to send his son to Philadelphia. "But before his Quaker father gave up his boy to the 'worldly occupation of painting'," wrote C. Edwards Lester in his book *The Artists of America*,* "he felt it to be his duty to lay the matter before the Society of which he was a member. The Society assembled and waited for the moving of the Spirit. It was a serious question with these serious men and women, whether they could give their consent that one of their own members should wander from the fold to pursue an Art which 'had hitherto been employed to embellish life, to preserve voluptuous images, and add to the sensual gratifications of man.'

"There is not so much to provoke a smile in this business as some persons may suppose. People that pray over such matters are not always the fools the world in our times takes them for. A great many men have laughed at the Puritans, Cromwellians, or Round-heads, as you please, but no man ever laughed at them after meeting them in the halls of debate, or crossing swords with them on the field of battle.

" 'The spirit of speech first descended on one John Williamson—"To John West and Sarah Persons" said this Western Luminary, "a man-child hath been born, on whom God hath conferred some remarkable gifts of mind; and you have all heard that, by something amounting to inspiration, the youth has been induced to study the art of painting. It is true that our tenets refuse to own the utility of that art to mankind; but it seemeth to me that we have considered the matter too nicely. God has bestowed on this youth a genius for art—shall we question His wisdom? Can we believe that He gives such rare gifts but for a wise and good purpose? I see the Divine hand in this; we shall do well to sanction the art and encourage this youth." '

"The assembly seems to have felt the force of these words, and the young painter was called in. He entered and took his station in the middle

---

The Artists of America: A Series of Biographical Sketches of American Artists, by C. Edwards Lester, New York, 1846, republished by Kennedy Galleries, Inc.—Da Capo Press, New York, 1970, pp. 74-77.

of the room, his father on his right hand and his mother on the left, surrounded by a company of simple-hearted worshippers. A female spoke—for in the Society of Friends the pride of man has fastened no badge of servitude upon women. There seemed to be but one opinion. If painting had been employed hitherto only to 'preserve voluptuous images, in wise and pure hands, it may rise in the scale of moral excellence, and display a loftiness of sentiment and a devout dignity worthy of the contemplation of Christians. Genius is given by God for some high purpose—what that purpose is, let us not inquire—it will be manifest in His own good time and way. He hath in this remote wilderness endowed with rich gifts of a superior spirit this youth, who has now our consent to cultivate his talents for Art. May it be demonstrated in his life and works, that the gifts of God have not been bestowed in vain, nor the motives of the beneficent inspiration which induces us to suspend the strict operation of our tenets prove barren of religious and moral effect!'

" 'At the conclusion of this address,' says Galt, who had the information from West himself, 'the women rose and kissed the young Artist and the men one by one laid their hands on his head.' I know of nothing more beautiful to the history of Art, or even of Religion. I know of no scene more worthy of the pencils of our painters, then this first, and, for aught I know, last consecration, in our country, of a young genius to Art. I am not certain, too, if this may not have been the first meeting ever convened in America to consider the high claims of Art upon citizens and Christians, and I should be inclined to doubt if any assembly has ever since been gathered, which has put forth so high, lasting, and noble an influence upon the Fine Arts.

"It was a scene the young painter himself never forgot. He assured Galt that from that hour he considered himself expressly dedicated to Art—and that this release from the strict tenets of his religious community implied a covenant on his part to employ his powers on subjects holy and pure. How sacredly he regarded this covenant the world knows—for no painter ever painted so much who always chose such pure and lofty themes. These honest men decided that the Lord had made Benjamin to be a painter. How well they judged, their neighbors had a fair opportunity of knowing when *Christ Healing the Sick* and *Death on a Pale Horse* were hung up in Philadelphia."

James Thomas Flexner in *America's Old Masters** described his appearance and manner: "The brilliant young painter seemed to have been endowed by nature with every requisite of success; he was even very handsome. Five feet eight inches tall and athletically built, he had strong harmonious features and light brown hair that shone over a remarkable pink and white complexion. He moved quickly and his eyes sparkled with an illusive vitality. All who met him were impressed by the contrast between the alertness of his look and his sedate remarks, which seemed more suitable to a Quaker preacher than to so radiant a young man. The quick repartee you expected never came, nor the sudden flash of emotion. West had great control over his temper, and on the rare occasions when it was aroused, he said nothing, working his clenched lips as if to hold in the fury. That his thoughts were methodical rather than brilliant pleased his neighbours, who would not have tolerated a genius of the Byronic stamp; moral in all his actions, never given to excess, he was the perfect type of Quaker youth inspired by God. Undoubtedly this was largely responsible for his amazing success in a proscribed profession."

Determined to go abroad to improve his art by study of the great masterpieces, West sailed for Italy in 1759, financed by a wealthy New Yorker, and given free passage by a Philadelphia merchant. He created a great sensation in Rome—the dilettanti there had thought of Americans as a savage people living in a primeval forest—and after three years there he became universally regarded as a great painter, elected to the Academies of Florence, Bologna, and Parma. Deciding his education to be complete, spent largely in study under Anton Raphael Mengs, he intended to return to Philadelphia after a visit to England.

Entering London in 1763, at twenty-five, he began modestly as a student of drawing at St. Martin's Lane Academy and painted an occasional portrait. An expert ice skater who had practiced often on the broad reaches of the Schuylkill, he left his studio when the weather grew cold for the basin in Kensington Gardens. Soon he was requested to give an exhibition of his brilliant skating which had caught the attention of the sports-loving aristocracy, who, discovering him to be a painter as well, went to see and praise his pictures. In 1764, he exhibited two classical pictures at the Society of Artists where all the leading British artists were represented. His pictures received the most praise from spec-

---

**America's Old Masters*, by James Thomas Flexner, Dover Publications, Inc., New York, 1967, pp. 38-39.

tators and newspaper critics alike. In less than three years, West became a popular artist, an important innovator in the neo-classical movement. His canvases of this period, such as *Agrippina Landing at Brundisium with the Ashes of Germanicus* (1766), were many years in advance of the French school that was to carry this style to its greatest height.

Recommended by Archbishop Drummond to the King, West's first meeting resulted in a commission, *The Departure of Regulus* (1767). The subject of the proposed picture was enthusiastically read from the text to the artist by the monarch himself. From this began the friendship that was one of the closest in history between a monarch and a painter.

Undertaking a recent historical subject in his painting, *The Death of General Wolfe* (1769), the artist revolted against the inflexible convention which then prevailed all over the western world and dictated that heroic figures be represented in ancient costumes; a convention which he himself had helped strengthen through his neo-classical pictures. Returning to the realism he had practiced in America copying from nature, he painted the soldiers in the red uniforms they had actually worn at the time, over everyone's objection, including the King's. The painting proved a triumph, and West had firmly established the practice of using modern dress in historical painting.

The King was sitting to him for his portrait in 1776, when a messenger brought in a dispatch box that announced the Declaration of Independence. All through the years of the Revolution that followed, West remained the intimate friend of George III despite his refusal to hide his sympathy for the American patriots.

It was nevertheless a difficult situation for West; Flexner describes an instance of his Christian character in handling it:* "The American loyalist exiles in London were furious that a rank traitor should be at the King's right hand, and indeed, when we consider George's usually unbending nature, it seems a strange phenomenon. The following incident, which is found in several contemporary documents, suggests an explanation. Lord Cathcart, whose wife was an American refugee, asked West in the presence of the King if he had heard the news of the British victory at Camden. The peer supposed, he cried in so loud a voice that the sovereign would certainly hear, that the victory would not give West as much pleasure as it gave His Majesty's loyal subjects in general! Silence filled the room as all the courtiers listened for West's reply. When the painter said, also loudly, that the calamities of his country never gave him pleasure, everyone waited for George to toss him from the court. But the King walked quietly over and put his hand on the American's shoulder. 'Right, right, West. I honour you for it.' Then he turned on Lord Cathcart and told him to remember that a man who did not love his native land could never be a faithful subject of another 'or a true friend.'

"Or a true friend—there lies the key to the mystery. A king, standing upright among his bowing courtiers, can trust and love a man who tells the truth even when it seems to his own disadvantage."

The defeat at Yorktown and the King's loss of control of Parliament made him deeply depressed, and he sought West's opinion on how America would act toward England if declared independent: ". . . the painter replied that the ill-will would soon subside and America would prefer England to all other European nations. Then George wondered whether Washington would proclaim himself king. When West answered that on the contrary he would return to private life, the King shook his head and said that if he did so he would be the greatest man in the world."†

Jubilant at the victory, West returned to his project of painting American history which he had begun in 1772 with *William Penn's Treaty with the Indians*. Writing to Charles Willson Peale in Philadelphia within a month after the signing of the peace, he said that he intended to compose "a set of pictures containing the great events which have effected the revolution of America. For the better enabling me to do this, I desire you to send whatever you thought would give me the most exact knowledge of the costume of the American armies, and [also] portraits in small, either painting or drawing, for the conspicuous characters necessary to be introduced into such a work."‡ Realizing afterwards that he could not publicly represent the King's defeats, he turned the project over to another of his pupils, John Trumbull.

There being no public gallery in London, nor an institution in either England or America to teach painting—the Royal Academy classes taught only drawing—West's studio and home became

---

*Ibid., pp. 68-69.

†Ibid., pp. 69-70.
‡Ibid., p. 70.

the first effective American art school. His Divine mission, of which he never lost a consciousness of having, was particularly fulfilled through his great gifts as an American Christian teacher of painting. His countrymen who came to him for instruction were later to paint many of the portraits and historical subjects that have kept for ever visible the men and events associated with the birth of America, the world's first Christian Republic.

As Flexner points out:* "Since almost every distinguished American artist of the next generation studied in his studio, he was incontrovertibly the father of American painting. Copley, Stuart, Charles Willson Peale, Rembrandt Peale, Pratt, Trumbull, Allston, Morse, Malbone, Leslie, Earle, Dunlap, Sully—West trained them all and many more besides. English painting too owed him a great debt. Contemporary art chroniclers tell us that every important British painter of the generation after Reynolds received instruction from West."

During his childhood, the Bible had been his primer; he was to exhibit almost a hundred Biblical pictures at the Royal Academy. Biblical, classical and historical themes with moral content were the constant sources of West's painting. In a letter of 1809 to Charles Willson Peale, he wrote: "Although I am friendly to portraying eminent men, I am not friendly to the indiscriminant waste of genius in portrait painting . . . the art of painting has powers to dignify man, by transmitting to posterity his noble actions, and his mental powers, to be viewed in those invaluable lessons of religion, love of country, and morality; such subjects are worthy of the pencil, they are worthy of being placed in view as the most instructive records to the rising generation."†

In 1780, the King had assisted West in overcoming the Church of England's objections to religious painting, and commissioned him to decorate the chapel at Windsor with thirty-five huge murals showing *The Progress of Revealed Religion*. Pleased with his plans for the chapel, he wrote the King on September 26, 1801: "I have finished three pictures, begun several others, and composed the remainder of the subjects for the chapel, on the progress of 'Revealed Religion', from its commencement to its completion; and the whole arrangement with the circumspection

from the Four Dispensations, into five and thirty compositions, that the most scrupulous amongst the various religious sects in this country, about admitting pictures into churches, must acknowledge them as truths, or the Scripture fabulous. They are subjects so replete with dignity, character, and expression as demanded the historian, the commentator, and the accomplished painter to bring them into view."‡ Because of the deterioration of the King's mind, the plans for the Chapel were eventually abandoned, and the completed pictures were returned to the painter.

During a visit to Paris in 1802, he exhibited *Death on a Pale Horse* at the Salon, whose color and composition anticipated the romantic movement in painting by a quarter of a century, which once again made him a leader in the progress of art. He played a major part in the foundation of the British Institution which formed the first important public collection of pictures in England. In 1810, when he was seventy-two, he completed in twenty days a picture of *Christ Requiring the Pure of Mind to Come to Him as Little Children*, in which all of the many figures were lifesized. The King finally went completely mad, and West at seventy-three was deprived of the means of support he had relied on during most of his life. Undaunted, he turned to the public, painting a huge canvas, *Christ Healing the Sick* (1811), which was purchased before it was completed for the largest sum ever paid in England for a contemporary picture. He then started on an even larger and more ambitious work, *Christ Rejected* (1812). Both paintings earned him small fortunes and great fame from traveling exhibitions and through the sale of engravings.

When he died on March 11, 1820, he had produced more than four hundred paintings and drawings which would cover a wall ten feet high and a quarter of a mile long. His body was enthroned in state in the great room of the Royal Academy; his right hand even in death had kept the position of holding a brush. He was buried in St. Paul's Cathedral with great ceremony.

JOHN SINGLETON COPLEY
1738–1815

While his life was divided almost equally between America and later England, it was in America that he created his greatest works of art. In isolation from the great art centers of the world, he

---

Ibid., p. 74.

†*Benjamin West and the Taste of his Times,* by Grose Evans, Southern Illinois University Press, 1959, p. 31.

‡Catalog, *Revealed Religion; A Series of Paintings by Benjamin West in the War Memorial Chapel,* Bob Jones University, Greenville, South Carolina, 1963.

was a seeker for perfection who worked with passionate intensity, reaching deep within himself to realize his own vision.

Born in or near Boston, a few months before Benjamin West, his gifts began to be expressed by the time he was seven or eight in a charcoal sketch of a group of martial figures. The Bible was an important source of inspiration to the boy who early painted scenes from it. In 1748, his mother, widowed shortly after Copley's birth, married Peter Pelham, a schoolteacher and the first well-trained mezzotint engraver to appear in the Colonies. He introduced the youth to an atmosphere where prints, paintings, and artists' supplies were familiar household accessories. Thus, through Providence, the home was one of the few in the Colonies where art was the predominant interest, in preparation for his mission to portray with powerful sincerity and fidelity the men and women of Massachusetts who figured so importantly in the Constitutional Debate Period.

His stepfather gave him some training in painting, and copies of old masters remaining in the studio at one time occupied by John Smibert gave him an idea of the traditions of European painting. At thirteen, his stepfather died, and to help support his mother and half-brother, he at once set up shop as a painter and engraver. He was painting professionally by the time he was fifteen, doing stiff but competent likenesses in the manner of John Greenwood (1727-1792) and Joseph Badger (1708-1765). The arrival of Joseph Blackburn (active in America 1754 to 1763) in New England in 1754 had an immediate effect on his style, and after several years of methodical industry Copley surpassed Blackburn and became the best painter in America. Determined to work in pastels, he wrote the famous pastellist, Jean-Etienne Liotard, in Geneva, asking him to send a set of pastels. When they arrived, he taught himself to use them, and then became the first important American draughtsman in pastel.

Chafing frequently at what he considered to be the limited opportunities for the practice and appreciation of art in the Colonies, he was consistently thrown back on his own resources. Cut off from access to the fluency of European styles, unable to learn brushwork from engravings, he developed his own technique through the laborious process of trial and error. Unable to receive more than a few hints on coloring from abroad, and having seen only a small number of copies of European pictures which were usually very inaccurate, he was forced to develop by experimentation his own personal palette. His drawing, his characterization—all had to be slowly worked out through intense application and steadfast vision. Finally setting aside his aspirations to produce the imaginative flights he understood to be the practice of great art through his correspondence with foreign-trained artists, he gave himself up to painting the likenesses his countrymen wanted; at heart a passionate realist, he gloried in painting things as they are—and made immortal pictures. His Boston portraits are the most authentic records of our pre-Revolutionary ancestors which have come down to us. John Adams wrote of Copley's portraits: "You can scarcely help discoursing with them, and asking questions and receiving answers."*

He reached middle age before he appreciated the advantages of making preliminary drawings. Up to that time he worked directly on the canvas, feeling his way with infinite pains. One contemporary account exclaimed that Copley had "painted a very beautiful head of my mother, who told me that she sat to him fifteen or sixteen times! Six hours at a time!! And that once she had been sitting to him for many hours, when he left the room for a few minutes, but requested that she would not move from her seat during his absence. She had the curiosity, however, to peep at the picture, and found it all rubbed out."†

In 1766, he sent his *Boy with Squirrel* to London for submission to the annual exhibition of the Society of Artists. When it arrived, Reynolds, West, and the other academicians were astonished and delighted that a twenty-eight year old American who had never been out of the provincial city of Boston could paint such a fine painting. After confusion over the identity of the artist, it was exhibited incorrectly as by "William Copley"; connoisseurs flocked to see it, and on the strength of this one picture, the unknown painter was elected a member of the Society of Artists, the highest honor that could be given by the English art world.

Both West and Reynolds urged him to study in England. However, his marriage in 1769 to Susannah Clarke, daughter of one of the leading Tory families of Boston, and his increasing prosperity discouraged him from giving up the security of his business and the twenty-acre farm with three houses on it—which took in most of

Three Hundred Years of American Painting, by Alexander Eliot, Time Incorporated, New York, 1957, p. 14.
†*Ibid.*

what is now Beacon Hill—for the uncertain benefits of foreign study and travel. His first long journey away from home was to New York, where he stayed six months painting many of the prominent people.

Copley had tried to be non-partisan in his politics during the events leading up to the Revolution, although at the time of the Stamp Act resistance his letters showed his sympathy to be with the patriots. However, his father-in-law, Richard Clarke, was an agent for the East India Company and one of the consignees of the tea that figured in the Boston Tea Party. Copley was also friendly with John Hancock and Samuel Adams. About half of his sitters were Whigs, and the other half were Tory. His own background was Whig and his wife's was Tory. Soon he found himself called upon to try to mediate a conciliation between both sides over the tea; though he failed in the task, it was a charge he felt he had done everything possible to accomplish and he thus became a participant in a turning point in American history.

In 1774, he sailed for Europe, and while in Rome, painted *The Ascension*, the first complicated composition he had ever attempted and also his first original essay into history painting. His Christian faith was deeply stirred. Writing to his half-brother, Henry Pelham, he expressed his feelings: ". . . I have always, as you may remember, considered the Ascension as one of the most Sublime Subjects in Scripture. I considered how the Apostles would be affected at that Instant . . . no one who reads the Account in the first Chapter of the Acts can be a moment's loss to decide that they would be so astonish'd, and after crowding together to hear what Christ said to St. Peter with vast attention in their countenances, they would (keeping their places) and their attention to the Ascending Christ absorbed in holy Adoration, worship him as he rose from the Earth, and so far from speaking to one another that not one of them would reflect that he had a companion with him. No thought could at that Instant intrude itself into their minds, already fully possessed with Holy wonder . . . It would be just to observe that the Apostolic Character forbids to make the expression of Astonishment very great. It should be tempered with Love and contain Majesty of behavior acquired by many times being spectators of the Power of Christ exercised in Miracles of a Stupendous nature."*

In the same letter, he also noted: ". . . but my utmost vigilence to make good what I have

acquired and at least (to support what I have gained) shall be made use of, and I hope in this to be bless'd as I have by the goodness of God in all my important concerns through life. Could anything be more fortunate than the time of my leaving Boston? Poor America! I hope for the best but I fear the worst. Yet certain I am She will finally emerge from her present Calamity and become a Mighty Empire. And it is a pleasing reflection that I shall stand amongst the first of the Artists that shall have led that Country to the Knowledge and cultivation of the fine Arts, happy in the pleasing reflection that they will one Day shine with a luster not inferior to what they have done in Greece or Rome in my Native Country."†

After a journey through many of the leading cities of Europe, he arrived in London in 1775 where he was reunited with his family. Lack of immediate success in England convinced him that he had to abandon the approach he had worked out so painstakingly for himself in isolation, and in his middle age learn to paint like the fashionable British painters. He was so successful in his application that his work underwent an almost complete change. When he carried his new technique into historical painting, he won great acclaim following the exhibition of *The Death of Chatham* (1781), which took two years to complete, and included the portraits of more than fifty noblemen, most of them painted from life. It is regarded by many as the greatest historical painting ever done in England.

In 1776, he was elected an Associate of the Royal Academy, and in 1783 he became a full member. Although in the full tide of prosperity, he grew increasingly homesick for America; profoundly affected by the unending denunciations he heard of his countrymen, he became a staunch patriot. When he painted the American merchant Elkanah Watson in 1782, he determined to place in the background "a ship bearing to America the acknowledgments of our independence," but left off the stars and stripes. The painting stood for a long time unfinished against the wall. On December 5, he accompanied Watson to the House of Lords to hear King George III acknowledge American independence. Afterwards in great excitement, Copley invited Watson to return to his studio. "There," wrote Watson in

---

Letters and Papers of John Singleton Copley and Henry Pelham, 1739-1776, The Massachusetts Historical Society, 1914, republished by Kennedy Graphics, Inc.—Da Capo Press, New York, 1970, pp. 295-296.
†*Ibid.*, p. 301.

his diary, "with a bold hand, a master's touch, and I believe an American heart, he attached to the ship the stars and stripes. This, I imagine, was the first American flag hoisted in England."*

His portraits and historical paintings continued to bring him substantial income and renown. Creating a vast canvas twenty-five feet by twenty, *The Repulse of the Floating Batteries of Gibraltar*, he completed it in 1791 after six years of laborious work. There was no gallery large enough to contain it and he finally set up in a tent near Buckingham Palace. The royal family attended the opening, followed by some sixty thousand people.

Biblical subjects were also a continuing inspiration to him: *The Nativity*, 1777; *Samuel Relating to Eli the Judgements of God upon Eli's House*, 1780; *The Tribute Money*, 1782; *Abraham Offering Up His Son Isaac*, 1796; *Hagar and Ishmael in the Wilderness*, 1798; *Saul Reproved by Samuel for Not Obeying the Commandments of the Lord*, 1798.

His later years after 1798 were difficult ones of professional setbacks, loss of popularity, financial troubles, and an increasing conviction that he had made a mistake by leaving America to learn the manner of the old masters. He told his wife that his American portraits, which he had once scorned as crude, were better than any of the highly polished works of his English career.

He continued to paint until his seventy-eighth year. Before his death in London on September 9, 1815, "He was perfectly resigned and willing to die, and expressed his firm trust in God, through the merits of the Redeemer."

CHARLES WILLSON PEALE
1741–1827

Known to his contemporaries as "the ingenious Mr. Peale," he was a painter, inventor, saddler, upholsterer, harness maker, silversmith, sign painter, watch and clock repairer, engraver, soldier, politician, taxidermist, dentist, scientist, museum proprietor, writer, and naturalist—an outstanding example of the ingenuity developed by the Colonists when every homestead had to manufacture its own needs. As a craftsman, Peale was so able that he became a universal genius, belonging to the select company of men like Franklin and Jefferson. Like them, he also took a prominent part in the Revolution, his interests

were as varied as theirs, and he left as they did an enduring mark on almost every field he touched.

He was born in St. Paul's Parish, Queen Anne County, Maryland, and showed an early propensity to draw. His father died when he was eight; Mrs. Peale moved to Annapolis where she supported herself and her four children sewing dresses, and soon Charles was making "patterns for the ladies to work after." He amused the family by copying two prints in oil colors using the expedient of putting them under the glass on which he painted. The earliest original design he could remember having made was a schoolboy painting of Adam and Eve. Withdrawn from school at thirteen, he was apprenticed to a saddler; when he was twenty he was released early from his apprenticeship as a reward for special diligence. Soon after, he married and was persuaded to accept a substantial loan from his former master to set himself up in business. This initiated a series of debts over a period of time that caused him much anguish and nearly landed him in debtor's prison on several occasions. "All that can be said in mitigation of my indiscretion is that I engaged in so many labors of Body and mind with my several mechanical undertakings, that I allowed myself no time for reflections of any kind. I did not seem to regard the future, being wholly occupied with the present, or feared danger until I was overtaken with difficulties."† He vowed to earn the needed sums and return in triumph, and although it was to take eleven years, with his creditor's money accumulating at six per cent, he paid them off in the summer of 1775.

He soon broadened his activities to include upholstery, harness-making, watch and clock repairing, and silversmithing. During a trip to Norfolk, Virginia, he saw several amateurish landscapes and a portrait. "They were miserably done; had they been better, perhaps they would not have led me to the idea of attempting anything in that way."‡ After producing a landscape and several portraits of members of his family, he began a sign painting business. Having no idea how artists prepared and put on colors, and having never seen a palette or easel, he worked out these details for himself, just as he had designed his own watchmaking and silversmithing tools.

Searching for more knowledge in his new trade,

America's Old Masters, by James Thomas Flexner, Dover Publications, Inc., New York, 1967, p. 156.

†*Charles Willson Peale*, by Charles Coleman Sellers, Charles Scribner's Sons, New York, 1969, p. 43.

‡*America's Old Masters*, by James Thomas Flexner, Dover Publications, Inc., New York, 1967, p. 178.

he went to Philadelphia where he visited the studios of several artists, acquired a volume on painting, *The Handmaid to the Arts* (1758) by Robert Dossie, and bought some paints. Becoming aware that painting was a much more complicated craft than he had thought, he traded John Hesselius (1728-1778) a saddle in exchange for lessons in portrait painting. In 1765, he sailed from Annapolis to Boston where the paintings in the old studio of John Smibert (1668-1751) impressed him deeply. He then continued on to Newburyport, where he painted several portraits. While there, he associated with the patriot leaders, and during the Stamp Act agitation, he wrote that he "assisted in making emblematic designs showing with what unanimity of detestation the people viewed that odious act of Parliament."*

Returning to Boston, he paid a visit to John Singleton Copley who gave him encouragement—"The sight of Mr. Copley's picture room was a great feast to me"†—and he was soon busy painting miniatures. When back in Annapolis, his work so impressed the leading citizens that Governor Sharpe and ten members of the Council subscribed the funds necessary to send him to study in London; a merchant gladly furnished free passage and Chief Justice Allen of Pennsylvania, who had financed Benjamin West's trip to Italy, gave Peale a letter to that artist.

He arrived in London early in 1767, and hurried immediately to West's studio, who, when told that an American student waited to see him, rushed downstairs with his brush still in his hand to greet his fellow countryman. West immediately took responsibility for his welfare, found him lodgings nearby and helped him in every way he could; Peale always remembered with gratitude the kindness of his reception. The master was thirty, only three years older than his pupil, and Peale was greatly impressed by him and his work. However, he did not enjoy London, and struggled to learn as much as possible as quickly as he could in order to return home soon: "I was not content to learn to paint in one way, but engaged in the whole circle of arts, except painting on enamel."‡ His studies included oil and miniature painting, modeling in plaster, and mezzotint scraping. He exhibited three miniatures and two oil portraits at the Royal Academy shows of 1768 and 1769. His major English work was a full-length portrait of William Pitt, from which he made his first mezzotint. Reacting strongly against his entire English environment, he became more than ever an American patriot, and, convinced that the Colonies should develop their own manufactures, refused to take any English clothes with him when he sailed back to Annapolis in the spring of 1769.

He returned to considerable success, and in 1772 was called to Mount Vernon to paint the first portrait ever made of George Washington. It has become one of the artist's best known works. Peale executed a miniature of Martha Washington at the same time, which was set in a gold frame in a pendant, and it is said Washington wore it round his neck till the last days of his life. The artist continued to receive advice from West and also Benjamin Franklin, whom he had looked up in England. Franklin urged him not to become depressed over any lack of encouragement he might receive: "The arts have always travelled westward, and there is no doubt of their flourishing hereafter on our side of the Atlantic as the number of wealthy inhabitants shall increase."§

After a season spent in Baltimore and another at Charlestown, Peale settled in Philadelphia in 1776. "Yesterday morning I took a walk into Arch Street to see Mr. Peale's painter's room," wrote John Adams to Abigail, "Peale is from Maryland, a tender, soft, affectionate creature. He showed me a large picture containing a group of figures, which, upon inquiry, I found were his family: his mother and his wife's mother, himself and his wife, his brothers and sisters, and his children, sons and daughters, all young [*The Peale Family*, 1773]. There was a pleasant, a happy cheerfulness in their countenances, and a familiarity in their air towards each other.

"He showed me one moving picture. His wife, all bathed in tears, with a child about six months old laid out upon her lap [*Rachel Weeping*, 1772]. This picture struck me prodigiously . . . He showed me several imitations of heads, which he had made in clay, as large as the life, with his hands only. Among the rest, one of his own head and face, which was a great likeness. He is ingenious. He has vanity, loves finery, wears a sword, gold lace, speaks French, is capable of friendship, and strong family attachments and natural affections."¶

He had long been active among the Sons of

Ibid., p. 183.
†*Ibid.*
‡*Ibid.*, p. 186.

§*Ibid.*, p. 191.
¶*Familiar Letters of John Adams and his Wife, Abigail Adams during the Revolution*, New York, 1876, pp. 215-216.

Liberty, and on August 9, 1776, wrote in his diary: "Entered as a common soldier in Captain Peter's company of militia. Went on guard that night."* Within two months, his fellow soldiers elected him to second lieutenant; several weeks later they promoted him to first lieutenant; by June, 1777, he was made a captain. He saw active duty in the battles of Princeton and Trenton, an officer who foraged and cooked for his men, and made fur-lined moccasins with his own hands to replace their worn-out boots. At Valley Forge, Peale executed miniatures of some forty officers on ivory for them to send back home as momentos. Using bed ticking for canvas, he also portrayed Washington, Lafayette, Nathanael Greene, and dozens of other leaders.

After the British evacuated Philadelphia, he was among the first Whigs back in the city. Before long, he became deeply involved in politics, which soon alienated his wealthy patrons and adversely affected his business. In 1778, he was elected to the Assembly and became chairman or member of thirty-two legislative committees, but at the end of his term declined to run again. Looking back on it in his autobiography, he felt he had been launched "into that dangerous and troublesome Political Sea, subject to like troubles by every blast, and very often in contrary directions . . . for the difference of opinion here made me enemies of those whom before I had considered my friends."† By the time of little Rembrandt Peale's christening on August 26, 1779, Peale had changed his denominational allegiance to Presbyterian, whose members by and large supported the constitution of 1776, while those of the Church of England had opposed it.

To secure portrait commissions, he attracted public attention by painting life-size portraits of revolutionary heroes from the small pictures he had painted of them between battles, and collected them together in the first public picture gallery in America. His other activities included the construction of a triumphal arch celebrating the end of the war; a representation of the engagement of the *Bon Homme Richard* and the *Serapis* through a series of six scenes of "moving pictures", mechanically devised and operated by Peale with backstage sound effects; a series of mezzotints after portraits of historical figures; transparencies—oil paintings on paper lit from behind by many candles—for public celebrations.

In 1786, he conceived the idea of expanding his picture gallery into a natural history museum, a project which was to occupy all his later years although he continued to paint as well. Fascinated by some mastodon bones of which he had been asked to make drawings, he soon broadened his interest to many other aspects of the natural world. He collected a great variety of birds and animals, having taught himself taxidermy, and then discovered the methods employed by modern institutions; he did not simply stuff but used his abilities as a sculptor to model the body on which the pelts were placed. The practice of mounting them in natural attitudes in habitat settings was also his invention. To collect specimens of plants, minerals, fossils and other natural curiosities, he made frequent trips to the countryside. An especially popular exhibit was the assembled skeleton of a mastodon, which Peale himself helped excavate in Ulster County, New York, in 1801. He moved his museum from the building of the American Philosophical Society to the second floor of Independence Hall in 1802 where it remained until 1826. More than 100,000 objects were eventually assembled, which he arranged in an orderly system in advance of his times.

Desiring to organize the artists of Philadelphia into an academy where their work could be on public view, he formed the Columbianum, or American Academy of the Fine Arts, in 1795. This proved short-lived, but he persevered; and in 1805 he was one of the founders of the Pennsylvania Academy of the Fine Arts, which still exists.

When his son Rembrandt returned from a trip to England in 1803, well versed in new techniques learned in West's studio, Peale, who had not painted for six years, revived his interest in painting, taking lessons from Rembrandt almost daily. Later, when in his seventieth year, he completely changed his style of painting to follow the techniques of the disciples of David which Rembrandt had newly brought back from his studies in Paris. Some critics regard these pictures as his best. In 1821, when he was eighty, he began one of his largest pictures, *Christ Healing the Sick at the Pool of Bethesda*, eight feet wide and more than six feet high. An adaptation of a print by Christian Wilhelm Ernst Dietrich, he finished it in three months, falling from a scaffold in mid-course while working on the upper part, and breaking one or more ribs. He could not be persuaded by his wife to stop, explaining that while at work he could feel no pain.

He made a number of inventions, including an improved kitchen chimney, a new kind of wooden

*Flexner, *Op. Cit.*, p. 194.
†Sellers, *Op. Cit.*, p. 171.

bridge, a stove that consumed its own smoke, and a steam bath. He also improved the polygraph for making copies of documents, made false teeth, and conducted experimental farming. He corresponded frequently with Thomas Jefferson, wrote an unpublished autobiography, published an *Essay on Building Wooden Bridges*, 1797; *An Epistle to a Friend on the Means of Preserving Health*, 1803; *An Essay to Promote Domestic Happiness*, 1812. He painted Washington from life more often than any other artist—fourteen times in all.

He out-lived three wives, and was courting a fourth when he died at 86. Of seventeen sons and daughters, eleven lived to maturity, many of whom were named after famous painters and naturalists. It has been said that if the documents were not there, if the paintings did not hang on museum walls, who would believe that Peale had really lived?

REMBRANDT PEALE
1778–1860

The second son and third child of Charles Willson Peale, Rembrandt Peale was born February 22, 1778, in a farm house in Bucks County, Pennsylvania, where his mother had fled from the approach of the British army. His father was at that time a captain of a volunteer company with Washington's army.

He began drawing at the age of eight, between school hours; he was later to say that his eagerness to return to his drawing was so great that he had swallowed his food without chewing, affecting his health. His father gave him his earliest instruction, and by the time he was thirteen, he left school to devote himself day and night to his art, painting a *Self-Portrait at Thirteen* (1791), now in a private collection.

Having been born on the same birth day as Washington, he had a childhood worship of Washington; he venerated his character and aspect, and sought every occasion to see him. His great desire to paint a portrait of the President was finally realized at age seventeen, when a series of three sittings of three hours each were granted, having been arranged by his father who also planned to paint a canvas of his own. At the second sitting, they were joined by James Peale (1749-1831), brother of the father, and Raphaelle Peale (1774-1825), Rembrandt's brother. Rembrandt worked in front, slightly to the sitter's left, his father taking a three-quarters view on Washington's left and Rembrandt's right

hand. James on the other side, began a three-quarters view on ivory, and beyond him, on Washington's right, Raphaelle began a profile on paper. Gilbert Stuart (1755-1828), for whom the President had just previously sat, was told by Mrs. Washington of the scene. He replied by warning her earnestly to take good care of her husband, for he stood in danger of being "Pealed all around."

While in Charleston, South Carolina, Peale painted a number of leading citizens for his father's museum, among them *David Ramsay*, done when the artist was between seventeen to nineteen years old. He left Charleston for London in 1801, accompanied by his wife and two children, to assist his brother Rubens in an exhibition of a mastodon which he had helped his father excavate in Ulster County, New York. While in London he published two treatises on the mastodon, which were commented on favorably by Cuvier. He also took the opportunity to study under Benjamin West, painted portraits for his father's gallery in Philadelphia, and exhibited several pictures at the Royal Academy.

Peale returned to America in 1803 and opened a studio in Philadelphia, having gained much success. He was one of the founders of the Pennsylvania Academy of the Fine Arts in 1805. Trips to Paris in 1808 and 1809 followed, where he painted portraits of many of the French leaders for his father's museum.

In 1814 he opened a natural history museum and picture gallery in Baltimore. To light his museum with gas in 1816, he became involved with the formation of a gas company, which inaugurated this industry in America. During a period of nine years with his museum, he painted many portraits, and composed a number of large canvases such as *The Ascent of Elijah*. To recoup operating losses, he painted a historical composition on a huge canvas twenty-four feet long and thirteen feet high containing 23 full sized figures, called *The Court of Death* (1820). Termed "A Moral Allegory", the idea was taken from a poem by an English clergyman, Bishop Beilby Porteus. It was the first large picture of its size executed in America, conceived as a mural painting without a wall to be toured to the principal cities. Exhibited over a period of thirteen months with very favorable acclaim, it was seen by 32,000 people. In New York it was recommended from the pulpits, and by the Corporation of the city, who went in a body to see it. Large touring pictures by other artists, which pointed up a moral or Biblical teaching, became a unique cultural phenomenon in America during this period.

Peale disposed of his museum in 1822, after which it was managed by his brother, Rubens, until 1830 when it was sold to the city and was long known as the Old City Hall. Restored, it is now The Peale Museum, and is the oldest museum building in the United States.

From 1822 to 1823, he worked in a studio he established in New York, then returned to Philadelphia. There he labored to perfect an ideal portrait of Washington. After sixteen attempts he created his well-known "port-hole" portrait which was considered a great success and was purchased by the United States Government in 1832. Because of the number of copies (76) he made of this picture—which he reproduced with various modifications until the end of his life—it is his most famous portrait.

Succeeding Trumbull as President of the American Academy of Fine Arts in 1825, he spent the next few years in New York and Boston painting portraits and experimenting with lithography. He was among the first to practice this medium in America and his large head of Washington was awarded a silver medal at the Franklin Institute.

He went abroad again in 1828 for two years, described in his *Notes on Italy*, published in 1831. His manual, *Peale's Graphics*, setting forth a system for teaching drawing and writing was published in 1835.

He continued to paint portraits throughout his later years, producing replicas of his *Washington*, and writing his recollections which appeared in *The Crayon*. By then he had become the dean of American painting, the last living painter from the period of the Founding Fathers. Macgill James, writing in the catalog to an exhibition of paintings by Rembrandt Peale, observed: "The Americans of the fifties must have felt a certain awe for the aged artist when he ascended the platform to deliver his well known lecture on *Washington and His Portraits*, for he had actually looked upon the great man who had become a legend."*

Among his many portrait paintings are: *Christopher Gadsen*, c. 1795-1797; *Thomas Jefferson*, 1800; *Rubens Peale and the First Geranium*, 1801; *Henry Clay*; *Andrew Jackson*; *Robert Hare*, 1820-1825; *The Marquis de Lafayette*, 1825.

*Catalog, *An Exhibition of Paintings by Rembrandt Peale*, The Municipal Museum of Baltimore, 1937, Introduction by Macgill James, p. 5.

EDWARD LAMSON HENRY
1841–1919

A painter of 18th- and early 19th-century American historical events and genre themes, his art always told a story. He was born in Charleston, South Carolina and raised in New York City. His wife, Francis L. Henry, was later to write of his childhood in her biography of the artist: "A little older, when children ask for toys and playthings, he asked for brushes and paint. In church, to keep him quiet during the long sermons of that day, he was given a pencil, and Bibles, hymn books and prayer books were filled with battles, boats, horses and wagons. And if the minister happened to be preaching about the warriors and heroes of old, they too were generally to be found among the drawings . . ."†

After leaving school, his training in business was begun as a messenger on Wall Street. Assigned to deliver some bonds in a great hurry to a bank, he became so interested in an engraving of early American history hanging on the wall of the bank, that time flew. On his way back, he again stopped to look at pictures in windows, and so returned to the office long after closing hours, his interest in bonds for that day lost. His family soon gave up hopes of a business career for him and allowed him to follow his artistic inclinations. He studied in New York with the landscapist W. M. Oddie (c.1818-1865) and then at the Pennsylvania Academy of Fine Arts in Philadelphia in 1858. "He was greatly interested in keeping the old landmarks of the city for coming generations. With Mr. Kulp, a noted antiquarian, he made the restoration of Independence Hall as it is today."‡ He was nineteen years old when he went to Paris to study.

"Even in those early days of hard study, his great interest was centered in life around him; but the greatest interest was American history. In school days the lesson in history was always read so far beyond the given lesson that the teacher would be compelled to stop him at recitation . . . He never forgot dates: ask him at any time when such and such an event happened, instead of mentioning a number of years he would tell the exact date of the event."§

†*A Memorial Sketch* by Francis L. Henry, in *The Life and Work of Edward Lamson Henry N.A.*, by Elizabeth McCausland, N.Y. State Museum Bulletin No. 339, 1945, republished by Kennedy Galleries, Inc.—Da Capo Press, New York, 1970, p. 313.
‡*Ibid.*, p. 324.
§*Ibid.*, pp. 314-315.

Elected to the National Academy of Design in 1869, at age 26, his paintings appealed greatly to his countrymen—they were sold even before they were shown in the annual Academy exhibitions. In later life, he had the reputation of always selling on varnishing day.

He frequently used his friends and neighbors as models in his paintings. Dr. Howard Crosby, the Henrys' pastor and close friend coming to call one day, was chosen as the clergyman in Henry's painting *A Virginia Wedding* (1890), and is seen standing in the door.

His paintings were crafted with affection for his subjects and careful attention to detail and research. "His large library of books, mostly Americana, travels, costumes and customs of the early American habits and life that our forefathers led, was one evidence of his interest. He was always searching through the country for their homes, sparing no pains or expenses in getting all and everything that could help him make his work as perfect as possible; for he always felt and others often said, his paintings would live and be used as references long after he had gone. So, he wanted to make them as perfect and as true to the time they represented as was possible."* He often drew upon his own large collection of historical carriages and costumes. He had an enthusiasm for all forms of transportation, as well as architecture, antiques, photography and music.

Trips to Europe in 1860-1862, 1871, 1875, and 1881 gave him the opportunity to study with the leading artists there of the time: Suisse, Gleyre and Gustave Courbet. The critic, Will Low, wrote in 1919 that his work would remain unique, ". . . and a typical American product little affected by his early training in France, devoted to the perpetuation of truly national types and forming, when the day comes for its better appreciation, a life work of which an American artist may well be proud . . ."†

A memorial of the artist read at the April 28, 1920 meeting of the National Academy of Design, noted: "No one can doubt the peculiar historic interest as well as the genuine charm of the paintings of E. L. Henry—a full fledged Academician for over half a century . . . Mr. Henry's art has a characteristic American quality, no doubt enhanced by his subjects, yet not wholly due to them. In depicting on canvas the manners and customs, the inventions and habitations, the

politics and pioneering of his native country during the first half of the nineteenth century, Mr. Henry stands unrivalled . . ."‡

Among his many works are: *Old Clock on the Stairs*, 1868; *St. Paul's Church: 1766*, 1868; *Independence Hall*, 1870; *The Meeting of General Washington and Rochambeau*, 1873; *Mountain Stage*, 1880; *In Sight of Home*, 1882; *Studying Her Sunday School Lesson*, 1890; *Sir William Johnson Presenting Medals to the Indian Chiefs of the Six Nations at Johnstown, N.Y., 1772*, 1903; *Carriage Ride on a Country Lane*, 1906.

JAMES EDWARD KELLY
1855–1933

A student of history all of his life, Kelly's mother, an Irishwoman, had early directed his patriotism toward the land in which he had been born in freedom. His father, of Scottish birth and by trade an optician, recognized the capabilities of the boy, reading to him from the newspapers and illustrated periodicals of the civil war period, and taking him everywhere with him in New York. Together they watched the many kinds of ships from the old Battery, witnessed the military and naval processions, identified eminent soldiers and sailors, and in other ways absorbed the activity and excitement of the times. A direction was begun towards an artistic career for the boy, with American history and its outstanding participants as the leading themes.

His first pictures were historical compositions, and from his earliest childhood he had studied everything he could find touching American history. It can be said that he was the only artist and sculptor who during so long and active a life in his chosen profession always adhered firmly to his original boyhood resolution to draw and model only American subjects.

In 1871, he was apprenticed to a wood engraver and studied in the Academy of Design. He was one of the founders of the Art Students' League. After working in the art department of Harper & Brothers in 1873, he opened a studio with Edwin A. Abbey where they began illustrating for the magazines. He never studied abroad or absorbed any European influences, going directly to individual and authoritative sources whenever possible for inspiration and guidance in developing his themes.

Long before the magazine world awoke to the

Ibid., p. 312.
†McCausland, *Op. Cit.*, p. 65.

‡*Ibid.*, p. 66.

fact that material relating to the civil war was rapidly disappearing, Kelly had searched out dozens of the men whose names were written in history, and using his special aptitude for interviewing had made sketches of them from life, and had taken down from them their stories in their own words. This resulted in the only series of portraits of military and naval leaders of the Civil War for which the subjects sat or were otherwise sketched from life, and who, in nearly all instances, approved and signed them as soon as the artist had finished.

His first piece of sculpture was a statuette of *Sheridan's Ride* which he set about modeling in wax after gaining a few hints from his friend Hartley, the sculptor, and using sketches he had made of Sheridan plus his thorough knowledge of horses.

Chosen to model the five bas-reliefs around the base of the Monmouth monument, Kelly's first large order, his designs were accepted over those of sixty competitors. They represent *Ramsey Defending His Guns, Washington Rallying His Troops, Molly Pitcher, The Council of War at Hopewell,* and *Wayne's Charge.*

His bronze bas-relief, *Washington in Prayer at Valley Forge,* originally placed in the New York West Side Y.M.C.A., was subsequently transferred by direction of President Theodore Roosevelt to the East front of the U.S. Sub-Treasury, Wall and Broad Streets, and unveiled there with appropriate ceremonies, February 22, 1907. This was one of his favorite subjects, for which he made careful researches among the less well-known narratives of the Valley Forge encampment of 1777-78, and was fully convinced of its historic basis and authenticity on all points. The work created an immense amount of interest throughout the country; and fac-similes in various forms were requested by and supplied to a great many colleges, schools, churches, historical societies and other institutions. It is more widely known than any other of his works.

Diffident by nature, he worked quietly—almost aloof—and seldom did anything to attract general notice. Those seeking works from his studio had to hunt to locate him. Writing in *Munsey's Magazine,* Anna Leach noted: "The most striking characteristic of his work is its pure Americanism. It belongs to no school. Mr. Kelly has been trained in no school. The conventions of sculpture are to him a sealed book. When somebody made a polite inquiry concerning his technique, Mr. Kelly looked gravely in his face, and said, 'I do not know what you mean by "technique".'

. . . While he is the sternest realist in form, he is a brilliant idealist in the spirit of conception."*

His other works include: *Arnold Wounded in the Trenches; Paul Revere's Ride; Schuyler Giving His Plans to Gates Before the Battle of Saratoga,* for the Saratoga monument; statue of *General Grant at Donelson,* for which the general posed; statue of *Call to Arms,* for the Troy monument; statue of *General Buford at Gettysburg; Knowlton at Harlem Heights,* at Columbia College for the Sons of the Revolution.

JOHN WESLEY GROSSMAN, JR.
(1932–   )

Born in Des Moines, Iowa, the eldest of six children, his parents became aware of his artistic abilities by the time he was five. His first instructor at seven was a neighbor boy who showed him how to draw Mickey Mouse. When ten, he began drawing and writing the first "issue" of a 20 page homemade comic book called *Sea Comics,* which gave his family amusement and some puzzlement—it being a combination of an interest in undersea life and science fiction adventures. Twenty-four issues resulted between 1942 and 1946 in which he taught himself drawing styles by copying *Buck Rogers* and science fiction pulp magazine illustrators.

As a boy he received early religious training and was baptized in the Open Bible Church in Des Moines. By the time he reached high school, he was majoring in commercial art, and working after school hours in a small Des Moines studio. A series of Scholastic Art Awards conducted by Scholastic Magazines were received by him and his work exhibited in their annual National High School Art Exhibitions, held in the Fine Arts Galleries of the Carnegie Institute, Pittsburgh, in 1947, 1949 and 1950. He was also awarded a scholarship by them to the Minneapolis School of Art where he studied briefly in 1950; he was soon working on his own as a freelance professional lettering artist in Minneapolis, having developed an interest in letterforms.

After service in the U.S. Army 1952-54, and a three month generalized summer course at the College of Arts and Crafts, Oakland, California, he was again working as a lettering artist in a studio in San Francisco. A two year trip to Europe ensued, 1956-58, spent mostly in Paris where he attended the Cours de la Civilization

---

*Article, *A Sculptor of American History,* by Anna Leach, *Munsey's Magazine,* Vol. XIV, 1896, p. 452.

Française at the Sorbonne, and during which he also travelled, sketched and visited the museums.

Returning to San Francisco, he married Margaret Andrea Clausen in 1959, an artist whom he had met previously in 1955, and together they began freelancing, offering a complete design service. Their son, Jason was born in 1964. A graphic designer until 1971, examples of his work were exhibited in a number of west coast artist and art director shows. Grossman was also a lettering and design instructor at the San Francisco Art Institute 1960-66.

His return to America had made him realize how deeply he loved his own country, and he and Andrea had soon begun a study of the principles of the American form of government. In 1962, they were led to attend a study group meeting of *The Christian History of the Constitution* and there found the understanding they had been seeking. Grossman was later to become the designer of the Christian History series of books and related material.

By 1964, he had become convinced that he must ultimately make a change of careers to that of painting, working from the original Christian base of western art. A six year transition period followed, during which he taught himself oil painting, exhibited, and practiced graphic design at the same time. His first paintings were exhibited in 1966, and he had his first one-man show in San Francisco in 1968, followed by one in 1969, and another in 1972. A major showing spanning six years of his work was mounted at the Pioneer Museum and Haggin Galleries in Stockton, California, also in 1972.

He was appointed by Governor Reagan to the California Arts Commission in 1967, serving first as vice-chairman, and then as chairman 1969-70. Among his activities on the commission, he was particularly instrumental in conceiving and implementing a touring exhibition. *Horizons: A Century of California Landscape Painting*, in which paintings borrowed from the State's museums were toured to 30 communities throughout California. They were mounted on specially designed modular walls that were set up in the lobbies of the financial institutions who provided most of the funds for the program. Over 150,000 Californians from neighborhoods and small communities saw the exhibition in the course of the year it was on tour. By 1973, however, Grossman had become convinced that State funding and administration of the arts was a throwback to the centralized forms of government which America's

founding had originally replaced, and he resigned.

Governor Reagan presented one of his paintings to the Emperor and Empress of Japan in 1971, and also to President Escheverría of Mexico in 1972. By that year, the artist was painting full time and had constructed a studio adjacent to his home in Woodacre, California. His works, which are in many private collections, include: *Ranunculi*, 1968; *"The Strength of the Hills is His Also"*, 1969; *Presence*, 1969; *From the Breadrack*, 1970; *California Golden Hills*, 1971; *Spring Psalm*, 1972; *Psalm 23*, 1973; *Portraits of Old-Fashioned Roses*, 1973; *Mt. Whitney, California*, 1974; *Morning in the Lucas Valley*, 1975; *Psalm 25:4*, 1975.

ALLAN RAMSAY
1713–1784

A Scottish painter born in Edinburgh, his art became one of the most distinctive contributions to the classical age of British portraiture. Arriving in London about 1733, he studied at St. Martin's Lane Academy, returned to Edinburgh, then set out for Italy in 1736. It was there that he discontinued studies in historical painting and began to devote himself entirely to portraits.

He settled in London about 1762, where he became the most sought-after portrait painter in England. The classical learning and knowledge of European literature which he had acquired made him one of the most cultivated painters of his time. He corresponded with Voltaire, Rousseau, and Hume, and painted a portrait of Rousseau for Hume.

"In a period when likenesses were in extraordinary demand," wrote Alastair Smart in the catalog to a major exhibition of Ramsay's work in 1958, "the fashionable portrait painter found it difficult to satisfy all his patrons. His solution when he was overburdened with work was to confine himself to painting his sitter's head; the canvas would then be dispatched to the drapery-man, who would add a suitable body. Sometimes the patron would be asked to select a pose, or even a costume, from a volume of drawings, many of them copies of portraits by earlier painters such as Rubens, Van Dyck, Maratta or Kneller.

"At times Ramsay accepted this mechanical convention as it stood; but on other occasions, when he was especially interested in a particular commission, he introduced important modifications, and in such cases he supplied his drapery-painter, Joseph Van Haeken, with drawings of his own from which to work, either radically altering a stock pose or inventing an entirely new composition."*

After becoming vice-president of the Society of Artists in 1766, he was appointed Painter in Ordinary to George III, the highest honor to which a British portrait painter could aspire until the formation of the Royal Academy in 1768.

According to Alastair Smart, "The King could scarcely be persuaded to sit to any other painter: as he himself remarked to Lord Eglinton, who was pleading the cause of [the painter] Sir Joshua Reynolds, 'Mr. Ramsay is my painter, my Lord'. According to Allan Cunningham, the King treated Ramsay like a brother, and sometimes would ask him to take his easel and canvas to the dining-room, so that he might criticize his work as he ate, 'and have the pleasure of his conversation'. Ramsay would then speak 'freely and without disguise' about the affairs of Europe, of which he had considerable knowledge."†

By the end of the 1760's, he was so occupied with the labor of satisfying the enormous demand for copies of his royal portraits, that he required a band of assistants to aid him, and was rarely able to accept other commissions. As a matter of record, there is only one known portrait by Ramsay, apart from the replicas of the royal portraits (which ran into hundreds), that is dated after 1769. The years 1754-1766 represented the crown of his achievement.

By 1788 he was devoting himself increasingly to literary pursuits, and at his death in 1784 he was to be remembered chiefly as a writer, particularly as the author of a work on *The Constitution of England*, (1766), his other works having been mostly concerned with political events of the moment. His interest in politics became so strong that at one time he seemed to have considered the possibility of standing for Parliament.

Because of a lifelong devotion to drawing, over three hundred of his drawings are known to exist. He painted nearly one thousand portraits. Among his major works are: *George III*; *Queen Charlotte*; *Lord Chesterfield*; *Dr. Mead* at the National Portrait Gallery in London; *David Hume*; *Artist's Wife* at the National Gallery in Edinburgh.

---

*Catalog, *An Exhibition of Paintings by Allan Ramsay*, The Iveagh Bequest, Kenwood, England, 1958, Introduction by Alastair Smart, p. 5.

†*Ibid.*, p. 15.

DESIGN OF THE VOLUME

John Grossman

Of the many elements which compose the design of this book, certainly the designs of the individual letters themselves which form the words the reader is now reading must be considered fundamental. The typeface in which the entirety of *The Christian History of the American Revolution* has been set is Caslon, designed by William Caslon (1692-1766). He was the greatest of the English letter-founders, and he so changed the history of English type-cutting, that after his appearance most of the types used in England in the eighteenth century were cut by Caslon himself, or else were fonts modelled on the styles he made popular.

Early typographic material in American printing houses was almost all foreign, with Dutch and English faces in the majority. The later types were English, and chiefly those of Caslon—although after 1775 type was being made in North America. Primers and books, newspapers and broadsides; all were mostly printed in Caslon old style types in the mid-eighteenth century and up to the Revolution. *The Declaration of Independence* itself was printed in the Caslon letter. It continued to be the face most commonly in use until about 1800. Benjamin Franklin admired and recommended Caslon's types, and equipped his own office with them.

Daniel Berkeley Updike, in his comprehensive book, *Printing Types* (1922), analyzed why Caslon's types have endured down through the years: "His letters when analyzed, especially in the smaller sizes, are not perfect individually; but in mass their effect is agreeable. That is, I think, their secret—a perfection of the whole, derived from harmonious but not necessarily perfect individual letter forms. To say precisely *how* Caslon arrived at his effects is not simple; but he did so because he was an artist. He knew how to make types, if ever a man did, that were . . . 'friendly to the eye,' or 'comfortable' . . . Caslon types are, too, so beautiful in mass, and above all so legible and 'common-sense,' that they can never be disregarded, and I doubt if they will ever be displaced."

There have been a number of different subsequent cuttings of Caslon. The text of this book was set in Linotype Caslon by Colonial Press, Clinton, Massachusetts, and Maryland Linotype Composition Co., Baltimore, Maryland. The headings were handset in Caslon 540 by Spartan Typographers, Oakland, California, and Caslon 471 by Falk Typography, San Francisco, California.

The layout of the book is based on classical axial symmetry—the elements centered and balanced—rather than the current asymmetric post-Bauhaus style frequently seen. This is in keeping with the restoration of Christian balance and symmetry to the understanding of the American Revolution.

Paul Revere (1735-1818) cast the gilded iron eagle adapted to embossing for the cover. The original measures sixty-six inches long from wing tip to wing tip, is thirty-two inches high, and weighs two hundred pounds. It is believed to be one of four commissioned in 1789 by General Henry Knox for his mansion at Thomaston, Maine, and is now in a private collection in Plymouth, Massachusetts. The embossing dies were engraved by Claud Davis Engraving, Inc., Osawatomie, Kansas. The proportion and shape of the debossed oval was taken from the ox-eye window in the pediment above the entrance of Mount Vernon, as designed by George Washington. Colonial Press, Clinton, Massachusetts, executed the embossing, debossing, and gold stamping, as well as the binding. The cover material is Roxite C Vellum Finish, the color specially mixed to match the blue of the American Flag, and was manufactured by Holliston Mills, Kingsport, Tennessee.

The small eagle identifying the Editor's notes was adapted from no. 5 of the ornamental cuts shown in a *Specimen of Printing Types from the Foundry of Binny & Ronaldson*, Philadelphia, 1812. Binny & Ronaldson are said to have issued the first specimen book by an American type founder.

The book was printed by offset lithography by Colonial Press, on 50# Warren's 1845, Medium Finish, Cream, manufactured by S. D. Warren Division of Scott Paper Company, Westbrook, Maine. The endpapers were printed on 80# Superfine Cover, Regular, Soft White, made by Mohawk Paper Company, Cohoes, New York.

Photo retouching to restore the appearance of some of the documents was done by Don Peters, Walnut Creek, California. Andrea Grossman did the assembly and paste-up of the camera-ready pages. The book was designed by John Grossman, Woodacre, California.

SCRIPTURAL REFERENCES

Prepared by
Rosalie J. Slater

INDEX OF
LEADING IDEAS

If thou canst answer me,

set thy words in order before me, stand up.

(Job 33:5)

EXPLANATION AND USE

OF THE INDEX

Prepared by
Rosalie J. Slater

"There is no one system of indexing; if the general underlying principle is grasped thoroughly each piece or work can be treated individually . . . An index is not necessarily only a summary of what is contained in the book; it may become its complement."
—Mary Petherbridge, London, 1904.

The Index of Leading Ideas to *Consider and Ponder* is designed to be an educational tool for the reader or student. It is representative of the Christian method of teaching and learning, namely, the Principle Approach. This method was first introduced in my volume *Teaching and Learning America's Christian History*, see page 88. The study of "Leading Ideas" was incorporated into the Christian History Study Course in this same volume as a step in developing the Principle Approach, see pages 305–352.

The ability to identify basic principles and leading ideas and to reason therefrom was typical of our colonial education. The Index of Leading Ideas reflects a return to this American Christian philosophy of education and government.

If the student or reader of *Consider and Ponder* can see the relationship of Biblical principles and Leading Ideas to the establishment of America's Christian form of civil government, a further step may be taken. The individual himself can relate the same governmental principles which brought about the establishment of the American Christian Republic to his or her own life. Only as Christian character and Christian self-government are restored on an individual level will the nation return to its Christian constitutional basis of government.

The Index of Leading Ideas should provide each reader or student with the following:

FACILITY in identifying the Biblical principles or Leading Ideas which constitute America's Christian character and government
VISIBILITY of historic Christianity's influence through church polity upon the form of American civil government
IRREFUTABILITY of the Bible as the major influence in American education and government'
AVAILABILITY of the names and contributions of individual men and women to the founding years of America
ORGANIZATION of pertinent historical information leading to the American Revolution

Letters a, b, c, d following page numbers indicate first, second, third, fourth quarters of page—

a	c
b	d

597

Leading Ideas are both indexed and outlined for the convenience of the reader or student. All entries are alphabetized. But, inasmuch as we are interested in the flow of ideas or the historical sequence of events, the internal arrangement of phrases, sentences or sub-headings are not always alphabetized. For example:

AMERICAN YOUTH: This phrase indexes the ardent admonition of Benson Lossing to the adults of each generation to educate their offspring in the principles and the price paid for American Liberty. The reader can glance at the key ideas as they unfold in the Lossing article.

BRITISH MINISTRY: This entry traces the innovation of that "darling idea" of American revenue which shattered one hundred and fifty years of American self government. It became the fatal rock "upon which the British Empire began to come apart". Once again the alphabetical order has been made secondary to the flow of the idea in the interest of the sequence of events which led to the separation between Britain and America.

CHRISTIANITY: As the irresistible force in the world, this entry includes a multiplicity of ideas. Therefore, each sentence or phrase is alphabetized and the total number of ideas can be said to represent a constellation of government internal and external, particularly as Christianity moved westward into America.

LEXINGTON AND CONCORD: Here where the "first blow for liberty" was struck, a chronological arrangement has been followed, enabling the reader to obtain a complete picture of the event. There are actually two accounts by two historians, Mercy Warren and David Ramsey. Each battle of the American Revolution is individually indexed.

Some words are linked together because united they constitute a powerful Leading Idea. Some of these are: BLESSINGS OF LIBERTY, DIVINE RIGHT OF KINGS, ENTERPRISING SPIRIT, FAST DAYS, LAW OF NATIONS, MINUTE MEN, RIGHT OF RESISTANCE, SECOND COMING OF CHRIST, SELF-DEFENSE, SELF-GOVERNMENT, STATE OF NATIONS, TAXATION WITHOUT REPRESENTATION, THRONE OF GRACE, TRIAL BY JURY. All of these mark the uniqueness of America, and they identify her Christian history, character and government.

Some Leading Ideas so permeate *Consider and Ponder* it was thought advisable to index and outline with sub-headings, for example:

AMERICA includes the following sub-headings: *Christian founding; Uniqueness of; Adopts children of all lands; Preparation in self-government;*

Attitude towards England; Preservation of.

Another example of a Leading Idea and its sub-headings is:

LIBERTY: *Civil and religious; Benefits of; History of; in the Old Testament; in the New Testament; after the Reformation; in America; in the American Revolution; Defense of; by the pen; by the sword; Destruction of; Individual responsibility for.*

A few individuals are dealt with through sub-headings, for example:

GEORGE WASHINGTON: *Christian Commitment and Character; Providential Preparation; Military Preparation; Administrative Preparation; Appointed Commander-in-Chief; Valley Forge; Winter of 1777–78; Dealings with Congress; Martha Washington; Retirement from Military Command; Our First American President; "Father of his Country".*

ACKNOWLEDGMENTS

Mr. William M. Hosmer and Mr. James B. Rose, indexers of *The Christian History of the Constitution of the United States of America* compiled by Miss Verna M. Hall, first suggested an index of ideas for the volumes on *The Christian History of the American Revolution*. Mr. Hosmer and Mr. Rose actually began the index but their own individual Christian histories required that they relinquish the task to me. Their pioneering work and encouragement has been much appreciated.

To my dear friend, Mrs. Lois Jenkinson, who has worked beside me so faithfully during the years of developing this index, I express my sincere thanks. Her care and accuracy, patience and persistence has considerably lightened my load in the detail of this work.

I also wish to express my appreciation for the expert help of Mrs. Gladys Soule in the alphabetization of the thousands of entry words and their subsequent placement. We thank God for supplying such friends and helpers who have contributed so generously of their talents.

To Miss Verna M. Hall, my Christian partner and associate in this ministry, I express appreciation for the amount of space which she has allowed for an index which has become, in many instances, an outline.

This indexer's prayer is that the Index of Leading Ideas may help those who read and study *Consider and Ponder* to catch a vision of America's contribution to the Chain of Christianity moving westward in its Gospel purpose for all mankind.

WHAT TO CONSIDER AND PONDER IN THE INDEX

For the new student of America's Christian history, the Index of Leading Ideas provides an overview of subjects covered in the volume *Consider and Ponder*. It is suggested that thumbing through the index may help one focus upon an area of interest—a door or window to look into the contents of *Consider and Ponder*. It might work like this:

Consider AMERICAN MARTYRS. This refers to the first brave men who fell in the cause of Liberty at Lexington and Concord on that fateful day of April 19, 1775. Turning to this record opens up a whole series of memorable events reported by two historians, a northern woman, Mercy Warren, and a southern physician, David Ramsey.

Just below is the entry, AMERICAN MATRONS. Turning to this page in *Consider and Ponder* opens up a series of cameo biographies of women whose physical courage contributed to the American Revolution.

Many will look up HOLY BIBLE. Note the coincidence of the appearing of the English Bible in the stream of history and the opening up of America. The reader or student may want to read the wonderful testimony "The Hand of God in American History" by the Baptist minister, Reverend Foljambe, given at our Centennial in 1876.

Your interests and your requirements will dictate what you select to lead you into the volume *Consider and Ponder*. It will first introduce you to the philosophy of American Christian government and to the inseparability of the individual Christian walk from its effect upon the life of the nation. As you begin reading and studying, the Index of Leading Ideas will provide information and will often supply an outline or summary of the subject or Leading Idea which interests you.

Random words, Leading Ideas, which seem inconsequential at first glance may reveal the inner spirit of this volume. Some examples might be: BAREFOOT: this refers to the condition of the soldiers at Valley Forge during the terrible winter of 1777–78. PICTURE: refers to the theme picture at the front of the volume, *General George Washington in Prayer at Valley Forge*. Do you have pictures in your home to contemplate and reflect upon like this one? Who would think of PIDGEON-BOXES as having to do with church growth, but Benjamin Franklin thought so. VEIL: refers to God's reservation of the land of the thirteen colonies for centuries until He had a people ready for a permanent settlement. Thus words are Leading Ideas into the philosophy of American Christian history, education and government.

Above all, the Index of Leading Ideas provides a means by which you can reason and reflect upon the Hand of God in American history and the unique opportunity given to us as American Christians to extend the blessings of liberty through the Christian form of civil government to all the world.

It is my sincere hope that the Index of Leading Ideas may indeed be a complement to *Consider and Ponder*.

CONSIDER AND PONDER IN THE
AMERICAN CHRISTIAN HOME

Who should teach and learn America's Christian history? In America Christian homes played a major role in teaching the love of Christ and the Hand of God in our American history. Since the educational goal of the American Christian home in a republic is to build the foundation of American Christian character, is it surprising that patriotic mothers contributed to the nation's independence? "Patriotic mothers nursed the infancy of freedom. Their counsels and their prayers mingled with the deliberations that resulted in a nation's assertion of its independence. They animated the courage, and confirmed the self-devotion of those who ventured all in the common cause." (Page 73d, *Consider and Ponder*).

These same patriotic mothers also contributed to the teaching and learning of the fundamental principles of Christian liberty which America was to establish in Christian civil government. It was "in the domestic sanctuary" where "that love of civil liberty, which afterwards kindled into a flame, and shed light on the world" was first expressed. "The talk of matrons, in American homes, was of the people's wrongs, and the tyranny that oppressed them, until the sons who had grown to manhood, with strengthened aspirations towards a better state of things, and views enlarged to comprehend their invaded rights, stood up prepared to defend them to the utmost." (Page 73d *Consider and Ponder*).

It is hoped therefore, that present-day mothers will accept once again the confirmation of their importance in teaching and learning the lesssons of Christian liberty and that they will inspire their children to extend those principles into every avenue of their lives. Only in an American

Christian home has woman the privilege of working from her center of power as the first teacher of the family, the one who is "accountable for the character of the next generation."

Fathers, will you take back the first sphere of the government of this nation—that of the home? Mothers will not be able to move forward confidently unless you accept leadership for supplying the Biblical guidance for the growth of Christian character and the practice of Christian self-government in the home. "Home sentiment" of the father is best communicated by example. Where better to begin to turn our nation around economically than in the American Christian home where industry, frugality, prudence, economy—essentials of Christian self-government—need to be identified in the Christian walk by both father and mother. A study of our founding fathers indicates their consistent efforts for making home the religious and educational base. The community outreach of home will have greater impact than any other single feature in America, and it should, for home is God's primary institution. It is the Christian center from which the national circumference will take its character.

Parents can also take back the direction of the school education of their children by knowing what the school must build upon—America's Christian history and government. Control of school curricula and methodology springs from a knowledge of the underlying American Christian philosophy of education and government. This can be learned from a study of America's Christian history. When American homes and schools work from the same center of philosophy, each fulfilling its own distinct sphere, we shall begin to see dramatic results in the life of our nation and in the return to Christian government.

CONSIDER AND PONDER IN THE CHURCH AND SEMINARY

The American Christian Church can find in *Consider and Ponder* the documentation and inspiration for the leadership of the clergy during the founding period of America. How we need to recapture this important leadership—a leadership which was exercised in both education and government. If our Bible-trained clergy would extend their ministry to include the preservation of Biblical government in America we could, indeed, send forth the proper Christian representatives to the local, state and national spheres of external political representation. If Christians do not stand in the gap of government in America

we shall lose our liberties both religious and civil.

The Election Sermon documents the role of the leadership of the clergy in American civil government. From century to century they were invited to preach a sermon upon the election of the new civil officers. Unlike our present day political meetings where the clergy may be invited to offer an invocation or benediction, in earlier days of our Republic they delivered what might be termed a "state of Christendom" address. It was a lengthy discussion of Christian responsibility to the Biblical principles of government. These sermons were printed at the expense of the legislature and sent to each elected officer of civil government. Often these sermons were circulated throughout the colonies and many found their way to England.

The clergy also preached commemorative sermons for they were conscious of God as the Disposer of the events of history. It was important to them as men of God to keep the uniqueness of our Christian responsibility in America alive to each oncoming generation. The anniversary sermons of the Pilgrims, the centennial sermon honoring the Hand of God in American History and the Fast Day sermons all testify to the recognition that American Government is inseparable *internally* from the Christian principles, the Christian character and the Christian form of civil government found in the Holy Scriptures.

The professional educators who moved into the vacuum left by our American clergy have taken over the field of education and have led us astray. We need our clergy to take back the leadership of American Education. If our ministers of the Gospel will accept the importance of teaching and learning America's Christian History and recognize the relationship between Christian education and Christian government we shall have started on the rebuilding of the foundations. The Principle Approach of teaching and learning is Biblical. It will restore the reasoning and writing of leading ideas and principles which we have deleted from present educational systems predicated upon secular philosophies. But it requires Christian courage to cut through the *"philosophy and vain deceit, after the tradition of men, after the rudiments of the world, and not after Christ."* (Colossians 2:8)

Consider and Ponder includes Election Sermons, an Artillery Sermon, three commemorative sermons, and three Fast Day Sermons. In addition are to be found a number of significant dissertations delivered by the clergy on subjects of importance. Examples of these are Elisha Williams' "The Essential Rights and Liberties of Protestants"; Timothy Dwight's "A Dissertation on the History, Eloquence, and Poetry of the Bible"; Rev. Charles Inglis' "A Memorial Concerning the Iroquois" and others. All signify that the American clergy took an active part in Christian leadership in those fields which today are not being dealt with from Biblical principles.

Of particular interest to ministers of all denominations will be the three accounts of church history and government in *Consider and Ponder*. How startling to recognize that the understanding of *church polity* is the key to understanding American *civil polity*! How often have we traced the roots of American government to the pagan nations rather than to the unfolding story of the Christian church as it moved westward to these shores with the Pilgrims.

The rich treasury of *Consider and Ponder* for the home, church and school is such a small part of what our heritage consists. It is hoped that the rising ministry in Christian colleges and seminaries will research deeper into this Mother Lode of Christian documentation than they have in the past. It is all readily available for that American Christian who has caught the vision of America's Gospel purpose and unique contribution to the field of Christian civil government.

CONSIDER AND PONDER IN THE ELEMENTARY SCHOOL

Elementary teachers build upon the foundations of the American home—good or bad—and they have a unique opportunity to plant the first seeds of Christian self-government in the school during the early years. But they also need to replace the present school curriculum with America's Christian history and literature. We are still wasting valuable years in following meekly in the paths of progressive education. If Christian schools in America do not take back the leadership of education and re-form the philosophy, methodology and content of education, we shall continue to be passive participants in socialism.

Consider and Ponder provides the elementary teacher with the opportunity of learning what Christianity has contributed to the blessings of liberty which we now enjoy and which enable us to establish Christian schools. Like the widow woman of Zarephath who had only "an handful of meal in a barrel, and a little oil in a cruse", bake what you find in *Consider and Ponder* into a little cake and feed it to your classes. God will magnify your faith and your willingness and you, too, will find that "the barrel of meal shall not waste, neither shall the cruse of oil fail".

There are many articles of interest for elementary teachers in *Consider and Ponder*. Consider the "Primitive Christians". We all need to renew our link with these first challengers of worldliness and paganism. Every age has to deal with this challenge. What can we learn from this article that will help us with our battle today in Christian education?

You might pass by the article "Centennial Oration at Valley Forge, June 19, 1878." However this article is a thrilling testimony to America's life out of death during that terrible winter. It is never too early to introduce students to the bravery and heroism of our "ragged Continentals", those American soldiers who suffered and endured for our liberty. At this time you might introduce them to General George Washington as God's instrument prepared for the critical years of the American Revolution. Feelings and attitudes more than facts will teach his character to elementary boys and girls.

Elementary teachers will love the section on "Patriotic Women and Home Sentiment." This selection of biographies shows the influence of early education in Principles and Leading Ideas upon our people. Your students will be stirred by the accounts of the bravery of our American heroines. They will be touched by the tenderness of those founding fathers who describe the joys and values of domestic life.

For parents and teachers the section on "American Christian Education" will prove to be an invaluable encouragement and source of instruction in righteousness for years to come. Most of these articles are written by ministers of the Gospel. Reverend John Witherspoon's five letters on "The Education of Children" have some particularly pertinent points for elementary teachers because he demonstrates the Biblical basis of teaching authority and discipline—the foundation of learning Christian self-government. He also discusses the individuality of temper and disposition in children as well as piety and politeness—the latter so often absent in today's transactions. Above all, Dr. Witherspoon indicates the importance of the individual conduct and example of parents. The character and conduct of teachers and their influence upon the lives of their students is no less important. For it is in the early years that the foundations of character are laid. And it is America's Christian character which constitutes our Constitution.

CONSIDER AND PONDER IN THE
HIGH SCHOOL AND COLLEGE

As teachers, as parents perhaps, *Consider and Ponder* is first of all your rich inheritance. American education is founded upon self-education. We must return to this conviction once again and teachers can lead the way through their willingness to begin their own self-education. It will be a long time before Christian colleges will be prepared to teach America's Christian history.

There is much content in *Consider and Ponder* for your courses in history—World History, European History, English History, American History. But the riches of history go deeper than traditional secular curriculum. They must be mined as the gold of Christian character. As teachers we have sought the unification of all knowledge so that students might have an overwhelming conviction that "whither shall I go from thy spirit? or whither shall I flee from thy presence?"

From the vantage point of The Hand of God in American History we can watch God shaping the many scientific fields after the English Bible was in the hands of the individual. How exciting to see the inventions appearing so that the ocean avenues might be opened up for greater exploration and travel—just in time for the Pilgrims and their evangelical mission to America.

As we study history from the Providential approach, we can teach our students to see God's Hand in their own lives as well as in the life of the nation. Thus we free them from man's interpretation of history.

For students of literature what better place to begin than with the Graduation Address of Timothy Dwight, "A Dissertation on the History, Eloquence, and Poetry of the Bible". This unique article provides a Biblical standard for every individual form of literature. It also reaffirms our own conviction of the superiority of the Bible as literature.

We cannot overlook a unique American field of literature, that of oratory. Henry Armitt Brown's moving "Centennial Oration at Valley Forge, June 18, 1878" represents a high peak in the feelings of American Christians one hundred years ago as they contemplated the American Revolution.

Miss Hall has included two accounts of the same historical period in American history. Mercy Warren, our New England historian, and David Ramsey, our southern historian, confirm the unity and diversity which existed in the colonial mind among individuals from different geographic areas.

American Christian schools and colleges must first approach *Consider and Ponder* as their own declaration of faith in God's purpose for bringing forth this nation. Then, as the Lord leads, they can set their courses in new directions fortified with the testimony of what God has already done for us as a nation. American liberty is both evangelical and political. If the blessings of liberty are to be maintained, they need to be carefully identified and cherished by each generation. Let us not break faith with those whose blood was shed in behalf of us—their posterity. Let us be faithful to the next generations who follow us.

THE EDUCATION OF JOHN QUINCY ADAMS

THE CHARACTER FOR A CHRISTIAN REPUBLIC

Rosalie J. Slater

A COLONIAL EDUCATION IN LEADING IDEAS

One of the most critical changes we have witnessed in American education has been the change away from the reasoning, writing, reflecting ability so prominent in the generations that produced the Declaration of Independence, the Constitution of the United States of America, the Monroe Doctrine and other documents. This ability to define a philosophy of government in writing was the result of a colonial education in principles, leading ideas and their application to the field of civil government—America's unique contribution.

Modern scholarship informs us that the literacy level of the American colonists at the time of the American Revolution, was the highest ever achieved in the world. Thus, it is not surprising that the American State Papers would reflect this extension of the blessings of liberty. But what is perhaps more astonishing to secular scholars is the degree to which this education reflected the Biblical knowledge of our Founding Fathers and Mothers.

From the coming of the Pilgrims with the

602

Geneva Bible, the application of Biblical reasoning to civil government had confirmed the Gospel purpose of America. The *Mayflower Compact* was not only a document of government, it was a profession of Christian faith. For more than one hundred fifty years the clergy continued to provide leadership by preaching and teaching the Biblical principles of government from the pulpit, and in their election sermons at the seats of colonial civil government. Thus the Word of God became the American Political textbook.

"Above all, the colonists were acquainted with the Bible itself, principally in the Geneva Version but increasingly in the King James Version. The Bible was read and recited, quoted and consulted, early committed to memory and constantly searched for meaning. Deemed universally relevant, it remained throughout the century the single most important cultural influence in the lives of Anglo-Americans. . . .

"Though the Bible had been richly valued for generations, it was not until the seventeenth century that it was widely read and studied. The message of Protestantism was that men could find in Scripture the means to salvation, the keys to good and evil, the rules by which to live, and the standards against which to measure the conduct of prince and pastor."*

We have chosen to examine the education of John Quincy Adams of the generation following those who established the nation. John Adams contributed to the writing and adopting of the Declaration of Independence, to the diplomacy of the American Revolution and to the American presidency during its first two administrations. His son, John Quincy Adams, continued the stewardship of American government and gave more than half a century to the service of his country.

We are indebted to the consistency of our early statesmen in the faithful recording of their application of a philosophy of government in their letters, diaries, journals and published papers. It is these records which will trace the influences which shaped the mind and character of young John Quincy Adams—preparing him with a character to support a Christian Republic.

HOME, THE FIRST SPHERE OF GOVERNMENT

The year 1767 was notable in New England for two events—the beginning of the efforts of the

American Education, The Colonial Experience 1607–1683 by Lawrence A. Cremin, Harper and Row, Publishers, 1970, page 40.

British Ministry to raise revenue from America in the imposition of the Townshend Acts, and the birth of John Quincy Adams. Events were moving in rapid sequence to bring about a permanent separation between Great Britain and her American Colonies and young John Quincy Adams was to witness many of the sights and sounds of this unfolding history. When he was six, Boston became the first city to dispose of the fatally taxed tea. The Boston Port blockade which followed struck a note of warning throughout the colonies. It also brought them together again into a representative fellowship in the First Continental Congress. The boy saw his father depart for Philadelphia as an elected delegate from Massachusetts. That spring he stood by his mother's side, an eight year old, startled by the huge bursts of cannon from the British fleet reducing Charlestown to ashes, while patriots on Bunker's Hill retreated after taking devastating toll of British regulars.

But the young lad was no passive spectator of events. Braintree, the home town of the Adams family, was ten miles from Boston. John Quincy made this trip daily to bring news to his mother on the farm. He felt deeply the challenges to colonial liberty, and he was drawn irresistibly to an individual concern and consciousness of responsibility. Braintree was located close enough to Boston for many to seek refuge from the British occupation of that town. So the Adams' family farm became a center of news and hospitality. There was a sense of urgency in the air. Supplies for the newly created Continental army were needed and ammunition was precious. Even his mother's pewter spoons were surrendered for bullets. "I well recollect going into the kitchen and seeing some of the men engaged in running those spoons into bullets for the use of the troops. Do you wonder that a boy of seven years of age, who witnessed this scene, should be a patriot?"

Danger from enemy troops was always present and Johnny learned to drill with the local militia. But he also learned to dig and hoe in the fields with his brothers and sister to help Mamma harvest the crops. Like his father before him he learned the chores of tending cattle, chopping kindling and peforming other duties of farm life.

His mother, Abigail Adams, had accepted the responsibility for keeping up the education of her children—especially of her oldest son, John Quincy Adams, in the absence of his father. First came instruction in the Word of God. So well did his mother commit the Word to young John Quincy's heart that it became for him both compass and anchor in a long life of service.

From his mother he was also led into the love and inspiration of literature. He learned the poetry of Pope, read the plays of Shakespeare, struggled with Milton, and generally devoured the family library. He listened to his mother's talk of the economic concerns of the war. She strove valiantly to keep up the spirits of the little family in the absence of Papa. John Quincy responded to his mother's dependence upon him with a manliness which became characteristic. Duty and service were both engrained in his parents. He learned much from their example and personal conduct. His father felt very strongly about the qualities of Christian character needed for that representative form of government which the American colonies would adopt. Writing to their friend and neighbor, Mercy Warren, he had defined it thus:

"The Form of Government, which you admire, when its Principles are pure is admirable, indeed, it is productive of every Thing, which is great and excellent among Men. But its Principles are as easily destroyed, as human Nature is corrupted. Such a government is only to be supported by pure Religion or Austere Morals. Public Virtue cannot exist in a Nation without private, and public Virtue is the only Foundation of Republics. There must be a positive Passion for the public good, the public Interest, Honour, Power and Glory, established in the Minds of the People, or there can be no Republican Government, nor any real Liberty: and this public Passion must be Superiour to all private Passions. Men must be ready, they must pride themselves, and be happy to sacrifice their private Pleasures, Passions and Interests, nay, their private Friendships and dearest Connections, when they stand in Competition with the Rights of Society . . ."*

In addition to his studies in the Bible and his reading in the family library, Abigail Adams directed John Quincy's thoughts towards a knowledge of history. History was a passion with John Adams, and Abigail wanted to deepen her own knowledge in the absence of her partner. The months and years of her husband's absence needed buttressing with subjects of worthy contemplation so that her thoughts might not disintegrate into loneliness, fear or despair. She wrote, "I have taken a very great fondness for

reading Rollin's *Ancient History* since you left me. I am determined to go through with it, if possible, in these, my days of solitude. I find great pleasure and entertainment from it, and I have persuaded Johnny to read me a page or two every day and hope he will, for his desire to oblige me, entertain a fondness for it."

HISTORY WITH A CHRISTIAN PURPOSE

The study of history has a Christian purpose and fulfillment, and Charles Rollin, born in 1661, whose work on *Ancient History* was completed in 1730, defined it in these words:

"The study of profane history would little deserve to have a serious attention, and a considerable length of time bestowed upon it, if it were confined to the bare knowledge of ancient transactions, and an uninteresting inquiry into the eras when each of them happened. It little concerns us to know, that there were once such men as Alexander, Caesar, Aristides, or Cato, and that they lived in this or that period; that the empire of the Assyrians made way for that of the Babylonians, and the latter for the empire of the Medes and Persians, who were themselves subjected by the Macedonians, as these were afterwards by the Romans.

"But it highly concerns us to know by what methods those empires were founded; by what steps they rose to that exalted pitch of grandeur which we so much admire; what it was that constituted their true glory and felicity; and what were the causes of their declension and fall.

"It is of no less importance to study attentively the manners of different nations; their genius, laws, and customs; and especially to acquaint ourselves with the character and disposition, the talents, virtues, and even vices, of those by whom they were governed; and whose good or bad qualities contributed to the grandeur or decay of the states over which they presided.

"Such are the great objects which ancient history presents; causing to pass, as it were, in review before us, all the kingdoms and empires of the world; and at the same time, all the great men who were any ways conspicuous; thereby instructing us, by example rather than by precept, in the arts of empire and war, the principles of government, the rules of policy, the maxims of civil society, and the conduct of life that suits all ages and conditions. . . .

"But another object of infinitely greater importance, claims our attention. For although pro-

---

Warren-Adams Letters, Vol. I, 1743–1777, The Massachusetts Historical Society, 1917, page 222.

fane history treats only of nations who had imbibed all the absurdities of a superstitious worship: and abandoned themselves to all the irregularities of which human nature, after the fall of the first man, became capable; it nevertheless proclaims universally the greatness of the Almighty, his power, his justice, and, above all, the admirable wisdom with which His Providence governs the universe.

"If the inherent conviction of this last truth raised, according to Cicero's observation, the Romans above all other nations; we may, in like manner, affirm, that nothing gives history a greater superiority to many branches of literature, than to see in a manner imprinted, in almost every page of it, the precious footsteps and shining proofs of this great truth, *viz.* that God disposes all events as supreme Lord and Sovereign; that he alone determines the fate of kings and the duration of empires; and that he transfers the government of kingdoms from one nation to another because of the unrighteous dealings and wickedness committed therein."*

No doubt Johnny enjoyed reading from Rollin the story of Alexander the Great breaking the ungovernable horse which had been given as a gift to his ambitious father, Philip. But no one dared mount the fierce war horse. In a dramatic scene young Alexander turned the horse's head to the sun, away from his shadow which had frightened him. Then, leaping upon his back, Alexander displayed a remarkable skill in working with the horse until he was tamed. But in the discussion following this story of the world's youngest conqueror, Johnny must have learned of the sad death at 33 of this spirited, passionate man. He could lead conquering armies, but he was not able to govern himself and he died a victim of his own ungovernable passions and sins.

Such an approach to history coincided with the entire education of John Quincy Adams. It put the responsibility for the rise and fall of nations upon the character and conduct of its people and rulers. It made all the more remarkable the Christian era with its westward course, awaiting that moment in history when all the elements were ready for the establishment of the world's first Christian republic. Even as John and Abigail Adams contributed to the founding period of this republic so would their son, John Quincy Adams, perpetuate and extend their vision

of Christian leadership and responsibility for civil government.

LEARNING TO WRITE DOWN HIS OBSERVATIONS

The tender years of companionship with his mother were a touchstone to the life and character of John Quincy Adams. In later years he recalled leaping out of bed in the morning after saying his prayers, repeating with spirit the first lines from one of his mother's favorite poems, William Collins' ode to the patriot warriors of Scotland who fell in battle:

"How sleep the brave who sink to rest,
By all their country's wishes blest. . . ."

When about ten years of age, John Quincy Adams began the habit of writing. As Abigail figured her accounts of the farm, sewed by the fireside or encouraged the younger brothers and sister in their lessons, Johnny wrote to his father to review his character development and education and to ask for parental instruction. It is a unique commentary on his first ten years of living:

Braintree, June the 2d, 1777
"Dear Sir,
I love to receive letters very well, much better than I love to write them. I make but a poor figure at composition; my head is much too fickle. My thoughts are running after birds'-eggs, play, and trifles, till I get vexed with myself. Mamma has a troublesome task to keep me steady, and I own I am ashamed of myself. I have but just entered the third volume of Smollett, though I had designed to have got half through it by this time. I have determined this week to be more diligent, as Mr. Thaxter will be absent at court, and I can not pursue my other studies. I have set myself a stint, and determine to read the third volume half out. If I can but keep my resolution I will write again at the end of the week, and give a better account of myself. I wish, sir, you would give me some instructions with regard to my time, and advise me how to proportion my studies and my play, in writing, and I will keep them by me and endeavor to follow them. I am, dear sir, with a present determination of growing better,
Yours,
JOHN QUINCY ADAMS

"P.S.—Sir, if you will be so good as to favor me with a blank-book I will transcribe the most re-

Ancient History by Charles Rollin, 1842, Harper Brothers, Preface.

markable occurrences I meet with in my reading, which will serve to fix them upon my mind."*

Ten years at home were all the years that John Quincy Adams was to spend in close association with his beloved mother, Abigail Adams. But these first ten years were the foundation stones of his life, so consistently had precept been impressed by parental example. In the summer of 1777 John Adams had returned to Braintree full of expectations that he could now resume his provincial life in Massachusetts. But his talents were to be called into a larger sphere of service for the struggling new nation. Once again he made ready to depart for Europe. This time he took with him 11-year old John Quincy Adams. Despite the warm and affectionate companionship between mother and son each accepted the responsibility of the decision. Convinced that Johnny could be of service to his father, and knowing that the boy would profit by a closer association with the older Adams, Abigail relinquished him, though not without a keen realization of what his departure would mean to her personally. Yet, as one of New England's most accomplished correspondents she utilized her letters to her son to continue the education so well begun at Braintree. Through these letters she continued to keep before his eyes the spiritual and moral demands upon his life. Though separated by thousands of miles—sometimes for years at a time, this mother and son enjoyed a mutual devotion to Christian principles and Christian character. "The child is father of the man" and the new nation would have no better representative of its Christian character than in the life and service of John Quincy Adams.

But it was John Adams who first reassured the anxious mother that her young eaglet was ready to leave the nest. As he embarked on his mission as American Commissioner to France, he wrote to his wife on the eve of embarkation this tender message:

"Uncle Quincy's—
13 February, 1778

"DEAREST OF FRIENDS,

I had not been twenty minutes in this house, before I had the happiness to see Captain Tucker and a midshipman coming for me. We will be soon on board, and may God prosper our voyage in every stage of it as much as at the beginning,

and send to you, my dear children, and all my friends, the choicest blessings!

"So wishes and prays yours, with an ardor that neither absence, nor any other event can abate,

JOHN ADAMS

"P.S. Johnny sends his duty to his mamma, and his love to his sisters and brothers. He behaves like a man."†

John Adams was devoted to the education of his children. His thoughts were expressed many times in his correspondence to Mrs. Adams:

"Human nature, with all its infirmities and depravation, is still capable of great things. It is capable of attaining to degrees of wisdom and of goodness which we have reason to believe appear respectable in the estimation of superior intelligences. Education makes a greater difference between man and man, than nature has made between man and brute. The virtues and powers to which men may be trained, by early education and constant discipline, are truly sublime and astonishing. Newton and Locke are examples of the deep sagacity which may be acquired by long habits of thinking and study. . . .

"It should be your care therefore, and mine, to elevate the minds of our children, and exalt their courage, to accelerate and animate their industry and activity, to excite in them an habitual contempt of meanness, abhorrence of injustice and inhumanity, and an ambition to excel in every capacity, faculty, and virtue. If we suffer their minds to grovel and creep in infancy, they will grovel and creep all their lives.

"But their bodies must be hardened, as well as their souls exalted. Without strength, and activity and vigor of body, the brightest mental excellencies will be eclipsed and obscured."‡

Arrived in France and greeted warmly by Benjamin Franklin, John Adams placed his son in a private boarding school in Passy, just outside Paris. Here he found American schoolmates— the two grandsons of Benjamin Franklin, the son of Silas Deane, Jesse Deane, and Charles Cochran of South Carolina. Johnny's progress in Latin, but especially in French, was noteworthy. On weekends his father took him to visit the

---

*History of the Life, Administration, and Times of John Quincy Adams, Sixth President of the United States, by John Robert Irelan, 1887, page 16.

†Life and Public Services of John Quincy Adams by William H. Seward, 1849, page 31.
‡Ibid., pages 31-32.

Cathedral de Notre Dame, he walked the crooked streets of Paris, and climbed to the top of Montmartre. He walked along the banks of the Seine, and watched children play simple French classics in the Theatre des Petit Comediens in the Bois de Boulogne. Life was full of delightful sights and sounds and there was much to observe.

One only of Abigail's letters to her son can be given here but it is indicative of the quality of her continuing education of John Quincy Adams:

June, 1778

"MY DEAR SON,

'Tis almost four months since you left your native land, and embarked upon the mighty waters, in quest of a foreign country. Although I have not particularly written to you since, yet you may be assured you have constantly been upon my heart and mind.

"It is a very difficult task, my dear son, for a tender parent to bring her mind to part with a child of your years going to a distant land; nor could I have acquiesced in such a separation under any other care than that of the most excellent parent and guardian who accompanied you. You have arrived at years capable of improving under the advantages you will be likely to have, if you do but properly attend to them. They are talents put into your hands, of which an account will be required of you hereafter; and, being possessed of one, two, or four, see to it that you double your numbers.

"The most amiable and useful disposition in a young mind is diffidence of itself; and this should lead you to seek advice and instruction from him who is your natural guardian, and will always counsel and direct you in the best manner, both for your present and future happiness. You are in possession of a naturally good understanding, and of spirits unbroken by adversity and untamed with care. Improve your understanding by acquiring useful knowledge and virtue, such as will render you an ornament to society, an honor to your country, and a blessing to your parents. Great learning and superior abilities, should you ever possess them, will be of little value and small estimation, unless virtue, honor, truth, and integrity are added to them. Adhere to those religious sentiments and principles which were early instilled into your mind, and remember, that you are accountable to your Maker for all your words and actions.

"Let me enjoin it upon you to attend constantly and steadfastly to the precepts and instructions of your father, as you value the happiness of your mother and your own welfare. His care and attention to you render many things unnecessary for me to write, which I might otherwise do; but the inadvertency and heedlessness of youth require line upon line and precept upon precept, and, when enforced by the joint efforts of both parents, will, I hope, have a due influence upon your conduct; for, dear as you are to me, I would much rather you should have found your grave in the ocean you have crossed, or that any untimely death crop you in your infant years, than see you an immoral, profligate, or graceless child.

"You have entered early in life upon the great theater of the world, which is full of temptations and vice of every kind. You are not wholly unacquainted with history, in which you have read of crimes which your inexperienced mind could scarcely believe credible. You have been taught to think of them with horror, and to view vice as

'A monster of so frightful mien,
That, to be hated, needs but to be seen.'

"Yet you must keep a strict guard upon yourself, or the odious monster will soon lose its terror by becoming familiar to you. The modern history of our own times furnishes as black a list of crimes as can be paralleled in ancient times, even if we go back to Nero, Caligula, or Caesar Borgia. Young as you are, the cruel war, into which we have been compelled by the haughty tyrant of Britain and the bloody emissaries of his vengeance, may stamp upon your mind this certain truth, that the welfare and prosperity of all countries, communities, and, I may add, individuals, depend upon their morals. That nation to which we were once united, as it has departed from justice, eluded and subverted the wise laws which formerly governed it, and suffered the worst of crimes to go unpunished, has lost its valor, wisdom, and humanity, and, from being the dread and terror of Europe, has sunk into derision and infamy.

"But, to quit political subjects, I have been greatly anxious for your safety, having never heard of the frigate since she sailed, till, about a week ago, a New York paper informed, that she was taken and carried into Plymouth. I did not fully credit this report, though it gave me much uneasiness. I yesterday heard that a French vessel was arrived at Portsmouth, which brought news of the safe arrival of the *Boston*; but this wants confirmation. I hope it will not be long before

I shall be assured of your safety. You must write me an account of your voyage, of your situation, and of everything entertaining, you can recollect.

"Be assured I am most affectionately yours, ———".*

Passy, September the 27th, 1778

"HONORED MAMMA,

My papa enjoins it upon me to keep a journal, or a diary of the events that happen to me, and of objects that I see, and of characters that I converse with from day to day; and altho' I am convinced of the utility, importance, and necessity of this exercise, yet I have not the patience and perseverance enough to do it so constantly as I ought. My papa, who takes a great deal of pains to put me in the right way, has also advised me to keep copies of all my letters, and has given me a convenient blank book for this end; and altho' I shall have the mortification a few years hence to read a great deal of my childish nonsense, yet I shall have the pleasure and advantage of re-marking the several steps by which I shall have advanced in taste, judgment, and knowledge. A journal book and a letter book of a lad of eleven years old can not be expected to contain much of science, literature, arts, wisdom or wit, yet it may serve to perpetuate many observations that I may make, and may hereafter help me to recollect both persons and things that would otherwise escape my memory."†

Many New England homes encouraged the presence and attention of their children when the serious issues and events of the times were discussed. No wonder then, that John Quincy Adams in Paris, could thoroughly enjoy the association and conversation of men like Dr. Franklin, and Arthur Lee. They were interested in everything, the art of diplomacy no less than the arts and sciences themselves. This was characteristic of Americans. It was to be true of John Quincy Adams also. During his years of service to the rising nation, he did much to encourage the arts and sciences stating, "The founders of your constitution have left it as their dying commandment to you, to achieve, as the lawful sovereigns of the land, this resplendent glory to yourselves—to patronize and encourage the arts and sciences, and all good literature."

Johnny also enjoyed the enthusiastic friendship of Madame Lafayette whose charm and natural-ness was in contrast to the high style of other French ladies. Madame la Marquise de la Fayette had a bond of sympathy for that nation whose cause her husband had adopted. She was a re-freshing change from the painted ladies of the court and was kind and interested in the young lad.

But best of all John Quincy Adams enjoyed the companionship and supervision of his father, John Adams. Father and son spent time together reviewing Johnny's studies. His father's com-mendations were an added incentive to master his Latin and Greek and the ancient classics. He also made considerable progress in English history and literature, and was thoroughly informed in Euro-pean politics as well as in all matters connected with American questions. His father pronounced him a good penman—a legacy to those who would be able to read the writings and observa-tions of our founders.

John Adams' assignment in Paris was shorter than anticipated and father and son were back in Boston in a year. John Quincy Adams ex-pected now to enter Andover Academy in prepa-ration for Harvard. Unexpectedly a new call upon his father's services took both him and Charles, a younger brother, back to Europe.

The education of the two young Adamses was continued in the French school in Passy where Johnny had previously been enrolled. When John Adams left Paris for a mission to Holland, his sons accompanied him and while there, attended the Amsterdam Latin School. In Leyden the boys attended lectures on medicine, studied Homer, Greek grammar and the New Testament in the world-famous university where the Pilgrims' pastor, John Robinson, had studied and lectured.

A DIPLOMATIC APPOINTMENT AT FOURTEEN

The maturity of John Quincy Adams and his proficiency in reading, writing and speaking French resulted in 1781, in his appointment by Congress as diplomatic secretary to his friend, Francis Dana, just appointed Commissioner to the Court of Catherine the Great. Dana's in-structions to seek the friendship and sympathy of Russia included the fourteen-year old youth whose competency as an interpreter was extremely valuable in the mission. The boy resided in St. Petersburg for more than a year, a city to which he would return some twenty-eight years later as Ambassador from the United States.

Life, Administration and Times of John Quincy Adams, Sixth President of the United States, by John Robert Irelan, 1887, pages 20–22.

†*Ibid.*, page 17.

It was during this year in Petersburg that John Quincy Adams began actually to keep a diary—a habit which he maintained some sixty-seven years. He had already become aware of the relationship of character and a philosophy of government to the individual freedom and productivity expressed in the countries through which he travelled. He wrote, "this is not a very good place for learning the Latin or Greek languages, as there is no academy or school here, and but very few private teachers, who demand at the rate of 90 pounds sterling a year for an hour and a half each day. Mr. Dana don't chuse to employ any at that extravagant price without your positive orders, but I hope I shall be able to go on alone."

To his father he wrote, October 12, 1781:

"There is nobody here but Princes and Slaves, the Slaves cannot have their children instructed, and the nobility that chuse to have their's send them into foreign countries. There is not one school to be found in the whole city."*

There was an English library in St. Petersburg to which Mr. Dana subscribed, so Johnny continued his studies and reading, and began to teach himself German. In fourteen months the mission came to an end. Johnny decided not to wait until the winter was over, and at fifteen began a journey crossing a snow-bound Europe, alone—a journey which took him some six months. He took it upon himself to look into the prospects of future trade between Sweden and Denmark and his own country. With credentials from Dana he spent several months in Sweden. The Swedes "are in general good friends to America, but seem to be a little afraid for their mines; however they are very well disposed for carrying on commerce with America. . . . Mr. Brandenburg, in Stockholm, intends to send a Vessel to some part of America this spring. He desired me to let him know what would be the best articles he could send, and gave me a list of the exports of Sweden, a copy of which I have sent to Mr. Dana, desiring him to answer Mr. Brandenburg as I was not certain myself about the matter."†

Back in Paris as his father's secretary he wrote his mother his observations on the government of Russia:

*The Writings of John Quincy Adams, edited by Worthington Chauncey Ford, Vol. I, 1779–1796, page 6.
†Ibid., page 7.

"HONOURED MAMMA:

"As you have ordered me in a letter, which I have lately received, to give you my observations on the countries thro' which I have travelled, the following are some upon Russia; but, I must previously beg you will remember, that you say in your letter that you expect neither the precision of a Robertson, nor the elegance of a Voltaire; therefore, you must take them as they are.

"The government of Russia is entirely despotical; the sovereign is absolute in all the extent of the word. The persons, the estates, the fortunes of the nobility depend entirely upon his caprice. And the nobility have the same power over the people, that the sovereign has over them. The nation is wholly composed of nobles and serfs, or, in other words, of masters and slaves. The countryman is attached to the land in which he is born; if the land is sold, he is sold with it, and he is obliged to give to his landlord the portion of his time which he chooses to demand. . . .

"This form of government is disadvantageous to the sovereign, to the nobles and to the people, For first, it exposes the sovereign every moment to revolution, of which there have been *already* four in the course of this century . . . *Secondly*, as the nobles all depend wholly upon the sovereign, they are always in danger of their estates being confiscated and themselves sent into Siberia . . . And, *thirdly*, as to the people nobody, I believe, will assert that a people can be happy who are subjected to personal slavery. Some of these serfs are immensely rich, but they are not free, and, therefore, they are despised; besides they depend still upon the nobles, who make them contribute the more for their riches . . . The richer they are, the more the nobles prize them. Thus a common man costs but 80 or 100 rubles, at most; but I have seen a man, who gave to his landlord, for his liberty, and that of his descendants, 450,000 rubles. This proves the esteem they have for liberty, even where one would think they should not know that such a thing exists.

"As I am a little pressed for time, and as my letter has already run to a considerable length, I must, for the present subscribe myself,

Your most dutiful son".‡

A CRITICAL DECISION TO GO HOME

In 1784 the Adams family was reunited in England. Two Abigails, mother and sister, were

‡Ibid., pages 10–13.

coming to Europe to join two John Adamses. The American Revolution was over, and John Adams had once again played a conspicuous part with John Quincy Adams transcribing more than one of the historic peace documents for his father.

What a reunion it was. Mother Abigail hardly recognized her grown-up elegant son with waistcoat, small-clothes, hat and sword in the very latest style of Europe. And Sister Abigail, little Abby, now nineteen and vivacious, was eager to be escorted by her brother to the sights and sounds of London. It was a most satisfying time of re-acquaintance and approval. Then on to Paris.

As joint Commissioners in Paris, John Adams and Thomas Jefferson renewed their friendship. The young Adams' were charmed with Mr. Jefferson whose love of young people prompted him to plan many activities on their behalf. The studious John Quincy found a diversion from his books and he immensely enjoyed escorting both mother and sister to the salons of many eminent French friends.

But his mind began to turn on other things. Writing to a friend at the close of 1784 he said:

"You can imagine what an addition has been made to my happiness by the arrival of a kind and tender mother, and of a sister who fulfills my most sanguine expectations; yet the desire of returning to America still possesses me. My country has over me an attractive power which I do not understand. Indeed, I believe that all men have an attachment to their country distinct from all other attachments . . . But I have another reason for desiring to return to my native country. I have been such a wandering being these seven years, that I have never performed any regular course of studies, and am deficient on many subjects. I wish very much to have a degree at Harvard, and shall probably not be able to obtain it unless I spend at least one year there."*

It is a credit to the maturity of John Quincy Adams that he recognized the requirements for his preparation for a life of usefulness. Nevertheless, to his Diary, he confessed a reluctance to surrender his independent life to the discipline of a college quadrangle. He wrote:

"After having been traveling for these seven years almost all over Europe, and having been in the world and among company for three; to return to spend one or two years within the pale of a college, subjected to all the rules which I have so long been freed from; then to plunge into the dry and tedious study of the law for three years; and afterwards not expect (however good an opinion I may have of myself) to bring myself into notice under three or four years more, if ever. It is really a prospect somewhat discouraging for a youth of my ambition (for I have ambition, though I hope its object is laudable). But still,

' O, how wretched Is that poor man
that hangs on princes' favors! '

or on those of anybody else. I am determined that so long as I shall be able to get my own living in an honorable manner, I will depend upon no one. My father has been so much taken up all his life-time with the interests of the public, that his own fortune has suffered by it; so that his children will have to provide for themselves, which I shall never be able to do, if I loiter away my precious time in Europe, and shun going home until I am forced to it."†

So, despite the appointment of John Adams as Minister to London and the opportunities of living abroad with the family for a few more interesting years, John Quincy Adams responded to the same call that his father had always responded to—duty. Once again he set forth alone—this time homeward bound on an eight-week voyage to America. As he turned his steps towards Harvard, he carried a letter from his father to Cousin Samuel Adams:

"The child whom you used to lead out into the Common, to see with detestation the British troops, and with pleasure the Boston militia, will have the honor to deliver you this letter. He has since seen the troops of most nations in Europe, without any ambition, I hope, of becoming a military man. He thinks of the bar and peace and civil life, and I hope will follow and enjoy them with less interruption than his father could. If you have in Boston a virtuous club, such as we used to delight and improve ourselves in, they will inspire him with such sentiments as a young American ought to entertain, and give him less occasion for lighter company.

"I think it no small proof of his discretion, that he chooses to go to New England rather

---

Life, Administration and Times of John Quincy Adams, by John Robert Irelan, 1887, pages 29–30.

†Ibid., pages 30-31.

than to Old. You and I know, that it will probably be more for his honor and his happiness in the result; but young gentlemen of eighteen do not always see through the same medium with old ones of fifty . . ."*

John Quincy Adams also carried another letter which he delivered to Professor Waterhouse at Harvard College. It, too, was from his father and it endeavored to introduce an applicant whose preparation was unique and had been largely the result of determined self-education:

Auteuil, 24 April, 1785

"This letter will be delivered you by your old acquaintance John Quincy Adams, whom I beg leave to recommend to your attention and favor. He is anxious to study some time at your university before he begins the study of the law, which appears at present to be the profession of his choice. He must undergo an examination, in which I suspect he will not appear exactly what he is. In truth, there are few who take their degrees at college, who have so much knowledge. But his studies having been pursued by himself, on his travels, without any steady tutor, he will be found awkward in speaking Latin, in prosody, in parsing, and even, perhaps, in that accuracy of pronunciation in reading orations or poems in that language, which is often chiefly attended to in such examinations. It seems to be necessary, therefore, that I make this apology for him to you, and request you to communicate it in confidence to the gentlemen who are to examine him, and such others as you think prudent.

"If you were to examine him in English and French poetry, I know not where you would find anybody his superior; in Roman and English history, few persons of his age. It is rare to find a youth possessed of so much knowledge. He has translated Virgil's Aeneid, Suetonius, the whole of Sallust, and Tacitus's Agricola, his Germany, and several books of his Annals, a great part of Horace, some of Ovid, and some of Caesar's commentaries, in writing, besides a number of Tully's orations. These he may show you; and although you will find the translations in many places inaccurate in point of style, as must be expected at his age, you will see abundant proof that it is impossible to make those translations without understanding his authors and their language very well.

*The Works of John Adams, 1854, Vol. IX, page 532.

"In Greek his progress has not been equal; yet he has studied morsels in Aristotle's Poetics, in Plutarch's Lives, and Lucian's Dialogues, the choice of Hercules, in Xenophon, and lately he has gone through several books in Homer's Iliad.

"In mathematics I hope he will pass muster. In the course of the last year, instead of playing cards like the fashionable world, I have spent my evenings with him. We went with some accuracy through the geometry in the Preceptor, the eight books of Simpson's Euclid in Latin, and compared it, problem by problem and theorem by theorem, with le père de Chales in French; we went through plane trigonometry and plain sailing, Fenning's Algebra, and the decimal fractions, arithmetical and geometrical proportions, and the conic sections, in Ward's mathematics. I then attempted a sublime flight, and endeavored to give him some idea of the differential method of calculation of the Marquis de L'Hopital, and the method of fluxions and infinite series of Sir Isaac Newton; but alas! it is thirty years since I thought of mathematics, and I found I had lost the little I once knew, especially of these higher branches of geometry, so that he is as yet but a smatterer, like his father. However, he has a foundation laid, which will enable him with a year's attendance on the mathematical professor, to make the necessary proficiency for a degree.

"He is studious enough, and emulous enough, and when he comes to mix with his new friends and young companions, he will make his way well enough. I hope he will be upon his guard against those airs of superiority among the scholars, which his larger acquaintance with the world, and his manifest superiority in the knowledge of some things, may but too naturally inspire into a young mind, and I beg of you, Sir, to be his friendly monitor in this respect and in all others."†

In six months John Quincy Adams had prepared himself for entrance into Harvard College as a Junior. He entered a class of one hundred and forty and graduated second in the class of 1786, delivering one of the valedictory orations on the subject of "The Importance of Public Faith to the Well-Being of a Community." Now there remained only the reading of law in the office of the learned Theophilus Parsons at Newburyport, later of the Massachusetts Supreme Court. Three years later he was admitted to practice in Essex County, July 15, 1790. Now began the period of waiting which he had dreaded.

†Ibid., pages 530-531.

CHALLENGES PHILOSOPHY OF
FRENCH REVOLUTION

But John Quincy Adams did not let this three year period pass without an application of his philosophy of government. Thomas Paine's *Rights of Man* had just been published under the endorsement of Thomas Jefferson, serving Washington's administration as Secretary of State. John Quincy Adams in a series of essays signed PUBLICOLA challenged the fundamental doctrines of Paine's work. He denied that "whatever a whole nation chooses to do, it has the right to do" and he maintained that "nations, no less than individuals, are subject to the eternal and immutable laws of justice and morality." In effect, John Quincy Adams indicated "that Paine's doctrine annihilated the security of every man for his inalienable rights, and would lead in practice to a hideous despotism, concealed under the party-colored garments of democracy."

At this time Americans were to be tested severely in their friendship for their Revolutionary ally, France. Students of a philosophy of government could discern the direction of the nation, from the fall of the Bastille, the destruction of the French constitution, the execution of their king, and the succeeding anarchy and despotism which followed. John Quincy Adams challenged Paine's contention that the people of Great Britain should follow the example of France and "topple down headlong" their present government. But, at the same time he reiterated the distinctions between the American and the French Revolutions:

"Happy, thrice happy the people of America! whose gentleness of manners and habits of virtue are still sufficient to reconcile the enjoyment of their natural rights, with the peace and tranquillity of their country; whose principles of religious liberty did not result from an indiscriminate contempt of all religion whatever, and whose equal representation in their legislative councils was founded upon an equality really existing among them, and not upon the metaphysical speculations of fanciful politicians, vainly contending against the unalterable course of events, and the established order of nature."*

When in 1793 Great Britain declared war against France, the feelings in America seemed to be far from neutral. Traditional hostility towards Great Britain tended to make Americans take belligerent action against the commerce of Great Britain through privateering. Once again John Quincy Adams under pseudonym of MARCELLUS exposed the lawlessness, injustice and criminality of such interference in favor of one of the belligerents. He maintained that "impartial and unequivocal neutrality was the imperious duty of the United States." This position strengthened the hand of the administration of George Washington as it issued the Proclamation of Neutrality.

One more aspect of neutrality had to be challenged. This was the presence and conduct of the French minister, Genet, who, under the cloak of diplomatic immunity had challenged and insulted our national government for its advocacy of neutrality. Genet, through a chain of "democratic societies", appealed to the people outside their own government. John Quincy Adams exposed Genet's actions as a violation of the Law of Nations:

"When therefore the French Minister 'thanks God, that he has forgotten what GROTIUS, PUFFENDORF and VATTEL have written upon the laws of nations,' he ought to be told, that his forgetfulness 'is not a thing to thank God on.' . . . To insult the memory and slander the reputation of men like these, of men whose virtues and genius have deserved well of mankind, does as little credit to the head as to the heart of Mr. Genet."†

President Washington was indeed under obligation to John Quincy Adams, for his writings turned the tide of sentiment against Genet. His attention became fixed upon the young man and he began to make inquiries concerning his life and character. He saw in him a man of political knowledge who could effectively express a philosophy of government. His background of familiarity with the languages and customs of foreign courts seemed to mark him as a unique representative for his country.

Accordingly, in June of 1794 John Quincy Adams, aged 28, was summoned to Philadelphia where he received his commission as minister from the United States to the Netherlands. John Adams, then Vice President, had made no effort to secure this position for his son although President Washington had consulted him as to the

---

The Writings of John Quincy Adams, edited by Worthington Chauncey Ford, 1913, page 98.

†*Ibid.,* pages 165-166.

availability of the young man. Writing a few weeks before the appointment had been made official, John Adams informed Abigail Adams of the recognition of her son:

"It is proper that I should apprize you, that the President has it in contemplation to send your son to Holland, that you may recollect yourself and prepare for the event. I make this communication to you in confidence, at the desire of the President, communicated to me yesterday by the Secretary of State. You must keep it an entire secret until it shall be announced to the public in the journal of the Senate. But our son must hold himself in readiness to come to Philadelphia, to converse with the President, Secretary of State, Secretary of the Treasury, &c., and receive his commissions and instructions, without loss of time. He will go to Providence in the stage, and thence to New York by water, and thence to Philadelphia in the stage. He will not set out, however, until he is informed of his appointment."*

A CHARACTER TO SUPPORT A
CHRISTIAN REPUBLIC

A careful study of the public life and writings of John Quincy Adams is required to properly assess his application of character and philosophy of government. Here we can only briefly indicate the offices he held and some of his major accomplishments.

PUBLIC SERVICE OF JOHN QUINCY ADAMS

Age	Office	Dates
14	Diplomatic Secretary to Francis Dana, minister to Russia. Appointed by the Continental Congress	1781–2
27	Resident Minister to Holland. Appointed by George Washington	1794–7
30	United States Ambassador to Prussia. Appointed by John Adams under special urging from George Washington	1797–1801
35	Elected a member of the Massachusetts State Senate	1802
36	Elected to the United States Senate from Massachusetts	1803–1808
42	Minister to Russia. Appointed by President Madison	1809–15
48	Minister to England. Appointed by James Madison	1815–17
50	Secretary of State. Appointed by James Monroe	1817–25
58	President of the United States of America	1825–29
63	Elected to the United States Congress, House of Representatives, to fill the Plymouth seat from Massachusetts	1830–1848

OUTSTANDING ACCOMPLISHMENTS

1817:
Standardization of Weights and Measures of the United States
February 22, 1819:
Treaty with Spain for acquisition of Florida
1823:
The Monroe Doctrine—
written by John Quincy Adams
February 22, 1841:
The *Amistad* case argued before the United States Supreme Court
December 3, 1844:
Opening of the Twenty-Eighth Congress and the rescinding of the gag rule. The right of petition restored to the American people.

Perhaps the most notable accomplishment of John Quincy Adams during his years in Congress was his steadfast effort to maintain the right of petition. This effort became the focus of the pro and anti-slavery forces which brought upon his head the invective of both sides. John Quincy Adams was no abolitionist but steered a lonely course of principle. As a Christian his position on slavery brought his weight against the admission of slave states into the union. Doubtless God raised the voice of John Quincy Adams so that the conscience of American government could come to terms with this basic Biblical principle of the Declaration of Independence. Here are his sentiments on the subject:

"When our fathers abjured the name of Britons, and 'assumed among the nations of the earth the separate and equal station to which the laws of nature and of nature's God entitled them,' they tacitly contracted the engagement for themselves, and above all for their posterity, to contribute, in their corporate and national capacity, their full share, ay, and more than their

---

Life and Public Services of John Quincy Adams, by William H. Seward, 1849, page 62.

full share, of the virtues that elevate and of the graces that adorn the character of civilized man. They announced themselves as *reformers* of the institution of civil society. They spoke of the laws of nature, and in the name of nature's God; and by that sacred adjuration they pledged us, their children, to labor with united and concerted energy, from the cradle to the grave, to purge the earth of all slavery; to restore the race of man to the full enjoyment of those rights which the God of nature had bestowed upon him at his birth; to disenthrall his limbs from chains, to break the fetters from his feet and the manacles from his hands, and set him free for the use of all his physical powers for the improvement of his own condition. The God in whose name they spoke had taught them, in the revelation of the Gospel, that the only way in which man can discharge his duty to Him is by loving his neighbor as himself, and doing with him as he would be done by; respecting his rights while enjoying his own, and applying all his emancipated powers of body and of mind to self-improvement and the improvement of his race."*

CONCERN FOR THE CHARACTER OF
THE NEXT GENERATION

Concern for posterity distinguished the founding fathers of America. Every generation has the Biblical responsibility to remember what has been given to us through the inheritance received from our fathers. Likewise, we cannot live without regard for those who follow us. *"One generation shall praise thy works to another, and shall declare thy mighty acts."* Psalms 145:4.

We conclude this brief introduction to the education of John Quincy Adams with evidence of his concern for the character of the next generation. Raised in a Christian home he too wished to inculcate in his own children the teaching and learning of Biblical principles of life. Though absent from some members of his family, sometimes for years, as he served his country in foreign posts, his children were ever in his heart and in his prayers. Here is one of a series of letters to his son on "The Bible and Its Teachings." It is preceded by a brief biographical sketch and statement by James L. Alden who published the nine letters because of his own concern for the rising generation in America:

"The following letters were written by Mr.

Memoir of the Life of John Quincy Adams, by Josiah Quincy, 1858, pages 407-8.

Adams, while ambassador at St. Petersburgh, to one of his sons, who was at school in Massachusetts. Their purpose is the inculcation of a love and reverence for the Holy Scriptures, and a delight in their perusal and study. Throughout his long life, Mr. Adams was himself a daily and devout reader of the Scriptures, and delighted in comparing and considering them in the various languages with which he was familiar, hoping thereby to acquire a nicer and clearer appreciation of their meaning. The Bible was emphatically his counsel and monitor through life, and the fruits of its guidance are seen in the unsullied character which he bore through the turbid waters of political contention to his final earthly rest. Though long and fiercely opposed and condemned in life, he left no man behind him who would wish to fix a stain on the name he has inscribed so high on the roll of his country's most gifted and illustrious sons.

"The intrinsic value of these letters, their familiar and lucid style, their profound and comprehensive views, their candid and reverent spirit, must win for them a large measure of the public attention and esteem. But, apart from even this, the testimony so unconsciously borne by their pure-minded and profoundly learned author to the truth and excellence of the Christian faith and records, will not be lightly regarded.

"It is no slight testimonial to the verity and worth of Christianity, that in all ages since its promulgation, the great mass of those who have risen to eminence by their profound wisdom, integrity, and philanthropy, have recognized and reverenced Jesus of Nazareth as the Son of the living God. To the names of Augustine, Xavier, Fenelon, Milton, Locke, Lavater, Howard, Chateaubriand, and their thousands of compeers in Christian faith, among the world's wisest and noblest, it is not without pride that the American may add, from among his countrymen, those of such men as WASHINGTON, JAY, PATRICK HENRY, and JOHN QUINCY ADAMS.

St. Petersburg, Sept., 1811

"My dear Son:

In your letter of the 18th January to your mother, you mentioned that you read to your aunt a chapter in the Bible or a section of Doddridge's Annotations every evening. This information gave me real pleasure; for so great is my veneration for the Bible, and so strong my belief, that when duly read and meditated on, it is of all books in the world, that which contributes most to make men good, wise, and happy—that the earlier my children begin to read it, the more steadily they pursue the practice of reading it throughout their lives, the more lively and confident will be my hopes that they will prove useful citizens to their country, respectable members of society, and a real blessing to their parents. But I hope you have now arrived at an age to understand that reading, even in the Bible, is a thing in itself, neither good nor bad, but that all the good which can be drawn from it, is by the use and improvement of what you have read, with the help of your own reflection. Young people sometimes boast of how many books, and how much they have read; when, instead of boasting, they ought to be ashamed of having wasted so much time, to so little profit.

"I advise you, my son, in whatever you read, and most of all in reading the Bible, to remember that it is for the purpose of making you wiser and more virtuous. I have myself, for many years, made it a practice to read through the Bible once every year. I have always endeavored to read it with the same spirit and temper of mind, which I now recommend to you: that is, with the intention and desire that it may contribute to my advancement in wisdom and virtue. My desire is indeed very imperfectly successful; for, like you, and like the Apostle Paul, 'I find a law in my members, warring against the laws of my mind.' But as I know that it is my nature to be imperfect, so I know that it is my duty to aim at perfection; and feeling and deploring my own frailties, I can only pray Almighty God, for the aid of his Spirit to strengthen my good desires, and to subdue my propensities to evil; for it is from him, that every good and every perfect gift descends.

"My custom is, to read four or five chapters every morning, immediately after rising from my bed. It employs about an hour of my time, and seems to me the most suitable manner of beginning the day. But, as other cares, duties and occupations, engage the remainder of it, I have perhaps never a sufficient portion of my time in meditation, upon what I have read. Even meditation itself is often fruitless, unless it has some special object in view; useful thoughts often arise in the mind, and pass away without being remembered or applied to any good purpose— like the seed scattered upon the surface of the ground, which the birds devour, or the wind blows away, or which rot without taking root, however good the soil may be upon which they are cast. . . .

"I have thought if in addition to the hour which I daily give to the reading of the Bible, I should also from time to time (and especially on the Sabbath) apply another hour occasionally to communicate to you the reflections that arise in my mind upon its perusal, it might not only tend to fix and promote my own attention to the excellent instructions of that sacred Book, but perhaps also assist your advancement in its knowledge and wisdom. At your age, it is probable that you have still greater difficulties to understand all that you read in the Bible, than I have at mine; and if you have so much self-observation as your letters indicate, you will be sensible of as much want of attention, both voluntary and involuntary, as I here acknowledge in myself. I intend, therefore, for the purpose of contributing to your improvement and my own, to write you several letters, in due time to follow this, in which I shall endeavor to show you how you may derive the most advantage to yourself, from the perusal of the Scriptures. It is probable, when you receive these letters, you will not, at first reading entirely understand them; if that should be the case, ask your grand-parents, or your uncle or aunt, to explain them: if you still find them too hard, put them on file, and lay them by for two or three years, after which read them again, and you will find them easy enough.

"It is essential, my son, in order that you may go through life with comfort to yourself, and usefulness to your fellow-creatures, that you should form and adopt certain rules or principles, for the government of your own conduct and temper. Unless you have such rules and principles, there will be numberless occasions on which you will have no guide for your government but your passions. In your infancy and youth, you have been, and will be for some years, under the authority and control of your friends and instructors; but you must soon come to the age when you must govern yourself. You have already come to that age in many respects; you know the difference between right and wrong, and you know some of your duties, and the obligations you are under, to become acquainted with them all.

"It is in the Bible, you must learn them, and from the Bible how to practice them. Those duties are to God, to your fellow-creatures, and to yourself. 'Thou shalt love the Lord thy God, with all thy heart, and with all thy soul, and with all thy mind, and with all thy strength, and thy neighbor as thyself.' On these two commandments, Jesus Christ expressly says, 'hang all the law and the prophets;' that is to say, the whole purpose of Divine Revelation is to inculcate them efficaciously upon the minds of men. You will perceive that I have spoken of duties to *yourself,* distinct from those to God and to your fellow-creatures; while Jesus Christ speaks only of two commandments. The reason is, because Christ, and the commandments repeated by him, consider self-love as so implanted in the heart of every man by the law of his nature, that it requires no commandment to establish its influence over the heart; and so great do they know its power to be, that they demand no other measure for the love of our neighbor, than that which they know we shall have for ourselves. But from the love of God, and the love of our neighbor, result duties to ourselves as well as to them, and they are all to be learned in equal perfection by our searching the Scriptures.

"Let us, then, search the Scriptures; and, in order to pursue our inquiries with methodical order, let us consider the various sources of information, that we may draw from in this study. The Bible contains the revelation of the will of God. It contains the history of the creation of the world, and of mankind; and afterward the history of one peculiar nation, certainly the most extraordinary nation that has ever appeared upon the earth. It contains a system of religion, and of morality, which we may examine upon its own merits, independent of the sanction it receives from being the Word of God; and it contains a numerous collection of books, written at different ages of the world, by different authors, which we may survey as curious monuments of antiquity, and as literary compositions. In what light soever we regard it, whether with reference to revelation, to literature, to history, or to morality—it is an invaluable and inexhaustible mine of knowledge and virtue.

"I shall number separately those letters that I mean to write you upon the subject of the Bible, and as, after they are finished, I shall perhaps ask you to read them all together, or to look over them again myself, you must keep them on separate file. I wish that hereafter they may be useful to your brothers and sisters, as well as to you.

"As you will receive them as a token of affection for you, during my absence, I pray that they may be worthy to read by them all with benefit to themselves, if it please God, that they should live to be able to understand them.

"From your affectionate Father,

JOHN QUINCY ADAMS."*

Letters of John Quincy Adams to His Son on the Bible and Its Teachings, 1850, pages 6-21.

INDEX OF LEADING IDEAS

Prepared by
Rosalie J. Slater

providential training, 51b; saved the annihilation of the colonial charters, 461a; seventeen hundred and seventy-seven, the gloomiest period of, 56a; taught monarchs and statesmen a great moral lesson, 254c; to succeed where English Revolution of 1688 failed, 273b; turned on the hinge of taxation, 444a; turning point of, news of the French Alliance of 1778, 65d; unveiled political and religious truth, 254d; use of paper money in, 438c; was in the mind and the heart of the people, 251a; winter at Valley Forge, 1777-78, America's Life out of Death, 68c; yeoman of, persevered and kept the faith, 62c

AMERICAN RIGHTS: and liberties, reasserted by Georgia Provincial Congress, July 13, 1775, 530a; goal of 1st Continental Congress of 1774, to redress on constitutional principles, 475d

AMERICANS: claimed the rights and privileges of Englishmen, 393b; classes who were on the side of British administration, 365c; considered English legislators unfit to exercise unlimited supremacy over them, 482b; considered the tea party a duty they owed their country, 460d; denied legality of parliamentary taxation, 456c; determined to avoid beginning hostilities, 401d; discontinued importation of tea, 456d; effect of intolerable acts on minds of, 462d; entitled to same rights and liberties as Britons, 37d; exclusive right of taxation inherited from forefathers, 445b; exhorted not to forget obligations of Liberty, 67a; exhorted to remember holy ground of Valley Forge, 63a; feelings of, toward the name of Howe, 415b; firmly attached to monarchy before the Revolution, 398c; injured, sent petitions to His Majesty, King of England, 531d; introduced Christianity into families, business and education, 157a; not able to contend in arms on equal terms with parent state, 494a; on Bunker's Hill, reluctantly retreated, 498b; ready to defend their inheritance, purchased by blood of ancestors, 401d; remarkable Christian character of, 73a; resolved upon resistance, encouraged by pulpit, press, bench, bar, 505d; rights and liberties compared with the Apostle Paul's, 37d; saw their charters as a shield against all taxes not imposed by representatives, 446b; should honor the memory of Baron von Steuben, 64d; tastes and opinions of, pure and simple, 362d; their industry and invention, called forth by Providence, 422c; the spirit of, in the Suffolk Resolves, 399d; were underestimated by the ministerial majority in parliament, 464a

AMERICAN SETTLEMENT: *That century a remarkable era.* a period of great moral and social events, 47c; providential timing of influences shaping our national life and character, 48a; of invention, research, exploration, 48b; of copious learning and genius in literature, art, philosophy, theology, statesmanship, 48b; of changes in ecclesiastical and political world, 48c; the Reformation in purer form, 49a; development of religious liberty, 50a; growth of representative government, 50c

AMERICAN SETTLERS: and the love of freedom, 49d; disease smote them, but they fainted not, 49d; famine overtook them, but they feasted on roots, 49d; first, battled with dangers and hardships, 49c; first, laid foundations of our institutions, 49d; their rapid maturity and preparation to vie with Europe, 398b; their uniqueness in preparation for America, 398b

AMERICAN SLOGAN: *"don't shoot until you see the whites of their eyes,"* 497d

AMERICAN SOLDIER: at Valley Forge, an example of honor, 62c

AMERICAN STATES: one body in the community of

nations, 250c

AMERICAN SUNDAY SCHOOL UNION: anniversary meeting of, Boston, May 27, 1852, 21a

AMERICAN TAXATION: controversy on, defended by pens of Virginians, and New England writers, 440a; first published defense on, 440a; petitions of colonists against, treated with contempt, 368a; the darling measure of, pushed by systematic effort, 384a

AMERICAN TERRITORY: France and England contended for, 441a

AMERICAN TORIES: urged British administration to take more vigorous measures against their fellow Americans, 401b

AMERICAN TROUBLES: profits of West India Sugar planters, endangered by continuance of, 482c

AMERICAN UNION: early steps to promote, by election of delegates to Continental Congress, 393d

AMERICAN WAR: not the American Revolution, 251a

AMERICAN WHIG: feared episcopacy as a political importation, 143b

AMERICAN WOODS: and hard campaigns, not envisioned by ministers in England, 496c; ignorance of British Generals commanding in, 494c

AMERICAN WRITERS: demonstrated the financial contributions of the colonies to the empire, 453c; demonstrated that British monopoly of colonial trade would lead to slavery, 453c

AMERICAN YEOMAN: an example of devotion to duty, 62c

AMERICAN YOUTH: create in them patriotic emotions, 255a; let them be instructed in the vital principles of our Republic, 255a; let them be led by the hand of history, where our fathers acted and endured, 255c; let them be taught the price of our heritage, 255c; teach them to appreciate the blessings they enjoy, 255a; that our, be educated in the principles of Christianity, 28b

AMERICA'S CASE: resembled, Rehoboam's fight against the house of Israel, 546a

AMMUNITION: and arms, almost wholly deficient in the colonies, 496b; made by American patriots, 74d; New England men furnished themselves with, while exercising forebearance, 491c

ANARCHY: no part of American principles, 251d; resisteth the higher powers, 539a; the Apostle Paul, no friend to, 539a

ANCESTORS: *see also* FOREFATHERS, PILGRIM FATHERS Anniversary sermons preached in Plymouth, in commemoration of the Pilgrims' first landing, December 22, 1620, 30b; enjoin us to follow them with honor, 30a; great day of, 23c; concern for their descendants, 29a; convinced of the importance of public instruction, 222d; have been vilified, their religion questioned, 40c; influence of their parental education and examples, 218a; prevailed upon to accept monarchy, 247a; proud monument to our American Archives, 250b; wish us not to forsake the Gospel, 30a; would suffer again to bring us to repentance, 29d; received assistance from the clergy, 206a

ANCIENT WORLD: ideas alien to, man's universal rights, universal religious freedom, liberty of conscience, 11d; endeavored to suppress Christianity by force, 16a

ANDRE, JOHN, 1751-1780. British major, appointed to negotiate with Benedict Arnold for betrayal of West Point, captured by Americans; takes over Franklin's house in Philadelphia, 1777, 57d

ANDROS, SIR EDMUND, 1637-1714. British colonial governor in America. Imprisoned John Wise for his opposition to Province tax, 100a; during arbitrary government of, New Englanders reprinted Increase Mather's *Narrative of the miseries of New-England,*

and *Elijah's Mantle*, 252d; American colonies resumed their charters in 1689 in spite of, 272b

ANGELICAL: swiftness, and founding of Massachusetts Colony, 45b

ANGEL OF DEATH: sent by Lord of Hosts, to deliver Israel from Assyrian hosts, 542a

ANGELS: instrumentality of, used in God's care of the world, 23a

ANGLO-AMERICAN: people and nation of North America, formed in 1789, 248d

ANNIVERSARIES: of great events in our history should be kept, 67b

ANNIVERSARY: of election sermon, origin in charter of Massachusetts Bay, 1633, 191b; of our New England Fathers' arrival in Plymouth, ought to be observed, 41b; the 350th of the Pilgrims' landing, 22b; Thanksgiving sermon, preached at Plymouth, 22a; of Valley Forge, 55b

ANTAXERXES I, CALLED LONGIMANUS: King (464-424 B.C.) son of Xerxes I. appointed Nehemiah governor of Judea (445); permitted Nehemiah to go and build up the walls of Jerusalem, 536d

ANTI-CHRISTIANITY: and Christianity, issue of Revelation XII, 4d

ANTIOCH: city of, chosen for propagation of the Gospel, 11b

ANTITHESIS: Isaiah's most perfect examples of, 229d

ANVILLE, D', N. DE LA ROCHEFOUCAULD, 1700-1746: duke in command of French fleet sailing to lay waste the seacoast from Nova Scotia to Georgia in 1746, 50d

ANXIETY: of the people of Philadelphia awaiting the British Army, 56c

APARTMENT: humble, of George Washington, at Valley Forge, 75d

APHARSACHITES: their accusations by letter (Ezra 9:4) counterpart of, at New Plymouth, in Lyford and Oldham, 26b

APOCALYPSE: *See* REVELATION OF ST. JOHN

APOSTLES: after Christ, spoke of civil government, 36d; all of the, put hearers in mind of a judgement to come, 517d; and prophets, bare testimony against lawless oppressors, 41c; felt the necessity of preaching the Gospel, 5a; friendly to civil liberty, 38d; have labored for posterity, 213d; imitate the glorious pattern of their excellence, 226a; their travail over their children till Christ was formed in them, 5a

APOSTLES OF MATERIALISM: of science, of culture, of logical immorality, their teaching leads men to limit their worship to the visible and the tangible, 6c

APOSTROPHE: Isaiah's most perfect use of this figure of composition, 229d

APPEASEMENT: a policy of slavery between children or nations, 236b

APRIL 18, 1775: British grenadiers embarked from Boston for Lexington and Concord, 406c

APRIL 19, 1775: King's Order regarding Military stores will expire on, 325a; Battle of Lexington, 405d; 491c

APRON: used to bring gunpowder to soldiers, by unknown woman in North Carolina, 80c

APTHORPE, EAST, REVEREND, 1733-1765: Episcopal minister, missionary for the Society for Propagation of the Gospel, 178a; issued pamphlet on evangelization, in 1764, answered by Jonathan Mayhew, 178a

"ARBELLA": Ship which brought Winthrop and his company of Puritans to America, Rev. George Phillips, chaplain on, 90a

ARBITER OF THE UNIVERSE: acknowledged in the establishment of the American nation, 347

ARBITRARY: edicts, could not bind a free people, 247c; efforts of Stuarts in England, helped to spread colonization, 359b; principles of Scottish Bishops,

112d; rule in civil government, opposed by ministers, 191d

ARBITRARY GOVERNMENT: introduced with taxation without representation, 458d

ARBITRARY POWER: a virtuous and steady opposition to, duty of American freemen, 458d; in Roman and English history, discussed by Mercy Warren, 359a; not supported by the Gospel law of liberty, 519b; not vested in rulers by Christian religion, 518d; stretch of, seen in loss of Massachusetts' civil constitution, 462a; defense against, laws which secure every man's liberty and property, 539b

ARBITRARY RULER: endeavors to have a standing army at his command, 201b

ARCHEOLOGIST: prophetical, Book of Revelation not meant for, 4a

ARCHITECT: Admirable, of Massachusetts Bay Colony, 44b

"AREOPAGUS": Judges of the, hear eloquence of Paul at Athens, 228b

ARISTOCRACY: a conflict of feudal pretentions in the American Revolution, 253a; learned, of Greece and Rome, looked down with contempt on the Christians, 8c

ARISTOCRATIC: form of government, discussed by John Wise, 100d

ARISTOTLE: rules of, and Timothy Dwight's preference for St. Paul's address to Agrippa, 227c

ARITHMETIC BOOKS: early, contained rules for enabling pupil to translate the money of one colony to another, 327b

ARMED CUTTERS: British, became revenue ships, 442d

ARMED FORCE: presence of, against the British Constitution, 376d

ARMED FORCES: of Great Britain, augmented for use against the colonies, 484d

ARMIES: opposing, met as free citizens of the same realm, 546a; raised by American colonies for Great Britain, paid in paper money, 438b; Congress insisted on thirteen distinct colonial, 60c

ARMINIANISM: made great noise in the land in 1734, stated Jonathan Edwards, 121a; vigorous antagonism to, in the Great Awakening, 103b

ARM OF FLESH: General Thomas Gage proclaimed Martial law for Massachusetts, June 12, 1775, 415c; 497a; 508-509

ARMS: Americans not able to contend in, on equal terms with Britain, 494a; and ammunition prohibited for America, 399b; of Bostonians, surrendered at promise of Gage for their liberty, 411a; inadequate, of soldiers at Valley Forge, 58c; King's order on prohibition of, 322b; the country rose in, after first blow for liberty, 409b; United Provinces of Netherlands, join in prohibition of, 325c

ARMY: chaplains in, were Massachusetts ministers, 206d; Congress slow in admitting necessity for a permanent, 499b; few in the colonies understood the business of providing for an, 496b; in hands of wicked sovereign, the means of overturning the constitution of a country, 201b; kept from disbanding by extraordinary virtues of Washington, 64d; lack of a standing, often brought provincials to brink of destruction, 499c; of Cromwell and William of Orange, contrasts in recruits for, 270d; raising of, voted by Massachusetts Provincial Congress, after Lexington, 493a; Washington's first, not organized, 60d

ARNOLD, BENEDICT, 1741-1801: American army officer, traitor, with Ethan Allen, captured Ticonderoga, May 10, 1775, 414d

ARRIAN, FLAVIUS ARRIANUS: 2nd century A.D. Greek historian, stoic, judged the Christians as a philosopher, 16b

tian era, 320a

BARCLAY, HENRY, 1734-1764: Protestant-Episcopal rector of Trinity Church, N.Y. city, was for some years a missionary to the Mohawk Indians, 320c

BAREFOOT: Continental soldiers at Valley Forge, 58c

BAROMETER: invented during the era of the American Settlement, 48b

BARRE, COLONEL ISAAC, 1726-1802: member of Parliament, opposed taxation of colonies, comments on character of British hirelings sent to ravish America, 365c

BARRETT, JAMES, COLONEL: commander of the troops at Concord, ordered his men to begin no onset against the troops of their sovereign, 408a

BARROW, OR BARROWE, HENRY, D. 1593: Martyr of Congregationalism, 89d

BARROWISM: early form of New England Congregationalism, 95c; mild type of, William Brewster faithful to, 89d

BARTER: American colonists forced to, because of lack of staple currency, 332c

"BARTER CURRENCY": or "country pay" was legalized in many of the colonies, cereals and other farm products were taken in payment for all debts, 332c; worked infinite annoyance and confusion in the colonies, 332d

BARTRAM, JOHN, 1699-1777: American botanist, self-taught, admitted to the Royal Society before the American Revolution, 440b

BATTLEFIELD: triumphant, pictured in the Revelation of St. John, 3d

BATTLE OF THE AMERICAN REVOLUTION: it was the Lord's, 52c

BATTLES OF THE AMERICAN REVOLUTION: Lexington, April 19, 1775, Mercy Warren's account, 405d; David Ramsay's account, 491d; Ticonderoga, May 10, 1775, 414c; Bunker Hill, June 17, 1775, Mercy Warren's account, 417a; David Ramsay's account, 496d; attack on Fort Henry, Wheeling, Virginia, September 1, 1777, 81a; Brandywine, September 11, 1777, 56d; Cedar Spring, South Carolina, 1780, 79b

BATWELL, DANIEL: Episcopal clergyman, preached Fast Day Sermon, July 20, 1775, before Morgan's Rifle-Men, 543b

BAXTER, RICHARD, 1615-1691: English puritan scholar and writer, church of, reflected the diversity of congregationalism, 105d

BAYONET: men either controlled by, or by the Bible, 20b

"BAY PSALM BOOK": prepared by Richard Mather and John Eliot in 1640, a song sung from, at the 1648 meeting of the Synod, 93b

BAY SALTS: French method of making salt, recommended to American Manufacturer in 1774, 339c

BEACH, JOHN, 1700-1782: American Congregationalist, reordained by the Church of England, appointed to a Mission at Newton, Connecticut, divisions of the Great Revival, bring large increase to his church, 168b

BEAST POWER: worship of, is the worship of world-power, 6a; the worship of the visible and tangible, 6c; described in Revelation XIII, 5d

BEAUMONT, FRANCIS, 1584-1616: English dramatist in the era of the American Settlement, 48c

BEGINNINGS: of Plymouth, unpromising, 26d

BEHAVIOUR: of children should deserve parental tenderness, 236a

BELL: ringing of, or beating of a drum, to call people to public worship in New England, 94b

BENCH: the, the pulpit, the press, and the bar, all encouraged American resistance, 505d

BENEFITS: of the future, seen through the Christian spirit, 27d

BENEVOLENCE: an act of, to destroy the power of a

tyrant, 203a; principles of, cherished in America, 248c

BERKELEY, GEORGE, 1685-1753: Irish philosopher, Bishop, described state of religion in the English Colonies, 161c; described the English spiritual neglect of the Indians, 162a; commented in 1729 at growth of sects in Rhode Island, 170a; his scheme for a college for Indian scholars and missionaries, 176c; endeavored to secure charter for a college in Bermuda, 176d; lived in America 1728-1731, 177a; in Rhode Island, labored unsuccessfully for a college, 177b; left his college library in Rhode Island, 177c; his works bore a character of moderation, 290d; prophecies regarding America in verse "westward the course of Empire takes its way," 249b

BERNARD, FRANCIS, 1712-1779: Colonial governor in America, character of, described by Mercy Warren, 366c; his treatment of Massachusetts General Assembly after the Circular Letter, 371a; impeached by the Massachusetts General Assembly, 371d; applied for troops to be sent to Boston, 372a; refused to convoke Massachusetts General Assembly, 372d; refused to remove the King's troops surrounding the State House, 376c; censored by the Massachusetts General Assembly for acting against the constitution, 377b; repaired to England where he was royally rewarded for conduct, 377c; his property granted to him by Massachusetts was never confiscated, 377d

BEVERLY, ROBERT, 1675-1716: first native born historian of Virginia, 440a

BIBLE, THE HOLY: see also HOLY SCRIPTURES, WORD OF GOD;

The History of: coincidence of dates in the history of our country and the history of the Bible, 19d; in the hands of the Pilgrims at Plymouth, 20a; incorporated into American life, institutions and people, 53b

In American Government: furnish the best principles of civil liberty, the most effectual support of republican government, 21a; in the ascendancy, exerting its influence on the people and on the government, 156c; on the same shelf with the Constitution, 21d

In American Education: a dissertation on the history, eloquence, poetry of, 224; made the basis of American Christian education, 157a; parents exhorted to teach children true religion of, 218d; U.S. government cannot forbid it being taught in the public schools, 155d

In American Society: the first of all charities is that which brings the Bible home to every fireside, 19b; the greatest of all instrumentalities for social advancement, 20c; human reason left without a divine guide, would fill the world with disorder, crime, misery, 20b; the most perfect maxims and examples for regulating social conduct and domestic economy, 255d

BIBLE-READING: men settled America, 49b

BIBLES: study your, instruction to youth, 220c

BIBLICAL: foundations of, our Pilgrim Fathers, 23d; injunction for individual labor, disfavors slavery, 433a

BIBLICAL COMMENTARIES: names of those most frequently used by the New England Clergy, 548d

BIBLICAL EXAMPLES: worthy of imitation, recommended to youth, 220d

BIBLICAL LEARNING: New England Clergy, excelled in all branches of, 440c

BIBLICAL PROMISE: of success in the education of children, 233b

BIGOTS: found lessons of American Revolution, impossible to learn, 254d; Pilgrims and Puritans, con-

arbitrary act of Boston Port Bill, reduced them to distress, 389b; inhabitants, garrisoned in their own town, waited patiently, 401a; famine, rapine, pestilence faced them, 409d; requested Gage to open gates of the city, 411a; surrendered their arms to Gage, but he refused to let them leave, 411b; economic disaster threatened them, 470a

BOSTON DIVINES: *see also* CLERGY, MINISTERS; names of, who took popular side, 192d; role of, during one year of suspension of civil government in Massachusetts, 209

BOSTON HARBOR: Islands in, cleared of their livestock by General Putnam, 411b; lighthouse at entrance of, burnt by Americans, 411c

BOSTON HEIGHTS: covered with citizens as they watched the burning of Charlestown, 497d

BOSTON NECK: fortified by Governor Gage, 471d

BOTETOURT, BARON DE, 1718?-1770: Colonial Governor of Virginia, gave assurances to colonies of King's redress, 381a; reassured by Hillsborough regarding an American Revenue, 454a; Virginians' confidence in King's pledge not to raise an American Revenue, 454c

BOUNDARIES: ignorance of American Geography, laid foundation for disputes, 441c

BOWDOIN, JAMES, 1726-1790: American merchant and Revolutionary leader, chosen as a representative, his name erased by Governor Gage, 391d

BOYLE, ROBERT, 1627-1691: English physicist and chemist, founder of Boyle lectures for defense of Christianity, conducted Society for the Propagation of the Gospel, amongst natives in New England, lecture fund to convert infidels to faith in Christ, 159b

BOYLSTON, ZABDIEL, 1679-1766: American Physician, member of Royal Society of London, before the American Revolution, 440b

BRADDOCK, EDWARD, 1695-1755: General, Commander-in-Chief of British forces in America during French and Indian War, retreat of, covered by his aid-de-camp, George Washington in 1755, 504a

BRADFORD, WILLIAM, 1590-1657: Governor of New Plymouth, intercepted subversive letters of Lyford and Oldham, 26b; quote from his *History 'Of Plimoth Plantation'* on Pilgrims' design in coming to America, 24c; counsel sought by Winthrop's company on church polity, 90b; present at Cambridge Synod, June 1647, 93a

BRAHE, TYCHO, 1546-1601: Danish Astronomer, in the era of the American Settlement, 48b

BRANDYWINE, BATTLE OF, SEPTEMBER 11, 1777: Americans defeated, 56d; Lafayette wounded at, 64a; John Marshall bore rifle in, 64b

BRANT, JOSEPH, 1742-1807: Iroquois Mohawk Chief, Indian name *Thayendanegea*, educated in England by Sir William Johnson, aided English to influence Indians, 313d

BRANT, MOLLY: sister of Joseph Brant, became second wife of British Agent of Indian Affairs, Sir William Johnson, 313c

BRATTLE, THOMAS, 1658-1713: American merchant, treasurer of Harvard, member of Royal Society of London before the American Revolution, 440b

BRAVE MEN: for defence of country, furnished by the Ancient and Honorable Artillery Company in Boston, 204a

BRAVERY: of the Americans, not known to General Gage until the Battle of Lexington, 409c

BRAY, THOMAS, 1656-1730: sent by Bishop of London as a commissary to Maryland, 159d; his efforts to increase influence of episcopal church, 160b; laid foundations of Society for Promoting Christian Knowledge, and Society for Propagation of the Gospel, 160c

BRAZIL: gold mines of, furnished the Portuguese with large quantities of precious metal, 336b

BREASTPLATE: of faith and love, part of our Christian armour, 550c

BREED'S HILL: fortified instead of Bunker's Hill by the provincials, 417b; 497b

BREWSTER, WILLIAM, 1567-1644: Beloved Elder of the Plymouth Church, faithful to a mild type of Barrowism, 89d; counsel sought by Winthrop's company on church polity, 90b; remarks on the character of the Pilgrims at Leyden, 25c

BRIBERY: in elections, with decline of freeholders, 28d

BRIDE: of Christ, the Church, Revelation XII, 5a

BRIMSTONE: and sulpher, Continental Congress recommended the collection of, 342a

BRITAIN: power of, fully apprized by Americans, before the American Revolution, 493d

BRITISH: garrison, well-equipped, lived in luxury in New York, 56a; gold, bought country's produce, 56b; in control of Boston, when General George Washington took command, 504d; pretensions, opposed on British principles, 252b

BRITISH ADMINISTRATION: designs of, opposed by Boston divines, 192b

BRITISH AMERICA: calculated to be a nursery of heroes, 204c

BRITISH ARMY: *see also* BRITISH OFFICERS, BRITISH REGIMENTS, BRITISH SOLDIERS, BRITISH TROOPS; stationed in Massachusetts Province in 1770, 454d; in Boston, to be reinforced, news shocked populace, 1775, 404c: Second Continental Congress rendered supply of, precarious and expensive, 500b; under command of Pigot and Howe at Bunker Hill, 417c; cost dear to, at Bunker Hill, 417b; reinforced with fresh veteran troops, 1777, 56c; landed at Head of Elk, August 25, 1777, 56c; marched into city of Philadelphia, October, 1777, 56c; evacuated Philadelphia, June 18, 1778, 66c

BRITISH BATTERIES: floating in river, kept up a continual fire upon American entrenchments on Breed's Hill, 417b

BRITISH BOARD OF TRADE: *See* BRITISH WESTERN POLICY

BRITISH COLONIES: *see also* AMERICAN COLONIES; Bishop of St. Asaph, commented upon growth and progress of, 27a; cemented by similarity of civil institutions, 247b; no political connections with each other, 247a; so many independent states, 247a; prepared for the American Revolution, 249c

BRITISH CONSTITUTION: respected by the two great aristocratic parties of England, the Tories and the Whigs, they differed on privileges of, 271a; its superiority over other forms of government because the people had representation, and without their concurrence, no law binding on them could be enacted, 445a; Colonial charters sacred under, 462a; English Colonies had substance of, in their provincial governments, 437a; security of liberty and property to colonies, derived from, 430b; protected right of taxation by representation, and trial by a jury of peers, 430d; the proper basis for control of colonies, Burke, 487b; letter of, violated by the plan for a parliamentary tax, 444d; principles of, violated by a standing army in Boston, 374b; cited by Massachusetts General Assembly against presence of an armed force, 376d; Quebec Act, contrary to spirit and letter of, 463c; 532c; spirit of, justified conduct of colonists in Boston Tea Party, 459b; disregarded by the passing of the Boston Port Bill, 460a; "*superiour to every man or set of men whatever*", Georgia Resolves, July 10, 1775, 527c

BRITISH COUNCIL: enforcement of Acts of Trade, 1760, first stage of the American Revolution, 248b

BRITISH EMPIRE: began her own dismemberment after

1764, 442b rended by the paltry tax on tea, 1767, 453b; final dismemberment of, due to reciprocal jealousies of Great Britain and the Americans, 483d

BRITISH FISHERIES: difficulties in support of, by resolutions of Continental Congress, 500a

BRITISH FISHERMEN: resolutions of Continental Congress, interdicted all supplies to, 500b

BRITISH FLEET: watched the rebel coast in 1777, 56b

BRITISH INDIAN AFFAIRS: department organized with Guy Johnson, contained influential citizens of Tryon County, 313c; endeavored to influence Indians to side of Crown during the American Revolution, 313d

BRITISH LIBERTY: James Otis argued from principles in favor of, 368a

BRITISH LINES: Lydia Darrah of Philadelphia passed through, in order to warn General Washington of secret attack upon the American Army, 78c

BRITISH MANUFACTURERS: their clamors neglected as non-importation threatened in 1768, 374c; suffered from repeal of American duties, 452d; solicited repeal of American duties, 452d; 480d

BRITISH MINISTRY: impelled by necessity in the repeal of the Stamp Act, 363c; innovating spirit of, interrupted tranquillity of the provinces, 365b; advocated coercion for the American Colonies, 403c; made a treaty with the Dutch to prevent their help to the colonies, 404b; exposed by the writings of Benjamin Franklin, 455d; plan to force tea on colonies, a violent attack on liberties of America, 458d; flattered themselves that the majority of colonies would submit, 478c; disappointed at the Colonial union of the colonies, 478c; elected a new Parliament to deal with American acts, 479b; regarded resolutions of the First Continental Congress as idle clamours of a mob, 480a; Crown appointees abused the colonies in their official dispatches to England, 480b; friends of, insulted Franklin, called Chatham's Bill traitorous, 481d; wished to new-model the colonial constitutions, 482d; believed colonies wanted to renounce sovereignty of Great Britain, 483c; plans to coerce the American colonies, carried by great majorities in Parliament, 484b; Bill for restraint of trade of New England colonies, 485a; refusal to repeal Massachusetts Government Acts was "*the fatal rock*," 487d; colonists refused submission to tyranny of, 501d; effected a separation between Britain and America, 521d

BRITISH NAVIGATION LAWS: unfriendly to adventurous spirit of American Commerce, 453d

BRITISH OFFICERS: reared in the halls of nobility, made war a profession, 253b; bill making it lawful to quarter their troops in private homes in the colonies, passed by parliament, 368c; spirited conduct of, at Battle of Bunker's Hill, 498a; pushed British soldiers forward with their swords, 497d; singled out by Provincials on Bunker's Hill, 498c; large number of killed, due to good marksmenship of Provincials, 498c

BRITISH REGIMENTS: *see also* BRITISH ARMY, BRITISH SOLDIERS, BRITISH TROOPS; ordered to Boston in 1767 following Townshend Bill, 451d; peaceably received in Boston, 452a; the 29th, involved in the massacre of March 5, 1770, 454d; the Captain and six men of the 29th, acquitted in Boston trial, John Adams and Josiah Quincy, counsel for, 455a; Captain Wilson of the 29th, detected in exciting African Slaves to murder their masters, 381d; Colonel Dalrymple, consented that the 29th be sent to Castle Island, 382c; regiments identified in Philadelphia in October, 1777, 57c

BRITISH RULERS: convinced of right of colonial taxation, 456b

BRITISH SOLDIERS: *see also* BRITISH ARMY, BRITISH REGIMENTS, BRITISH TROOPS; Boston inhabitants suffered every species of insult from, 381b; illegality of quartering in town, exposed by Samuel Adams, 382c; thousands died, active to enslave their brethren in America, 534d; wounded and slaughtered by a handful of Provincials at Bunker's Hill, 417d

BRITISH SOVEREIGNTY: in America, not established on consent of the people, 208

BRITISH SUBJECTS: rights of, violated by transporting for trial in Great Britain, 389d; and right of, to grant or withhold taxes, 445a

BRITISH SUPERIORITY: Americans impressed with, before Lexington, 493c

BRITISH TAXATION: unfriendly to adventurous spirit of American commerce, 453d

BRITISH TRADE: greatly magnified by the American colonies, 444c

BRITISH TROOPS: *see also* BRITISH ARMY, BRITISH REGIMENTS, BRITISH SOLDIERS; mostly veteran warriors from continental battlefields, 253b; Samuel Adams exposed illegality of quartering in Boston, 382c; recall of, urged in Parliament, 403b; reach Lexington, on April 19, 1775, 406c; withdrew from Concord Bridge, 408a; committed barbarities on Americans, 408b; flew before raw, inexperienced militia, 408c; weakened by severe engagement at Bunker's Hill, 419a; did not consider Provincial troops to be their equals, 494c; recall of, in Georgia's Petition to the King, 533a; disappointment that they could slay their brethren in America, 534c; evacuation of, not end of the American Revolution, 250d

BRITISH WESTERN POLICY: kaleidoscopic changes in British ministry affect, 303b; ministerial policies not easily distinguishable, 304d; three periods of policy making, 304a; purpose of Proclamation of 1763, 304b; Lord Shelburne responsible for, 304c; Shelburne's policies followed by Hillsborough until 1768, 304d; Rockingham ministry favorable to Shelburne's policy, 305d; Chatham's "broad bottom ministry," weaknesses of, 306c; Shelburne's letter to Board of Trade forced issue on western lands, 309a; paramount issue, disposal of land in upper Ohio, 310c; positive and final action deferred until the Revolution, 304d

American Interest: Since 1763 settlers crowded into upper Ohio valley, 306d; Indians cheated because of failure of British to provide needed regulations, 307a; threat of Indian war, 307a; Americans pressured ministry to open up lands for colonization, 307a; Mississippi Company formed, Washington a member of, 307a; Philadelphia merchants, Franklin, promoted a colony in the Illinois, 307b; Hillsborough favored the Philadelphians and gave them every encouragement, 310c

Shelburne's Western Policy: responsible for wording of Proclamation of 1763, 304b; began in 1767 to put his plan into execution, 307b; Treaty at Fort Stanwix with Iroquois, set boundary line, 307c; outlined plans for raising revenue in America, 307d; recommended Indian trade be placed in control of colonies, 308b; his letter to Board of Trade, forced issue of the western lands, 309a

Hillsborough's Western Policy: adopted policies of Shelburne until 1768, 304d; accepted position of president of the Board of Trade under Shelburne, 306b; differences between Shelburne, discovered, 306c; appointed secretary of state for the colonies, 308d; inspired answer of Board of Trade to Shelburne's recommendations, 309b; letter to General Gage on, 309c; favored Philadelphians, as claimants for settlement of Ohio country, 310c

x, appointed for army by Provincial Congress of Massachusetts, May 20, 1775, 206c; under command of Hon. Artemus Ward, 206c; services offered by Congregational pastors, 207b; gentlemen to act as, on whose virtue, firmness, patriotism they can safely rely, 207d; provision for, by Committee of Supplies, 207d

CHARACTER: distinctions of, in John Wise, 100a; diversity of American, established with the Declaration, 250a; essential, of Christianity, of first century, should be studied, 16b; future, and parental instruction, 220d; man's, will be judged not by external appearance, but by inward reality, 516d; of a good member of society should speak out against follies, ignorance, or mistakes of those at the helm, 186c; of church membership, declined as a result of Half-Way Covenant, 98a; of Dr. Franklin, impressed the French people, 65c; of George Washington as a young man, 504a; of George Washington when he took command of the Continental Army, 421b; of George Washington, demonstrated in his dealings with Congress, 60c; of John Hancock, a gentleman of fortune, 416a; of James Warren, husband of Mercy Warren, described, 421d; of Dr. Joseph Warren, who fell at Bunker's Hill, 418d; of the New England colonists, 431b; of Quakers, and growth of Pennsylvania, 432a; of Samuel Adams, an example of patriotism, religion, virtue, 415d; of soldier and Christian, not incompatible, 198b; of the world, formed by education, 28c; our, in the judgement, will be tested by the law of the Gospel, 517a; pattern of, found in the prophets and patriarchs of the Bible, 226a; peculiar, of Christianity, 7d; real, of our Founding Fathers, requires a fair estimate, 105a; the key to understanding history, 358b

CHARACTER OF THE PEOPLE: behind their emissions of paper money, 504c

CHARIOT: plain, of Mrs. Washington, 75c

CHARITABLE: action, no reference to an outward end, 17c

CHARITIES: first of all, brings the Bible to every fireside, 19b

CHARLES I, STUART, 1600-1649: arbitrary measures of, drove the nation into rebellion, 107a; persecution of Scotch Presbyterians, 112a; conspired against the constitution he was bound to protect, 263b; and his contest with the British Parliament, 359b; resolved to govern without the aid of a parliament, 263d; attempted to levy revenues without consent of parliament, 433d; summoned Council of Peers at York, not representative, 263d; convened parliament in 1640, dissolves it, 263d; summoned new parliament, became Long Parliament, 264a; Long Parliament's manifesto against his arbitrary power, 264d; attempted with armed men to seize patriot leaders of Parliament, 265a; seized by Cromwell and the Independents, 1647, 266d; tried by Cromwell and a parliament which had prejudged his case, 267b; trial of, an act of tyranny, 267c; majority of English nation preferred a limited monarchy, 267c; executed on January 30, 1649, 267c; suffered death as an enemy of the constitution, 434a; his execution, the policy of Cromwell, not the nation's, 267d; many of his best subjects, fled to the colonies, 359b

CHARLES II, STUART, 1630-1685: it was hoped he had learned moderation in exile, 269d; restoration of in 1661, welcomed by all England, 270b; pursued same arbitrary measures as his father, 434a; conciliation of Presbyterians by a declaration, 107d; "scatters dust" in the eyes of the Presbyterians, 108a; cruelty and oppression of Scotch Presbyterians under, 112a; enhanced prerogatives of the crown,

359d; with restoration of, the Puritan or republican element lost all hope of dominion in England, 270b

CHARLESTOWN, MASSACHUSETTS: powder in arsenal, seized by Governor Gage, 1774, 472a; inhabitants of, opened doors, dressed wounds of British Troops, retreating from Lexington and Concord, April 19, 1775, 408d; town of, reduced to ashes by fire of the British on Bunker's Hill, June 17, 1775, 417d; fate of this unfortunate town beheld by many with regret, 418a; 497c: the burning of, did not discourage the provincials, 499a

CHARM-BINDING: the minds of men, the magicians of the second century A.D., 8d

CHARTER OF MASSACHUSETTS: changed by Massachusetts Government Act of 1774, 471c; efforts of British Parliament to new-model, 489d; Provincial Congress operated in spite of annihilation of, 400c; subject of Proclamation of January 23, 1776, "Phaenomenon without example in the political world, a large and populous colony, subsisting in great decency, for more than a year, under such a suspension of government," 209

CHARTERS, COLONIAL: validity of, a basic concern to American colonists, 429a; all English colonies had obtained between 1603-1688, except Georgia, 433d; no provision for taxation without consent, 252c; 443d; contained the principles on which the colonies were formed, 446a; granted by Britain, gave powers of government to the people, 461a; Parliament wished for opportunity to revoke, 461a; to be new-modeled by a jealous British ministry, 482d; Parliament's manner of depriving them, produced colonial opposition, 489c; saved by the American Revolution, 461b; a basis of the Declaration of Rights of the 1st Continental Congress, 446c

CHATHAM, EARL OF, WILLIAM PITT, 1708-1778: formed his "broad bottom ministry," in July, 1766, 306a; resumed his seat in House of Lords, after long absence, 480c; tried to dissuade his countrymen from effort to subdue America by arms, 480c; presented Bill for healing differences between Great Britain and the Colonies, 418b; would secure to colonies all privileges granted by their charters and constitutions, 481c; Lord Dartmouth tables Bill of, 481d; his bill attributed to Dr. Franklin by Lord Sandwich, 481d; friends of British ministry called it traitorous, 481d; rejected without a second reading in House of Lords, 482b; rejected by a majority of 64-32, 482b; rejection disappointing to Americans, 489a

CHAUCER, GEOFFREY, 1340?-1400: poet of Middle English, lent a charm to the hospitality of Catholic England, 290b

CHAUNCEY, CHARLES, 1592-1672: clergyman, had been professor of Greek at Cambridge University, 2nd President of Harvard College, 438d; opposer of Half-Way Covenant, 97b

CHAUNCEY, CHARLES, DR., 1705-1787: American clergyman, answered the appeal of Reverend Chandler for sending a bishop to America, 142b; took popular side in the American Revolution, 192d

CHEERFULNESS: of the common soldier at Valley Forge, 62b

CHEEVER, EZEKIEL, 1615-1708: teacher for seventy years in Boston Latin School, 222a

CHERISH: "those dear, ragged Continentals" cried John Laurens, 62d

CHIBUCTO, HALIFAX: sickness swept French Fleet off, in 1746, 51c

CHIEF: Martha Washington by the side of the, as he walked the difficult path Heaven opened before him, 75b

CHIEF JUSTICE OF MASSACHUSETTS: Peter Oliver, impeached by the Massachusetts General Assembly, March, 1774, 388d

CHIEF'S: the, humble dwelling at Valley Forge, 75d

CHILDREN: and patriotism, early vision of, x; attitude of Jesus towards them, 216c; blessed by knowing the Holy Scriptures, 215a; decorum of, in the house of God, 94a; education of, sermon on parental fidelity, 1792, 213; education of, six letters on by John Witherspoon, 1797, 232; first teacher of, mothers, 223d; forsake not the Gospel, 30a; happy, who received Christ's blessing, 216d; influence of, whose parents have neglected Christian education, 219b; instruction of her, a pleasure for Mercy Warren, 84b; instructions adapted to their age and capacities, 219d; obligations of, to receive parental instructions, 220a; open the doors of the schoolhouse to all the, 223b; our, should contemplate Washington at prayer, x; our, should not be ignorant of the cost of the American Republic, 255c; parents have rule and jurisdiction over, 184b; religious instruction of, and preservation of the Union, 21c; Remarks addressed to, by Levi Hart, minister, 220a; Solomon's, heard the tender instruction of a father, Book of Proverbs addressed to them, 219d; teach our, to acknowledge the God of our Fathers, x; to remove from corruption their, purpose of Pilgrim Fathers in coming to America

CHILDREN OF ISRAEL: distinguished as the Sabbath-keeping nation, 154b

CHRIST, JESUS: alone, the source of Christianity for the Christian, 188c; and His apostles, furnish most perfect examples of living, 256d; as typified by Melchizadek, in favor of a defensive war, 538a; birth of, and America, linked, 254a; bore testimony against tyranny in church and state, 37b; bride of, the Church, Revelation XII, 5a; crucifixion of, and style of divine writers, 227b; did not want Jews to find any treason against Rome in Him, 37a; foe of, found by preachers of Gospel, 5c; glorious pattern of excellence for mankind, 226b; His great intention, to introduce men to spiritual liberty, 39c; His sentiments on liberty and government, 37b; hope through, for pardon of our sins, 30a; in the Church, hated by the wicked one, 5c; is Lord of the conscience, King in own Kingdom, 189a; men partaking of spirit of, will support cause of liberty, 39c; mind and will of, laid down in Scriptures, 187d; miracles of, and fullness of Godhead, 10a; religion of, doctrines of, contained in Scriptures, 188d; second coming of, and triumph of church, 15d; sets men free from burden of law, 193b; the source of civil liberty, 197a; spirit of, and spirit of devil, irreconcilable principles at work in the world, 5c; submit to authority of, make Him our Director and Guide, 188b; the religion of, and civil liberty, 255b; victory of, over paganism seen in Book of Revelation, 3b; victory of, over wrong-heartedness, wrong-spiritedness, wrong-thoughtedness, seen in Book of Revelation, 3c; with, those who avoid yoke of his enemies, 4d; work of, laid upon His Universal Church, 103d

CHRIST CHURCH, PHILADELPHIA: Continental Congress, adjourned to, to hear Fast Day Sermon, July 20, 1775, 535d

CHRISTENDOM: mind of, aroused by Luther and the Reformation, 47d; survey this globe and you will find that liberty has only taken its seat in, 518c

CHRISTIAN: accomplishments, pray for increase in America, 27b; character of a good, and a good soldier, not incompatible, 198b; civilization, cannot spring out of chance, 47b; conscientiousness, needed in America's Second Century, 53d; deference to the judgement and attention of others, 240c; devout,

identifies cause of disease, 9b; every, has right of judgement regarding religion, 183d; has equal right with rulers, to search the Scriptures, 187a; has everything needful in the Scriptures, 187c; his influence upon government, 155d; institutions, and the influence of the Independents upon, 25b; legislation, restraints of, needed in America, 54a; Mercy Warren contemplated life as a, 358a; one who believes Christ's Doctrines is a, 188c; one who submits to Christ's Commands is a, 188c; principles, absent from Rome's rise to glory, 27d; Sacred Scriptures are a rule of faith for a, 183d; the follower and disciple of Christ is a, 188c; your duty as a, and the education of your children, 232a

CHRISTIAN APOLOGISTS: men who stood up for the defence of Christianity, 16c; two classes of, who spoke through their writings, 16d; effect on Roman authorities, 16d; Tertullian addressed the persecutors of the Christians, 10c

CHRISTIAN ARMOUR: needed in Christian Warfare, 548b

CHRISTIAN CHARACTER: American, and devotion to liberty, learned at home, 73d; follows the impulse from within, 17c; its qualities needed in home government, 82d; needed in leaders and legislators, 54a; of George Washington at Valley Forge, 64d; of Martha Washington, 75b; of our Pilgrim Fathers, 25b; of people of Massachusetts, during suspension of civil government, 208; of Primitive Christians, a reproach to any age, 10c; of the Founding generation, 29a; 45a; 55b; of the husbands of Abigail Adams and Mercy Warren, 85c; remarkable, of American Women, during the American Revolution, 73a

CHRISTIAN CHARITY: belonged to the office of the Christian Matron, 17c; collection of voluntary contributions in first century, 17b; communities in distant lands assisted, 17c; of inhabitants of Charlestown, towards the retreating British troops, 408d; Presbyterians urged to express, during American Revolution, 152a; towards those of different sentiments in religion, 184a

CHRISTIAN CHURCH: the Apocalypse, a revelation from Christ to, 3d; learning and religion, firmest pillars of, 439a; and state separate, with advantage to both, 53a; and state, united by law in early America, 50a; the Bride of Christ, Revelation XII, 5a; building and Franklin's pigeon-boxes, 221c; Christ in the, hated by the wicked One, 5c; formation of, after Cambridge Platform, 93d; establishments of, formal, in southern states, 50a; faith of, rises up like a song, 5c; free, and free state in America, 50c; her anguish, to bring forth Christ to world, 5a; importance of, in American Revolution, 73b; in exile, as true Prince of, unrecognized, 5c; is but one, her foes multiform, 5b; New England men educated for the service of the, 438d; newly formed, elected officers from membership, 94a; out of the, the American state developed, 191b; persecutor of, the dragon in Revelation, 5b; spiritual work of, Christian warfare, 4d; the law of her life, to bring forth Christ to the world, 5a; work of, to bring forth Christ to man, 5b

CHRISTIAN CIVILIZATION: America the scene of an advancing, 47b

CHRISTIAN FELLOWSHIP: of Primitive Christians, 10b; not comprehended by the world, 12d; striking to pagans, 17b

CHRISTIAN FLAG: let it go forth side by side with the American flag, 21a

CHRISTIAN HEALING: in first centuries of Christianity, 9c; roused paganism to deviltry, 9b; our Saviour overcomes power of darkness, 9b; sufferer delivered from dominion of evil, healed by the sanctifying

476a; gave equal representation to each province, 476b; first committee to consider rights infringed since 1763, 476c; agreed upon a declaration of their rights, 476c; resolves on peaceable measures to take until repeal of grievous acts, 477b; finished work and dissolved themselves, October 26, 1774, 477d; recommended that another congress meet on May 10, 1775, unless redress of grievances be obtained, 477d; transactions in Great Britain in consequence of, 479b

Action of colonies: its recommendations universally obeyed, 397b; measures of, approved by constitutional assemblies of colonies, 478a; New York the only legislature which withheld their approbation, 478a; first ratified by Pennsylvania Assembly despite Quakers, 478a; replied to people of Massachusetts regarding their resolves, recommended them to persevere in temperate conduct, 472c; measures and recommendation of, approved and adopted by Georgia, 524b

2nd Continental Congress, May 10, 1775: met after hostilities had commenced, on date fixed, 499c; chose Peyton Randolph, president, Charles Thomson, secretary, 499c; John Hancock chosen to succeed Randolph when he returned home after a few days, 500b; composed of men of equal character who ventured all in the cause of liberty for our sakes, 541b; depositions from Battle of Lexington, laid before, 499d; resolved itself into a committee of the whole to consider the state of America, 499d; resolutions in regard to the treatment of British troops, 499d; supply of British Army rendered precarious, 500b; published Articles of Confederation in May, 1775, 419b; recommended to Massachusetts the resumption of a regular government, 419c; advised her to be governed according to spirit of her charter, 501a; established a general post-office, made Franklin head of, 501b; once more made efforts for reconciliation, 501c; voted to raise a continental army, 420b; resolutions regarding the supply of the continental army with gun powder, by the several colonies, 341d; recommended the collection by the colonies of salt petre and sulphur for manufacture of gun powder, 342c; the command of the army by the unanimous voice of, vested in George Washington, June 15, 1775, 421b; 503c; a declaration of arms, July 6, 1775, 501c; received word from Georgia of her action in joining the other colonies in a provincial union, July 20, 1775; left Philadelphia, September, 1777, before British occupied the city, 57a; took refuge in frontier village of York, 59a; their incapacity, 60a; men of inferior rank in, by 1777, 60b; divided by sectional jealousies, united in jealousy of Washington and the army, 60b; insisted on 13 distinct state armies, 60c; failed to feed and clothe the Continental Army, 60d; Washington bore on his heart the weight of all, 64a; dealt with Congress as a statesman, 64c; rejected the Conciliatory Bills of 1778 under stirring influence of Washington's declaration "nothing short of independence would do," 66b

CONTINENTAL FAST DAY, July 20, 1775: recommended by Congress because of our sins, 542d; the pulpit, the press, the bar, unite in, 505d; coeval with resolutions for organizing an army, was appointment of a day of public humiliation, fasting and prayer to Almighty God, 506a

Continental Fast Day Sermons: a sermon preached at Tredyffryn, in Chester County, by the Revd. David Jones, A.M. Philadelphia, 536a; a sermon preached at York-Town before Captain Morgan's and Captain Price's Companies of Rifle-Men, by Daniel Batwell, A.M. Philadelphia, 543b; the Continental Congress adjourned to Christ Church, Philadelphia to hear a

sermon preached by Rev. Jacob Duche, 535d

CONTINENTAL MONEY: *See also* MONEY; depreciation of, caused George Washington problems in his accounts, 333b

CONTINENTAL SOLDIERS: *"Cherish these dear ragged Continentals"*; at Valley Forge during the winter of 1777-1778, 58b; description of, footsteps stained with blood, 58b; condition of arms, 58c; uniforms of, tattered, of every description, 58c; sufferings of, hunger, cold, disease, famine, death, 58d; built log huts at Valley Forge, 58d; steadfast despite sufferings, 58d; lacked all necessaries of life, blankets, overcoats, tents, 60d; four months of suffering, 60d; they persevered, they kept the faith, 62b

Statements of the suffering of: Dr. Waldo's accounts, 61a, 62a, 62b; Washington writes to Congress, 61a, 61b, 62a, 63a; Lafayette writes, 61c, 61d, 62c; Laurens writes, 61c, 62c; Greene writes to Knox 61c, 62c; Baron von Steuben, 61a; Wharton writes, 62d

Valley Forge is Holy Ground: orator calls upon Americans to consecrate this spot of holy deeds, 63a

CONTRABAND TRADE: of American colonies with Spanish and French colonies, legalized in 1764, 443a

CONTRACT: no, made on the Lord's Day is binding in a Christian nation, 156c

CONTRACTS: between colonists and king, violated, 247c

CONTRIBUTIONS: voluntary, of public assemblies, provided welfare, 17b

CONTROL: of men, by Bible or bayonet, 20b; over men, either internal or external, 21d

CONTROVERSY: between New England churches and American Presbyterians, 110a; between Synodists and Anti-Synodists, 97c; hinge of, absolute unlimited supremacy of Parliament, 476d; over Episcopal bishops, opposition to in colonies for years, 192b

CONVENTION: clergy in, at Watertown, offer services as chaplains for army, 207a; of Congregational ministers in 1760, heard sermon preached by Ezra Stiles, 103c; of Salem Church, conversion of Edward Gibbons, 45c; of Massachusetts ministers, declaration against itinerant preaching, 134d

CONVENTION OF TOWNS: held in Boston, September 22, 1768, deputies to, advised people to pay greatest deference to government and to wait patiently for redress of their grievances, 373a; 452a

CONVERSION: of heathen, design of Pilgrim Fathers, 24c; of Indians, civil effects of, 316c; of Indians pursued more vigorously by French than by English, 317b; of Indians and peace on the frontiers, 317c; of Iroquois, Inglis plan for, included education, 319a; of money units difficult, 327d; of world, sought through Monthly Concert of Prayer, 103b

CONVERSIONS: essential characteristics of genuine, during Great Revival, 126a; extensive, under Nerva, produced weak Christians, 14d

CONVULSIONS: hysterical, not part of conversions in Bible, 129d

CONWAY, THOMAS, 1735?-1800: soldier of fortune from Ireland, huts of, and the Pennsylvanians at Valley Forge, 63b; disgraceful intrigue to supplant Washington, the Conway Cabal, 63b

COOPER, SAMUEL, 1744-1783: Congregational minister, effects of the Great Revival on his ministry, 123d; took popular side in the Revolution, 192d

CORINTH: city of, chosen for propagation of Gospel, 11b

CORNELIUS: not directed to quit his military profession by the Apostle Peter, 198b

CORNWALLIS, CHARLES, 1738-1805: English Major General in the American War of Independence, arrived in Philadelphia with British Army, October, 1777,

man, a founder of New Haven, an earnest opposer of the Half-Way Covenant, 97b; called to the First Church in Boston, 97d; stigmatizes the *"parish way"* of Presbyterianism, 97c

DAVID: a man after God's own heart, spent his life in scenes of war, 538c; and Abigail, and style of divine writers, 227a; and Absalom, and style of divine writers, 227a; and importance of parental education, 216d; and Jonathan, and style of divine writers, 227a; believed a defensive war is sinless, 538c; character of, an exhaustless fund of instruction, 226a; delivered Israel by slaying Goliath, a proof that a defensive war is sinless, 538c; sensible of the relationship of civil and religious liberty, 33a

DAVIES, SAMUEL, 1723-1761: chosen to succeed Jonathan Edwards as president of College of New Jersey, 141c

DAVIS, ISAAC, 1745-1775: American patriot, in fight with British at Concord Bridge, killed in the first volley, April 19, 1775, 492a

DEACONESSES: responsibilities of, in New England church polity, 94a

DEACONS: responsibilities of, in New England church polity, 94a

DEAD: to world, Christians, 13b

DEADNESS: to world, of our Pilgrim Fathers, 25b

DEARBORN, HENRY, 1751-1829: officer at Valley Forge, 64a

DEATH: and tortures, despised by Primitive Christians, 10c; instruments of, for defence of liberty, 200d; of one half of the Pilgrims after landing, 23c; out of, America rose free, at Valley Forge, 68c; political, and slavery from luxury, 28a

DEATH PENALTY: for clipping coin in Maryland, 337c

DEBERDT, DENNIS, 1694?-1770: agent of province of Massachusetts in London, letter to from Convention of Towns at Boston, September 22, 1768, 373c

DEBT: national, of Great Britain after Peace of Paris, 444d; no, can be collected on Christian Sabbath, 156c; our, a concern for the liberty of our posterity, 202d

DEBTORS: honest, to be protected from prosecutors, in Georgia Resolves, July 10, 1775, 528b; instructions to Magistrates for recovery of, by Georgia Provincial Congress, 530d

DECEPTION: power of, second wild beast, Revelation XIII. 6a

DECLARATION: by Charles II to conciliate Presbyterians, 107d

DECLARATION OF ARMS: reasons for, published by the 2nd Continental Congress, 501c; colonists enumerated their injuries in, 501c; read to Washington's troops at Cambridge, 504c

DECLARATION OF INDEPENDENCE, July 4, 1776: and history of the American Revolution, 248d; liberties claimed could not be taken, altered, or abridged, without their consent, 477b; a declaration of religious as well as civil liberty, 146c; allowed diversity of American character with national unity, 250a

DECLARATION OF INDULGENCE, 1687: of James II, gave equal franchises to every sect, 271d

DECLARATION OF RIGHTS: 1765 statement by Stamp Act Congress, held in New York, Presbyterians agree to, 150a; the Magna Charta of America, 153b; 1774 statement, agreed upon by the 1st Continental Congress, 476c; declared the principles of the English constitution and the several charters the basis of life, liberty, property, 476c; no forfeit of rights of Englishmen by migrating to America, 476c; could not properly be represented in Parliament, 476c; entitled to power of legislation in taxation, 476c; independency of colonial legislatures maintained, 476c; consented to regulation of external

commerce by Britain, 476d; excluded every idea for raising of an American revenue, 476d; resolved that the colonists were entitled to Common Law of England, 477a; entitled to trial by jury of peers, 477a; entitled to benefit of English Statutes in existence at time of their colonization, 477a; entitled to immunities and privileges secured them by Royal charters and provincial laws, 477a; right to assemble peaceably and petition King to consider grievances, 477a; a standing army without consent of provincial legislatures was unlawful, 477a; constituent branches of legislature should be independent of each other, 477a; legislative power by Crown appointees, unconstitutional, 477a

DECLARATORY ACT, 1766: held suspended over heads of Americans, 366d; more hostile to American rights than Stamp Act, 450b; enacted Parliament's right to bind colonies, 450b; foundation of a precedent which threatened the liberties of America, warned by Dickenson of Pennsylvania, in a series of letters signed by a farmer, 450d

DEDICATION: of a public grammar school, Wilmington, 1773, 231; to the 350th Pilgrim anniversary, 22b

DEFEAT: of the dragon, result of Christian Warfare, 5c; overwhelming, of loyalists, at Cedar Spring, 80a

DEFECTION: from religion of state, is a crime against the state, 12a; of New York from sister colonies, hoped for by British ministry, 483a

DEFENCE: capacity for, impeded by slavery, 432d; of Christianity, against pagan writings, 16a; of liberty, found in the New Testament, 197d; of liberty, requires free internal government, 200b; of property, in the state of Nature, 185a; of the country, strongest motive for an army, 201d; true end, to protect and secure liberty of mankind, 205b

DEFENDERS: must not become offenders, 199d; of America, join in July 20, 1775, Fast Day, act of humiliation, 547a

DEFENSIVE: New York City advised to act on, by Continental Congress, 499d

DEFENSIVE WAR: only a, is justified in the sight of God, 199b; decreed by all kingdoms, whether Jew, Gentile, Barbarian or Christian, 537c; fought by people of England against James II, 538d; no more murder than a legal process against a criminal, 540b; our only redress against a foreign enemy, 540c; justified by reason and revelation, 540c; no choice but to fight, or submit to slavery, 540d; sinless, and consistent with the purest religion, 543a

DEFENSIVE WARS: fought by the Deliverers of Israel, raised up by the Lord, 538b

DEGENERACY OF THE AGE: due to decline of Christianity in parental education, 219b

DE KALB, BARON, JOHANN, 1721-1780: German officer, commissioned Major General in Continental Army, described Valley Forge as a "wilderness," 59b

DELAWARE: Puritan settlements scattered on the, 111a; counties of, to collect salt petre and sulphur, 342a; settled by Swedes, 437c; no established religion in, 437d; sent deputies to Stamp Act Congress, 449c; exempted from restraint of trade bill, 488a

DELIVERANCE: of a gracious Providence, hoped for, 29a from our political evils, may we expect that God will work with us and in us, 42d; God's, sought by Connecticut Legislature, 210c; of the Lord, in ages past, 542a; we rely for our, not on our merits, but on our Saviour's, 544d

DELIVERERS: of Israel, raised up by God to fight defensive wars, 538b; of Israel, Othniel, Ehud, Barak, Gideon, Japhtha and others, 538b

DELUGE: prevented battle at Warren Tavern, 56b

DELUSIONS: charm-binding the minds of men, 8d

DEMAGOGUES: educated, the greatest danger to a republic, 53c

DEMANDS: unjust, submitted to, fatal to liberty, 199c

DEMOCRACY: the form of government of New England churches, 100d; is Christ's government in church and state, 100d; and the congregationalism of John Wise, 105b; as the best government, 103b; of Greeks, seen as misnomer, compared to the American Revolution, 254b; a homicidal tyranny, as conceived by Rousseau, 283d

DEMOCRATIC: form of government, for both state and church, discussed by John Wise, 100d; forms of government in the English colonies, 435d

DEMOCRATIC CONSTITUTIONS: of the colonies, regretted by the friends of parliamentary supremacy, 461a

DEMOCRATIC LIBERTY: delayed by the Independent's execution of Charles I, 267d

DEMOCRATIC REVOLUTION: of 1660 in England, failed in its purposes, 263b

DEMOSTHENES, 385?-322 B.C.: Athenian orator and statesman, grandeur of, surpassed by the Bible, 224d; oratory of, surpassed by the Apostle Paul, 227c

DENOMINATIONS: historians of the, Henry Martyn Dexter, Charles Hodge, Bishop Samuel Wilberforce, 89b

DEPENDENCE: our, upon Almighty God, where we may hope for success, 541d

DEPORTMENT: of parent necessary to preserve his authority over children, 235d; of parents, influences future conduct of children, 243a; of parents, to convince children of religion's necessity, 243c

DEPOSITIONS: from Battle of Lexington, proving that the King's troops were the aggressors, laid before the Continental Congress by John Hancock, 499d

DEPRECIATION: *see also* MONEY; and wanton expenditure, concern of 1779, 248b; of Continental money, caused George Washington problems in his accounts, 333b; of money values, constant in the colonies, 337d

DEPUTIES: twenty-eight, at the Stamp Act Congress, 449c

DESCARTES, RENE, 1596-1650: French scientist and philosopher, in the era of the American Settlement, 48c; diffused philosophical freedom through his teachings, 275d; a denial to atheists in France, 280c

DESCRIPTION: of George Washington at Valley Forge, 64b

DESCRIPTIONS: outstanding examples from the Bible, 230c

DESIGN: Christ's, for New England, 44d

DESPOTIC: government, and a licentious spirit, 200b

DESPOTISM: of Rome, and fear of Christianity, 13a; in times of, contempt for laws of the state, 17d; in times of, slavish obedience to laws of the state, 17d: God's redemption of America from, 248d; vigilance in detection of, in the American Philosophy of government, 250d; and Christianity, incompatible, 518b; is bad, whether papist, or protestant, 540a

DESTRUCTION: our, not from foreign foe, but from within, 223b

DIALOGUE: spoken at opening of grammar school, Wilmington, 1773, 231

DICKINSON, JOHN, 1732-1808: American statesman, author, corresponded with Mercy Warren, 77b; efficient defender of the natural rights of mankind, 249d; wrote a series of letters signed a Farmer, proving danger threatened the liberties of America, 450d; carried through congress a masterly petition to the King, 502a; devoted to reconciliation on constitutional principles, 502a

DICKINSON, JONATHAN, 1688-1747: American Presbyterian minister, defender of its doctrines, 115b; a strict Calvinist, 115b

DISCIPLINE: in New England churches, after Cambridge Platform, 94a; early, of New England churches, nearer presbyterianism than congrega-

tionalism, 109a; those who keep strictest, give the fewest strokes, 233d; the problem of introducing, among free men habituated to think for themselves, 505b; in the Continental Army, instituted by Baron von Steuben, 65b

DISCIPLINING: rod of God, for repentance of our sins, 29a

DISCORD: between Great Britain and American Colonies, subject of July 20, 1775, Fast Day prayers, 547d

DISCORDANT PRINCIPLES: between patrician few and plebian many, 253a

DISCOURAGEMENT: no symptoms of, in our Pilgrim Fathers, 25c; in the present dispute and our prevailing sins, 542d

DISCOVERY: of America, and the Hand of God, 47b; physical and spiritual, God timed to each other, 48a

DISEASE: smote our American settlers, but they fainted not, 49d; infested the huts of soldiers at Valley Forge, 58d

DISMEMBERMENT: of British Empire, after 1764, 442b

DISOBEDIENCE: of one man, brought loss of liberty to all men, 32b

DISPENSATION MOSAIC: ceremonial law of, distinct from the law of liberty of the Gospel, 516a

DISPENSATIONS: of Providence, towards America, a warning, 28a

DISPOSITION: of children, a challenge to absolute authority over them, 235a; of a Christian, unites piety and politeness, 240b; of Iroquois, a factor in their conversion, 318b; man's inward, judged by his visible action, 517a

DISPOSITIONS: spiritual, are Godward and Christward, 4d; our, cause our happiness or misery, Martha Washington to Mercy Warren, 76c

DISSERTATION: on the Bible as literature, graduating address of Timothy Dwight, 224

DIVERSITY: of the colonies, misleading to the British Ministry, 478d; with unity, characteristic of a congregational church, 105c

DIVINE BLESSING: sought by a whole people, in the July 20, 1775, Fast Day, 506c

DIVINE CALL: to patriots of Massachusetts Colony, 44b

DIVINE GOODNESS: alone, has turned American wilderness into fruitful fields, 543b

DIVINE GRACE: freedom of, does not counteract importance of parental education, 216a

DIVINE GUIDE: of human reason, the Scriptures, 21b

DIVINE INTERPOSITION: saved the American cause from destruction, 52b; many signal instances of, in favor of our country, 347

DIVINE JUDGEMENTS: visited on New England, 98b

DIVINE LAW: importance of transmitting to posterity, 213b

DIVINE LIFE: the, shone forth in weak and despised vessels, 11a

DIVINE PROVIDENCE: assistance of, and the eyes of the Lord, 23b; aid of, implored to aid the colonies maintain liberties, 43a; history the record of, 46d; and historical development of self-government 50d; recognized by Washington in the American cause, 52c; submission to, and freedom from slavery, 362a

DIVINE RIGHT OF KINGS: James I educated in, 433d; assumption of, and the American Revolution, 253a; to govern wrong, taught by some Christian divines, 518c

DIVINE SCRIPTURES: excellency of, as fountain of fine writing, 224b; types of literature found in the, history, 225c; Orations, 227c; Poetry, 228c

DIVINE SPIRIT: power of, and supernatural effects, 9a

DIVINE WRITERS: abound in striking ways of communicating sentiments, 225a; the genuine offspring of elevated Genius, 225b; understood use of the imagination as inlet to the Soul, 225d; employ poetical descriptions in History of Israel, 225d; insert an endless variety of incidents and characters, 225d; present strongly marked characters, 226a; compared to Homer, 226b; use simple narration to bring forth character, 226b; make history inspiring, instructive, striking, 226c

DOCTRINE: purity of Christian, preserved by conduct, 8b; of Whitefield, challenged in Episcopal churches, 122c; not, but church polity, the source of conflict in New England, 192c; of representation and taxation, not American innovation, 251b; novel, of parliamentary power, degraded Americans, 445c

DOCTRINES: taught during the Great Revival, 125a; of New England churches, formal defence of, by President Thomas Clap of Yale College, 127b; prescribed by pope, council, church fathers, 188b; Christ's, believed as true, makes a Christian, 188c; odious, injurious to mankind, ascribed to Christianity, 518b

DOCTRINES OF GRACE: distinguishing, increased as pulpit themes, influence of the Great Awakening, 103b

DOLLAR: etymology or the origin of, traced, 336b

DOMESTIC: "*I grow more, as I increase in years.*" Samuel Adams to his wife Betsy, 84c

DOMESTIC AGRICULTURE: to be encouraged by the Province of Georgia, as recommended by the Continental Congress, 524d

DOMESTIC ECONOMY: your most perfect maxims and examples of, found in the Bible, 255d

DOMESTIC EDUCATION: of Martha Washington, 75a; of Mercy Warren, 76d

DOMESTIC ENJOYMENT: and civil and religious liberty, 357d

DOMESTIC FELICITY: learned from parental education, 214b; of parents, their duty as individuals, 218d

DOMESTIC MANUFACTURES: encouraged to aid non-importation agreement, 478b

DOMESTIC SANCTUARY: nurtured love of civil liberty, 73c

DOMESTIC TRADE: of the colonies, utilized all commodities, 332d

DOMINION: of men over one another, 184a; of Christ, invaded, when consciences governed by men, 189a; and revenue over colonies, claimed by Great Britain, 248a

DOMITIAN, 81-96 A.D.: despotic emperor, who encouraged informers against the Christians, 14b

DOUAY BIBLE: circulated before the King James version, 20a

DOUBLE AUTHORITY: of both parents, to enforce education of children, 232b

DRAGON: in Revelation, persecutor of the Church, 5b; one evil spirit, diverse in power, 5b; defeat of, result of Christian Warfare, 5c; inspires the wild beasts of Revelation XIII, 5d

DROUGHTS: visited upon New England, 98b

DRUM: beating of, to call people to public worship, 94b

DRYDEN, JOHN, 1631-1700: English poet, surpassed by the poetry of the Psalms, 229a; reproduced in his verse the wavering of the English court between Protestantism and Catholicism, 290c

DUBRYSON: French officer at Valley Forge, aid to De Kalb, 64a

DUCHE, JACOB, 1738-1798: Anglican clergyman, chaplain of the first Continental Congress, 1774, preached July 20, 1775 Fast Day Sermon in Christ Church, Philadelphia, 535d

DUDLEY, PAUL, 1675-1751: a learned naturalist, chief justice of Massachusetts Bay Colony, a member of the Royal Society of London, 440b

DUNMORE, 4TH EARL OF, JOHN MURRAY, 1732-1809: Scottish colonial administrator in America, Governor of Virginia, 1771-1775, 413a; dismantled fort in

Williamsburg, 413b; proclaimed emancipation of blacks and put arms in their hands, 413b; retired on board the *Fowey* man-of-war, 413c; carried on a predatory war upon Virginia, burned Norfolk, 413c; dissolved Virginia House of Burgesses in 1774, 467d

DUPLESSIS: French officer at Valley Forge, 64a

DUPONCEAU, PIERRE, 1760-1844: French officer at Valley Forge, accompanied Baron von Steuben to America as his secretary, 64a

DUPORTAIL, LOUIS, CHEVALIER, 1736-1802: French officer engineer, attached to Lafayette, at Valley Forge, 64a; built fortifications at Valley Forge, 59c

DUTCH: and French made up almost the entire New York population, 111d; settlers, Calvinists and presbyterian, 113b; treaty with, to prevent help to colonies, 404b; settled New York and New Jersey, 437c

DUTCH COINS: used in the American colonies, 336c

DUTIES: imposed on America, but no revenue laws before 1764, 444b; colonial, to be paid in specie, 443b; methods of collection, arbitrary, unconstitutional, 443b; on glass, paper, painters' colors, removed in 1767, 456c; five-sixths of American, repealed in 1770, 454c

DUTY: the will to ask "*Is it right?*", 6c; of all men, to stand fast in God's liberty, 193b; indispensable, of Christian minister, to warn nation, 203d; to God, King and country, prompted action of Boston patriots, 371c; stamp, introduced by Mr. Grenville into parliament, 447c; on tea, a respectable minority in parliament, for removal, 456c

DWIGHT, TIMOTHY, 1751-1817: American congregational clergyman and educator, grandson of Jonathan Edwards, gave as his graduating address at Yale, *A Dissertation on the History, Eloquence, Poetry, of the Bible,* 224: president of Yale 1795-1817

E

EARTH: in its products, given by God for the use of man, 184c

EAST INDIA COMPANY: confident of tea sales in the colonies, 458a; consignees, urged to resign their appointments, 459a; effect of Boston Port Bill on, 460a

EAST INDIA TEA: not to be imported by Georgia as part of the Non-Consumption agreement, 524c

EAST JERSEY: New England settlers in, Puritans, were both congregationalists and presbyterians, 110d; emigrants to, from Scotland, numerous and influential, 112d

EASTON, JAMES: a leader in the expedition which captured Ticonderoga, May 9, 1775

ECCLESIASTICAL: plan of our Pilgrim Fathers, rational and scriptural, 24c; matters, and civil, plummet line between, 27c; interference, by Presbyterian Parliament, 92c; censures, followed by forfeiture of civil rights, 107d; systems in Connecticut, compromise between presbyterians and congregationalists, 109a; supremacy of King in colonies feared, 144b; appointments in colonies, fell into disrepute, 172c

ECCLESIASTICAL COUNCILS: history of in New England, 103c; design of, falls into four classes, 104a

ECCLESIASTICAL ESTABLISHMENTS: of Europe, are corruptions of the Christian religion, 256c

ECCLESIASTICAL ORDER: rules of, and the Great Revival, 133c

ECCLESIASTICAL TYRANNY: in England, made men of Massachusetts deny church courts legitimate authority, 109d

ECONOMIC DISASTER: of Boston Port Bill on life, liberty and property, 470a

ECONOMY: encouraged by the Massachusetts Provincial

ENGINEERS: at Valley Forge, under Du Portail, 59c; country destitute of, and fortifications, 496b

ENGINERY: of world's progress, the Bible, 20c

ENGLAND: *see also* EUROPE; IN 1763 as the parent state, looked to for justice, 42b; true religion declined in, from accession of Charles II, 121b; stood alone in not establishing her church amongst her colonies, 174d; by Revolution of 1688 became the star of constitutional government, 272d; and France, long disputed the right to govern Iroquois territory, 313a; accepted the Spanish Dollar as a standard of value, 333d; furnished the original stock of the present population of the United States, 437c; contended with France for American Territory, 441a

ENGLISH: settlers, many Calvinists were presbyterian, 113b; names given to the Five Nations of the Iroquois, 310d; compared to the French in their concern for the conversion of the Indians, 317b

ENGLISH COINS: values of, in the American Colonies, 336c

ENGLISH COLONIES: *see also* AMERICAN COLONIES; uniqueness of in their colonization, 428c; security of liberty and property, derived from the English Constitution, 430b; at liberty to govern themselves, 430c; trade open to every individual, 430c; wealth of, not in proportion to physical resources, 430d; amazing growth and progress under wise policy of Great Britain, 430d; prospered with English principles, 433c; obtained their charters between 1603-1688, 433d; settled by those opposed to the prerogative, 434a; and the Revolution of 1688, God's timetable, 434b; religion of, nurtured a love for liberty, 434d; state of society in, favored liberty and independence, 435c; were communities of independent individuals, 436c; provincial constitutions of, nurtured spirit of liberty, 437a; enjoyed a government, little short of being independent, 437a; and constitutional rights of Englishmen, 438a; fiscal history of, different from parent state, 438a; established on principles of commercial monopoly, 446d

ENGLISH COLONISTS: devoted to fundamental English principles, 434a; reading of, favored the cause of liberty, 435b; a majority of, were farmers, 436d; but remotely affected by bustlings of Old World, 437b

ENGLISH COMMON LAW: respected in the colonies, 438a

ENGLISH CONSTITUTION: and taxation and representation, 251b; principles of, referred to in the Declaration of Rights of the First Continental Congress, 476c; the work of centuries, overturned by Cromwell, 268d

ENGLISH CONSTITUTIONAL LAW: principles of the American Revolution, based upon, 251c

ENGLISH DEISTS: were forerunners of German Rationalists, 284a

ENGLISH FREE-THINKERS: led reaction to the letter of the Bible, 284a

ENGLISH INSTITUTIONS: reflected in enduring works in English Literature, 290a

ENGLISHMEN: who refused to bear arms against the Americans, 404a; did not see the severity of the Fishery Bill to the Americans, 489b

ENGLISH MONEY SYSTEM: American colonies cut loose from, 338d

ENGLISH PHILOSOPHERS: bore a character analogous to English Institutions, 290d

ENGLISH POUND: ignored by the colonists, except when buying English goods, 326c

ENGLISH REPRESENTATION: represented the land of England but not the men, 228b; arbitrarily distributed among cities, towns and boroughs, 288c; disproportionate as to size or wealth or population, 288c

ENGLISH REPUBLIC: there could be no, not sufficient

political knowledge for, 267c

ENGLISH REVOLUTION: fundamental principles settled in 1688, 434b

ENGLISH SETTLERS: and vices taught to the Indians, 318b

ENGLISH STATUTES: colonists entitled to benefit of, 477a

ENGLISH TOLERATION ACTS: protects other denominations than episcopal in Virginia, 111a

ENGLISH UNIVERSITIES: many of the first settlers educated in, 438d

ENGLISH WHIGS: hoping to save the privileges of nobility, invited William of Orange to England, 272a

ENTERPRISING SPIRIT: of the American colonists, and the trade of America, 442c; produced by prospects of individual liberty, 436c; restrictive trade measures endeavored to check, 360b

ENTHUSIASM: was a mine of gold and silver for the colonies, 496c

EPHESUS: city of, chosen for propagation of the Gospel, 11b

EPISCOPAL CHURCH IN AMERICA: history of the denomination, 159; church polity of and its relationship to civil polity, 89b; and to the American Constitution, 89b

Early History: could not flourish in America, 159b; Sir Robert Boyle and the Society for the Propagation of Gospel to New England, 159b; Dr. Blair sent to Virginia, 159b; Dr. Bray sent to Maryland, 159d; became established church of Maryland, 1692, 160b; resisted by Romanists and Quakers, 160b; came into New York when Dutch ceded to English, 1667, 161a; into Boston, King's Chapel, 1679, 161b; Bishop Berkeley on religion in English colonies, 161c; spiritual statistics of, 161d; efforts of George Keith, 162d; toils and dangers of missionaries, 165b; movement in Yale College, 165c; Dr. Cutler ordained in England, 165d; Cutler's answers to the Bishop of London, 166a; persecutions, 167a

The Great Revival: George Whitefield in New England, 167c; astonishing effects attended Whitefield's meetings, 167d; many sought shelter of episcopal church, 168b; gained upon the sects in Connecticut, 168d; state of clergy in Virginia, 169d; Whitefield's labors in, 169b; more restrained, more useful than in New England, 169b; clergy lost support in, 169d; no college, only one school in, 169d

Efforts for an American Episcopate: spiritual statistics for North America, 170b; uniqueness of church's planting in America, 170c; teachers but no bishops before the Revolution, 171a; American colonies separated from control and discipline of Church of England, 172a; moral and social corruption in Virginia, 172c; want of bishops felt, 173b; unsuccessful efforts under Charles II, 175a; under Queen Anne, 175d; Bishop Berkeley on spiritual destitution of America, 176c; his efforts for college in Bermudas, 177a; in Rhode Island, 177a; Seeker's reply to Mayhew on American bishopric, 178a; voice of episcopal clergy in America for bishop, 181a; opposition to English institutions and episcopacy grows, 181c; Virginia clergy, 181c; change of attitude toward church and state evident, 182a; time of American Revolution grows near, 182c

EPOCH: Christianity, a new and great, in history, 7b

EQUALITY: of rights, principles of in Scriptures, 21a; of all men, in respect to each other, 184a; and to the preservation of their persons and property, 184c; of all men under God in America, 248c; the colonies unaccustomed to distinction of rank, they looked up to Heaven as the source of their rights, 435d; were composed of communities of separate, independent individuals, 436c

ERA: a new, in the science of government, inaugurated

tures," 53b

EVERLASTING GOSPEL: false revelation of, ascribed to Joachim of Calabria, 3b

EVIL: cannot be legislated out of the world, 54a; resistance to, not forbidden in Scripture, 199a

EVIL ONE: called the Prince of this world, 5c

EVILS: great, have always confronted the world's earnest workers, 54b; thirteen, specified by the Synod of 1679, 98d

EVIL SPIRIT: dragon in Revelation, diverse in varieties of power, 5b

EVIL SPIRITS: kingdom of, destroyed by Jesus, 9c

EXAMPLE: the single, in modern history, of George Washington retiring as a successful military leader, voluntarily, 60c; generous, of Lafayette and the French Alliance, 65c; its importance in parental education, 216b; importance of, to enforce instruction in education of children, 239d; of parents, influences future conduct of children, 243a; deemed a politic measure to make Massachusetts the first colony to measure the sword with the veterans of Britain, 399c

EXODUS: of our Founders from England, 45b

EXPENSE: of war, let it not discourage us, 543b

EXPENSES: George Washington kept his, during the Revolutionary War, 327d

EXTERNAL: appearance of man's character, not the basis of the Gospel judgement, 516d; the American Revolution not, 251a

EXTERNAL TAX: by East India Company and Parliament, made to answer all the purposes of an internal tax, 489c

EXTRAVAGANCE: and corruption of second century of America, 53d

EXTRAVAGANCIES: a danger to America, 28b; our, and vices, a hazard to our liberties, 30a

EYES OF THE LORD: and assistance of divine Providence, 23b; run to and fro, 29a

EZEKIEL: reproved the Shepherds of Israel for not feeding the flock, 39a

EZEKIEL'S: description of the Cherubims, and the style of the Bible, 230c

EZRAS: we had our, in our famous Founders, 45a

F

FACTS: striking, needed to reach men's hearts, 8d; undeniable, in Christian phenomena, 9a

FAIR TRADE: and contraband trade, 442c

FAITH: of the Church, rises up like a song, 5c; heroism of, of Primitive Christians, 10c; they kept the, the Continental Army at Valley Forge, 62b; faith productive of good works, desired by Franklin, 190b; works of kindness, charity, mercy and public spirit, 190b; is the shield of the Christian, 551a; is the victory over the world of the Christian, 551a; can quench the fiery darts of the wicked one, 551a

FAITHFUL: preserved and cared for by God, 15b

FAITHFULNESS: out of, to God, defence of our rights and liberties, 202c

FAITH OF OUR FATHERS: professed by the majority of New England ministers at time of Whitefield, 133b

FALL: of man, brought a reverse of his liberty 32b

FALLING OUT: any, between Christians indicates a need for revival of religion, 104b

FALSE PROPHET: second wild beast of Revelation XIII, 6a

FAMILIES: contemplate the picture of Washington at prayer, x, Christianity diffused through, 11b; from Burke County, N.C. march toward fort, 80b; at Fort Henry, defended by soldiers, 81b

"THE FAMILY CIRCLE": article in 1847 on Washington at Prayer, x

FAMILY EXAMPLE: should unite piety and politeness, 241a

FAMILY FOUNTAIN: every, nourished American Freedom, 251a

FAMINE: of the Word of God, greatest disaster to mankind, 21a; overtook our first American settlers, 49d; stood guard with soldiers at Valley Forge, 58d; at Valley Forge, Washington reports to Clinton on, 61d; threatened Bostonians shut up in Boston by General Gage, 409d; brought to colonies forbidden to fish on their own coasts, 491a

FAMOUS FOUNDERS: our, instruments of God, 45a

FANATICISM: enemy of Christianity, 8c

FANEUIL HALL, BOSTON, MASSACHUSETTS: scene of meeting to prepare remonstrance against the tea ships, 384d

FARMERS: attracted to the rich soil of the Great Valley of Valley Forge, 59a; furnished little to the Continental Army, 60a; a majority of English Colonists were, 436d; gave a cast of independence to the English Colonies, 436d; in Massachusetts were discouraged from selling to British Soldiers, 473c

FAST, THE: sanctified by the Jews, brought public redress, 545a

FAST DAYS: appointed by Primitive Christians to supply common wants in the community, 17c; annual and special, in New England churches, 94d; called for often by the American Presbyterian Church during the American Revolution, 150c; a New England institution, 440d; Governor Wright of Georgia agrees to appoint, 546a; Reverend Hadden Smith, censured by Georgia Provincial Congress for not joining in, 534a

Particular Fast Days Observed: churches of Massachusetts Colony for God's blessing on the Synod of 1679, 98c; in New England on the 16th of October, 1746, when the French Fleet was repelled, 51d

June 1, 1774: the day when the Boston Port Bill began to operate was observed in most of the colonies as a day of fasting and prayer, 392c; in Virginia set apart by the House of Burgesses, 467d; in Philadelphia it was solemnized with every manifestation of public calamity and grief, 469d

April 19, 1775: Governor Trumbull of Connecticut appointed April 19, 1775, as a day of public fasting and prayer throughout the colony, 407

July 20, 1775: appointed by the Continental Congress as a day of public humiliation, fasting and prayer to Almighty God to bless their rightful sovereign king George . . . that America might soon behold a gracious interposition of heaven for the redress of her many grievances, the restoration of her invaded rights, a reconciliation with the parent state, on terms constitutional and honourable to both." 506a; observed in Georgia in accord with the other colonies, 535c

Fast Day Sermons of July 20, 1775: by Reverend David Jones at Tredyffryn, Chester County, Pa., 536; by Reverend Daniel Batwell at Yorktown before Captain Morgan's and Captain Price's Companies of Rifle Men, 543b; by Reverend Jacob Duche, at Christ Church, Philadelphia, before the Continental Congress, 535d

Fast Day Proclamation: full-page of Governor Francis Bernard's March 8th, 1769, proclamation for a General Fast, 375

FATALITY: which led the British Ministry to pass the Stamp Act, 252b

FATAL ROCK, THE: that broke the Empire in twain, Parliament's refusal to repeal the Massachusetts Government Acts, 487d

FATHER: (God) gives to all men equal right to liberty, 193d

revival, 133c

FRUITS OF HIS LABOR: man's natural right to, in society, a principle of the Physiocrats, 282c

FULLER, SAMUEL, d. 1633: Pilgrim physician and Deacon, summoned from Plymouth to attend the Puritans, 90a; writes to Bradford and Brewster from Salem, 90b; indicated separatist inclinations of Puritans, 90c

FUNERALS: a recoil from papal ways, in New England churches, 95a

FURNITURE: American manufacture of, encouraged, 339a

G

GADSDEN, CHRISTOPHER, 1724-1805: delegate to the Continental Congress from South Carolina, 494d; his comment on liberty and property, 494d

GAGE, THOMAS, 1721-1787: selected as Commander-in-Chief of British forces in America, 391b

First Years in America: married a lady in New York, held with considerable reputation for several years a military employment in the colonies, 391c

Underestimated Colonial ability for self-government: fresh applications made to for troops after seizure of Hancock's sloop, *Liberty*, June, 1768, 372c; arrival in Boston, forced quarters for soldiers, state house improved for barracks, interference with colonial government, 374a; censured by Mass. Assembly for acting against the constitution, 1769, 377b; appointed Governor of Mass. in May, 1774, received with respect in Boston, 391c; 469d; address from inhabitants of Salem after Boston Port Bill, their refusal to be rivals in commerce to Boston, 470c; erased names of representatives chosen by the people, 391d; Mass. General Assembly in secret conference proposed congress of all the colonies, reported to Gage, 393b; he dissolved the Mass. Assembly, 393c; Mass. charter abolished under act to new model her government, orders to arrest and deport leading characters in opposition, 395b; the virtue of the people of Mass. prevent anarchy during suspension of civil government, 396a

Underestimated Colonial ability for self-defence: Britain viewed with alarm training of voluntary *minutemen*, Gage did not find disarmament practical, 399b; Suffolk Resolves recommended people to perfect themselves in art of war, 399d; legislative body dissolved by Gov. Gage, 400b; continued to act as a provincial congress, appointed committees of safety, 400d; difficulties of Bostonians, their determined spirit, 401a; Leslie's errand to Salem discovered American determination to avoid beginning hostilities, 401d; cause of colonies advocated in parliamentary debates, 403b; vote to increase forces in America, 403d; Gage determined to destroy colonial military stores, 491c; April 18, 1775, Smith informed Gage country was arming, 408a; Battle of Lexington and consternation of Gage who knew little of bravery of country, 409c; Bostonians betrayed into a resignation of their arms, 411b; Gage proclaimed martial law, June 12, 1775, pardon to all except Samuel Adams and John Hancock, 415c; Gage proclamation a prelude to immediate action, 417c

Proclamations by: against the solemn league and covenant to suspend commercial intercourse with Great Britain, which he styled *"an unlawful, hostile, and traitorous combination,"* 471c; a proclamation for *"the encouragement of piety and virtue,"* considered a studied insult by the inhabitants, 471d; proclamation for suspending the meeting of the Mass. Provincial Congress, legality denied, newly elected members met, 472c; a proclamation holding forth alternative of peace or war, pardon to all except Samuel Adams and John Hancock, 415c; 497a; text of this proclamation for martial law, June 12, 1775, 508-509

GALATIANS: the Apostle Paul admonished to stand fast in liberty, 193b

GALILEO, 1564-1642: Italian astronomer and physicist, represented Science in the era of the American Settlement, 48b

GALLOWAY, JOSEPH, 1729-1803: loyalist, lawyer, member Continental Congress, opposed independency, returned to Philadelphia behind British bayonets, 57c; ascribed the American Revolution to the action of the Presbyterian clergy, 149a

GARDEN, ALEXANDER, 1730?-1791: South Carolina naturalist and physician, member Royal Society of London, 440b

GARRISON: British, well-equipped in New York, 56a

"GASPEÉ": British revenue cutter, set on fire, June 9, 1772, 405c; court of inquiry set up by illegal procedure in the affair of, 405c

GATES, HORATIO, 1728?-1806: American Revolutionary officer under Washington, 421d; a Major General in the Continental Army, 505c; his military preparation for the American Revolution, 249d

GENERAL INTELLIGENCE: a distinctive of the American Republic, 254c

GENERATION: our Founding Fathers judged in the light of our, 104d; importance of the rising, 213b; education of the present, influence on succeeding ages, 217a; to mortgage privileges of another, is not practicable, 246d; one, includes the American Revolution, 1760-1790, 249a

GENEVA BIBLE: circulated before the King James version, 20a

GENIUS: in divine writers, unparalleled in force, and sublimity, 225b; young Indians distinguished for, should have college education, 319b

GENIUSES: of God, need encouragement through education, 28d

GENOA: republic of, no example for the American Republic, 254b

GEOGRAPHICAL: position of America, helped the Republican Idea, 65b; advantages, of location of Valley Forge, 59c; bounds of the Five Nations from Hudson to Genesee, likened to a Long House covering its outmost limits, 310d; individuality of America, the natural seat of freedom, 434d

GEORGE I, GEORGE LOUIS, 1660-1727: King of Great Britain and Ireland, first king of House of Hanover, appealed to for an American bishop by the Society for the Propagation of the Gospel, 176b

GEORGE II, GEORGE AUGUSTUS, 1683-1760: King of Great Britain and Ireland, son of George I, encroachments of the crown, 360a

GEORGE III, GEORGE WILLIAM FREDERICK, 1738-1820: King of Great Britain and Ireland, grandson of George II, continued arbitrary direction of the Stuarts, 360a; his supremacy in ecclesiastical matters in the colonies feared, 144b; received joint address of Parliament February, 1769, in support of his measures towards the colonies, 452c; prohibited the exportation of arms and ammunition to America, October 19, 1774, 322a; speech to new parliament on American resistance, Nov. 30, 1774, blasted hopes of colonies, 404a; 479c; assurances to parliament for enforcing obedience of colonies, 484c; refused to answer second petition of the Second Continental Congress, Sept. 4, 1775, 502d; many petitions addressed to, from injured American colonies, 531d; petition from Georgia Provincial Congress, 532b; July 14, 1775; honored and prayed for, in July 20, 1775 Continental Fast Day, 547b

clared war against, 5d; labored to establish unjust sovereignty in America, 208; commercial and political interests opposed to America, 247b; revenue and dominion over colonies, claimed, 248a; attitude towards the Indians' right to the soil, 428d; government of, held no patronage in America, 437a; wars of, and active part taken by the colonies, 438b; regarded provinces as instruments of commerce, 441d; changes in colonial policy, commenced in year 1764, 442b; benefits from commercial intercourse of colonies, 442c; revenue from colonies by direct internal taxes, a novel idea, 443d; union with, might have lasted for ages, had she repealed claim to right of taxation, 453a; people of, regarded tea party as a defiance of that country, 460d; granted charters when she was indifferent to the colonies, 461a; numbers in, censured the King's refusal to answer the American Petition, 503a

"GREAT ENGINERY OF WORLD'S PROGRESS": the Bible, 20c

GREAT EVENTS: anniversaries of, should be kept, 67b

GREAT LAKES: control of, retained by England after Treaty of 1764, 313b

GREAT MEN: indebted to their wives, mothers, sisters, 74a

GREAT REVIVAL, 1740-1745: See EPISCOPAL CHURCH IN AMERICA, PRESBYTERIAN CHURCH IN AMERICA

GREAT WAR: the, between evil and good, Revelation XII, 4c

GREECE: learned aristocracy of, contempt for Christians, 8c

GREEK: language, first preachers of the Gospel used in the cities, 11c; the dream of the, safe in America, 67a

GREEKS: democracy of, a misnomer when compared to the birth of this Republic, 254b; originally more rude and savage than the Iroquois, 320a

GREEK VERBS: the study of, compared in difficulty to the translation of colonial money units, 327c

GREENE, NATHANIEL, 1742-1786: General in the American Revolution, a Quaker blacksmith from Rhode Island who was second to Washington, 64a; his appointment to Quartermaster brought relief to the army, 66a; military preparation of, for the American Revolution, 249d; writes to General Knox of the starvation, nakedness, and suffering of the soldiers at Valley Forge, 61c; 62c

GRENADIERS: famous British, who marched into Philadelphia, September 1777, 57b

GRENVILLE, GEORGE, 1712-1770: English statesman credited for the bill laying a stamp duty on America, 447c

GRIEVANCES: on the Stamp Act, detailed by the Freeholders of Plymouth in their town meeting of October 21, 1764, 361d; settled only by forcible means, after failure of all constitutional means of redress, 434b

GROSSMAN, JOHN W., JR., 1932- : American Christian painter and graphic designer; designer of The Christian History Series; Biographies of the Artists, 574

GROUND: hard and frozen at Valley Forge, 58c

GUIDE: to us and to our posterity, our American Archives, 250b

GUNLOCKS: American manufacture of, encouraged, 339a

GUNPOWDER: shortage of in siege at Fort Henry, Virginia, 81b; Elizabeth Zane risked her life for, 81c; one hundred barrels of, taken from William and Mary Castle, Portsmouth Harbour, New Hampshire, 323c; American manufacture of, encouraged, 339b; powder mills of New York Colony to manufacture, 342a; supplied to Washington's army by Governor Trumbull, 342b; salt petre and sulphur to be supplied for manufacture of, by colonies and inhabitants,

342c; sent by New York Provincial Congress to General Wooster's regiment in Connecticut, 342d; Governor Trumbull pleaded to the Continental Congress for, to be spared to General Washington's army in Cambridge, 343a; United Colonies could not depend upon foreign importations, 343b; needs of the American colonies for, critical, 343c; Continental Congress recommended to the several colonies that they erect mills for making, 343d

GURNET POINT: inside, the Mayflower came to her moorings, 89b

H

HABAKKUK THE PROPHET: his description of God surpasses Homer, 230b

HABITS: forming of, and parental education, 214d; of vice, add contempt to the knowledge of God, 215a; bad, more easily prevented than cured, 221b; of virtue, and knowledge and free institutions, 224a

HADRIAN, 76-138 A.D.: Roman Emperor (117-138), during his reign the laws of the state were brought against the Christians, 15a

HAGGAI THE PROPHET: flourished during reign of Darius I (c. 520 B.C.) labored to animate the Jews and encourage them, 23a

HALF-WAY COVENANT, 1662: controversy originated in Connecticut Colony, 96b; first innovations in church polity in 1657, 96d; distinguished between partial and full membership, in church, 97a

HALL, VERNA M.: American Christian scholar and historian; compiler of The Christian History of the Constitution of the United States of America; Self-Government with Union; The Christian History of the American Revolution, Vol. I, Consider and Ponder, Introduction to, XXIII

HALLAM, HENRY, 1777-1869: English historian Constitutional History of England, 1827, comments on Charles II declaration to conciliate Presbyterians, 108a

HAMILTON, ALEXANDER, 1757 or 1753?-1804: American statesman, a youth at Valley Forge, aide-de-camp to General Washington, 64b

HAMPDEN, JOHN, 1594-1643: English Puritan statesman, prevented from embarking to America by a royal edict from Charles I, 359d

HANCOCK, JOHN, 1737-1793: American Revolutionary merchant and stateman, enlisted early in the cause of his country, 416a; patriotic exertions in artillery company, 205a; on committee to impeach Governor Bernard, July 1, 1768, 371d; his sloop, Liberty, seized to promote a ferment, 372b; 451b; called on by Governor Hutchinson to assist in the landing of the tea, 384d; resigned his commission, continued opposed to ministerial system, 385a; president of the Massachusetts Provincial Congress, 1774, 339d; 472d; stigmatized by the name of rebel or insurgent by Gage, 1775, 415c; repaired to Philadelphia after his escape from Lexington, 416b; promised condign punishment from General Gage, 497a; laid depositions from Battle of Lexington before the Continental Congress, May 10, 1775, 499c; successor to Peyton Randolph in the presidency of the Continental Congress, 416c; 500b; continued in presidential chair until October, 1779, 416c; occupied in his own state of Massachusetts for residue of his life, 416d

HANDEL, GEORGE FREDERICK, 1685-1759: German composer, other Handels predicted for America, 231d

HAND OF GOD: let us acknowledge, for His merciful favor to our Pilgrim Fathers, 26c; American freedom in the, 28b; a chosen theme in American history, 46d; observed in the wise timing of events,

46d; in the discovery and preparation of America, 47b; in the development of our national life, 49a; France repelled by the, in 1746, 50b; in the American Revolution as in the Reformation, 52a; seen in the unity of the colonists, 52a; in the preparation of the men for the American Revolution, 52a; guided in forming the American Republic, 52d; impressed them with the belief that no design formed against them could prosper, 252b; seen in the rapidity of events leading to America's separation, 404c; able to deliver America from her alarming affairs, 520d

HAPPINESS: temporal, an individual responsibility, 202d; of children, the duty and comfort of parents, 236c

HARDSHIPS: of our Pilgrim Fathers, let us reflect upon, 25b; and dangers, faced by America's first settlers, 49c; endured by the people under the Boston Port Bill, 470b

HART, LEVI: pastor in Norwich, Connecticut, reviewed thirty years of his ministry with the parents and children of his congregation, 218b; 220a

HARTLEY, DAVID, 1705-1757: English philosopher, his writings analogous to English institutions, 290d; his plan of conciliation for the American Colonies also rejected, 487c

HARVARD COLLEGE: founded by the Massachusetts legislature in 1637, first American college began to confer degrees in 1642, 439a; censored by George Whitefield during the Great Revival, 130d; vindication of by Rev. Edward Wigglesworth, 130d

HARVARD, JOHN, 1608-1638: a worthy minister who left a legacy to the infant seminary which was named in honour of him, 439a

HATFIELD, MASS.: refused to join in the Massachusetts Convention of Towns, 452a

HAWKINS, JOHN, 1532-1595: English naval commander, first to engage in the slave trade to the West Indies in 1563, 428a

HAWKS, FRANCIS LISTER, 1798-1866: American Episcopal layman and church historian, his comments on the state of religion in Virginia before the Great Revival, 169a

HAWLEY, JOSEPH, 1723-1788: American political leader, active in the colonial cause, 371d

HEAD OF ELK, MD.: British army landed at, August 25, 1777, 56c

HEATH, WILLIAM, 1737-1814: American Revolutionary officer, appointed a general officer of the Massachusetts Minute Men, 473b

HEATHEN: conversion of, design of the Pilgrim Fathers, 24c

HEAVEN: powers of, invoked in aid of the sick, by the Primitive Christians, 9c; triumph of, in care of our ancestors, 26b; we shall be unworthy of the blessings of, if we submit to tyranny, 74d; gratitude to, by unknown woman of courage in North Carolina, 80d; an appeal to, began our civil year, 191b; and hell, should be mentioned in the education of children, 243c; hand of, seen in the prosperity of the colonies, 252b; American Colonists looked up to, as the source of their rights, 423; regarded as the source of the rights and liberties of the colonists, 435d; an appeal to, for the vindication of their rights, 494d

HEAVENLY GUIDANCE: sought by Lydia Darrah, 78b

HEBREW'S: the, prophecy, safe in America, 67a

HEBRON, CONN.: religion in a desirable state in the midst of a general decline, 128a

"HE COMES": the key to the Book of Revelation, 3d

HELL: and heaven, should be mentioned in the education of children, 243c

HEMP: and flax, recommended to be raised by the people, 339a

HENRY, MATTHEW, 1662-1714: English Nonconformist clergyman and Bible commentator, his Commentaries on the Bible used by the New England Clergy as a source of political theory, 548d

HENRY, PATRICK, 1736-1799: found by God for the new nation, 52a; efficient defender of the natural rights of mankind, 249d; oratorical powers first brought to notice over the value of tobacco in the salaries of Virginia parsons, 333a; ushered in resolves against the Stamp Act in the Virginia House of Burgesses, May 30, 1765, 361b; 448a

HENRY VIII, 1491-1547: of the house of Tudor, King of England (1509-47), involved in conflict with papal power, originating in his wish to divorce Catherine. Do we condemn him for refusing obedience to the pope?, 539d

HERBERT, GEORGE, 1593-1633: English clergyman and poet, 44d; his poem *The Church Militant* sees the Chain of Christianity moving westward, 45a

HEROES: armed for victory, by the American Christian home, 73b; nursery of, in British America, 204c; of literature, compared to the Hero of Scriptures, 230d

HEROIC DEEDS: have consecrated the ground of Valley Forge, 63a

HEROIC RESISTANCE: of Americans on Bunker's Hill, 417c

HEROISM: of faith, of Primitive Christians, 10c; of our Pilgrim Fathers, 25c; and self-sacrifice of women in the American Revolution, 74a

HESSIAN MERCENARIES: defeated by Washington at Trenton, Christmas 1776, 57c; march with the British into Philadelphia, 1777, 57c

HEZEKIAH, 740?-692 B.C.: King of Judah (720?-692 B.C.) in the days of, the Lord delivered Israel from the Assyrian host, 542a

HIERARCHY: episcopal, prevented in America, 28c

HIGGINSON, FRANCIS, 1587-1630: Puritan clergyman, established the church at Salem, Massachusetts, 45c

HIGGINSON, JOHN, 1616-1708: American Congregational clergyman, one of New England's greatest ministers, one of the writers of *Elijah's Mantle*, stating the Christian purpose of New England, 252d

HIGHER POWERS: what is meant by, respecting civil government, 539a; the just, good, wholesome and constitutional laws of a land, 539a; obedience to, designed to secure the property and happiness of the community, 539a; obedience to, as binding on princes as on the people, 539a; does not enjoin submission to wicked, oppressive laws, 539a

HIGHLANDS: of the Hudson, guarded by ill-equipped American army in 1777, 56a

HILLSBOROUGH, EARL AND VISCOUNT OF, 1718-1793: English statesman, Secretary of State for the colonies, opposed concession, followed Lord Shelburne's western policy until 1768, 304d; assisted by Indian Agent, Sir William Johnson, 305a; his letter to General Gage revealed indecision in regard to the disposition of western lands, 309d; his haughty tone assuring Bernard he is above the provincial legislature, May 24, 1768, 371a; wrote letters to the provincial governors regarding the Massachusetts Circular Letter which was both injudicious and irritating, 451a; assured Governor Botetourt of parliament's relinquishment of American Revenue, May 14, 1769, 454a

HIRELINGS: accumulated swarms of, sent from Great Britain to ravish rights of the colonies, 365b

HISTORIAN: of the American Revolution, must rely upon Omnipotent Wisdom, 255c

HISTORIC SPOTS: of our nation, should be visited by thousands, 67b

HISTORY: of world, divergent principles in conflict, 4d; the new and great epoch in, Christianity, 7b; progress of, seen as Christianity victorious, 15d; of America, and history of Bible coincident, 19d; of a nation, dealt with thoroughly reveals the Hand of God, 46b; of a nation, superficial study of, leads to irreligion, 46c; events of, not accidental, 46d; American, and the Hand of God seen in the timing of events, 46d; is the autobiography of God, 47a; of liberty and its defence described, 66d; of George Washington, includes Martha Washington, 75a; drawn to Mercy Warren's attention, 77a; of America and the crimes of Europe, 112a; of New England, habitual study of political ethics, 192c; of mankind, filled with encroachments on liberty, 197b; in the Bible, contains truths, instructive, moral and divine, 226c; of the American Revolution, in three stages, 248b; is philosophy, teaching by example, 250b; requires a just knowledge of character, 358b

HOLLAND: *see also* EUROPE IN 1763; in the era of the American Settlement, 48d; furnished original stock for the present population of the United States, 437c

HOLY SCRIPTURES: *see also* BIBLE, THE, WORD OF GOD; contain principles of obedience to God, 18a; King James Version of 1611, everywhere received, 19d; general diffusion of, begins with the King James Version, 20a; an examination of them, and God's regard for liberty, 35b; liberty is the spirit and genius of the sacred writings, 40a; their authority is directly opposed to all disorders, 129d; instruction in, a blessing of childhood, 215a; taught to Timothy from a child, 217c; opposition to, often laid in youth by parental education, 217d; ministers of New England, excelled in knowledge of, 440c; is our only rule of faith and practice for a defensive war, 537d; indicate examples of people refusing obedience to arbitrary kings, 538d

HOLY SPIRIT: magnetick influence of, in the planting of Massachusetts Colony, 44c; earliest manifestation of, in the Great Revival, 121b; work of during the Great Revival, 121b; work of, confused with a lively imagination during the Great Revival, 129a

HOME: a picture for, *Washington at Prayer*, x; conditions for wives and children, severe in 1777-1778, 62a; importance of, a source of power in the American Revolution, 73b; Christian character learned at, from patriotic mothers, 73d; guardianship of, from tyranny, and the American Revolution, 254a

HOME GOVERNMENT: discussed by Samuel Adams in a letter, 82d

HOME MANUFACTURE: encouraged by the First Continental Congress, 396d; as recommended by the Continental Congress, to be encouraged by Georgia, 524d

HOMER: Ancient Greek author of the *Iliad* and the *Odyssey*, could be spared from literature, but not the Bible, 20d; "*the Father of Poetry*" surpassed by the Bible, 224d; compared to the divine writers in examples of character, 226b

HOME SENTIMENT: power of, in the American Revolution, 73b; sustained the hero and the statesman, 73b; of the Founding Fathers, 81d

HOOKER, RICHARD, 1554?-1600: English theologian, represented theology, in the era of the American Settlement, 48c

HOOKER, THOMAS, 1586?-1647: Congregational clergyman, active in framing the Connecticut Constitution, 110a; comments on the consent of the people, 94b

HORN: blowing of, to call people to public worship, 94b

HORN-SMITHS: encouraged for American Manufacturing, 339c

HORSES: hundreds of, starved to death at Valley Forge, 61c

HOSIERY: American Manufacture of encouraged, 339c

HOSPITALITY: Children learn from the behaviour of their parents, 241d

HOSTILITIES: Americans determined to avoid beginning, 401d; commenced by the British, produced an American Army, 493b; without blood, as people endeavored to secure military supplies, 399c; had already commenced when the Second Continental Congress met, 500c

HOUR: of darkness and danger at Valley Forge, x; darkest hour at Valley Forge relieved, 64d

HOUSE FOR GOD: built first by American settlers, 49c

HOUSEHOLD DUTIES: and literary pursuits of Mercy Warren, 77a

HOUSE OF BURGESSES: early tendency to self-government in Virginia, 1620, 50c; Virginia's, resolved a Fast Day on June 1st, 1774, the day on which the operation of the Boston port bill was to commence, 467d

HOUSE OF COMMONS: invaded by the army of Cromwell, 266d; represented the land of England but not the men, 288b; few voters out of entire population required to elect, 288c; claimed freedom of speech as an inherited right in 1621, 433d; debated answer to George III on American Resistance, 479d; evaded action on petitions from merchants regarding coercion of America, 480d

HOUSE OF DEPUTIES: in Massachusetts, an early tendency of self-government in 1643, 50c

HOUSE OF LORDS: protest by some Lords against measures of the British Ministry, 479d; Lord Chatham resumed his seat in, spoke against attempts to subdue Americans by arms, 480c; names of those lords who were for Lord Chatham's conciliatory bill, 482a; names of lords protesting the joint address to his majesty on the coercion of the American colonies, 484b

HOWE: the name of, was once revered, beloved and dreaded in America, 415b

HOWE, GEORGE AUGUSTUS, 1724-1758: older brother of Richard and William, killed at Ticonderoga, 415b

HOWE, RICHARD, 1726-1799: English naval officer who undertook the conquest of America, 415d

HOWE, SIR WILLIAM, 1729-1814: 5th viscount Howe, succeeded Gage as Commander-in-Chief in America, 415b; arrived in Boston in 1775, 496d; British Commander in Battle of Bunker's Hill, 417c; 497d; commanded victorious army in Philadelphia in 1777, 58a; left Valley Forge untouched, 66b; comment by John Adams on the influence of his wife, 74b

HUGUENOTS (FRENCH PROTESTANTS): struggles of in France, during the era of the American Settlement, 48d; persecution of, during the reign of Louis XIV consumated by the revocation of the Edict of Nantes in 1685 drove hundreds of thousands from their native country, large numbers of them came to this country, 111c; 437c

HULL, WILLIAM, 1753-1825: officer at Valley Forge, 64a

HUMAN CHARACTER: of man, found in the history of the Jews, 255d

HUMAN LAWS: must not differ in principle from those in the Gospel, 256b

HUMAN REASON: guide of, the Holy Scriptures, 21b

HUMAN SOCIETY: improves only under liberty, 35a

HUME, DAVID, 1711-1776: Scottish philosopher and historian, his works bore a character analagous to English institutions, 291a

HUNGER: the constant guest of soldiers at Valley Forge, 58d

HUNTER, ROBERT, d. 1734: Governor of New York, brought with him in 1730 German emigrants from England who had fled persecution in Germany, 111b

HUNTING SHIRT: became the uniform of the Provincial Army, 504d

to freedom of speech, 433d; educated in the divine right of kings, 433d; of blessed memory for the translation of the Bible if for nothing else, 19d

JAMES II, 1633-1701: King of England, Scotland, and Ireland 1685-88; pursued the same arbitrary measures as his father, 434a; would not be subject to higher powers, 539d; his persecution of the Scotch Presbyterians, 112a; did not comprehend the value of constitutional law, 271c; depended on a standing army, 271c; endeavored to win favor for Roman Catholics, 271c; willing to persecute Protestant dissenters 271c; the Declaration of Indulgence suspended all laws against dissenters, deemed a death blow to the church, 271d; departed from the Constitution, was forced to abdicate, 538d; deserted by all he fled England, 272a; during his reign emigration to America increased, 360a

JAMESTOWN: plantation of, and the diffusion of the Holy Scriptures, 20a; germ of our national life, planted in, 49c

JEALOUSIES: mutual, of Great Britain and the colonies, destroyed confidence to the final dismemberment of the empire, 483d

JEFFERSON, THOMAS, 1743-1826: Virginia statesman, Third President of the United States, found by God for the new nation, 52a; he acknowledged he owed everything to his mother's rearing, 74b; corresponded with Mercy Warren, 77b; prepared the people for the American Revolution, 249d; notes on the establishment of a money unit for the United States, 326d; author A Summary View of the Rights of British America, 1774, 440a

JEPHTHAH: the ninth Judge of Israel, history of, and the style of the divine writers, 227a; a deliverer of Israel, died in the faith that a defensive war is sinless, 538c

JEREMIAH; PROPHET: Lamentations of, in the solf, tender strain of Elegy, where are simplicity and grief so finely united, 229a

JERSEY: settlers in, inclined to congregationalism, and presbyterianism, 113b

JERUSALEM: return of the Jews to, after captivity, 22d

JESUS CHRIST: infant, efforts of the evil one to destroy, 5c; in the name of, evil spirits adjured in Primitive Christianity, 9c; doctrines of, spread despite persecutions, 15c; the chief corner stone, referred to in Revelation, 23d; the chief corner stone of our Pilgrim Fathers, 24a; brethren in, Pilgrims and planters of the Massachusetts colony, 25d; the truth as it is in, and the character of the clergy, 27c; disciples of, transported into futurity, 27d; his obedience, brought liberty for all mankind, 32c; growth in the knowledge of, animated by liberty, 34b; the author of our liberty from the bondage of satan, 36c; did not say many things on civil government and political liberty, 36d; gave general rules for guidance of civil government, 37c; a prayer that the aboriginal nations shall bow the knee to, 43d; and church government, distinct from civil magistrate, 107d; sinners flee to, during the Great Revival, 121c; our righteousness, the conviction of Whitefield, 122d; preaching of, not followed by convulsions or ravings, 129c; acknowledged as Saviour by the first settlers, 157a; set apart the Sabbath for instruction, 158a; preferred doers of the word to mere hearers, 190c; and the defence of his spiritual kingdom, 198a; statement about children, 216c; his love of children, impressions on parents, 216d; blessed at age of twelve, subject to his parents, 220d; may his pure religion be perpetuated till his second coming, 221a; by grace and truth brought in the law of liberty, 515b; shall judge men according to his Gospel, 516d; our deliverer, our prayer calls upon him, 544d;

soldiers of, must be stout-hearted and well armed, 549a

JEWISH: captivity, restored by Cyrus, 22b; religion, and despotism, 518d; religion, whole system of, against injustice and oppression, 518d; religion, and an extraordinary regard for property, 518d; sect, work of the Apostle Paul to separate Christians from, 13d; temple, rose with blessing of Providence, 23b

JEWS: methods used to expel demoniacal powers, 9b; banished by Emperor Claudius, Christians also, 13d; returning to Jerusalem, dispirited, 22d; feeble state of, in Jerusalem, 23a; the nature of their civil government, a free government, 35d; civil government of, wise laws for the preservation of liberty, 35d; government of, calculated to keep alive the spirit of liberty, 36a; changed to a monarchy, God's warning of the loss of liberties, 36a; request for a King divested them of the liberty they had enjoyed, 36b; should they be required to respect the Christian Sabbath in America, 154c; in America, admitted to equal rights and privileges, 157a; attitude toward law, after becoming Christians, 193b; genius of, different from Greeks and Romans, 225a; the history of, presents the true human character of man, 255d; God's covenant with, 544d

JOAQUIN OF CALABRIA, 1145?-?1202: Abbott, false revelation of so-called Everlasting Gospel, 3b

JOB: history of, his attention to the good of his children, 216d; the restoration of, finest example of Epic in the Bible, 229b

JOHNSON, GUY, 1740?-1788: British Superintendent of Indian Affairs, 1774-1782, 313b; his map of 1771 shows principal Indian Trails, 313b; called a Council at Oswego of the Six Nations in May, 1775, fourteen hundred Indians agreed to enter the service of the King, 314a; used his influence with the Mohawks against us, 541d

JOHNSON HALL: site of Indian Treaty in 1764, 313b

JOHNSON, SIR JOHN, 1742-1830: son of Sir William, succeeded to his title and estate, 313c; Superintendent of Indian Affairs from 1782, 313c; secretly organized royalists and Indians against America, 314c; placed under arrest by General Schuyler, 314c

JOHNSON, SAMUEL, 1696-1772: American Presbyterian clergyman and educator, 165d; a tutor at Yale, affected toward episcopacy by reading, 165d; abandoned ministry at Yale, sailed to England for re-ordination in the Church of England, 165d; his answers to queries by the Bishop of London, 165d; on the need for bishops, 173d; first president of King's now Columbia College, New York, 221d

JOHNSON, SIR WILLIAM, 1715-1774: British Superintendent of Indian Affairs, 1755-74, 305a; correspondence with Hillsborough on Indian trade, 305a; member of Illinois Company for western land settlement, 307b; associated with Mohawks, took for his second wife, Molly Brant, an Indian girl, 313c; acquired powerful influence over the Six Nations, 313c

JOHNSTONE, GEORGE, D. 1787: English Governor of West Florida, letters to from the Georgia Provincial Congress, 531c; 532b; an appeal to his former conduct in establishing West Florida, 531d; set forth reasons for their petition to the King, 531d

JONSON, BENJAMIN, 1573?-1637: English playwright and poet, in the era of the American Settlement, 48c

JOSEPH: his example recommended to youth's imitation, 220d; an example of character for unwary youth, 226a; history of, and style of divine writers, 226c; his history and example, one of the best for mankind, 256d

JOSEPH II, 1741-1790: King of Germany, Holy Roman

Emperor, in full control of Austria on death of his mother, Maria Theresa, 277d; inclined to scepticism and unbelief, 277d

JOSHUA: a magnificent example of the general and hero, 226a

JOSHUAS: we had our, in our famous Founders, 45a

JUDAISING TEACHERS: urged Galatians to submit to the law, 193b

JUDGEMENT DAY: all nations shall appear in, 517b; a particular day when the whole Creation stands before God, 517c; extends to all of our thoughts, words, actions, 517d

JUDGEMENTS OF GOD: not stayed by the Synod of 1679, 99c

JUDGES: of the Supreme Court of Massachusetts called upon to receive grants for their services from the treasury of the province, to renounce all unconstitutional salaries, 388b; of the Admiralty Courts, a creature of the crown, 443b; of Massachusetts, made independent of the province, 455b; new, appointed by the crown, rendered incapable of performing their official duty, 471d

JURISPRUDENCE: a classic model of, the American Republic, 254d

JUSTICE: principle of, towards the natives, discovered by our ancestors, 23d; often successful against great odds, 203c; proof of the impartial, of Massachusetts, in the case of Captain Preston and the Boston Massacre, 462c; and religion, consistent, 540c

K

KALB, JOHANN, 1721-1780: Bavarian officer, served under Washington's command, self-sacrificing and generous, died in American service, 63d

KANT, IMMANUEL, 1724-1804: German philosopher, Prussia gave its youth to the teachings of, 276c

KEITH, GEORGE, 1638-1716: Scotch Quaker who became an Anglican evangelist, 162b; disputed the Quakers, 162c; historian of Virginia, 440a

KEPLER, JOHANNES, 1571-1630: German astronomer, represented science in the era of the American Settlement, 48b

KINGCRAFT: clouded minds of monarchs and statesmen to the lessons of the American Revolution, 254d

KINGDOM: a, of this world, not the aim of Christianity, 7d; of evil spirits, destroyed by Jesus, said Justin Martyr, 9c; temporal, our Lord charged with setting up, 198a; temporal, our Lord allows it to fight for its liberty, 198a; of our Lord, cannot be injured or defended by the sword, 198a; an individual, or a, bound to preserve God-given liberty, 202b

KINGDOM OF JESUS: oh that it was come, then we shall learn war no more, 540b

KING OF KINGS: Washington pleaded the cause of the nation before, x

KINGS: when Jews came under power of earthly, God let them know how they would be likely to be deprived of their liberties, 36a; disobeyed in Scripture when they became oppressive, 538d; Paul taught us to pray for, 544b

KING'S CHAPEL: in Boston, the first Episcopal church in New England, 161b

KING'S COLLEGE: now Columbia, Samuel Johnson first president of, 221d

KING'S LETTER: of 1662, required franchise to orthodox freeholders, 98b

KINGS OF ISRAEL: in the chain of history, believed a defensive war is sinless, 538c

KING'S ORDER: of October 19, 1774, prohibited exportation of arms and ammunition to America, 322a; prohibiting military stores, caused New Hampshire men to act, 323d; regarding arms and ammunition

into the colonies was to expire, April 19, 1775

KING'S TROOPS: arrival of in Boston, shocked with grief the population, 373d; disembarked in Boston October 1, 1778, 373d; arrival of, expected to lead to violent resistance, met with the appearance of decent submission, 373d; sent out in small parties to seize military stores, 399b; retreated to Boston after Lexington and Concord, pressed by the provincial militia, 492a

KIRKLAND, SAMUEL, 1741-1808: missionary to the Iroquois, helped to keep Indians friendly to the Americans, 313d

KNOWLEDGE: used to teach men to worship the beast by the apostles of materialism, 6c; may be a power for evil, as much as good, 53c; and virtue, and instruction of youth, 222b; and virtue, the security for the duration of our free institutions, 224a; useful, Washington's acquisition of in youth, prepared him to serve his country, 503d

KNOX, HENRY, 1750-1803: American Revolutionary officer, brave and faithful advisor to Washington, 64a; corresponded with Mercy Warren, 77b

KNOX, JOHN, 1505-1572: Scottish reformer, writer, and statesman, author of the 1561 Confession of Faith, 112b

KNYPHAUSEN, BARON WILHELM VON, 1716-1800: Commander of Hessian troops in America, 57d; in 1777 quartered at Henry Lisle's house in Philadelphia, 57d

L

LABOUR: of man's body, the work of his hands, is his property, 184d

LACEY, JOHN, 1755-1815: American General who endeavored to prevent supplies going to the British in Philadelphia, 60a

LAFAYETTE, MARQUIS DE, 1757-1834: French statesman and officer who volunteered his services for the American Revolution, 63d; the French boy of twenty with an old man's head, 64a; God was certainly present in the life of, 52c; wounded at Brandywine in 1777, 56d; testifies to the lack of provisions at Valley Forge, 61c; reports on the lack of clothing at Valley Forge, 61d; in his old age he remembers the patience and endurance of the soldiers at Valley Forge, 62d; his example, influenced the French Alliance of 1778, 65c

LAMB: wild beasts of Revelation XIII in opposition to Him who is the, 5d; second wild beast resembles a, 6a

LAND: Christ will heal our, 30a

LANDING: of our Pilgrim Fathers, hardships of, 25b

LAND POLICY: of New England colonies, favorable to their rapid growth, 431b

LANGDON, JOHN, 1741-1819: American Revolutionary leader, seized his majesty's castle at Portsmouth, 473d

LANGDON, SAMUEL, 1723-1797: American Congregational clergyman, president of Harvard (1774-1780); moderator convention of ministers 1775, 207c

LANGUAGE: sacred, to praise the Lord, 30c; expressive, of Old Testament, used by American settlers, 48d

LATHROP, JOHN, 1740-1816: Boston divine who took the popular side in the American Revolution, 192d

LATIN: language or Greek, the Gospel preached in, in the cities, 11c

LAUD, WILLIAM, 1573-1645: English prelate, opposed to Calvinism and Puritanism, Archbishop of Canterbury under Charles I, 263d; supported the King's prerogative in conflict with parliament, 263d

LAURENS, HENRY, 1724-1792: American Revolutionary statesman, president of Provincial Congress of South Carolina, 413d; his virtue and independence of spirit, 413d

LAURENS, JOHN, 1754-1782: young American officer at Valley Forge, 64a; writes of alarming conditions at Valley Forge, 1777-78, 61c; an aide to George Washington, commanded men of South Carolina, 63d; busy with scheme to raise negro troops, 63d; "*Cherish those dear ragged Continentals,*" 62d

LAW: of God, men are making void in America's second century, 53d; and Gospel, distinctions between, 515b; and liberty are consistent, 515c; all men are under some, 516c; and liberty in the English colonies, 435a; must exist wherever there is society, 514c; is a schoolmaster to bring us to Christ, 515b; is spiritual, 517a; of the Gospel, in the judgement our character will be brought to, 517a

LAW AND ORDER: Presbyterians urged to maintain during the American Revolution, 152a; American clergymen supporters of, 256c; observed during the suspension of government in Massachusetts, 398a; 461d

LAWFUL AUTHORITY: respect for, in the American Philosophy of Government, 250d

LAWFUL CURRENCY: accounts of George Washington are translated into for Congress, 332a

LAWLESS: self-will, secured by the spirit of Christianity, 17d; conduct, not in accord with the Gospel law of liberty, 522c

LAW OF GOD: people follow after Great Revival, states William Tennant, 122a; declared to be the Law of Nature, by Elisha Williams, 183b

LAW OF LIBERTY: is not a law of man, but of God, 515a

LAW OF NATIONS: restrains nations, states and communities, 197a; natural liberty consistent with, 197a; charters agreeable to, inferred protections to colonies from king, 429c; not the law of the sword, 441d

LAW OF NATURE: declared to be the Law of God, by Elisha Williams, 183b; within the bounds of, man free to act, 184c; not binding to some, in state of nature, 185a; forbids all injustice and wickedness, 194a; within bounds of, God-given liberty, 194a; cannot be transgressed in civil government, 194b; transgressed, if natural liberties are given up, 194c; relationship of independent states to each other, 194d; consistent with liberty, in civil government, 197a; and revelation, imply responsibility for family support, 202d; obligations of, after Declaration of Independence, 250a; and British Constitution, protect property, stated in the Georgia Resolves, July 10, 1775, 527c

LAW OF THE LAND: in America is Protestant Christianity, 156b

LAWS: of state, assault Christians under Hadrian, 15a; and liberties of America will be extended to the world, 54c; to oblige the church of Christ, only from Christ, 188d; power of making, intrusted to some in civil society, 194a; immoral, violate liberty of conscience, 194d; of society, must be consistent with law of nature, 194d; submission to, and defence of liberty, 200a; of a nation, show influence of parental education, 217d; are good, when they secure every man's liberty and property, 539b; in America, acknowledged in Europe as most equitable on earth, 546d

LAWYERS: no order of men more favorable to liberty, 435b; one half the delegates of the Continental Congress of 1774 were, 476a

LEADERS: early of Congress, replaced by inferior men by 1777, 60b: Christian principles and lofty personal character needed in our, 54a

LEARNED, EBENEZER, 1721-1801: officer at Valley Forge, a Massachusetts man, 63d

LEARNING: was cultivated in America before the American Revolution, 398b; and personal character of New England clergy, 438d; and religion, firmest pillars of church and commonwealth, 439a; in

Virginia, ruling powers averse to encouragement of, 439b

LEE, ARTHUR, 1740-1792: Virginia statesman, author *The Monitor's Letters*, 1769, 440a; efficient defender of the natural rights of mankind, 249d; colonial agent, offered petition from First Continental Congress to Parliament, 481a; presented petition to king, September 1, 1775, 502c

LEE, CHARLES, 1731-1782: American Military Commander under Washington, 421d; military preparation of, for the American Revolution, 249d; intercepted confidential letter from Lord Germaine to Governor Eden, 414a; commanded left wing of the American army at Prospect Hill during siege of Boston, 505c

LEE, HENRY, (LIGHT HORSE HARRY), 1756-1818: calvary officer at Valley Forge, 64a; "Lee's Legion" unable to prevent supplies going to the British in Philadelphia, 60a; destined to be famous in Senate, Cabinet and field, 64a

LEE, RICHARD HENRY, 1732-1794: American Revolutionary statesman, Virginia delegate to the Continental Congress from 1774-1779, 342c; on committee to promote manufacture of salt petre, 342c

LEGALITY: of parliamentary taxation, denied by Americans, 456c

LEGAL RESTRAINTS: needed because of the depravity of man, 539a

LEGAL TENDER: everything was appraised and became, in the colonies, 332c; paper money being made, the problems and opportunities, 438c

LEGISLATION: Christian, holds every man responsible, 54a; in the colonies, required the assent of the people, 438a

LEGISLATIVE ASSEMBLIES: colonial, acknowledged God, 157a; colonial, dissolved when colonial governors found energy, enterprise, or patriotism, 387a

LEGISLATIVE POWER: exercised by Crown appointees, declared unconsitutional in the Declaration of Rights, 477a

LEGISLATIVE VENGEANCE: taken by Parliament on the town of Boston, 460a

LEGISLATOR: can apply to life and laws of Moses for instruction, 226a

LEGISLATORS: Christian principles and character needed in our, 54a

LESLIE, ALEXANDER, 1740-1794: British military officer, his secret expedition to Salem to seize cannon was foiled by the people, 401c

LESSING, GOTTHOLD EPHRAIM, 1729-1781: German dramatist and critic with wide hope for universal brotherhood on earth, 276c

LESSONS: of Bible, are fresh for every period of history, 19d; can be learned from American Christian character during the Revolution, 73b; in colonization from Great Britain, 441d

LETTERS: from home, disheartening to soldiers at Valley Forge, 62a; on the education of children by John Witherspoon, 232; Hutchinson-Oliver, contained unfavorable representation of public affairs in Massachusetts, 455c; from a Pennsylvania farmer written by John Dickinson to warn the public of the Townshend Bill, 450d

LEVERETT, JOHN, 1662-1724: President of Harvard, 1707-1724, member of Royal Society of London, 440b

LEXINGTON AND CONCORD, April 19, 1775: action between the King's troops and some Americans, 405d; here the American Revolution began, 409a; the glory of, can be ours if we will, 67b; God was on their side, the people believed, 193c; British Troops under Colonel Smith reached at dawn on April 19, 1775, 406c; an excursion to capture Hancock and Samuel Adams, 416b; the company of Militia was commanded by Colonel John Parker, 406d; they assembled at two in the morning to oppose the royal army, 491d; British troops fired on the militia at, 406d; British regulars under Lord Percy added 900 men to the troops, 492a; the perseverance and tenacity of the Minute Men at, 249d; number of British regular and provincials killed or wounded at, 492b; colonists forced to the sword as a last appeal against the power of Britain, 409a; blood of those killed at, proved the firm cement of an extensive union, 492c

LIBERTIES: Americans jealous of their, and the exclusive right of taxing themselves, 445b; built only by virtue, courage, patriotism, by these only can we hope to keep them, 67c; chartered, annihilated by the intolerable acts, 462d; Continental Congress declared they could not submit to these grievous acts and measures, 477b; hazard to, our vices and extravagancies, 30a; no monarch should deprive people of, and expect God's approbation, 514a; not parted with, by entering into civil government, 186b; of America, civil and religious, prayed for on July 20, 1775, the Continental Fast Day, 506c; 536b; 543b; of Christians, and the right of resistance, authority for in the New Testament, 548b; of Englishmen, dependent on their consent to grants of monies by their representatives, 360b; of our Pilgrim Fathers, let us improve and maintain, 26d; of the people, subverted by unconstitutional tax on tea, 460d

"LIBERTY, THE": name of the sloop owned by John Hancock, seized to provoke a riot, June 10, 1768, 372b; 451b

LIBERTY,

Civil and religious: genuine, preserved by Biblical principles, 21c; these two senses of, become one, 33a; New England clergy found the liberty of the Gospel a source of political ethics, 192c; friends of, preachers of the Gospel, 206a; preservation of, entrusted to magistrates, 208; rests on the virtue and intelligence of the community, 223c; great principle of, men are by nature free, accountable to Him, 246b; representation and taxation indissolubly connected, 251b; the palladium of, exclusive disposal of property, 456b; the American colonies counted everything else cheap in comparison, 479b; the Gospel as a law of liberty does not countenance despotism, 518b

Benefits of: requisite to the growth of every good seed in a commonwealth, 35a; spirit of, prompted the industry and growth of the New England colonies, 431c; effect of slavery upon, in the Southern Colonies, 432d; upon its industry and wealth, 433a

History of, in the Old Testament: miraculous deliverance of the children of Israel from Egyptian bondage, 35c; in the civil government of the Jews, 35d; the ancient Prophets endowed with the spirit of, 36c

in the New Testament: liberty of conscience unknown until Christianity, 11d; Christians set at liberty under Nerva, 14c; writings of the New Testament friendly to the cause of liberty, 36c; Christ's sentiments on the subject of civil liberty, 37b; Apostle Paul manifested his sense of both civil and religious liberty, 37c

after the Reformation: liberty of conscience proclaimed by the Reformers, 47d; Cromwell made use of the enthusiasm for liberty for his advancement, 269b; Turgot would concede liberty to industry, 282d; the framework of English constitutional government had for its end, personal liberty, the security of property, 284c

in America: the main principles of that scriptural and religious liberty for which the Pilgrims suffered, 24d; America, the chosen refuge of, in the West, 67a;

the breath of life to the people, 273c; the religion of, nurtured a love for liberty, 434d; reading of, favored liberty, 435b; provincial constitutions nurtured the spirit of, 437a

in the American Revolution: first emigrants to these shores brought the principles of, 251a; drawn from the pure fountains of Liberty, 251b; it was Liberty herself they had in keeping at Valley Forge, 66d; Presbyterians thank God for the particular manner in which He established the independence of the United States of America, 153c; the Continental Congress established American Manufactures to aid our independence, 340a; Americans determined to resist in blood rather than become slaves to arbitrary power, 404d; preferring death to thraldom, 415a; the principles of liberty, the basis of colonial opposition to taxation without consent, 443d; in our present struggle for, no lasting happiness without reformation and a life worthy of the glorious gospel, 543a

Defense of, by the pen: liberty is both the spirit and genius of the sacred writings, 40a; writers who defended the cause of liberty, 435b; 548d; every man born into the world is born to liberty, Locke, 41c; Dickinson, Letters by the Farmer, proving dangers to the liberties of America, 450d; the fire of liberty blazed from the press, 448a; every newspaper teemed with dissertations in favor of liberty, 466d; the publication of the Declaration of Rights stated the principles of American liberty, 476c

by the sword: the history of liberty and its defence through the ages, 66d; duty of all men to stand fast in, 193b; a defensive war for a just cause is sinless, 536a

Destruction of: still crushed by tyrants, the nimrods of the earth, 34d; prevalence of a licentious spirit may destroy, 200b; our destruction from the inattention of the people, their carelessness and negligence, 223c

Individual responsibility for: youth must be educated in the principles of our most holy faith, 28b; men of wealth should found professorships of liberty in universities, 28d; improved by the faithful study of the scriptures, 34c; this natural freedom is not a liberty for every one to do what he pleases, 184c

LIBRARIES: large, uncommon in the New World, 435b

LIBRARY: 800 volumes sent to Yale from England began the move towards episcopacy, 165d; of Bishop Berkeley, intended for his college, left at Rhode Island, 177c

LICENTIOUSNESS: in government, not Christ's liberty, 205c; prevented by proper instruction of youth, 222b; of Catherine the Great, blended with the voluptuousness of Asiatic despotism, 277c

LICENTIOUS SPIRIT: and despotic government, 200b

LIFE: Christian, a contrast to paganism, 17a; America's life out of death at Valley Forge, 68c; preservation of, entrusted to magistrates, 208; our, should be free from the precarious will of Britain, 340c; and liberty and property, referred to in the Declaration of Rights, of the First Continental Congress, 476c

LIGHTHOUSE: at entrance of Boston Harbor, burnt by the Americans, 411c

LIMITED MONARCHY: preferred by the majority of the English nation at the time of Charles I, 267c

LINEN: American manufacture of, urged, 339d; manufactories in this country, and liberty, 340a; our climate more favorable for, than England or Ireland, 341c

LINE OF PROPERTY: boundary of Iroquois territory, fixed by Treaty of 1768, 313b

LINK: each age, in Christianity's chain, 68a; the defaulting, in the American Chain, Georgia had been, 529a

LITERACY: in New England, the highest in the world, 222c

LITERARY: pursuits of Mercy Warren, and household duties, 77a

LITERATURE: of the world, can be spared, but not the Bible, 20d; which has journeyed westward has arrived on our shores, 27a; in the era of the American settlement, God's gift to the world, 48c; love of, Mercy Warren cherished her, 77a; or learning, fostered by the first settlers of New England, 438d

LITERATURE OF THE BIBLE: displayed as fine writing, 222d; compared to pagan or secular writers, 224d; contains poetry more sublime than Homer, more correct and tender than Virgil, 224d; contains eloquence greater than Cicero and Demosthenes, 224d; a divine morality unsurpassed by Plato, 224d; contains history more majestic and spirited than Livy and Robertson, 224d; on every page the boldest metaphors, the most complete images, the liveliest descriptions, 225a; critics and their rules cannot surpass, 225b; Inspired writers manifest the presence of God, 225b; human manners exhibited as instructive and delightful, 225d; patterns of character found in Prophets, Patriarchs, Apostles, 226a; the glorious pattern of excellence, Jesus Christ, 226b; General History of, made striking by writers of Inspiration, 226b; Historical writings abound in a noble, manly eloquence, 227b; conspicuous examples of Poetry in the sacred writings, 228c; many Comparisons to be found, 229d; matchless excellence of sacred Descriptions, 230a; Prophecies always certain, their Hero, the Messiah, 230d; every Reader a candidate for immortal existence, 230d

History: something more than cold relation of distant events, 225c; use of imagination as an inlet into the Soul, 225d; characters naturally drawn, strongly marked, examples for the Legislator and Prince, 226a; confine themselves to simple narration, 226b; truths, instructive, moral and divine, 226c; exact relation of single events, example Elijah and prophets of Baal, 226d; other examples, 227a; each treated in masterly manner, 227d

Character: excellent patterns in the Prophets and Patriarchs, 226a; Joseph, an example to unwary youth, 226a; woman's beauty and virtue in Ruth and Esther, 226a; whom should every man imitate but the Apostles, the glorious pattern of excellence, Jesus Christ, 226a

Eloquence: historical writings abound in a noble, manly, 227b; Apostle Paul, a Christian orator, compared to pagan orators, pagan rules, 227c; Paul's address to Agrippa, 227d; his speech to Elymas the Sorcerer, 228a; his oration to the Athenians, 228a; his force and eloquence made Felix tremble, converted half the world, 228b

Poetry: examples of the most remarkable species, 228c; Song of Solomon, the most complete Pastoral, 228b; the 104th Pslam, most perfect example of the Ode, 228c; finest example of the Elegy, Jeremiah's Lamentations, 229a; Book of Job, finest example of a dramatic Epic poem, 229a; Prophecy gives weight and dignity to Poetry, Virgil outshown by Isaiah and John, 230c

Style: genius of the Jews different from that of the Greeks and Romans, 225a; though many illiterate, they transcended all others in style and sentiment, 225a; elevated Genius finds the shortest passage to the human soul, 225b; breathed a transporting enthusiasm into every production, 225c; writers of Inspiration gave a plain concise account of everything necessary to be known, 226c; the power of simplicity of writing finely demonstrated in Paul's Farewell to the Ephesians, 227d; a Comparison con-

verted into an exquisitely beautiful Allegory, instance of seen in the 5th chapter of Isaiah, 229d; matchless excellence of sacred descriptions, 230a; Homer compared to Habbakkuk, 230b; the advantage to every possible Reader, as compared to subjects of pagan writers, 230d

LIVY, TITUS LIVIUS, 59-17, B.C.: Roman historian, surpassed by the Bible, 224d

LOCKE, JOHN, 1632-1704: English philosopher, member of the vast Whig party, 271b; his writings and English Institutions, 290d

Christian Philosopher of the American Revolution: a writer in defense of the cause of liberty read by the Colonists, 435b; his works a source of the philosophy of government for the New England clergy, 548d; quoted by Rev. Williams on essential rights and liberties, 185a; his treatise *Of Civil Government,* referred to, 185d; quoted in artillery-election sermon on the state of nature and God-given liberty, 194a; quoted in Plymouth sermon of 1774, on the obligations of liberty, *"to spread the love of it among mankind, and defend it, against tyrants and oppressors,"* 41c; new LOCKES predicted for America in opening of a public grammar school in 1773, 231d

LOGAN, JAMES, 1674-1751: American statesman from Philadelphia, member of Royal Society of London before the American Revolution, interested in botany, 440b

LOGICAL IMMORALITY: apostles of, can lead men to worship the beast who is the adversary of the servants of the Lamb, 6c

LOIS: grandmother of Timothy, spoken of by the Apostle Paul, as a source of his faith and knowledge of the Holy Scriptures, 217c

LONDON COFFEE HOUSE: where the British celebrated their capture of Philadelphia in 1777, 57d

LONDON, ENGLAND: great joy in, at the repeal of the Stamp Act against the American Colonies, 449d

LONDON MERCHANTS: their petition in favor of the American Colonists evaded by Parliament, 480d

LONG HOUSE: a form of dwelling peculiar to the Iroquois Indian nations, 310b

LONGINUS, DIONYSIUS, CASSIUS, d. 273 A.D.: Greek Philosopher and rhetorician of the 3rd century, placed Paul's name on list with world's great orators, 227b; his observation on the epic poet and heroes, 226b

LONG ISLAND: the retreat of Washington from, and Colonel Glover and his Marblehead men, 63c

LONG PARLIAMENT, of 1640: derived its origin from the influence of Puritans, 264b; was designed to curb the power of monarchy, 264a; included moderate royalists united with friends of the people, 264b; death of the Earl of Strafford in 1641 revealed the weakness of the monarch, 264c; proceeded without control to its work of reform, 264c; became a tyrant, usurped constitutional authority, 264d; threatened overthrow of the throne and subjection of the people, 264d; its duration depended upon its own will, 265b; contest between a permanent parliament and an arbitrary king, 265b; individual selfishness at last prevailed, 265c; commons divided into Presbyterians and Independents in 1644, 265c; struggle for ascendency between Presbyterians and Independents, 266c; Presbyterians purged from Parliament by army of Independents, 267c; execution of Charles I delayed popular enfranchisements, 267c; abolished peerage, ruled by absolute power, 267d; a collective, self-constituted perpetual dictatorship, 267d; in control of the Independents, resisted by all others, 268a; failure of counterrevolution against, 268b; went from absolute monarchy to military despotism, 268c; dissolved in

1659 by Cromwell's son, Richard, 269d; is re-assembled, Charles II is restored to the throne, 270a

LORD MAYOR OF LONDON: his petition declared the Boston Port Bill "repugnant to every principle of law and justice," 461a

LORD, OUR, JESUS CHRIST:
described to his disciples the mark of their fellowship with Him and the Father in heaven, 17b; the eyes of, run to and fro in the earth, 29a; His assistance towards those whose heart is perfect towards Him, 541d

LORD'S DAY: venerated by our Pilgrim Fathers, 23d; observance of, and the preservation of our Union, 21c; and the civil government of the United States, 154c; the United States government cannot require its officers to labor on, 155d; public business cannot be transacted on, 155d; its effect on the transaction of worldly business in America, 156b; and unbelievers in America, 156d

LORD'S HOUSE: we shall meet again in, to celebrate His returning mercies, 546b

LORD'S SUPPER: administered in New England churches once a month, 94c; advocated in 1700 by Solomon Stoddard as a means of Regeneration, 98b

LOST WORLD: God's marvellous design for a, 32c

LOTTERIES: no, in the foundation of Massachusetts Colony, 44b

LOUISBURG, CANADA: capture of, and the military preparation for the American Revolution, 249d; successful expedition to, in 1745 for England, compensated to some of the colonies, 360c

LOUIS XIV, 1638: the revocation of the Edict of Nantes during reign of, drove hundreds of thousands of protestants out from their native country, 111c

LOUIS XVI, 1754-1793: had no love for the American Rebellion, 65c

LOVE: the hearty, fraternal, of the Primitive Christians, contrasted with the selfishness and distrust of the pagans, 10b; of country, not shaken at Valley Forge, 58d; of little children, shown by Christ Jesus, 216d

LOYALISTS: encouraged to pillage and plunder in South Carolina, 79c; defeat of, at Cedar Spring brought about by the courage of Jane Thomas, 80a; Governor Tryon put himself at head of in New York and New Jersey, 412b

LOYAL SUBJECTS: the Colonists were, as well as freemen who could not tamely submit, 500d

LOYALTY: and affection expressed to the king, in petitions against the Stamp Act, 362b; strong professions of to the Mother country contained in the instructions to the delegates to the First Continental Congress, 475c; of the American colonists asserted in their second petition to the king, 502d; to the king, and Provincial Union not deemed incompatible by the colonists, 532a; of the American colonists, their contributions to the King enumerated, 542b

LOYOLA, ST. IGNATIUS OF, 1491-1556: Spanish soldier and ecclesiastic, founder of Society of Jesus or Jesuits, 279b

LUCIAN: Greek satirist and wit of 2nd century, placed Christianity with fanaticism and magic, 16b; wrote life of the magician, Alexander of Abonoteichus, 13c

LUTHER, MARTIN, 1483-1546: discovered a new world in theology, 47d; principles of liberty begun in his day, further developed in America, 50a; and Calvin, believed in resistance to higher powers, only when religion was affected, 539d

LUXURY: degree of in North America, a threat to the American character, 28a; operates slavery and political death, 28a; not part of the New England colonies, 431c; one of the baneful consequences of slavery in the southern colonies, 432d

LYFORD, REV. JOHN: insidious foe of the Pilgrims, 26b

MACAULAY, CATHERINE, 1731-1791: English historian, quoted by Mercy Warren on vices of royalty, 366d

MACEDONIAN CALL, "Come over and help us" (Acts 16:9): and the planting of the Massachusetts colony, instamped in the seal of this colony, 44d

MACHIAVELLI, NOCCOLO, 1469-1527: Italian statesman and political philosopher of statecraft, studied by Governor Thomas Hutchinson, 378b; quoted by Mercy Warren on the dangers of deviation from original principles of government, 420d

MACHINE: for spinning cotton, instruction offered to spinning wheel makers by James Stewart of Virginia, 341a

MADDER: needed for American dye business, 339c; American farmers encouraged to grow, 339c; seeds and roots of from England, brought by James Stewart of Virginia, 340d

MAGAZINES: forts and arsenals, taken possession of by provincial militia after Lexington, 492d

MAGICIANS: pretended exhibition of supernatural powers, 8d; tricks exposed by Christianity, 13c

MAGISTRATES: in New Testament times: Roman, knew they had injured the liberties of Paul and Silas when they beat them and cast them into prison, 37d; Paul always submissive to, although he yielded no rights, he resigned no liberties, 38c

In England and Scotland: Presbyterians declared civil magistrate distinct from church government, 107d; arbitrary power of, limited by the Scotch General Assembly of 1649, 112b

In America: subordination to, and principles of Scripture, extremely important to our nation, 21b; needed to excel in piety and public virtue, 27c; divine right of to do wrong, supported by tories, 192b; duties of explained by New England ministers, 192d; vested with preservation of life, liberty, property of the people, 208; those who destroy life, liberty, property, to be resisted, 208; given authority by the Gospel, to be ministers for good of the subject, 519a; those who abuse their authority, not to be thought of as ministers of God, 519a

MAGNA CHARTA: of America, the Declaration of Rights, First Continental Congress, September 5, 1774, 153b; a plan like the, the Continental Congress hoped the Mother Country would propose for the colonies, 502c

"MAGNALIA CHRISTI AMERICANA": by Cotton Mather, 1072, quoted from on bishops, 109b

"MAGNETICK INFLUENCE": of the Holy Spirit in the planting of the Massachusetts Colony, 44c

MAGUS, SIMON: a magician and charm-binder of the 2nd century, 8d

MAINSPRING: of motion in the planting of the Massachusetts Colony, the Macedonian Call, Acts 16:9, 44b

MAJORITY: of both houses in parliament were against the Americans and resolved to compel them to obedience, 480d

MAKEMIE, FRANCIS, 1658?-1708: founder of Presbyterianism in America, organized first American Presbytery in 1706 in Philadelphia, 114a

MAN: his place and rank among the works of God, 31a; violated the law of his liberty at the fall, 32b; a moral being accountable to his maker, 187a; his relation to the state secured by Christianity, 17d; controlled either by God or the state, either by the Bible or by the bayonet, 20b

MANNERS: progress in and liberty, 34d; and usefulness of posterity, 214a; human, an instructive field in the literature of the Bible, 225d; gentleness of, and the humility of the Gospel, 240c; and conversation, must be formed by example and association, 241c

MARBLEHEAD, MASS.: men of, under Colonel John Glover, who manned the boats in the retreat of Washington from Long Island, 63c; people of, offer their harbor and ware-houses to Boston during the closing of their harbor under the Boston Port Act, 470b

MARCH 5, 1770: date of the Boston Massacre, details by Mercy Warren, 381c; by David Ramsey, 454d

MARCUS AURELIUS, 121-180 A.D.: Emperor of Rome when Celsus attacked Christianity, 16c

MARIA THERESA, 1717-1780: Archduchess of Austria, Queen of Hungary and Bohemia, a devotee of the church, venerated the prerogatives of aristocracy, 277d

MARION, FRANCIS, 1732?-1795: the "Swamp Fox," American Revolutionary commander, 52c; God was present in the life of, 52c

MARRIAGE: Samuel Adams writes to his future son-in-law on, 82c; a civil contract in New England churches, 95a

MARSHALL, JOHN, 1755-1835: a youth in the Third Virginia at Brandywine and Valley Forge, 64b

MARTIAL LAW: established for Massachusetts by General Gage's Proclamation of June 12, 1775, 415c; 497a

MARTIAL SPIRIT: became conspicious throughout the American Colonies, 399a; young and old fired with, the sounds of drums and fifes to be heard in all directions, 475b; pervaded all the colonies in 1775, they believed their liberties were in danger, 494c; of Israel, lost through vice and immorality, 536b; stirred up in Saul by the Spirit of the Lord, 542c

MARTIN, JOSIAH, 1737-1786: Governor of North Carolina 1771-1775, held up the supreme authority of parliament, 413c; negotiated with the Indians and encouraged insurrection of the negroes, 413d; for his own safety repaired to the king's ships, 413d

MARTYR: first, to American Freedom, James Otis, 379c

MARTYR, JUSTIN, 110-165 A.D.: witness to Christian healing, 9c; testified that Christianity is found among barbarians and Nomads, 15d

MARYLAND: one of first states for religious liberty, 50b; settled as a Catholic colony upon principles of general toleration, 110d; 159d; 437d; French Protestants settled in provinces of, 111d; large number of Scotch settled in, 113b; Dr. Blair sent as an episcopal missionary in 1685, held this office for 53 years, 159b; the established church deterred other denominations, 432b; number of grains of pure silver in local pound of, 326d; substitute for money found in tobacco as a medium of exchange, 332d; sent deputies to the Stamp Act Congress, October 1765, 449c; counties of, collected salt petre and sulphur for Philadelphia, 342a; dangers from large numbers of African slaves, 412d; Governor Sir Robert Eden obliged by Congress to quit, 414a; incapable of defence in 1777, 56b

MASON, GEORGE, 1798-1871: sagacious and learned, found by God for the new nation, 52a

MASSACHUSETTS BIBLE SOCIETY: Annual Meeting of May 28, 1849, address on the Bible, its influence upon society and civil government, by Robert C. Winthrop, 19b

MASSACHUSETTS COLONY:

Planting of: Scottow's narrative of, 44a; main spring of motion, the Macedonian call, *"Come over and help us," Acts 16:9,* 44d; Macedonian call instamped in the seal of this colony, 44d; the congregational church system was manifestly the policy of the founders, 50a; spontaneous growth of representative government, a House of Deputies appeared in 1643, 50c; established by original compact, powers of government stated by the Constitution, 208

Education in: first colony to make legislative provision for education, 438c; founded Harvard College in 1637, 439a; passed first education law in 1647 for towns to set up grammar schools, 223a

Money in: grains of pure silver in its local pound, 326d; at one time abated 25% of all taxes payable in grain to all who would advance cash, 332d; the Massachusetts Mint a great boon to the people, 333c; the famous pine tree coinage the only native colonial silver money of any importance, 333c; first paper money put out by Massachusetts in 1690, 333a; Bills of credit first authorized in Massachusetts in 1690, 438b

Manufacturing in: Massachusetts Provincial Congress Thursday, December 8, 1774, encouraged agriculture, manufactures, economy, so as to render the state independent of every other state, 338d; resolves of the Continental Congress regarding American Manufacture carried out voluntarily by the colonies, 340a; Massachusetts House of Representatives, August 24, 1775, heard report of Committee appointed to put in practice the making of salt petre, 344a

Government in:

MASSACHUSETTS GENERAL ASSEMBLY: instructions from constituents against the Stamp Act, 361c; called for a Stamp Act Congress of all the colonies, 449b; sent deputies to Stamp Act Congress meeting in New York, October, 7, 1765, 362c; 449c; agreed on bill for compensation to sufferers of Stamp Act crisis, 363c; granted general pardon to all offenders in late tumults, king disallowed the act, 363d; promoted circular letter to other provincial assemblies, 451a; text of circular letter, 369d; Hillsborough called on Mass. Assembly to rescind proceedings on Revenue Acts of 1767, 451a; dissolved after vote not to rescind, 370d; 451b; resolved an armed force in realm unconstitutional, 376d; uneasy presence of royal troops resulted in Boston Massacre, March 5, 1770, 381c; 454d; called upon Hutchinson to relinquish unconstitutional stipend, accept free gifts of the general assembly, 379a; judges and governor made independent of colony, provision made for paying their salaries by the crown, 455b; requested king to impeach both Hutchinson and Oliver, 387a; 455c; executive government taken out of the hands of the people by the Mass. Government Act, 461c; mutilation of Mass. Charter convinced other colonies of the common cause of Massachusetts, 462b; Governor Gage erased names chosen by the people, 391d; directed to meet in Salem, 392a; chose delegates for the Continental Congress, 393a; 470c; Massachusetts Government Act caused the Massachusetts General Assembly to resolve itself into the Massachusetts Provincial Congress and to adjourn to Concord, 472d

MASSACHUSETTS PROVINCIAL CONGRESS: chose John Hancock president, 472d; appointed committees of safety, of supplies, 400c; 473a; formed the minute men for the defence of the province, 473a; resolved to get in readiness twenty thousand men, 473b; requested help of neighboring colonies, 473b; voted to raise an army after Lexington, 493a; drew up rules and orders for the army, 409c; sent congratulatory address to Washington on his appointment to the chief command, 421d; circular letter sent to clergy for assistance in resisting slavery, 473b; British ministry refused to repeal the fatal rock of altering the laws and charter of Massachusetts, 487d

"Phaenomenon of mankind": Proclamation of January 23, 1776 by the General Court of Massachusetts testifying to the Colony of Massachusetts subsisting in decency and order for more than a year with a

the American colonists of, 494c; encouraged by artillery company, 204a; arrangements of the colonists for defence turned against the parent state, 492d

Military Discipline: problems of introducing in the Continental Army, 505b; experience of Baron von Steuben made most valuable contribution in, 65a; distinctions of rank present in European armies, absent in new world, 494a

Military Preparation: of the leaders of the American Revolution, 249d; of George Washington, 421c; 503d; school of Valley Forge under von Steuben, 65a

Military Profession: not condemned by John Baptist, 197d; Cornelius not directed to quit, 198b; not inconsistent with Christianity, 198b

MILITIA: equal veteran troops in determination, 201d; fights in defence of their lives, liberty, property, 201d; should not be made an instrument of tyranny, 201d; subject to discipline and order, 201d; considered a band of rustics by British, 399a; learn of Gage's plan to destroy stores at Concord, 491d; carried on all the military regulations of the Americans, 492d; conduct of at Bunker's Hill, caused neglect of an army, 499b; lost much of its first ardor in the progress of hostilities, 499b

MILLS: for making gun powder, recommended by the Continental Congress, 343d

MILTON, JOHN, 1608-1674: English poet, in the era of the American Settlement, 48c; men had a natural right to read in the State of Nature, 186c; his statement on militia and a free nation, 201d; on loss of liberty and virtue, 203b; gained from Isaiah first thoughts of *Paradise Lost,* 230a; new MILTONS predicted for America, 231a; ranged himself on the side of the Independents, 266a; his scheme of government for England, not practicable, 261c; the stately representative, of English republicanism, 290c

MIND: and spirit, fashioned by mothers, 224a

MINDS: men's, agitated by wild communistic dreams, 3b; of men, and Christ's miracles, 10a; great, of early leaders of the American Revolution, 60b

MINISTER: excellent, John Robinson, of our Pilgrim Fathers, 24a; of parish, supplied Mercy Warren with books, 76d; a, of the devil, father of falsehood, confusion, rebellion, 203d

MINISTERIAL: majority in parliament, precipitated nation into war, 463d

MINISTERS: *see also* CLERGY, NEW ENGLAND; duty of, to explain Scriptures, duty of people to search Scriptures, 187d; of New England, attached to principles of liberty, 191d; explained duties of magistrates and rulers, 192d; gave sanction of religion to cause of freedom, 193c

Of Massachusetts: to serve as chaplains in the army, 206d; role of, during year of suspension of civil government, their virtuous labors, public ministry, private example, commended in the Proclamation of Jan. 23, 1776 by the General Court of Massachusetts, 209

Of Connecticut: urged by General Assembly to call the people to repentence and prayer for deliverance, 207b; assistance of, requested by legislature, 210a

MINISTRY: a seminary for training Indians for, proposed in Iroquois Memorial, 319b

MINORITY: in parliament, contended for removal of tea tax, 456c; party in parliament, opposed the Intolerable Acts, 462c; a respectable, in parliament, in favor of the American Colonies, 480d

MINT: for silver coins, attempts to set up in Colonies, 333c

MINUTE MEN: of Lexington, and Bunker Hill, pre-

pared by a superintending Providence, 249d; courage of, compared to soldiers of Alexander or Caesar, 249d; from every town, youth trained in military art, 399a; formed by the Massachusetts Provincial Congress, 473a; of *Lexington:* ordered by Major Pitcairn to throw down their arms, 491d; *of Concord:* ordered not to give first fire, that they might not be the aggressors, 492a; did great execution by a scattering fire against retreating British troops, 492b

MIRACLES: of Christ, from the Godhead dwelling in him, 10a

MISERIES: of mankind, come from neglecting precepts of the Bible, 256b

MISERY: of the human race, from disobedience of unfallen man, 31d; spread, by submission to tyrants, 203a

MISREPRESENTATIONS: of the American contest, 251d

MITCHELL, JOHN, d. 1768: physician, botanist, cartographer, member Royal Society of London, 440b

MITCHELL, JONATHAN, 1624-1668: American Congregational clergyman, one author of *Elijah's Mantle,* reprinted by the Colonies, 252d

MITE: woman's, important during the American Revolution, 74c

MOB: Washington commanded a disorganized, at the beginning of the American Revolution, 60d

MODEL: for a church of Christ, laid down by Him in His word, 188d

MOHAMMEDANS: should they be required to respect the Christian Sabbath in America, 154c

MOHAWKS: one of the Iroquois Nations, 310d; geographical bounds between the Mohawks and Hudson Rivers, 310d; Joseph Brant recognized by William Johnson as the War Chief of the, 313d; persuaded by Joseph Brant to join the king's forces in the American Revolution, 314d; gained ascendancy over other tribes in bravery, 316a; brought to Christianity by the Society for the Propagation of the Gospel, 316a; bravest warriors perished in our victories as our allies, 316a; civilized by Christianity, 317d; benefits of Christianity for, vices of civilization, 318a; progress towards civilized life through religion, 320b; incited by Guy Johnson against the American Colonists, 541d

MOLIERE, JEAN BAPTISTE, 1622-1673: French actor and playwright, in the era of the American Settlement, 48c

MOLYNEUX, WILLIAM, 1656-1698: Irish Protestant patriot, philosopher, friend of Locke, 299c; asserted in the press that Ireland was not bound by acts of a legislative body in which it was not represented, 299d

MONARCH: who deprives the people of their liberties, must not expect approbation of God, 514a

MONARCHIC: aristocratic and democratic forms of government, both for church and state, discussed by John Wise in his treatise, 100c

MONARCHY: and episcopacy, suited to each other, stated Dr. Chandler, 145c; the American Revolution a war of principle between, and faith in the capacity of man for self-government, 253a; armies of, superior in experience and numbers, 253b

MONEY: Colonists forbidden to coin, 322c; and money units, differed for each colony, 326a; differences in standards of value of the different colonies, a cause of inconvenience, 327a; transactions, between colonies, difficult and annoying, 327b; problems of colonial times, 327c; rules for translating from one colony to another contained in an English publication in 1765, 327c; exclusive right of granting, the palladium of the people's liberty, 445b; American Colonies possessed no, to fight the American Revolution, 496a

"MONITOR'S LETTERS, THE": by Dr. Arthur Lee in 1769, discussed the great question of American taxation, 440a

MONOPOLY: of trade, Great Britain's use of colonies, 441d; of colonial trade and economic slavery, 453d

MONROE, JAMES, 1758-1831: a boy of twenty at Valley Forge, 64a

MONTESQUIEU, CHARLES DE SECONDAT, 1689-1755: French lawyer, man of letters, and political philosopher, praised England's constitutional government, 272d; discovered the *"title deeds of humanity"* in Christianity, 281d; sketched a government with liberty as its end, 284b

MORAL: antagonisms, which produced the American Revolution, 253b; deterioration, precursor of political downfall, 20c; diseases, diagnosed by Synod of 1679 of New England, 98d; dispositions, of young, dependent upon parental education, 214a; effect, of French Alliance, its greatest asset, 65d; faculties, of men and childhood education, 85b; law of Israel, centered in the Ten Commandments, 515b; law, necessity of obedience to, by civil governments, 155a; lessons, to be learned from the American Revolution, 254c; liberty, provided us by the religion of God and civil liberty, 39d; liberty, and self-government, connected, 40a; life, not merely a, the Gospel asks, 4d; obligation, of a nation, cannot be set aside, 155a; order, of the Universe established by the Creator, 21b; principles of Scriptures, ought to form the basis of our civil constitutions and laws, 256b; restraint, in society, less reliance on public law or physical force, 20b; Ruler, is the Creator of the universe and the Judge of man, 516c

MORALITY: cannot exist without religion, 158a; best rules of, found in Bible, 255d

MORGAN, DANIEL, 1736-1802: American Revolutionary soldier, leader of famed Rifle Company, 543b; July 20, 1775 Fast Day Sermon, preached before his rifle company at Yorktown, 543b

MORGAN, JOHN, 1735-1789: American physician, founded Medical College of University of Pennsylvania, member of Royal Society of London, 440b

MORRIS, ROBERT, 1734-1806: American financier and statesman, found by God for the new nation, 52a

MORTALITY: incredible, at Valley Forge, 62b

MORTGAGE: should one generation, the privileges of another, 246d

MORTON, NATHANIEL, 1613-1685: nephew of William Bradford, Plymouth historian, member of Royal Society of London, 440b

MOSAIC DISPENSATION: reenacted the observance of the Sabbath, 154b

MOSAIC LAW: a spirit of bondage unto fear, whereas the Gospel dispensation, breathes a spirit of confidence, 516b

MOSES: and divine injunctions for parental education, 217a; life and laws of, an example to the Legislator, 226a; his farewell sermon, an example of the manly eloquence of the Bible, 227b; the servant of God, often engaged in bloody battles, 538a; his defensive war against Sihon, king of the Amorites, 538b; we had our, in our famous founders, 45a

MOTHER: of Peyton Randolph, her influence upon him, 74b; of Thomas Jefferson, her influence upon him, 74b; of George Washington, her influence upon him, 74b; of Lord Bacon, her influence upon him, 74b; Mercy Warren writes of the sacred trust given to a, by Providence, 85a; should not cross father's efforts to teach habits of submission, 234c

MOTHER COUNTRY: ties to, weakened first in New England, 434d; authorized and controlled the trade of the American colonies, 443d; retained the tax on tea as Americans denied the legality of taxing them,

456c; wished for absolute submission to her authority, 503b

MOTHERS: debt to, of great men, 74a; training of, produce great men, 74b; arduous work of, to impress the youthful mind, 84d; of a nation, work on immortal beings, 223d; impress upon children exercise of the franchise, 224c; influence of, upon a free republic, 224c

MOTTO: for Christian warfare, Matthew 12:30 *"He that is not with me is against me,"* 4d; of worldliness, *"Might is right,"* 6c; of faith *"Right is might,"* 6c; of American states *"E Pluribus Unum,"* 250c; on most colonial money *"To counterfeit is death,"* 337c

MOUNT JOY: at Valley Forge, a wilderness wrapped in forest, 59b; location of redoubt on, 59d

MOUNT VERNON: Martha Washington returned to, during campaigns, 75c; George Washington's industry and success in arts of peaceful life at, 504a

MUHLENBERG, HENRY MELCHIOR, 1711-1787: founder of Lutheranism in America, his observation of the Christian testimony of George Washington, 68c

MUHLENBERG, JOHN PETER GABRIEL, 1746-1847: son of Henry Melchior, Virginia clergyman, turned brigadier general, 63d

MUSKETS: discharged, used as clubs by provincials on Bunker's Hill, 498a

MUTILATED MONEY: played havoc with colonial trade, 337b

MUTUAL DEFENCE: some part of natural liberty is given up for, 185d

MYSTERIOUS: work of Providence, in founding New England, 45b

N

NAILS: American manufacture of, encouraged by the Provincial Congress of Massachusetts, December 8, 1774, 339a

NAKEDNESS: of soldiers at Valley Forge, hundreds of men unfit for duty only for want of clothes and shoes, 61d

NAPOLEON I, BONAPARTE, 1769-1821: Military commander, Emperor of the French, asked Madame de Stael in what manner he could best promote the happiness of France, 223d

"NARRATIVE OF THE MISERIES OF NEW-ENGLAND": by Increase Mather; was reprinted during arbitrary government of Sir Edmund Andros, 252d

NASSAU HALL: first name of the college in New Jersey, commemorative of King William, Prince of Orange and Nassau, 439c

NATION: American, given us by our founders to preserve, 67d; every, has to survive misrule and mischief, 54b; every, should give due attention to this important lesson, Proverbs 14:34 *"Righteousness exalteth a nation: but sin is a reproach to any people,"* 545b; importance to our, of the authority of Scripture, 21a; magnitude of a, English Colonies nearly advanced to, under their provincial constitutions, 437b; mothers of a, fashion character, 223d; not long happy, when it becomes a voluntary slave to sin, 536b; the more thoroughly it deals with its history, the more will it recognize and own an overruling Providence therein, 46b

NATIONAL: existence, Providential Springs of our, 49a; faith, of the Roman Empire, polytheism, 12c; freedom, our, indebted to women, 74a; life, our, the Hand of God in the development of, 49a; religion, Christianity not a, 12c; character, and national manners, John Witherspoon on, 239d; character, diversities of, merged into American citizens, 113c; character, represents a nation and its religious base, 154b; church, not acceptable to the American Col-

gress of Georgia, 524b; local committees appointed in Georgia to deal with violators of, 525b; Georgia resolved not to trade with colonies who should violate the Association for, 525c

NON-RESISTANCE: and passive obedience, unlike spirit and temper of Christianity, 518b; Scripture texts thought to enjoin, 538d; Scripture text used to enforce doctrine of, 539c

NORFOLK, VIRGINIA: burning of, completed disgraceful campaign by Lord Dunmore, 413c

NORTH, FREDERICK, 1732-1792: 2nd Earl of Guilford, statesman, known as Lord North, Member of King's Council when order was passed, October 19, 1774, to prohibit exportation of arms and ammunition to America, 322d; ushered into the House of Commons the Boston Port Bill and the bill for regulating the government of Massachusetts, 389a; proposed bill to restrain trade of New England colonies, 484d; endeavored to punish New England states by extension of penal acts, 489b; refused representation of New York Assembly, 488c; his scheme of American Revenue and conciliation, 486a; objected to on principle of parliament's right of taxation, 486b; parliamentary supremacy, not American Revenue the real issue, 486b; his scheme did not produce disunion of colonies, but helped unite them, 486d

NORTH AMERICA: settlement of, and the King James Bible, 20a; British Colonies in, and the progress of the Gospel, 27a

NORTH CAROLINA: emigrations of Scotch and Irish into, 113a; ahead of any colony in opposition to British authorities, 152c; issued the *Mecklenburg Declaration* more than a year before Congress issued the *Declaration of Independence*, 152d; prevented by their governor from representation at the Stamp Act Congress, 449c; exempted from restraint of trade bill, 488a; spurned the proffered favor and submitted to the restraints imposed on their neighbors, 488b; Josiah Martin, governor of 1771-1775, upheld the supreme authority of parliament, 413c; number of grains of pure silver in local pound of, 326d; money units rated in terms of the Spanish Dollar, 327a; recommended by the Continental Congress to collect salt petre and sulphur to manufacture into gun powder, 342c; patriotism and courage of an unknown woman in, 80a

NORTON, JOHN, 1606-1663: Puritan preacher, minister of the church at Ipswitch, Massachusetts, active in Cambridge Synod of 1646, 93a; his sermon on Moses and Aaron promoted unity in the churches, 93a; pastor First Church Boston, 97c

NURSERY: picture for, *Washington at Prayer*, x, of heroes, in British America, 204c; America a, of science and truth, 231d

O

OAKES, URIAN, 1631-1681: New England clergyman, president of Harvard, 98c; moderator of Synod of 1679, 98c

"OATH OF A FREE MAN": and the spirit of the Colonists in 1776, 253a; earliest printed document in America, 253a

"OATH OF ALLEGIANCE TO THE UNITED STATES": taken by Bishop White of the American Episcopal Church after July 4, 1776, 149b

OBEDIENCE: to God, removes fear and lawlessness, 17d; to tyrants would condemn action of Biblical characters, 539c

OBLIGATION: to submit to civil government, and natural liberty, 186d; of every one, to search the Scriptures for the will of God, 187a; of children and youth to receive parental instruction, 220a

OBSTACLES: became the means of advancing Christianity, 7d; fail to hinder progress of Christianity, 15c

OCCUM, SAMSON, 1723-1792: educated Indian preacher, influenced the Indians to be friendly to the Americans, 313d

ODES: examples of, found amongst the Psalms, 228d

"OF CIVIL GOVERNMENT": John Locke's treatise on government, 185d

OFFICERS: of government, what our country needs in its leaders, 54a; write of the patience and fidelity of soldiers at Valley Forge, 62c; names of, at Valley Forge, 63a; of New England church, duties designated, 94a; of American Colonial Army, called because of their excellence as patriots, men to be relied on, 253d

OHIO VALLEY: subject of settlement and boundary dispute since 1763, 306d; George Washington, Commander-in-Chief of forces in Virginia against incursions of French and Indians active in, 504a

OLD SOUTH CHURCH, BOSTON: formed by a secession of members from First Church in Boston, 97d; meeting in, December 16, 1773, to decide action on the Tea Ships in Boston Harbor, 385b

OLD TESTAMENT: expressive language of, used by American Settlers, 48d; during the dispensation of, the law was a schoolmaster to bring us to CHRIST, 515b; furnished the clergy with many illustrations of government, 548b

OLIVE BRANCH: Americans hoped the British Sovereign would hold out, with redress of grievances, 414d

OLIVER, ANDREW, 1706-1774: Secretary of the Province of Massachusetts, in opposition to the patriotic party, 374d; his treasonable letters to undercut American non-importation efforts, 374d; his letter to British ministry to remove American leaders, 379c; his letters exposed by Franklin, 455c; as Lieutenant-Governor, the Massachusetts General Assembly requested his removal from the colony, 387a; obliged by the people to resign, 472a

OLIVER, PETER, 1713-1791: brother of Andrew, Chief Justice of Massachusetts Province, his lack of qualifications, 388d; impeached by the assembly, 455b; attempted to open the superior court regardless of the impeachment that lay against him, 401a

OLYMPIAS, d. 316 B.C.: the mother of Alexander the Great, her influence upon her son, 74c

OMNIPOTENCE: of parliament, and illegality of taxation, 447b

OMNIPOTENT WISDOM: historian of the American Revolution must rely upon, 255c

OPEN-AIR PREACHING: of George Whitefield, in Philadelphia, 1739, when pulpits were closed against him, 122d

OPPRESSION: of man, seen as an enemy to civil and religious liberty, 33a; and its effects upon mankind, 34a; and tyranny, began to work early in family of Cain, 35b; Colonial, commenced in 1764, 442b

OPPRESSORS: eventually reap destruction, 203c

OPULENCE: enervating of Europe, had not yet reached the colonists, 436c

ORATION: celebrating the Centennial Anniversary of Valley Forge, June 19, 1878, 55a

ORATORS: many of best in England, came to defence of America, 383b

ORATORY: quality and scope of, in America, 55b; of Apostle Paul, surpassed Cicero, Demosthenes, Eschines, 227c

ORIGEN, ADAMANTIUS, 185?-254 A.D.: Christian writer and teacher of Alexandria, his defence against Celsus, 9d; recorded trials of Primitive Christian Church, 15b

OTIS, JAMES, 1725-1783: American Revolutionary statesman, brother of Mercy Warren, impassioned defender of popular rights, 52a; found by God for the new nation, 52a; his tender relationship to his sister, 77a; efficient defender of natural rights of mankind, 249d; a religious adherence to the rights of his country, 362c; proposed a Stamp Act Congress, 362c; first champion of American Freedom, 367d; author of first tract while Stamp Act hung suspended, *Rights of the British Colonies Asserted and Proved*, 367d; his arguments against the Writs of Assistance, 368a; argued from principle in favor of *British Liberty*, 368a; resigned from his office of judge advocate, 368a; on committee to impeach Governor Bernard, 371d; the attempted assassination of, made him the first martyr to American Freedom, 379c; the consequences of the attack, worse than death, 380b; forgave the murderous band of his attackers, 380c; lived to see the Independence of America, 380c; his soul set free by flash of lightning, 380c; tributes to, after his death, 380d

OUTWARD: life of Primitive Christians, 8a; force, of no effect against inward power of divine truth, 10c; Christianity working, from within, 15d

OVERRULING: of God in the affairs of men, 47a

P

PACIFISM: inconsistent with the Christian principle of self-defence, 199a

PAGANISM: victory of Christ over, seen in the Book of Revelation, 3b; fall of, included in visions of Revelation, 3d; stern repulsion of, by Primitive Christians, 8b; vices of, contrasted with Christian virtues, 10b; Christianity's contrast with, seen in the life of the individual, 17a; Plymouth church erected on the ruins of, 30b

PAGANS: methods used to expel demoniacal powers, 9b; were struck by the *Christian Mark* of fellowship and love, 17b; cowardly selfishness of, in times of public calamity, and the self-sacrificing brotherly love of the Christians, 17c

PAINE, ROBERT TREAT, 1731-1814: American jurist, member of the Continental Congress, 1774-1778, on committee to devise means for manufacture of salt petre, 342c

PAINE, THOMAS, 1737-1809: Political pamphleteer, letters to Franklin, written with the sound of the cannon as the British Army approached Philadelphia, 56c; recorded the building of huts by the American Army at Valley Forge, 59d

PALLADIUM OF LIBERTY: the exclusive right of the people to the disposal of their property, 445b

PANEGYRIC: upon wisdom, found in Job, unequalled by any poet, 229b

PAOLI, PA.: Anthony Wayne's brigade massacred at, September 24, 1777, 57a

PAPER: manufacture of, from linen, before discovery of America, made books available to many, 47c; American manufacture of, encouraged by the Massachusetts Provincial Congress in 1774, 339b

PAPER MONEY: was the largest currency of the American colonies, issued by each of the colonies, later by the Continental Congress, 333a; 438c; colonists long experience with, because of a deficiency of gold and silver, 438c; first issued by Massachusetts in 1690, other colonies followed, 333a; Benjamin Franklin wrote a convincing pamphlet on, 333c; most, bore the device "*To counterfeit is death*," 337c; regulations adopted by the British against Colonial paper money in 1764, 443b; emissions made on faith in the people, later consequences of, 504c; for upwards of two years, produced more advantage to the colonies than Spain derived from her superabounding

gold and silver, 496c; in Virginia we see the effects of, on the money of account, 338a; Virginia tried to legalize depreciated paper money, 338c; paper currency issued by the Continental Congress obeyed natural rather than artificial laws and fell 400%, 56b

PAPIST: in America, admitted to equal rights and privileges, 157a; if despotism is bad in a, it cannot be good in a protestant, 540a

"PARADISE LOST": by John Milton; quoted on the loss of liberty, virtue and religion, 203b

PARDON: promised by General Gage after the Battle of Lexington, to all who would lay down arms, except Samuel Adams and John Hancock, 497a

PARENTS:

Parental Affection: should be purified by principles and precepts of religion, 232c

Parental Authority: and love, and the influence of pious example, 216b; parents have rule and jurisdiction over their children, 184b; should establish absolute authority early, 233c; ease of preserving authority when once established, 233d; indulgent parents, correct children more frequently and more severely, 233d; parents who have no, are a disgusting sight, 234a; diversity in the temper and disposition of children, require prudence and resolution of parents, 235a; no opposition between parental tenderness and, 236a; directed to the glory of God and the salvation of their children, 236c; increased, when it is in obedience to God, 236d

Parental Conduct: parents should be watchful of, 235d; efforts to conceal their character, exposed to their children, 240a; respectable conduct ought to be maintained as a proof of your own integrity, 244c

Parental Education: principles and practice of God's testimonies to posterity, 214a; instruction of posterity in Word of God, 214d; foundations laid for redemption, 215a; untaught children can despise religious knowledge, 215a; and reciprocal affections between parents and children, 215c; original sin, not an argument against, 215c; and injunction from Scriptures to instruct children, 215d; importance of, not counteracted by freedom of divine grace, 216a; a course of faithful and well directed instructions, 216b; of Noah, and his sons Ham and Shem, 217b; received by Abram, improved with his children, 217b; influence of, upon the laws, politics, religion of our country, 217d; should teach their children *Washington at Prayer*, x; particulars of, given to parents by minister, Levi Hart, 218c; greatest joy as Christians in leading children to God, 219a; neglect of, brings age of degeneracy, 219b; Solomon's instruction to his children, 219d; and obligation of children and youth to receive, 220a; marked, in future character of Timothy, 220d; evident in the life of the blessed Jesus, 220d

Founding Generation on Parental Education: Mercy Warren, the attention of a devoted mother to her children, 77a; she considered it "*the sacred trust by Providence delivered on every mother*," 85a; Samuel Adams to his daughter Hannah, on obedience to God and the purchase of our redemption by his Son, 82b; Samuel Adams to his future son-in-law on the Christian home, 82d; Benjamin Franklin on the importance "*to form and train up youth in wisdom and virtue*," 221b; Daniel Webster on the importance of mothers in moulding and fashioning the youth of a nation, 223d; Noah Webster, his advice to the young on the Scriptures as the source for instruction "*in social, religious, and civil duties*," 256d

Parental Example: should be a speaking lesson to his children, 243b; all meannesses, whether of sentiment, conversation, dress, manners, or employment, are carefully to be avoided, 244d

Parental Fidelity: called for by inspired writer of the 78th Psalm, 213b; dangers of neglect of religious education, 219b; time is short for, 220a

Parental Indulgence: restrained by precepts of religion, 232d

Parental Language: sudden anger, loud clamorous scolding, are at once contrary to piety and dignity, 244d

Parental Piety: happy parents, who brought their children to Christ for His blessing, 216d; exhorted to acquaint themselves with God first, 218c; consistency of precept and practice in religion, 218d; duty to exemplify Christianity in domestic felicity, 218d; let this divine religion be exemplified in your profession and lives, 218d; greatest joy of, to hear their children walk in truth, 219a; is despised by children and youth, consequences, 220b; the blessed Jesus subject to his parents, 220d; parents should be more displeased at sin than folly, 236d

PARKER, JOHN, 1729-1775: American Revolutionary patriot, commanded a company of militia at Lexington, April 19, 1775, ordered them to appear at the beat of drum on the parade at Lexington, 406d; 491d

PARLIAMENT:

In English History: Charles I, his belief in unlimited right of king, 263b; resolved to govern without parliament, 263d; his contest with the despotism of the Long Parliament, 264a; civil war between the Presbyterians and Independents, 265b; triumph of Independents under Cromwell, 266a; execution of Charles I, 267c; the counter revolution, sovereignty from king to parliament, from parliament to the commons, from the commons to the army, from the army to its commander, Cromwell, 268d; death of Cromwell, all classes demand restoration of monarchy, 269d; Long Parliament dissolved after 20-year standing, 270a; Charles II, and James II restored the prerogative of monarchy, 270c; the rise of Whigs and Tories for the defense of privilege, 271a; James II declaration of indulgence to suspend all laws against Roman Catholics and Dissenters alarmed the Church of England, 271d; William of Orange invited to save the English church and take throne of England, 272a; James' daughter Mary ascended throne, 272a; this Revolution of 1688 restored to England her free legislature, she became the star of constitutional government, 272d; Revolution of 1688 recovered for Parliament the sole right of taxing England, 272d;

In the American colonies: the Revolution of 1688 permitted the resumption of legislative rights by every colony curtailed under the Stuarts, 272d; as the British Parliament claimed the sole right of taxing England, the analogous right was reclaimed by the legislatures of America, 273a

Mercy Warren traces the *"darling point of an American Revenue":* the contest between the American Colonies and Parliament over taxation without representation, 360c; it was deemed essential to the liberties of Englishmen, that no grants of monies be made without consent of the people by their representatives, 360b

Encroachments by Parliament upon the Colonies: the Stamp Act, the first innovation for raising a revenue for the Crown, 360d; Stamp Act repealed, 363a; but the darling point of an American Revenue not relinquished by the ministry, 365c; imperceptible taxes of the Townshend bills, 367b; crown officers made independent of the representative body, 367c; suspension of all powers of legislation in New York, 368d; Parliament's Revenue Acts seen as infringe-

ments of constitutional rights, 370b; Bernard's unconstitutional actions, a standing army brought to Boston, 374a; Hutchinson convicted as the Grand Incendiary in his abridgement of English liberties, 383a; Hutchinson continued to urge taxation without representation as a parliamentary right, 387b; Lord North's bills, for closing port of Boston, for regulating the government of Massachusetts, 389a; General Gage appointed governor of Massachusetts, 390d; English Parliament divided on treatment of American colonies, 403d; General Gage proclaimed martial law, 415c; conduct of British administration and its deviation from first principles of government caused change in attitude of colonists, 421a

Principles of the Constitutional Debate with Parliament: Plymouth Town Meeting, set forth the spirit of the Pilgrim principles of liberty and property, 361d; James Otis, with energy and strength of argument, opposed in writing the Writs of Assistance, 367d; he argued from principle and in favor of *British liberty*, 368a; Massachusetts Circular Letter of February 1768, a review of the difficulties they faced and the steps taken, their determination to continue a free but loyal people, 369b

Constitutional Redress Sought by Colonies: Stamp Act Congress at New York, October 7, 1765, to justify their claims to the rights of Englishmen, 362c; all colonies petitioned against any American taxation, 368b; Massachusetts Circular Letter began to build continental union, 369c; all the American continent in combination against further importations from England, 374c; Bostonians dump tea in harbor, people ready to make compensation for damages when unconstitutional duty removed, 385d; committees of correspondence cement the union of the colonies in principle and purpose, 386a; Boston Port Bill went into effect with prayer and fasting in the colonies, and steps for a continental union, 392c

1st Continental Congress, September 5, 1774: met at Philadelphia, delegates from all colonies except Georgia, 396b; their first wish reconciliation on terms of reciprocity, justice, honor, 396b; agreed on a declaration of rights and bound themselves to suspend all intercourse with Great Britain, 397a; carefully avoid beginning hostilities, 401d; the action at Lexington compelled the colonists to resort to the sword against the mighty power of Britain, 409a; Georgia acknowledged themselves the last link in the American Chain, approved action of 1st Continental Congress, chose delegates for the 2nd Continental Congress, 414b

David Ramsay traces *"the whole ground of the American Controversy,"* 427a

English Colonies in relation to Parliament: Colonial Charters a voluntary compact with their sovereign, not an obligation of obedience to a parliament in which they were unrepresented, 429b; 12 of the 13 colonies settled at no expense to British government, 429d; local assemblies in same relation as Parliament stood to the people in England, 430b; full liberty to govern themselves during first 150 years, 430c; devoted to English ideas, and principles of liberty, 434a; looked up to Heaven as the source of their rights, 435d; provincial constitutions had sole direction of the internal government of the colonies, 437a

Colonial Oppression Commenced: first act of revenue, 1764, unique on parliamentary statute book, 443a; a dangerous innovation, direct internal taxes laid by parliament, 443d; Stamp Act not repealed on American principles, 450a; Declaratory Act, more hostile to American rights than Stamp Act, 450b; Townshend Bill established a dangerous precedent,

the present dangerous crisis of affairs, 544c

PEACEABLE: demeanor of Boston Citizens with arrival of King's Troops, 373d; measures of the First Continental Congress, 477b

PEACE OF PARIS, 1763: reduced Indian massacres in the New World for about twelve years, 441b; and British national debt, 444d

PEMBERTON, EBENEZER, 1704-1779: Boston divine, took popular side in the American Revolution, 192d

PENAL ACTS OF 1774: extended to include more New England states than Massachusetts, 489b; acted in favor of union of the colonists, 489b

PENN, RICHARD, d. England 1811: grandson of William, governor of Pennsylvania 1771-73; chosen to carry petition of Continental Congress to king, 421b; presented the American petition to king, September 1, 1775, 502c

PENN, WILLIAM, 1644-1718: Founder of Pennsylvania, 231d; as a Quaker championed for religious toleration, 271d; advocated views of the third party in England, 271b; had unusually correct ideas of religious liberty, 437d

PENNSYLVANIA: *see also* PHILADELPHIA; *Settlement of:* first settled by Quakers, 431d; one of first civil communities that ever incorporated religious liberty into its original constitution, 50b; perfect liberty of conscience in, 432a; its progressive improvement and increase of trade, 432b

Character of settlers: Quaker character of simplicity, industry, frugality contributed much to flourishing of province, 432a; German settlers, their character, 432a; by 1772, one third of population German, 111b; Welsh settled on left bank of Schuylkill, 111c; French Protestants settled in provinces of, 111d; largest emigrations of Scotch and Irish came to, 113a

In the American Revolution: peculiar difficulties to struggle with, most Quakers opposed to the American cause, 412d; sent deputies to the Stamp Act Congress in 1765, 449c; Mr. John Dickinson of Pennsylvania, presented series of letters signed A Farmer, proving the extreme danger which threatened the liberties of America, 450d; patriot's moderation in, saw the common cause of Boston, 466d; general assembly of inhabitants of, adopted resolutions against the Boston Port Bill, June 18, 1774, 467a; thus, without tumult or divided counsels, the whole province of, brought into the opposition, 467c; delegates to the Continental Congress given instructions most precise, 475d; Assembly of Pennsylvania, though composed of a majority of Quakers, was first legal body of representatives that ratified unanimously the acts of the general congress, 478a; appointed members for the Second Continental Congress, 478a; the Continental Congress recommended the collection of salt petre and sulphur for the manufacture of gun powder for the use of the continent, 342a; Franklin's pamphlet on paper money turned resistance to paper money, 333c

PENNSYLVANIANS: patriotism and courage of Lydia Darrah saved Washington's army at Whitemarsh, 77c; served at Valley Forge under Conway, 63b; and Anthony Wayne, "The Mad," one of the most brilliant soldiers of the Revolution, 63c

PEOPLE: privileges of, in America, 27a; God's, fed and led in the American wilderness, 45a; right of, to make the laws that govern them, 185b; are the fountain of civil power, 185b; educated by ministers in principles of polity, 192a; capacity of, to defend themselves against encroachments, 199d; overtaxed, diminish defensive power of the state, 200c; urged to skill in arms by clergy, 200d; power of civil government resides in, 208; educated in principles

of the American Revolution, 249d; assent of, necessary to all acts of legislation in colonies, 438a; share of, in government constituted superiority of British Constitution, 445a; opposition to tea tax on purest principles of patriotism, 458b; powers of government given to, in colonial charters, 461a; were brought into the dispute with Great Britain by the Boston Tea Party, 464b; rights of the, set forth by the 1st Continental Congress, 476c; cheerfully obeyed recommendations of 1st Continental Congress, 477d

PEOPLE OF FRANCE: stirred by the American Revolution, 65c

PEOPLE OF GREAT BRITAIN: revolted against the claims of the American people, 445c; were educated in habits of submission to parliamentary taxation, 445c

PEOPLE OF MASSACHUSETTS: body of, animated as with one soul, 44d; distresses of, relieved by liberal collections made throughout the colonies, 478b; encouraged to perseverance by the Continental Congress, 472a; enjoined to religious lives, 209; fired with martial spirit of preparation, 475b; knew no court independent of ancient charter, 471d; obliged Oliver and counsellors to resign, 472a; possessed a high regard for liberty, 470d; religion and morality enabled them to subsist without civil government, for more than twelve months, 419d; 475a

PEOPLE OF PENNSYLVANIA: unanimous in that fundamental principle of the American controversy *"that the parliament of Great Britain had no right to tax them,"* 467c; anxiety of people of Philadelphia in 1777, awaiting the entry of the British Army, 56c

PEOPLE OF RHODE ISLAND: seized military stores from the public battery, December 13, 1774, 473c

PERCY, HUGH, DUKE OF NORTHUMBERLAND, 1742-1817: led the reinforcements sent to Lexington by Gage, 408a; near the fields of Menotomy barbarities were committed by the king's army, 408b

PERFECTABILITY OF MAN: hides true liberty, 394c

PERICLES, d. 429 B.C.: Athenian statesman, the influence of his wife, Aspasia, 74a

PERSECUTION: of Primitive Christians, result of pagan espionage, 10b; causes of, 11d; did not all proceed from the state, 13b; first impulse given by Nero, 13d

PERVADING MIND: preceded the American Revolution, 249b; inspired the prophetic verse of Bishop Berkeley, 249b

PETER, APOSTLE: prohibited elders from lording it over God's heritage, 39a

PETER, HUGH, 1598-1660: English clergyman, appointed in 1641 to represent Massachusetts Bay Colony in England, preached to parliament on the rooting up of monarchy, 267a

PETITION: for redress of grievances, an English right, 434b; 1st Continental Congress reaffirmed right of the colonists to petition, 477a; from agents Bollan, Franklin, Lee to parliament from 1st Continental Congress, declared illegal, 481a; discredited by friends of ministry, 481b; from London merchants and traders, disregarded by parliament, 485c; second petition to King from 2nd Continental Congress, written by John Dickinson, 502b; final, to the King, sent by agent Richard Penn, 421b; king refused an answer, 502d; Georgia Provincial Congress sent, on July 14, 1775, to king, 532b

PETITIONS: of colonists treated with contempt, 208; 368b; to House of Commons from Merchants of London consigned to the Committee of Oblivion, 481a

PHAENOMENON: *"without Example in the political World, a large and populous Colony, subsisting in great Decency and Order, for more than a Year, under such a Suspension of Government,"* 208

POLITICAL APOSTATES: endeavor to cut up the liberties of America, 41d

POLITICAL CONNECTIONS: of British Colonies to each other, 247a

POLITICAL CREED: of an American, centered in God as the Author of liberty, 436a

POLITICAL DEATH: and slavery, springs from luxury, 28a

POLITICAL ETHICS: liberty of the Gospel, 192c

POLITICAL INSTITUTIONS: striking similarity of, in the American Colonies, 369a

POLITICAL KNOWLEDGE: of English Colonists increased under favorable circumstances, 437b

POLITICAL LIBERTY: and JESUS CHRIST, 36d; should be supported by the clergy, 41c

POLITICAL LIFE: and religion, Witherspoon on, 245c

POLITICAL OPINIONS: of American Colonies, divided into three classes, 471a

POLITICAL POWER: lacking in the State of Nature, 185a; given up in civil society, for preservation of person and property, 186a; committed to rulers, limited by design of government, 194c; resides in the people, 208; granted to the people in the colonial charters, 461a

POLITICAL REFORMER: John Wise, writing on church polity, 103b

POLITICAL SERMON: *A Sermon on American Affairs*, preached by Reverend John Zubly to the Georgia Provincial Congress, July 4, 1775, 513b

POLITICAL THEORIES: of New England Clergy, chiefly derived from the Bible, 548b; John Locke a source of, 548d; Bible Commentaries a source of, 548d

POLITICS: of a nation, show influence of parental education, 217d

POLYGAMY: laws against, because America is a Christian nation, 157c

POMEROY, SETH, 1706-1777: American Revolutionary officer, in command of Minute Men, 473a

POOLE, MATTHEW, 1624-1679: non-conformist clergyman, his commentaries on the Bible used by New England clergy, 548d

POOR, ENOCH, 1736-1780: Commander of New Hampshire men, 63c

POOREST: member in a Christian flock, helped to supply others in distant lands, 17c

POPE: the, cannot invade the rights of conscience, 187b; issued many bulls against Henry VIII, but he refused obedience to, 539d

POPE, ALEXANDER, 1688-1744: the cherished poet of English aristocratic life, 290c; quoted by Reverend Simeon Howard in a sermon, 203d

POPERY: French converted Indians to, retained their friendship, 317a; toleration of in Canada, injurious to the rights of mankind, 532c; established by Parliament in one half of North America, 541a

POPISH BISHOP: his residence in Canada, promoted discontent among the Indians, 317a

POPISH MISSIONARIES: supported by the English government, 317b

POPISH PRIESTS: Americans feared Parliament might oblige them to support, 541a

POPULAR INSTITUTIONS: impossible in England in the 17th century, people not yet capable of taking lead, 268a

POPULATION: rapidity of, in British Colonies in North America, 27a; growth, and decline of Christian virtues, 27b; tremendous increase of, during Colonial period, 49d; causes of increase in Colonial America, 431a; in New England provinces, 431b; in New York and Pennsylvania, 431d; in Maryland and Virginia, 432b; in southern colonies, 432c

PORTUGUESE MONEY: and Spanish money, the only coin in the American colonies, 332b; the johannes or

"*joe*," the most celebrated gold coin, 336b; obtained from Brazil, 336b; coinage of famous johannes series began in 1722, 336c

POSTERITY:

And the Pilgrim Fathers: concern for, and our Pilgrim Fathers, 24c; love of, and liberty, and our Pilgrim Fathers, 25c; improvement of, when men are at liberty, 35a; their religion and liberties transmitted to, 41b; of the Pilgrims, opposed the Stamp Act, 361d

And Valley Forge: we should "*cherish those dear ragged Continentals*," 62d; they served here for, 66d *parental education of:* importance of transmitting divine law to, 213d; and the work of redemption, 214a; and instruction in the Holy Scriptures, 215a; testimony of domestic felicity of parents to, 218d; of Solomon, received his parental education, 219d; time is short for parental education, 220a

And our nation's history: an invaluable guide to, our American Archives, 250b; Mercy Warren speaks to, concerning their history, 358a

Our responsibility to: happiness and liberty of, entrusted to us, 202d; if you submit to arbitrary measures, you endanger, 541c

POSTMASTER GENERAL: office of, held by Benjamin Franklin, dismissed after he exposed the Hutchinson-Oliver letters, 455d

POST OFFICE: established by Congress, with Dr. Franklin appointed head of department, 501b

POTTS'S FORGE: located at Valley Forge, description given, 59b

PRAISE: the Lord for the wonderful things He has done, 30c

PRAYER: *see also* FAST DAYS x; Washington at Valley Forge, x; for deliverance of New England, in 1746, 57b; for Heavenly guidance, by Lydia Darrah, 78b; of thanksgiving by an unknown woman of North Carolina, 80d; and intercession, urged on Presbyterians during the American Revolution, 152b; and repentance, urged by Connecticut legislature, 207b; fervent, and the American Revolution, 254a; a day of fasting and, kept at Williamsburg, Philadelphia and Boston, June 1, 1774, the day for shutting up the port of Boston, 469d; Jonathan Trumbull's Proclamation for the April 19, 1775, day of fasting and, for Connecticut, 407; Continental Congress set July 20, 1775, for a day of public humiliation, fasting and, for the 13 colonies, 506a; of Pastor Batewell, before his July 20, 1775, Fast Day Sermon, 543b; a disposition to, needed in our Christian Warfare, 551c

PREACHERS: of the Gospel, find the foe of Christ, 5c; of the Gospel, gave their first messages in cities, 11c; of election sermons, friends of liberty, their sermons circulated by means of newspapers, 192a; of the Gospel, friends of civil and religious liberty, their assistance sought during the American Revolution, 206b

PRECEDENT: danger of, taxation without representation, Americans warned by John Dickinson in his *Farmer's Letters*, 450d; dangerous, of the Boston Port Bill, Americans act against, 464d; of suffering of sister colony of Boston, disposed the colonies to union, 479a

PREPARATION: of America and the Hand of God, 47b

PREROGATIVE: induced by episcopacy, 28d; power of, enabled Scotch bishops to prevail over the will of the people, 112d; and privilege, a struggle in England, termination in the Revolution of 1688, 433d; of the monarch, limited by the people's liberty of granting their own money, 445b; asserted by titled aristocracy in the American Revolution, 253a

PRESBYTERIAN CHURCH IN AMERICA: history of the denomination, 106; church polity of and its rela-

to glory, 27d; Christian, of obedience, sometimes difficult to apply, 18a; distinguishing, of Congregationalism from Independency, 103d; distinguishing, which make a church congregational, 105a; divergent, in conflict, in history of world, 4d; first, revolutions bring governments back to, 461b; first, taught by mother to child, 223d; of Presbyterians in New England, 109a; irreconcilable, Spirit of Christ and spirit of devil, 5c; life-giving, of the American Revolution, 75a; living, Revelation a book of, 4a; noble, of husbands of Abigail Adams and Mercy Warren, 85d; of all genuine liberty, drawn from the Bible, 21c; of Christianity, our youth educated in, 28b; of liberty, and colonial opposition to taxation without consent, 443d; of obedience to God, in Holy Scriptures, 18a; scriptural, of liberty and the Pilgrim Fathers, 25a; of polity, people instructed by ministers, 192c; of purest patriotism, the opposition of the people to the tea tax, 458b; of the American Revolution, brought by first emigrants, 251a; of the Christian religion and civil liberty, 255b; of the two wild beasts of Revelation XIII, 6a; Protestant, and our Pilgrim Fathers, 23d; reconciliation on honourable, the goal of delegates from Georgia Provincial Congress, 535a; regularly defined, of history, 46d; that do not change, the basis of society, 282a; two fundamental, characterize a Congregational church, 105c; vital, of our Republic, let our youth be instructed in, 255a

PRINTING: discovered when world in deep ignorance and bondage, 427b

PRIVATE CAPITAL: settled twelve of the colonies, no colony except Georgia, was settled at government expense, 429d

PRIVATE ECONOMY: the remedy for the financial derangement of 1779, 248b

PRIVILEGE: and duty, go hand in hand in America, 67a; and prerogative, a struggle in England, terminating in the Revolution of 1688, 433d

PRIVILEGES: of the people, and power of the rulers, 27c; our rights and, preserved by the Continental Congress, 547a

PROCLAMATIONS: *British Western Policy*, issued by the King, 1763, 304a; *For a General Fast*, issued by Governor Francis Bernard, March 8, 1769, 375; *King's Prohibition of Arms and Ammunition*, October 19, 1774, 325a; 473c; *General Gage*, 1774, against suspension of commerce with Great Britain, 471c; *General Gage*, against the meeting of members at Salem, 472c; *Governor Trumbull for a Day of Fasting and Prayer*, February 1, 1775, 495; *United Colonies of Netherlands*, March 20, 1775, to prohibit exportation of arms to America, 325c; *Governor Trumbull for a Day of Public Fasting and Prayer*, issued March 22, 1775, 407; *General Gage Proclaims Martial Law*, June 12, 1775, 415c; 497a; 508; 509; *Continental Congress Proclaims a Continental Fast Day*, June 12, 1775, 510a; *General Court of Massachusetts*, January 23, 1776, on the suspension of civil government, 208; 209

PROFANENESS: of language, one God-provoking sin which prevails, 542d

PROFESSORSHIPS: of liberty, should be founded in universities by gentlemen of large estates and public spirit, 28d

PROGRESS: of world, dependent upon the Bible, 20c; all our, based upon education with a religious spirit, 53c

PROPERTY:
Biblical principle of: an extraordinary regard for in the Jewish religion, 518d; the Gospel has regard to, 519a; Zacchaeus, after his conversion returns stolen, 519b

In England: given only by consent, settled by English Revolution of 1688, 434b; security of, and personal liberty, end of English government in 1763, 284c

Defined in writings and sermons of American clergy: the natural right to, Elisha Williams, 183b; enjoyment of, not very safe in the state of nature, 185a; preservation of, end of civil government, 185b; of conscience, cannot be transferred, 187b; from an artillery-election sermon, injury to, forbidden under the law of nature, 194a; life, liberty and, depend upon, self-preservation, 202d; freedom to acquire, the result of Christianity, Witherspoon, 157a

Defense of in America: preservation of, entrusted to magistrates, 208; security of, in English colonies in America, derived from the English Constitution, 430b; and liberty, promoted the growth of the New England colonies, 431c; constitutional protection of, thrown down by the Revenue Acts, 443b; the palladium of the people's liberty is the exclusive privilege of granting their own, 445b; property of the colonists endangered by the Stamp Act, 448b; outrages to, produced by frenzy of patriotism, 451d; no security for, if taxed by a British parliament in which colonies not represented, 453c; right to exclusive disposal of, ground of the American Controversy, 456b; right of disposal, an inherent right of freemen, 458c; life, liberty and, referred to by the First Continental Congress in their Declaration of Rights, 476c; protected by the British Constitution, the Revenue Acts go against, 527d

Of the Indian in America: land purchased before settlement, 546d

And liberty: the love of, absorbed in the love of liberty, 494d; patriots willing to sacrifice for liberty, 496a; colonial indifference to, when put in competition with liberty, 499a; a general wreck of, rather than loss of liberties, 504c

PROPHECIES: of the Bible, their Hero is the Messiah, 230d

PROPHECY OF ISAIAH: what an aching void without the, 20d

PROPHET: surpasses Poet, as Habakkuk surpasses Milton, 230b

PROPHETICAL ARCHAEOLOGIST: the book of Revelation not a treasure house of marvels for the, 4a

PROPHETS: writings of, and the spirit of liberty, 36b; promoted civil and religious liberty, 36c; denounced tyrants as deceivers of mankind, 36c; before Christ, spoke of civil government, 36d; and Apostles, bare testimony against lawless oppressors, 41c; and patriarchs and apostles, have labored to promote the best good of posterity, 213b

PROSPERITY: source of corruption of the American Christian church, 25c; religious, of New England, a concern of the grandfathers, 96a; material, men absorbed in, in America's second century, 53d; cannot hide critical need for liberty, 67c

PROTESTANT: principles, and our Pilgrim Fathers, 23d; despotism, is as bad as papist despotism, 540a

PROTESTANT CHRISTIANITY: principles of, influence the government of the United States, 155c; is the law of the land, 156b

PROTESTANT CHRISTIANS: settled America, 156b

PROTESTANTISM: spirit of, and our Pilgrim Fathers, 24a; and the triumph of the Seven Year's War in Europe, 275b; broke the conformity of the Catholic system into sects and fragments, 276a; founded on a strong claim to natural liberty, 434d

PROTESTANT MISSIONARIES: would counteract efforts of Romish missionaries among the Indians, 317c

PROTESTANT NATION: reasons why America is, 156a

PROTESTANT REPUBLIC: established in the Netherlands,

677

phia, leaving the American Army encamped at Valley
Forge untouched, 66b

SAVANNAH, GEORGIA: town of, sent Resolutions to
Georgia Provincial Congress July 5, 1775, 523b;
"that this Province . . . will forthwith join the other
Provinces in every just and legal measure to secure
and restore the liberties of all *America,* and for
healing the unhappy divisions now subsisting between *Great Britain* and her Colonies . . .", 524a

SAVING WORK: a, in the Salem church upon a Gentleman of quality, 45c

SAVIOUR: our, forbids us to resist evil in small injuries,
198d; on His merits do we depend for mercy, 544d;
power of our, over all forms of evil, 9b; referred to
the signs of the times as witnessing of Him, 7b

SAY, LORD, WILLIAM FIENNES, 1582-1662: Parliamentary
leader and presbyterian patron of Connecticut, 108d;
indebted to, for the restoration of the charter of
Connecticut, 108d; prevented from embarking to
America, 359d

SAYBROOK PLATFORM: Colonial Synod held at Saybrook
in 1703, by legislative command, 108d; included
sentiments of presbyterians and congregationalists,
109a; came close to presbyterian model of church
government, 110a; approved by the Assembly which
prepared it in 1708, 110b; adopted by legislature as
discipline of churches, 110b

SAYLE, WILLIAM, in 1669: first governor of South Carolina, a presbyterian, 111a

SCAMMELL, ALEXANDER, 1747-1781: American general,
testified to days without provisions at Valley Forge,
61c

SCANDANAVIANS: discovered American continent in the
tenth century, 47c

SCARCITY: of real money, a chief annoyance of the
American Colonies, 332a

SCEPTICISM: progress of, in Europe after Seven Year's
War, 276a; the authority of reason, rather than the
authority of the Bible, 276a; its tendency was to
revolution, 276a; colossal genius of, Frederick the
Great of Prussia, 277a; the enemy of good government, no love of man, 281d

SCHISM OF 1741: *see also* CHURCH POLITY, PRESBYTERIAN
CHURCH; and source of authority in church government, 110a; a result of the Great Revival, 135b; act
regarding the ordination of ministers by Synod, 137b;
conclusions of, 137c

SCHOOL: military, of Baron von Steuben, at Valley
Forge, 65a

SCHOOLMASTERS: proposed plan for education and conversion of Iroquois, 318c; should be men of character,
318d

SCHOOLS: *see also* EDUCATION IN AMERICA; care to support both public and private, in New England, 29b;
lack of in Virginia, 169d; children in the, and early
arithmetics, to enable them to translate money of one
colony into that of another, 327b; of England, pervaded by cast of aristocracy, 291c

SCHUYLER, PHILIP JOHN, 1733-1804: Major General in
the Continental Army, commanding the northern department, 314c; placed Sir John Johnson under arrest in January 1776, 314c

SCHUYLKILL RIVER: Pott's Forge on creek of, at Valley
Forge, 59b

SCIENCE: apostles of, can lead men to worship the
beast, 6c; represented by Galileo, Brache, Kepler, in
the age of American Settlement, 48b; sacred, shall
pour her best gifts o'er the western world, 231b

SCIENCES: and arts, flourish in British Ameria, 27a

SCOTCH: Presbyterians persecuted under reign of James
II, and Charles I, 112a; emigrated to America in
considerable numbers, 112c; largest emigrations of,
to Pennsylvania, 113a; also settlers into Virginia

and North Carolina, 113a; a large number of, settled
in Maryland, 113b; early settlers of Georgia, 113b

SCOTCH BISHOPS: cruel efforts of, to impose episcopacy
on Scotland, 112a; principal authors of arbitrary
laws, 112b

SCOTCH-IRISH: emigrants from Pennsylvania, settled in
Virginia, 111a

SCOTLAND: cruelty and oppression in, for thirty years,
112a; parliament of, never a fair representation of
the people, 112b; prelacy and despotism inseparable
in, 112d; England's treaty with, 107b; feared the
sovereignty of the Long Parliament, and triumph of
the Independents, it loved liberty, but it loved its
nationality, 268a; a decay in power of religion in,
before the Great Revival, 121a; furnished original
stock of the present population of the United States,
437c

SCOTT, CHARLES, 1739?-1813: commanded 1st Virginia
regiment at Valley Forge, 63b

SCRIPTURAL: principles of liberty and the Pilgrim
Fathers, 25a; model of church government, needed
by New England churches, 92d; drawn up by John
Cotton, 93a

SEAL: of Massachusetts Colony, the Macedonian Call,
44d

SECKER, DR. THOMAS, 1693-1768: Archbishop of Canterbury, answered charge of Jonathan Mayhew on need
for an American Episcopate, 178b

SECOND CENTURY: of America, entered amid deepening
responsibilities, 53d

SECOND COMING OF CHRIST: seen as only means of
church's triumph, 15d; until the, continue parental
education, 221a

SECOND GENERATION: of colonists, did not all confess
Christ, 95d

SECRECY: of British troop movement on April 19, 1775,
406c

SECRET: attack on American Army at White Marsh,
prevented by a woman, 79a; compacts, Christians
accused of, by Celsus, 12d; negotiations, for French
Alliance, had been going on for several years, 65c

SECRET COMMITTEE: appointed by Province of Georgia,
to gather intelligence to frustrate the evil designs
of wicked men, 526b

SECTIONAL: feeling smothered itself in 1774, 1775, 1776,
and asserted itself in 1777, 60b

SECULAR SPIRIT: when nations are animated by, they
are against Christ, 6c

SECURITY: of property, the sole end of civil government, 185c; greatest, under God, will be our capacity
to defend ourselves, 204c

SEED: of New England congregationalism, sown in
prayer and hope, grew to a useful harvest, 95c

SELDEN, JOHN, 1584-1654: English jurist and statesman,
in ear of the American Settlement, 48c

SELF-DEFENCE: attention to means of, only recourse of
colonists when convinced of the fallacy of their hopes
of reconciliation, 489a; denial of, in New Testament,
seen by some Christians, 198d; by force of arms,
does not render evil for evil, 199a; necessary, by
those who value liberty, 203c; of western country,
due to its settling by freemen, 433b; universal principle of self-preservation, 197c

SELF-GOVERNMENT: one's actions, property, persons,
within bounds of God's law, 194a; allowed to English Colonies in America for 150 years, 430c; America, a grand demonstration of, 254d; development of,
in New England, an indication of Divine Providence, 50c; faith in the capacity of man for, and the
American Revolution, 253b; the Massachusetts Mint,
illustrated their ability for, 333d; the outcome of
moral liberty, 40a; support of, by the clergy of
Massachusetts during suspension of civil govern-

ment, 209; the more individual, the less state government, 20b

SELF-GOVERNMENT WITH UNION: distinguishing principle of Congregationalism, 103d; and individual enterprise of first emigrants, 251b; sought by the Continental Congress, 419b; established by the Declaration of Independence, 250a

SELFISH: a, individual, one overanxious about his trade and business, 478b

SELFISHNESS: cowardly, of pagans in times of public calamity, 17c; of American merchants, in their opposition to tea tax of East India Company, 458b

SELF-LOVE: argues no ill will against any man, 199a

SELF-PRESERVATION: allows everything necessary to self-defence, 197c; and our duty to God, 202c; neglect of, and loss of life, liberty, property, 202d

SELF-SACRIFICE: and brotherly love of Christians, 17c; and womanly examples of heroism, 74a; and the defense of liberty, 67c

SEMLER, JOHANN SALOMO, 1725-1791: German Protestant theologian, called "father of German rationalism", held the Bible under the light of criticism, 276c

SENSUALITY: and worldly-mindedness, dead to the importance of liberty, 29d

SENTINEL: ragged, kept watch for liberty at Valley Forge, 55d

SEPARATION OF CHURCH AND STATE: accomplished in America, 53a; not violated by the influence of Protestant Christianity, 155d

SERMON ON THE MOUNT: what an aching void without the, 20d and our Saviour's words on war, 198c

SERMONS: See ELECTION SERMON; An Artillery-Election Sermon, June 7, 1773, Boston, Mass., 193a; Provincial Congress of Georgia hears A Sermon on American Affairs, July 4, 1775, Savannah, 513b; Continental Fast Day Sermons, preached July 20, 1775, at Tredyffryn, Chester County, Pa., 536b; at Yorktown, Pa., before Captain Morgan's and Captain Price's Companies of Rifle-Men, 543b; Plymouth Anniversary Thanksgiving Sermons, preached at Plymouth, Mass., 1773, 22a; 1774, 30b

SERVANTS: Christianity gave inward freedom first, 18d; slothful, who yield to oppressive power, 202c; their relation to their masters, improved through the law of liberty, 519a

SERVICE: of my country, no fortune raised in the, 84c

SERVICES: of Baron von Steuben to America, most valuable of all, 65b

SETTLEMENT: of America, coincident with diffusion of the Bible, 20a

SEVENTEEN: infamous, names of those who refused to impeach Governor Bernard, 371d

SEVENTEEN SEVENTY-FIVE: a determined system of coercion by the British began the war, 403a

SEVENTEEN SEVENTY-SIX: Washington defeated the Hessians in a surprise attack Christmas night, 57c

SEVENTEEN SEVENTY-SEVEN: the gloomiest period of the American Revolution, 56a; condition of country after two years of war, 56a; condition of American and British armies, 56a; British garrisoned in New York in luxury, 56a; British fleet watched the rebel coast, 56b; Rhode Island was in the hands of the British, 56b; Georgia, Virginia, the Carolinas open to British invasion, 56b; Tory intrigue and British gold bought country's produce, 56b; a deluge prevented a battle at Warren Tavern, 56b; at Germantown, fog robbed Washington of victory, 56b; the Continental Army, suffering but steadfast, lay on the frozen ridges of Whitemarsh, 56c; the British Army was reinforced with veteran troops, 56c; in August the American Army marched through Philadelphia, 56c; the British Army landed at Head of Elk, 56c; anxiety of people in Philadelphia, 56c; capture of Phila-

delphia, 56c; the Battle of Brandywine, a defeat for the Americans, 56d; Anthony Wayne's brigade massacred at the Paoli, September 24, 57a; September 27, the Continental Congress left Philadelphia for York, 57a; the Whigs left Philadelphia at approach of the British Army, 57a; Tories returned to Philadelphia behind British bayonets, 57c; the Quaker City in riotous revelry with British occupation, 57d; condition and suffering of the Continental Army at Valley Forge, 58b; problems of the Continental Army with Congress, 60a; Continental Army in dire need of food, clothing, supplies, 60a; men of second rank in the Continental Congress, 60b; sectional feelings in Continental Congress, 60b; Continental Army persevered, they kept the faith, 62b; in this year of, a number of savage forays upon Virginia settlements, 81a; the campaigns of Burgoyne and Vaughan caused terror in Connecticut, 210a

SEVENTEEN SEVENTY-EIGHT: winter months of, dragged on at Valley Forge, 66a; March 23, Greene appointed Quartermaster General, under his management relief and succor came, 66a; Conciliatory Bills offering all but independence rejected by Continental Congress, 66b; on May 4th, news of French Alliance reached Headquarters, 66b; religious services and rejoicing 66b; on May 18, Lafayette took post at Barren Hill, 66b; June 18, news of British evacuation of Philadelphia, 66c; Continental Army left Valley Forge leaving the hills with their glory and their dead, 66c

SEVENTEEN SEVENTY-NINE: the Independence of America secured, now the need to secure America from the conditions of financial derangement, 248a

SEVEN YEARS' WAR: European: a triumph of the life-giving truth of the Reformation, the right of private judgment, 275a; American: needed the character of George Washington, 52b

SEWALL, JONATHAN MITCHELL, 1748-1808: lawyer, and poet, employed to vindicate conduct of Governor Bernard, 367d

SEX: appropriate duties assigned to each, 357d

SHADRACH: can we condemn his disobedience to higher powers, 539c

SHAFTESBURY, EARL OF, ANTHONY ASHLEY COOPER, 1621-1683: English statesman, granted Carolina by Charles II, invited to Carolina, believers of every creed, 111d; Independent party, member of Cromwell's Council of State, member of the vast Whig party, 271b

SHAKESPEARE, WILLIAM, 1564-1616: English dramatist and poet, could be spared from literature, but not the Bible, 20d; poet of the human race, in the era of the American Settlement, 48c; unfolded the panorama of English history and Protestant liberty, 290b

SHELBURNE, 2ND EARL OF, SIR WILLIAM PETTY, 1737-1805: and the Proclamation of 1763, 304c; western policy of, followed by Lord Hillsborough until 1768, 304d; his plans for raising revenue in America through quit rents, 307d; recommended in 1767 Indian Trade be placed in control of colonists, 308b

SHELL: blowing of a, to call people to public worship, 94b

SHEM: son of Noah, transmitted parental instruction of his father, 217b

SHEPARD, WILLIAM, 1737-1817: Commander at Fort William Henry, Virginia, refused to yield Fort to the white renegade, Simeon Girty, and his savage Indians, 81b

SHEPHERDS: of Israel, reproved by the Prophet Ezekiel for not feeding the flock, 39a

SHERMAN, JOHN, 1616-1685: pastor of church at Watertown, Mass., fellow of Harvard college, moderator of Synod of 1679, 98c

by Jonathan Mayhew, Congregational minister of Boston, 178a; sent missionaries to Mohawks, 316a

SOCIETY OF FRIENDS: a religious society founded by George Fox, called *Quakers*, William and Lydia Darrah of Philadelphia, members of, 77c

SOCIETY OF JESUS: called *Jesuits,* founded in 1534 by Loyola as a spiritual army against Protestantism, 279b

SOLDIER: common, description of, at Valley Forge, 62b; character of a, and a good Christian, not incompatible, 198b; necessary qualification for a good, religion, 205c

SOLDIERS: find woman of courage still on her knees in prayer, 80d; and their property of wages, dealt with by the gospel, 519a; join in act of humiliation on July 20, 1775, Fast Day, 543b

SOLDIERY: religiously educated, need chaplains, the concern of George Washington, VIII; in Massachusetts, regarded as instruments of tyranny, 454d

SOLEMN LEAGUE AND COVENANT: Parliament's treaty with Scotland for uniformity of religion, 107b; set forth by Massachusetts to suspend commercial intercourse with Britain, 471b

SOLOMON: and the importance of parental education, 216d; choice of wisdom over riches, result of parental education, 219d; addressed the Book of Proverbs to his children, 219d; it contains a complete system of wisdom, 256a; a proper example to a prince, 226a

SON OF GOD: a life lived by faith in, the gospel asks, 4d; His purchase of our eternal life, 82b

SONG OF MOSES AND THE LAMB: from Revelation, sung at the Cambridge Synod of 1648, 93b

SOUL: conflicts of, and forms of disease, 9d; propensities of, open to eye of parent, 85b; immortality of, its importance and parental education, 213d; shortest passage to, the genius of the divine writers, 225b; the care and loss of, the one thing needful in the education of a Christian, 243d

SOURCES: of American greatness, at Valley Forge, 55b

SOUTH CAROLINA: settled in 1670 under proprietors, first governor Presbyterian, settled mostly by episcopalians, 111a; in 1752, 1600 foreign protestants arrived, 112a; seconded call for Stamp Act Congress, 1765, 449c; sent deputies, 449c; elected representatives to a Continental Congress, 1774, 468a; people of, expressed resolutions against unconstitutionality of Boston Port Bill, 468b; Lord William Campbell, governor of, in 1775, 413c; Henry Laurens, president of Provincial Congress of, in 1775, 413d; Continental Congress recommended the collection of salt petre and sulphur in, for manufacture of gun powder, 342c; men of, at Valley Forge, commanded by John Laurens, 63d; patriotism and courage of Jane Thomas of, 79b; *Money Units:* rated in terms of the Spanish Dollar, 327a

SOUTHERN COLONIES: Puritan settlements there, of small influence, 110d; and African slavery, 428a; 432c; superior in resources, inferior in wealth and industry, 433b; long credit of British merchants, source of prosperity, 433b

SOUTHERN STATES: and formal church establishments, 50a

SOVEREIGN: country appealed to, in vain, VIII

SOVEREIGNS: authority of, exercised for the good of the people, 434b

SOVEREIGNTY: of God in the heart, the religion of Christianity, 8a; Roman, attributed to religious conciliation, 12b; without consent of the people, is tyranny, 208; of individual states, preserved under the Articles of Confederation, 419b; of Mother Country, acknowledged in British trade restrictions, 443d; total renunciation of Britain's, brought about by acts of the ministry, 489d

SOVEREIGNTY OF GOD: appealed to by the inhabitants of Georgia, in petition to King, 533b

SOVEREIGNTY OF THE PEOPLE: advocated by Jean Jacques Rousseau, 283c

SOVEREIGN WILL: of God, acknowledged in the affairs of men, 544a

SPAIN: the citadel of Catholicism under Philip II, 279a; desired to make the Gulf of Mexico and the Caribbean its own seas, 279d

SPANISH AMERICA: great care to establish forms of faith and worship amongst the colonists, 174d

SPANISH COLONIES: bought British manufactures from American Colonies, 442c; provided a market for produce of American Colonies, 442d

SPANISH DOLLAR: or piece of eight, most celebrated silver coin known to world trade, 336a; common to all local currencies in the colonies, 326d; with Portuguese money, comprised all the real money in the colonies, 332b; the basis of our present American coinage, 336a; *Spanish Coins: Silver,* subdivisions of the Spanish Dollar, 336c; *Gold,* Spanish Gold Doubloon, Spanish pistole, 336c; Jefferson's notes on Spanish coins, 336d; note in *The American Negotiator,* published in 1765 on, 337a

SPARKS, JARED, 1789-1866: American historian, note on Dr. Samuel Johnson, American educator, 221d

SPENCER, EDMUND, 1552?-1599: English poet, in era of the American Settlement, 48c

SPINNERS: needed in Philadelphia, to promote American manufactory, 340a; Scriptural description of, in Proverbs, 340b

SPINNING WHEEL MAKERS: to be instructed to make machine for spinning cotton, 341a

SPIRIT OF LIBERTY: in the Frenchman, made him sympathetic to America, 65c; chosen refuge in the west, in America, 67a

SPIRITUAL LIBERTY: Christ's great intention to introduce men into state of, 39c

SPIRITUAL STATISTICS: for continent of North America, in 1761, transmitted to the Bishop of London, 170b

SPIRITUAL WICKEDNESS: in high places, our Christian warfare, 549d

STAEL, MME DE, *nee* NECKER, 1766-1817: French writer, her remarks to Napoleon on the importance of mothers, 223d

STAGES: three, in the history of the American Revolution; first, the struggle for the preservation and recovery of rights and liberties, 248b; second, the War of Independence, 248d; third, the formation of the Anglo-American People and the Nation of North America, 248d

STAMP ACT: became law on March 22, 1765, 447c; purpose of, to raise a revenue to the crown, 360d, 447b; duty on all bonds, bills of lading, public papers, etc. was to be levied, 360d; first thought of the, that the Colonies would be obliged to submit, 447d; called a self-executing law, 447d; opposition to, from Virginia and New England, 448a; opposition to, and the fire of liberty blazed from the press, 448a; the Colonial Assemblies asserted their right to tax themselves, 449b; lower classes broke out into excesses of riot and tumult, 360d; effect of, described by Mercy Warren, 360d; universal reaction to, throughout the Colonies, 361a; first opposition to, by Patrick Henry of Virginia, 448a; Virginia Resolves against, ushered into house of burgesses by Patrick Henry, May 30, 1765, 361b; reaction to, in the West Indies, 361b; meeting of Massachusetts General Assembly, spirited opposition to, 361c; text of instructions from freeholders of Plymouth to their representative in the Mass. General Assembly, 361d; petitions to the King from colonial assemblies, coupled expressions of loyalty, 362b; contribution of Benjamin Franklin's

687

philosophy of government, 250b; to mother country, marked in their provincial constitutions, making no laws repugnant to her laws, 437a; Colonies represented as manifesting a disposition to throw off, 452c

SUFFERING: of our New England Fathers for religious liberty, 41a; of the soldiers at Valley Forge, 58d

SUFFOLK, MASS.: the convention which met at, prepared for resistance by arms, 399d

SUFFOLK RESOLVES: September 9, 1774, revealed the spirit of Americans, 399d; considered as overt acts of treason by the government, 400a; opposition to the Intolerable Acts of Parliament, 472b; sent to the Continental Congress at Philadelphia, 472b; approved by the 1st Continental Congress, brought them to the point of conflict, 484c

SUGAR PLANTERS: in West Indies, petition Parliament in 1775 regarding the American Acts, 482c

SULLIVAN, JOHN, 1740-1795: American Revolutionary officer, seized powder at Portsmouth, New Hampshire, 473d; officer at Valley Forge, 63d

SULPHUR: the collecting of, recommended by Continental Congress, 343d; premiums for the refining of, in respective provinces, 343d; Massachusetts House of Representatives recommended committee buy up, 344b

SUNDAY LAWS: objected to by foreign-born citizens, 154b

SUPERIOR COURT: of Massachusetts, closed by inhabitants, 401a

SUPERNATURAL: aspects of Christian warfare, Revelation XII, 4d; powers, pretended by magicians, 8d; interposition, the cause of the church's triumph, 15d

SUPERSTITION: the enemy of Christianity, 8c

SUPPLIES: sent by Providence to the Pilgrims when ready to perish, 26a; total failure of, for the American Army at Valley Forge, 61a; of countryside, go to the British Army in Philadelphia, in 1777, 60a; forwarded to the people of Boston, from the other colonies, 478b

SUPREMACY: oath of, imposed by Scottish Bishops for Kings, 112d; of Parliament, should be acknowledged by the Colonists, in Lord Chatham's proposed bill of reconciliation, 481b; unlimited, of Parliament, by legislators on other side of globe, unthinkable to Americans, 482c; of Parliament, in control of Colonial trade, stretched, 489d

SUPREME BEING: a belief in, helpful in the civilization of savage peoples, 320d; awe of, discovered by Iroquois before they knew Christianity, 321a; contest with Great Britain, intended by the, 340a

SURGEONS: and physicians, diligence of, at Valley Forge, 62a

SURVEY: historical, of our Founding Fathers, to do them justice, 104c

SUSPENSION: of civil government in Massachusetts Colony, a phenomenon without example, 208

SWANSON, MARY ELAINE: American Christian writer and biographer; See BIOGRAPHIES OF THE WRITERS, 557

SWEDEN: furnished original stock for present population of the United States, 437c

SWEDES: among the early settlers near the Delaware River, 437c

SWITZERLAND: furnished original stock for the present population of the United States, 437c

SWORD: small injuries not to be resisted by the, 199b; cannot injure or defend the kingdom of our Lord, 198b; defence of liberty by, passages in the New Testament, 197d; Dr. Joseph Warren, first victim of rank to fall by the, in the American Revolution, 418d; may rust, while liberty is left undefended, 199b; of defence, placed in hands of men with strongest motives, 201d; of the Christian, is the Word of God, 551b; of the wilderness, Pilgrims preserved from, 26a; settled claims of English in

North America, 441d

SYNOD OF 1646: called for by Massachusetts Court, to consider questions of church government, 92d

SYNOD OF 1662: met in Boston, to debate church membership, 97a

SYNOD OF 1679: met at Boston, to consider God's judgements, 98c; reported its results to the General Court of Massachusetts, 98d

SYNOD OF PHILADELPHIA: twice resolved against itinerant preaching, 134c

SYNODS: power of, differences between congregationalism and presbyterianism, 95b; authority of, and influence of presbyterianism, 109a; their relationship to church organization in New England, 109a; role and authority of, defined by the Cambridge Platform of 1648, 109b; carried beyond presbyterian doctrine, 109c

T

TALENTS: for the education of youth, the gift of God, 221b

TAR AND FEATHERS: applied by an intemperate populace, to persons going against the general good, 478c

TARLETON, SIR BANASTRE, 1754-1833: British officer of renowned cruelty and butchery, 79b

TASKMASTERS: in Egypt, God delivered the children of Israel from, 35d

TASSO, TORQUATO, 1544-1595: Italian poet, in era of American Settlement, 48c

TASTE: of America, comparatively pure and simple, 362d

TAXATION WITH REPRESENTATION: the hinge on which the American Revolution turned, 444a; its origin in the English Constitution, 251b; protected by the British Constitution, 430d; reclaimed by colonial legislatures after Revolution of 1688, 273a; only through provincial assemblies, 429d; people not represented in British Parliament, 445a; principle of, annulled by Declaratory Act, 450b; Lord Chatham's Bill declared "no tax, or other charge, should be levied in America, except by common consent in their provincial assemblies," 481c; principle declared in the Resolves of Georgia Provincial Congress, July 10, 1775, 527d; in their Petition to the King, July 14, 1775, 532c

TAXATION WITHOUT REPRESENTATION: Governor Hutchinson communicated this question to Parliament, 387b; subjection of the colonies by Parliament, commenced in 1764, 442b; 1st act of revenue, 1764, considered a dangerous act of innovation, 443a; John Dickinson's *Farmer's Letters* demonstrated that a small tax was a dangerous precedent in the Townshend Bill of 1767, 450d; duty on tea left, after partial repeal of Revenue Act of 1767, 456d; Lord North's scheme acknowledged the supremacy of Parliament, 486a; added to Great Britain's monopoly of trade, would leave Colonies in a state of slavery, 453d; Declaration of Rights of 1st Continental Congress, 1774, reaffirmed the principles of the British Constitution, that they had never ceded a right to dispose of their property without their consent, 476d

TAXES: "the free gifts of the people to their rulers," 434b; abated 25% in Massachusetts if paid in cash rather than grain, 332d; in Colonial America could be paid in tobacco, 332d

TAXING POWER: of Parliament, if it had assumed a judicial instead of a political character, would have been declared illegal, 251c

TEA: duty on, to be retained in America, 1770, 453a; removal of duty on, contended for in Parliament, rejected by a great majority, 456c; expected revenue from, failed in consequence of the American Associa-

against America, 438b; monopoly of, Great Britain's use of colonies as instruments of commerce, 441d; Colonial, was restricted by enforcement of Navigation Act, 442b; England's monopoly of Colonial, ran through 29 acts of Parliament from 1660-1764, 444b; of New England Colonies, to be restrained by bill proposed by Lord North, 484d; Restraint Bill, would operate against the people of New England and Great Britain, 485b; petition from merchants and traders of London in regard to bill, disregarded by British Ministry, 485c; coercion of the American Colonists the goal of the British Ministry by restraint of, bill, 485d; combinations, by American Colonies against Great Britain, Ireland, and the West Indies, 489d; Georgia Provincial Congress suspended Non-Exportation for a period in hopes of British Parliament's repeal of restrictive acts of, 524d

TRAJAN, MARCUS ULPIUS, 52-3-117: Roman Emperor, inaugurated legal persecution of Christians, 14d; Christianity condemned by law by the rescript of, 15a

TRANSLATIONS OF THE BIBLE: Wickliff's version, Tyndale's version, Coverdale's version, Cranmer's version, 19d; the Geneva Bible, and the Douay Bible, 20a; the authorized and standard version of King James, 20a

TREASON: high, accusation brought against Christians, 13b; under the Emperor Domitian, charge of, for embracing Christianity, 14c; in America, any man liable on slightest suspicion of, to be dragged from family to England for trial, 395b; 452d; the Suffolk Resolves considered as overt acts of, by the British government, 400a; and rebellion, the charge of General Gage against Samuel Adams and John Hancock, 415c, 497a

TREATY OF PARIS 1763: By this, France relinquished her right to Iroquois soil, 313a; England assumed jurisdiction of Iroquois soil by this, 313a

TREATY OF 1764: held at Johnson Hall, by this, England recognized Iroquois title to all lands claimed by them in the Colony of New York, excepting for strategic areas, 313b

TREATY AT FORT STANWIX, November 5, 1768: with the Iroquois, established boundary line for western lands, 307c; known as "The Line of Property" it fixed a line of separation between Iroquois and Crown colonies, 313b

TREATY OF ALLIANCE: signed by Franklin with the French, February 6, 1778, 64d; Franklin also prepared treaties of Amity, Commerce and Alliance, 65d

TREATY OF PEACE: preliminary, concluded at Paris, November 30, 1782, 284d

TRENCHARD, JOHN, 1662-1723: English publicist, widely read by the American Colonials, 201d; Trenchard's History of Standing Armies in England, quoted, 201d; author Cato's Letters, and the Independent Whig, 435b

TRENTON, NEW JERSEY: Washington defeated the Hessians at, on December 25, 1776, 57c

TRIAL BY JURY: protected by the British Constitution, 430d; offenders in Massachusetts might be transported to Britain for, 389c; 452c; lost to the colonists in Admiralty Courts, 443c; Act for Trial In England, May 20, 1774, 462b; 489c; of British soldiers in Boston Massacre, given favorable verdict, 455a; John Adams and Josiah Quincy counsel for the prisoners, 455a; of peers, reaffirmed in the Declaration of their Rights, by the Continental Congress of 1774, 477a

TRIBES: of every language and hue, congregated in the New World, 231a

TRIBUNAL OF GOD: no substitutions before, 187b

TRUMBULL, BENJAMIN, 1735-1820: American Congregational clergyman and historian, his comments on the Assembly which drew up Saybrook Platform, 108d; his comments on decline of religion in New England, 120d; his History of Connecticut quoted on Great Revival, 124c; his comments on decline of religion in Connecticut, 128a; the desirable state of religion in Hebron, mentioned by, 128a

TRUMBULL, JONATHAN, 1710-1785: American statesman, Royal and Colonial Governor of Connecticut, his reports to the Continental Congress, on barrels of powder sent from Connecticut to the Continental Army before Boston, 342b; on estimated needs of Connecticut Militia for guns, powder, ammunition, 342d; on proposals to manufacture salt petre, 343a; his pleading for powder for George Washington's Cambridge Army, 343a; on the critical need of gun powder in the Colonies, 343c; gave leave of the Connecticut Assembly for surprise attack on Ticonderoga, May 10, 1775, 414c; his July 13, 1775 letter to George Washington, 511

TRUST: a sacred, by Providence, a mother's education of her children, 85a; a, committed to us by Heaven, our God-given liberty, 202b

TRUTH: love of, first principle of education, 85a; sick healed by the enlightening and sanctifying power of, 9c

TRYON, WILLIAM, 1729-1788: last Crown governor of New York, 411d; endeavored to influence New York to decline union with other colonies, 412a; apprehensive for his safety, went on board Halifax packet, 412b; put himself at head of loyalists, annoyed inhabitants of New York and New Jersey, 412b

TURGOT, ANNE ROBERT JACQUES, BARON DE L'AULNE, 1727-1781: French statesman and economist, 282d; advocate of the free market economy, 283a

TURNER, CHARLES, 1732-1813: Congregational minister, preached Pilgrim Anniversary Sermon of 1773, 22b

TURNING POINT: of the American Revolution, news of the French Treaty, 65d

TUSCARORAS: or Shirt Wearing People, driven out of North Carolina in 1715, settled with the Iroquois, 313a; became the Sixth Nation of the Iroquois Confederacy, 313a

TYNDALE, WILLIAM, 1492?-1536: English translator of the Bible, 19d

TYPE: movable type, invention of, before discovery of America, 47c

TYRANNY: a complete system of, formed by British intolerable acts: Boston Port Bill, March 31, 1774, 460a; Act to Change Constitution of Massachusetts, May 20, 1774, 461c; Act for Trial in England, May 20, 1774, 462b; Quebec Act, June 22, 1774, 463b; a homicidal, democracy, as conceived by Rousseau, 283d; an act of, the execution of Charles I, 267c; and anarchy, are essentially the same, each resists the higher powers, 539a; and episcopacy, a menace to America, 28c; and oppression, a departure from the Holy Scriptures, 40a; and vengeance, failed to subdue the patriots, 79c; apparent to American Women, 74d; colonists must choose submission to, or resistance by force, 501d; comes from the atheist and free-thinker, 157c; escape from English, civil and prelatical, 23c; has no connection with the all-wise and alljust God, 546c; instances of, when checks of conscience are thrown aside, 358c; instruments of, soldiery, 454d; is the exercise of sovereignty without consent of the people, 208; is tyranny, by whomsoever it is imposed, 540a; Jesus Christ bore testimony against all forms of, 37b; must cease in church and state, where freedom from sin and the virtues of the Gospel prevail, 39d; of rulers, and the right and duty of the people to resist, asserted by John Knox, in the Confession of Faith, 112b; resistance to, a Christian duty, and issue of the Revolution

of 1688, 271a; scepter of, leaves a heritage of slavery,
203a; the encroachments of, and American Manufactures, 340c; we must not strengthen the hands of,
520a

TYRANTS: and oppressors, denounced by the Prophets,
36b; eventually reap destruction, 203c; frowned on
by God, as seen in the deliverance of the children
of Israel, 35c; maxim of, *divide et impera*, 200a;
obedience to, not the meaning of the Apostle Peter,
539c; submission to, strengthens their hands, 203a

U

UNCONSTITUTIONAL: acts against Massachusetts, brought
to the attention of the people by a series of letters,
466d; appointments of counsellors in Massachusetts,
people demanded resignation of, 395a; draughts on
the public treasury, Plymouth representatives instructed to prevent, 362b; innovation, opposed by
American freemen, 483c; methods for collection of
duties, resented by the people, 443b; statutes, excited
a combination of twelve colonies against trade with
Great Britain, Ireland, and the West Indies, 489d;
stipend received by Governor Hutchinson, the people
called on him to relinquish, 379a; events, reviewed
by Zubly in his political sermon to the Georgia
Provincial Congress, 520b; tax on tea, imposed by
Great Britain, 458c; tax on tea, cause of the Boston
Tea Party, 460d; trials, to be conducted in England,
452d

UNDER GOD: the basis of American rights and liberties,
530a

UNDISCIPLINED: Americans were, and without experienced officers before the American Revolution, 494b

UNION: advantages of, not in conflict with individual
enterprise, 251b; and self-government of the colonies after the Declaration of Independence, 250a;
as well as separateness, principle of congregationalism, 105c; boundaries of, from sea to sea, because
of Valley Forge, 67c; brotherly, of Christians, incomprehensible to pagans, 12d; continental, produced
by the agency of Providence, 469a; growing, of
colonies, observed by Gage, 401c; motives to, effect
of British Intolerable Acts, 462a; of action and principles, brought about by Committees of Correspondence, 386b; of all the colonies desired, with sovereignty of each state preserved, 419b; of American
Colonies, produced by Great Britain's attempts for
raising revenue, 468c; of the American Colonists,
aided by the King's refusal of their petition, 502d;
preservation of, and observation of the Lord's Day,
21c

UNITED STATES GOVERNMENT: must be administered on
principles of Protestant Christianity, 155c; cannot
forbid that the Bible be taught in its public schools,
155d; cannot disregard the Lord's Day, 155d; cannot require its officers to labor on the Lord's Day,
155d; when Christianity is ignored, atheists and infidels control, 155d

UNITED STATES OF AMERICA: are a Christian and Protestant nation, 156a; reasons why, 156a

UNIVERSAL FLOOD: one common ruin for the whole human race, 35c

UNIVERSE: the moral order of, left with a divine guide,
the Holy Scriptures, 21b

UNIVERSITIES: *English:* Oxford and Cambridge, had
proved their independence and had resisted kings,
291d; *American:* professorships of liberty, should
be founded in, by gentlemen of large estates and
public spirit, 28d

UNIVERSITY: *see also* AMERICAN CHRISTIAN COLLEGES;
established for education of the professions, 223a;
our obligation to our ancestors who began building

up this institution, 223a

UNKNOWN: graves at Valley Forge, and anniversaries
of great events, 67b; woman, patriot of North Carolina, 80a; thanked heaven for deliverance, 80d

UNLIMITED POWER: of government, never given to men
by their Great Creator, 208

UNMARKED: graves at Valley Forge, still lie in yonder
field, 55d

UNSECTARIAN: American education, not divorced from
religion, 53c

UNVEILING: of America, and God's hour, 47c

USSHER, JAMES, 1581-1656: Irish theologian and scholar,
archbishop of Armagh, his scheme for moderate
episcopacy, 107a

V

VALLEY FORGE: George Washington prayed at, *frontis-
piece*; "Foes were strong, and friends were few at,
x; June 19, 1878, anniversary of, oration written and delivered by Henry Armitt Brown, 55a;
sources of American greatness seen at, 55b; the
Continental Army entered, in December, 1777, 58b;
description of country of, 58d; Washington's strategy
in selection of site of, 59b; four months of suffering
recorded at, 60d; meatless and breadless days at,
61c; horses by the hundreds starved to death at, 61c;
nakedness, starvation, sickness, death at, 61d; incredible mortality at, 61d; diligence of physicians
and surgeons at, 62a; Christmas at, 63a; ground of,
holy, 63a; officers at, 63a; description of George
Washington and his burden at, 64b; military school
of Baron von Steuben at, 65a; must not forget
Franklin's work for America and French Alliance,
65b; winter days dragged on in 1778 at, 66a; news
of French Alliance received at, May 4, 1778, 66a;
religious services in celebration of French Treaty
at, 66b; Continental Army left, June 19, 1778, for
Monmouth, 66c; hills of, left with their glory and
their dead, 66c; blood spilled at, from a suffering
people, 66d; Americans exhorted not to forget, their
obligations for the Present, 67b; memory of, should
be honored by our actions in the present, 67b; what
was accomplished for America at, 67c; sacrifice at,
gave us a nation, 67c; "Virtue, Honor, and Love of
Country," established at, 67d; America rose from
death into life at, 68c

VANDYKE, SIR ANTHONY, 1599-1641: Flemish painter, in
era of the American Settlement, 48c

VANE, HENRY, 1613-1662: English Puritan statesman,
better represented the principles of the Independents,
266a

VARNUM, JAMES MITCHELL, 1748-1789: American lawyer and Revolutionary officer, commanded men of
Rhode Island at Valley Forge, 63d; his scheme to
raise negro troops, 63d

VAUGHAN, SIR JOHN, 1738-1795: British General, his
expedition up North River in 1777, filled country with
terror and despondency, 210a

VEIL: of waters, concealed America for centuries, 47b

VENDERS: of goods and manufactures, shall not take
advantage of the people, 525a

VENGEANCE: legislative, taken by Parliament on town
of Boston, 460a

VENICE: republic of, no example for the American Republic, 254b

VENISON: woods stored with, for our Pilgrim Fathers,
25d

VICE: powerful barrier to, a sacred regard to veracity,
85a; makes men timorous and cowardly, 202a; and
rebellion against God, brought Israel into slavery,
536b

VICES: of paganism, and Christian virtues, 10b; and

luxury, will hasten our ruin, 30a; taught to the Indians by English Settlers, 318b

VICTORY: God of our Fathers, alone giveth, x; Christ's coming and, proclaimed in the Revelation of St. John, 3b; of Christ, over wrong-thoughtedness, 3c; wrong-heartedness, wrong-spiritedness, seen in Revelation, 3d

VIGILANCE: eternal, is the price of liberty, 223c; eternal, to prevent episcopacy in America, 28c; unceasing, the defense of liberty, 67c; in detection of despotism, in the American Philosophy of Government, 250d; sacred trust of, an individual duty for every American citizen, 252c

VINDICATION: of our ancestors, furnished in the American Archives, 250b

VIOLENCE: appeal to, convenient course against Christians, 13c; combined with intellectual weapons, against Christianity, 16a; political fabric secure against, 222b; of people of Massachusetts caused Crown officers to flee to Boston, 472a

VIRGIL, OR VERGIL, PUBLIUS VERGILIUS MARO, 70-19 B.C., Roman poet, author of *The Aneid*, majesty of, surpassed by the Bible, 224d; writings of, compared specifically to the inspired writings, 225b; excellent as he is, the prophets shine without a competitor, 230c

VIRGINIA COLONY:

Settlement of: an episcopal province, few traces of Puritans in early history, 110d; 437d; later settlements in, included Puritan families, 110d; large body of French Protestants settled in, 1690-99, 11d; emigrations of Irish into, 113a

Religion in: growth of Episcopal church in, for 150 years, 169a; established church in, deterred other denominations, 432c; Dr. Blair sent as an episcopal missionary to, 159d; ministers of established church in, unfit before the Great Revival, 123b; Whitefield preached at seat of government in, 169b; difficulties of growth of the Episcopal church in, 169c; clergy lost right to be supported, 169d; people of, Independents, Episcopalians alike, opposed American episcopacy, 182c

Government in: House of Burgesses established in 1620, spontaneous growth of representative government, 50c; House of Burgesses, opposed episcopacy on political grounds, 143b

Education in: poverty of education in, 169d; education and free schools neglected in, 173a; charter from crown in 1691 for establishment of a college in, 439a; called William and Mary in honor of throne, 439b; learning of, in low state, before William and Mary College, 439b

Literature of: historians published works, names of, 440a; pens of, used in twelve years of paper war that preceded the American Revolution, 440a

Slavery in: from an early time the curse of slavery had rested upon, 172d; negro slavery added in 1620 to other forms in, 172d; dangers from large numbers of African slaves during the American Revolution, 412d; Governor Dunmore armed the blacks against their masters, 413a

Economics in: substitute for money found in tobacco in, 332d; parsons received their salaries in tobacco, 333a; from 1633, tobacco principal medium of exchange in, 333a; problems in regulation of money values in, effect of paper currency on money of account, 338a; James Stewart, inhabitant of, returned from England to introduce dye manufacture to America, 340b

In the American Revolution: led opposition to the Stamp Act, 447d; Virginia Resolves ushered into House of Burgesses by Patrick Henry, 361b; 448a; prevented by their governor from representation at Stamp Act Congress, 449c; her response to the Boston Port Bill, 252b; 467d; Governor Dunmore dissolved House of Burgesses on Virginia's resolution to recognize Boston's plight by a day of fasting, 467d; made opposition to parliamentary measures on different grounds than Massachusetts, 362d; between Virginia and Massachusetts a remarkable coincidence of opinion, energy and zeal, 393b; attached to Massachusetts, by their selection of a Commander-in-Chief from Virginia, 503c

Virginians: patriotism and courage of Elizabeth Zane, 80d; men of Virginia commanded at Valley Forge by William Woodford, and Charles Scott, 63b; Henry Ernest Muhlenberg, clergyman, and officer in the Continental Army, 63d

VIRTUE: and honor, and love of country, established at Valley Forge, 67d; and industry of Mohawks, after Christianization, 318a; and knowledge, and early instruction of youth, 222b; and manners, related to knowledge of Christianity, 316c; an example of, a community should be to its neighboring communities, 202b; loss of every principle of, by becoming slaves to Europe, 340c; loss of, soon follows loss of liberty, 203a; obtained from education of youth, 221b; of the people, and a free constitution, 223c; of the people, and the encouragement of agriculture, manufacture, and economy, 338d; of the people, during the suspension of government in Massachusetts, 208; 209; 396a; rather than outward station, 242a; Roman decline of, overturned their republic, 359a; and the defense of liberty, 67c

VIRTUES: of Primitive Christians, contrasted with vices of pagans, 10b; prominent, of Christians, 17b; public, needed in magistrates, 27c; extraordinary, of George Washington, kept army from disbanding, saved his country's cause, 64d; Christian, of Mrs. Washington, 76b

VIRTUOUS: education, influence of upon history of a nation, 218a

VOLTAIRE, *assumed name of* FRANCOIS MARIE AROUET, 1694-1778: French writer, invited to Prussia by Frederick the Great, 276c; prince of scoffers, idol of sceptics in society, 281b; his conviction that the people of France had no capacity for self-government, 281c; ripened in the atmosphere of England, 284b; his joy in England's Constitutional form of government, 272d

VOLUMES: dedication of these, to the Pilgrims, 22b

VOX DEI VOX POPULI: the great moral lesson of the American Revolution, that the legitimate source of power is the people and cannot be denied, 254d

VULTUROUS EYE: God's ways high above the, 45b

W

WALDO, ALBIGENCE, DR. 1750-1794: American Surgeon, at Valley Forge, writes of Colonel Prentice's Connecticut Regiment, of conditions of suffering, 60d; writes of effect of disheartening letters from home on officers at Valley Forge, 62a; his diary description of the common soldier in the American Revolution and his cheerfulness in the face of sickness and cold, 62b

WAR: art of, and men of affluence, 204d; arts of, forbidden to Quakers, 77c; calamities of, steps taken by colonists to avert, 246b; consistency of, with the spirit of the gospel, 199b; declared on, Great Britain by France after her alliance with America, 65d; defensive, not inconsistent with gospel, 198c; 543a; devouring sword of, has been unsheathed by our brother, 544a; expence of, let it not discourage us, 543b; French and Indian, made the weight and magnitude of America visible, 247d; horrors of, feared less than submission to parliamentary supremacy, 502c; not agreeable, to souls newly converted to Christ, 540a; knowledge of the science and discipline of, possessed by British troops, 494b; necessity of, because of depravity of human nature, 200d; no necessity of, when earth filled with knowledge of the Lord, 540b; not the business of the British colonies, 494b; of extermination against Christians, prevented by God, 15b; of principle, the American Revolution, 253a; on women and children by Indians, 441b; preferable to concessions to liberty, 199c; religion forbids, unless ncessary, 199b; seven long years of, needed a Washington, 52b; state of, those who invade liberty, 203b; passages in New Testament, which seem to forbid, 198c

WARD, ARTEMAS, 1727-1800: American Revolutionary Commander, chaplains in Massachusetts, appointed under command of, 206c; elected a general officer of Massachusetts Minute Men and Militia, 473a; 493b; given command of provincial army raised in Massachusetts, 493b; commanded right wing of American army at Roxbury around Boston, 505c

WAR OF INDEPENDENCE: begun 15 months before the Declaration of Independence, 248d

WARREN, JAMES, 1726-1808: Massachusetts political leader, 77a; husband of Mercy Warren, and merchant of Plymouth, 77a; on committee to impeach Governor Bernard, 371d; first proposed committees of correspondence to Samuel Adams, 386b; chosen for a secret council by Massachusetts General Assembly, 392d; his comments on the action at Lexington, 406a; as president of Massachusetts Provincial Congress, called for elections, as Massachusetts resumed government under the Articles of Confederation, 419c; presented George Washington with an address from Massachusetts Provincial Congress of their esteem and support of his new role as Commander-in-Chief of the American Army, 421d; character of, described, 421d

WARREN, JOSEPH, 1741-1775: American physician and Revolutionary officer, 207a; President of Massachusetts Provincial Congress in 1775, 207a; first victim of rank to fall at Bunker Hill, 418d; character and patriotism of, 418d; death of, deeply regretted, 498d; eulogy for, written by Dr. Benjamin Rush, 499a

WARREN, MERCY, nee OTIS, 1728-1814: American woman of letters, of Plymouth Colony, 76c; the most remarkable woman of the Revolutionary period, 76c; family history of, 76c; domestic education of, 76d; improved her mind by careful study, 76d; education of, not in schools, 76d; supplied with books by minister of parish, 76d; cultivated a taste for history, influenced by Raleigh's *History of the World*, 77a; her brother, James Otis, her companion and literary advisor, 77a; her marriage and children, 77a; literary pursuits and household duties, 77a; gave valuable instruction to her children, 77a; her interest in political affairs, 77b; deep religious feelings of, 77c

New England Historian Cotemporary with the American Revolution: her *Prelude to the American Revolution, 1765-1775*, 357; speaks of her qualifications as an historian of this period, 357b; speaks to posterity concerning their history, 358a; contemplates life and history as a Christian, 358a; history requires a just knowledge of character, 358b; character requires the checks of conscience, 358c; Nimrod, the beginning of depredation and ruin on earth, 358d; examples of deception and despotism in Roman history, 358d; describes the effect of the Stamp Act on the Colonists, 360d; describes the American Colonies at time of the American Revolution and the similarity of their political institutions, 369a; Independence was a plant of later growth than 1768, 369c; discusses a

standing army as an engine in the hand of despotism, 372d; reviews events of March 5, 1770, Boston Massacre, 381c; masterly writers in America, in defence of constitutional principles, 383c; describes the Boston Tea Party, 384a; defines history of committees of correspondence, 386a; describes Boston Port Bill, 389c; discusses the instruments of Providence for design of American Independence, 390d; Proposal for a Congress of all the Colonies to meet at Philadelphia, 393a; political ability which marked the First Continental Congress, 396d; influence of its transactions and resolves on Americans, 397a; ideals and courage of Americans risking life for liberty, 393b; discusses conditions under suspension of government and the virtue of the people of Massachusetts, 395c; describes differences between the American and French Revolutions, 397d; describes America's preparation for the American Revolution, 398b; Americans determined to avoid beginning hostilities, 401d; a Superintending Providence led to American Independence, 404c; the spirit and character of the American people, 404d; Battle of Lexington described, 405d; response of country to, 409b; Ticonderoga taken, 414c; Battle of Bunker Hill described, 417a; grief at death of General Joseph Warren at Bunker Hill, 418c; his courage and patriotism described, 419d; the raising of a Continental Army, 420a; hostilities commenced, American reliance on Providence, 422b

"History requires a just knowledge of character": Governor Bernard did not promote the interest of the people, 366c; Bernard impeached by the Massachusetts General Assembly, 371d; Bernard repaired to England, royally rewarded for his conduct in Massachusetts, 377c; treasonable letters of Andrew Oliver, Secretary of the Province of Massachusetts, 374d; depicts the character of Governor Hutchinson, 378a; his duplicity revealed in his letters to individuals in the British cabinet, 382d; Massachusetts General Assembly requested impeachment of Andrew Oliver and Thomas Hutchinson, 387a; Hutchinson urged Parliamentary taxation without representation, 387b; Governor Hutchinson left Massachusetts for England, 390a; he lived long enough to repent in bitterness his part against America, 390c; attempted assassination of Mr. James Otis, 379c; consequences of attack on Otis, 380b; James Otis lived to see the independence of America, 380c; tributes after his death, 380d; a sister's efforts at impartiality, 380d; General Gage appointed Governor of Massachusetts, 390d; Gage erased names of representatives chosen by the people, 391d; character of the royal governors described, 411d; Samuel Adams, his character, early nurtured in the principles of civil and religious liberty, 415d; John Hancock, a young gentleman of fortune, 416a; Joseph Warren, his character, 418b; George Washington, his character and background of preparation, 421b

British Bureaucracy: Mercy Warren notes the swarms of hirelings sent from Great Britain to ravish the colonies, 365b; describes the establishment of the Board of Customs, 367b; large salaries annexed to their office, 365b; salaries to be paid out of the revenue chest, officers made independent of the general assembly, 367c; no check left on wanton exercise of power, 367c; dispensed with trial by jury, annihilated the privileges of Englishmen, 367c; dangerous aspect of admiralty court challenged by James Otis, 367d

Rich Correspondence: names of men who asked her opinion in political matters, acknowledged the excellence of her judgment, 77b; letters from Martha Washington, 75d; 76c; letters to Abigail Adams, 84b; 85c